The File New command gives you access to predesigned templates that you can use as a starting point for common tasks. You can add your own templates, and you can even create special tabs in the File New dialog box.

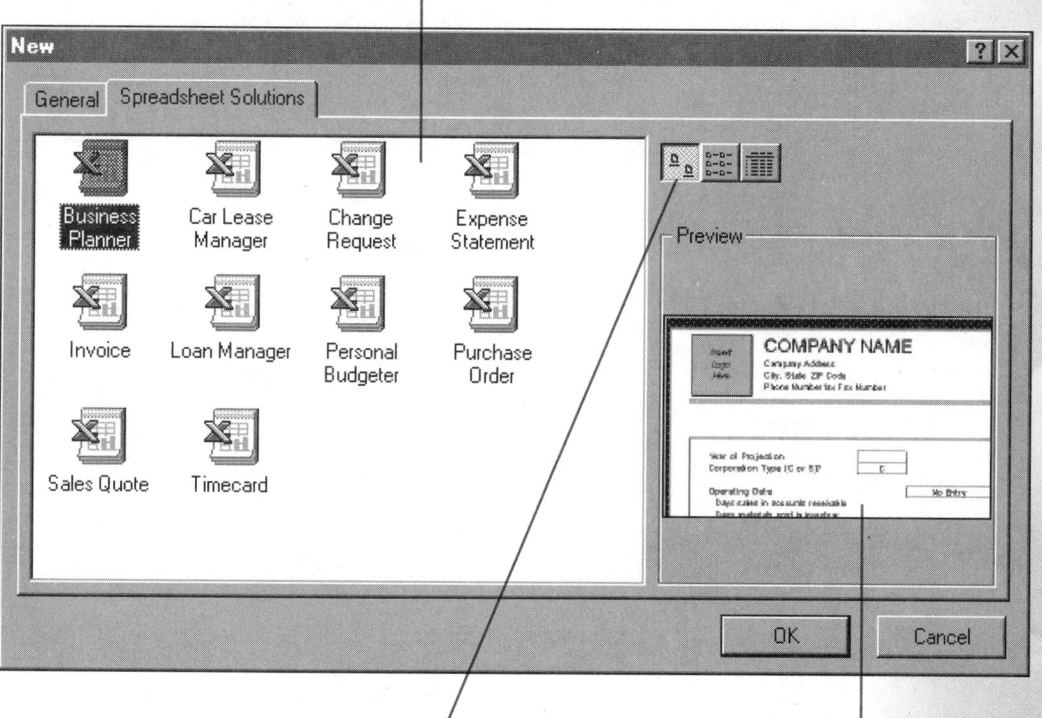

Use these buttons to quickly change the view of your files from icon view, to list view, to list view with details, such as file size and date.

The Preview area gives you a glimpse of the selected template.

Mark Dodge Mark Dodge's life experience as a cost accountant, small-business owner, one-man advertising agency, street fair organizer, live sound engineer, commercial fisherman, cake decorator, and professional musician somehow conspired to create the bit-based wordsmith he is today. He has been honored with five awards from the Society for Technical Communication, most recently for his written contributions to both print and online documentation for Microsoft Excel 5. He was previously technical editor of over a dozen books on Microsoft applications, coauthor of the two Microsoft Press editions of the *Microsoft Excel Companion*, as well as coauthor of the third and fourth editions of *Running Microsoft Excel*. He is currently a senior technical writer for the Microsoft Office User Assistance group and is working on getting his recording studio built while still musically adroit.

Chris Kinata Chris Kinata learned his fourth programming language at USC 25 years ago, remembers the installation of the first Internet terminal there, and in perverse moments (always after midnight, past a deadline, with a flaky beta) reminisces about programming with punch cards. He has designed biofeedback devices, converted brainwaves into computer art, shown conceptual art in real art galleries, and was in Peru looking for UFOs before Shirley MacLaine. Blah, blah, blah. He was employee #720 at Microsoft, worked there up to 120 hours a week for 5 years as a technical editor and writer, and then bailed out to home-school his kids in glorious Ballard, USA. He loves children, dreaming, archery, and jumping off the tops of mountains with a paraglider.

Craig Stinson Craig Stinson is a contributing editor of *PC Magazine* and editor of the Spreadsheets section of *PC Magazine*'s Solutions column. An industry journalist since 1981, Stinson was formerly editor of *Softalk for the IBM Personal Computer*. He is the author of *Running Windows 95* (Microsoft Press, 1995) and coauthor of *Running Windows NT* (Microsoft Press, 1993). In addition to his numerous computer publications, he has written music reviews for publications such as *Billboard*, the *Boston Globe*, the *Christian Science Monitor*, and *Musical America*. He lives with his wife and children in Eugene, Oregon.

The Cobb Group The Cobb Group, a leader in computer training and support, is well known for its bestselling, high-quality computer books and for its series of critically acclaimed newsletters that cover popular software.

In-Depth Reference

and Inside Tips from

the Software Experts

RUNNING

Microsoft® EXCEL for Windows® 95

MARK DODGE, CHRIS KINATA, AND CRAIG STINSON WITH THE COBB GROUP

Microsoft® Press

PUBLISHED BY
Microsoft Press
A Division of Microsoft Corporation
One Microsoft Way
Redmond, Washington 98052-6399

Library of Congress Cataloging-in-Publication Data
Dodge, Mark.
Running Microsoft Excel for Windows 95 / Mark Dodge, Chris Kinata, Craig Stinson.
p. cm.
Includes index.
ISBN 1-55615-831-9
1. Microsoft Excel for Windows. 2. Business--Computer programs.
3. Electronic spreadsheets. I. Kinata, Chris. II. Stinson, Craig, 1943- III. Title.
HF5548.4.M523D63 1995
005.369--dc20 95-30590
CIP

Printed and bound in the United States of America.

2 3 4 5 6 7 8 9 QMQM 0 9 8 7 6 5

Distributed to the book trade in Canada by Macmillan of Canada, a division of Canada Publishing Corporation.

A CIP catalogue record for this book is available from the British Library.

Microsoft Press books are available through booksellers and distributors worldwide. For further information about international editions, contact your local Microsoft Corporation office. Or contact Microsoft Press International directly at fax (206) 936-7329.

Acquisitions Editor: Lucinda Rowley
Project Editor: John Pierce
Technical Editor: Editorial Services of New England

Chapters at a Glance

Table of Contents

Acknowledgments

Creating a high-quality computer book requires a surprising expenditure of human energy. The image of the contemplative, reclusive writer ruminating in cerebral, Walden-like solitude is antithetic to reality for a computer book author. As we say in meeting-speak around here, it takes a lot of "bandwith" to write, edit, design, and produce a book like this, and the unsung often contribute as much to the process as the "sung." With this in mind, here follows the litany of saints whose contributions to this project were salt-essential. Many thanks to Lucinda Rowley, Peggy McCauley, John Pierce, Kim Eggleston, and Mary DeJong of Microsoft Press, as well as Bonnie Jo Collins, Michelle Neil, Nan Fritz, Kate Chambers, Emma Gibson, Jackie Fesler, Matthew Spence, Peter Whitmer, and many others at Editorial Services of New England for feats of editorial beauty. Special thanks to Carl Chatfield, Mike Mraz, and Kevin Browne for random acts of kindness. A tip of the fedora to Will Sibbald and Kathryn Hamilton for perennial indulgence. Thanks to Vicki, Max, and Regina for waiting. And the "you wreak me, baby" award for outstanding audio stimulation during stressful deadline-dancing goes to Tom Petty for stopping to chew the *Wildflowers*.

Mark Dodge

I'd like to thank the conspicuously expeditious and adroit folk at Editorial Services of New England for a particularly smooth revision: Tech Editors Kate Chambers and Emma Gibson (whose steadfast courage in pursuit of Truth put the lie to Independence Day); Project Editor Bonnie Jo Collins; Copy Editor Jackie Fesler; and Desktop Publishing Wiz Peter Whitmer. Also great gratitude to Lucinda Rowley and especially John Pierce of Microsoft Press, the latter of which hath made my nose grindstone-shiny yet feeling curiously fulfilled.

Chris Kinata

Once again I'd like to thank the editorial and production team that conceived and designed this book and then did the necessary pushing and pulling to get it completed: Lucinda Rowley, John Pierce, and Peggy McCauley of Microsoft Press; and Michelle Neil, Kate Chambers, Emma Gibson, Bonnie Jo Collins, Peter Whitmer, Jackie Fesler, Mark Heffernan, Vanessa Moore, Erin Harpe, Patricia Porter, Bettina Burch, and Bernadette Murphy of Editorial Services of New England. And, as always, I thank my wife and kids for their unfailing patience and support.

Craig Stinson

Introduction

Ever since its debut in 1985, Microsoft Excel has enjoyed critical acclaim as the world's most powerful, sophisticated, and usable electronic spreadsheet. Over the past decade, while competitors strove to imitate Excel's features, Excel was constantly innovating. With each revision, the designers of Excel have come up with brilliant new ways to make their spreadsheet more versatile and easier to use. With each revision, despite the best efforts of other companies to catch up, Excel has always managed to surge ahead of the pack.

What's New in Microsoft Excel 7.0

The newest version, Microsoft Excel for Windows 95, version 7.0, continues this remarkable tradition. Excel 7 is brimming with great ideas and great spreadsheet technology. If you're coming to Excel from another spreadsheet program, or if you're a new spreadsheet user, you have many treats in store. If you're moving up from Excel 5, you'll find that this already-great program has improved on nearly every front. Here is a partial list of Excel 7's new features.

Support for Windows 95

Excel 7 is a 32-bit application written expressly for Windows 95. The new operating environment brings several important benefits:

Long Filenames. In Excel 7, you no longer have to save workbooks under cryptic eight-letter filenames. You can use up to 218 characters to provide a descriptive and distinct name for every workbook on your hard disk.

Faster Performance. Microsoft devoted approximately 25 percent of the Excel 7 development effort toward making critical operations quicker. Formula recalculation is about 50 percent faster in Excel 7 than in Excel 5. Speed improvements involving other common operations — such as creating charts, moving data via the Clipboard, and opening and saving files — range from 20 percent faster to more than 100 percent faster.

Plug and Play. As a Plug and Play–aware application, Excel 7 responds appropriately to changes in the configuration of your system.

Improvements in System Resource Usage. Architectural changes in Windows 95 have dramatically reduced the likelihood that you will run low on system resources while working with Excel. As a result, you can open more workbooks, create more charts and other graphic objects, and keep more applications running at once.

Support for UNC Path Constructions. The Universal Naming Convention (UNC) allows formulas and macros to reference network resources using simple path constructions, without first mapping network drives.

An Improved Help System, with Full-Text Indexing. Microsoft redesigned the Help system in Windows 95 so that it would be easier to navigate and would provide a clear distinction between overview topics and specific details. The overviews appear on a table-of-contents page, while the details are accessible via an index-style list. Users also have the option of creating a complete index of an application's help text, which can then be used to find particular words or phrases in help messages.

Usability Enhancements

Excel 7 incorporates many small changes that add up to greater ease of use and ease of learning. These include:

FastFind. Like the other applications in the Microsoft Office 95 suite, Excel 7 offers FastFind, an optional facility for indexing the contents of your workbooks.

With FastFind, you don't have to remember the name or whereabouts of the workbook that contains some particular bit of text. You can simply let FastFind locate that workbook for you.

The Answer Wizard. With the Answer Wizard, Excel 7 goes beyond the Help improvements provided by Windows 95. The Answer Wizard lets you query the Help system with plain-English phrases, such as "How do I add a header to a report?" or "How do I delete a column?" The Answer Wizard also can provide quick "demos" to help you understand its answers.

AutoCorrect. Microsoft's AutoCorrect feature, first introduced in Word 6.0, is now available in Excel. AutoCorrect fixes common spelling errors, changing "teh" to "the," for example, or "THis" to "This." You can tell it what errors *you* are most likely to make, so that the feature becomes your own personal faulty-typing corrector. Or you can simply use it to expand abbreviations.

AutoComplete and Pick Lists. Excel 7 can save you keystrokes and help ensure consistency when you enter repetitive information into lists. As you type, it looks at the contents of the cells above the active cell. If it sees that you're beginning to type an entry that you've already typed, it offers to complete that entry for you. Alternatively, it lets you pop up a list of all the entries that you've already entered in the current column. From that pop-up list you can select an entry to repeat.

Scroll Tips. Moving from one part of a worksheet to another is easier now, thanks to scroll tips — navigational signposts that pop up along- side Excel 7's scroll bars.

Improved Drag and Drop. You can now drag data from one worksheet to another, or from a worksheet to a chart sheet. Adding new data points to a chart on its own sheet, for example, no longer requires copy and paste. You can simply drag the new data and drop it on the chart.

Pop-up Cell Notes. The Insert Note command is now a more effective way to annotate worksheets. If you hover your mouse over a cell to which you've attached a note, the note appears in a pop-up window.

Simpler Numeric Formatting. Excel has always had powerful numeric formatting options. Thanks to a redesigned dialog box, those formatting options are now easy to use.

Office Binders. A new Binder utility lets you store and print documents from different applications as a single file. For example, you can store documents from Excel, Word, and PowerPoint and print them as a single document, with consecutive page numbers.

Improved Analytic Tools

The current revision brings new analytic muscle to Excel:

Spreadsheet Solution Templates. Excel 7 includes ten professionally designed, customizable templates to help you get started with common applications. The templates cover invoicing, purchase orders, time sheets, expense tracking, financial reports and cash flow, personal budgeting, mortgage calculation, car leasing, sales quotes, and tracking change requests.

AutoFilter with Top 10. Excel 5's AutoFilter feature, which lets you focus a list to display records of interest, has been expanded in Excel 7 to include the Top 10 option. This provides an easy way to see the highest or lowest items in a list.

AutoCalculate. To see the sum, average, or count of any block of cells, simply select it. Thanks to AutoCalculate, the information you need appears on the status bar.

Template Wizard with Data Tracking. A new wizard makes it easy to turn your worksheets into reusable templates. If you want, the wizard also sets up a database (in Excel or another ODBC-compliant application) that tracks the values entered into particular cells of your template.

Data Mapping. A new addition to Excel's charting capability, data mapping lets you turn geographic information into color-coded maps.

New Workgroup Features

Excel 7 includes some new features to help with collaborative applications:

Shared Lists. Excel 7 lets two or more users work in the same workbook at once, each with read/write privileges. The program uses a unique conflict-resolution method to resolve mutually exclusive changes.

Post to Exchange Folder. Users who have Microsoft's Exchange Server can store Excel files in Exchange folders, rather than storing them as disk files. Exchange folders, which can be replicated across wide-area networks, serve as repositories for shared worksheets.

Custom OLE Properties. Users can attach custom OLE properties to Excel documents. OLE-aware applications, such as Exchange Server, can use these properties as the basis for document search and retrieval.

Integration with Microsoft Access

Excel users who also have Microsoft Access 7 have new ways to take advantage of Access's data-management power while working in Excel.

Access Forms. With Access Forms, you can create data-entry forms that prompt and validate user input.

Access Reports. You can use Access's powerful report capability to create highly structured and formatted reports (including mailing labels) from your Excel lists.

Convert to Microsoft Access. When you find yourself entering the same list data repeatedly, it may be time to convert your list to a relational database. Excel 7's Convert to Microsoft Access feature will do that for you.

About This Book

This book is a user's guide, tutorial, and comprehensive reference for Microsoft Excel 7.0. It is designed to help you gain the deepest possible understanding of Excel in the shortest possible time. This book assumes that you have a working knowledge of Microsoft Windows 95.

The book has eight parts, including three appendixes. The first part, which consists of Chapters 1 through 3, introduces Excel. Here we cover the basics of the Excel environment—the menu system, the toolbars, the Help system, the procedures for opening and closing files, and the use of Excel on a local-area network.

Part 2, which consists of Chapters 4 through 10, covers the Excel worksheet. We show you how to lay out, format, and edit a worksheet; how to navigate from one part of a workbook to another; and how to create links between workbooks. We also discuss printing worksheets and the services available to users who have moved to Excel from Lotus 1-2-3.

Part 3 consists of Chapters 11 through 15 and describes Excel's function library and other analytical tools. Chapter 11 provides an overview of the most commonly used functions, Chapter 12 deals with the modeling of dates and times, Chapter 13 covers financial analysis, Chapter 14 surveys the Analysis ToolPak, and Chapter 15 tells you how to use the Solver to find optimal solutions to complex problems.

Part 4 includes Chapters 16 through 19, which cover Excel's charting capabilities. Chapter 16 introduces the ChartWizard, Chapter 17 shows you how to customize the appearance of your charts, Chapter 18 explains how to edit chart data, and Chapter 19 describes Excel's new data mapping feature.

Part 5, which consists of Chapters 20 through 22, discusses Excel's list and database management features. Chapter 20 focuses on the commands and procedures for sorting, filtering, and subtotaling lists. Chapter 21 describes the use of Microsoft Query for retrieving data stored in external database files.

And, in Chapter 22, you'll meet the PivotTable Wizard, a sophisticated cross-tabulating report generator that lets you look at your data from many different perspectives.

Part 6, covering Chapters 23 through 25, explains macros. Chapter 23 tells you how to record, edit, and run macros. Chapter 24 explains how, with the help of Excel's macro language, you can add your own functions to the Excel function library. And Chapter 25 provides an overview of Visual Basic for Applications, the macro language introduced with Excel 5.

Part 7 includes Chapters 26 and 27, which address the interaction of Excel with other Windows-based and non–Windows-based applications. Chapter 26 discusses the use of the Windows Clipboard and OLE. Chapter 27 covers the ins and outs of file exchange with other spreadsheet and database programs.

Finally we include some useful appendixes in Part 8. Appendix A provides a reference guide to Excel's toolbars, and Appendix B covers the installation of Excel. If you haven't yet installed Microsoft Excel on your computer, read Appendix B first. The third appendix, "PSS Q&A: Troubleshooting Tips from Microsoft Support Services," responds to some frequent user issues and provides troubleshooting tips.

Using This Book

In this book, when you see a key combination written with a hyphen, like this:

Ctrl-A

it means "hold down the first key, and then press the second key." For example, Ctrl-A means "Hold down the Ctrl key and press A." When you see two key names separated by a comma, like this:

Alt, F

it means "Press and release the first key, and then press the second."

TIP Throughout this book you'll find loads of tips on better use of Excel. They are marked with this icon so you can't miss them.

Finally, wherever you encounter the "See Also" icon, you'll find references to other sections in the book that provide additional, related information.

Part 1

Getting Started with Microsoft Excel

Chapter 1

Getting Your Bearings

When you start a new learning experience, the first task is to learn the language. You need to know what the basic elements are called and where to find them. This chapter will help you learn the language of Microsoft Excel. Even if you're an experienced Microsoft Excel user, you'll need some new vocabulary for Excel 7 for Windows 95 — so let's get started.

Starting Microsoft Excel

If you haven't yet installed Microsoft Excel on your computer, you can refer to Appendix B, "Installing Microsoft Excel," for hardware requirements and installation information. After you've installed Excel, click the Start button on the Windows taskbar. To start the program, from the Start menu, choose Programs, and then Microsoft Excel. Excel opens and displays a blank workbook.

Excel's on-screen appearance varies depending on the type of monitor you're using. Figure 1-1, for example, shows a blank Excel workbook on a

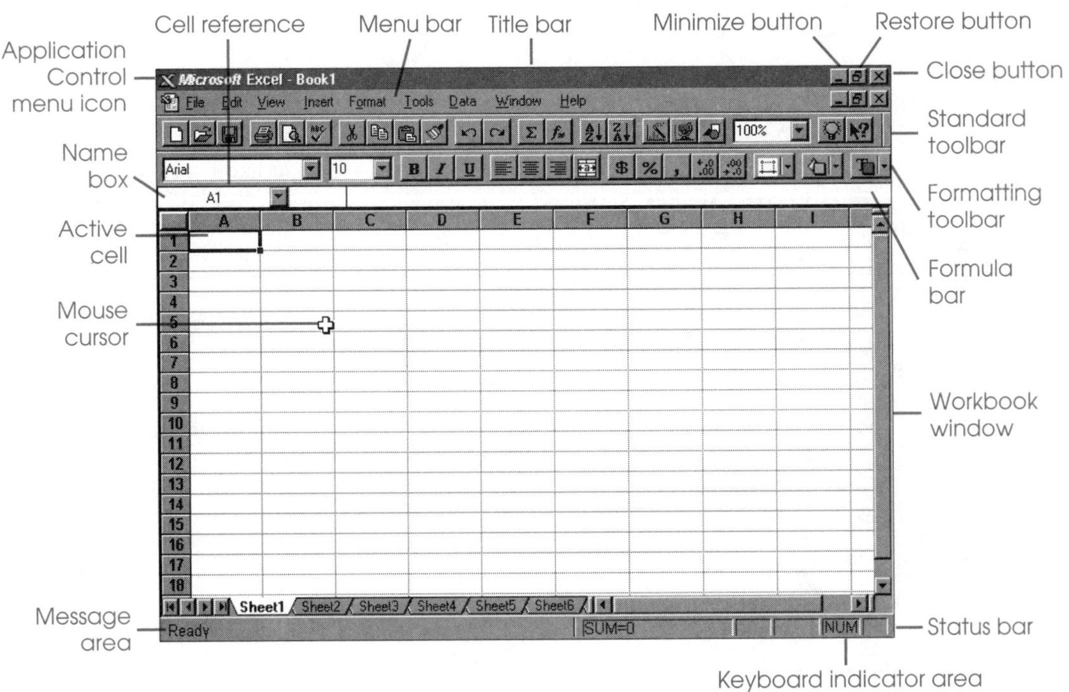

FIGURE 1-1

If you have a 14-inch VGA monitor, your screen looks like this when you start Microsoft Excel.

14-inch VGA monitor. If you have another type of monitor, your screen might look slightly different. Throughout this book, we use graphics taken from a 14-inch VGA monitor.

When you start the Excel program, the first blank workbook Excel displays is called *Book1*. If you open another new workbook during the same work session, Excel names it *Book2*. You can have several workbooks open at the same time, and you can subsequently save each workbook under a different name.

An Excel *workbook* can contain five types of *sheets:* worksheets, like the one visible in Figure 1-1; chart sheets; Visual Basic modules; dialog sheets; and Microsoft Excel macro sheets. In Parts 1 and 2 of this book, you work only with worksheets. After you've learned how to build a worksheet, we'll show you how to plot worksheet data in a chart and how to work with Visual Basic modules and dialog sheets so that you can automate your work.

See Also For information about saving and renaming documents, see Chapter 3, "Managing Files," page 52.

A Tour of the Microsoft Excel Workspace

When you start Microsoft Excel, your screen consists of five areas: the workbook window, which occupies most of the screen; the menu bar; two or more toolbars; the formula bar; and the status bar. (The menu bar, toolbars, formula bar, and status bar appear on the screen even when a workbook is not visible.) Collectively, these five areas are known as the Excel *workspace*.

See Also For information about toolbars, see Chapter 2, "Toolbars and Buttons," page 33.

The Workbook Window

As mentioned, the workbook window dominates the Excel workspace. Navigational controls appear at the bottom of the workbook window, and a title bar is displayed at the top. The window also includes borders, worksheets, and scroll bars. A new workbook, shown in Figure 1-2 on the next page, originally consists of 16 individual worksheets.

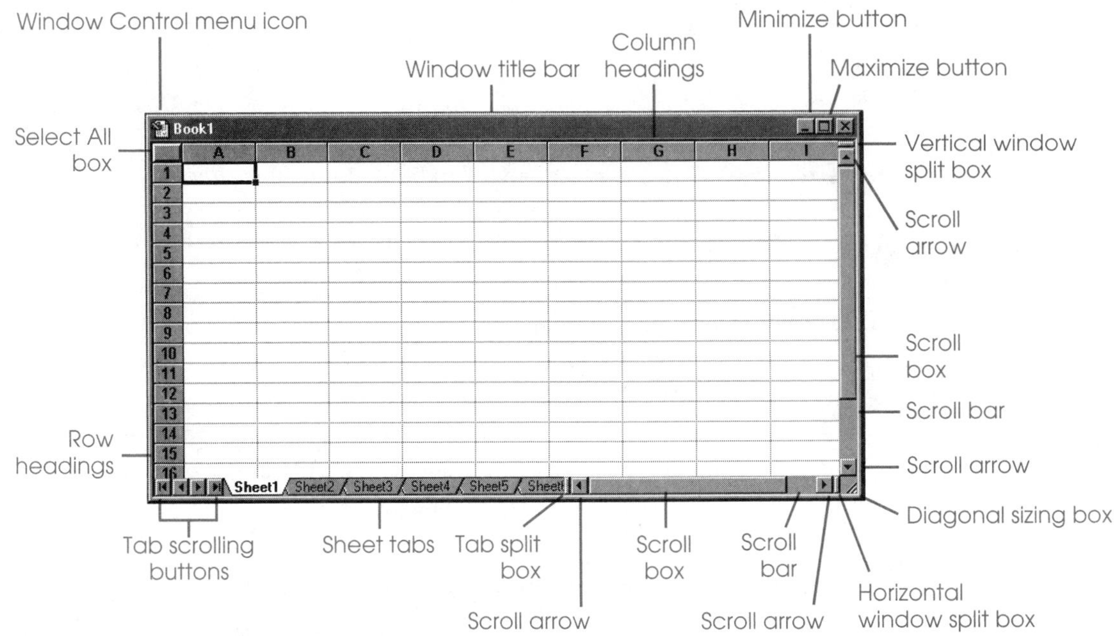

FIGURE 1-2

An Excel workbook normally consists of 16 individual worksheets, but you can add more.

Workbooks are great organizational tools. For example, you can keep together in the same workbook all the documents that relate to a specific project or all the documents maintained by an individual. Workbooks can eliminate a considerable amount of clutter on your hard drive, as well as reduce the number of steps necessary to set up your workspace each day. The more documents you have to manage, the more valuable workbooks become.

You can use workbooks as a multiuser management tool. For example, you can organize documents in discrete groups for individual tasks or individual users.

You can also share a workbook so that more than one person can work on it at the same time. See "Sharing Files with Others," page 75.

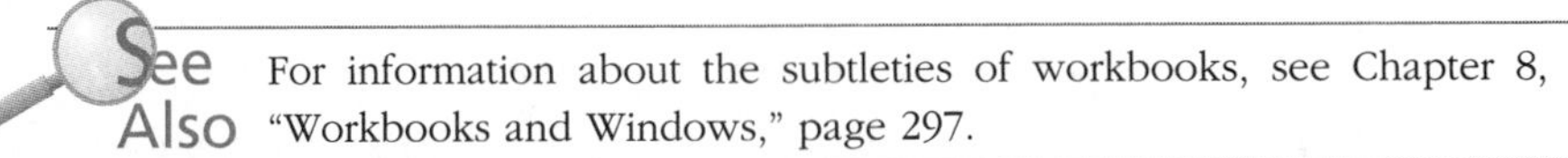

See Also For information about the subtleties of workbooks, see Chapter 8, "Workbooks and Windows," page 297.

Navigating in a Workbook

At the bottom of the workbook window are a number of controls that you can use to move from sheet to sheet in a workbook. Figure 1-3 shows these navigational controls.

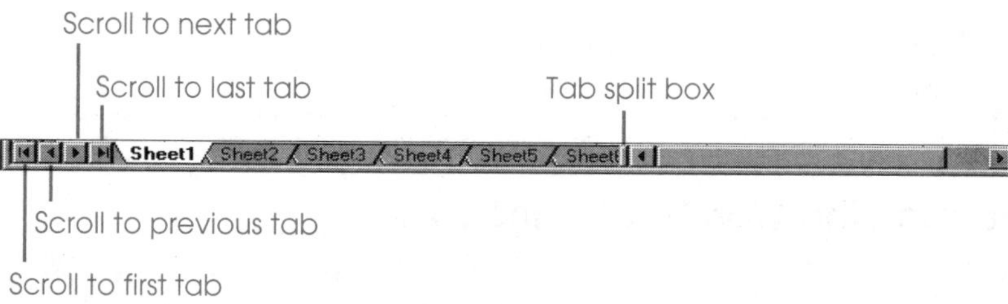

FIGURE 1-3
The workbook navigational controls.

You use the four *tab scrolling buttons* in the lower left corner to scroll through the sheet tabs in your workbook, allowing you to view the workbook's contents. The two tab scrolling buttons in the middle scroll the tabs one sheet at a time in the indicated direction. The two outermost tab scrolling buttons scroll directly to the first or last tab in the workbook. You can drag the *tab split box* to change the number of sheet tabs displayed. To reset the tab display, simply double-click the tab split box.

These tab scrolling buttons and the tab split box do not activate the sheets, however. To do so, you must click the tab of the sheet you want to activate after you have scrolled to the sheet using the tab scrolling buttons. For example, to activate Sheet4, click the tab labeled *Sheet4,* as shown in Figure 1-4.

You can also use the keyboard to move from sheet to sheet in a workbook. Press Ctrl-PgUp to move to the previous sheet in the workbook and Ctrl-PgDn to move to the next sheet.

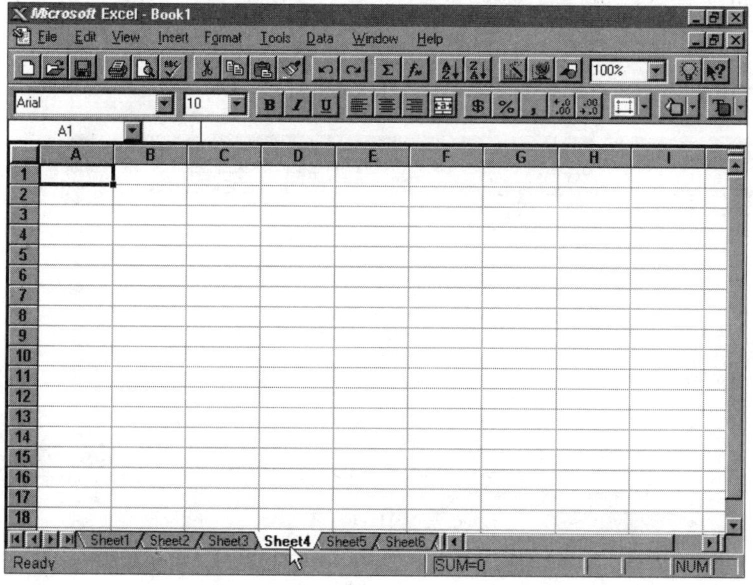

FIGURE 1-4
When you click a tab, you activate the corresponding sheet.

For more information about using workbooks, see Chapter 8, "Workbooks and Windows," page 297.

Resizing the Workbook Window

At the right end of the workbook window's title bar in Figure 1-2, you'll notice three buttons. These are the *Minimize, Maximize,* and *Close buttons.* When your workbook window is maximized, the active window is displayed at full size in the Excel workspace, as shown in Figure 1-4.

After you maximize the window, a button with two small boxes — the *Restore button* — appears in the menu bar. When you click the Restore button, the window changes to a "floating" window, as shown in Figure 1-5.

When you click the Minimize button (the one with a small line at the bottom), the workbook collapses to what looks like a small title bar, as shown in Figure 1-6. Minimizing workbooks is a handy way to reduce workspace clutter when you have several workbooks open at the same time. Click the Restore button on the bar to redisplay the workbook at its former size.

As you can see in Figure 1-4, these three buttons also appear at the top of the screen in the Microsoft Excel title bar. They resize the Excel application window in the same ways.

You can also drag the window borders to control the size of the workbook window. The smaller the window, the less you see of the worksheet; however, because you can open multiple windows for the same workbook,

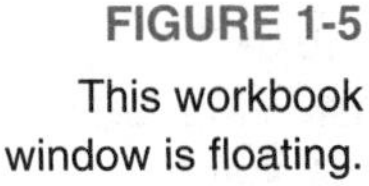
FIGURE 1-5
This workbook window is floating.

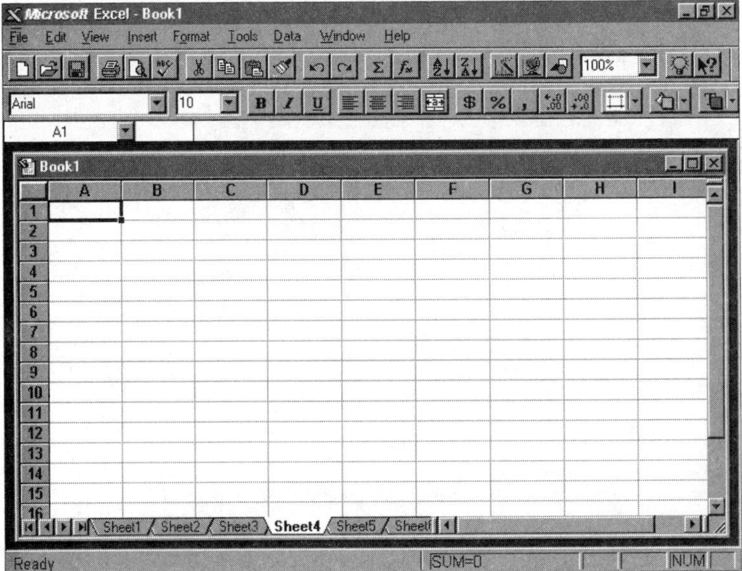

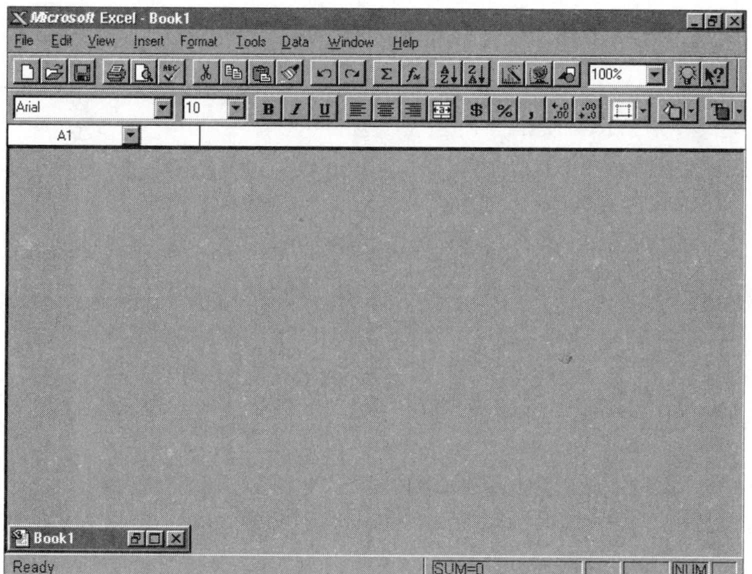

FIGURE 1-6
This workbook window is minimized.

you might find it more convenient to view different parts of the workbook, or even of an individual worksheet, side by side in two small windows rather than to switch between sheets or scroll back and forth in one large window.

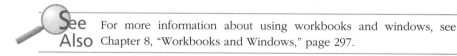

TIP Want to see more rows on your screen? The Windows 95 taskbar at the bottom of the screen can be set to automatically hide itself when not in use. Click the taskbar's Start button, then choose Settings, Taskbar. On the Taskbar Options tab, click the Auto Hide check box, then click OK. Now the taskbar stays hidden and pops up only when you drag the mouse pointer to the bottom of the screen.

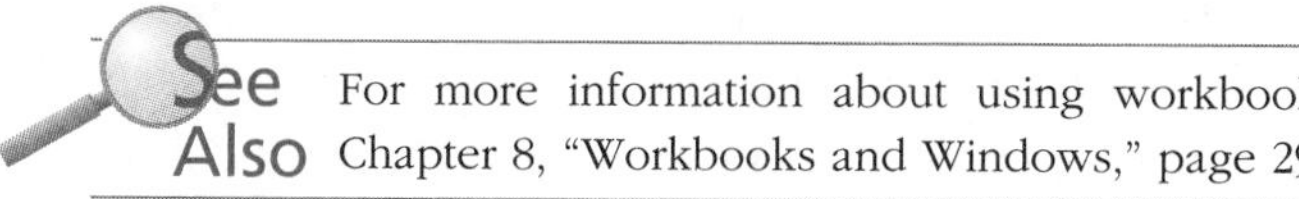

For more information about using workbooks and windows, see Chapter 8, "Workbooks and Windows," page 297.

The Title Bar

At the top of the Excel workspace is the *title bar,* which displays the application name along with the name of the workbook in which you are currently working. When you load Excel, the title bar displays *Microsoft Excel—Book1* unless you start Excel by opening a previously saved workbook.

If your worksheet is floating, as in Figure 1-5, the title (here, *Book1*) appears at the top of the workbook window. When you open additional windows and display workbooks in them, the names of the workbooks in those windows are displayed in their respective title bars.

The title bar of the window in which you are working is displayed in a solid color, indicating that the window is active. You can reposition the active window on your screen by dragging its title bar.

The Worksheet

Like a traditional accounting ledger, a *worksheet* (also referred to as a *sheet* in Parts 1 and 2 of this book) is divided into a grid of columns and rows. A letter is assigned to each column and appears as a column heading above the worksheet grid. The column letters range from A through IV. (After column Z comes column AA, after AZ comes BA, and so on, up to IV.) A number is assigned to each row and appears as a row heading to the left of the worksheet grid. The row numbers range from 1 through 16,384.

At the intersection of each column and row is a *cell*. Cells are the basic building blocks of every worksheet. Each cell occupies a unique location on the worksheet where you can store and display information, and each cell is assigned a unique set of coordinates, called the *cell reference*. For example, the cell at the intersection of column A and row 1 has the cell reference A1. The cell at the intersection of column Z and row 100 has the cell reference Z100. The currently selected cell is referred to as the *active cell*. The cell reference for the active cell appears at the left end of the formula bar in the *Name box*.

Looking at Your Data Through Windows

The workbook window is like a porthole through which you can see only a limited portion of the worksheet.

To illustrate, suppose you were to cut a small, square hole in a piece of cardboard and then place the cardboard over this page. At any given time, you could see only a portion of the page through the hole. By moving the cardboard around on the page, however, you could eventually read the entire page through the "window" in your piece of cardboard.

Viewing worksheets in Excel is much the same, except that you move around the worksheet to see different sections of it in the window. You can also open another window to view different sections of the same worksheet simultaneously. For more information about windows, see Chapter 8, "Workbooks and Windows," page 297

With 256 columns and 16,384 rows, your worksheet contains more than 4 million individual cells. Before you try to unravel the mysteries of the universe on a single worksheet, however, remember that the number of cells you can use at any one time is limited by the amount of memory your computer has. Although Excel allocates memory only to cells containing data, you probably won't be able to use all the cells in one worksheet.

The Scroll Bars

To change your view of the worksheet, you can use the *scroll bars* along the right and bottom sides of the workbook window to move around the worksheet. Only the active workbook window — the one you are currently working in — has scroll bars.

Talking Scroll Bars

The scroll bars in Excel 7 for Windows 95 work a little differently than in previous versions. The size of the scroll box (sometimes called the "thumb") changes depending on the size of the scrollable area. For example, the scroll boxes shown in Figure 1-2 on page 6 are nearly as large as the scroll bars themselves, indicating that there is little more to see in the active area of the workbook — nothing, in fact, because this is a blank workbook. As you add data to more rows and columns than can be displayed on a single screen, the scroll boxes get proportionally smaller, as shown here, giving you immediate feedback about the size of the worksheet.

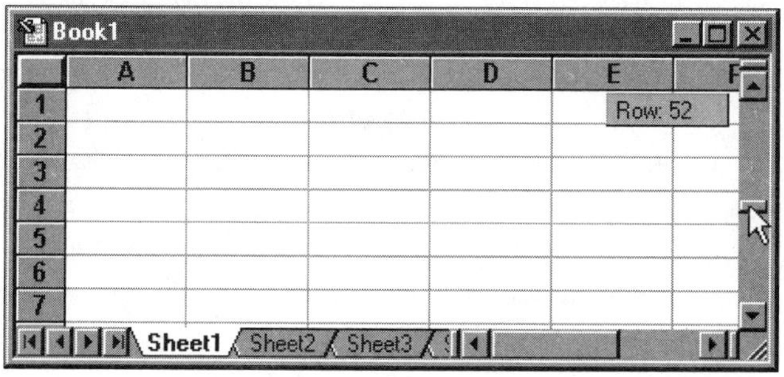

In addition, when you click a scroll box, a small *screen tip* box appears, as shown above. This box displays the name of the row or column that will appear in the upper-right corner of the window when you release the mouse button. You can use these screen tips to help position the scroll box more precisely.

The *scroll arrows* at either end of the scroll bars allow you to move through the worksheet one row or column at a time. Clicking the up or down arrow in the vertical scroll bar has the effect of scrolling the sheet up or down one row at a time. Similarly, clicking the right or left arrow in the horizontal scroll bar has the effect of scrolling the worksheet to the right or left one column at a time.

To move a long way through the worksheet, you can drag the *scroll boxes* in the scroll bars to positions that correspond to the position of the window over the worksheet. To move a new screenful of information into view, click the shaded area of the scroll bar. Note that the Name box at the left end of the formula bar always displays the active cell reference, regardless of where you scroll the window.

Scrolling Beyond the Active Area The *active area* of a worksheet is the area that contains the data you've entered. In a new worksheet, Excel considers the default active area as roughly columns A through J and rows 1 through 20 even before you enter any data. For example, if you drag the scroll box to the bottom of the vertical scroll bar in a new worksheet, the worksheet scrolls to approximately row 20, depending on the type of display you're using. To move beyond the active area of the worksheet, you have several methods at your disposal. In very large worksheets, you can quickly scroll distant columns or rows into view by pressing Shift while you drag. For example, by holding down Shift and dragging to the right end of the horizontal scroll bar, you can bring the last column of the worksheet — column IV — into view. Similarly, holding down Shift and dragging to the bottom of the vertical scroll bar allows you to bring row 16,384 into view. Because this method scrolls the worksheet quickly, keep a close eye on the column or row reference in the screen tip box as you scroll.

TIP As you scroll the worksheet, you might lose sight of the active cell. To quickly bring the active cell back into view, press Ctrl-Backspace or type an entry for that cell. You can press one of the direction keys to simultaneously move to an adjacent cell and bring the active cell into view.

Scrolling with the Keyboard The direction keys let you scroll up, down, left, and right, one column or row at a time; the PgUp and PgDn keys let you move a new screenful of data into view. Scrolling with the keyboard relocates the active cell. To scroll the worksheet without changing the active cell, press Scroll

Lock and then press a direction, PgUp, or PgDn key. For example, to scroll up or down one row at a time without moving the active cell, press Scroll Lock and then press the Up or Down direction key. To scroll left or right a screenful at a time, press Scroll Lock and then press Ctrl-PgUp to move left or Ctrl-PgDn to move right.

The Menu Bar

At the top of the Excel workspace is the *menu bar*. Here, you select Excel commands to manipulate the information you have entered in your worksheet. Excel's menu bar has nine menus: File, Edit, View, Insert, Format, Tools, Data, Window, and Help. You display Excel's menus the same way you display those of any Windows-based program: Point to the menu you want to use and click the mouse button.

When you display a menu, some commands are displayed in black, while others might be displayed in gray, or dimmed. Excel monitors the status of your worksheet and allows you to choose only those commands that are applicable at any given time. The black commands are available for use; the dimmed commands are unavailable.

Some commands on the menus have an arrow after them, indicating that a list of additional commands, called a *submenu,* is available for each of those commands, as shown in Figure 1-7.

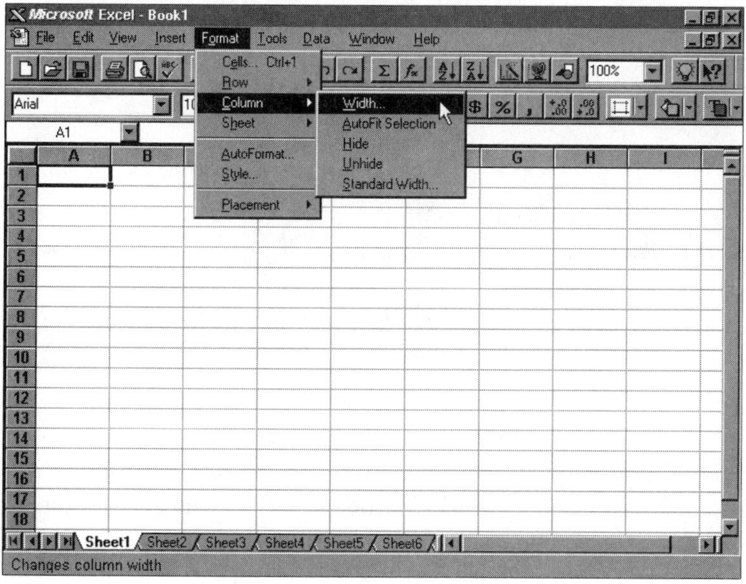

FIGURE 1-7
When you choose a command with an arrow next to it, a submenu is displayed.

Dialog Boxes and Tab Dialog Boxes

Some commands have an ellipsis (...) after them, indicating that you must supply more information before Excel can carry out the command. You supply this information in a *dialog box*. For example, Figure 1-8 shows the dialog box that appears when you choose the Delete command from the Edit menu.

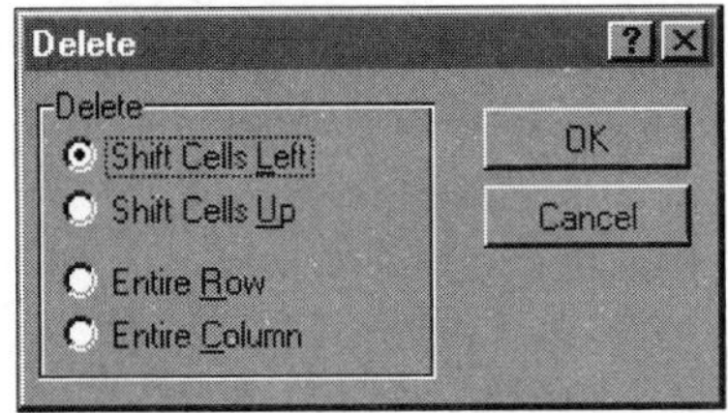

FIGURE 1-8
Menu commands followed by an ellipsis (...) display a dialog box to prompt you for more information.

Some commands are more universal in nature. For these commands, Excel provides *tab dialog boxes,* which present several unique sets of options for the same command. Figure 1-9 shows the tab dialog box that appears when you choose the Options command from the Tools menu.

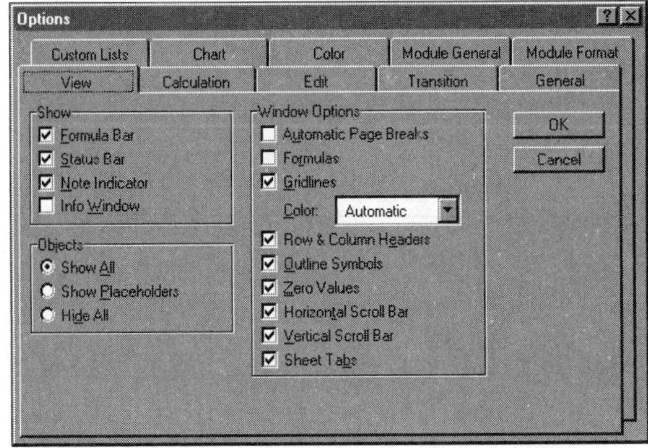

FIGURE 1-9
Some commands display tab dialog boxes, which provide two or more sets of options for the corresponding command.

To activate a set of options in a tab dialog box, click the name of the tab you want to use. You can specify settings in one tab and then click another tab to set more options.

When you are finished with a dialog box or a tab dialog box, click OK or press Enter to activate the settings and options you specified. If you change your mind, click Cancel or press Esc to cancel the settings and options.

The Options Dialog Box

The tab dialog box that appears when you choose the Options command from the Tools menu is probably the most important dialog box of all. As you can see in Figure 1-9, the Options dialog box contains 10 tabs that control nearly every aspect of Excel, including general settings such as how many worksheets appear in a default workbook and the name and point size of the default font. The Options dialog box also provides special settings for charts, Lotus 1-2-3 transition, and macro modules, among others. If you take a moment to click each tab and look through the options available in this dialog box, you'll get an idea of the scope of the program as well as the degree of control you have over your workspace. If you're unsure about what a particular setting or option does, simply click the Help button (the question mark) in the title bar, and then click the setting or option to display information about it.

Choosing Commands with the Keyboard

Some commands on Excel's menus are followed by their keyboard equivalents. For example, notice the keyboard equivalents following the commands on the Edit menu shown in Figure 1-10. These key combinations allow you to choose a command without first displaying an Excel menu. In other words, to choose the Copy command, you can simply press Ctrl-C.

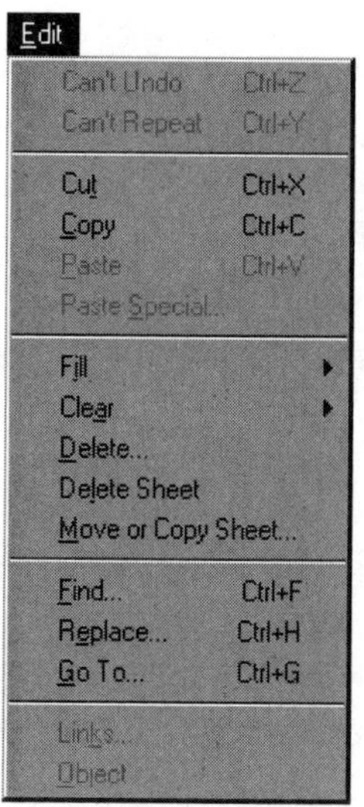

FIGURE 1-10
Use the keyboard equivalents displayed to the right of command names to choose a command without displaying the menu.

Accessing the Menu Bar Using the Keyboard

Sometimes you might find it more convenient to choose commands from menus using the keyboard instead of the mouse. Pressing the Alt key or the slash (/) key — the default Microsoft Excel Menu or Help key — lets you display the menus using the keyboard. When you press either key, Excel activates the menu bar. Pressing the Down direction key or Enter displays the Window Control menu. Pressing the Right direction key highlights the next menu to the right, the File menu. Repeatedly pressing the Right or Left direction key displays each menu in turn. When the menu you need is highlighted, press the Down direction key or Enter to display it, press the Down direction key to highlight the desired command, and then press Enter to choose the command.

For example, to use the keyboard to choose the Options command from the Tools menu, press the slash key, press the Right direction key six times to highlight Tools in the menu bar, press the Down direction key to display the menu, and continue to press the Down direction key until the Options command is highlighted. To choose the command and display the Options dialog box, press Enter.

You might have also noticed the underlined letter in each of the menu names on the menu bar. The underlined letter designates the letter key you can press to display that particular menu, as an alternative to using the direction keys. For example, after you press the slash key to activate the menu bar, you can press the T key to display the Tools menu. Then, to choose a particular command such as Options, press the O key — the underlined letter in *Options* — to display the Options dialog box.

TIP Instead of pressing the slash key to activate the menu bar, you can also press the Alt key along with the underlined letter to display a menu. Then, with the menu displayed, type the underlined letter of the command you want.

The Microsoft Excel Menu Or Help Key Option

If you prefer, you can assign the slash key's menu-accessing function to another key. From the Tools menu, simply choose Options and click the Transition tab. Then type the key you want to use in the Microsoft Excel Menu Or Help Key edit box and click OK. (Don't use a key that you will use in a worksheet, such as A or 2.) The new key allows you to access the menu bar, just as the slash key did before you replaced it.

Shortcut Menus

Shortcut menus contain only those commands that apply to the item indicated by the position of the mouse pointer when you activate the menu. Shortcut menus provide a handy way to access the commands you need with a minimum of mouse movement. Excel has many shortcut menus, each offering the commands most likely to be useful at the pointer's current location.

You access a shortcut menu by clicking the right mouse button. The shortcut menu pops up adjacent to the mouse pointer, as shown in Figure 1-11, which shows the shortcut menu that appears when you click a column heading with the right mouse button. You choose the command you want with the mouse or keyboard just as you would choose a command from a regular menu.

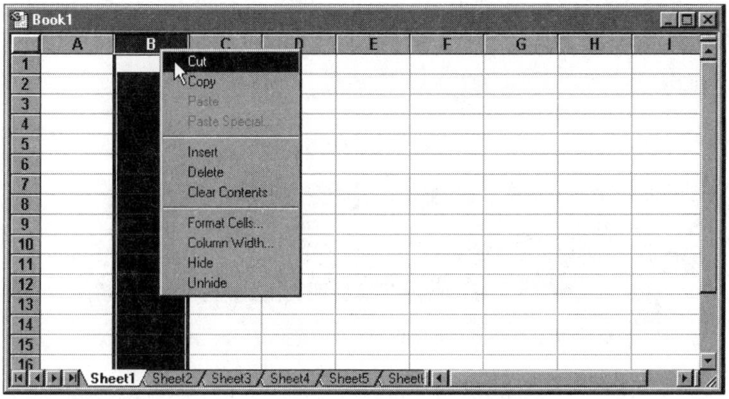

FIGURE 1-11
Clicking the right mouse button activates a shortcut menu.

The shortcut menu can contain many combinations of commands, depending on the position of the pointer and what type of sheet you are working on. For example, if you display a shortcut menu when the pointer is over a cell, a menu like the one shown in Figure 1-12 appears.

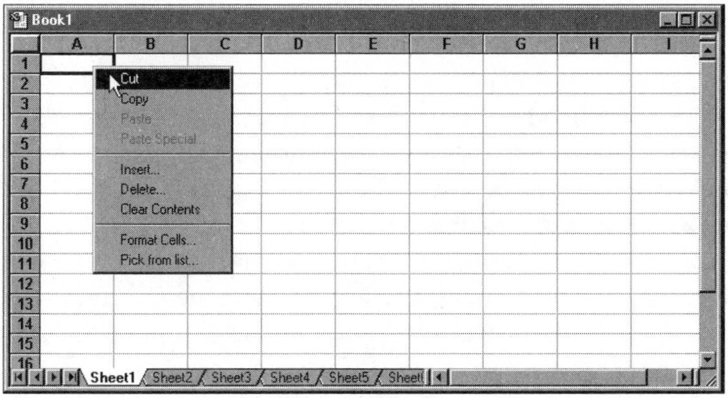

FIGURE 1-12
This shortcut menu appears when you click the right mouse button while the pointer is over a cell.

TIP Press Shift-F10 to display a shortcut menu for the selected item. The shortcut menu appears on the left side of the workbook window. For example, if you press Shift-F10 when a cell or range of cells is selected, the shortcut menu shown in Figure 1-12 appears.

The Formula Bar

We mentioned earlier that worksheet cells are Excel's building blocks. They store and display the information you enter in an Excel worksheet and allow you to perform worksheet calculations. You can enter information directly in a cell on the worksheet, or you can enter information through the *formula bar*. The contents of the active cell always appear in the formula bar, as shown in Figure 1-13.

FIGURE 1-13
The formula bar displays the contents of the active cell.

Although you can enter information directly in a cell, using the formula bar has some advantages. If you move the pointer into the formula bar and click, three buttons appear in the formula bar, as shown in Figure 1-13. The button containing the *X* is called the *Cancel button,* and the button containing the check mark is called the *Enter button*. When you click the Enter button, Excel "locks in" the information you have typed in the formula bar and transfers that information to your worksheet. Clicking the Enter button is similar to pressing the Enter key except that pressing Enter activates the cell directly below the one in which you entered the data. If you make a mistake while typing, clicking the Cancel button tells Excel to delete what you have typed. Clicking the Cancel button is similar to pressing the Esc key.

The third button is called the *Function Wizard button*. When you click this button, the Function Wizard dialog box appears, allowing you to insert any of Excel's built-in worksheet functions in the active cell.

At the left end of the formula bar is the Name box. In Figure 1-13, the Name box displays the reference A1, which tells you that cell A1 is active and that any information you type in the formula bar will be transferred to that cell. When the formula bar is inactive and you click the arrow to the right of the Name box, a drop-down list appears, displaying any names defined for the current workbook.

TIP By default, Excel displays the formula bar in your workspace. If you prefer to hide the formula bar, you can choose the Formula Bar command from the View menu. To redisplay the formula bar, simply repeat this process.

See Also For information about names and the Function Wizard, see Chapter 5, "Building Formulas," page 111.

The Status Bar

The *status bar* displays the condition of your workspace. For example, most of the time, Excel displays the word *Ready* at the left end of the status bar, meaning that the worksheet is ready to accept new information. As you type new information, Excel displays the word *Edit* in the status bar. To return to Ready mode, you need to "lock in" the information you just typed by clicking the Enter button or pressing Enter on the keyboard.

Another function of the status bar is to let you know what a highlighted menu, command, or toolbar button does, as shown in Figure 1-14 on the next page. As you scroll through the commands on a menu, you'll notice a brief description of each command in the status bar. This feature is helpful if you forget the function of a command that you use infrequently. Also, when you move the mouse pointer over a toolbar button, a short description of the button's functionality appears in the status bar.

TIP Excel displays the status bar by default. If you want to hide it, choose the Status Bar command on the View menu. To redisplay the status bar, simply choose this command again.

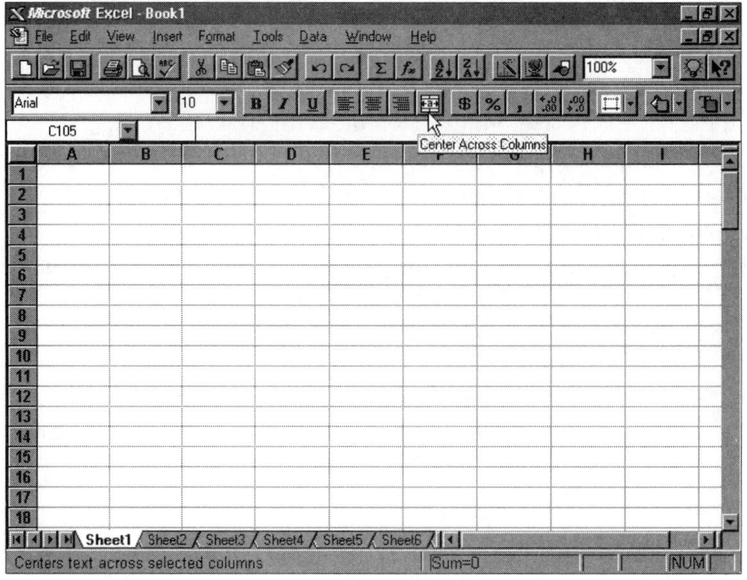

FIGURE 1-14 The status bar displays a brief description of the selected menu, command, or toolbar button.

The boxes at the right end of the status bar display various keyboard modes that you can turn on or off. For example, CAPS appears in this area of the status bar when you press the Caps Lock key. When you press the Num Lock key to activate the numeric keypad (to use it for numeric entry rather than navigation), NUM appears in this area of the status bar.

What Does SUM=0 Mean?

When a blank cell is selected, "SUM=0" appears toward the right side of the status bar. This is the new AutoCalculate feature, which instantly displays the total of the currently selected cells — in this case, a blank cell. The AutoCalculate area of the status bar normally displays the sum of the selected values, but if you click the right mouse button over the area, as shown in the following illustration, you can also get an average of the selected values, a count of the number of selected nonblank cells, a count of selected cells that contain only numbers, or the minimum or maximum value in the selection.

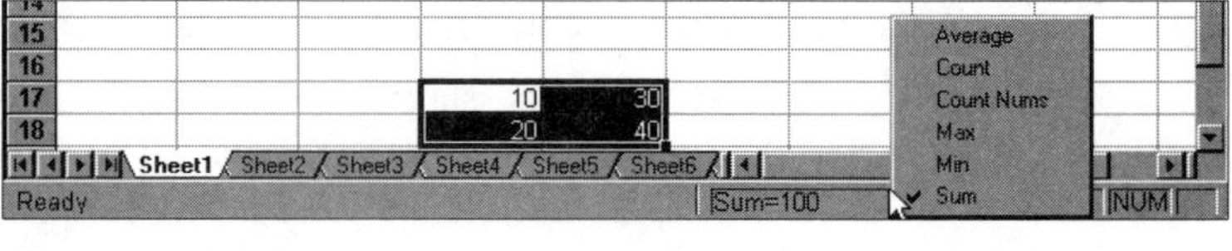

For more information about keyboard modes, see the sidebar titled "Keyboard Modes," page 89.

The Pointer

You should already be familiar with the basic technique of using the mouse to move the pointer around the screen. In Excel, the pointer serves different functions in different areas of the worksheet.

When you move the pointer to the menu bar, the pointer appears as an arrow so that you can point to the command you want. When you move the pointer to the formula bar, the pointer's shape changes to an I-beam. When you see the I-beam, you click to set an insertion point where you want to edit or enter information in your worksheet.

When you move your pointer over the worksheet grid, the pointer's shape changes to a plus sign. If you move the plus sign over cell C5 and click the mouse button, a border appears around the cell and the Name box at the left end of the formula bar displays the cell reference C5, indicating that you have selected this cell.

You'll see the pointer take on other shapes as you begin using it to manipulate the worksheet and its window. We explain the different functions of the pointer in subsequent chapters as we address various worksheet operations.

Getting Help

While you are using Microsoft Excel, help is never more than a moment away. If you become confused, forget what a particular command does, or even if you need some general guidance, you can get assistance by choosing commands from the Help menu. The Help menu commands include Microsoft Excel Help Topics, Answer Wizard, The Microsoft Network, Lotus 1-2-3 Help, and About Microsoft Excel. You can also activate the Help system by pressing the F1 key.

Navigating Through the Help System

When you choose the Microsoft Excel Help Topics command from the Help menu, a Microsoft Excel Help window like the one in Figure 1-15 (on the next page) appears, showing the general organization of Help.

FIGURE 1-15
The Microsoft Excel Help window shows the Contents tab by default.

The new Help dialog box has four tabs that you use in different ways to get the information you need: Contents, Index, Find, and Answer Wizard. The Contents tab is similar to the table of contents in a book. When you activate the Contents tab, each "chapter" is represented by a title next to a small closed-book icon, as shown in Figure 1-15.

Double-click one of the titles to display more detail under that heading, as shown at the bottom of Figure 1-16.

If you find a topic that interests you, double-click it to display it. You can never be sure exactly what type of topic you'll get. Sometimes it will be a topic containing numbered step-by-step procedures. Sometimes you'll see a large graphic "card" with a visual example. Occasionally you'll get a "ghosted" procedure where instructions appear in floating yellow notes telling you each step along the way. And other times you'll see a simple topic like the one shown in Figure 1-17. The Help system is set up so that you don't need to worry about the form of help you'll get — the most appropriate approach is automatically used, depending on the nature of the topic.

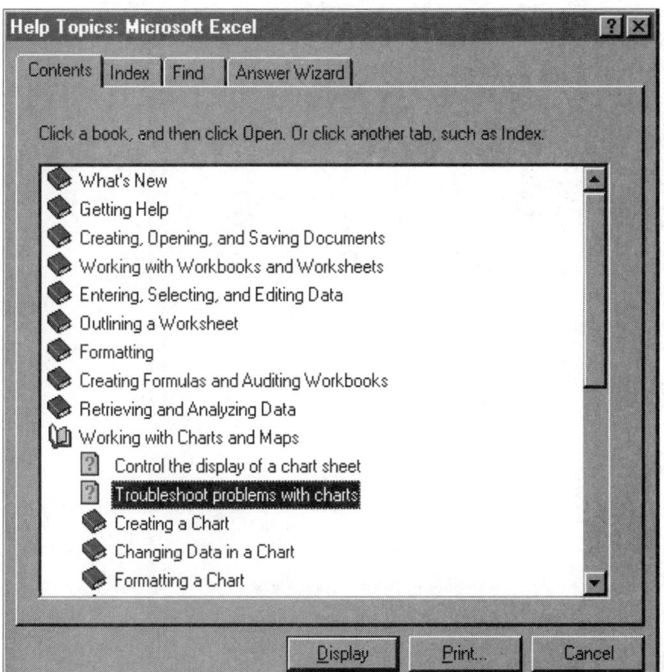

FIGURE 1-16

Double-click a heading to display subordinate headings and topics.

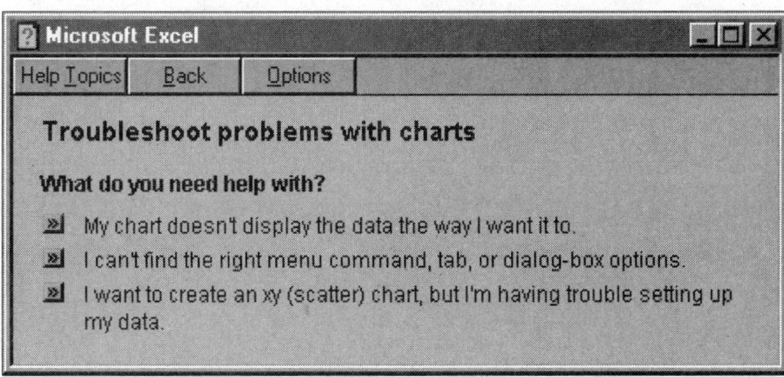

FIGURE 1-17

Help topics often contain pointers to other topics.

If the Contents tab doesn't suit your fancy, try the Find tab or the Index tab. The Help index is much like that of a book. Type a keyword about the subject you need help with, and the index list snaps to the corresponding alphabetic index location, as shown in Figure 1-18 on the next page. Again, double-clicking the topic name displays the corresponding Help topic.

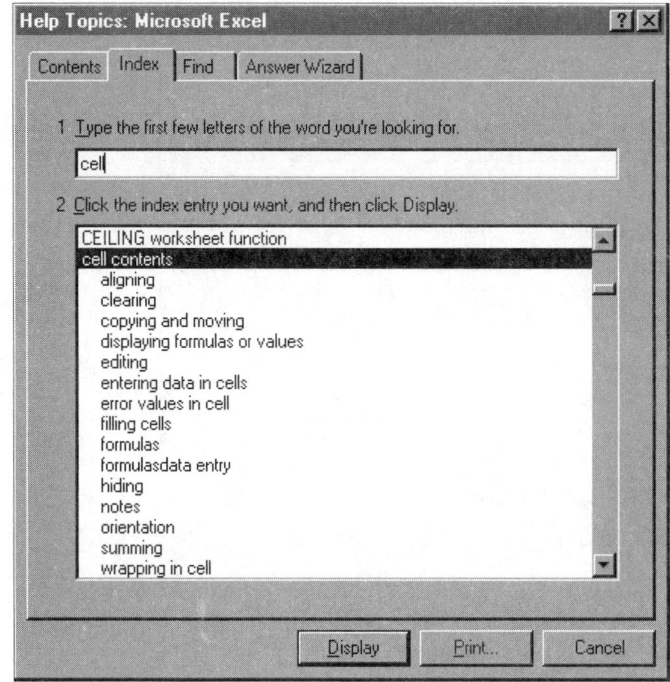

FIGURE 1-18 Type a word in the box at the top of the Index tab to display index entries quickly.

You also use keywords on the Find tab, but here you see a list of all topics in Help that contain the words you type. For example, typing "cell" in the Find tab yields over 900 topics! Adding the word "reference" narrows it down to a mere 200 entries, as shown in Figure 1-19. Click the Options button to add criteria that can help narrow your search. The Files button displays a dialog box you can use to narrow your search a bit more by specifying Help files to look in. For example, select only the Visual Basic Reference if you're looking for some help with macro programming.

The Answer Wizard

The last tab in the Help Topics dialog box represents the latest in online help technology. (It's so new and innovative that Microsoft has a patent pending.) The Answer Wizard allows you to enter questions in full or partial sentences, using natural language, just as if you were talking to the Excel guru down the hall. The Wizard then takes your question and, based on key words, juxtaposition of words, and verbs used, returns a list of topics that is generated by a sophisticated system of probabilities built into the Wizard. It is complicated, but only *under* the surface. Using the Wizard is simplicity itself — just type in a question, like the one shown in Figure 1-20.

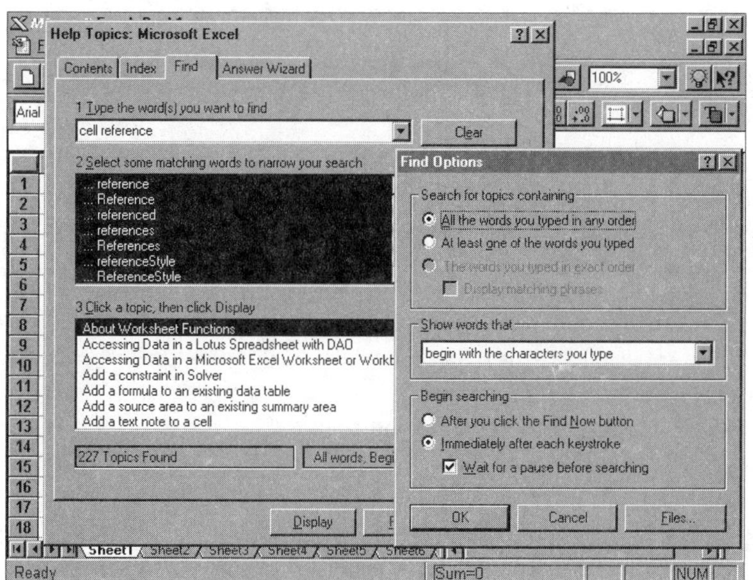

FIGURE 1-19

Use the Find tab to search for occurrences of a word or phrase anywhere in the Help system.

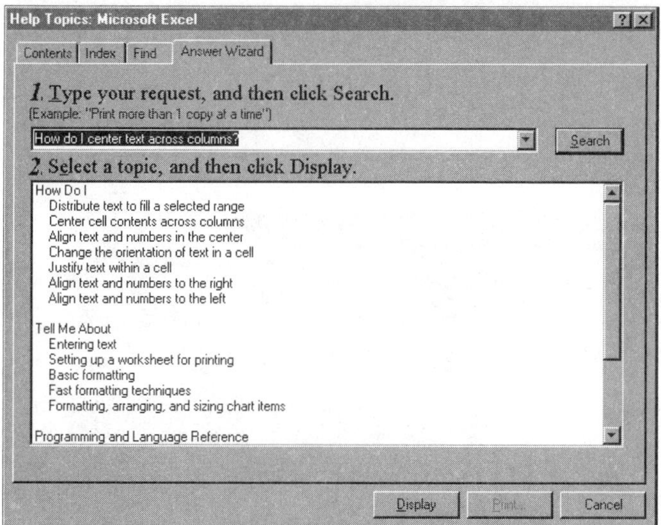

FIGURE 1-20

Using the Answer Wizard tab, you can ask questions in plain English.

When you ask a question, the Wizard finds up to seven likely topics in each of three categories: "How Do I," which lists procedural topics; "Tell Me About," which contains reference and conceptual topics; and "Programming and Language Reference," which lists topics dealing specifically with the macro programming aspects of your question. If the topic list doesn't return exactly what you're looking for, try rephrasing the question using a different word or two.

TIP You can go directly to the Answer Wizard tab by choosing the Answer Wizard command on the Help menu.

Using Help Procedures

In the "How Do I" section of the Answer Wizard tab shown in Figure 1-20, there is a topic named "Justify text within a cell." In this case, double-clicking the topic name displays step-by-step instructions for that topic in a special Help window, as shown in Figure 1-21.

This Help procedure window includes an Options button. When you click this button and choose the Keep Help On Top command and then choose On Top, the Help procedure window remains open even when you return to the workbook. This lets you follow the numbered steps while you work. To return to the workbook, click anywhere in the workbook. If you choose the On Top command, the Help procedure window remains visible. The result is shown in Figure 1-21.

As you choose commands and enter data in Excel, the Help procedure window remains visible. You can resize the window, drag the title bar to move the window out of the way, and choose commands on the Options menu to copy and print the instructions. Click the Close button to close the Help procedure window when you are finished.

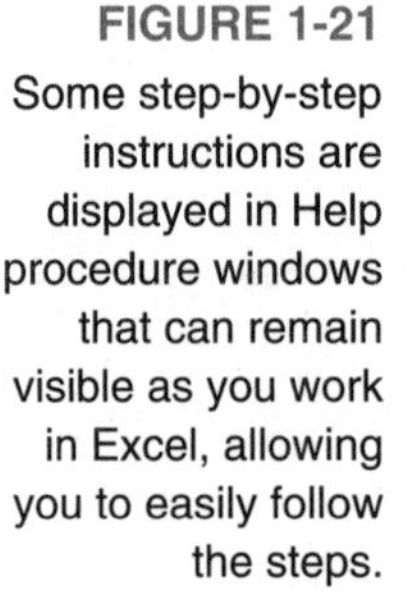

FIGURE 1-21
Some step-by-step instructions are displayed in Help procedure windows that can remain visible as you work in Excel, allowing you to easily follow the steps.

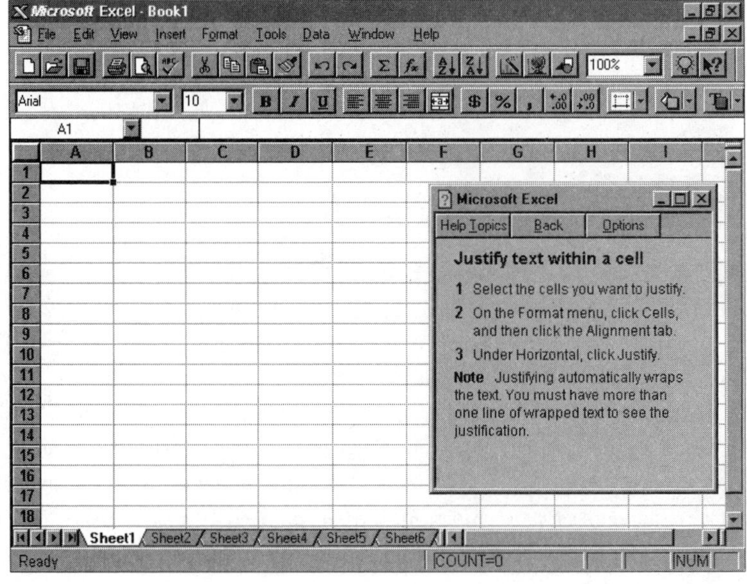

> **Before You Call Product Support**
>
> We encourage you to use the Excel documentation, the online Help system, and this book to find the answers to your questions before you reach for your telephone. Also read through the new appendix, "Troubleshooting Tips from Microsoft Product Support Services," on page 955. When you have exhausted these resources, it's time to call Microsoft Product Support. But before you do, choose About Microsoft Excel from the Help menu and click the System Info button. Doing so displays a dialog box that lists your computer's current system configuration, the applications running, display information, and much more. If you want, you can print the information in a report. When you talk to Product Support, having this information at your fingertips will assist the representative in diagnosing your problem and will save you both

Help for Lotus 1-2-3 Users

The Lotus 1-2-3 Help command on the Help menu eases the transition of Lotus 1-2-3 users to Excel. When you choose this command, Excel displays a dialog box in which you can type the key sequence you would use to choose a particular command in Lotus 1-2-3, as shown in Figure 1-22.

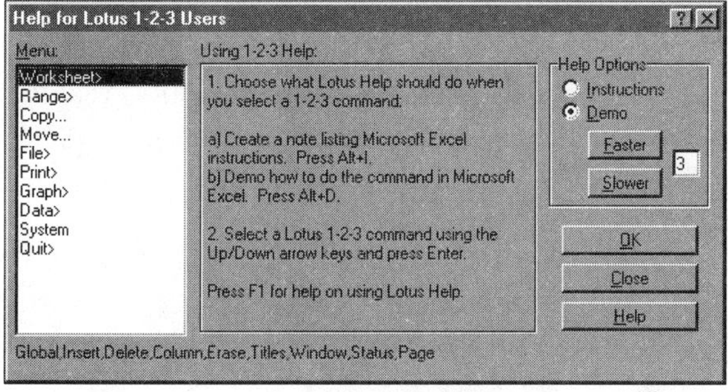

FIGURE 1-22
The Lotus 1-2-3 command displays the Help for Lotus 1-2-3 Users dialog box.

Getting Context-Sensitive Help

Excel also allows you to ask for information about a command without using the Help menu. Simply click the Help button (the arrow with a question mark) on the Standard toolbar (see Chapter 2, "Toolbars and Buttons," for information about toolbars), and use the question mark pointer shown in Figure 1-23 to choose a command or click an object about which you want help. Excel then displays the Help topic that applies to the selected command or object. This

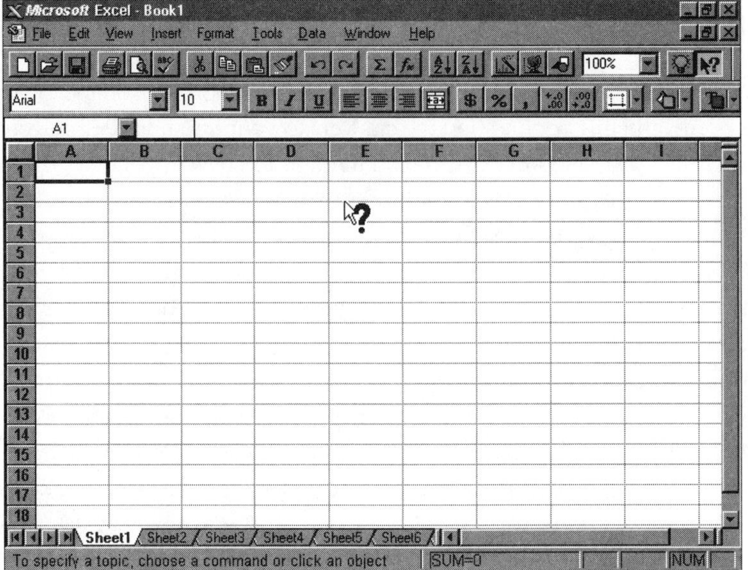

FIGURE 1-23 When you click the Help button on the Standard toolbar, the question mark pointer lets you access context-sensitive help.

type of help is called *context-sensitive* help because it relates to what you are actually doing in the worksheet.

For example, suppose you want to erase the contents of a group of cells. You think you need to use the Clear command, but you're not sure. To display information about the Clear command in a Help window, click the Help button on the Standard toolbar, pull down the Edit menu, choose Clear, and click All.

Dialog-Box Help

You can click the Question Mark button that is present in most dialog boxes and tab dialog boxes to display a question-mark cursor similar to the one in Figure 1-23. Then click an option or area in the dialog box to display a tip for that item, as shown in Figure 1-24.

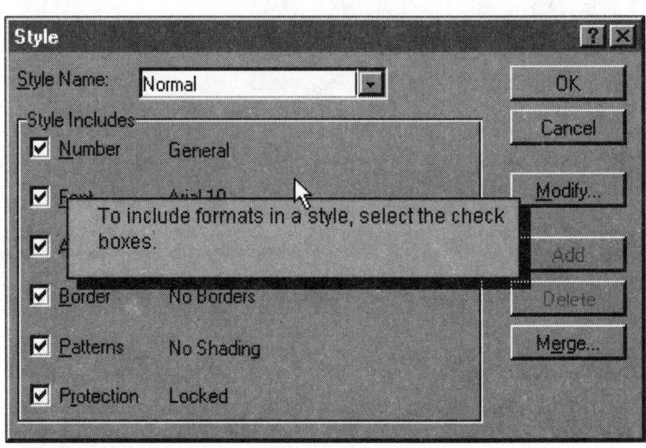

FIGURE 1-24 Click the Question Mark button in the dialog box title bar, and then click the item you want help on.

Accessing Tips and Tricks with the TipWizard

Microsoft Excel provides so many options and shortcuts that you might at times wonder if you're missing out on a tip or trick that would save you time. Well, you probably are, which is why the *TipWizard* was created. The TipWizard notifies you when an alternative, and better, way to perform a particular task exists.

The TipWizard monitors your work habits, and when it has a suggestion for you, the TipWizard button on the Standard toolbar (the button with a light bulb on it) "lights up." You can click the TipWizard button to display the TipWizard toolbar, which contains a brief but helpful hint.

TIP The TipWizard keeps track of the tips that it has displayed during the current session. Once a tip has been offered, the Wizard will not display it again. You can reset the TipWizard so that it displays all the tips. To do so, choose Options from the Tools menu, click the General tab, and select Reset TipWizard.

For example, select a cell and then choose the Copy command from the Edit menu. Immediately the light bulb on the TipWizard button becomes yellow, if it is not already. (On a monochrome display, a question mark appears inside the light bulb.) Click the button, and the TipWizard toolbar appears with your helpful hint displayed, as shown in Figure 1-25 on the next page.

To hide the TipWizard toolbar and conserve valuable screen space, click the TipWizard button on the Standard toolbar. As soon as another helpful hint becomes available, the TipWizard button lights up again. During an Excel session, your tips accumulate and are numbered as they appear in the TipWizard box. To browse through the tips, click the up and down arrow buttons to the right of the TipWizard box. If a tip involves a toolbar button, the button appears on the TipWizard toolbar. In Figure 1-25, the Copy button appears. This functional button remains until another tip involving a button appears, but you can redisplay it by using the arrow buttons.

Identifying Toolbar Buttons with ToolTips

For those of us who have trouble remembering what all those toolbar buttons do, Excel 7 provides ToolTips. With ToolTips activated, a descriptive label appears when you move the mouse pointer over a toolbar button, as shown in Figure 1-26. Toolbar buttons are also described in the message area of the status bar.

ToolTips are active by default. To deactivate them, choose Toolbars from the View menu and deselect Show ToolTips.

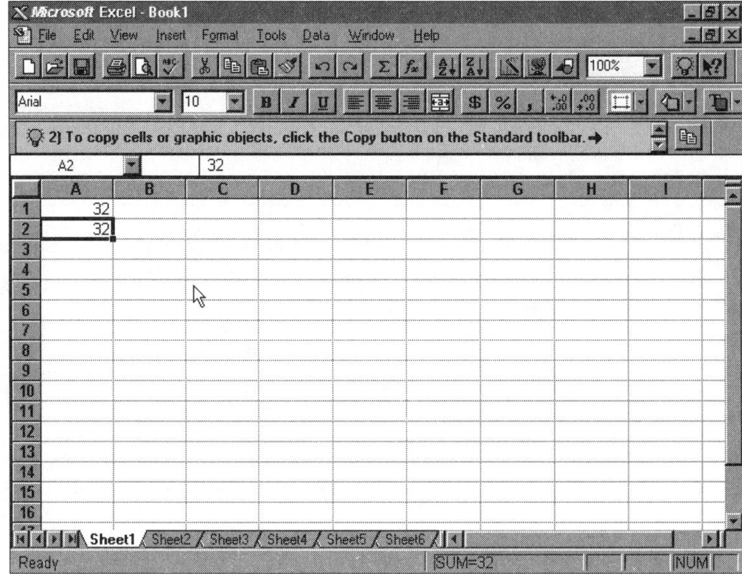

FIGURE 1-25
The TipWizard gives you helpful hints about better ways to perform certain tasks in Excel.

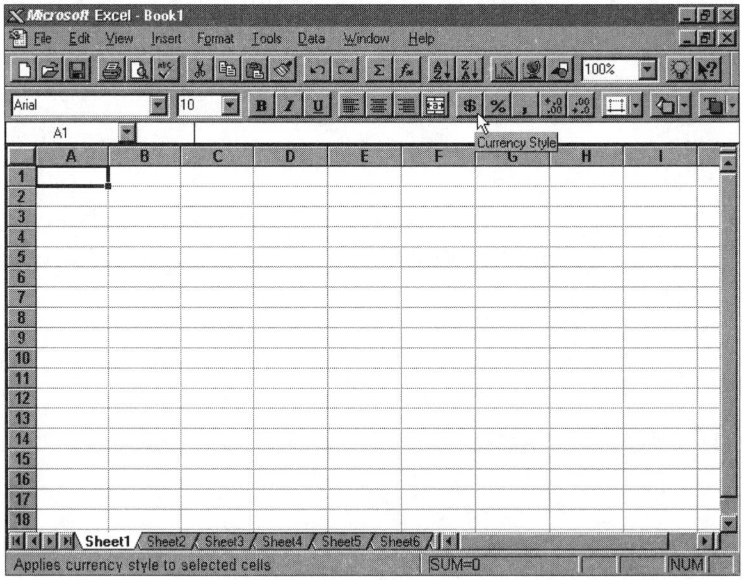

FIGURE 1-26
With ToolTips activated, a descriptive label appears when you move the mouse pointer over a toolbar button.

For information about toolbars, see Chapter 2, "Toolbars and Buttons," page 33.

Exiting Microsoft Excel

When you are finished with your Microsoft Excel session, choose the Exit command from the File menu or click the Close button. Excel asks if you want to save any changes you made to each open workbook. If you click Yes, you can specify a new filename for any unsaved workbook and then save it. If you click No, any changes you've made are lost when you exit Excel. Clicking the Cancel button cancels the Exit command and returns you to the program.

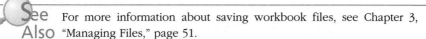

For more information about saving workbook files, see Chapter 3, "Managing Files," page 51.

Chapter 2

Toolbars and Buttons

When you first start Microsoft Excel, two toolbars are visible on the screen — the Standard and Formatting toolbars. These toolbars contain a lot of helpful buttons, but they are only the tip of the iceberg. Excel has many more toolbars, and you can place a staggering number of additional buttons on them. In this chapter, we'll show you how to use and create toolbars that fit your needs.

Introducing Toolbars

Microsoft Excel offers a smorgasbord of toolbars filled with buttons designed to simplify repetitive operations. You can build your own toolbars, choosing from over 200 predefined buttons or using buttons that you create yourself. In this chapter, we'll describe some of these buttons, explore the existing toolbars, and show you how to create and customize toolbars to suit your needs.

Excel gives you the option of displaying additional toolbars below the menu bar or in other locations in the workspace. Excel includes a number of built-in toolbars, which provide handy shortcuts for many common actions.

When you first start Excel, the Standard and Formatting toolbars are displayed. The Standard toolbar, shown in Figure 2-1, provides buttons that are useful in day-to-day operations. The Formatting toolbar includes buttons for formatting text, numbers, and cells.

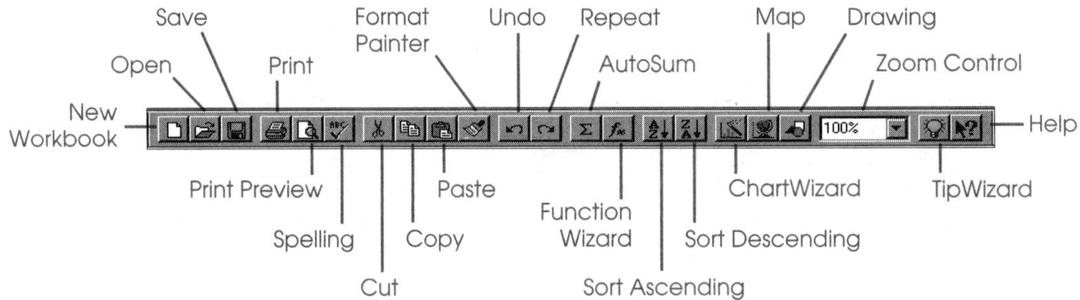

FIGURE 2-1

The Standard toolbar. Toolbars provide shortcuts for editing, formatting, drawing, charting, and other common activities.

Some of the other toolbars are displayed automatically when you need them. For example, Excel displays the Chart toolbar when you are working on a chart.

For information about the Formatting toolbar, see Chapter 6, "Formatting a Worksheet," page 155.

For more information about the Chart toolbar, see "Modifying an Embedded Chart," page 594.

Adding More Toolbars to Your Screen

You can display additional toolbars at any time, and you can have as many toolbars active as you want — at the expense of your worksheet's window size, of course. To activate another toolbar, choose Toolbars from the View menu and select the desired toolbar from the Toolbars dialog box. To quickly activate another toolbar, use the toolbar shortcut menu. First position the mouse pointer over any displayed toolbar and click the right mouse button to display the shortcut menu, as shown in Figure 2-2.

The most useful toolbars are listed on the toolbar shortcut menu, along with the Toolbars and Customize commands. Check marks indicate toolbars that are already active. To activate another toolbar, simply click its name. For example, click Drawing to display the Drawing toolbar.

You can hide a toolbar by opening the toolbar shortcut menu and reselecting the toolbar you want to hide. For example, open the toolbar shortcut menu and click Drawing (which now has a check mark next to it) to remove the Drawing toolbar from the workspace. Alternatively, you can deselect the name of the toolbar in the Toolbars dialog box.

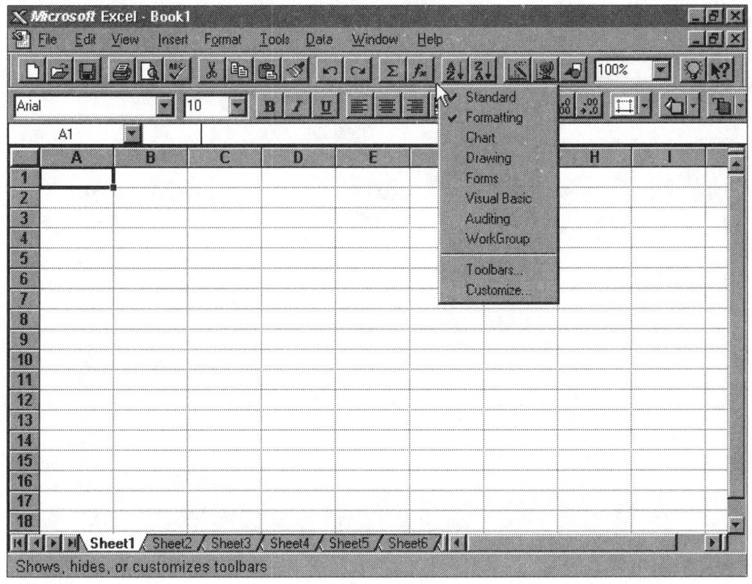

FIGURE 2-2

Click the right mouse button while the mouse pointer is over any toolbar to display the toolbar shortcut menu.

Positioning Toolbars on Your Screen

Excel allows you to relocate your toolbars. When you first start Excel, the Standard and Formatting toolbars are located at the top of the screen, where they are said to be *docked*. You can undock a toolbar by clicking it and dragging it to another location. (Be careful not to click one of the buttons by mistake.)

When you relocate a toolbar, its appearance changes slightly. For example, if you drag the Standard toolbar from its default location to the middle of the screen, the toolbar looks like a miniature window, with a title bar and a *Close button* in the upper right corner (which you click once to remove the toolbar from the screen). When you undock a toolbar, you can change its shape by dragging its borders, as shown in Figure 2-3.

TIP You can double-click a toolbar's gray background to dock and undock it. But if you double-click the *border* of a toolbar, such as the line between the Standard and Formatting toolbars, the Toolbars dialog box appears. (Double-clicking a border takes a deft hand.) If a docked toolbar does not extend across the whole screen, you can also double-click the gray background next to the toolbar to display the Toolbars dialog box.

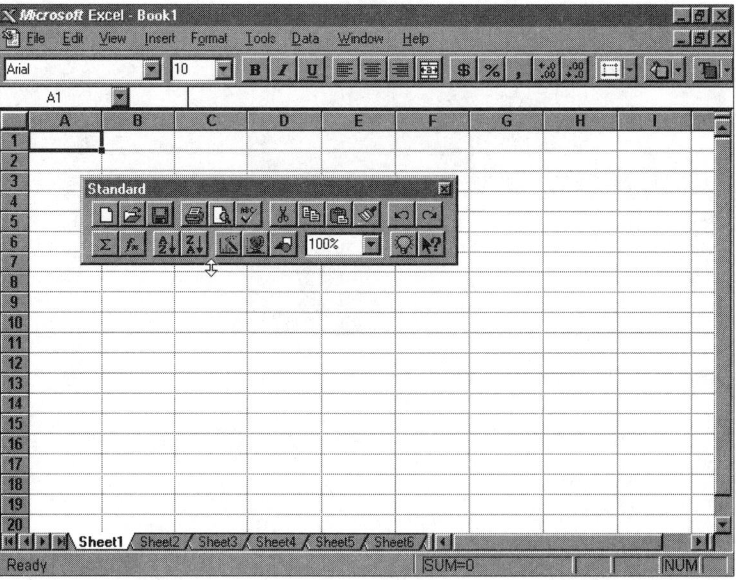

FIGURE 2-3
You can change both the location and the shape of toolbars.

Excel remembers the location and shape of the toolbar. The next time you start Excel, the toolbar will appear as it did when you quit the program. You can dock or redock a toolbar by dragging it to the top or bottom of the screen, or by double-clicking the toolbar. (Again, be careful to avoid clicking a button.) If you drag the toolbar shown in Figure 2-3 to the bottom of the screen, it reshapes itself into a single row, and the title bar and Close button disappear. The borders of the toolbar merge with those of the status bar, as shown in Figure 2-4. If you undock the toolbar again, it assumes the shape it had before you docked it. Each time you double-click the toolbar, it alternates between its most recent docked and undocked locations.

Note that you can also dock a toolbar that contains only buttons on the right or left side of the screen. For example, you cannot dock the Standard toolbar on the side of the screen because it contains a list box (the Zoom Control box), which is too wide, but you can dock the Auditing toolbar on either side because it contains only buttons. Likewise, toolbars containing palette buttons, such as the first button on the Chart toolbar, cannot be docked on the right or left side of the screen.

If Your Toolbar Looks Different from Those in This Book

Perhaps your computer was used previously by someone else or you share a computer with other people. Because Excel has so many toolbars that can be customized in so many ways, the copy of Excel you are using might already have been modified. You can use the toolbar shortcut menu to redisplay a toolbar that is not currently active. If any built-in toolbar has been modified, you can restore its default appearance by choosing the Toolbars command on the toolbar shortcut menu, selecting the toolbar in the list (if necessary), and then clicking Reset. (If the selected toolbar is not one of Excel's built-in toolbars, the Reset button changes to Delete.)

Alternatively, you might want to make some modifications of your own using the Customize command. (See the next section, "Customizing Toolbars.")

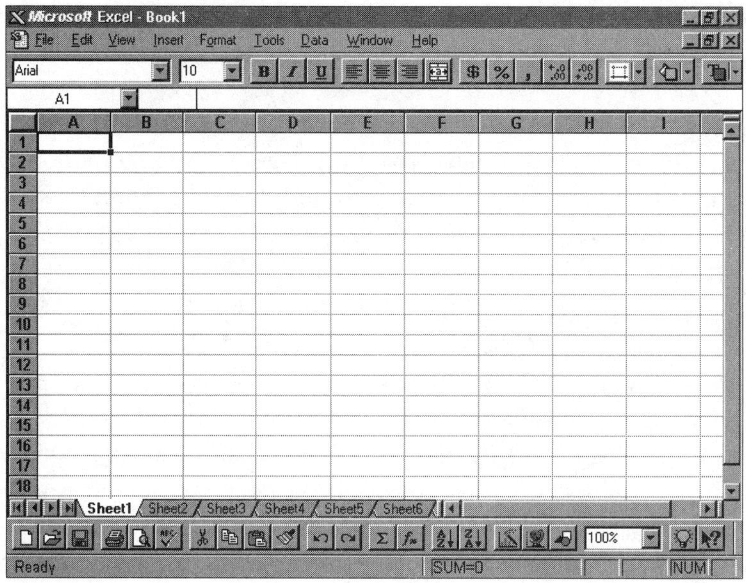

FIGURE 2-4
You can dock a toolbar at the bottom of the screen.

See Also

For a complete list of all the available toolbar buttons, see "Toolbar Buttons and Boxes," page 931.

Customizing Toolbars

In Microsoft Excel, the predefined toolbars contain a wealth of buttons. Many other buttons, which are not on any of the predefined toolbars, are also available for use on the toolbars. In addition, you can create your own toolbar buttons to add to the list. In this section, we'll tell you how to remove buttons from toolbars, add buttons to toolbars, rearrange toolbar buttons, change the display format of toolbars, and create new toolbars.

Removing and Adding Buttons

Displaying the Customize dialog box is like flipping the switch that allows you to modify toolbars. Though you might not need to use the dialog box itself, it must be active before you can move toolbar buttons.

To remove a button from a toolbar, follow these steps:

1. From the View menu, choose Toolbars and click Customize (or choose Customize from the toolbar shortcut menu).

2. The Customize dialog box must be open, but you remove the button from the toolbar, not from the dialog box. Click the button that you want to remove, drag it anywhere outside the toolbar, and release the mouse button.
3. Click Close to close the dialog box.

For example, to remove the Cut button (the button with the scissors on it) from the Standard toolbar, first display the Customize dialog box and then drag the Cut button off the toolbar, as shown in Figure 2-5.

TIP When you click any button, either in the Customize dialog box or on a displayed toolbar, the button's outline changes to gray, and the button's description appears in the Description section of the Customize dialog box. This way, you can be sure that you selected the correct button for removal.

To add a button, follow these steps:

1. From the View menu, choose Toolbars and click Customize (or choose Customize from the toolbar shortcut menu).
2. From the Categories list box in the Customize dialog box, select the category of the button you want to add. Excel displays all the buttons available in that category in the Buttons section of the dialog box.

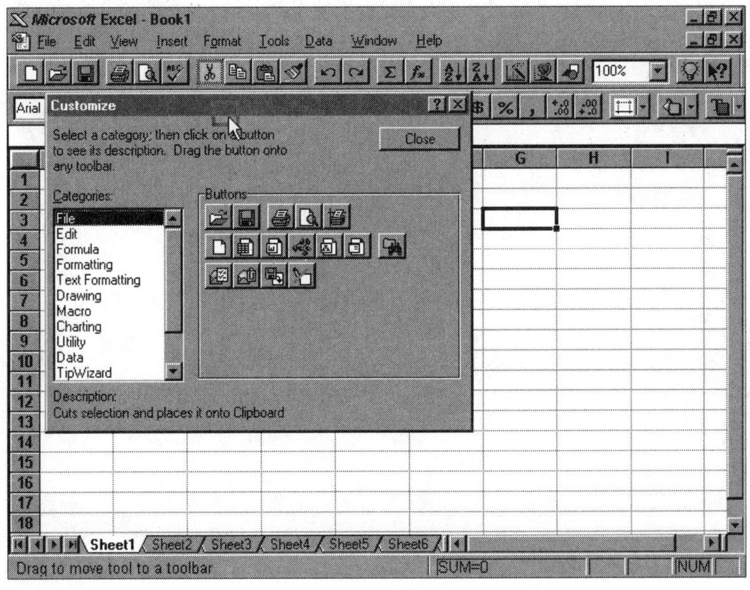

FIGURE 2-5

Drag a button away from a toolbar to remove it. We removed the Cut button from the Standard toolbar.

3. Click the button you want to add and drag it to the position on the toolbar where you want it to appear. Any existing buttons move to the right to accommodate the new button.

   NOTE It is possible to add more buttons to a toolbar than can be displayed while the toolbar is docked.

To add the Clear Contents button to the newly modified Standard toolbar, follow these steps:

1. With the Customize dialog box open, select the Edit category from the Categories list box.
2. Click the Clear Contents button (with the eraser on it) and drag it to the Standard toolbar, to the same location from which we removed the Cut button — to the left of the Copy button (the button with the two small pages on it). The result looks something like the toolbar in Figure 2-6.

Rearranging Toolbar Buttons

You can also rearrange buttons on a toolbar while the Customize dialog box is displayed. Using our Standard toolbar example, drag the Clear Contents button that we just added to the right until the button's outline overlaps the right half of the Format Painter button (the button with the paintbrush on it). The result looks something like Figure 2-7.

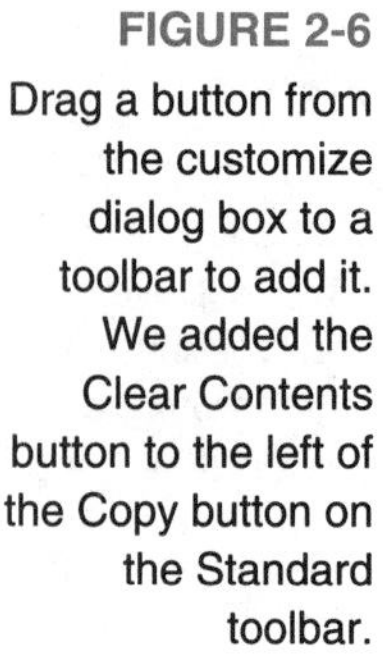

FIGURE 2-6
Drag a button from the customize dialog box to a toolbar to add it. We added the Clear Contents button to the left of the Copy button on the Standard toolbar.

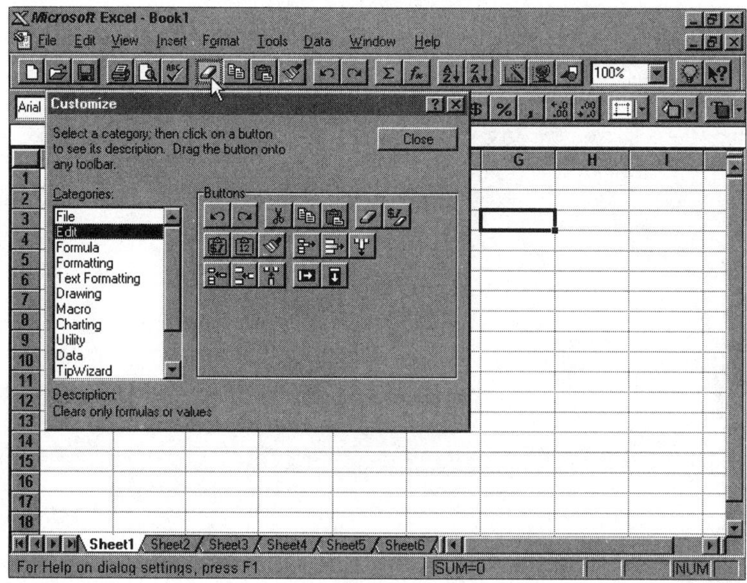

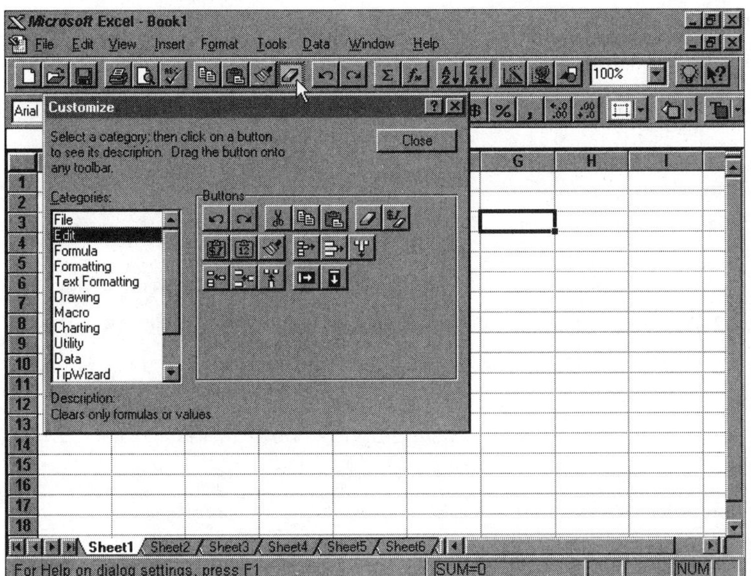

FIGURE 2-7
We moved the Clear Contents button to the right of the Format Painter button.

In addition, you can rearrange the spaces between buttons by removing spaces or adding new ones. It takes a little practice, but the basic techniques are simple. To add a space to the left of a button, drag the button to the right until it partially overlaps the adjacent button. To add a space to the right of a button, drag the button to the left. Similarly, you can remove a space by dragging an adjacent button over the space until the button is approximately centered over the space.

You can also rearrange toolbars by dragging buttons between displayed toolbars. For example, with both the Standard and Formatting toolbars displayed, choose the Customize command from the toolbar shortcut menu. With the Customize dialog box displayed, drag any button from one toolbar to the other. The button disappears from its original location and reappears in the new location.

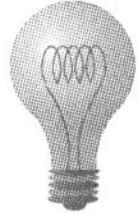

TIP You can also copy buttons between toolbars. With the Customize dialog box open, hold down Ctrl while you drag the button you want to copy to the new location. (A small plus sign appears next to the mouse pointer.) The button remains on the original toolbar, and a duplicate button appears in the new location. If you change your mind, simply drag the duplicate button off the toolbar.

Restoring Default Toolbars

To return your modified toolbar to its original condition, follow these steps:

1. From either the View menu or the toolbar shortcut menu, choose Toolbars.
2. Select the name of the toolbar you want to restore from the Toolbars list and then click Reset. The toolbar returns to its default configuration. Click OK when you are finished.

Changing the Size and Color of Toolbar Buttons

If you want, you can enlarge all the toolbar buttons for easy selection and improved legibility. You simply select the Large Buttons option in the Toolbars dialog box. Note, however, that magnifying the buttons reduces the number of buttons that can be displayed on a docked toolbar.

You can also make toolbars monochrome by deselecting the Color Toolbars option in the Toolbars dialog box.

When the Show ToolTips option is selected, a small label appears when you move the mouse pointer over any toolbar button.

For information about changing a toolbar button's appearance, see "Changing the Look of Toolbar Buttons," page 45.

For more information about ToolTips, see "Identifying Toolbar Buttons with ToolTips," page 29.

Creating New Toolbars

It's easy to create customized toolbars. To do so, follow these steps:

1. From either the View menu or the toolbar shortcut menu, choose Toolbars.
2. When the Toolbars dialog box appears, highlight the name of the toolbar that appears in the Toolbar Name edit box and then type the name of the toolbar you want to create. Click New.
3. The Customize dialog box appears, along with a small toolbar, which is currently empty and floating on the screen, as shown in Figure 2-8.
4. Add buttons to the empty toolbar by dragging buttons from the Customize dialog box or by copying or moving buttons from other toolbars.

After you define a custom toolbar and close the Customize dialog box, its name appears on the toolbar shortcut menu and in the Toolbars list in the

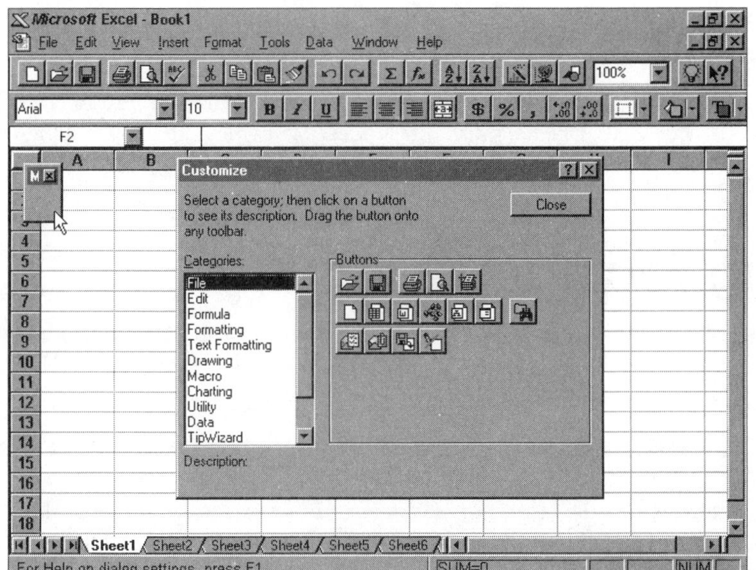

FIGURE 2-8

When you type a new name in the Toolbars dialog box and click the New button, the Customize dialog box appears along with an empty toolbar.

Toolbars dialog box. You can choose to display, hide, and dock a custom toolbar just like any predefined toolbar.

TIP A quicker method for creating a new toolbar is to drag a button from the Customize dialog box. If you release the mouse button anywhere outside the dialog box except on an existing toolbar, Excel creates a new toolbar and calls it *Toolbar 1*. Subsequent toolbars created in this manner are named *Toolbar 2, Toolbar 3,* and so on.

Deleting Custom Toolbars

It's as easy to remove a custom toolbar as it is to create one. To remove a custom toolbar, follow these steps:

1. From the toolbar shortcut menu, choose Toolbars.
2. In the Toolbars dialog box, select the name of the custom toolbar you want to remove. You cannot remove any of Excel's built-in toolbars.
3. Click Delete and then click OK at the prompt. (The Reset button, which is available when a built-in toolbar is selected, changes to the Delete button when a custom toolbar is selected.)

After you delete a toolbar, you cannot use the Undo command or button to restore it.

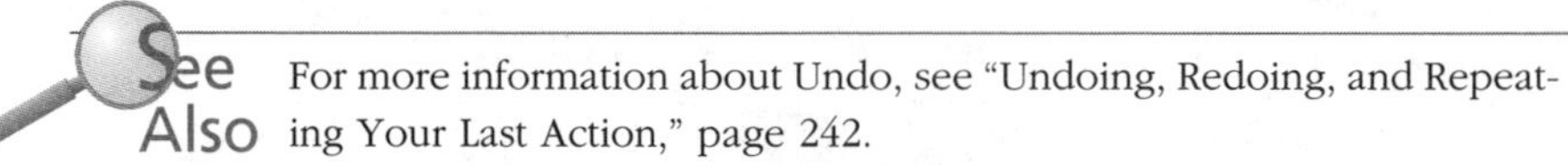

For more information about Undo, see "Undoing, Redoing, and Repeating Your Last Action," page 242.

Saving Toolbar Settings

When you exit Microsoft Excel, any predefined toolbars you changed or any custom toolbars you created are saved in the condition and position they were in when you quit. Each time you start Excel, your custom and modified toolbars are ready for use. Excel saves your custom toolbar settings in the Windows folder, in a special file with the extension .XLB. The filename is created from your Windows logon user name, for example, MARKDOD.XLB. To create different combinations of toolbar settings, you can save modified and custom toolbar variations by renaming the .XLB file.

Whenever you quit Excel, the .XLB file saves any changes you have made to the toolbar configuration. To save your current settings as well as another custom configuration, follow these steps:

1. Exit Excel by clicking the Close button at the right corner of the Excel window title bar or by choosing Exit from the File menu.
2. Start the Windows Explorer.
3. Change the name of the .XLB file, which is located in your Windows directory, by using the Rename command on the File menu. If you don't see file extensions in the Windows Explorer, choose Options from the View menu and clear the Hide MS-DOS File Extensions check box.

The settings that were active when you exited Excel are saved under the new filename, and any modifications you make during the next Excel session are saved in a new .XLB file, again using your name. You can subsequently rename this new .XLB file, if you like. In this way, you can create any number of toolbar configurations, which you can access by opening the .XLB file using the Open command on Excel's File menu. Alternatively, you can double-click your custom .XLB file in the Windows Explorer when you want to start Excel with a particular toolbar configuration. You can even create a shortcut for it in the Windows Explorer, or add it to the Windows taskbar Start menu.

If more than one person uses the same computer, each person's toolbar settings are saved in a separate .XLB file. Excel automatically uses the .XLB file for the correct user, based on the name the user enters when logging on to Windows.

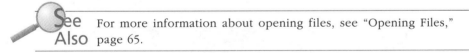

For more information about opening files, see "Opening Files," page 65.

Changing the Look of Toolbar Buttons

If you want, you can change the way a toolbar button looks by changing its face with Excel's Button Editor, by copying another face and pasting it onto the button, or by creating your own button face from scratch. For example, the Custom category in the Customize dialog box contains a number of *button faces* — that is, buttons with images on them — that you can use to create custom toolbar buttons. You can copy these faces onto existing buttons. Note, however, that when you drag a Custom category button to a toolbar, a dialog box appears allowing you to assign a macro to it. For now, click the Cancel button. For more information about assigning macros to custom toolbar buttons, see "Other Ways to Run Macros," page 841. To change the face of a button, follow these steps:

1. With the Customize dialog box open, position the mouse pointer over the button on the toolbar you want to edit and click the right mouse button to display the button shortcut menu, as shown in Figure 2-9.

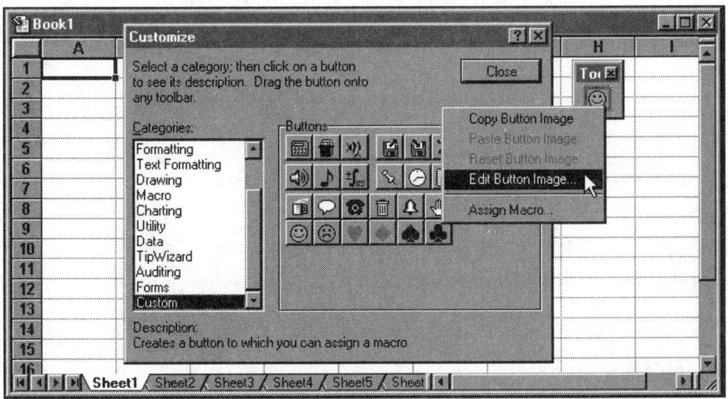

FIGURE 2-9
Position the mouse pointer over a toolbar button and then click the right mouse button to display the button shortcut menu.

2. From the button shortcut menu, choose Edit Button Image. The Button Editor dialog box appears, as shown in Figure 2-10.
3. Using the controls in the Button Editor dialog box, create the button face you want and then click OK.

FIGURE 2-10
You can use the Button Editor to change the face of any toolbar button.

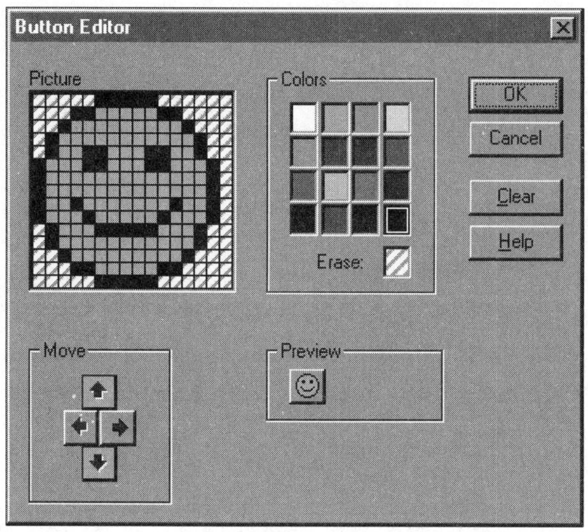

The small squares in the Picture section of the Button Editor dialog box correspond to *pixels,* which are the units of resolution on your computer screen. To erase only some of the existing pixels, click the Erase square in the Colors section and then click or drag through the pixels in the Picture section you want to remove.

Creating a Custom Button

To create a new button face from scratch follow the steps in the previous procedure to open the Button Editor dialog box and then click Clear. Next, click a color square in the Color section and then click or drag through the pixel squares in the Picture section, as if you were dipping your "brush" in paint and then applying it to the canvas. Use the arrow buttons in the Move section to shift the image in the corresponding direction. The arrow buttons work only if there are blank pixels in the direction you want to shift, however. In Figure 2-10, for example, there is room to shift the image to the right one pixel by clicking the right button. The Preview box shows the button as it will appear in its actual size.

NOTE When you create toolbar buttons with custom button faces, those buttons are available on a toolbar only. In other words, these buttons are not included in the Customize dialog box.

If you're not satisfied with your custom button face, restore the original button face using the Reset Button Image command on the button shortcut menu.

Copying Button Faces

To copy a button face from one button to another, follow these steps:

1. Open the Customize dialog box. If necessary, drag the button you want to copy to a toolbar. You can copy a button only when it is on a toolbar.
2. With the Customize dialog box still open, position the mouse pointer over the button you want to copy, and then click the right mouse button to display the button shortcut menu.
3. From the button shortcut menu, choose Copy Button Image.
4. Position the mouse pointer over the button you want to change and display the button shortcut menu.
5. From the button shortcut menu, choose Paste Button Image. The face of the copied button image replaces the face on the current button.
6. If necessary, drag the button from which you copied the image off the toolbar to delete it. Click OK.

Editing and Button Size

The default dimensions of Excel's toolbar buttons are 16 pixels wide by 15 pixels high. These are also the dimensions of the pixel grid in the Picture section of the Button Editor dialog box shown in Figure 2-10. But what happens when you choose the Toolbars command from the View menu and then select the Large Buttons option in the Toolbars dialog box? The dimensions of the displayed toolbar buttons change to 24 pixels wide by 23 pixels high, and the dimensions of the pixel grid in the Button Editor's Picture section change accordingly.

All of Excel's existing buttons include faces designed especially for both small and large button sizes. However, if you edit a small button face and then select the Large Buttons option, the button face image stays the same size, centered in the button, which expands around it. If you want your image to adjust with the button size, select the Large Buttons option before you edit the button face. Excel then reduces the image as best it can for the small button size and expands it again when you switch back to the large button size. You might want to experiment a bit, however, because the image can become distorted when reduced.

Attaching a Toolbar to a Workbook

Earlier in this chapter, we described how toolbar settings, including custom toolbars, are saved when you exit Microsoft Excel. Then when you reload Excel, those settings are reactivated and ready for use. Excel also allows you to attach a custom toolbar to a workbook so that the toolbar is activated whenever the corresponding workbook is opened. That way, you can create many different toolbars for specific tasks in specific workbooks. Because the toolbars are attached to the workbooks, you can then eliminate them from the Toolbars list box in the Toolbars dialog box, thereby reserving the list for more "universal" toolbars.

To attach a toolbar to a workbook, you must include a module sheet in the workbook. (A module sheet is a special worksheet that helps you customize workbooks. You'll learn more about module sheets in Chapter 23, "Creating Macros.") To add a new module sheet and attach a toolbar to your workbook, follow these steps:

1. From the Insert menu, choose Macro and then Module. (Skip this step if your workbook already contains a module sheet.)
2. With the module sheet active, choose the Attach Toolbars command from the Tools menu. (When you insert a sheet, it becomes active automatically; if your workbook already contains a module sheet, you must activate it yourself.)
3. In the Attach Toolbars dialog box, select the toolbar you want to attach to your workbook from the Custom Toolbars list box. (Only custom toolbars can be attached to workbooks.)
4. Click the Copy button to add the toolbar to the Toolbars In Workbook list box, as shown in Figure 2-11.

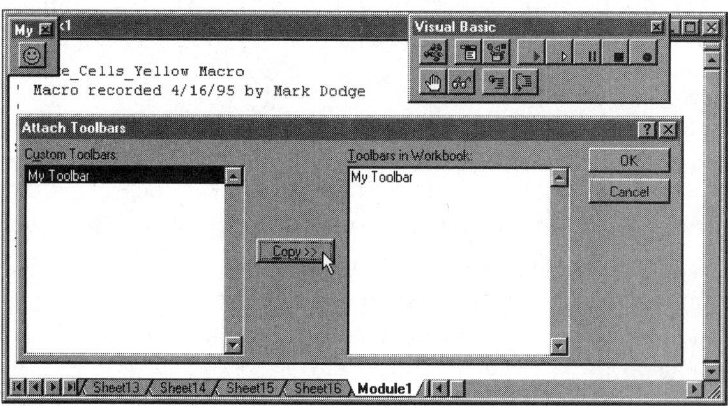

FIGURE 2-11
Attach toolbars to workbooks using the Attach Toolbars dialog box.

5. Click OK to attach the toolbar to your workbook and close the dialog box.

After you attach a custom toolbar to a workbook, you can delete the toolbar in the Toolbars dialog box if you don't need it. Then whenever you open the workbook, the custom toolbar is automatically activated. When you close the workbook, the attached custom toolbar remains, allowing you to customize or remove it as needed.

To delete the custom toolbar, choose the Toolbars command from the View menu, select the toolbar's name in the Toolbars list box, click Delete, and then click OK in the alert box.

To "unattach" a custom toolbar from a workbook, you must use the Attach Toolbars dialog box again, except this time, select the toolbar in the Toolbars In Workbook list, and then click the Delete button. (The Copy button changes to Delete when you select an attached toolbar.) If you do not "unattach" a toolbar in this way, it will reappear every time you open the workbook, even if you use the Toolbars command to remove it.

See Also For more information about saving your toolbar settings, see "Saving Toolbar Settings," page 44.

For more information about recording macros, see "Recording Macros," page 830.

Chapter 3

Managing Files

One of the advantages of working with computers is that you can save your work on disk, in an electronic file. When your work is saved on disk, it's always at your fingertips, and with Microsoft Excel's Find File feature, you'll never have trouble locating your files. You can easily share work you've saved on disk with others, without having to produce paper copies. In this chapter, we describe all the ways you can save, open, find, and share your Excel files.

Managing Files

You use the File menu to save and retrieve your workbook files. Microsoft Excel "remembers" the last four files you worked on and includes their names at the bottom of the menu so that you can open them quickly. The File menu is shown in Figure 3-1.

FIGURE 3-1
At the bottom of the File menu, Excel displays the four files you most recently worked on so that you can quickly open any one of them.

Creating a New File

You can create a new workbook quickly by clicking the New Workbook button on the Standard toolbar. Figure 3-2 shows the file-management buttons available on the Standard toolbar.

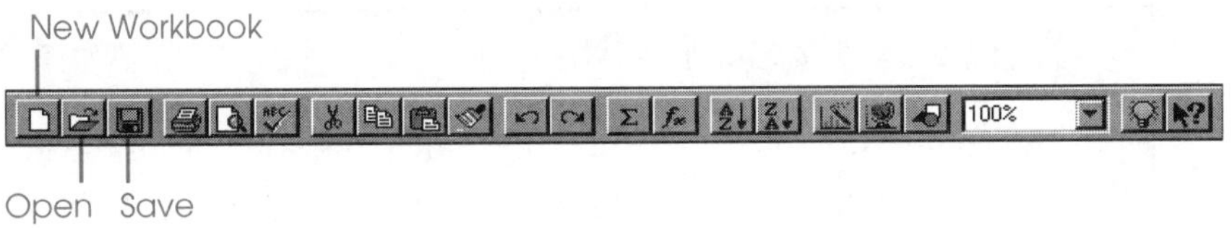

FIGURE 3-2

Use the first three buttons on the Standard toolbar to help manage your files.

If you create a new workbook when another workbook is already open, the new workbook window appears on top of the existing window. If the previous workbook was named Book1, the new workbook is named Book2. Later workbooks are numbered sequentially: Book3, Book4, and so on. You use the commands on the Window menu to switch from one workbook to another.

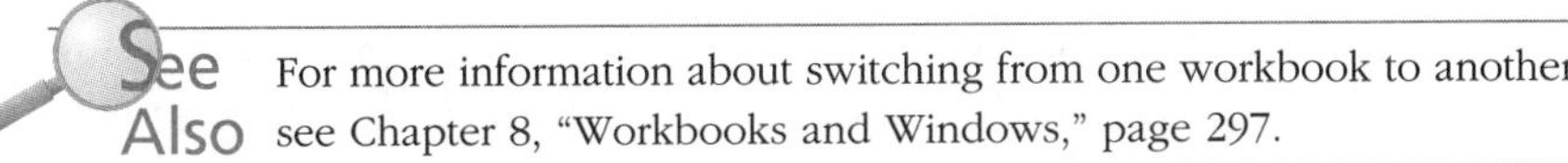

For more information about switching from one workbook to another, see Chapter 8, "Workbooks and Windows," page 297.

Creating a New File Based on an Existing File

When you use the New command on the File menu instead of the New Workbook button on the toolbar, the New dialog box appears, as shown in Figure 3-3. Workbooks that appear in the New dialog box become the basis for your new workbooks. The General tab in the New dialog box contains a "Workbook" icon. Selecting the Workbook icon creates a new blank workbook, as if you had clicked the New Workbook toolbar button. The Spreadsheet Solutions tab contains several workbook template icons. These templates give you a head start on many common spreadsheet tasks. When you select one of these icons and click OK, Excel opens a *copy* of the workbook.

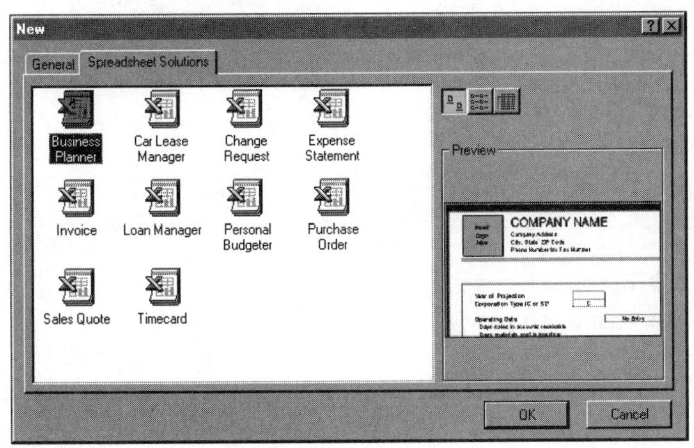

FIGURE 3-3

You can open a copy of any file that appears in the New dialog box.

Adding Your Own Templates and Tabs

The contents of the New dialog box mirror the contents of the MS Office\Templates folder that is created when you first install Excel. (If the templates are not installed, you'll need to rerun the Setup program to add the templates to your installation. For installation information, see Appendix B.) Any files that are placed in the Templates folder appear on the New dialog box's General tab. So, if you put into the Templates folder a workbook that you frequently use as the basis for new workbooks, it will always appear on the General tab in the New dialog box. When you use the New dialog box to "open" the workbook, Excel creates a copy, leaving the original intact.

The Spreadsheet Solutions tab appears in the New dialog box because there is a folder named Spreadsheet Solutions, which contains Excel files, inside the Templates folder. You can also create your own tab in the New dialog box by creating a folder inside the Templates folder and saving Excel files in it using the Save As command on the File menu (see "Saving Files," on page 55). The following figure shows the New dialog box with a tab added.

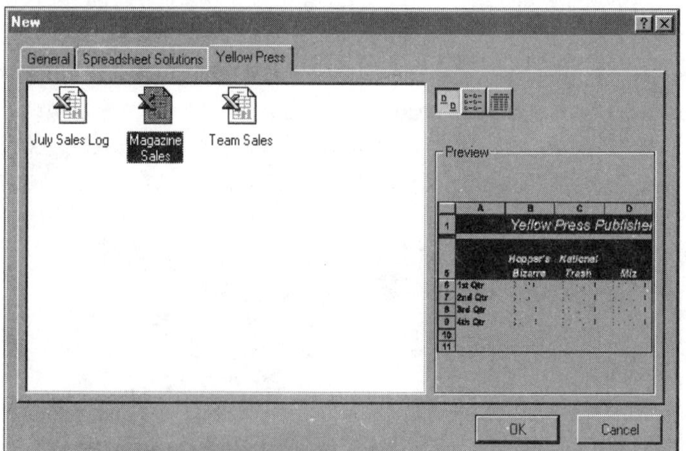

NOTE You can create as many folders as you want to add to the Templates folder, but only folders that contain Excel files appear as tabs in the New dialog box.

Adding Your Own Templates and Tabs

The figure on the previous page shows standard workbook icons, which look different from the template icons shown in Figure 3-3. This lets you tell at a glance if a file is a regular workbook or if it was saved in template format. It really makes no difference, however; the New dialog box creates a copy of either file type, essentially treating them both as templates.

Figure 3-3 shows the New dialog box with one of the new Spreadsheet Solutions templates selected. A thumbnail preview of the selected file appears to the right of the file list. The three buttons above the preview let you choose how to view the file list: icon view (as shown in Figure 3-3), list view, or list view with details such as file size and date last modified. Notice that the Spreadsheet Solutions icons look like little pads of paper. These pad icons indicate files that have been saved in template format (see File Formats, page 59). For example, if you double-click the Business Planner template icon, Excel creates and opens a copy of the workbook, and names it "Business Planner1." Excel treats this file as a new file: No matter how you first save the file, the Save As dialog box appears, reminding you to give it a new name.

TIP Files do not have to be saved in template format to be used as templates. When you place a regular workbook in the Template folder, it appears in the New dialog box. When you select it, Excel opens a copy of the workbook, because the New dialog box treats all workbooks it displays as templates.

See Also For more information about templates, see "Using Template Files," page 206.

Saving Files

After you invest time and energy in creating a workbook, you'll probably want to save it so that you can retrieve it later. When you save a workbook file, you not only save the data you've entered in it but you also save the settings you assigned to the workbook, including the window configuration and display characteristics, formulas, functions, fonts, and styles.

On the File menu, five commands let you save your Excel files — Save, Save As, Save Workspace, Close, and Exit. Each of these commands works in a slightly different way. Generally, you use the Save As command to save a document for the first time or to modify the way Excel saves your document, and you use the Save command to save changes to existing documents. To ensure against accidental loss of your work, however, Excel also asks if you want to save your changes when you choose the Close or Exit command. You can also save the current document quickly by clicking the Save button on the Standard toolbar; this is the same as choosing the Save command from the File menu.

When you save a workbook file with one of the Save commands, the workbook remains open. When you close a workbook file with the Close command or quit Excel with the Exit command, however, Excel removes the file from the screen.

See Also For information about the Save Workspace command, refer to "Saving the Entire Workspace," page 65.

Saving a File for the First Time

Before you can save a workbook file for the first time, you must assign it a name and indicate where you want Excel to store the file. To name your document, choose either Save or Save As from the File menu, or click the Save button on the Standard toolbar. When you save a file for the first time, the Save As dialog box appears, as shown in Figure 3-4.

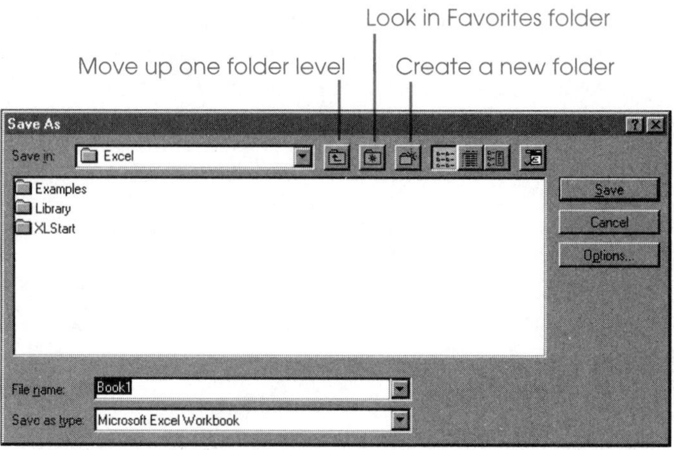

FIGURE 3-4

The Save As dialog box appears when you save a file for the first time.

NOTE The Look in Favorites folder button you see in Figure 3-4 activates a special folder called Favorites. For more information about the Favorites folder, see "Opening Files," page 65.

In Figure 3-4, the suggested filename, Book1, appears in the File Name edit box because you haven't yet assigned a new name to the document. To change the filename, simply type a new name. (You don't have to type the extension .XLS; Excel adds that for you.) The original contents of the edit box disappear as soon as you begin typing. Click Save when you are finished entering the filename. After you save the file, the workbook window remains open on the workspace and Excel displays the workbook's new name in the title bar.

TIP If you use the same folder for the majority of your file-management operations, you can designate that folder as the default folder. From the Tools menu, simply choose the Options command and then click the General tab. Click the Default File Location edit box and type the full pathname for the folder. The folder you specify in the Default File Location edit box is used as the default folder each time you choose the Open, Save, or Save As command.

Filename Rules

File naming in Excel 7 follows the same basic rules you use in other Microsoft Windows 95 applications. Filenames and paths can have up to 218 characters and can include any combination of alphanumeric characters, spaces, and the special characters &, $, %, ', (,), -, @, ~, !, and _. Although you can use any combination of uppercase and lowercase letters, keep in mind that Excel does not distinguish case in your filenames. For example, the names MYFILE, MyFile, and myfile are identical as far as Excel is concerned.

The familiar MS-DOS three-character file extension helps identify your Excel files, and it is added automatically when you save a file. Note, however, that file extensions may not appear with Windows filenames. The following table lists some of Excel's default extensions.

Document Type	Extension
Add-in	.XLA
Backup	.XLK
Template	.XLT
Workbook	.XLS
Workspace	.XLW

Occasionally, you might want to create your own file extensions to flag special files. To do so, simply type the filename, a period, and then the extension. For example, you might create a file called MYFILE.EXT.

TIP Depending on your Windows installation, the MS-DOS file extensions such as .XLS may or may not appear. They are still there, but in Windows 95 you can choose to display them or turn them off. From the Windows Explorer, choose the Options command on the View menu, and on the View tab, select or clear the "Hide MS-DOS file extensions for file types that are registered" check box. For more information, see your Windows 95 documentation.

If you want to accept the program's default file extension, simply type the filename without a period or extension name. You might, however, find the new Properties dialog box more helpful than using extensions. For more information, see "Adding Summary Information to Files," page 62.

Unless you specify otherwise, Excel saves your file in the current folder. As shown earlier in Figure 3-4, the path to the current folder appears above the File Name edit box in the Save As dialog box. To save your file in a different folder, you can specify the path along with your filename in the File Name edit box, or you can select the folder you want from the Folders list box. The current folder is displayed in the Save In box above the list box. To change folders, double-click the folder you want from the list box. The selected folder remains open until you make a new selection.

If you want to save a file to another disk drive, click the arrow to the right of the Save In drop-down list box to display a list of all the disk drives connected to your system. Then select the desired drive from the list box. You can also save files on a network drive if your computer is connected to a network.

Document Types in Previous Versions of Excel

In Excel 7, as well as in Excel 5, worksheets, chart sheets, dialog sheets, and macro sheets are all contained in workbooks. In previous versions of Excel, worksheets, chart sheets, and macro sheets were saved separately. When you open one of these earlier sheet types in Excel 7, it is automatically converted to an Excel 7 workbook, which you can then choose to save in the new Excel 7 format or keep in its original format. You can also combine sheets from a previous version of Excel in a single Excel 7 workbook. For more information about working with workbooks, see Chapter 8, "Workbooks and Windows," page 297.

Excel 5 workbooks are compatible with Excel 7, and vice-versa. This means you can save a workbook in Excel 7, and then open it in Excel 5 without problems.

For more information about saving files on a network drive, see "Sharing Files with Others," page 75.

File Formats

In addition to providing the filename and location, you can specify a different file format in the Save As dialog box. Click the arrow to the right of the Save As Type drop-down list box. The list expands to reveal all the formats in which you can save your files.

The default format is Microsoft Excel Workbook, and you'll almost always use this option. If you want to export an Excel file to another program, however, you can use one of the other options to convert the file to a format that is readable by that program.

The Template format allows you to save files to be used as the basis for multiple new files. This format is particularly useful when sharing templates with other Excel users working with Excel 5.

NOTE To open a Template file in order to modify the original template, simply use the Open command.

For more information about Excel's export formats, see Chapter 27, "Importing and Exporting," page 909.

Creating Backup Files Automatically

You can have Excel always create a duplicate copy of your file on the same disk and in the same directory as the original. Choose the Save As command and click the Options button to display the Save Options dialog box shown in Figure 3-5. Then select the Always Create Backup option.

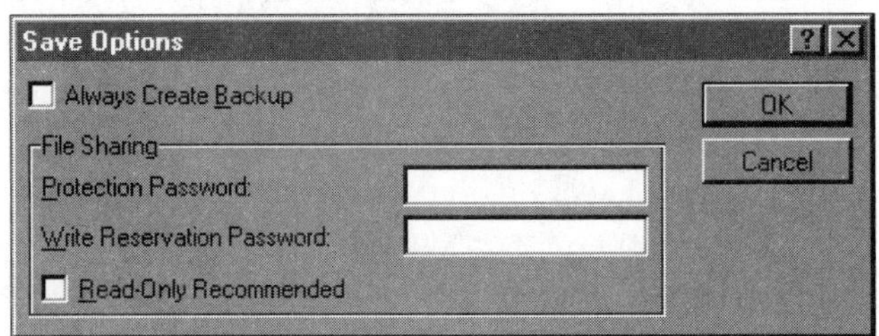

FIGURE 3-5
The Save Options dialog box gives you control of various file-security features.

The backup file is a duplicate file that carries the same name as your original, but the name is preceded by "Backup of" and has the file extension .XLK. If this is the first time you've saved the file, the backup file and the workbook file are identical. If you saved the file previously with the Always Create Backup option selected, Excel renames the last saved version of your file, giving it a .XLK extension, and overwrites the existing .XLK file.

NOTE Keep in mind that Excel always uses a .XLK extension when creating backup files, regardless of the file type. Suppose you work with a workbook named Myfile.XLS as well as a template file on disk named Myfile.XLT, and you select the Always Create Backup option for both. Because only one Myfile.XLK can exist, the most recently saved file is saved as the .XLK file, and Excel overwrites the other file's backup, if one exists.

Protecting Files

You can password-protect your files with two types of passwords: protection and write reservation. Passwords can have up to 15 characters, and capitalization matters. Thus, if you assign the password *Secret* to a file, you can't reopen that file by typing *SECRET* or *secret*. For added security, Excel does not display passwords on the screen when you type them to open a protected file.

When you assign a protection password to a file and close it, Excel prompts you to supply that password before reopening the file.

When you assign a write reservation password, anyone can open the file, but they cannot save the file if they haven't opened it using the password.

A third protection option, the Read-Only Recommended option, augments the security provided by passwords. If less-stringent security meets your needs, you can check this option to *suggest* that the user open the file as a read-only file, rather than to force the issue by setting a password.

To assign any of these protection options to your files, follow these steps:

1. Choose Save As from the File menu and type a filename in the File Name edit box, if necessary.
2. Click the Options button.
3. Select the options you want to use and enter passwords, if necessary.
4. Click OK to close the Save Options dialog box.
5. Click Save to close the Save As dialog box.

Resaving a File

After you save a file for the first time, you need not use the Save As command again unless you want to resave the file under a new name or in a new location, or you want to use one of the options in the Save Options dialog box. To save your changes to a file that you have already saved, simply select Save from the File menu or click the Save button on the Standard toolbar. Excel overwrites the last saved version of the file with the current contents of the workbook and leaves the window open in the workspace.

Having Excel Save Your Workbooks Automatically

Sometimes we get wrapped up in our work and forget to save our files regularly. The AutoSave command on the Tools menu allows you to specify an interval (such as every 15 minutes) in which Excel will automatically save the current workbook or all open workbooks. You can also specify whether Excel displays a dialog box asking if you want to save any changes.

The AutoSave command is an add-in, so if you didn't include it when you installed Excel on your computer, it won't appear. To find out, choose the Add-Ins command from the Tools menu and see whether AutoSave appears in the list of available add-ins. If it does not appear, you must rerun the Excel Setup program. For more information about installing add-ins, see Appendix B, "Installing Microsoft Excel," page 951.

Saving a File with a Different Name

If you choose the Save As command while a file that has already been saved is open, you can save the file under a new name. (You can also add or change options for the file in the Save Options dialog box.) When you choose Save As to store a previously saved file, you'll see the same Save As dialog box shown in Figure 3-4 on page 56, except that Excel displays the name under which you last saved the file. If you type a new name before pressing Enter or clicking Save, Excel saves the current workbook under the new name and leaves the previous version of the file intact under the old name. If you don't change the name before clicking Save, Excel asks you whether you want to overwrite the existing file. If you choose to overwrite the old version and the Always Create Backup option is active, Excel creates a .XLK file or updates the existing .XLK file.

Adding Summary Information to Files

When you choose the Properties command on the File menu, Excel displays a Properties dialog box that you use to record general information about the active workbook file. The Properties dialog box is shown in Figure 3-6.

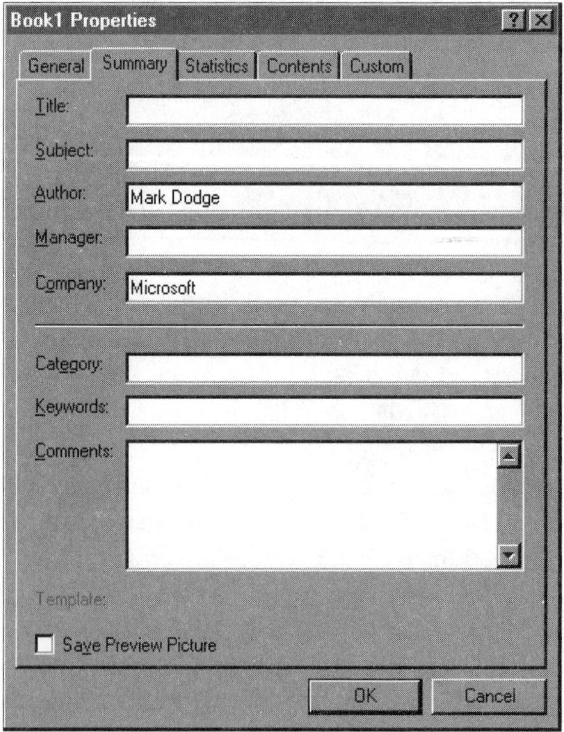

FIGURE 3-6

The Properties dialog box lets you record information about your workbook.

The information you enter in the Properties dialog box can be used later for file identification or clarification. For example, you can use properties as search criteria in the Advanced Find dialog box to search for files with a particular entry or combination of entries in any of the Properties edit boxes.

Linking Custom Properties to Cells

You can link a custom property to a named cell in your worksheet. When you do, the value of the custom property becomes whatever the named cell contains and changes whenever the value in the cell changes. First you must name a cell (see "Naming Cells and Ranges," on page 126), which makes available the Link To Content checkbox on the Custom tab in the Properties dialog box. When the Link To Content box is checked, the workbook's defined names appear in a drop-down list in the Value edit box (whose name changes to Source when linking content), as shown here.

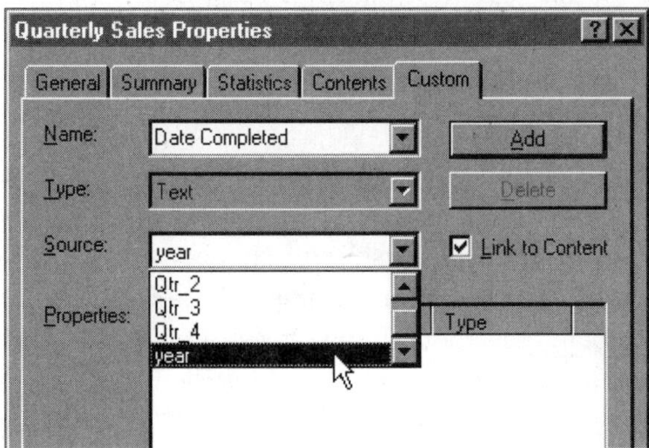

Select or create a name for the custom property in the Name box. (The Type box becomes inactive when linking to content). When you've specified a Source (the named cell to which you want to link), click the Add button and the custom property appears in the Properties list box.

The Properties dialog box contains five tabs. The General tab displays information about the file, including size, location, attributes, creation date, and date of last modification. The Summary tab, shown in Figure 3-6, allows you to enter your own property values. The Author and Company values are filled in for you, based on the information you supplied when you first installed Excel.

TIP To change the default Author name shown on the Summary tab of the Properties dialog box, choose Options from the Tools menu, click the General tab, and type the new name in the User Name box.

The Statistics tab lists helpful information such as the name of the last person who made modifications to the file and total editing time, so you can see how much of your life went into a particular piece of work. The Statistics tab also includes a Revision Number field that indicates how many times the file has been saved while open for multiuser editing (see "Sharing Files with Others," on page 75).

The Contents tab lists the names of each worksheet that the workbook contains.

Use the Custom tab to create your own properties. You can create a property using a new name, or you can select one from a list of possibilities. Then you can assign it a data type: Text, Date, Number, or "Yes or No." Finally, assign a value to your custom property that is consistent with your data type. For example, you could create a custom text property called Client (which is one of the suggested possibilities), and type the client's name in the values field. Then, using the Find File features in the Open dialog box (see "Opening Files," on page 65), you can locate all the files with a particular client name in this custom property field.

You can have Excel automatically display the Properties dialog box whenever you save a workbook for the first time by following these steps:

1. Choose Options from the Tools menu and click the General tab.
2. Click the Prompt For File Properties option to select it.
3. Click OK to return to the workbook window.

Saving the Entire Workspace

You can use the Save Workspace command on the File menu to save a snapshot of your current Excel environment. When you choose the Save Workspace command, the dialog box in Figure 3-7 appears.

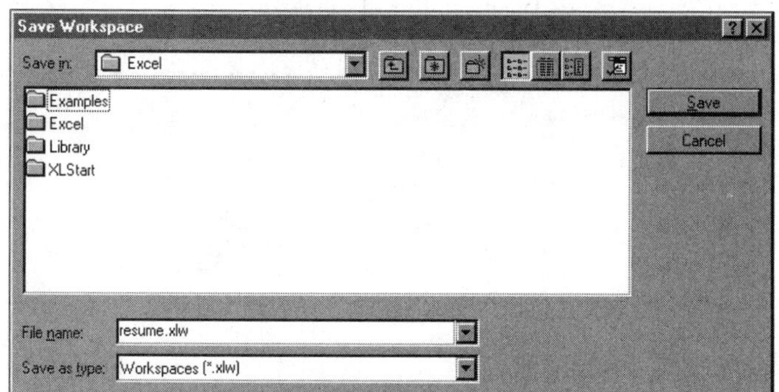

FIGURE 3-7
Save a snapshot of your Excel workspace with the Save Workspace command.

When you save a workspace, Excel notes the locations of all the workbooks that are currently open, as well as many of the workspace settings, so that you can retrieve your workspace in the same condition it was in when you saved it. That is, all the workbooks that were open when you saved the workspace file will be opened, and all the applicable settings will be activated. Settings that are saved with workspaces include many of the display and calculation settings available in the tab dialog box that appears when you choose the Options command from the Tools menu. The default filename suggested for a workspace file is Resume.XLW, but you can use a different name as long as you follow the file naming rules.

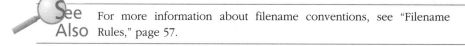

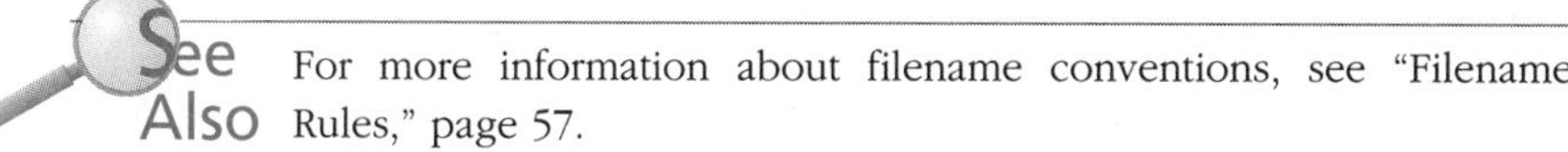

For more information about filename conventions, see "Filename Rules," page 57.

Opening Files

To retrieve a file from disk, choose the Open command from the File menu or click the Open button on the Standard toolbar. Excel displays a dialog box, like the one shown in Figure 3-8 on the next page, that contains a list of the Excel files (files with the extension .XL*) stored in the current folder.

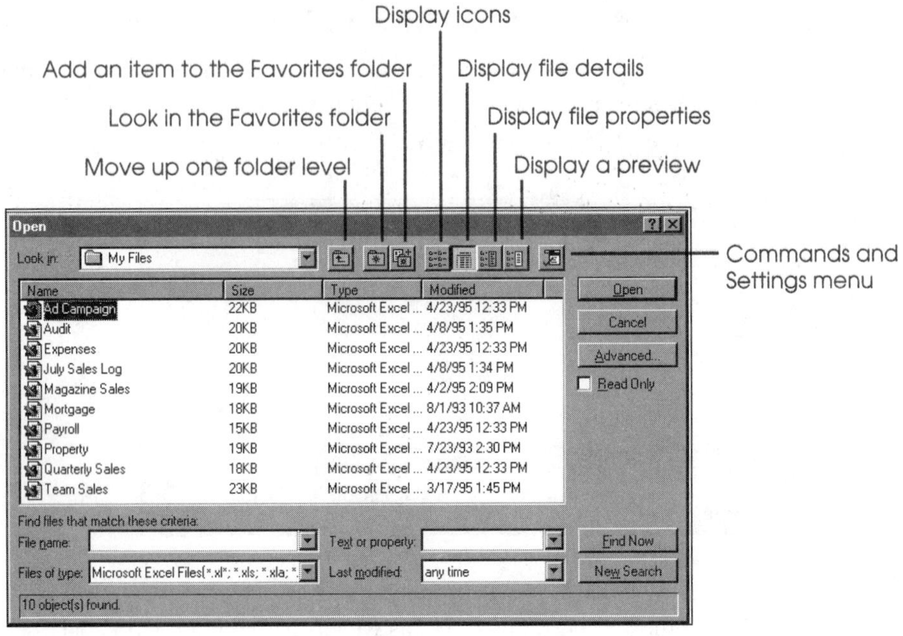

FIGURE 3-8

Use the Open command to retrieve files stored on disk.

TIP You can have as many files open at a time as your computer's memory allows. Each file you open occupies memory, however, regardless of the amount of data it contains. For that reason, you should limit the number of files you have open at any one time, especially if some of them contain large amounts of data (such as a workbook in which you have filled thousands of cells).

The Files Of Type list box near the bottom of the Open dialog box determines which files are available for selection. The default entry is Microsoft Excel Files, which tells the program to display only Excel files in the Open dialog box — that is, only those files whose extensions begin with the characters XL. You can display specific types of files or display all files by selecting an option from the Files Of Type drop-down list box. For example, to show all files in the current directory, select All Files from the Files Of Type drop-down list box. To display only Lotus 1-2-3 files, select the Lotus 1-2-3 Files option.

To open a file, double-click its icon in the list box, or type the file's name in the File Name edit box and click Open. If the file is located in the current folder, Excel opens it when you click Open. If you want to retrieve a file in another folder without changing the current folder, type the file's full pathname in the File Name edit box, or use the Look In list box and the Up One Level button to look through the available drives and folders.

TIP You can open several files simultaneously using the Open dialog box. To open several files, hold down the Ctrl key and click the names of all the files that you want to open. When you click Open, Excel opens all the selected files.

The Open dialog box includes a set of view buttons similar to the ones found in the Save As dialog box shown in Figure 3-4, with the addition of a button that displays a preview of the selected file. The Open dialog box shown in Figure 3-8 shows the file list displayed in Details view. Notice the headings that appear over each section of file information. When you click one of these headings, the files are sorted in order, based on that heading. For example, if you click the Modified heading, the files are sorted in date order. You can also change the width of the columns displayed in Details view by dragging the lines between headings, similar to the way you can drag to change column width in a worksheet.

TIP You can click the right mouse button on most files listed in the Open, New, or Save As dialog boxes to display a shortcut menu that contains commands you can use on the selected file. For example, you can delete a file displayed in the Open dialog box using this shortcut menu.

Click the Commands and Settings menu button to display a drop-down menu (shown in Figure 3-9 on the next page) that contains additional commands you can use on selected files, as well as a few, such as the Open Read Only and Sorting, that are also available elsewhere in the dialog box. When you choose the Print command from this location, Excel both opens and prints the file without further actions on your part. This is equivalent to opening the file and then clicking the Print button on the Standard toolbar, which prints the active workbook using the default settings in the Print dialog box. The Properties command displays the Properties dialog box without closing the Open dialog box. The Map Network Drive command lets you connect to a remote drive on a network.

FIGURE 3-9
The Commands And Settings menu appears when you click the Commands And Settings Menu button.

The Search Subfolders, Group Files By Folder, and Saved Searches commands pertain to the file-finding features discussed in "Searching for Files" on page 71.

Opening Files as Read Only

Selecting the Read Only option on the right side of the Open dialog box prevents changes to the saved version of the file on disk. If you have selected this option, you can view and even edit the file, but you can't save it under its current name. Instead, you must use the Save As command to save the edited file under a new filename. (If you choose the Save command, Excel automatically displays the Save As dialog box.)

The Read Only option is most useful when you're working on a network. If you open a file without selecting the Read Only option, others on the network must select the Read Only option to view that file. Naturally, you can still save your changes, but the other users would have to use the Save As command and save their changes under a new filename. If other users try to open the same file without using the Read Only option, they'll receive an error message unless the Allow Multi-User Editing option is turned on. See "Sharing Workbooks on a Network," page 77.

Reopening a Recently Opened File

Near the bottom of the File menu, you'll find the names of up to four files you've worked with most recently, even in previous sessions. To reopen one of these files, simply choose its name from this menu.

What's a "Favorites"?

Two buttons shown in the Open dialog box in Figure 3-8 give you control over a folder named Favorites. The Favorites folder is created when you install Excel and is located in your Windows folder. The Look in Favorites button immediately activates the Favorites folder, giving you single-click access to the files you have stored there. Usually, the Favorites folder contains only shortcuts to files and folders — not the files and folders themselves—unless you move or save files there. You can add shortcuts to files located anywhere on your computer or on any computer to which you have a network connection.

The Add to Favorites button displays a small menu that contains two oddly-named commands. The Add "Look In" Folder To Favorites command creates a shortcut to the folder currently displayed in the Look In box and places it in the Favorites folder. The Add Selected Item To Favorites command creates a shortcut to the selected item and places the shortcut in the Favorites folder, rather than actually moving the item.

Use the Add "Look In" Folder To Favorites command to create shortcuts to other frequently-used folders in the Favorites folder. This way, you can easily jump from folder to folder without having to move up and down the folder hierarchy each time. Just click the Look in Favorites button first, and jump to the other folders from there.

TIP You can turn off the display of the most recently used files by choosing Options from the Tools menu, clicking the General tab, and clearing the Recently-Used File List check box.

Opening Files Automatically When You Start Excel

You can use several methods to open one or more files automatically when you start Excel. First, from the Start menu on the Windows taskbar, choose the Run command. When the Run dialog box appears, type *c:\MS Office\Excel\Excel* (assuming that "excel" is the name of your Excel folder) followed by the names of any files you want to open. If those files are not stored in the current folder, be sure to include their full pathnames.

For example, to start Excel with the worksheet files C:\Regions\North.xls and C:\Regions\South.xls, choose Run from the Start menu and then type the following in the Run dialog box:

```
C:\MSOffice\Excel\Excel C:\Regions\North.xls C:\Regions\South.xls
```

Secondly, if you have a file or set of files you work with regularly, you can store them in a special folder called XLStart. This folder must be a subfolder of the folder that contains your Excel program files. (Microsoft Excel's Setup program automatically creates the XLStart folder for you when it installs Excel on your hard disk.) When you start Excel, the files in the XLStart folder are automatically opened. You can use the Save As command to save files to the XLStart folder, or you can move the files to this folder with the Windows Explorer.

If you want to work with several workbooks for an extended period of time, you can save a workspace file in the XLStart folder so that the entire workspace is automatically loaded each time you start Excel.

For more information about creating template files, see "Using Template Files," page 206.

For more information about workspace files, see "Saving the Entire Workspace," page 65.

The Alternate Startup Folder

If you want to start Excel and simultaneously open files that are located in a folder other than the XLStart folder, you can specify an alternate startup folder. Simply choose Options from the Tools menu, click the General tab, and type the full pathname of the folder you want in the Alternate Startup File Location edit box. This option is particularly useful if your computer is connected to a network and you want to open files in a shared folder.

Starting Excel with No Workbook Displayed

You might prefer not to see Book1 every time you start Excel. To do this, you can add a /e switch to the command line for Excel.

Choose the run command on the Windows taskbar's Start menu, and type *c:\MS Office\Excel\Excel /e* in the edit box. (See the Microsoft Windows documentation for details.)

TIP Sometimes you can use a trick to recover data that you thought was lost from a corrupted workbook. If you try to open a workbook without success, try the following. First, open two new workbooks. Select cell A1 in one of the workbooks and then press Ctrl-C to copy. Activate the second workbook, choose Paste Special on the Edit menu, and then click Paste Link. Next, choose Links on the Edit menu, click Change Source, locate the corrupted workbook on your hard disk, select it, and click OK. Click OK again in the Links dialog box. If luck is with you, data from cell A1 in the lost workbook appears in cell A1, thanks to the linking formula. If so, press F2 to activate Edit mode and press F4 three times to change the absolute reference $A$1 to its relative form, A1. Now you can copy the formula down and across until you can see all of the data you need to retrieve. Repeat for each sheet in the workbook.

See Also For more information about network issues, see "Sharing Files with Others," page 75.

Searching for Files

If you're unsure about the location of a particular file, you can use the file-finding features in the Open dialog box to search any drive that is connected to your system — and you can use a variety of search criteria to narrow your search. The file-finding features are divided into two levels: The "fast find" controls at the bottom of the Open dialog box, shown in Figure 3-10, and the Advanced Find features.

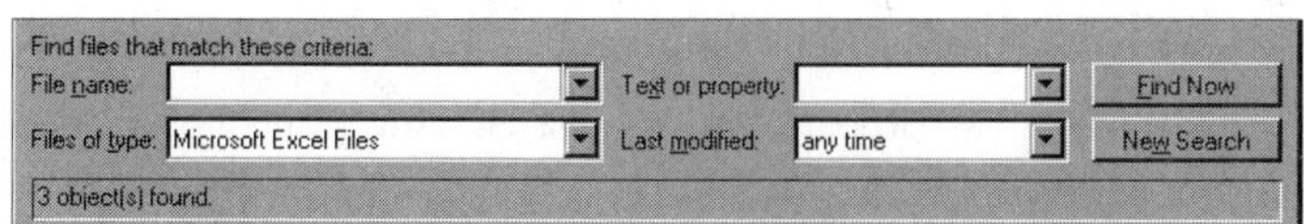

FIGURE 3-10
The "fast find" controls might be all you need.

The controls located under Find Files That Match These Criteria at the bottom of the Open dialog box are the basic tools you need to find a particular file on any disk drive connected to your computer system. To find a specific file, type a filename directly in the File Name edit box. To find all files with a particular three-character extension, type an asterisk and the extension, including wildcards, such as *.XL* or *.DOC, in the File Name edit box, and click the Find Now button. You can also use the File Name edit box to search for several different types of files at the same time. Simply enter the filename extensions, separating them with semicolons. For example, if you enter **.xl*;*.doc* in the File Name edit box, Excel finds all files with these extensions.

TIP In addition to the file-finding features in the Open dialog box, Excel offers several other places you can use file-finding features. The WorkGroup toolbar contains a Find File button, and the same find-file features are also available in the dialog boxes that appear when you click the Browse button in many other dialog boxes.

You can use the Look In box in the Open dialog box to specify the disk drive and directory you want to search.

There are three commands on the Commands and Settings menu shown in Figure 3-9 that help you find files. The Search Subfolders command is an option that toggles on or off each time you choose it. When it is selected, Excel searches the active folder plus any subfolders it contains. Group Files By Folder is linked to the Search Subfolders option and displays the folder hierarchy for any files found. This option is inactive unless Search Subfolders is selected. The Saved Searches submenu lists the names of the searches you saved most recently in the Advanced Find dialog box. Simply choose the name of a search from this submenu to repeat it.

Use the Files Of Type drop-down list to specify file types other than the default, Microsoft Excel Files, which appears automatically when you display the Open dialog box. The arrow to the right of the list box drops down a list of file types for which there is built-in support, including Lotus 1-2-3, Quattro Pro, or more specific Excel file types such as Templates or even Excel 4.0 Macro Sheets.

The Last Modified list box includes a list of timeframes such as today, this week, and last month.

The Text Or Property box is a great place to turn if all you can remember is a few words somewhere in the file. Type the text in this box, and Excel will locate any files that contain the text (and that also match any other criteria, of course). If you entered something in the Property dialog box, you can type that here as well. For example, if you are sure that the file you want to find contains the word "advisor" in either the Properties dialog box or somewhere in the worksheet itself, type it in the Text or Property box and Excel will locate it.

To find a file when you have specified the criteria you need, click Find Now.

Using Advanced Search Criteria

When you click the Advanced button in the Open dialog box, the Advanced Find dialog box appears, as shown in Figure 3-11.

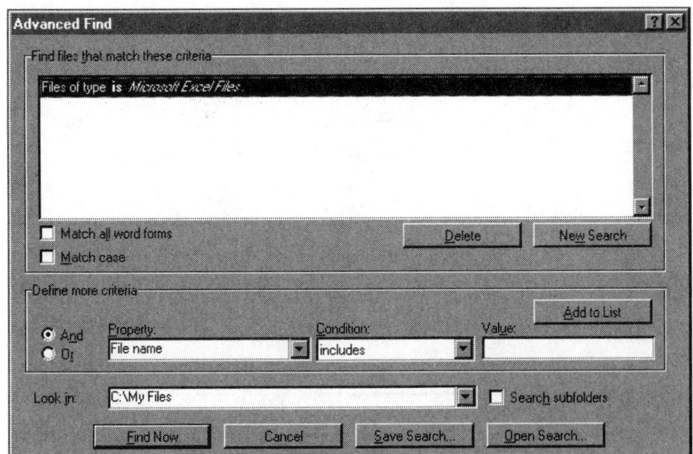

FIGURE 3-11
The Advanced Find dialog box lets you refine your search criteria.

You can use the Look In box of the Advanced Find dialog box to specify the folder you want to search. The Search Subfolders check box extends the search to include any folders subordinate to the one you specify. When Search Subfolders is selected, the Open dialog box displays all files matching the specified criteria anywhere in the path you specify whenever you display the Open dialog box. For example, say you "look in" the root of the C drive using the default criteria at the bottom of the Open dialog box, which are "Microsoft Excel Files" and "Last Modified Any Time." The dialog box displays all the Excel files on your hard disk in one big list. If you're not sure what folder to look in, adding a few more criteria might be helpful.

TIP When you use the Search Subfolders option, you might want to view files in the Open dialog box using the detail view by clicking the Details button. This displays all found files along with the folder structure, so you can easily tell where the files are stored. In List view, found files appear all together with no visible folder hierarchy.

NOTE When you select the Search Subfolders option, it remains selected even when you exit and restart Excel.

The list at the top of the Advanced Find dialog box in Figure 3-11 shows the default criterion, "Files Of Type is *Microsoft Excel Files.*" This list reflects any criteria specified at the bottom of the Open dialog box. If you specified additional criteria in the Open dialog box, such as a filename, property, or modification time, these are also listed here.

Adding Advanced Search Criteria

You use the Define More Criteria area of the Advanced Find dialog box to add criteria to the list. The Property box lists most of the properties available in the Properties dialog box (on the File menu). If, for example, you enter "SUM Corporation" as the Company property in every workbook you create that relates to that company, select Company in the Property list box, and type *SUM Corporation* in the Value box. Clicking the Add To List button adds the criterion to the list at the top of the dialog box, as well as clearing the Value box for the next criterion.

TIP To get into the habit of entering properties to help identify groups of files, you can have the Properties dialog box appear automatically each time you save a file for the first time. On the Tools menu, choose Options, click the General tab, and click the Prompt For File Properties option.

The Condition list box contains a number of text operators that change depending on the property you specify. For example, text properties such as Company have conditions such as "includes phrase," "begins with," and even "is not." (In Excel 5, these kinds of conditions were specified using wildcard codes.) Conditions for date properties such as Last Printed include "last week" and "anytime between," and numeric conditions like Number of Characters include "equals," "at least," and "more than."

The And and Or buttons allow you to specify whether each criterion you add is "in addition to" or "instead of" the previous criterion. You can add quite a few criteria, but some property types allow only one "And." For example, if you attempt to add another Files Of Type criterion with the And button selected, a dialog box informs you that a file type already appears in the criteria list, and asks if you want to change it to an "Or" criteria.

Use the Delete button to single out and remove individual criteria in the list. Click the New Search button to clear all the criteria from the list, except for the default Files Of Type criterion. The Find Now button dismisses the Advanced Find dialog box, carries out the search, and displays the results in the Open dialog box.

The Match All Word Forms option is a remarkable feature that finds variations of words in any text-based criterion *except* filenames. For example, entering "bite" as the value for the Contents property finds any files that contain the words bite, bites, biting, bit, or bitten. Excel normally ignores capitalization of criteria text, but selecting the Match Case option allows you to specify the case of text you're looking for.

Saving and Reusing Search Criteria

The Save Search button in the Advanced Find dialog box displays the Save Search dialog box, where you can type a name for the current search criteria. This name is displayed in the dialog box that appears when you click the Open Search button. The names of saved searches also appear in the Saved Searches submenu of the Commands and Settings menu (see Figure 3-9), making it easy to revisit a previous search without opening the Advanced Find dialog box.

See Also For more information about the Properties dialog box, see "Adding Summary Information to Files," page 62.

Sharing Files with Others

Microsoft Excel provides features that help you work more efficiently in workgroups. If you're connected to a network or you're running Microsoft Mail or Microsoft Exchange, using the features described in this section can make sharing information a lot easier.

Using the Save In drop-down list in the Save As dialog box, you can save a workbook on any available network drive.

The dialog box that is displayed when you choose the Open command on the File menu contains a Look In dropdown list that is similar to the Save In list. You can use this list box to retrieve workbooks saved on the network.

See Also For more information about network connections, see your Microsoft Windows or network software documentation.

Retrieving Busy Files Automatically

When you try to open a file that resides on a network drive while another user has the file open, Excel displays the File Reservation dialog box, which allows you to open the file as read only. If the file was saved using the password-protection options available in the Save Options dialog box, you must also enter the appropriate password.

The File Reservation dialog box that appears when you attempt to open a file that is either in use or protected is shown in Figure 3-12.

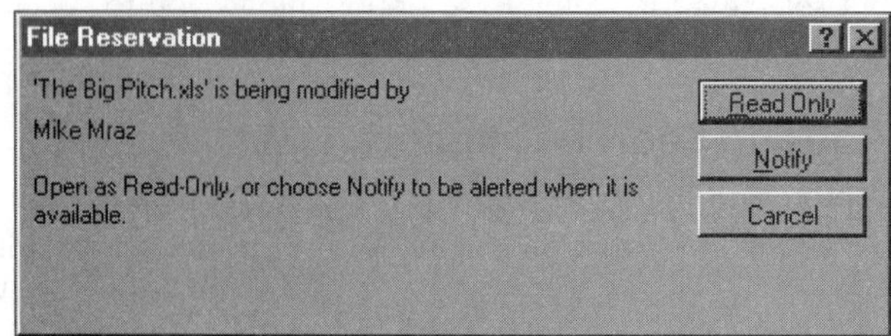

FIGURE 3-12
The File Reservation dialog box appears when you attempt to open a busy or protected file on a network drive.

If you click the Notify button in the File Reservation dialog box, you will automatically be alerted when the file becomes available. If either protection or write reservation passwords are required, the corresponding label in the dialog box is undimmed so that you can type the password to open the file.

If the file is in use by another person on the network, a similar dialog box appears when the file becomes available, as shown in Figure 3-13. This version of the File Reservation dialog box contains a Read-Write button instead of a Notify button. If the file was saved with the Read-Only Recommended option selected, a Read-Only button also appears, with the suggestion that you open the file as read only. If the file was saved as read only, the Read-Write button is dimmed, and you must use the Read-Only button to open the file.

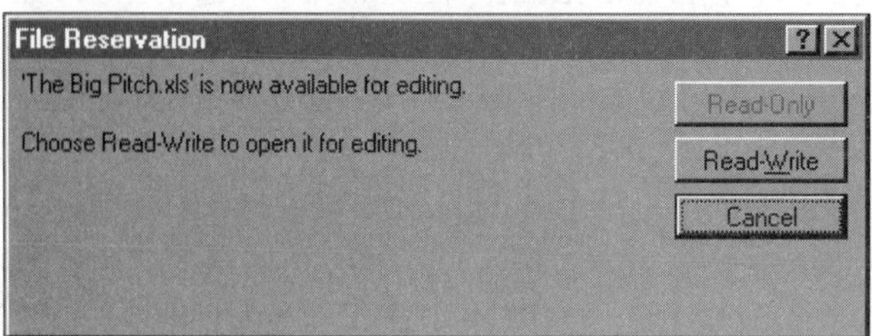

FIGURE 3-13
The File Reservation dialog box lets you know when you can use the file.

See Also For information about password-protection options, see "Protecting Files," page 60.

Sharing Workbooks on a Network

It has always been possible to share files on a network. You just had to make sure that you coordinated your efforts to avoid having more than one person open a file at the same time. But now, Excel 7 allows two or more people to work on the same workbook simultaneously, using the Shared Lists command on the File menu. The Shared Lists dialog box is shown in Figure 3-14.

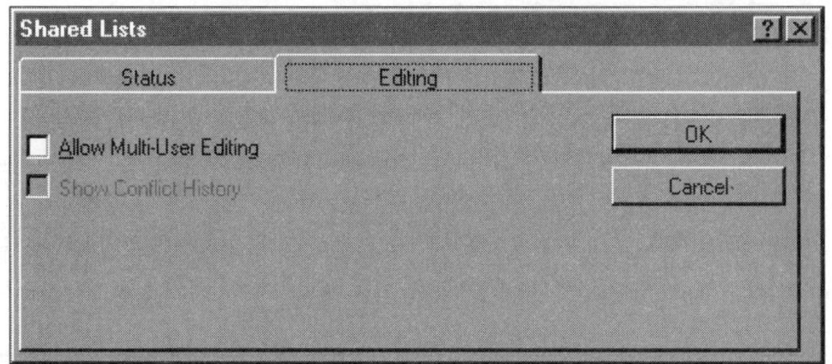

FIGURE 3-14

The Shared Lists command makes it possible for several people to work on a workbook at the same time.

When you check the Allow Multi-User Editing box and click OK, an alert box appears to let you know that the workbook will be saved in order to consummate the command (you can change your mind and click Cancel before the deed is done). This is necessary because the workbook in the shared location must be saved as "sharable" before another user can open it. Once the workbook is saved, the bracketed word [Shared] appears in the title bar whenever anyone opens the workbook, and it persists unless the Allow Multi-User Editing option is turned off, which again causes the workbook to be saved.

The first time you use the Shared Lists command, a dialog box appears that allows you to change the name that other users see when the workbook is being shared, as shown in Figure 3-15. Excel suggests the name that appears in the User Name box on the General tab of the Options dialog box (Tools menu). You can see the names of all who have the workbook open at any given moment by choosing the Shared Lists command and clicking the Status tab, as shown in Figure 3-16 on the next page.

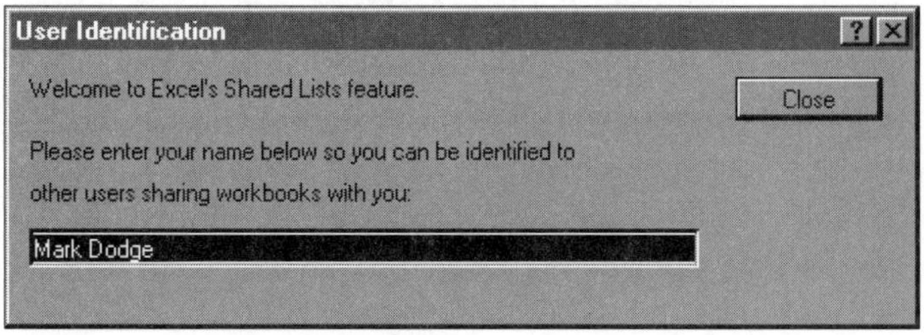

User Identification

Welcome to Excel's Shared Lists feature.

Please enter your name below so you can be identified to other users sharing workbooks with you:

Mark Dodge

Close

FIGURE 3-15

The User Identification dialog box confirms your name as it was entered when Excel was first installed.

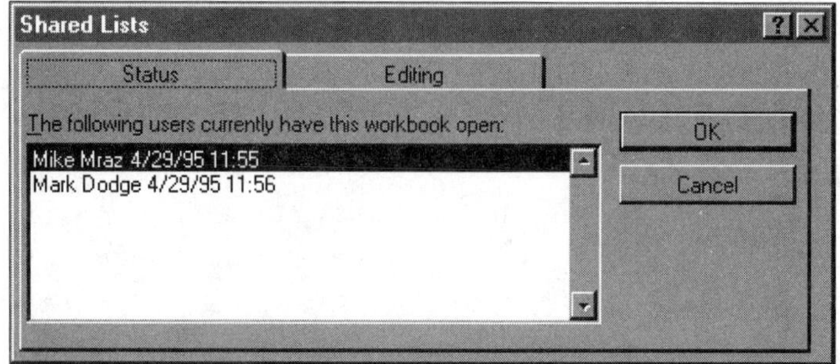

FIGURE 3-16 The Status tab of the Shared Lists dialog box displays the names of all who have the workbook open.

Of course, there are inherent risks when several people work at the same time in the same place. Inevitable conflicts arise when several people are making changes that affect the same cells. When someone saves changes, Excel not only saves the workbook but also updates it if any changes have been saved by other users. If so, a dialog box informs you

What You Can't Do with a Shared List

You might wonder why the multi-user workbooks feature is called "Shared Lists" rather than shared workbooks. In this release of Excel, there are limitations on what you can do when a workbook is shared. Maintaining a "list" (or rudimentary database) is a task that is fairly representative of what can be accomplished with the available multi-user functionality.

When a workbook is activated for multi-user editing, you can enter text and numbers, as well as copy, paste, and move data by dragging with the mouse. You can even insert rows and columns. But you can't change cell formatting and you can't save formulas. The formatting commands and controls are disabled for a workbook in shared mode. If you enter a formula or copy one from another location, a dialog box appears telling you that new formulas cannot be saved while the workbook is in shared mode (even if no one else currently has the workbook open). When you save the workbook, any formulas you entered in shared mode remain visible, but when you close and reopen it, the formulas and the resulting values are gone.

Realistically, using the multi-user functionality available, you can do a lot more than just maintain a list. For example, you could share a budgeting worksheet among the people responsible for each departmental budget, as long as the formulas and formatting are done before (or after) sharing the workbook.

that changes have been incorporated (although you won't know exactly what was changed). In the process, Excel checks for conflicts and determines if any "mediation" is called for. Most times, a dialog box appears after saving that simply informs you that changes made by other users have been incorporated. However, if others' changes involve any of the same cells you changed, the "mediator" arrives in the form of the Conflict Resolution dialog box shown in Figure 3-17.

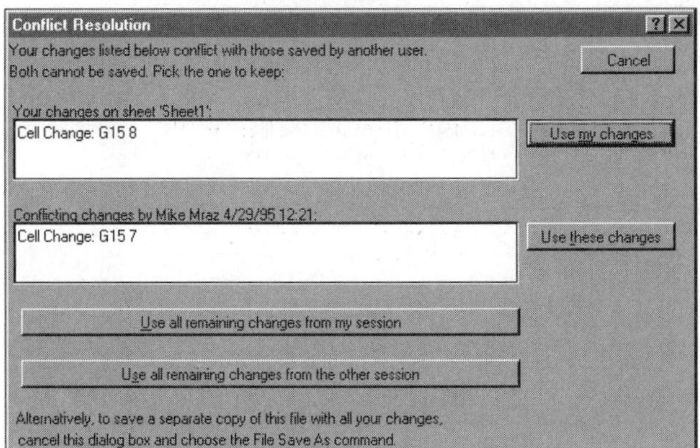

FIGURE 3-17
If more than one person changes the same cells, the last person to save changes gets to decide which ones to keep.

For each conflict identified, the Conflict Resolution dialog box specifies the cells involved and allows you to decide whose changes to keep. If there is more than one conflict, this dialog box reappears. You decide each conflict individually, or you can use the buttons at the bottom of the dialog box to use all the changes entered by one person or the other.

TIP When setting up a multi-user workbook, establish some working guidelines and design the workbook for maximum safety. For example, each person could have a separate named worksheet in the workbook, each worksheet reflecting their specific areas of responsibility. Everyone must agree not to make changes to other worksheets. Create a separate consolidation worksheet that pulls all the relevant data from the personal sheets in order to present it in the necessary format. For more information, see Chapter 8, page 297.

Note that conflicts can exist only between the last saved version and the version you are trying to save. If more than two users have made changes to the same cells, each person who saves the workbook gets to decide who wins the conflict at the moment of saving. If you want to see the history, click Show Conflict History on the Editing tab of the Shared Lists dialog box. When you click OK, Excel adds a new worksheet after the last worksheet, as shown in Figure 3-18. The worksheet keeps track of conflicts only, not of all edits made to the workbook.

FIGURE 3-18
The Conflict History worksheet keeps track of any conflicting changes made to the workbook.

Ad Campaign [Shared]

	A	B	C	D	E	F
1	Action Type	Date	Time	Who	Change	Sheet Location
2						
3	Won	4/29/95	12:11:21 PM	Mike Mraz	Cell Change	Sheet1
4	Lost	4/29/95	12:11:45 PM	Mark Dodge	Cell Change	Sheet1
5	Won	4/29/95	12:21:15 PM	Mark Dodge	Cell Change	Sheet1
6	Lost	4/29/95	12:22:52 PM	Mike Mraz	Cell Change	Sheet1

Sheet14 / Sheet15 / Sheet16 / Conflict History

The Conflict History worksheet is a special locked worksheet that can be displayed only when a worksheet is in shared mode — the worksheet disappears when you clear the Allow Multi-User Editing option in the Shared Lists dialog box. If you subsequently reselect multi-user editing for the workbook, the conflict history starts fresh, and any conflicts recorded in previous multi-user sessions are lost.

TIP To keep track of conflicts after discontinuing multi-user editing, copy the contents of the locked Conflict History worksheet and paste them into another worksheet.

Mailing Workbooks Using Electronic Mail

Excel provides built-in features to take advantage of electronic mail. If Microsoft Mail, Microsoft Exchange, Lotus cc:Mail, or another mail program is present, the Send and Add Routing Slip commands become available on Excel's File menu. When you choose the Send command, Excel activates the Send screen of the mail application, with a copy of the current workbook attached, as shown in Figure 3-19 (Microsoft Exchange is shown).

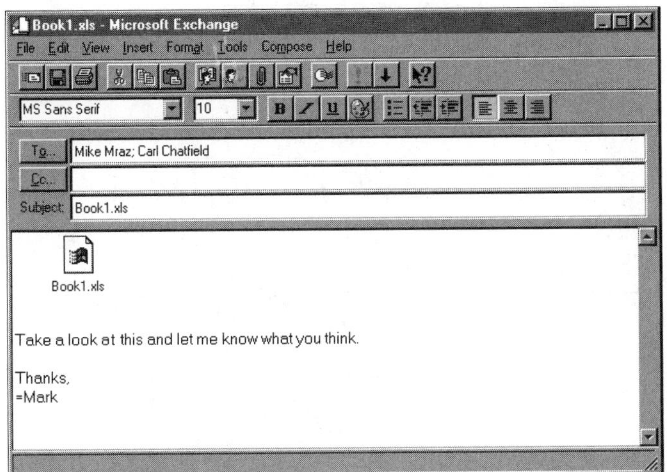

FIGURE 3-19
The Send command activates the mail program and attaches a copy of the current workbook.

TIP You can send mail using the Send Mail button on the WorkGroup toolbar.

When you click the Send Mail button, the message and attached copy of the workbook are sent to the recipients listed in the To edit box. When the message is received, the recipients simply double-click the Excel icon in the mail message to open the workbook. Note that any changes you make to the workbook after sending the message are not reflected in the sent copy.

Routing Workbooks to a Workgroup Using Electronic Mail

If you are working on a project that involves a group of people whose input is crucial, you can route a workbook to a group using electronic mail. When you choose the Add Routing Slip command from Excel's File menu, the Routing Slip dialog box shown in Figure 3-20 (on the next page) is displayed.

TIP You can click the Routing Slip button on the WorkGroup toolbar to display the Routing Slip dialog box.

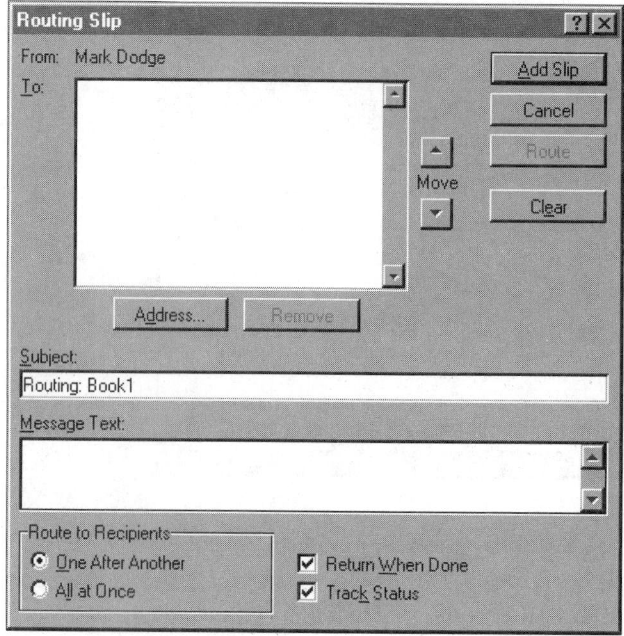

FIGURE 3-20
Route a workbook to a group using the Add Routing Slip command.

The Add Routing Slip command offers several advantages over the Send command. For example, the Add Routing Slip command allows you to specify sequential routing. That is, if you construct a list of recipients using the Address button and select the One After Another option, the workbook will be sent to the first person on the list. When that person replies, the workbook will automatically be forwarded to the next person on the list. The To list box shows you the sequence, which you can modify by selecting a name in the list and clicking the Move buttons. Alternatively, you can choose to route the workbook to all recipients at the same time by selecting All At Once.

To send the message off on its appointed rounds, click the Route button in the Routing Slip dialog box. To simply attach the routing slip to the workbook, click the Add Slip button. Using the latter method allows you to continue working. Then, when you're ready to send the message, choose the Send command. (This method also allows you to edit the routing slip itself to include more or fewer people in the distribution because after you add a routing slip, the Add Routing Slip command changes to Edit Routing Slip.)

If the Track Status option in the Routing Slip dialog box is selected, you will receive notification each time the workbook is forwarded so that you can keep track of its progress. If the Return When Done option is selected, the workbook is returned to you in the mail after it has made its rounds.

Posting to Microsoft Exchange

If you have Microsoft Exchange installed, the Post To Exchange Folder command appears on the File menu. When you post a workbook, a copy of the workbook is placed in the location you specify. This is a handy way to make workbooks available for review to a large audience, without having to burden the mail system with large workbooks or extensive lists of reviewers.

Part 2

Worksheets

Chapter 4

Worksheet Basics

Microsoft Excel gives you a lot of visual clues to help you as you work with your data. But Excel is an extremely powerful program and includes many ways to do things — even things that appear to be very simple. In this chapter, we'll first explain the basics of selection, navigation, data entry, and data protection. Then we'll show you some tricks that can make the simple stuff even simpler.

Moving Around the Worksheet

Before you can work with cells, you must select a cell or a group of cells. When you select a single cell, it becomes active, and its reference appears in the Name box at the left end of the formula bar. Although only one cell can be active at a time, you can often speed operations by selecting groups of cells called *ranges*. You can move among the cells in a selected range (but not those outside the range) without changing your range selection.

In this chapter, we describe both mouse and keyboard techniques for selecting cells and ranges. In subsequent chapters, we won't differentiate between mouse and keyboard instructions; instead, we'll simply tell you, for example, to select a cell or click OK.

Selecting with the Mouse

To select a single cell, point to it and click the mouse button. The active cell border appears around the cell, and the cell reference appears in the Name box.

To select a range of cells, for example A1:B5, follow these simple steps:

1. Point to cell A1.
2. Hold down the left mouse button and drag down and to the right to cell B5.

   Figure 4-1 shows the selected range.

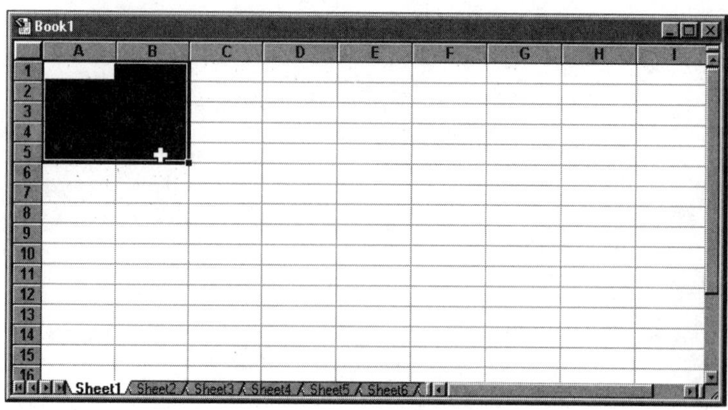

FIGURE 4-1 The selected cells are highlighted as you drag through a range.

Excel describes the range in terms of the cells located at the upper left and lower right corners of the range. For example, the range in Figure 4-1 is A1:B5. The active cell always occupies one corner of the range.

Extending a Selection

Instead of dragging through all the cells you want to work with, you can indicate any two diagonal corners of the range. This technique is known as *extending a selection*. For example, to extend the selection A1:B5 so that it becomes A1:C10, hold down the Shift key and click cell C10. When you need to select a large range, you may find this technique more efficient than dragging the mouse across the entire selection.

Keyboard Modes

The right side of the status bar displays the following indicators when one of the corresponding modes is active:

EXT	Extend Mode. Press F8 to extend the current selection using the keyboard. This is the keyboard equivalent of holding down Shift and selecting cells with the mouse.
ADD	Add mode. Press Shift-F8 to add more cells to the current selection using the keyboard. The cells need not be adjacent. This is the keyboard equivalent of holding down Ctrl and selecting cells with the mouse.
NUM	Num Lock mode. This mode is on by default and locks the keypad in numeric-entry mode. To turn off Num Lock, press the Num Lock key.
FIX	Fixed Decimal mode. Choosing the Options command from the Tools menu, clicking the Edit tab, and selecting the Fixed Decimal option adds a decimal point to numeric entries, in the location you specify in the Places edit box. For example, if you turn on Fixed Decimal mode and specify two decimal places, the entry 12345 is entered in the cell as 123.45.
CAPS	Caps Lock mode. Pressing the Caps Lock key allows you to enter text in all capital letters. The number and symbol keys are not affected.

(continued)

(continued)

Keyboard Modes

Three other keyboard modes don't show indicators in the status bar:

- Scroll Lock mode. Normally, when you use the PgUp and PgDn keys, the active cell moves a page at a time as you scroll through the worksheet. Pressing the Scroll Lock key allows you to use the PgUp and PgDn keys without moving the active cell.
- Overwrite mode. Normally, when you type in the formula bar, new characters are inserted between existing characters. With Overwrite mode turned on, the characters you type replace any existing characters you type over. To activate Overwrite mode, press the Ins key while the Formula bar is active.
- End mode. Pressing the End key and then pressing a direction key moves the selection to the next region in the direction of the arrow on the key, or to the last worksheet cell in that direction.

As an alternative to holding down the Shift key, you can press F8. For example, to select A1:H20, follow these steps:

1. Click cell A1.
2. Press F8. The EXT indicator appears in the status bar, showing that you have activated Extend mode.
3. Click cell H20.
4. To turn off Extend mode, press F8 again.

Selecting Beyond the Window Borders

If you need to select a range that extends beyond your workbook window, you can simply drag the mouse pointer past the window border, or you can use the View menu's Zoom command. For example, to select the range A14:A25, follow these steps:

1. Click cell A14.
2. Drag the mouse pointer down through cell A25. (When the pointer reaches the bottom of the window, the worksheet begins scrolling up.)
3. Release the mouse button. Figure 4-2 shows the result.

To select the range A3:A12 in Figure 4-2, click cell A12 and drag the mouse pointer up toward the title bar. When you reach cell A3, release the mouse button.

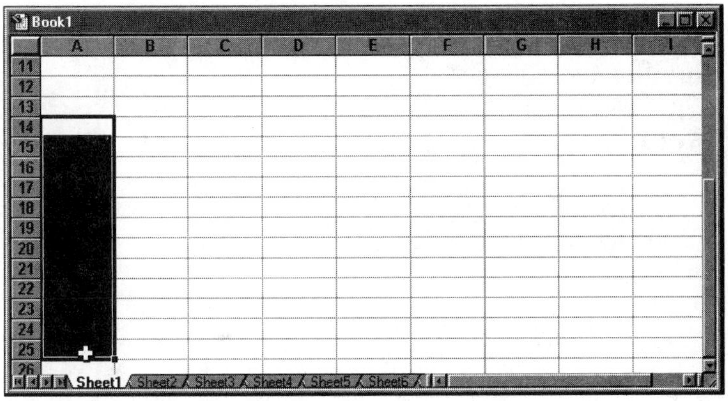

FIGURE 4-2
You can drag past the window borders to bring additional cells into view as you make your selection.

You can also drag past the left and right borders of the workbook window to bring additional columns into view as you make your selection.

When you need to select large ranges, the dragging technique can be too time-consuming. Here is an alternative for selecting A1:M38:

1. Click cell A1.
2. Use the scroll bars to bring cell M38 into view.
3. Hold down Shift or press F8.
4. Click cell M38.

You can also use the Go To command on the Edit menu to select ranges.

See Also For more information about the Go To command, see "Using the Go To Command," page 96.

Selecting Multiple-Area Ranges

Multiple-area ranges are cell ranges that do not encompass a single rectangular area. To select multiple-area ranges with the mouse, use the Ctrl key. For example, to add the range C7:E10 to the already selected range A1:B6, hold down Ctrl and drag through cells C7:E10. As you can see in Figure 4-3 at the top of the next page, the first cell you click in the new range becomes the active cell.

You can also use Add mode to select multiple-area ranges. After selecting the first area of your range, press Shift-F8 to turn on Add mode. When the ADD indicator appears at the right end of the status bar, drag through the cells of the new range. Press Esc or Shift-F8 to turn off Add mode.

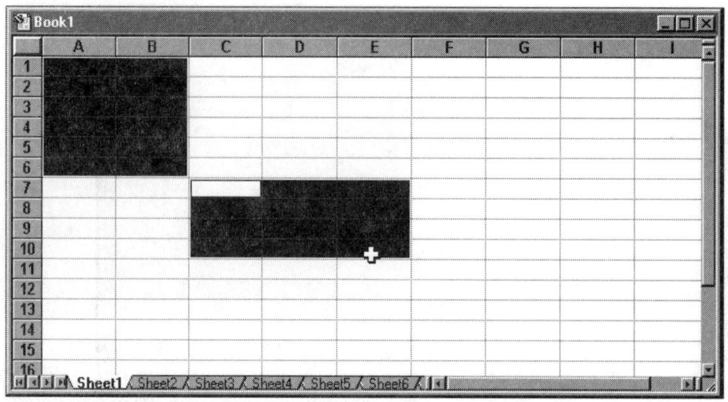

FIGURE 4-3
Hold down Ctrl to select multiple-area ranges with the mouse.

Selecting Columns and Rows

To select an entire column or row, click the column or row heading. The first visible cell becomes the active cell. For example, to select B1 through B16384, click the heading for column B. The first visible cell in the column is the active cell. To select more than one adjacent row or column at a time, drag through the row or column headings, or click the heading at one edge of the range, press Shift or F8, and then click the heading at the opposite edge. To select nonadjacent rows or columns, use Ctrl or Shift-F8 as already described.

You can also select entire columns and rows at the same time. For example, to select column A and rows 1, 2, and 3, follow these steps:

1. Click row heading 1.
2. Drag down to row heading 3.
3. Press Ctrl and click column heading A.

Figure 4-4 shows that Excel highlights all of column A and all of rows 1, 2, and 3.

Sales.xls

	A	B	C	D	E	F	G	H	I
1	ABC Company Sales								
2									
3	1995	Qtr 1	Qtr 2	Qtr 3	Qtr 4		Total	Average	
4	Product 1	1000	1050	1100	1150		4300	1075	
5	Product 2	1100	1150	1200	1250		4700	1175	
6	Product 3	1200	1250	1300	1350		5100	1275	
7	Product 4	1300	1350	1400	1450		5500	1375	
8									
9	Total	4600	4800	5000	5200		19600	4900	
10	Average	1150	1200	1250	1300		4900	1225	
11									
12									
13									
14									
15									
16									

Sheet1 Sheet2 Sheet3 Sheet4 Sheet5 Sheet6

FIGURE 4-4
You can select entire columns and rows by clicking their headings.

TIP At times you will want to select all the cells in a worksheet to change the format for the entire worksheet or to copy the contents of one worksheet to another. To select the entire worksheet at once, simply click the Select All box in the upper left corner of your workbook window, where the column and row headings intersect.

Selecting and Moving Within Regions

A *region* is a range of cell entries bounded by blank cells or row and column headings. For example, in Figure 4-5, the range A3:E7 is a region, as are the ranges G3:H7, A9:E10, and G9:H10. To select or move around regions, choose the Options command from the Tools menu, and then click the Edit tab. The Allow Cell Drag And Drop option should be selected by default. If it is not, select the option and then click OK. As shown in Figure 4-5, a small square, called the *fill handle,* appears at the lower right corner of the active cell's border.

Fill handle

Sales.xls

	A	B	C	D	E	F	G	H	I
1	ABC Company Sales								
2									
3	1995	Qtr 1	Qtr 2	Qtr 3	Qtr 4		Total	Average	
4	Product 1	1000	1050	1100	1150		4300	1075	
5	Product 2	1100	1150	1200	1250		4700	1175	
6	Product 3	1200	1250	1300	1350		5100	1275	
7	Product 4	1300	1350	1400	1450		5500	1375	
8									
9	Total	4600	4800	5000	5200		19600	4900	
10	Average	1150	1200	1250	1300		4900	1225	
11									
12									
13									
14									
15									
16									

Sheet1 / Sheet2 / Sheet3 / Sheet4 / Sheet5 / Sheet6

FIGURE 4-5
The small square at the lower right corner of the cell border indicates that the Allow Cell Drag And Drop option is active.

When the Allow Cell Drag And Drop option is active, moving the mouse pointer over the edge of a cell border changes the plus sign to an arrow. With the arrow pointer visible, double-click the bottom edge of the cell border. Excel selects the cell at the bottom of the current region. If the active cell is already at the bottom of a region, double-clicking the bottom edge of the cell border selects the cell above the next lower region. For example, if you double-click the bottom edge of the active cell in Figure 4-6, Excel selects cell A8. Double-clicking the top, bottom, left, or right edge of a cell border selects a cell in that direction.

FIGURE 4-6
Double-click the edge of a cell border to select a cell at the end of a region.

Sales.xls

	A	B	C	D	E	F	G	H	I
1	ABC Company Sales								
2									
3	1995	Qtr 1	Qtr 2	Qtr 3	Qtr 4		Total	Average	
4	Product 1	1000	1050	1100	1150		4300	1075	
5	Product 2	1100	1150	1200	1250		4700	1175	
6	Product 3	1200	1250	1300	1350		5100	1275	
7	Product 4	1300	1350	1400	1450		5500	1375	
8									
9	Total	4600	4800	5000	5200		19600	4900	
10	Average	1150	1200	1250	1300		4900	1225	
11									
12									
13									
14									
15									
16									

Sheet1 / Sheet2 / Sheet3 / Sheet4 / Sheet5 / Sheet6

If you hold down Shift as you double-click the edge of a cell border, Excel selects all cells from the current cell to the next edge of the region. For example, with cell A3 active, double-clicking the bottom edge of the cell border while holding down Shift selects the range A3:A7, as Figure 4-7 shows.

FIGURE 4-7
Holding down Shift while double-clicking the edge of a range border extends the selection in that direction to the region's edge.

Sales.xls

	A	B	C	D	E	F	G	H	I
1	ABC Company Sales								
2									
3	1995	Qtr 1	Qtr 2	Qtr 3	Qtr 4		Total	Average	
4	Product 1	1000	1050	1100	1150		4300	1075	
5	Product 2	1100	1150	1200	1250		4700	1175	
6	Product 3	1200	1250	1300	1350		5100	1275	
7	Product 4	1300	1350	1400	1450		5500	1375	
8									
9	Total	4600	4800	5000	5200		19600	4900	
10	Average	1150	1200	1250	1300		4900	1225	
11									
12									
13									
14									
15									
16									

Sheet1 / Sheet2 / Sheet3 / Sheet4 / Sheet5 / Sheet6

The cell from which you start the selection remains the active cell. If you double-click the right edge of the border around the range A3:A7 while holding down Shift, Excel then selects the range A3:E7, as Figure 4-8 shows.

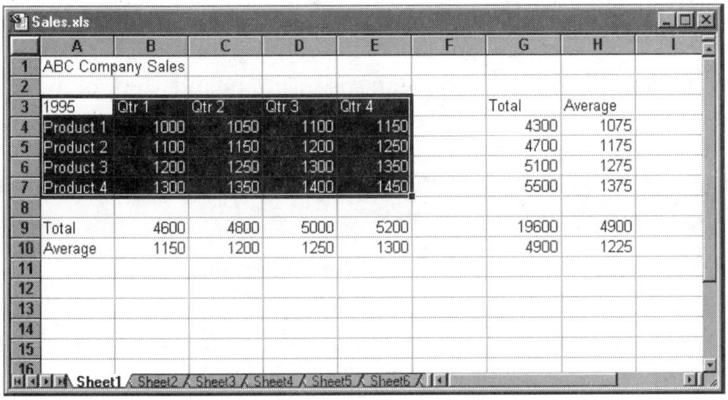

FIGURE 4-8

You can select blocks of cells with only a few mouse clicks.

Selecting with the Keyboard

You can also use the keyboard to select cells and move around your worksheet. To select a single cell, use the direction keys. For example, if cell A1 is active, press the Down direction key once to select cell A2. Press the Right direction key to activate the cell immediately to the right of the active cell; press the Left direction key to activate the cell immediately to the left.

Moving Between Cell Regions

To move through cell regions, use Ctrl with the direction keys. For example, if cell A3 is the active cell, press Ctrl and the Right direction key to activate cell E3, as shown in Figure 4-9. If a blank cell is active when you press Ctrl and a direction key, Excel moves to the first cell in the corresponding direction that contains a cell entry, or to the last cell in that direction in the worksheet, if there are no cells containing entries in that direction.

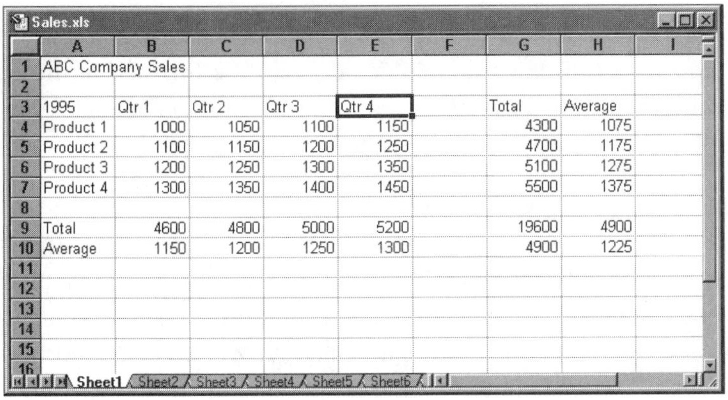

FIGURE 4-9

You can use the Ctrl key and the direction keys to move between cell regions.

Using Home and End

The Home and End keys are valuable for selecting and moving around. The following table shows how you can use Home and End alone and in conjunction with other keys to make selections and move around a worksheet.

Press	To
Home	Move to the first cell in the current row.
Ctrl-Home	Move to cell A1.
Ctrl-End	Move to the last cell in the last column in the active area.
End	Activate End mode. Then use the direction keys to move between cell regions.
Scroll Lock-Home	Move to the first cell entirely in the current window.
Scroll Lock-End	Move to the last cell entirely in the current window.

The *active area* is a rectangle that encompasses all the rows and columns in a worksheet that contain entries. For example, in Figure 4-9, pressing Ctrl-End while any cell is active selects cell H10. Pressing Ctrl-Home selects cell A1.

You use End with the direction keys to move between cell regions. To activate End mode, press End; to turn off End mode, press End again. Press End and the Right direction key to select the rightmost cell in the current region, or the first cell in the next region if you're already in the rightmost cell in the current region. Press End and the Down direction key to select the bottom cell in the current region. After you press a direction key, End mode is automatically turned off.

When you turn on Scroll Lock, movement is relative to the window rather than to the active cell. For example, to move to the first cell in the current window, press Scroll Lock and then press Home. To turn off Scroll Lock, simply press Scroll Lock again.

Using the Go To Command

To quickly move to and select a cell or a range of cells, choose the Go To command from the Edit menu (or press F5), enter the cell or range reference in the Reference edit box, and click OK. You can also use the Go To command to extend a selection. For example, to select A1:Z100, you could click A1, choose the Go To command, type *Z100,* and then hold down the Shift key while pressing Enter.

To move to another worksheet in the same workbook, choose Go To and type the name of the worksheet, followed by an exclamation point and a cell name or reference. For example, to go to cell D5 in a worksheet called Sheet2, type *Sheet2!D5*.

When you use the Go To command, Excel lists in the Reference edit box the cell or range from which you just moved. This way, you can easily move back and forth between two locations by repeatedly pressing F5 and then Enter. Excel also keeps track of the last four locations from which you used the Go To command and lists them in the Go To dialog box. You can use this list to move among these locations in your worksheet. Figure 4-10 shows the Go To dialog box with four previous locations displayed.

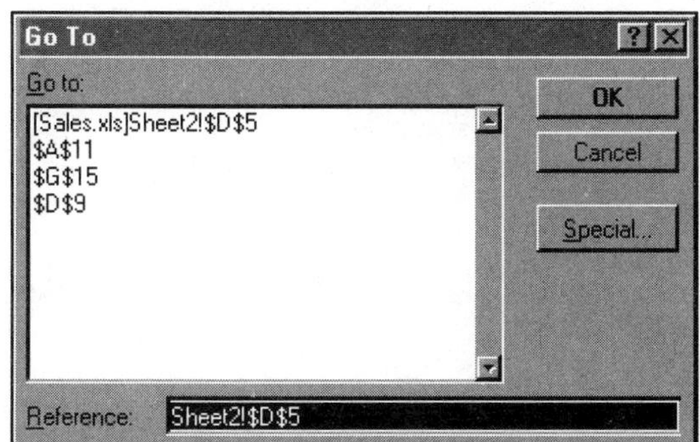

FIGURE 4-10
The Go To dialog box keeps track of the last four locations from which you used the Go To command.

For more information about moving to other worksheets in the same workbook, see "References to Other Worksheets in the Same Workbook," page 117.

For more information about cell names, see "Naming Cells and Ranges," page 126.

Extending a Selection

As when you're using the mouse, you can extend a keyboard selection by using Shift or F8. (You cannot extend a selection with the Tab key.)

For example, to select the range A1:B5 with Shift, follow these steps:

1. Select cell A1.
2. Hold down Shift, press the Right direction key once, and press the Down direction key four times.
3. Release Shift.

Your screen should look like the one shown earlier in Figure 4-1.

Now select the range A1:C12 using F8 by following these steps:

1. Select cell A1.
2. Press F8 to turn on Extend mode. (The EXT indicator appears in the status bar.)
3. Press the Right direction key twice and press the Down direction key 11 times.
4. Press F8 again to turn off Extend mode.

To extend a selection beyond the window border, you use Shift and the direction keys. For example, to select the range A1:C40, follow these steps:

1. Select cell A1.
2. Hold down Shift and press the Right direction key twice.
3. Continue to hold down Shift and press the PgDn key twice.
4. Continue to hold down Shift and use the direction keys to move the selection up or down until cell C40 is included in the selected range. (PgDn scrolls down one screen at a time. The distance differs, depending on your computer's display.)

Selecting Multiple-Area Ranges

To select multiple-area ranges, use Add mode. For example, to add the range C7:E10 to the already selected range A1:B6, follow these steps:

1. With the range A1:B6 selected, press Shift-F8 to turn on Add mode.
2. Use the direction keys to select cell C7.
3. To select the range C7:E10, hold down Shift and use the direction keys, or press F8 and use the direction keys.

Selecting Columns and Rows

You can select an entire column by selecting a cell in the column and pressing Ctrl-Spacebar. To select an entire row with the keyboard, select a cell in the row and press Shift-Spacebar.

To select several entire adjacent columns or rows, highlight a range that includes cells in each of the columns or rows and then press Ctrl-Spacebar or Shift-Spacebar. For example, to select columns B, C, and D, select B4:D4, or any range that includes cells in these three columns, and then press Ctrl-Spacebar.

TIP To select the entire worksheet with the keyboard, press Ctrl-Shift-Spacebar.

Entering Data

Microsoft Excel accepts two basic types of cell entries: *constants* and *formulas*. Constants fall into three main categories: numeric values, text values (also called labels or strings), and date and time values. In this section, we look at numeric and text values.

Excel also recognizes two special types of constants called *logical values* and *error values*.

See Also For more information about formulas and error values, see Chapter 5, "Building Formulas," page 111.

For more information about date and time values, see Chapter 12, "Dates and Times," page 459.

For more information about logical values, see Chapter 11, "Common Worksheet Functions," page 397.

Simple Numeric and Text Values

An entry that includes only the numerals 0 through 9 and certain special characters (+ – E e ( ) . , $ % and /) is a numeric value. An entry that includes almost any other character is a text value. The following table lists some examples of numeric and text values.

Numeric Values	Text Values
123	Sales
345678	Hello
$9999.99	A Label
1%	123 Main Street
1.23E+12	No. 324

Entering Numeric Values

To enter a numeric value, select the cell and type the number. As you type, the number appears in the formula bar and in the active cell. The flashing vertical bar that appears in the cell or in the formula bar is called the *insertion point*.

Locking In the Entry

When you finish typing, you must lock in the entry to store it permanently in the cell. The simplest way to lock in an entry is to press Enter after you type the entry. The insertion point disappears, and Excel stores the entry in the cell.

If you press Tab, Shift-Tab, Enter, Shift-Enter, or a direction key after you type the entry, Excel locks in the entry and activates an adjacent cell.

TIP Pressing Enter normally causes the active cell to move down one row. You can change this, however, so that the active cell stays the same when you press Enter. To do so, choose Options from the Tools menu, click the Edit tab, and deselect the Move Selection After Enter option.

As mentioned in Chapter 1, when you begin typing an entry, three buttons appear on the formula bar: the Cancel button, the Enter button, and the Function Wizard button. These buttons are shown in Figure 4-11. The Cancel button, which contains an X, provides a way to leave the formula bar without locking in an entry. If you change your mind while typing, you can click the Cancel button. (To cancel an entry with the keyboard, press Esc.) Clicking the Enter button, which contains a check mark, is another way to lock in your cell entry. If you press the Function Wizard button, Excel displays a dialog box from which you can select one or more of Excel's built-in functions.

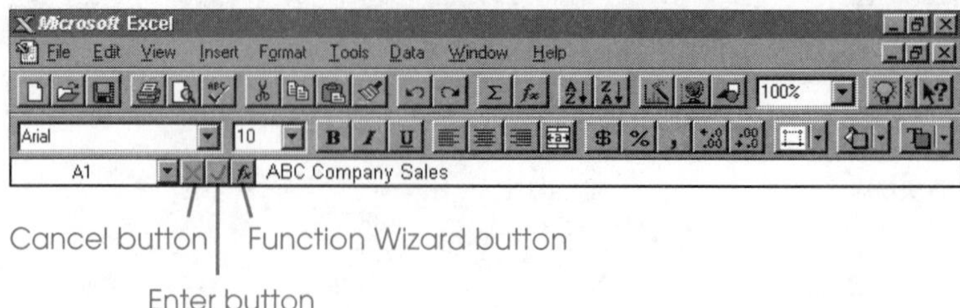

FIGURE 4-11

You can lock in a cell entry by clicking the Enter button or cancel a cell entry by clicking the Cancel button on the Formula bar.

For more information about the Function Wizard, see Chapter 11, "Common Worksheet Functions," page 397.

Special Characters

If you begin a numeric entry with a plus sign (+), Excel drops the plus sign. If you begin a numeric entry with a minus sign (–), Excel interprets the entry as a negative number and retains the sign.

You use the character *E* or *e* to indicate scientific notation. For example, Excel interprets 1E6 as 1,000,000 (1 times 10 to the sixth power).

Excel interprets numeric constants enclosed in parentheses as negative numbers, which is a common accounting practice. For example, Excel interprets (100) as –100.

You can use decimal points as you normally do. You can also use commas to separate hundreds from thousands, thousands from millions, and so on. When you enter numbers that include commas as separators, the numbers appear with commas in the cell but without them in the formula bar. For example, if you enter *1,234.56,* the formula bar displays 1234.56. Meanwhile, the cell displays the number with the comma in place, as if you had applied one of Excel's built-in Number formats.

If you begin a numeric entry with a dollar sign, Excel assigns a Currency format to the cell. For example, if you enter $123456, Excel displays $123,456 in the cell, and the formula bar displays 123456. In this case, Excel adds the comma to the worksheet display because it is part of Excel's Currency format.

If you end a numeric entry with a percent sign (%), Excel assigns a percentage format to the cell. For example, if you enter 23%, Excel displays 23% in the formula bar and assigns a Percentage format to the cell, which displays 23%.

If you use a forward slash (/) in a numeric entry and the string cannot be interpreted as a date, Excel interprets the number as a fraction. For example, if you enter *11 5/8,* Excel displays 11.625 in the formula bar and assigns a Fraction format to the cell. The cell displays 11 5/8.

TIP To make sure a fraction cannot be interpreted as a date, precede the fraction with a zero and a space. For example, to enter 1/2, type *0 1/2.*

See Also For more information about Excel's built-in Number formats, see "Assigning and Removing Formats," page 158.

Displayed Values Versus Underlying Values

Although you can type as many as 255 characters in a cell, a numeric cell entry can contain a maximum of 15 digits. If you enter a number that is too long to appear in a cell, Excel converts it to scientific notation. Excel adjusts the precision of the scientific notation to display such an entry in a cell, as shown in Figure 4-12. However, if you enter a very large or a very small number, Excel also displays it in the formula bar using scientific notation with up to 15 digits of precision.

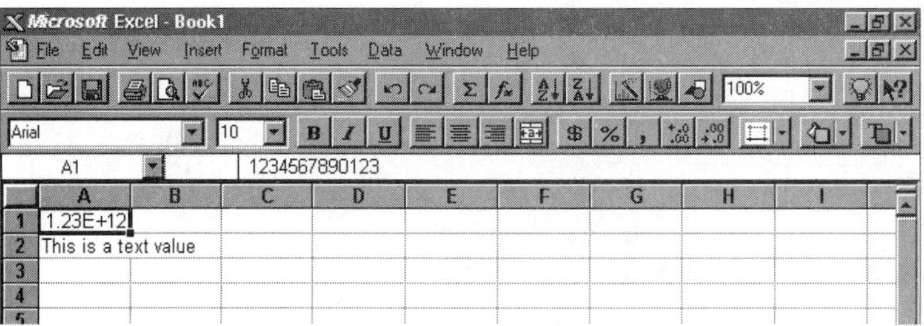

FIGURE 4-12
The number 1234567890123 is too long to fit in cell A1, so Excel displays it in scientific notation.

The values that appear in cells are called *displayed values;* the values that are stored in cells and that appear in the formula bar are called *underlying values*. The number of digits that appear in a cell depends on the width of the column. If you reduce the width of a column that contains a long entry, Excel might either display a rounded-off version of the number or a string of pound signs (#), depending on the display format you're using. If you see a series of pound signs in a cell where you expect to see a number, simply increase the width of the cell.

See Also For more information about increasing the width of a cell, see "Controlling Column Width," page 192.

For more information about precision, see "Precision of Numeric Values," page 151.

Entering Text Values

Entering text is similar to entering numeric values. To enter text in a cell, select a cell, type the text, and lock in the entry by pressing Enter or clicking the Enter button. To cancel an entry, press Esc or click the Cancel button.

Long Text Entries

If you enter text that is too long to be displayed in a single cell, Excel allows the text to overlap the adjacent cells. However, the text is stored in the single cell. If you then type text in a cell that is overlapped by another cell, the overlapping text appears truncated, as shown in cell A2 in Figure 4-13.

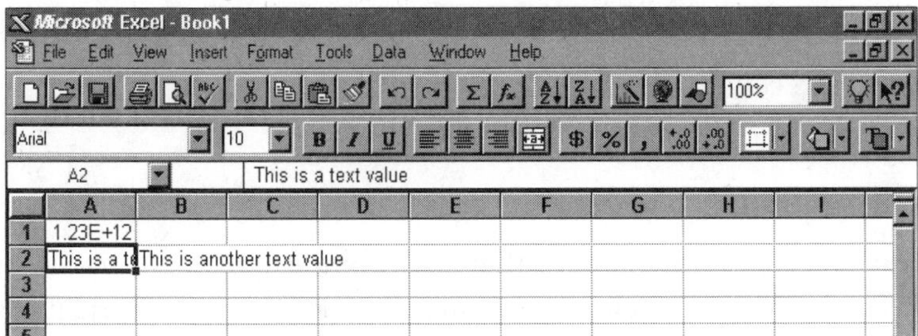

FIGURE 4-13
When the cell to the right of a long text value contains an entry, the text value cannot spill over and appears truncated.

TIP The easiest way to alleviate overlapping text is to widen the column by double-clicking the column border in the heading. For example, in Figure 4-13, when you double-click the line between the A and the B in the column heading, the width of column A adjusts to accommodate the longest entry in the column.

See Also For more information about adjusting columns to accommodate entries, see "Controlling Column Width," page 192.

Using Wordwrap

If you have long text entries, Wordwrap makes them easier to read. Select the cells, choose Cells from the Format menu, click the Alignment tab, and select the Wrap Text box; then click OK. The Wrap Text option lets you enter long strings of text that wrap onto two or more lines within the same cell rather than overlapping across adjacent cells. To accommodate the extra lines, Excel increases the height of the row that contains the formatted cell.

See Also For more information about wrapping text in cells, see "Aligning Cell Contents," page 178.

Numeric Text Entries

A numeric text entry consists of text and numbers or all numbers. To enter text and numbers, select the cell, type the entry, and press Enter. Because this entry includes nonnumeric characters, Excel interprets it as a text value.

To create a text entry that consists entirely of numbers, precede the entry with an equal sign and enclose it with quotation marks, or precede the entry with an apostrophe. For example, to enter the part number 1234, follow these steps:

1. Select the cell.
2. Type = *"1234"* or *'1234*
3. Press Enter.

The equal sign and the quotation marks or the apostrophe appear in the formula bar but not in the cell. While numeric entries are normally right-aligned, the numeric text entry is left-aligned in the cell as shown in Figure 4-14.

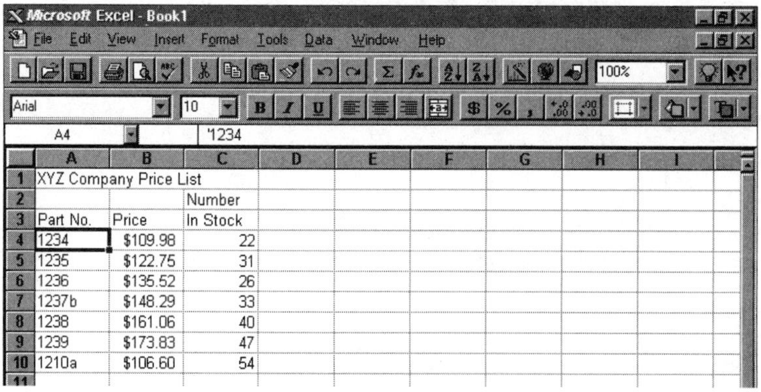

FIGURE 4-14
The part numbers in column A were entered as text.

	A	B	C
1	XYZ Company Price List		
2			Number
3	Part No.	Price	In Stock
4	1234	$109.98	22
5	1235	$122.75	31
6	1236	$135.52	26
7	1237b	$148.29	33
8	1238	$161.06	40
9	1239	$173.83	47
10	1210a	$106.60	54

Making Entries in Ranges

To make a number of entries in a range of adjacent cells, you first select those cells. Then you use Enter, Shift-Enter, Tab, and Shift-Tab to move the active cell within the range, as follows:

Press	To Activate
Enter	The cell below the active cell
Shift-Enter	The cell above the active cell
Tab	The cell one column to the right of the active cell
Shift-Tab	The cell one column to the left of the active cell

For example, to make entries in the range B2:D4, follow these steps:

1. Select from cell B2 to cell D4 so that cell B2 is active.
2. Type *100* in cell B2 and press Enter.
3. In cell B3 (now the active cell), type *200* and press Enter.
4. In cell B4 (now the active cell), type *300* and press Enter. Cell C2 becomes the active cell, as shown in Figure 4-15.

You can continue to make entries in this way until you fill the entire range.

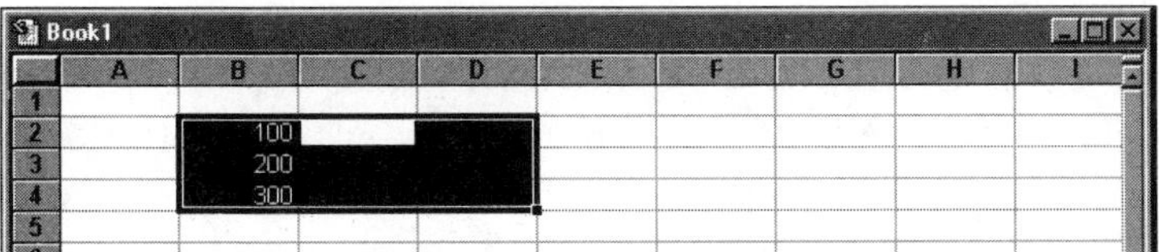

FIGURE 4-15
You can fill a range of selected cells by making entries and pressing Enter.

TIP To enter the same value in several cells at once, first select the cells. Then type your entry and hold down Ctrl while you press Enter or click the Enter button.

Correcting Errors in Entries

You can correct typing mistakes before you lock in the entry, and you can change the contents of a cell after you lock in the entry.

Correcting Errors Before You Lock In the Entry

To correct simple errors as you type, press Backspace, which erases the character to the left of the insertion point. To correct an earlier error, select the cell and then click the formula bar, or double-click the cell and position the insertion point at the error. Erase, insert, or replace characters. To delete several adjacent characters, select the characters by dragging across them in the formula bar and then press Backspace or Del.

You can also correct typing errors using only the keyboard. To do so, select the cell you want to edit and press F2. The lower left corner of the status bar indicates that the mode has changed from Ready to Edit, and the insertion point appears at the end of the cell entry. Use the direction keys to position the insertion point to the right of the character or characters you want to change, press Backspace, and then type any new characters.

To replace several characters, position the insertion point just before or just after the characters you want to replace, hold down Shift, and then press the Left or Right direction key to extend your selection. To erase the characters, press Backspace or Del; to overwrite them, type the new characters.

TIP To move from one end of a cell entry to the other, press Home or End. To move through an entry one word at a time, hold down Ctrl and press the Left or Right direction key.

Correcting Errors After You Lock In the Entry

To erase the entire contents of the active cell, press Del or press Backspace and then press Enter. Backspace lets you confirm the deletion: if you press Backspace accidentally, click the Cancel button or press Esc to restore the contents of the cell. You can also select the cell and type the new contents. Excel erases the previous entry as soon as you begin typing. To revert to the original entry, click the Cancel button or press Esc before you lock in the new entry.

To restore an entry after you press Delete or if you have already locked in a new entry, choose the Undo command from the Edit menu or press Ctrl-Z.

Protecting Your Data

In addition to password protection for your files, Excel offers several commands that let you protect workbooks, workbook structures, individual cells, graphic objects, charts, scenarios, and windows from access or modification by others.

By default, Excel "locks" (protects) cells, graphic objects, charts, scenarios, and windows, but the protection is not in effect until you choose Protection and then Protect Sheet from the Tools menu. Figure 4-16 shows the dialog box that appears when you choose this command. The protection status you specify applies to the current worksheet only.

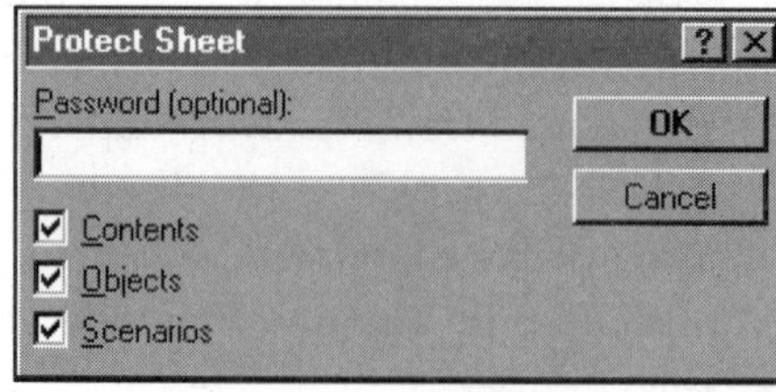

FIGURE 4-16
You can enable or disable protection for a particular worksheet in a workbook.

After protection is enabled, you cannot change a locked item. If you try to change a locked cell, Excel displays the error message *Locked cells cannot be changed*.

The Contents option in the Protect Sheet dialog box applies protection to the contents of cells in the current worksheet. The Objects option applies protection to any graphic objects in the current worksheet. The Scenarios option applies protection to any settings you have saved using the Scenario Manager.

Unlocking Individual Cells

Most of the time you will not want to lock every cell in a worksheet. Before you protect a worksheet, select the cells you want to keep unlocked, and then from the Format menu, choose the Cells command and click the Protection tab. Click the Locked check box to deselect it. Figure 4-17 shows the dialog box after you choose the Protection tab of the Format Cells command.

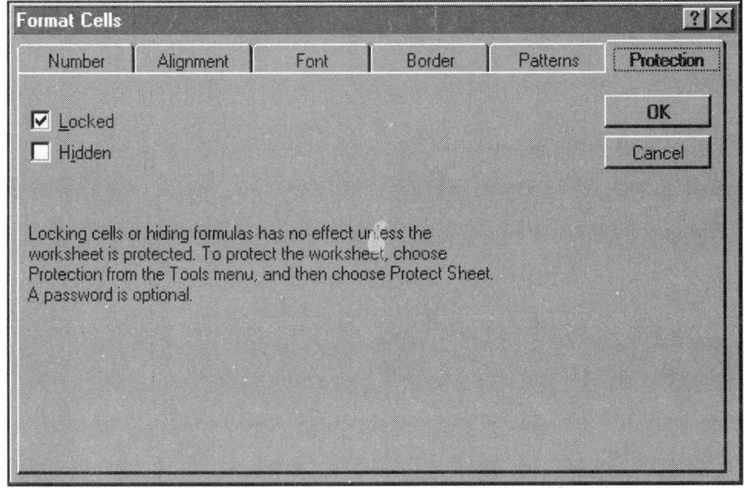

FIGURE 4-17
The Protection tab of the Format menu's Cells command lets you set the protection status for individual cells.

TIP Keep in mind that Excel does not provide any on-screen indication of the protection status of individual cells. To distinguish unlocked cells from the protected cells in the worksheet, change their format; for example, you can change cell color or add borders.

You can also use the Protect Workbook command on the Protection submenu of the Tools menu to prevent the alteration of a workbook's structure and to lock in the position of the workbook window itself. The dialog box that appears when you choose the Protect Workbook command is shown in Figure 4-18.

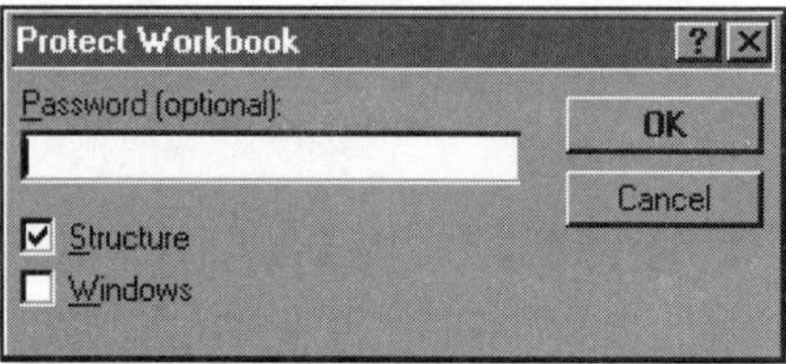

FIGURE 4-18 The Protect Workbook dialog box lets you set the protection status for the workbook itself.

Selecting the Structure option in the Protect Workbook dialog box prevents modification of the worksheet arrangement in a workbook. Selecting the Windows option prevents moving or resizing the workbook window.

For information about graphic objects, see Chapter 9, "Graphics," page 345.

For information about scenarios, see "The Scenario Manager," page 551.

For information about formatting see Chapter 6, "Formatting a Worksheet, page 155.

Hiding Cells and Sheets

If you apply the Hidden protection format to a cell that contains a formula, the formula remains hidden in the formula bar when you select that cell. Formulas in these cells are still available; they are simply hidden from view. Unless you also apply the "hidden" number format, however, the result of the formula is still visible. To apply the Hidden protection format, follow these steps:

1. Select the cells you want to hide.
2. From the Format menu, choose the Protection tab of the Cells command, and select Hidden.
3. From the Tools menu, choose Protection and then Protect Sheet.

You can also hide entire worksheets in a workbook. Any data or calculations in a hidden worksheet are still available; the worksheet is simply hidden from view. To hide a worksheet in a workbook, follow these steps:

4. Click the tab of the worksheet you want to hide.
5. Choose Sheet and then Hide from the Format menu.

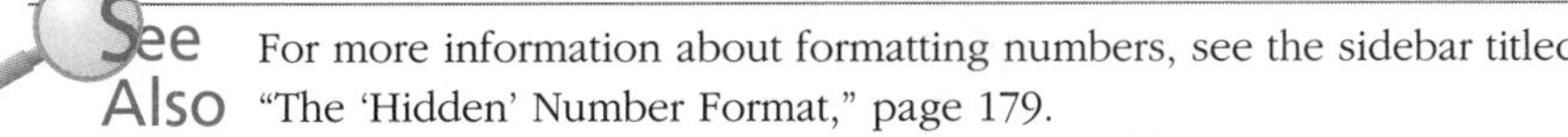

See Also For more information about formatting numbers, see the sidebar titled "The 'Hidden' Number Format," page 179.

Entering Passwords

In the dialog box that appears when you choose Protect Sheet or Protect Workbook from the Tools menu, you can assign a password that must be used in order to release Sheet or Workbook protection. (You can use a different password for each.) To assign a password, follow these steps:

1. Choose Protection and then Protect Sheet or Protect Workbook from the Tools menu.
2. Type a password and click OK.
3. When prompted, reenter the password and click OK to return to the worksheet or workbook.

CAUTION Password protection in Excel is serious business. Once you assign a password, there is no way to unprotect the sheet or workbook without it. Don't forget your passwords!

Removing Protection

If protection is activated for a worksheet or a workbook, or both, the Protection command on the Tools menu changes to Unprotect Sheet or Unprotect Workbook, or both. To remove protection, choose the appropriate Unprotect command.

If you supplied a password when you protected the worksheet or workbook, you cannot remove protection until you type the password. Typing the wrong password generates the message *Incorrect password.* The password you type must match the worksheet or workbook protection password in every detail, including capitalization.

Chapter 5

Building Formulas

If you didn't need formulas, you could use a word processor to build your spreadsheets. Formulas are the heart and soul of a spreadsheet, and Microsoft Excel offers a rich environment in which to build complex formulas. Armed with a few mathematical operators and rules for cell entry, you can turn your worksheet into a powerful calculator.

Creating Formulas

Let's walk through some rudimentary formulas to see how they work. First select blank cell A10 and type

=10+5

TIP ALL FORMULAS IN MICROSOFT EXCEL MUST BEGIN WITH AN EQUAL SIGN. The equal sign tells Excel that the succeeding characters constitute a formula. If you omit the equal sign, Excel interprets the characters as text (even 10 + 5) unless the entry is a valid numeric value.

Now press Enter. The value 15 appears in cell A10, but when you select cell A10, the formula bar displays the formula you just entered. As mentioned in Chapter 4, what appears in the cell is the displayed value; what appears in the formula bar is the underlying value. Now enter the following simple formulas and press Enter after you type each one:

=10–5

=10*5

=10/5

Each of the preceding formulas uses a mathematical operator: the plus sign (+), the minus sign (–), the multiplication sign (*), or the division sign (/).

Precedence of Operators

The term *precedence* refers to the order in which Excel performs calculations in a formula. Excel follows these rules:

- Expressions within parentheses are processed first.
- Multiplication and division are performed before addition and subtraction.
- Consecutive operators with the same level of precedence are calculated from left to right.

Let's enter some formulas to see how these rules apply. Select an empty cell and type

=4+12/6

Press Enter and you see the value 6. Excel first divides 12 by 6 and then adds the result (2) to 4. Select another empty cell and type

=4*12/6

Press Enter and you see the value 8. In this case, the answer is the same whether Excel multiplies or divides first.

To change the order of precedence, you can use parentheses. The following formulas contain the same values and operators, but the placement of parentheses is different in each one, and hence the results are also different.

Formula	Result
=3*6+12/4–2	19
=(3*6)+12/(4–2)	24
=3*(6+12)/4–2	11.5
=(3*6+12)/4–2	5.5
=3*(6+12/(4–2))	36

If you are unsure of the order in which Excel will process a sequence of operators, use parentheses — even if the parentheses aren't actually necessary.

Matching Parentheses

If you do not include a closing parenthesis for each opening parenthesis in a formula, Excel displays the message *Parentheses do not match* and highlights the erroneous portion of the formula. After you type a closing parenthesis, Excel briefly displays that pair of parentheses in bold. This feature is handy when you're entering a long formula and you're not sure which pairs of parentheses go together.

Using Cell References in Formulas

A *cell reference* identifies a cell or a group of cells in your workbook. When you create a formula that contains cell references, you link the formula to other cells in your workbook. The value of the formula is then dependent on the values in the referenced cells and changes when the values in the referenced cells change.

For practice, let's enter a formula that contains a cell reference. First select cell A1 and enter the formula

=10*2

Now select cell A2 and enter the formula

=A1

The value in both cells is 20. If at any time you change the value in cell A1, the value in cell A2 also changes. Now select cell A3 and type

=A1+A2

Excel returns the value 40. You'll find that cell references are extremely helpful as you create and use complex formulas.

Entering Cell References with the Mouse

You can save time and increase accuracy when you enter cell references in a formula by selecting them with the mouse rather than typing them. For example, to enter references to cells A9 and A10 in a formula in cell B10, follow these steps:

1. Select cell B10 and type an equal sign.
2. Click cell A9 and type a plus sign.
3. Click cell A10 and press Enter.

When you click each cell, a flashing border called a *marquee* surrounds the cell, and a reference to the cell is inserted in cell B10. After you finish entering a formula, be sure to press Enter. If you do not press Enter and you select another cell, Excel assumes you want to include the cell reference in the formula.

The active cell does not have to be visible in the current window for you to enter a value in that cell. You can scroll through the worksheet without changing the active cell and click cells in remote areas of your worksheet as you build formulas. The formula bar displays the contents of the active cell, no matter where you are in the worksheet.

TIP If you scroll through your worksheet and the active cell is no longer visible, you can redisplay the active cell by holding down Ctrl and pressing Backspace.

Relative, Absolute, and Mixed References

Relative references — the type we've used so far in the sample formulas — refer to cells by their position in relation to the cell that contains the formula; for example, "the cell up two rows from this cell." *Absolute references* refer to cells by their fixed position in the worksheet; for example, "the cell located in column A and row 2." A *mixed reference* contains a relative reference and an absolute reference; for example, "the cell located in column A and up two rows." Absolute and mixed references are important when you begin copying formulas from one location to another in your worksheet.

The following is a relative reference to cell A1:

=A1

An absolute reference to cell A1 looks like this:

=$A$1

You can combine the relative and absolute references to cell A1 to create these mixed references:

=$A1

=A$1

If the dollar sign precedes the letter (A, for example), the column coordinate is absolute and the row is relative. If the dollar sign precedes the number (1, for example), the column coordinate is relative and the row is absolute.

You can press F4 to change reference types quickly. The following steps show how:

1. Select cell A1 and type

   =B1+B2

2. Press F4 to change the reference in the formula bar that is nearest the insertion point to absolute. The formula becomes =B1+$B$2.
3. Press F4 again to change the reference to mixed (relative column coordinate and absolute row coordinate). The formula becomes =B1+B$2.
4. Press F4 again to reverse the mixed reference (absolute column coordinate and relative row coordinate). The formula becomes =B1+$B2.
5. Press F4 again to return to the original relative reference.

See Also For more information about copying cell references, see Chapter 7, "Editing a Worksheet," page 227.

What Are Mixed References Good For?

Sometimes you want to copy formulas across rows and down columns, but the formulas refer to other cells in the same rows or columns. Relative references automatically adjust when you copy them, and absolute references don't. Using relative or absolute references, you'd probably end up modifying each formula individually. But using mixed references, you can make the formula do the work for you. When you copy a mixed reference, the part of the reference preceded by a dollar sign does not adjust, while the other part adjusts to reflect the relative location of the copied formula.

The following worksheet displays formulas that calculate monthly interest payments for fixed principal amounts in row 2 and fixed interest rates in column A.

	A	B	C
1			
2		10000	20000
3	0.07	=-PMT($A3/12 * B$2)	=-PMT($A3/12 * C$2)
4	0.08	=-PMT($A4/12 * B$2)	=-PMT($A4/12 * C$2)
5			

To create this worksheet, you enter the formula shown in cell B3, then copy it to the right and down as far as you need. The mixed references in the formula adjust to use the correct principal amount and interest rate for each cell. The first component of the formula is a mixed reference to the annual interest rate (divided by 12 to represent a monthly rate), $A3/12. Copy the formula anywhere, and it will always refer to a value in column A, but the row letter will adjust so that you can enter different interest rates in column A to see the effect of various rates. The second component is a mixed reference to the loan amount, B$2. Copy the formula anywhere, and it will always refer to a value in row 2, but the column number will adjust to refer to the principal amount in row 2 of the same column.

References to Other Worksheets in the Same Workbook

You can refer to cells in other worksheets within the same workbook just as easily as you refer to cells in the same worksheet. For example, to enter a reference to cell A9 in Sheet2 into cell B10 in Sheet1, follow these steps:

1. Select cell B10 in Sheet1 and type an equal sign.
2. Click the Sheet2 tab at the bottom of the Book1 window.
3. Click cell A9 and then press Enter.

   After you press Enter, Sheet1 is reactivated, and the formula

   =Sheet2!A9

appears in cell B10. Notice that the worksheet portion of the reference is separated from the cell portion by an exclamation point. Notice also that the cell reference is relative. When you direct-select references to other worksheets, the default cell reference is relative. If you want, you can change the cell reference to an absolute or mixed reference by pressing F4. Keep in mind that you can also construct interworksheet references like the one in the example by typing them, but the direct-selection technique is easier and more reliable.

References to Worksheets in Other Workbooks

In the same way that you can refer to cells in other worksheets within the same workbook, you can also refer to cells in worksheets located in separate workbooks. These references are called *external* references. For example, to enter a reference to cell A9 in Sheet2 of Book2 into cell B10 in Sheet1 of Book1, follow these steps:

1. Create a new workbook — Book2 — by clicking the New Workbook button on the Standard toolbar (the first button on the left).
2. Choose the Arrange command from the Window menu and then choose Vertical. (Both workbooks appear, side by side on your screen.)
3. Select cell B10 in Sheet1 of Book1 and type an equal sign.
4. Click anywhere in the Book2 window to activate the workbook.
5. Click the Sheet2 tab at the bottom of the Book2 window.
6. Click cell A9 and press Enter.

   After you press Enter, Sheet1 of Book1 is reactivated, and the formula

   =[Book2]Sheet2!$A$9

appears in cell B10. Notice that the workbook reference appears first in the formula and is enclosed in brackets. Notice also that external references entered in this fashion are absolute. As with other references, you can type an external reference yourself, but direct selection with the mouse is easier and more accurate.

R1C1 Reference Style

Worksheet formulas usually refer to cells by a combination of column letter and row number, such as A1 or Z100. If you use R1C1 reference style, however, Excel refers to cells by row and column *numbers* instead. The cell reference R1C1 means row 1, column 1, so R1C1 refers to the same cell as A1. To activate R1C1 reference style, choose the Options command from the Tools menu, click the General tab, and select the R1C1 option.

About Reference Syntax

So far, we've used Excel's default worksheet and workbook names for the examples in this book. When you save a workbook, you must specify a permanent name for it. If you create a formula first and then save the workbook with a new name, the formula is adjusted accordingly. For example, if you save Book2 as SALES.XLS, the reference

```
=[Book2]Sheet2!$A$9
```

automatically changes to

```
=[SALES.XLS]Sheet2!$A$9
```

And if you rename Sheet2 of SALES.XLS to February, the reference automatically changes to

```
=[SALES.XLS]February!$A$9
```

If the referenced workbook is closed, the full pathname to the directory where the workbook is stored appears in the reference, as shown in the example,

```
='C:\EXCEL\[SALES.XLS]February'!$A$9
```

In the above example, notice that single quotation marks surround the workbook and worksheet portion of the reference. Excel automatically adds the quotation marks around the pathname when you close the workbook. Remember, if you type a new reference to a closed workbook, you must add the single quotation marks yourself.

When you select the R1C1 option, all the cell references in your formulas change to R1C1 format. For example, cell M10 becomes R10C13, and cell IV16384, the last cell in your worksheet, becomes R16384C256.

When you use R1C1 notation, relative cell references are displayed in terms of their relationship to the cell that contains the formula rather than by their actual coordinates. This can be helpful when you are more interested in the relative positions of cells than in their absolute positions. For example, suppose you want to enter a formula in cell R10C2 (B10) that adds cells R1C1 and R1C2. After selecting cell R10C2, type an equal sign, select cell R1C1, type a plus sign, select cell R1C2, and then press Enter. Excel displays

=R[–9]C[–1]+R[–9]C

Negative row and column numbers indicate that the referenced cell is above or to the left of the formula cell; positive numbers indicate that the referenced cell is below or to the right of the formula cell. The brackets indicate relative references. So, this formula reads *Add the cell nine rows up and one column to the left to the cell nine rows up in the same column.*

A relative reference to another cell must include brackets around the numbers in the reference. If you don't include the brackets, Excel assumes you're using absolute references. For example, the formula

=R8C1+R9C1

uses absolute references to the cells in rows 8 and 9 of column 1.

Editing Formulas

You edit formulas the same way you edit text entries. To delete a cell reference or other character from a formula, drag through the reference or character in the cell or the formula bar and press Backspace or Del. To replace a cell reference with another one, highlight the reference you want to replace and click the replacement cell.

To undo your changes if you have not locked them in, click the cancel button or press Esc. If you have locked in the entry but have not chosen another command or typed in another cell, use the Undo command on the Edit menu, press Ctrl-Z, or click the Undo button in the Standard toolbar.

You can also insert additional cell references in a formula. For example, to insert a reference to cell B1 in the formula

=A1+A3

simply move the insertion point between A1 and the plus sign and type

+B1

or type a plus sign and click cell B1. The formula becomes

=A1+B1+A3

Using Numeric Text in Formulas

You can perform mathematical operations on numeric text values as long as the numeric string contains only the characters

0 1 2 3 4 5 6 7 8 9 . + – E e

In addition, you can use the / character in fractions. You can also use the five number-formatting characters

$, % ( )

but you must enclose the numeric string in double quotation marks. For example, if you enter the formula

=$1234+$123

Excel displays the message *Error in formula*. However, the formula

="$1234"+"$123"

produces the result 1357 (without the dollar sign). Excel automatically translates numeric text entries into numeric values when it performs the addition.

Text Values

You manipulate most text values in the same way that you manipulate numeric values. For example, if cell A1 contains the text ABCDE and you enter the formula

=A1

in cell A10, cell A10 also displays ABCDE. Because this type of formula treats a string of text as a value, it is sometimes called a *string value* or *text value*.

You use the special operator & (ampersand) to *concatenate,* or join, several text values. For example, if cell A2 contains the text FGHIJ and you enter the formula

=A1&A2

in cell A3, cell A3 displays ABCDEFGHIJ. To include a space between the two strings, change the formula to

=A1&" "&A2

This formula uses two concatenation operators and a literal string, or *string constant* — a space enclosed in double quotation marks.

You can also use the & operator to concatenate strings of numeric values. For example, if cell A3 contains the numeric value 123 and cell A4 contains the numeric value 456, the formula

```
=A3&A4
```

produces the string 123456. This string is left-aligned in the cell because it is a text value. (Remember, you can use numeric text values to perform any mathematical operation as long as the numeric string contains only the numeric characters listed in the section titled "Using Numeric Text in Formulas" on page 120.)

In addition, you can use the & operator to concatenate a text value and a numeric value. For example, if cell A1 contains the text ABCDE and cell A3 contains the numeric value 123, the formula

```
=A1&A3
```

produces the string ABCDE123.

Using Functions: A Preview

A *function* is a predefined formula that operates on a value or values and returns a value or values. Many Excel functions are shorthand versions of frequently used formulas. For example, the SUM function lets you add a series of cell values by simply selecting a range. Compare the formula

```
=A1+A2+A3+A4+A5+A6+A7+A8+A9+A10
```

with the formula

```
=SUM(A1:A10)
```

Obviously, the SUM function makes the formula a lot shorter and easier to create.

Some Excel functions perform extremely complex calculations. For example, using the NPER function, you can calculate the number of periods required to pay off a loan at a given interest rate and payment amount.

All functions consist of a function name followed by a set of *arguments* enclosed in parentheses. (In the previous example, A1:A10 is the argument in the SUM function.) If you omit a closing parenthesis when you enter a function, Excel will add the parenthesis after you press Enter, as long as it is obvious where the parenthesis is supposed to go. (Relying on this feature can produce unpredictable results, however; so for accuracy, always double-check your parentheses.)

For more information about functions, see Chapter 11, "Common Worksheet Functions," page 397.

For more information about the NPER function, see "The NPER Function," page 487.

The AutoSum Button

The SUM function is used more often than any other function. To make this function more accessible, Excel includes a button on the Standard toolbar, shown in Figure 5-1.

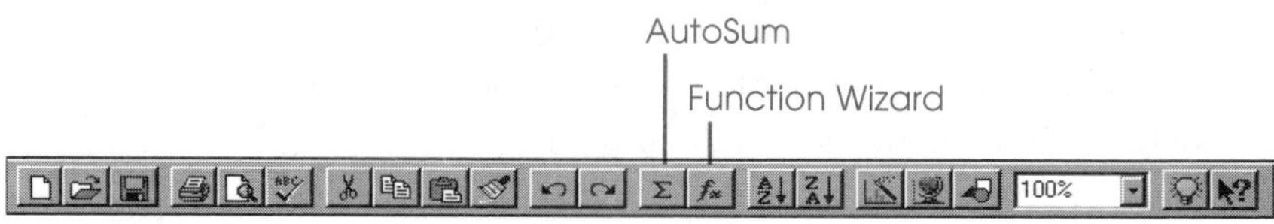

FIGURE 5-1

The Standard toolbar includes two buttons — the AutoSum button and the Function Wizard button — that make Excel's built-in functions easier to use.

In Figure 5-2, we selected the cell below the numbers in column A and clicked the AutoSum button to calculate the sum of the numbers in the column.

Notice in Figure 5-2 that the AutoSum button inserts the entire formula for you and suggests a range to sum. Often the suggested range is correct, but if not, you can simply drag through the correct range before you press Enter.

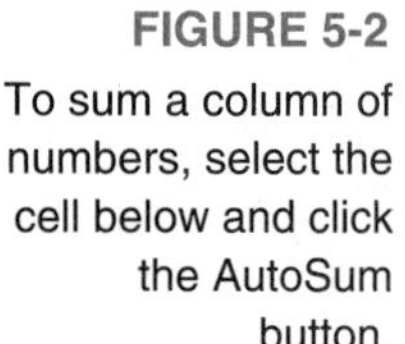

FIGURE 5-2

To sum a column of numbers, select the cell below and click the AutoSum button.

For more information about the AutoSum button, see "The SUM Function," page 407.

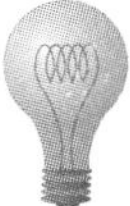

TIP Get a quick sum by selecting the cells you want to sum and looking at the AutoCalculate box in the status bar, where the total of the selected cells appears. Click the right mouse button on the AutoCalculate box to choose whether selected cells are summed, averaged, or counted or the maximum or minimum value is displayed in the status bar. See the sidebar "What Does SUM=0 Mean?" in Chapter 1 on page 20.

Accessing Built-In Functions with the Function Wizard

When you want to use a built-in function, Excel's Function Wizard button, shown in Figure 5-1, is the best approach. For example, to calculate the current net value of an investment using the NPER function mentioned earlier, follow these steps:

1. Click the Function Wizard button on the Standard toolbar.
2. When the first Function Wizard dialog box appears, as shown in Figure 5-3, select Financial from the Function Category list box.

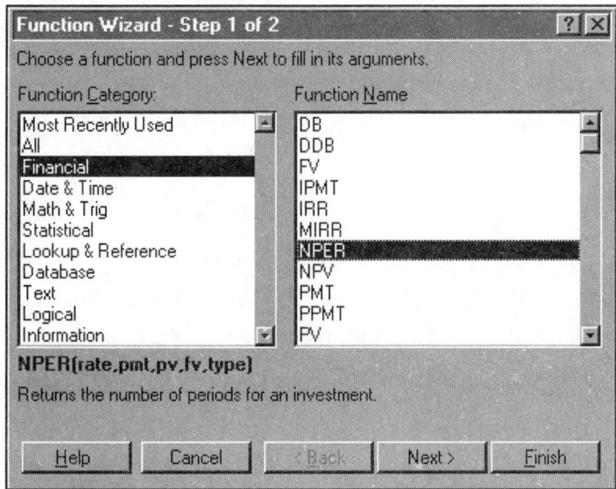

FIGURE 5-3
When you click the Function Wizard button, this dialog box appears.

3. Select NPER from the Function Name list box and click Next to display the second Function Wizard dialog box shown in Figure 5-4 on the next page.

FIGURE 5-4

The Function Wizard's Step 2 dialog box appears when you click the Next button.

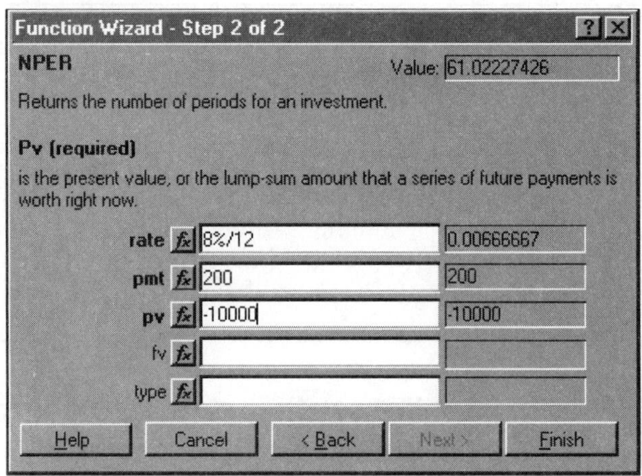

4. In the Rate edit box, type *8%/12* (8% yearly interest, divided by 12 months).
5. In the Pmt edit box, type *200* (your monthly payment).
6. Finally, in the Pv edit box, type *–10000* (the invested amount, preceded by a minus sign) and then click the Finish button.

The formula is entered in the selected cell, and the resulting value is displayed on the worksheet.

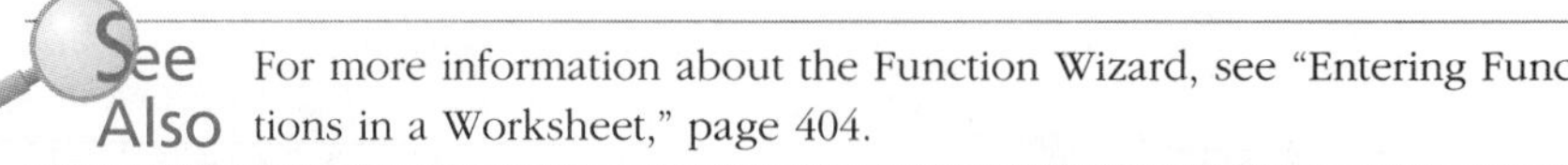

For more information about the Function Wizard, see "Entering Functions in a Worksheet," page 404.

Using Functions to Create Three-Dimensional Formulas

You've seen how you can use references to cells in a worksheet and to cells in another worksheet within the same workbook. You can also use references to cells that span a range of worksheets in a workbook. These references are called *3-D references*. Suppose you set up 12 worksheets in the same workbook — one for each month — with a year-to-date summary sheet on top. If all the monthly worksheets are laid out identically, you could use 3-D reference formulas to summarize the monthly data on the summary sheet. For example, the formula

```
=SUM(Sheet2:Sheet13!B5)
```

adds all the values contained in cell B5 on all the worksheets between and including Sheet2 and Sheet13. To construct this three-dimensional formula, follow these steps:

1. Type *=SUM(* in cell B5 of Sheet1.
2. Click the Sheet2 tab and then click the next tab scrolling button (located to the left of the worksheet tabs) until the Sheet13 tab is visible.
3. Hold down the Shift key and click the Sheet13 tab.
4. Select cell B5 and press Enter.

Notice that when you hold down the Shift key and click the Sheet13 tab, all the tabs from Sheet2 through Sheet13 change to white, indicating that they are selected for inclusion in the reference you are constructing.

You can use the following functions with 3-D references:

SUM	MIN	VAR
COUNTA	PRODUCT	VARP
AVERAGE	STDEV	COUNT
MAX	STDEVP	

See Also For more information about working with workbooks, see Chapter 8, "Workbooks and Windows," page 297.

Formula Bar Formatting

You can enter spaces, tabs, and line breaks in a formula to make it easier to read without affecting the calculation of the formula. To enter tab characters, press Ctrl-Alt-Tab. To enter line breaks, press Alt-Enter. Figure 5-5 shows a formula that contains both tabs and line breaks.

FIGURE 5-5
You can enter tabs and line breaks in a formula to make it more readable.

Naming Cells and Ranges

You can assign names to cells and cell ranges and then use those names in your formulas. Using names instead of cell references is convenient because it eliminates the need to type complex cell references. In addition, when you want to make changes to your formulas, you can simply change the named cells rather than change the references in each formula.

How Excel 7 Handles Name Conflicts When Importing Excel 4 Workbooks

Although names apply to all worksheets in an Excel 7 or Excel 5 workbook, each worksheet in an Excel 4 workbook has its own set of names. Excel 7 creates special names when you open an Excel 4 workbook file that contains worksheets with duplicate names. For example, suppose an Excel 4 workbook contains 12 worksheets, Jan through Dec, each containing the name gross_profit. When you open this workbook in Excel 7, the duplicate names are converted using the forms *Jan!gross_profit, Feb!gross_profit,* and so on.

After you define names in a worksheet, those names are made available to any other worksheets in the workbook. A name defining a cell range in Sheet6, for example, is available for use in formulas in Sheet1, Sheet2, and so on in the workbook. As a result, each workbook contains its own set of names.

You can also define special "sheet level" names that are available only on the worksheet in which they are defined.

Also For more information about sheet-level names, see "Defining Sheet-Level Names," page 130.

Using Names in Formulas

You can use the name of a cell or range in a formula. The result is the same as it would be if you entered the reference of the cell or the range. For example, suppose you enter the formula

```
=A1+A2
```

in cell A3. If you define the name Mark as cell A1 and the name Vicki as cell A2, the formula

=Mark+Vicki

returns the same value.

Defining Names with the Name Box

The easiest way to define a name is to use the Name box in the formula bar, which is shown in Figure 5-6.

To define a name for cell C5 using the Name box, follow these steps:

1. Select cell C5.
2. Click the Name box in the formula bar.
3. Type *Test_Name* and press Enter.

If a selected cell or range is named, the name takes precedence over the cell reference and is displayed in the Name box. For example, the Name box displayed C5 at the beginning of the exercise, but now the Name box displays Test_Name when C5 is selected. Note that you cannot use spaces in a name.

When you define a name for a range of cells, the range name does not appear in the Name box unless the entire range is selected.

NOTE When you define a name, the worksheet name is part of the definition, and the cell reference is absolute. For example, when you define the name Test_Name for cell C5 in Sheet1, the actual name definition is recorded as Sheet1!$C$5.

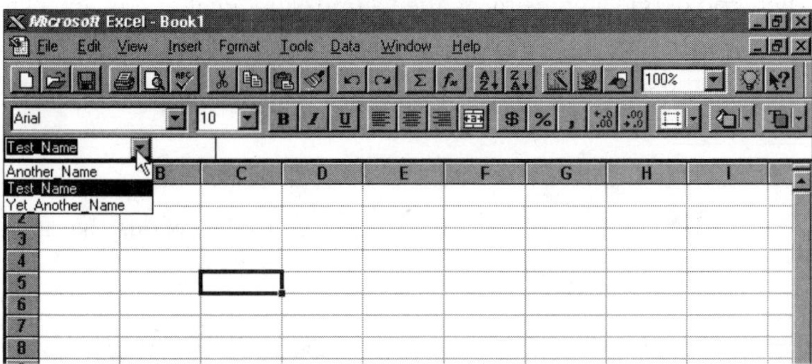

FIGURE 5-6

Use the Name box in the formula bar to define names in your worksheet.

For more information about naming cells and ranges, see "Rules for Naming Cells and Ranges," page 131.

For more information about absolute references, see "Relative, Absolute, and Mixed References," page 115.

Moving to a Named Cell or Range

You can move to a named cell or range by clicking the arrow next to the Name box and selecting the cell or range name from the drop-down list. Also, if you type a name in the Name box that is already defined, Excel simply moves to the named cell or range in the worksheet.

Defining Names with the Name Command

The Name command on the Insert menu lets you use the text in adjacent cells to define cell and range names. You can also use this command to redefine existing names.

Suppose cell A4 contains the text Product 1 and you want to use this text as the name for the adjacent cells B4:E4. To define a name using the text in cell A4, follow these steps:

1. Select the range B4:E4.
2. From the Insert menu, choose Name and then Define to display the Define Name dialog box. Notice that Excel inserts the text Product_1 in the Names In Workbook edit box and inserts the cell reference Sheet1!$B$4:$E$4 in the Refers To edit box.
3. Press Enter.

When you define a name using the Define Name dialog box, Excel inserts a text label in the Names In Workbook edit box if the selected cell or the cell immediately to the left or above the selected cell contains a text label that can serve as a cell name, as shown in Figure 5-7.

TIP You can quickly display the Define Name dialog box by pressing Ctrl-F3.

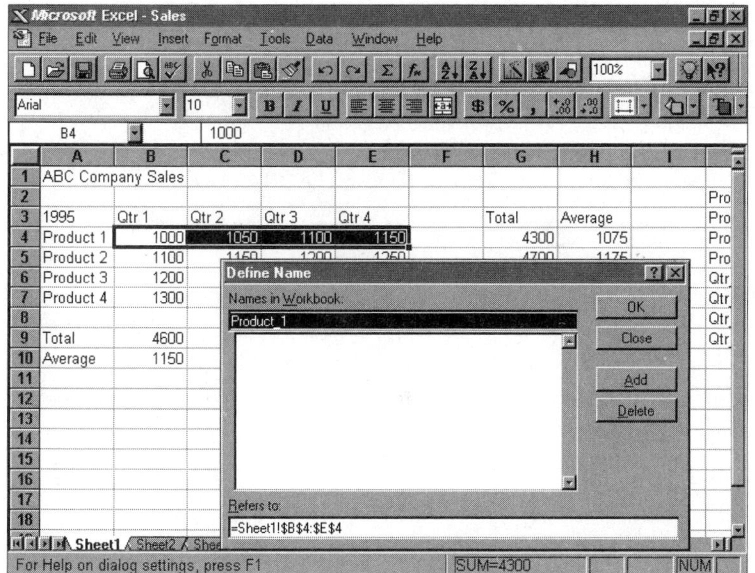

FIGURE 5-7
Excel suggests a name for a cell or range.

The next time you open the Define Name dialog box, the name appears in the Names In Workbook list box, which displays all the defined names for the workbook.

You can also define a name without first selecting a cell or range in the worksheet. To define cell D20 with the name Test2, follow these steps:

1. From the Insert menu, choose Name and then Define.
2. Type *Test2* in the Names In Workbook edit box and then type *=D20* in the Refers To edit box.
3. Click the Add button.

The Define Name dialog box remains open, and the Refers To edit box displays the name definition =Sheet1!D20. Excel adds the worksheet reference for you, but note that the cell reference stays relative, just as you entered it. If you do not enter the equal sign preceding the reference, Excel interprets the definition as text. For example, if you entered *D20* instead of *=D20,* the Refers To edit box would display the text constant ="D20" as the definition of the name Test2.

When the Define Name dialog box is open, you can also insert references in the Refers To edit box by selecting cells in the worksheet. In addition, to name several cells or ranges in the Define Name dialog box, be sure to click the Add button after entering each definition. (If you click OK, Excel closes the dialog box.)

TIP The Define Name dialog box is one of the few in Excel that allows you to select cells or worksheets while the dialog box is open. Click the Refers To box at the bottom of the dialog box, and then select the worksheet tab and cell range you want instead of typing the reference.

Defining Sheet-Level Names

As mentioned earlier, names in Excel are normally "book-level"; that is, a name defined in one worksheet is available to other worksheets in the same workbook. But you can also create "sheet-level" names that are available only on the worksheet in which they are defined. To define a sheet-level name for a cell or range of cells, precede the name with the name of the worksheet, followed by an exclamation point. For example, to define SheetName as a sheet-level name in Sheet1, follow these steps:

1. Select the cell or range you want to name.
2. Choose Name and then Define from the Insert menu. Type *Sheet1!SheetName* in the Names In Workbook edit box.
3. Click OK.

When you select a cell or range that you have defined with a sheet-level name, the name of the cell or range (SheetName, for example) appears in the Name box on the formula bar, but the name of the worksheet (Sheet1!, for example) is hidden. If you want to see a sheet-level name in its entirety, activate the worksheet in which the name is defined and choose Name and then Define from the Insert menu. When the Define Name dialog box appears, the entire sheet-level name is displayed in the Names In Workbook list box. Because sheet-level names are available only on the worksheet in which they are defined, Excel only displays the sheet-level names for the active worksheet in the Define Name dialog box. Thus, in the example above, if you first select Sheet2 and choose Name and then Define from the Insert menu, Sheet1!SheetName no longer appears in the Define Name dialog box.

When a worksheet contains a duplicate book-level and sheet-level name, the sheet-level name takes precedence over the book-level name. For example, if in Sheet1 you define the names SheetName (book-level) and Sheet1!SheetName (sheet-level) using different cell ranges, SheetName is available on every worksheet in the workbook *except* Sheet1, where Sheet1!SheetName takes precedence. Keep in mind that Excel does not allow you to use a duplicate book-level name in the worksheet where the sheet-level name is defined. Thus, in the example, you cannot use SheetName in Sheet1. You can, however, refer to a sheet-level name in another worksheet by including the name, in its entirety, in a formula. For example, you could enter the formula *=Sheet1!SheetName* in a cell in Sheet2.

Redefining Names in the Define Name Dialog Box

To redefine an existing cell or range name in the Define Name dialog box, first select the name in the Names In Workbook list box and then edit the cell or range reference in the Refers To edit box. You can either type a new reference or select a new cell or range while the Define Name dialog box is open.

Rules for Naming Cells and Ranges

The following is a list of rules that will come in handy when you name cells and ranges in Excel.

- All names name must begin with a letter, a backslash (\), or an underscore (_).
- Numbers can be used.
- Symbols other than backslash and underscore cannot be used.
- Indicate blank spaces in range names with an underscore.
- Names that resemble cell references cannot be used.
- Single letters, with the exception of the letters R and C, can be used as names.

Editing Names

You can use any of the editing techniques already described to change the contents of the Refers To edit box in the Define Name dialog box. For example, to change the cells associated with a range name, follow these steps:

1. From the Insert menu, choose Name and then Define.
2. Select the name from the Names In Workbook list box.
3. In the Refers To edit box, drag through the cell references you want to change and type the new references.
4. Click OK.

As mentioned, you can also change the contents of the Refers To edit box by selecting cells directly in the worksheet while the Define Name dialog box is open. If the cells you want to select are hidden behind the dialog box, simply click anywhere on the title bar of the dialog box and drag the dialog box out of the way.

To delete a name in the Define Name dialog box, select the name from the Names In Workbook list box and then click Delete. Keep in mind that when you delete a name, any formula in the worksheet that refers to that name returns the error value #NAME?.

Creating Names from Text Cells

You can also use the Name command on the Insert menu to name several individual cells or adjacent ranges at once. This is particularly useful when you need to define many names in a region on your worksheet. When you choose Name and then Create from the Insert menu, Excel uses the labels in the row or column (or the row and column) adjacent to the range you want to define to name the other cells in the range.

The worksheet in Figure 5-8 contains a series of labels in column A and row 3.

FIGURE 5-8 We'll use this worksheet to demonstrate Excel's name-creation procedures.

Sales

	A	B	C	D	E	F	G	H	I
1	ABC Company Sales								
2									
3	1995	Qtr 1	Qtr 2	Qtr 3	Qtr 4		Total	Average	
4	Product 1	1000	1050	1100	1150		4300	1075	
5	Product 2	1100	1150	1200	1250		4700	1175	
6	Product 3	1200	1250	1300	1350		5100	1275	
7	Product 4	1300	1350	1400	1450		5500	1375	
8									
9	Total	4600	4800	5000	5200		19600	4900	
10	Average	1150	1200	1250	1300		4900	1225	
11									
12									
13									
14									
15									

Sheet1 / Sheet2 / Sheet3 / Sheet4 / Sheet5 / Sheet

To assign names to the cell ranges in columns B through E that correspond to the labels in column A, follow these steps:

1. Select cells A4:E7.
2. From the Insert menu, choose Name and then Create to display the Create Names dialog box, shown in Figure 5-9. (You can also display the Create Names dialog box by pressing Ctrl-Shift-F3.)
3. The Left Column option is selected by default, so click OK.

Now when you click the arrow to the right of the Name box in the formula bar, you see the names Product_1, Product_2, Product_3, and Product_4 listed. (The name Product_1 is defined as the range $B$4:$E$4, for example.)

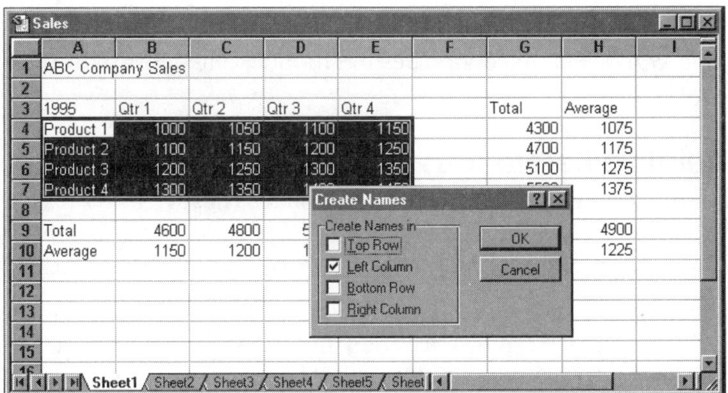

FIGURE 5-9
Use the Create Names dialog box to name several cells or ranges.

If you select a range with labels for both rows and columns, the Top Row and Left Column options in the Create Names dialog box are selected, allowing you to create two sets of names at once. For example, in Figure 5-8, if you select the range A3:E7, you can create the names Qtr_1, Qtr_2, Qtr_3, and Qtr_4 at the same time. (The name Qtr_1, for instance, is defined as the range $B$4:$B$7.) In addition, if the selected range includes a label in the upper left corner, Excel uses the label to name the entire group of cells. So, in Figure 5-8, selecting the range A3:E7 not only creates named ranges for each product and quarter, but also defines the range B4:E7 as _1995 because cell A3 contains the label '1995.

Naming Constants and Formulas

You can create names to define constants and formulas, even if the constants and formulas don't appear in any cell in your worksheet. For example, if you often use the value 5% to calculate sales tax, you can use the name Tax in your calculations. To do so, follow these steps:

1. From the Insert menu, choose Name and then Define.
2. When the Define Name dialog box appears, type *Tax* in the Names In Workbook edit box and type *5%* or *.05* in the Refers To edit box.
3. Click OK.

Now you can use the name Tax in a formula like =Price+(Price*Tax) to calculate the cost of items with a 5 percent sales tax. Note that named constants and formulas do not appear in the Name box in the formula bar, but they do appear in the Define Name dialog box.

You can also enter a formula as a name definition in the Refers To edit box. For example, you might want to define the name Tax with a formula like =Sheet1!$B$22+1.2%. If you enter a formula in the Refers To edit box that refers to a cell in a worksheet, Excel updates the formula whenever the value in the cell changes.

Using Relative References in Named Formulas

When you are creating a named formula that contains relative references, such as =Sheet1!B22+1.2%, Excel interprets the position of the cells referenced in the Refers To edit box as relative to the cell that is active. Later, when you use such a name in a formula, the reference is relative to the cell containing the formula that uses the name. For example, if cell B21 was the active cell when you defined the name Tax as =Sheet1!B22+1.2%, the name Tax will always refer to the cell one row below the cell in which the formula is currently located.

Three-Dimensional Names

In Excel 7, you can create three-dimensional names, which use 3-D references as their definitions. For example, to define a three-dimensional name for the 3-D reference we created earlier in "Using Functions to Create Three-Dimensional Formulas" (see page 124), follow these steps:

1. Select cell B5 on Sheet1.
2. Choose Name and then Define from the Insert menu.
3. Type *Three_D* in the Names In Workbook edit box and type *=Sheet2:Sheet13!B5* in the Refers To edit box.
4. Press Enter.

Now you can use the name Three_D in formulas that contain any of the functions listed on page 125. For example, the formula

```
=SUM(Three_D)
```

totals the values in the three-dimensional range named Three_D. Since you used relative references in step 3, the definition of the range Three_D changes as you select different cells in the worksheet. For example, if you select cell C3 and display the Define Name dialog box, you will see =Sheet2:Sheet13!C3 in the Refers To edit box.

Pasting Names into Formulas

After you define one or more names in your worksheet, you can use the Name and Paste commands on the Insert menu to insert the names in your formulas. For example, to paste the name Product_2 into a formula, follow these steps:

1. Begin entering a formula by typing an equal sign, then type the operators, functions, or constants of your formula. (We entered the SUM function.)
2. Choose Name and then Paste from the Insert menu, or press F3.
3. When the Paste Name dialog box appears, as shown in Figure 5-10, select Product_2.
4. Click OK to insert the name Product_2 in the formula.
5. Type any other operands and operators, and press Enter.

You can use the Paste Names button instead of the menu command, but you must customize a toolbar to include this tool.

TIP You can also paste a name into a formula by selecting it in the Name box on the Formula bar.

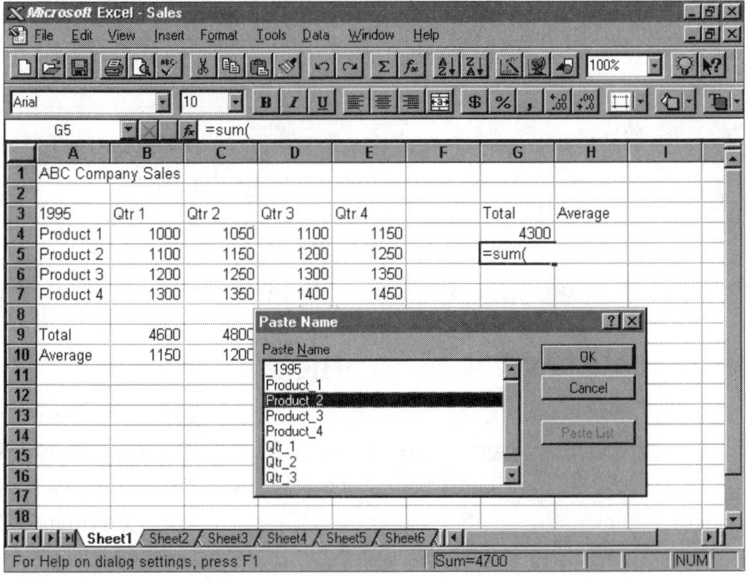

FIGURE 5-10

Use the Paste Name dialog box to insert names in your formulas.

For more information about customizing toolbars, see Chapter 2, "Toolbars and Buttons," page 33.

For more information about the Name box, see "Defining Names with the Name Box," on page 127.

The Paste List Option

You can paste a list of defined names in your worksheet by clicking the Paste List option in the Paste Name dialog box. As shown in Figure 5-11, Excel pastes the list in your worksheet beginning at the active cell.

When Excel pastes the list in your worksheet, it overwrites any existing data. If you inadvertently overwrite data, choose Undo List Names from the Edit menu.

Sales

	J	K	L	M	N	O	P	Q	R
1									
2		_1995	=Sheet1!$B$4:$E$7						
3		Product_1	=Sheet1!$B$4:$E$4						
4		Product_2	=Sheet1!$B$5:$E$5						
5		Product_3	=Sheet1!$B$6:$E$6						
6		Product_4	=Sheet1!$B$7:$E$7						
7		Qtr_1	=Sheet1!$B$4:$B$7						
8		Qtr_2	=Sheet1!$C$4:$C$7						
9		Qtr_3	=Sheet1!$D$4:$D$7						
10		Qtr_4	=Sheet1!$E$4:$E$7						
11									
12									
13									
14									
15									
16									

Sheet1 / Sheet2 / Sheet3 / Sheet4 / Sheet5 / Sheet6

FIGURE 5-11
Use the Paste List option to paste a list of the names and definitions in your worksheet.

TIP If you want to quickly locate a named cell reference in a workbook, select the name in the Name box on the formula bar. Excel activates the corresponding worksheet and selects the named cell or range.

Applying Names to Formulas

To replace references in formulas with the corresponding names, choose Name and then Apply from the Insert menu. When you choose this command, Excel locates in formulas all the cell and range references for which you have defined names. If you select a single cell before you choose the Apply command, Excel applies names throughout the active worksheet; if you select a range of cells, Excel applies names only to the selected cells.

About Range Intersections

To understand the Use Row And Column Names option (and the choices that appear if you click the Options button), you need to know a little more about how Excel handles range names.

In the worksheet in Figure 5-8, we assigned the name Qtr_1 to the range B4:B7 and the name Product_1 to the range B4:E4. If at cell I4, we enter the formula

```
=Qtr_l*4
```

Excel assumes that we want to use only one value in the range B4:B7 — the one that lies in the same row as the formula that contains the reference.

This is called *implicit intersection*. Because we entered the formula in cell I4, Excel uses the value in B4. If we copy this formula to the range I5:I7, each cell in that range contains the formula =Qtr_1*4, but at I5 the formula references B5, at I6 it references B6, and so on.

You can also use this technique to reference individual cells in a named row.

What happens if we enter the formula

```
=Qtr_1*4
```

in I15 instead of I4? Excel returns an error value because no cell within the range named Qtr_1 lies on the same row or column as the referencing formula. We can, however, reference B4 by name with the help of the *intersection operator*. The intersection operator is the space character that appears when you press the Spacebar.

If we enter the formula

```
=Qtr_1 Product_1*4
```

Excel knows that we want to reference the value that lies at the intersection of the range named Qtr_1 and the range named Product_1. In others words, cell B4.

Figure 5-12 shows the Apply Names dialog box, which lists all the cell and range names you have defined. To apply more than one name, hold down Shift as you click each name.

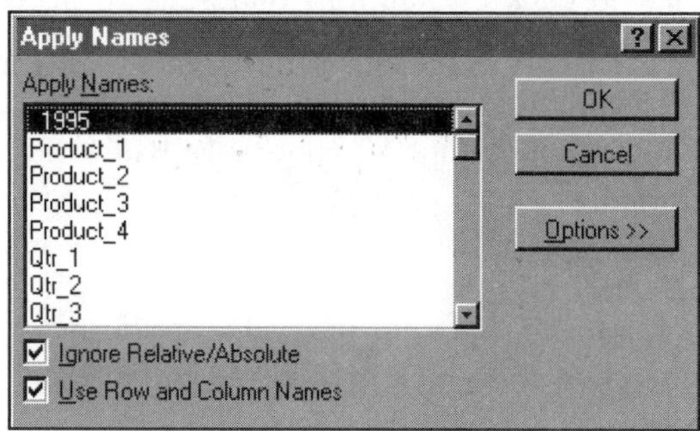

FIGURE 5-12
Use the Apply Names dialog box to substitute names for cell and range references in your formulas.

Use the Ignore Relative/Absolute option to replace references with names regardless of the reference type. In general, leave this check box selected. Most name definitions use absolute references (the default when you define and create names), and most formulas use relative references (the default when you paste cell and range references in the formula bar). If you deselect this option, Excel replaces absolute, relative, and mixed references only with name definitions that use the corresponding reference style.

If you find that typing range names (especially range names in formulas that require intersection operators — see the sidebar on page 137) is tedious work, leave the Use Row And Column Names option selected (the default) in the Apply Names dialog box. Excel will then insert the range names for you. Referring back to Figure 5-8, for example, if you enter the formula =B4*4 (without names) in cell I4 and use the Apply Names dialog box with the Use Row And Column Names option selected, Excel changes the formula to read =Qtr_1*4. Without the Use Row And Column Names option, Excel does not apply names to the formula. Similarly, if you enter the formula =B4*4 in cell I15 and then use the Apply Names dialog box, Excel changes the formula to read =Product_1 Qtr_1*4, but only if you leave the Use Row And Column Names option selected.

Other Options in the Apply Names Dialog Box

Clicking the Options button in the Apply Names dialog box makes additional choices available, as shown in Figure 5-13.

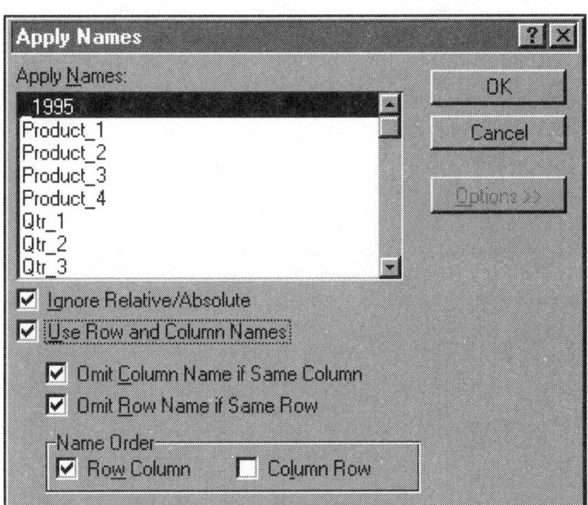

FIGURE 5-13

Click the Options button to make additional choices available.

When you apply names to formulas using the Apply Names dialog box, by default Excel does not apply the column or the row name if either is superfluous. To include the column or row name, deselect the appropriate option.

You can use the Name Order options to control the order in which row and column components appear when Excel applies two names connected by an intersection operator.

Using Range Names with the Go To Command

When you choose the Go To command from the Edit menu (or press F5), range names appear in the list box at the left side of the Go To dialog box, as shown in Figure 5-14. To go to one of these ranges, simply select the range name and click OK.

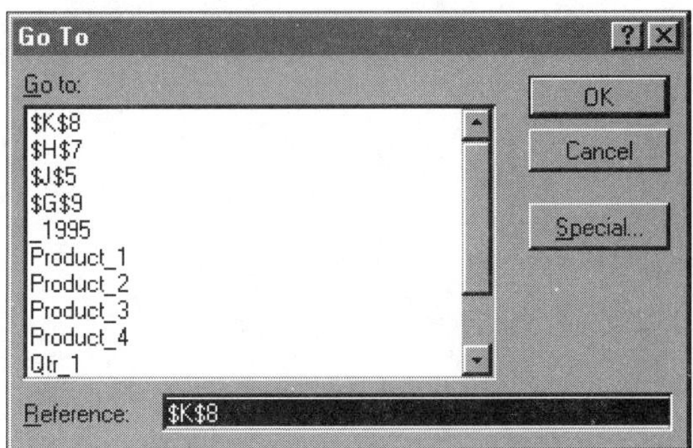

FIGURE 5-14

Use the Go To dialog box to select a cell or range name so that you can move to that cell or range quickly.

TIP The Go To dialog box remembers the last four places you "went to," as shown in Figure 5-14. The latest location is always in the Reference box when you display the dialog box, so you can jump back and forth between two locations by pressing F5, and then pressing Enter.

Understanding Error Values

An error value is the result of a formula that Excel cannot resolve. The seven error values are #DIV/0!, #NAME?, #VALUE!, #REF!, #N/A, #NUM!, and #NULL!. The table below lists each of these error values and what they mean.

Error Value	Means
#DIV/0!	You attempted to divide a number by zero. This error usually occurs when you create a formula with a divisor that refers to a blank cell.
#NAME?	You entered a name in a formula that is not in the Define Name dialog box list. You may have mistyped the name or typed a deleted name. Excel also displays this error value if you do not enclose a text string in double quotation marks.
#VALUE!	You entered a mathematical formula that refers to a text entry.
#REF!	You deleted a range of cells whose references are included in a formula.
#N/A	No information is available for the calculation you want to perform. When building a model, you can enter #N/A in a cell to show that you are awaiting data. Any formulas that reference cells containing the #N/A value return #N/A.
#NUM!	You provided an invalid argument to a worksheet function. #NUM! can also indicate that the result of a formula is too large or too small to be represented in the worksheet.
#NULL!	You included a space between two ranges in a formula to indicate an intersection, but the ranges have no common cells.

Arrays

Arrays are calculating tools you can use to build formulas that produce multiple results or to operate on groups of values rather than on single values. An *array formula* acts on two or more sets of values, called *array arguments,* to return either a single result or multiple results. An *array range* is a block of cells that share a common array formula. An *array constant* is a specially organized list of constant values that you can use as arguments in your array formulas.

Using Arrays

The easiest way to learn about arrays is to look at a few examples. For instance, using arrays, you can calculate the sum of the values in rows 1 and 2 for each column in Figure 5-15 by entering a single formula. Follow these steps:

1. Select the range A3:E3.
2. Type

   =A1:E1+A2:E2

3. Press Ctrl-Shift-Enter.

   Figure 5-15 shows the results.

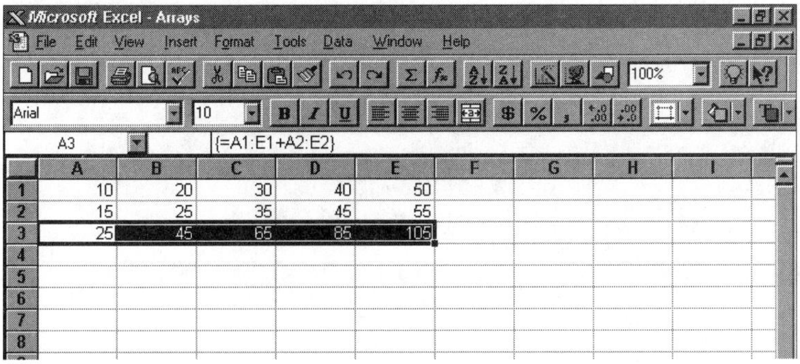

	A	B	C	D	E	F	G	H	I
1	10	20	30	40	50				
2	15	25	35	45	55				
3	25	45	65	85	105				
4									
5									
6									
7									
8									

FIGURE 5-15

We used an array formula to total the values in each column.

As you can see in Figure 5-15, a single array formula computes the sum of each group of values. This "single formula" exists in five cells at once. Although it seems to be five separate formulas, you cannot make any changes to it without selecting the entire formula — that is, the entire range A3:E3. Cells A3:E3 serve as the array range, and the array formula is stored in each cell of the array range. (Excel adds the braces, which are visible in the formula bar, when it distributes the array formula throughout the cells of the array range.) The array arguments are the range references A1:E1 and A2:E2.

The array formula in Figure 5-15 occupies a horizontal array range. The array formula in Figure 5-16 occupies a vertical array range.

FIGURE 5-16
In this worksheet, a vertical array formula calculates the products of the values in each row.

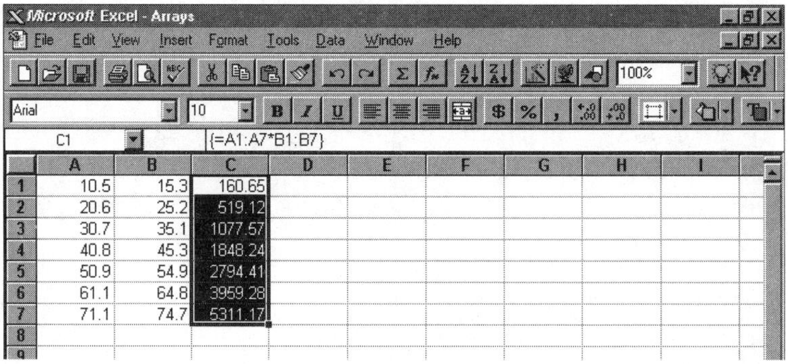

In Figure 5-16, you can use an array formula and the AVERAGE function to compute the average of the products of each pair of values in the worksheet. For example, to average A1*B1, A2*B2, A3*B3, and so on, follow these steps:

1. Select any blank cell.
2. Type *=AVERAGE(A1:A7*B1:B7)*
3. Press Ctrl-Shift-Enter.

Figure 5-17 shows the result.

FIGURE 5-17
We used an array formula in cell D1 to compute the average of the products of the pairs of values in columns A and B.

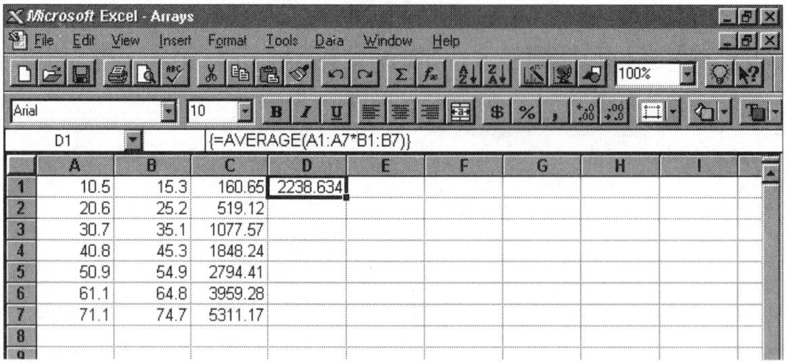

Two-Dimensional Arrays

In the previous example, the array formulas resulted in horizontal and vertical one-dimensional arrays. You can also create arrays that include two or more rows and columns, otherwise known as two-dimensional arrays. For example, to calculate the integer values of each entry in cells A1:C7 of Figure 5-17, you can create a two-dimensional array range. Here are the steps:

1. Select a range the same size and shape as the range you want to work with. (In this case, you would select a range with seven rows and three columns, such as E1:G7.)
2. Type *=INT(A1:C7)*
3. Press Ctrl-Shift-Enter.

As you can see in Figure 5-18, each cell in the range E1:G7 displays the integer value of the corresponding cell in the range A1:C7. In fact, Excel has entered the array formula

{=INT(A1:C7)}

in each cell in the range E1:G7. (The INT function simply changes a number to its integer value.)

Microsoft Excel - Arrays

E1 {=INT(A1:C7)}

	A	B	C	D	E	F	G	H	I
1	10.5	15.3	160.65	2238.634	10	15	160		
2	20.6	25.2	519.12		20	25	519		
3	30.7	35.1	1077.57		30	35	1077		
4	40.8	45.3	1848.24		40	45	1848		
5	50.9	54.9	2794.41		50	54	2794		
6	61.1	64.8	3959.28		61	64	3959		
7	71.1	74.7	5311.17		71	74	5311		
8									

FIGURE 5-18
We used a two-dimensional array formula to compute the integer value of each of the entries in cells A1:C7.

NOTE: You cannot create three-dimensional arrays across multiple worksheets in workbooks.

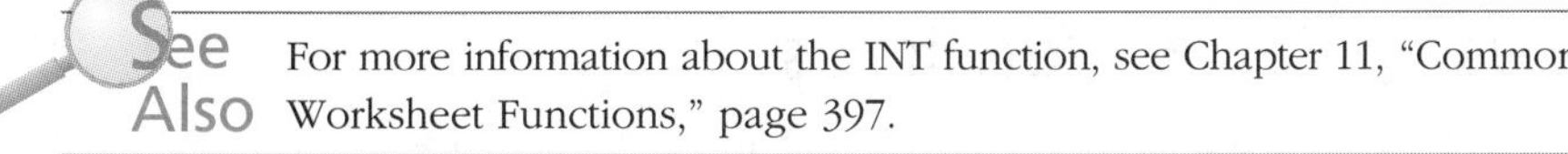

For more information about the INT function, see Chapter 11, "Common Worksheet Functions," page 397.

Array Formula Rules

To enter array formulas, first select the cell or range that will contain the results. If the formula produces multiple results, you must select a range the same size and shape as the range or ranges on which you perform your calculations.

Press Ctrl-Shift-Enter to lock in an array formula. Excel then places a set of braces around the formula in the formula bar to indicate that it is an array formula. Don't type the braces yourself; if you do, Excel interprets your entry as a label.

You cannot edit, clear, or move individual cells in an array range, nor can you insert or delete cells. You must treat the cells in the array range as a single unit and edit them all at once.

To edit or clear an array, select the entire array and activate the formula bar. (The braces around the formula disappear.) Edit or clear the formula and then press Ctrl-Shift-Enter.

TIP To select an entire array, click any cell in the array and press Ctrl-/.

To move the contents of an array range, select the entire array and choose the Cut command from the Edit menu. Then select the new location and choose the Paste command from the Edit menu. You can also use the mouse to drag the selection to a new location.

You cannot cut, clear, or edit part of an array, but you can assign different formats to individual cells in the array. You can also copy cells from an array range and paste them in another area of your worksheet.

For more information about the Cut and Paste commands, see Chapter 7, "Editing a Worksheet," page 227.

For more information about moving a selection with the mouse, see "Moving and Copying with the Mouse," page 232.

Using Array Constants

An array constant can consist of numbers, text, or logical values. You must enclose an array constant in braces ({}) and separate its elements with commas and semicolons. Commas indicate values in separate columns, and semicolons indicate values in separate rows.

Suppose you want to compute the integer values of the three numbers 123.456, 1.234, and 12345.678. You can perform these three computations with a single array formula, like this:

1. Select any horizontal three-cell range.

2. Type *=INT({123.456,1.234,12345.678})*. Be sure to type the braces yourself this time to indicate that the enclosed values make up an array constant.

3. Press Ctrl-Shift-Enter.

   Figure 5-19 shows the results.

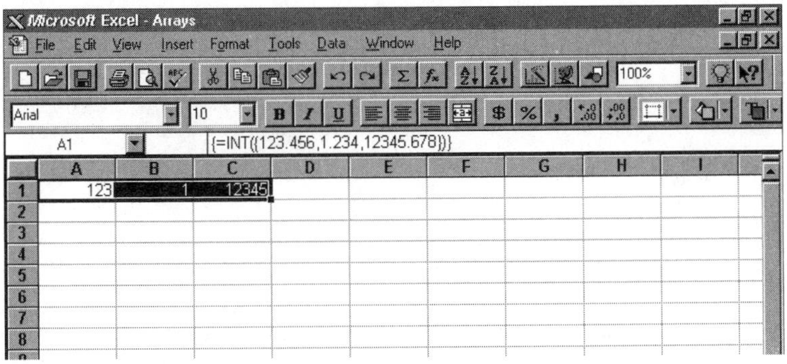

FIGURE 5-19
We used an array constant as the argument for this array formula.

You can also create vertical array constants, in which elements are separated by semicolons.

In addition, you can create two-dimensional array constants. Commas place the elements in separate columns in the same row, and semicolons separate the rows. For example, to calculate the square roots of a series of 12 values and display them as a block, you use the SQRT function with the following array formula:

=SQRT({4,9,16,25;36,49,64,81;100,121,144,169})

To enter this formula, select a range with four columns and three rows and then type the formula with the array constant in braces. When you press Ctrl-Shift-Enter to lock in the formula, Excel supplies the outer set of braces. Figure 5-20 shows the results.

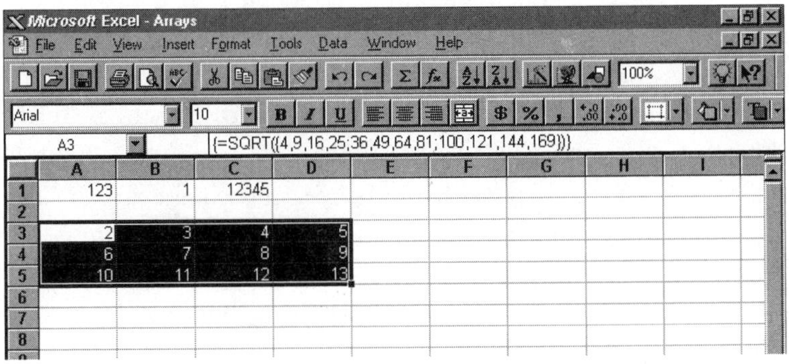

FIGURE 5-20
This array formula uses a four-column-by-three-row array constant.

See Also

For more information about the SQRT function, see Chapter 11, "Common Worksheet Functions," page 397.

Array Expansion

When you use arrays as arguments in a formula, all your arrays should have the same dimensions. If the dimensions of your array arguments or array ranges don't match, Excel often expands the arguments. For example, to multiply all the values in cells A1:B5 by 10, Excel uses the following array formula

{=A1:B5*10}

or these array constants

{={1,2;3,4;5,6;7,8;9,10}*10}

Notice that these two formulas are not balanced; ten values are on the left side of the multiplication operator, and only one is on the right. Excel can expand the second argument to match the size and shape of the first. In the preceding example, the first formula is equivalent to

{=A1:B5*{10,10;10,10;10,10;10,10;10,10}}

and the second is equivalent to

{={1,2;3,4;5,6;7,8;9,10}*{10,10;10,10;10,10;10,10;10,10}}

When you work with two or more sets of multivalue arrays, each set must have the same number of rows as the argument with the greatest number of rows, and the same number of columns as the argument with the greatest number of columns.

Calculating the Worksheet

Calculating is the process of computing formulas and then displaying the results as values in the cells containing the formulas. When you change the values in the cells to which these formulas refer, Microsoft Excel updates the values of the formulas as well. This updating process is called *recalculating,* and it affects only those cells containing references to the cells that have changed.

By default, Excel recalculates whenever you make changes that affect cell entries. If a large number of cells have to be recalculated, the words Calculating Cells and a number appear at the left end of the status bar. The number indicates the percentage of recalculation completed. During recalculation, the mouse pointer might assume the shape of an hourglass, which means you have to wait before you can use another command or make a cell entry. You can interrupt the recalculation process, however. Even if the mouse pointer appears as an hourglass, you can still use commands or make cell entries. Excel simply pauses in its recalculation and then resumes when you're done.

What If You Have a Pentium Processor?

In short: don't worry. For previous versions of Excel, you need a software "patch" from Microsoft to ensure accuracy. But Excel 7 checks for flawed Pentium processors at startup, so it doesn't need a patch. If it detects a flawed chip, Excel performs floating-point division in software. Since Excel checks the processor each time you start up, you can upgrade the chip at any time, and Excel will recognize it.

Manual Recalculation

To save time, particularly when you're entering changes in a large workbook with many formulas, you can switch from automatic to manual recalculation; that is, Excel will recalculate only when you tell it to. To set manual recalculation, follow these steps:

1. From the Tools menu, choose Options.
2. Click the Calculation tab, as shown in Figure 5-21.

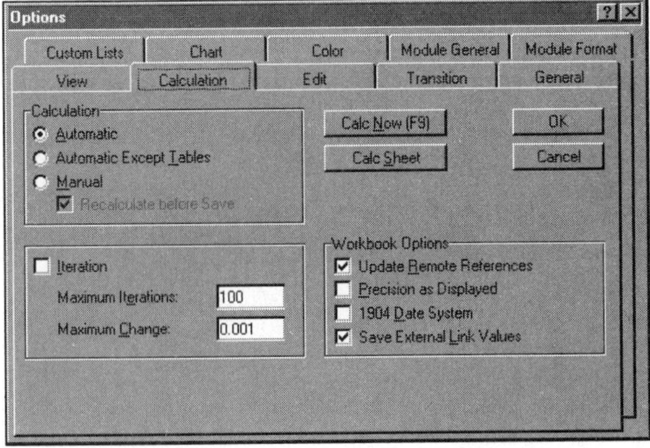

FIGURE 5-21
The Calculation tab of the Options dialog box controls worksheet calculation and iteration.

3. In the Calculation section, select the Manual option and then click OK.

Now if you make a change that normally initiates recalculation, the status bar displays *Calculate*. To see the effects of your cell entries, press F9. Excel then calculates all the cells in all the worksheets that are affected by the changes you've made since the last recalculation.

TIP If you want to calculate only the active worksheet, press Shift-F9.

You can also use the Calc Now or Calc Sheet buttons on the Calculation tab. To recalculate all open workbooks, click Calc Now. To calculate only the active worksheet in a workbook, click Calc Sheet. In addition, you can recalculate all open workbooks by using the Calculate Now toolbar button, which you can add to a toolbar.

Even if you have set recalculation to Manual, Excel normally recalculates your entire workbook when you save it to disk. To prevent this recalculation, deselect the Recalculate Before Save option on the Calculation tab of the Options dialog box. If you select the Automatic Except Tables option, Excel automatically recalculates all the affected cells in your workbook except data tables.

For more information about data tables, see Chapter 15, "What-If Analysis," page 543.

For more information about customizing toolbars, see Chapter 2, "Toolbars and Buttons," page 33.

Replacing Formulas or Parts of Formulas with Their Resulting Values

To replace a formula or a range of formulas with their resulting values, use the Paste Special command on the Edit menu. For example, suppose cell A1 contains the value 100, cell A2 contains the value 200, and cell A3 contains the value 300. If cell A6 contains the formula

```
=A1+A2+A3
```

its resulting value is 600. If you want to eliminate the calculation but retain the value 600, follow these steps:

1. Select cell A6 and choose Copy from the Edit menu.
2. Choose Paste Special from the Edit menu.
3. When the Paste Special dialog box appears, select Values in the Paste box and press Enter twice.

   The formula in cell A6 is replaced by the value 600.

To change part of a formula to a value, select the part you want to change and press F9. For example, let's modify the formula

=A1+A2+A3

in cell A6 of the previous example. To replace the reference A1 with its value, highlight the cell reference in the formula bar and press F9. The formula then becomes

=100+A2+A3

To replace individual cell references with their values, highlight each one and press F9. Then lock in the value by pressing Enter. To return the formula to its original state, click the Cancel button in the formula bar or press Esc.

Circular References

A *circular reference* is a formula that depends on its own value. The most obvious type is a formula that contains a reference to the same cell in which it is entered. For example, if you enter the formula

=C1–A1

in cell A1, Excel displays the message *Cannot resolve circular references.* When you click OK to acknowledge the error, the formula returns the value 0.

Many circular references, however, can be resolved. The worksheet in Figure 5-22 (on the next page) displays the underlying formulas in each cell. This set of formulas is circular because the formula in A1 depends on the value in A3, and the formula in A3 depends on the value in A1. The status bar displays the first circular reference Excel finds: Circular: A3.

TIP To switch between displaying resulting values (the default) and displaying the underlying formulas on a worksheet, press Ctrl-‘ (backwards apostrophe on the tilde key). This key is usually located above the Tab key at the left end of the numbers row.

To resolve this kind of circular reference, select the Iteration option on the Calculation tab of the Options dialog box. Excel then recalculates a specified number of times all the cells in open worksheets that contain a circular reference. Each time Excel recalculates the formulas, the results in the cells get closer to the correct values.

When you select the Iteration option, Excel sets the Maximum Iterations option to 100 and the Maximum Change option to 0.001. Thus, Excel recalculates a maximum of 100 times or until the values change less than 0.001 between iterations, whichever comes first. In Figure 5-22, we selected the Iteration option and accepted the default settings for Maximum Iterations and Maximum Change. As a result, the first iteration of the formula in cell A3 returns 999.9995, and the Calculate message in the status bar tells you that more iterations are possible. Pressing F9 recalculates the value, bringing it closer to 1000. The initial iteration returned 999.9995 because Excel calculated the value to within 0.001; each recalculation brings the value closer. If Maximum Change was set to 0.0001, the value would immediately appear as 1000.

Excel does not repeat the *Cannot resolve circular reference* message if it fails to resolve the reference. You must determine when the answer is close enough.

FIGURE 5-22

This worksheet contains a circular reference.

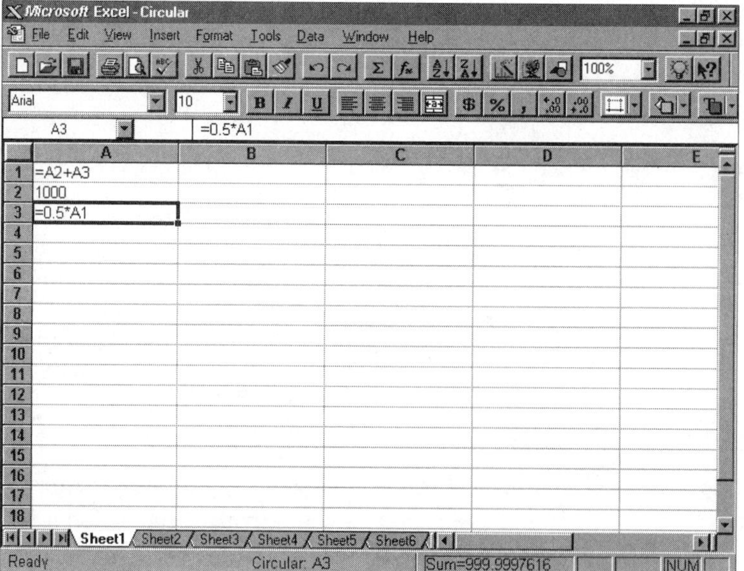

The process just described is called *convergence:* The difference between results becomes smaller with each iterative calculation. In the opposite process, *divergence,* the difference between results becomes larger with each iterative calculation. In this case, Excel continues iterations until it completes the maximum number you specify. Excel can perform 100 iterations in seconds, but be sure the Calculation option is set to Manual; otherwise, Excel recalculates the circular references every time you make a cell entry.

The circular reference warning usually indicates that you made an error in a formula. Click OK and look at the formula. If the error is not obvious, check the cells that the formula references.

Precision of Numeric Values

Excel stores numbers with as much as 15-digit accuracy and converts any digits after the fifteenth to zeros. Excel drops any digits after the fifteenth in a decimal fraction. In addition, Excel displays numbers that are too long for their cells in scientific notation. Here are some examples of how Excel treats integers and decimal fractions longer than 15 digits when they are entered in cells with the default column width of 8.43 characters:

Entry	Displayed Value	Underlying Value
123456789012345678	1.23E+17	123456789012345000
1.23456789012345678	1.234568	1.23456789012345
1234567890.12345678	1.23E+09	1234567890.12345
123456789012345.678	1.23E+14	123456789012345

Excel can calculate positive values approximately as large as 9.99E+307 and approximately as small as 1.00E–307. If a formula results in a value outside this range, Excel stores the number as text and assigns a #NUM! error value to the formula cell.

The Precision As Displayed Option

Your worksheet can appear erroneous if you use rounded values. For example, if you use cell formatting to display numbers in currency format with two decimal places, the value 10.006 is displayed as the rounded value $10.01. If you add 10.006 and 10.006, the correct result is 20.012. However, if all these numbers are formatted as currency, the worksheet displays the rounded values $10.01 and $10.01, and the rounded value of the result is $20.01. The result is correct, as far as rounding goes, but its appearance may be unacceptable for a particular purpose, such as a presentation.

You can correct this problem by selecting the Precision As Displayed option on the Calculation tab of the Options dialog box. However, you should exercise caution when you use this option, because the underlying values in your worksheet are actually changed to their displayed values. In other words, if a cell containing the value 10.006 is formatted as currency, selecting the Precision As Displayed option *permanently* changes this value to 10.01.

See Also For more information about number formatting, see Chapter 6, "Formatting a Worksheet," page 155.

Lotus 1-2-3 Transition Options

The Options command on the Tools menu contains a tab labeled Transition. When you click this tab, you see several Lotus 1-2-3 transition options, including Transition Formula Evaluation and Transition Formula Entry. The first option controls the way Excel handles the calculation of Lotus 1-2-3 worksheets when those worksheets are opened in Excel. The second option changes the way Excel interprets entries.

When the Transition Formula Entry option is selected, you can enter any Lotus 1-2-3 function using Lotus 1-2-3 syntax and the function automatically is converted to the equivalent Excel function. For example, type the following Lotus 1-2-3 formula in Excel with the Transition Formula Entry option selected:

```
@AVG(A1..A5)
```

When you press Enter, the formula changes to

```
=AVERAGE(A1:A5)
```

Excel interprets text and logical values differently from Lotus 1-2-3. In Excel, if you average a column that contains both numbers and text entries, the text entries are ignored. In contrast, Lotus 1-2-3 treats cells that contain text as zero values. For example, in Lotus 1-2-3, the average of 4, 6, and 8 is 6, and the average of 4, 6, 8, and 0 is 4.5. Differences like this cannot be ignored when you're making the transition from Lotus 1-2-3 to Excel. So when you open a Lotus 1-2-3 worksheet in Excel, keep in mind that the Transition Formula Evaluation option is automatically activated, and as a result, Excel will interpret text as zero values. Excel also interprets TRUE as 1 and FALSE as 0 when these values are referred to in formulas.

Note that Excel allows you to use Lotus 1-2-3 range operators at any time, converting them to Excel-style operators. For example, when you type the Lotus-style range

```
A1..A3
```

in Excel, it is converted to

```
A1:A3
```

after you press Enter.

Transition Navigation Keys

The Transition tab of the Options dialog box includes the Transition Navigation Keys option, which modifies the functionality of the keyboard shortcuts and function keys as shown in the following table.

Keys	Transition Navigation Keys Action	Normal Excel Action
Ctrl-Left Direction	Left one page	Left to the edge of the current region
Ctrl-Right Direction	Right one page	Right to the edge of the current region
Tab	Right one page	Right one cell
Shift-Tab	Left one page	Left one cell
Home	Selects the cell in the upper left corner of the worksheet	Selects the cell in the first column of the current row
F6	Activates the next window of the same workbook	Activates the next pane of the current window
Shift+F6	Activates the previous pane of the same window	Activates the previous pane of the current window

Text-Alignment Prefix Characters

When the Transition Navigation Keys option is turned on, you can use the following text-alignment prefix characters to assign alignment formats to text entries in your worksheet. To use a text-alignment prefix character, select a cell, type the desired character, and then type the text entry and press Enter. The text-alignment character appears in the formula bar but not in the cell.

Character	Transition Navigation Keys Action	Normal Excel Action
' (apostrophe)	Aligns data in the cell to the left	Same
" (double quotation mark)	Aligns data in the cell to the right	None
^ (caret)	Centers data in the cell	None
\ (backslash)	Repeats characters across the cell	None

Chapter 6

Formatting a Worksheet

In this chapter, you'll learn how to assign and change the formats, alignments, and fonts of text and numeric cell entries. (We'll save the Format menu's Sheet command for Chapter 8 and the Placement command for Chapter 9.) You'll also learn how to put template files to good use and how to change the way Microsoft Excel appears on your computer's screen. Later in the chapter, we'll explain Excel's outlining features.

Why use formats? Compare Figure 6-1 with Figure 6-2, and you'll have the answer. Although the information is basically the same in both worksheets, the worksheet in Figure 6-2 is formatted and therefore much easier to read and interpret.

WWWW-CO 1995 Sales

	A	B	C	D	E	F
1	1995 Sales: WWWW Company, Inc.					
2		Product				
3	Month	Widgets	Wombats	Woofers	Whatzits	Total by Month
4	January	433.33	3084.03	3501.77	6385.43	13404.56
5	February	4827.84	5005.87	9837.37	4093.03	23764.11
6	March	1674.16	7154.01	7619.9	2842.43	19290.5
7	April	443	1756.27	775.85	5099.14	8074.26
8	May	464.61	5997.18	4967.3	3704.59	15133.68
9	June	8525.77	9201.34	5693.62	4193.42	27614.15
10	July	3880.67	3927.47	8174.5	5013.34	20995.98
11	August	8389.46	8722.76	2547.25	673.09	20332.56
12	Septembe	7950.16	5033.68	9006.5	1141.11	23131.45
13	October	8853.37	1717.41	6148	4668.97	21387.75
14	November	6508.76	4087.6	3582.32	644.68	14823.36
15	December	245.24	8356.39	2053.37	2857.13	13512.13
16	Total by P	52196.37	64044.01	63907.75	41316.36	221464.5

Sheet1 / Sheet2 / Sheet3 / Sheet4 / Sheet5 / Sheet6

FIGURE 6-1

All entries in this worksheet are displayed in their default formats.

WWWW-CO 1995 Sales

	A	B	C	D	E	F
1	1995 Sales: WWWW Company, Inc.					
2				*Product*		
3	***Month***	**Widgets**	**Wombats**	**Woofers**	**Whatzits**	**Total by Month**
4	**January**	$433.33	$3,084.03	$3,501.77	$6,385.43	$13,404.56
5	**February**	$4,827.84	$5,005.87	$9,837.37	$4,093.03	$23,764.11
6	**March**	$1,674.16	$7,154.01	$7,619.90	$2,842.43	$19,290.50
7	**April**	$443.00	$1,756.27	$775.85	$5,099.14	$8,074.26
8	**May**	$464.61	$5,997.18	$4,967.30	$3,704.59	$15,133.68
9	**June**	$8,525.77	$9,201.34	$5,693.62	$4,193.42	$27,614.15
10	**July**	$3,880.67	$3,927.47	$8,174.50	$5,013.34	$20,995.98
11	**August**	$8,389.46	$8,722.76	$2,547.25	$673.09	$20,332.56
12	**September**	$7,950.16	$5,033.68	$9,006.50	$1,141.11	$23,131.45
13	**October**	$8,853.37	$1,717.41	$6,148.00	$4,668.97	$21,387.75
14	**November**	$6,508.76	$4,087.60	$3,582.32	$644.68	$14,823.36
15	**December**	$245.24	$8,356.39	$2,053.37	$2,857.13	$13,512.13
16	**Total by Product**	$52,196.37	$64,044.01	$63,907.75	$41,316.36	$221,464.49

Sheet1 / Sheet2 / Sheet3 / Sheet4 / Sheet5 / Sheet6

FIGURE 6-2

The formatted worksheet is easier to read.

Formatting Before You Copy

When you copy a cell, you copy both its contents and its formats. If you then paste this information into another cell, the formats of the source cell replace the old formats. You can take advantage of this time-saver by formatting your source cell before you choose the Copy and Paste commands or buttons, or the Fill command. (For more information about copying and pasting, see Chapter 7, "Editing a Worksheet," page 227.)

We'll discuss the menu and toolbar methods of applying formats as we go through this chapter.

Assigning and Removing Formats

The Cells command on the Format menu controls most of the formatting you'll apply to the cells in your worksheets. Formatting is easy: Simply select the cell or range and choose the appropriate Format menu commands. For example, to format cells B4:F16 in Figure 6-1, we followed these steps:

1. Select cells B4:F16.
2. From the Format menu, choose Cells.
3. Click the Number tab, if it is not already active.
4. From the Category list box, select Currency.
5. Set the Decimal Places box to 0.
6. Click OK to return to the worksheet.

As you can see in Figure 6-2, Microsoft Excel changes the numbers in selected cells to display currency values. (You might need to increase the column width to see the currency values.)

TIP If you want to quickly display the Format Cells dialog box, press Ctrl-1.

A formatted cell remains formatted until you apply a new format or remove the format. When you overwrite or edit an entry, you need not reformat the cell. To remove all assigned formats, follow these steps:

1. Select the cell or range.
2. From the Edit menu, choose Clear, and then Formats.

   To also remove the values in cells, you select All from the Clear submenu.

   NOTE To format a common set of cells in two or more worksheets in the same workbook, you can use the group editing feature. (See "Editing Groups of Sheets Simultaneously," page 326.)

See Also For more information about changing column widths, see "Controlling Column Width," page 192.

For more information about the Clear command, see "Clearing Cell Contents and Formats," page 245.

Formatting with Toolbars

Figure 6-3 shows the Standard toolbar, which contains the Format Painter button. This button lets you copy formats from selected cells to other cells and worksheets in the current workbook and even in other workbooks.

FIGURE 6-3
With the Format Painter button on the Standard toolbar, you can copy the formats of selected cells to other cells.

To copy formats to another location, follow these steps:

1. Select the cell or cells you want to copy formats from.
2. Click the Format Painter button. (The pointer appears with a small paintbrush icon next to it.)
3. Select the cell or cells you want to copy formats to.

If you copy formats from a range of cells and then select a single cell when you paste, the Format Painter pastes the entire range of formats, from the selected cell down and to the right. If, however, you select a range of cells when you paste formats, the Format Painter follows the shape of the copied range. If the range you want to format is a different shape than the copied range, the pattern is repeated or truncated as necessary.

Build Your Own "Super Formatting" Toolbar

Using Microsoft Excel's toolbar customization features, you can create a toolbar for just about any purpose. After you get the hang of it, you'll want to create a few toolbars containing buttons for the commands you use most often. For example, we created this "Super Formatting" toolbar that contains a number of useful formatting buttons, including some that are not available on any other toolbar:

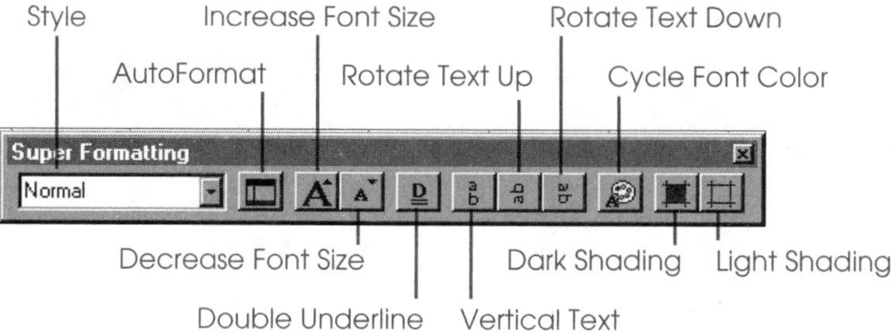

To construct the "Super Formatting" toolbar, follow these steps:

1. From the View menu, choose Toolbars to display the Toolbars dialog box.
2. Highlight the entry in the Toolbar Name edit box, type *Super Formatting,* and click the Customize button.
3. Select the Formatting option from the Categories list box.
4. Select a button you want to add and drag it to the new toolbar. Repeat for each additional button. (We added the Style box, the AutoFormat button, and the two shading buttons from this category.)
5. Select the Text Formatting category.

(continued)

Build Your Own "Super Formatting" Toolbar

6. Select each button you want to add, in turn, and drag it to the new toolbar. (We added the Increase and Decrease Font Size buttons, the Double Underline button, the three vertical and rotate text buttons, and the Cycle Font Color button from this category.)
7. Click Close.

Now you can display the "Super Formatting" toolbar along with the regular Formatting toolbar whenever you are constructing a new worksheet. For more information about customizing toolbars, see Chapter 2, "Toolbars and Buttons," page 33.

As Figure 6-4 shows, Excel also provides the Formatting toolbar, which is, as its name suggests, designed specifically for formatting.

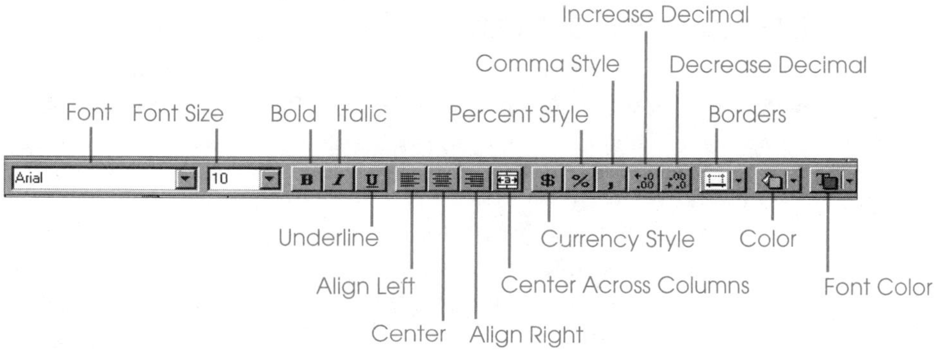

FIGURE 6-4
The Formatting toolbar.

To apply a format with a toolbar button, select a cell or range and then click the button with the mouse. To remove the format, click the button again.

Formatting Individual Characters

You can apply formatting to the individual characters of a text entry in a cell as well as to the entire cell. Select the individual characters and then choose the Cells command from the Format menu. Select the attributes you want and click OK. Press Enter to see the results of formatting individual characters, as shown in Figure 6-5 on the next page.

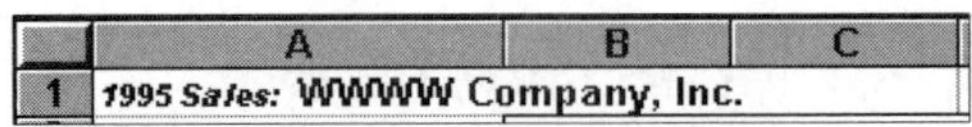

	A	B	C
1	*1995 Sales:* WWWWW Company, Inc.		

FIGURE 6-5
You can format characters differently within a cell.

NOTE If you try to apply formats to the individual characters of a numeric entry, the formats disappear when you press Enter and are overridden by the numeric format of the cell. If you want, you can convert a numeric entry to a text entry by preceding it with a single quotation mark.

See Also For more information about editing directly in cells, see "Editing Directly in Cells," page 241.

For more information about font styles, see "Formatting Fonts," page 183.

For an example of formatting individual characters, see "Selecting Font Styles and Effects," page 184.

Using AutoFormat

You can save a lot of time by using the AutoFormat command on the Format menu. Excel's automatic formats are predefined combinations of formats: number, font, alignment, border, pattern, column width, and row height.

NOTE You can also use the AutoFormat button, which corresponds to the AutoFormat command, except that it applies only to the last-selected format from the AutoFormat dialog box. You can add the AutoFormat button by selecting the Formatting category in the Customize dialog box. For information about customizing toolbars, see Chapter 2, "Toolbars and Buttons," page 33.

The AutoFormat command uses existing formulas and text labels to determine how to apply formatting. You can use other formatting commands after you use AutoFormat to adjust the overall appearance. If you don't like the way something looks, choose Undo AutoFormat from the Edit menu and then try adding blank columns or rows to set off areas you don't want AutoFormat to change. You can also select only those regions of a worksheet that you want AutoFormat to affect.

To use AutoFormat, follow these steps:

1. Enter data in your worksheet, such as that shown earlier in Figure 6-1.

2. Specify the current region by selecting any cell in the group of cells you want to format. (The *current region* is the contiguous block of cells that contains the active cell and is surrounded by blank columns, blank rows, or worksheet borders.) Alternatively, you can select the specific range of cells you want to format.

3. From the Format menu, choose the AutoFormat command. The cell selection expands to include the entire current region, and a dialog box like the one in Figure 6-6 appears.

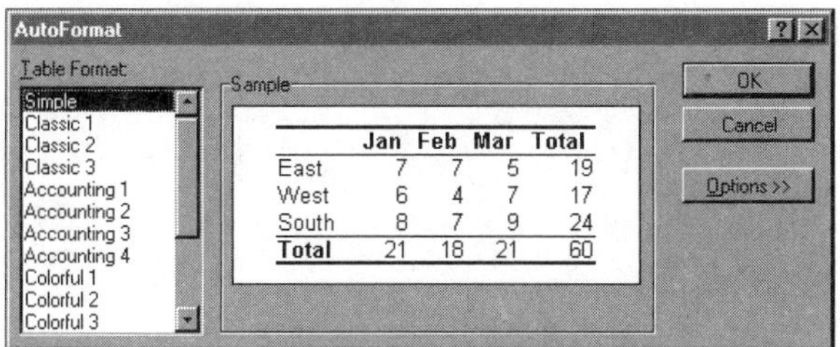

FIGURE 6-6

The AutoFormat dialog box offers a selection of predefined formats you can apply to your worksheet data.

4. In the AutoFormat dialog box, click Options to display the Formats To Apply section. (If you click an option to deselect a format type, the Sample display adjusts accordingly.)

5. Select a format from the Table Format list box and then click OK. For example, if you entered the data as shown in Figure 6-1 and selected the Classic 2 table format, your worksheet would look like the one in Figure 6-7.

WWWW-CO 1995 Sales

	A	B	C	D	E	F	G
1	1995 Sales: WWWW Company, Inc.						
2		Product					
3	Month	Widgets	Wombats	Woofers	Whatzits	Total by Month	
4	January	$433.33	$3,084.03	$3,501.77	$6,385.43	$13,404.56	
5	February	$4,827.84	$5,005.87	$9,837.37	$4,093.03	$23,764.11	
6	March	$1,674.16	$7,154.01	$7,619.90	$2,842.43	$19,290.50	
7	April	$443.00	$1,756.27	$775.85	$5,099.14	$8,074.26	
8	May	$464.61	$5,997.18	$4,967.30	$3,704.59	$15,133.68	
9	June	$8,525.77	$9,201.34	$5,693.62	$4,193.42	$27,614.15	
10	July	$3,880.67	$3,927.47	$8,174.50	$5,013.34	$20,995.98	
11	August	$8,389.46	$8,722.76	$2,547.25	$673.09	$20,332.56	
12	September	$7,950.16	$5,033.68	$9,006.50	$1,141.11	$23,131.45	
13	October	$8,853.37	$1,717.41	$6,148.00	$4,668.97	$21,387.75	
14	November	$6,508.76	$4,087.60	$3,582.32	$644.68	$14,823.36	
15	December	$245.24	$8,356.39	$2,053.37	$2,857.13	$13,512.13	
16	Total by Product	$52,196.37	$64,044.01	$63,907.75	$41,316.36	$221,464.49	

Sheet1 / Sheet2 / Sheet3 / Sheet4 / Sheet5 / Sheet6

FIGURE 6-7

In seconds, you can transform a raw worksheet into a presentation-quality table with the AutoFormat command.

6. Select a cell outside the table to remove the highlight from the current region and see the effect of your changes.

Formatting Numbers and Text

Excel's Format commands let you control the display of numeric values and modify the display of text entries. From the Format menu, choose the Cells command (or simply press Ctrl-1) and then click the Number tab in the Format Cells dialog box. The Number tab, as shown in Figure 6-8, offers 12 categories of formats.

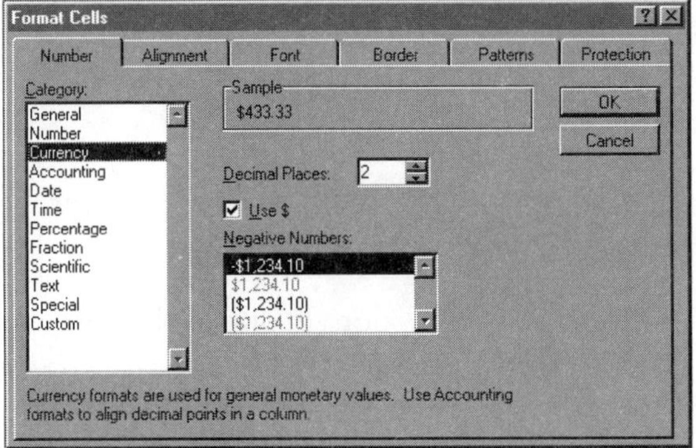

FIGURE 6-8

The Format Cells dialog box includes the Number tab, which offers a wealth of built-in numeric formats.

When you select a category from the Category list box, the right side of the dialog box displays the formats and options available for that category type. The sample area at the top of the dialog box shows you how the selected format will affect the contents of the active cell.

TIP Always select a cell that contains a number you want to format before opening the Format Cells dialog box. That way, you can see the results in the sample box.

Keep in mind the difference between underlying and displayed worksheet values. Formats do not affect the underlying numeric or text values in cells. For example, if you enter a number with 6 decimal places, in a cell that is formatted with 2 decimal places, the number is displayed with only two decimal places, but the underlying value is not changed. Excel uses the underlying value in calculations.

See Also For information about built-in date and time formats, see Chapter 12, "Dates and Times," page 459.

For information about creating numeric formats, see "Creating Custom Numeric Formats," page 170.

For information about creating text formats, see "Formatting Positive, Negative, Zero, and Text Entries," page 175.

The General Format

The General format is the first category in the Format Cells dialog box. Unless you specifically change the format of a cell, Excel displays any text or numbers you enter in the General format. With the three exceptions listed below, the General format displays exactly what you type. For example, if you enter *123.45,* the cell displays 123.45.

The first exception concerns numbers too long to display in a cell. For example, the General format displays the number *12345678901234* (an integer) as 1.23E+13 in a standard-width cell. Long decimal values are rounded or displayed in scientific notation. For example, if you enter *123456.7812345* in a standard-width cell, the General format displays the number as 123456.8.

Second, the General format does not display trailing zeros. For example, the number *123.0* is displayed as 123.

Third, a decimal fraction entered without a number to the left of the decimal point is displayed with a zero. For example, *.123* is displayed as 0.123.

The Number Formats

The Number category contains options that display numbers in integer, fixed-decimal, and punctuated formats. Figure 6-9 shows the Numbers option.

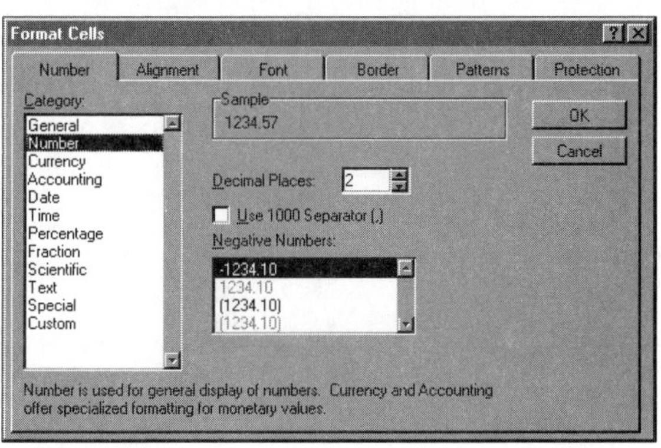

FIGURE 6-9

Excel's simplified number formatting is easier than ever.

Select the number of decimal places to display (0 to 30) by typing or scrolling the value in the Decimal Places box. For example, selecting 2 decimal places displays *1234.567* as 1234.57 and displays *1234.5* as 1234.50. If the number is an integer, Excel adds a decimal point and two trailing zeros.

The Use 1000 Separator option adds commas between hundreds and thousands, thousands and millions, and so on. For example, with 1000 Separators and two decimal places selected, Excel displays *1234.567* as 1,234.57.

The Negative Numbers option allows you to display negative numbers preceded by a minus sign, in red, in parentheses, or in both red and parentheses.

The Currency Formats

The four Currency formats are similar to the formats in the Number category except that instead of using them to control the display of commas, you use them to control whether a dollar sign precedes the number.

All the currency formats produce a blank space (the width of a close parenthesis) on the right side of positive values, ensuring that decimal points align in a column of similarly formatted positive and negative numbers.

The Accounting Formats

Excel provides special formats that address the needs of accounting professionals. When these formats are used with the accounting underline font formats, you can easily create P & L statements, balance sheets, and other schedules that conform to generally accepted accounting principles.

The Accounting format corresponds roughly to the Currency formats — you can display numbers with and without dollar signs and decimal places. The big difference is that the Accounting format displays any dollar signs in the cells aligned to the left, whereas the numbers are aligned to the right as usual as shown in Figure 6-10. The result is that both the dollar signs and the numbers are vertically aligned in the same column. Numbers with similar dollar-sign and non-dollar-sign formats line up properly in a column.

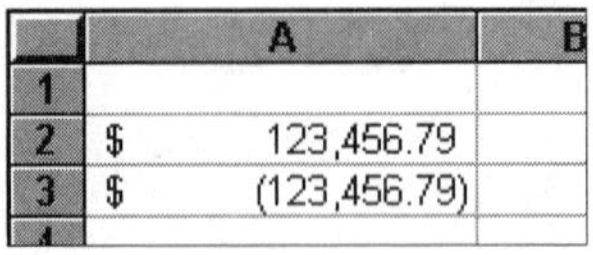

	A	B
1		
2	$ 123,456.79	
3	$ (123,456.79)	

FIGURE 6-10

The Accounting format aligns dollar signs to the left of a cell and numbers to the right.

The Accounting format treats zero values as dashes. The spacing of the dashes depends on whether you select decimal places. If you include two decimal places, the dashes line up under the decimal point.

TIP You apply a two-decimal-place Accounting format without dollar signs when you click the Comma Style button on the Formatting toolbar. You apply a two-decimal-place Accounting format with dollar signs when you click the Currency Style button on the Formatting toolbar.

NOTE For information about Date and Time formats, see "Dates and Times," page 459.

For more information about the accounting underline font formats, see "Formatting Fonts," page 183.

The Percentage Formats

The formats in the Percentage category display numbers as percentages. The decimal point of the formatted number shifts two places to the right, and a percent sign appears at the end of the number. For example, a percentage format without decimal places displays *0.1234* as 12%; selecting two decimal places displays *0.1234* as 12.34%.

TIP You can also apply a percentage format without decimals by clicking the Percentage Style button on the Formatting toolbar.

The Fraction Formats

The formats in the Fraction category shown in Figure 6-11 on the next page display fractional amounts as actual fractions rather than as decimal values. These formats are particularly useful for entering stock prices. As shown in Figure 6-11, the first three Fraction formats use single-digit, double-digit, and triple-digit numerators and denominators. For example, the single-digit format displays *123.456* as 123 1/2, rounding the display to the nearest value that can be represented as a single-digit fraction. If you enter the same number in a cell to which the double-digit format has been applied, Excel uses the additional precision allowed by the format and displays 123 26/57. The underlying value does not change in either case.

The remaining six fraction formats allow you to specify the exact denominator you want. For example, if you enter 123.456 in a cell formatted using the As Sixteenths format, Excel displays 123 7/16. If you enter 123.5 into the same cell, Excel displays 123 8/16.

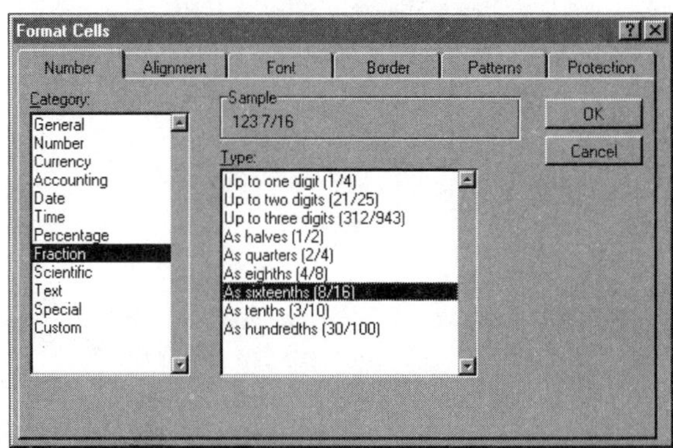

Figure 6-11
Excel now provides more fraction formatting options.

The Scientific (Exponential) Formats

The Scientific formats display numbers in exponential notation. For example, the two-decimal-place Scientific format displays the number *98765432198* as 9.88E+10.

The number 9.88E+10 is 9.88 times 10 to the tenth power. The symbol E stands for the word *exponent,* a synonym here for the words *10 to the* n*th power*. The expression *10 to the tenth power* means ten times itself ten times, or 10,000,000,000. Multiplying this value by 9.88 gives you 98800000000, an approximation of 98765432198. Increasing the decimal places allows you to increase the precision of the display, but at the possible cost of making the displayed number wider than the cell.

You can also use the Scientific format to display very small numbers. For example, this format displays *0.000000009* as 9.00E–09, which is 9 times 10 to the negative ninth power. The expression *10 to the negative ninth power* means 1 divided by 10 to the ninth power, 1 divided by 10 nine times, or 0.000000001. Multiplying this number by 9 gives our original number, 0.000000009.

The Text Format

Applying the Text format to a cell indicates that the entry in the cell is to be treated as text. For example, a numeric value is normally right-aligned in its cell. If you apply the Text format to the cell, however, the value is left-aligned as if it were a text entry.

For all practical purposes, a numeric constant formatted as text is still considered a number because of Excel's inherent ability to recognize numeric values. However, if you apply the Text format to a cell that contains a formula, the formula is considered text and is displayed as such in the cell. Any other formulas that refer to a formula formatted as text return the #VALUE error value.

TIP Formatting a formula as text is useful as a way of seeing the effects of "removing" a formula from a worksheet model without actually deleting it. You can format a formula as text so that it is visible on the worksheet and then locate the other dependent formulas that produce error values. After you apply the Text format, however, you must click the formula bar and press Enter to "recalculate" the worksheet and change the formula to a displayed text value. To restore the formula to its original condition, apply the desired numeric format to the cell, click the formula bar again, and press Enter.

See Also For information about creating custom formats, see "Creating Custom Numeric Formats," page 170.

The Special Formats

The four Special formats are a result of many requests from users. These generally noncalculated numbers include two zip code formats, a phone number format (complete with the area code in parentheses), and a Social Security Number format. Each of these special formats lets you quickly type numbers without having to enter the punctuation characters. For example, if you type 2065551212 and apply the Phone Number format, the cell displays the number as (206) 555-1212, as shown in the Sample box in Figure 6-12 on the next page.

Excel applies the parentheses and the dash for you in the format, which makes it much easier to enter a lot of numbers at once, since you don't have to move your hand from the keypad. In addition, the numbers you enter actually remain numbers instead of becoming text entries, which would be the case if you entered parentheses or dashes in the cell. Also, the leading zeros that often appear in zip codes are retained. Normally, if you enter 04321, Excel drops the zero and displays 4321. But if you use the Zip Code format, Excel correctly displays the code as 04321.

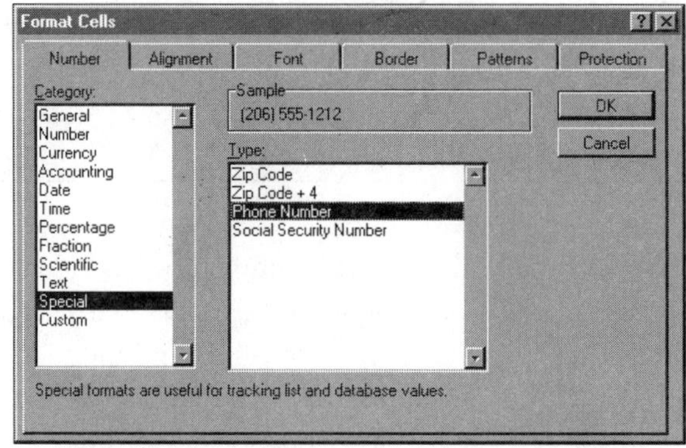

FIGURE 6-12
Excel provides several frequently requested number formats in the Special category.

Formatting Numbers As You Type

You can include special formatting characters such as dollar signs, percent signs, commas, or fractions to format numbers as you enter them. When you type in a numeric entry characters that represent a format Excel recognizes, Excel applies that format to the cell. For example, if you type *$45.00,* Excel interprets your entry as the value 45 formatted as currency with two decimal places. Only the value 45 appears in the formula bar, but the formatted value, $45.00, appears in the cell. If you type *1 3/8* (with a single space between the 1 and the 3), 1 3/8 appears in the cell and 1.375 appears in the formula bar. If you type *3/8,* however, 8-Mar appears in the cell. Assuming you make the entry in 1995, 3/8/1995 appears in the formula bar. To display 3/8 in the cell as a fraction, so that 0.375 appears in the formula bar, you must type *0 3/8* (with a space between the 0 and the 3).

For information about entering dates, see Chapter 12, "Dates and Times," page 459.

Creating Custom Numeric Formats

You use the Number tab in the Format Cells dialog box to create custom formats by selecting the Custom category and typing special formatting symbols in the Type edit box. Excel adds your new format to the bottom of the list of formatting codes in the Custom category. Use the symbols in the following table to create custom formats.

Symbol	Meaning
0	Digit placeholder. Ensures that a specified number of digits appears on each side of the decimal point. For example, if the format is 0.000, the value .987 is displayed as 0.987. If the format is 0.0000, the value .987 is displayed as 0.9870. If a number has more digits to the right of the decimal point than 0s specified in the format, the number is rounded. For example, if the format is 0.00, the value .987 is displayed as 0.99; if the format is 0.0, .987 is rounded to 1.0.
#	Digit placeholder. Works like 0, except that extra zeros do not appear if the number has fewer digits on either side of the decimal point than #s specified in the format. This symbol shows Excel where to display commas or other separating symbols. The format #,###, for example, tells Excel to display a comma after every third digit to the left of the decimal point. If you want Excel to include commas and display at least one digit to the left of the decimal point in all cases, specify the format #,##0.
?	Digit placeholder. Follows the same rules as the 0 placeholder, except that space is left for insignificant zeros on either side of the decimal point. This placeholder allows you to align numbers on the decimal points. For example, 1.4 and 1.45 would line up on the decimal point if both were formatted as 0.??.
.	Decimal point. Determines how many digits (0 or #) appear to the right and left of the decimal point. If the format contains only #s to the left of this symbol, Excel begins numbers smaller than 1 with a decimal point. To avoid this, use 0 as the first digit placeholder to the left of the decimal point instead of #.
%	Percentage indicator. Multiplies by 100 and inserts the % character.
/	Fraction format character. Displays the fractional part of a number in a nondecimal format. The number of digit placeholders that surround this character determines the accuracy of the display. For example, the decimal fraction 0.269 when formatted with # ?/? is displayed as 1/4, but when formatted with # ???/??? is displayed as 46/171.

(continued)

continued

Symbol	Meaning
,	Thousands separator. Uses commas to separate hundreds from thousands, thousands from millions, and so on, if the format contains a comma surrounded by #s, 0s, or ?s. In addition, the comma acts as a *rounding* and *scaling agent.* One comma at the end of a format is used by Excel to tell it to round a number and display it in thousands; two commas tells Excel to round to the nearest million. For example, the format code #,###,###, would round 4567890 to 4,568, whereas the format code #,###,###,, would round it to 5.
E– E+ e– e+	Scientific format characters. Displays the number in scientific notation and inserts E or e in the displayed value if a format contains one 0 or # to the right of an E–, E+, e–, or e+. The number of 0s or #s to the right of the E or e determines the minimum number of digits in the exponent. Use E– or e– to place a negative sign by negative exponents; use E+ or e+ to place a negative sign by negative exponents and a positive sign by positive exponents.
$ – + / ( ) *space*	Standard formatting characters. Enter these characters directly into your format.
\	Literal demarcation character. Precede each character you want to include in the format (except for : $ – + / ( ) and *space*) with a backslash. Excel does not display the backslash. For example, the format code #,##0" "\D;–#,##0" "\C displays positive numbers followed by a space and a *D* and negative numbers followed by a space and a *C*. To insert several characters, use the quotation-mark technique described in the *"Text"* table entry.
_	Underscore. Leaves space equal to the width of the next character. For example, _) leaves a space equal to the width of the close parenthesis. Use this formatting character for alignment purposes.
"Text"	Literal character string. Works like the backslash technique except that all text can be included within one set of double quotation marks without separate demarcation characters for each literal character.
*	Repetition initiator. Repeats the next character in the format enough times to fill the column width. Use only one asterisk in a format.

(continued)

continued

Symbol	Meaning
@	Text placeholder. If the cell contains text, the placeholder inserts that text in the format where the @ appears. For example, the format code "This is a "@"." displays *This is a debit.* in a cell containing the text *debit.*

See Also For a complete listing of date and time formatting symbols, see Chapter 12, "Dates and Times," page 459.

Creating New Formats

Often, you can use one of Excel's existing custom formats as a starting point for creating your own format. To build on an existing format, first select the cells you want to format. From the Format menu, choose the Cells command (or press Ctrl-1), click the Number tab and click the Custom category. Select the format you want to change from the Type list box, as shown in Figure 6-13, and then edit the contents of the edit box. The original format is not affected, and the new format is added to the list in the Type list box.

For example, to create a format to display a date with a long-format day, month, and year, follow these steps:

1. Click Custom in the Category list box and select the d-mmm-yy format.
2. In the Type edit box, edit the format to read dddd, mmmm dd, yyyy.
3. Click OK.

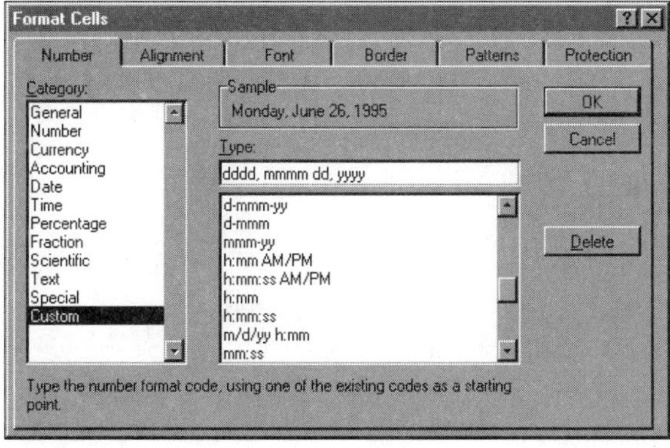

FIGURE 6-13

Create new custom formats based on existing ones.

TIP Saving your workbook saves new formats, but to carry special formats from one workbook to another, you must copy and paste a cell with the Custom format. To easily access special formats, consider saving them in one workbook.

The following table lists Excel's built-in codes for the Custom category and indicates how these codes relate to the other categories on the Number tab. (Note that this table does not list Date and Time codes, which are covered in Chapter 12.)

Category	Format Codes
General	No specific fornat
Number	0
	0.00
	#,##0
	#,##0.00
	#,##0_);(#,##0)
	#,##0_);[Red](#,##0)
	#,##0.00_);(#,##0.00)
	#,##0.00_);[Red](#,##0.00)
Currency	$#,##0_);($#,##0)
	$#,##0_);[Red]($#,##0)
	$#,##0.00_);($#,##0.00)
	$#,##0.00_);[Red]($#,##0.00)
Percentage	0%
	0.00%
Scientific	0.00E+00
	##0.0E+0
Fraction	# ?/?
	# ??/??
Date	See Chapter 12
Time	See Chapter 12
Text	@
Accounting	_($* #,##0_);_($* (#,##0);_($* "-"_);_(@_)
	_(* #,##0_);_(* (#,##0);_(* "-"_);_(@_)

Creating a Part-Number Format

Suppose you're creating an inventory worksheet and you want all the entries in the range A5:A100 to appear in the format *Part XXX-XXXX*. To create this format, follow these steps:

1. Select the range A5:A100.
2. From the Format menu, choose the Cells command and click the Number tab.
3. Click the Custom category, select the contents of the Type edit box, and type *"Part" ###-####*.
4. Click OK.

Now begin making entries in column A. (You might have to widen the column. After you make an entry or two, select the entire column. From the Format menu, choose Column and then AutoFit Selection.) Type the numbers for each part; Excel will add the word *Part* and the hyphen. For example, if you select cell A10 and enter *1234567,* Excel displays the entry as Part 123-4567.

For more information about copying and pasting between workbooks, see "Copying and Pasting Between Workbooks," page 335.

Formatting Positive, Negative, Zero, and Text Entries

Excel assigns different formats to positive and negative currency values in your worksheet. You can also specify formats for positive and negative values when you create custom formats, and you can specify how you want zero and text values to appear.

You can create custom formats with as many as four parts, with the portions separated by semicolons, like this:

Positive format; Negative format; Zero format; Text-value format

If your custom format includes only one part, Excel applies that format to positive, negative, and zero values. If your custom format includes two parts, the first part applies to positive and zero values; the second part applies only to negative values. Text-value formatting instructions must be the last element in the format specification, and unless you include text-value formatting, your format has no effect on text entries.

For example, suppose you create a billing statement worksheet, and you want to format the entries in the Amount Due column so that they display differently depending on the value in each cell. You might create this format:

"Amount due: "$#,##0.00_);"Credit: "($#,##0.00);"Let's call it even.";"Please note: "@

The following table shows the effects of this format on various worksheet entries:

Entry	Display
12.98	Amount due: $12.98
–12.98	Credit: ($12.98)
0	Let's call it even.
This is not a bill	Please note: This is not a bill

Again, you would probably need to widen the column to display the results.

TIP The Sample box at the top of the Format Cells dialog box shows how the value in the active cell appears in each format.

Adding Color to Formats

You can also use the Number formats to change the color of selected cell entries. For example, you might use color to distinguish categories of information or to make totals stand out. You can even assign colors to selected numeric ranges so that, for example, all values above or below a specified threshold appear in a contrasting color. Of course, colors don't appear on printed worksheets unless you have a color printer.

NOTE You can also change the color of a cell entry with the Font tab in the Format Cells dialog box or the Font Color button on the Formatting toolbar; however, the colors you specify with the Number tab take precedence over the colors you specify with the Font tab or Font Color button.

To change the color of an entry, type the name of the new color, in brackets, in front of the definition of the Custom format in the Type edit box.

For example, if you want the totals in row 16 of the worksheet shown earlier in Figure 6-2 to appear in blue and in Currency format with two decimal places, edit the $#,##0.00_);($#,##0.00) format as follows:

[Blue]$#,##0.00_);($#,##0.00)

When you apply this format to a worksheet, positive and zero values appear in blue; text and negative values appear in black (the default).

You can simply type the colors in the Type edit box. For example, the format

[Blue];[Red];[Yellow];[Green]

displays positive values in blue, negative values in red, zero values in yellow, and text in green.

You can specify the following color names in your formats: Black, Blue, Cyan, Green, Magenta, Red, White, and Yellow. You can also specify a color as COLOR*n,* where *n* is a number in the range 1 through 16. Excel selects the corresponding color from your worksheet's current 16-color palette. If that color is *dithered* (combines dots of two or more solid colors), Excel uses the nearest solid color.

TIP You can suppress all zero values in a worksheet. From the Tools menu, choose Options and click the View tab. Then click the Zero Values option in the Window Options section to deselect it.

See Also For more information about Excel's color palette, see "Changing the Available Colors," page 215.

Conditional Formatting

You can also display numbers that depend on comparison values. To do so, you add a condition to the first two parts of the standard four-part custom format, replacing the positive and negative formats. The third format becomes the default format for values that don't match the other two conditions. You can use the conditional operators <, >, =, <=, >=, or <> with any number to define a format.

For example, suppose you are tracking accounts receivable balances. To display accounts with a balance of more than $50,000 in blue, negative values in parentheses and in red, and all other values in the default color, create this format:

[Blue][>50000]$#,##0.00_);[Red][<0]($#,##0.00);$#,##0.00_)

Conditional formatting can also be a powerful aid if you need to scale numbers. For example, if your company produces a product that requires a few milliliters of a compound for each unit and you make thousands of units every day, you will need to convert from milliliters to liters and kiloliters when you budget the usage. Excel can make this conversion with the following numeric format:

[>999999]#,##0,,_m"kl";[>999]#4,_k_m"l";#_k"ml"

The following table shows the effects of this format on various worksheet entries:

Entry	Display
72	72 ml
7286957	7 kl
5876953782	5,877 kl

As you can see, using a combination of the conditional format, the thousands separator, and the proportional space indicator can improve both the readability and effectiveness of your worksheet, without increasing the number of formulas.

Deleting Custom Formats

To delete a custom format, select the format on the Number tab of the Format Cells dialog box and click Delete. You cannot delete built-in formats.

Aligning Cell Contents

The Alignment tab in the Format Cells dialog box positions text and numbers in cells. You can also use this tab to create multiline text labels, repeat a series of characters within one or more cells, and format text vertically in cells. Figure 6-14 shows the seven mutually exclusive Horizontal alignment options: General, Left, Center, Right, Fill, Justify, and Center Across Selection. The Vertical and Orientation sections control vertical alignment. You can select the Wrap Text option with any alignment option.

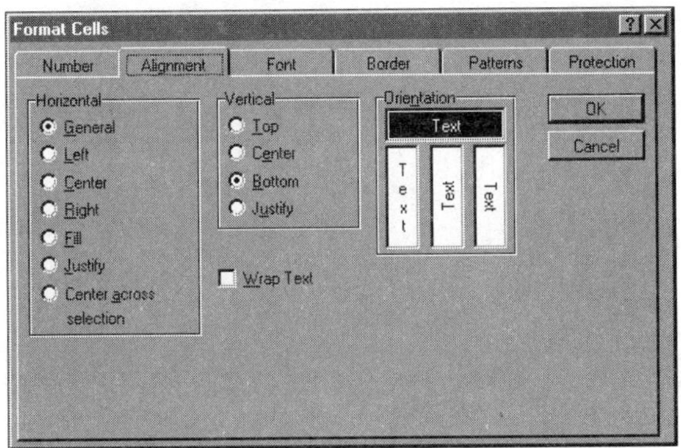

FIGURE 6-14
Excel offers many alignment options.

When you select General, the default Horizontal alignment option, numeric values are right-aligned and text values are left-aligned.

The Left, Center, and Right Options

The Left, Center, and Right options align the contents of the selected cells to the left, center, or right of the cell, overriding the default cell alignment. For example, in Figure 6-15, the entries in cells A1:C1 have the General alignment, so the number in cell B1 is right-aligned and the label in cell C1 is left-aligned. The entries in cells A2:C2 are left-aligned, the entries in cells A3:C3 are right-aligned, and the entries in cells A4:C4 are centered.

The "Hidden" Number Format

To hide values in a worksheet, assign a null format to them. To create a null format, enter only the semicolon separator for that portion of the format. For example, to hide negative and zero values only, use this format:

```
$#,##0.00;;
```

To hide all entries in a cell, use this format:

```
;;;
```

The null format hides the cell contents in the worksheet, but the entry is still visible in the formula bar. To hide the cell contents so that they don't appear in the worksheet or the formula bar, use Excel's protection features. For more information about Excel's protection features, see "Protecting Your Data," page 106.

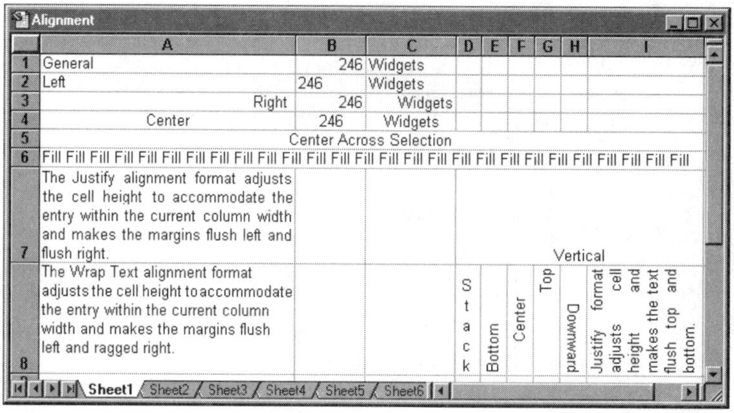

FIGURE 6-15
Use the Alignment tab to change the alignment of cell entries.

Alignment

	A	B	C	D	E	F	G	H	I
1	General	246	Widgets						
2	Left	246	Widgets						
3	Right	246	Widgets						
4	Center	246	Widgets						
5	Center Across Selection								
6	Fill Fill Fill Fill Fill Fill Fill Fill Fill Fill Fill Fill Fill Fill Fill Fill Fill Fill Fill Fill Fill Fill Fill Fill Fill Fill Fill Fill								
7	The Justify alignment format adjusts the cell height to accommodate the entry within the current column width and makes the margins flush left and flush right.			Vertical					
8	The Wrap Text alignment format adjusts the cell height to accommodate the entry within the current column width and makes the margins flush left and ragged right.			Stack	Bottom	Center	Top	Downward	Justify format adjusts cell height and makes the text flush top and bottom.

Sheet1 / Sheet2 / Sheet3 / Sheet4 / Sheet5 / Sheet6

Centering Text Across Columns

The Center Across Selection option centers text from one cell across all selected blank cells to the right, or to the next cell in the selection containing text. For example, in Figure 6-15, the Center Across Selection format was applied to the range A5:I5. The centered text is in cell A5.

In Figure 6-16, the Center Across Selection format was applied to cells B2:E2, with the word *Product* entered in cell B2.

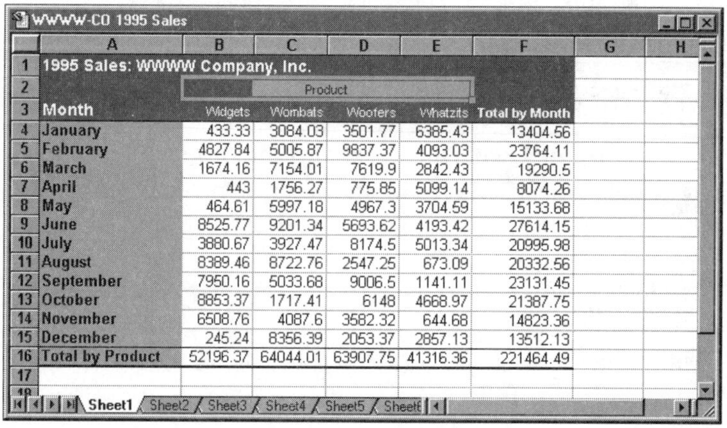

FIGURE 6-16
The Center Across Selection alignment option is used to center the label across the range B2:E2.

WWWW-CO 1995 Sales

	A	B	C	D	E	F
1	1995 Sales: WWWW Company, Inc.					
2		Product				
3	Month	Widgets	Wombats	Woofers	Whatzits	Total by Month
4	January	433.33	3084.03	3501.77	6385.43	13404.56
5	February	4827.84	5005.87	9837.37	4093.03	23764.11
6	March	1674.16	7154.01	7619.9	2842.43	19290.5
7	April	443	1756.27	775.85	5099.14	8074.26
8	May	464.61	5997.18	4967.3	3704.59	15133.68
9	June	8525.77	9201.34	5693.62	4193.42	27614.15
10	July	3880.67	3927.47	8174.5	5013.34	20995.98
11	August	8389.46	8722.76	2547.25	673.09	20332.56
12	September	7950.16	5033.68	9006.5	1141.11	23131.45
13	October	8853.37	1717.41	6148	4668.97	21387.75
14	November	6508.76	4087.6	3582.32	644.68	14823.36
15	December	245.24	8356.39	2053.37	2857.13	13512.13
16	Total by Product	52196.37	64044.01	63907.75	41316.36	221464.49

Sheet1 / Sheet2 / Sheet3 / Sheet4 / Sheet5 / Sheet6

Vertical and Orientation Options

The Vertical options include four alignment options — Top, Center, Bottom, and Justify — and four Orientation options. The Orientation section lets you format your entries to read horizontally, vertically from top to bottom, or sideways with the letters rotated 90 degrees either counterclockwise or clockwise. Excel automatically adjusts the height of the row to accommodate vertical orientation unless you previously or subsequently set the row height. If you want to return selected cells to their normal orientation, click the horizontal option at the top of the Orientation section. Figure 6-15 shows examples of all these alignment options.

See Also For information about changing row heights, see "Controlling Row Height," page 197.

The Fill Option

The Fill option repeats your cell entry to fill the width of the column. For example, in Figure 6-17, cell H9 contains a formula that averages the entries in cells H4 through H7. You can enter a row of greater-than signs to fill cells C9:G9 by following these steps:

1. Enter a single > (greater-than sign) in cell C9.
2. Select cells C9:G9.
3. From the Format menu, choose Cells and click the Alignment tab.
4. Select the Fill option and click OK.

Excel repeats the greater-than sign across cells C9:G9, as shown in Figure 6-17 on the next page. Although the cell range seems to contain many greater-than signs, the formula bar reveals that it actually contains a single greater-than sign. Like the other Format commands, the Alignment tab's Fill option affects only the appearance, not the underlying contents, of the cell. Excel repeats the characters across the entire range, with no breaks between cells. Although they appear to contain entries, cells D9:G9 are empty.

Selecting Alignment from the Toolbars

You can select Left, Center, Right, or Center Across Selection alignment by clicking the corresponding buttons on the Formatting toolbar, shown earlier in Figure 6-4.

When you "turn on" one of the toolbar alignment options, its button appears as if it has been pressed to show that the option is activated. As a result, you can always glance at the toolbar to see if one of these alignment options has been applied to the active cell.

To turn an alignment option off (and return the active cell to General alignment), click the button a second time.

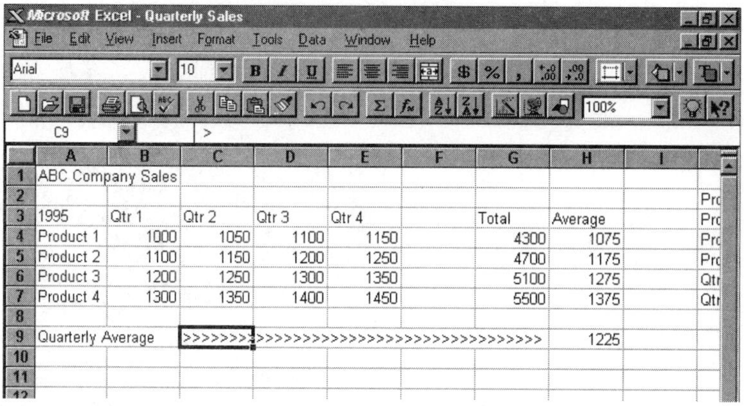

FIGURE 6-17

Use the Fill option to repeat a character across cells.

Usually the entries you repeat with the Fill alignment option are single characters such as a hyphen (–), an asterisk (*), or an equal sign (=); however, you can also repeat multicharacter entries. For example, in Figure 6-15, cell A6 contains the word *Fill* and the Fill option on the Alignment tab has been applied to cells A6:I6.

You might think it would be just as easy to type the repeating characters as it is to use Fill. However, the Fill option gives you two important advantages. First, if you adjust the column width, Excel increases or decreases the number of characters in the cell to accommodate the new column width. Second, you can repeat a single character or multiple characters across several adjacent cells.

NOTE Because the Fill option on the Alignment tab affects numeric values as well as text, it can cause a number to look like something it isn't. For example, if you apply the Fill option to a 10-character-wide cell that contains the number 3, the cell will appear to contain 3333333333.

The Wrap Text and Justify Options

If you enter a label that's too wide for the active cell, Excel extends the label past the cell border and into adjacent cells — provided those cells are empty. If you then select the Alignment tab's Wrap Text option, however, Excel displays your label entirely within the active cell. To accommodate the entire label, Excel increases the height of the row in which the cell is located and then "wraps" the text onto additional lines. As shown in Figure 6-15 on page 180, cell A8 contains a multiline label formatted with the Wrap Text option. You can use the Wrap Text option along with other Alignment options.

The Alignment command provides two Justify options — one in the Horizontal section and one in the Vertical section of the Alignment dialog box.

The Horizontal Justify option wraps text in the active cell, adjusts the row height accordingly, and forces the text to align flush with the right margin, as shown earlier in cell A7 in Figure 6-15.

TIP Do not confuse the Horizontal Justify alignment option with the Justify command on the Fill submenu of the Edit menu. The Horizontal Justify alignment option wraps text within a cell and adjusts the row height as necessary, displaying the cell contents with flush left and right margins. In contrast, the Justify command on the Fill submenu redistributes a text entry in as many cells below it as necessary, actually dividing the text into separate chunks. For more information about the Justify command on the Fill submenu, see "The Justify Command," page 271.

If you create a multiline label and subsequently deselect the Wrap Text or Horizontal Justify option, Excel readjusts the row to its original height.

The Justify option in the Vertical section on the Alignment tab does essentially the same thing as its Horizontal counterpart, except that it adjusts cell entries relative to the top and bottom of the cell rather than the sides, as shown in cell I8 of Figure 6-15, shown earlier. For example, if a cell contains two lines of text and the current row height is greater than the two lines of text require, the Vertical Justify option forces the top line of text to the top of the cell and the bottom line of text to the bottom of the cell. This version of the Justify option is particularly useful for adjusting text that is oriented vertically.

See Also For more information about adjusting row height manually, see "How Wrapping and Justifying Text Affects Row Height," page 198.

Formatting Fonts

Technically, the term *font* refers to a combination of typeface (for example, Helvetica), size (for example, 10 point), and character style (for example, bold). In Excel, you use the Font tab in the Format Cells dialog box to select the font and color of your cell entries. The Font tab includes Font, Font Style, and Size edit and list boxes, as well as Underline, Color, and Effects options. You can revert to the default font by selecting the Normal Font option.

You use fonts in a worksheet just as you do in printed text: to emphasize headings and to distinguish different kinds of information. To specify a font for a cell or for a range, first select the cell or range. From the Format menu, choose the Cells command (or press Ctrl-1) and click the Font tab. The Format Cells dialog box appears, as shown in Figure 6-18.

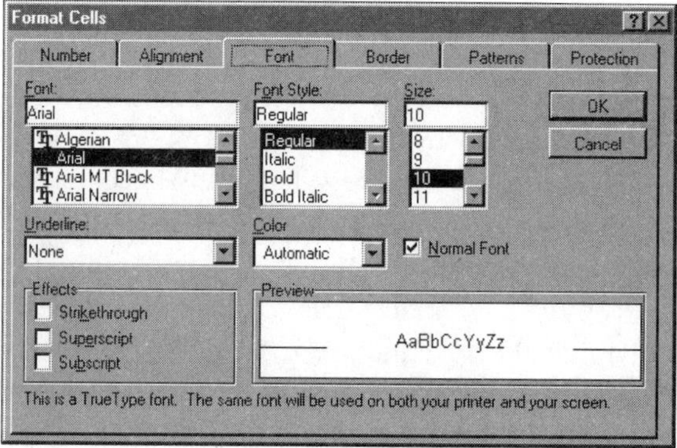

FIGURE 6-18
The Font tab in the Format Cells dialog box lets you assign typefaces, character styles, sizes, colors, and effects to your cell entries.

Selecting a Typeface and a Size

To select a typeface, click its name in the Font list box or type its name in the Font edit box. The numbers in the Size list box then change to show the sizes at which Excel can optimally print the selected typeface. You can use the Size list box scroll bar to see all the possible sizes. To specify a size, simply click it. When specifying a size, keep in mind that type sizes are given in points, such as 10 point, and that one point is 1/72 of an inch. Unless you preset the row height, Excel automatically adjusts it to accommodate larger point sizes.

To specify a size not listed, select the contents of the Size edit box and type a new number. You will usually get the best output if you select sizes that appear in the Size list box, but Excel will do its best to print at any size you specify. Some combinations of typeface and size will be more satisfactory than others. You might want to experiment to see the results you get with your own printer and screen display.

Selecting Font Styles and Effects

The available font styles vary depending on the typeface you select in the Font list box. In addition to regular, most fonts offer italic, bold, and bold italic styles. For example, all these styles are available for the Arial font, but regular and italic are the only styles in which you can actually print Arial MT Black. Simply select the style you want to use from the Font Style list box on the Font tab. You can see the effects of the options you select in the Preview section.

TIP To return to the font and size defined by the Normal style, simply select the Normal Font option. For more information about the Normal style, see "Formatting with Styles," page 199.

The Font tab includes four Underline options (Single, Double, Single Accounting, and Double Accounting) and three Effects options (Strikethrough, Superscript, and Subscript). Figure 6-19 shows examples of each of these options.

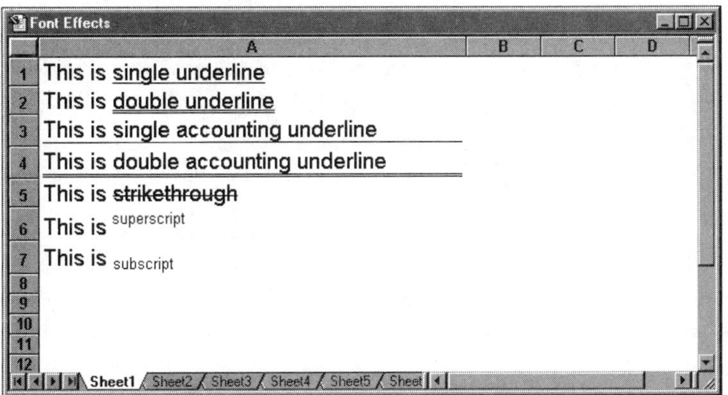

FIGURE 6-19
You can apply Underline options, Strikethrough, Superscript, and Subscript to cells or to selected text in cells.

Applying Font Formats with Toolbars

You can apply the following font format options using a box and buttons on the Formatting toolbar: Font, Font Size, Bold, Italic, Underline, and Font Color. (The Underline button applies the single underline style.) You can use the box and buttons individually or in combination. To remove a toolbar-applied format from a cell or range, select the cell or range and then click the toolbar box or button again to turn the format off. You activate the font list in the Formatting toolbar by clicking the downward-pointing arrow next to the box. See Figure 6-4 on page 161 for the Formatting toolbar.

The two accounting underlines differ from their normal counterparts in two ways. Accounting underlines are applied to the entire width of the cell, whereas regular underlines are applied only under characters in a cell. If the cell contains a text entry that extends beyond the cell border, the accounting underlines stop at the cell border. Also, the Accounting underline formats appear in a cell, unlike the Single and Double underline, which draw lines through the descenders of letters such as "g" and "p."

Selecting a Color

To see your color choices, click the downward-pointing arrow beside the Color drop-down list box on the Font tab in the Format Cells dialog box.

If you select Automatic (the default color option), Excel displays the contents of your cell in black. The other 55 choices represent your current color palette. If you don't see the color you want there, you can customize the palette.

You can also apply font colors using the Font Color button on the Formatting toolbar. Clicking this button applies the color shown in the rectangle to your selection. When you click the arrow to the right of the Font Color button, a palette of colors drops down. Click one of the colored squares to apply the color to the contents of the selected cells. This button is a tear-off palette, which means that you can click and drag the button and the palette will float, separate from the toolbar.

After you select a color in the palette, the color in the Font Color button changes so that you can apply the color again without using the palette.

Also For more information about customizing the color palette, see "Changing the Available Colors," page 215.

Adding Custom Borders

Borders and shading can be effective devices for defining areas in your worksheet or for drawing attention to important cells.

> **NOTE** Borders often make a greater visual impact when worksheet gridlines are removed. From the Tools menu, choose the Options command and click the View tab. Click the Gridlines option to remove gridlines from your worksheet. For more information, see "Controlling the Display of Gridlines," page 212.

Figure 6-20 shows the Format Cells dialog box after you click the Border tab. Here you specify the placement of the borders as well as the style and color of the line.

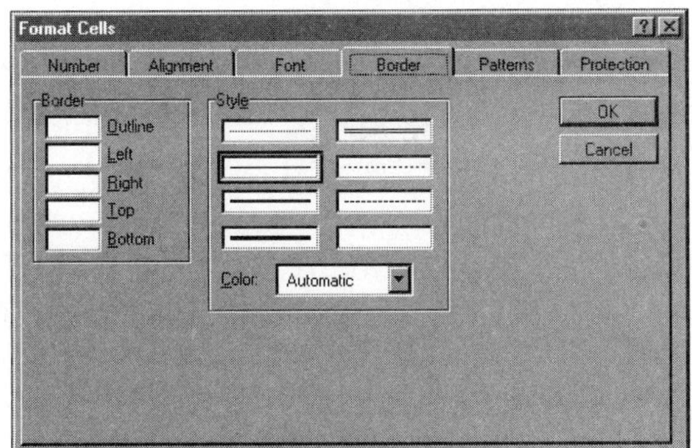

FIGURE 6-20
The Border tab in the Format Cells dialog box lets you assign seven styles of borders in 56 colors.

Selecting a Line Style

The seven border styles include four solid lines in different weights, a double line, and two kinds of broken lines. (The first finely-dotted line is actually a solid hairline when printed.) The double line is particularly useful for underscoring columns of numbers above a total. To select a line style, click the box in the Style section that contains the type of line you want to use.

Selecting Line Color

The default color for borders is black, which appears as Automatic in the Color box on the View tab of the Options dialog box.

To select a color other than black, click the downward-pointing arrow at the right end of the Color box. The color list drops down, revealing the current 56-color palette. You can use one of these colors, or you can modify the palette to change these choices.

For more information about the View tab, see "Controlling Display Options," page 208.

For more information about changing the color palette, see "Changing the Available Colors," page 215.

Selecting Border Placement

After you select a line style and color, you need to place the border. The options are Outline, Left, Right, Top, and Bottom. Selecting Outline places a line around the perimeter of the current selection, whether it is a single cell or a block of cells. Selecting Left draws a line along the left edge of each cell in your selection — and so on.

Click a placement option to select it. A sample of the line appears in the adjacent box. If the line sample is not satisfactory, click a different style or color option.

Applying Two or More Borders at Once

You can apply more than one kind of border to a cell selection. For example, you can apply a heavy outline border to a block of cells and, at the same time, apply a set of lightweight lines to the right border of each cell in the selection. The worksheet in Figure 6-21 shows another possible combination of border styles.

FIGURE 6-21 This budget worksheet makes use of several border styles.

borders

1996 Budget Summary					
Cost Center	1st Qtr	2nd Qtr	3rd Qtr	4th Qtr	Total
100	7,951.00	7,861.00	9,052.00	6,798.00	31,762.00
110	7,893.00	8,086.00	1,969.00	8,820.00	26,878.00
120	8,330.00	5,838.00	1,773.00	9,601.00	25,662.00
130	9,949.00	8,361.00	3,069.00	2,589.00	24,098.00
140	6,135.00	1,503.00	894.00	7,308.00	15,980.00
150	7,859.00	4,686.00	965.00	7,523.00	21,183.00
160	8,979.00	4,669.00	4,849.00	6,673.00	25,330.00
170	2,595.00	7,396.00	5,282.00	4,377.00	19,820.00
180	4,320.00	6,805.00	3,553.00	3,933.00	18,791.00
Total	64,011.00	55,205.00	31,406.00	57,622.00	208,244.00

Sheet1 / Sheet2 / Sheet3 / Sheet4 / Sheet5 / Shee

Changing or Removing Borders

If you change your mind about a border style, reselect the cell block and then redisplay the Border tab in the Format Cells dialog box. The Border tab then shows the border styles that have already been applied. To change an existing solid bottom border to a double line, for example, follow these steps:

1. Select the cells with the border you want to change.
2. From the Format menu, choose Cells and click the Border tab.
3. Select the double-line style, select Bottom, and then click OK.

To remove the solid bottom border, you can select Bottom without selecting another style, which makes the solid line disappear from the box, and click OK. Alternatively, you can select the "null" line style (the empty box in the lower right of the Style section), reselect Bottom, and click OK.

If solid gray appears in the box to the left of one or more placement options on the Border tab, the cells in your selection do not all share the same border style for the placement option in question. For example, if you select cells B2:G13 in the worksheet shown in Figure 6-21 and then click the Border tab in the Format Cells dialog box, the dialog box appears as shown in Figure 6-22.

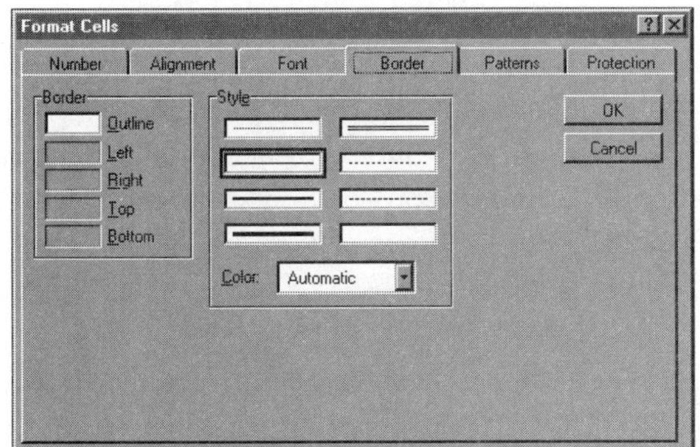

FIGURE 6-22
Solid gray next to an option means that the format applies to some, but not all, of the selected cells.

In this case, the cells in column B have a heavy border on their left. Those in column C do not. Therefore, Excel displays gray instead of either line style in the box next to the Left option. The Right, Top, and Bottom placement options are gray for the same reason.

In this example, to change all the left borders to the same style, such as a dotted line, first select the dotted-line option in the Style section and then reselect the Left placement option. Excel replaces the gray with a dotted line.

To remove all left borders from all the cells in the selection, either click the Left placement option twice (until the box next to Left is empty) or select the null line style and then reselect Left.

Applying Border Formats with the Borders Button

You can apply many combinations of border formats using the Borders button on the Formatting toolbar. When you click the small arrow on the Borders button, Excel displays a tear-off palette from which you can select a border style. If you click the arrow and then click the palette's border and drag away from the toolbar, the Borders palette "tears off" the toolbar and floats independently of the toolbar, as shown in Figure 6-23.

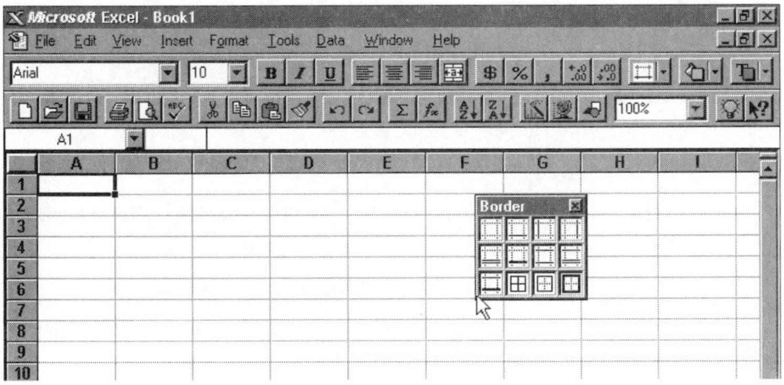

FIGURE 6-23
Click the arrow next to the Borders button and then click and drag the palette's border to "tear off" the Borders palette.

As you can see, the Borders palette offers 12 border options, including combinations of border styles such as single top border and double bottom border. The first option in the palette removes all border formats from a selected cell or range. The other options in the palette show, in miniature, the border combinations available when you select them. The last option you select appears on the face of the Borders button. To return the Borders palette to the Formatting toolbar, simply click the Close box in the upper right corner of the palette.

Adding Colors and Patterns

You use the Patterns tab in the Format Cells dialog box to add colors and shading to selected cells. The Patterns tab includes the current color palette (as specified on the Color tab of the Options dialog box) and a drop-down list box of colors and shading, as shown in Figure 6-24.

The Color section on the Pattern tab controls the background of the selected cells. When you choose a color from the Color section and do not select any pattern, a colored background appears in the selected cells.

FIGURE 6-24
The Patterns tab of the Format Cells dialog box lets you select colors and patterns for cell backgrounds.

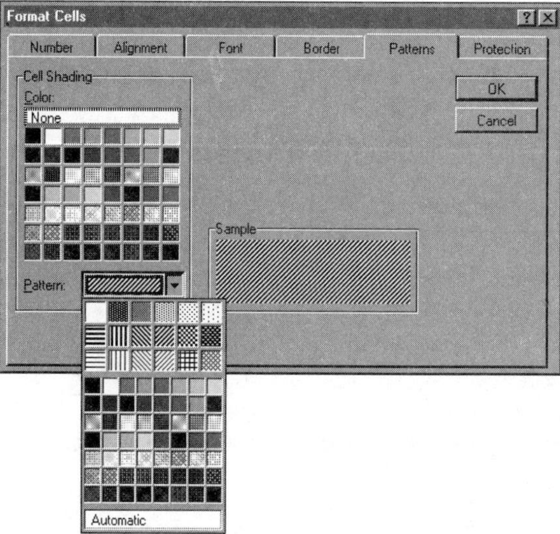

TIP You can use the Color button on the Formatting toolbar to apply a background color to a cell or range. When you click the arrow on the Color button, a tear-off palette appears from which you can select a color.

If you pick a color from the Color section and then select a pattern from the Pattern drop-down list box, the pattern is overlaid on the solid background. For example, if you select red from the Color section and then click one of the dot patterns, the result is a cell that has a red background and black dots. The Sample section lets you preview your selection before you apply it. To return the background color to its default state, click None in the Color section.

The color options in the Pattern drop-down list box control the color of the pattern itself. For example, if you leave the Color section set to None and select both red and the dot pattern from the Pattern drop-down list box, the cell will have a white background with red dots. If you then pick yellow in the Color section, the result is a cell with a yellow background and red dots. Figure 6-25 shows different patterns assigned to the cells in a worksheet.

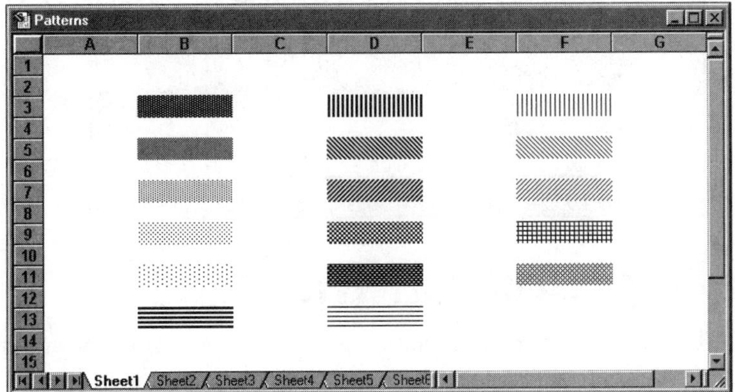

FIGURE 6-25
Using the Patterns tab, a different pattern has been assigned to each of these cells.

Of course, the way colors look when printed depends on the capabilities of your printer.

See Also For more information about modifying the color palette, see "Changing the Available Colors," page 215.

Using Shading

You can use the shading styles available on the Patterns tab to add emphasis to selected cells in your worksheet. For example, you might use shading to set apart worksheet totals or to draw attention to cells in which you want the user to make an entry in a worksheet template. Figure 6-26 on the next page shows how you can use shading to create a "banded" effect. In this case, the shading helps the reader follow a row of numbers while reading from left to right. Bands are particularly useful when you want to print wide reports without gridlines.

When selecting a color for the cell's background, you should pick a color that allows you to easily read text and numbers in the default color, black. Another option is to select a complementary color for text and numbers by clicking the Font tab in the Format Cells dialog box or the Font Color button on the Formatting toolbar. For example, yellow is an excellent background color for red text. Unless you have a color printer, however, you should test-print the worksheet to be sure the colors you select are acceptable when printed in black and white.

FIGURE 6-26 Shading can be used for emphasis or, as in this example, to distinguish rows of numbers.

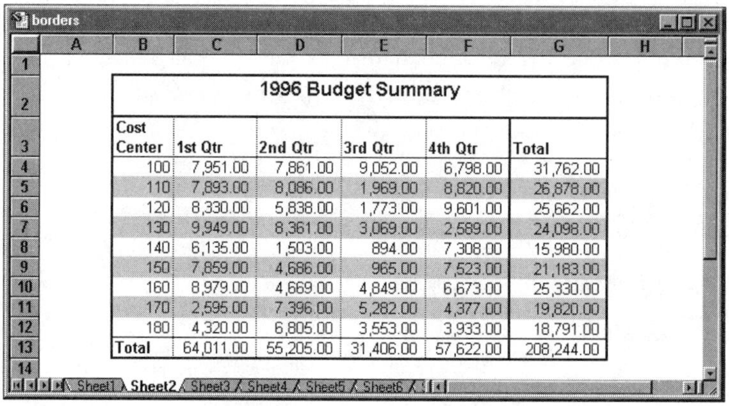

1996 Budget Summary					
Cost Center	1st Qtr	2nd Qtr	3rd Qtr	4th Qtr	Total
100	7,951.00	7,861.00	9,052.00	6,798.00	31,762.00
110	7,893.00	8,086.00	1,969.00	8,820.00	26,878.00
120	8,330.00	5,838.00	1,773.00	9,601.00	25,662.00
130	9,949.00	8,361.00	3,069.00	2,589.00	24,098.00
140	6,135.00	1,503.00	894.00	7,308.00	15,980.00
150	7,859.00	4,686.00	965.00	7,523.00	21,183.00
160	8,979.00	4,669.00	4,849.00	6,673.00	25,330.00
170	2,595.00	7,396.00	5,282.00	4,377.00	19,820.00
180	4,320.00	6,805.00	3,553.00	3,933.00	18,791.00
Total	64,011.00	55,205.00	31,406.00	57,622.00	208,244.00

Controlling Column Width

Microsoft Excel's default column width is 8.43 characters. This does not mean that each cell in your worksheet can display 8.43 characters, however. Because Excel uses proportionally spaced fonts (such as Arial) as well as fixed-pitch fonts (such as Courier), different characters can take up different amounts of space. A default-width column, for example, can display about seven numerals in most 10-point fixed-pitch fonts.

Often, the standard column width is not wide enough to display the complete contents of a cell. As you have already seen, a label that is too long runs over into adjacent cells; if the adjacent cell contains an entry, the label is truncated. When you enter a long number in a narrow column that has the General numeric format, that number appears in scientific notation. If a cell's entry is too long to fit after you assign a numeric format, a series of pound signs (#) appears. To display the entire contents of the cell, you must change the width of the column or columns that contain the long entries. You can change column width in several ways.

Adding Graphic Backgrounds to Your Worksheets

Excel now allows you to add background images to worksheets by choosing the Sheet command from the Format menu, and then choosing Background from the submenu. When you do so, Excel displays a dialog box, similar to that displayed by the Open command (File menu), that you use to open a graphic file stored on disk. The graphic image is then applied to the background of the active worksheet, much like a watermark might be used on a piece of paper.

The graphic image is "tiled" in the background of your worksheet, which means that the image is repeated as necessary to fill the worksheet. Be careful when using backgrounds behind data, however. As you can see in the figure above, it could be very difficult to read cell entries with the wrong background applied.

Cells to which you have assigned a color or pattern on the Patterns tab of the Format Cells dialog box display the color or pattern rather than the graphic background. You could, for example, apply a white or yellow solid color to cells containing data, allowing the text and numbers to stand out, while the background pattern decorates the rest of the worksheet.

For more information about the General numeric format, see "The General Format," page 165.

Using the Mouse to Change Column Widths

To change column widths with the mouse, place the mouse pointer in the column-heading area on the line that divides the column you want to change from its neighbor to the right. For example, to widen or narrow column C, place the pointer in the column-heading area on the line separating column C from column D. Your mouse pointer changes to a double-headed arrow as shown in Figure 6-27. Now hold down the mouse button and drag the column divider to the right or left. As you drag, the width of the column is displayed in the Name box on the formula bar. When the width is correct, release the mouse button.

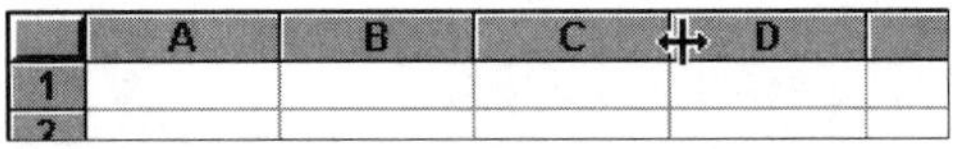

FIGURE 6-27

Use the double-headed arrow cursor to adjust column width and row height.

To change the width of more than one column at a time, drag through the column headings of the columns you want to change. (You can select nonadjacent columns by holding down Ctrl as you click the column headings.) Next, change the width of one of the columns as we just described. When you release the mouse button, all of the columns change simultaneously, and they are all exactly the same width.

Automatically Fitting a Column to Its Widest Entry

You can change a column's width to accommodate its widest cell entry by double-clicking the column divider to the right of the column. To see how this works, enter the label *Total by Month* in cell A1 of a new worksheet. Next, move the mouse pointer to the column-headings area and double-click the divider line between column A and column B. The column snaps to the width necessary to accommodate the label you just typed.

If you add a longer entry to a column after automatically adjusting its width, you will need to use the automatic-adjustment feature again. Also, depending on the font you are using, characters that appear to fit within a column on your screen may not fit within a column when you print a work- sheet. You can preview your output before printing by choosing the Print Preview command from the File menu.

TIP You can also adjust a column's width to its widest entry by selecting the entry and then using the AutoFit Selection command on the Column submenu of the Format menu.

For information about the Print Preview command, see Chapter 10, "Printing and Presenting," page 373.

Using the Column Commands

From the Format menu, choose Column to display a submenu that includes five commands — Width, AutoFit Selection, Hide, Unhide, and Standard Width. To assign a column width, simply select cells in each column you want to change (you need not select entire columns), and then choose the Width command. To change the widths of all the columns in the current worksheet, click one of the row headings at the left edge of the worksheet (or select any cell and press Shift-Spacebar) and then choose the Width command.

When you choose the Width command, the Column Width dialog box shown in Figure 6-28 appears. If all the columns you select are the same width, that width appears in the Column Width edit box; if the columns you select are of different widths, the edit box is blank. In either case, type a number from 0 through 255 in integer, decimal, or fraction form. (The old width setting is erased as soon as you begin typing.) When you click OK, Excel adjusts the widths of the selected columns.

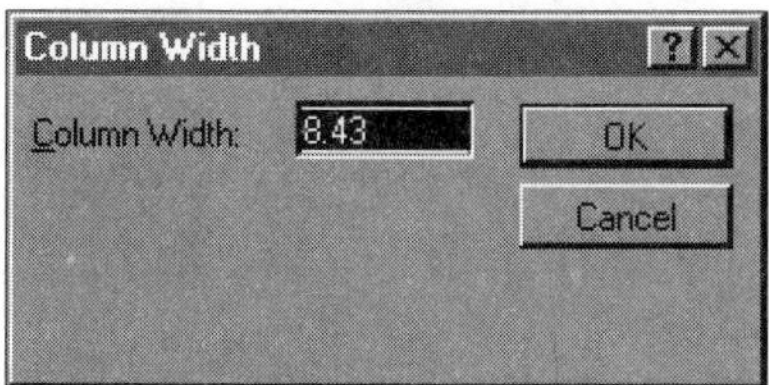

FIGURE 6-28
Use the Column Width dialog box to specify the widths of columns.

You can use the AutoFit Selection command on the Column submenu to adjust a column's width to the longest entry among the selected cells. Choosing this command is similar to double-clicking the column divider with the mouse except that it adjusts the column width to fit the longest entry in the selected cells, rather than the longest entry in the entire column (unless the entire column is selected).

To restore the default width of one or more columns, select any cells in those columns and choose the Standard Width command from the Column submenu. As shown in Figure 6-29, the default column width appears in the Standard Column Width edit box, so all you have to do is click OK. To change the standard width, simply type a new value in the edit box. All columns currently set to the default width in your worksheet then adjust to the new setting.

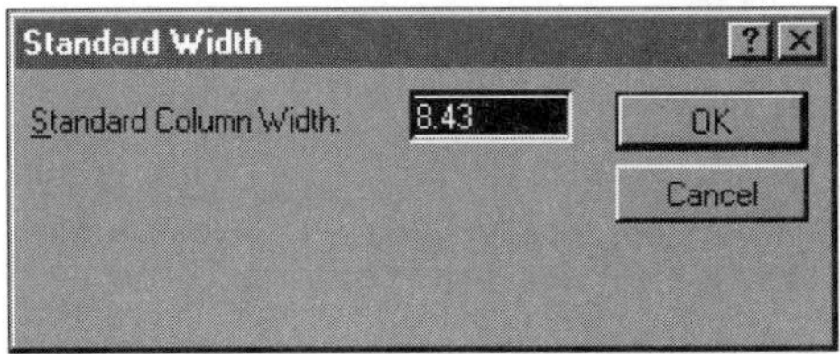

FIGURE 6-29

Use the Standard Width dialog box to restore the default column width or to change the standard width.

Hiding a Column or Row

You might, on occasion, want to hide information in your worksheet — for example, employee salaries in a departmental budget worksheet. Fortunately, Excel allows you to hide entire columns or rows. (The Hidden option on the Protection tab of the Format Cells dialog box, when used in conjunction with the Protection command on the Tools menu, hides only formulas in the formula bar.)

To hide a column, first select a cell in the column you want to hide. From the Format menu, choose Column and then Hide. When you choose the Hide command, Excel sets the width of the selected column to 0. You can also hide a column by dragging the line between the column headings to the left until you have narrowed the column to nothing; or you can enter *0* in the Column Width dialog box. When a column's width is set to 0, Excel skips over that column when you move the active cell, and the column's letter disappears from the top of the worksheet. For example, if you hide column C, the column heading line reads A, B, D, and so on.

To redisplay a column, first drag across the column headings on both sides of the hidden column. Next, from the Format menu, choose Column and then click Unhide.

You can use the mouse and the commands on the submenu that appears when you choose Row on the Format menu to hide and redisplay rows in a similar manner.

For more information about the Protection command, see "Protecting Your Data," page 106.

Controlling Row Height

Microsoft Excel automatically adjusts the standard height of a row to accommodate the largest font used in that row. For example, when the largest font in row 1 is 10-point Arial, the standard height for that row is 12.75. If you apply 12-point Times New Roman to a cell in row 1, however, the standard height of the entire row automatically becomes 15.75. (Like font size, row height is measured in points. Remember that one point equals $\frac{1}{72}$ of an inch, so a row with a height of 13 is a little over $\frac{1}{6}$ inch.)

If you don't adjust any row heights yourself, Excel generally uses its standard row height. Thus, you don't usually need to worry about characters being too tall to fit in a row.

Using the Mouse to Change Row Heights

Adjusting the height of a row is similar to adjusting the width of a column. In the row-heading area, position the mouse pointer on the line under the number of the row you want to change. When the pointer takes on the double-headed arrow shape (see Figure 6-27), hold down the mouse button, drag the line that divides the rows to the new position, and then release the mouse button.

To change the height of more than one row at a time, drag through the headings of the rows. (To select nonadjacent rows, hold down Ctrl as you click the row headings.) Next, change the height of one of the rows as described. When you release the mouse button, all the rows change simultaneously, and all are exactly the same height.

Automatically Adjusting Row Height

If you have changed a row's height, you can reset it to fit the tallest entry in the row by double-clicking the row divider below the row you want to change. To see how this works, click the bottom divider of row 1 — the divider between row headings 1 and 2 — and drag it down to make the row taller. Next, double-click the divider line you just dragged. The row snaps back to the standard height. If a row contains text that is larger than standard size, double-clicking the divider below the row adjusts the row height as necessary to fit the tallest entry. Note that if you delete the text from the cell, the row height is still determined by the largest font size format applied to any cell in that row.

Using the Row Commands

Similar to the Column command, the Row command on the Format menu includes a submenu with four commands — Height, AutoFit, Hide, and Unhide. You can use the Height command to change the heights of several rows at once. Simply select at least one cell in each row and choose the Height command to display the dialog box shown in Figure 6-30. To change the height of all the rows in the worksheet, click one of the column headings (or select any cell and press Ctrl-Spacebar) before you choose the Height command. If all the rows you select are the same height, that height appears in the Row Height edit box; if the rows are different heights, the edit box is blank. Either way, to change the height of all selected rows, enter a new row height and then click OK.

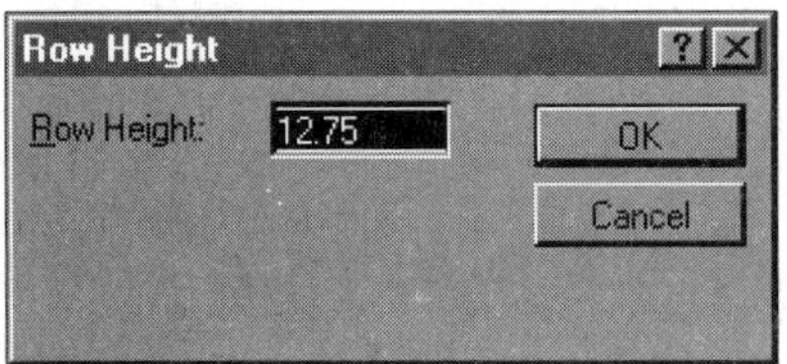

FIGURE 6-30
Use the Row Height dialog box to change the height of selected worksheet rows.

To reset a row's height to its tallest entry after you've changed it, choose the AutoFit command from the Row submenu.

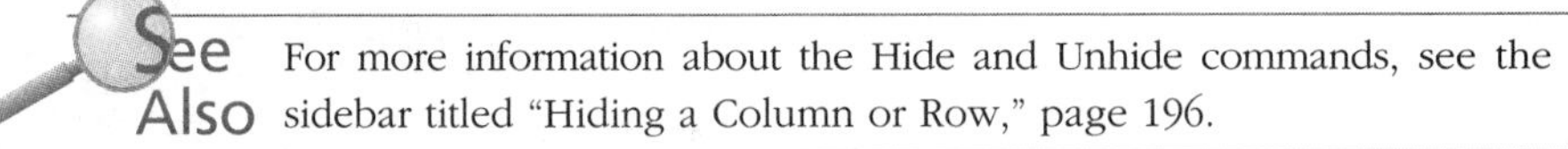
See Also For more information about the Hide and Unhide commands, see the sidebar titled "Hiding a Column or Row," page 196.

How Wrapping and Justifying Text Affects Row Height

When you create a multiline text entry using the Wrap Text or the Justify options on the Alignment tab of the Format Cells dialog box, Excel automatically adjusts the row height to accommodate your multiline entry. If you subsequently add words to make that entry longer or increase the point size of the font you're using, Excel adjusts the row height again — so that your text never spills out of the cell in which it's entered. Similarly, if you reduce the size of a multiline entry, Excel readjusts the row height accordingly.

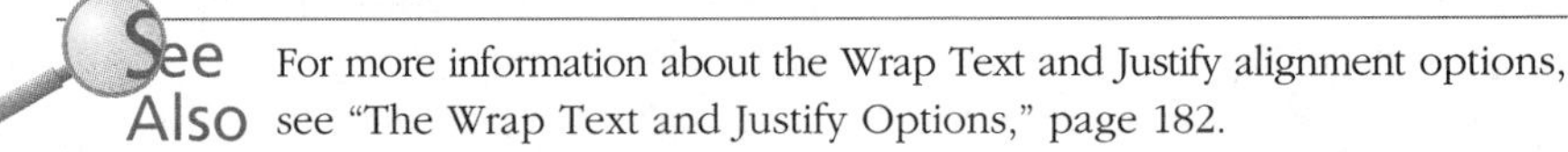
See Also For more information about the Wrap Text and Justify alignment options, see "The Wrap Text and Justify Options," page 182.

Formatting with Styles

Microsoft Excel's style feature allows you to assign names to combinations of formatting attributes. You can then apply those attributes by selecting the name from a list. Styles help you achieve consistency in formatting, both within a worksheet and across worksheets and workbooks. You can easily use styles to modify the formatting characteristics of many cells at once.

Every new workbook has six predefined styles: Comma, Comma [0], Currency, Currency [0], Normal, and Percent. (The Comma and Currency formats use two decimal places; the Comma [0] and Currency [0] formats round to the nearest integer value.) These six predefined styles have the same characteristics on each worksheet in a workbook and in each new workbook you create, but you can change them for any workbook, and you can add styles of your own. When you save a workbook, all its style definitions are saved along with the rest of your data.

You define styles using the Style command on the Format menu. As the Style dialog box in Figure 6-31 shows, the Normal style has the following six attributes:

- The numeric format is General.
- The font is 10-point Arial by default.
- The horizontal alignment is General (numbers flush right, labels flush left), and the vertical alignment is Bottom.
- No borders are assigned.
- No custom shading patterns are defined.
- The protection status is "locked."

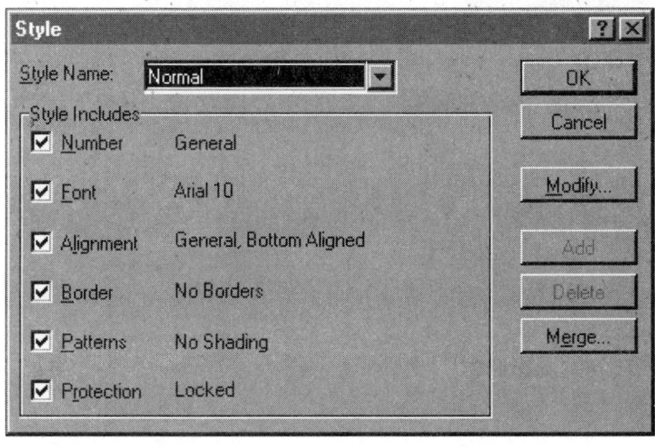

FIGURE 6-31
Excel's predefined Normal style includes these attributes.

Styles can have a minimum of one and a maximum of six attributes. All the predefined styles except Normal have only one attribute — a number format. The predefined Currency style, for example, has the Accounting number format with 2 decimal places.

The predefined Normal style has one important characteristic: It is automatically applied to every cell in every new workbook. Thus, if you want a cell to have the standard set of formatting attributes, you don't need to do anything. If, however, you want to change the default attributes, you can redefine the Normal style.

For information about protecting your data, see "Protecting Your Data," page 106.

For information about redefining the Normal style, see "Modifying a Style," page 203.

Applying a Style

To apply a defined style (either a predefined style or one that you have created) to a cell or a range, first select the cell or range and then follow these steps:

1. From the Format menu, choose the Style command to display the Style dialog box.
2. Click the downward-pointing arrow at the right end of the Style Name box and select a style, as shown in Figure 6-32.
3. Click OK.

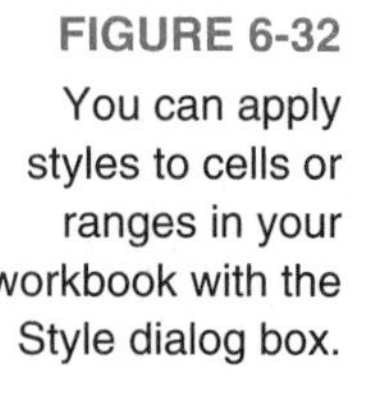

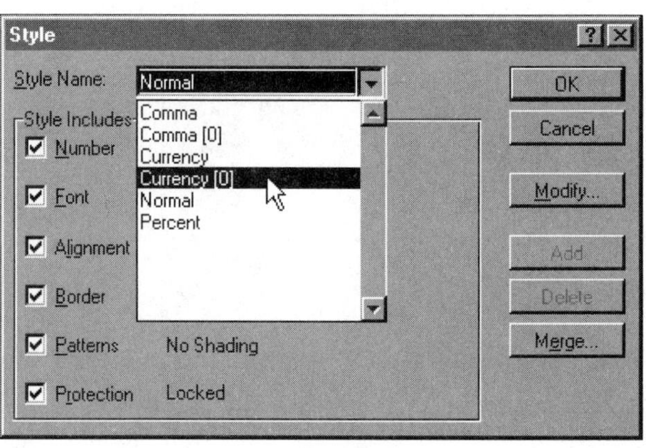

FIGURE 6-32
You can apply styles to cells or ranges in your workbook with the Style dialog box.

Applying Styles with Toolbars

Excel includes a Style box, similar to the one in the Style dialog box, that you can place on a toolbar. You can add the Style box (in the Formatting category) to an existing toolbar or to a toolbar that you create using the methods described in Chapter 2, "Toolbars and Buttons," page 31.

When the Style box is available on a toolbar, you can use it to determine whether a style has been applied to any cell in your workbook. Simply select the cell and then check the name of the style that appears in the Style box on the toolbar.

The predefined Currency [0] style, for example, uses an Accounting format with no decimal places and parentheses for negative values. If you want dollar values to appear with this style, select the cells you want to apply the style to, choose the Style command from the Format menu, select Currency [0], and click OK. (You might have to widen the columns to make room for the extra digits.)

TIP To quickly display the Style dialog box, press Alt-' (single quotation mark). If you have a toolbar that includes the style box, this key combination moves to the box, instead of opening the dialog box.

Defining a Style

You can define a style in either of two ways: by providing an example of the style attributes you want or by choosing the Style command from the Format menu and filling out the Style dialog box. After you define a new style, you can use it anywhere in the current workbook. You can also copy it to another workbook.

See Also For more information about copying styles to other workbooks, see "Merging Styles from Different Workbooks," page 204.

Defining Styles by Example

If you have already used commands on the Format menu or buttons on the Formatting toolbar to apply formatting attributes to a cell or a range, you can use the style-by-example procedure to encapsulate those commands in a new style. For example, suppose you format a cell with right alignment and 18-point Helvetica bold. To make this combination of attributes a new style — in this case called *MyStyle* — follow these steps:

1. Select the cell that contains the formatting you want. (In this case, right alignment and 18-point Helvetica bold.)
2. From the Format menu, choose the Style command.
3. When the Style dialog box appears, type *MyStyle* in the Style Name edit box.
4. Deselect the Number, Border, Patterns, and Protection options in the Style Includes section and click OK. The name of the new style will now appear in the Style dialog box and in the Style box's drop-down list.

The safest way to create a style by example is to select only one cell — one that you know has all the attributes you want to assign to the new style. If you select two or more cells that are not formatted identically, the new style assumes only those attributes that all cells in the selection have in common.

TIP You can also define a style by example with the Style box. First add the Style box to a toolbar. Then, select a cell with the formats you want to name, click the contents of the Style box, and enter a name for the new style. Press Enter to save the custom style, which will appear in both the Style drop-down list box on your toolbar and in the Style Name drop-down list box in the Style dialog box.

Defining Styles from Scratch

To create a new style without first formatting a cell, follow these steps:

1. From the Format menu, choose the Style command.
2. In the Style Name edit box, type the name of the style you want to define.
3. Click the Modify button. The Format Cells dialog box appears, as shown in Figure 6-33. The changes you make in the Format Cells dialog box apply to your new style definition.

4. Select format options from the Number, Alignment, Font, Border, Patterns, and Protection tabs, and then click OK to return to the Style dialog box. The Style Includes section of the dialog box reflects the formats you added.
5. Deselect the options you don't want to include in the style definition.

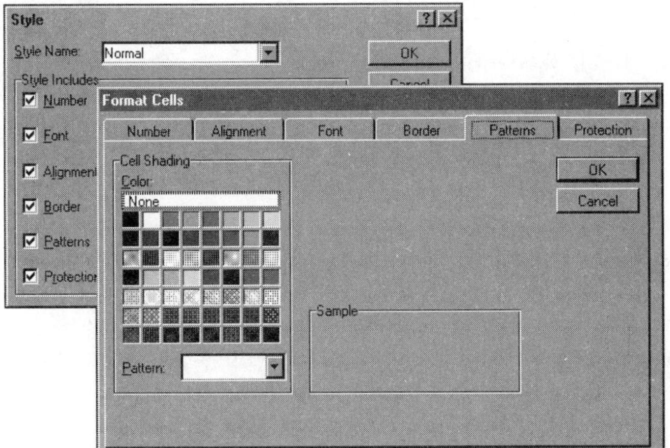

FIGURE 6-33
Clicking the Modify button in the Style dialog box displays the Format Cells dialog box. Excel applies changes made here to the current style.

6. After you're satisfied with the formatting attributes you selected, click the Add button. Your new style appears among all the others defined for the current workbook, and you can apply it at any time from the Style Name drop-down list box (or the Style box if you add it to a toolbar). Click OK to close the Style dialog box.

Modifying a Style

A major advantage to formatting with styles is that if you change your mind about the appearance of a particular element in your workbook, you can revise every instance of that element at once simply by redefining the style. For example, if you'd like the font in the MyStyle style — which is now 18-point Helvetica bold — to be italic as well as bold, you can simply redefine MyStyle.

To modify a style definition — to add italic to the definition of MyStyle, for example — follow these steps:

1. From the Format menu, choose the Style command.
2. Select the style — in this case MyStyle — from the Style Name drop-down list box and then click Modify to display the Format Cells dialog box.

3. Select the appropriate format options. For this example, click the Font tab and select the Bold Italic option in the Font Style list box.
4. Click OK to return to the Style dialog box and then click OK to confirm your changes.

Redefining a Style with Toolbars

You can also redefine a style using the toolbar Style box. (For more information, see the sidebar titled "Applying Styles with Toolbars," page 201.) To redefine a style with the Style box, follow these steps:

1. Select a cell that is formatted with the style you want to redefine.
2. Make your formatting changes.
3. Click the name in the toolbar Style box and press Enter. Excel asks you to confirm that you want to redefine the existing style based on the style in the selected cell.
4. Click Yes. Excel then redefines the style and changes every instance of the style in the worksheet to match the new definition.

Overriding a Style with Direct Formatting Changes

You can change the appearance of any cell or range in your worksheet, whether or not you have applied a style to that cell or range, by using the Cells command on the Format menu to access the Number, Alignment, Font, Border, and Patterns tabs or by using the buttons on the Formatting toolbar. (The Cells command is discussed earlier in this chapter.)

Merging Styles from Different Workbooks

To maintain formatting consistency across a group of worksheets, you can keep them all in the same workbook. If this is impractical but you still want to maintain stylistic consistency, you can copy style definitions between workbooks. (Another way to achieve consistency is with templates.)

To copy a style from one workbook to another, follow these steps:

1. Open both the source workbook (the one you're copying from) and the destination workbook (the one you're copying to).

2. Click the destination workbook to make it the active window.
3. Choose the Style command from the Format menu and click the Merge button. Excel displays a list of all other open workbooks, as shown in Figure 6-34.

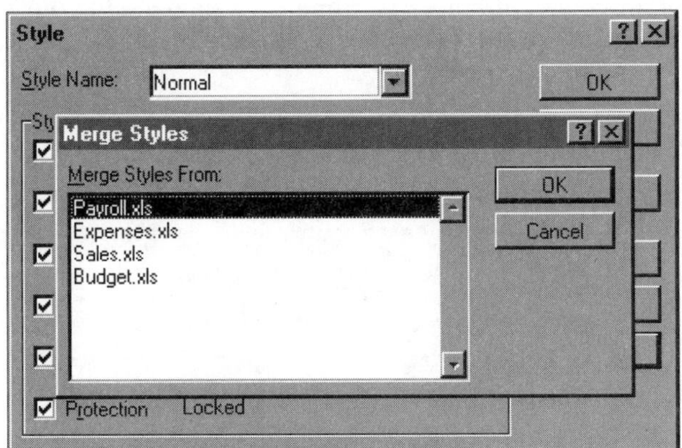

FIGURE 6-34
When you copy styles from one workbook to another, Excel displays a list of all other open workbooks.

4. Select the name of the workbook you want to copy styles *from* and click OK.

If a style in your source workbook has the same name as one already in your destination workbook, an alert box asks if you want to merge styles that have the same name from the source workbook. You will receive this warning only once, however, no matter how many duplicate style names exist. If you choose Yes, the styles from the source workbook override those with the same names in the destination workbook.

For more information about templates, see "Using Template Files," page 206.

For more information about opening multiple windows, see Chapter 8, "Workbooks and Windows," page 297.

Deleting a Style

To delete a style's definition, choose the Style command from the Format menu, select the style in the Style Name drop-down list box, and then click Delete. Any cells that were formatted with the deleted style will revert to the Normal style. (You cannot delete the Normal style.) Any cell that was formatted with a deleted style and was then also formatted directly, however, retains all the direct formatting.

Using Template Files

A *template file* is a model that can serve as the basis for many worksheets. A template might include both data and formatting information. Template files are great time-savers. They're also an ideal way to ensure a consistent look among reports, invoices, and other documents you create in your workbooks. Figure 6-35 shows an example of a template file.

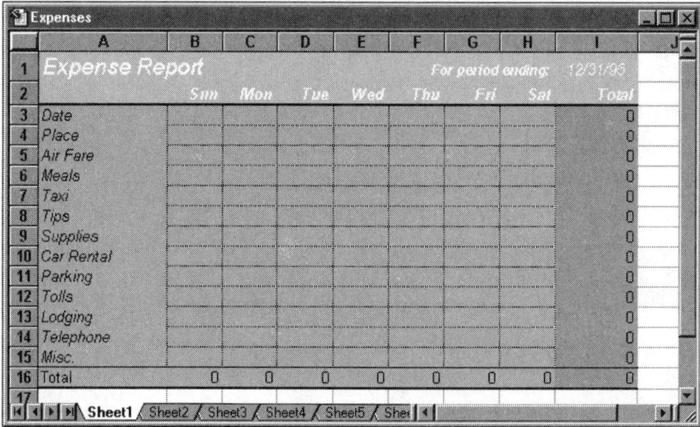

FIGURE 6-35
This template file serves as the basis for creating expense reports.

Starting with Excel 7, any Excel workbook can become a template. When you installed Excel, both the Excel folder and a folder named Templates were installed within the Office folder on your hard disk. Any workbook in the Templates folder, whether it was actually saved in Template format or not, can be used as the basis for new workbooks when you choose the New command from the File menu.

Workbooks you place in the Templates folder appear on the General tab of the New dialog box. This is important and a little confusing, so here it is again: Any workbooks in the Templates folder will appear on the General tab of the New dialog box, whether you saved them in template format or not. When you use the New command to "open" any workbook that appears on the General tab (that is, in the Templates folder), rather than opening the workbook itself, a new copy of the workbook is created.

In Excel 7, there is no real functional difference between regular workbooks and those saved in template format. Using the template format can be essential, however, if you share workbook templates with others who are still using Excel 5. (The file formats of Excel 5 and 7 are compatible.) In addition, in Windows 95, you can show the old MS-DOS three-character extension so you can tell at a glance if you intended a workbook to serve as a template (.XLT) or a regular workbook (.XLS).

TIP If you only want to create a new blank workbook, simply click the New Workbook button on the Standard toolbar. This does the same thing as clicking the Workbook icon on the General tab in the New dialog box.

To create a template file, follow these steps:

1. Create a workbook with all the data and formatting that is common to all the workbooks you will create, such as the information shown in Figure 6-35.
2. From the File menu, choose the Save As command and supply a filename.
3. Click the arrow to the right of the Save as type drop-down list box and select Template. Excel automatically switches to the template folder so that your new template will always be available when you choose New from the File menu.
4. Click Save.

To use a template file, choose New from the File menu. Excel displays only template files (designated by the .XLT extension), rather than ordinary worksheets, and opens a *working copy* of the selected template, leaving the original template intact on disk. The copy is given a temporary name made up of the original template name plus a number. If the template file is named Expenses.xlt, for example, the working copy appears with the name Expenses1. When you save the file, Excel opens the Save As dialog box so that you can assign a different name to the template file. Excel then appends the .XLS extension to the name.

Modifying a Template File

To change a template file, follow these steps:

1. From the File menu, choose the Open command and select the template file in the File Name list box.
2. Make the desired changes to the template.
3. To resave the workbook as a template file, choose the Save command. To save it as a regular workbook, choose the Save As command, select Microsoft Excel Workbook in the Save as type drop-down list box, and click OK.

Note that you no longer have to hold down Shift to open the template itself, as was the case in previous versions of Excel.

Adding Templates to the XLStart Folder

If you want your template file to be displayed as an option whenever you create a new workbook, save it in the Templates folder, as described earlier, or in the XLStart folder. This folder was created when you installed Excel and is located in the same folder as your Excel program. If any template files are present in the XLStart folder when you choose the New command from the File menu, they appear on the General tab in the New dialog box. For example, Expenses is a template saved in the XLStart folder and appears listed in the new dialog box.

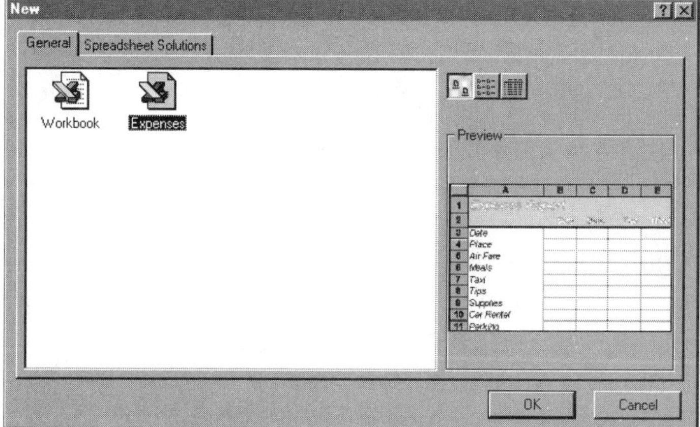

Note that regular workbooks (those *not* saved in Template format) you save in the XLStart folder are opened automatitcally when you first start Excel.

Controlling Display Options

In addition to the commands on the Format menu, the Options command on the Tools menu includes three important tabs that you can use to control the way your documents appear on screen: the View tab, the General tab, and the Color tab.

The commands on the Format menu affect only selected worksheet cells, while the tabs in the Options dialog box are global in scope. The View tab controls the overall appearance of the current workbook. The General tab specifies the default font. The Color tab allows you to modify the set of 56 colors available for any given workbook.

The View tab controls the display of the formula and status bars as well as the appearance of automatic page breaks, formulas, gridlines, column and row headings, outline symbols, zero values, and graphic objects, among other things. When you choose the Options command from the Tools menu, you see the dialog box shown in Figure 6-36.

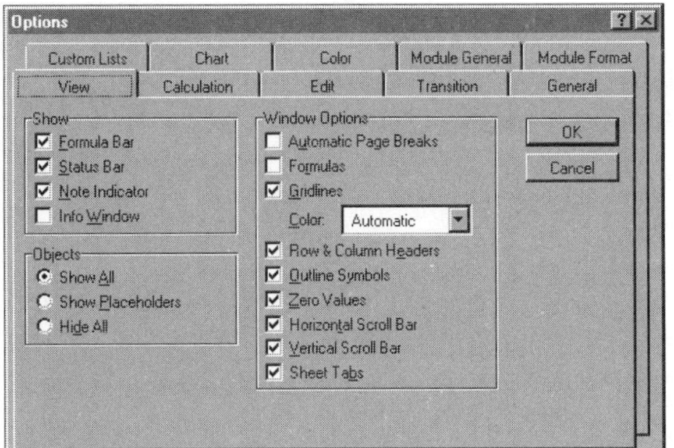

FIGURE 6-36

The View tab, the General tab, and the Color tab in the Options dialog box control the appearance of your workbook.

Spreadsheet Solutions Templates

The Spreadsheet Solutions tab in the New dialog box provides several predesigned templates for your personal and business number-crunching needs. These templates include Loan Manager, Car Lease, Personal Budgeter, and Business Planner. In addition, the Invoice, Expense Statement, Sales Quote, Timecard, Purchase Order, and Change Request templates have associated database workbooks, located in the Library folder in your Excel folder. These templates work with the Template Wizard, allowing you to use these templates as forms to load data into databases.

Note that many of the Spreadsheet Solutions templates, as well as the Template Wizard, are options that might not be installed on your computer. If your Spreadsheet Solutions tab does not contain all the templates listed, rerun the Setup program to install them. For more information about running Setup, see Appendix B, "Installing Microsoft Excel." For more information about the Template Wizard, see "Using the Template Wizard to Create Templates and Databases," page 752.

For information about outlining and outline symbols, see "Outlining Your Worksheets," page 217.

For information about automatic page breaks, see "Inserting and Removing Manual Page Breaks," page 386.

For information about graphic objects, see Chapter 9, "Graphics," page 345.

Controlling the Display of the Formula Bar and Status Bar

You can use the Formula Bar and Status Bar options in the Show section of the Options dialog box's View tab to suppress the display of the formula bar and status bar. (These options are the same as the Formula Bar and Status Bar commands on the View menu.) Figure 6-37 shows how your screen looks if you deselect these two options.

Although you can function in Excel without the formula bar and status bar, you'll probably want to leave these options selected as a convenience. You can always hide them for display purposes when you complete a worksheet.

The Window Options

The options you select in the Window Options section on the Options dialog box's View tab affect only the active workbook; they do not change the display of other workbooks. If you use the New Window command on the

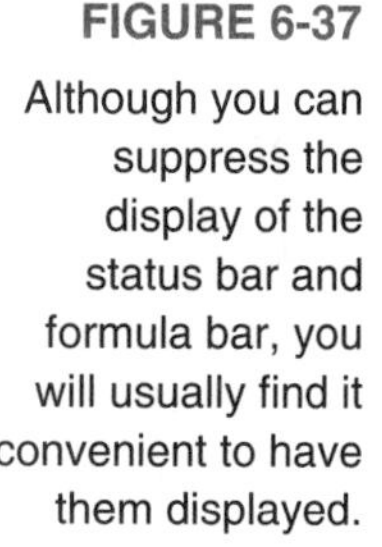

1995 Sales: WWWW Company, Inc.

Month	Widgets	Wombats	Woofers	Whatzits	Total by Month
	Product				
January	$433.33	$3,084.03	$3,501.77	$6,385.43	$13,404.56
February	$4,827.84	$5,005.87	$9,837.37	$4,093.03	$23,764.11
March	$1,674.16	$7,154.01	$7,619.90	$2,842.43	$19,290.50
April	$443.00	$1,756.27	$775.85	$5,099.14	$8,074.26
May	$464.61	$5,997.18	$4,967.30	$3,704.59	$15,133.68
June	$8,525.77	$9,201.34	$5,693.62	$4,193.42	$27,614.15
July	$3,880.67	$3,927.47	$8,174.50	$5,013.34	$20,995.98
August	$8,389.46	$8,722.76	$2,547.25	$673.09	$20,332.56
September	$7,950.16	$5,033.68	$9,006.50	$1,141.11	$23,131.45
October	$8,853.37	$1,717.41	$6,148.00	$4,668.97	$21,387.75
November	$6,508.76	$4,087.60	$3,582.32	$644.68	$14,823.36
December	$245.24	$8,356.39	$2,053.37	$2,857.13	$13,512.13
Total by Product	$52,196.37	$64,044.01	$63,907.75	$41,316.36	$221,464.49

FIGURE 6-37

Although you can suppress the display of the status bar and formula bar, you will usually find it convenient to have them displayed.

Window menu to create two or more windows in which to view the same workbook, you can even use different display options in each. For example, you can view formulas in one window and see the results of those formulas in another window.

See Also For more information about using multiple windows, see Chapter 8, "Workbooks and Windows," page 297.

Displaying the Underlying Formulas

Normally, when you enter a formula in a cell, you see the results of that formula, not the formula itself. Similarly, when you format a number, you no longer see the underlying (unformatted) value displayed in the cell. You can see the underlying values and formulas only by selecting individual cells and looking at the formula bar.

The Formulas option on the Options dialog box's View tab lets you display all the underlying values and formulas in your worksheet. As you can see in Figure 6-38 on the next page, the underlying contents of each cell appear, and all cells are now left-aligned. (Excel ignores any alignment formatting when you select the Formulas option.) In addition, the width of each column in the worksheet approximately doubles to accommodate the underlying formulas. When you deselect the Formulas option, Excel restores all columns to their former widths. (The actual width of the column remains unchanged; columns only appear wider on the screen.)

TIP You can quickly display formulas in your worksheet by pressing Ctrl-‘ (the single left quotation mark, which is usually located on the tilde key above the Tab key on the top left of most keyboards). To redisplay values, press Ctrl-‘ again. This keyboard shortcut is handy when you need to toggle the display back and forth for auditing purposes.

The Formulas option is particularly helpful when you need to edit a large worksheet. You can see your formulas without having to activate each cell and view its contents in the formula bar. You can also use the Formulas option to document your work: After you select Formulas, you can print your worksheet with the formulas displayed for archiving purposes.

FIGURE 6-38
Use the Formulas option to view underlying values and formulas.

WWWW-CO 1995 Sales

	A	B	C	
1	1995 Sales: WWWW Com			
2				*Product*
3	***Month***	**Widgets**	**Wombats**	**Woofe**
4	**January**	433.33	3084.03	3501.7
5	**February**	4827.84	5005.87	9837.3
6	**March**	1674.16	7154.01	7619.9
7	**April**	443	1756.27	775.85
8	**May**	464.61	5997.18	4967.3
9	**June**	8525.77	9201.34	5693.6
10	**July**	3880.67	3927.47	8174.5
11	**August**	8389.46	8722.76	2547.2
12	**September**	7950.16	5033.68	9006.5
13	**October**	8853.37	1717.41	6148
14	**November**	6508.76	4087.6	3582.3
15	**December**	245.24	8356.39	2053.3
16	**Total by Product**	=SUM(B4:B15)	=SUM(C4:C15)	=SUM

Sheet1 / Sheet2 / Sheet3 / Sheet4 / Sheet5 / Sheet6

See Also For more information about printing worksheets, see Chapter 10, "Printing and Presenting," page 373.

Controlling the Display of Gridlines

Typically, Excel displays a grid to mark the boundaries of each cell in the worksheet. Although this grid is usually helpful for selection and navigation, you might not want it displayed all the time. To suppress gridline display, deselect the Gridlines option on the Options dialog box's View tab.

TIP You can increase the on-screen effectiveness of your border formats dramatically by eliminating the display of gridlines in your worksheet.

Turning off the Gridlines option removes the gridlines from your screen and also suppresses them for printing. If you want gridlines printed but not displayed (or vice-versa), use the Page Setup command. To control the printing of gridlines, from the File menu, choose the Page Setup command, click the Sheet tab, and then select or deselect the Gridlines option in the Print section.

See Also For more information about printing a document without gridlines, see Chapter 10, "Printing and Presenting," page 373.

Changing the Color of Gridlines

To change the color of the gridlines in your workbook, select a color from the Color drop-down list box on the Options dialog box's View tab and click OK. Select the Automatic option to return to the default color.

Controlling the Display of Row and Column Headers, Scroll Bars, and Sheet Tabs

If you deselect the Row & Column Headers option on the View tab in the Options dialog box, the row numbers and column letters disappear. Similarly, if you deselect the Horizontal Scroll Bar, Vertical Scroll Bar, or Sheet Tabs options, those window items disappear from view for the current workbook. You can use these options to polish your finished workbooks for display purposes; they do not affect the way the worksheets in the current workbook will look when you print them. Figure 6-39 shows a worksheet without row and column headings, scroll bars, or sheet tabs. (The display of gridlines has also been suppressed.)

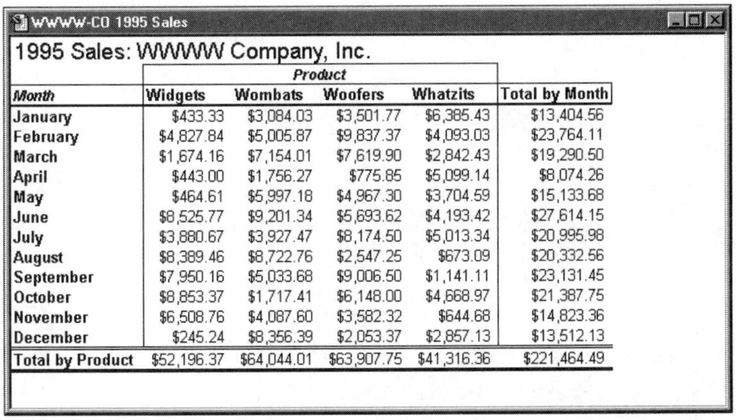

WWWW-CO 1995 Sales

1995 Sales: WWWWW Company, Inc.

	Product				
Month	**Widgets**	**Wombats**	**Woofers**	**Whatzits**	**Total by Month**
January	$433.33	$3,084.03	$3,501.77	$6,385.43	$13,404.56
February	$4,827.84	$5,005.87	$9,837.37	$4,093.03	$23,764.11
March	$1,674.16	$7,154.01	$7,619.90	$2,842.43	$19,290.50
April	$443.00	$1,756.27	$775.85	$5,099.14	$8,074.26
May	$464.61	$5,997.18	$4,967.30	$3,704.59	$15,133.68
June	$8,525.77	$9,201.34	$5,693.62	$4,193.42	$27,614.15
July	$3,880.67	$3,927.47	$8,174.50	$5,013.34	$20,995.98
August	$8,389.46	$8,722.76	$2,547.25	$673.09	$20,332.56
September	$7,950.16	$5,033.68	$9,006.50	$1,141.11	$23,131.45
October	$8,853.37	$1,717.41	$6,148.00	$4,668.97	$21,387.75
November	$6,508.76	$4,087.60	$3,582.32	$644.68	$14,823.36
December	$245.24	$8,356.39	$2,053.37	$2,857.13	$13,512.13
Total by Product	$52,196.37	$64,044.01	$63,907.75	$41,316.36	$221,464.49

FIGURE 6-39
You can suppress the display of row and column headings, horizontal and vertical scroll bars, and sheet tabs, as well as gridlines.

Navigating Without Headers or Scroll Bars

When Row & Column Headers is deselected, you must use the Format menu to change the width of a column. Also, to keep track of where you are on the current worksheet, you must rely on the cell reference display in the Name box at the left end of the formula bar. To scroll around the worksheet without scroll bars, you must use the keyboard-navigation options or choose the Go To command on the Edit menu (or press F5) and type the cell reference to which you want to move. To switch to another worksheet when the sheet tabs are hidden, press Ctrl-PgUp to move to the previous sheet or Ctrl-PgDn to move to the next sheet. You can also use the Go To command to move to other worksheets in a workbook. Simply type the worksheet name and a cell reference, such as *Sheet5!A1,* in the Reference edit box.

See Also For information about the keyboard-navigation options, see "Scrolling with the Keyboard," page 12.

The Zero Values Option

Normally, zero values are displayed in your worksheet. To hide those values, deselect the Zero Values option on the View tab in the Options dialog box. Any cells containing only zeros or formulas that result in zero values appear blank. The underlying entries are unaffected, however. If you edit an entry or if the result of a formula changes so that the cell no longer contains a zero value, the value immediately becomes visible. If the Formulas option on the View tab is selected, deselecting Zero Values has no effect on the display.

Changing the Standard Font

The General tab in the Options dialog box controls many aspects of your workspace, as you can see in Figure 6-40. Most of these options are discussed elsewhere in this book.

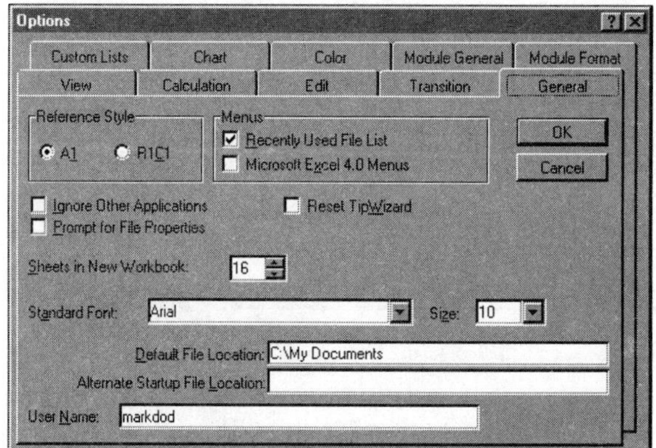

FIGURE 6-40
The General tab of the Options dialog box controls the standard font used in new workbooks.

You use the General tab to set the standard font, which Excel uses in several ways. All new workbooks are created with column and row headings displayed in the standard font, and any entries you make in a new workbook are displayed in this font. In addition, the standard font is used as the font definition in the Normal style.

To redefine the standard font, select the font name and size you want from the corresponding drop-down list boxes on the General tab of the Options dialog box. When you click OK, a dialog box informs you that the new standard font will not become active until you quit and restart Excel, enabling you to save changes to any open workbooks. The next time you start Excel, all new workbooks you create are displayed with the new standard font. In the Style dialog box that appears when you choose Style from the Format menu, the Normal style now includes the new standard font as well. If you change the Font definition of the Normal style for a workbook, the worksheet display changes accordingly. However, each new workbook you open will continue to use the standard font defined on the General tab until you redefine it again.

For information about R1C1 references, see "R1C1 Reference Style," page 118.

For information about opening a file you have used recently, see "Reopening a Recently Opened File," page 68.

For information about summary information, see "Adding Summary Information to Files," page 62.

For information about the TipWizard, see "Accessing Tips and Tricks with the TipWizard," page 29.

For information about the number of sheets in a workbook, see "Working with Sheets," page 309.

For information about loading files automatically, see "Opening Files Automatically When You Start Excel," page 69.

Changing the Available Colors

In Excel's Format Cells dialog box, the Font, Border, and Patterns tabs all offer a choice of 56 colors, which constitute your default color palette. This palette is also available for gridlines on the View tab of the Options dialog box and the tear-off palettes of the Color and Font Color buttons on the Formatting toolbar. Using the Color tab in the Options dialog box, you can modify any color in the palette. The Color tab is shown in Figure 6-41.

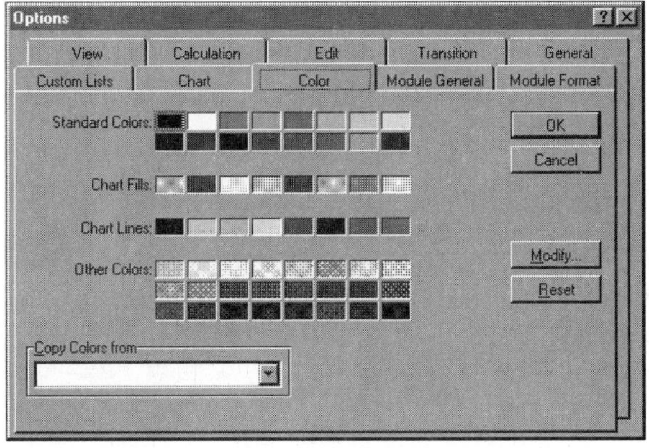

FIGURE 6-41
The Color tab in the Options dialog box controls the colors in the default color palette.

The Color tab presents samples of each solid color in the current palette in the Standard Colors section. The Chart Fills and Chart Lines sections reflect the default colors and order that Excel uses for chart elements. The Other Colors section offers other "blended" colors that are available on the current palette.

To substitute a different color for one of the current colors, select the current color and then click Modify. You'll see the Color Picker dialog box, as shown in Figure 6-42.

FIGURE 6-42
You can edit the colors in Excel's default color palette with the Color Picker dialog box.

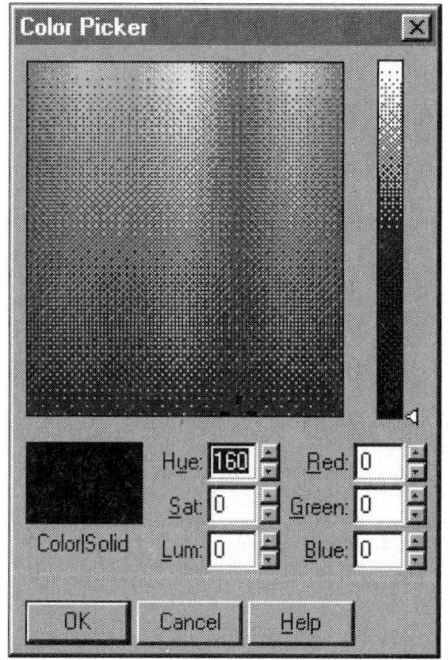

Colors displayed on your screen are defined by three parameters — their red, green, and blue values. An alternative system of specification uses three different parameters, called *hue, saturation,* and *luminescence* (labeled *Hue, Sat,* and *Lum* in the Color Picker dialog box). You can specify a new color by modifying the values of any of these parameters. Simply click the arrows next to or type new values in the appropriate edit boxes.

If you have a mouse, you can define a new color more directly by dragging either or both of two pointers. The first pointer is in the large square that dominates this dialog box. This pointer controls hue and saturation. The second pointer is the arrowhead beside the vertical scale to the right of the large square. This pointer controls luminescence. By experimenting with these two pointers and looking at the samples that appear in the Color|Solid box (in the lower left corner of the dialog box), you can come up with new colors without having to know anything about the parameters that define them.

Any colors you define that are not among your system's repertoire of solids are achieved by a mixture of dots from solid colors. Such "blended" colors, which are said to be *dithered,* work well for shading. But for text and lines, Excel always uses the nearest solid color in preference to a dithered color. When you define a color that can be achieved only by dithering, the Color|Solid box shows you both the dithered shade and the nearest solid alternative that Excel uses when necessary.

Click OK in the Color Picker dialog box when the color is changed to your satisfaction. The modified color replaces the original on the Color tab.

After you edit the color palette, click OK to save it. Your customized palette then becomes a permanent attribute of the current workbook. Click the Reset button on the Color tab to revert to the original color palette.

Copying Palettes from Other Workbooks

To achieve a consistent look among workbooks, you can copy your custom palette. To do so, follow these steps:

1. Open both the destination workbook (the one to which you're copying) and the source workbook (the one from which you're copying).
2. Make the destination workbook active.
3. From the Tools menu, choose the Options command and click the Color tab.
4. Click the arrow for the Copy Colors From drop-down list box to see a list of all other open workbooks.
5. Select your source workbook and then click OK.

Outlining Your Worksheets

Many typical spreadsheet models are built in a hierarchical fashion. For example, in a monthly budget worksheet, you might have a column for each month of the year, followed by a totals column. For each line item in your budget, the totals column adds the values in each month column. In this kind of structure, you can describe the month columns as subordinate to the totals column because their values contribute to the outcome of the totals column. Similarly, the line items themselves might be set up in a hierarchical manner, with groups of expense categories contributing to category totals. Microsoft Excel can turn worksheets of this kind into outlines.

Figure 6-43 shows a table of sales figures before outlining. Figure 6-44 shows the same worksheet as an outline, and Figure 6-45 shows how you can change the level of detail displayed after you outline a worksheet.

FIGURE 6-43

This worksheet is an excellent candidate for outlining.

Team Sales

	A	B	C	D	E	F	G	H	I	J
1		Jan	Feb	Mar	Q1	Apr	May	Jun	Q2	Jul
2	Team A									
3	Adams	706	274	674	1654	104	148	942	1195	170
4	Alexander	964	909	19	1892	437	993	78	1508	397
5	Ameling	734	315	37	1086	392	948	193	1533	60
6	Andrews	884	906	920	2709	997	387	70	1453	548
7	Arthur	917	894	766	2577	186	682	652	1520	446
8	Team A Total	4205	3298	2415	9918	2116	3158	1934	7208	1621
9										
10	Team B									
11	Bailey	119	202	128	449	868	816	812	2495	228
12	Baker	361	84	569	1014	108	152	313	573	785
13	Barnes	294	681	442	1417	599	831	7	1436	646
14	Beckman	927	866	769	2562	725	554	204	1484	507
15	Bukowski	269	395	313	977	110	822	87	1019	413
16	Team B Total	1970	2228	2220	6419	2409	3175	1423	7007	2579

Sheet1 / Sheet2 / Sheet3 / Sheet4 / Sheet5 / Sheet6

FIGURE 6-44

The worksheet in Figure 6-43 is now in outline form.

Team Sales

	A	B	C	D	E	F	G	H	I
1		Jan	Feb	Mar	Q1	Apr	May	Jun	Q2
2	Team A								
3	Adams	706	274	674	1654	104	148	942	1195
4	Alexander	964	909	19	1892	437	993	78	1508
5	Ameling	734	315	37	1086	392	948	193	1533
6	Andrews	884	906	920	2709	997	387	70	1453
7	Arthur	917	894	766	2577	186	682	652	1520
8	Team A Total	4205	3298	2415	9918	2116	3158	1934	7208
9									
10	Team B								
11	Bailey	119	202	128	449	868	816	812	2495
12	Baker	361	84	569	1014	108	152	313	573
13	Barnes	294	681	442	1417	599	831	7	1436

Sheet1 / Sheet2 / Sheet3 / Sheet4 / Sheet5 / Sheet6

The only difference between the worksheets in Figures 6-44 and 6-45 is that the columns and rows listing the months and individual team members are hidden in Figure 6-45. Without outlining, you would have to hide each group of columns and rows manually; with outlining, you can collapse the outline to change the level of detail instantly.

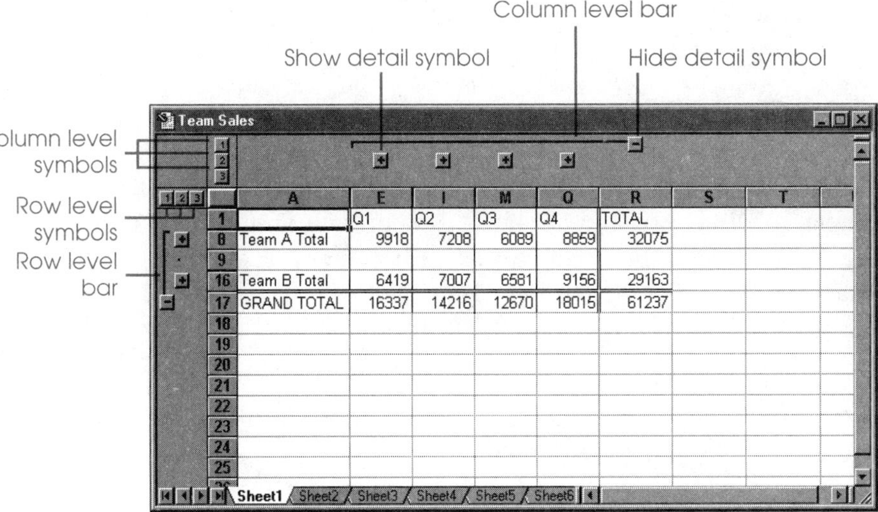

	A	E	I	M	Q	R	S	T
1		Q1	Q2	Q3	Q4	TOTAL		
8	Team A Total	9918	7208	6089	8859	32075		
9								
16	Team B Total	6419	7007	6581	9156	29163		
17	GRAND TOTAL	16337	14216	12670	18015	61237		

FIGURE 6-45

Two clicks of the mouse button transformed the worksheet in Figure 6-44 into this quarterly overview.

Outlining has two additional benefits. First, you can more easily reorganize an outlined worksheet than one that is not outlined. In Figure 6-45, for example, if you hold down Shift while clicking the show detail symbol (the button with a plus sign) at the top of column E and use standard editing techniques to move that column, the subordinate columns B, C, and D automatically move as well.

Second, in an outlined worksheet you can easily select only those cells that share a common hierarchical level. For example, to graph the quarterly sales totals in Figure 6-44 (omitting the monthly details), first collapse the outline as shown in Figure 6-45, and then individually select columns E, I, M, and Q (the quarterly totals) without selecting the intervening columns. (Again, you can accomplish this by hiding columns individually, but, in most cases, outlining is considerably faster.)

The outline in Figure 6-45 is a simple one. It uses three levels each for columns and rows. You can create much more complex outlines — Excel can handle a maximum of eight outline levels each for columns and rows.

Creating an Outline

To outline part of your worksheet automatically, first select the area to outline. From the Data menu, choose the Group And Outline command, and then choose Auto Outline. To outline your entire worksheet, select only one cell and then choose Auto Outline. In a moment or two, depending on the complexity of your worksheet, your outline appears.

Outlining with Toolbar Buttons

The outlining buttons offer some shortcuts for working with an outline. Figure 6-46 shows a custom toolbar containing the six outlining buttons. You can use these buttons to display outline symbols, ungroup and group the current selection, display or hide the detail columns or rows, and select only those cells that are visible.

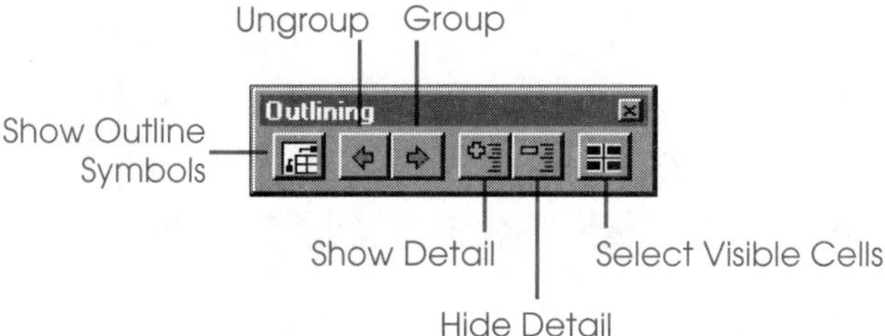

FIGURE 6-46

This custom toolbar has six buttons that can be used in outlining.

To create this custom toolbar, follow these steps:

1. From the View menu, choose Toolbars.
2. In the Toolbars dialog box, highlight the contents of the Toolbar Name edit box, type *Outlining,* and then choose the New button.
3. In the Customize dialog box, select Utility in the Categories list box.
4. From the Buttons section, drag the Show Outline Symbols and Select Visible Cells buttons to the new toolbar.
5. Select Data in the Categories list box.
6. Drag the Ungroup, Group, Show Detail, and Hide Detail buttons to the new toolbar.
7. Click the Close button.

To create an outline using toolbar buttons, select the range to outline and then click the Show Outline Symbols button. An alert box asks if you want to create an outline, if none yet exists. Click OK. Excel creates your outline automatically. If you click the Show Outline Symbols button again, the outline symbols disappear from the screen. The outline is still there; it's just hidden. Click the button again, and the outline reappears. The Show Outline Symbols button corresponds to the Outline Symbols option on the View tab of the Options dialog box that appears when you choose Options from the Tools menu.

The Ungroup and Group buttons allow you to modify the hierarchies in your outline. If you select entire columns or rows and click the Ungroup button, the outline level is removed. Similarly, if you select entire columns or rows, the Group button creates a new outline level; the selected columns and rows become the detail data. The Ungroup and Group buttons correspond to the commands of the same name on the submenu that appears when you choose the Group And Outline command on the Data menu.

The Show Detail and Hide Detail buttons operate when you select cells in summary columns or rows. The Show Detail button expands the outline level subordinate to the selected summary cell; the Hide Detail button does just the opposite. These two buttons also correspond to commands of the same name on the submenu that appears when you choose Group And Outline on the Data menu.

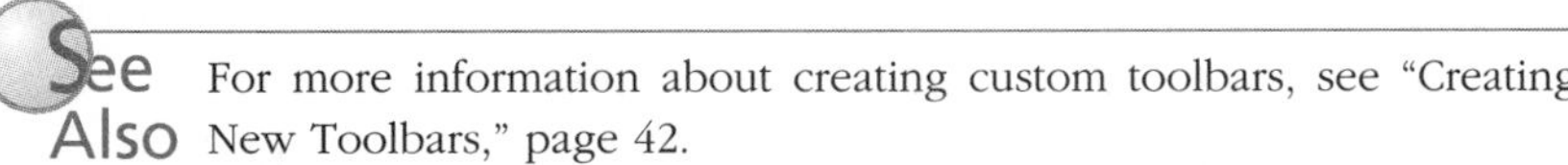

See Also For more information about creating custom toolbars, see "Creating New Toolbars," page 42.

Using Automatic Styles

Excel can automatically apply a predefined set of styles to cells at the various levels of your outline. Figure 6-47 shows the outline from Figure 6-44 (shown earlier) with automatic styles applied. As you can see, these automatic styles have names such as ColLevel_1, RowLevel_1, and so on. When you apply automatic styles, Excel adds the names of these styles to the Style Name list box in the Style dialog box for the current workbook. You can then work with these styles — and modify their definitions — the same way you work with other styles.

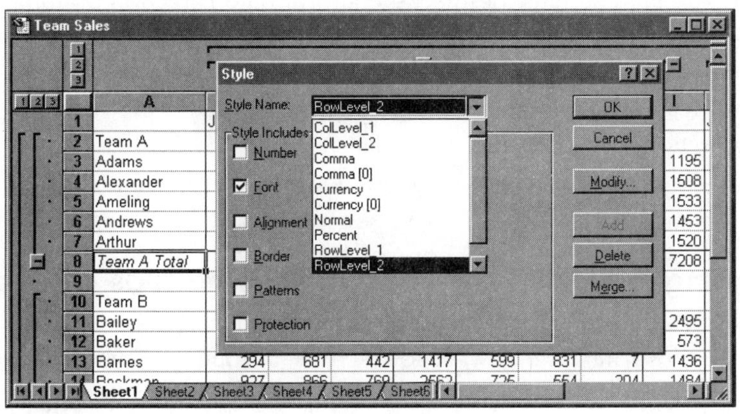

FIGURE 6-47
Excel can automatically apply predefined styles to the summary levels of an outline.

You can tell Excel that you want to use automatic styles before you create the outline. From the Data menu, choose the Group And Outline command, and then click Settings. Select the Automatic Styles option in the Outline dialog box, as shown in Figure 6-48.

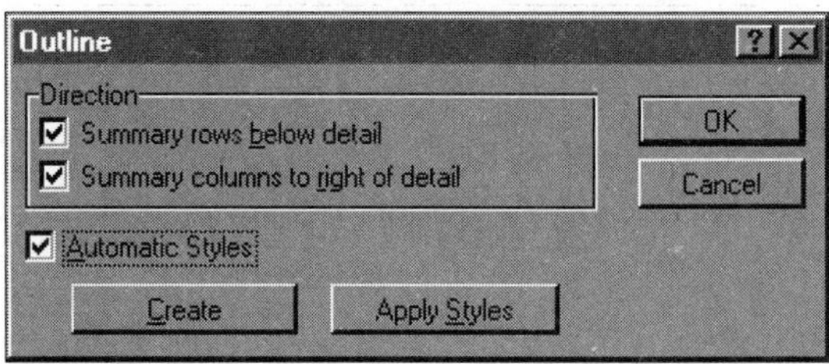

FIGURE 6-48
The Outline dialog box controls outline settings and provides a way to apply automatic outline styles.

If you create an outline without automatic styles and then change your mind, first select the area of your worksheet to which you want to apply automatic styles. Then choose Group And Outline from the Data menu, and choose Settings to display the Outline dialog box. Click Apply Styles.

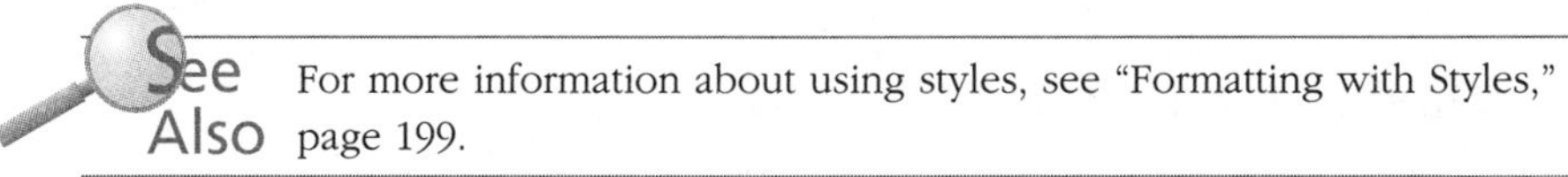

For more information about using styles, see "Formatting with Styles," page 199.

Outlining a Worksheet with a Nonstandard Layout

The Direction options in the Outline dialog box — Summary Rows Below Detail and Summary Columns To Right Of Detail — are selected by default and reflect the most common worksheet layout. If your worksheet is constructed with rows of SUM formulas (or other types of summarization formulas) in rows above the detail rows, or with columns of formulas to the left of detail columns, deselect the appropriate Direction option before outlining. If you do use nonstandard worksheet layouts, be sure that the area you want to outline is consistent to avoid unpredictable and possibly incorrect results; that is, be sure all summary formulas are located in the same direction relative to the detail data.

After you select one or both Direction options, click the Create button to create the outline.

Extending the Outline to New Worksheet Areas

At times, you might create an outline and then add more data to your worksheet. You might also want to re-create an outline if you change the organization of a specific worksheet area. To include new columns and rows in your outline, simply repeat the procedure you followed to create the outline in the first place: Select a cell in the new area, then from the Data menu, choose Group And Outline and then Auto Outline. Excel asks you to confirm that you want to modify the existing outline; click OK.

Suppressing the Outline Display

When you outline a worksheet, Excel displays some additional symbols above and to the left of the row and column headings. These symbols indicate the structure of your outline, and you can use them to change the level of detail that Excel displays. However, these symbols do take up screen space. If you want to suppress them, you can click the Show Outline Symbols button if you created a custom Outlining toolbar like the one described on page 220. Alternatively, you can choose the Options command from the Tools menu. Click the View tab and deselect the Outline Symbols option.

To redisplay the outline symbols, click the Show Outline Symbols button a second time, or reselect the Outline Symbols option on the View tab of the Options dialog box.

Collapsing and Expanding Outline Levels

When you first create an outline, the areas above and to the left of your worksheet are marked by one or more brackets that terminate in *hide detail symbols,* which have minus signs on them. The brackets are called *level bars.* Each level bar indicates a range of cells that share a common outline level. The hide detail symbols appear above or to the left of each level's *summary* column or row.

For example, if you translate columns B through E shown earlier in Figure 6-44 into a traditional outline, it looks like this:

I. Q1 (column E)
- A. January (column B)
- B. February (column C)
- C. March (column D)

Excel indicates this structure by drawing a level bar across columns B through D, terminating the level bar in a hide detail symbol above column E.

To collapse an outline level so that only the summary cells show, click that level's hide detail symbol. For example, if you no longer need to see the sales numbers for January, February, and March in Figure 6-44, click the hide detail symbol above column E. The worksheet then looks like Figure 6-49 on the next page.

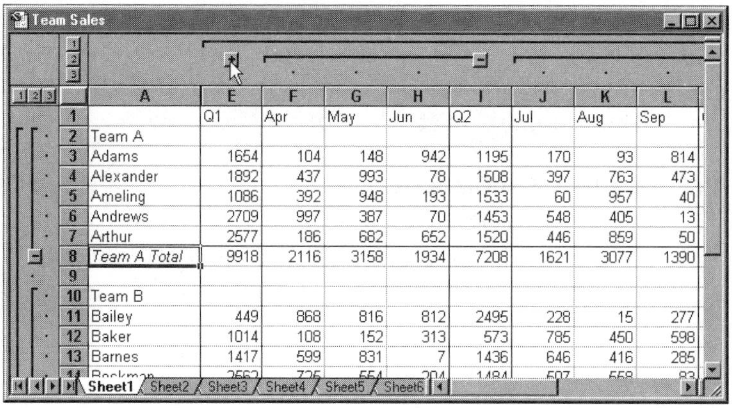

Team Sales

	A	E	F	G	H	I	J	K	L
1		Q1	Apr	May	Jun	Q2	Jul	Aug	Sep
2	Team A								
3	Adams	1654	104	148	942	1195	170	93	814
4	Alexander	1892	437	993	78	1508	397	763	473
5	Ameling	1086	392	948	193	1533	60	957	40
6	Andrews	2709	997	387	70	1453	548	405	13
7	Arthur	2577	186	682	652	1520	446	859	50
8	*Team A Total*	9918	2116	3158	1934	7208	1621	3077	1390
9									
10	Team B								
11	Bailey	449	868	816	812	2495	228	15	277
12	Baker	1014	108	152	313	573	785	450	598
13	Barnes	1417	599	831	7	1436	646	416	285

Sheet1 / Sheet2 / Sheet3 / Sheet4 / Sheet5 / Sheet6

FIGURE 6-49
We have hidden the details for January through March by clicking the hide detail symbol above Q1. Excel now displays a show detail symbol above Q1.

A *show detail symbol* with a plus sign on it now replaces the hide detail symbol above the Q1 column (column E). To redisplay the hidden monthly details, click the show detail symbol.

Displaying a Specific Outline Level

To collapse each quarter so that only the quarterly totals and annual totals appear, you can click the hide detail symbols above Q1, Q2, Q3, and Q4. But the *level symbols* — the squares with numerals at the upper left corner of the worksheet — provide an easier way. An outline usually has two sets of level symbols, one for columns and one for rows. The *column level symbols* appear above the worksheet, and the *row level symbols* appear to the left of the worksheet.

You can use the level symbols to set an entire worksheet to a specific level of detail. The worksheet shown earlier in Figure 6-44 has three levels each for both columns and rows. By clicking both of the number 2 level symbols in the upper left corner of the worksheet, you can transform the outline shown in Figure 6-44 to the one shown in Figure 6-45. By clicking the number 1 level symbols, you can further reduce the level of detail displayed by the worksheet so that only the grand total sales figure for the year, in cell R17, is shown.

When you collapse part of an outline, Excel hides the columns or rows that you don't want to see. In Figure 6-45, for example, rows 2 through 7 and 10 through 15, as well as columns B through D, F through H, J through L, and N through P, are hidden. Normally, when you select a range that includes hidden cells, those hidden cells are included in the selection. If you drag the mouse from E8 to Q8 in Figure 6-45, for example, Excel selects the entire range, including the hidden cells. Whatever you do with these cells also happens to the hidden cells. By clicking the Select Visible Cells button on our custom Outlining toolbar, however, you can restrict a selection to only the visible cells within a range.

For example, to add a formula in cell S8 of the worksheet in Figure 6-45 to compute the averages of your four quarterly sales figures, follow these steps:

1. Make S8 the active cell and type

   =AVERAGE(

2. Drag the mouse from E8 to Q8. The formula bar now reads

   = AVERAGE(E8:Q8

3. Click the Select Visible Cells button on our Custom Outlining toolbar. Excel changes the formula in the formula bar to read

   = AVERAGE(E8,I8,M8,Q8

4. Type a close parenthesis and press Enter to calculate the quarterly average for row 8.

The Select Visible Cells button is ideal for copying, charting, or performing calculations on only those cells that occupy a particular level of your outline. But you can use this option with any set of visible cells in an outline, even if they're not at the same hierarchical level. You can also use the Select Visible Cells button with worksheets that contain columns or rows that have been hidden manually. Select Visible Cells works the same way in worksheets that have not been outlined; it excludes any cells in hidden columns or rows from the current selection.

TIP You can also use the Go To command on the Edit menu to restrict a selection to a range of visible cells. In the Go To dialog box, click the Special button to display the Go To Special dialog box, where you can select the Visible Cells Only option.

Also For more information about the AVERAGE function, see "The AVERAGE Function," page 505.

Ungrouping and Grouping Columns and Rows

In most cases, Excel's automatic outlining procedure interprets the structure of your worksheet correctly and sets up your outline with the right levels in the right places. If the default outline doesn't give you the structure you expect, however, you can adjust it by ungrouping or grouping particular columns or rows.

You can easily change the hierarchy of outlined columns and rows using the Group and Ungroup commands on the Group And Outline submenu of the Data menu (or the buttons of the same name on our custom Outlining toolbar). Simply select the columns or rows you want to change and choose one of the commands. For example, you could select row 8 in the worksheet shown earlier in Figure 6-44, choose the Ungroup command (or click the Ungroup button on the Outlining toolbar), and then click OK to change row 8 from level 2 to level 1. The outlining symbol to the left of the row moves to the left under the row level 1 button. To restore the row to its proper level, simply choose the Group command (or click the Group button). The outlining symbol then returns to its original level 2 position.

NOTE You cannot ungroup or group a nonadjacent selection, and you cannot ungroup a selection that's already at the highest hierarchical level. If you want to ungroup a top-level column or row to a higher level so that it is displayed separately from the remainder of the outline, you have to group all the other levels of the outline instead.

Removing an Outline

It's easy to remove an outline from a worksheet. From the Data menu, choose Group And Outline and then Clear Outline.

You can also remove either the column or row levels (or both) from an outline by ungrouping all of the outline's levels to the highest level. If your outline is many levels deep and your worksheet is large, this process can be laborious. Another way to make your worksheet behave as though it is not outlined is to display all the levels of detail (by clicking the highest numbered level button for both columns and rows) and then suppress the display of Excel's outline symbols. You can do this by clicking the Show Outline Symbols button on the custom Outlining toolbar described on page 220.

For more information about suppressing the display of outline symbols, see "Suppressing the Outline Display," page 223.

Chapter 7

Editing a Worksheet

Microsoft Excel's many editing features take the place of old-fashioned erasers, scissors, and glue, so you can delete, copy, cut, and paste cells and ranges in your worksheets. In this chapter, we discuss the Edit menu commands: Undo, Redo, Repeat, Cut, Copy, Paste, Paste Special, Fill, Clear, Delete, Find, and Replace. We also cover the Insert menu commands: Cells, Rows, Columns, and Note, as well as the Spelling, Auditing, and AutoCorrect commands on the Tools menu. Many of these commands are included as buttons on the Standard toolbar, shown in Figure 7-1. Finally we examine some other important editing and auditing features, including direct cell manipulation (cell drag and drop), the tracer tools, the Info window, and the Select Special dialog box.

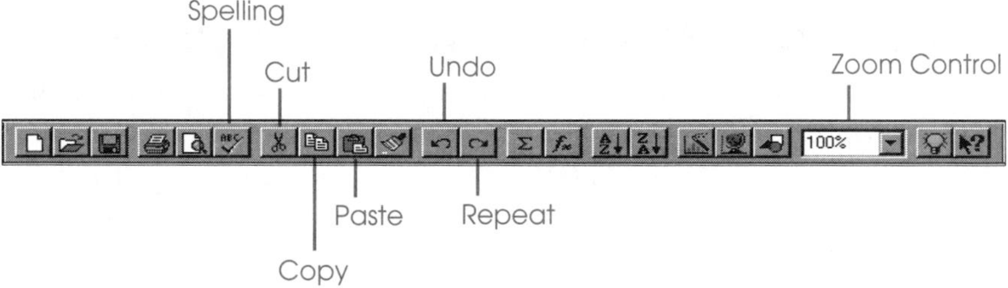

FIGURE 7-1

The Standard toolbar includes many buttons you can use to make editing easier.

In this chapter we discuss how to use these commands and features on a single worksheet. You can also edit two or more worksheets simultaneously. Chapter 8, "Workbooks and Windows," discusses the group editing feature.

Setting Workspace Options for Editing

As you've already seen, the Options command on the Tools menu displays a stellar dialog box in the Microsoft Excel universe. The importance of the Options dialog box is further underscored by the Edit tab, which contains an assortment of options that allow you to control editing-related workspace settings, as shown on the next page in Figure 7-2.

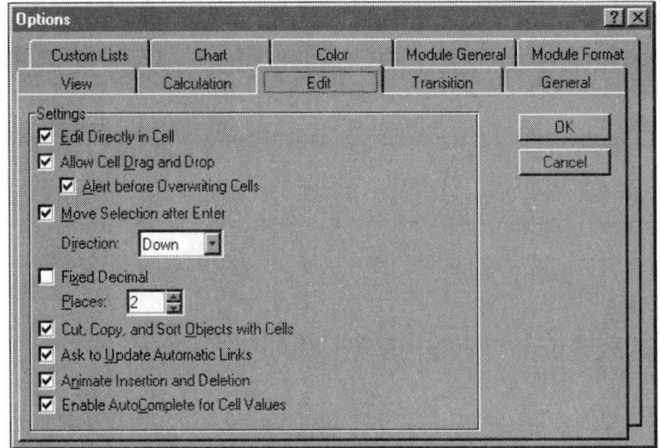

FIGURE 7-2 From the Tools menu, choose the Options command and click the Edit tab to display a list of options that let you control editing-related workspace settings.

The Move Selection After Enter Option

When the Move Selection After Enter option is active and Down is displayed in the Direction drop-down list (the default setting), pressing Enter after typing a cell entry locks in the entry and activates the cell below. To change the direction of the selection after you press Enter, use the Direction drop-down list. The other options are for the cell to the right, up, or to the left. When you deselect this option, pressing Enter simply locks in the entry and leaves the same cell active.

The Fixed Decimal Option

The Fixed Decimal option on the Edit tab of the Options dialog box is handy when you need to enter long lists of numeric values. (It's equivalent to the floating decimal feature available on most 10-key calculators.) For example, if you're entering multiple values that contain two decimal places, select the Fixed Decimal option and type 2, if necessary, in the Places edit box. (The FIX indicator appears in the status bar after you close the Options dialog box.) After you type each numeric value, Excel adds a decimal point at the specified position. If the setting in the Places edit box is 2 and you enter the number 12345 in your worksheet, for example, your entry will be converted to 123.45; if you enter a single-digit value, such as 9, it will be converted to 0.09.

The Fixed Decimal option does not affect existing entries in your worksheet; it applies only to entries you make after you select the option. Thus, you can select or deselect the option at any time or change the number of decimal places without altering your existing data. The Fixed Decimal option applies only when you do not type a decimal point. If you type a number with a decimal point, the Fixed Decimal option has no effect.

The Animate Insertion And Deletion Option

When Animate Insertion And Deletion is selected, as it is by default in Excel 7, inserting or deleting entire rows or columns appears animated on your screen. That is, the rows or columns appear to roll in the direction of the action. For example, when you delete, rows appear to roll upward and columns seem to roll to the left. When you insert, rows appear to roll down, and columns seem to roll to the right. This offers a visual cue that confirms what you've done. Without this option, inserting and deleting rows or columns occurs instantaneously, making it difficult to tell if you did the right thing. If you keep an eye on the worksheet, you can watch the animation and tell immediately if you deleted when you meant to insert. Keep in mind, however, that this occurs only for entire rows and columns — inserting and deleting cells is not animated.

We'll discuss the other options available on the Edit tab throughout this chapter.

For information about the Cut, Copy, And Sort Objects With Cells option, see Chapter 9, "Graphics," page 345.

For information about the Ask To Update Automatic Links option, see Chapter 26, "Integrating Applications with the Clipboard and OLE," page 889.

Shortcuts for Entering and Editing

In Excel, you can perform many of the most common editing tasks without using commands. Using the mouse in combination with the Shift and Ctrl keys, you can cut, copy, paste, clear, insert, delete, and move cells. In addition, you can duplicate much of the functionality of the Fill commands with simple mouse movements.

You turn the direct cell-manipulation feature on and off by choosing the Options command from the Tools menu and selecting the Allow Cell Drag And Drop option on the Edit tab. (To safeguard against mistakes, be sure the Alert Before Overwriting Cells option is also selected.) When the direct cell-manipulation feature is turned on (which is the default condition), a small black square, called the *fill handle,* is visible in the lower right corner of the selection rectangle, as shown in Figure 7-3.

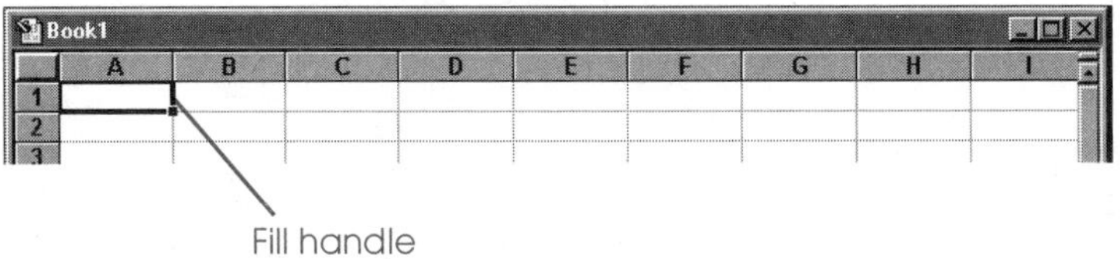

FIGURE 7-3

When Allow Cell Drag And Drop is turned on, a fill handle appears in the lower right corner of the selection rectangle.

With the Allow Cell Drag And Drop option selected, try moving the mouse pointer around the selection rectangle border. When you position the mouse pointer over the fill handle, it changes to a bold cross hair, as shown in Figure 7-4. When you position the pointer over the border, it changes to an arrow, as shown in Figure 7-5.

FIGURE 7-4

The pointer changes to a bold cross hair when you move it over a fill handle.

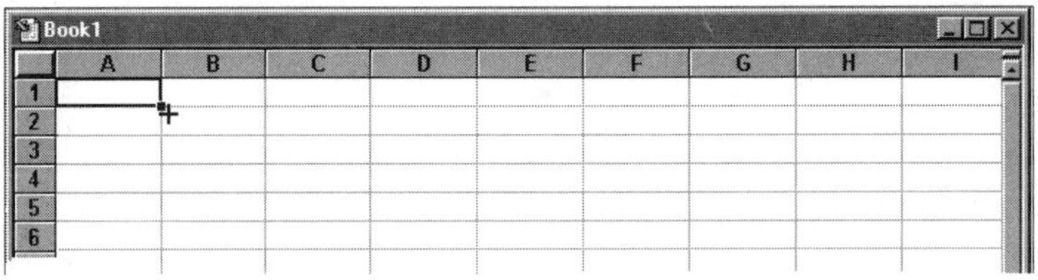

Moving and Copying with the Mouse

To quickly move a cell or range to a new location, select the cell or range and drag it to the new position. For example, in Figure 7-5, the mouse pointer is positioned over the border that surrounds cells A1:A4. When the arrow pointer appears, click the border and drag it to column C.

FIGURE 7-5

Position the pointer over the selection rectangle border to move these cells elsewhere by dragging.

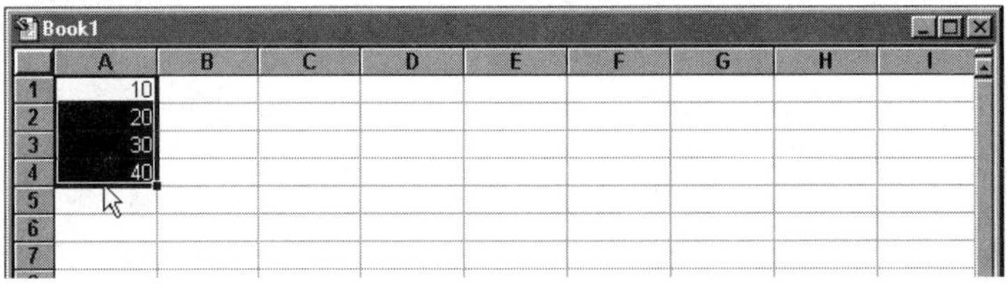

As you drag, an outline of the range appears. You can use this to help you position the range correctly. When the outline is over cells C1:C4, release the mouse button. The result is shown in Figure 7-6.

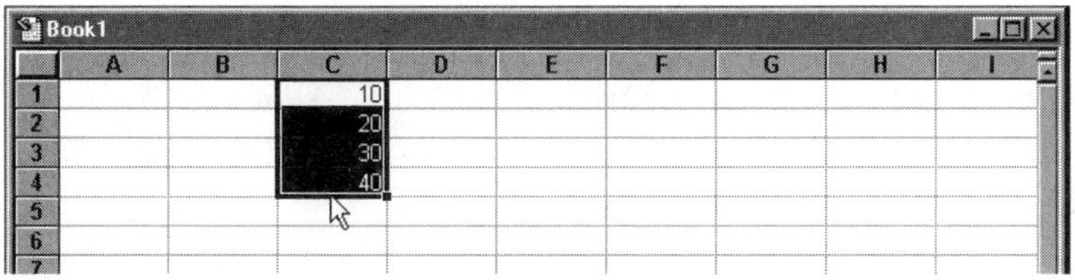

FIGURE 7-6
Using the mouse, we dragged the selected cells to a new location.

To copy the selection (copy and paste) rather than move it (cut and paste), press the Ctrl key before you release the mouse button. The mouse pointer then appears with a small plus sign next to it, as shown in Figure 7-7, which indicates you are copying rather than moving the selection.

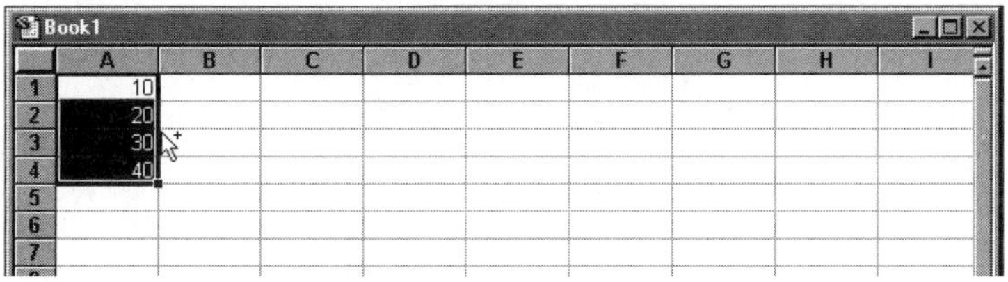

FIGURE 7-7
Before you finish dragging, press Ctrl to copy the selection. Notice the plus sign next to the pointer.

You can also use direct cell-manipulation to insert cells in your worksheet. For example, in Figure 7-8, we first selected cells A1:A2 and then dragged the selection while holding down the Shift key. As you can see, a gray I-beam indicates where the selected cells will be inserted when you release the mouse button. The I-beam appears whenever the arrow pointer passes over a horizontal or vertical cell border. In this case, the vertical border between cells C1:C2 and D1:D2 is indicated, but we could just as easily insert the cells horizontally, *between* cells C1 and C2.

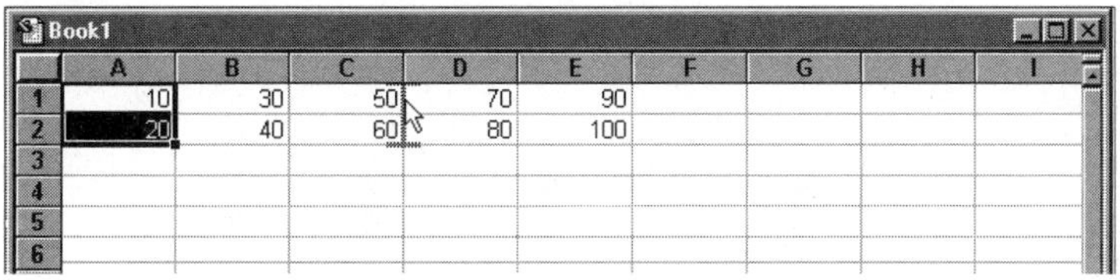

FIGURE 7-8
The I-beam indicates where the selected cells will be inserted.

To insert the cells, release the mouse button while still pressing the Shift key. When you release the mouse button, the selected cells move to the new location, as shown in Figure 7-9 on the next page. In addition, the cells in columns B and C move to the left to fill the space vacated by A1:A2.

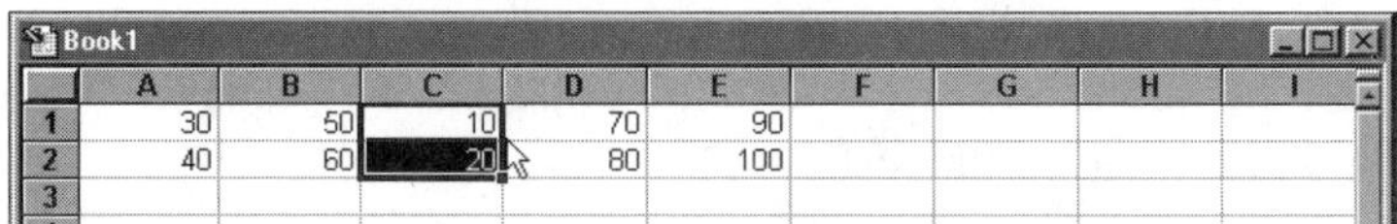

FIGURE 7-9
The selected cells are inserted in their new location.

If you press Ctrl-Shift while dragging, the selected cells are copied instead of moved to the insertion point. Again, a small plus sign appears next to the arrow pointer, and a copy of the selected cells is inserted in the new location, while the original selected cells are left intact.

You can also use these techniques to select entire columns or rows and then move or copy them to new locations.

Inserting, Deleting, and Clearing Cells with the Mouse

To perform the next group of operations, you use the fill handle. If you select a cell or range, the fill handle appears in the lower right corner of the selection rectangle. If you select an entire column (or columns), the fill handle appears next to the column heading. If you select an entire row (or rows), the fill handle appears next to the row heading. Using the worksheet in Figure 7-8, suppose you want to add some numbers between columns A and B. First select either cells A1:A2 or the entire column A. Next click the fill handle and drag one column to the right while holding down the Shift key. As you drag, the mouse pointer becomes a double line with a pair of outward-pointing arrows. Figure 7-10 shows the worksheet after you release the mouse button and Shift.

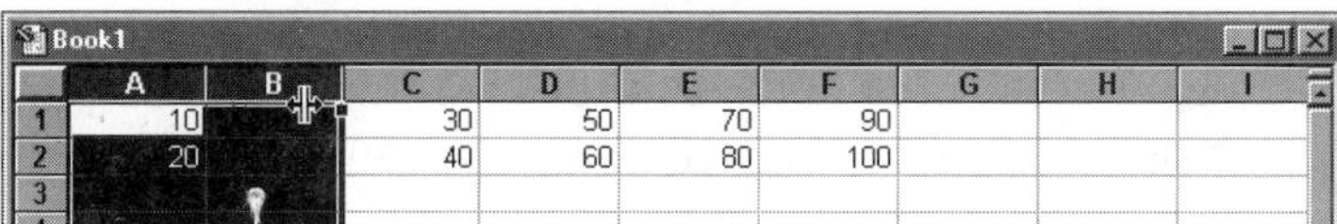

FIGURE 7-10
Use the mouse to insert blank cells or columns.

You can just as easily delete cells, columns, or rows using the same technique. For example, to delete the column we just inserted, select column B and then, while holding down Shift, drag the fill handle one column to the left. The selection turns a medium shade of gray, and the mouse pointer changes to a double line with a pair of inward-pointing arrows, as shown in Figure 7-11. When you release the mouse button, the selection is deleted. (This mouse action is equivalent to choosing the Delete command from the Edit menu.)

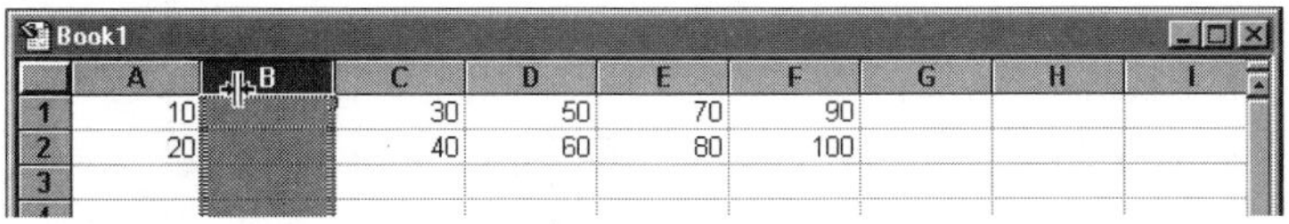

FIGURE 7-11
You can use the mouse to delete cells or columns.

NOTE If you don't hold down Shift while you drag back over the selected cells, you clear the cell contents instead of deleting the cells. This mouse action is equivalent to choosing the Contents command from the Clear submenu of the Edit menu, which clears formulas, text, and numbers only. If you hold down the Ctrl key while dragging back over the selection, you perform an operation that is equivalent to choosing the All command from the Clear submenu, which clears the entire contents of a cell, including formats and notes.

For more information about the Delete command, see "Deleting Cells, Columns, and Rows," page 245.

For more information about the Clear command, see "Clearing Cell Contents and Formats," page 245.

Dragging with the Right Mouse Button

If you select cells and then drag the selection rectangle using the right mouse button, a shortcut menu is displayed when you release the button, as shown in Figure 7-12. You can use the commands on the shortcut menu to manipulate your cell selection in a variety of ways.

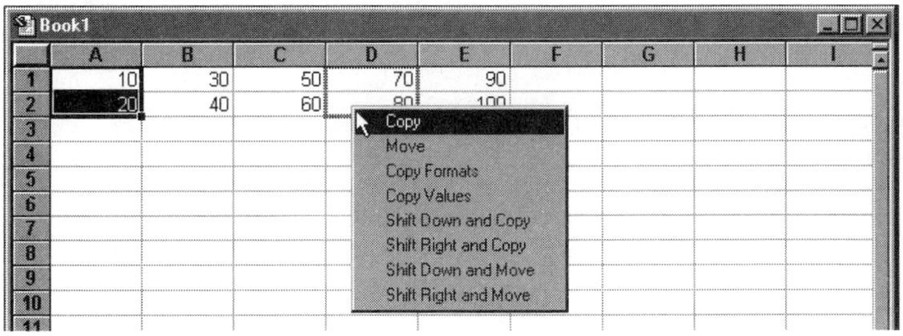

FIGURE 7-12
If you use the right mouse button to drag selected cells, this shortcut menu appears when you release the button.

As you might expect, the Copy command on the shortcut menu copies the selected, or *source,* cells — both contents and formats — to the location, or *destination,* where you release the mouse button. The Move command cuts the source cells from their original location and places them in the destination cells.

The Copy Formats command copies to the destination cells all the formats that were applied to the source cells; the contents of neither the source cells nor the destination cells are affected. The Copy Values command, on the other hand, copies the contents of the source cells to the destination cells but does not affect the formats of either.

The four Shift commands on the shortcut menu perform a variety of copying and moving functions. For example, if in Figure 7-12 we choose either of the Shift Down commands, cells D1:D2 and all the cells below them move down to accommodate the two cells we dragged (cells A1:A2). If we choose either of the Shift Right commands, cells D1:D2 and all the cells to their right move to the right to accommodate the two cells we dragged.

Filling and Creating Series with the Mouse

You can use the fill handle to quickly and easily fill cells and create series using Exel's AutoFill feature. You can perform most of the functions available in the Series dialog box that appears when you choose the Series command from the Fill submenu.

When you select a single cell, click the fill handle, and then drag in any direction, the contents of that cell are copied to the selected range. When you select a range of cells, either the range is copied in the direction you drag the mouse, or the series is extended in the direction you drag, depending on the cell contents, the shape of the selection, and whether or not you are holding down Ctrl.

For example, using the worksheet shown earlier in Figure 7-8, if you select cell A2 and drag the fill handle down to cell A5, the contents of cell A2 are copied to cells A3 through A5. Figure 7-13 shows the results.

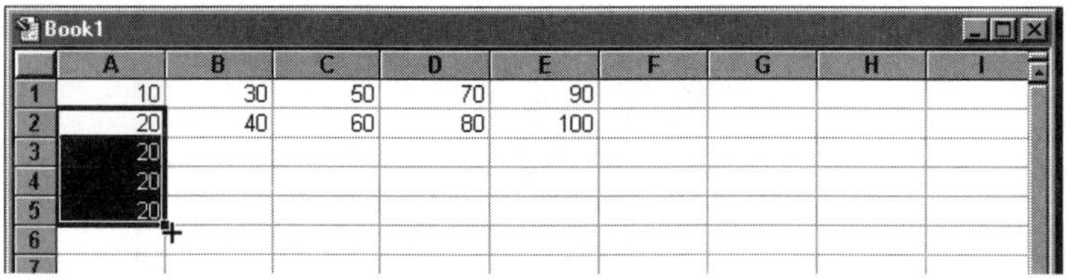

Book1

	A	B	C	D	E	F	G	H	I
1	10	30	50	70	90				
2	20	40	60	80	100				
3	20								
4	20								
5	20								
6									

FIGURE 7-13
You can copy the contents of a cell to adjacent cells by dragging the fill handle.

However, if you select the range A1:A2 and drag the fill handle down to cell A6, you create a *series* using the interval between the two selected values, as shown in column A of Figure 7-14. Alternatively, if you select cells C1:C2 and hold down the Ctrl key while you drag the fill handle down to cell C6, you copy the selected cells, repeating the pattern as necessary to fill the range, as shown in column C of Figure 7-14. Notice the small plus sign next to the mouse pointer, indicating a copy operation.

Book1

	A	B	C	D	E	F	G	H	I
1	10	30	50	70	90				
2	20	40	60	80	100				
3	30		50						
4	40		60						
5	50		50						
6	60		60						
7									

FIGURE 7-14
We created a series in column A and copied a range in column C.

TIP Generally, when you create a series, you drag the fill handle down or to the right, and the values increase accordingly. You can also create a series of decreasing values, however, by simply dragging the fill handle either up or to the left. Enter the starting values in the cells at the bottom or to the right of the range you want to fill and then drag the fill handle back to the beginning of the range.

If you select a text value and drag the fill handle, the text is copied to the cells where you drag. If, however, the selection contains both text and numeric values, the AutoFill feature takes over and extends the numeric component while copying the text component. You can also extend dates in this way, using a number of date formats, including Qtr 1, Qtr 2, and so on. If you enter text that describes dates, even without numbers (such as months or days of the week), Excel treats the text as a series.

Figure 7-15 shows some examples of series created using the fill handle with various selected values. The values in column A were typed in, and the values to the right of column A were extended by AutoFill using the fill handle.

Autofill

	A	B	C	D	E	F	G	H	I
1	1/1/95	1/2/95	1/3/95	1/4/95	1/5/95	1/6/95	1/7/95	1/8/95	
2	19:00	20:00	21:00	22:00	23:00	0:00	1:00	2:00	
3	1995	1996	1997	1998	1999	2000	2001	2002	
4	Qtr 1	Qtr 2	Qtr 3	Qtr 4	Qtr 1	Qtr 2	Qtr 3	Qtr 4	
5	Product 1	Product 2	Product 3	Product 4	Product 5	Product 6	Product 7	Product 8	
6	Mon	Tue	Wed	Thu	Fri	Sat	Sun	Mon	
7	Monday	Tuesday	Wednesday	Thursday	Friday	Saturday	Sunday	Monday	
8	Jan	Feb	Mar	Apr	May	Jun	Jul	Aug	
9	August	September	October	November	December	January	February	March	
10									

FIGURE 7-15
The values in columns B through H were extended by selecting the values in column A and dragging the fill handle to the right.

In Figure 7-16, columns A and B contain entries with different intervals, and columns C through H show how AutoFill can extrapolate a series based on a selected interval, even when text and numeric values are mixed in cells.

FIGURE 7-16
The values in columns C through H were extended using the intervals between the starting values in columns A and B.

Autofill

	A	B	C	D	E	F	G	H
1	1/1/95	1/5/95	1/9/95	1/13/95	1/17/95	1/21/95	1/25/95	1/29/95
2	19:00	19:30	20:00	20:30	21:00	21:30	22:00	22:30
3	1995	1997	1999	2001	2003	2005	2007	2009
4	Qtr 1	Qtr 4	Qtr 3	Qtr 2	Qtr 1	Qtr 4	Qtr 3	Qtr 2
5	Product 1	Product 4	Product 7	Product 10	Product 13	Product 16	Product 19	Product 22
6	Mon	Wed	Fri	Sun	Tue	Thu	Sat	Mon
7	Monday	Wednesday	Friday	Sunday	Tuesday	Thursday	Saturday	Monday
8	Jan	Apr	Jul	Oct	Jan	Apr	Jul	Oct
9	1 1/2	1 3/4	2	2 1/4	2 1/2	2 3/4	3	3 1/4
10								

AutoFill normally increments various date and time values when you drag the fill handle, even if you initially select only one cell. For example, if you select a cell that contains Qtr 1 or 1/1/94 and drag the fill handle, AutoFill extends the series as Qtr 2, Qtr 3, or 1/2/94, 1/3/94, and so on. But if you hold down Ctrl while you drag, the AutoFill feature is suppressed, and the selected values are simply copied to the adjacent cells.

Conversely, Excel normally copies a single selected value like 100 to adjacent cells when you drag the fill handle. But if you hold down Ctrl while you drag, Excel extends the series 100, 101, 102, and so on.

Sometimes you can double-click the fill handle to automatically extend a series from a selected range. AutoFill determines the size of the range by matching an adjacent range. For example, in Figure 7-14, we filled column A with a series of values. You can fill column B by simply entering series values in B1 and B2, and then selecting the range B1:B2 and double-clicking the fill handle. The newly created series stops at cell B6 to match the filled cells in column A. The result is shown in Figure 7-17.

FIGURE 7-17
We extended a series into B3:B6 by selecting B1:B2 and double-clicking the fill handle.

Book1

	A	B	C	D	E	F	G	H	I
1	10	30	50	70	90				
2	20	40	60	80	100				
3	30	50	50						
4	40	60	60						
5	50	70	50						
6	60	80	60						

When the selected cells contain something other than a series, such as simple text entries, double-clicking the fill handle copies the selected cells to the adjacent range. For example, if the range D1:D2 contained text and you double-clicked the fill handle, the text entries would be copied down through cell D6.

For more information about the Series command, see "The Series Command," page 269.

For more information about Date formats, see Chapter 12, "Dates and Times," page 459.

Dragging the Fill Handle with the Right Mouse Button

When you use the right mouse button to fill a range or extend a series, a shortcut menu appears when you release the button, as shown in Figure 7-18. You can use the commands on the shortcut menu to control the way ranges are filled or the way series are extended.

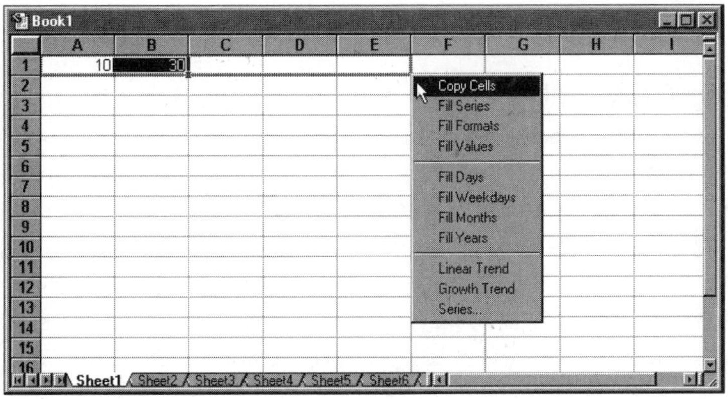

FIGURE 7-18

If you use the right mouse button to drag the fill handle, this shortcut menu appears when you release the button.

The Copy Cells command on the shortcut menu simply copies the selected, or source, cells — both contents and formats — to the destination range where you drag, repeating the pattern of the source cells as necessary. If in Figure 7-18 we choose the Fill Series command, the sequence of selected numbers is extended as if we had used the fill handle normally with the left mouse button. If we choose the Fill Formats command, only the formatting of the source cells is copied — the contents of the cells are not affected. If we choose the Fill Values command, on the other hand, the contents of the source cells are copied (or a series is extended, depending on the contents), but the formats of the source cells and the destination cells remain intact.

If the source cells contain dates, the Fill Days, Fill Weekdays, Fill Months, and Fill Years commands on the shortcut menu are made available, allowing you to extend a series where only the corresponding component of the date is incremented.

The Linear Trend command creates a simple linear trend series similar to that which is created by dragging the fill handle with the left mouse button. The Growth Trend command creates a simple nonlinear growth series, using the selected cells to extrapolate points along an exponential growth curve. In Figure 7-19, rows 3 through 6 in column A contain a series created with the Linear Trend command, and the same rows in column B contain a series created with the Growth Trend command.

When you choose the Series command, the Series dialog box appears, allowing you to create custom incremental series. The Series command is explained in more detail on page 269.

FIGURE 7-19
We created a linear trend series in column A and a growth trend series in column B.

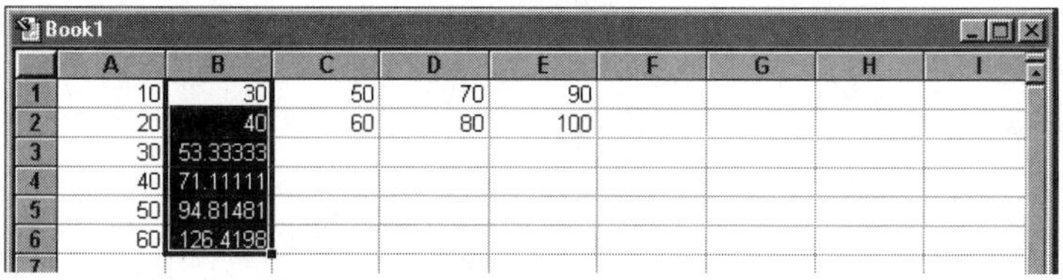

Book1

	A	B	C	D	E	F	G	H	I
1	10	30	50	70	90				
2	20	40	60	80	100				
3	30	53.33333							
4	40	71.11111							
5	50	94.81481							
6	60	126.4198							

Creating Custom Lists

If you find yourself repeatedly entering a particular sequence in your worksheets, such as a list of names, you can use Excel's Custom Lists feature to make entering that sequence as easy as dragging the mouse. After you've created the sequence, you can enter it in an adjacent range of cells by simply typing any item from the sequence in a cell and then dragging the fill handle.

For example, Figure 7-20 shows the single name we entered in cell A1 and the custom list we entered in cells A2:A5 by simply dragging the fill handle.

FIGURE 7-20
You can create custom lists that you can enter automatically by dragging the fill handle.

Autofill

	A	B	C
1	Vicki		

Autofill

	A	B	C
1	Vicki		
2	Max		
3	Mark		
4	Regina		
5	Mac		

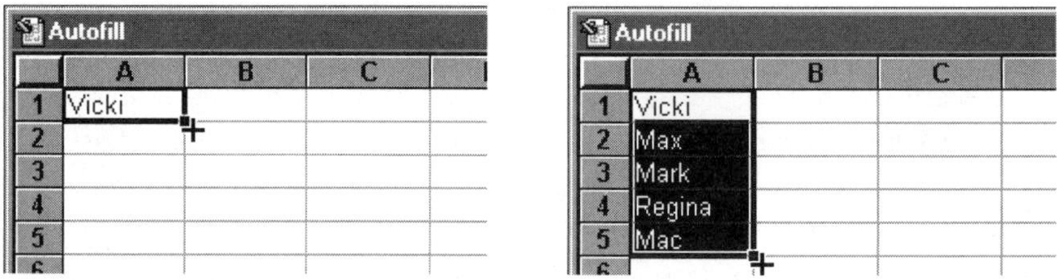

To create a custom list, follow these steps:

1. From the Tools Menu, choose Options and click the Custom Lists tab.
2. With NEW LIST selected in the Custom Lists list box, type the items you want to include in your list in the List Entries list box. Be sure to type the items in the order you want them to appear.
3. Click OK to return to the worksheet.

Importing Custom Lists

You can also create a custom list by importing the entries in an existing cell range. To import the entries shown in Figure 7-20, we first selected the range A1:A5 and clicked the Custom Lists tab of the Options dialog box. Then we clicked the Import button to add the selected entries as a new list, as shown in Figure 7-21. Then click OK to close the dialog box.

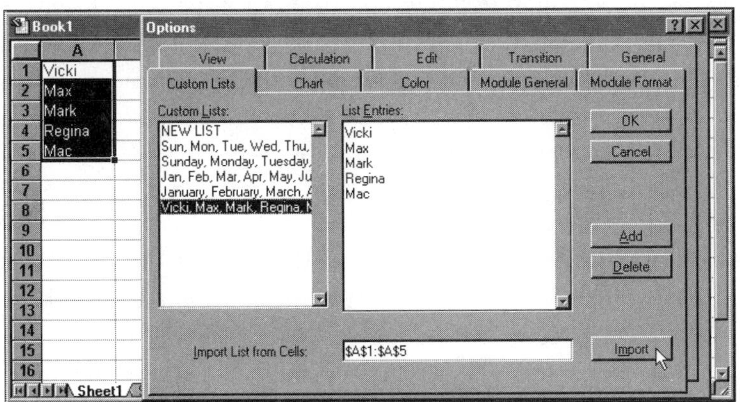

FIGURE 7-21
Use the Import buttons on the Custom Lists tab to define existing cell entries as custom lists.

Editing Directly in Cells

You can edit the contents of cells without using the formula bar. By double-clicking a cell, you can perform any normal formula-bar editing procedure directly in the cell. Figure 7-22 shows a cell that is being edited in this fashion.

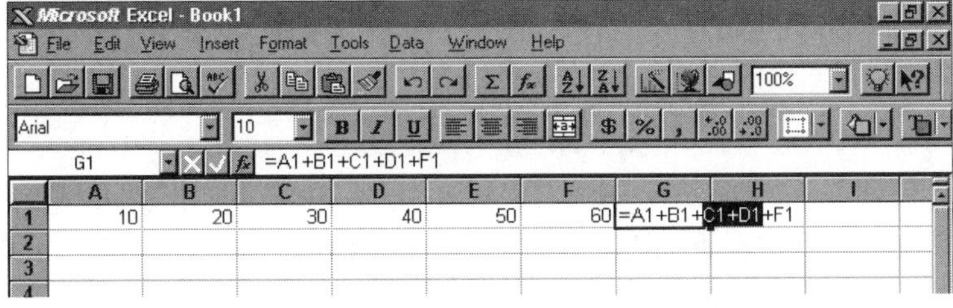

FIGURE 7-22
You can edit a cell directly in the worksheet by double-clicking the cell.

NOTE To edit directly in cells, the Edit Directly In Cell option must be selected. If this option, which is on by default, has been turned off, you can activate it by choosing the Options command from the Tools menu, clicking the Edit tab, and then selecting the Edit Directly In Cell option.

Undoing, Redoing, and Repeating Your Last Action

You can use the Undo command to recover from editing mistakes without having to reenter data or patch information back in place. To use this command, you must catch your mistake before you use another command or make an entry. Simply choose Undo from the Edit menu or press Ctrl-Z to reverse the previous action. You can also click the Undo button on the Standard toolbar.

Undo reverses the effect of most commands on the Edit menu and restores any entry in the formula bar. For example, if you accidentally delete a range of data, choose Undo to replace the entries. If you edit the contents of a cell and subsequently discover that your changes are incorrect, choose Undo to restore the original cell entry. In addition, you can use Undo to reverse formatting and many other types of commands.

The Undo command changes to indicate the action it's currently able to reverse. For example, suppose you choose the All command from the Clear submenu of the Edit menu to erase the contents of a range of cells and then discover that you have cleared the wrong range. If you catch your error before you choose another command or make an entry, you can choose the Undo Clear command from the Edit menu to correct the mistake. Likewise, if you enter a formula in a cell, the Edit menu displays Undo Entry.

Unfortunately, Excel has many commands that Undo can't reverse. After you choose one of these commands, Can't Undo appears dimmed on the Edit menu.

CAUTION A few commands are irreversible. For example, you cannot reverse Delete Sheet on the Edit menu. If you aren't sure whether you need a worksheet, activate it and look at it before you delete it. Similarly, you cannot reverse the Worksheet command on the Insert menu. Be sure to save your workbook before you use either of these commands. If you later find that you deleted or inserted worksheets in error, you can always retrieve your original workbook.

If you're working with a large range, Excel might not be able to undo your actions because not enough memory is available. For example, suppose you try to use the Cut and Paste commands to move all the cells in column A (cells A1:A16384) to column C (cells C1:C16384), and you see the alert message *Selection too large. Continue without Undo?* If you click OK, Excel disables Undo and attempts to carry out the operation (although successful completion of the task still isn't guaranteed). A better choice is to click Cancel and then move several smaller blocks of cells. By breaking the cut-and-paste operation into more manageable portions, you can achieve the desired effect and still have Undo available.

See Also For more information about the Cut and Paste commands, see "Cutting and Pasting," page 251.

Actions That Don't Affect Undo

As we mentioned earlier, you can undo an action only if you haven't used another command or made an entry. By the same token, you can perform certain tasks in the worksheet without affecting Undo. For instance, you can use the cell pointer and scroll bars to move through your worksheet and activate other cells. (After you activate a cell for editing, however, Undo becomes Can't Undo and is dimmed.) Also, commands that move the cell pointer do not affect Undo. For instance, you can use Go To and Find on the Edit menu without affecting Undo. And you can move to other worksheets and workbooks using commands or the mouse without affecting Undo.

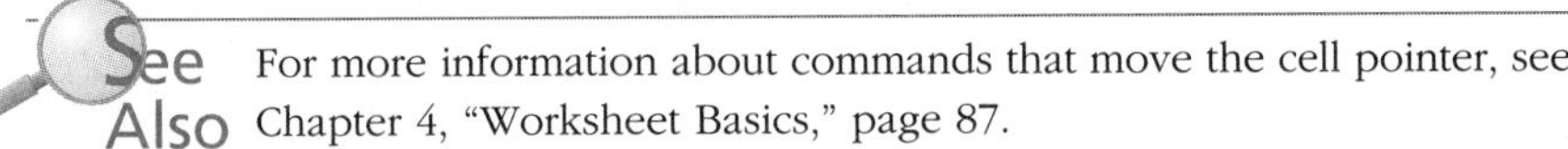
See Also For more information about commands that move the cell pointer, see Chapter 4, "Worksheet Basics," page 87.

Redoing What You've Undone

After you use Undo, the command name changes to Redo. Redo reverses Undo, restoring the worksheet to its condition before you used Undo. For example, when you pull down the Edit menu after you use Undo Clear, the command appears as Redo (u) Clear. (The underlined *u* that appears after the word *Redo* indicates that you can simply press Alt, then *e*, and then this letter to choose the command.) If you choose this command, Microsoft Excel again clears the contents of the selected range and changes the name back to Undo Clear.

The Undo button on the Standard toolbar essentially undoes Undo. It becomes a Redo button immediately after you undo an action.

You can take advantage of the Undo/Redo command to see the effects of an editing change in your worksheet. Suppose you edit a cell that is referenced in several formulas. To see the effects of your change, scroll through the worksheet and view the other cells. If you don't remember what a cell looked like before the change, you can use Undo and Redo to get a "before and after" view.

TIP An easy way to check out the before and after versions of a worksheet is to repeatedly click the Undo button on the Standard toolbar or press Ctrl-Z to toggle back and forth.

Repeating Your Last Action

You can use the Repeat command to repeat an action — a great time-saver when you need to perform the same action in several areas. Repeat is particularly handy with commands such as Insert and Delete, which you cannot perform on nonadjacent multiple cell or range selections.

Click the Repeat button on the Standard toolbar to repeat the last action.

In some ways, Repeat is similar to Undo. The name of the command changes to reflect your most recent action. For example, suppose you choose the Formats command from the Clear submenu of the Edit menu. When you pull down the Edit menu a second time, the Repeat command appears as Repeat Clear. If you select another cell or range and choose Repeat Clear or click the Repeat button, Microsoft Excel assumes that you want to perform the same action — clearing formats, in this case — on the new selection.

Unlike Undo, Repeat works with most commands. The only exceptions are those commands that can't logically be repeated. For example, if you save a file using the Save command on the File menu, you can't repeat the action. In this case, Repeat reflects the last repeatable command.

Using Editing Commands

While you can use direct cell manipulation, as described earlier in this chapter, to quickly and easily perform many common editing operations, menu commands sometimes offer advantages and additional functionality. This section describes Excel's editing commands and covers the rules and regulations that apply to editing operations.

Clearing Cell Contents and Formats

You can use the Clear commands on the Edit menu to erase the contents of a cell or range, the format assigned to that cell or range, or both. You can also use Clear with cell notes and charts.

The Clear submenu offers four commands: All, Formats, Contents, and Notes. The All command erases the contents of the selected cells, any formats (other than column width and row height), and any notes attached to those cells. The Formats command removes the formats from the selected cells but leaves their contents and notes in place; the selected cells then revert to the General format and the Normal style. The Contents command erases the contents of the selected cells but leaves their formats and notes intact. The Notes command removes any notes from the selected cells but leaves their contents and formats in place.

For example, to clear the contents of a cell or range, follow these steps:

1. Select the cell or range.
2. Choose Clear and then Contents from the Edit menu (or you can press the Del key).

The contents of the cell or range are immediately erased, but the formatting remains.

NOTE If you're working in the formula bar or editing directly in a cell, pressing Del erases the selected characters or the character to the right of the insertion point.

See Also For information about cell notes, see "Adding Notes to Cells," page 288.

Deleting Cells, Columns, and Rows

You can use the Delete command to remove cells from your worksheet. Unlike Clear, which erases the formats, contents, or notes in a cell but leaves the cell in place, Delete removes the selected cell or range from the worksheet. In other words, Clear works like an eraser, and Delete works like a pair of scissors.

Deleting Entire Columns and Rows

You can use the Delete command to remove entire columns and rows from your worksheet and to eliminate wasted space. For example, in the worksheet shown in Figure 7-23 on the next page, three blank rows appear between the last items in the lists in columns A through G and the totals in row 13. To delete these blank rows, drag through the row headings for rows 10, 11, and 12 and then choose Delete from the Edit menu.

FIGURE 7-23

Three extra rows appear above the totals row in this worksheet.

Magazine Sales

	A	B	C	D	E	F	G
1	Yellow Press Publishers: 1995 Sales						
5		Hopper's Bizarre	National Trash	Miz	Wall Street Jungle		Total
6	1st Qtr	$3,200.00	$3,932.00	$4,102.00	$2,310.00		$13,544.00
7	2nd Qtr	$4,501.00	$4,872.00	$5,432.00	$3,429.00		$18,234.00
8	3rd Qtr	$3,714.00	$4,321.00	$4,981.00	$3,012.00		$16,028.00
9	4th Qtr	$4,374.00	$5,012.00	$5,612.00	$3,001.00		$17,999.00
10							
11							
12							
13	Total	$15,789.00	$18,137.00	$20,127.00	$11,752.00		$65,805.00
14							
15					1994 Goal:	$80,000	
16					% of Goal:	82%	
17							

Sheet1 / Sheet2 / Sheet3 / Sheet4 / Sheet5 / Sheet6

As you can see in Figure 7-24, after you delete rows 10 through 12, every entry in the rows below the deleted rows is shifted upward so that the totals originally in row 13 now appear in row 10.

In addition, Excel adjusts the formulas in row 10 to account for the deleted rows. Before we deleted the extra rows, the formula in cell B13 (now in cell B10) was

=SUM(B6:B12)

FIGURE 7-24

When we delete rows 10 through 12, the remaining rows in the worksheet move up to fill the gap.

Magazine Sales

	A	B	C	D	E	F	G
1	Yellow Press Publishers: 1995 Sales						
5		Hopper's Bizarre	National Trash	Miz	Wall Street Jungle		Total
6	1st Qtr	$3,200.00	$3,932.00	$4,102.00	$2,310.00		$13,544.00
7	2nd Qtr	$4,501.00	$4,872.00	$5,432.00	$3,429.00		$18,234.00
8	3rd Qtr	$3,714.00	$4,321.00	$4,981.00	$3,012.00		$16,028.00
9	4th Qtr	$4,374.00	$5,012.00	$5,612.00	$3,001.00		$17,999.00
10	Total	$15,789.00	$18,137.00	$20,127.00	$11,752.00		$65,805.00
11							
12					1994 Goal:	$80,000	
13					% of Goal:	82%	
14							
15							
16							
17							

Sheet1 / Sheet2 / Sheet3 / Sheet4 / Sheet5 / Sheet6

However, cell B10 now contains the formula

=SUM(B6:B9)

You can also use Delete to remove columns. Simply select the column and choose Delete. Your column disappears from the worksheet, and all subsequent columns shift one column to the left. Again, Excel updates any formulas affected by the deletion.

You can't delete multiple selections in one operation. For example, if you select columns A and F and choose Delete, you'll see the alert message *Cannot use that command on multiple selections.*

Deleting Partial Columns and Rows

You can delete partial columns and rows — and even a single cell. Simply select the cell or cells and choose Delete.

For example, to delete cells F6:F10 from the worksheet in Figure 7-24 without changing the remaining cells in column F, select cells F6:F10 and then choose Delete from the Edit menu. Excel displays the dialog box in Figure 7-25. As you can see, Excel needs more information before it can carry out the Delete command. You can use the Delete dialog box to shift remaining cells left or up to fill the gap or to delete entire rows and columns. For this example, leave Shift Cells Left selected and click OK. Excel deletes only the selected range — F6:F10. Excel then adjusts the worksheet so that the cells in G6:G10 move to F6:F10, those in H6:H10 move to G6:G10, and so on. Figure 7-26 on the next page shows how the worksheet looks after this deletion. Note that Excel widens the column.

If you select F6:F10, choose Delete, and then select Shift Cells Up, Excel still removes only the range F6:F10. It then moves the remainder of column F — the entire range F11:F16384 — up five cells.

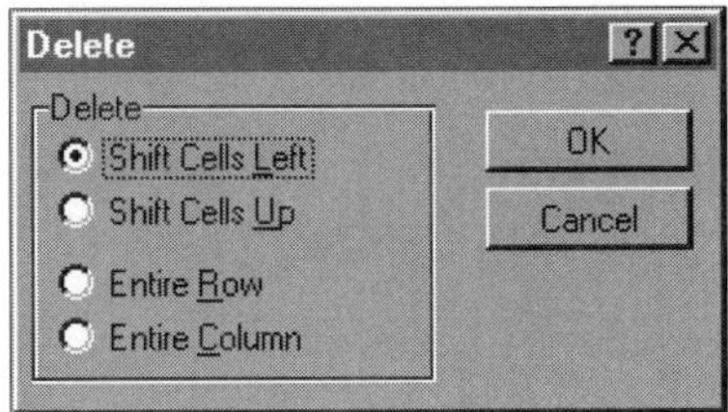

FIGURE 7-25
The Delete command deletes specific cells as well as entire rows and columns.

FIGURE 7-26
The Shift Cells Left option deleted cells F6:F10.

Magazine Sales

	A	B	C	D	E	F	G
1	Yellow Press Publishers: 1995 Sales						
5		Hopper's Bizarre	National Trash	Miz	Wall Street Jungle		Total
6	1st Qtr	$3,200.00	$3,932.00	$4,102.00	$2,310.00	$13,544.00	
7	2nd Qtr	$4,501.00	$4,872.00	$5,432.00	$3,429.00	$18,234.00	
8	3rd Qtr	$3,714.00	$4,321.00	$4,981.00	$3,012.00	$16,028.00	
9	4th Qtr	$4,374.00	$5,012.00	$5,612.00	$3,001.00	$17,999.00	
10	Total	$15,789.00	$18,137.00	$20,127.00	$11,752.00	$65,805.00	
12					1994 Goal:	$80,000	
13					% of Goal:	82%	

Sheet1 / Sheet2 / Sheet3 / Sheet4 / Sheet5 / Sheet6

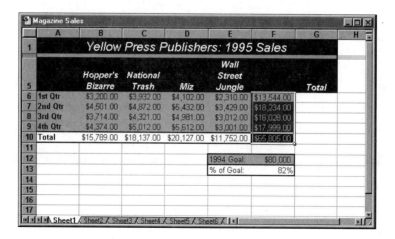

When you delete a partial row or column, it's easy to misalign data. For example, in Figure 7-26, the label *Total* in column G did not move left with the other data in that column. As a result, the heading for the data in column F now appears in the wrong column. We could have avoided this problem by deleting cells F1:F10 instead of F6:F10 as shown in Figure 7-27.

TIP Although you can generally use Undo to cancel a deletion, you should take heed of the following:

First, before you delete an entire column or row, scroll through your worksheet to be sure you're not erasing important information that is not currently visible.

Second, if you delete a cell upon which formulas in other cells depend, a *#REF!* error message appears in those formulas. Deleting cells that are referred to by formulas can be disastrous. You can use Undo to correct this problem, but only if you catch the error before you choose another command or make an entry.

Third, when you delete a column or row referred to by an argument of a function, Excel modifies the argument, if at all possible, to account for the deletion. This adaptability is a compelling reason to use functions instead of formulas where possible.

	A	B	C	D	E	F
1	Yellow Press Publishers: 1995 Sales					
5		Hopper's Bizarre	National Trash	Miz	Wall Street Jungle	Total
6	1st Qtr	$3,200.00	$3,932.00	$4,102.00	$2,310.00	$13,544.00
7	2nd Qtr	$4,501.00	$4,872.00	$5,432.00	$3,429.00	$18,234.00
8	3rd Qtr	$3,714.00	$4,321.00	$4,981.00	$3,012.00	$16,028.00
9	4th Qtr	$4,374.00	$5,012.00	$5,612.00	$3,001.00	$17,999.00
10	Total	$15,789.00	$18,137.00	$20,127.00	$11,752.00	$65,805.00
12					1994 Goal:	$80,000
13					% of Goal:	82%

FIGURE 7-27
Another column needs to be inserted in this worksheet.

Inserting Columns and Rows

You can use the commands on the Insert menu to add cells, columns, and rows to a worksheet. For example, suppose that after you've made adjustments and put the finishing touches on the worksheet shown in Figure 7-27, you discover that the company has acquired another magazine, whose sales figures are to be combined with the others. (Guess you should have left that extra column after all.) Fortunately, with the Columns command on the Insert menu, you can fix things up in a hurry without a lot of shuffling and recalculation.

To insert space for the new magazine, simply select a column heading, column F in this case, and choose the Columns command from the Insert menu. The contents of column F move to column G, leaving the inserted column F blank and ready for new information, as shown in Figure 7-28.

	A	B	C	D	E	F	G
1	Yellow Press Publishers: 1995 Sales						
5		Hopper's Bizarre	National Trash	Miz	Wall Street Jungle		Total
6	1st Qtr	$3,200.00	$3,932.00	$4,102.00	$2,310.00		$13,544.00
7	2nd Qtr	$4,501.00	$4,872.00	$5,432.00	$3,429.00		$18,234.00
8	3rd Qtr	$3,714.00	$4,321.00	$4,981.00	$3,012.00		$16,028.00
9	4th Qtr	$4,374.00	$5,012.00	$5,612.00	$3,001.00		$17,999.00
10	Total	$15,789.00	$18,137.00	$20,127.00	$11,752.00		$65,805.00
12					1994 Goal:		$80,000
13					% of Goal:		82%

FIGURE 7-28
The Columns command on the Insert menu added a column for a new magazine.

The newly inserted cells take on the same formats as the cells in the column to the left, and the formulas in cells G6:G13 are adjusted to account for the expanded range.

Similarly, to insert a row, select the row above which you want the new row inserted and choose the Rows command from the Insert menu. You can also insert cells rather than entire rows or columns by choosing the Cells command on the Insert menu, which displays the dialog box shown in Figure 7-29.

The Insert and Delete Buttons

Excel provides six buttons for inserting and deleting. These buttons are not located on any toolbar, so to use them you must either create a custom toolbar or modify an existing toolbar. If you do a lot of inserting and deleting, you might want to create an Insert/Delete custom toolbar, containing all six tools, like the one shown below.

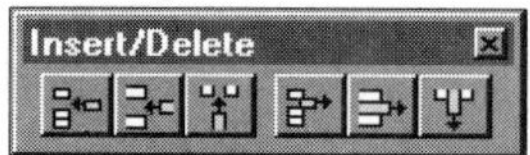

The buttons are, from left to right, Insert, Insert Row, Insert Column, Delete, Delete Row, and Delete Column. (For information about how to create custom toolbars, see Chapter 2, "Toolbars and Buttons," page 33.)

You won't see the Insert or Delete dialog box when you use the Insert or Delete button. Instead, Excel uses common-sense rules to determine the direction in which to shift the surrounding cells. If the selection is wider than it is tall, (2 cells wide by 1 cell high, for example), the Insert button automatically shifts cells down, and the Delete button shifts cells up.

Using the Insert Row, Insert Column, Delete Row, and Delete Column buttons is equivalent to selecting the Entire Row or Entire Column options in the Insert and Delete dialog boxes. You need not first select entire rows or columns to use these buttons. Instead, simply select one or more cells below each row or to the right of each column you want to insert, or select one or more cells in each row or column you want to delete.

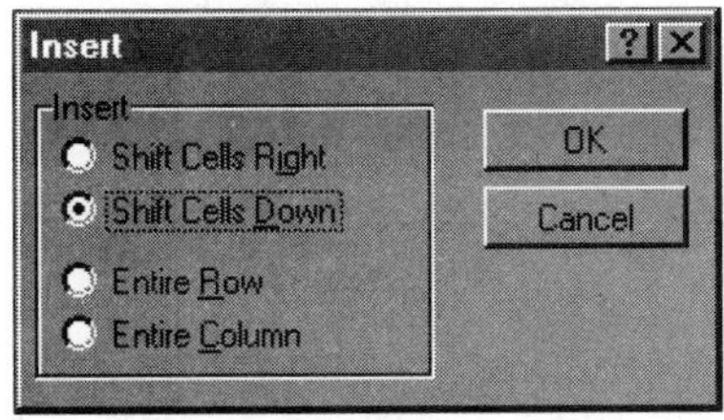

FIGURE 7-29
The Cells command on the Insert menu displays this dialog box.

The options in the Insert dialog box are similar to those in the Delete dialog box shown earlier in Figure 7-25. However, when a cell is inserted in a worksheet, the remaining cells (or columns) shift to the right, rather than the left, or the remaining cells (or rows) move down, rather than up. You can also use the options in the Insert dialog box to add entire rows or columns to your worksheet.

If you recently used the Cut or Copy command to transfer some information from your workbook to the Windows *Clipboard* (an area of memory that holds data temporarily), the Cells command on the Insert menu is replaced by the Cut Cells or the Copied Cells command. You can use either of these commands to simultaneously insert the necessary number of cells and paste the contents of the Clipboard into the new cells. To insert blank cells under these circumstances, first press Esc to clear the Clipboard's contents and then open the Insert menu. The Cells command reappears.

As with the Delete command, you can't choose a multiple nonadjacent selection when you use the Insert command. If you attempt to do so, you'll see the alert message *Cannot use that command on multiple selections.*

See Also

For more information about the Cut and Copy commands, see "Cutting and Pasting," page 251.

For more information about inserting cut cells, see "Inserting Cut Cells," page 254.

Cutting and Pasting

You can use the Cut and Paste commands on the Edit menu to move entries and formats from one place to another. Unlike Delete and Clear, which remove cells and cell entries, the Cut command puts a dotted-line *marquee* around the selected cells and places a copy of your selection on the Clipboard, which stores it so that you can paste it in another location.

When you select the range to which you want to move the cut cells, the Paste command places them in their new location, clears the contents of the cells within the marquee, and removes the marquee.

TIP Keyboard shortcuts are available for the Cut and Paste commands. You can press Ctrl-X for the Cut command and Ctrl-V for the Paste command. Alternatively, you can click the Cut and Paste buttons on the Standard toolbar to execute these commands. You can also use the mouse to cut and paste cells and cell ranges directly. For more information about cutting and pasting with the mouse, see "Shortcuts for Entering and Editing," page 231.

When you use the Cut and Paste commands to move a range of cells, Excel clears both the contents and the formats of the cut range and transfers them to the cells in the paste range. For example, to move the contents of the range A1:A5 in Figure 7-30 to cells C1:C5, select cells A1:A5 and then choose Cut from the Edit menu. A marquee appears around the cells you selected, as shown in Figure 7-30. Next select cell C1 and choose Paste from the Edit menu. Figure 7-31 shows the result: Both the contents and the formats assigned to cells A1:A5 are transferred to cells C1:C5, and cells A1:A5 are blank. Now if you enter values in cells A1:A5, those cells revert to their default formats.

FIGURE 7-30
Use the Cut and Paste commands to move the contents of the range A1:A5 to cells C1:C5.

Cut and Paste

	A	B	C	D	E	F	G	H	I
1	$10	$20		$30					
2	$20	$30		$40					
3	$30	$40		$50					
4	$40	$50		$60					
5	$100	$140		$180					
6									
7									

When you move a cell, Excel adjusts any formulas outside the cut area that refer to that cell. For example, in Figure 7-30, cell A5 contains the formula

=SUM(A1:A4)

When we moved cells A1:A5 to cells C1:C5 (Figure 7-31), the move had no apparent effect on the cell contents. However, the formula in cell C5 now reads

=SUM(C1:C4)

FIGURE 7-31
The contents and formats of cells A1:A5 now appear in cells C1:C5.

Cut and Paste

	A	B	C	D	E	F	G	H	I
1		$20	$10	$30					
2		$30	$20	$40					
3		$40	$30	$50					
4		$50	$40	$60					
5		$140	$100	$180					
6									
7									

Cut and Paste Rules

When you use the Cut and Paste commands, remember the following rules:

- The cut area you select must be a single rectangular block of cells. If you try to select more than one range, you'll see the message *Cannot use that command on multiple selections.*
- You can paste only once after you use Cut. To paste the selected data in two or more locations, use the Copy command. You can then use the commands on the Clear submenu to erase the contents of the original cell or range.
- You don't have to select the entire paste range before you choose Paste. When you select a single cell as your paste range, Excel extends the paste area to match the size and shape of the cut area. The cell you select becomes the upper left corner of the paste area. If you do select the entire paste area, however, be sure the range you select is the same size and shape as the cut area. If the cut and paste areas are not identical in size and shape, an alert box appears, displaying the message *Cut and paste areas are different shapes.* To correct the problem, click OK in the alert box and select a new paste area.
- Excel overwrites the contents and formats of any existing cells in the paste range when you use Paste. If you don't want to lose existing cell entries, be sure your worksheet has enough blank cells below and to the right of the cell you select as the upper left corner of the paste area to hold the entire cut area.

Using Overlapping Cut and Paste Ranges

Suppose you want to move cells A1:B5 in the worksheet on the left in Figure 7-32 to cells B1:C5 to fill the empty column C. You could select cells A1:A5 and choose the Columns command from the Insert menu, but then all the cells in rows 1 through 5 would shift one column to the right.

Fortunately, Excel offers a way around this problem. Because Excel transfers the contents of your cut area to your paste area before it erases them from the cut area, you can specify overlapping cut and paste areas without losing information in the overlapping cells.

In the worksheet on the left in Figure 7-32, shown on the next page, if you select cells A1:B5 as your cut area and cells B1:C5 as your paste area, the entries in A1:B5 move as you expect, but the entries to the right of column C in rows 1 through 5 do not move. The worksheet on the right in Figure 7-32 shows the result.

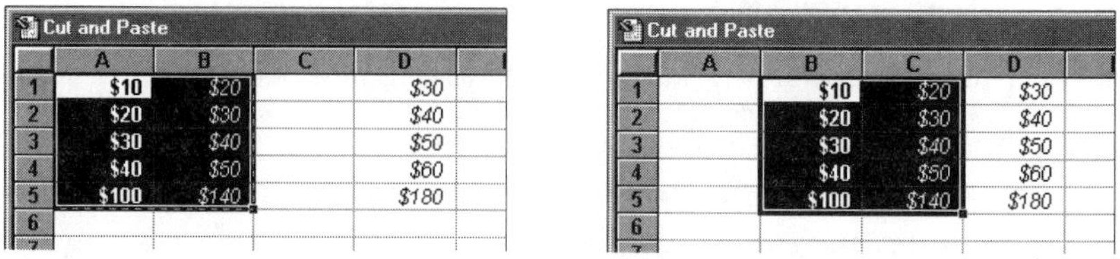

FIGURE 7-32

You can use overlapping cut and paste areas when moving information.

Cut and Paste

	A	B	C	D
1	$10	$20		$30
2	$20	$30		$40
3	$30	$40		$50
4	$40	$50		$60
5	$100	$140		$180
6				

Cut and Paste

	A	B	C	D
1		$10	$20	$30
2		$20	$30	$40
3		$30	$40	$50
4		$40	$50	$60
5		$100	$140	$180
6				

Inserting Cut Cells

When you use the Paste command, Excel pastes cut cells into the selected area of your worksheet. If the selected area already contains data, that data is replaced by the data that you paste.

Under some circumstances, you can insert material from the Clipboard *between* existing worksheet cells instead of pasting it *over* existing cells. To do this, use the Insert menu's Cut Cells command instead of the Edit menu's Paste command. The Cut Cells command replaces the Cells command and appears only after you have cut data to the Clipboard. (You can also use the mouse to perform this operation on cells and cell ranges directly. See "Shortcuts for Entering and Editing," page 231.)

For example, to rearrange the names of the months shown in Figure 7-33 so that they start with September and end with August, follow these steps:

1. Select A10:A13 and choose Cut from the Edit menu.
2. Make A2 the active cell.
3. From the Insert menu, choose Cut Cells.

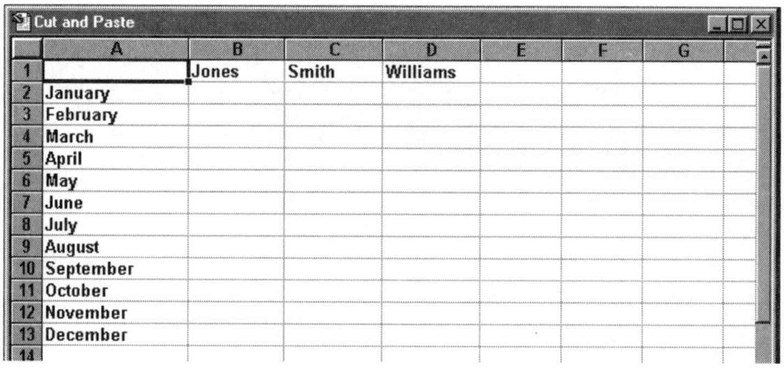

FIGURE 7-33

We want to rearrange the sequence of months in this worksheet.

Cut and Paste

	A	B	C	D	E	F	G
1		Jones	Smith	Williams			
2	January						
3	February						
4	March						
5	April						
6	May						
7	June						
8	July						
9	August						
10	September						
11	October						
12	November						
13	December						
14							

Excel puts the data from A10:A13 in cells A2:A5 and then moves the rest of column A down to accommodate the insertion, as shown in Figure 7-34.

Cut and Paste

	A	B	C	D	E	F	G
1		Jones	Smith	Williams			
2	September						
3	October						
4	November						
5	December						
6	January						
7	February						
8	March						
9	April						
10	May						
11	June						
12	July						
13	August						
14							

FIGURE 7-34
Using the Cut command on the Edit menu with the Cut Cells command on the Insert menu, we transferred four months from the bottom of the list without changing the rest.

For more information about using the mouse to insert cut cells, see "Shortcuts for Entering and Editing," page 231.

Copying and Pasting

You can use the Copy and Paste commands on the Edit menu to duplicate the contents and formats of selected cells in another area of your worksheet without disturbing the contents of the original cells. You use the Copy command (or the Copy button on the Standard toolbar) to indicate the range of cells you want to copy, and you use the Paste command (or the Paste button on the Standard toolbar) to indicate where you want the copies to be placed. You can also press the Enter key instead of choosing the Paste command, but only if you want to paste just a single copy. Pressing Enter after you choose Copy pastes one copy and then removes the copied cells from the Clipboard.

You can also use the mouse to copy and paste cells and cell ranges directly in your worksheet.

The Paste command pastes everything from the copied cells — entries, formats, and notes. To paste only certain elements, use the Paste Special command.

For more information about copying and pasting with the mouse, see "Shortcuts for Entering and Editing," page 231.

For more information about the Paste Special command, see "Selective Pasting," page 263.

Copying a Single Cell

Suppose cell A1 of your worksheet contains the value 100. To copy the contents of cell A1 to cell C1, follow these steps:

1. Select cell A1.
2. Choose Copy from the Edit menu or click the Copy button on the Standard toolbar. A marquee appears around the selected cell.
3. Select cell C1.
4. Choose Paste from the Edit menu or click the Paste button on the Standard toolbar.

The marquee around cell A1 does not disappear after you use Paste. This marquee indicates that the copy area is still active. As long as the marquee appears, you can continue to use Paste to create additional copies of the cell. You can even use the commands on the Window menu and the Open and New commands on the File menu to access other workbooks and windows without losing your copy area. For example, you might copy a cell to another area of your worksheet, use the Open command on the File menu to access a second workbook, and then paste the cell into the new workbook as well. To finish pasting and remove the contents of the copy area from the Clipboard, press Enter, or press Esc to abort the operation.

By specifying paste areas of different sizes and shapes, you can create multiple copies of the contents of the copy area. For example, if you specify the range C1:E2 as the paste range, Excel copies the contents of cell A1 to all the cells in the range C1:E2, as shown in Figure 7-35.

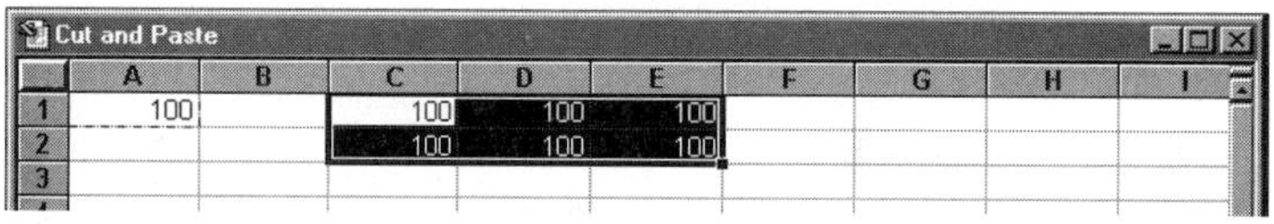

Cut and Paste

	A	B	C	D	E	F	G	H	I
1	100		100	100	100				
2			100	100	100				
3									

FIGURE 7-35

You can create multiple copies of a single cell.

You can also specify multiple nonadjacent paste areas. For example, to copy the contents of cell A1 to cells C1, C3, and D2, follow these steps:

1. Select cell A1.
2. Choose Copy from the Edit menu or click the Copy button.
3. Select cell C1 and then hold down Ctrl and click cells D2 and C3.

4. Choose Paste from the Edit menu or click the Paste button.

   Your worksheet now looks like the one shown in Figure 7-36.

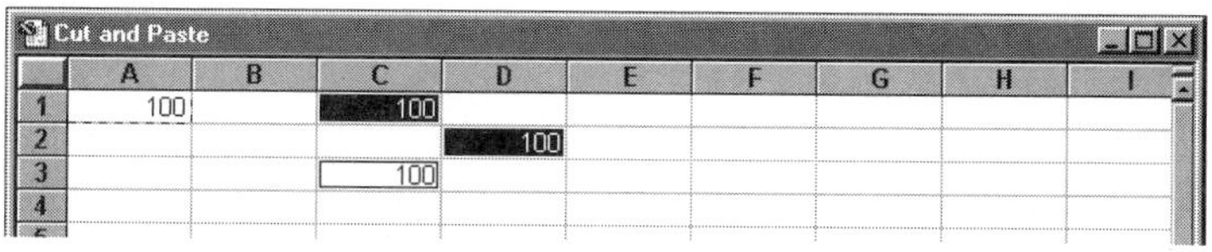

FIGURE 7-36

You can select multiple nonadjacent paste areas.

Copying Ranges

You can use the Copy command to copy ranges as well as single cells. For example, to copy the contents of cells A1:A3 to cells C1:C3, follow these steps:

1. Select cells A1:A3 and choose the Copy command or click the Copy button. A marquee appears around the range of cells to be copied.
2. Select cell C1 and choose the Paste command or click the Paste button.

As with the Cut and Paste commands, you don't have to select the entire paste area when you copy a range of cells. You need only indicate the upper left corner of the range by selecting a single cell.

The marquee remains active. You can continue to paste the contents of the copy area into new paste areas until you press Enter or Esc. Pressing Enter or Esc turns off the marquee and clears the contents of the copy area from the Clipboard.

You can also create multiple copies of the copy range. For example, you can select C1:D1 as the paste range to create two copies of A1:A3, side by side, in columns C and D. You can achieve the same result by selecting the range C1:D3. Not every paste range works when you're copying cell ranges, however. For example, if you copy cells A1:A3 and then designate the range C1:C2, C1:D2, C1:C4, or C1:E5, the alert message *Copy and paste areas are different shapes* appears. In other words, you must either select only the first cell in each paste area or select one or more paste ranges of exactly the same size and shape as the copy area.

Inserting Copied Cells

When you use the Paste command, Excel pastes copied cells into the selected area of your worksheet. If the selected area already contains data, that data is replaced by the data that you paste.

With the help of the Copied Cells command on the Insert menu, you can insert material from the Clipboard *between* existing worksheet cells, instead of pasting it *over* existing cells. The Copied Cells command appears only after you have copied data to the Clipboard.

The Copied Cells command works the same way as the Cut Cells command. If Excel needs more information about how to adjust the worksheet, it will present a dialog box similar to the one shown earlier in Figure 7-29. Select either Shift Cells Right or Shift Cells Down and then click OK to finish the operation.

You can also use the mouse to insert copied cells and cell ranges directly in your worksheet.

See Also For more information about inserting cut cells, see "Inserting Cut Cells," page 254.

For more information about using the mouse to insert copied cells, see "Shortcuts for Entering and Editing," page 231.

Copying Relative, Absolute, and Mixed References

As you learned in Chapter 5, Excel uses two types of cell references: relative and absolute. These two types of references behave very differently when you use the Copy command.

Relative References When you copy a cell that contains relative cell references, the formula in the paste area doesn't refer to the same cells as the formula in the copy area. Instead, Excel changes the formula references in relation to the position of the pasted cell.

Returning to a worksheet like the one shown earlier in Figure 7-27 (on page 249), suppose you enter the formula

=AVERAGE(B6:E6)

in cell G6. This formula averages the values in the four-cell range that begins five columns to the left of cell G6. Of course, you want to repeat this calculation for the remaining categories as well. Instead of typing a new formula in each cell in column G, select cell G6 and choose Copy from the Edit menu. Next select cells G7:G10 and choose Paste from the Edit menu. The results are shown in Figure 7-37. Because the formula in cell G6 contains a relative reference, Excel adjusts the references in each copy of the formula. As a result, each copy of the formula calculates the average of the cells in the corresponding row. For example, cell G7 contains the formula

=AVERAGE(B7:E7)

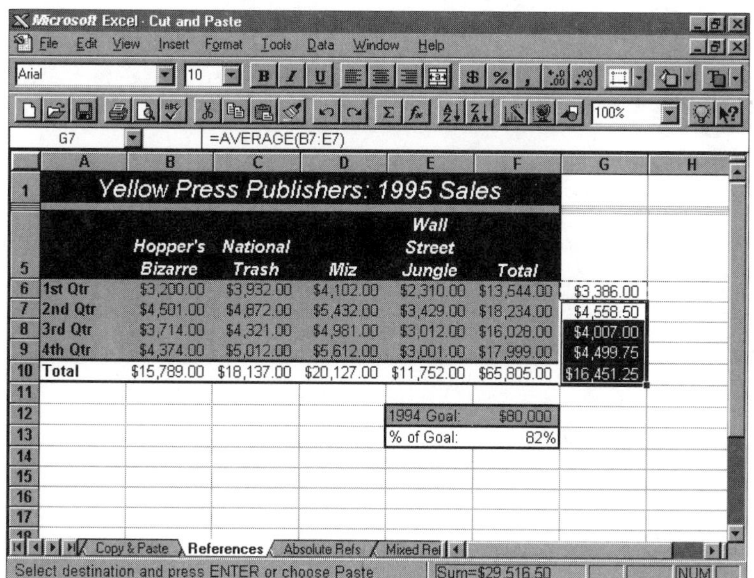

	A	B	C	D	E	F	G
1	Yellow Press Publishers: 1995 Sales						
5		Hopper's Bizarre	National Trash	Miz	Wall Street Jungle	Total	
6	1st Qtr	$3,200.00	$3,932.00	$4,102.00	$2,310.00	$13,544.00	$3,386.00
7	2nd Qtr	$4,501.00	$4,872.00	$5,432.00	$3,429.00	$18,234.00	$4,558.50
8	3rd Qtr	$3,714.00	$4,321.00	$4,981.00	$3,012.00	$16,028.00	$4,007.00
9	4th Qtr	$4,374.00	$5,012.00	$5,612.00	$3,001.00	$17,999.00	$4,499.75
10	Total	$15,789.00	$18,137.00	$20,127.00	$11,752.00	$65,805.00	$16,451.25
12					1994 Goal:	$80,000	
13					% of Goal:	82%	

FIGURE 7-37
We copied the relative references from cell G6 to cells G7:G10.

Absolute References To ensure that cell references do not change when you copy them, use absolute references.

For example, in the worksheet in Figure 7-38, cell B2 contains the hourly rate at which employees are to be paid, and cell C5 contains the formula

=B2*B5

	A	B	C
2	Hourly Rate	15.75	
4	*Name*	*Hours Worked*	*Wages Due*
5	Johnson	27	$425
6	Smith	32	
7	Trent	40	
8	Watson	29	

FIGURE 7-38
The entry in cell C5 is a formula that contains relative references.

Suppose you want to copy the formula in C5 to the range C6:C8. Figure 7-39 shows what happens if you copy the existing formula to this range. The formula in cell C6 returns the value 0, and cell C7 contains the #VALUE! error value. If you take a closer look at the formulas in cells C6:C8, you'll see that none of them refers to cell B2. For instance, the formula in cell C6 is

=B3*B6

FIGURE 7-39
We incorrectly copied the relative formula in cell C5 to cells C6:C8.

	A	B	C
1			
2	Hourly Rate	15.75	
3			
4	*Name*	*Hours Worked*	*Wages Due*
5	Johnson	27	$425
6	Smith	32	$0
7	Trent	40	#VALUE!
8	Watson	29	$783

Because cell B3 is empty, the formula returns a 0 value. Similarly, cell C7 contains the formula

=B4*B7

Because cell B4 contains a label rather than a value, the formula in cell C7 returns an error value.

Because the reference to cell B2 in the original formula is relative, it changes as you copy the formula to other cells in the worksheet. To apply the wage rate in cell B2 to all the calculations, you must change the reference to cell B2 to an absolute reference before you copy the formula.

You can change the reference style by activating the formula bar and typing a dollar sign ($) in front of the column and row references or by using the F4 key. The $ symbol tells Excel to "lock in" the reference. For example, in the worksheet in Figure 7-38, you can select cell C5 and type dollar signs before the B and the 2. The formula becomes

=$B$2*B5

TIP You can adjust references in a formula by placing the insertion point anywhere adjacent to the reference and pressing F4. Each time you press F4, Excel switches the nearest reference to the next type.

When you copy the modified formula to cells C6:C8, the second cell reference, but not the first, is adjusted within each formula. In Figure 7-40, cell C6 now contains the formula

=$B$2*B6

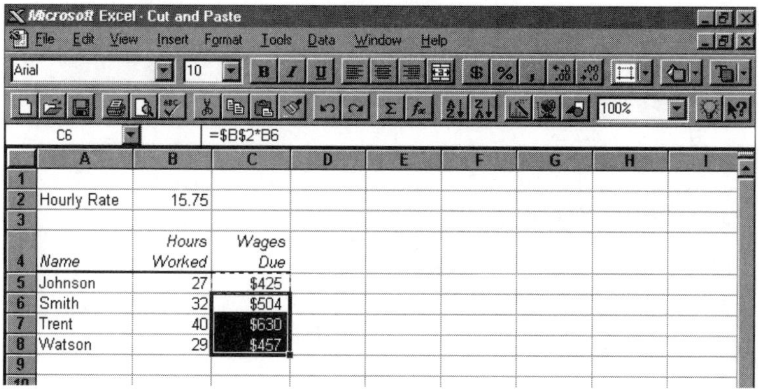

FIGURE 7-40
We created an absolute reference to cell B2.

Mixed References You can also use mixed references in your formulas to anchor only a portion of a cell reference. In a mixed reference, one portion is absolute and the other is relative. When you copy a mixed reference, Excel anchors the absolute portion and adjusts the relative portion to reflect the location of the cell to which you copied the formula.

In a mixed reference, a dollar sign appears before the absolute portion. For example, $B2 and B$2 are mixed references. Whereas $B2 uses an absolute column reference and a relative row reference, B$2 uses a relative column reference and an absolute row reference. To create a mixed reference, type the $ symbol in front of the column or row reference, or use the F4 key to cycle through the four combinations of absolute and relative references — from B2 to $B$2 to B$2 to $B2.

The loan payment table in Figure 7-41 on the next page shows a situation in which mixed references are convenient. Cell C5 uses the formula

= –PMT($B5,10,C$4)

to calculate the annual payments on a $10,000 loan over a period of 10 years at an interest rate of 7 percent. We copied this formula to cells C5:E8 to calculate payments on three loan amounts using four interest rates.

The first cell reference, $B5, indicates that we always want to refer to the values in column B. The row reference remains relative, however, so that the copied formulas in rows 6 through 8 refer to the appropriate interest rates in cells B6 through B8. Similarly, the second cell reference, C$4, indicates that we always want to refer to the loan amounts displayed in row 4. In this case, the column reference remains relative so that the copied formulas in columns C through E refer to the appropriate loan amounts in cells C4 through E4. For example, cell E8 contains the formula

= –PMT($B8,10,E$4)

FIGURE 7-41

This loan payment table uses formulas that contain mixed references.

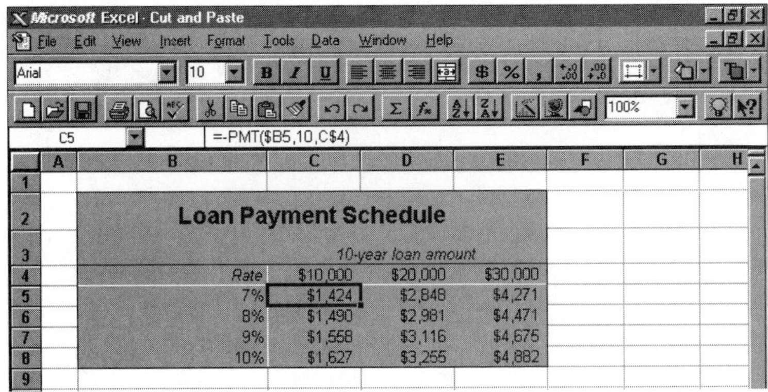

Without mixed references, we would have to edit the formula manually for each column or row of the calculations in cells C5 through E8.

Using Cut, Copy, Paste, and Clear in the Formula Bar

You can also use Cut, Copy, Paste, and Clear to edit entries in the formula bar. Often, simply reentering a value or formula is easier, but the Edit menu commands are convenient when you're working with a long, complex formula or label. For example, to add another *very* to the label

This is a very, very long label.

place the insertion point to the left of the space before the word *long,* type a comma and a space, and then type the word *very*. Alternatively, you can follow these steps:

1. Select the first instance of the word *very,* the comma, and the space after the comma in the formula bar.
2. Choose the Copy command from the Edit menu or click the Copy button on the Standard toolbar.
3. Place the insertion point in front of the *v* in the second *very*.
4. Choose the Paste command from the Edit menu or click the Paste button on the Standard toolbar.
5. Press Enter to lock in the revised entry.

   Your label now reads

   This is a very, very, very long label.

You can also use this capability to copy all or part of a formula from one cell to another. For example, suppose cell A10 contains the formula

=IF(NPV(.15,A1:A9)>0,A11,A12)

and you want to enter

=NPV(.15,A1:A9)

in cell B10. Follow these steps:

1. Select cell A10.
2. In the formula bar, select the characters you want to copy — in this case, NPV(.15,A1:A9).
3. Choose Copy from the Edit menu (or click the Copy button) and then press Enter or Esc.
4. Select cell B10, type = to begin a formula, and choose Paste from the Edit menu (or click the Paste button).

The formula's cell references are not adjusted when you cut, copy, and paste in the formula bar.

Selective Pasting

At times, you might want to move or copy the value in a cell without carrying over the underlying formula on which the value is based. Or you might want to copy the formula but not the format of a cell. The Paste Special command on the Edit menu offers a convenient way to paste only certain elements of a copied cell.

For example, cell F4 in Figure 7-42 contains the formula

=AVERAGE(B4:E4)

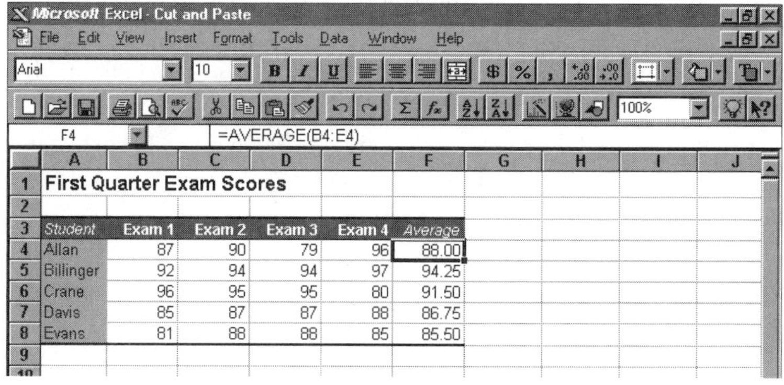

FIGURE 7-42

We want to use the value from cell F4 in cell G4.

To use the value from cell F4 in cell G4 without copying the actual formula from cell F4 to the new location, follow these steps:

1. Select cell F4 and choose Copy from the Edit menu or click the Copy button on the Standard toolbar. (You must choose Copy to use Paste Special. When you choose Cut, Paste Special is dimmed.)
2. Select cell G4 and choose Paste Special from the Edit menu.
3. In the Paste Special dialog box, shown in Figure 7-43, select the Values option and click OK.
4. Press Esc to clear the marquee and clear the clipboard.

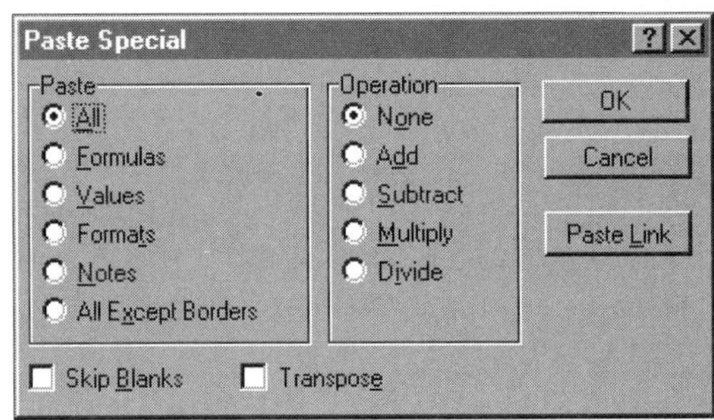

FIGURE 7-43
The Paste Special dialog box lets you paste formulas, values, formats, or notes.

When you select the Values option in the Paste Special dialog box, Excel pastes only the value of the formula in cell F4 into cell G4. After the operation is complete, cell G4 contains the number 88. Excel does not paste the formula or the format of the original cell, so if you later change any of the values in cells B4:E4, the value in cell G4 will remain unchanged.

The Formulas option transfers only the formulas from the cells in the copy range to the cells in the paste range. Any formats or notes in the paste range remain unaffected.

The Formats option transfers only the formats in the cells in the copy range to the paste range. This option has the same effect as selecting a range of cells and choosing the appropriate commands from the Format menu. For example, in Figure 7-42, cells A3:A8 are formatted with several border and font formats; cells H3:H8 are unformatted. If you copy cells A3:A8 and paste their formats into cells H3:H8 using the Formats option in the Paste Special dialog box, the worksheet looks like Figure 7-44. The formats in the copied cells have been pasted into cells H3:H8, but the contents have not.

Sometimes you might want to copy cells from one place to another, but you don't want to disturb the borders you spent so much time applying. The All Except Borders option makes this easy.

Cut and Paste

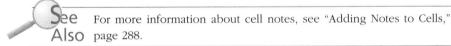

	A	B	C	D	E	F	G	H	I
1	First Quarter Exam Scores								
2									
3	Student	Exam 1	Exam 2	Exam 3	Exam 4	Average			
4	Allan	87	90	79	96	88.00			
5	Billinger	92	94	94	97	94.25			
6	Crane	96	95	95	80	91.50			
7	Davis	85	87	87	88	86.75			
8	Evans	81	88	88	85	85.50			
9									

FIGURE 7-44
Only the formats of cells A3:A8 are pasted into cells H3:H8 using the Formats option in the Paste Special dialog box.

TIP You can quickly copy and paste formats from a single cell or from a range of cells using the Format Painter button on the Standard toolbar. For more information about the Format Painter button, see "Formatting with Toolbars," page 159.

The All option pastes the formulas, values, formats, and cell notes from the copy range into the paste range. Because selecting All has the same effect as selecting Paste, you may wonder why Excel offers this option. That question brings us to our next topic — the Operation options.

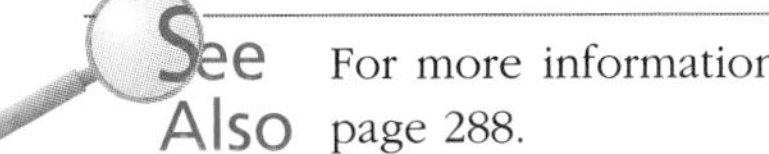

See Also For more information about cell notes, see "Adding Notes to Cells," page 288.

The Operation Options

You use the options in the Operation section of the Paste Special dialog box to mathematically combine the contents of the copy area with the contents of the paste area. When you select any option other than None, Excel does not overwrite the paste range. Instead, it uses the specified operator to combine the copy and paste ranges. For example, say we want to calculate each student's final score. We'll need to add the average exam scores and bonus points in columns F and G of Figure 7-45. To combine the contents of these two areas, follow these steps:

1. Select cells F4:F8 and choose Copy from the Edit menu.

2. Select cell H4 and choose Paste Special from the Edit menu.
3. Select the Values option and click OK in the Paste Special dialog box to paste only the values in cells F4:F8 into cells H4:H8. (Because the pasted cells are still selected, you can now use the Cells command on the Format menu to apply the Number format.)
4. Select the range G4:G8 and choose Copy again.
5. Select cell H4 and choose Paste Special.
6. In the Paste Special dialog box, select the Values and Add options and then click OK.

FIGURE 7-45
This worksheet contains average exam scores and bonus points.

Cut and Paste

	A	B	C	D	E	F	G	H
1	First Quarter Exam Scores							
2								
3	Student	Exam 1	Exam 2	Exam 3	Exam 4	Average	Bonus	Combined
4	Allan	87.00	90.00	79.00	96.00	88.00	2	
5	Billinger	92.00	94.00	94.00	97.00	94.25	3	
6	Crane	96.00	95.00	95.00	80.00	91.50	4	
7	Davis	85.00	87.00	87.00	88.00	86.75	2	
8	Evans	81.00	88.00	88.00	85.00	85.50	3	
9								

As you can see in Figure 7-46, Excel adds the values in cells F4:F8 to the values in cells H4:H8.

The other options in the Operation section of the Paste Special dialog box combine the contents of the copy and paste ranges using different operators. The Subtract option subtracts the contents of the copy range from the contents of the paste range, the Multiply option multiplies the contents of the ranges, and the Divide option divides the contents of the paste range by the contents of the copy range.

FIGURE 7-46
We used the Values and Add options in the Paste Special dialog box to combine the average scores with the bonus points.

Cut and Paste

	A	B	C	D	E	F	G	H
1	First Quarter Exam Scores							
2								
3	Student	Exam 1	Exam 2	Exam 3	Exam 4	Average	Bonus	Combined
4	Allan	87.00	90.00	79.00	96.00	88.00	2	90.00
5	Billinger	92.00	94.00	94.00	97.00	94.25	3	97.25
6	Crane	96.00	95.00	95.00	80.00	91.50	4	95.50
7	Davis	85.00	87.00	87.00	88.00	86.75	2	88.75
8	Evans	81.00	88.00	88.00	85.00	85.50	3	88.50
9								

TIP As a rule, avoid using the All option with any of the Operation options in the Paste Special dialog box when the copy range includes formulas. In fact, you'll probably want to avoid the Operation options altogether if the paste range contains formulas.

You'll usually select the Values option from the Paste section of the Paste Special dialog box when you take advantage of the Operation options. As long as the entries in the copy range are numbers, you can use the All option, instead of Values, to copy both the numbers and the formats of the copy range to the paste range. If the copy range contains formulas, however, you might get unexpected results using All.

If the copy range contains text entries and you use Paste Special with an Operation option (other than None), Excel does not paste the text entries into the paste range. For example, if you copy cell A4 in Figure 7-46 and use Paste Special with the Values and Multiply options selected to combine the text value with the numeric value in cell B4, nothing happens.

Blank spaces in the copy and paste ranges are assigned the value 0, regardless of which Operation option you select.

Skipping Blank Cells

The Paste Special dialog box contains a Skip Blanks option that you use when you want Excel to ignore any blank cells in the copy range. Generally, if your copy range contains blank cells, Excel pastes those blank cells over the corresponding cells in the paste area. As a result, the contents, formats, and notes in the paste area are overwritten by the empty cells. When you use the Skip Blanks option, however, the corresponding cells in the paste area are unaffected.

Transposing Entries

You use the Transpose option in the Paste Special dialog box to reorient the contents of the copy range in the selected paste range: The entries in rows appear in columns, and the entries in columns appear in rows. To illustrate, let's use the Transpose option to reorient the contents of cells B3:E3 shown earlier in Figure 7-42. If we copy cells B3:E3, specify cell H3 as the beginning of the paste range, and use Paste Special with Transpose selected, the worksheet looks like the one in Figure 7-47.

If the transposed cells contain formulas, Excel transposes the formulas as well as the values and adjusts cell references. To ensure that the transposed formulas refer to the correct cells, you can use absolute cell references.

FIGURE 7-47
The Transpose option reorients a pasted selection.

Cut and Paste

	A	B	C	D	E	F	G	H	I
1	First Quarter Exam Scores								
2									
3	Student	Exam 1	Exam 2	Exam 3	Exam 4	Average		Exam 1	
4	Allan	87	90	79	96	88.00		Exam 2	
5	Billinger	92	94	94	97	94.25		Exam 3	
6	Crane	96	95	95	80	91.50		Exam 4	
7	Davis	85	87	87	88	86.75			
8	Evans	81	88	88	85	85.50			
9									

For more information about absolute cell references, see "Using Cell References in Formulas," page 113.

Using Paste Special with Arrays

As with any other formula, you can convert the results of an array formula to a series of constant values by selecting the entire array range, choosing Copy, and — without changing your selection — choosing Paste Special. If you select the Values option in the Paste Special dialog box, Excel overwrites the array formulas with constant values. Because the range now contains constant values rather than formulas, Excel no longer treats the selection as an array.

Filling Cell Ranges with Data

The Fill command on the Edit menu displays a submenu with several commands. The Down, Right, Up, and Left commands are handy when you want to copy one or more cells to an adjacent set of cells. Before choosing these commands, select the range you want to fill, including the cell or cells containing the formulas, values, and formats that you want to fill the selected range with. (Notes are not included when you use the Fill commands.)

TIP You can quickly fill a selected range of cells using keyboard shortcuts. Press Ctrl-D to fill selected cells below, and press Ctrl-R to fill selected cells to the right.

For example, suppose the range A1:A4 contains the values 10, 20, 30, and 40. You can use the Right command on the Fill submenu to copy these cells across your worksheet. In Figure 7-48, we copied the contents of cells A1:A4 to cells B1:C4 by selecting cells A1:C4 and choosing Fill and then Right from the Edit menu.

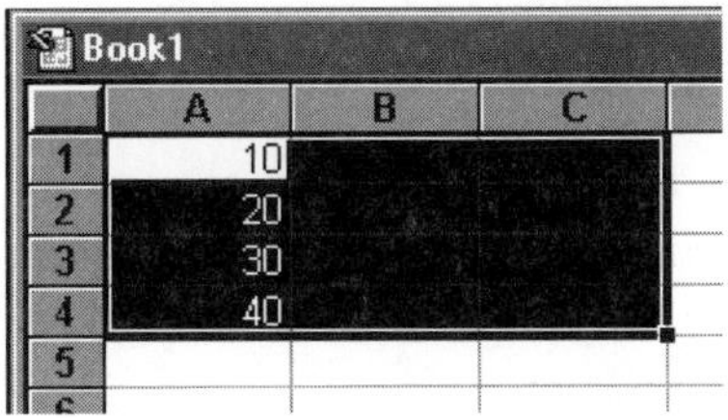

FIGURE 7-48
We chose Right from the Fill submenu of the Edit menu to copy data in cells A1:A4 to B1:C4.

If any cells in the range B1:C4 contain entries, they are overwritten as a result of the Fill command. You can also use the mouse to fill cell ranges directly in your worksheet.

For more information about using the mouse to fill cell ranges, see "Shortcuts for Entering and Editing," page 231.

The Across Worksheets Command

The Across Worksheets command on the Fill submenu allows you to copy cells from one worksheet in a workbook to other worksheets in the same workbook.

For more information about the Across Worksheets command, see "Editing Groups of Sheets Simultaneously," page 326.

The Series Command

You can use the Series command on the Fill submenu to quickly create a regular series of numbers or dates. You supply a starting value, the range to be filled, an interval with which to increment the series *(step value)*, and, if you want, a maximum value for the series *(stop value)*.

Let's look at the Series command in action. Suppose cells A1 and A2 contain the values 10 and 20. If you select cells A1:A10 and choose Series from the Fill submenu of the Edit menu, Excel displays a dialog box like the one in Figure 7-49 at the top of the next page.

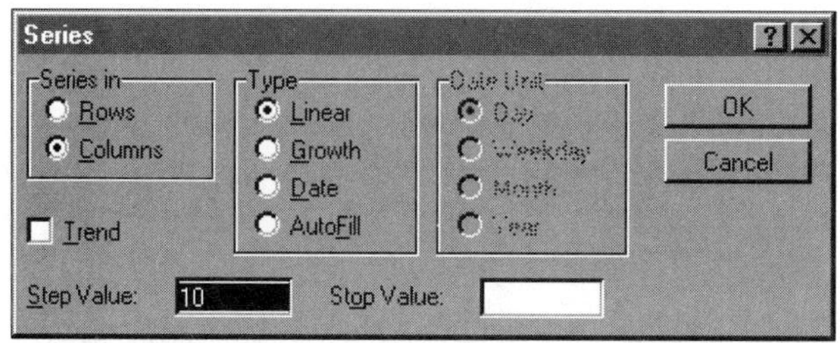

FIGURE 7-49
Use the Series dialog box to create a regular series of numbers.

To create a series, first tell Excel whether you want to create the series in columns or in rows. The Rows option tells Excel to use the first value in each row to fill the cells to the right; the Columns option tells Excel to use the first value in each column to fill the cells below. In this case, the selection is taller than it is wide, so the Columns option is selected automatically.

Next select the type of data series you want to create. Excel uses the Type options in conjunction with the start values in cells A1:A2 and the value in the Step Value edit box to create your data series. The Linear option adds the value specified in the Step Value edit box to the values in your worksheet. The Growth option multiplies the first value in the selection by the step value. If you select the Date option, you can specify the type of date series from the options in the Date Unit section. For now, click OK to accept the suggested value of 10 in the Step Value edit box.

Now enter the same two starting values (10 and 20) in cells C1 and C2, select the range C1:C10, and then choose the Series command again. This time, use the Growth option with the suggested Step Value of 10. The resulting two series are shown in Figure 7-50.

FIGURE 7-50
Starting with identical values in both columns, we created a linear series in column A and a growth series in column C.

Book1

	A	B	C	D	E	F	G	H	I
1	10		10						
2	20		100						
3	30		1000						
4	40		10000						
5	50		100000						
6	60		1000000						
7	70		10000000						
8	80		1E+08						
9	90		1E+09						
10	100		1E+10						
11									

The AutoFill option in the Series dialog box provides a powerful way to create data series. If you enter one or more values as an example, AutoFill will extend the series using the interval between the selected values. You can also use the mouse to create series of numbers or dates directly in your worksheet.

For more information about using the mouse to create series, see "Shortcuts for Entering and Editing," page 231.

For more information about the Date options in the Series dialog box, see "Entering a Series of Dates," page 462.

For more information about AutoFill, see "Filling and Creating Series with the Mouse," page 236.

The Justify Command

You can use the Justify command on the Fill submenu to split a cell entry and distribute it into two or more adjacent rows. Unlike other Fill commands, Justify affects the contents of the original cell.

For example, cell A1 in Figure 7-51 contains a long label. To divide this label up into cell-sized parts, select cell A1 and choose Fill and then Justify from the Edit menu.

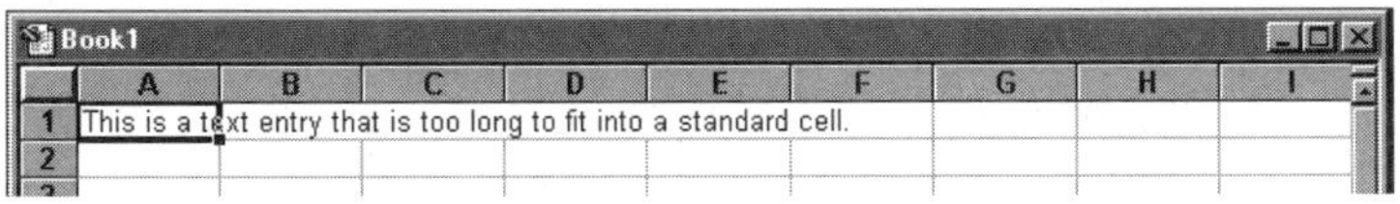

FIGURE 7-51
Cell A1 contains a long label.

When you choose the Justify command, Excel displays the message *Text will extend below selected range*. Clicking OK in the alert box extends the length of the selected range to the length required for justification, overwriting the contents of any cells within the extended range in the process. The result is shown in Figure 7-52. To avoid overwriting, click Cancel in the alert box, widen the column that contains the range, and choose the Justify command again.

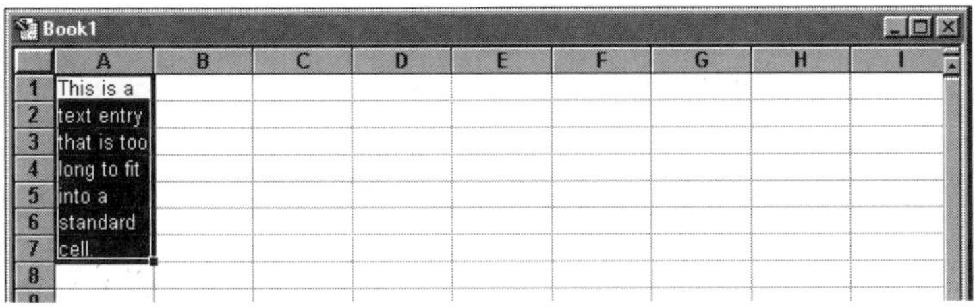

FIGURE 7-52
The Justify command distributed the label from cell A1 to cells A1:A7.

If you later decide to edit the entries in cells A1:A7 or to change the width of the column that contains those labels, you can use the Justify command again to redistribute the text. For example, you can widen column A in Figure 7-52. Select the range A1:A7, and choose Fill and then Justify. Figure 7-53 shows the result.

FIGURE 7-53
After widening column A, we used Justify again to redistribute the text.

If you select a multicolumn range when you choose Justify, Excel justifies the entries in the leftmost column of the range, using the total width of the range you select as its guideline for determining the length of the justified labels. The cells in adjacent columns are not affected. As a result, some of your label displays might be truncated by the entries in subsequent columns.

TIP You can use the Text To Columns command on the Data menu to distribute cell entries horizontally. The Text To Columns command is located on the Data menu because you use it most often when you import database information into Excel from other programs. For more information about converting text to columns, see "Parsing Pasted Text with the Convert Text To Columns Wizard," page 894.

Any blank cells within the leftmost column of the text you are justifying serve as "paragraph" separators. That is, Excel groups the labels above and below the blank cells when it justifies text entries.

Finding and Replacing Data

Suppose you've built a large worksheet and you now need to find every occurrence of a particular character string or value in that worksheet. (A character string is defined as any series of characters you can type in a cell — text, numbers, math operators, or punctuation symbols.) You can use the Find command on the Edit menu to locate any string of characters, including cell references and range names, in the formulas or values in a worksheet. This command is particularly useful when you want to find linked formulas or error values such as #NAME? or #REF! What's more, you can use the Replace command to overwrite the strings you locate with new entries.

See Also For more information about linked formulas and error values, see Chapter 5, "Building Formulas," page 111.

Using Find

If you want to search the entire worksheet to locate a string of characters, you select a single cell. Excel begins its search from that cell and travels through the entire worksheet. To search only a portion of the worksheet, select the appropriate range.

When you choose the Find command, you see a dialog box like the one in Figure 7-54. First specify the Find What string — the string of characters you want to search for.

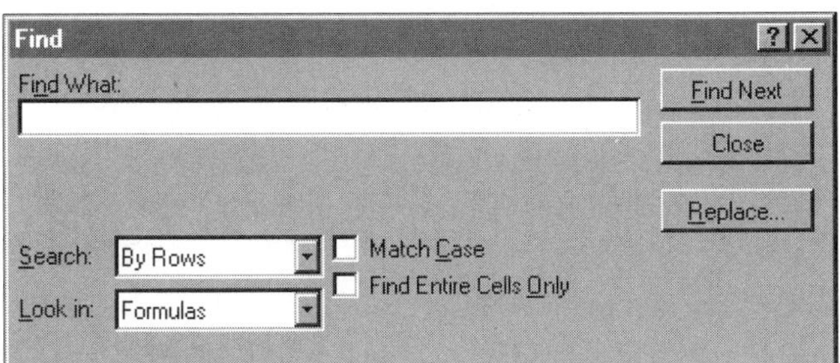

FIGURE 7-54
Use the Find dialog box to locate a character string.

The Search Options

You can use the Search options in the Find dialog box to search by rows or by columns. When you select the By Rows option, Excel looks through the worksheet horizontally, row by row, starting with the currently selected cell. If it finds an occurrence of the string specified in the Find What entry box, Excel highlights the cell that contains that occurrence and stops searching. If it doesn't find an occurrence before it reaches the last cell in the active portion of the worksheet, Excel returns to cell A1 and continues to search through the worksheet until it either finds an occurrence or returns to the originally selected cell. Select the By Rows option if you think the string is located to the right of the selected cell.

The By Columns option searches through the worksheet column by column, beginning with the selected cell. Select the By Columns option if you think the string is below the selected cell.

The Look In Options

The Look In options in the Find dialog box tell Excel whether to search formulas, values, or notes for the string in the Find What entry box. When you select Formulas, Excel searches in the formulas contained in the worksheet cells. When you select Values, on the other hand, Excel searches in the displayed results of formulas in the worksheet. In either case, Excel searches in the constant values in the worksheet. When you select Notes, Excel examines any text attached as a note to a cell.

The nuances of the Formulas and Values options can be confusing. Remember that the underlying contents of a cell and the displayed value of that cell are often not the same. When using the Formulas and Values options, you should keep in mind the following:

- If a cell contains a formula, the displayed value of the cell is usually the result of that formula (a number such as 100 or a character string if the formula involves text).
- If a cell contains a numeric value, the displayed value of the cell might or might not be the same as the cell's underlying contents.
- If a cell has the General format, the displayed value of the cell and the cell's contents are usually the same.
- If a cell contains a number that has a format other than General, the contents of the cell and its displayed value are different.
- The underlying and displayed values of a cell that contains a text entry are usually the same.

In the simple worksheet in Figure 7-55, cells B2 and B3 contain the number 1000. The entry in cell B2 has the General format, and the entry in cell B3 has a currency format. Cell C2, which contains the value 600, has been assigned the name Test. Cell C3 contains the value 400. Cell C4 contains the formula

=Test+C3

which returns the value 1000. Cell E5 contains the label *Test*.

FIGURE 7-55 We'll use this worksheet to show how to search for a string in a value or formula.

Find

	A	B	C	D	E	F	G	H	I
1									
2		1000	600						
3		$1,000	400						
4			1000						
5					Test				
6									

Suppose you select cell A1, choose Find from the Edit menu (or press Ctrl-F), and type *1000* in the Find What edit box. If you select Values as the Look In option and click Find Next, Excel looks at what is displayed in each cell. It first finds the occurrence of the string 1000 in cell B2. If you click Find

Next or press Enter, Excel finds the next occurrence of the string in the displayed value of cell C4. Excel ignores the entry in cell B3 because the displayed value, $1,000, does not precisely match the Find What string, 1000. Because you're searching through values and not formulas, Excel ignores the fact that the underlying content of the cell is the number 1000.

TIP If you close the Find dialog box and want to search for the next occurrence of the Find What string in your worksheet, you can press F4, the keyboard shortcut for repeating the last action.

Now suppose you select cell A1 again and repeat the search, this time selecting the Formulas option. As before, Excel first finds the occurrence of the Find What string in cell B2. If you click Find Next, Excel now highlights cell B3, which contains the number 1000 formatted as currency. Because you're searching through formulas and not displayed values, Excel ignores the format assigned to this cell. Instead, it matches the Find What string to the underlying contents of the cell.

If you click Find Next again, Excel returns to cell B2. During this search, Excel ignored the value in cell C4. Even though this cell displays the value 1000, it actually contains the formula =Test+C3, which does not match the Find What string.

Let's look at one more example. If you specify *Test* as the Find What string and select Formulas as the Look In option, Excel first finds the string *Test* in the formula =Test+C3 and highlights the cell that contains that formula, C4. Notice that this search is not case-sensitive. If you click Find Next, Excel highlights cell E5, which contains the label *Test*. If you repeat the search but this time select Values as the Look In option, Excel finds only the occurrence of the text entry *Test* in cell E5. To find the defined cell name *Test* in cell C2, you must use the Go To command on the Edit menu or select the name in the Name box on the formula bar.

For more information about notes, see "Adding Notes to Cells," page 288.

For more information about the Go To command, see "Using the Go To Command," page 96.

The Match Case Option

If you select the Match Case option in the Find dialog box, Excel distinguishes capital letters from lowercase letters. It finds only those occurrences that match the uppercase and lowercase characters of the search string exactly. If you leave this box unselected, Excel disregards the differences between uppercase and lowercase letters.

The Find Entire Cells Only Option

You can use the Find Entire Cells Only option in the Find dialog box to specify a search for only complete and individual occurrences of the string. Normally, Find searches for any occurrence of a string, even if it is part of another string. For example, say a worksheet contains only two entries: the number 998 and the number 99. If you specify 99 as the Find What string, Excel finds the entry 99, which matches the Find What string exactly, and the entry 998, which contains a string that matches the Find What string. However, if you specify 99 as the Find What string and select the Find Entire Cells Only option, Excel finds only the entry 99.

Wildcard Characters

You can use the wildcard characters ? and * to widen the scope of your searches. Wildcards are helpful when you're searching for a group of similar but not identical entries or when you're searching for an entry you don't quite remember.

The ? character takes the place of any single character in a Find What string. For example, the Find What string *100?* matches the values 1000, 1001, 1002, 1003, and so on up to 1009. (It also matches entries such as 100A, 100B, and so on.)

The * character takes the place of one or more characters in a Find What string. For example, the string *1** matches the entries 10, 15, 100, 1111, 10001, 123456789, 123 Maple Street, and 1-800-MSPRESS.

You can use the wildcard characters anywhere within a Find What string. For example, you can use the string **s* to find all entries that end with *s*. Or you can use the string **es** to find each cell that contains the string sequence *es* anywhere in its formula or value.

To search for a string that contains either ? or *, enter a tilde (~) before the character. For example, to find the string *Who?* — but not Whom — enter *Who~?* as your Find What text.

For more information about wildcard characters, see "Adding Advanced Search Criteria," page 74.

Using Replace

In addition to locating characters, you can replace a specified character string with a new string. The Replace command works much like the Find command. When you choose Replace from the Edit menu (or press Ctrl-H or click the Replace button in the Find dialog box), you see a dialog box like the one in Figure 7-56. Type the character string you want to search for in the Find What edit box and the string you want to substitute in the Replace With edit box.

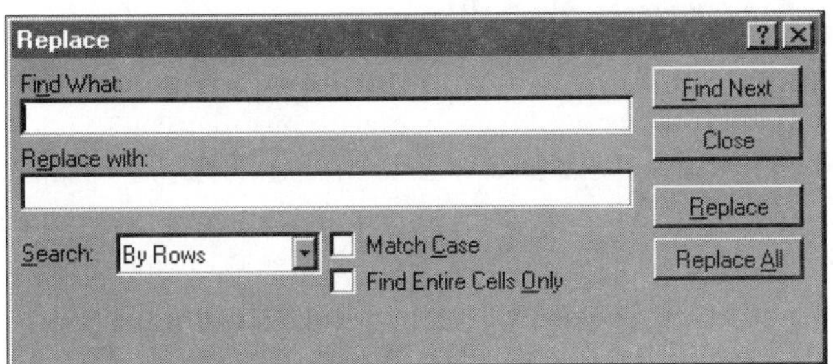

FIGURE 7-56
Use the Replace command to replace a specified string with a new string.

For example, to replace each occurrence of the name *Joan Smith* with *John Smith,* type *Joan Smith* in the Find What edit box and *John Smith* in the Replace With edit box. Click the Find Next button or press Enter to move from one occurrence of the Find What string to the next without changing the contents of the current cell. When you locate an occurrence you want to change, click the Replace button to substitute the Find What string with the Replace With string. After replacing the character string in the current cell, Excel moves to the next occurrence.

To replace every occurrence of the Find What string with the Replace With string, click the Replace All button. Instead of pausing at each occurrence to allow you to change or skip the current cell, Excel locates all the cells that contain the Find What string and replaces them.

You can also use wildcard characters (? and *) in the Find What string to broaden your search. For example, to change all occurrences of the names *Joan Smith* and *John Smith* to *John Smythe,* type *Jo?n Smith* in the Find What edit box and *John Smythe* in the Replace With edit box and then click the Replace All button. Excel changes all occurrences of both *Joan Smith* and *John Smith* to *John Smythe.*

NOTE Although you can use wildcards in the Find What edit box to aid in your search, if you enter wildcard characters in the Replace With edit box, Excel uses a literal ? or * symbol when it replaces each occurrence of your Find What text.

Getting the Words Right

Spreadsheets are not all numbers, of course, so Excel includes several features to help make entering and editing text easier. The new AutoCorrect command helps you fix common typing errors even before they become spelling problems. For the rest of the words in your worksheets, the Spelling command helps make sure you've entered your text according to Webster. Finally, you might be able to get the new AutoComplete feature to do some of the typing for you.

Fix Typing Errors on the Fly

Perhaps you always have to stop and think "i before e except after c" before you type "receive." Or perhaps you're such a fast typist that you're constantly typing the second letter of a capitalized word before the Shift key snaps back. Excel's new AutoCorrect feature helps fix this kind of chronic problem for you as you type. Choose the AutoCorrect command on the Tools menu to display the AutoCorrect dialog box shown in Figure 7-57.

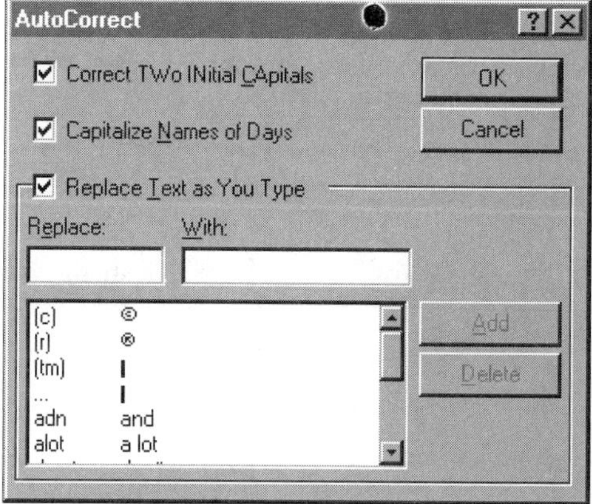

FIGURE 7-57
You can add your most common typing errors to the AutoCorrect dialog box.

If the Correct TWo INitial CApitals check box is selected (as it normally is), you couldn't even type the name of the option as it appears in the dialog box. Most of the time, you wouldn't want to anyway, which is what makes this such a helpful feature. As you finish typing a word and press the space bar, Excel checks to see if the word contains capital letters. If the word is all caps, Excel leaves it alone (assuming that this was intentional), but if it contains both uppercase and lowercase characters, AutoCorrect makes sure that there's only one cap ital letter at the beginning of the word. If not, subsequent uppercase characters are changed to lowercase. Apparently due to their increasing usage, AutoCorrect does not attempt to modify "mid-cap" words such as AutoCorrect.

AutoCorrect is smart enough to know the days of the week, and if it finds one, it makes sure it's capitalized, as long as the Capitalize Names Of Days option is selected. The Replace Text As You Type option turns on the replacement list at the bottom of the dialog box, where a number of common replacement items are listed. In addition to correcting common typing errors like replacing "adn" with "and," AutoCorrect also provides a few useful shorthand shortcuts in its replacement list. For example, instead of searching for the right font and symbol to add a copyright mark, you can simply type (c) and AutoCorrect automatically replaces it with ©. You can add your own common typing errors and shorthand shortcuts to the list by typing the before-and-after text into the Replace and the With boxes, then clicking the Add button.

NOTE If you have other Microsoft Office programs installed, anything you add to the AutoCorrect list will also appear in other Office programs' AutoCorrect lists.

AutoCorrect works when entering text in cells, formulas, text boxes, on-sheet controls, and chart labels. AutoCorrect does not work when entering text in dialog boxes.

Let Excel Help with the Typing

Often, when entering data in lists, you end up typing the same things over and over. For example, a worksheet that tracks sales transactions might contain columns for products and salespeople associated with each transaction. Usually, you'll have far more transactions than either products or salespeople, so inevitably you'll enter multiple transactions for each salesperson and each product. AutoComplete can help cut down the amount of typing you do, as well as help increase the accuracy of your entries by at least partially automating them. You turn AutoComplete on by choosing Options from the Tools menu, clicking the Edit tab, and selecting the Enable AutoComplete For Cell Values option. (It is turned on by default.)

When you begin typing a cell entry, AutoComplete scans all the entries in the same column and, as each character is typed, determines whether there is a possible match in the column. For example, in Figure 7-58 on the next page, as soon as we typed "Wha" into cell B10, AutoComplete completed the entry with the unique match in the same column: "Whatsit." Note in the figure that the text added by AutoComplete is highlighted. You can either continue typing, hit Backspace or Del to delete the suggested completion, or press Enter or an arrow key to accept the completion and move to another cell.

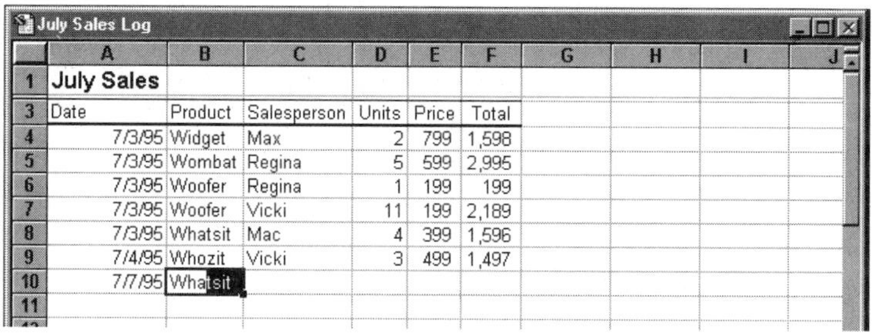

FIGURE 7-58

AutoComplete finishes the entry "Whatsit" in cell B10.

July Sales Log

	A	B	C	D	E	F
1	July Sales					
3	Date	Product	Salesperson	Units	Price	Total
4	7/3/95	Widget	Max	2	799	1,598
5	7/3/95	Wombat	Regina	5	599	2,995
6	7/3/95	Woofer	Regina	1	199	199
7	7/3/95	Woofer	Vicki	11	199	2,189
8	7/3/95	Whatsit	Mac	4	399	1,596
9	7/4/95	Whozit	Vicki	3	499	1,497
10	7/7/95	Whatsit				
11						

AutoComplete matches only complete cell entries, not individual words in a cell, although an entry may consist of multiple words. For example, if you begin typing "A Whatsit" in column B of the worksheet, AutoCorrect doesn't find a match even after you get to the "Wha" in Whatsit, because the complete cell entry is not a match. As soon as it finds a unique match, AutoComplete suggests an entry. For example, in column C of the same worksheet, we could simply type V in cell C10, and AutoComplete would immediately suggest Vicki as the entry we were after, since it is the only entry beginning with the letter V in the column. AutoComplete does not work when editing formulas.

Instead of relying on automatic matching, you can use the Pick From List command to select an entry from the same column without typing. To do so, select a cell, click the right mouse button, and choose the Pick From List command at the bottom of the shortcut menu that appears, as shown in Figure 7-59. (If your shortcut menu looks different from the one shown in the figure, it's because you weren't already editing in the cell. It's OK. The Pick From List command appears at the bottom of the menu either way.) Once the pick list is displayed, simply click the entry you want, and Excel immediately enters it in the cell.

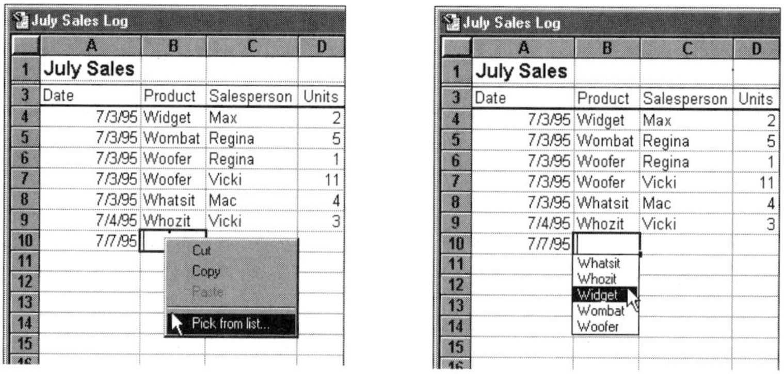

FIGURE 7-59

Click the right mouse button and choose the Pick From List command to display a list of unique entries in the column.

July Sales Log

	A	B	C	D
1	July Sales			
3	Date	Product	Salesperson	Units
4	7/3/95	Widget	Max	2
5	7/3/95	Wombat	Regina	5
6	7/3/95	Woofer	Regina	1
7	7/3/95	Woofer	Vicki	11
8	7/3/95	Whatsit	Mac	4
9	7/4/95	Whozit	Vicki	3
10	7/7/95			

Cut
Copy
Paste
Pick from list...

July Sales Log

	A	B	C	D
1	July Sales			
3	Date	Product	Salesperson	Units
4	7/3/95	Widget	Max	2
5	7/3/95	Wombat	Regina	5
6	7/3/95	Woofer	Regina	1
7	7/3/95	Woofer	Vicki	11
8	7/3/95	Whatsit	Mac	4
9	7/4/95	Whozit	Vicki	3
10	7/7/95			

Whatsit
Whozit
Widget
Wombat
Woofer

TIP If you have activated a cell by double-clicking it or by clicking the formula bar, you can also display the pick list by pressing Alt-Down arrow key.

Checking Your Spelling

If errors remain despite AutoCorrect and AutoComplete, you don't have to rely on your own proofreading skills when it comes to correct spelling. Instead, you can use the Spelling command on the Tools menu to check for typing errors. (You can also use the Spelling button on the Standard toolbar.)

Use the Spelling command to check the entire worksheet or any part of it. If you select a single cell, Excel checks the entire worksheet, including all cells, notes, Excel graphic objects, and page headers and footers. If you select more than one cell, Excel checks the selected cells only. If the formula bar is active, Excel checks only its contents, and if you select words within the formula bar, Excel checks the selected words only. If the range you select for spell checking contains hidden or outlined cells that are not visible, Excel checks these as well. Cells that contain formulas are not checked, however.

TIP You can press F7 to instantly begin a spell check. If Excel finds any unrecognized words, the Spelling dialog box appears.

Figure 7-60, on the next page, shows the dialog box that appears after choosing the Spelling command from the Tools menu to check a worksheet that contains a typographical error.

Excel highlights the cell that contains the misspelled word *rane* and displays a list of suggested corrections. To correct the word, you can type the word as you want it spelled in the Change To edit box and press Enter, or select the correct word from the Suggestions list box and then click Change to substitute the word. If the misspelled word appears in other cells, you can click Change All to correct it throughout the document.

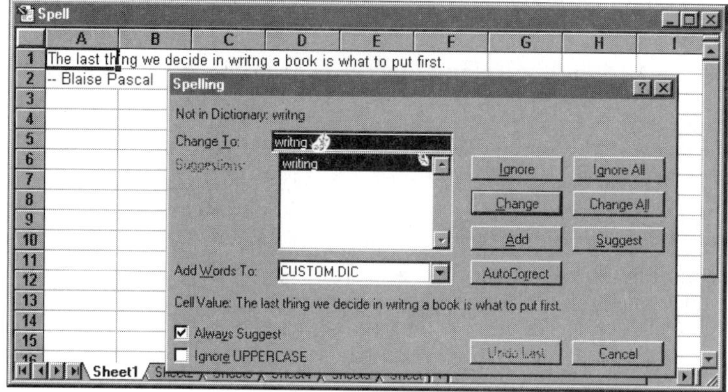

FIGURE 7-60
The Spelling dialog box not only checks your spelling but suggests possible corrections.

If Excel finds a word that its dictionary does not recognize but is nonetheless correctly spelled, you can click Ignore or Ignore All to ignore the single instance or all the occurrences of the selected word and continue the spell check. If you use the unrecognized word often in your worksheets, you can click Add to add the word to your custom dictionary.

In our example, we selected the word *rain* from the Suggestions list box and clicked Change. If *rane* is actually a word we want to use, we could click Add to include the word in our custom dictionary. In addition, proper names are often flagged as being misspelled. If a proper name appears frequently in your worksheets, add it to your custom dictionary.

You can tell Excel to skip words that contain only capital letters by selecting the Ignore UPPERCASE option. To undo a correction, click the Undo Last button.

If you choose the Spelling command and Excel finds no incorrectly spelled words, an alert box says either *Finished spell checking entire sheet* or *Finished spell checking selected cells*. If you start the spell check in the middle of the worksheet, Excel prompts you when it reaches the end of the active area to see if you want to continue at the beginning of the worksheet.

For more information about toolbars and buttons, see Chapter 2, "Toolbars and Buttons," page 33.

For information about headers and footers, see "Creating a Header and Footer," page 380.

Auditing and Documenting a Worksheet

Microsoft Excel has a number of powerful and flexible features that help you audit and debug your worksheets and document your work. In this section, we'll discuss the cell tracers, the Note command, the Info window, and the Go To Special feature.

Most of Excel's auditing features can be accessed via the Auditing toolbar, which is shown in Figure 7-61.

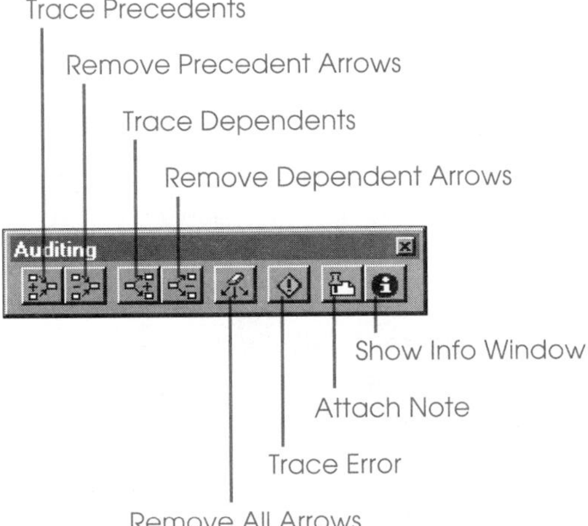

FIGURE 7-61

The Auditing toolbar contains buttons you can use to control the cell tracers, cell notes, and the Info window.

Tracing Cell References

If you've ever looked at a large worksheet and wondered how you could get an idea of the data flow — that is, how the formulas and values relate to one another — you'll appreciate the *cell tracers*. You can also use the cell tracers to help find the source of those pesky errors that occasionally appear in your worksheets.

The Auditing toolbar contains six buttons that control different functions of the cell tracers. To demonstrate how the cell tracers work, we'll use the Auditing toolbar. However, if you prefer, you can use the commands on the Auditing submenu of the Tools menu to control the cell tracers and to display the Auditing toolbar.

Understanding Precedents and Dependents

The terms *precedent* and *dependent* crop up quite often in this section. They refer to the relationships that cells containing formulas create with other cells. A lot of what a spreadsheet is all about is wrapped up in these concepts, so here's a brief description of each term.

Precedents are cells whose values are used by the formula in the selected cell. A cell that has precedents always contains a formula.

Dependents are cells that use the value in the selected cell. A cell that has dependents can contain either a formula or a constant value.

Figure 7-62 shows a simple worksheet that we'll use in our discussion of the cell tracers. Although this worksheet is not too difficult to figure out, you should consider the ramifications of using the cell tracers in a large and complex worksheet.

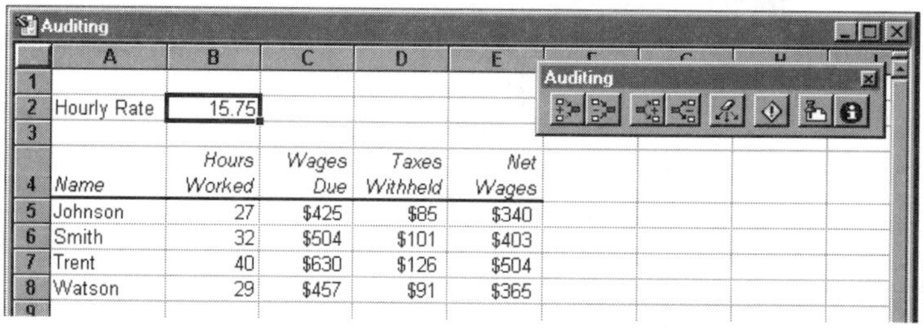

	A	B	C	D	E
1					
2	Hourly Rate	15.75			
3					
4	*Name*	*Hours Worked*	*Wages Due*	*Taxes Withheld*	*Net Wages*
5	Johnson	27	$425	$85	$340
6	Smith	32	$504	$101	$403
7	Trent	40	$630	$126	$504
8	Watson	29	$457	$91	$365

FIGURE 7-62
We'll use this worksheet and the Auditing toolbar to demonstrate how the cell tracers work.

Tracing Dependent Cells

In the worksheet in Figure 7-62, we selected cell B2, which contains the hourly rate value. To find out which cells contain formulas that use this value, click the Trace Dependents button on the Auditing toolbar (or choose the Trace Dependents command from the Auditing submenu of the Tools menu). Figure 7-63 shows the results.

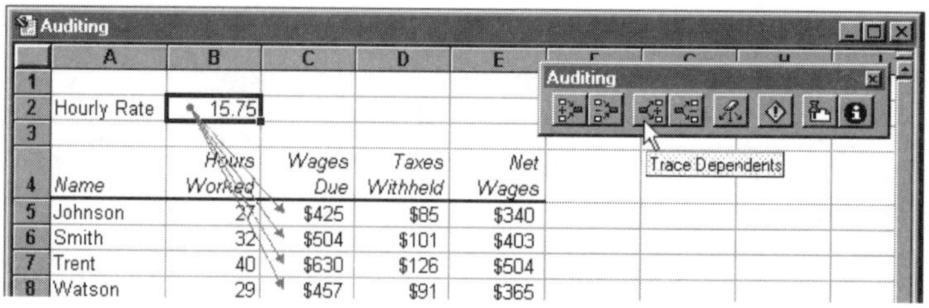

	A	B	C	D	E
1					
2	Hourly Rate	15.75			
3					
4	*Name*	*Hours Worked*	*Wages Due*	*Taxes Withheld*	*Net Wages*
5	Johnson	27	$425	$85	$340
6	Smith	32	$504	$101	$403
7	Trent	40	$630	$126	$504
8	Watson	29	$457	$91	$365

Trace Dependents

FIGURE 7-63
When you trace dependents, arrows point to formulas that directly refer to the selected cell.

The *tracer arrows* indicate that cell B2 is directly referred to by the formulas in cells C5, C6, C7, and C8. A dot appears in cell B2, indicating that it is a precedent cell in the data flow. Now, if you click the Trace Dependents button again (or choose the Trace Dependents command), another set of arrows appears, indicating the next level of dependencies — or *indirect dependents.* Figure 7-64 shows the results.

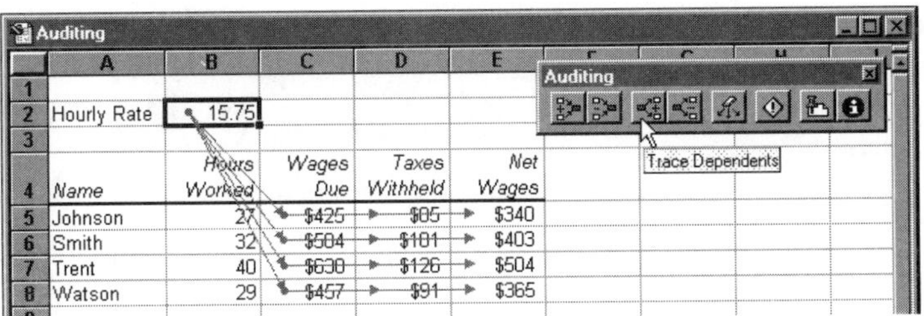

Auditing
Hourly Rate
15.75
Hours Worked
Wages Due
Taxes Withheld
Net Wages
Name
Johnson
Smith
Trent
Watson
27
32
40
29
$425
$504
$630
$457
$85
$101
$126
$91
$340
$403
$504
$365
Trace Dependents

FIGURE 7-64
When you trace dependents again, arrows point to the next level of formulas — ones that indirectly refer to the selected cell.

One handy feature of the tracer arrows is that you can use them to navigate, which can be a real advantage in a large worksheet. For example, in Figure 7-64 with cell B2 still selected, double-click the arrow pointing from cell B2 to cell C8. (When you move the mouse pointer over a tracer arrow, it becomes arrow-shaped.) The selection jumps to the other end of the arrow, and cell C8 becomes the active cell. Now if you double-click the arrow pointing from cell C8 to cell E8, the selection jumps to cell E8. If you double-click the same arrow again, the selection jumps back to cell C8 at the other end. Double-click the arrow from cell C8 to cell B2, and you're back where you started.

If you double-click on an arrow that extends beyond the screen, the window shifts to display the cell at the other end. You can use this feature to jump from cell to cell along a path of precedents and dependents.

Clearing Tracer Arrows

Each time you trace another cell's precedents or dependents, additional tracer arrows appear. You'll find, however, that your screen quickly becomes cluttered, making it difficult to discern the data flow for particular cells. It's a good idea to start fresh each time you want to trace cells. To remove all the tracer arrows from the screen, simply click the Remove All Arrows button on the Auditing Toolbar (or choose the Remove All Arrows command from the Auditing submenu).

Tracing Precedent Cells

You can also trace in the opposite direction by starting from a cell that contains a formula and tracing the cells that are referred to in the formula. In Figure 7-65, we selected cell E5, which contains one of the net wages formulas. To find out which cells this formula refers to, we clicked the Trace Precedents button. (You could also use the Trace Precedents command on the Auditing submenu.)

FIGURE 7-65
When you trace precedents, arrows point from all the cells that the formula in the selected cell directly refers to.

	A	B	C	D	E
1					
2	Hourly Rate	15.75			
3					
4	*Name*	*Hours Worked*	*Wages Due*	*Taxes Withheld*	*Net Wages*
5	Johnson	27	$425	$85	$340
6	Smith	32	$504	$101	$403
7	Trent	40	$630	$126	$504
8	Watson	29	$457	$91	$365

This time, an arrow appears with dots in cells C5 and D5. The dots identify these cells as precedents in the data flow. (The appearance of dots in both C5 and D5 indicates that both cells are equally precedent to the selected cell.) Notice that the arrow still points in the same direction — toward the formula and in the direction of the data flow — even though we started from the opposite end of the path. To continue the trace, click the Trace Precedents button again (or choose the Trace Precedents command). Figure 7-66 shows the results.

FIGURE 7-66
When you trace precedents again, arrows point from the next (indirect) level of cells that the formula in the selected cell refers to.

	A	B	C	D	E
1					
2	Hourly Rate	15.75			
3					
4	*Name*	*Hours Worked*	*Wages Due*	*Taxes Withheld*	*Net Wages*
5	Johnson	27	$425	$85	$340
6	Smith	32	$504	$101	$403
7	Trent	40	$630	$126	$504
8	Watson	29	$457	$91	$365

Tracing Errors

Suppose your worksheet displays error values, like the ones shown in Figure 7-67. To trace one of these errors back to its source, select the cell that contains the error and click the Trace Error button (or choose the Trace Error command from the Auditing submenu).

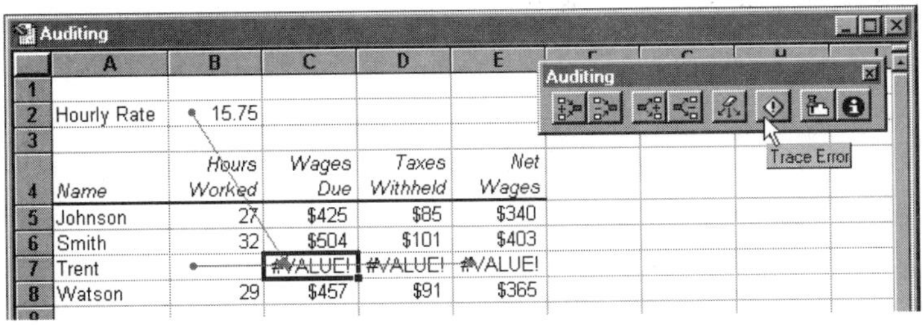

FIGURE 7-67
Select a cell that contains an error value and click the Trace Error button to display arrows that trace the error back to its source.

Excel selects the cell that contains the first formula in the error chain, draws arrows from that cell to the cell you selected, and displays a message box. (On a color monitor, you'll notice that the arrows are red.) After you choose OK, Excel draws arrows to the cell that contains the first erroneous formula from the values the formula uses. (On a color monitor, you'll notice that the arrows are blue.) At this point, it's up to you to determine the reason for the error; Excel simply takes you back to the source formula and shows you the precedents. In our example, it turns out that the error is caused by a space character that was inadvertently entered in cell B7, replacing the hours worked figure.

Tracing References to Other Worksheets

If a cell contains a reference to a different worksheet or to a worksheet in another workbook, a dashed tracer arrow appears with a small icon attached, as shown in Figure 7-68.

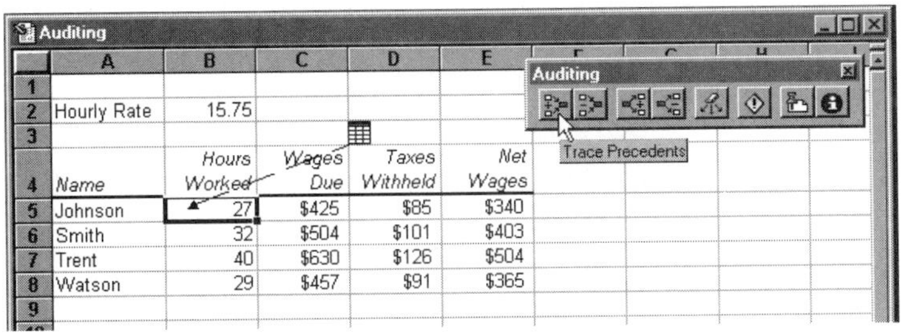

FIGURE 7-68
If you trace the precedents of a cell that contains a reference to another worksheet or workbook, a special tracer arrow appears.

You cannot continue to trace precedents from the active cell when a dashed tracer arrow appears. If you want, you can activate the referenced worksheet or workbook and then start a new trace from the referenced cell. If you double-click a dashed tracer arrow, the Go To dialog box appears, with the reference displayed in the Go To list box. You can select the reference in the list box and click OK to activate the worksheet or workbook. However, if the reference is to another workbook that is not currently open, an error message appears.

Adding Notes to Cells

You can attach notes to cells to document your work, explain calculations and assumptions, or provide reminders. Select the cell you want to annotate and then select the Note command from the Insert menu to display the Cell Note dialog box. (You can also click the Attach Note button on the Auditing toolbar to display the Cell Note dialog box.) The active cell's reference appears in the Cell edit box at the top of the dialog box. Type your entry in the Text Note edit box, as shown in Figure 7-69, and click Add or OK to attach the note to the active cell. When you click Add, the dialog box remains open so that you can edit or add additional notes. When you click OK, Excel closes the dialog box and returns to the worksheet.

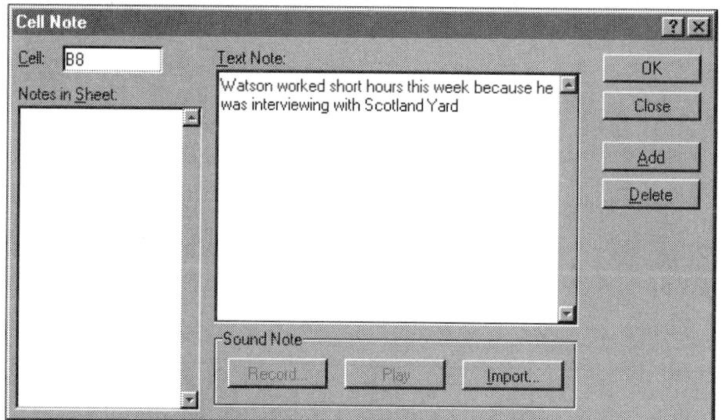

FIGURE 7-69
Use the Cell Note dialog box to attach a note to a cell.

Although you can attach only one note to a cell, you can make your note text as long as you like. As you make entries in the Text Note edit box, Excel automatically wraps text from one line to the next. If you want to begin a new paragraph in the Text Note edit box, press Enter.

Creating extremely long notes seems to defeat their purpose, but you can use the scroll bar or the direction keys to move through long notes.

After you add a note to a cell, the cell reference and the first few characters of the note appear in the Notes In Sheet list box on the left side of the Cell Note dialog box. To edit a note, select it from the list box, activate the Text Note edit box, and make your changes. Click Delete and then choose OK to delete the selected note. (You can also use the Notes command on the Clear submenu of the Edit menu to remove notes from a cell or range of cells.)

While the Cell Note dialog box is open, you can select other cells in order to edit their notes or add new notes. First activate the Cell edit box and type a cell reference or use the mouse or direction keys to select a cell. (If the Cell Note dialog box blocks your view of the cell that you want to select, you can move it around on the screen by dragging its title bar.) Next edit or enter the contents of the Text Note edit box just as you would the formula bar.

You can also close the Cell Note dialog box by clicking the Close button. Clicking Close doesn't undo any additions or deletions you've already locked in; it simply cancels any new entries in the Text Note edit box and removes the Cell Note dialog box from your screen.

A small square (red on a color monitor) in the upper right corner of a cell indicates an attached note. You can suppress the display of this indicator by choosing the Options command from the Tools menu, clicking the View tab, and clearing the Note Indicator option. When you move the cursor over a cell displaying a note indicator, the note pops up in a box called a cell tip, similar to the ToolTips that display the button names for toolbar buttons. A cell tip is shown in Figure 7-70.

Auditing

	A	B	C	D	E
1					
2	Hourly Rate	15.75			
3					
4	*Name*	*Hours Worked*	*Wages Due*	*Taxes Withheld*	*Net Wages*
5	Johnson	27	$425	$85	$340
6	Smith	32	$504	$101	$403
7	Trent	40	$630	$126	$504
8	Watson	29	$457	$91	$365

Watson worked short hours this week because he was interviewing with Scotland Yard

FIGURE 7-70
A cell tip displays the note attached to a cell containing a note indicator when you move the cursor over the cell.

To print cell notes, choose the Page Setup command from the File menu, click the Sheet tab, and select the Notes option, or print the contents of the Info window.

For more information about printing, see Chapter 10, "Printing and Presenting," page 373.

For more information about the Info window, see "Monitoring Cell Properties with the Info Window," page 290.

Sound Notes

You can also include audio information in cell notes. To record sound notes, you must have recording hardware, such as SoundBlaster, and a microphone.

To create sounds, use the Record and Play buttons in the Cell Note dialog box. When you click Record, a dialog box appears that contains buttons labeled Record, Stop, Pause, and Play. To record a sound note, click the Record button and begin recording. When you are finished, click Stop. You can use the Pause button to interrupt your recording and the Play button to review the recording you just made. When you are satisfied with your sound note, click OK, or click Cancel to discard the sound note.

If you click OK, the Record button in the Cell Note dialog box becomes the Erase button, allowing you to remove sound notes from individual cells. After you add a sound note to a cell, an asterisk (*) appears next to the cell address in the Notes In Sheet list box of the Cell Note dialog box, indicating that a sound note is attached to that cell.

You can also import a previously recorded sound to use as a sound note. To do this, click Import in the Cell Note dialog box. The Import Sound dialog box appears, allowing you to switch to the directory that contains your sound files. You can then select the file containing the sound you want to import.

You can record voice, music, sound effects — anything you like, limited only by the system resources available. The amount of time used by each recording is shown in the scale at the bottom of the Record dialog box. Keep in mind that sound notes take a considerable amount of disk space, so use them judiciously.

Monitoring Cell Properties with the Info Window

You can use the Info window to monitor the status of the cells in your worksheet. The easiest way to open the Info window is to click the Show Info Window button on the Auditing toolbar. You can also display the Info window by choosing Options from the Tools menu, clicking the View tab, and selecting the Info Window option. Figure 7-71 shows the Info window adjacent to the workbook about which it is reporting. The word *Info* followed by the names of the currently active workbook and worksheet appears in the title bar of the Info window.

Notice that the menu bar changes when the Info window is active. The Info menu bar includes five menus: File, Info, Macro, Window, and Help. Initially, you see only three pieces of information in the Info window: the cell reference, the underlying formula in the cell, and any note attached to the cell. However, you can use the commands on the Info menu to display more information. The Info menu offers nine display commands: Cell, Formula, Value, Format, Protection, Names, Precedents, Dependents, and Note. All of the commands on the Info menu are toggle commands. (A check mark appears beside those currently selected.) To clear a command on the Info menu, simply choose that command again. (Figure 7-71 shows the results of choosing all nine display commands.)

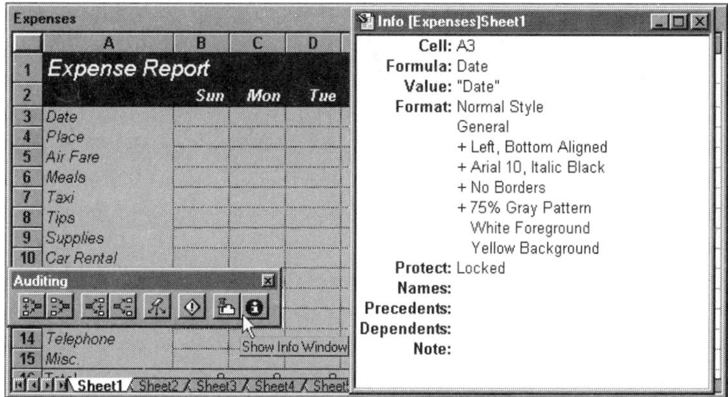

FIGURE 7-71
The Info window lets you monitor the status of your cells.

To switch between the workbook and the Info window, choose one or the other from the list of active documents at the bottom of the Window menu. Alternatively, if you want to keep the Info window in view as you work in your workbook, resize and reposition the workbook and Info windows so that they don't overlap. To quickly arrange the windows on your screen, use the Arrange command on the Window menu.

To print the contents of the Info window, select the cell or range for which you want to print information, activate the Info window, and choose the Print command from the File menu.

The Info window remains open until you click its Close box in the upper right corner (or turn off the Info Window option in the Options dialog box). The status of the Info window is not preserved when you exit Excel, so each time you start Excel, you must redisplay the Info window.

For more information about arranging windows, see Chapter 8, "Workbooks and Windows," page 297.

For more information about printing, see Chapter 10, "Printing and Presenting," page 373.

Using the Go To Special Dialog Box

The options in the Go To Special dialog box provide powerful debugging tools that let you quickly find cells that meet certain specifications.

To access the Go To Special dialog box, shown in Figure 7-72, choose the Go To command from the Edit menu, or press F5, and then click the Special button.

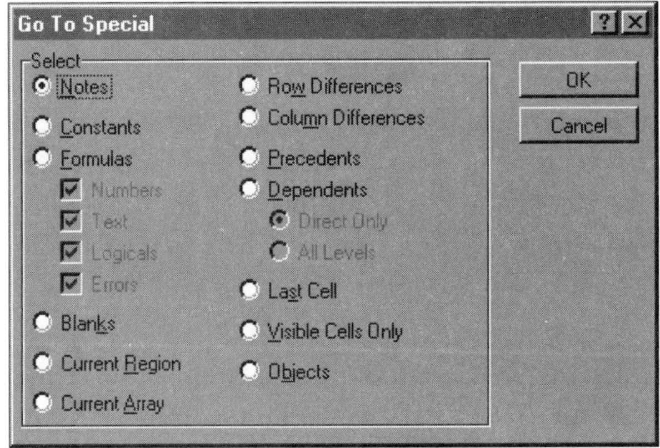

FIGURE 7-72
Choose the Go To command from the Edit menu and click the Special button to display the Go To Special dialog box — a handy auditing and debugging tool.

After you specify one of the Go To Special options and click OK, Excel highlights the cell or cells that match the criteria. With a few exceptions, if you select a range of cells before you open the Go To Special dialog box, Excel searches only the selected range; if the current selection is a single cell or one or more graphic objects, Excel searches the entire active worksheet.

Some of the Go To Special options, such as Notes, Precedents, and Dependents, might cause Excel to select multiple nonadjacent ranges. To navigate through these selections, you can use Enter to move down or to the right one cell at a time. Shift-Enter lets you move up or to the left one cell at a time.

TIP To quickly select all cells on the current worksheet to which a note is attached, press Ctrl-Shift-?.

The Constants, Formulas, and Blanks options locate cells that contain the specified type of entries. When you select the Constants or Formulas option, Excel activates the Numbers, Text, Logicals, and Errors options in addition to Constants and Formulas. Use these options to narrow your selection criteria.

The Current Region option is handy when you're working in a large, complex worksheet and need to select blocks of cells. (Recall that a region is defined as a continuous rectangular block of cells bounded by blank rows, blank columns, or worksheet borders.) When you choose Current Region, your selection is set to that area of the worksheet.

TIP You can use the keyboard to quickly select the region to which the selected cell belongs. To select the current region, press Ctrl-Shift-*.

If the selected cell is part of an array range, you can use the Current Array option to select all the cells in that array.

TIP You can also use a keyboard shortcut to select the array to which the selected cell belongs. To select the current array, press Ctrl-/.

Choose Row Differences or Column Differences to compare the entries in a range of cells to spot potential inconsistencies. To use these debugging options, select the range before displaying the Go To Special dialog box. The position of the active cell in your selection determines which cell or cells Excel uses to make its comparisons. When searching for row differences, Excel compares the cells in the selection with the cells in the same column as the active cell. When searching for column differences, Excel compares the cells in the selection with the cells in the same row as the active cell.

For example, you've selected the range B10:G20, and cell B10 is the active cell. If you select the Row Differences option, Excel compares the entries in cells C10:G10 with the entry in cell B10, the entries in cells C11:G11 with the entry in cell B11, and so on. If you use the Column Differences option, Excel compares the entries in cells B11:B20 with the entry in cell B10, the entries in cells C11:C20 with the entry in cell C10, and so on.

Among other things, Excel looks for differences in your cell and range references and selects those cells that don't conform to the comparison cell. Suppose cell B10 is your comparison cell and contains the formula

=SUM(B1:B9)

If you select cells B10:G10 and then select the Row Differences option, Excel scans this range to check for any formulas that don't fit. For example, to follow the pattern in cell B10, the formula in cells C10 and D10 should be

=SUM(C1:C9)

and

=SUM(D1:D9)

If any of the formulas in row 10 don't match this pattern, Go To Special selects the cells containing those formulas. If they all match, Excel displays a *No cells found* message.

The Row Differences and Column Differences options also verify that all the cells in the selected range contain the same type of entries. For example, if the comparison cell contains a SUM function, Excel flags any cells that contain a function, formula, or value other than SUM. If the comparison cell contains a constant text or numeric value, Excel flags any cells in the selected range that don't exactly match the comparison value. The options, however, are not case sensitive.

TIP You can also use keyboard shortcuts to select Column Differences or Row Differences. To search for column differences, select the range you want to search and press Ctrl-Shift-|. To quickly search for row differences, select the range you want to search and press Ctrl-\.

To use the Precedents and Dependents options, first select the cell whose precedents or dependents you want to trace, press F5, click the Special button, and select Precedents or Dependents. Excel then activates the Direct Only and All Levels options. Use these options to set the parameters of your search: Direct Only finds only those cells that directly refer to or that directly depend on the active cell; All Levels locates direct precedents and dependents plus those cells that are indirectly linked to the active cell. When searching for precedents or dependents, Excel always searches the entire worksheet.

TIP You can also use these keyboard shortcuts to quickly select precedents and dependents of the active cell:

Ctrl-[	Selects direct precedents
Ctrl-Shift-{	Selects all precedents
Ctrl-]	Selects direct dependents
Ctrl-Shift-}	Selects all dependents

The Last Cell option in the Go To Special dialog box selects the cell in the lower right corner of the range that encompasses all cells that contain data, notes, or formats. When you select Last Cell, Excel finds the last cell in the active area of the worksheet, not the lower right corner of the current selection.

The Visible Cells Only option excludes from the current selection any cells in hidden rows or columns.

TIP You can also press Alt-; to quickly select only the visible cells in the current selection.

The Objects option selects all graphic objects in your worksheet, regardless of the current selection.

See Also For more information about working with graphic objects, see Chapter 9, "Graphics," page 345.

Chapter 8

Workbooks and Windows

In Chapter 1, we introduced you to both the workbook and the worksheet and showed you the basics of how to get around. In this chapter, we'll show you how to work with more than one workbook at a time. We'll also show you how to open multiple windows for the same workbook. (You'll find this capability beneficial when you want to see two widely separated regions of a worksheet at the same time.) Along the way, we'll survey the commands and shortcuts for opening, navigating, manipulating, hiding, saving, and closing multiple windows.

In addition, we'll show you how to add and remove worksheets, name them, and split them into *windowpanes*. We'll also examine Microsoft Excel's powerful *group editing* feature, which allows you to format and edit two or more worksheets in the same workbook at once. We'll take a look at the Zoom command, with which you can reduce or enlarge the display of your workbooks, and *named views,* which let you customize combinations of display, workspace, and print settings and save them for easy retrieval.

Working with Workbook Windows

In early versions of Microsoft Excel, worksheets, charts, and macro sheets were stored on disk as separate documents. Since Excel 5, however, all these types of data, and more, peacefully coexist in workbooks. You can keep as many sheets containing various types of data in a workbook as you want, you can have more than one workbook open at the same time, and you can have more than one window open for the same workbook. The only limitations to these capabilities are those imposed by your computer's memory and system resources.

Managing Multiple Workbooks

Generally, when you start Excel, a blank workbook opens with the provisional title Book1. The exception is when you load Excel and an existing file simultaneously. For example, if you start Excel by double-clicking a document icon — or if you have one or more worksheet files stored in the XLStart directory so that they open automatically — Excel does not start with a blank Book1.

To open an additional file, choose New or Open from the File menu or use the New Workbook or Open button on the Standard toolbar (the first two buttons on the left).

You can open as many workbooks as you like until your computer runs out of memory. The new workbook appears on top of the last active workbook window and becomes the active (or current) workbook window. The active window appears with scroll bars.

Note that if you use the Open command or the Open button to open a workbook that is already open, the copy that is on your screen is replaced by the version last saved to disk. (If any changes were made to the open workbook, an alert box asks you to confirm that you want to revert to the saved version by clicking Yes.) To work with two or more windows on the same workbook, choose the New Window command from the Window menu.

For more information about the XLStart directory, see "Opening Files," page 65.

For more information about working with multiple windows, see "Opening Multiple Windows for the Same Workbook," page 305.

Navigating Between Open Workbooks

To move from one open workbook window to another, you can click a window to activate it, and then shuffle through a "stack" of windows using a keyboard shortcut, or you can choose a window name from the Window menu.

For example, three workbooks — Products, Expenses, and Sales — overlap, as in Figure 8-1. To switch from Products to Sales, click anywhere in the Sales workbook.

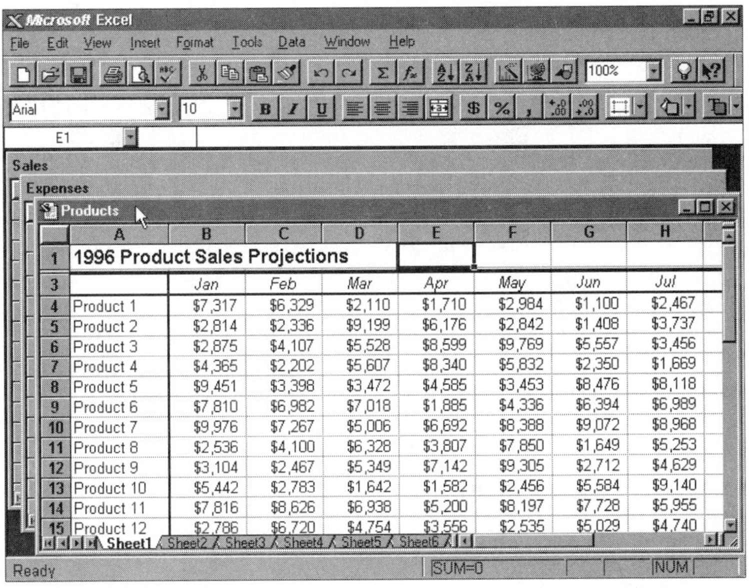

FIGURE 8-1

To move to a window that's at least partially visible, position the mouse pointer anywhere in the window and click.

TIP If the workbook you want is open, but not even partially visible on the screen, you can cycle through the open windows by pressing Ctrl-F6. To switch from workbook to workbook in the opposite direction, hold down Shift and press Ctrl-F6.

If you have many windows open, the Window menu is the easiest route from one window to another. As shown in Figure 8-2, the bottom section of the Window menu lists the open workbooks by name. To move directly to a workbook, choose its name.

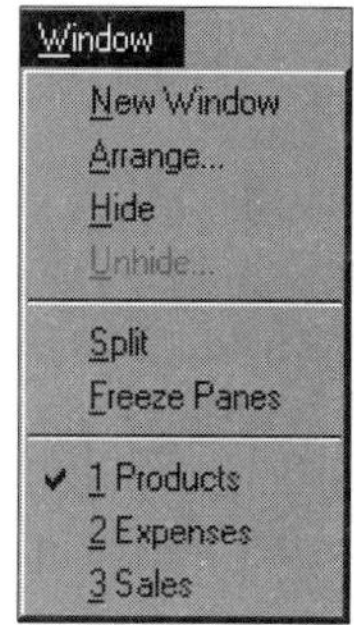

FIGURE 8-2 The Window menu is your best navigational tool when you have many workbooks open.

The Window menu can list a maximum of nine workbooks. If you have more than nine open, the Window menu includes a command called More Windows. When you choose this command, a dialog box appears, listing the names of all open workbooks. Simply select a name and click OK.

Arranging Workbook Windows

To see two or more workbooks at once, choose the Arrange command from the Window menu. Excel displays the dialog box shown in Figure 8-3. The Arrange command arranges all open windows into one of four possible configurations: Tiled, in which the screen is divided among the open documents, as shown in Figure 8-4; Horizontal, as shown in Figure 8-5; Vertical, as shown in Figure 8-6 on page 302; or Cascade, as previously shown in Figure 8-1.

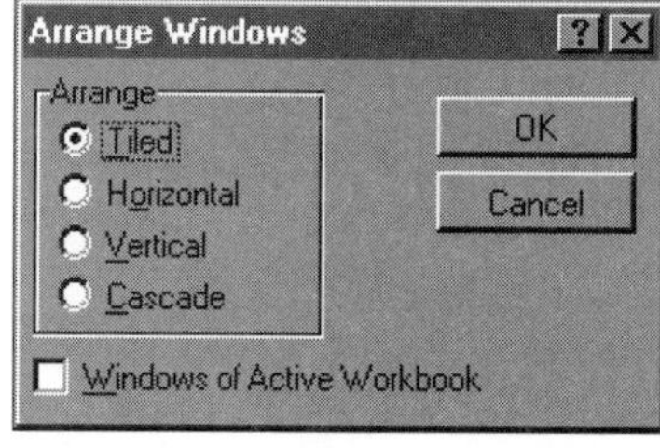

FIGURE 8-3 The Arrange command on the Window menu gives you a choice of four different configurations.

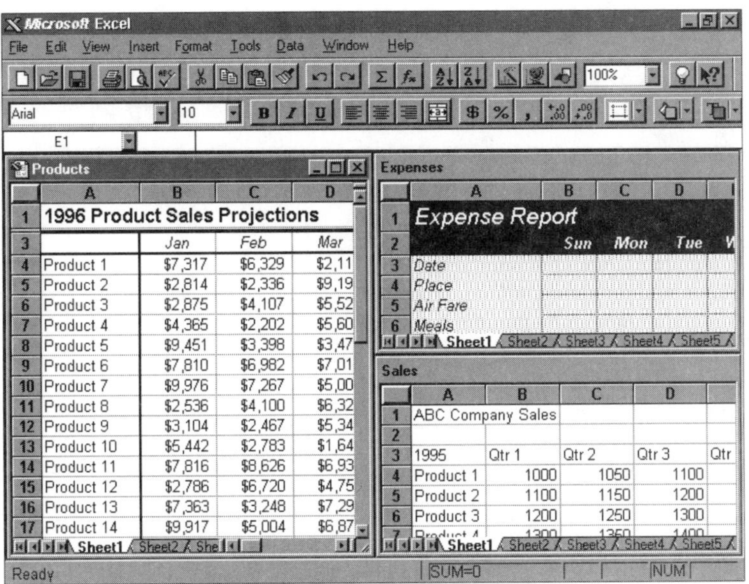

FIGURE 8-4
These worksheets are tiled.

If you select the Windows Of Active Workbook option in the Arrange Windows dialog box, the active window is maximized, or if more than one window is open for the same workbook, only those windows are arranged according to the option set in the Arrange section of the dialog box. This is handy when you have several workbooks open, but you want to arrange only the active workbook's windows without closing the others.

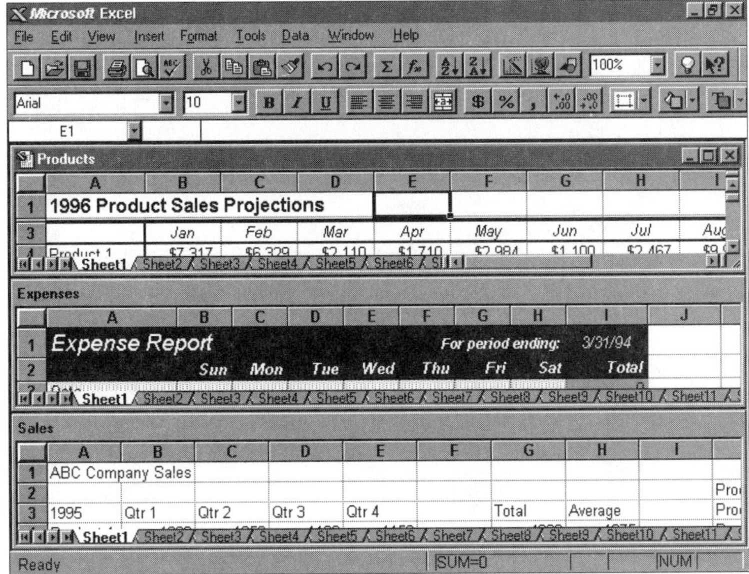

FIGURE 8-5
These worksheets are arranged horizontally.

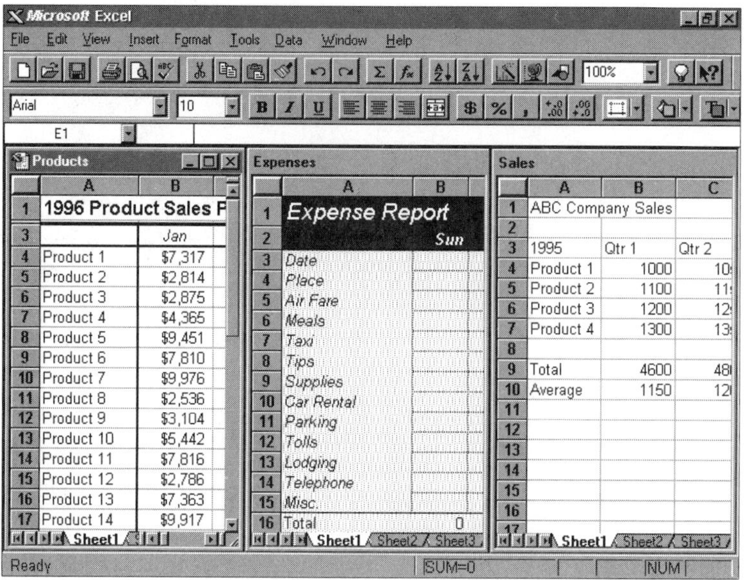

FIGURE 8-6
These worksheets are arranged vertically.

See Also For more information about working with multiple windows, see "Opening Multiple Windows for the Same Workbook," page 305.

Maximizing and Minimizing Workbook Windows

Even with your windows neatly arranged, as shown in Figure 8-6, you can still maximize a window by clicking its Maximize button at the right end of the window's title bar, shown in Figure 8-7. When you want the side-by-side view once more, click the Restore button (which was formerly the Maximize button), and Excel restores your screen to its former configuration. When a window is not maximized, it is floating.

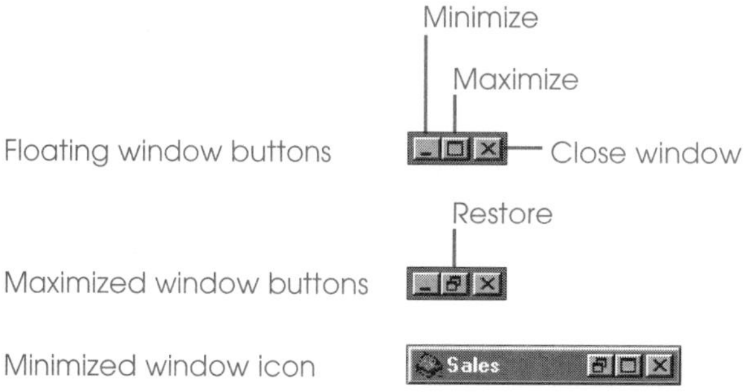

FIGURE 8-7
The Maximize button changes to the Restore button once a window is maximized.

Maximizing the Whole Enchilada

You can maximize the workbook window if you need to see more of the active worksheet, but if that still isn't enough, you can use the Full Screen command on the View menu. When you choose this command, Excel removes the formula bar, status bar, toolbars, and title bars from your computer screen — everything except the menu bar, the Full Screen button, and the maximized workbook window — as shown in the following figure.

	A	B	C	D	E	F	G	H	I
1	1996 Product Sales Projections								
3		Jan	Feb	Mar	Apr	May	Jun	Jul	
4	Product 1	$7,317	$6,329	$2,110	$1,710	$2,984	$1,100	$2,467	$9,9
5	Product 2	$2,814	$2,336	$9,199	$6,176	$2,842	$1,408	$3,737	$1,7
6	Product 3	$2,875	$4,107	$5,528	$8,599	$9,769	$5,557	$3,456	$4,6
7	Product 4	$4,365	$2,202	$5,607	$8,340	$5,832	$2,350	$1,669	$5,0
8	Product 5	$9,451	$3,398	$3,472	$4,585	$3,453	$8,476	$8,118	$5,7
9	Product 6	$7,810	$6,982	$7,018	$1,885	$4,336	$6,394	$6,989	$2,0
10	Product 7	$9,976	$7,267	$5,006	$6,692	$8,388	$9,072	$8,968	$5,9
11	Product 8	$2,536	$4,100	$6,328	$3,807	$7,850	$1,649	$5,253	$3,9
12	Product 9	$3,104	$2,467	$5,349	$7,142	$9,305	$2,712	$4,629	$3,9
13	Product 10	$5,442	$2,783	$1,642	$1,582	$2,456	$5,584	$9,140	$7,9
14	Product 11	$7,816	$8,626	$6,938	$5,200	$8,197	$7,728	$5,955	$1,7
15	Product 12	$2,786	$6,720	$4,754	$3,556	$2,535	$5,029	$4,740	$7,0
16	Product 13	$7,363	$3,248	$7,295	$9,822	$2,076	$8,372	$1,846	$1,2
17	Product 14	$9,917	$5,004	$6,873	$8,719	$8,399	$4,204	$8,290	$2,6
18	Product 15	$6,593	$8,499	$1,404	$1,749	$5,999	$4,398	$9,773	$1,1
19	Product 16	$2,036	$5,359	$8,656	$4,240	$2,690	$2,211	$4,893	$1,2
20	Product 17	$733	$5,814	$2,773	$4,464	$2,067	$8,424	$1,337	$1,4
21	Product 18	$1,831	$1,422	$1,572	$5,771	$6,611	$9,131	$9,121	$1,2
22	Product 19	$1,533	$2,938	$5,923	$9,180	$7,783	$1,542	$5,745	$5,9
23	Product 20	$9,688	$3,310	$4,472	$3,065	$4,700	$6,384	$9,079	$6,9
24	Product 21	$1,251	$2,433	$5,082	$7,202	$1,237	$7,456	$9,631	$2,2
25	Product 22	$2,156	$5,623	$8,960	$5,829	$6,495	$4,953	$1,921	$2,9

The Full Screen command provides a convenient way to display the most information on the screen without changing the magnification of the data. (For more information about changing the magnification, see "Zooming Worksheets," page 322.) To return the screen to its former configuration, simply click the Full Screen button that appears in the upper-right corner of the screen, or choose the Full Screen command again.

One other important point: When you maximize one window, you maximize all other open windows. If Products, Expenses, and Sales are open, for example, and you maximize Products, Excel also maximizes Expenses and

Sales. You won't see these other windows because they lie behind Products, but you can move to them using Ctrl-F6 or the Window menu.

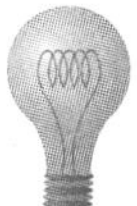

TIP If you're working with several workbooks in a particular arrangement that is often useful, choose the Save Workspace command on the File menu. You can save the current settings and set everything up the same way by simply opening one file. See "Saving the Entire Workspace," page 65.

A window always includes a Minimize button. When you click the Minimize button, the window is reduced to an icon that resembles a short title bar. To restore the window, click the Maximize button.

Moving and Sizing Workbook Windows

To move a workbook window with the mouse, position the mouse pointer on the title bar of the window, hold down the mouse button, drag the window to a new position, and release the mouse button. To change a window's size, drag the window borders.

See Also For more information about resizing windows, see "Resizing the Workbook Window," page 8.

Saving and Closing Workbooks

When you save a workbook using the Save or Save As command on the File menu or the Save button on the Standard toolbar, characteristics such as the window's size, position on the screen, and display settings are also saved in the same file. The next time you open the file, the workbook window looks exactly the same as it did the last time you saved it. Even the same cells that were selected when you saved the file are selected when you open it.

To close an individual workbook window, choose the Close command from the File menu or click the Close box at the right end of the title bar (or to the right of the menu bar if the window is maximized). The Close box is the small button with the "x" on it. If you've made changes since the last time you saved your work, a dialog box asks whether you want to save the workbook before you close it. If you did not intend to close the workbook, simply click the Cancel button.

Opening Three-Dimensional Lotus 1-2-3 Files and Microsoft Excel 4 Workbook Files

A Lotus 1-2-3 file that includes multiple worksheets is opened as a workbook in Excel 7. Three-dimensional formulas are converted to the corresponding Excel formulas.

Workbook files created with Excel 4 can contain *bound* and *unbound* worksheets. Bound worksheets in a workbook are opened as individual sheets in a single Excel 7 workbook. However, each individual unbound worksheet in an Excel 4 workbook is opened as a separate workbook.

For information about the transition from Lotus 1-2-3, see "Lotus 1-2-3 Transition Options," page 152. For information about getting help with your transition from Lotus 1-2-3 to Excel, see "Help for Lotus 1-2-3 Users," page 27. For information about importing Lotus 1-2-3 files, see Chapter 26, "Importing and Exporting," page 889.

See Also For information about saving files and saving and opening groups of workbooks, see Chapter 3, "Managing Files," page 51.

Opening Multiple Windows for the Same Workbook

Suppose you've created a workbook called Products, like the one shown earlier in Figure 8-1. Even if you maximize the workbook window, only cells A1:H18 are likely to be completely visible (this may vary depending on your monitor). If you need to see another area of the workbook simultaneously, open a second window for the workbook. To open another window, choose the New Window command from the Window menu. To view both windows together on your screen, choose the Arrange command from the Window menu and select one of the Arrange options. If you select the Vertical option, your screen then looks like the one in Figure 8-8 on the next page.

Notice that Excel assigns the name Products:2 to the new workbook window. It also changes the name of the original workbook window to Products:1. In addition, Products:2 becomes the active window as indicated by the solid color of its title bar and the presence of scroll bars.

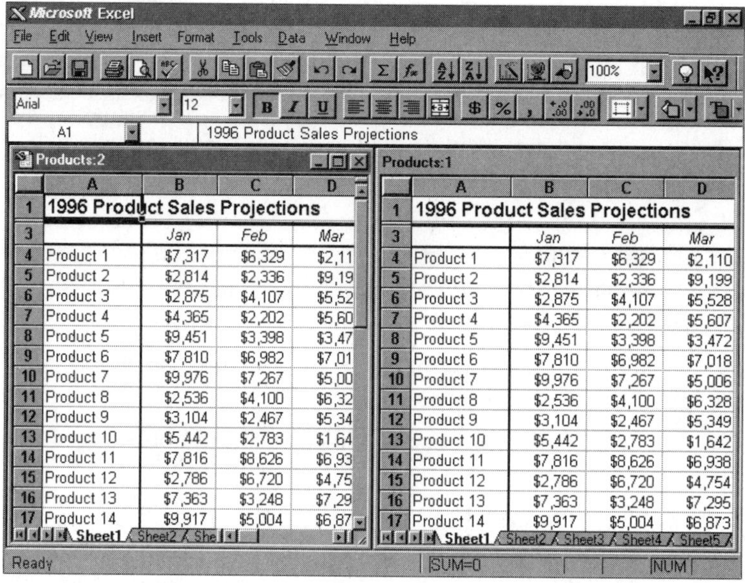

FIGURE 8-8
Use the New Window command to open a second window for the same workbook, and then use the Arrange command to view both windows simultaneously.

It's important to understand the difference between the File menu's New command and the Window menu's New Window command. The File menu's New command creates a new workbook, which is displayed in a new window. The workbook that results from the New command is completely separate from any preexisting workbooks. The New Window command, however, simply creates a new window for the active workbook.

Any work you do in a window affects the entire workbook, not just the portion of the workbook viewed in that window. For instance, when you make an entry in one workbook window, you can view that entry in any window associated with that workbook. By the same token, if you edit or erase the contents of a cell in one workbook window, you can see the change when you look at the same cell, or any cell dependent upon that cell, in another window of the same workbook.

You can scroll through the new window to look at another section of the workbook. For example, if you click the down and right scroll arrows in Products:2 a few times, you can move cells L24:N38 into view, as shown in Figure 8-9. You can also use Go To on the Edit menu (or press F5) to move to a different location in the new window.

TIP If other windows are open but you want to view only the windows on the active workbook, select the Windows Of Active Workbook box on the Arrange Windows dialog box.

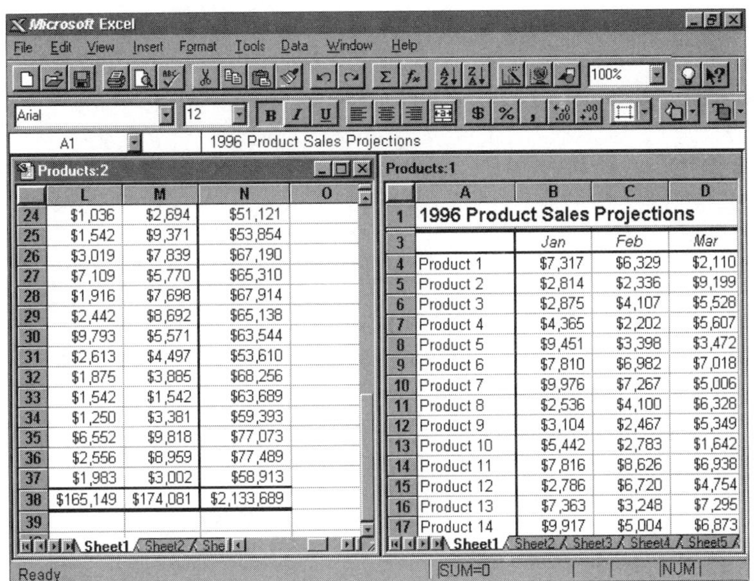

FIGURE 8-9

Cells L24:N38 now appear in the second window.

See Also

For more information about navigating in a workbook, see "Navigating in a Workbook," page 6.

For more information about navigating with the Go To command, see "Using the Go To Command," page 96.

Hiding and Protecting Workbooks

Sometimes, you might want to keep certain information out of sight or simply protect it from inadvertent modification. You can conceal and protect data by hiding workbook windows, workbooks, or individual worksheets, from view.

See Also

For information about protecting the workbook file itself, see "Protecting Files," page 60.

For information about protecting individual cells, see "Protecting Your Data," page 106.

For information about hiding columns and rows, see the sidebar titled "Hiding a Column or Row," page 196.

Hiding Workbook Windows

At times you might need to keep a workbook open so that you can use the information it contains, but you don't want that window to take up room on your screen. When several open workbooks clutter your workspace, you can use the Hide command on the Window menu to conceal some of them. Excel can still work with the information in the hidden workbooks, but they don't take up space on your screen, nor do their filenames appear on the Window menu.

To hide a workbook window, simply activate it and choose Hide from the Window menu. Excel removes the window display from your workspace, but the workbook remains open. To bring the hidden window into view, choose Unhide from the Window menu. (This command appears dimmed unless a window is hidden.) If you have hidden the only open workbook window, you must choose Unhide from the File menu. In either case, a dialog box like the one shown in Figure 8-10 lists all the hidden workbook windows.

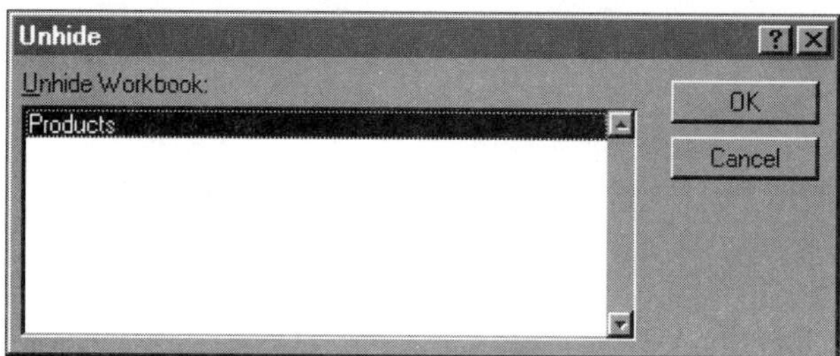

FIGURE 8-10
The Unhide dialog box lists all the workbook windows that are currently hidden.

Select the workbook you want to view and click OK. The hidden workbook appears and becomes active.

If you've protected the hidden workbook by choosing the Protect Workbook command from the Protection submenu of the Tools menu and then selecting the Windows option, you must enter your password before you can hide or unhide the workbook.

Saving Workbooks as Hidden

Sometimes, you might want to hide a particular workbook, even when it is first opened, perhaps to prevent others from opening and viewing its sensitive contents in your absence. You can save a workbook as hidden by following these steps:

1. With the workbook you want to hide active, choose Hide from the Window menu.
2. While holding down Shift, choose Close All from the File menu.
3. When a message appears asking if you want to save changes to the workbook, click Yes.

The next time you open the workbook, it opens as hidden. To ensure that the workbook cannot be unhidden by others, you might want to assign a password using the Protect Workbook command on the Protection submenu of the Tools menu before hiding and saving the workbook.

TIP The opposite of hiding and protecting a workbook would be to make it available to others for editing. Excel's new Shared Lists command on the File menu allows muti-user editing. See "Sharing Files with Others," page 66.

Hiding Individual Worksheets

If you want to hide a particular worksheet in a workbook, you can use the Hide command on the Sheet submenu of the Format menu. When you choose the Hide command, the active worksheet no longer appears in the workbook. To unhide a hidden worksheet, choose the Unhide command from the Sheet submenu. (The Unhide command appears dimmed when there are no hidden worksheets in the active workbook.) As shown in Figure 8-11, the Unhide dialog box for worksheets is similar to the Unhide dialog box for workbooks.

FIGURE 8-11
Use the Unhide command on the Sheet submenu of the Format menu to unhide individual worksheets.

If the structure of your workbook is protected using the Protect Sheet command on the Protection submenu of the Tools menu, you cannot hide or unhide individual worksheets.

See Also For information about hiding just the formulas and values in cells, see the sidebar titled "The 'Hidden' Number Format," page 179.

For information about hiding entire columns and rows, see the sidebar titled "Hiding a Column or Row," page 196.

Working with Sheets

The workbook is the binder for all your sheets, and like a binder, it can contain a variety of different kinds of sheets that you can insert, remove, or move anywhere you want. Unlike a binder, you can also copy sheets as well as name and rename sheets. Finally, you can select groups of sheets and edit them together — that is, enter data and apply formats to all selected sheets at once.

NOTE Up to now, we have only discussed worksheets; however, Excel 7 actually has several different kinds of sheets. For the purposes of this discussion, we will use the generic term "sheet" in this section, but we will return to the term "worksheet" for the more specific discussions later in this chapter and throughout the remainder of Part 2.

Sheet Basics

A new workbook, by default, contains 16 worksheets, named Sheet1 through Sheet16. You can change the default number of sheets that appear in a new work- book by choosing the Options command from the Tools menu and clicking the General tab. The General tab of the Options dialog box is shown in Figure 8-12.

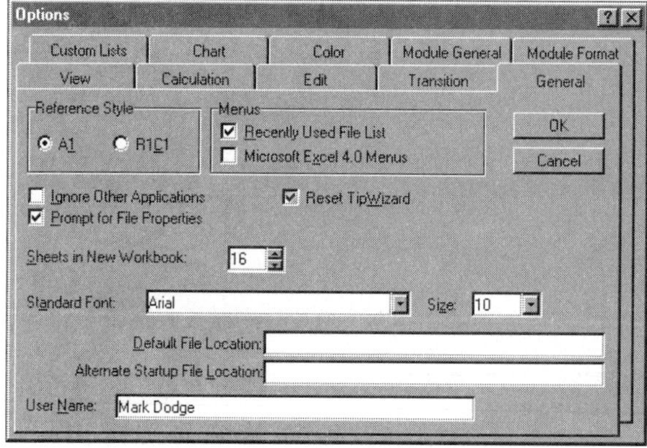

FIGURE 8-12
You can control the number of sheets that appear in a new workbook by using the General tab of the Options dialog box.

The General tab contains the Sheets In New Workbook edit box, where you can type the number or click the up and down arrows to indicate how many sheets you want all new workbooks to contain, up to a maximum of 255.

TIP Each blank sheet in a workbook consumes additional disk space, so you might want to create new workbooks with a small number of sheets and add new sheets only when necessary. You should also be sure to delete unused sheets in your workbooks to conserve disk space.

NOTE Although you can specify that new workbooks are created with up to 255 sheets, you can add as many sheets to an existing workbook as you want, subject only to the limitations of your computer's memory and system resources.

A workbook can contain the following types of sheets:

- Worksheets
- Chart sheets (see Part 4, page 581)
- Visual Basic modules (see Part 6, page 827)
- Dialog sheets
- Microsoft Excel 4.0 macro sheets (see Part 6, page 827)

Inserting and Deleting Sheets in a Workbook

It's easy to change the number of sheets in a workbook. For example, to insert a new sheet in an existing workbook, follow these steps:

1. Select a sheet tab in the workbook before which you want to insert a new sheet, such as Sheet2 in Figure 8-13.

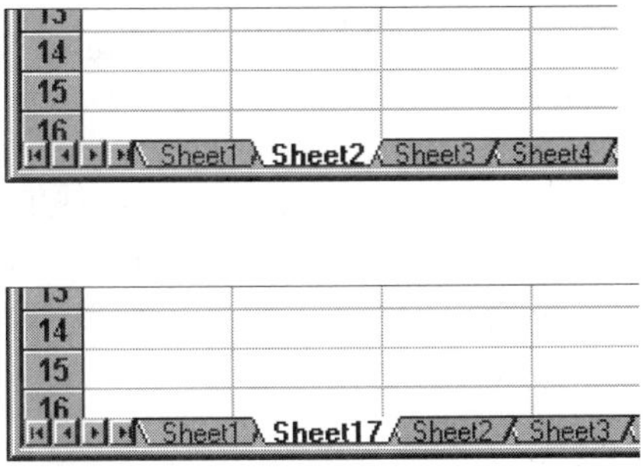

FIGURE 8-13
You can use the Worksheet command on the Insert menu to add a new sheet before the selected sheet.

2. Then choose the Worksheet command from the Insert menu.

   Figure 8-13 shows the new sheet, Sheet17, inserted before Sheet2.

Using the same technique, you can also add several sheets to a workbook at the same time. To add more than one sheet, select a sheet tab, press Shift, and then select a range of sheets — the same number that you want to insert — before choosing the Worksheet command. (Notice that [Group] has been added to the workbook title in the window title bar, indicating that you have selected a group of sheets for editing.) Excel inserts the same number of new sheets before the first sheet in the selected range, as illustrated in Figure 8-14.

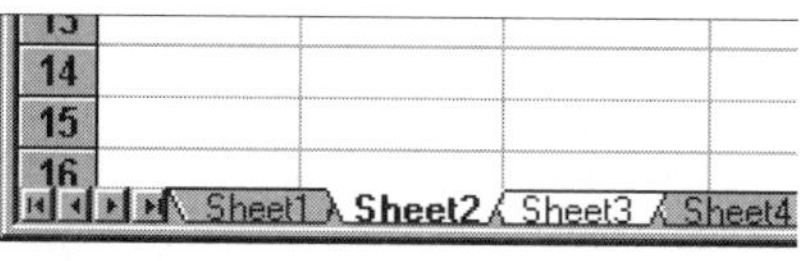

FIGURE 8-14
To insert two new sheets at once, hold down Shift and select two existing sheets. Then choose Worksheet from the Insert menu.

Notice that Excel numbers the new sheets based on the number of sheets in the workbook — in this case, 16. The first sheet you insert is Sheet17, the next is Sheet18, and so on. Keep in mind that you cannot undo the Worksheet command on the Insert menu.

> **NOTE** You can insert other types of sheets in your workbooks using the Chart and Macro commands on the Insert menu. The Chart command is discussed in Chapter 16, "Basic Charting Techniques," page 583, and the Macro command is discussed in Chapter 23, "Creating Macros," page 829.

To delete a sheet, you can use the Delete Sheet command on the Edit menu. Simply select the sheet you want to delete, choose Delete Sheet, and click OK at the prompt to permanently remove it from your workbook. If you want to delete more than one sheet, you can hold down Shift to select a range of sheets, or you can hold down Ctrl and select nonadjacent sheets before you choose the Delete Sheet command. You cannot undo the Delete Sheet command.

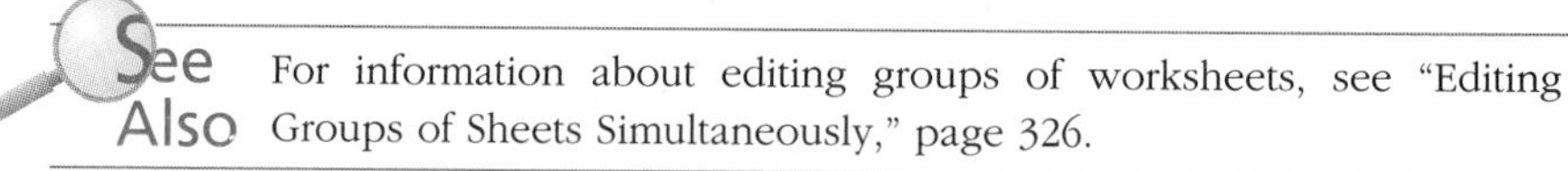

For information about editing groups of worksheets, see "Editing Groups of Sheets Simultaneously," page 326.

Naming and Renaming Sheets in a Workbook

If you grow weary of seeing Sheet1, Sheet2, and so on, in your workbooks, you can give your sheets more imaginative and helpful names using the Rename command on the Sheet submenu of the Format menu. When you choose this command, the dialog box in Figure 8-15 appears.

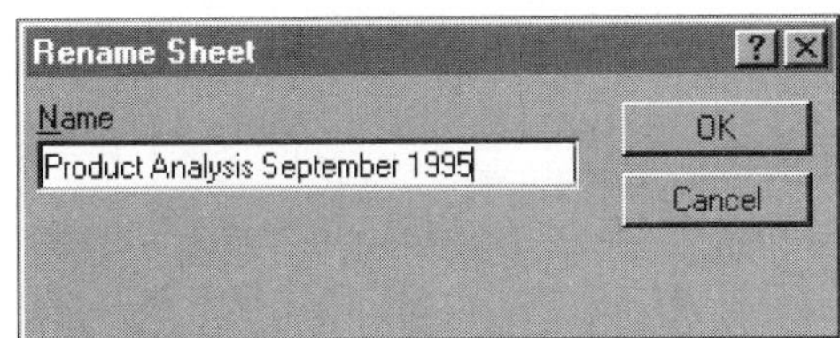

FIGURE 8-15
To rename a sheet, choose Sheet and then Rename from the Format menu.

As you can see in Figure 8-15, you are not limited to eight-character names for your sheets. In fact, you can use up to 31 characters in your sheet names. Remember, though, that the name you use determines the width of the corresponding tab at the bottom of the workbook window, as shown in Figure 8-16. Therefore, you might still want to keep your sheet names concise so that you can see more than two or three tabs at a time.

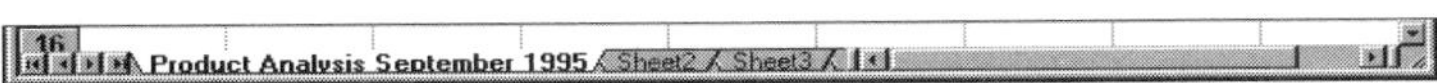

FIGURE 8-16
The name you give to a sheet appears in the tab for that sheet.

TIP You can double-click a sheet tab to quickly display the Rename Sheet dialog box and then enter a new name for the sheet in the Name edit box.

Moving and Copying Sheets in a Workbook

As you might expect, Excel provides a very easy way to move a sheet from one place to another in the same workbook. In fact, all you have to do is click the sheet tab you want to move with the mouse and then drag the sheet to its new location. Figure 8-17 shows this process.

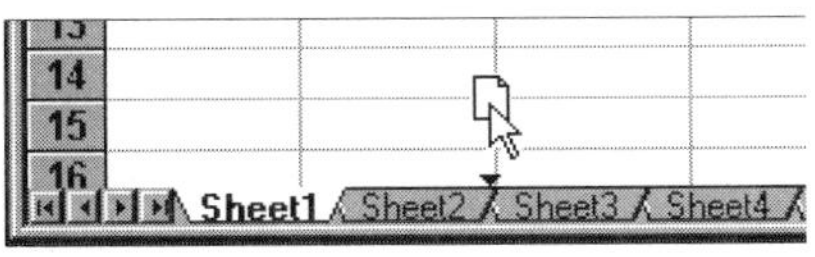

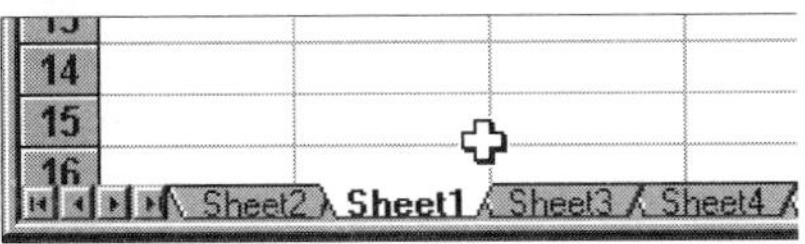

FIGURE 8-17
To move a sheet, select a sheet tab and drag it to the new location.

When you drag a sheet, a small worksheet icon appears, and a tiny arrow indicates where the sheet will be inserted in the tab order. If you want to move the sheet to a new location that is not currently visible on your screen, simply drag past the visible tabs in either direction. The tabs scroll automatically in the direction you drag.

Using this technique, you can also move several sheets at the same time. In Figure 8-18, we selected Sheet1, and, while holding down Shift, we clicked Sheet3 to select the range Sheet1:Sheet3. We then dragged to the right to move the range of sheets to a new location.

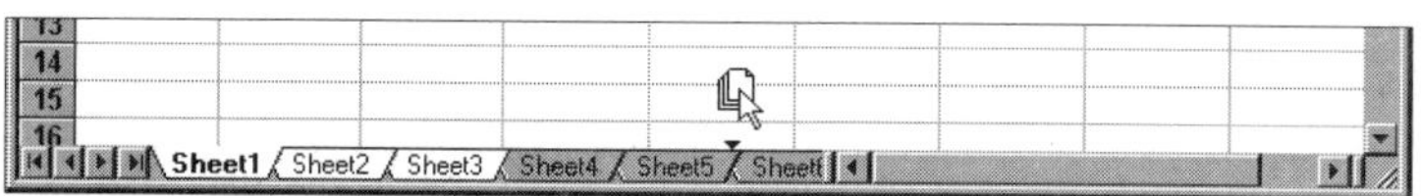

FIGURE 8-18
You can select several adjacent sheets and move them together.

You can also move several nonadjacent sheets at the same time by holding down Ctrl while you select the sheets. Notice that when you release the mouse button to drop the sheets in their new location, the formerly nonadjacent sheets are inserted together.

In addition, you can copy sheets using similar mouse techniques. First select the sheet or sheets you want to copy and then hold down Ctrl while you drag the sheet or sheets to the new location. As you drag, a plus sign appears in the small worksheet icon, as shown in Figure 8-19.

FIGURE 8-19
When you hold down Ctrl and drag, Excel copies the selected sheet or sheets to the new location.

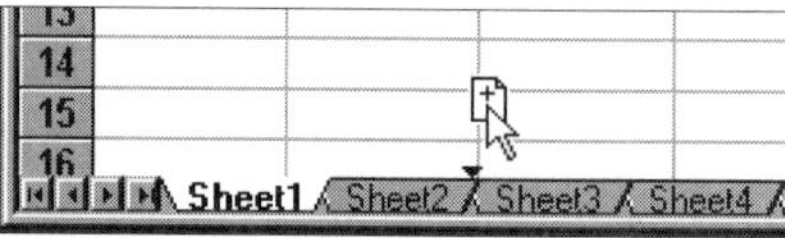

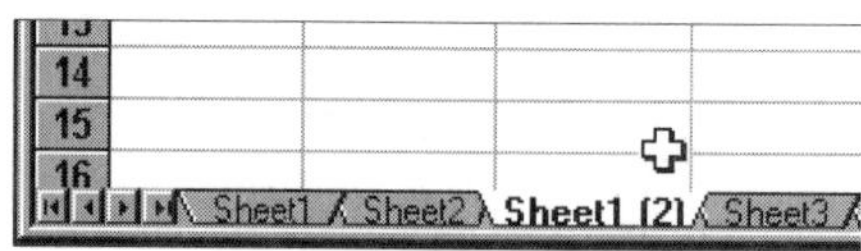

When you copy a sheet, the identical sheet appears in the new location; however, a number in parentheses is appended to the copy's name to distinguish it from the original sheet. For example, as shown in Figure 8-19, the name of the Sheet1 copy is Sheet1 (2).

Excel also provides the Move Or Copy Sheet command on the Edit menu, which performs similar sheet-management functions, including moving and copying sheets between workbooks. When you choose this command from the Edit menu, the Move Or Copy dialog box in Figure 8-20 appears.

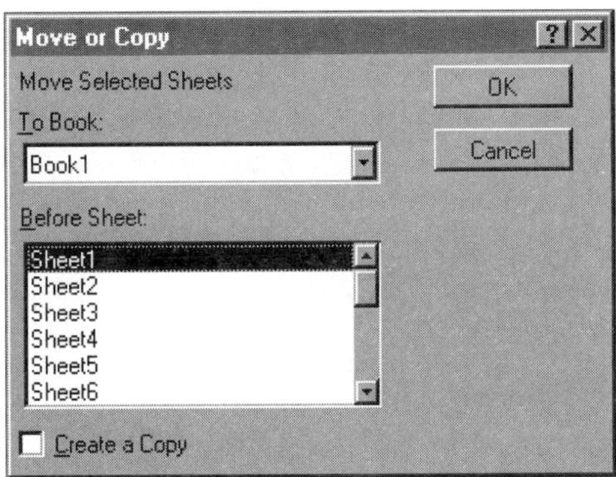

FIGURE 8-20
Use the Move Or Copy dialog box to move or copy sheets in the same workbook or to other workbooks.

This dialog box performs the same operations as the mouse methods already described. Before you choose the Move Or Copy Sheet command, select the sheet or sheets you want to move or copy. Then, in the Move Or Copy dialog box, you can move the selection before a specific sheet by selecting the sheet in the Before Sheet list box. You can create a copy of your selection by specifying a sheet in the list box and then selecting the Create A Copy option.

The Sheet Tab Shortcut Menu

If you position the mouse pointer over the sheet tabs in a workbook and click the right mouse button, the following menu appears.

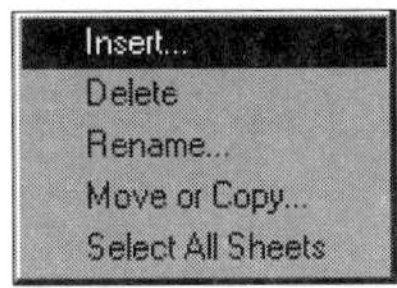

In addition to providing a convenient method for inserting, deleting, renaming, moving, and copying sheets, this shortcut menu provides the Select All Sheets command. As its name indicates, you use this command to select all the sheets in a workbook, which comes in handy if you want to perform certain functions, such as copying, on all the sheets at once.

Another advantage of using this menu to insert sheets is that the Insert dialog box lets you choose the type of sheet you want to insert.

Moving and Copying Sheets Between Workbooks

One of the more exciting features of Excel is the ability to move and copy sheets *between workbooks* by dragging. You can use the same methods to move and copy that you use for worksheets in the same workbook. For example, suppose you have two workbooks arranged vertically in the workspace and you want to copy Sheet1 in Book1 to Book2. First rename Sheet1 to *Sheet from Book 1* and then hold down the Ctrl key and drag the sheet to Book2. *Sheet from Book 1* is copied and inserted in Book2 without using a single command! (See Figure 8-21.)

You can also move or copy worksheets from one workbook to another using the Move Or Copy Sheet command on the Edit menu. For example, to move a sheet or sheets from one workbook to another, select the sheet or sheets you want to move and choose the Move Or Copy Sheet command. Then, when the Move Or Copy dialog box appears, select the name of the workbook to which you want to move your selection in the To Book drop-down list box. You can also simultaneously move the sheets and create a new workbook by selecting New Book from the To Book drop-down list box. If you want to copy sheets instead of move them, select the Create A Copy option before clicking OK in the Move Or Copy dialog box.

FIGURE 8-21

You can drag a sheet or sheets directly to another visible workbook.

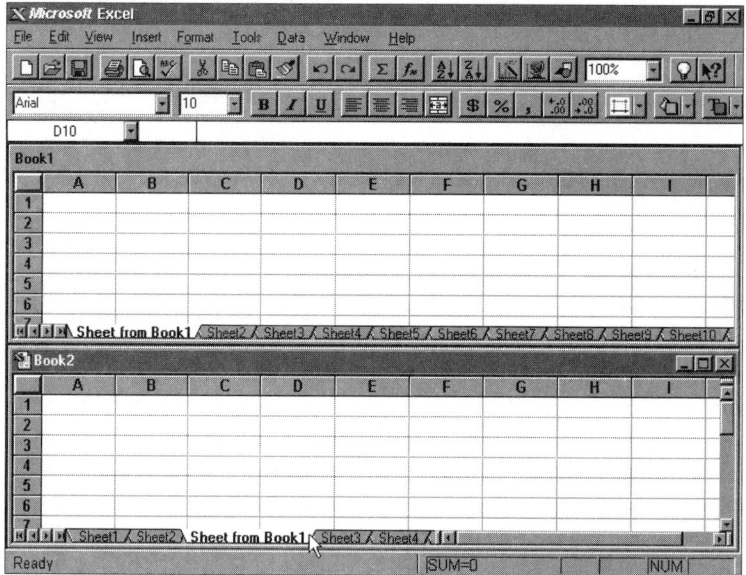

Splitting Sheets into Panes

Windowpanes are another way to view different areas of your worksheet simultaneously. You can split any sheet in a workbook vertically, horizontally, or both vertically and horizontally.

The windowpane feature offers synchronized scrolling capability. For example, in the worksheet in Figure 8-22, Columns B through M and rows 4 through 37 contain product sales data. Column N and row 38 contain totals.

Products

	A	B	C	D	E	F	G	H
1	1996 Product Sales Projections							
3		Jan	Feb	Mar	Apr	May	Jun	Jul
4	Product 1	$7,317	$6,329	$2,110	$1,710	$2,984	$1,100	$2,467
5	Product 2	$2,814	$2,336	$9,199	$6,176	$2,842	$1,408	$3,737
6	Product 3	$2,875	$4,107	$5,528	$8,599	$9,769	$5,557	$3,456
7	Product 4	$4,365	$2,202	$5,607	$8,340	$5,832	$2,350	$1,669
8	Product 5	$9,451	$3,398	$3,472	$4,585	$3,453	$8,476	$8,118
9	Product 6	$7,810	$6,982	$7,018	$1,885	$4,336	$6,394	$6,989
10	Product 7	$9,976	$7,267	$5,006	$6,692	$8,388	$9,072	$8,968
11	Product 8	$2,536	$4,100	$6,328	$3,807	$7,850	$1,649	$5,253
12	Product 9	$3,104	$2,467	$5,349	$7,142	$9,305	$2,712	$4,629
13	Product 10	$5,442	$2,783	$1,642	$1,582	$2,456	$5,584	$9,140
14	Product 11	$7,816	$8,626	$6,938	$5,200	$8,197	$7,728	$5,955
15	Product 12	$2,786	$6,720	$4,754	$3,556	$2,535	$5,029	$4,740
16	Product 13	$7,363	$3,248	$7,295	$9,822	$2,076	$8,372	$1,846
17	Product 14	$9,917	$5,004	$6,873	$8,719	$8,399	$4,204	$8,290

Sheet1 / Sheet2 / Sheet3 / Sheet4 / Sheet5 / Sheet6

Vertical split box

Horizontal split box

FIGURE 8-22

It will be easier to keep track of where we are in this worksheet when we split it into panes.

There are several ways to split a sheet into panes:

- Drag either split box with the mouse to split the window vertically or horizontally.
- Double-click either split box to split the window vertically or horizontally.
- From the Window menu, choose the Split command to split the window into vertical and horizontal panes simultaneously.

In the worksheet in Figure 8-22, in order to keep an eye on the totals in column N as you work with the monthly sales figures in columns B through M, you can split the window into two panes: one 7 columns wide and the other 1 column wide.

To create a vertical pane, point to the vertical split box — the black box at the right end of the horizontal scroll bar (just to the right of the right scroll arrow). When your mouse pointer is over the vertical split box, it changes to a double-headed arrow, as shown in Figure 8-23 on the next page.

$3,472	$4,585	$3,453	$8,476	$8,118
$7,018	$1,885	$4,336	$6,394	$6,989
$5,006	$6,692	$8,388	$9,072	$8,968
$6,328	$3,807	$7,850	$1,649	$5,253
$5,349	$7,142	$9,305	$2,712	$4,629
$1,642	$1,582	$2,456	$5,584	$9,140
$6,938	$5,200	$8,197	$7,728	$5,955
$4,754	$3,556	$2,535	$5,029	$4,740

Sheet5 / Sheet6

FIGURE 8-23 When you move the mouse pointer over a split box, the pointer changes to a double-headed arrow.

TIP Before choosing the Split command or double-clicking one of the split boxes, select a cell in the sheet where you want the split to occur. The sheet is split immediately to the left or above the selected cell. For example, in Figure 8-22, cell B4 is selected. When you double-click the vertical split box, the split occurs between columns A and B — to the left of the selected cell. If cell A1 is active, the split occurs in the center of the sheet.

You can select any cell in column H and double-click the vertical split box. Your worksheet now looks like the one in Figure 8-24. Notice that the window displays two horizontal scroll bars — one for each pane. Next use the horizontal scroll bar below the right pane to scroll column N into view. Your worksheet now looks like the one in Figure 8-25.

Products

	A	B	C	D	E	F	G	H
1	1996 Product Sales Projections							
3		Jan	Feb	Mar	Apr	May	Jun	Jul
4	Product 1	$7,317	$6,329	$2,110	$1,710	$2,984	$1,100	$2,467
5	Product 2	$2,814	$2,336	$9,199	$6,176	$2,842	$1,408	$3,737
6	Product 3	$2,875	$4,107	$5,528	$8,599	$9,769	$5,557	$3,456
7	Product 4	$4,365	$2,202	$5,607	$8,340	$5,832	$2,350	$1,669
8	Product 5	$9,451	$3,398	$3,472	$4,585	$3,453	$8,476	$8,118
9	Product 6	$7,810	$6,982	$7,018	$1,885	$4,336	$6,394	$6,989
10	Product 7	$9,976	$7,267	$5,006	$6,692	$8,388	$9,072	$8,968
11	Product 8	$2,536	$4,100	$6,328	$3,807	$7,850	$1,649	$5,253
12	Product 9	$3,104	$2,467	$5,349	$7,142	$9,305	$2,712	$4,629
13	Product 10	$5,442	$2,783	$1,642	$1,582	$2,456	$5,584	$9,140
14	Product 11	$7,816	$8,626	$6,938	$5,200	$8,197	$7,728	$5,955
15	Product 12	$2,786	$6,720	$4,754	$3,556	$2,535	$5,029	$4,740
16	Product 13	$7,363	$3,248	$7,295	$9,822	$2,076	$8,372	$1,846
17	Product 14	$9,917	$5,004	$6,873	$8,719	$8,399	$4,204	$8,290

Sheet1 / Sheet2 / Sheet3 / Sheet4 / Sheet5

FIGURE 8-24 We split the window into two vertical panes.

Products

	A	B	C	D	E	F	G	N
1	**1996 Product Sales Projections**							
3		*Jan*	*Feb*	*Mar*	*Apr*	*May*	*Jun*	***Total***
4	Product 1	$7,317	$6,329	$2,110	$1,710	$2,984	$1,100	$68,007
5	Product 2	$2,814	$2,336	$9,199	$6,176	$2,842	$1,408	$55,038
6	Product 3	$2,875	$4,107	$5,528	$8,599	$9,769	$5,557	$64,558
7	Product 4	$4,365	$2,202	$5,607	$8,340	$5,832	$2,350	$62,438
8	Product 5	$9,451	$3,398	$3,472	$4,585	$3,453	$8,476	$61,437
9	Product 6	$7,810	$6,982	$7,018	$1,885	$4,336	$6,394	$71,618
10	Product 7	$9,976	$7,267	$5,006	$6,692	$8,388	$9,072	$78,208
11	Product 8	$2,536	$4,100	$6,328	$3,807	$7,850	$1,649	$51,267
12	Product 9	$3,104	$2,467	$5,349	$7,142	$9,305	$2,712	$61,722
13	Product 10	$5,442	$2,783	$1,642	$1,582	$2,456	$5,584	$47,997
14	Product 11	$7,816	$8,626	$6,938	$5,200	$8,197	$7,728	$66,915
15	Product 12	$2,786	$6,720	$4,754	$3,556	$2,535	$5,029	$64,086
16	Product 13	$7,363	$3,248	$7,295	$9,822	$2,076	$8,372	$63,689
17	Product 14	$9,917	$5,004	$6,873	$8,719	$8,399	$4,204	$76,061

Sheet1 / Sheet2 / Sheet3 / Sheet4 / Sheet5

FIGURE 8-25
We scrolled column N into view in the right pane.

Now you can use the left pane's horizontal scroll bar to scroll between columns A and M without losing sight of the totals in column N. In addition, when you scroll vertically between rows 1 and 38, you'll always see the corresponding totals in column N. For example, if you scroll down to view rows 18 through 33 in the left pane, those same rows are visible in the right pane.

If you also want to keep an eye on the monthly totals in row 38, you can create a horizontal pane. Select any cell in row 38 and double-click the horizontal split box. Your worksheet now looks similar to Figure 8-26.

Products

	A	B	C	D	E	F	G	N
24	Product 21	$1,251	$2,433	$5,082	$7,202	$1,237	$7,456	$51,121
25	Product 22	$2,156	$5,623	$8,960	$5,829	$6,495	$4,953	$53,854
26	Product 23	$7,412	$6,020	$7,572	$9,404	$6,670	$1,237	$67,190
27	Product 24	$5,543	$6,617	$2,162	$5,924	$2,833	$3,214	$65,310
28	Product 25	$5,573	$3,323	$7,267	$5,053	$7,493	$6,250	$67,914
29	Product 26	$8,413	$2,571	$6,143	$7,898	$2,902	$9,117	$65,138
30	Product 27	$3,684	$8,349	$1,237	$4,666	$7,075	$1,916	$63,544
31	Product 28	$2,704	$8,279	$7,292	$6,997	$4,631	$7,928	$53,610
32	Product 29	$7,546	$3,960	$7,582	$2,839	$7,823	$8,110	$68,256
33	Product 30	$8,589	$9,424	$3,965	$3,556	$3,610	$4,245	$63,689
34	Product 31	$5,456	$8,638	$9,322	$7,071	$1,237	$1,542	$59,393
35	Product 32	$9,648	$8,636	$6,259	$3,506	$4,668	$8,434	$77,073
36	Product 33	$9,079	$2,357	$5,007	$2,205	$7,941	$5,649	$77,489
37	Product 34	$2,312	$7,225	$2,423	$9,927	$1,067	$1,542	$58,913
38	**Total**	$185,352	$176,366	$182,192	$188,361	$173,954	$173,318	$2,133,689
39								

Sheet1 / Sheet2 / Sheet3 / Sheet4 / Sheet5

FIGURE 8-26
We created a horizontal pane so that we could keep an eye on the totals in row 38.

TIP To create both vertical and horizontal windowpanes quickly, choose the Split command from the Window menu. For example, you can split the window as shown in Figure 8-26 by selecting cell N38 and choosing Split from the Window menu.

You can then reposition the split bars as you like by dragging them with the mouse. After you split a window, the Split command changes to Remove Split, which returns one or both split bars to their default "unsplit" position. You can also remove a split by double-clicking a split bar or by dragging it back to the top or right side of the window.

To move from pane to pane using the keyboard, press F6. Each time you do so, the active cell moves to the next pane in a clockwise direction, activating the upper right cell in each pane, unless you specifically select a cell in each pane. If so, pressing F6 moves to the last cell you selected in each pane. Shift-F6 moves counterclockwise to the next pane.

Freezing Panes

After you've split a window into panes, you can freeze the left panes, the top panes, or both by choosing the Freeze Panes command from the Window menu. For example, if you've split a window vertically, the Freeze Panes command "locks in" the columns that are in view in the left pane so that you can scroll through the worksheet without losing sight of these columns. Similarly, if you've split a window horizontally, the Freeze Panes command locks in the rows that are in view in the top pane. If you've split a window both vertically and horizontally, both the columns in the left panes and the rows in the top panes are frozen.

In Figure 8-27, we selected cell B4 and chose the Split command to split the window vertically and horizontally. We want to freeze the product entries in column A and the month entries in row 3. To keep this information in view as we enter and edit data in the worksheet, we chose the Freeze Panes command from the Window menu. Figure 8-28 shows the result, with the data scrolled to display the grand total in cell N38.

Products

	A	B	C	D	E	F	G	H
1	1996 Product Sales Projections							
3		Jan	Feb	Mar	Apr	May	Jun	Jul
4	Product 1	$7,317	$6,329	$2,110	$1,710	$2,984	$1,100	$2,467
5	Product 2	$2,814	$2,336	$9,199	$6,176	$2,842	$1,408	$3,737
6	Product 3	$2,875	$4,107	$5,528	$8,599	$9,769	$5,557	$3,456
7	Product 4	$4,365	$2,202	$5,607	$8,340	$5,832	$2,350	$1,669
8	Product 5	$9,451	$3,398	$3,472	$4,585	$3,453	$8,476	$8,118
9	Product 6	$7,810	$6,982	$7,018	$1,885	$4,336	$6,394	$6,989
10	Product 7	$9,976	$7,267	$5,006	$6,692	$8,388	$9,072	$8,968
11	Product 8	$2,536	$4,100	$6,328	$3,807	$7,850	$1,649	$5,253
12	Product 9	$3,104	$2,467	$5,349	$7,142	$9,305	$2,712	$4,629
13	Product 10	$5,442	$2,783	$1,642	$1,582	$2,456	$5,584	$9,140
14	Product 11	$7,816	$8,626	$6,938	$5,200	$8,197	$7,728	$5,955
15	Product 12	$2,786	$6,720	$4,754	$3,556	$2,535	$5,029	$4,740
16	Product 13	$7,363	$3,248	$7,295	$9,822	$2,076	$8,372	$1,846

FIGURE 8-27
Column A and row 3 are displayed in separate windowpanes.

Notice that the double-line pane dividers have changed to single-line pane dividers. Now we can scroll through the remainder of the worksheet without losing sight of the entries in column A and row 3.

Products

	A	I	J	K	L	M	N	O
1	**1996 Produ**							
3		*Aug*	*Sep*	*Oct*	*Nov*	*Dec*	***Total***	
26	Product 23	$2,603	$2,501	$8,753	$3,019	$7,839	$67,190	
27	Product 24	$5,130	$6,123	$6,827	$7,109	$5,770	$65,310	
28	Product 25	$9,523	$6,319	$1,250	$1,916	$7,698	$67,914	
29	Product 26	$8,783	$2,647	$4,293	$2,442	$8,692	$65,138	
30	Product 27	$4,425	$4,209	$7,456	$9,793	$5,571	$63,544	
31	Product 28	$1,727	$4,163	$1,542	$2,613	$4,497	$53,610	
32	Product 29	$9,111	$8,539	$4,208	$1,875	$3,885	$68,256	
33	Product 30	$6,720	$8,134	$5,653	$1,542	$1,542	$63,689	
34	Product 31	$7,052	$7,731	$2,375	$1,250	$3,381	$59,393	
35	Product 32	$4,782	$4,114	$2,463	$6,552	$9,818	$77,073	
36	Product 33	$9,873	$9,457	$7,250	$2,556	$8,959	$77,489	
37	Product 34	$6,991	$6,162	$7,318	$1,983	$3,002	$58,913	
38	**Total**	$163,779	$181,090	$179,051	$165,149	$174,081	$2,133,689	

Sheet1 / Sheet2 / Sheet3 / Sheet4 / Sheet5 / Sheet6

FIGURE 8-28
The Freeze Panes command locks in the data in the left and top panes.

TIP To activate another sheet in the workbook if the sheet tabs are not visible, press Ctrl-PgUp to activate the previous sheet, or Ctrl-PgDn to activate the next sheet. You can also use the Go To command on the Edit menu or press F5. In the Go To dialog box, enter the sheet reference and any cell reference, using the following syntax:

Sheet2!A1

When you press Enter or click OK, Sheet2 is activated, with cell A1 selected.

Notice also that in Figure 8-27, the sheet tabs are nearly invisible because the horizontal scroll bar for the lower left pane is so small. After freezing the panes in Figure 8-28, however, a single horizontal scroll bar appears, and the sheet tabs reappear.

After you use the Freeze Panes command, it is replaced by the Unfreeze Panes command on the Window menu. Simply choose this command so that you can scroll all the windows again.

Splitting and Freezing Panes Simultaneously

You can also use the Freeze Panes command directly, without first splitting the sheet into panes. For example, if you select cell B4 in the Products worksheet and then choose Freeze Panes, the window splits, and the panes above and to the left of the active cell freeze. When you use this method, subsequently choosing Unfreeze Panes both unfreezes the panes and removes the panes.

NOTE After you choose Freeze Panes, you cannot scroll the upper left pane in any direction. You can scroll only the columns in the upper right pane and only the rows in the lower left pane. You can scroll the lower right pane in either direction.

Zooming Worksheets

You can use the Zoom command on the View menu to change the size of your worksheet display. For example, to see the entire active worksheet area to check its overall appearance, use the Zoom command to reduce the on-screen display to the necessary size. When you choose Zoom from the View menu, the dialog box in Figure 8-29 appears.

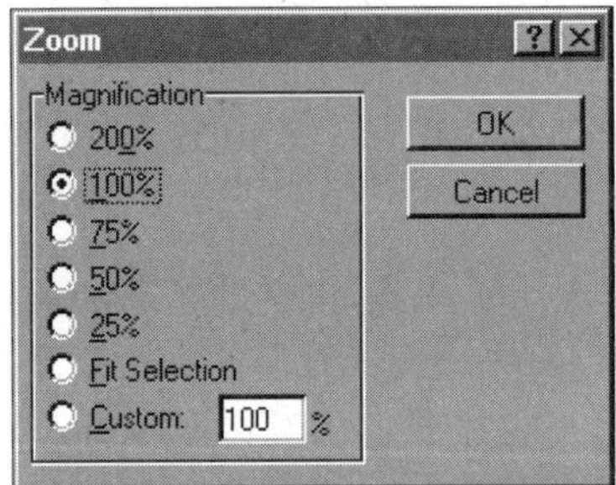

FIGURE 8-29 The Zoom command gives you control over the size of your on-screen display.

The Zoom dialog box has one enlargement option; three reduction options; a Fit Selection option that determines the necessary reduction or enlargement for you (based on the size of the currently selected cells and the size of the window); and a Custom edit box, in which you can specify any percentage from 10% reduction to 400% enlargement.

NOTE The Zoom command affects all selected sheets, so if you group several sheets together, they are all displayed at the selected Zoom percentage.

For example, to view the entire Products worksheet (shown earlier in Figure 8-22) on one screen, follow these steps:

1. Select the entire active area of the worksheet — in this case, cells A1:N38.
2. Choose the Zoom command from the View menu.
3. Select the Fit Selection option and click OK. Now the entire worksheet is displayed on the screen, as shown in Figure 8-30.

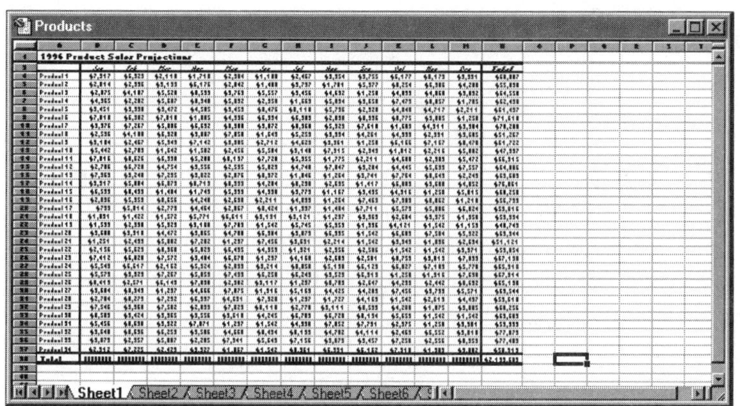

FIGURE 8-30
Using the Zoom command, you can view the entire worksheet on one screen.

Of course, reading the numbers is a problem at this size, but you can select other reduction or enlargement sizes for that purpose. You can still select cells, format them, and enter formulas as you normally would. Choose the Zoom command again and notice that the Custom option, not the Fit Selection option, is activated, with 44% entered in the edit box (the actual percentage depends on the size of the selection and the type of display your computer uses). When you select the Fit Selection option, Excel determines the proper reduction and displays it here. The next time you want to display the entire worksheet, you can simply type this number in the Custom edit box instead of preselecting the current region.

With the Zoom dialog box still open, select the 200% option and click OK. The worksheet changes to look like the one in Figure 8-31.

The Zoom option that is in effect when you save the worksheet is active again when you reopen the worksheet.

Products

	A	B	C	D
1	1996 Product Sales Projections			
3		*Jan*	*Feb*	*Mar*
4	Product 1	$7,317	$6,329	$2,110
5	Product 2	$2,814	$2,336	$9,199
6	Product 3	$2,875	$4,107	$5,528
7	Product 4	$4,365	$2,202	$5,607
8	Product 5	$9,451	$3,398	$3,472

Sheet1 / Sheet2 / Sheet3 / Sheet4 / Sheet5 / Sheet6

FIGURE 8-31
You can enlarge your worksheets for easier viewing or presentation purposes.

The Zoom Control Box and Buttons

You can use the Zoom Control box and the Zoom In and Zoom Out buttons to change the display size of your sheets quickly. The Zoom Control box appears on the Standard toolbar. Because the Zoom In and Zoom Out buttons are not on any toolbar, you must either add them to an existing toolbar or create a toolbar like the one shown in the next figure. The Zoom In and Out buttons appear in the Utility category in the Customize dialog box.

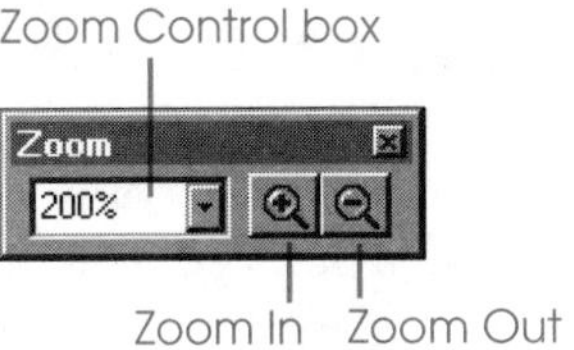

When you click the arrow next to the Zoom Control box, a list with the default reduction and enlargement options appears. It includes the Selection option, which is the same as Fit Selection in the Zoom dialog box. When you click a Zoom button, the display changes to the next default reduction or enlargement option in that direction. For example, if you click the Zoom Out button when a sheet is at 100%, the display changes to 75% reduction. For more information about toolbars, see Chapter 2, "Toolbars and Buttons," page 33.

Named Views

Suppose you want your sheet to have particular display characteristics and print settings for one purpose, such as editing, but different display characteristics and settings for another purpose, such as an on-screen presentation. Using the View Manager command on the View menu, you can assign names to different sets of options. You can then save these options and select one by name when you need it, rather than manually implementing the changes in your sheet.

When you choose the View Manager command, the View Manager dialog box, shown in Figure 8-32, offers you instant access to these sets of options, known as *named views*.

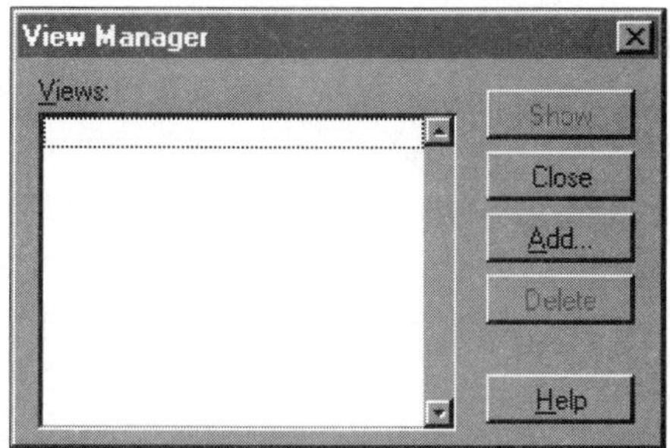

FIGURE 8-32
The View Manager dialog box lets you store different sets of display and print settings with your sheet.

NOTE The View Manager is an Excel add-in. If the View Manager command does not appear on your View menu, you need to install the View Manager add-in. You can run the Excel Setup program again or see Appendix B, "Installing Microsoft Excel," page 951.

The settings that are stored in named views include column widths, row heights, display options, window size and position on the screen, windowpane settings, the cells that are selected at the time the definition is created, and, optionally, the print settings.

When you first choose the View Manager command, the View Manager dialog box is empty. To define a named view, follow these steps:

1. Set up your sheet with the display settings you want.
2. Choose the View Manager command from the View menu and click Add. You'll see a dialog box like the one in Figure 8-33.

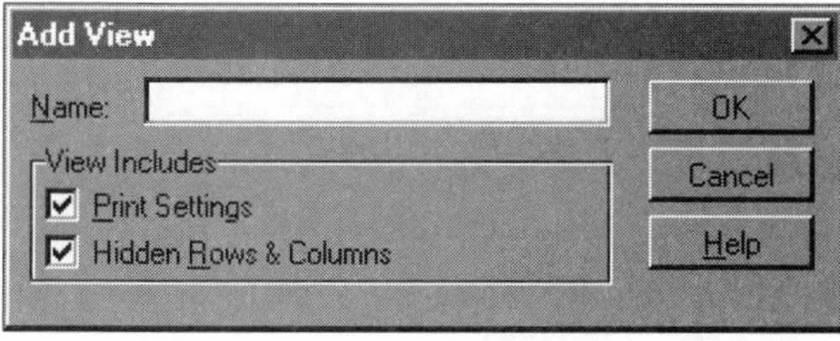

FIGURE 8-33
You define a name for the current set of display and print settings with the Add View dialog box.

3. Type a name in the Name edit box, select the options you want, and click OK. The Print Settings and Hidden Rows & Columns options let you include the corresponding settings in your named view definition. The next time you choose the View Manager command, the name you entered in the Add View dialog box appears in the Views list box.

See Also For more information about print settings, see Chapter 10, "Printing and Presenting," page 373.

Editing Groups of Sheets Simultaneously

You can group together multiple sheets in a workbook and then add, edit, or format data in all the sheets in the group at the same time. You'll find this group editing feature particularly useful when you're creating or modifying a set of worksheets that are similar in purpose and structure — a set of monthly reports or departmental budgets, for example.

You can select and group sheets using one of these methods:

- Select the tab of the first sheet in a range of adjacent sheets you want to group, hold down Shift, and click the tab of the last sheet in the range.
- Select the tab of the first sheet you want to group, hold down Ctrl, and click the tabs of each sheet you want to include, whether or not the sheets are adjacent.
- Choose Select All Sheets from the sheet tab shortcut menu.

To see how the group editing feature works, imagine that you want to add the same set of formatting options to the worksheets Exams 1, Exams 2, Exams 3, and Exams 4, which are contained in the workbook Exams shown in Figure 8-34. (We entered data in the Exams 1 worksheet only — the other three worksheets are blank.) You can add formats to one worksheet and then use the Copy command to re-create them in the other worksheets. But a simpler approach is to group all four worksheets and then format all members of the group at the same time. As Figure 8-34 shows, we have already grouped the worksheets in the Exams workbook. (Excel indicates group editing mode by adding [Group] to the title bar of the workbook.)

Exams [Group]

	A	B	C	D	E	F
1	First Quarter Exam Scores					
2						
3	Student	Exam 1	Exam 2	Exam 3	Exam 4	Average
4	Allan	87	90	79	96	88
5	Billinger	92	94	94	97	94.25
6	Crane	96	95	95	80	91.5
7	Davis	85	87	87	88	86.75
8	Evans	81	88	88	85	85.5

Exams 1 / Exams 2 / Exams 3 / Exams 4

FIGURE 8-34
We'll use this workbook as an example for group editing.

Now that we have a group of worksheets, we can add formatting, formulas, or any other data to the active worksheet, and all member worksheets will be modified simultaneously. For example, we applied formatting to the Exams 1 worksheet using the AutoFormat command. We also adjusted some font sizes and column widths to arrive at the worksheet in Figure 8-35.

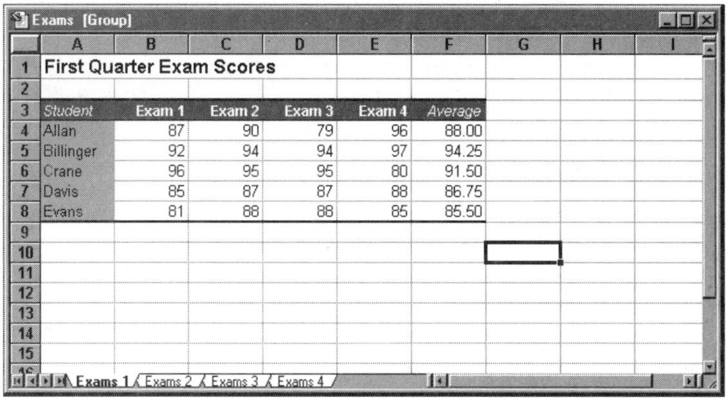

Exams [Group]

First Quarter Exam Scores

Student	Exam 1	Exam 2	Exam 3	Exam 4	Average
Allan	87	90	79	96	88.00
Billinger	92	94	94	97	94.25
Crane	96	95	95	80	91.50
Davis	85	87	87	88	86.75
Evans	81	88	88	85	85.50

Exams 1 / Exams 2 / Exams 3 / Exams 4

FIGURE 8-35
Any formatting, formulas, or data you add to the active worksheet in a group is added to the other group members at the same time.

If we select the Exams 2 tab, as shown in Figure 8-36, we can see that all the formats we applied to the Exams 1 worksheet are also applied to the other worksheets in the group.

NOTE You can select other sheets in the group without leaving group editing mode. If you click a worksheet tab outside the group, Excel leaves group editing mode and removes the (Group) indicator from the title bar of the workbook. If all sheets in the workbook are included in the group, clicking any sheet tab except that of the active sheet exits group editing mode.

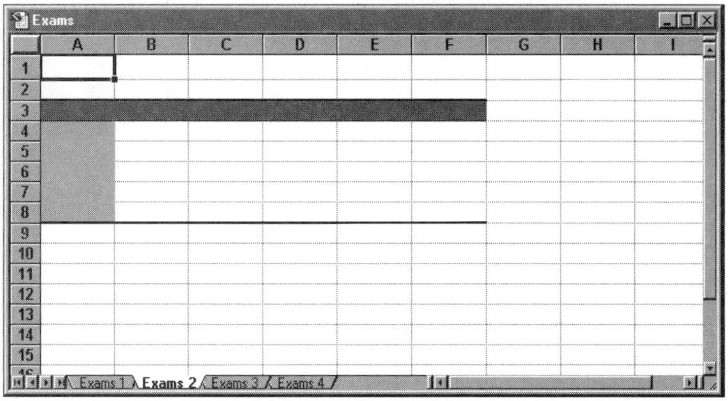

Exams

Exams 1 / Exams 2 / Exams 3 / Exams 4

FIGURE 8-36
The formats we applied to Exams 1 are also applied to the other worksheets in the group.

For more information about the AutoFit command, adjusting font sizes, and changing column widths, see Chapter 6, "Formatting a Worksheet," page 155.

Filling a Group

When you establish a group of sheets, the Across Worksheets command on the Fill submenu of the Edit menu becomes available. The dialog box that appears when you choose this command is shown in Figure 8-37.

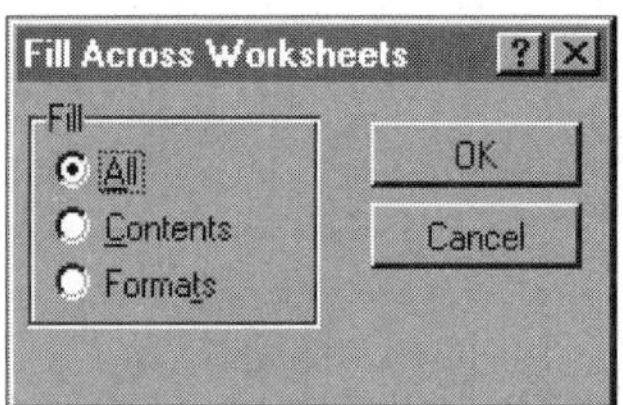

FIGURE 8-37 The Across Worksheets command lets you copy data to all the sheets in a group.

Using this command is similar to using the Copy and Paste commands, except that it's a lot simpler. For example, we selected the range A1:F8 in Figure 8-37 and chose the Across Worksheets command from the Fill submenu of the Edit menu. (Remember, this command is not available until you select a group of sheets.) We then selected the Contents option and clicked OK to copy the text and values entered in Exams 1 to Exams 2, Exams 3, and Exams 4. Now all we have to do is edit the First Quarter Exam Scores headings in Exams 2, Exams 3, and Exams 4 to read Second Quarter, Third Quarter, and Fourth Quarter, and enter the proper scores for each student. Even the formulas in column F were copied correctly using the Across Worksheets command.

Other Group Editing Actions

Excel's group editing feature lets you perform a number of other actions on the same cells of all member sheets simultaneously.

Entering Text Whatever you type in one sheet is duplicated in all sheets belonging to the group.

Printing When editing a group, all printing commands on the File menu are applied to every sheet in your group at the same time.

Format Menu Commands Any formatting changes you make with the Number, Alignment, Font, Border, Patterns, and Protection tabs in the Format Cells dialog box are applied to all group members at the same time. The results of the Row, Column, AutoFormat, and Style commands are also applied across sheets in group editing mode.

For example, if you assign the Number format to cells F4:F8 in the active worksheet, that format is also applied to cells F4:F8 in the other group worksheets, overriding any other numeric format you previously applied.

Similarly, if you assign a style to a range of cells in one worksheet, that style is assigned to the same range in the other worksheets.

Edit Menu Commands All commands on the Edit menu except Find and Replace are applied to every sheet in the group at the same time.

Insert Menu Commands You can use the Cells, Rows, Columns, and Function commands to insert the corresponding items in every sheet in the group at the same time.

Working with Linked Workbooks

Creating dynamic links between workbooks with external reference formulas provides a number of advantages. First, you can break large, complex models into more manageable portions. For example, instead of placing all your company's budget data in one model, you can create several departmental budgets. You can then create a master budget workbook to draw relevant data from the individual departmental models, which are called *supporting* workbooks. Links between worksheets in workbooks also provide a flexible means of extracting any number of reports and analyses from a group of supporting worksheets in other workbooks.

In addition to creating more manageable and flexible models, linked workbooks can save recalculation time and memory.

To establish links between workbooks, you can either build an external reference formula yourself (by typing, pointing with the mouse, or using Paste Special from the Edit menu and clicking the Paste Link button), or you can use automatic consolidation. Automatic consolidation is particularly useful for linking two or more workbooks that contain worksheets that store the same kind of information and have a similar structure. This section discusses some special considerations to be aware of when working with workbooks that are linked by external reference formulas.

For information about creating external reference formulas, see "References to Worksheets in Other Workbooks," page 117.

For information about automatic consolidation, see "Consolidating Worksheets," page 337.

For information about linking workbooks, see Chapter 5, "Building Formulas," page 111.

Saving Linked Workbooks

As mentioned in Chapter 3, you use the Save As command to give your workbooks descriptive names when you save them. For example, suppose you're modeling your company's 1996 budget in a workbook called Book1. When you save the workbook, you can use the Save As command to give the workbook a name like Budget 1996.

Now suppose that you have another active workbook in which you plan to enter actual (as opposed to budgeted) expenditures, and that you have already saved it with the name Actual 1996. This Actual workbook contains links to your Budget workbook and, therefore, is dependent on the Budget workbook for some of its information. When you created them, these links identified the Budget workbook as Book1. If you save Book1 as Budget 1996 *while the Actual workbook is still open,* all the references to Book1 in the Actual workbook change to *Budget 1996*. Thus, if Actual contains the reference

```
=[Book1]Sheet1!$A$1
```

the reference changes to

```
='[Budget 1996.xls]Sheet1'!$A$1
```

If, on the other hand, you close the dependent Actual workbook *before* you save the supporting Book1 (Budget) workbook, you see the warning *Save 'Actual 1996' with references to unsaved documents?* If you click OK, Excel saves and closes Actual 1996. However, if you then save Book1 as Budget 1996, the references to Book1 in the Actual workbook are not updated, and the dependent formulas in the Actual workbook continue to assume that the name of the Budget workbook is Book1. When you reopen Actual 1996, Excel displays a message box asking *This document contains links. Reestablish links?* If you click Yes, Excel is unable to find Book1 and opens the File Not Found dialog box (similar to the Open dialog box), with which you can locate and open the workbook you want. Normally, you would select the file or insert the disk that contains the file for which Excel is searching. However, Book1 doesn't exist anymore (its new name is Budget 1996), and Excel will never be able to update any references to that workbook. When you use the File Not Found dialog box to find the renamed workbook, Excel displays an alert box with the message *Cannot find 'Book1'.* When you click OK and then Cancel, Excel opens the Actual workbook but you must manually change the external reference formulas from Book1 to Budget 1996.

TIP You may or may not see the .xls File extensions on your computer. This is controlled in the Windows Explorer. To hide the File extensions, choose the Options command on the Explorer's Tools menu and click the "Hide MS-DOS File extensions for File types that are registered" option.

You can choose the Links command on the Edit menu to update or permanently redirect the links. The Links dialog box lists the original link to Book1 and provides two buttons: Update Now and Change Source. If you select the link and click Update Now, Excel opens the File Not Found dialog box. You can select Budget 1996 in the File Name list box and click OK to update the values in Actual 1996. In this case, the external reference formulas do not change — they still refer to Book1.

To modify the formulas themselves as well as update the values in the Actual workbook, select the existing link and click Change Source in the Links dialog box. Next select Budget 1996 in the Change Links dialog box and click OK. Select the appropriate sheet in the Select Sheet dialog box and click OK again. The formulas in the Actual workbook now refer to the correct Budget workbook.

When you create a set of linked workbooks, always save the supporting workbooks before you save the dependent workbooks. If you save the workbooks in the wrong order, you'll have to use the Links command on the Edit menu to redirect the links.

For more information about the Links command, see "Opening Supporting Workbooks," page 332.

For more information about changing the source file, see "Redirecting Links," page 333.

Opening a Dependent Workbook

When you save a workbook that contains dependent formulas, Excel stores the most recent results of those formulas. If you open and edit the supporting workbook after closing the dependent workbook, the values of some cells in the supporting workbook might be different. When you open the dependent workbook again, it contains the old values of the external references in the dependent formulas, but Excel displays an alert box with the message *This document contains links. Re-establish links?* The alert box lets you tell Excel whether to read the current values from the closed workbook on the disk.

If you click No, Excel opens the dependent workbook without updating any references to the supporting workbook. All dependent formulas retain their last saved values.

If you click Yes, Excel searches for the supporting workbook. If found, Excel reads the supporting values and updates the dependent formulas in the dependent workbook. Excel does not open the supporting workbook; it merely reads the appropriate values from it.

If Excel can't find the supporting workbook, it displays the File Not Found dialog box, as described earlier. From this dialog box, you can cancel the update process, change the current directory, or identify the file.

Opening Supporting Workbooks

In addition to using the Open command on the File menu and the Open button on the Standard toolbar, you can open supporting workbooks by using the Links command on the Edit menu. The Links command becomes available only when an external or remote reference formula exists in the active worksheet.

You can use the Links command to open the workbooks on which another workbook depends. The main difference between the Links and Open commands is that Open presents a list of all files in the current directory, whereas Links lists only those files that support the active workbook, regardless of the directory in which they are stored.

NOTE Using the Links command is a handy way to look up the names of all the supporting workbooks of a dependent workbook. The Links dialog box lists the links that exist for the entire workbook, not only for the active worksheet.

For example, to open a workbook that contains values that support Actual 1996, choose Links from the Edit menu. You'll see a dialog box like the one in Figure 8-38. Select the name of the workbook you want and click Open Source.

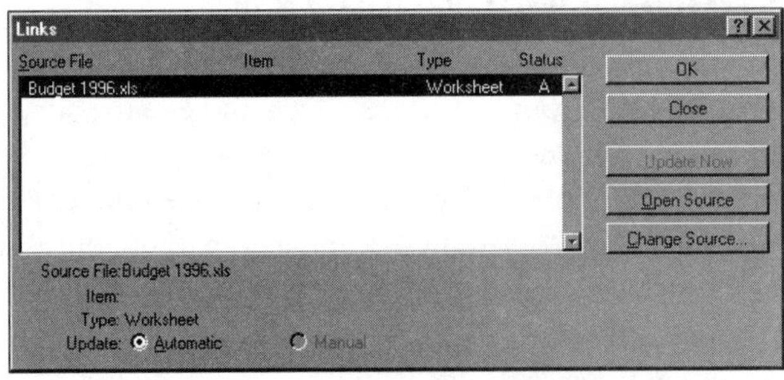

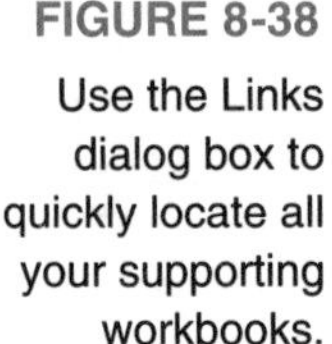

FIGURE 8-38
Use the Links dialog box to quickly locate all your supporting workbooks.

The list in the Links dialog box displays the name of the source file and the status of the link. An *A* in the Status column indicates a link that is updated automatically. An *M* in the Status column indicates a manual link that is not updated until you click the Update Now button.

Be careful — the order in which you open files is important. For example, if you select Budget 1996 in the Links dialog box and then click Open Source, Budget 1996 appears as the active document. If you then try to use the Links command to open another workbook that supports Actual 1996, you'll get a list of workbooks that support Budget 1996 instead, because it is now the active workbook. To see a list of the workbooks that support Actual 1996, you must reactivate that workbook *after* you open Budget 1996 and *before* you choose the Links command.

See Also For more information about remote references, see "Linking Microsoft Excel to Another Application," page 334.

Updating Links Without Opening Supporting Workbooks

You can also use the Links command to update dependent formulas without opening the supporting workbooks. This is useful if you use Excel on a network and one of your colleagues is working with a supporting workbook. When you choose Links, select the workbook name in the Links dialog box and then click the Update Now button. Excel gets the necessary values from the last-saved version of the supporting workbook.

Redirecting Links

If you rename a supporting workbook or move it to another directory or drive, you must redirect your workbook links to let Excel know where to find the supporting data. To redirect your workbook links, select the original name of the supporting workbook or workbooks in the Links dialog box and then click the Change Source button. In the resulting dialog box, shown in Figure 8-39, type the name of the renamed or moved workbook referenced by your dependent formulas in the File Name edit box or select it from the list box. If necessary, you can select another directory or drive. When you click OK, Excel changes all references to the supporting workbook to reflect the new workbook name or location. Click OK in the Links dialog box to return to the worksheet.

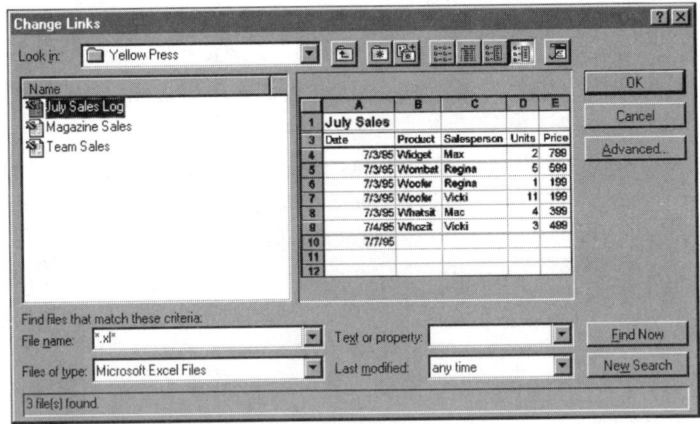

FIGURE 8-39
When you use the Change Source button to redirect your workbook links, you see a dialog box like this one.

Linking Microsoft Excel to Another Application

The Links dialog box includes a Type field in the Source File list box. In Figure 8-38, the Links dialog box displayed Worksheet as the Type; however, you can also link objects and documents created in other applications, such as Microsoft Word, to Excel worksheets and charts. When you use the Links command in an Excel document that has been linked to another application, the Type field displays the application name and the object type.

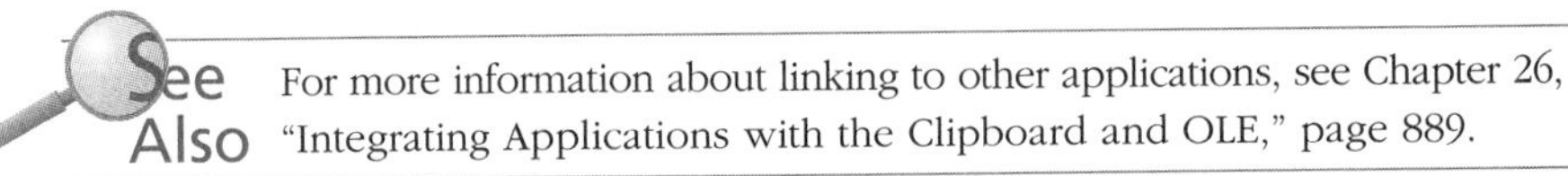

For more information about linking to other applications, see Chapter 26, "Integrating Applications with the Clipboard and OLE," page 889.

Copying, Cutting, and Pasting in Linked Workbooks

You can use relative or absolute references to cells in other workbooks the same way you use relative or absolute references within a single workbook. Relative and absolute references to cells in supporting workbooks respond to the Copy, Cut, and Paste commands and toolbar buttons in much the same way as references to cells in the same workbook.

For example, suppose you create the formula

=[Form2]Sheet1!Z1

in cell A1 in Sheet1 of Form1 and use Copy and Paste to copy this formula to cell B1. The formula in cell B1 becomes

=[Form2]Sheet1!AA1

The original formula changed when it was copied to cell B1 because the reference to cell Z1 in Form2 is relative. However, if the formula in cell A1 of Form1 contains an absolute reference to cell Z1 in Form2, as in

=[Form2]Sheet1!$Z$1

the result of copying and pasting the formula in cell B1 would still be

=[Form2]Sheet1!$Z$1

Copying and Pasting Between Workbooks

When you copy a dependent formula from one workbook to another and that formula includes a relative reference to a third workbook, the reference is adjusted to reflect the new position of the formula. For example, cell A1 in Form1 contains the formula

=[Form2]Sheet1!A1

If you copy and paste that formula from cell A1 in Form1 to cell B5 in Form3, the result is the formula

=[Form2]Sheet1!B5

The formula is adjusted to reflect its new relative position.

If you copy a formula that contains an absolute reference to another workbook, that formula remains the same. For example, cell A1 in Form1 contains the formula

=[Form2]Sheet1!$A$1

If you copy and paste that formula into cell B5 in Form3, the result is still

=[Form2]Sheet1!$A$1

Even if you copy a dependent formula to the workbook to which the formula refers, it is still a dependent formula. For example, if you copy the formula

=[Form2]Sheet1!$A$1

from cell A1 of Form1 to cell A3 on Sheet1 of Form2, the resulting formula is essentially the same, except that the book reference is not necessary because the formula is in the same workbook. As a result, the formula becomes

=Sheet1!$A$1

Cutting and Pasting Between Workbooks

You can cut a dependent formula and paste it in another workbook. Cutting and pasting dependent formulas is the same as cutting and pasting regular formulas.

Excel does not adjust the relative references in a formula when you cut it from one workbook and paste it in another, as it does when you copy a formula. For example, cell A1 in Sheet1 of Form1 contains the formula

=[Form2]Sheet1!A1

If you cut that formula and paste it in cell B5 of Form3, the result is still the formula

=[Form2]Sheet1!A1

Cutting and Pasting Cells Referred to by Dependent Formulas

As we mentioned in Chapter 7, when you cut and paste cells, Excel adjusts any references to those cells in the formulas of the workbook. Dependent formulas do not follow the same rules. When you cut and paste a cell referred to by a dependent formula in a closed workbook, that formula is not adjusted to reflect the change.

For example, suppose you create the formula

=[Form2]Sheet1!A10

in cell A1 in Form1. If you close Form1 and use Cut and Paste to move the entry in cell A10 of Form2 to cell B10 of Form2, the formula in cell A1 of Form1 remains the same. You might expect the link to be broken because the worksheet containing the formula was closed when you modified the referenced cell. However, Excel manages to keep track of everything. When you open the workbook, the message *"This document contains links. Re-establish links?"* alerts you that data the workbook depended on has changed.

Severing Links Between Workbooks

To sever the links between workbooks, you use the Paste Special command on the Edit menu to change the external references in your dependent formulas to constant values. Then you won't be able to update the references because all ties to the supporting workbooks are removed.

To sever links using the Paste Special command, follow these steps:

1. Select the cell containing the dependent formula.
2. Choose Copy and then Paste Special from the Edit menu.
3. In the Paste Special dialog box, select the Values option, click OK, and press Esc to clear the Clipboard.
4. As a precaution, use the Find command on the Edit menu to look for any dependent formulas you might have missed. Enter the exclamation

point (!) required in all dependent formulas in the Find What edit box and then select Formulas from the Look In drop-down list box.

5. Click Find Next, and Excel searches your worksheet for any references to supporting workbooks.

You can change an external reference in a dependent formula to a constant value without eradicating the formula. To do this, select the cell and, in the formula bar, select the portion of the formula that contains the external reference, press F9, and then press Enter. Excel changes the external reference to a value without changing the rest of the formula.

See Also

For more information about the Paste Special command, see "Selective Pasting," page 263.

For more information about the Find command, see "Finding and Replacing Data," page 272.

Consolidating Worksheets

The Consolidate command on the Data menu can assemble information from as many as 255 supporting worksheets into a single master worksheet. The supporting worksheets can be in the same workbook as the master worksheet or in different workbooks. For example, if you have financial information for each of your company's divisions in separate workbooks, you can use the Consolidate command to create a master worksheet that totals the corresponding items in each divisional workbook.

You can use the Consolidate command in a number of ways. You can link the consolidated data to the supporting data so that subsequent changes in the supporting worksheets are reflected in the consolidation worksheet. Or you can simply consolidate the source data, without creating a link.

You can consolidate *by position* or *by category*. If you consolidate by position, Microsoft Excel gathers information from the same cell location in each supporting worksheet. If you consolidate by category, Excel uses column or row labels as the basis for associating worksheets. Consolidating by category gives you more flexibility in the way you set up your supporting worksheets. For example, if your January column is column B in one worksheet and column D in another, you can still gather the January numbers when you consolidate by category.

You can consolidate worksheets using any of the functions listed in the Function drop-down list box in the Consolidate dialog box. As shown in

Figure 8-40, the default function is Sum, which adds the data items from each supporting worksheet and places their totals in the consolidation worksheet. You can also use any of the following functions: Count (which corresponds to the COUNTA function), Average, Max, Min, Product, Count Nums (which corresponds to the COUNT function), StdDev, StdDevp, Var, and Varp.

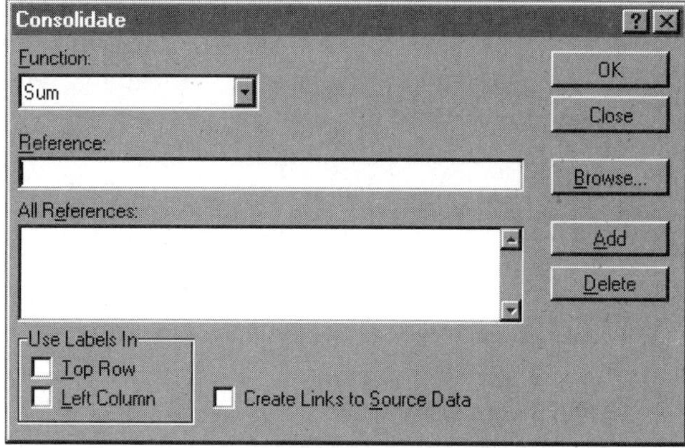

FIGURE 8-40
The default function in the Consolidate dialog box is Sum.

You can consolidate worksheets in workbooks that are currently open or in workbooks that are stored on disk. The workbook containing the worksheet that receives the consolidated data must be open, but supporting workbooks can be closed — provided you give Excel the correct locations so that it can find each workbook file. You must save all supporting workbooks before you begin consolidation.

The following sections provide three examples of consolidation: consolidation by position, consolidation by category, and consolidation by category with links created to the source data. In these examples, we'll consolidate worksheets in the same workbook, but you can just as easily consolidate worksheets in separate workbooks.

For more information about functions, see Chapter 11, "Common Worksheet Functions," page 397.

Consolidating by Position

When you consolidate by position, Excel applies the consolidation function (Sum, Average, or whatever else you select) to the same cell references in each supporting worksheet. This is the simplest way to consolidate, but your supporting worksheets must have exactly the same layout.

Figure 8-41 shows a simple example of a workbook containing a master worksheet — Averages — that matches the layout of four supporting worksheets. These worksheets — Exams 1, Exams 2, Exams 3, and Exams 4 — can be consolidated by position because each has five columns and five rows of identically structured data.

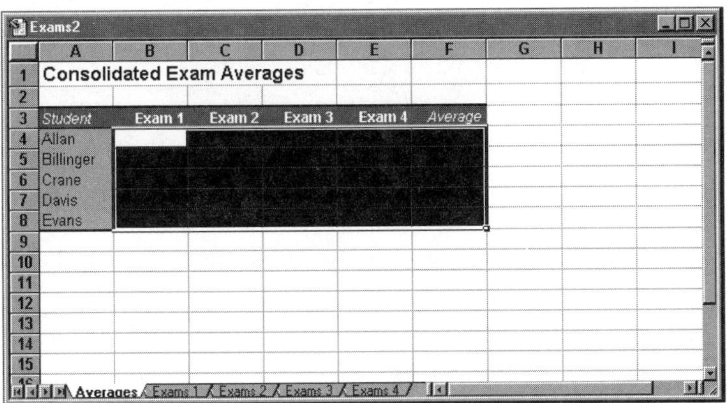

FIGURE 8-41
We'll use the Consolidate command on the Data menu to consolidate information from the worksheets named Exams 1, Exams 2, Exams 3, and Exams 4 into the worksheet named Averages.

To consolidate the supporting worksheets into the worksheet named Averages, follow these steps:

1. Activate the consolidation worksheet and select the *destination area* — the block of cells that will receive the consolidated data. In Figure 8-41, the destination area is the range B4:F8 of Averages.
2. Choose the Consolidate command from the Data menu.
3. You will average values from each source worksheet, so select Average from the Function drop-down list box in the Consolidate dialog box. Leave the options in the Use Labels In section unselected. Because you're not going to create a link with the source worksheets, leave the Create Links To Source Data option unselected as well.
4. Type a reference for each source range in the Reference edit box or select each range with the mouse.

   Although using the mouse is easier, if you have any references to source worksheets that are not currently open, you will have to type them. (You can use the Browse button to locate and enter a filename and then manually enter the cell reference.)

   If you type a reference, it must have the following form:

   [Filename]Sheetname !Reference

If the reference is in the same workbook, the filename is unnecessary. If the source range has already been assigned a name, you can use this name in place of *Reference*.

If you use the mouse to select your source ranges, you can drag the Consolidate dialog box out of the way by clicking its title bar and dragging it off to one side. You can activate a worksheet by clicking its tab. If a workbook is open but obscured by other workbooks on the screen, you can get to it by choosing its name from the Window menu. All of these window maneuvers can be performed while you make your selections in the Consolidate dialog box; the dialog box remains active until you close it.

5. Click the Add button in the Consolidate dialog box. Excel transfers the reference from the Reference edit box to the All References list box. Figure 8-42 shows the completed dialog box.

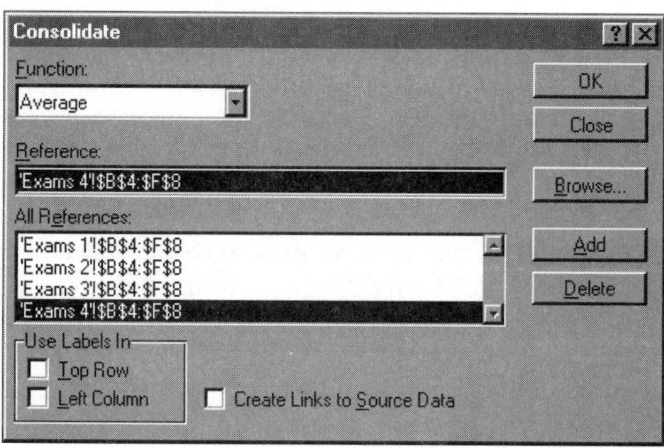

FIGURE 8-42

The Consolidate command uses the references in the All References list box to create the consolidated averages.

Notice that we selected B4:F8 in each of our source worksheets. Because we're consolidating by position and our consolidation worksheet has the appropriate column and row headings, our source references should include only the actual values we want to consolidate.

6. Click OK. Excel averages the source numbers in the destination area, as shown in Figure 8-43.

The averages in our example produced some noninteger results, as Figure 8-43 shows, so we might want to apply an appropriate Number format to the destination cells.

Exams2

	A	B	C	D	E	F
1	Consolidated Exam Averages					
2						
3	Student	Exam 1	Exam 2	Exam 3	Exam 4	Average
4	Allan	89.75	93	81.75	94.75	89.81
5	Billinger	92.5	93.25	88.5	96.5	92.69
6	Crane	92.5	92.5	93.25	84.75	90.75
7	Davis	86.25	88.25	88	88.25	87.69
8	Evans	82	88	89.25	91	87.56

Averages / Exams 1 / Exams 2 / Exams 3 / Exams 4

FIGURE 8-43
Range B4:F8 in the Averages worksheet now contains the averages of the corresponding cells in the four supporting worksheets.

NOTE After you perform a consolidation, the references you enter in the Consolidate dialog box are retained when you save the workbook. The next time you open the workbook and want to refresh the consolidated values, rather than entering the references again, you can simply choose the Consolidate command and click OK.

Consolidating by Category

Now let's look at a more complex example. We averaged grades from worksheets similar to those in our previous examples, except that this time each worksheet included a few different students and different numbers of students, as shown in Figure 8-44.

The consolidation worksheet has column headings for Exam 1 through Exam 4 — each worksheet is the same in this respect. However, the consolidation worksheet has no row headings. We need to omit the row headings because they are not consistently arranged in the source worksheets. As you'll see, the Consolidate command enters the row headings for us.

To consolidate by category, follow these steps:

1. Select the destination area.

   This time the destination area must include column A so that Excel will have somewhere to enter the consolidated row headings. But how many rows should the destination area include? To answer that, we can look at each source worksheet and determine how many unique line items we have. An easier way, however, is to select cell A4 as the destination area. When you specify a single cell as your destination area,

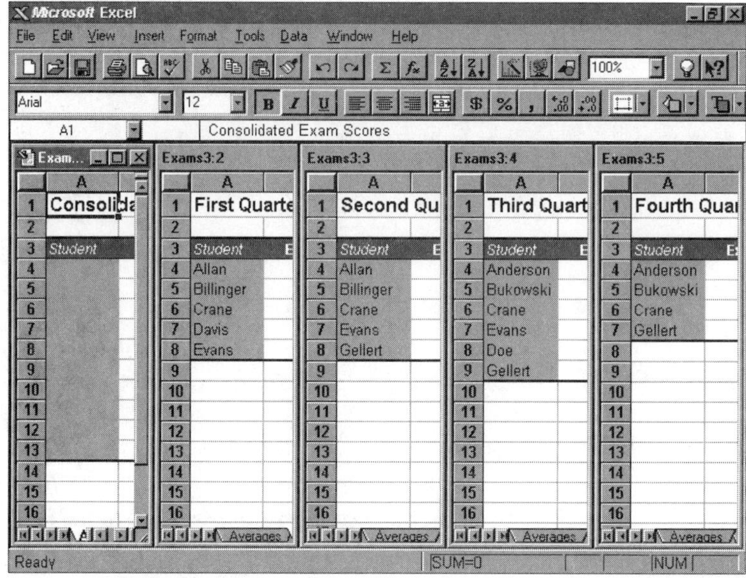

FIGURE 8-44

We'll use the categories (students) in the left column of each source worksheet as the basis for this consolidation.

the Consolidate command fills out the area below and to the right of that cell as needed. In our example, we inserted more than enough rows to accommodate the data, in order to preserve the formatting. Alternatively, you could consolidate first and then use the AutoFormat command on the Format menu to quickly reformat the new data.

2. Choose the Consolidate command from the Data menu and complete the Consolidate dialog box. Select Average in the Function drop-down list box. To consolidate by row categories in this example, select the Left Column option in the Use Labels In section.

3. The consolidation worksheet already has column labels, so we can omit them from the source worksheet references. But our source references must include each row heading and extend from column A to column F (from the row headings column to the Average column). Therefore, in the Reference edit box, enter or select the following source references:

    ='Exams 1'!$A$4:$F$8

    ='Exams 2'!$A$4:$F$8

    ='Exams 3'!$A$4:$F$9

    ='Exams 4'!$A$4:$F$7

4. Click OK, and Excel fills out the Averages worksheet, as shown in Figure 8-45.

Exams3

Student	Exam 1	Exam 2	Exam 3	Exam 4	Average
Allan	88	94	79	96	88.75
Billinger	93	92	89	95	92.13
Anderson	92	93	85	94	90.88
Bukowski	93	95	88	98	93.25
Crane	93	93	93	85	90.75
Davis	85	87	87	88	86.75
Evans	85	88	89	86	86.92
Doe	90	88	94	97	92.25
Gellert	84	89	88	94	88.58

Consolidated Exam Scores

Averages / Exams 1 / Exams 2 / Exams 3 / Exams 4

FIGURE 8-45
The Consolidate command created a separate line item in the consolidation worksheet for each unique item in the source worksheets.

The consolidation worksheet now includes a line item that corresponds to each unique line item in the source worksheets. If two or more worksheets have the same line item, the consolidation worksheet performs the selected mathematical operation on the corresponding figures for each column position. For this example, we applied Number formats to the destination cells after consolidation.

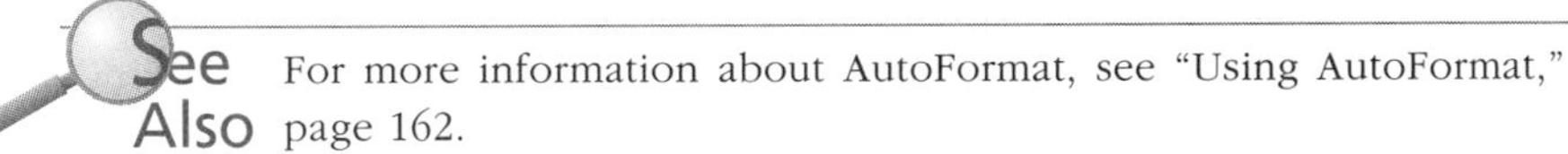

For more information about AutoFormat, see "Using AutoFormat," page 162.

Creating Links to the Source Worksheets

In the previous examples, we simply consolidated numbers with the Average function. The result has been a series of constants in the consolidation worksheet. Subsequent changes to the source worksheets will not affect the consolidation worksheet until we repeat the consolidation.

You can also use the Consolidate command to forge a permanent link between the consolidation and the source worksheets. To create the link, select the Create Links To Source Data option in the Consolidate dialog box and then consolidate the same way you would without the links.

When you consolidate with this option selected, Excel creates an outline in the consolidation worksheet, as shown in Figure 8-46 on the next page.

Each source item is linked separately to the consolidation worksheet, and Excel creates the appropriate summary items. You might have to adjust formatting after you perform a linking consolidation because additional columns and rows are created.

FIGURE 8-46
When you create links to the source worksheets, your consolidation worksheet is outlined automatically with linking formulas hidden in subordinate outline levels.

Exams3

Consolidated Exam Scores

Student	Exam 1	Exam 2	Exam 3	Exam 4	Average
Allan	88	94	79	96	88.75
Billinger	93	92	89	95	92.13
Anderson	92	93	85	94	90.88
Bukowski	93	95	88	98	93.25
Crane	93	93	93	85	90.75
Davis	85	87	87	88	86.75
Evans	85	88	89	86	86.92
Doe	90	88	94	97	92.25
Gellert	84	89	88	94	88.58

Averages / Exams 1 / Exams 2 / Exams 3 / Exams 4

See Also For more information about outlining worksheets, see "Outlining Your Worksheets," page 217.

Chapter 9

Graphics

With Microsoft Excel, you can create a variety of graphic objects — boxes, lines, circles, ovals, arcs, freeform polygons, text boxes, and buttons. You can specify font, pattern, color, and line formats, and you can position objects in relation to the worksheet or to other objects. You can also take pictures of your worksheets and use them in other Excel documents or in documents created in other applications. If you've already created graphics in other applications, Excel lets you import those graphics as well.

Throughout this chapter, we add graphics to worksheets, but you can also add the same kinds of graphics to chart sheets. In addition, you can apply the techniques discussed in this chapter to a variety of graphic objects called *controls* that you create using Microsoft Excel Visual Basic for Applications.

For more information about charts, see Part 4, "Charts," page 581.

For more information about Visual Basic for Applications, see Chapter 25, "An Overview of Visual Basic," page 861.

Creating Graphic Objects

Before we get started, you might want to display the Drawing toolbar, which contains all of the drawing buttons we describe in this chapter. You might also want to hide the Standard and Formatting toolbars to free up as much screen space as possible. The easiest way to display the Drawing toolbar is to click the Drawing button on the Standard toolbar. You can also position the mouse pointer over any displayed toolbar, click the right mouse button, and choose Drawing from the shortcut menu that appears. Use the shortcut menu to hide both the Standard and Formatting toolbars as well.

If you have ever used a drawing program, such as Windows Paint or CorelDRAW, you already know how to create lines, boxes, ellipses, and arcs. In Excel, you simply click the button you want on the Drawing toolbar and then drag the pointer to create the object. Figure 9-1 identifies the buttons on the Drawing toolbar.

For example, you can select the Filled Rectangle button and then drag the cross-hair pointer anywhere on the worksheet or chart to draw a simple box shape. The result looks something like Figure 9-2. Notice that Excel displays *Rectangle 1* at the left end of the formula bar. Excel refers to new graphic objects by category, in the order in which you create them.

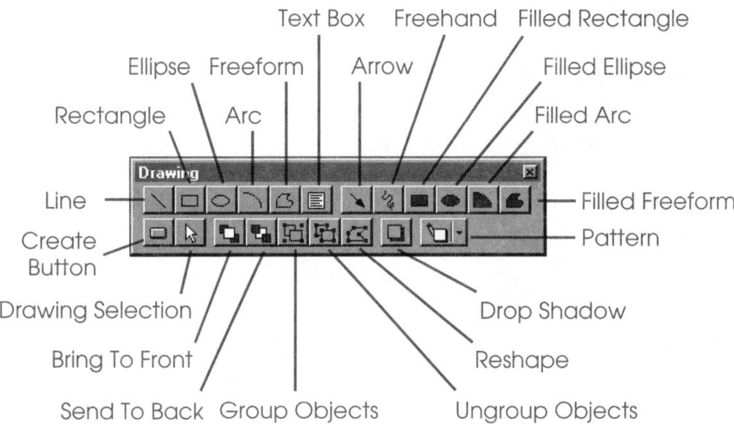

FIGURE 9-1
The buttons on the Drawing toolbar.

The regular Rectangle, Ellipse, Arc, and Freeform buttons create transparent shapes; their filled counterparts produce opaque shapes to which you can add background shading.

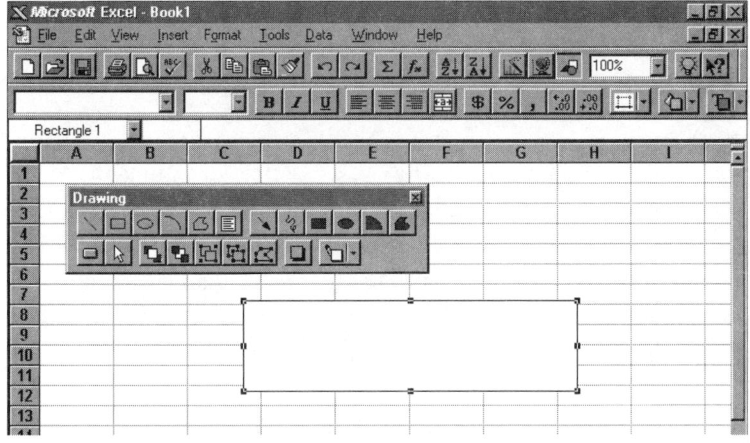

FIGURE 9-2
You can create a simple box using the Filled Rectangle button.

You can use both the regular and Filled Rectangle, Ellipse, and Arc buttons. Select the button, click and hold one corner of the intended shape, drag the mouse to the opposite corner of the intended shape, and then release the mouse button. The Line and Arrow buttons work essentially the same way.

When you release the mouse button and move the mouse pointer away from the object you are drawing, Excel assumes you are finished and the pointer resumes its usual plus-sign shape, indicating that you are no longer in drawing mode. Excel automatically leaves drawing mode each time you finish drawing an object. You can also cancel drawing mode after you click a drawing button by simply clicking anywhere in the worksheet or chart without dragging.

TIP To draw several objects one after the other, double-click the button when you first select it to lock Excel into drawing mode. The button you double-click then remains active until you cancel the drawing session or select another button. To cancel the drawing session, simply click the button again.

Any objects you create appear to "float" over the worksheet or chart in a separate layer. Objects are separate from the worksheet or chart and can be grouped and formatted as discrete items. You can also click an object you have created, choose the Object command on the Format menu, and then select options on the Properties tab in the Format Objects dialog box to adjust the relationship of objects to a worksheet.

Assigning Macros to Objects

You can "attach" a macro to any object so that you can activate the macro by simply clicking the object. To attach a macro to an object, first select the object and then choose the Assign Macro command from the Tools menu. When the Assign Macro dialog box appears, specify whether you want to record a new macro or assign an existing macro to the object. For information about macros, see Part 6, "Macros and Visual Basic," page 827.

You can also use the Create Button button on the Drawing toolbar to create a button object. As soon as you create the button object, the Assign Macro dialog box opens. For information about button objects, see "Using a Button on a Worksheet or Chart," page 843.

After you've created a graphic, you can manipulate it in a variety of ways. When you move the mouse pointer inside the perimeter of a filled object or inside the border that defines a nonfilled object, the pointer changes to the standard arrow. You can then select the object or move it elsewhere by dragging. If you select the object and point to one of the handles that appears on its perimeter, the pointer changes to a double-headed arrow. You can use this pointer to stretch and resize the object. If you drag a center handle, you can change the object's height or width. If you hold down Shift while dragging a corner handle, you can resize the object both vertically and horizontally while retaining its shape, as Figure 9-3 illustrates.

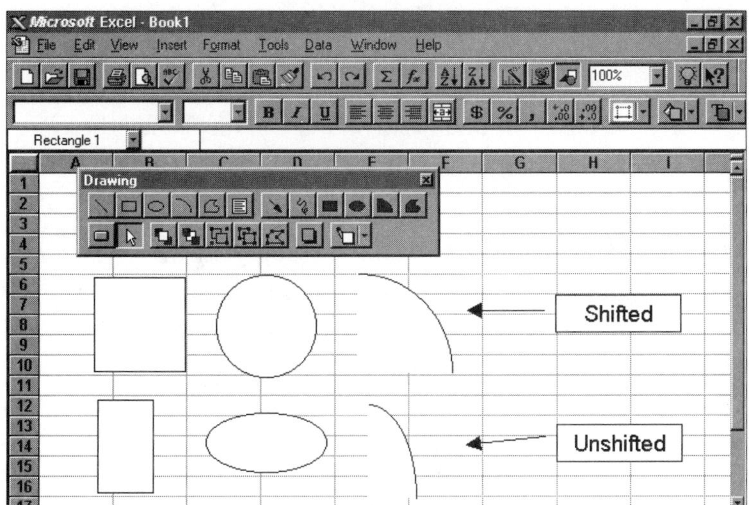

FIGURE 9-3
When you create or size objects, hold down Shift to constrain them along horizontal, vertical, or diagonal lines. (The labels at the right of the worksheet are text boxes created with the Text Box button.)

See Also For more information about using the Object command, see "Positioning Objects," page 360.

Drawing Constrained Objects

You can hold down Shift while creating objects to *constrain* the objects. When you constrain objects, you can achieve the following effects:

- The Line and Arrow buttons draw horizontal, vertical, or diagonal lines.
- The Rectangle and Filled Rectangle buttons draw perfect squares.
- The Ellipse and Filled Ellipse buttons draw perfect circles.
- The Arc and Filled Arc buttons draw perfect 90-degree arcs.

Figure 9-3 shows objects drawn with and without the Shift key.

Pressing Shift or Alt while using certain buttons on the Drawing toolbar has other special effects that we will point out later in this chapter.

Using Cells as a Drawing Grid

You can hold down Alt while creating objects to use the gridlines on a worksheet as a drawing grid. The edges of your objects are then forced to follow the gridlines. If you use Shift and Alt together to draw a square or a circle aligned to the grid, Excel does its best, but the result might not be perfect. This is because the default height and width of the cells on a worksheet do not provide an ideal grid for perfect squares or circles.

TIP To make a copy of an object you have created, press Ctrl and then drag the object with the mouse. You can also use the Copy and Paste buttons on the Standard toolbar.

Drawing Freehand Lines and Polygons

The Freehand button lets you use your mouse to draw unconstrained lines. If you hold down Shift while drawing with this button, Excel fills the inside of the object you create. You can also create a freehand-type line with the Freeform and Filled Freeform buttons. The difference between using the Freehand button and the Freeform buttons in this instance is that releasing the mouse button does not end the drawing. To complete the freeform polygon shape and leave drawing mode you must click the beginning point of your drawing or double-click where you want to stop drawing.

For example, if you click the Freeform button and then click anywhere on the worksheet or chart to begin drawing, the line created by the button remains anchored to the point you clicked. If you release the mouse button, the line stretches from the anchor point to the cross-hair mouse pointer like a rubber band. If you stretch out the line and click again, you create a straight line between the first anchor point and the second point you clicked. You can continue this as long as you want, creating lines between each anchor point. (This is how we created the starburst image you'll see later in Figure 9-10.) You can also hold down the mouse button while using either Freeform button to add a freehand line. In this way, you can create a hybrid object with both straight and curved lines. As mentioned, you complete the freeform polygon by clicking the point where you began drawing to close up the shape or by double-clicking to create an open shape.

The Reshape Button

Drawing an attractive freehand line or freeform polygon shape with a mouse can be challenging. For those times when you have difficulty creating the shape you want, Excel includes a Reshape button that changes a freehand line or a freeform polygon to a series of points, which you can drag to reshape the object.

When you select a freeform polygon, eight handles appear around it, just as they do around objects drawn with the Rectangle, Arc, or Ellipse buttons. Eight handles also appear around objects drawn with the Freehand button. To adjust the shape of a freehand line or a freeform polygon, select it and then click the Reshape button. A new set of handles appears, following the curves and corners of the image; only two handles appear at the end points of straight lines. You can then drag as many of the handles as necessary to new positions.

TIP After you click the Reshape button, you can delete handles on an object. If you want to clean up your drawing by eliminating some of the corners, press Ctrl and click each handle you want to delete.

For example, we used the Filled Freeform button to create the shape on the left in Figure 9-4, and then we selected the shape. The shape on the right is the same freeform polygon after we clicked the Reshape button.

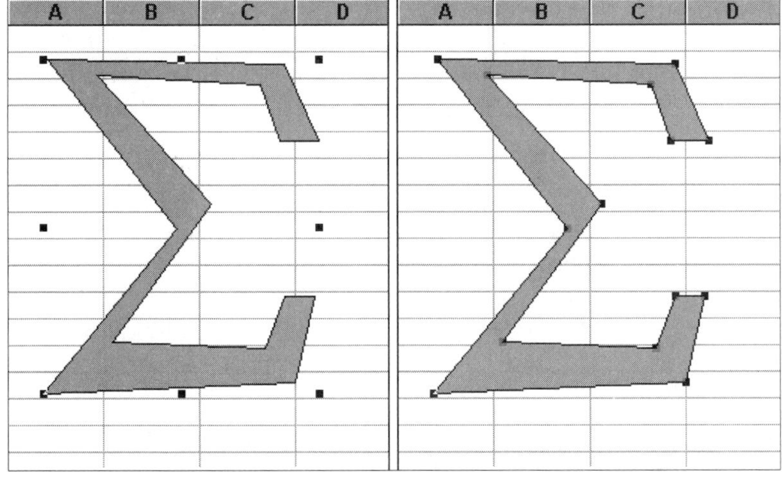

FIGURE 9-4
When you click the Reshape button, handles appear at each corner, as in the image on the far right.

Using the Text Box Button

You can use the Text Box button on the Drawing toolbar to add comments, headings, legends, and other text to your worksheets and charts to give them more impact or to clarify them.

When you select the Text Box button and draw a box, a blinking insertion point appears in the box, indicating that you can begin typing. Text is left-aligned by default, but you can use the alignment tools on the Formatting toolbar or the Object command on the Format menu to realign the text. The worksheet in Figure 9-5 contains two text boxes.

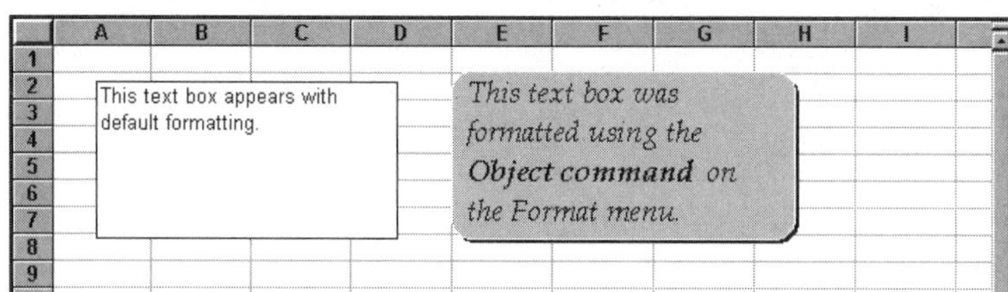

FIGURE 9-5 These two text boxes were created using the Text Box button.

Keep in mind that you can use the Spelling command on the Tools menu to check spelling in text boxes. When you use this command with a single cell selected, all the text in the current worksheet is checked, including text in text boxes. If you choose this command when a text box (or any object) is selected, only that text box (or object) is checked.

TIP You can link a text box to a cell. First, draw a text box. Next, with the text box selected, type an equal sign and then type a cell reference in the formula bar. For example, suppose cell D3 contains a formula that returns the value $123.45. When you type

=$D$3

in the formula bar while the text box is selected, the value $123.45 appears in the text box.

When you link a text box in this way, you cannot type additional text into it. To remove the link, select the text box and delete the reference formula in the formula bar.

Selecting and Grouping Objects

Sometimes you'll find it convenient to move, resize, or even reformat more than one object at a time. You might want to move several objects at once while preserving their positions relative to one another. For these purposes, Excel includes the Drawing Selection, Group Objects, and Ungroup Objects buttons on the Drawing toolbar. It also provides the Group and Ungroup commands on the Placement submenu of the Format menu.

The Drawing Selection button has a few special properties that help you work with objects. After you click the button, the Drawing Selection arrow appears, with which you can select only objects, not cells. The Drawing Selection button remains active until you click it again. When you use the Drawing Selection button, your cell selections disappear on the worksheet, making it easier to distinguish the objects. Also, if an object has a macro assigned to it and the macro is normally activated when the object is clicked, you can use the Drawing Selection arrow to select the object without activating the macro. You can then edit the object itself. Finally, you can use the Drawing Selection arrow to select a group of objects by dragging a rectangle around them, as shown in Figure 9-6.

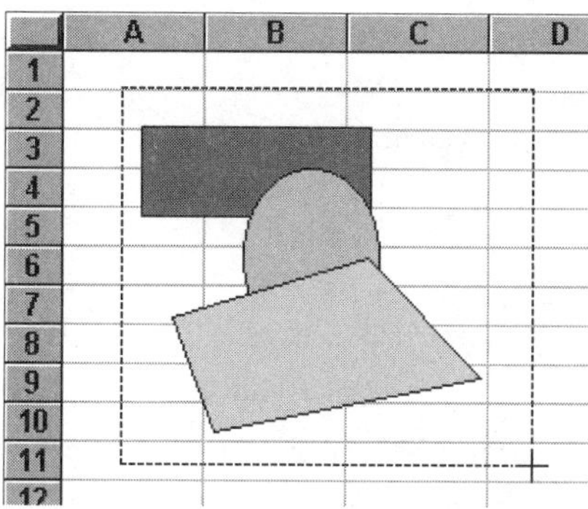

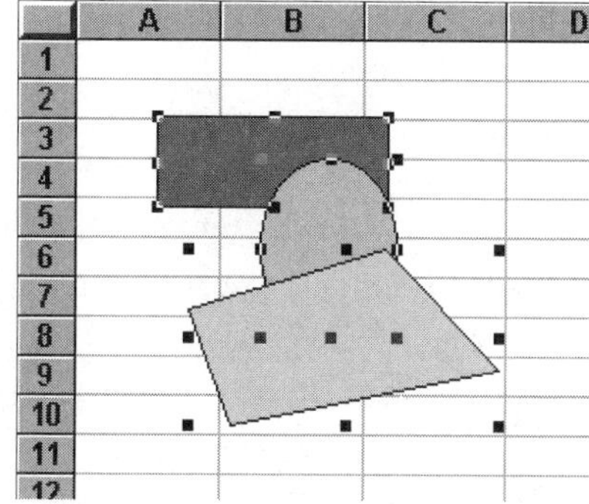

FIGURE 9-6

You can use the Drawing Selection button to drag a rectangle around the objects you want to select. After you select the objects, selection handles appear around each object.

You can also group objects together by clicking each object while holding down Shift. In addition, you can select all the objects on the current worksheet or chart by choosing the Go To command from the Edit menu, clicking the Special button, and then selecting the Objects option.

After you select a group of objects, you can lock them together using either the Group Objects button on the Drawing toolbar or the Group command on the Placement submenu of the Format menu. The sets of handles around each selected object are then replaced by a single set of handles for the entire group, as shown in Figure 9-7 on the next page.

After you group a set of objects, you can manipulate them as though they were a single object. You can resize them, move them, and apply formatting to them as a group. When you apply formatting, however, the separate objects might behave differently, especially if you have grouped different kinds of objects with different formats. It is best to apply formatting before you group objects together, unless the objects you want to work with are similar.

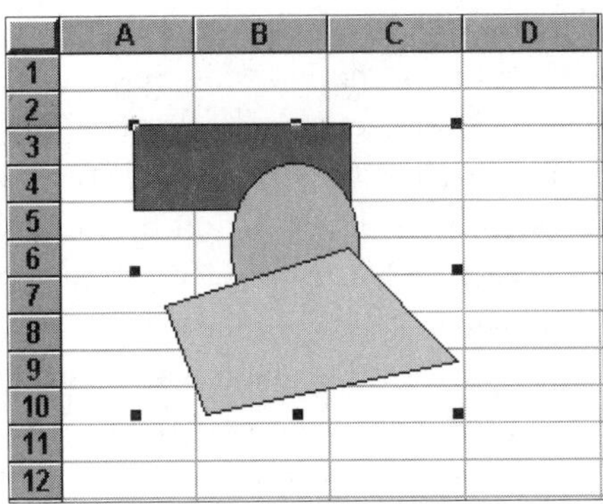

FIGURE 9-7

These objects are grouped together.

To ungroup a set of objects, select the group and then click the Ungroup Objects button on the Drawing toolbar. You can also use the Ungroup command on the Placement submenu of the Format menu. (This command replaces the Group command when a group of objects is selected.)

Selecting a Text Box

Unlike other objects, when you first select a text box by clicking it, a gray border appears around the box to indicate that it is selected. You can then manipulate the text box as you would any other object. When you click the text box a second time, however, a flashing insertion point appears in the text area, giving you the opportunity to edit the text inside the box. If you want to move a text box while its text area is active, you must click and drag the text box's border; otherwise, you end up selecting the text inside the box instead.

Formatting Objects

In Chapter 6, we discussed using the Cells command on the Format menu to add patterns, colors, and shading to cells. You can apply the same formats to objects using the Object command on the Format menu.

When you choose the Object (or Selected Object) command from the Format menu or when you double-click the object, the Format Object dialog box appears. The Patterns tab of this dialog box gives you control over the style, color, and weight of the object's border, as well as over its fill color and pattern. Figure 9-8 shows the Format Object dialog box as it appeared after we double-clicked the trapezoid-shaped object in Figure 9-7.

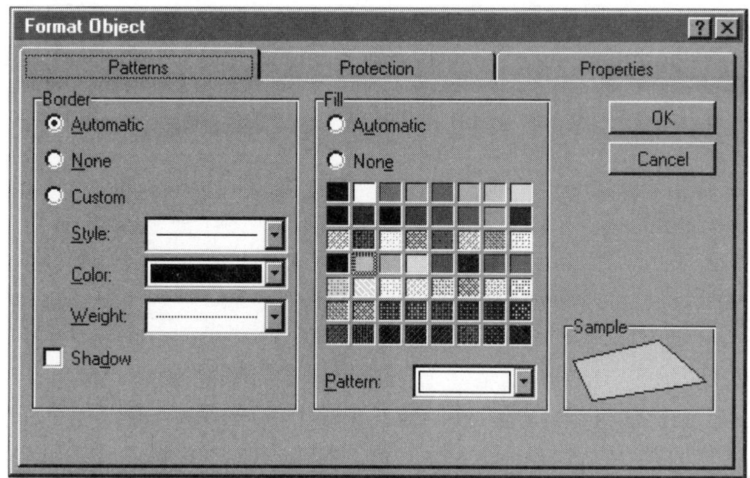

FIGURE 9-8
The Format Object dialog box appears when you choose the Object command from the Format menu or when you double-click an object.

NOTE If a chart sheet is active, the Cells command changes to the Selected Object command. The name of the actual command varies depending on which object is selected. Similarly, the name of the Format Object dialog box changes. For example, if a chart's legend is selected, the command on the Format menu appears as Selected Legend and opens the Format Legend dialog box.

If a rectangle, embedded chart, or text box is selected, an additional option — Round Corners — appears below the Shadow check box on the Patterns tab of the Format Object dialog box. If an ellipse, circle, freeform polygon (as in Figure 9-8), or freehand line is selected, the Round Corners option is not available. If an arc is selected, neither the Shadow nor the Round Corners option is available. Figure 9-5, shown earlier, displays an example of a text box with both the Shadow option and the Round Corners option applied.

TIP To display the Format Object dialog box for a text box, double-click the text box's border. When you do, two additional tabs appear in the dialog box, Font and Alignment.

Selecting the Automatic border style (the default) on the Patterns tab of the Format Object dialog box produces a thin, solid black line. You can customize borders using the Style, Color, and Weight options, along with the Shadow and Round Corners options. You can select from eight Style options, including four types of dotted lines and three levels of shading. The Color options include the

The Color Palette

The palette of colors available for use with objects is determined by the Color tab of the Options dialog box. To display the Options dialog box, choose the Options command from the Tools menu. You can then click the Color tab, select the Edit option, and modify the existing color palette. For more information about the Color tab, see "Changing the Available Colors," page 215.

56 colors that appear on the Color tab of the Options dialog box. The available border Weight options are hairline (the dotted line), thin, medium, and thick.

You can use the Fill section of the Patterns tab to select a fill color, pattern, and pattern color for the selected object. You use the Pattern drop-down list box to select both a pattern and a pattern color. The color you select for the pattern is assigned to the black areas of the pattern. The color you select for the fill is assigned to the white areas. For example, if you select dark green as your fill color and the default pattern — white, or none — the object is displayed in a solid dark green. If, on the other hand, you select cyan as your fill color, a dot pattern, and magenta as your pattern color, the object will be cyan with magenta dots.

You can see the effects of combinations of Border and Fill options, including Patterns, by looking at the Sample section in the lower right corner of the Format Object dialog box. The Sample box also renders an approximation of the selected object's shape, as you can see in Figure 9-8.

The Color and Patterns Buttons

The Color button on the Formatting toolbar and the Pattern button on the Drawing toolbar are tear-off palettes. If you click and drag them away from the toolbar, they become little floating toolbars similar to the color palette in Figure 9-8. Both buttons can be used to format either cells or objects.

The Color button duplicates the palette in the Fill section that controls the fill, or background color. The Pattern button duplicates the palette that controls pattern and pattern color (the one that appears when you display the Pattern drop-down list box in the Fill section on the Patterns tab).

To hide a floating palette, click the tiny close box in its upper right corner.

If you select a line or an arrow and then choose the Object command from the Format menu, or if you double-click a line or an arrow, the options on the Patterns tab change, as you can see in Figure 9-9. In addition to the Style, Color, and Weight options, the Patterns tab lets you attach or remove arrowheads. If you draw a line to which you want to add an arrowhead, remember that the arrowhead will appear at the end of the line — that is, the place where you release the mouse button.

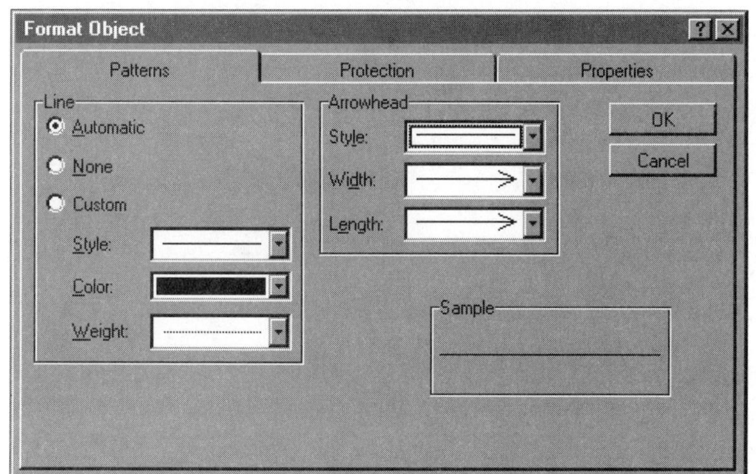

FIGURE 9-9
When a line is selected, the Patterns tab of the Format Object dialog box lets you turn lines into arrows and vice versa.

The options in the Arrowhead section let you tailor the arrows to your liking. The Style options are no arrow, open head, closed head, and open or closed double-head. The Width options let you create narrow, medium, or wide arrowheads, and the Length options let you create short, medium, or long arrowheads.

For more information about embedded charts, see "Creating Embedded Charts," page 586.

For more information about worksheet pictures, see "Taking Pictures of Your Worksheets," page 364.

For more information about the color palette, see "Changing the Available Colors," page 215.

The Drop Shadow Button

You can use the Drop Shadow button on the Drawing toolbar to add depth to any graphic object except a line, an arrow, or an arc. Selecting this button is equivalent to selecting the Shadow option on the Patterns tab of the Format Object dialog box.

In Figure 9-10, we created the box on the left by using the Filled Rectangle button. We created the starburst shape on the right by using the Filled Freeform button, adding a diagonal pattern, and using the Drop Shadow button. We then drew the text boxes, entered the text, and created the arrows with the Arrow button by holding down Shift while dragging to create straight lines.

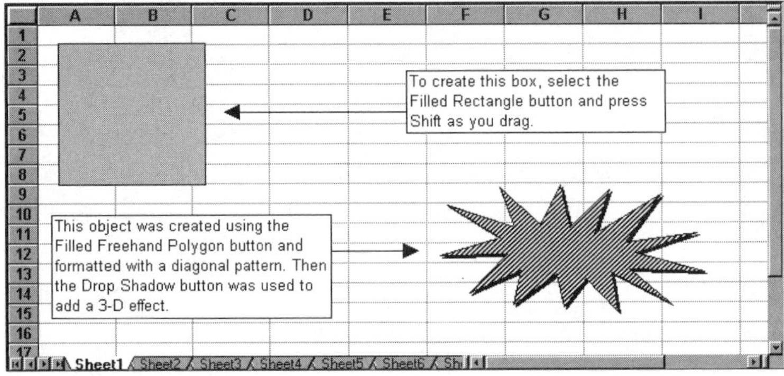

FIGURE 9-10
We created these graphic objects using the Drawing toolbar and the Format Object dialog box.

Formatting a Text Box

When you select a text box and then display the Format Object dialog box, the Font and Alignment tabs appear in the dialog box, in addition to the Patterns, Protection, and Properties tabs. Figure 9-11 shows the Font tab of the Format Object dialog box after we selected a text box; Figure 9-12 at the top of the next page shows the Alignment tab.

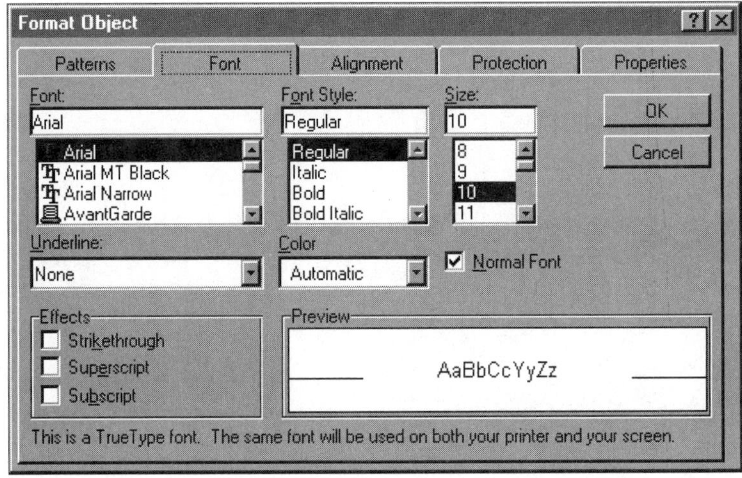

FIGURE 9-11
The Format Object dialog box provides a Font tab with options for objects drawn with the Text Box button.

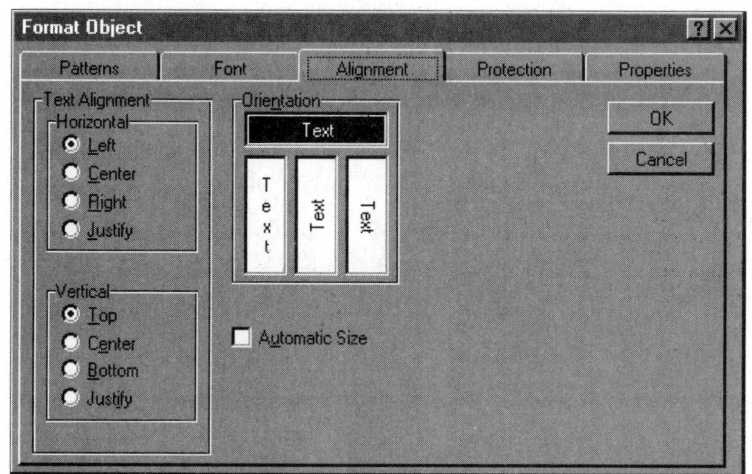

FIGURE 9-12

The Format Object dialog box also provides an Alignment tab with options for objects drawn with the Text Box button.

The Font tab is identical in both appearance and function to the Font tab of the Format Cells dialog box. Because you can rotate the text in a text box, the Alignment tab offers both Horizontal and Vertical alignment options, similar to the options available on the Alignment tab of the Format Cells dialog box.

We formatted the text boxes in Figure 9-13 with various alignment and orientation options. In addition, we selected the Automatic Size option for the three boxes containing the *Center center* label. The Automatic Size option automatically adjusts the size of the text box to fit the text it contains.

FIGURE 9-13

These alignment and orientation options are among those available on the Alignment tab. The three *Center center* boxes were formatted with the Automatic Size option turned on.

For more information about the Font tab, see "Formatting Fonts," page 183.

For more information about the Alignment tab, see "Aligning Cell Contents," page 178.

Positioning Objects

Think of the objects on a worksheet as being stacked on top of each other. You can adjust the position of objects in relation to each other using the Bring To Front and Send To Back buttons on the Drawing toolbar or the commands of the same names on the Placement submenu of the Format menu. Figure 9-14 shows two identical sets of ungrouped objects. In the set on the right, we positioned the rectangle in front of the other objects using the Bring To Front button, and we positioned the trapezoid behind the other objects using the Send To Back button.

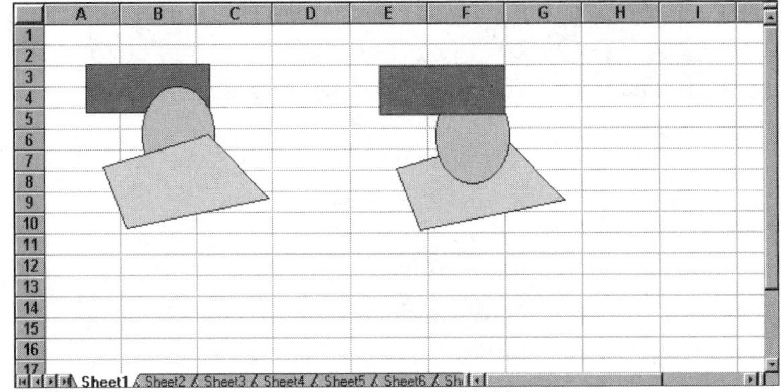

FIGURE 9-14 You can reposition objects in relation to each other with the Bring To Front and Send To Back buttons or commands.

You can change the way objects are attached to a worksheet by using the options on the Properties tab of the Format Object dialog box, which is shown in Figure 9-15.

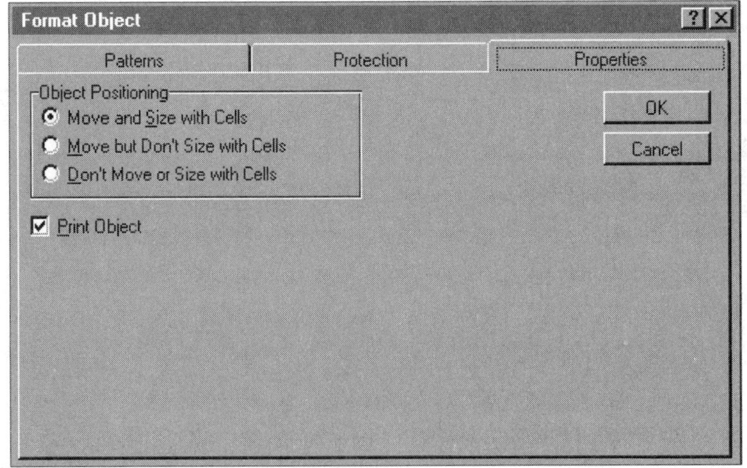

FIGURE 9-15 You can use the Properties tab of the Format Object dialog box to control how cell changes affect graphics.

The default placement option is Move And Size With Cells, meaning that if you do anything to change the size or shape of the underlying cells, the object adjusts accordingly. For example, Figure 9-16 on the next page shows how the size and shape of three objects, which were originally identical, changed as we changed the width and height of the underlying cells.

An *underlying cell* is any cell whose right or bottom border is between the upper left corner and the lower right corner of the object. In Figure 9-16, notice that the object in the middle is just touching the top border of cell D8, which is not an underlying cell, whereas the top of the object breaks across the bottom border of cell D3, which therefore qualifies as an underlying cell.

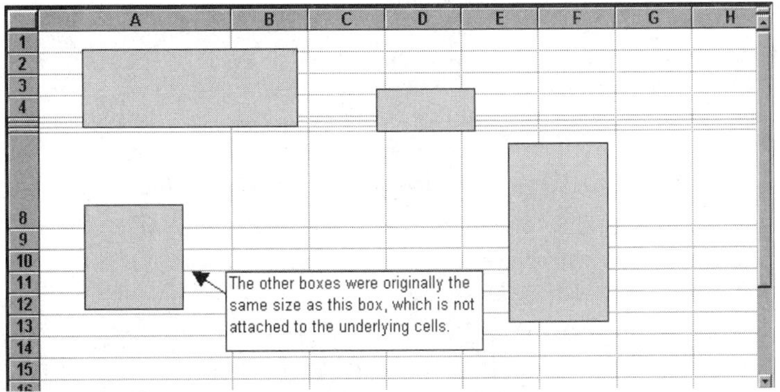

The other boxes were originally the same size as this box, which is not attached to the underlying cells.

FIGURE 9-16
When you select the Move And Size With Cells option, the object responds to any changes made to the underlying cells.

If you insert columns or rows before an object formatted with the Move And Size With Cells option, the object moves accordingly. If you insert columns or rows between the first and last underlying cells, the object stretches to accommodate the insertion. If you select the Move But Don't Size With Cells option and then insert or delete columns or rows, the object moves but retains its shape and proportion. If you select the Don't Move Or Size With Cells option, the object floats above the worksheet and is not affected by any changes you make to the underlying cells.

The Print Object option at the bottom of the Properties tab is normally turned on. If you turn off this option, the selected object is not printed when you print the worksheet.

See Also For more information about printing, see Chapter 10, "Printing and Presenting," page 373.

Cutting, Copying, and Sorting Objects with Cells

In addition to moving and sizing objects with cells, Excel allows you to cut, copy, and sort objects that are attached to cells. This capability is controlled by the Cut, Copy, And Sort Objects With Cells option on the Edit tab of the Options dialog box. To activate or deactivate this option, choose the Options command from the Tools menu, click the Edit tab, and then select or deselect the Cut, Copy, And Sort Objects With Cells option.

When Cut, Copy, And Sort Objects With Cells is turned on, you can easily construct "databases" of the objects that you create in Excel or that you import from other applications. For example, Figure 9-17 at the top of the next page shows a rudimentary database of objects whose names are entered in the underlying cells. (Each corresponding object is drawn adjacent to the name so that the same cell becomes the underlying cell to which the object is attached.) In Figure 9-17, the window on the right shows what happens when you select any cell in the list, choose the Sort command from the Data menu, and click OK. The cells and attached objects are sorted according to the text in the cells.

You can also use the Delete command on the Edit menu to simultaneously delete a cell and any objects attached to the cell. Similarly, if you copy a cell, any attached objects are also copied.

FIGURE 9-17
You can sort objects along with cells, as shown in the window on the far right.

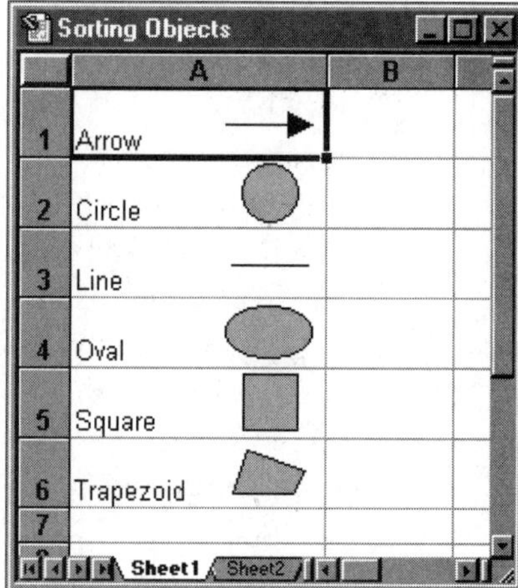

See Also For more information about importing objects from other applications, see "Using Graphics from Other Programs," page 367.

For more information about the Sort command, see "Sorting Lists and Other Ranges," page 718.

Controlling the Display of Objects

To speed up the scrolling of your worksheet, you can choose the Options command from the Tools menu and click the View tab. In the Objects section of the View tab, the Show All option is normally active. Selecting the Show Placeholders option reduces text boxes, button objects, and embedded charts to simple patterns that indicate their locations on the worksheet. The Show Placeholders option increases your scrolling speed because Excel doesn't have to redraw the objects every time you scroll to a new screen. You must reactivate the Show All option before you print.

The Hide All option suppresses the display of objects entirely, increasing screen redraw speed even more. Although you cannot directly modify objects when Hide All is activated, some actions will still change them. If anything other than Don't Move Or Size With Cells is selected on the Properties tab of the Format Object dialog box, the object will respond to adjustments made to the column width or row height of underlying cells.

Protecting Objects

You can prevent objects from being selected, moved, formatted, or sized by choosing the Object command from the Format menu (or the Selected Object command, if the object is on a chart sheet), clicking the Protection tab, and selecting the Locked option, as shown in Figure 9-18. You can also use the Lock Text option, which is visible only when a text box is selected, to protect the text contents of a text box. Newly drawn objects are automatically assigned Locked protection. However, to turn on worksheet security and actually activate protection for both text boxes and new objects, you must also choose the Protect Sheet command from the Protection submenu of the Tools menu.

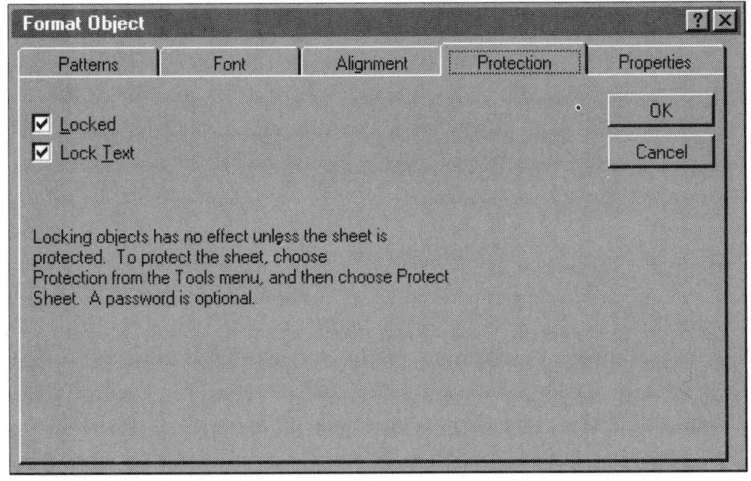

FIGURE 9-18
Choose the Object command from the Format menu, or double-click an object, and then click the Protection tab to check the object's protection status. The Lock Text option is available only when a text box is selected.

For more information about protecting your work, see "Protecting Your Data," page 106.

Taking Pictures of Your Worksheets

Microsoft Excel provides two techniques for taking "pictures" of your worksheets: the Camera button (which you can add to a toolbar) and the Copy Picture command (which appears on the Edit menu when you press Shift).

Using the Camera Button

With the Camera button, shown in Figure 9-19, you can copy an image of a range of cells and paste the image anywhere in the same worksheet, another worksheet in the same workbook, or another workbook. Copying an image is not the same as copying the same range of cells with the Copy command on the Edit menu. When you use the Camera button, you copy a linked image of the cells, not their contents. As a result, the image changes dynamically as the contents of the original cells change.

FIGURE 9-19
The Camera button.

To display the Camera button, choose the Toolbars command from the View menu and click the Customize button. In the Customize dialog box, select the Utility category and drag the Camera button onto any toolbar. (If you don't drag the Camera button onto a toolbar, it creates its own toolbar.)

Figure 9-20 shows two worksheets side by side. If you select the range A3:B6 in Exams Quarter 3 and click the Camera button, the pointer changes from a plus sign to a cross hair. Click anywhere in Book4 to select it and then click the cross-hair pointer where you want the upper left corner of the picture to appear. Excel embeds the picture as shown on the right in Figure 9-20. Any graphic objects within the range A3:B6 or that overlap the range are also included in the embedded picture.

After you paste the picture, you can change its size and proportions by dragging its selection handles, and you can treat it just like any other graphic object. Changes in shape, size, or formatting do not affect the dynamic updating of the data displayed in the picture.

If we select the embedded picture in Figure 9-20, the formula bar displays a formula much like any other cell-linking formula. After you create the picture, you can change the formula in the formula bar, and the

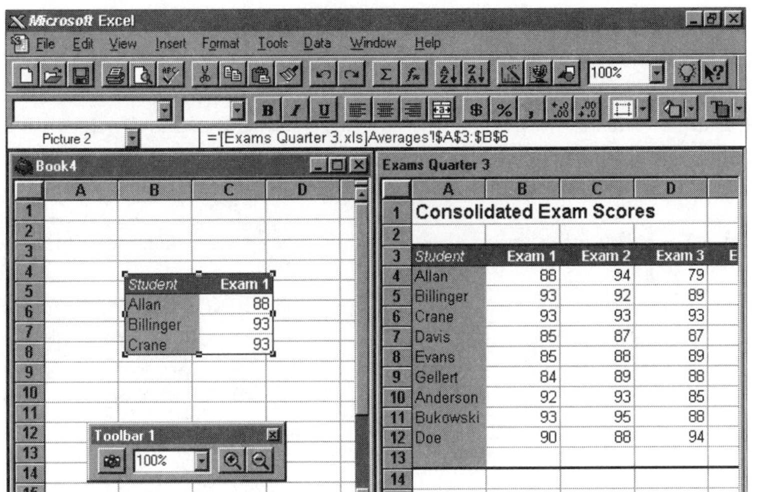

FIGURE 9-20

The Camera button creates a linked image of a selected range.

picture will change accordingly. You can even change the reference formula to link a completely different worksheet or workbook.

For example, if we select the embedded picture in Book4 in Figure 9-20, the Name box in the formula bar displays the name Picture 2 and the formula shown for the object is

='[Exams Quarter 3.xls]Averages'!$A$3:$B$6

If you change the formula to

='[Exams Quarter 3.xls]Averages'!$A$3:$B$9

the picture adjusts to include the additional rows, as shown in Figure 9-21.

Book4

Student	Exam 1
Allan	88
Billinger	93
Crane	93
Davis	85
Evans	85
Gellert	84

Sheet1 Sheet2 Sheet3

FIGURE 9-21

If you change the cell references in a formula for a picture created with the Camera button, the picture changes accordingly.

The link between the source and destination documents has another distinctive and useful characteristic. Suppose you close the Exams Quarter 3 worksheet in Figure 9-20. If you then double-click the embedded image in Book4, Exams Quarter 3 opens automatically, with the pictured range selected. This response is a feature of Dynamic Data Exchange (DDE).

For more information about cell links, see "References to Worksheets in Other Workbooks," page 117.

For more information about Dynamic Data Exchange, see Chapter 26, "Integrating Applications with the Clipboard and OLE," page 889.

Using the Copy Picture Command

The Copy Picture command creates an image just as the Camera button does, but with an important difference. The copied picture is static, with no links to any worksheet. Static pictures are useful when you don't need to update data or when the speed with which Excel recalculates the worksheet is more important than updating. You can use the Copy Picture command to add images of worksheets and charts to reports or other documents via the Clipboard. After you take the picture, you can paste it in another Excel document or in a document from any application that accepts Clipboard images.

To use the Copy Picture command, select the cells, object, or chart you want to copy, hold down Shift, and choose Copy Picture from the Edit menu (where the Copy command has become the Copy Picture command and the Paste command has become the Paste Picture command). Excel displays the dialog box shown in Figure 9-22.

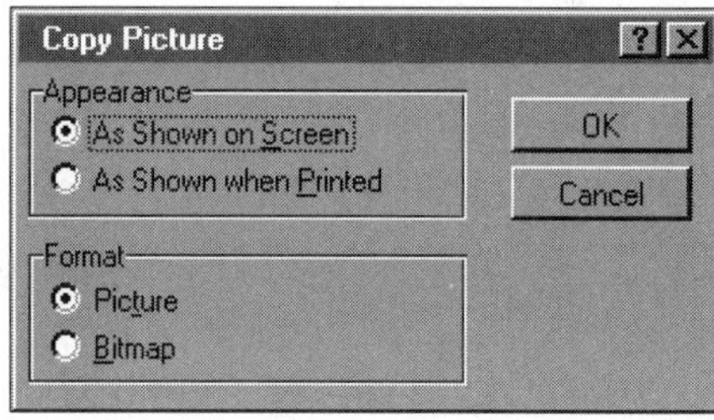

FIGURE 9-22
The Copy Picture dialog box lets you control the appearance of the picture.

The default option, As Shown On Screen, reproduces the selection at the moment you take the picture. The As Shown When Printed option reproduces the selection according to the settings in the Page Setup dialog box that control the printing of gridlines and row and column headings. For example, the worksheet in Figure 9-23 contains two pictures of the same area. We created the top one with the As Shown On Screen option selected and the bottom one with the As

Shown When Printed option selected and the Page Setup options for printing gridlines turned off, and the option for printing row and column headings turned on.

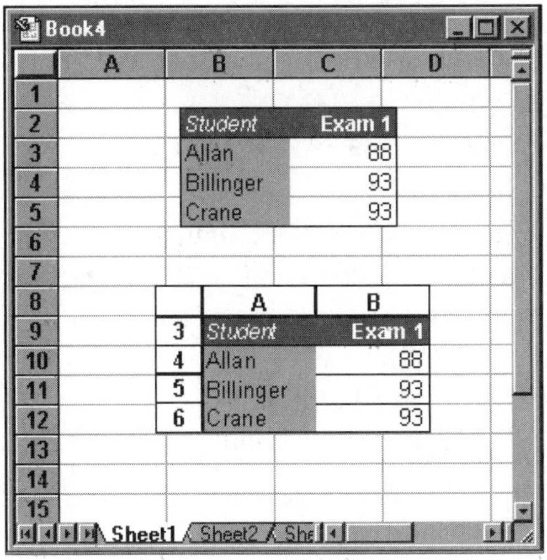

FIGURE 9-23
The top picture was created with the Copy Picture command's As Shown On Screen option, and the bottom picture was created with the As Shown When Printed option.

The Picture and Bitmap options are useful if your workbook will be viewed on different computers. The Picture option copies the picture in a format that can be displayed on monitors with different resolutions, whereas the Bitmap option copies the picture in a format that appears to be correct only when the display resolution is the same as the screen from which it was copied.

After you copy an image of the selection to the Clipboard, you can paste the image anywhere you want — in another location on the worksheet, in another worksheet, or even in a document from another application. You can paste the image into an Excel document with the Paste command, the Paste Picture command, or the Paste button on the Standard toolbar.

Using Graphics from Other Programs

You can import graphics into Microsoft Excel from other programs that produce files compatible with the Windows Clipboard, such as Windows Paint in Windows 95.

If the application used to create the graphic you want to import into Excel supports Dynamic Data Exchange (DDE) or OLE, you might be able to establish a link between the source file and the graphic. After you import the graphic into Excel, the link allows the graphic to be updated automatically if the source document changes.

To import a graphic from another application, begin by opening the file that contains the graphic in the source application and copying the image you want using the Copy command. Next, in Excel, open the workbook into which you want to paste the graphic and choose the Paste or Paste Special command (or click the Paste button on the Standard toolbar).

As with other graphic objects, you can size, position, and protect pasted-in images. You can also add borders with the Object command on the Format menu.

To export an image of an Excel worksheet or chart, use the Copy Picture command and then paste the image, via the Clipboard, into any other application that supports the Clipboard.

For more information about Dynamic Data Exchange and OLE, see Chapter 26, "Integrating Applications with the Clipboard and OLE," page 889.

The Picture Command

The Picture command on the Insert menu allows you to embed in your workbooks graphics that have been saved in a variety of file formats. (The actual formats supported depend on your computer's configuration.) When you choose the Picture command, a dialog box like the one in Figure 9-24 appears.

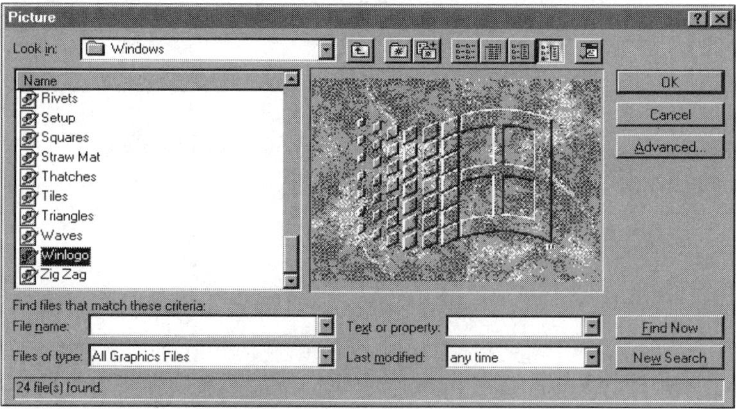

FIGURE 9-24
Using the Picture dialog box, you can insert graphic files from other applications into your workbook.

Use the Name box in the Picture dialog box to locate a particular graphic that is saved on disk. The Files Of Type drop-down list box allows you to zero in on a particular file type, but normally displays All Graphics Files. A thumbnail representation of the selected file appears in the preview box. If you click the button, the Advanced Find dialog box appears to help you sift through the files on your computer's disk drives. When you find the file, click Insert to insert the graphic in the worksheet.

For more information about searching for files, see "Searching for Files," page 71.

The Object Command

The Object command on the Insert menu gives you direct access to other applications you can use to create objects or edit existing objects that you will subsequently insert in your worksheet. The difference between inserting a picture and inserting an object is that a picture is always static and cannot be edited or updated, whereas an object retains a connection to its source application. You can open an embedded object for editing by double-clicking it, and you can choose to link an object to the source file so that it is updated automatically if the source file changes.

When you choose the Object command from the Insert menu, a dialog box appears with two tabs — Create New and Create From File. The Create New tab, shown in Figure 9-25, allows you to activate an application and then create the object directly in the selected application. You select an application from the Object Type list box. The contents of this list box vary depending on the configuration of your system and the applications you have installed.

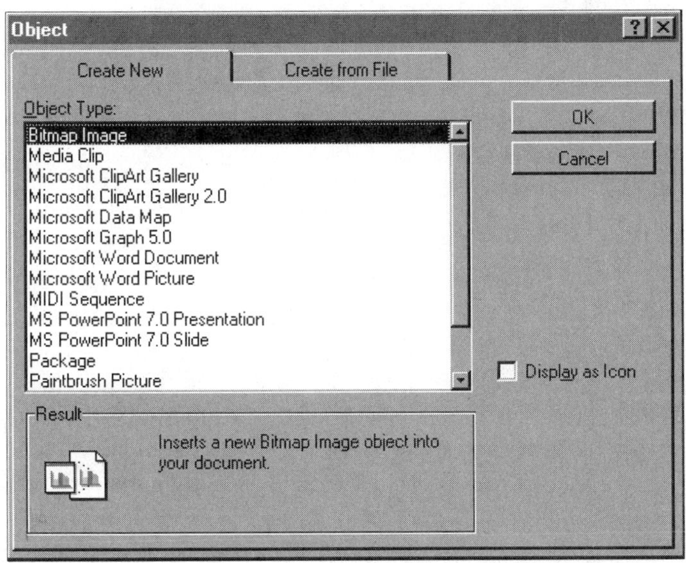

FIGURE 9-25
You can use the Create New tab of the Object dialog box to simultaneously insert an object and activate the application.

When you select an item from the Object Type list box, a small frame is inserted in the current worksheet at the location of the active cell, and the application needed to create or edit that object type is started. For example, if you select Paintbrush Picture from the Object Type list box, Microsoft Paint starts, and you can then create a new drawing or edit an existing one. When you are finished, click any cell in the worksheet. The object you created is inserted at the location of the active cell.

The Object dialog box's Create From File tab is shown in Figure 9-26. You can use this tab to insert an existing file as an object, rather than create a new object with the Create New tab. (The object types you can actually embed depend on the applications installed in your computer.)

FIGURE 9-26 With the Create From File tab of the Object dialog box, you can insert existing documents in your workbooks.

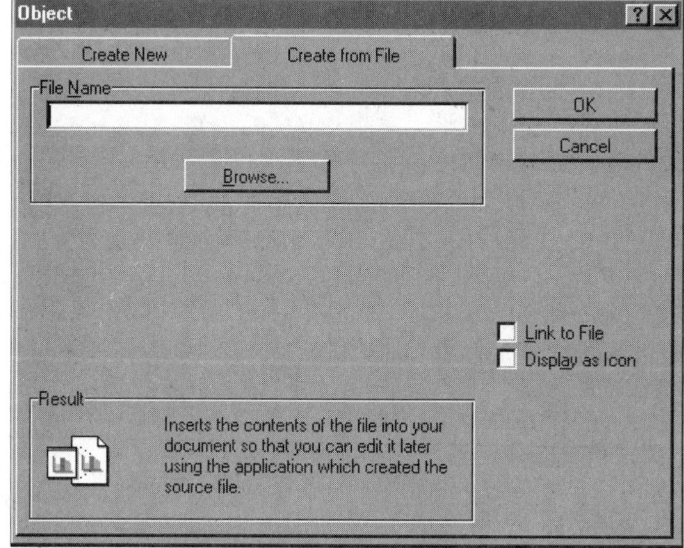

Although the Link To File option on the Create From File tab is not selected by default, you can still open the object in its source application by double-clicking it. If you select the Link To File option, the object is automatically updated when the source file changes. The Display As Icon option embeds the selected file in your workbook as an icon. This option is particularly convenient when an embedded object is very long or large and is more easily viewed in its source application. However, if you distribute the workbook to other users, be sure the same application is available on their computers, or they will not be able to open the embedded icon for viewing.

To make changes to any embedded object, simply double-click the object. The source application starts and the object file opens, allowing you to make modifications.

See Also For more information about linking objects, see Chapter 26, "Integrating Applications with the Clipboard and OLE," page 919.

Chapter 10

Printing and Presenting

Microsoft Excel makes it easy for you to produce polished, professional-looking reports from worksheets. This chapter explains how to use the Page Setup command to define the layout of your printed pages. It also explains how to restrict your print range, define print titles, control page breaks, and use Excel's Print Preview feature. This chapter concentrates on printing worksheets, but with a few of the refinements discussed in Chapter 16, you can apply the procedures covered here to the printing of charts.

This chapter also covers the Report Manager. You use the Report Manager to assign names to combinations of print areas and print settings, making it easy to re-create a printout at any time.

Specifying What to Print

Unless you tell Microsoft Excel to do otherwise, choosing the Print command from the File menu and clicking OK prints one copy of the entire populated area of the current worksheet. You do not have to specify a print range as you do in some other spreadsheet programs. As you can see from the Print dialog box shown in Figure 10-1, however, you can specify what portion of your document Excel should print.

- To print the entire workbook, not just the current worksheet, select Entire Workbook in the Print dialog box.
- To print a group of worksheets, but not the entire workbook, select those worksheets as a group before choosing Print from the File menu. Then click the Selected Sheet(s) option in the Print dialog box.

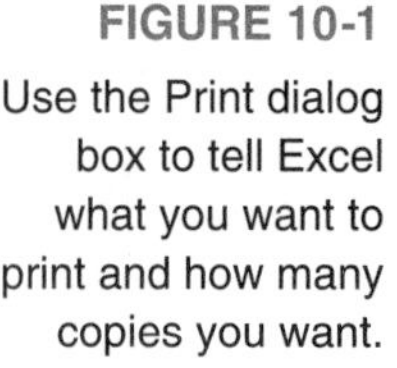

FIGURE 10-1
Use the Print dialog box to tell Excel what you want to print and how many copies you want.

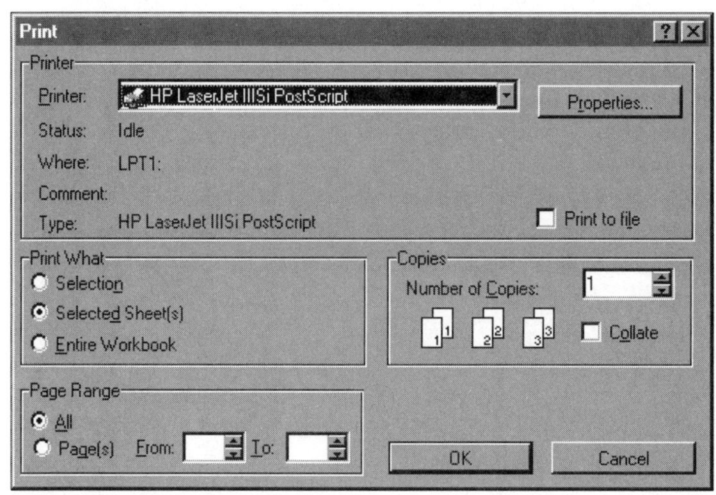

- To print part of a worksheet, first select what you want to print and then click the Selection option in the Print dialog box. (Alternatively, you can define an area on the Sheet tab of the Page Setup dialog box.)
- To print only a particular range of pages, enter the starting and ending page numbers in the From and To edit boxes.
- To print more than one copy, enter the number of copies you want in the Copies edit box. If you select the Collate option, Excel will print one complete copy of the document at a time.

The top line of the Print dialog box tells you which printer will handle your output. To use a different printer, click the down arrow to display the drop-down list and then select the printer you want from the list of those available.

Defining an Area to Print

When you choose the Selected Sheet(s) option in the Print dialog box, Excel checks to see if the range name *Print_Area* has been assigned on each worksheet. If this name has been assigned, Excel prints only the range to which you've assigned the name. Otherwise, it prints the entire populated area of the sheet. Thus, if you want to print the same area of a given sheet repeatedly, you can save yourself some steps by giving that area the name *Print_Area*. You can do that either by choosing Print Area and then Set Print Area from the File menu or by following these steps:

1. Choose Page Setup from the File menu and then click the Sheet tab.
2. Specify the range you want to print in the Print Area edit box.

You can assign the name *Print_Area* on as many sheets as you like. If you select two or more sheets and print using the Selected Sheet(s) option, Excel will print only the *Print_Area* range of any sheet where that name is defined and will print the entire populated area of any remaining selected sheets.

TIP To bypass the Print dialog box, click the Print button on the Standard toolbar or Shift-click the Print Preview button. Excel prints using the Selected Sheet(s) option.

Printing Multiple Ranges on the Same Page

Unlike some other spreadsheet programs, Microsoft Excel instructs your printer to eject the current page at the end of a print job. If you select multiple ranges and then click the Selection option in the Print dialog box, Excel breaks pages between each region of your selection. Even if you use the Report Manager to combine different areas of a worksheet into a named report, Excel still starts each region on a new page.

Normally, the automatic ejection of the page at the end of a print job is a convenience because you don't have to bother with issuing Align and Page commands, as you do in Lotus 1-2-3 Release 2 or Release 3. However, 1-2-3's approach has the virtue of letting you "gang" several print ranges onto a single page.

If you want to print separate ranges together on one page in Excel, first try using Format menu commands to hide the intervening rows or columns. For example, you might print A1:D14 together with H1:K14 by hiding columns E, F, and G and selecting the range A1:K14. If that approach isn't satisfactory (for example, because you want H1:K14 to be printed below A1:D14), you can use the Camera button, which you can add to any toolbar by choosing Toolbars from the View menu and selecting the Camera button from the Utility category of the Customize dialog box. Take a snapshot of the print range, paste it below the first range, select the entire region — first range plus snapshot — choose the Print command, and then click the Selection option. For more information about the Camera tool, see "Taking Pictures of Your Worksheets," page 364.

See Also For more information on defining names, see "Naming Cells and Ranges," page 126.

Printing Multiple Copies

Microsoft Excel normally prints one copy of whatever you tell it to print. If you want more than one copy, enter the number of copies you want in the Number Of Copies edit box of the Print dialog box (shown earlier in Figure 10-1).

If you want collated copies of your document, select the Collate option in the Print dialog box. Collated copies are more convenient but take longer to print. When you print collated copies, Windows 95 regards each trip through the pages of your document as a separate print job. As a result, Windows 95 spends more time preparing spool files, and you have to wait longer before you can get back to work.

For more information about selecting a group of worksheets, see "Working with Sheets," page 309.

For more information about specifying worksheet print areas, see "Defining an Area to Print," page 375.

Controlling the Appearance of Your Pages

The various sections of the Page Setup dialog box let you specify factors that affect the appearance of your printed pages, such as the orientation, scaling, paper size, print quality, and the number that prints on the first page of your document. Figure 10-2 shows the Page tab of the Page Setup dialog box, which you can display in any of the following ways:

- By choosing the File menu's Page Setup command
- By clicking the Setup button in Print Preview

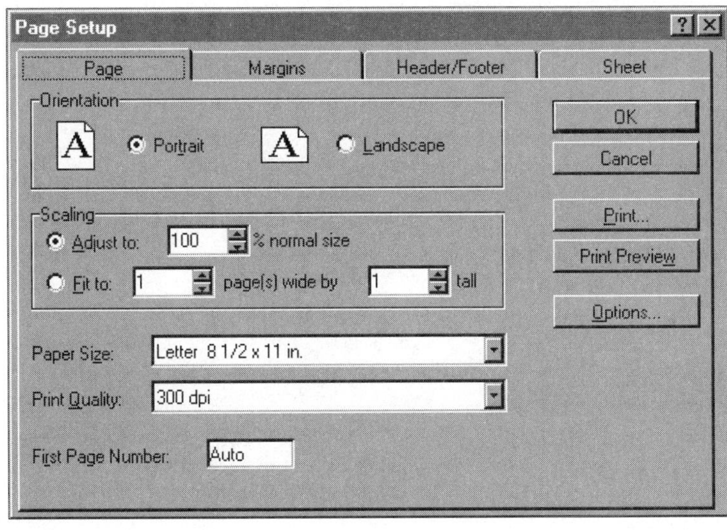

FIGURE 10-2
The Page tab of the Page Setup dialog box lets you choose between portrait and landscape orientation, apply a scaling factor, select paper size and print quality, and specify a starting page number.

For information about the Print dialog box, see "Specifying What to Print," page 374.

For information about Print Preview, see "Using Print Preview," page 388.

Printing Wide or Tall

The Orientation setting determines whether your worksheet prints horizontally (wide) or vertically (tall). When you select the Portrait orientation option, Microsoft Excel prints your worksheet with each row running horizontally from left to right across the page. When you select the Landscape orientation option, Excel prints the worksheet so that each row runs vertically from the top of the page to the bottom. Portrait is the default, and you will probably use it most of the time.

Landscape orientation is useful for printing worksheet pages that are wider than they are long on 8½-by-11-inch paper. For example, you could use this option to print on one sheet of paper a schedule that is 15 columns wide but only 8 rows deep.

Setting a Reduction Ratio

Excel lets you override the default size of your printouts in two ways: by specifying a scaling factor (from 10 percent through 400 percent) or by automatically fitting the report to a specified number of pages. These scaling options are available for any printer installed on your Windows system.

Be aware that Excel always applies a scaling factor in both the horizontal and vertical dimensions. For example, if your full-size printout is two pages deep by one page wide and you tell Excel to scale it to a single page, the resulting printout will be narrower as well as shallower.

If you want to return to a full-size printout after selecting a scaling option, choose the Page Setup command from the File menu, select the Adjust To option, and type *100* in the % Normal Size edit box.

Specifying Paper Size and Print Quality

The Paper Size and Print Quality drop-down lists include the options available for your printer driver. Most laser printers, for example, let you select print-quality settings of 300 dpi (dots per inch), 150 dpi, or 75 dpi. The higher dpi settings look better but take longer to print.

The First Page Number Setting

The First Page Number edit box is meaningful only if you plan to include page numbers in your printout's header or footer. If you plan to print page numbers, you can start them at any number you want, including 0 or a negative number.

See Also For more information about headers and footers, see "Creating a Header and Footer," page 380.

Setting Margins

The Margins tab of the Page Setup dialog box gives you control over the top, bottom, left, and right margins of your printed worksheets. As shown in Figure 10-3, the default settings are 1 inch for the top and bottom margins and 0.75 inch for the left and right margins. You'll probably find these default settings acceptable for printing most worksheets; however, you can easily change any margin setting by entering a new value in the corresponding edit box.

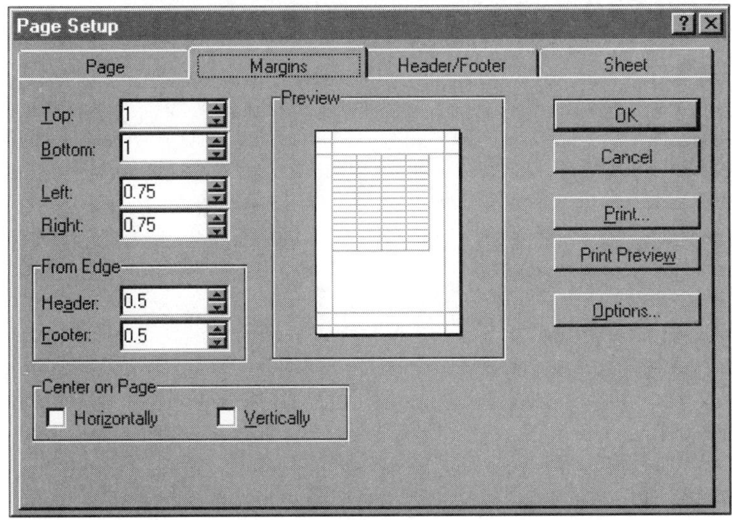

FIGURE 10-3
The Margins tab of the Page Setup dialog box lets you override the default margin settings and select centering options.

Centering Your Work on the Page

If you want your printout to be centered either vertically or horizontally on the page, don't worry about margin settings. Tell Excel to center it automatically by selecting one or both of the Center On Page options at the bottom of the dialog box shown in Figure 10-3.

Creating a Header and Footer

A header is a line or block of text printed at the top of each page. A footer is a line or block of text printed at the bottom of each page. By default, Excel creates a centered header and a centered footer on each page. The header, positioned one-half inch from the top edge, includes the name of the worksheet you're printing. The footer, printed one-half inch from the bottom edge, includes the word *Page* followed by the current page number. You can change the position of the header and footer by using the Margins tab of the Page Setup dialog box, and you can change the content of the header and footer in a variety of ways. Excel includes a number of predefined headers and footers, some of which automatically include your name or the name of your company, and you can create other headers and footers to suit your needs.

You specify a header or a footer (or remove the default header or footer) in the Header/Footer tab of the Page Setup dialog box, shown in Figure 10-4. This dialog box includes Header and Footer drop-down lists and sample boxes that display the current header and footer as they'll look on your printed page.

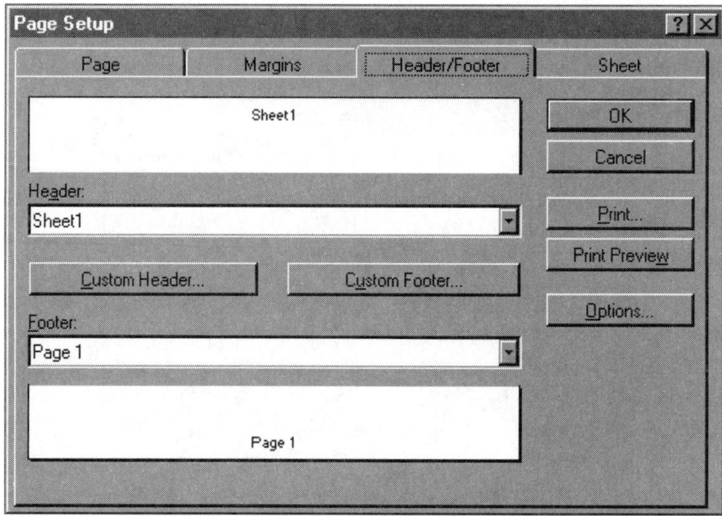

FIGURE 10-4

The Header/Footer tab of the Page Setup dialog box makes it easy to put text at the top and bottom of your printed pages.

Initially, both drop-down lists include the same set of options. If you have created any custom headers or footers for the current workbook, they also appear in the drop-down lists. To see the list of predefined headers, follow these steps:

1. Click the arrow at the right end of the Header option.
2. Press Home to go to the top of the list.

3. Keep your eye on the corresponding example box as you press the Down direction key to move through the list.

To switch to a different predefined header or footer, simply open the appropriate drop-down list and click the header or footer you want.

Creating Custom Headers and Footers

If you don't find exactly what you need in Excel's supply of predefined headers and footers, you can create your own or modify one of Excel's by clicking the Custom Header or Custom Footer button on the Header/Footer tab of the Page Setup dialog box. When you do this, you'll see the dialog box shown in Figure 10-5.

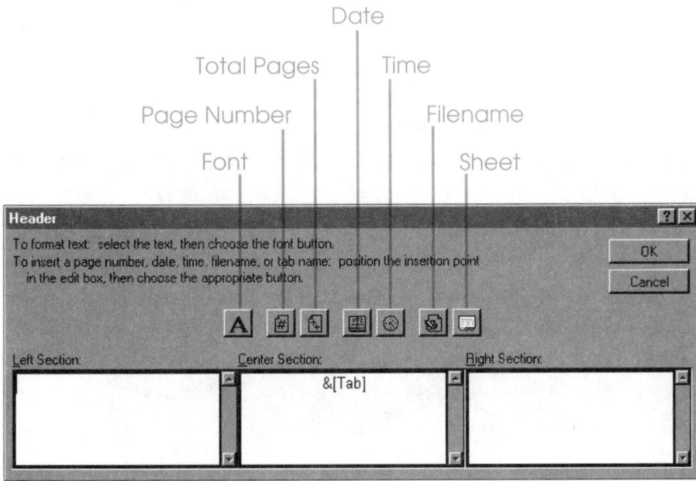

FIGURE 10-5

Excel lets you create custom headers and footers by clicking the buttons in this dialog box.

TIP To override Excel's default header and footer, create a new workbook and set the header and footer as you want them. Then save the workbook as a template under the name BOOK. Store this template file in the XLStart folder of your Excel folder. You can use this technique to override other Excel defaults, too.

Excel's code for printing the current sheet name is *&[Tab]* in the Center Section edit box, as shown in Figure 10-5. In this case, the text *Sheet1* would be printed. Excel uses various codes that begin with an ampersand and are enclosed in brackets to represent information that you might want to put in your headers and footers — such as the current time, current date, and current page number. Fortunately, you don't have to learn these codes to create headers and footers. Simply click the appropriate edit box (Left Section, Center Section, or Right Section), and then click the buttons above the section edit boxes.

To specify text in your header or footer, click the appropriate section edit box and type your text. To divide the text between two or more lines, press Enter at the end of each line. To include an ampersand in your text, type two ampersands.

For example, to create a header that contains three elements — the text *Dewey, Cheatum & Howe,* flush left; the current sheet name in the center of the page; and the current date flush right — follow these steps:

1. Click the Left Section edit box and type *Dewey, Cheatum && Howe.* The current sheet name code, in this case &[Tab], already appears in the Center Section edit box, so you can leave it as is.
2. Click the Right Section edit box and click the Date button — the one with the icon that looks like a miniature desk calendar. The dialog box now looks like the one in Figure 10-6.

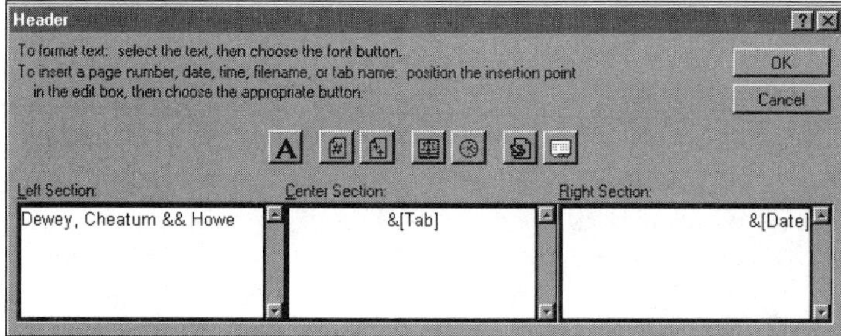

FIGURE 10-6
This header prints *Dewey, Cheatum, & Howe* at the left, the current sheet name in the center, and the current date at the right.

Changing Fonts

Excel's default font for headers and footers is 10-point Arial. To select a different typeface, point size, and style, click the Font button — the one with the capital A on it. The Font dialog box appears. (To assign a different font to text that you've entered in one of the Section edit boxes, first select the text and then click the Font button.) Excel displays the header and footer text in the font and style you select. Note, however, that font options apply to the current Section edit box only.

Setting Print Titles

On many worksheets, the column and row labels that identify information categories are located in only the leftmost columns and top few rows. When Excel breaks a large report into pages, those important column and row labels might appear only on the first page of the printout. You can use the Sheet tab of the Page Setup dialog box to print the contents of one or more columns, one or more rows, or a combination of columns and rows on every page of a report. The Sheet tab of the Page Setup dialog box is shown in Figure 10-7.

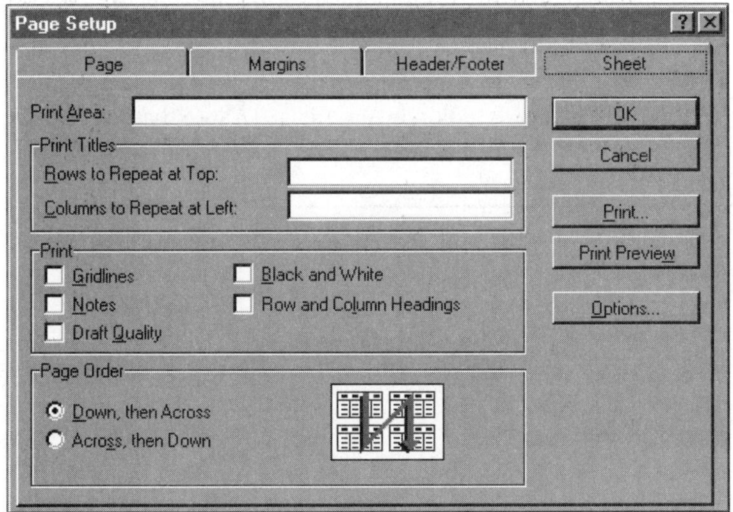

FIGURE 10-7

The Sheet tab of the Page Setup dialog box lets you specify print titles and select various other printing options.

TIP You can specify separate print titles for each worksheet in your workbook. Excel remembers the titles for each worksheet.

In some earlier versions of Excel, you had to be careful to exclude print title columns and rows from the area of the worksheet that you were asking Excel to print. Otherwise, your titles would appear twice: once as titles and once as part of the print area. The current version of Excel is smart enough to recognize when print titles fall within the print area, so you no longer have to worry about duplicated titles.

Suppose you want to print the contents of column A and rows 3 and 4 on all pages of a lengthy report. Follow these steps:

1. Choose Page Setup from the File menu.
2. Click the Sheet tab.
3. Click the Rows To Repeat At Top edit box.
4. Select the headings or any cells in rows 3 and 4 in the worksheet window. (If necessary, drag the dialog box out of the way.)
5. Click the Columns To Repeat At Left edit box.
6. Select the heading or any cell in column A in the worksheet window.

If you prefer to type these entries, you can simply enter the row numbers or column letters in the edit boxes. To specify rows 3 and 4, for example, type *3:4*. To specify column A, type *A:A*. Note that for a single row or column, you have to type the number or letter twice, with a colon in between.

TIP To remove print titles, you can go back to the Page Setup dialog box and delete the title specifications. But you might find it quicker to use the Define Name dialog box. Simply press Ctrl-F3 and delete the name that ends in *Print_Titles*. Excel records your title settings as range names, using the format *Sheet1!Print_Titles, Sheet2!Print_Titles,* and so on. Deleting the name associated with the current worksheet is equivalent to removing the specification in the Page Setup dialog box.

Setting the Printing Order of Large Print Ranges

When you print a large report, Excel breaks the report into page-sized sections based on the current margin and page-size settings. If the print range is both too wide and too deep to fit on a single page, Excel normally works in "down, then across" order. For example, if the print range measures 120 rows by 20 columns and Excel can fit 40 rows and 10 columns on a page, Excel prints the first 40 rows and first 10 columns on page 1, the second 40 rows and first 10 columns on page 2, followed by the third 40 rows and first 10 columns on page 3. On page 4, it prints the first 40 rows and second 10 columns, and so on.

If you prefer to have Excel print each horizontal chunk before moving down to the next vertical chunk, select the Across, Then Down option.

Printing Gridlines

By default, Excel does not print gridlines regardless of whether they're displayed. If you want gridlines printed, select the Gridlines option in the Page Setup dialog box's Sheet tab.

See Also For information about turning gridlines on and off, see "Controlling the Display of Gridlines," page 212.

Printing Cell Notes

Cell notes are annotations created using the Note command on the Insert menu. To include cell notes with your printout, select the Notes option. Excel then adds a new page at the end of your printout and prints all your notes together, starting on that new page.

See Also For information about creating cell notes, see "Adding Notes to Cells," page 288.

Draft Quality

If your printer offers a draft-quality mode, you can obtain a quicker, if less beautiful, printout by selecting the Draft Quality option. This option has no effect if your printer has no draft-quality mode and is most useful for dot-matrix or other slow printers.

Translating Screen Colors to Black and White

If you've assigned background colors and patterns to your worksheet but you're using a black-and-white printer, you'll probably want to select the Black And White option, which tells Excel to ignore any background colors and patterns when printing.

Printing Row and Column Headings

If you select the Row And Column Headings option, Excel prints row letters to the left of and column numbers above worksheet data. This option is handy when you're using printouts to document the structure of a worksheet.

Setting Printer Driver Options

Occasionally while working in Microsoft Excel, you might need to set options that only your printer driver provides. You might, for example, need to switch from automatic to manual paper feed, or from one paper tray to another. You can change settings such as these by going to the Windows Control Panel and choosing Printers. But you can also get to the relevant dialog box from within Excel's own menu system by selecting the printer from the Printer drop-down list in the Print dialog box, which displays a list of your computer's installed printers. Then click the Properties button to access the setup dialog box for the selected printer.

Inserting and Removing Manual Page Breaks

When you print a report that is too large to fit on a single sheet of paper, Microsoft Excel breaks that report into page-size sections based on the current settings in the Page Setup dialog box. As you can see in Figure 10-8, Excel's automatic page breaks are indicated on the screen by light dashed lines.

TIP If you don't want to see automatic page breaks, choose Options from the Tools menu, click the View tab, and deselect the Automatic Page Breaks check box.

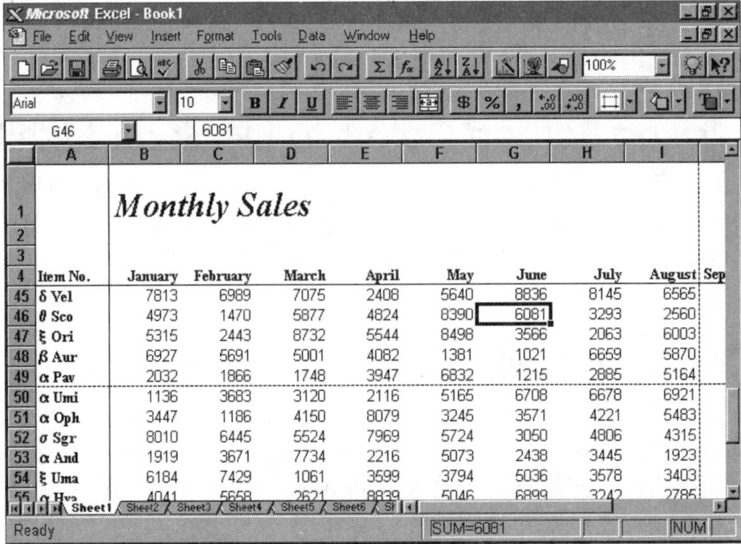

FIGURE 10-8
Automatic page breaks appear on the screen as light dashed lines.

You'll often want to specify page breaks yourself rather than leave the decisions to Excel. Use the Insert menu's Page Break command to place vertical and horizontal page breaks in your printed report. Excel honors these manual page breaks even if you add or delete cells above or to the left of the breaks.

To insert a manual page break, follow these steps:

1. Select the cell below and to the right of the place where you want the break. This cell will become the upper left corner of a new page.
2. From the Insert menu, choose Page Break.

As Figure 10-9 shows, Excel marks manual page breaks with a bold dashed line.

To add a horizontal page break without affecting the vertical breaks in your worksheet, select the cell in column A of the row with which you want to begin a new page and then insert the break. To insert a vertical break without affecting the horizontal breaks, select the cell in row 1 of the column with which you want to begin the new page and then insert the break.

To delete a forced page break, follow these steps:

1. Select the cell below or to the right of the bold dashed line.
2. From the Insert menu, choose Remove Page Break.

If you don't see the Remove Page Break command on the Insert menu, the cell you have selected is not below or to the right of a forced page break.

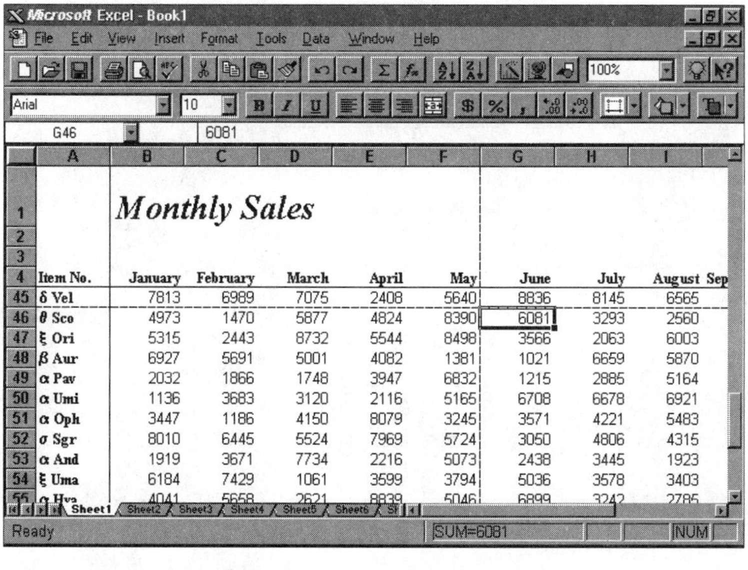

FIGURE 10-9
Manual page breaks are indicated by bold dashed lines.

Using Print Preview

Microsoft Excel's Print Preview lets you look at page breaks, margins, and the format of your printout before you begin printing. To get to Print Preview, use one of the following methods:

- Click the Print Preview button on the Standard toolbar.
- Shift-click the Print button on the Standard toolbar.
- Choose the Print Preview command from the File menu.
- Click the Print Preview button in either the Print or Page Setup dialog box.

Figure 10-10 shows an example of a worksheet in Print Preview.

If you're not satisfied with the layout of your report, you can change the margins and column widths without leaving Print Preview. (You need a mouse to do this.) You can also display the Page Setup dialog box directly from within Print Preview and then change any page settings.

TIP You can move forward or backward a page at a time by clicking the Next or Previous button or by pressing PgUp and PgDn. To move more quickly through a long document, drag the scroll box. As you drag, Excel displays the current page number in the lower left corner of the Print Preview screen.

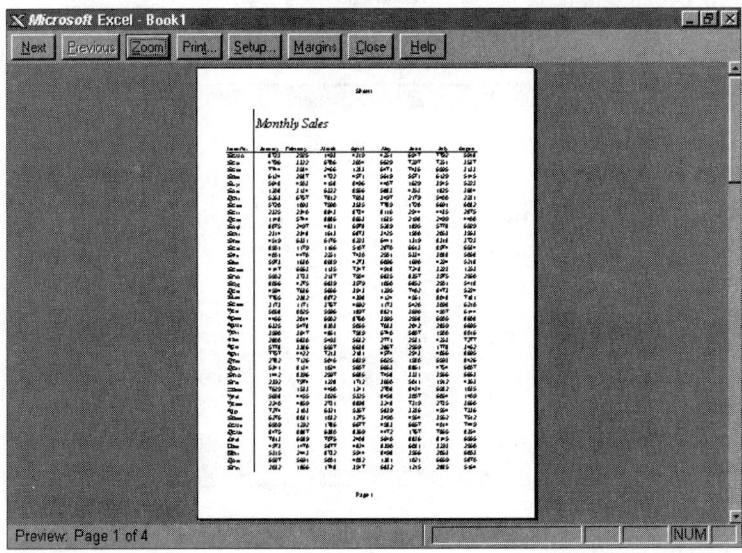

FIGURE 10-10
A worksheet displayed in Print Preview.

After you're satisfied with the appearance of your document, you can click the Print button to print the document, or you can click Close to leave Print Preview and print the document using the File menu's Print command.

Zooming In or Out

Excel turns your mouse pointer into a magnifying glass while Print Preview is in effect so you can zoom in on any portion of the page. For example, to check the formatting of your header, point to the header and click the mouse button. Your screen looks like the one shown in Figure 10-11. To return to the full-page preview, simply click the page.

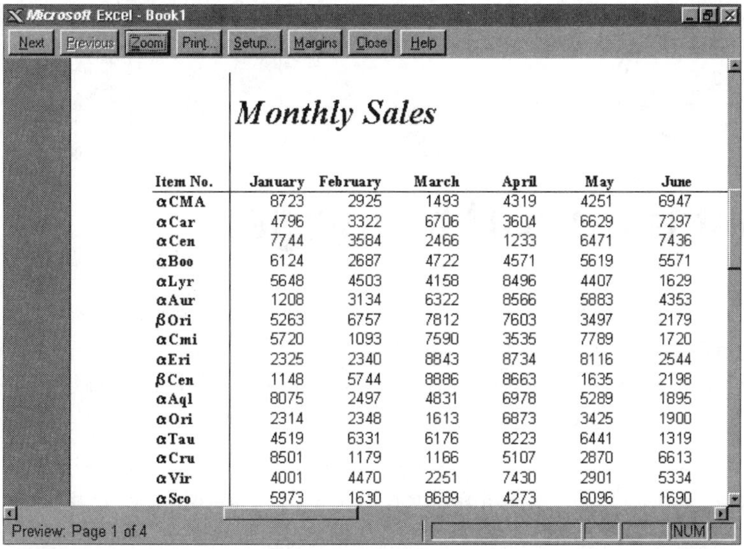
Microsoft Excel - Book1
Next
Previous
Zoom
Print...
Setup...
Margins
Close
Help
Monthly Sales
Item No. January February March April May June
αCMA 8723 2925 1493 4319 4251 6947
αCar 4796 3322 6706 3604 6629 7297
αCen 7744 3584 2466 1233 6471 7436
αBoo 6124 2687 4722 4571 5619 5571
αLyr 5648 4503 4158 8496 4407 1629
αAur 1208 3134 6322 8566 5883 4353
βOri 5263 6757 7812 7603 3497 2179
αCmi 5720 1093 7590 3535 7789 1720
αEri 2325 2340 8843 8734 8116 2544
βCen 1148 5744 8886 8663 1635 2198
αAql 8075 2497 4831 6978 5289 1895
αOri 2314 2348 1613 6873 3425 1900
αTau 4519 6331 6176 8223 6441 1319
αCru 8501 1179 1166 5107 2870 6613
αVir 4001 4470 2251 7430 2901 5334
αSco 5973 1630 8689 4273 6096 1690
Preview: Page 1 of 4
NUM

FIGURE 10-11

Click the mouse button to magnify the Print Preview screen. Click the mouse button again to restore the normal display.

Adjusting Margins and Column Widths

If you have a mouse, you can use Print Preview to adjust any of the four margins, the width of any column, or the positions of your headers and footers. Start by clicking the Margins button. As Figure 10-12 shows on the next page, Excel displays dotted lines to represent your margins and header and footer placement. Handles at the top of the page mark the right boundary of each column.

To adjust a margin, drag the appropriate dotted line. As you drag, the page-number indicator in the lower left corner of the screen changes to display the name of the margin and its current setting.

To adjust a column width, click the column's handle and drag. Again, the indicator at the bottom of the screen assists you by reporting the current column width.

FIGURE 10-12
Clicking the Margins button displays lines that let you change margins and handles that let you change column widths.

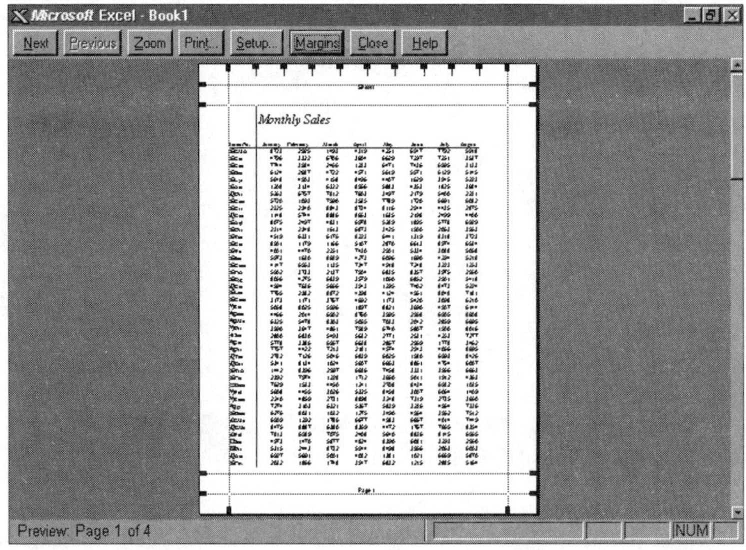

Using the Report Manager

The Report Manager lets you define a particular printout or collection of printouts as a named report. You can then re-create that report by selecting its name and clicking the Print button. You'll find the Report Manager invaluable when you need to create multiple reports from the same worksheet or when you have to create a particular report on a recurring basis. Instead of constantly switching print settings, you can define your report once and regenerate it at will.

The Report Manager is an add-in that works hand-in-hand with the View Manager (another add-in) and the Scenario Manager. If you did a full installation of Excel, you can invoke the Report Manager by choosing the Report Manager command from the View menu, the View Manager by choosing the View Manager command from the View menu, and the Scenario Manager by choosing Scenarios from the Tools menu. If these commands do not appear on your menu, you need to install the add-ins by rerunning the Excel Setup program and selecting the Complete Custom option.

For more information about the View Manager, see " Named Views," page 324.

For more information about the Scenario Manager, see "The Scenario Manager," page 551.

Defining the Report

A *report* consists of one or more elements, each of which can be a workbook page, a view created with the View Manager, or a scenario created with the Scenario Manager. Let's look at a simple example.

Suppose that from the worksheet shown in Figure 10-13, you want to print five separate printouts at the end of each month — one for each of your four divisions and one of the entire worksheet. To define each of your regular printouts as a named report, start by using normal Excel procedures to prepare the first printout. On the Sheet tab of the Page Setup dialog box, specify the area you want to print in the Print Area edit box. Also use Page Setup to specify your print titles, headers, footers, margins, and any other settings you want to use for this report.

When you have set up Excel to print your Division 1 sales figures, choose the View Manager command from the View menu to invoke the View Manager, click the View Manager's Add button, and supply a name (such as *Division 1*) in the Add View dialog box. Be sure the Print Settings check box is selected. Note that it doesn't matter which part of your worksheet is visible when you create this named view; you'll (presumably) use the view only for the purpose of specifying a named report, so the current print settings are all that matter.

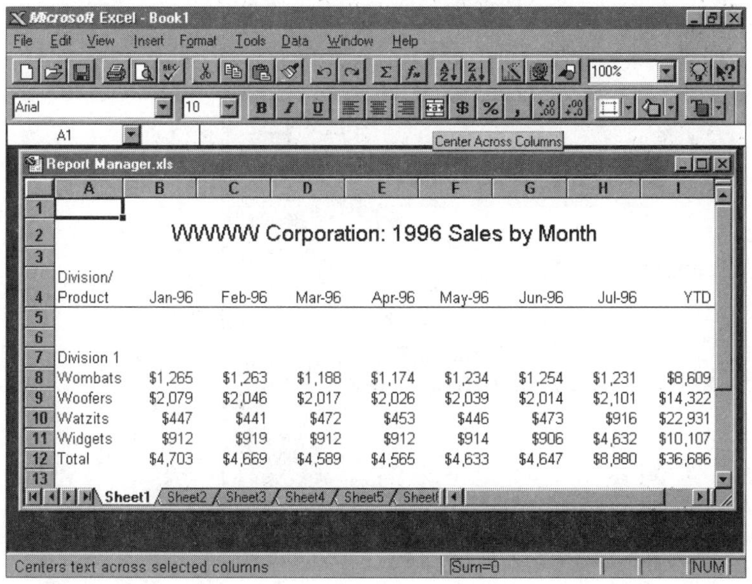

FIGURE 10-13
We'll use the Report Manager to define each of several divisional sales printouts as a named report.

After you create a named view for your first divisional printout, repeat these steps for printouts of each of the remaining divisions and for a printout of the entire worksheet. When you finish, you have five named views, one for each combination of print settings that you commonly use.

Now choose Report Manager from the View menu to invoke the Report Manager. The Report Manager dialog box, shown in Figure 10-14, appears.

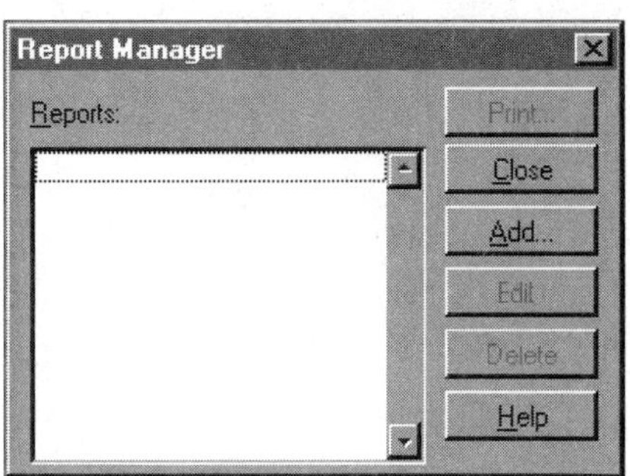

FIGURE 10-14 When you first invoke the Report Manager with a new worksheet, you see an empty Reports list box.

Because you haven't defined any reports yet, the Report Manager's initial dialog box presents an empty list. To define your first report, click the Add button to display the Add Report dialog box shown in Figure 10-15.

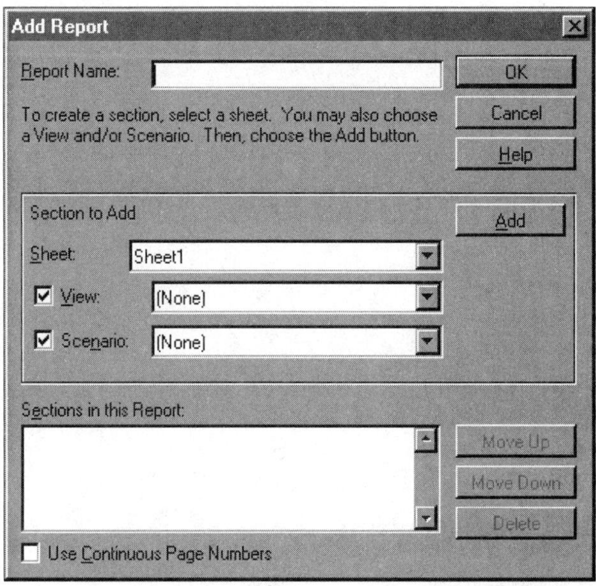

FIGURE 10-15 To define a report, enter a name in the Report Name edit box and use the drop-down lists to indicate the named views and scenarios you want your report to include.

All you need to do is enter a name in the Report Name edit box at the top of the dialog box, drop down the View list box, and select the view that you want to include in your report. Then click Add to add the view as a section.

Repeat these steps for each report you want to create. Now when you return to the Print Report dialog box, the list includes all your defined reports. To print one of them, simply select a report name and click the Print button.

We've deliberately kept this example simple for illustrative purposes. Bear in mind, however, that you can define a report that consists of many pages, views, or scenarios, or a combination of any of these elements.

Part 3

Analyzing Data

Chapter 11

Common Worksheet Functions

Worksheet functions are special tools that perform complex calculations quickly and easily. They are like the special keys on sophisticated calculators that compute square roots, logarithms, and statistical evaluations.

Microsoft Excel has more than 300 built-in functions that perform a wide range of calculations. Some functions, such as SUM, SIN, and FACT, are the equivalent of lengthy mathematical formulas that you might create by hand. Other functions, such as IF and VLOOKUP, cannot be duplicated by formulas.

Excel offers several groups of functions not discussed in this chapter. We'll cover date and time functions in Chapter 12, financial functions in Chapter 13, statistical functions and the statistical tools available in the Analysis ToolPak in Chapter 14, and database statistical functions in Chapter 20.

When none of the built-in functions is quite what you need, you can create custom functions, as explained in Chapter 24.

Getting More Help with Worksheet Functions

While preparing this book, we had to make some tough choices. Fully describing each of the 300 or so worksheet functions would fill an entire book. To provide the greatest benefit, we had to judge which functions to focus on and which to mention only briefly. For those who want more information about the functions we do not cover in detail, the Excel online Help system includes a detailed description of each worksheet function.

The easiest way to get more information about functions is to choose Microsoft Excel Help Topics from the Help menu and browse through the various categories of help topics for worksheet functions, as follows:

1. Click the Contents tab at the top of the Help window and then double-click the book icon that appears next to Reference Information. Double-click the Worksheet Functions book icon.
2. Double-click the book icon for the function category you want to browse through.
3. Double-click the question mark icon for the worksheet function you want information about to jump to its description.

You can also get quick information about functions by using the Function Wizard, described on page 404.

The Power of Functions

Let's look at an example that demonstrates the power of Microsoft Excel functions. The worksheet in Figure 11-1 shows monthly pet sales for a 12-month period. To find the total yak sales for the year, you could enter the formula

=B4+B5+B6+B7+B8+B9+B10+B11+B12+B13+B14+B15

in cell B16, but this formula is very cumbersome. You can use the SUM function to create

=SUM(B4:B15)

which tells Excel to add the numbers stored in the range B4 through B15. The result of this formula and that of the longer version are identical: $8,094.

Formulas can contain more than one function, and you can nest functions within formulas. For example, the formula

=A1*SUM(A4:A7)

returns the product of the value in cell A1 and the total of the values in the range A4:A7.

FIGURE 11-1
The SUM function calculates yak sales for a 12-month period.

The Syntax of Functions

Worksheet functions have two parts: the name of the function followed by one or more arguments. Function names — such as SUM and AVERAGE — describe the operation the function performs. Arguments specify the values or cells to be used by the function. For example, in the formula

```
=SUM(C3:C5)
```

SUM is the function's name, and C3:C5 is its single argument. This formula sums, or totals, the numbers in cells C3, C4, and C5.

> **NOTE** The equal sign (=) at the beginning of the formula indicates that the entry is a formula, not text (such as a comment or table heading). If you leave out the equal sign, Excel interprets the entry as the text SUM(C3:C5).

Notice that parentheses surround the function's argument. The opening parenthesis marks the beginning of the argument and must appear immediately after the name of the function. If you enter a space or some other character between the name and the opening parenthesis, the error value #NAME? appears in the cell.

A few functions, such as PI and TRUE, have no arguments. (As you'll see, these functions are usually nested in other formulas or functions.) Even though they have no arguments, they must be followed by an empty set of parentheses, as in

```
=A1*PI()
```

Using Arguments

When you use more than one argument in a function, you separate the arguments with commas. For example, the formula

```
=PRODUCT(C1,C2,C5)
```

tells Excel to multiply the numbers in cells C1, C2, and C5.

You can use as many as 30 arguments in a function, as long as the total length of the formula does not exceed 1024 characters. However, a single argument can be a range that refers to any number of cells in your worksheet. For example, the function

```
=SUM(A1:A5,C2:C10,D3:D17)
```

has three arguments but totals the numbers in 29 cells. (The first argument, A1:A5, refers to the range of five cells from A1 through A5, and so on.) The referenced cells can, in turn, contain formulas that refer to more cells or ranges. Using arguments, you can easily create complex chains of formulas to perform powerful worksheet operations.

Expressions as Arguments

You can use combinations of functions to create an *expression* that Excel evaluates to a single value and interprets as an argument. For example, in the formula

```
=SUM(SIN(A1*PI( )),2*COS(A2*PI( )))
```

the SIN(A1*PI( )) and 2*COS(A2*PI( )) are expressions that are evaluated and used as the arguments to the SUM function.

Types of Arguments

In the examples presented so far, all the arguments have been cell or range references. You can also use numbers, text, logical values, range names, arrays, and error values as arguments. Some functions return values in these data types, and you can then use these values as arguments to other functions.

Numeric Values

The arguments to a function can be numeric. For example, the SUM function in the formula

```
=SUM(327,209,176)
```

totals the numbers 327, 209, and 176. Usually, however, you enter the numbers you want to use in cells of a worksheet and then use references to those cells as arguments to your functions.

Text Values

You can use text as an argument to a function. For example, in the formula

```
=TEXT(NOW( ),"MMM D, YYYY")
```

in the second argument to the TEXT function, "MMM D, YYYY", is a text argument that specifies a pattern for converting the serial date value returned by NOW into a text string. Text arguments can be text strings enclosed in double quotation marks or references to cells that contain text.

Logical Values

The arguments to a few functions specify only that an option is either set or not set; you can use the logical values TRUE to set an option and FALSE to specify that the option isn't set. A logical expression returns the value TRUE or FALSE to the worksheet or the formula containing the expression. For example, the first argument to the IF function in the formula

```
=IF(A1=TRUE,"Future", "Past")&"History"
```

is a logical expression that uses the value in cell A1; if the value is TRUE, the expression A1=TRUE evaluates to TRUE, the IF function returns Future, and the formula returns Future History to the worksheet.

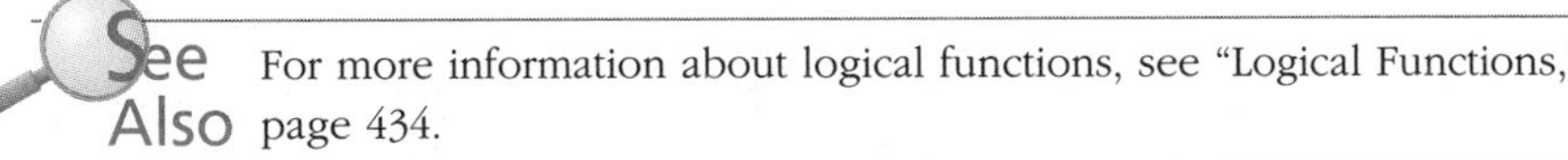

See Also For more information about logical functions, see "Logical Functions," page 434.

Named References

You can use a range name as an argument to a function. For example, if you use the Define command from the Name submenu of the Insert menu to assign the name QtrlyIncome to the range C3:C6, you can use the formula

```
=SUM(QtrlyIncome)
```

to total the numbers in cells C3, C4, C5, and C6.

Arrays

You can use an array as an argument in a function. Some functions, such as TREND and TRANSPOSE, require array arguments; other functions don't require array arguments but will accept them. Arrays can be composed of numbers, text, or logical values.

Error Values

Excel accepts error values as arguments to a few functions.

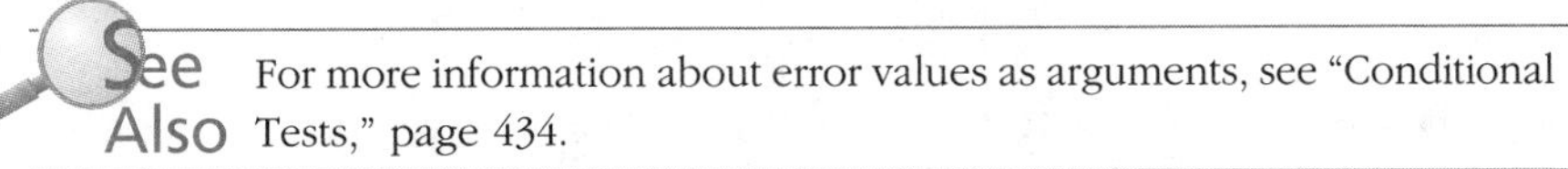

See Also For more information about error values as arguments, see "Conditional Tests," page 434.

Mixed Argument Types

You can mix argument types within a function. For example, the formula

```
=AVERAGE(Group1,A3,5*3)
```

uses a range name (Group1), a cell reference (A3), and a numeric expression (5*3) to arrive at a single value. All three arguments are acceptable.

Entering Functions in a Worksheet

You can enter functions in a worksheet by typing the function from the keyboard or by choosing the Function command from the Insert menu. If you type the function, use lowercase letters. When you finish typing the function and press Enter or select another cell, Microsoft Excel changes the name of the function to uppercase letters if you entered it correctly. If the letters don't change, you probably entered the name of the function incorrectly.

Using the Insert Function Command

When you select a cell and choose Function from the Insert menu, Excel displays the first Function Wizard dialog box, as shown in Figure 11-2. To select a function, first select a category from the Function Category list (or select All) and then scroll through the alphabetic Function Name list and select the function. Alternatively, you can select any function name from the Function Name list and then press the first letter of the name you want until the name is highlighted. To enter the function, click Next or press Enter. Excel enters an equal sign (if you're inserting the function at the beginning of a formula), the function name, and a set of parentheses. Excel then moves to the second Function Wizard dialog box, shown in Figure 11-3.

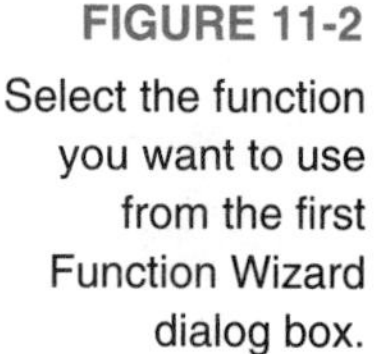

FIGURE 11-2
Select the function you want to use from the first Function Wizard dialog box.

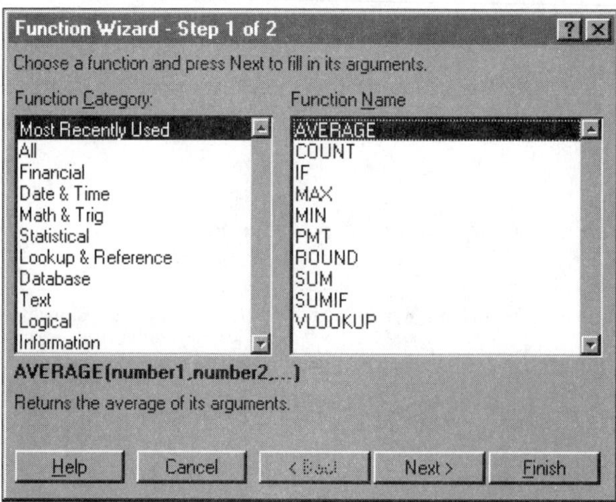

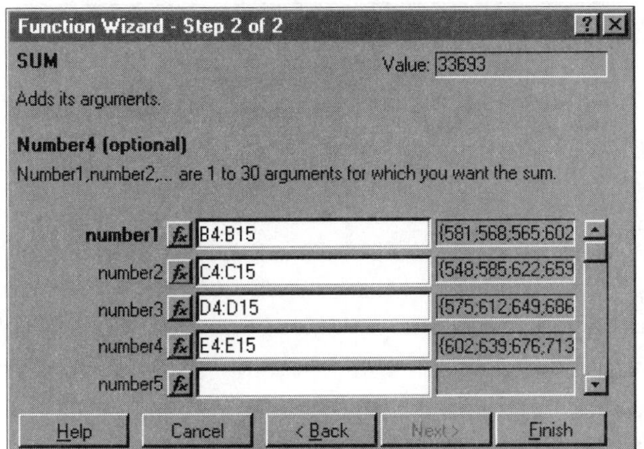

FIGURE 11-3
The second Function Wizard dialog box helps you enter the arguments to the function.

The second Function Wizard dialog box contains one edit box for each argument of the function you selected. If the function accepts a variable number of arguments, the dialog box grows as you enter optional arguments. A description of the argument edit box containing the insertion point appears in the top of the dialog box.

To the right of each argument edit box, a display area shows the current value of the argument. This display is very handy when you are using references or defined names. The current value of the function appears in the upper right corner of the dialog box.

When you click Finish or press Enter, the completed function appears in the formula bar.

Some functions, such as INDEX, have more than one form. When you select a function with more than one form from the Function Name list, Excel presents an additional Function Wizard dialog box, like the one shown in Figure 11-4, in which you select the form you want to use.

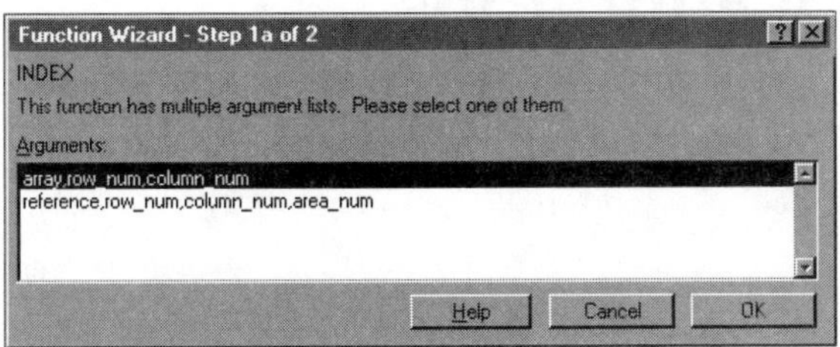

FIGURE 11-4
If a function has more than one form, the Function Wizard lets you choose the one you want.

Inserting Arguments with the Keyboard

If you know the name of the function you want to use but you can't remember all its arguments, you can use a keyboard shortcut to paste the argument names in the formula bar. Type an equal sign followed by the function's name in the formula bar and then press Ctrl-A. Excel jumps directly to the second Function Wizard dialog box. This feature is particularly useful when you're working with functions that have easy-to-remember names and long strings of arguments.

Inserting References

As with any other formula, you can insert cell references and defined names into your functions. For example, to enter a function in cell C11 that averages the cells in the range C2:C10, first select cell C11 and type *=average(*. Next select the range C2:C10. A marquee appears around the selected cells and a reference to the selected range appears in the formula bar. When you press Enter to lock in the formula, the marquee disappears and Excel supplies a closing parenthesis for you. (When you type the function name rather than use Insert Function, you must add the closing parenthesis only if you nest the function within a formula. However, Excel's parentheses can sometimes cause unexpected results; always double-check them.)

If you define named ranges, constants, or formulas in your worksheets, you can insert them into your formulas by choosing the Paste command from the Name submenu of the Insert menu and then selecting the name from the list in the Paste Name dialog box. When you click OK, the name appears at the insertion point in the formula.

Mathematical Functions

Several Microsoft Excel mathematical functions are available for carrying out specialized calculations quickly and easily. Other mathematical functions are available in the Analysis ToolPak add-in.

For information about the Analysis ToolPak, see Chapter 14, "Statistical Analysis," page 503.

The SUM Function

The SUM function totals a series of numbers. It takes the form

=SUM(*numbers*)

The *numbers* argument is a series of as many as 30 entries that can be numbers, formulas, ranges, or cell references that result in numbers. SUM ignores arguments that reference text values, logical values, or blank cells.

Because SUM is such a commonly used function, Excel provides a special button on the Standard toolbar for entering it. If you select a cell and click the AutoSum button, which is labeled Σ, Excel creates a =SUM( ) formula and guesses which numbers you want to total. For example, if you select cell C16 in Figure 11-1 (shown earlier) and then click the AutoSum button, Excel proposes the formula shown in Figure 11-5 and draws a marquee around the cells used as the argument in the formula.

If the proposed SUM function argument is correct, you can click the AutoSum button a second time or press Enter to lock in the formula and remove the marquee. If the proposed argument is not correct, you can edit it by selecting the correct range of cells while the proposed argument is still highlighted and the marquee is still present. Excel then replaces the proposed argument with the selected range and redraws the marquee around your selection.

Easy Function Entry for Lotus 1-2-3 Users

Lotus 1-2-3 worksheet functions use the "at" symbol (@) as a prefix and two dots (..) as a range operator; Excel functions and formulas use the equal sign (=) as a prefix and the colon (:) as a range operator. In Excel, you can use either @ or = when entering formulas, and you can use either .. or : as a range operator. Excel translates the @ prefix and the .. range operator into the Excel equivalents. For example, if you enter *@SUM(B2..B4),* Excel translates the function into =SUM(B2:B4) when you press Enter.

However, Excel does not translate Lotus 1-2-3 functions into Excel functions. For example, if you enter the Lotus function *@AVG(B2..B4)*, Excel does not translate it into =AVERAGE(B2:B4); instead, Excel displays the *Function Is Not Valid* error message.

You can use the AutoSum button to enter several SUM functions at one time. For example, if we selected cells C16:E16 in Figure 11-5 instead of only cell C16 and then clicked the AutoSum button, Excel would propose a SUM formula for C16 using arguments similar to those of the formula in B16. When we clicked the AutoSum button a second time to accept the formula, Excel would lock the formula into C16 and replicate it across the row in D16 and E16. (You can also use this technique to replicate a SUM formula up or down a column.)

Expanding a SUM range to include a new value is much easier than expanding a range totaled with ordinary addition operators. Suppose cell F4 in Figure 11-6 contains the formula

=B4+C4+D4+E4

If, after entering this formula, you discover that you omitted the Bats category, you can select column C and then choose the Columns command from the Insert menu to insert a column of cells for the new category. Excel adjusts the TOTALS formulas, which now appear in column G, to account for the shift of the columns, but it won't include the new column in the formulas. As Figure 11-7 shows, the formula in cell G4 now reads

=B4+D4+E4+F4

If, instead of using addition operators, you had used the SUM function to create the formula

=SUM(B4:E4)

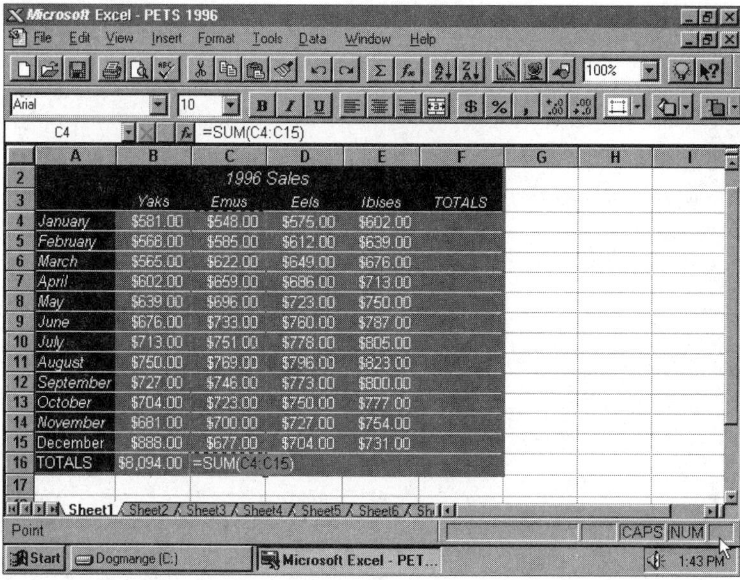

FIGURE 11-5
When you click the AutoSum button with cell C16 selected, Excel enters the formula =SUM(C4:C15).

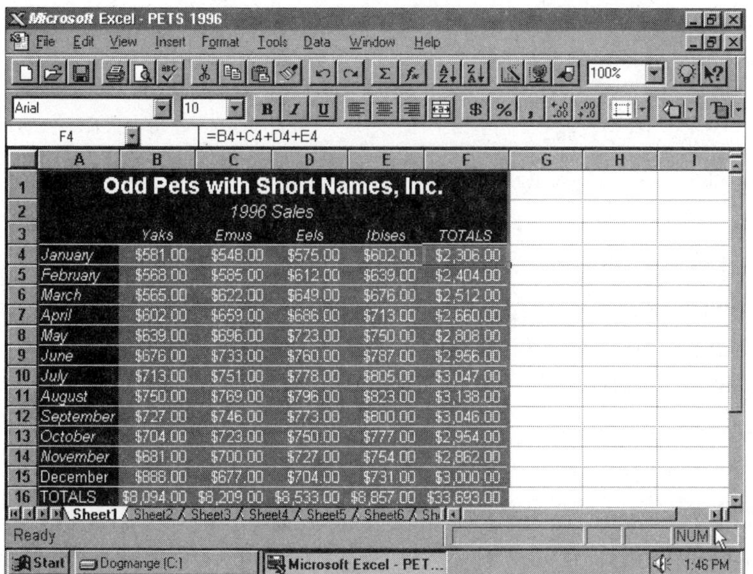

FIGURE 11-6
The formula =B4+C4+D4+E4 calculates total sales for January.

Microsoft Excel - PETS 1996

G4 =B4+D4+E4+F4

Odd Pets with Short Names, Inc.

1996 Sales

	Yaks	Bats	Emus	Eels	Ibises	TOTALS
January	$581.00	$400.00	$548.00	$575.00	$602.00	$2,306.00
February	$568.00	$387.00	$585.00	$612.00	$639.00	$2,404.00
March	$565.00	$422.00	$622.00	$649.00	$676.00	$2,512.00
April	$602.00	$388.00	$659.00	$686.00	$713.00	$2,660.00
May	$639.00	$402.00	$696.00	$723.00	$750.00	$2,808.00
June	$676.00	$333.00	$733.00	$760.00	$787.00	$2,956.00
July	$713.00	$444.00	$751.00	$778.00	$805.00	$3,047.00
August	$750.00	$431.00	$769.00	$796.00	$823.00	$3,138.00
September	$727.00	$388.00	$746.00	$773.00	$800.00	$3,046.00
October	$704.00	$415.00	$723.00	$750.00	$777.00	$2,954.00
November	$681.00	$400.00	$700.00	$727.00	$754.00	$2,862.00
December	$888.00	$389.00	$677.00	$704.00	$731.00	$3,000.00
TOTALS	$8,094.00	$4,799.00	$8,209.00	$8,533.00	$8,857.00	$33,693.00

FIGURE 11-7
Although a new category was added, the totals do not change because the formula references the individual cells.

in cell F4 of Figure 11-6, Excel would have expanded the range of the *numbers* argument to include the inserted column. Because Excel always adjusts cell ranges when you insert or delete rows and columns within the range, the formula would have been updated to read

=SUM(B4:F4)

Keep in mind that arguments do not have to consist of continuous ranges of cells. For example, to total the numbers in cells A3, B12, and G13 through H15, you enter each reference as a separate argument, like this:

=SUM(A3,B12,G13:H15)

Alternatively, you can assign a range name to a set of cells and use the name instead. To assign a name to the cells in the previous formula, follow these steps:

1. Click cell A3, hold down the Ctrl key (to make a discontinuous selection), and click cell B12.
2. Without releasing Ctrl, select cells G13 through H15. (From the keyboard, press Shift-F8 to use Add mode.)
3. Choose Name and then Define from the Insert menu to assign a range name, such as Group1, to this collection of cells, and then use the range name in the formula

   =SUM(Group1)

The ABS Function

The ABS function returns the absolute value of a number or formula and takes the form

=ABS(*number*)

The *number* argument is a number, a reference to a cell that contains a number, or a formula that results in a number. For example, if cell A1 contains the number –75, the formula

=ABS(A1)

returns 75. If the number referred to by the argument is positive, ABS returns that number unchanged.

The SIGN Function

The SIGN function determines whether an argument results in a negative, positive, or zero value and takes the form

=SIGN(*number*)

The *number* argument can be a number, a reference to a cell that contains a number, or a formula that results in a number. If *number* is positive, the SIGN function returns the value 1; if *number* is negative, SIGN returns the value –1;

Using Extra Cells in Ranges

Formulas that use the SUM function are more flexible than those that use the addition operator (+), but you will still have problems if you add a cell to the beginning or end of a range. For example, cell A7 of the following worksheet contains the formula

=SUM(A1:A5)

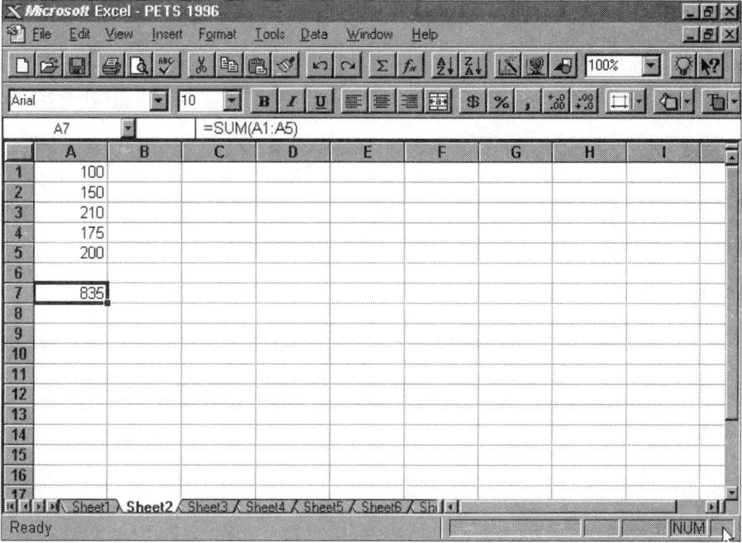

Suppose you insert a row below row 5 by selecting cell A6 and then choosing Rows from the Insert menu. You then enter the value 100 in cell A6. Because the formula, which is now in cell A8, refers only to the range A1:A5, the formula doesn't change when you insert the new row, and the new number in cell A6 is not included in the total.

Because Excel ignores text entries and blank cells when it calculates the SUM function, you can enter the formula

=SUM(A1:A6)

in cell A7 and get the same result as the original formula. (The function ignores the blank cell A6.)

Using Extra Cells in Ranges

However, when you select A6 and insert the new row, the formula changes to

```
=SUM(A1:A7)
```

Now cell A6 is included in the formula, and cell A7 is blank.

An alternative technique involves defining a name for the relative reference of the cell above the active cell. Using this technique, you can select cell A7, which will contain the SUM function, choose Name and then Define from the Insert menu to display the Define Name dialog box, and define the name *up1* as =A6 (meaning *the cell that is one cell above the active cell*). The reference must be relative; don't make it absolute by using the $ symbol. You can then enter a SUM function that uses this name in cell A7, like this

```
=SUM(A1:up1)
```

Now when you select cell A6 and insert a new row, the formula automatically includes the new row.

if *number* is 0, SIGN returns 0. For example, suppose cells A1 through A3 contain the numbers 10, –20, and –5. The formula

```
=SIGN(SUM(A1:A3))
```

adds the three numbers (resulting in the value –15) and returns the value –1.

The ROUND, ROUNDDOWN, and ROUNDUP Functions

The ROUND function rounds the number referred to by its argument to a specified number of decimal places. Round takes the form

=ROUND(*number,num_digits*)

The *number* argument can be a number, a reference to a cell that contains a number, or a formula that results in a number. The *num_digits* argument, which can be any positive or negative integer, determines how many places will be rounded. Specifying a negative *num_digits* argument rounds that number of places to the left of the decimal, and specifying a *num_digits* argument of 0 rounds to the nearest integer. Excel rounds digits less than 5 down and rounds digits greater than or equal to 5 up. The following table shows several examples of the ROUND function:

Entry	Returns
=ROUND(123.4567,–2)	100
=ROUND(123.4567,–1)	120
=ROUND(123.4567,0)	123
=ROUND(123.4567,1)	123.5
=ROUND(123.4567,2)	123.46
=ROUND(123.4567,3)	123.457

Rounding Versus Formatting

Don't confuse the ROUND function with fixed formats such as 0 and 0.00, which are available when you choose Cells from the Format menu and then click the Number tab. When you use Number to round the contents of a cell to a specified number of decimal places, you change only the *display* of the number in the cell; you don't change the *value*. When performing calculations, Excel always uses the underlying value, not the displayed value.

The ROUNDDOWN and ROUNDUP functions take the same form as the ROUND function. As their names imply, they always round down or up.

Rounding with the EVEN and ODD Functions

You can use the EVEN and ODD functions to perform rounding operations. The EVEN function rounds a number up to the nearest even integer. The ODD function rounds a number up to the nearest odd integer. Negative numbers are correspondingly rounded down. These functions take the forms

=EVEN(*number*)

and

=ODD(*number*)

The following table shows some examples of these functions in action:

Entry	Returns
=EVEN(23.4)	24
=EVEN(2)	2
=EVEN(3)	4
=EVEN(–3)	–4
=ODD(23.4)	25
=ODD(3)	3
=ODD(4)	5
=ODD(–4)	–5

Rounding with the FLOOR and CEILING Functions

The FLOOR and CEILING functions can be used to carry out rounding operations. The FLOOR function rounds a number down to the nearest given multiple, and the CEILING function rounds a number up to the nearest given multiple. These functions take the forms

=FLOOR(*number,multiple*)

and

=CEILING(*number,multiple*)

In both cases, the values of *number* and *multiple* must be numeric and have the same sign. If they have different signs, Excel returns the #NUM! error value. The following table shows some examples of rounding operations performed with these functions:

Entry	Returns
=FLOOR(23.4,0.5)	23
=FLOOR(5,3)	3
=FLOOR(5,–1)	#NUM!
=FLOOR(5,1.5)	4.5
=CEILING(23.4,5)	25
=CEILING(5,3)	6
=CEILING(–5,1)	#NUM!
=CEILING(5,1.5)	6

The INT and TRUNC Functions

The INT function rounds numbers down to the nearest integer and takes the form

=INT(*number*)

The *number* argument is the number for which you want to find the next lowest integer. For example, the formula

=INT(100.01)

returns the value 100, as does the formula

=INT(100.99999999)

even though the number 100.99999999 is essentially equal to 101.

When *number* is negative, INT also rounds that number down to the nearest integer. For example, the formula

=INT(–100.99999999)

results in the value –101.

The TRUNC function truncates everything to the right of the decimal point in a number, regardless of its sign. The optional *num_digits* argument truncates everything after the digit specified. It takes the form

=TRUNC(*number,num_digits*)

For example, the function

=TRUNC(13.978)

returns the value 13.

> **NOTE** ROUND, INT, and TRUNC all eliminate unwanted decimals, but the three functions work differently. ROUND rounds up or down to the number of decimal places you specify; INT rounds down to the nearest integer; TRUNC truncates decimal places with no rounding. The primary difference between INT and TRUNC is in the treatment of negative values. If you use the value –100.99999999 in an INT function, the result is –101, but using the same value in a TRUNC function results in –100.

The RAND and RANDBETWEEN Functions

The RAND function generates a random number between 0 and 1 and takes the form

=RAND( )

The RAND function is one of the few Excel functions that doesn't take an argument. As with all functions that take no arguments, you must still enter the parentheses after the function name.

The result of a RAND function changes each time you recalculate your worksheet. If you use automatic recalculation, the value of the RAND function changes each time you make a worksheet entry.

The RANDBETWEEN function, which is available when you install the Analysis ToolPak add-in, provides more control than RAND. With RANDBETWEEN you can specify a range of numbers within which to generate random integer values.

This function takes the form

=RANDBETWEEN(*bottom,top*)

The *bottom* argument represents the smallest integer, and the *top* argument represents the largest integer the function should use. The values you use for these arguments are inclusive; that is, they are values that the function might return. For example, the formula

=RANDBETWEEN(123,456)

can return any integer from 123 up to and including 456.

See Also For more information about the Analysis ToolPak add-in, see Chapter 14, "Statistical Analysis," page 503.

The FACT Function

The FACT function calculates the factorial of any number. (The factorial of a number is the product of all the positive integers from 1 up through the specified number. For example, 3 factorial, or 3!, is the equivalent of 1*2*3, or 6.) This function takes the form

=FACT(*number*)

The *number* argument must be a positive integer. For example, FACT(1) returns 1, but FACT(–1) returns the #NUM! error value. If *number* is not an integer, FACT truncates decimal places without rounding to create an integer before evaluating FACT.

For example, to calculate 10!, use the formula

=FACT(10)

This formula returns the value 3628800.

The PRODUCT Function

The PRODUCT function multiplies all the numbers referenced by its arguments and takes the form

=PRODUCT(*number1, number2, . . .*)

The PRODUCT function can take as many as 30 arguments. Excel ignores any arguments that are text, logical values, or blank cells.

The MOD Function

The MOD function returns the remainder of a division operation and takes the form

=MOD(*number,divisor*)

The result of the MOD function is the remainder produced when *number* is divided by *divisor*. For example, the function

=MOD(9,4)

returns 1, the remainder that results from dividing 9 by 4.

If *number* is smaller than *divisor,* the result of the function equals *number*. For example, the function

=MOD(5,11)

returns 5. If *number* is exactly divisible by *divisor,* the function returns 0. If *divisor* is 0, MOD returns the #DIV/0! error value.

The SQRT Function

The SQRT function returns the positive square root of a number and takes the form

=SQRT(*number*)

The *number* argument must evaluate to a positive number. For example, the function

=SQRT(4)

returns the value 2.

If *number* is negative, SQRT returns the #NUM! error value.

The COMBIN Function

The COMBIN function determines the number of possible combinations, or groups, that can be taken from a pool of items. It takes the form

=COMBIN(*number,number_chosen*)

The *number* argument is the total number of items in the pool, and the *number_chosen* argument is the number of items you want to group in each combination. For example, to determine how many 12-player football teams can be created with 17 players, use the formula

=COMBIN(17,12)

The result, 6188, indicates that 6188 teams could be created.

The N Function

The N function translates values into numbers. With most Excel functions, when you enter an argument that doesn't generate the correct type of data, the program automatically translates it, so you don't generally need to use N in formulas. Excel includes this function for compatibility with other worksheet programs. The N translation function takes the form

=N(*value*)

If *value* is a number or a reference to a cell that contains a number, N returns that number. If *value* is the logical value TRUE or a reference to a cell that evaluates to TRUE, N returns 1. If *value* is a date with one of the Excel date formats, N returns that date's serial number. If *value* is anything else, N returns 0.

The ISNUMBER Function

The ISNUMBER function determines whether a value is a number and takes the form

=ISNUMBER(*value*)

Suppose you want to know if the entry in cell A5 is a number. The formula

=ISNUMBER(A5)

returns TRUE if cell A5 contains a number or a formula that results in a number; otherwise, it returns FALSE.

See Also

For more information about this and other IS functions, see "The ISTEXT and ISNONTEXT Functions," page 430; "Trapping Errors: The ISERR, ISERROR, and ISNA Functions," page 438; "The ISLOGICAL Function," page 439; "The ISREF Function," page 457; and "The ISBLANK Function," page 457.

Logarithmic Functions

Excel's five logarithmic functions are LOG10, LOG, LN, EXP, and POWER. The Analysis ToolPak add-in provides several other advanced logarithmic functions.

See Also For more information about the Analysis ToolPak, see Chapter 14, "Statistical Analysis," page 503.

The LOG10 Function

The LOG10 function returns the base 10 logarithm of its argument and takes the form

=LOG10(*number*)

The *number* argument must evaluate to a positive number. If *number* is negative, the function returns the #NUM! error value. For example, the formula

=LOG10(100)

returns the value 2.

The LOG Function

The LOG function returns the logarithm of a positive number using a specified base. This function takes the form

=LOG(*number,base*)

For example, the formula

=LOG(5,2)

returns the value 2.321928095, or the base 2 logarithm of 5. If you don't include the *base* argument, Excel assumes the base is 10.

The LN Function

The LN function returns the natural (base *e*) logarithm of the positive number referred to by its argument. This function takes the form

=LN(*number*)

For example, the formula

=LN(2)

returns the value 0.693147181.

The EXP Function

The EXP function computes the value of the constant *e* (approximately 2.71828183) raised to the power specified by its argument. It takes the form

=EXP(*number*)

For example, the formula

=EXP(2)

returns 7.389056099 (2.718281828*2.718281828).

The EXP function is the inverse of the LN function. For example, if cell A1 contains the formula

=LN(8)

then the formula

=EXP(A1)

returns 8.

The POWER Function

The POWER function raises a number to the specified power and takes the form

=POWER(*number,power*)

The *number* argument is the number you want to raise to *power*. This function is the equivalent of using the ^ operator; for example, the formulas

=POWER(3,2)

and

=3^2

both return the value 9.

Trigonometric Functions

Excel lists more than 50 functions in the Math & Trig category in the Function Wizard dialog box, but we'll cover only the most common functions in this section. The Analysis ToolPak contains additional functions.

See Also For more information about the Analysis ToolPak, see Chapter 14, "Statistical Analysis," page 503.

The PI Function

The PI function returns the value of the constant *pi* (π) accurate to 14 decimal places: 3.14159265358979. This function takes the form

=PI()

PI has no arguments, but you must still enter the empty parentheses after the function name.

Usually the PI function is nested within a formula or function. For example, to calculate the area of a circle, you multiply π by the square of the circle's radius. The formula

=PI( )*(5^2)

computes the area of a circle with a radius of 5. The result of this formula rounded to two decimal places is 78.54.

The RADIANS and DEGREES Functions

The trigonometric functions measure angles in radians rather than in degrees. Radians measure the size of an angle based on the constant π, where a 180-degree angle is defined as π radians. Excel provides two functions, RADIANS and DEGREES, that make trigonometric life easier for you.

You can convert radians to degrees using the DEGREES function, which takes the form

=DEGREES(*angle*)

where *angle* is a number that represents an angle measured in radians. You can convert degrees to radians using the RADIANS function, which takes the form

=RADIANS(*angle)*

where *angle* is a number that represents an angle measured in degrees. For example, the formula

=DEGREES(3.14159265)

returns 179.9999998, whereas the formula

=RADIANS(179.9999998)

returns 3.14159265.

The SIN Function

The SIN function returns the sine of an angle and takes the form

=SIN(*number*)

where *number* is the angle in radians. For example, the formula

=SIN(1.5)

returns the value 0.997494987.

The COS Function

The COS function, the complement of the SIN function, calculates the cosine of an angle and takes the form

=COS(*number*)

where *number* is the angle in radians. For example, the formula

=COS(1.5)

returns the value 0.070737202.

The TAN Function

The TAN function computes the tangent of an angle and takes the form

=TAN(*number*)

where *number* is the angle in radians. For example, the formula

=TAN(1.5)

returns the tangent of an angle of 1.5 radians: 14.10141995.

The ASIN and ACOS Functions

The ASIN and ACOS functions are the inverse of the SIN and COS functions. Given the sine of an angle in radians, the ASIN function computes the angle's arcsine. Given the cosine of an angle in radians, the ACOS function computes the angle's arccosine. These functions take the forms

=ASIN(*number*)

where *number* is the size of the angle, between –1 and 1, and

=ACOS(*number*)

where *number* is the cosine of the angle, between –1 and 1. To help you remember this distinction, think of the phrase "the angle whose" when you refer to the results of these functions. For example, the function

=ASIN(0)

returns 0, or the radian measure of "the angle whose" sine is 0. The function

=ACOS(0)

returns 1.570796327, or the radian measure of "the angle whose" cosine is 0.

The argument of the ACOS and ASIN functions must be in the range –1 through 1, inclusive. Any value outside this range results in the #NUM! error value. ASIN always returns a value between $-\pi/2$ and $\pi/2$ radians. ACOS always returns a value between 0 and π radians.

The ATAN and ATAN2 Functions

The ATAN function computes the arctangent of a tangent value and takes the form

=ATAN(*number*)

where *number* is the tangent of the angle.

ATAN always returns a value between $-\pi/2$ and $\pi/2$ radians. For example, the function

=ATAN(2)

returns the radian measure of the angle whose tangent is 2. The result is 1.107148718.

ATAN2 returns the four-quadrant arctangent of the tangent described in the argument. This function takes the form

=ATAN2(*x-num,y-num*)

The *x-num* argument is the x-axis coordinate of a point, and the *y-num* argument is the y-axis coordinate of a point. This function returns the radian measure of the angle from the origin to the specified point, in the range $-\pi$ through π, excluding $-\pi$. Either *x-num* or *y-num* can be 0; if both values are 0, the function returns the #DIV/0! error value.

The SINH Function

The SINH function returns the hyperbolic sine of a number and takes the form

=SINH(*number*)

For example, the function

=SINH(2)

returns 3.626860408.

The COSH Function

The COSH function returns the hyperbolic cosine of a number and takes the form

=COSH(*number*)

For example, the function

=COSH(1.5)

returns 2.352409615.

The TANH Function

The TANH function returns the hyperbolic tangent of a number and takes the form

=TANH(*number*)

For example, the function

=TANH(1)

returns 0.761594156.

The ASINH, ACOSH, and ATANH Functions

The ASINH, ACOSH, and ATANH functions are the inverse of the SINH, COSH, and TANH functions. Each function takes a single numeric argument. For example, the ASINH function returns the angle in radians of a hyperbolic sine argument.

Engineering Functions

The Analysis ToolPak contains dozens of functions that are of interest mostly to engineers and scientists. These functions fall into three main groups: functions for working with complex numbers (also called *imaginary numbers*); functions for converting between the decimal, hexdecimal, octal, and binary numbering systems and between systems of measurement; and various forms of the Bessel function.

See Also For more information about the Analysis ToolPak, see Chapter 14, "Statistical Analysis," page 503.

Text Functions

Text functions convert numeric text entries into numbers and number entries into text strings and let you manipulate the text strings themselves.

The VALUE Function

If you enter numbers in your worksheet in text format (enclosed in quotation marks), you can use the VALUE function to convert that text into a numeric value. This function takes the form

=VALUE(*text*)

The *text* argument can be a string enclosed in double quotation marks or a reference to a cell that contains text. The text string to be converted can be in any recognized format, including custom formats you create. If *text* is not in one of these formats, Excel displays the #VALUE! error value.

For example, the formula

=VALUE("40205")

returns the numeric value 40205. If cell A10 contains the text entry ="40205", the formula

=VALUE(A10)

also returns 40205.

The VALUE function can also convert text entries in the form of dates and times into numeric date values. For example, the formula

=VALUE("1/1/87")

returns the serial date value 31778.

Because Excel converts numeric text into numbers for calculations, you generally don't have to use VALUE with numbers entered as text in formulas.

For more information about text formats, see Chapter 6, "Formatting a Worksheet," page 155.

For more information about how Excel handles dates, see Chapter 12, "Dates and Times," page 459.

The TEXT Function

The TEXT function converts a number into a text string with a specified format. This function takes the form

=TEXT(*value,format_text*)

The *value* argument can be any number, formula, or cell reference. The *format_text* argument designates how the resulting string is displayed. You can use any of Excel's formatting symbols ($, #, 0, and so on) except the asterisk (*) to specify the format you want; you cannot use the General format.

For example, the formula

=TEXT(98/4,"0.00")

returns the text string 24.50.

The DOLLAR Function

Like the TEXT function, the DOLLAR function converts a number into a string. However, DOLLAR formats the resulting string as currency with the number of decimal places you specify. This function takes the form

=DOLLAR(*number,decimals*)

For example, the formula

=DOLLAR(45.899,2)

returns the text string $45.90, and the formula

=DOLLAR(45.899,0)

returns the text string $46. Notice that Excel rounds the number when necessary. If you omit the *decimals* argument for the DOLLAR function, Excel uses two decimal places. If you use a negative number for the *decimals* argument, Excel rounds to the left of the decimal point.

The FIXED Function

The FIXED function rounds a number to the specified number of decimal places, formats the result with commas and a period, and displays the result as text. This function takes the form

=FIXED(*number,decimals,no_commas*)

The *number* and *decimals* arguments are the same as those described for the DOLLAR function. The *no_commas* argument is a logical value (TRUE or FALSE) that specifies whether commas should be included in the result. If you omit it, Excel assumes a default value of FALSE and includes commas in the result. For example, the formula

=FIXED(4798.786,2,TRUE)

returns the text string 4798.79.

If you omit the *decimals* argument, Excel uses two decimal places. If you use a negative number for *decimals,* Excel rounds to the left of the decimal point. For example, the formula

=FIXED(4798.786,–1,FALSE)

returns the text string 4,800.

The LEN Function

The LEN function returns the number of characters in an entry and takes the form

=LEN(*text*)

The *text* argument can be a literal number, a literal string enclosed in double quotation marks, or a reference to a cell. For example, the formula

=LEN("Test")

returns 4. If cell A1 contains the label *Test,* the formula

=LEN(A1)

also returns 4.

The LEN function returns the length of the displayed text or value, not the length of the underlying cell contents. For example, suppose cell A10 contains the formula

=A1+A2+A3+A4+A5+A6+A7+A8

and its result is the value 25. Then the formula

=LEN(A10)

returns the value 2, the length of the value 25. The LEN function ignores trailing zeros.

The cell referenced as the argument of the LEN function can contain another string function. For example, if cell A1 contains the function

=REPT("-*",75)

then the formula

=LEN(A1)

returns the value 150.

The ASCII Functions: CHAR and CODE

Every computer uses numeric codes to represent characters. The most prevalent system of numeric codes is called *ASCII,* or *American Standard Code for Information Interchange.* ASCII uses a number from 0 to 127 (in some systems, to 255) to represent each number, letter, and symbol.

The CHAR and CODE functions deal with these ASCII codes. The CHAR function returns the character that corresponds to an ASCII code number; the CODE function returns the ASCII code number for the first character of its argument. These functions take the forms

=CHAR(*number*)

and

=CODE(*text*)

For example, the formula

=CHAR(83)

returns the letter *S.* (Note that you can enter the argument without a leading zero.) The formula

=CODE("S")

returns the ASCII code 83. Similarly, if cell A1 contains the letter *S,* the formula

=CODE(A1)

also returns the code 83.

Because numerals are also characters, the argument for CODE can be a numeral. For example, the formula

=CODE(8)

results in 56, the ASCII code for the character 8.

If you type a literal character as the *text* argument, be sure to enclose the character in double quotation marks; otherwise, Excel returns the #NAME? error value.

The Clean-Up Functions: TRIM and CLEAN

Often leading and trailing blank characters prevent you from correctly sorting entries in a worksheet or database. If you use string functions to manipulate text in your worksheet, extra spaces can prevent your formulas from working correctly. The TRIM function eliminates leading, trailing, and extra blank characters from a string, leaving only a single space between words. This function takes the form

=TRIM(*text*)

For example, if cell A1 of your worksheet contains the string *Fuzzy Wuzzy Was A Bear*, the formula

=TRIM(A1)

returns *Fuzzy Wuzzy Was A Bear* as its result.

The CLEAN function is similar to TRIM, except that it operates only on nonprintable characters such as tabs and program-specific codes. CLEAN is especially useful if you import data from another program and some entries contain nonprintable characters. (These characters might appear in your worksheet as bold vertical bars or small boxes.) You can use CLEAN to remove these characters from the data. This function takes the form

=CLEAN(*text*)

The EXACT Function

The EXACT function is a conditional function that determines whether two strings match exactly, including uppercase and lowercase letters. Formatting differences are ignored. This function takes the form

=EXACT(*text1,text2*)

If *text1* and *text2* are identical, including uppercase and lowercase letters, EXACT returns TRUE; otherwise, EXACT returns FALSE. The *text1* and *text2* arguments must be either literal strings enclosed in double quotation marks or references to cells that contain text. For example, if cell A5 and cell A6 of your worksheet both contain the text *Totals,* the formula

=EXACT(A5,A6)

returns TRUE.

See Also For more information about comparing two strings while ignoring case differences, see "Conditional Tests," page 434.

The Case Functions: UPPER, LOWER, and PROPER

Three functions manipulate the case of characters in text strings: UPPER, LOWER, and PROPER. The UPPER function converts a text string to all uppercase letters. The LOWER function converts a text string to all lowercase letters. The PROPER function capitalizes the first letter in each word and any other letters in the text string that do not follow another letter; all other letters are converted to lowercase. These functions take the forms

=UPPER(*text*)

and

=LOWER(*text*)

and

=PROPER(*text*)

Suppose you enter a series of names in a worksheet and you want all the names to appear in capital letters. If cell A1 contains the text *john Johnson,* you can use the formula

=UPPER(A1)

to return *JOHN JOHNSON*. Similarly, the formula

=LOWER(A1)

returns *john johnson,* and

=PROPER(A1)

returns *John Johnson*.

Unexpected results can occur when the text contains punctuation, however. For example, if cell A1 contains *a two-thirds majority wasn't possible,* the previous formula produces *A Two-Thirds Majority Wasn'T Possible.*

The T Function

The T function translates values into text. With most Excel functions, when you enter an argument that doesn't generate the correct type of data, the program automatically translates it, so you don't generally need to use T in formulas. Excel includes this function for compatibility with other spreadsheet programs. The T translation function takes the form

=T(*value*)

If the *value* argument of a T function is text, the function returns that text. If the argument is anything else, the T function returns a null text string ("").

The ISTEXT and ISNONTEXT Functions

The ISTEXT and ISNONTEXT functions test whether an entry is text. These functions take the forms

=ISTEXT(*value*)

and

=ISNONTEXT(*value*)

Suppose you want to determine whether the entry in cell C5 is text. If you use the formula

=ISTEXT(C5)

and the entry in C5 is text or a formula that returns text, Excel returns the logical value TRUE. If you test the same cell using the formula

=ISNONTEXT(C5)

Excel returns the logical value FALSE.

The Substring Functions

The following functions locate and return portions of a text string, or assemble larger strings from smaller ones: FIND, SEARCH, RIGHT, LEFT, MID, SEARCH, SUBSTITUTE, REPT, REPLACE, and CONCATENATE.

The FIND and SEARCH Functions

You use the FIND and SEARCH functions to locate the position of a substring within a string. Both functions return the number of the character where Excel first finds the text. (Excel counts blank spaces and punctuation marks as characters.)

These two functions work the same way, except that FIND is case-sensitive and SEARCH allows wildcards. The functions take the forms

=FIND(*find_text,within_text,start_num*)

and

=SEARCH(*find_text,within_text,start_num*)

The *find_text* argument identifies the text sought, and the *within_text* argument indicates where to look for it. You can use either literal text enclosed in double quotation marks or a cell reference for either argument. The optional *start_num* argument specifies the character position in *within_text* where you want to begin the search. The *start_num* argument is helpful when *within_text* contains more than one occurrence of *find_text*. If you omit *start_num,* Excel reports the first match it locates.

You get a #VALUE! error value if *find_text* isn't contained in *within_text,* if *start_num* isn't greater than zero, or if *start_num* is greater than the number of characters in *within_text* or greater than the position of the last occurrence of *find_text.*

For example, to locate the *p* in the string *A Night At The Opera*, use the formula

```
=FIND("p","A Night At The Opera")
```

This formula returns 17, because *p* is the seventeenth character in the string.

If you're not sure of the character sequence you're searching for, you can use the SEARCH function and include wildcards in your *find_text* string. To search for a single character that occupies a specific position, use a question-mark character (?); to search for any sequence of characters that occupies a specific position, use an asterisk (*).

Suppose you've used the names Smith and Smyth in your worksheet. To determine whether either name is in cell A1, use the formula

```
=SEARCH("Sm?th",A1)
```

If cell A1 contains the text *John Smith* or *John Smyth*, the SEARCH function returns the value 6 — the starting point for the string *Sm?th*. If you're not sure of the number of characters, use the * wildcard. For example, to find the position of *Allan* or *Alan* within the text stored in cell A1 (if any), use the formula

```
=SEARCH("A*an",A1)
```

The RIGHT and LEFT Functions

The RIGHT function returns the rightmost series of characters from a string argument, whereas the LEFT function returns the leftmost series of characters from a string argument. These functions take the forms

=RIGHT(*text,num_chars*)

and

=LEFT(*text,num_chars*)

The *num_chars* argument indicates the number of characters to extract from the *text* argument. These functions count blank spaces in the *text* argument as characters; if *text* contains leading or trailing blank characters, you might want to use a TRIM function within the RIGHT or LEFT function to ensure the expected result.

The *num_chars* argument must be greater than or equal to zero. If you omit *num_chars,* Excel assumes it is 1. If *num_chars* is greater than the number of characters in *text,* RIGHT and LEFT return the entire *text* argument.

For example, suppose you enter *This is a test* in cell A1 of your worksheet. The formula

```
=RIGHT(A1,4)
```

returns the word *test*.

The MID Function

You can use the MID function to extract a series of characters from a text string. This function takes the form

=MID(*text,start_num,num_chars*)

The *text* argument is the string from which you want to extract the substring, *start_num* is the place in the string where the substring begins (relative to the left end of the string), and *num_chars* is the number of characters you want to extract.

For example, suppose cell A1 contains the text *This Is A Long Text Entry*. You can use the formula

```
=MID(A1,11,10)
```

to extract the characters *Long Text* from the entry in cell A1.

The REPLACE and SUBSTITUTE Functions

These two functions substitute new text for old text. The REPLACE function replaces one string of characters with another string of characters and takes the form

=REPLACE(*old_text,start_num,num_chars,new_text*)

The *old_text* argument is the text string in which you want to replace characters. The next two arguments, *start_num* and *num_chars,* specify which characters to replace (relative to the left end of the string). The *new_text* argument specifies the text string to insert.

Suppose cell A3 contains *Millie Potter, Psychic*. To place this text in cell A6, replacing the first six characters with the string *Mildred,* select A6 and use the formula

```
=REPLACE(A3,1,6,"Mildred")
```

The new text is *Mildred Potter, Psychic*. The label in A3 remains unchanged, and the new label appears only in cell A6, where you entered the formula.

With the SUBSTITUTE function, you don't specify the starting number and number of characters to replace; instead, you simply specify the text to replace. The SUBSTITUTE function takes the form

=SUBSTITUTE(*text,old_text,new_text,instance_num*)

Suppose cell A4 contains the text *candy* and you want to place it in cell D6 and change it to *dandy*. Use the formula

=SUBSTITUTE(A4,"c","d")

When you enter this formula in cell D6, the text in cell A4 remains the same. The new text appears only in D6, the cell that contains the formula.

The *instance_num* argument is optional. It tells Excel to replace only the specified occurrence of *old_text*. For example, if cell A1 contains the text *through the hoop* and you want to substitute *loop* for *hoop*, the 4 in the formula

=SUBSTITUTE(A1,"h","l",4)

tells Excel to substitute an *l* for the fourth *h* in the text in cell A1. If you don't include *instance_num,* Excel changes all occurrences of *old_text* to *new_text*.

The REPT Function

The REPT function lets you fill a cell with a string of characters repeated a specified number of times. This function takes the form

=REPT(*text,number_times*)

The *text* argument specifies the string in quotation marks to be repeated. The *number_times* argument specifies how many times to repeat the text string; it can be any positive number, but the result of the REPT function is limited to 255 characters. If you enter 0 for the *number_times* argument, REPT leaves the cell blank; if *number_times* is not an integer, REPT ignores the decimal portion of the number.

Suppose you want to create a row of asterisks 150 characters wide. Enter the formula

=REPT("*",150)

The result is a string of 150 asterisks.

The *text* argument can be more than one character. For example, the formula

=REPT("-*",75)

results in a row of asterisks and hyphens 150 characters wide. The *number_times* argument specifies the number of times you want *text* repeated, not the total number of characters you want to create. If the text string has two characters, the length of the resulting string is two times the *number_times* argument.

The CONCATENATE Function

Using the CONCATENATE function is the equivalent of using the & character to assemble larger strings from smaller strings. This function takes the form

=CONCATENATE(*text1,text2, ...*)

You can use up to 30 *text* arguments, which are the pieces of text you want to assemble.

For example, if cell B4 contains the text *Strained*, the formula

=CONCATENATE("The Koala Tea Of Mercy, Australia, Is Not ",B4,".")

returns *The Koala Tea Of Mercy, Australia, Is Not Strained.*

Logical Functions

Microsoft Excel has a rich set of logical functions, including some that are included in the Analysis ToolPak add-in. Most logical functions use conditional tests to determine whether a specified condition is true or false.

For more information about the Analysis ToolPak, see Chapter 14, "Statistical Analysis," page 503.

Conditional Tests

A conditional test is an equation that compares two numbers, functions, formulas, labels, or logical values. For example, each of these formulas performs a conditional test:

```
=A1>A2
=5–3<5*2
=AVERAGE(B1:B6)=SUM(6,7,8)
=C2="Female"
=COUNT(A1:A10)=COUNT(B1:B10)
=LEN(A1)=10
```

Every conditional test must include at least one logical operator. Logical operators define the test relationship between elements of the conditional test. For example, in the conditional test A1>A2, the greater-than (>) logical operator compares the values in cells A1 and A2. The following table lists Excel's six logical operators.

Operator	Definition
=	Equal to
>	Greater than
<	Less than
> =	Greater than or equal to
< =	Less than or equal to
< >	Not equal to

The result of a conditional test is either the logical value TRUE (1) or the logical value FALSE (0). For example, the conditional test

=Z1=10

returns TRUE if the value in Z1 equals 10 and FALSE if Z1 contains any other value.

The IF Function

The IF conditional function takes the form

=IF(*logical_test,value_if_true,value_if_false*)

For example, the formula

=IF(A6<22,5,10)

returns 5 if the value in cell A6 is less than 22; otherwise, it returns 10.

You can nest other functions within an IF function. For example, the formula

=IF(SUM(A1:A10)>0,SUM(A1:A10),0)

returns the sum of A1 through A10 if it is greater than 0; otherwise, it returns 0.

You can use text arguments in IF functions. For example, the worksheet in Figure 11-8 on the next page lists exam scores for a group of students. The formula

=IF(F4>80%,"Pass","Fail")

entered in cell G4 tells Excel to test whether the average test score contained in cell F4 is greater than 80. If it is, the function returns the text *Pass*; if the average is less than or equal to 80, the function returns text *Fail*.

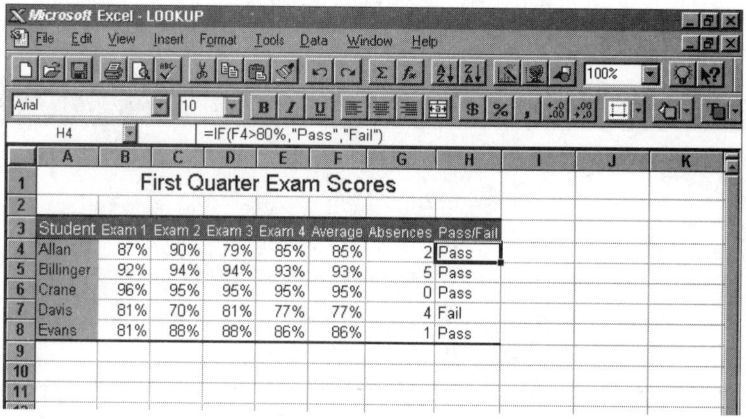
Microsoft Excel - LOOKUP
File Edit View Insert Format Tools Data Window Help
H4
=IF(F4>80%,"Pass","Fail")
First Quarter Exam Scores
Student Exam 1 Exam 2 Exam 3 Exam 4 Average Absences Pass/Fail
Allan 87% 90% 79% 85% 85% 2 Pass
Billinger 92% 94% 94% 93% 93% 5 Pass
Crane 96% 95% 95% 95% 95% 0 Pass
Davis 81% 70% 81% 77% 77% 4 Fail
Evans 81% 88% 88% 86% 86% 1 Pass

FIGURE 11-8
You can use the IF function to return a text string.

You can use text arguments in IF functions to return nothing, instead of 0, if the result is false. For example, the formula

=IF(SUM(A1:A10)>0,SUM(A1:A10),"")

returns nothing ("") if the conditional test is false.

The *logical_test* argument of an IF function can also consist of text. For example, the formula

=IF(A1="Test",100,200)

returns the value 100 if cell A1 contains the string *Test* and 200 if it contains any other entry. The match between the two text entries must be exact except for case.

The AND, OR, and NOT Functions

Three additional functions help you develop compound conditional tests: AND, OR, and NOT. These functions work in conjunction with the simple logical operators =, >, <, >=, <=, and <>. The AND and OR functions can have as many as 30 logical arguments each and take the forms

=AND(*logical1,logical2,...,logical30*)

and

=OR(*logical1,logical2,...,logical30*)

The NOT function has only one argument and takes the form

=NOT(*logical*)

Arguments for AND, OR, and NOT can be conditional tests, or they can be arrays or references to cells that contain logical values.

Suppose you want Excel to return the text *Pass* only if the student has an average score above 80 *and* fewer than 5 unexcused absences. In Figure 11-9, we use the formula

```
=IF(AND(G4<5,F4>80%),"Pass","Fail")
```

Microsoft Excel - LOOKUP

H4 =IF(AND(G4<5,F4>80%),"Pass","Fail")

First Quarter Exam Scores

Student	Exam 1	Exam 2	Exam 3	Exam 4	Average	Absences	Pass/Fail
Allan	87%	90%	79%	85%	85%	2	Pass
Billinger	92%	94%	94%	93%	93%	5	Fail
Crane	96%	95%	95%	95%	95%	0	Pass
Davis	81%	70%	81%	77%	77%	4	Fail
Evans	81%	88%	88%	86%	86%	1	Pass

FIGURE 11-9
You can create complex conditional tests using the AND function.

Although the OR function takes the same arguments as AND, the results are radically different. For example, the formula

```
=IF(OR(G4<5,F4>80%),"Pass","Fail")
```

returns the text *Pass* if the student's average test score is greater than 80 *or* if the student has fewer than 5 absences. Thus, the OR function returns the logical value TRUE if any *one* of the conditional tests is true; the AND function returns the logical value TRUE only if *all* the conditional tests are true.

The NOT function negates a condition, so it is usually used in conjunction with other functions. NOT instructs Excel to return the logical value TRUE if the argument is false and the logical value FALSE if the argument is true. For example, the formula

```
=IF(NOT(A1=2),"Go","NoGo")
```

tells Excel to return the text *Go* if the value of cell A1 is not 2.

Nested IF Functions

At times, you cannot resolve a logical problem using only logical operators and the AND, OR, and NOT functions. In these cases, you can nest IF functions to create a hierarchy of tests. For example, the formula

```
=IF(A1=100,"Always",IF(AND(A1>=80,A1<100),"Usually",
IF(AND(A1>=60,A1<80),"Sometimes","Who cares?")))
```

uses three separate IF functions. If the value in cell A1 is always an integer, the formula can be read: *If the value in cell A1 is 100, return the string* Always; *otherwise, if the value in cell A1 falls between 80 and 100 (that is, 80 through 99), return the string* Usually; *otherwise, if the value in cell A1 falls between 60 and 80 (60 through 79), return the string* Sometimes; *and, finally, if none of these conditions is true, return the string* Who cares?

You can nest as many as seven IF functions, as long as you don't exceed the 255-character limit for single-cell entries.

Other Uses for Conditional Functions

You can use all the conditional functions described in this section as stand-alone formulas. Although you usually use functions such as AND, OR, NOT, ISERROR, ISNA, and ISREF within an IF function, you can also use formulas such as

```
=AND(A1>A2,A2<A3)
```

to perform simple conditional tests. This formula returns the logical value TRUE if the value in A1 is greater than the value in A2 *and* the value in A2 is less than the value in A3. You might use this type of formula to assign TRUE and FALSE values to a range of numeric database cells and then use the TRUE and FALSE conditions as selection criteria for printing a specialized report.

The TRUE and FALSE Functions

The TRUE and FALSE functions offer alternative ways to represent the logical conditions TRUE and FALSE. Neither of these functions accepts arguments. They take the forms

```
=TRUE( )
```

and

```
=FALSE( )
```

For example, suppose cell B5 contains a conditional test formula. The formula

```
=IF(B5=FALSE( ),"Warning!","OK")
```

returns Warning! if the result of the conditional test formula in cell B5 is FALSE. It returns OK if the result of the formula in cell B5 is TRUE.

Trapping Errors: The ISERR, ISERROR, and ISNA Functions

If a formula in your worksheet refers to a cell that returns an error, that formula also returns an error. For example, if cell A1 returns an error, the formula

```
=A1/10
```

also returns an error. The same thing happens if the formula refers to a cell that returns the #N/A error value.

Three specialized logical functions, ISERR, ISERROR, and ISNA, test the value of an argument or cell to determine whether it contains an error value. ISERR tests for all error values except #N/A; ISERROR tests for all error values, including #N/A; and ISNA tests for #N/A values only. These functions let you selectively "trap" errors and #N/A values, preventing them from filtering through the worksheet. These functions take the forms

=ISERR(*value*)

and

=ISERROR(*value*)

and

=ISNA(*value*)

Although *value* can be a number, a formula, or literal text, it is usually a reference to a cell or range. Only one cell within a range — the one in the same column or row — is tested.

Typically, ISERR, ISERROR, and ISNA are used as conditional tests in IF functions. For example, the formula

=IF(ISERROR(A1/A2),0,A1/A2)

tests the formula A1/A2. If A1/A2 returns an error (as it will if A2 is blank or contains the value 0), the ISERROR function returns the logical value TRUE and the IF function returns the value 0. If A1/A2 does not return an error, the ISERROR function returns the logical value FALSE and the IF function returns the result of A1/A2. Similarly, the formula

=IF(ISNA(A1),0,A1*10)

tests the value in cell A1. If that value is #N/A, the IF function returns 0; otherwise, it returns the product of A1 and 10.

See Also For more information about other IS functions, see "The ISNUMBER Function," page 418; "The ISTEXT and ISNONTEXT Functions," page 430; "The ISREF Function," page 457; "The ISBLANK Function," page 457; and "The ISLOGICAL Function," in the next section.

The ISLOGICAL Function

The ISLOGICAL function determines whether a cell contains a logical value and takes the form

=ISLOGICAL(*value*)

If the cell specified by the *value* argument contains a logical value, Excel returns TRUE; otherwise, it returns FALSE.

See Also For more information about the IS functions, see "The ISNUMBER Function," page 418; "The ISTEXT and ISNONTEXT Functions," page 430; "Trapping Errors: The ISERR, ISERROR, and ISNA Functions," page 438; "The ISREF Function," page 457; and "The ISBLANK Function," page 457.

Lookup and Reference Functions

Several functions "look up" information stored in a list or a table or manipulate references.

The ADDRESS Function

The Address function provides a handy way to build a reference from numbers. ADDRESS takes the form:

=ADDRESS(*row_num,column_num,abs,a1,sheet_text*)

The *row_num* and *column_num* arguments designate the row and column values for the address. The *abs* argument is a logical value. If *abs* is TRUE, the resulting address uses absolute references. The *a1* argument is also a logical value. If *a1* is TRUE, the resulting address will be in the a1 form; if *a1* is FALSE, the resulting address will be in the R1C1 form. The *sheet_text* argument allows you to specify the name of the sheet for the beginning of the address. Excel places single quotation marks around the sheet text.

The CHOOSE Function

You use the CHOOSE function to retrieve an item from a list of values stored as the arguments to the function. CHOOSE takes the form

=CHOOSE(*index_num,value 1,value 2,...,value 29*)

The *index_num* argument is the position in the list of the item you want to look up, and *value 1, value 2,* and so on are the elements of the list. The *index_num* value must always be positive and cannot exceed the number of elements in the list. If you use an *index_num* value less than 1 or greater than the number of values in the list, Excel returns the #VALUE! error value.

The CHOOSE function returns the value of the element of the list that occupies the position indicated by *index_num*. For example, the function

=CHOOSE(2,6,1,8,9,3)

returns the value 1, because 1 is the second item in the list. (The *index_num* value itself is not counted as part of the list.)

The arguments of CHOOSE can be cell references. If you use a cell reference for *index_num,* Excel selects an item from the list according to the value stored in that cell. Suppose cell A11 contains the formula

=CHOOSE(A10,0.15,0.22,0.21,0.21,0.26)

If cell A10 contains the value 5, the CHOOSE function returns the value 0.26; if cell A10 contains the value 1, the function returns the value 0.15.

Similarly, if cell C1 contains the value 0.15, cell C2 contains the value 0.22, and cells C3, C4, and C5 all contain the value 0.21, the formula

=CHOOSE(A10,C1,C2,C3,C4,C5)

returns 0.15 if cell A10 contains the value 1 and returns 0.21 if cell A10 contains the value 3, 4, or 5.

You cannot specify a range as a single item in the list. You might be tempted to create a function such as

=CHOOSE(A10,C1:C5)

to take the place of the longer function in the previous example. If you do, however, the result is a #VALUE! error value.

The elements in the list can be text strings. For example, the function

=CHOOSE(3,"First","Second","Third")

selects the third item from the list and returns the string *Third.*

The MATCH Function

The MATCH function is closely related to the CHOOSE function. However, where CHOOSE returns the item that occupies the position in a list specified by the *index_num* argument, MATCH returns the position of the item in the list that most closely matches a lookup value. This function takes the form

=MATCH(*lookup_value,lookup_array,match_type*)

The *lookup_value* argument is the value or string to look up, and *lookup_array* is the range that contains the values with which to compare *lookup_value.*

In the worksheet in Figure 11-10 on the next page, if you enter the formula

=MATCH(10,A1:D1,0)

in cell E1, the result is 1, because the cell in the first position of *lookup_array* contains a value that matches *lookup_value.*

FIGURE 11-10
The MATCH function locates the position of a value in a list.

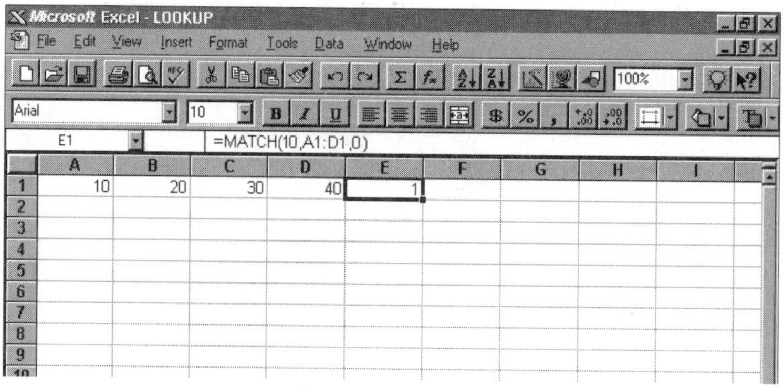

The *match_type* argument defines the rules for the search and must be 1, 0, or –1. If *match_type* is 1 or is omitted altogether, the MATCH function looks for the largest value in the range that is less than or equal to *lookup_value*. The *lookup_array* must be sorted in ascending order. For example, in the worksheet in Figure 11-10, the formula

=MATCH(19,A1:D1,1)

would return the value 1, because 10, the first item in the range, is the largest value in the range that doesn't exceed the *lookup_value* 19. If no items in the range are less than or equal to *lookup_value*, the function returns the #N/A error value.

To see what happens if you do not sort the *lookup_array* in ascending order, look at Figure 11-11. The formula

=MATCH(20,A1:D1,1)

now returns the value 1 instead of 4, the value you probably expected.

FIGURE 11-11
The MATCH function does not work properly with a *match_type* argument of 1 if the *lookup_array* is not in ascending order.

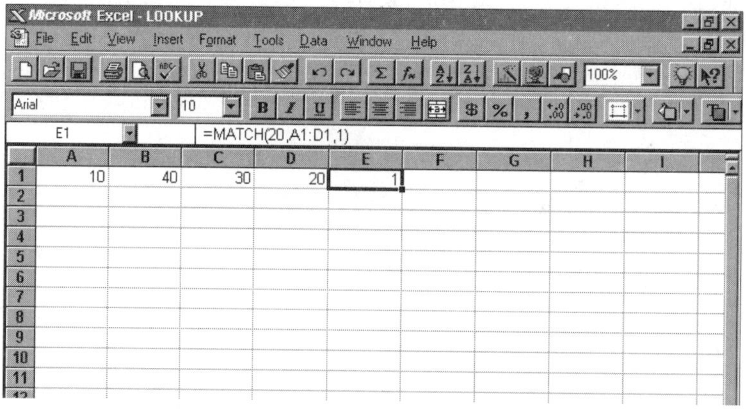

If *match_type* is 0, the MATCH function finds the first value in the range that exactly matches *lookup_value*. The *lookup_array* does not need to be sorted. If no items in the range exactly match *lookup value*, the function returns #N/A.

If *match_type* is –1, MATCH looks for the smallest value in the range that is greater than or equal to *lookup_value*. When *match_type* is –1, the items in the list must be sorted in descending order. If no items in the range are greater than or equal to *lookup_value,* the function returns the #N/A error value.

The *lookup_value* argument and the items in the range can also be text strings. For example, if cells A1:D1 contain the text entries shown in Figure 11-12, the formula

```
=MATCH("Twenty",A1:D1,0)
```

returns the value 2. When you use MATCH to locate text strings, you usually specify a *match_type* argument of 0 (an exact match). You can then use the wildcards * and ? in the *lookup_value* argument.

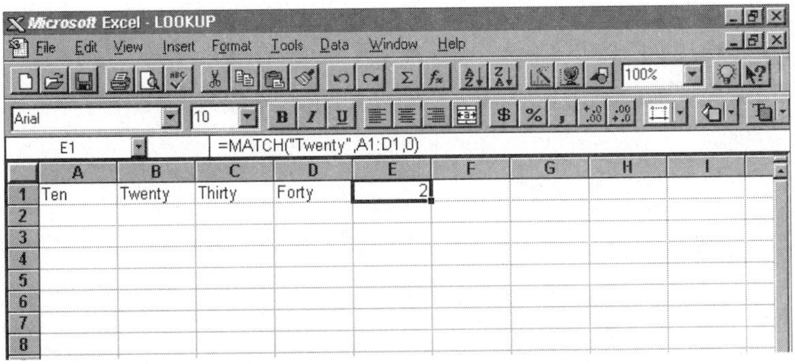

FIGURE 11-12
You can use MATCH to locate the position of a text string.

The VLOOKUP and HLOOKUP Functions

VLOOKUP and HLOOKUP are nearly identical functions that look up information stored in tables you've constructed. When you look up information in a table, you normally use a row index and a column index to locate a particular cell. Excel uses this method with a slight variation: It derives the first index by finding the largest value in the first column or row that is less than or equal to a *lookup_value* argument you supply and then uses a *row_index_num* or *col_index num* argument as the other index. This method allows you to look up a value based on information in the table, rather than having to know exactly where the value is.

These functions take the forms

=VLOOKUP(*lookup_value,table_array,col_index_num,range_lookup*)

and

=HLOOKUP(*lookup_value,table_array,row_index_num,range_lookup*)

The *lookup_value* argument is a value to look up in the table to find the first index, *table_array* is an array or range name that defines the table, and *row_* or *col_index_num* designates the row or column of the table (the second index) from which to select the result. Because *lookup_value* is compared to the first column or row of data to determine the first index, we call the data in that first column or row the *comparison values.* The *range_lookup* argument is a logical value that determines whether the function matches the lookup_value exactly or approximately. Use FALSE for the *range_lookup* argument to match the *lookup_value* exactly.

The difference between VLOOKUP and HLOOKUP is the type of table each function uses: VLOOKUP works with vertical tables (tables arranged in columns); HLOOKUP works with horizontal tables (tables arranged in rows).

Whether a table is considered vertical or horizontal depends on where the comparison values are located. If they are in the leftmost column of the table, the table is vertical; if they are in the first row of the table, the table is horizontal. The comparison values can be numbers or text. In either case, they must be arranged in ascending order. In addition, no comparison value should be used more than once in a table.

The *index_num* argument (sometimes called the *offset*) provides the second table index and tells the lookup function which column or row of the table to look in for the function's result. The first column or row in the table has an index number of 1, so if the index number is 1, the result of the function is one of the comparison values. The *index_num* argument must be greater than or equal to 1 and must never be greater than the number of rows or columns in the table; that is, if a vertical table is three columns wide, the index number cannot be greater than 3. If any value does not meet these rules, the function returns an error value.

The VLOOKUP Function

You can use the VLOOKUP function to retrieve information from the table in Figure 11-13. The formula

=VLOOKUP(41,A3:C7,3)

returns the value 14.

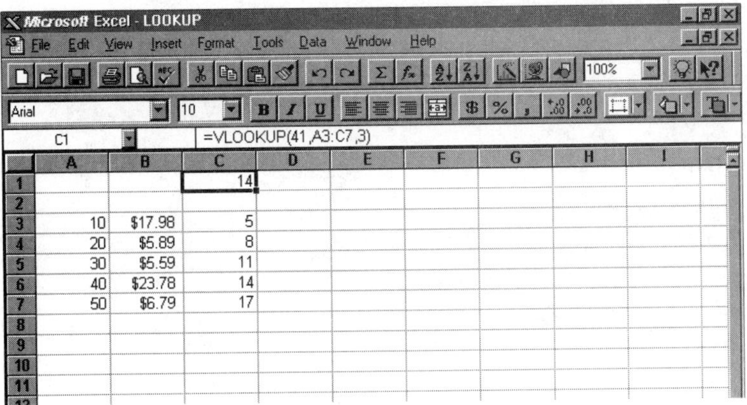

	A	B	C
1			14
2			
3	10	$17.98	5
4	20	$5.89	8
5	30	$5.59	11
6	40	$23.78	14
7	50	$6.79	17

FIGURE 11-13
You can use the VLOOKUP function to retrieve information from a vertical table like this one.

Let's see how Excel came up with this result. The function first locates the column that contains the comparison values — in this case, column A. Next it scans the comparison values to find the largest value that is less than or equal to the *lookup_value*. Because the fourth comparison value, 40, is less than the *lookup_value* of 41, and the fifth comparison value, 50, is greater than the *lookup_value,* Excel uses the row containing 40 (row number 6) as the row index. The column index is the *col_index_num* argument; in this example, *col_index_num* is 3, so column C contains the data you want. The function, therefore, returns the value from cell C6, which is 14.

The *lookup_value* argument in a lookup function can be a value, a cell reference, or text enclosed in double quotation marks. The *lookup_array* can be indicated by cell references or a range name. If we assign the name *Table* to the range A3:C7 in Figure 11-13 and enter the number 41 in cell A1, the formula

```
=VLOOKUP(A1,Table,3)
```

returns the same result as the previous example.

Remember that these lookup functions search for the greatest comparison value that is less than or equal to the lookup value (unless you use FALSE as the *range_lookup* argument), not for an exact match between the comparison values and the lookup value. If all the comparison values in the first row or column of the table range are greater than the lookup value, the function returns the #N/A error value. If, however, all the comparison values are less than the lookup value, the function returns the value that corresponds to the last (largest) comparison value in the table.

You can also use the lookup functions to look up text. For example, the formula

```
=VLOOKUP(8,B2:E6,4)
```

returns the string *Barb* from the table in Figure 11-14 on the next page.

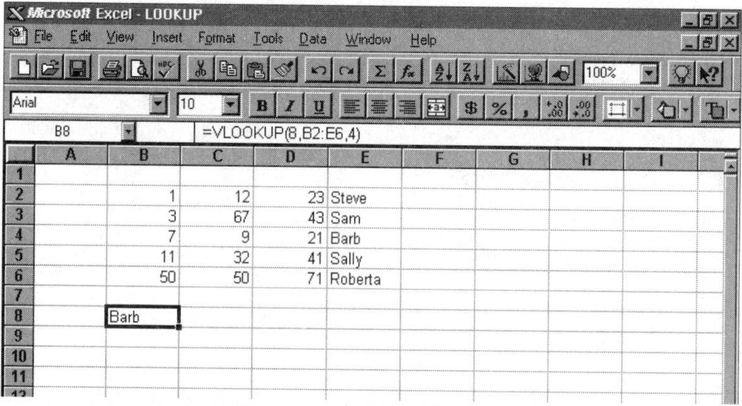

FIGURE 11-14
You can use VLOOKUP with text comparison values.

The *lookup_value* and comparison values can also be text strings. Figure 11-15 shows a lookup table that uses text comparison values. For example, the formula

=VLOOKUP("doug",B2:C6,2)

returns the value 46000. (If you use a text string as the *lookup value,* you must enclose it in double quotation marks.)

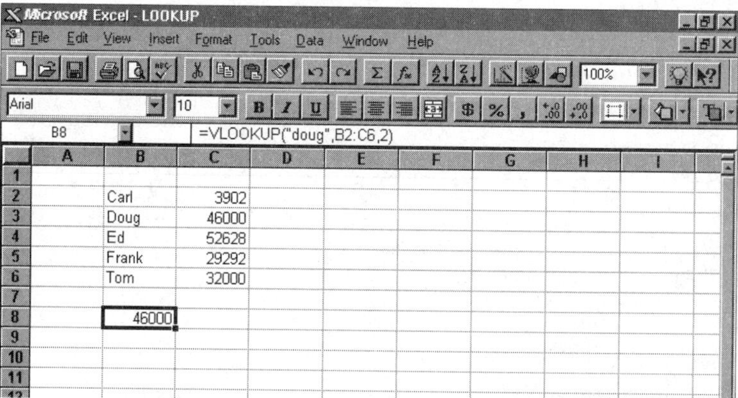

FIGURE 11-15
This vertical lookup table uses text comparison values.

The usefulness of text comparison values is limited in Excel because the comparison values must be arranged in alphabetic order. In addition, unless you include the *range_lookup* argument of FALSE to specify an exact match, Excel finds the comparison value that is less than or equal to the *lookup_value,* rather than an absolute match. Thus, the formula

=VLOOKUP("Steve",B2:C6,2)

returns the value 29292 from Figure 11-15. This value corresponds to the comparison value *Frank*, which is the "greatest" comparison value that is "less than" the lookup value *Steve*. Although this method is consistent, it does not yield the expected result.

You can combine numbers, text, and logical entries in the comparison range, but you still must arrange the elements in the range in ascending order according to the Excel sorting rules: numbers, text, and then logical values.

In Figure 11-16, the VLOOKUP function fails because the comparison values in column B are not in ascending order. The formula

=VLOOKUP(4,B2:C6,2)

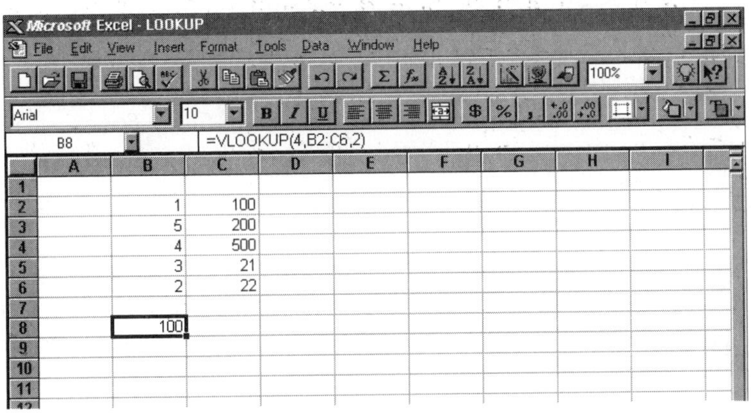

B8 =VLOOKUP(4,B2:C6,2)

	A	B	C
1			
2		1	100
3		5	200
4		4	500
5		3	21
6		2	22
7			
8		100	

FIGURE 11-16
The VLOOKUP function works properly only when the comparison values are in ascending order.

returns the value 100 instead of 500, because it searches the comparison value list only until it comes to a number greater than the lookup value. In this example, the function stops the search when it finds 5, backs up to the previous comparison value, and uses that row to obtain the result. The comparison values below 5 are ignored unless you provide a FALSE *range_lookup* argument.

The HLOOKUP Function

The HLOOKUP function is identical to the VLOOKUP function except that it works with horizontal tables. The worksheet in Figure 11-17 on the next page shows an example of a horizontal lookup table. The formula

=HLOOKUP(6,B2:E7,3)

returns the value 101 because the lookup value, 6, equals the comparison value in column C, and the index number, 3, tells the function to look in the third row of the table (row 4) for the correct item.

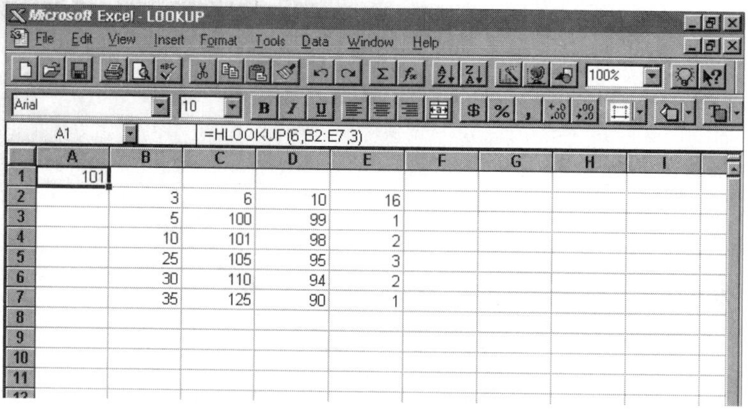

FIGURE 11-17 You can use the HLOOKUP function to retrieve information from a horizontal table like this one.

Microsoft Excel - LOOKUP

A1 =HLOOKUP(6,B2:E7,3)

	A	B	C	D	E
1	101				
2		3	6	10	16
3		5	100	99	1
4		10	101	98	2
5		25	105	95	3
6		30	110	94	2
7		35	125	90	1

The LOOKUP Function

The LOOKUP function has two forms. In both forms, it is similar to VLOOKUP and HLOOKUP, and follows the same rules.

The First Form The first form (or vector form) of LOOKUP is

=LOOKUP(*lookup_value,lookup_vector,result_vector*)

The *lookup_value* argument is a value to find in the comparison values given by *lookup_vector,* and *result_vector* contains the possible results. Each range consists of a single row or column.

Like HLOOKUP and VLOOKUP, LOOKUP searches *lookup_vector* for the largest comparison value that is not greater than *lookup_value.* It then selects the result from the corresponding position in *result_vector.* Although *lookup_vector* and *result_vector* are often parallel in the worksheet, they don't have to be. They can be located in separate areas of the worksheet, and one range can be horizontal and the other vertical. The only requirement is that they must have exactly the same number of elements.

For example, consider the worksheet in Figure 11-18. The formula

=LOOKUP(3,B3:B7,E3:E7)

compares the *lookup_value,* 3, with the values in the *lookup_vector,* B3:B7. The third cell of the *lookup_vector,* B5, contains the largest value that is not greater than the *lookup_value,* so the function returns the contents of the third cell of the result range, E5, as the result 300.

Now consider Figure 11-19, where the ranges are not parallel. The formula

=LOOKUP(3,A1:A5,D6:H6)

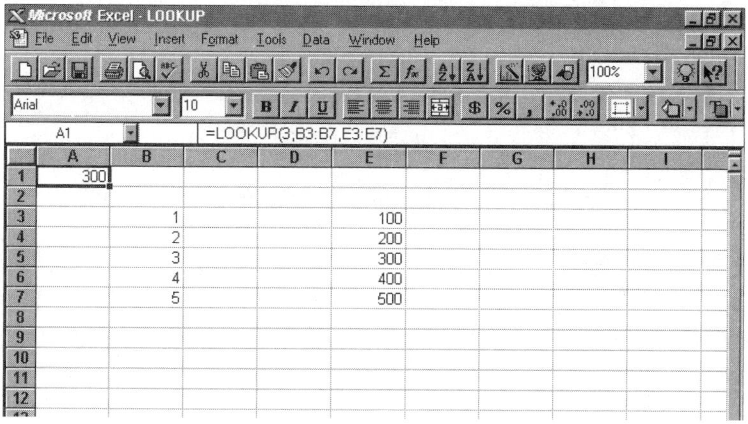

FIGURE 11-18
You can use the LOOKUP function to retrieve information from a range.

returns 300. Both the *lookup_vector,* A1:A5, and the *result_vector,* D6:H6, have five elements. The *lookup_value,* 3, matches the entry in the third cell of the *lookup_vector,* so the result of the formula is the entry in the third cell of the result range: 300.

The Second Form The second form (or array form) of LOOKUP is

=LOOKUP(*lookup_value,array*)

The *lookup_value* argument is a value to find in the table defined by *array.* This form of the LOOKUP function has no *index_num* or *result_vector* argument. The result is always taken from the last row or column of *array.*

You can use this form of LOOKUP with either a horizontal or a vertical table. LOOKUP uses the dimensions of the table to figure out where the comparison values are. If the table is taller than it is wide, or if the table is

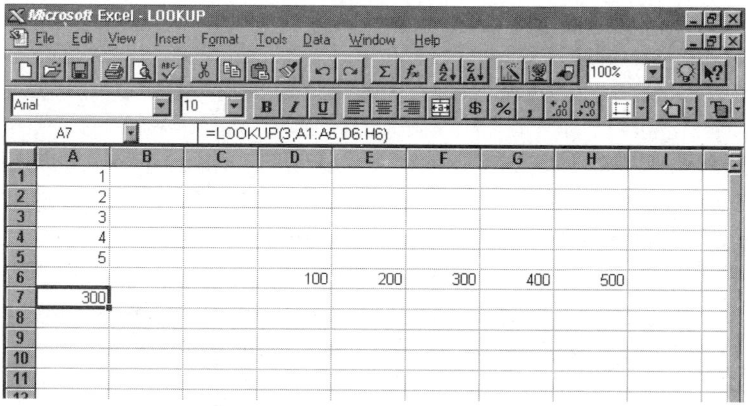

FIGURE 11-19
The LOOKUP function can retrieve information from a nonparallel cell range.

square, the function treats it as a vertical table and assumes that the comparison values are in the leftmost column. If the table is wider than it is tall, the function views the table as horizontal and assumes the comparison values are in the first row of the table.

Because HLOOKUP and VLOOKUP are more predictable and controllable, you'll generally find using them preferable to using LOOKUP.

The INDEX Function

Like CHOOSE and LOOKUP, INDEX is a lookup function. It has two forms: an array form, which returns the value or values in those cells, and a reference form, which returns an address, or reference (not a value) to a cell or range of cells in the worksheet. We'll discuss the array form first.

The First Form The first form (or array form) of the INDEX function works only with array arguments and it returns the *values* of the results, not their cell references. This form of the function is

=INDEX(*array,row_num,column_num*)

The result is the value at the position in the *array* argument indicated by the *row_num* and *column_num* arguments.

For example, the formula

=INDEX({10,20,30;40,50,60},1,2)

returns the value 20, because 20 is the value in the cell in the second column and first row of the array.

The Second Form The second form (or reference form) of INDEX returns a cell address and is useful when you want to perform operations on a cell (such as changing the cell width), rather than on its value. This function can be confusing, however, because if an INDEX function is nested in another function, that function can use the value in the cell whose address is returned by INDEX. Furthermore, the reference form of INDEX doesn't display its result as an address; it displays the value(s) in that address. The important thing to remember is that the result is actually an address, even if it doesn't look that way.

The INDEX function has two advantages: You can give it multiple, discontiguous areas of the worksheet as a lookup range argument, which in this case is called the *index range* argument; and it can return a range (more than one cell) as a result. The reference form of this function is

=INDEX(*reference,row_num,column_num,area_num*)

The *reference* argument can be one or more ranges, which are called *areas*. Each area must be rectangular and can contain numbers, text, or formulas. If the areas are not adjacent, the *reference* argument must be enclosed in parentheses.

The *row_num* and *column_num* arguments must be positive numbers (or references to cells that contain numbers) that designate a cell in the *reference* argument. If the *row_num* argument is greater than the number of rows in the table or if the *column_num* argument is greater than the number of columns, the INDEX function returns the #REF! error value.

If every area in *reference* consists of only one row, the *row_num* argument is optional. Similarly, the *column_num* argument is optional if every area consists of only one column. If you enter 0 as the *row_num* or *column_num* argument, INDEX returns a reference for the entire row or column, respectively.

The *area_num* argument is needed only if more than one area is included in *reference*. It identifies which area in *reference* the *row_num* and *column_num* arguments are to be used with. The first area specified in *reference* is designated area 1, the second area 2, and so on. If the *area_num* argument is omitted, it is assumed to be 1. The *area_num* argument must always be a positive integer. If *area_num* is less than 1, the function returns the #REF! error value.

Let's consider some examples to see how all this works. Figure 11-20 shows an example of an INDEX function. The formula in cell A1

=INDEX(C3:E6,A2,A3)

uses the row coordinate in cell A2,3, and the column coordinate in cell A3,2, to return the address of the cell in the third row and the second column of the range C3:E6, which is D5. However, because Excel displays the value of the result, the number 700 — the contents of cell D5 — are displayed in cell A1.

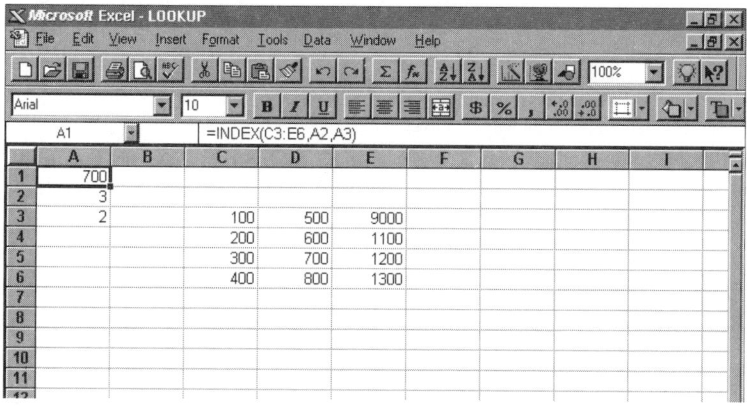

FIGURE 11-20
You can use the INDEX function to retrieve the address of the cell where information is located.

Here's another example that's a bit more tricky. Using the worksheet in Figure 11-20, the formula

=INDEX(C3:E6,0,2)

displays the #VALUE! error value because the *row_num* argument of 0 causes INDEX to return a reference to the entire column specified by the *column_num* argument of 2, which is the range D3:D6. You see the #VALUE! error value because Excel can't display the value as a range result. However, if we nest this formula in another function, as follows:

=SUM(INDEX(C3:E6,0,2))

the result is 2600, the sum of the values in D3:D6. Now you can see the utility of obtaining a reference result with INDEX.

If *reference* is only one row deep or one column wide, you can use only one index to select a value. Using Figure 11-20 again, the formula

=INDEX(C3:C6,2)

returns the value 200. Similarly, the formula

=INDEX(C3:E3,2)

returns the value 500. (The INDEX function is similar to the CHOOSE function when used with a one-dimensional table.)

Now let's see how the INDEX function works with multiple ranges in the *reference* argument. (Remember, when more than one range is used, you must enclose the argument in parentheses.) For example, in the formula

=INDEX((A1:C5,D6:F10),1,1,2)

the reference range is composed of two areas: A1:C5 and D6:F10. The area_num argument, 2, tells INDEX to work on the second of these areas. This formula returns the address D6, which is the cell in the first column and first row of the range D6:F10. The displayed result is the value in that cell.

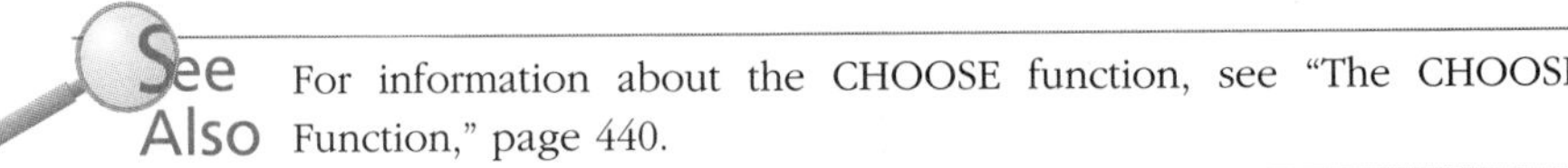

For information about the CHOOSE function, see "The CHOOSE Function," page 440.

The OFFSET Function

The OFFSET function returns a reference of a specified height and width, located at a specified position relative to another reference. This function takes the form

=OFFSET(*reference,rows,cols,height,width*)

The *reference* argument specifies the position from which the offset is calculated. The *rows* and *cols* arguments specify the vertical and horizontal distances between the *reference* argument and the reference returned by the function. Positive values for *rows* and *cols* specify offsets below and to the right of *reference,* respectively. Negative values specify offsets above and to the left of *reference,* respectively. The *height* and *width* arguments specify the shape of the reference returned by the function. The *height* and *width* arguments are optional. If you omit them, the function returns a reference of the same dimensions as *reference*. If you include them, *height* and *width* must be positive.

The INDIRECT Function

You can use the INDIRECT function to find out the contents of a cell from its reference. INDIRECT takes the form

=INDIRECT(*ref_text,a1*)

The *ref_text* argument is an A1 reference, an R1C1 reference, or a cell name, and *a1* is a logical value that indicates which of these types of reference you're using. If *a1* is FALSE, Excel interprets *ref_text* as the R1C1 format; if *a1* is TRUE or is omitted, Excel interprets *ref_text* as the A1 format. If your entry for *ref_text* isn't valid, INDIRECT returns the #REF! error value.

For example, if cell C6 of your worksheet contains the text value *B3*, and cell B3 contains the value 2.888, the formula

=INDIRECT(C6)

returns the value 2.888. If your worksheet is set to display R1C1-style references, cell R6C3 contains a text reference to cell R3C2, and cell R3C2 contains the value 2.888, then the formula

=INDIRECT(R6C3,FALSE)

also returns the value 2.888.

The ROW and COLUMN Functions

Although the names of the ROW and COLUMN functions are nearly the same as the names of the ROWS and COLUMNS array functions, the functions are quite different. These functions take the forms

=ROW(*reference*)

and

=COLUMN(*reference*)

The result of these functions is the row or column number of the cell or range referred to by the function's argument. For example, the formula

=ROW(H5)

returns the result 5.

If the *reference* argument is omitted, the result is the row or column number of the cell that contains the function.

If the *reference* argument is a range or a range name and the function is entered as an array, the result of the function is an array that consists of the row or column numbers of each of the rows or columns in the range. For example, if you select cells B1:B10, type the formula

=ROW(A1:A10)

and then press Ctrl-Shift-Enter to enter the formula in all of the cells of the range B1:B10, that range will contain the array result {1;2;3;4;5;6;7;8;9;10}, the row numbers of each cell in the argument.

The ROWS and COLUMNS Functions

The ROWS function returns the number of rows in a reference or an array and takes the form

ROWS(*array*)

The *array* argument is an array constant, a range reference, or a range name.

For example, the result of the formula

ROWS({100,200,300;1000,2000,3000})

is 2, because the *array* argument contains two "rows." The formula

ROWS(A1:A10)

returns 10, because the range A1:A10 contains ten rows.

The COLUMNS function is identical to the ROWS function except that it returns the number of columns in the *array* argument. For example, the formula

COLUMNS(A1:C10)

returns 3, because the range A1:C10 contains three columns.

The AREAS Function

An area is a single cell or a rectangular block of cells. You can use the AREAS function to determine the number of areas in a range. This function takes the form

=AREAS(*reference*)

The *reference* argument can be a cell reference, a range reference, or several range references. (If you use several range references, you must enclose them in a set of parentheses so that Excel doesn't interpret the commas that separate the ranges as argument separators.) The result of the function is the number of areas referred to by the argument.

For example, suppose you assign the name *Test* to the group of ranges A1:C5,D6,E7:G10. The function

=AREAS(Test)

returns the number 3, the number of areas in the group.

The TRANSPOSE Function

The TRANSPOSE function changes the horizontal or vertical orientation of an array. This function has the form

=TRANSPOSE(*array*)

If the *array* argument is vertical, the resulting array is horizontal. If the *array* argument is horizontal, the resulting array is vertical. The first row of a horizontal array argument becomes the first column of the vertical array result, and vice versa. The TRANSPOSE function must be entered as an array formula in a range that has the same number of rows and columns as the *array* argument has columns and rows, respectively.

Suppose you want to transpose a vertical array in cells A1:C7 of a worksheet so that it fills a horizontal array in cells A10:G12. Select the range A10:G12, type

=TRANSPOSE(A1:C7)

and then press Ctrl-Shift-Enter to enter the function in each cell of the selected range. Figure 11-21 shows the results.

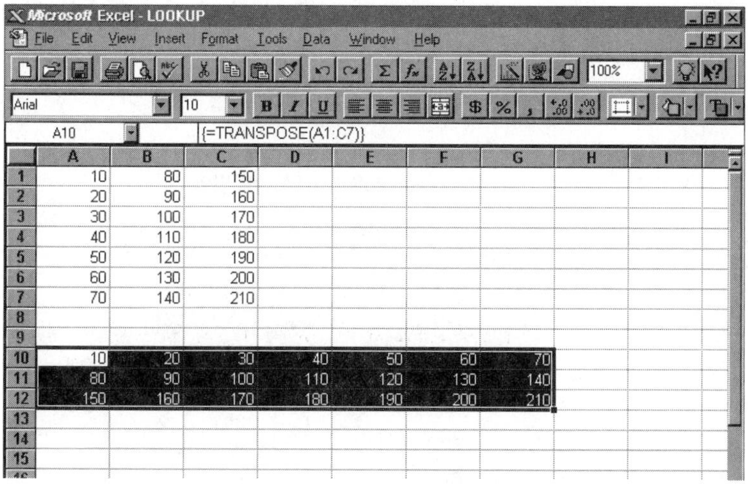

FIGURE 11-21

Use the TRANSPOSE function to change the vertical array in cells A1:C7 into a horizontal array in cells A10:G12.

The COUNTBLANK Function

The COUNTBLANK function simply counts the number of empty cells in the specifed range and takes the form

=COUNTBLANK(*range*)

The *range* argument is the range you want to check. This function is a little tricky, because a formula that evaluates to text, such as ="" or =" ", might seem empty but really isn't. In contrast, a formula that isn't technically empty but evaluates to zero, such as =100–A1 where A1 contains the number 100, isn't counted.

The TYPE Function

The TYPE function determines whether a cell contains text, a number, a logical value, an array, or an error value. This function takes the form

=TYPE(*value*)

The result of the TYPE function is a code for the type of entry in the referenced cell: 1 for a number, 2 for text, 4 for a logical value (TRUE or FALSE), 16 for an error value, and 64 for an array.

For example, if cell A1 contains the number 100, the formula

=TYPE(A1)

returns 1. If A1 contains the text *Microsoft Excel,* the formula returns 2.

The NA Function

NA is a placeholder function. You'll use NA primarily for marking blank cells to help you avoid including those cells in calculations. When you enter the NA function in a cell, that cell and all formulas that refer to that cell return the result #N/A. (Some functions return the #N/A value as a type of error.) The NA function is included for compatibility with other spreadsheet programs. This function takes the form

=NA( )

Unlike most functions, NA takes no arguments, but you must include empty parentheses with it.

Suppose several formulas in your worksheet depend on the value in a cell, but you are not certain of the value the cell should contain. Instead of entering a guess, you can enter the NA function in the cell as a placeholder. Until you replace the NA function with the correct value, any formula in the worksheet that refers to that cell displays the result #N/A.

You can also enter the value #N/A directly into a cell instead of using the NA function. The result is the same.

The ISREF Function

The ISREF function returns the logical value TRUE if the cell specified by its argument contains a reference. ISREF takes the form

=ISREF(*value*)

If the cell specified by the *value* argument is not a reference, the function returns the logical value FALSE.

For more information about the IS functions, see "The ISNUMBER Function," page 418; "The ISTEXT and ISNONTEXT Functions," page 430; "Trapping Errors: The ISERR, ISERROR, and ISNA Functions," page 438; "The ISLOGICAL Function," page 439; and "The ISBLANK Function," page 457.

The ISBLANK Function

You can use the ISBLANK function to determine whether a referenced cell is blank. ISBLANK takes the form

=ISBLANK(*value*)

The *value* argument is a reference to a cell or range. If *value* refers to a blank cell or range, the function returns the logical value TRUE; otherwise, it returns FALSE.

For more information about the IS functions, see "The ISNUMBER Function," page 418; "The ISTEXT and ISNONTEXT Functions," page 430; "Trapping Errors: The ISERR, ISERROR, and ISNA Functions," page 438; "The ISLOGICAL Function," page 439; and "The ISREF Function," page 457.

Chapter 12

Dates and Times

With Microsoft Excel, you can enter date values and time values in your worksheet to date stamp documents or to perform date and time arithmetic. As a result, creating a production schedule or a monthly billing system is relatively easy. Although Microsoft Excel uses numeric values to count each nanosecond, starting from the turn of the century, we can use formatting to display those numbers in forms we can more easily recognize.

How Microsoft Excel Records Dates and Times

The basic unit of time in Microsoft Excel is the day. Each day is represented by a serial date value from 1 through 65380. The base date, represented by the serial value 1, is Sunday, January 1, 1900. The maximum serial value, 65380, represents December 31, 2078. When you enter a date in your worksheet, Excel records the date as a serial value that represents the number of days between the base date and the specified date. For example, the date January 1, 1996, is represented by the serial value 35065, because there are 35065 days between the base date — January 1, 1900 — and January 1, 1996.

The time of day is a decimal value that represents the portion of a day between its beginning — 12:00 midnight — and the specified time. The time 12:00 noon, for example, is represented by the value 0.5, because the difference between midnight and noon is exactly half a day. The time/date combination 2:09:03 PM, October 25, 1996, is represented by the serial value 35363.5896180556.

By assigning serial values to days, hours, minutes, and seconds, Excel enables you to perform sophisticated date and time arithmetic. You can manipulate dates and times in your worksheet formulas just as you manipulate other types of values.

Entering Dates and Times

Although Microsoft Excel records dates and times as serial date values, you don't have to enter them that way. In Chapter 6, you learned that you can enter a number in a cell and format that number in one step by typing the number "in format." Generally, you use this "in format" technique to enter dates and times. Simply select the cell in which you want to make the entry and type the date in one of the following formats: m/d/yy, d-mmm-yy, d-mmm, or mmm-yy.

NOTE An additional built-in format, m/d/yy h:mm, combines a date and a time.

The 1904 Date System Option

You can change the base date (the date that corresponds to the serial value 1) from January 1, 1900 — the base date used by Microsoft Excel for Windows — to January 2, 1904 — the base date used by Microsoft Excel for the Macintosh. To switch to the 1904 Date System, choose Options from the Tools menu, click the Calculation tab, and select the 1904 Date System option. When you turn on the 1904 Date System option, the serial date values in your worksheet remain the same, but the display of all dates changes, and the serial values of any dates you enter in your Excel for Windows worksheets match corresponding serial values from Excel for the Macintosh worksheets. If you transfer information into Excel for Windows from a worksheet created in Excel for the Macintosh, turning on this option ensures that the serial date values in the worksheet are evaluated correctly. In this book, we use the 1900 Date System, which is the standard for Windows and MS-DOS programs.

If you transfer documents between Excel for the Macintosh and Excel for Windows, the proper date system for the worksheet is automatically set for you. When the date system changes, existing serial date values display different dates, but the underlying values do not change. As a result, if you change date systems after you have begun entering dates in a worksheet, all your dates will be off by four years.

For example, to enter the date December 1, 1996, select the cell and type *12/1/96* or *12-1-96*. (You can use either forward slashes or hyphens as separators.) Excel does not display the date's serial value in the formula bar; instead, it assigns the m/d/yy format to the cell (if the cell isn't already formatted differently) and displays 12/1/96 in the formula bar.

You can use any built-in date format to enter dates in this way. (You can also create your own date formats.) If your entry doesn't exactly match a built-in format, Excel picks the format that is most similar to your entry. For example, if you enter *1 Dec*, you see the formatted entry 1-Dec in the cell. In the formula bar, the entry appears as 12/1/1996 (assuming the current year is 1996) so that you can edit the date more easily.

TIP You can enter the current date in a cell or formula by holding down Ctrl and pressing the semicolon (;) key. The date is entered in m/d/yy format.

NOTE When you enter a date between 1920 and 2010, you need enter only the last two digits of the year value. To enter a date outside this range, however, you must use the full year. For example, to enter the date January 1, 2030, enter *1/1/2030.*

You can also enter times "in format." Select the cell in which you want to make the entry and type the time in one of the following forms: h:mm AM/PM, h:mm:ss AM/PM, h:mm, h:mm:ss, mm:ss, mm:ss.0, [h]:mm:ss, or the combined date and time format, m/d/yy h:mm. Notice that the hours, minutes, and seconds of the time entries must be separated by colons. (You cannot enter minutes "in format.")

For example, to enter the time 2:15 PM in a cell, select the cell and type *2:15 PM* or *14:15*. Either way, Excel recognizes the time as the decimal value equivalent of 0.59375 and displays it on the worksheet in the Time format you used for the entry. (If you don't include AM, PM, am, or pm with the time, Excel uses the 24-hour, or military, time convention. On the 24-hour clock, 3:00 AM is 300 hours, 2:00 PM is 1400 hours, and 11:00 PM is 2300 hours.)

TIP You can enter the current time in a cell or formula by holding down Ctrl and Shift together and pressing the colon (:) key. The time is entered in h:mm AM/PM format.

See Also For more information about custom formats, see "Creating Your Own Date and Time Formats," page 468.

Entering a Series of Dates

You can create an evenly spaced series of dates in a row or column in several ways, but the job is especially easy when you use the Series command on the Fill submenu of the Edit menu. With this command, you can build a series of dates that are days, weeks, months, or years apart.

Suppose you want to create a series of dates in cells A1 through A16. The series begins with March 1, 1996, and the dates must be exactly one month apart. Follow these steps:

1. Type the starting date in the first cell of the range in which you want the series to appear — in this case, type *3/1/96* in cell A1.
2. Select the range — in this case, A1:A16 — and choose Fill and then Series from the Edit menu.
3. In the Series dialog box, shown in Figure 12-1, accept the default options in the Series In and Type sections. (Columns creates a columnar series, and Date creates a date series.)

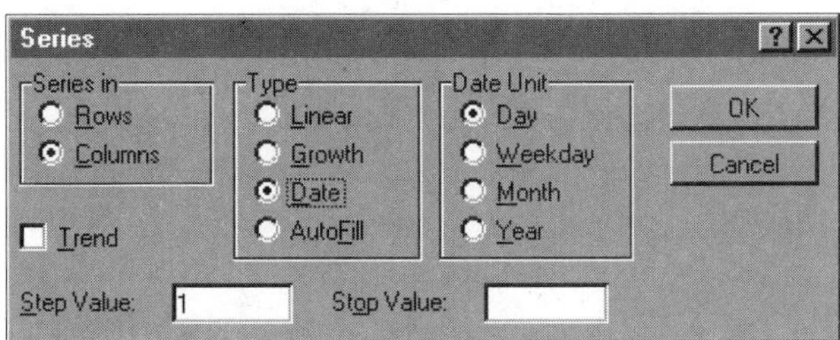

FIGURE 12-1
Use the Series dialog box to create date series.

4. In the Date Unit section, select Month to specify the interval. Then check that the Step Value is 1, and click OK.

Figure 12-2 shows the result. The range A1:A16 contains a series of dates exactly one month apart.

	A	B	C	D	E	F	G	H	I
1	3/1/96								
2	4/1/96								
3	5/1/96								
4	6/1/96								
5	7/1/96								
6	8/1/96								
7	9/1/96								
8	10/1/96								
9	11/1/96								
10	12/1/96								
11	1/1/97								
12	2/1/97								
13	3/1/97								
14	4/1/97								
15	5/1/97								
16	6/1/97								

Sheet1 / Sheet2 / Sheet3 / Sheet4 / Sheet5 / Sheet6 / Sh

FIGURE 12-2
Using the Series command on the Fill submenu of the Edit menu, we created a series of dates one month apart.

The other options in the Date Unit section of the Series dialog box let you specify different intervals for your date series. The Day option builds a series of dates one or more days apart (depending on the step value); the

Weekday option creates a series of dates using only the five working days of the week. The Year option builds an annual date series.

The Step Value option lets you specify the interval between cells. For example, by typing *2* in the Step Value edit box and selecting Date in the Type section and Month in the Date Unit section, you can create a series of dates for every other month. By typing a negative number in the Step Value edit box, you can create a series that goes backward (decreases) in time.

To set an ending date for the series, you can enter a date in the Stop Value edit box. For example, to enter a series of dates that extends from 1/1/96 through 12/31/97, type *1/1/96* in a cell, display the Series dialog box, select the Columns option, and type *12/31/97* in the Stop Value edit box. Excel interprets the entry as the serial date value 35795.

See Also For more information about the Series command, see "Filling Cell Ranges with Data," page 268.

Entering a Date Series Using AutoFill

In Chapter 7, we introduced you to AutoFill, which lets you create a series of data with the mouse. This feature also lets you create date series quickly and easily. For example, to quickly create the same one-month date series shown in Figure 12-2, follow these steps:

1. Enter the starting date — in this case, *3/1/96* — in A1 (the first cell of the range) and the second date in the series, *4/1/96*, in A2 (the second cell).
2. With the mouse, select the two cells.
3. Move the mouse pointer over the small black fill handle in the lower right corner of the selection. (If the fill handle is not visible, choose Options from the Tools menu, click the Edit tab, and turn on the Allow Cell Drag And Drop option.) The mouse pointer changes to a bold cross hair when it is over the fill handle.
4. Drag the fill handle until the range you want to fill with dates — in this case, cells A1:A16 — is selected.
5. Release the mouse button. AutoFill analyzes the two selected cells, determines that their entries are one month apart, and creates the same one-month data series shown in Figure 12-2.

AutoFill uses the selected cells to determine the type of series you intend to create with the fill handle. As described in Chapter 7, it copies text and nonsequential values and automatically increments sequential numeric values. Because dates are stored as serial values, AutoFill extends them sequentially, as illustrated in Figure 12-3.

	A	B	C	D	E	F	G	H	I
1	Selected value(s)		Resulting AutoFill series						
2									
3	1/1/96	2/1/96	3/1/96	4/1/96	5/1/96	6/1/96	7/1/96		
4	1/1/96	3/1/96	5/1/96	7/1/96	9/1/96	11/1/96	1/1/97		
5	1-Jan	2-Jan	3-Jan	4-Jan	5-Jan	6-Jan	7-Jan		
6	Dec-96	Dec-97	Dec-98	Dec-99	Dec-00	Dec-01	Dec-02		
7	Dec-96	Dec-98	Dec-00	Dec-02	Dec-04	Dec-06	Dec-08		
8									
9									
10	1/1/96	1/2/96	1/3/96	1/4/96	1/5/96	1/6/96	1/7/96		
11	Qtr 1	Qtr 2	Qtr 3	Qtr 4	Qtr 1	Qtr 2	Qtr 3		
12	Jan	Feb	Mar	Apr	May	Jun	Jul		
13	January	February	March	April	May	June	July		
14	Day 1	Day 2	Day 3	Day 4	Day 5	Day 6	Day 7		
15	Mon	Tue	Wed	Thu	Fri	Sat	Sun		
16									

FIGURE 12-3

Using AutoFill, we started with the values in the Selected value(s) section of the worksheet and created the values to the right.

Row 3 contains a common one-month date series, and row 4 contains a bimonthly series created using 1/1/96 and 3/1/96 as starting values. Rows 5 and 6 illustrate different formats and increments, and row 7 contains an every other year series.

The examples in rows 10 through 15 in Figure 12-3 show how even a single cell can provide enough information for AutoFill to determine a series. When you use the fill handle on single-cell values like the ones in rows 10 through 15, Excel assumes you want to increment the numeric value in each cell. (If you want to copy the cell instead, hold down Ctrl while dragging the fill handle.) Notice, however, that the entries in rows 11 through 15 contain text values. AutoFill recognizes text entries for days and months and extends them as if they were numeric values. In addition, when a cell contains a mixed text and numeric entry, AutoFill automatically copies the text portion (if it is not the name of a month or day). AutoFill also increments the numeric portion if it occurs at either end of the entry (but not in the middle). The results are shown in rows 11 and 14 of Figure 12-3.

See Also For more information about AutoFill, see "Filling and Creating Series with the Mouse," page 236.

Formatting Dates and Times

After you enter a date, you can use the Cells command on the Format menu to change its format. The following table shows how the date February 24, 1996, looks in the first five built-in Date formats:

Format	Display
m/d	2/24
m/d/yy	2/24/96
mm/dd/yy	02/24/96
d-mmm	24-Feb
d-mmm-yy	24-Feb-96

To assign a Date format to a cell, follow these steps:

1. Select the cell you want to format.
2. From the Format menu, choose Cells (or press Ctrl-1) and click the Number tab in the Format Cells dialog box.
3. Select the Date category, as shown in Figure 12-4.

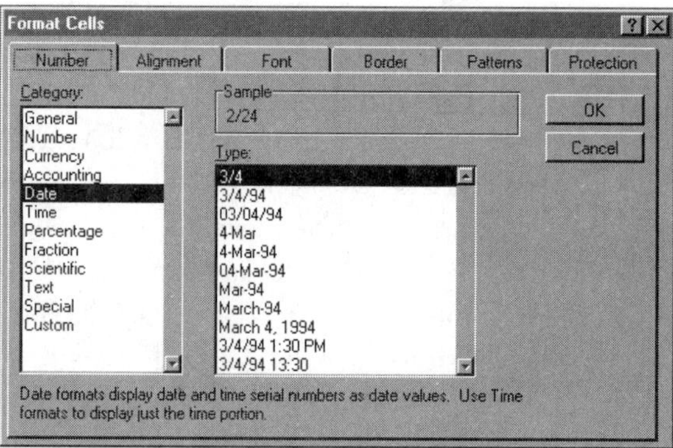

FIGURE 12-4 Use the Number tab in the Format Cells dialog box to apply Date formats to cells.

4. Select the format you want to use from the Type list box.
5. Click OK.

Similarly, you can change the format of a time entry. The following table shows the results of formatting the entry 13:52:32.44 using the first eight Time formats:

Format	Display
h:mm	13:52
h:mm PM	1:52 PM
h:mm:ss	13:52:32
h:mm:ss PM	1:52:32 PM
mm:ss.0	52:32.4
[h]:mm:ss	13:52:32
m/d/yy h:mm PM	1/0/00 1:52 PM
m/d/yy h:mm	1/0/00 13:52

Notice that some formats use the traditional 12-hour time convention and other formats use the 24-hour time convention. In addition, the last two formats display the date as 1/0/00 because the entry does not include a date.

The fifth format displays only minutes and seconds, allowing you to measure times to a decimal fraction of a second.

To assign a Time format to a cell, follow these steps:

1. Select the cell you want to format.
2. From the Format menu, choose Cells (or press Ctrl-1) and click the Number tab.
3. Select the Time category, as shown in Figure 12-5.

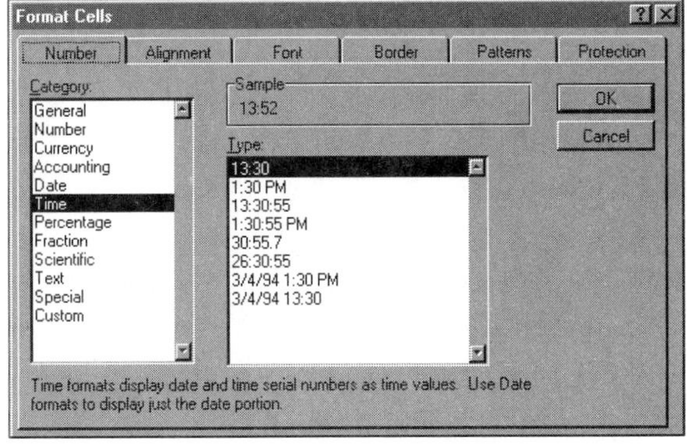

FIGURE 12-5
Use the Cells command on the Format menu to apply Time formats to cells.

4. Select the format you want to use from the Type list box.
5. Click OK.

See Also For more information about the [h]:mm:ss format, which appears in the Type list box as 26:30:55, see "Measuring Elapsed Time," page 469.

Combining Date and Time Formats

In addition to the built-in formats that display dates and times, the combined format — m/d/yy h:mm — displays the date and time in one cell. For example, if a cell contains the serial value 35260.125 and you apply the m/d/yy h:mm format to that entry, the date and time display as 7/14/96 3:00.

When you enter a combination date and time in format, you can type either *7/14/96 3:00* or *3:00 AM 7-14-96*. In the formula bar, 7/14/96 3:00 is displayed as 7/14/1996 3:00:00 AM because the value for seconds and the AM or PM designation are part of the underlying value of dates and times.

Creating Your Own Date and Time Formats

To supplement the standard Date and Time formats, you can create custom formats. The general technique is the same as the technique for creating custom numeric formats.

For example, to create a format that displays a date in the most complete form, so that the date entry July 14, 1996, appears as Sunday, July 14, 1996, follow these steps:

1. Select the cell that contains the date.
2. From the Format menu, choose Cells (or press Ctrl-1) and click the Number tab.
3. Select the Custom category.
4. Highlight the entry in the Type edit box and type your custom format — in this case, *dddd mmmm d, yyyy*.
5. Click OK. Excel stores the new format in the Type list box for the Custom category and displays the date with the new format in the selected cell.

You can use the same technique to display only a portion of a date or a time. For example, if you enter the format *mmmm,* Excel displays the date July 14, 1996, as the word *July*.

After you add a custom Date or Time format to the Type list box, you can apply it to any date or time entry. You simply select the cell that contains the entry, choose the Cells command from the Format menu (or press Ctrl-1), click the Number tab, select the Custom category, select the format from the Type list box, and click OK to apply the format.

The table on the next page shows the formatting codes you can use to create custom date and time formats. Keep in mind two points. First, when you enter the code *m* immediately after an *h* or the code *mm* immediately after an *hh,* Excel displays minutes instead of months; otherwise, Excel assumes that *m* means months. Second, if you include one of the codes AM/PM, am/pm, A/P, or a/p in a time format, Excel uses the 12-hour time convention; if you omit these codes, Excel uses the 24-hour time convention.

See Also For more information about custom formats, see "Creating Custom Numeric Formats," page 170.

Measuring Elapsed Time

The brackets listed at the bottom of the table on the next page deserve some special discussion. You can enclose time codes in brackets to display more than 24 hours, more than 60 minutes, or more than 60 seconds in a time value. The brackets must always appear around the first code in the format. Excel provides one built-in elapsed time code, [h]:mm:ss. Other valid bracketed time codes are

[mm]:ss

[ss]

Bracketed codes have no effect if used in any other position. For example, the code h:[mm]:ss simply indicates the normal h:mm:ss format.

Suppose you want to determine the elapsed time between two dates and you enter the following in cells A1, A2, and A3, respectively:

11/23/96 13:32

11/25/96 23:59

=A2–A1

If you apply the built-in format [h]:mm:ss to cell A3, the result of the formula in that cell is 58:27:00, the elapsed time between the two dates. If you apply the standard h:mm:ss format to cell A3 instead, the result is 10:27:00, the difference in the times, without regard to the difference in dates. The [h]:mm:ss format is also available in the Time category, where it appears in the Type list box as 26:30:55.

Code	Display
General	Number in General format
d	Day number without leading zero (1–31)
dd	Day number with leading zero (01–31)
ddd	Day-of-week abbreviation (Sun–Sat)
dddd	Day-of-week name (Sunday–Saturday)
m	Month number without leading zero (1–12)
mm	Month number with leading zero (01–12)
mmm	Month name abbreviation (Jan–Dec)
mmmm	Complete month name (January–December)
yy	Last two digits of year number (00–99)
yyyy	Entire year number (1900–2078)
h	Hour without leading zero (0–23)
hh	Hour with leading zero (00–23)
m	Minute without leading zero (0–59)
mm	Minute with leading zero (00–59)
s	Second without leading zero (0–59)
ss	Second with leading zero (00–59)
s.0	Second and tenth of second without leading zero
s.00	Second and hundredth of second without leading zero
ss.0	Second and tenth of second with leading zero
ss.00	Second and hundredth of second with leading zero
AM/PM	Time in AM/PM notation
am/pm	Time in am/pm notation
A/P	Time in A/P notation
a/p	Time in a/p notation
[ ]	When used to enclose a time code, as in [h], displays the absolute elapsed time; allows you to display more than 24 hours, 60 minutes, or 60 seconds.

Using Date and Time Arithmetic

After you enter a date, you can use it in formulas and functions as you would any other value. Suppose you want to calculate the date 200 days after July 4, 1996. If cell A1 contains the entry 7/4/96, you can use the formula

```
=A1+200
```

to compute the date 200 days later, which is 35450, or 1/20/97.

As another example, suppose you want to find the number of weeks between October 31, 1996, and May 13, 1997. Use the formula

```
=(("5/13/97")–("10/31/96"))/7
```

which results in approximately 27.7 (weeks).

TIP To display a date or time's serial value, just reformat the cell in the General format. You can quickly apply the General format by pressing Ctrl-Shift-~ (tilde). Press Ctrl-Z if you want to undo the formatting change.

You can use times in formulas and functions just as you can use dates. However, the results of time arithmetic are not as easy to understand as the results of date arithmetic. For example, you can determine how much time has elapsed between 8:22 AM and 10:45 PM with this formula

```
="22:45"–"8:22"
```

The result is .599306, which can be formatted as 2:23 PM. Excel displays the result in relation to 12 midnight, therefore 2:23 PM indicates that there are 14 hours and 23 minutes between the two times.

Suppose you want to determine the time that is 2 hours, 23 minutes, and 17 seconds after 12:35:23 PM. The formula

```
=("12:35:23 PM")+("2:23:17")
```

returns the correct answer: .624074, which can be formatted as 2:58 PM. In this formula, 2:23:17 represents not an absolute time (2:23:17 AM) but an interval of time (2 hours, 23 minutes, and 17 seconds). This format is perfectly acceptable to Excel.

NOTE Excel's default format doesn't display the seconds, but the time's full value — 0.624074074074074 — includes them.

Date and Time Functions

Microsoft Excel's date and time functions let you perform worksheet calculations quickly and accurately. For example, if you use your workseet to calculate your company's monthly payroll, you might use the HOUR function to determine the number of hours worked each day and the WEEKDAY function to determine whether employees should be paid at the standard rate (for Monday through Friday) or at the overtime rate (for Saturdays and Sundays).

The DATE Function

You can use the basic date function, DATE, to enter a date in a cell. DATE is particularly useful when all or part of a date is the result of a formula and not a known value. This function takes the form

=DATE(*year,month,day*)

The arguments in the DATE function must appear in descending order of magnitude: years, months, days.

The result of DATE is a serial value that represents the number of days that have elapsed between the base date and the specified date. For example, if you use the formula

=DATE(96,6,19)

to enter the date June 19, 1996, the result is the serial value 35235, which Excel displays as 6/19/96.

Excel liberally interprets DATE function arguments. If you enter a DATE function with a day argument that is higher than the last day of the month, Excel simply counts forward into the next month. For example, if you enter the formula

=DATE(96,7,50)

Excel stores the serial date value for August 19, 1996. This flexibility comes in handy when you are performing date arithmetic.

Your day argument can be as high as you want, as long as it does not exceed the maximum serial date value of 65380. Similarly, your month argument can be higher than 12. Excel simply counts forward into subsequent years to interpret a DATE function whose month argument is 13 or higher.

If you use 0 as the day argument in a DATE function, Excel interprets the value as the last day of the previous month. For example, if you enter

=DATE(96,3,0)

Excel stores the serial value for the displayed date February 29, 1996. Similarly, if you enter 0 for the month, December of the previous year is displayed. For example, if you enter

=DATE(96,0,0)

Excel moves both the month and the day back and stores the serial value for November 30, 1995.

You can use a negative number as the day argument to "count backward" in the previous month. For example, if you enter

=DATE(96,8,–6)

Excel stores the serial value for July 25, 1996.

Excel can also calculate the value of a DATE argument. For example, to display the date that is 26 days before September 3, 1996, you enter the formula

=DATE(96,9,3–26)

The result is 35285, or 8/8/96.

The TODAY Function

The TODAY function is a special form of the DATE function. Whereas DATE returns the serial value of any date, TODAY always returns the serial value of the current date. The TODAY function takes the form

=TODAY( )

Although this function takes no argument, you must remember to include the empty parentheses.

Use this function when you want a date on your worksheet to always reflect the current date.

The TIME Function

You can use a function to enter the appropriate time in a cell and then use one of Excel's built-in Time formats to make the result presentable. The primary time function is TIME, which takes the form

=TIME(*hour, minute, second)*

The *hour* argument is the hours, *minute* the minutes, and *seconds* the seconds. The *seconds* argument is optional. If you omit it, you must include a comma after the *minute* argument, like this:

=TIME(*hour, minute,*)

The result of the TIME function is a decimal value that represents the portion of the day between midnight and the specified time. The TIME function uses the 24-hour time convention. Thus, 2:15 PM is represented by the formula

=TIME(14,15,)

As with the DATE function, you can use large numbers and negative numbers as arguments in the TIME function. For example, the formula

=TIME(12,60,)

returns 1:00 PM. Normally, the maximum value for the minute argument is 59, so when Excel encounters a minute value of 60, it increases the hour value by one.

You can also have Excel calculate the value of an argument. For example, if you want to know the time 35 seconds before 5:00:14, you can use the formula

```
=TIME(5,0,14–35)
```

Excel returns 4:59:39 AM.

For more information about codes and measuring time, see "Measuring Elapsed Time," page 469.

For more information about using dates and times in formulas and functions, see "Using Date and Time Arithmetic," page 470.

The NOW Function

You can use the NOW function to enter the current date and time in a cell. This function takes the form

```
=NOW( )
```

Like the TODAY function, the NOW function has no argument. The result of the function is a serial date and time value that includes an integer (the date) and a decimal value (the time). For example, if today is July 21, 1996, and the time is 11:45 AM, the NOW function returns the value 35267.49.

Excel doesn't update the value of NOW continuously. If the value of a cell that contains the NOW function is not current, you can update the value by recalculating the worksheet. (You calculate the worksheet by making an entry, by clicking the Calc Now button on the Calculation tab of the Options dialog box, or by pressing F9 or Ctrl-=.) Excel also updates the NOW function whenever you open the worksheet.

The NOW function is an example of a *volatile* function; that is, a function whose calculated value is subject to change. If you open a worksheet that contains one or more NOW functions and then immediately close the work- sheet, Excel prompts you to save your changes even though you haven't made any, because the current value of NOW has changed since the last time you used the worksheet. (Another example of a volatile function is RAND.)

For more information about the RAND function, see "The RAND and RANDBETWEEN Functions," page 415.

The WEEKDAY Function

The WEEKDAY function returns the day of the week for a specific date and takes the form

=WEEKDAY(*serial_number,return_type*)

The *serial_number* argument can be a serial date value, a reference to a cell that contains either a date function or a serial date value, or text, such as 1/27/96 or January 27, 1996. If you use text, be sure to enclose it in quotation marks.

The WEEKDAY function returns a number that represents the day of the week that the specified date falls on. The optional *return_type* argument determines the way the result is represented. If *return_type* is 1 or omitted, the function returns a number from 1 through 7 where 1 is Sunday and 7 is Saturday. If *return_type* is 2, the function returns a number from 1 through 7 where 1 is Monday and 7 is Sunday. If *return_type* is 3, the function returns a number from 0 through 6 where 0 is Monday and 6 is Sunday.

TIP You might want to format a cell containing the WEEKDAY function with a custom day-of-week format, such as *dddd*. This formatting lets you use the result of the WEEKDAY function in other functions and still have a meaningful display on the screen.

The YEAR, MONTH, and DAY Functions

The YEAR, MONTH, and DAY functions return the value of the year, month, and day portions of a serial date/time value. These functions take the form

=YEAR(*serial_number*)

and

=MONTH(*serial_number*)

and

=DAY(*serial_number*)

The *serial_number* argument can be a serial date value, a reference to a cell that contains either a date function or a serial date value, or a text date enclosed in quotation marks.

The result of these functions is the value of the corresponding part of the specified *serial_number* argument. For example, if cell A1 contains the date

3/25/1996

the formula

=YEAR(A1)

returns the value 1996, the formula

=MONTH(A1)

returns the value 3, and the formula

=DAY(A1)

returns the value 25.

The HOUR, MINUTE, and SECOND Functions

Just as the YEAR, MONTH, and DAY functions let you extract the year, month, and day portions of a serial date/time value, the HOUR, MINUTE, and SECOND functions extract the hour, minute, and second portions of a serial date/time value. These functions take the form

=HOUR(*serial_number*)

and

=MINUTE(*serial_number*)

and

=SECOND(*serial_number*)

The result of these functions is the value of the corresponding part of the specified *serial_number* argument. For example, if cell B1 contains the time

12:15:35 PM

the formula

=HOUR(B1)

returns the value 12, the formula

=MINUTE(B1)

returns the value 15, and the formula

=SECOND(B1)

returns the value 35.

The DATEVALUE and TIMEVALUE Functions

Excel's DATEVALUE function translates a date into a serial value. It is similar to the DATE function, except that you must enter a text argument. The DATEVALUE function takes the form

=DATEVALUE(*date_text*)

The *date_text* argument represents any date between January 1, 1900 and December 31, 2078 in any of Excel's built-in Date formats. (You must add quotation marks around the text.) For example, the formula

=DATEVALUE("3/25/96")

returns the serial value 35149. If you enter *date_text* without a year, Excel uses the current year from your computer's internal clock.

The TIMEVALUE function translates a time into a decimal value. It is similar to the TIME function, except that you must enter a text argument. The TIMEVALUE function takes the form

=TIMEVALUE(*time_text*)

The *time_text* argument represents a time in any of Excel's built-in Time formats. (You must add quotation marks around the text.) For example, if you enter

=TIMEVALUE("4:30 PM")

the function returns the decimal value 0.6875.

The DAYS360 Function

Certain date calculations routinely used in the securities industry are based on an artificial 360-day year, which consists of twelve 30-day months. If you need to make such calculations, use the DAYS360 function instead of subtracting one date from another. This function takes the form

=DAYS360(*start_date,end_date,method*)

For example, to determine the number of days between July 1, 1996, and December 15, 1996, based on the 360-day year, use the formula

=DAYS360("7-1-96","12-15-96")

which results in 164. Note that if you use dates entered "in format" instead of serial values as the *start_date* and *end_date* arguments, you must enclose them in quotation marks. Alternatively, you can use references to cells that contain the start and end dates. For example, if cell A1 contains the value 7/1/96 and cell A2 contains the value 12/15/96, you can find the interval between these dates by using the formula

=DAYS360(A1,A2)

The optional *method* argument accepts either 1 (TRUE) or 0 (FALSE). If you enter *1,* the European method of calculation is used. If the starting date is the 31st, the 30th is used. If the ending date is the 31st, the first of the next month is used (except when the starting date is the 30th). February 30 is always used instead of February 28 or 29.

Specialized Date Functions

A set of specialized date functions perform operations such as calculations for the maturity dates of securities, for payroll, and for work schedules. The functions described in this section are available only when you install the Analysis ToolPak add-in.

For more information about the Analysis ToolPak, see "Accessing the Analysis ToolPak," page 504.

The EDATE and EOMONTH Functions

You use the EDATE function to calculate the exact date that falls an indicated number of months before or after a given date. This function takes the form

=EDATE(*start_date,months*)

The *start_date* argument is the date you want to calculate from, and *months* is an integer value that indicates the number of months before or after the start date. If the *months* argument is positive, the EDATE function returns a date after the start date; if the *months* argument is negative, the function returns a date before the start date.

For example, to find the date that falls exactly 23 months after June 12, 1996, enter the formula

=EDATE("6/12/96",23)

which returns the value 35927, or May 12, 1998.

The EOMONTH function returns a date that is an indicated number of months before or after a given date. EOMONTH is similar to EDATE, except that the value returned is always the last day of the month. The EOMONTH function takes the form

=EOMONTH(*start_date,months*)

For example, to calculate the serial date value that is the last day of the month and 23 months after June 12, 1996, enter the formula

=EOMONTH("6/12/96",23)

which returns 35946, or May 31, 1998.

The YEARFRAC Function

The YEARFRAC function calculates a decimal number that represents the portion of a year that falls between two given dates. This function takes the form

=YEARFRAC(*start_date,end_date,basis*)

The *start_date* and *end_date* arguments specify the period of time you want to convert to a fractional year. *Basis* is the type of day count you want to use. A *basis* argument of 0 (or omitted) indicates a basis of 30/360, or 30 days per month and 360 days per year, as established in the United States by the National Association of Security Dealers (NASD). A basis of 1 indicates actual/actual, or the actual number of days in the month(s)/actual days in the year. Similarly, a basis of 2 indicates actual/360, and a basis of 3 indicates actual/365. A basis of 4 indicates the European method of determining the basis, which also uses 30 days per month/360 days per year.

For example, to determine the fraction of a year that falls between 4/12/96 and 12/15/96, enter the formula

```
=YEARFRAC("4/12/96","12/15/96")
```

which returns 0.675, based on the default 30-day month and 360-day year.

The WORKDAY and NETWORKDAYS Functions

The WORKDAY and NETWORKDAYS functions are invaluable for anyone who calculates payroll and benefits or who determines work schedules. Both functions return values that are based on working days only, excluding weekend days. In addition, you can choose whether to include holidays and specify the exact dates.

The WORKDAY function returns the date that is exactly the indicated number of working days before or after a given date. This function takes the form

=WORKDAY(*start_date,days,holidays*)

The *start_date* argument is the date you want the function to count from, and *days* is the number of workdays before or after the start date, excluding weekends and holidays. Use a positive value for *days* to count forward from the start date; use a negative value to count backward. For example, to determine the date that is 100 working days from the current date, use the formula

```
=WORKDAY(NOW( ),100)
```

The optional *holidays* argument can be an array or a reference to a cell range that contains the dates you want to exclude from the calculation. Simply enter any dates that you want to exclude in the array or range specified as this argument. If you leave *holidays* blank, the function counts all weekdays from the start date. For example, to exclude holidays for 1996, the following formula uses the serial date values for January 1, February 19, May 27, July 4, September 2, October 7, November 21, and December 25 as the *holidays* argument, entered in array style:

```
=WORKDAY(NOW( ),100,{"1/1/96","2/19/96","5/27/96","7/4/96","9/2/96",
"10/7/96","11/21/96","12/25/96"})
```

Similarly, the NETWORKDAYS function calculates the number of working days between two given dates. This function takes the form

=NETWORKDAYS(*start_date,end_date,holidays*)

The *end_date* argument is the last date you want to include in the range. Again, you can choose to exclude holidays. For example, to determine the number of working days (holidays included) between January 15, 1996, and June 30, 1996, use the formula

=NETWORKDAYS("1/15/96","6/30/96")

which results in a value of 120.

Chapter 13

Financial Analysis

The Microsoft Excel financial functions allow you to perform common business calculations, such as net present value and future value, without building long and complex formulas. For example, suppose you're considering a real-estate purchase and want to calculate the net present value of the purchase price to determine whether the investment is worthwhile. To find this value without using functions, you would have to build a formula similar to this one:

```
=(A1/(1+.08))+(B1/(1+.08)^2)+(C1/(1+.08)^3)+(D1/(1+.08)^4)
```

Using the NPV function, you can perform the same calculation with only 15 keystrokes:

```
=NPV(.08,A1:D1)
```

NOTE Many of the financial functions discussed in this chapter are supplied with the Analysis ToolPak add-in. For information about accessing the Analysis ToolPak add-in, see "Accessing the Analysis ToolPak," page 522.

Functions for Calculating Investments

Most financial functions accept similar arguments. To streamline this section, we'll define the common arguments in the following table and explain any differences in how they are used in the individual function descriptions. Another list of common arguments accompanies the section on depreciation.

Argument	Description
future value	Value of investment at end of term (0 if omitted)
inflow 1, inflow 2, ..., inflow n	Periodic payments when individual amounts differ
number of periods	Term of investment
payment	Periodic payments when individual amounts are the same
type	When payment is to be made (0 if omitted) 0 = at end of period 1 = at beginning of period

(continued)

continued

Argument	Description
period	Number of an individual periodic payment
present value	Value of investment today
rate	Discount rate or interest rate

The PV Function

Present value is one of the most common methods for measuring the attractiveness of a long-term investment. Basically, present value is today's value of the investment. It is determined by discounting the inflows (payments received) from the investment back to the present time. If the present value of the inflows is greater than the cost of the investment, the investment is a good one.

The PV function computes the present value of a series of equal periodic payments or of a lump-sum payment. (A stream of constant payments is often called an *ordinary annuity.*) This function takes the form

=PV(*rate,number of periods,payment,future value,type*)

For definitions of these arguments, see the table on this page. To compute the present value of a series of payments, use *payment,* and to compute the present value of a lump-sum payment, use *future value.* For an investment with both a series of payments and a lump-sum payment, you use both arguments.

Suppose you are presented with an investment opportunity that returns $1,000 each year over the next five years. To receive this annuity, you must invest $4,000. Are you willing to pay $4,000 today to earn $5,000 over the next five years? To decide whether this investment is acceptable, you need to determine the present value of the stream of $1,000 payments you will receive.

Assuming that you could invest your money in a money-market account at 4.5 percent, we'll use 4.5 percent as the discount rate of the investment. (Because this discount rate is a sort of "hurdle" over which an investment must leap before it becomes attractive to you, it is often called the *hurdle rate.*) To determine the present value of this investment, use the formula

=PV(4.5%,5,1000)

This formula uses a *payment* argument, has no *future value* argument, and has no *type* argument, indicating that payments occur at the end of the period (the default). This formula returns the value –4389.98, meaning that you should be willing to spend $4,389.98 now to receive $5,000 over the next five years. Because your investment is only $4,000, you decide that this is an acceptable investment.

Now suppose you're offered $5,000 at the end of five years, rather than $1,000 for each of the next five years. Is the investment still as attractive? To find out, use the formula

=PV(4.5%,5,,5000)

You must include a comma as a placeholder for the unused *payment* argument so that Excel knows that 5000 is a *future value* argument. Again, no *type* argument is used. This formula returns the present value –4012.26, which means that, at a hurdle rate of 4.5 percent, you should be willing to spend $4,012.26 to receive $5,000 in five years. Although the proposal is not as attractive under these terms, it is still acceptable because your investment is only $4,000.

The NPV Function

Net present value is another common method for determining the profitability of an investment. In general, any investment that yields a net present value greater than zero is considered profitable. This function takes the form

=NPV(*rate,inflow 1,inflow 2,...,inflow 29*)

For definitions of these arguments, see the table on pages 482 and 483. As many as 29 *inflow* values are allowed as arguments. (Any number of values can be plugged into the formula by using an array as an argument.)

NPV differs from PV in two important respects. Whereas PV assumes constant *inflow* values, NPV allows variable payments. The other major difference is that PV allows payments and receipts to occur at either the beginning or end of the period, whereas NPV assumes that all payments and receipts are evenly distributed and occur at the end of the period. If the cost of the investment must be paid up front, you should not include the cost as one of the function's *inflow* arguments but should subtract it from the result of the function. On the other hand, if the cost must be paid at the end of the first period, you should include it as a negative first *inflow* argument. Let's consider some examples to help clarify this distinction.

Suppose you are contemplating an investment on which you expect to incur a loss of $55,000 at the end of the first year, followed by gains of $95,000, $140,000, and $185,000 at the ends of the second, third, and fourth years. You will invest $250,000 up front, and the hurdle rate is 12 percent. To evaluate this investment, use the formula

=NPV(12%,–55000,95000,140000,185000) –250000

The result, – 6153.65, tells you not to expect a net profit from this investment. Note that the negative values in this formula indicate the money you spend on your investment. (To determine what initial cost or interest rate would justify the investment, you can use the Goal Seek command.)

This formula does not include the up-front cost of the investment as an argument for the NPV function. However, if you make the initial $250,000 investment at the end of the first year, the formula is

=NPV(12%,(–250000–55000),95000,140000,185000)

See Also For more information about the Goal Seek command, see "The Goal Seek Command," page 565.

The FV Function

Future value is essentially the opposite of present value, and the FV function computes the value at some future date of an investment that makes payments as a lump sum or as a series of equal periodic payments. This function takes the form

=FV(*rate,number of periods,payment,present value,type*)

For definitions of these arguments, see the table on pages 482 and 483. You use *payment* to compute the future value of a series of payments and *present value* to compute the future value of a lump-sum payment.

Suppose you're thinking about starting an IRA. You plan to deposit $2,000 at the beginning of each year in the IRA, and you expect the average rate of return to be 11 percent per year for the entire term. Assuming you're now 30 years old, how much money will your account accumulate by the time you're 65? Use the formula

=FV(11%,35,–2000,,1)

to learn that your IRA balance will be $758,328.81 at the end of 35 years.

Now assume that you started an IRA account three years ago and have already accumulated $7,500 in your account. Use the formula

=FV(11%,35,–2000,–7500,1)

to learn that your IRA will grow to $1,047,640.19 at the end of 35 years.

In both of these examples, the *type* argument is 1 because payments occur at the beginning of the period. Including this argument is particularly important in financial calculations that span many years. If you omit the *type* argument in the formula above, Excel assumes that you add money to your account at the end of each year and returns the value $972,490.49 — a difference of more than $75,000!

The PMT Function

The PMT function computes the periodic payment required to amortize a loan over a specified number of periods. This function takes the form

=PMT(*rate,number of periods,present value,future value,type*)

For definitions of these arguments, see the table on pages 482 and 483.

Suppose you want to take out a 25-year mortgage for $100,000. Assuming an interest rate of 8 percent, what will your monthly payments be? First divide the 8 percent interest rate by 12 to arrive at a monthly rate (approximately 0.67 percent). Next convert the number of periods into months by multiplying 25 by 12 (300). Now plug the monthly rate, number of periods, and loan amount into the PMT formula

=PMT(0.67%,300,100000)

to compute the monthly mortgage payment, which turns out to be –$774.47. (The result is negative because it is a cost to you.)

Because 0.67 percent is an approximation, you could use the formula

=PMT((8/12)%,300,100000)

for a more accurate result. This formula returns –$771.82.

The IPMT Function

The IPMT function computes the interest part of the payment required to repay an amount over a specified time period, with constant periodic payments and a constant interest rate. This function takes the form

=IPMT(*rate,period,number of periods,present value,future value,type*)

For definitions of these arguments, see the table on pages 482 and 483.

As in the previous example, suppose you borrow $100,000 for 25 years at 8 percent interest. The formula

=IPMT((8/12)%,1,300,100000)

tells you that the interest component of the payment due for the first month is –$666.67. The formula

=IPMT((8/12)%,300,300,100000)

tells you that the interest component of the final payment of the same loan is –$5.11.

The PPMT Function

The PPMT function is similar to the IPMT function, except that it computes the principal component of the payment when a loan is repaid over a specified time period with constant periodic payments and a constant interest rate. If you compute both IPMT and PPMT for the same period, you can add the results to obtain the total payment. The PPMT function takes the form

=PPMT(*rate,period,number of periods,present value,future value,type*)

For definitions of these arguments, see the table on pages 482 and 483.

Again suppose you borrow $100,000 for 25 years at 8 percent interest. The formula

=PPMT((8/12)%,1,300,100000)

tells you that the principal component of the payment for the first month of the loan is –$105.15. The formula

=PPMT((8/12)%,300,300,100000)

tells you that the principal component of the final payment of the same loan is –$766.70.

The NPER Function

The NPER function computes the number of periods required to amortize a loan, given a specified periodic payment. This function takes the form

=NPER(*rate,payment,present value,future value,type*)

For definitions of these arguments, see the table on pages 482 and 483.

Suppose you can afford mortgage payments of $1,000 per month and you want to know how long it will take to pay off a $100,000 loan at 8 percent interest. The formula

=NPER((8/12)%,–1000,100000)

tells you that your mortgage payments will extend over 165.34 months.

If the *payment* argument is too small to amortize the loan at the indicated rate of interest, the function returns an error value. The monthly payment must at least be equal to the period interest rate times the principal amount; otherwise, the loan will never be amortized. For example, the formula

=NPER((8/12)%,–600,100000)

returns the #NUM! error value. In this case, the monthly payment must be at least $666.67 (or $100,000 * (8/12)%) to amortize the loan.

Functions for Calculating the Rate of Return

The RATE, IRR, and MIRR functions compute the continuously paid rates of return on investments.

The RATE Function

The RATE function lets you determine the rate of return of an investment that generates a series of equal periodic payments or a single lump-sum payment. This function takes the form

=RATE(*number of periods,payment,present value,future value,type,guess*)

For definitions of these arguments, see the table on pages 482 and 483. You use *payment* to compute the rate for a series of equal periodic payments and *future value* to compute the rate of a lump-sum payment. The *guess* argument, which like *type* is optional, gives Excel a starting place for calculating the rate. If you omit the *guess* argument, Excel begins with a guess of 0.1 (10 percent).

Suppose you're considering an investment that will pay you five annual $1,000 payments. The investment costs $3,000. To determine the actual annual rate of return on your investment, use the formula

=RATE(5,1000,–3000)

This formula returns 20%, the rate of return on this investment. The exact value returned is 0.198577098, but because the answer is a percent, Excel formats the cell as a percent.

The RATE function uses an iterative process to compute the rate of return. The function begins by computing the net present value of the investment at the *guess* rate. If that first net present value is greater than zero, the function selects a higher rate and repeats the net present value calculation; if the first net present value is less than zero, the function selects a lower rate for the second iteration. RATE continues this process until it arrives at the correct rate of return or until it has gone through 20 iterations.

If you receive the #NUM! error value when you enter the RATE function, Excel probably cannot calculate the rate within 20 iterations. Try entering a different *guess* rate to give the function a running start. A rate between 10 percent and 100 percent usually works.

The IRR Function

The internal rate of return of an investment is the rate that causes the net present value of the investment to equal zero. In other words, the internal rate of return is the rate that causes the present value of the inflows from an investment to exactly equal the cost of the investment.

Internal rate of return, like net present value, is used to compare one investment opportunity with another. An attractive investment is one whose net present value, discounted at the appropriate hurdle rate, is greater than zero. Turn that equation around and you can see that the discount rate required to generate a net present value of zero must be greater than the hurdle rate. Thus, an attractive investment is one for which the discount rate required to yield a net present value of zero — that is, the internal rate of return — is greater than the hurdle rate.

The IRR function is closely related to the RATE function. The difference between RATE and IRR is similar to the difference between the PV and NPV functions. Like NPV, IRR accounts for investment costs and unequal payments. The IRR function takes the form

=IRR(*values,guess*)

The *values* argument is an array or a reference to a range of cells that contain numbers. Only one *values* argument is allowed, and it must include at least one positive and one negative value. IRR ignores text, logical values, and blank cells. IRR assumes that transactions occur at the end of a period and returns the equivalent interest rate for that period's length.

As with RATE, the *guess* argument gives Excel a starting place for its calculations and is optional. If you receive the #NUM! error value when you enter an IRR function, include a *guess* argument in the function to help Excel reach the answer.

Suppose you agree to buy a condominium for $120,000. Over the next five years, you expect to receive $25,000, $27,000, $35,000, $38,000, and $40,000 in net rental income. You can set up a simple worksheet that contains your investment and income information. Enter the six values into cells A1:A6 of the worksheet. (Be sure to enter the initial $120,000 investment as a negative value.) Then the formula

=IRR(A1:A6)

returns the internal rate of return of 11 percent. If the hurdle rate is 10 percent, you can consider this condominium purchase a good investment.

The MIRR Function

The MIRR function is similar to IRR in that it calculates the rate of return of an investment: the modified internal rate of return. The difference is that MIRR takes into account the cost of the money you borrow to finance the investment and assumes that you'll reinvest the cash it generates. MIRR assumes that transactions occur at the end of a period and returns the equivalent interest rate for that period's length. The MIRR function takes the form

=MIRR(*values,finance rate,reinvestment rate*)

The *values* argument must be an array or a reference to a range of cells that contain numbers, and it represents a series of payments and income occurring at regular periods. You must include at least one positive and one negative value in the *values* argument. The *finance rate* argument is the rate at which you borrow the money you need for the investment. The *reinvestment rate* argument is the rate at which you reinvest the cash.

Continuing with the example from the IRR function, use the formula

```
=MIRR(A1:A6,10%,8%)
```

to calculate a modified internal rate of return of 10 percent, assuming a cost of funds rate of 10 percent and a reinvestment rate of 8 percent.

Functions for Calculating Depreciation

Five functions help you determine the depreciation of an asset for a specific period: the SLN, DDB, DB, VDB, and SYD functions. The following table lists four arguments commonly used in these functions:

Argument	Description
cost	Initial cost of asset
life	Length of time asset will be depreciated
period	Individual time period to be computed
salvage	Asset's remaining value after it has been fully depreciated

The SLN Function

The SLN function lets you determine the straight-line depreciation for an asset for a single period. The straight-line depreciation method assumes that depreciation is uniform throughout the useful life of the asset. The cost or basis of the asset, less its estimated salvage value, is deductible in equal amounts over the life of the asset. This function takes the form

=SLN(*cost*,*salvage*,*life*)

Suppose you want to depreciate a machine that costs $8,000 new and has a life of 10 years and a salvage value of $500. The formula

```
=SLN(8000,500,10)
```

tells you that each year's straight-line depreciation is $750.

The DDB and DB Functions

The DDB function computes an asset's depreciation using the double-declining balance method, which returns depreciation at an accelerated rate — more in the early periods and less later. Using this method, depreciation is computed as a percentage of the net book value of the asset (the cost of the asset less any prior years' depreciation). The function takes the form

=DDB(*cost,salvage,life,period,factor*)

For definitions of the first four arguments, see the table on page 490. All DDB arguments must be positive numbers, and you must use the same time units for *life* and *period;* that is, if you express *life* in months, *period* must also be in months. The *factor* argument is optional and has a default value of 2, which indicates the normal double-declining balance method. Using 3 for the *factor* argument specifies the triple-declining balance method.

Suppose you want to depreciate a machine that costs $5,000 new and that has a life of five years (60 months) and a salvage value of $100. The formula

=DDB(5000,100,60,1)

tells you that the double-declining balance depreciation for the first month is $166.67. The formula

=DDB(5000,100,5,1)

tells you that the double-declining balance depreciation for the first year is $2,000.00. The formula

=DDB(5000,100,5,5)

computes the double-declining balance depreciation for the last year as $259.20.

The DB function is similar to the DDB function except that it uses the fixed declining balance method of depreciation and can calculate the depreciation for a particular period in the asset's life. This function takes the form

=DB(*cost,salvage,life,period,month*)

For definitions of the first four arguments, see the table on page 490. The *life* and *period* arguments must use the same units. The *month* argument is the number of months in the first year. If you omit this argument, Excel assumes *month* to be 12, a full year. For example, to calculate the real depreciation for the first period on a $1,000,000 item with a salvage value of $100,000, a life of six years, and seven months in the first year, use the formula

=DB(1000000,100000,6,1,7)

which returns $186,083.33.

The VDB Function

The VDB function calculates the depreciation of an asset for any complete or partial period, using either the double-declining balance or another accelerated-depreciation factor that you specify. (VDB stands for *variable declining balance.*) This function takes the form

=VDB(*cost,salvage,life,start,end,factor,no_switch*)

For definitions of the first three arguments, see the table on page 490. The *start* argument is the period after which depreciation will be calculated, and *end* is the last period for which depreciation will be calculated. These arguments let you determine the depreciation for any length of time during the life of the asset. The *life, start,* and *end* arguments must all use the same units (days, months, years, and so on). The *factor* argument is the rate at which the balance declines. The *no_switch* argument is a value that specifies whether to switch to straight-line depreciation when the straight-line depreciation is greater than the declining balance.

The last two arguments are optional. If you omit *factor,* Excel assumes that the argument is 2 and uses the double-declining balance method. If you omit *no_switch* or set it to 0 (FALSE) Excel switches to straight-line depreciation when the depreciation is greater than the declining balance. To prevent Excel from making this switch, specify a *no_switch* value of 1 (TRUE).

Suppose you purchased a $15,000 asset at the end of the first quarter of the current year and that this asset will have a salvage value of $2,000 after five years. To determine the depreciation of this asset next year (the fourth to seventh quarters of its use), use the formula

=VDB(15000,2000,20,3,7)

The depreciation for this period is $3,670.55. The units used here are quarters. Notice that the *start* argument is 3, not 4, since we are jumping over the first three periods to start in the fourth. This formula does not include a *factor* argument, so Excel calculates the depreciation using the double-declining balance method. To determine the depreciation for the same period using a *factor* of 1.5, use the formula

=VDB(15000,2000,20,3,7,1.5)

With this rate, the depreciation for the same period is $3,180.52.

The SYD Function

The SYD function computes an asset's depreciation for a specific time period with the sum-of-the-years'-digits method. Using the sum-of-the-years'-digits method, depreciation is calculated on the cost of the item less its salvage value. Like the double-declining balance method, the sum-of-the-years'-digits method is an accelerated depreciation method. The SYD function takes the form

=SYD(*cost,salvage,life,period*)

For definitions of these arguments, see the table on page 490. You must use the same units for *life* and *period*.

Suppose you want to depreciate a machine that costs $15,000 and has a life of three years and a salvage value of $1,250. The formula

=SYD(15000,1250,3,1)

tells you that the sum-of-the-years'-digits depreciation for the first year is $6,875. The formula

=SYD(15000,1250,3,3)

tells you that the sum-of-the-years'-digits depreciation for the third year is $2,291.67.

Functions for Analyzing Securities

Excel offers a group of functions designed for specific tasks relating to the computation and analysis of various types of securities. All of these functions are part of the Analysis ToolPak. If these functions are not available, you have not installed the Analysis ToolPak add-in. To install this add-in, choose the Add-ins command from the Tools menu, select Analysis ToolPak-VBA from the Add-ins Available list box, and click OK. If this option is not listed, you will need to run the Microsoft Excel Setup program again to add the ToolPak.

TIP If you think you might want to modify or add to the functions in the Analysis ToolPak but are more familiar with Excel's older macro language than with the newer Visual Basic, consider choosing the Analysis ToolPak option instead of the Analysis ToolPak-VBA option. The Analysis ToolPak add-in's functions were written in the older macro language so that you can more easily read and edit them. For more information about using add-ins, see Chapter 14, "Statistical Analysis," page 503, and Chapter 25, "An Overview of Visual Basic," page 861.

Many of these functions share similar arguments. We'll describe the most common ones in the following table to avoid revisiting the same information in the function discussions that follow.

Argument	Description
basis	Day count basis of the security. If omitted, defaults to 0, indicating US (NASD) 30/360 basis. Other basis values: 1 = actual/actual 2 = actual/360 3 = actual/365 4 = European 30/360
coupon	Annual coupon interest rate of the security
frequency	Number of coupon payments made per year: 1 = annual 2 = semiannual 4 = quarterly
investment	Initial purchase price of the security
issue	Issue date of the security
maturity	Maturity date of the security
par	Par value of the security; $1000 if omitted
price	Security's price per $100 of face value
rate	Interest rate of the security at the issue date
redemption	Value of the security at redemption
settlement	Settlement date of the security (the day you have to pay for it)
yield	Annual yield of the security

Excel calculates functions using serial date values. You can enter dates in a function in three ways: by entering the serial number, by entering the date enclosed in quotation marks, or by entering a reference to a cell that contains a date. For example, June 30, 1996 can be entered as the serial date value 35246, or as "6/30/96." If you enter the date in a cell as 6/30/96 and then reference that cell in the function rather than entering the date itself, Excel uses the serial date value. (To convert dates into serial values, you can use the DATEVALUE function.) If the security-analysis function results in a #NUM! error value, check that the dates are in the correct form.

The *maturity* date value must be greater than the *settlement* date value, which must be greater than the *issue* date value. Also, the *yield* and *rate* arguments must be greater than or equal to zero, and the *redemption* argument must be greater than zero. If any of these conditions is not met, the #NUM! error value is displayed in the cell containing the function.

See Also For more information about the DATEVALUE function, see "The DATEVALUE and TIMEVALUE Functions," page 476.

The DOLLARDE and DOLLARFR Functions

One of this pair of functions converts the familiar fractional pricing of securities to decimals, and the other converts decimals to fractions. These functions take the forms

=DOLLARDE(*fractional_dollar, fraction*)

and

=DOLLARFR(*decimal_dollar, fraction*)

The *fractional_dollar* argument is the value you want to convert expressed as an integer followed by a decimal point and then the numerator of the fraction. *Decimal_dollar* is the value you want to convert expressed as a decimal fraction, and *fraction* is an integer indicating the denominator to be used as a rounding unit. For the DOLLARDE function, *fraction* is the actual denominator of the fraction you are converting. For the DOLLARFR function, *fraction* is the unit the function is to use when converting the decimal value, which effectively rounds the decimal number to the nearest half, quarter, eighth, sixteenth, thirty-second, or whatever the value specified by *fraction*.

For example, the formula

=DOLLARDE(1.03,32)

translates as 1+3/32, which is equivalent to 1.09375. The formula

=DOLLARFR(1.09375,32)

returns the result 1.03.

The ACCRINT and ACCRINTM Functions

The ACCRINT function returns the interest accrued by a security that pays interest on a periodic basis. This function takes the form

=ACCRINT(*issue,first interest date,settlement,coupon,par, frequency,basis*)

For definitions of these arguments, see the table on page 494.

For example, suppose a Treasury bond has an issue date of March 1, 1996, a settlement date of April 1, 1996, a first interest date of September 1, 1996, a

7 percent coupon with semiannual frequency, a par value of $1,000, and a basis of 30/360. The accrued interest formula is

=ACCRINT(35125,35309,35156,0.07,1000,2,0)

which returns 5.833333, indicating that $5.83 accrues between March 1, 1996 and April 1, 1996.

Similarly, the ACCRINTM function returns the interest accrued by a maturity security that pays interest on a periodic basis. This function takes the form

=ACCRINTM(*issue,maturity,coupon,par,basis*)

Using the previous example with a maturity date of July 31, 2001, the accrued interest formula is

=ACCRINTM(35125,37103,0.07,1000,0)

which returns 379.1667, indicating that the $1,000 bond will pay $379.17 interest on July 31, 2001.

The INTRATE and RECEIVED Functions

The INTRATE function calculates the rate of interest, or discount rate, for a fully invested security. This function takes the form

=INTRATE(*settlement,maturity,investment,redemption,basis*)

For definitions of these arguments, see the table on page 494. For example, suppose a bond has a settlement date of March 31, 1996, and a maturity date of September 30, 1996. The $1,000,000 investment will have a redemption value of $1,032,324, using the default 30/360 basis. The bond's discount rate formula is

=INTRATE("3/31/96","9/30/96",1000000,1032324,0)

which returns 0.064648, or 6.46%.

Similarly, the RECEIVED function calculates the amount received at maturity for a fully invested security. The form of this function is

=RECEIVED(*settlement,maturity,investment,discount,basis*)

Using the previous example with a 5.5 percent discount rate, the formula is

=RECEIVED("3/31/96","9/30/96",1000000,.055,0)

which returns 1028277.635, or $1028277.63.

The PRICE, PRICEDISC, and PRICEMAT Functions

The PRICE function calculates the price per $100 of face value of a security that pays interest on a periodic basis. This function takes the form

=PRICE(*settlement,maturity,rate,yield,redemption,frequency,basis*)

For definitions of these arguments, see the table on page 494. For example, suppose a bond's settlement date is March 31, 1996, and its maturity date is July 31, 1996. The interest rate is 5.75 percent, with semiannual frequency. The security's annual yield is 6.50 percent, its redemption value is $100, and it is calculated using the standard 30/360 basis. The bond price formula is

=PRICE("3/31/96","7/31/96",0.0575,0.065,100,2,0)

which returns 99.73498.

Similarly, the PRICEDISC function returns the price per $100 of face value of a security that is discounted instead of paying periodic interest. This function takes the form

=PRICEDISC(*settlement,maturity,discount,redemption,basis*)

Using the preceding example with the addition of a discount amount of 7.5 percent, the formula is

=PRICEDISC("3/31/96","7/31/96",0.075,100,0)

which returns 97.5.

Finally, the PRICEMAT function returns the price per $100 of face value of a security that pays its interest at the maturity date. This function takes the form

=PRICEMAT(*settlement,maturity,issue,rate,yield,basis*)

Using the previous example with an issue date of March 1, 1996, and the maturity date changed to July 31, 1997, the formula is

=PRICEMAT("7/31/96","7/31/97","3/31/96",0.0575,.065,0)

which returns 99.17879.

The DISC Function

The DISC function calculates the discount rate for a security and takes the form

=DISC(*settlement,maturity,price,redemption,basis*)

See the table on page 494 for the definitions of these arguments.

For example, suppose a bond has a settlement date of June 15, 1996, a maturity date of December 31, 1996, a price of 96.875, and a $100 redemption value, and uses the standard 30/360 basis. The bond discount rate formula is

=DISC("6/15/96","12/31/96",96.875,100,0)

which returns 0.057398, or 5.74%.

The YIELD, YIELDDISC, and YIELDMAT Functions

The YIELD function determines the annual yield for a security that pays interest on a periodic basis. It takes the form

=YIELD(*settlement,maturity,rate,price,redemption,frequency,basis*)

For definitions of these arguments, see the table on page 494. For example, suppose a bond has a settlement date of February 15, 1996, a maturity date of December 1, 1996, a coupon rate of 5.75 percent with semiannual frequency, a price of 99.2345, and a $100 redemption value, and uses the standard 30/360 basis. The annual bond yield formula is

=YIELD("2/15/96","12/1/96",0.0575,99.2345,100,2,0)

which returns 0.067406, or 6.741%.

The YIELDDISC function, on the other hand, calculates the annual yield for a discounted security. It takes the form

=YIELDDISC(*settlement,maturity,price,redemption,basis*)

Using the preceding example but changing the price to 96.00, the bond yield formula is

=YIELDDISC("2/15/96","12/1/96",96,100,0)

which returns 0.052448, or 5.245%.

The YIELDMAT function calculates the annual yield for a security that pays its interest at maturity. This function takes the form

=YIELDMAT(*settlement,maturity,issue,rate,price,basis*)

Using the arguments from the YIELD example but adding an issue date of January 1, 1994, and changing the price to $99.2345, the yield-at-maturity formula is

=YIELDMAT("2/15/96","12/1/96","1/1/96",0.0575,99.2345,0)

which returns 0.067178, or 6.718%.

The TBILLEQ, TBILLPRICE, and TBILLYIELD Functions

The TBILLEQ function calculates the bond-equivalent yield for a Treasury bill. It takes the form

=TBILLEQ(*settlement,maturity,discount*)

See the table on page 494 for definitions of these arguments. For example, suppose a Treasury bill has a settlement date of February 1, 1996, a maturity date of July 1, 1996, and a percent discount rate of 8.65. The formula for calculating the Treasury bill yield that is equivalent to the yield of a bond is

=TBILLEQ("2/1/96","7/1/96",0.0865)

which returns 0.091, or 9.1%.

You use the TBILLPRICE function to calculate the price per $100 of face value for a Treasury bill. This function takes the form

=TBILLPRICE(*settlement,maturity,discount*)

Using the previous example, the formula to calculate the price per $100 of face value is

=TBILLPRICE("2/1/96","7/1/96",0.0865)

which returns 96.3718, or $96.37.

Finally, the TBILLYIELD function calculates a Treasury bill's yield. It takes the form

=TBILLYIELD(*settlement,maturity,price*)

Using the previous example with its result, a price of $96.37, the yield formula is

=TBILLYIELD(96.37)

which returns the yield 0.898, or 8.98%.

The COUPDAYBS, COUPDAYS, COUPDAYSNC, COUPNCD, COUPNUM, and COUPPCD Functions

The following group of functions perform calculations relating to bond coupons. For all the sample formulas in this section, we'll use as our example a bond with a settlement date of March 1, 1996, and a maturity date of December 1, 1996. Its coupons are payable semiannually, using the actual/actual basis (that is, a basis argument of 1).

The COUPDAYBS function calculates the number of days from the beginning of the coupon period to the settlement date. This function takes the form

=COUPDAYBS(*settlement,maturity,frequency,basis*)

For definitions of these arguments, see the table on page 494.

Using our sample data, the formula looks like this:

=COUPDAYBS("3/1/96","12/1/96",2,1)

and returns 91.

The COUPDAYS function calculates the number of days in the coupon period that contains the settlement date. This function takes the form

=COUPDAYS(*settlement,maturity,frequency,basis*)

Using our sample data, the formula looks like this:

=COUPDAYS("3/1/96","12/1/96",2,1)

and returns 183.

The COUPDAYSNC function calculates the number of days from the settlement date to the next coupon date. This function takes the form

=COUPDAYSNC(*settlement,maturity,frequency,basis*)

Using our sample data, the formula looks like this:

=COUPDAYSNC("3/1/96","12/1/96",2,1)

and returns 92.

The COUPNCD function calculates the next coupon date after the settlement date. This function takes the form

=COUPNCD(*settlement,maturity,frequency,basis*)

Using our sample data, the formula looks like this:

=COUPNCD("3/1/96","12/1/96",2,1)

and returns 35217, or June 7, 1996.

The COUPNUM function calculates the number of coupons payable between the settlement date and the maturity date and rounds the result to the nearest whole coupon. This function takes the form

=COUPNUM(*settlement,maturity,frequency,basis*)

Using our sample data, the formula looks like this:

=COUPNUM("3/1/96","12/1/96",2,1)

and returns 2.

The COUPPCD function calculates the coupon date previous to the settlement date. It takes the form

=COUPPCD(*settlement,maturity,frequency,basis*)

Using our sample data, the formula looks like this:

=COUPPCD("3/1/96","12/1/96",2,1)

and returns 35034, or December 1, 1995.

The DURATION and MDURATION Functions

The DURATION function calculates the annual duration for a security whose interest payments are made on a periodic basis. Duration is the weighted average of the present value of the bond's cash flows and is used as a measure of how a bond's price responds to changes in yield. This function takes the form

=DURATION(*settlement,maturity,coupon,yield,frequency,basis*)

See the table on page 494 for definitions of these arguments.

For example, suppose a bond has a settlement date of January 1, 1994, a maturity date of December 31, 1999, a semiannual coupon rate of 8.5 percent, a yield of 9.5 percent, and uses the default 30/360 basis. The resulting formula is

=DURATION(34335,36525,0.085,0.095,2,0)

which returns a duration of 4.78708.

The MDURATION function calculates the annual modified duration for a security with interest payments made on a periodic basis, adjusted for market yield per number of coupon payments per year. This function takes the form

=MDURATION(*settlement,maturity,coupon,yield,frequency,basis*)

Using the values from the DURATION formula, the modified duration formula looks like this:

=MDURATION(34335,36525,0.085,0.095,2,0)

and returns a value of 4.570005.

The ODDFPRICE, ODDFYIELD, ODDLPRICE, and ODDLYIELD Functions

This group of functions is used to improve the accuracy of formulas that determine price and yield for securities whose first or last period is unusual. These functions use two arguments in addition to those listed in the table on page 494. The *first_coupon* argument is the security's first coupon due date as a serial date value, and the *last_interest* argument is the security's last coupon due date as a serial date value.

The ODDFPRICE function returns the price per $100 of face value for a security having an odd (short or long) first period. This function takes the form

=ODDFPRICE(*settlement,maturity,issue,first_coupon,rate,yield,redemption, frequency,basis*)

The ODDFYIELD function calculates the yield of a security that has an odd (short or long) first period and takes the form

=ODDFYIELD(*settlement,maturity,issue,first_coupon,rate,price,redemption, frequency,basis*)

The ODDLPRICE function calculates the price per $100 face value of a security having an odd (short or long) last coupon period. This function takes the form

=ODDLPRICE(*settlement,maturity,last_interest,rate,yield,redemption, frequency,basis*)

The ODDLYIELD function calculates the yield of a security that has an odd (short or long) last period and takes the form

=ODDLYIELD(*settlement,maturity,last_interest,rate,price,redemption, frequency,basis*)

Chapter 14

Statistical Analysis

Microsoft Excel provides a wide range of features that can help you analyze statistical data. Built into the program are a number of functions such as AVERAGE, MEDIAN, and MODE that assist in simple analysis tasks. When the built-in statistical functions aren't enough, you can turn to the Analysis ToolPak.

The Analysis ToolPak, an add-in module, provides a collection of functions and tools to augment Excel's built-in analytic capabilities. You can use the ToolPak to create histograms, produce rank-and-percentile tables, extract random or periodic samples from a data set, perform regression analysis, derive statistical measures of a data sample, generate random-number sets that are not uniformly distributed, apply Fourier and other transformations to your data, and more.

Accessing the Analysis ToolPak

The capabilities of the Analysis ToolPak are broad enough to warrant a book of their own. In this chapter, we'll focus on the capabilities that apply to the analysis of statistical data. For details about specific commands and functions not covered here, consult Microsoft Excel's excellent online Help system.

If you performed a complete installation of Excel, the Analysis ToolPak is available each time you start Excel. You can use the ToolPak functions just as you would other Excel functions, and you can access the ToolPak tools by following these steps:

1. Choose Data Analysis from the Tools menu. The first time you choose this command, you'll have to wait a moment while Excel reads a file from disk, and then you'll see the dialog box shown in Figure 14-1.

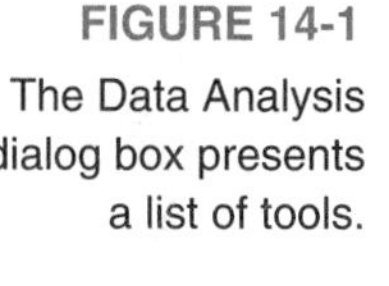

FIGURE 14-1
The Data Analysis dialog box presents a list of tools.

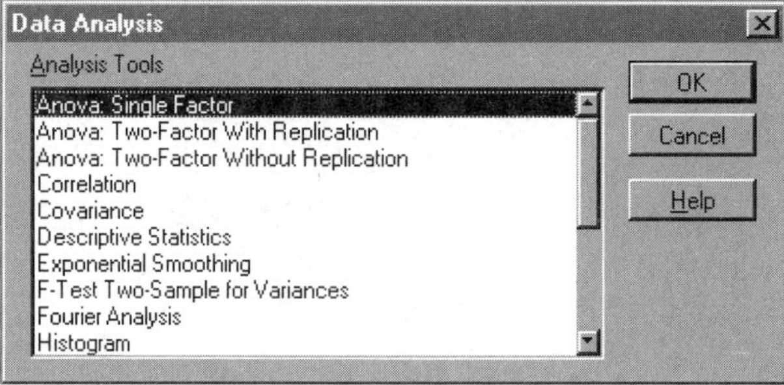

2. To use an analysis tool, select its name from the list box and click OK.
3. Complete the dialog box that appears. In most cases, this means identifying the data you want to analyze by specifying the input range,

telling Excel where you want it to put its analysis by specifying the output range, and selecting the options you want.

If the Data Analysis command does not appear on the Tools menu or if a formula that uses a ToolPak function returns a #NAME? error value, choose Add-Ins from the Tools menu and then select Analysis ToolPak-VBA from the Add-Ins Available list and click OK. If Analysis ToolPak-VBA is not listed in the Add-Ins Available list, you must install it by double-clicking the Microsoft Excel Setup icon.

Analyzing Distributions of Data

In statistics, a collection of measurements is called a *distribution*. With Microsoft Excel, you can analyze distributions using several tools: the built-in statistical functions; the sample and population statistical functions; the Descriptive Statistics tool, which automates the reporting of Descriptive Statistics functions; the Histogram tool; and the rank and percentile functions together with the Rank and Percentile tool.

Built-In Statistical Functions

You use Microsoft Excel's built-in statistical functions to analyze a group (or *population*) of measurements. In this section, we limit the discussion to the most commonly used statistical functions. Excel also offers the advanced statistical functions LINEST, LOGEST, TREND, and GROWTH, which operate on arrays of numbers.

See Also For information about LINEST, LOGEST, TREND, and GROWTH, see "Linear and Exponential Regression," page 534.

The AVERAGE Function

The AVERAGE function computes the arithmetic mean, or average, of the numbers in a range by summing a series of numeric values and then dividing the result by the number of values.

This function takes the form

=AVERAGE(*number1,number2,...*)

AVERAGE ignores blank, logical, and text cells and can be used instead of long formulas. For example, to calculate the average of the sales figures in cells B4 through B15 of Figure 14-2 on the next page, you could use the formula

=(B4+B5+B6+B7+B8+B9+B10+B11+B12+B13+B14+B15)/12

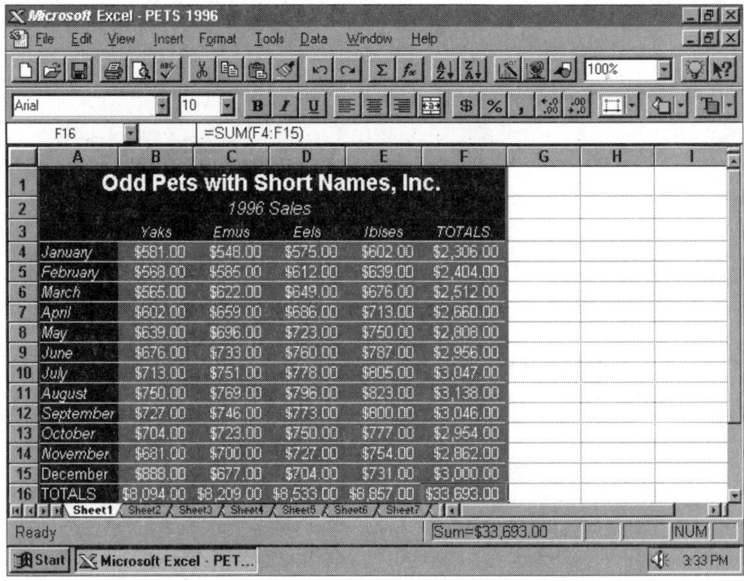

FIGURE 14-2 We'll use this worksheet to demonstrate some of Excel's built-in statistical functions.

to arrive at the result $674.50. This method has the same drawbacks as using the + operator instead of a cell range with the SUM function: You must edit the cell references and the divisor each time you change the range to be averaged. It's obviously more efficient to enter

=AVERAGE(B4:B15)

The MEDIAN Function

The MEDIAN function computes the median of a set of numbers and takes the form

=MEDIAN(*number1,number 2,...*)

The median is the number in the middle of the set; that is, an equal number of values is higher and lower than the median. If *numbers* includes an even number of values, the value returned is the average of the two that lie in the middle of the set.

The MODE Function

The MODE function determines which value occurs most frequently in a set of numbers and takes the form

=MODE(*number1,number 2,...*)

For example, the formula

=MODE(1,3,3,6,7)

returns 3. If the number of values in the range is zero, or exceeds 8191, or contains #N/A, the function returns the #NUM! error value. If the number contains #NA, or no number occurs more than once, MODE returns the #N/A error value.

The MAX Function

The MAX function returns the largest value in a range and takes the form

=MAX(*number1,number 2,...*)

For example, in the worksheet shown earlier in Figure 14-2, you can use the formula

=MAX(B4:B15)

to determine the highest monthly yak sales: $888.

The MIN Function

The MIN function returns the smallest value in a range and takes the form

=MIN(*number1,number 2,...*)

For example, in the worksheet shown earlier in Figure 14-2, you can determine the lowest monthly yak sales — $565 — by using the formula

=MIN(B4:B15)

The COUNT and COUNTA Functions

The COUNT function tells you how many cells in a given range contain numbers, including dates and formulas that evaluate to numbers. This function takes the form

=COUNT(*value1,value2,...*)

For example, in the worksheet in Figure 14-3 on the next page, the formula in cell E3

=COUNT(B4:B15)

returns the value 8 — the number of cells in the range B4:B15 that contain numbers.

The COUNT function counts only the numbers in a range and ignores blank cells and cells that contain text, logical, or error values. To count all nonblank cells (regardless of what they contain), you can use the COUNTA function. This function takes the form

=COUNTA(*value1,value2,...*)

FIGURE 14-3
The COUNT function ignores cells that don't contain numbers.

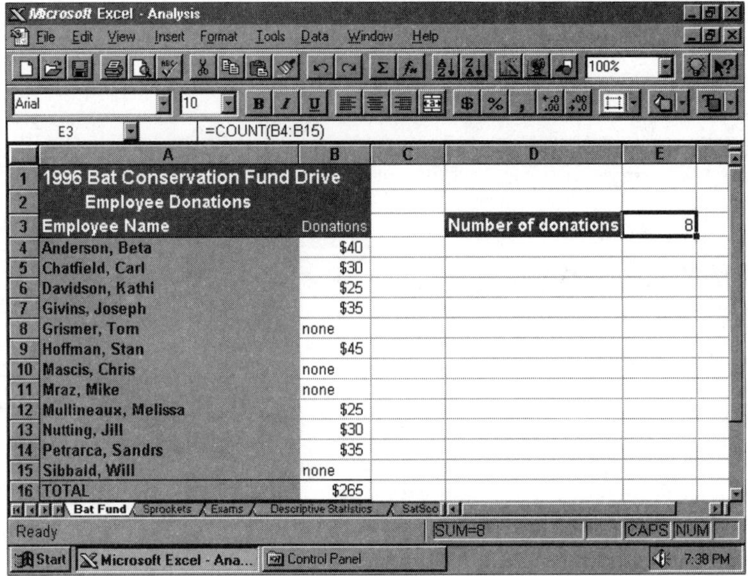

Using the worksheet in Figure 14-3, the formula

=COUNTA(B4:B15)

returns the value 12 because the range B4:B15 contains eight numbers and four text values.

The SUMIF and COUNTIF Functions

The SUMIF function is similar to SUM but tests each cell in a range before adding it to the total. This function takes the form

=SUMIF(*range,criteria,sum_range*)

The *range* argument specifies the range you want to test, *criteria* specifies the test to be performed on each cell in the range, and *sum_range* specifies the corresponding numbers to be totaled. For example, in Figure 14-2 (shown on page 506), if the column containing the names of the months has the defined name *monthNames* and the column containing yak sales has the defined name *yakSales,* you can find the sales for June with the formula

=SUMIF(monthNames,"June",yakSales)

which returns the number 676.

Similarly, COUNTIF counts the cells that match the specified criteria and takes the form

=COUNTIF(*range,criteria*)

For example, you can find the number of months in which yak sales fell below $600 with the formula

=COUNTIF(yakSales,"<600")

which returns the number 3. Notice that you can use relational operators in the *criteria* argument to test for complex conditions.

The SUMPRODUCT and SUMSQ Functions

The SUMPRODUCT function multiplies the corresponding members of each of two or more arrays (sets of numbers), totals the products, and then returns the sum of the products. Nonnumeric values in the arguments are treated as zeros. This function takes the form

=SUMPRODUCT(*array1,array2,array_3,...*)

Figure 14-4 shows a worksheet that uses SUMPRODUCT. The formula in F6

=SUMPRODUCT(B2:G2,B3:G3)

determines the total number of sprockets needed to produce the desired number of all six widget types. It does this by multiplying B2*B3, C2*C3, and so on through G2*G3, and then totaling the six products.

The SUMPRODUCT function can accept as many as 30 array arguments. Each array must have the same dimensions; otherwise, SUMPRODUCT returns the #VALUE! error value.

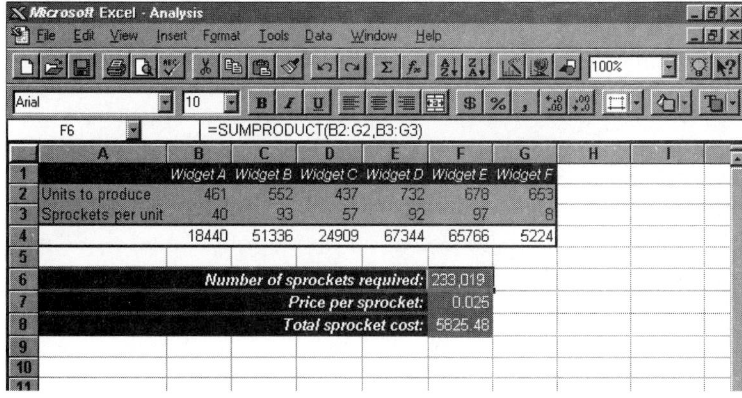

FIGURE 14-4
This worksheet uses SUMPRODUCT to calculate how many sprockets are needed to produce the desired numbers of all six types of widgets.

The SUMSQ function is similar to the SUMPRODUCT function, except that it squares the numbers in the arguments and returns the sum of the squares, rather than the products. This function takes the form

=SUMSQ(*number1,number2,...*)

For example, the formula

=SUMSQ(5,6)

returns the value 61 (25+36).

Sample and Population Statistical Functions

Variance and standard deviation are statistical measurements of the dispersion of a group, or population, of numbers. The standard deviation is the square root of the variance. As a rule, about 68 percent of a normally distributed population falls within one standard deviation of the mean, and about 95 percent falls within two standard deviations. A large standard deviation indicates that the population is widely dispersed from the mean; a small standard deviation indicates that the population is tightly packed around the mean.

Four statistical functions — VAR, VARP, STDEV, and STDEVP — compute the variance and standard deviation of the numbers in a range of cells. Before you calculate the variance and standard deviation of a group of values, you must determine whether those values represent the total population or only a representative sample of that population. The VAR and STDEV functions assume that the values represent only a sample of the total population; the VARP and STDEVP functions assume that the values represent the total population.

Calculating Sample Statistics: VAR and STDEV

The VAR and STDEV functions take the forms

=VAR(*number1,number2,...*)

and

=STDEV(*number1,number2,...*)

The worksheet in Figure 14-5 shows exam scores for five students and assumes that the scores in cells B4:E8 represent only a part of the total population. Cell C12 contains the formula

=AVERAGE(B4:E8)

which returns the average of the exam scores: 87.35. Cell C13 uses the VAR function to calculate the variance for this sample group of test scores:

=VAR(B4:E8)

Cell C14 uses the STDEV function to calculate the standard deviation:

=STDEV(B4:E8)

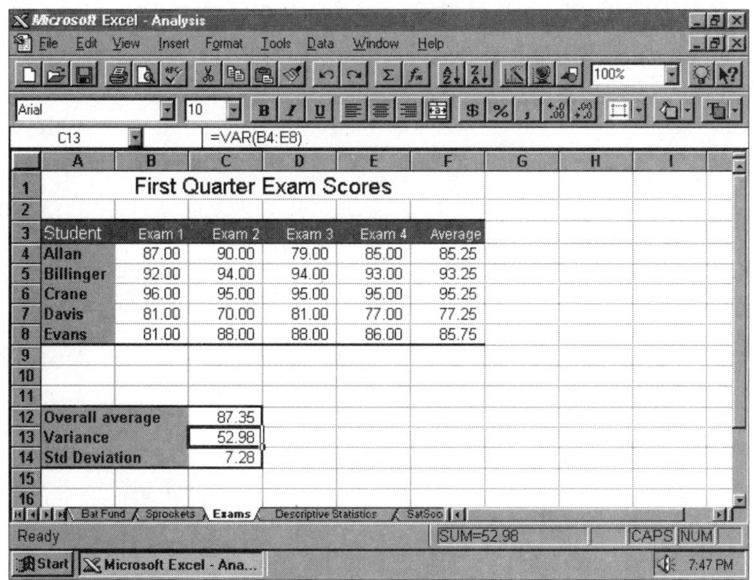

First Quarter Exam Scores

Student	Exam 1	Exam 2	Exam 3	Exam 4	Average
Allan	87.00	90.00	79.00	85.00	85.25
Billinger	92.00	94.00	94.00	93.00	93.25
Crane	96.00	95.00	95.00	95.00	95.25
Davis	81.00	70.00	81.00	77.00	77.25
Evans	81.00	88.00	88.00	86.00	85.75

Overall average	87.35
Variance	52.98
Std Deviation	7.28

FIGURE 14-5
THE VAR and STDEV functions measure the dispersion of sample exam scores.

As displayed, the VAR function returns 52.98, and the STDEV function returns 7.28. Assuming that the test scores in the example are normally distributed, we can deduce that about 68 percent of the students achieved scores between 80.07 (87.35-7.28) and 94.63 (87.35+7.28).

Calculating Total Population Statistics: VARP and STDEVP

If the numbers you're analyzing represent an entire population rather than a sample, you use the VARP and STDEVP functions to calculate variance and standard deviation. To compute the variance for the total population, use the formula

=VARP(*number1,number2,...*)

To find the standard deviation, use the formula

=STDEVP(*number1,number2,...*)

Assuming that cells B4:E8 in the worksheet shown in Figure 14-5 represent the total population, you can calculate the variance and standard deviation with the formulas

=VARP(B4:E8)

and

=STDEVP(B4:E8)

After formatting, the VARP function returns 50.33, and the STDEVP function returns 7.09.

The SUMX2PY2, SUMX2MY2, and SUMXMY2 Functions

The SUMX2PY2, SUMX2MY2, and SUMXMY2 functions let you perform three variations on sum-of-the-sum-of-the-squares operations, which are used in many statistical calculations. The SUMX2PY2 function calculates the sum of the sum of the squares of the corresponding values in X and Y, where X and Y are arrays that contain the same number of elements. The SUMX2MY2 function calculates the sum of the differences of the squares of the corresponding values in X and Y. And finally, the SUMXMY2 function calculates the sum of the squares of the differences of the corresponding values in X and Y. These functions take the forms

=SUMX2PY2(*array_x,array_y*)

and

=SUMX2MY2(*array_x,array_y*)

and

=SUMXMY2(*array_x,array_y*)

For example, using the same two arrays for all three functions, you can build the following formulas:

=SUMX2PY2({1,2,3,4},{2,4,6,8})

which returns 150;

=SUMX2MY2({1,2,3,4},{2,4,6,8})

which returns –90; and

=SUMXMY2({1,2,3,4},{2,4,6,8})

which returns 30.

See Also

For more information about using arrays, see "Arrays," page 141.

The Descriptive Statistics Tool

The Descriptive Statistics tool provides a table of descriptive statistics for one or more sets of input values. As shown in Figure 14-6, for each variable in the input range, this tool's output range includes the following information: the mean, standard error, median, mode, standard deviation, sample variance, kurtosis, skewness, range, minimum, maximum, sum, count, *k*th largest and smallest values (for any value of *k* you specify), and the confidence level for the mean.

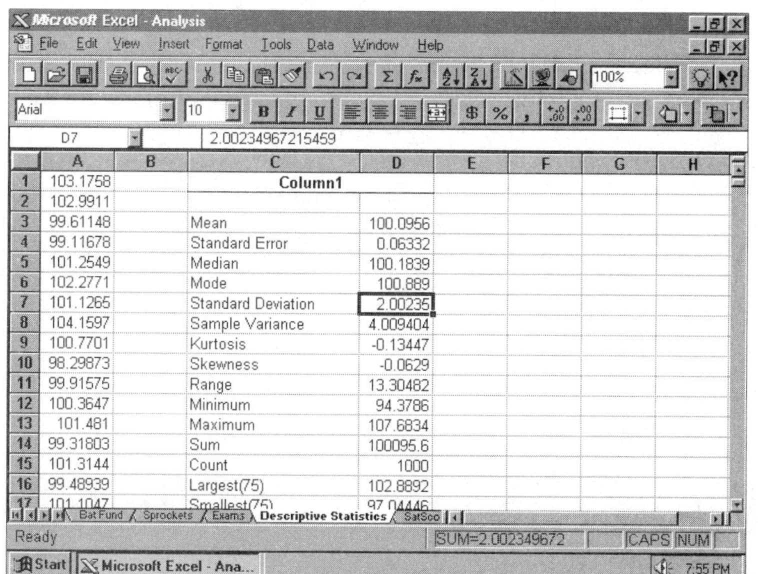

	A	B	C	D
1	103.1758		Column1	
2	102.9911			
3	99.61148		Mean	100.0956
4	99.11678		Standard Error	0.06332
5	101.2549		Median	100.1839
6	102.2771		Mode	100.889
7	101.1265		Standard Deviation	2.00235
8	104.1597		Sample Variance	4.009404
9	100.7701		Kurtosis	-0.13447
10	98.29873		Skewness	-0.0629
11	99.91575		Range	13.30482
12	100.3647		Minimum	94.3786
13	101.481		Maximum	107.6834
14	99.31803		Sum	100095.6
15	101.3144		Count	1000
16	99.48939		Largest(75)	102.8892
17	101.1047		Smallest(75)	97.04446

FIGURE 14-6

We generated 1000 normally distributed random numbers, using 100 as the mean and 2 as the standard deviation, and then verified their "normalcy" with the Descriptive Statistics tool.

To use the Descriptive Statistics tool, choose Data Analysis from the Tools menu, select the Descriptive Statistics option from the Data Analysis dialog box, and click OK. The dialog box shown in Figure 14-7 appears.

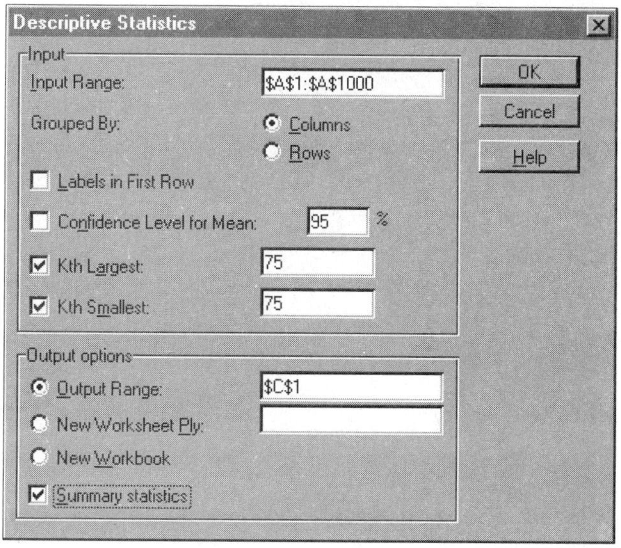

FIGURE 14-7

Use the Descriptive Statistics tool to create a table of descriptive statistics.

The Descriptive Statistics tool requires an input range that consists of one or more variables and an output range. You must also indicate whether the variables are to be arranged by column or by row. If you include a row of labels, be sure to select the Labels In First Row option. Excel then uses the labels to identify the variables in its output table. Select the Summary Statistics option only if you want a detailed output table; otherwise, leave this check box empty and select the check boxes of individual items to tell Excel which information you want.

Like the other tools in the Analysis ToolPak, Descriptive Statistics creates a table of constants. If a table of constants doesn't suit your needs, you can get most of the same statistical data from other Analysis ToolPak tools or from formulas that use Excel's worksheet functions. The statistics and formulas are listed in the following table:

Statistic	Formula
Mean	=AVERAGE(*number1,number2,...*)
Median	=MEDIAN(*number1,number2,...*)
Mode	=MODE(*number1,number2,...*)
Standard deviation (sample)	=STDEV(*number1,number2,...*)
Standard deviation (population)	=STDEVP(*number1,number2,...*)
Variance (sample)	=VAR(*number1,number2,...*)
Variance (population)	=VARP(*number1,number2,...*)
Kurtosis	=KURT(*number1,number2,...*)
Skewness	=SKEW(*number1,number2,...*)
Range	=MAX(*number1,number2*)–MIN(*number1,number2,...*)
Minimum	=MIN(*number1,number2,...*)
Maximum	=MAX(*number1,number2,...*)
Sum	=SUM(*number1,number2,...*)
Count	=COUNT(*value1,value2,...*)
*k*th largest	=LARGE(*array,k*)
*k*th smallest	=SMALL(*array,k*)

For information about random number generation, see "Generating Random Numbers" on page 524.

The Histogram Tool

A histogram is a chart (usually a simple column chart) that takes a collection of measurements and plots the number of measurements (called the *frequency*) that fall within each of several intervals (called *bins*).

To see how Microsoft Excel's Histogram tool works, we'll use the table of scores shown in Figure 14-8, which consists of 1000 scores that fall within the range 600 to 1500. (The input range must contain numeric data only.) To see a breakdown of the total scores at 50-point intervals, start by setting up the distribution "bins" shown in column F of Figure 14-9 on the next page.

The bins don't have to be equally spaced, as these are, but they must be in ascending order. (If they are equally spaced, you can create the bins easily by using the AutoFill feature or by choosing Fill and then Series from the Edit menu.)

Microsoft Excel - Analysis

	A	B	C	D
1	Student ID	Verbal	Math	Total
2	763-24-1607	550	444	994
3	444-07-9997	533	534	1067
4	157-86-9638	632	599	1231
5	244-38-7923	577	586	1163
6	374-20-1477	501	458	959
7	125-90-0492	651	557	1208
8	983-16-4737	607	578	1185
9	949-04-2211	614	525	1139
10	285-52-1925	603	571	1174
11	492-15-3068	582	435	1017
12	022-30-3704	435	458	893
13	130-49-9848	548	460	1008
14	760-27-1502	552	439	991
15	367-33-8523	558	465	1023
16	444-98-9797	528	555	1083
17	828-93-9121	287	485	772

Descriptive Statistics / SatScore 1 / SatScore 2 / SatScore 3

FIGURE 14-8
We'll use this table to demonstrate Excel's Histogram tool.

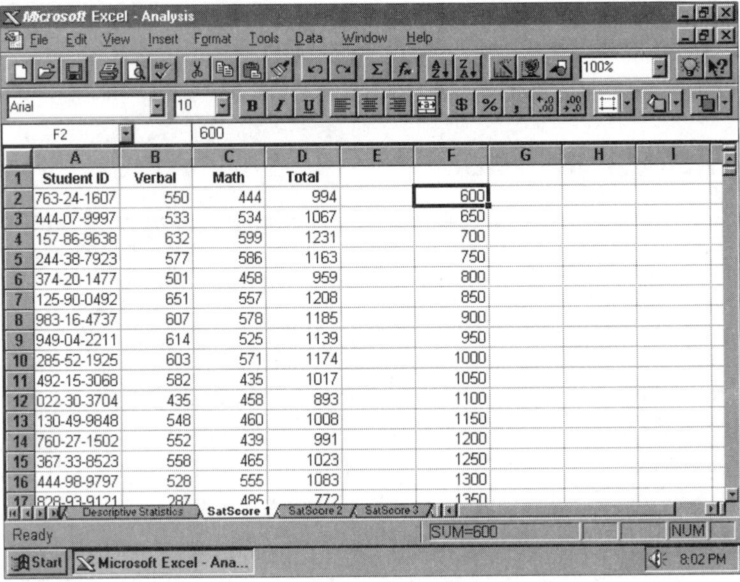

	A	B	C	D	E	F
1	Student ID	Verbal	Math	Total		
2	763-24-1607	550	444	994		600
3	444-07-9997	533	534	1067		650
4	157-86-9638	632	599	1231		700
5	244-38-7923	577	586	1163		750
6	374-20-1477	501	458	959		800
7	125-90-0492	651	557	1208		850
8	983-16-4737	607	578	1185		900
9	949-04-2211	614	525	1139		950
10	285-52-1925	603	571	1174		1000
11	492-15-3068	582	435	1017		1050
12	022-30-3704	435	458	893		1100
13	130-49-9848	548	460	1008		1150
14	760-27-1502	552	439	991		1200
15	367-33-8523	558	465	1023		1250
16	444-98-9797	528	555	1083		1300
17	828-93-9121	287	485	772		1350

FIGURE 14-9 Column F contains the distribution bins.

Next choose Data Analysis from the Tools menu, select the Histogram tool, and click OK. The Histogram dialog box appears, as shown in Figure 14-10.

Histogram

Input
Input Range: $D$2:$D$1001
Bin Range: $F$2:$F$20
☐ Labels

Output options
◉ Output Range: $G$1
○ New Worksheet Ply:
○ New Workbook
☐ Pareto (sorted histogram)
☐ Cumulative Percentage
☑ Chart Output

OK
Cancel
Help

FIGURE 14-10 This dialog box appears when you select the Histogram tool from the Data Analysis dialog box.

The Histogram tool can take three items of information: the location of the data (in this case, D2:D1001), the location of the bins (F2:F20), and the upper left cell of the range where you want the analysis to appear (G1).

NOTE If you want, you can leave the Bin Range edit box blank. Excel then creates evenly distributed bin intervals using the minimum and maximum values in the input range as beginning and end points. The number of intervals is equal to the square root of the number of input values.

Optionally, the Histogram tool can create a pareto (sorted) analysis, include cumulative percentages, and generate a chart. For now, select the Chart Output option and skip the other options. (We'll come back to them in a moment.) When you click OK, Excel creates a chart and writes its analysis in columns G and H, as shown in Figure 14-11.

In the Frequency column, the Histogram tool reports the number of input values that are equal to or greater than the bin value but less than the next bin value. The last value in the table reports the number of input values equal to or greater than the last bin value.

Notice that the Histogram tool duplicates your column of bin values in the Bin column, which is convenient if you place the output somewhere other than next to the bin values. Unfortunately, you'll get an error message if you try to overwrite the bin-value range with the output range. If you're placing the output right next to the bins, as we did in Figure 14-11, you might want to drag the output range one column to the left and overwrite the duplicate bin values using Excel's direct cell manipulation feature.

	A	B	C	D	E	F	G	H
1	Student ID	Verbal	Math	Total			Bin	Frequency
2	763-24-1607	550	444	994		600	600	0
3	444-07-9997	533	534	1067		650	650	1
4	157-86-9638	632	599	1231		700	700	2
5	244-38-7923	577	586	1163		750	750	7
6	374-20-1477	501	458	959		800	800	11
7	125-90-0492	651	557	1208		850	850	21
8	983-16-4737	607	578	1185		900	900	75
9	949-04-2211	614	525	1139		950	950	111
10	285-52-1925	603	571	1174		1000	1000	133
11	492-15-3068	582	435	1017		1050	1050	153
12	022-30-3704	435	458	893		1100	1100	148
13	130-49-9848	548	460	1008		1150	1150	105
14	760-27-1502	552	439	991		1200	1200	113
15	367-33-8523	558	465	1023		1250	1250	52
16	444-98-9797	528	555	1083		1300	1300	46
17	828-93-9121	287	485	772		1350	1350	11

FIGURE 14-11

This analysis tells us that 1 score was at least 600 but less than 650, 2 are at least 650 but less than 700, and so on.

Because the Histogram tool copies the bin-value range, it's best to fill the range with numeric constants rather than formulas. If you do use formulas, be sure they don't include relative references; otherwise, when Histogram copies the range, the formulas might produce unwanted results.

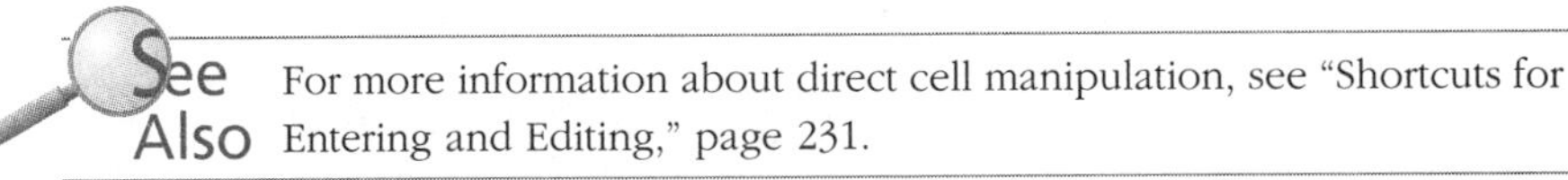

For more information about direct cell manipulation, see "Shortcuts for Entering and Editing," page 231.

Charting a Distribution Analysis

Because you selected the Chart Output option in the Histogram dialog box, the Histogram tool generated a chart (shown in Figure 14-12) at the same time it performed its analysis. The chart was created from the data in Figure 14-9 on page 516. (We enlarged the chart to make it easier to see.) This standard Excel column chart can be manipulated just like any other chart.

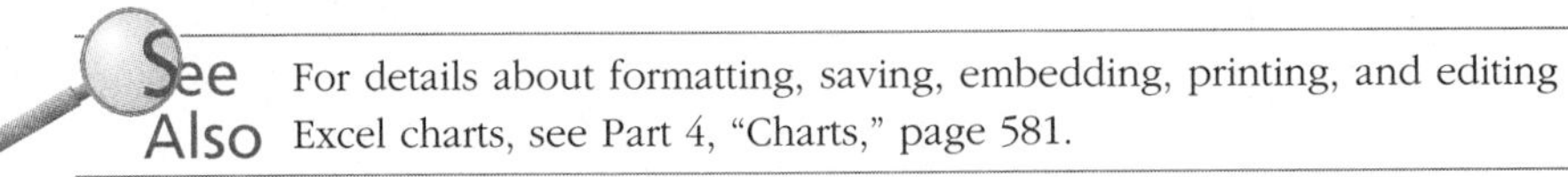

For details about formatting, saving, embedding, printing, and editing Excel charts, see Part 4, "Charts," page 581.

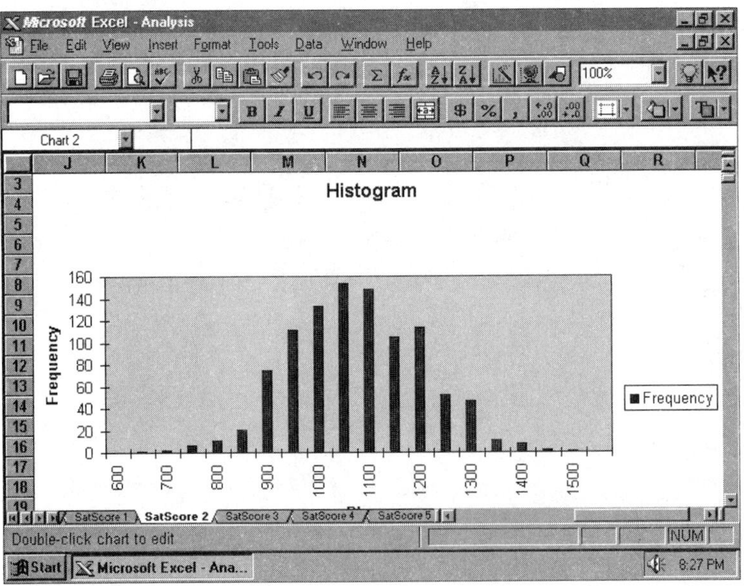

FIGURE 14-12
The Histogram tool can automatically create a column chart like this one.

The Pareto and Cumulative Percentage Options

You use the Pareto option in the Histogram dialog box to sort the output (in descending order) and the Cumulative Percentage option to create a table that lists the cumulative percentages of each bin level. For example, creating a table of cumulative percentages with the data shown earlier in Figure 14-8 tells you that 66.1 percent of the student population scored below 1100.

Analyzing Distribution with the FREQUENCY Function

The Histogram tool generates a set of numeric constants. If you'd rather create formulas linked to the input values, you can use the Analysis ToolPak's FREQUENCY array function, which takes the form

=FREQUENCY(*data_array,bins_array*)

To use the FREQUENCY function, follow these steps:

1. Set up a column of bin values, just as you would with the Histogram tool.
2. Select the entire range where you want the output to appear. This range must be a column of cells; the FREQUENCY function can't use a row or multicolumn range as its output range.
3. Enter the formula, specifying the input range as the first argument and the bin range as the second. Press Ctrl-Shift-Enter to lock in the array formula.

Figure 14-13, shown at the top of the next page, shows the FREQUENCY function applied to the data shown earlier in Figure 14-8 (on page 515).

See Also For more information about using formulas that work with arrays, see "Array Formula Rules," page 143.

Functions That Analyze Rank and Percentile

The Analysis ToolPak includes several functions that extract rank and percentile information from a set of input values: PERCENTRANK, PERCENTILE, QUARTILE, SMALL, LARGE, and RANK.

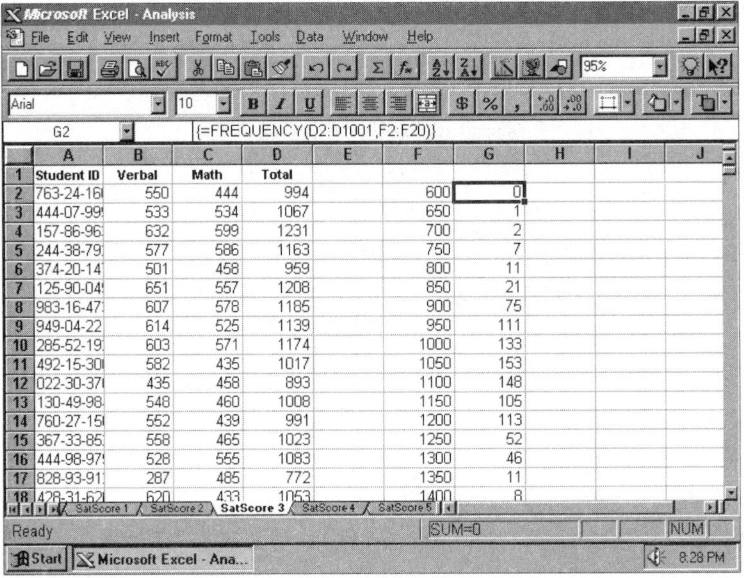

FIGURE 14-13 Use the FREQUENCY function to link the distribution analysis to the input data.

The PERCENTRANK Function

The PERCENTRANK function returns a percentile ranking for any member of a data set. You can use this function to create a percentile table that's linked to the input range so that the percentile figures are updated if the input values change. We used this function to create the percentile ranking in column E of Figure 14-14.

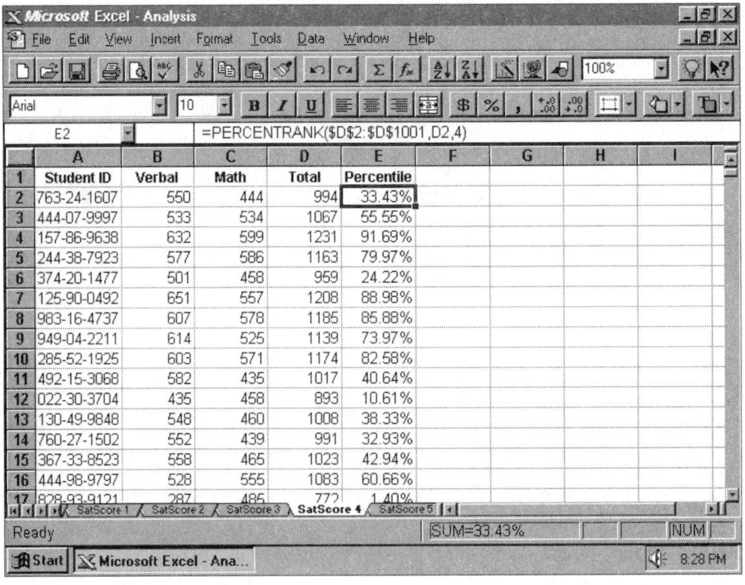

FIGURE 14-14 PERCENTRANK links percentile figures to input values.

The PERCENTRANK function takes the form

=PERCENTRANK(*array,x,significance*)

The first argument specifies the input range (which is D2:D1001, in our example), and the second specifies the value whose rank you want to obtain. The third argument, which is optional, indicates the number of digits of precision you want; if omitted, results are rounded to three digits (0.*xxx* or *xx.x*%).

The PERCENTILE and QUARTILE Functions

You use the PERCENTILE function to determine which member of an input range stands at a specified percentile ranking. It takes the form

=PERCENTILE(*array,k*)

For example, to find out which score in Figure 14-14 represents the 87th percentile, you can use the formula

=PERCENTILE(D2:D1001,0.87)

You must express the percentile as a decimal fraction between 0 and 1.

The QUARTILE function, which takes the form

=QUARTILE(*array,quart*)

works much like the PERCENTILE function, except that it returns only the lowest, the 25th-percentile, the median, the 75th-percentile, or the highest value in the input set. The function's first argument specifies the input range. The second argument, which must be 0, 1, 2, 3, or 4, specifies the value to be returned, as shown in the following table:

Argument	Returns
0	Lowest value
1	25th-percentile value
2	Median (50th-percentile) value
3	75th-percentile value
4	Highest value

Note that you can use the MIN function instead of the QUARTILE(*range*,0) function, the MEDIAN function instead of the QUARTILE(*range*,2) function, and the MAX function instead of the QUARTILE(*range*,4) function. These functions are faster than QUARTILE, particularly with large data sets.

The SMALL and LARGE Functions

The SMALL and LARGE functions return the *k*th smallest and *k*th largest values in an input range and take the forms

=SMALL(*array,k*)

and

=LARGE(*array,k*)

To find the 15th highest score in Figure 14-14, you can use the formula

=LARGE(D2:D1001,15)

The RANK Function

The RANK function, which takes the form

=RANK(*number,ref,order*)

returns the ranked position of a particular number within a set of numbers. For example, to find out which ranking the score 1200 has in the data set in Figure 14-14, you can use the formula

=RANK(1200,D2:D1001)

By default, the highest value is ranked 1, the second highest is ranked 2, and so on. If you want the values ranked from the bottom instead of the top, add a third argument that is any number other than 0.

If RANK can't find an exact match between its first argument and an input value, it returns the #N/A error value.

The Rank and Percentile Tool

Suppose you want to rank the scores shown earlier in Figure 14-8. You could rank the scores by sorting the data in descending order, with the best score at the top and the worst score at the bottom of the column. To find the rank of any score, you might want to create an ascending series of numbers beside the sorted scores, with 1 beside the best score and 1000 beside the worst.

The Analysis ToolPak includes a Rank and Percentile tool that not only performs these tasks for you but also creates percentile figures for each value in your input range. To use this tool, choose Data Analysis from the Tools menu, select the Rank And Percentile option, and click OK. The dialog box that appears asks for input and output ranges. As with the Histogram tool, the input range must contain numeric data only.

Columns E through H in Figure 14-15 show the result of using the Rank and Percentile tool to analyze column D of the test-score data in Figure 14-8 (on page 515). The first row of this report tells us that the 421st item in the

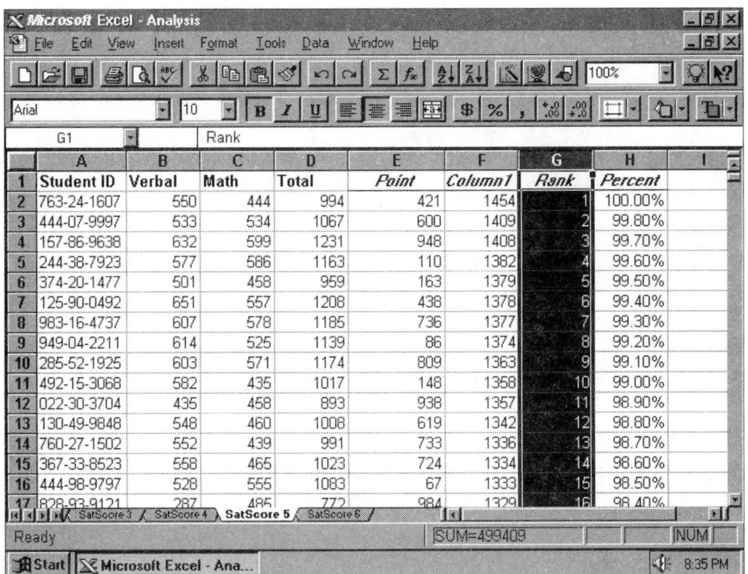

	A	B	C	D	E	F	G	H
1	Student ID	Verbal	Math	Total	*Point*	*Column1*	*Rank*	*Percent*
2	763-24-1607	550	444	994	421	1454	1	100.00%
3	444-07-9997	533	534	1067	600	1409	2	99.80%
4	157-86-9638	632	599	1231	948	1408	3	99.70%
5	244-38-7923	577	586	1163	110	1382	4	99.60%
6	374-20-1477	501	458	959	163	1379	5	99.50%
7	125-90-0492	651	557	1208	438	1378	6	99.40%
8	983-16-4737	607	578	1185	736	1377	7	99.30%
9	949-04-2211	614	525	1139	86	1374	8	99.20%
10	285-52-1925	603	571	1174	809	1363	9	99.10%
11	492-15-3068	582	435	1017	148	1358	10	99.00%
12	022-30-3704	435	458	893	938	1357	11	98.90%
13	130-49-9848	548	460	1008	619	1342	12	98.80%
14	760-27-1502	552	439	991	733	1336	13	98.70%
15	367-33-8523	558	465	1023	724	1334	14	98.60%
16	444-98-9797	528	555	1083	67	1333	15	98.50%
17	828-93-9121	287	485	772	984	1329	16	98.40%

FIGURE 14-15

Use the Rank and Percentile tool to analyze the totals in column D.

input range is a score of 1454. The report also tells us that this score ranks first and is better than 100 percent of the other scores. The second row of the report indicates that the second-best score is 1409, it is the 600th item in the input range, and it is better than 99.80 percent of the competition — and so on.

Suppose you want to know the student ID number of the person whose total test score was the 421st item in the input range, the ID number of the student whose score was the 600th item, and so on. One easy way to obtain this information is to insert a new column next to the Rank column, add the heading Student ID, and then use the INDEX function to get the ID numbers from the table shown earlier in Figure 14-8. Figure 14-16, on the top of the next page, shows the result.

In this example, we used the Rank and Percentile tool to analyze a single column of data. We could also use this tool to analyze all three scores — verbal, math, and total. In that case, we would specify the range B1:D1001 as the input range, and the tool would generate 12 columns of output, 4 for each input column.

NOTE Be sure that the data you analyze consists only of numeric constants or formulas that use absolute references. If the input cells contain formulas with relative references, these references might become scrambled in the output range when they're sorted.

See Also For more information about the INDEX function, see "The INDEX Function," page 450.

FIGURE 14-16
Use the INDEX function to match student ID numbers with the ranked scores.

Microsoft Excel - Analysis

G2 =INDEX($A$2:$A$1001,E2,0)

	A	B	C	D	E	F	G	H	I
1	Student ID	Verbal	Math	Total	*Point*	*Column1*	*Student ID*	*Rank*	*Perc*
2	763-24-1607	550	444	994	421	1454	557-48-9140	1	100.0
3	444-07-9997	533	534	1067	600	1409	265-13-3555	2	99.8
4	157-86-9638	632	599	1231	948	1408	930-05-3292	3	99.7
5	244-38-7923	577	586	1163	110	1382	118-98-9172	4	99.6
6	374-20-1477	501	458	959	163	1379	940-91-3929	5	99.5
7	125-90-0492	651	557	1208	438	1378	665-07-3831	6	99.4
8	983-16-4737	607	578	1185	736	1377	661-81-0509	7	99.3
9	949-04-2211	614	525	1139	86	1374	211-02-8672	8	99.2
10	285-52-1925	603	571	1174	809	1363	218-01-1242	9	99.1
11	492-15-3068	582	435	1017	148	1358	320-36-4193	10	99.0
12	022-30-3704	435	458	893	938	1357	909-43-7511	11	98.9
13	130-49-9848	548	460	1008	619	1342	736-39-1057	12	98.8
14	760-27-1502	552	439	991	733	1336	301-02-6934	13	98.7
15	367-33-8523	558	465	1023	724	1334	780-64-2850	14	98.6
16	444-98-9797	528	555	1083	67	1333	753-50-2173	15	98.5
17	828-93-9121	287	485	772	984	1329	754-38-1789	16	98.4

SatScore 3 | SatScore 4 | SatScore 5 | SatScore 6

Ready SUM=0 NUM

Generating Random Numbers

Microsoft Excel's built-in random-number function, RAND, generates a uniform distribution of random real numbers between 0 and 1. In other words, all values between 0 and 1 share the same probability of being returned by a set of formulas based on the RAND function. Figure 14-17 illustrates the distribution

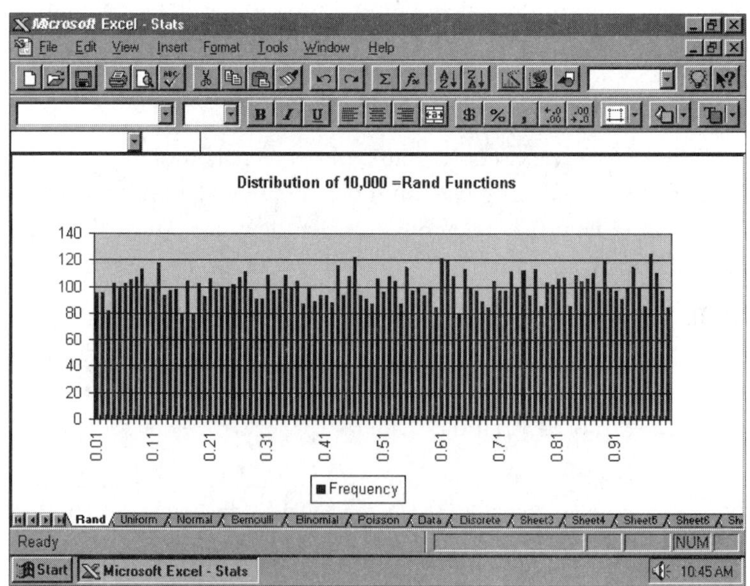

FIGURE 14-17
Excel's RAND function returns uniformly distributed real numbers between 0 and 1.

of one particular trial of 10,000 RAND formulas. Because the sample is relatively small, the distribution is by no means perfectly uniform. Nevertheless, repeated tests of this kind demonstrate that the RAND function doesn't favor any position within its spectrum of distribution.

You can use the random-number component of the Analysis ToolPak to create sets of random numbers that are not uniformly distributed. These random-number sets are useful for Monte Carlo decision analysis and other kinds of simulations. Six distribution types are available: Uniform, Normal, Bernoulli, Binomial, Poisson, and Discrete (user-defined). In addition, you can use the Patterned Distribution option to create nonrandom numbers at specified intervals. (The Patterned Distribution option can serve as an alternative to Excel's Series command from the Fill submenu of the Edit menu.)

To use the Random Number Generation tool, choose Data Analysis from the Tools menu, select the Random Number Generation option in the Data Analysis dialog box, and click OK. Excel presents a dialog box like the one shown in Figure 14-18.

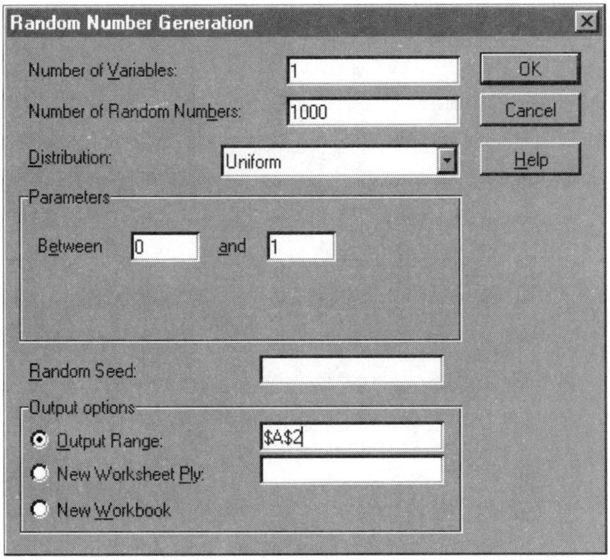

FIGURE 14-18
The Parameters section of the Random Number Generation dialog box changes to reflect the distribution type you select.

For all distribution types, you use the Output Range edit box to tell Excel where you want the random numbers to go. If the range you specify already contains data, you'll see a warning message before the data is overwritten.

In the Number Of Variables and Number Of Random Numbers boxes, you indicate how many columns of numbers you want and how many numbers you want in each column. For example, if you want 10 columns of 100 numbers each, specify 10 in the Number Of Variables edit box and 100 in the Number Of Random Numbers edit box.

You can also specify a seed value. However, each time you generate a random-number set with a particular distribution type using the same seed value, you get exactly the same sequence of numbers, so you should specify a seed value only if you need to be able to reproduce a random-number sequence.

The Parameters section of this dialog box changes, depending on the type of distribution you select. As Figure 14-18 shows, when you select the Uniform Distribution option, you can specify the end points of the distribution.

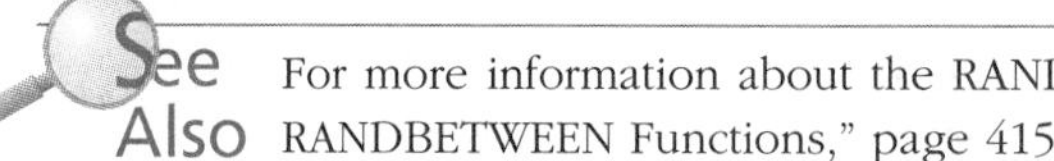

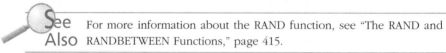

For more information about the RAND function, see "The RAND and RANDBETWEEN Functions," page 415.

The Uniform Distribution Option

The Uniform Distribution option works much the same way as the RANDBETWEEN function, generating an evenly distributed set of real numbers between specified beginning and end points, as shown in Figure 14-19.

You can use this option as a more convenient alternative to RAND when you want end points other than 0 and 1 or when you want sets of numbers to be based on the same seed value.

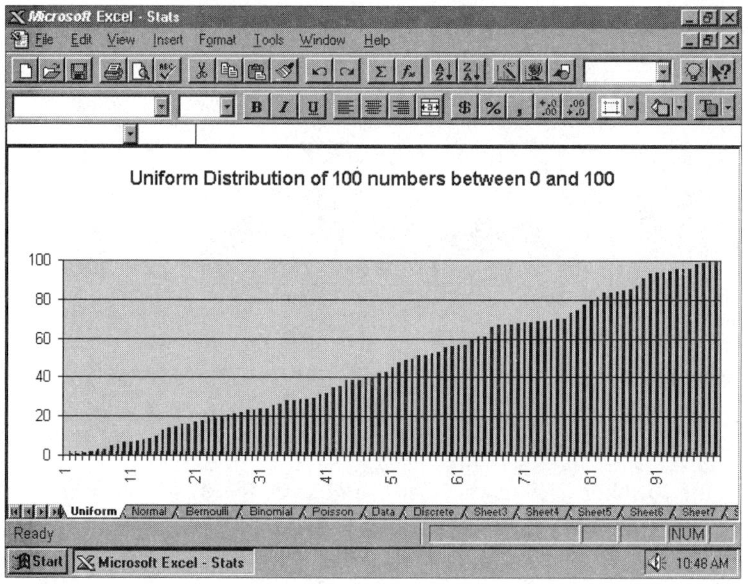

FIGURE 14-19

We asked for 100 uniformly distributed random numbers between 0 and 100.

For more information about the RANDBETWEEN function, see "The RAND and RANDBETWEEN Functions," page 415.

The Normal Distribution Option

A normal distribution has the following characteristics:

- One particular value, the mean, is more likely to occur than any other value.
- Values above the mean are as likely to occur as values below it.
- Values close to the mean are more likely to occur than values distant from the mean.

The chart in Figure 14-20 shows the effects of the Normal Distibution option.

To generate normally distributed random numbers, you specify two parameters: the mean and the standard deviation. The standard deviation is the average absolute difference between the random numbers and the mean. Approximately 68 percent of the values in a normal distribution will fall within one standard deviation of the mean.

You can use the Descriptive Statistics tool to verify the "normalcy" of a normally distributed set of random numbers. For example, Figure 14-6 (shown earlier on page 513) shows a table of descriptive statistics and a distribution

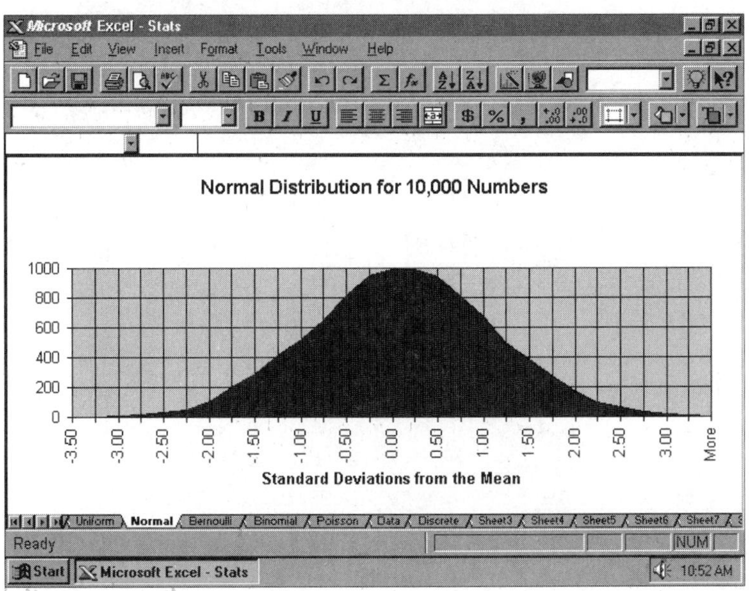

FIGURE 14-20

We made a histogram of 10,000 normally distributed numbers.

curve for a set of 1000 random numbers generated with the Normal Distribution option, using a mean of 100 and a standard deviation of 2. Because the sample is small, the output does not accord perfectly with statistical theory.

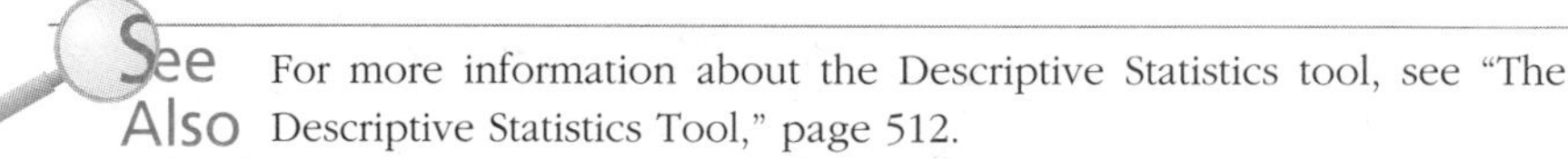

See Also For more information about the Descriptive Statistics tool, see "The Descriptive Statistics Tool," page 512.

The Bernoulli Distribution Option

The Bernoulli Distribution option simulates the probability of success of a number of trials, given that all trials have an equal probability of succeeding and that the success of one trial has no impact on the success of subsequent trials. (Note that "succeed" in this context has no value implication. In other words, you can use this distribution to simulate failure as readily as success.) All values in the Bernoulli distribution's output are either 0 or 1.

The probability that each cell will return a 1 is given by the distribution's sole parameter, p, which must be a number from 0 to 1. For example, if you want a sequence of 100 random Bernoulli values whose most likely sum is 27, you define a 100-cell output range and specify a p value of 0.27. The chart in Figure 14-21 shows how the successes (value of 1) are spaced randomly among the failures (value of 0).

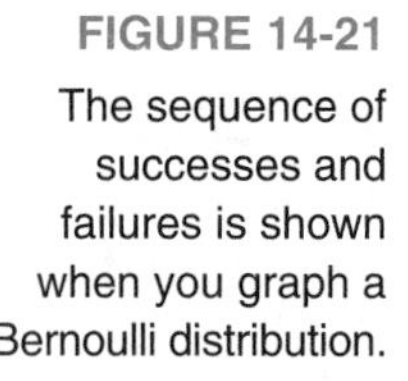

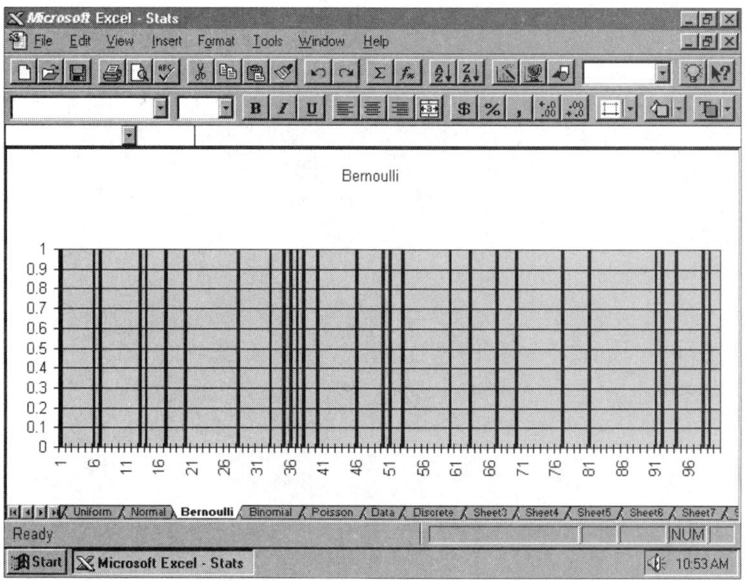

FIGURE 14-21
The sequence of successes and failures is shown when you graph a Bernoulli distribution.

The Binomial Distribution Option

The Binomial Distribution option simulates the number of successes in a fixed number of trials, given a specified probability rate. As with the Bernoulli Distribution option, the trials are assumed to be independent; that is, the outcome of one has no effect on any other.

To generate binomially distributed numbers, you specify the probability — the *p* argument — that any trial will succeed and the number of trials. (Notice that "succeed" in this context has no value implication. In other words, you can use this distribution to simulate failure as readily as success.) For example, suppose you make 10 sales presentations a week; you close the sale 20 percent of the time; and you would like to know what your success rate might be over the next year. You enter *50* (for 50 working weeks in the year) in the Number Of Random Numbers edit box, *0.2* in the P value box, and *10* in the Number Of Trials edit box to learn that you can expect to make no sales four times in the coming year. We used the Histogram Data Analysis tool to chart the data in Figure 14-22.

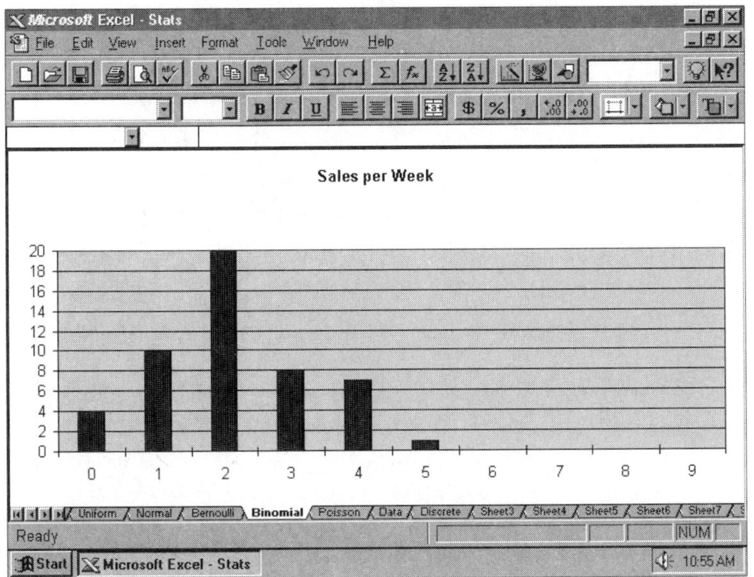

FIGURE 14-22
We used a binomial distribution to predict sales per week for the next year.

The Poisson Distribution Option

The Poisson Distribution option simulates the number of times an event occurs within a particular time span, given a certain probability of occurrence. The occurrences are assumed to be independent; that is, each occurrence has no effect on the likelihood of others.

The Poisson Distribution option takes a single parameter, *lambda*, which represents the expected outcome of an individual occurrence. For example, suppose you expect to receive an average of 10 service calls a day. You want to know how often you can expect to get 18 or more service calls in a day over a year. To get this information, you enter *260* (52 weeks times 5 days) in the Number Of Random Numbers edit box and *10* in the Lambda edit box. Figure 14-23 shows a histogram of the output and tells us that you'll have about 10 days on which you can expect 18 or more service calls.

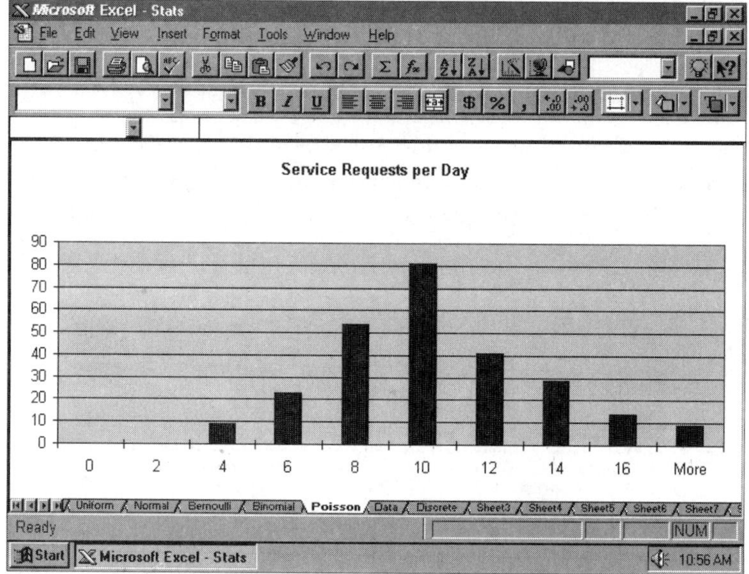

FIGURE 14-23

The Poisson distribution can help you plan manpower needs.

The Discrete Distribution Option

You use the Discrete Distribution option to create a custom distribution pattern by specifying a table of possible outcomes along with the probability associated with each outcome. The probability values must be between 0 and 1, and the sum of the probabilities in the table must equal 1. To use the Discrete Distribution option, you specify the possible outcomes and their probabilities as a two-column range whose reference is the only parameter used by this option.

The Patterned Distribution Option

The Patterned Distribution option in the Random Number Generation dialog box generates nonrandom numbers. Selecting the Patterned Distribution option displays the dialog box shown in Figure 14-24.

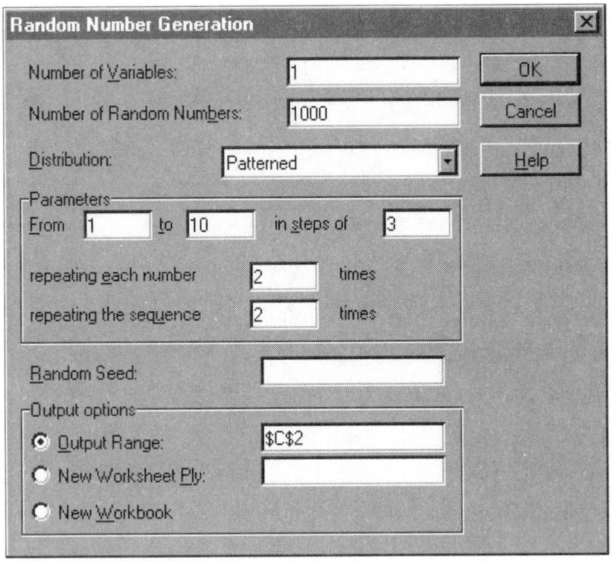

FIGURE 14-24

The Patterned Distribution option lets you create an arithmetic series with operational repetitions.

You can think of the Patterned Distribution option as a fancy Series command. It lets you create one or more arithmetic series with optional internal repetitions. For example, to create the series 1, 1, 4, 4, 7, 7, 10, 10, 1, 1, 4, 4, 7, 7, 10, 10, complete the dialog box as shown in Figure 14-24, requesting two sequences of the numbers 1 through 10, using a step interval of 3, and repeating each number twice within each cycle.

If the step interval takes the series beyond the specified upper value, the Patterned Distribution option includes the upper value by truncating the last interval. For example, if you specify a step interval of 4 and the numbers 1 through 10, Excel creates the series 1, 5, 9, and 10.

Sampling a Population of Numbers

The Sampling tool extracts a subset of numbers from a larger group (or *population*) of numbers. From an input range, you can sample a specified number of values either at random or at every *n*th value. The Sampling tool copies the extracted numbers to an output range that you specify.

To use the Sampling tool, choose Data Analysis from the Tools menu, select the Sampling option in the Data Analysis dialog box, and click OK. Figure 14-25 on the next page shows the dialog box that appears.

The values in the input range must be numeric. They can include blank values and dates, provided the dates are entered as numbers, not text. For example, to simplify a chart of daily commodity prices, you can use the Sampling tool to extract every *n*th data point and then create a new plot from the extracted data.

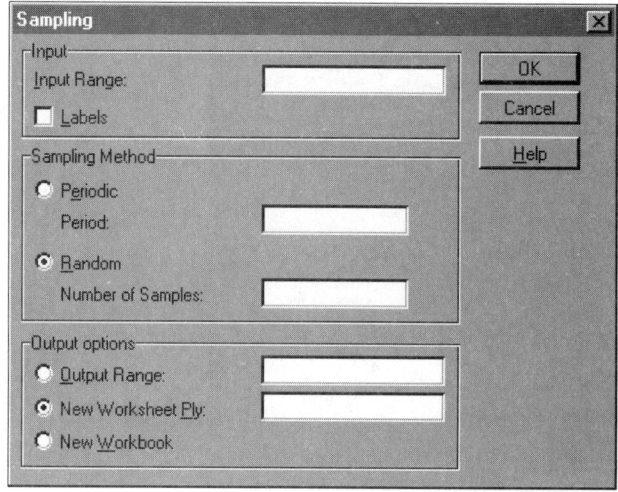

FIGURE 14-25 The Sampling tool lets you extract a random or periodic subset of a numeric population.

Sampling Text Values

To perform the equivalent of sampling from a range containing text values, follow these steps:

1. Set up a series of ascending integers beginning at 1 in a column alongside the text values.
2. Use the Sampling tool to extract numbers from this series.
3. Extract the text values by using the resulting numbers as arguments to the INDEX function. (See "The LOOKUP Function," page 448.)

Calculating Moving Averages

A moving average is a forecasting technique that simplifies trend analysis by smoothing fluctuations that occur in measurements taken over a period of time. These fluctuations can be caused by random "noise" that is often a by-product of the measurement technique. For example, measurements of the height of a growing child will vary with the accuracy of the ruler and whether the child is standing straight or slouching. You can take a series of measurements, however, and smooth them over time, resulting in a curve that reflects the child's actual growth rate.

Fluctuations in measurements can result from other temporary conditions that introduce bias. Monthly sales, for example, might vary with the number of working days in the month or the absence of a star salesperson who takes a vacation.

Suppose you have created the three-year demand curve shown in Figure 14-26. To generate a less "noisy" trend line from this data, you can plot a six-month moving average. The first point in the moving average line is the average of the first six monthly figures (January through June 1995). The next point averages the second-through-seventh monthly figures (February through July 1995), and so on. You can use the Moving Average tool to perform this analysis for you.

To use the Moving Average tool, choose Data Analysis from the Tools menu, select the Moving Average option in the Data Analysis dialog box, and click OK. The Moving Average tool requires three pieces of information: the range that contains the data you want to analyze, the range where the averaged data will appear, and the interval over which the data is averaged. To determine a three-month moving average, for example, you specify an interval of 6.

Figure 14-27 on the next page shows a six-month moving average superimposed over the original demand curve in Figure 14-26. The Moving Average tool produced the data in column C, which was used to create the

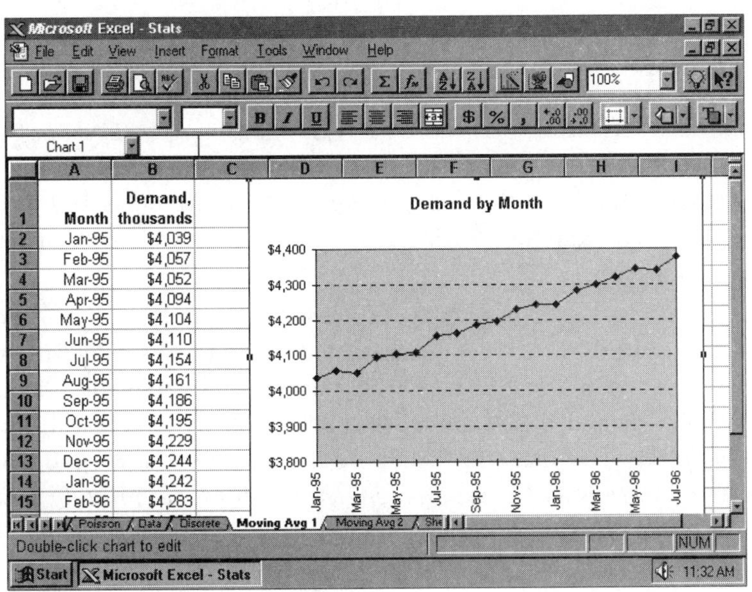

FIGURE 14-26

We'll use this three-year demand curve to demonstrate Excel's Moving Average tool.

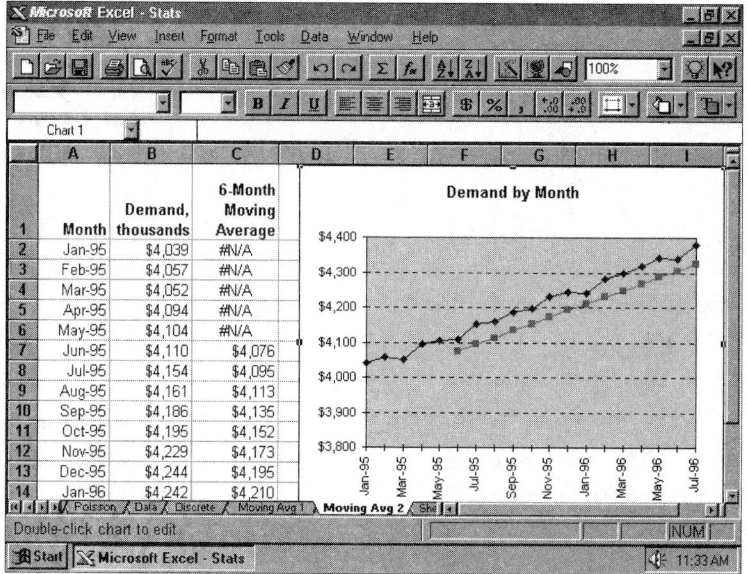

	A	B	C
1	Month	Demand, thousands	6-Month Moving Average
2	Jan-95	$4,039	#N/A
3	Feb-95	$4,057	#N/A
4	Mar-95	$4,052	#N/A
5	Apr-95	$4,094	#N/A
6	May-95	$4,104	#N/A
7	Jun-95	$4,110	$4,076
8	Jul-95	$4,154	$4,095
9	Aug-95	$4,161	$4,113
10	Sep-95	$4,186	$4,135
11	Oct-95	$4,195	$4,152
12	Nov-95	$4,229	$4,173
13	Dec-95	$4,244	$4,195
14	Jan-96	$4,242	$4,210

FIGURE 14-27 The Moving Average tool provides a better perspective of the overall trend.

straighter plot line in the chart. Notice that the first five cells in the tool's output range contain #N/A error values. Where the interval is n, you will always have n–1 #N/A error values at the beginning of the output. Including those values in a chart presents no problem, because Excel simply leaves the first area of the plot line blank.

Linear and Exponential Regression

Excel includes several array functions for performing linear — LINEST, TREND, FORECAST, SLOPE, and STEYX — and exponential — LOGEST and GROWTH — regression. These functions are entered as array formulas and produce array results. You can use each of these functions with one or several independent variables.

The term *regression,* as it is used here, might be confusing to some people because regression is commonly associated with a movement backward, whereas in the world of statistics, regression is often used to predict the future. To better understand the concept, we advise you to erase the dictionary definition from your mind and start fresh with the following definition: *Regression is a statistical technique that lets you find the equation that best describes a set of data.*

Often businesses try to predict the future by using sales and percent-of-sales projections based on past history. A simple percent-of-sales technique identifies the assets and liabilities that vary along with sales, determines the proportion of each, and assigns them appropriate percentages. Although using simple percent-of-sales forecasting is often sufficient for slow or steady short-term growth patterns, the technique rapidly loses accuracy as growth accelerates.

Regression analysis uses more sophisticated equations to analyze larger sets of data and translate them into coordinates on a line or curve. In the past, regression analysis was not widely used because of the large numbers of calculations involved. Since spreadsheet applications such as Microsoft Excel began offering built-in regression functions, the use of regression analysis has become much more widespread.

Linear regression produces the slope of a line that best fits a single set of data. Based on a year's worth of sales figures, linear regression can tell you the projected sales for March of the following year by giving you the slope and y-intercept (that is, the point where the line crosses the y axis) of the line that best fits the sales data. By following the line forward in time, you can estimate future sales, assuming linear growth.

Exponential regression produces an exponential curve that best fits a set of data that you suspect does not change linearly with time. For example, a series of measurements of population growth will nearly always be better represented by an exponential curve than by a line.

Multiple regression is the analysis of more than one set of data, which often produces a more realistic projection. You can perform both linear and exponential multiple regression analyses. For example, suppose you want to project the appropriate price for a house in your area based on square footage, number of bathrooms, lot size, and age. Using a multiple regression formula, you can estimate a price, based on a database of information gathered from existing houses.

Calculating Linear Regression Statistics

The following equation algebraically describes a straight line for a set of data with one independent variable:

$$y = mx + b$$

where x is the independent variable, y is the dependent variable, m represents the slope of the line, and b represents the y intercept.

When a line represents the contribution of a number of independent variables in a multiple regression analysis to an expected result, the equation of the regression line takes the form

$$y = m_1x_1 + m_2x_2 + \ldots + m_nx_n + b$$

where y is the dependent variable, x_1 through x_n are n independent variables, m_1 through m_n are the coefficients of each independent variable, and b is a constant.

The LINEST Function

The LINEST function uses this more general equation to return the values of m_1 through m_n and the value of b, given a known set of values for y and a known set of values for each independent variable. This function takes the form

LINEST(*known_y's,known_x's,const,stats*)

The *known_y's* argument is the set of y-values you already know. This argument can be a single column, a single row, or a rectangular range of cells. If *known_y's* is a single column, each column in the *known_x's* argument is considered an independent variable. Similarly, if *known_y's* is a single row, each row in the *known_x's* argument is considered an independent variable. If *known_y's* is a rectangular range, you can use only one independent variable; *known_x's* in this case should be a rectangular range of the same size and shape as *known_y's*.

If you omit *known_x's,* Excel uses the sequence 1, 2, 3, 4, and so on.

The *const* and *stats* arguments are optional. If either is included, it must be a logical constant — either TRUE or FALSE. (You can substitute 1 for TRUE and 0 for FALSE.) The default settings for *const* and *stats* are TRUE and FALSE, respectively. If you set *const* to FALSE, Excel forces b (the last term in the straight-line equation) to be 0. If you set *stats* to TRUE, the array returned by LINEST includes the following validation statistics:

se_1 through se_n	Standard error values for each coefficient
se_b	Standard error value for the constant b
r^2	Coefficient of determination
se_y	Standard error value for y
F	F statistic
df	Degrees of freedom
ss_{reg}	Regression sum of squares
ss_{resid}	Residual sum of squares

Before creating a formula using LINEST, you must select a range large enough to hold the result array returned by the function.

If you omit the *stats* argument (or set it explicitly to FALSE), the result array encompasses one cell for each of your independent variables and one cell for *b*. If you include the validation statistics, the result array looks like this:

m_n	m_{n-1}	...	m_2	m_1	b
se_n	se_{n-1}	...	se_2	se_1	se_b
r^2	se_y			,	
F	df			,	
ss_{reg}	ss_{resid}			,	

After selecting a range to hold the results array, type the function and press Ctrl-Enter to enter the function in each cell of the result array.

Note that, with or without validation statistics, the coefficients and standard error values for your independent variables are returned in the opposite order from your input data. If you have four independent variables organized in four columns, LINEST evaluates the leftmost column as x_1, but it returns m_1 in the fourth column of the result array.

Figure 14-28 shows a simple example of the use of LINEST with one independent variable. The entries in column B of this worksheet represent monthly product demand for a small business. The numbers in column A represent the months in the period. Suppose you want to compute the slope and y-intercept of the regression line that best describes the relationship between the demand and the months. In other words, you want to describe the trend of the data. To do this, select the range F6:G6, type the formula

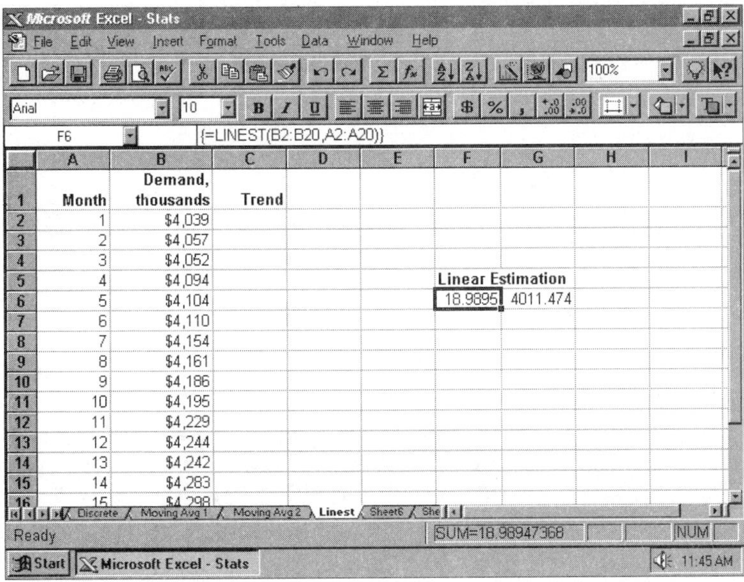

FIGURE 14-28
The LINEST function computes the slope and y-intercept of a regression line.

```
=LINEST(B2:B20,A2:A20)
```

and press Ctrl-Shift-Enter. The resulting number in cell F6, 18.9895, is the slope of the regression line; the number in cell G6, 4011.474, is the y-intercept of the line.

The TREND Function

LINEST returns a mathematical description of the straight line that best fits known data. TREND enables you to find points that lie along that line. You can use the array of numbers returned by TREND to plot a trend line — a straight line that helps make sense of actual data. You can also use TREND to extrapolate; that is, to make intelligent guesses about future data based on the tendencies exhibited by known data. (Be careful. Although you can use TREND to plot the straight line that best fits the known data, it can't tell you whether that line is a good predictor of the future. The validation statistics returned by LINEST can help you make that assessment.)

The TREND function accepts four arguments:

=TREND(*known_y's,known_x's,new_x's,const*)

The first two arguments represent the known values of your dependent and independent variables, respectively. As in LINEST, the *known_y's* argument is a single column, a single row, or a rectangular range. The *known_x's* argument also follows the pattern described for LINEST on page 536.

The third and fourth arguments are optional. If you omit *new_x's*, the TREND function considers *new_x's* to be identical to *known_x's*. If you include *const,* the value of that argument must be TRUE or FALSE (or 1 or 0). If *const* is TRUE, TREND forces *b* to be 0.

To calculate the trend-line data points that best fit your known data, simply omit the third and fourth arguments from this function. The results array will be the same size as the *known_x's* range. In Figure 14-29, we used TREND to find the value of each point on the regression line that describes the data set from the example in Figure 14-28. To create these values, we selected the range C2:C20 and entered the following as an array formula using Ctrl-Shift-Enter:

```
=TREND(B2:B20,A2:A20)
```

To extrapolate from existing data, you must supply a range for *new_x's*. You can supply as many or as few cells for *new_x's* as you want. The result array will be the same size as the *new_x's* range. In Figure 14-30 we used

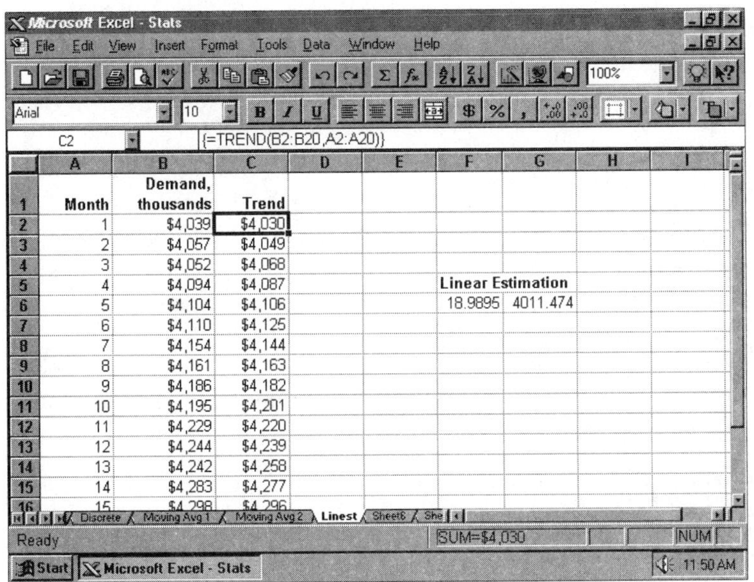

Microsoft Excel - Stats

C2 {=TREND(B2:B20,A2:A20)}

	A	B	C	D	E	F	G
1	Month	Demand, thousands	Trend				
2	1	$4,039	$4,030				
3	2	$4,057	$4,049				
4	3	$4,052	$4,068				
5	4	$4,094	$4,087			Linear Estimation	
6	5	$4,104	$4,106			18.9895	4011.474
7	6	$4,110	$4,125				
8	7	$4,154	$4,144				
9	8	$4,161	$4,163				
10	9	$4,186	$4,182				
11	10	$4,195	$4,201				
12	11	$4,229	$4,220				
13	12	$4,244	$4,239				
14	13	$4,242	$4,258				
15	14	$4,283	$4,277				
16	15	$4,298	$4,296				

Discrete / Moving Avg 1 / Moving Avg 2 / Linest / Sheet6 / She

Ready SUM=$4,030 NUM

Start Microsoft Excel - Stats 11:50 AM

FIGURE 14-29 The TREND function creates a data series that can be plotted as a line on a chart.

TREND to calculate demand for the 20th, 21st, and 22nd months. To arrive at these values, we entered the numbers 20 through 22 in A22:A24, selected C22:C24, and entered the following as an array formula:

=TREND(B2:B20,A2:A20,A22:A24)

Microsoft Excel - Stats

C22 {=TREND(B2:B20,A2:A20,A22:A24)}

	A	B	C	D	E	F	G
1	Month	Demand, thousands	Trend				
2	1	$4,039	$4,030				
3	2	$4,057	$4,049				
4	3	$4,052	$4,068				
5	4	$4,094	$4,087			Linear Estimation	
6	5	$4,104	$4,106			18.9895	4011.474
17	16	$4,318	$4,315				
18	17	$4,342	$4,334				
19	18	$4,340	$4,353				
20	19	$4,378	$4,372				
21							
22	20		$4,391				
23	21		$4,410				
24	22		$4,429				
25							

Discrete / Moving Avg 1 / Moving Avg 2 / Linest / Linest 2 / Sh

Ready SUM=$4,391 NUM

Start Microsoft Excel - Stats 12:01 PM

FIGURE 14-30 TREND can predict the sales figures for months 20, 21, and 22.

The FORECAST Function

The FORECAST function is similar to TREND, except that it returns a single point along a line rather than returning an array that defines the line. This function takes the form

=FORECAST(*x*,*known_y's*,*known_x's*)

The *x* argument is the data point for which you want to extrapolate a value. For example, instead of using TREND, we can use the FORECAST function to extrapolate the value in cell C24 in Figure 14-30 by entering the formula

=FORECAST(22,B2:B20,A2:A20)

where the *x* argument refers to the 22nd data point on the regression line. We can use this function to calculate any point in the future.

The SLOPE Function

The SLOPE function returns the slope of the linear regression line. The slope is defined as the vertical distance divided by the horizontal distance between any two points on the regression line. Its value is the same as the first number in the array returned by the LINEST function. In other words, SLOPE calculates the trajectory of the line used by the FORECAST and TREND functions to calculate the values of data points. The SLOPE function takes the form

=SLOPE(*known_y's*,*known_x's*)

To find the slope of the regression line that describes the data set from the example shown earlier in Figure 14-24, we can use the formula

=SLOPE(B2:B20,A2:A20)

which returns a value of 18.9895.

The STEYX Function

The STEYX function calculates the standard error of a regression, a measure of the amount of error accrued in predicting a *y* for each given *x*. This function takes the form

=STEYX(*known_y's*,*known_x's*)

If we apply this function to the worksheet shown earlier in Figure 14-24, the formula

=STEYX(B2:B20,A2:A20)

returns a standard error value of 9.43198.

Calculating Exponential Regression Statistics

The equation that describes an exponential regression curve is

$$y = b * m_1^{x_1} * m_2^{x_2} * \ldots * m_n^{x_n}$$

If you have only one independent variable, the equation is

$$y = b * m^x$$

The LOGEST Function

The LOGEST function works like the LINEST function, except that you use it to analyze data that is nonlinear. LOGEST returns coefficient values for each independent variable plus a value for the constant *b*. This function takes the form

= LOGEST(*known_y's,known_x's,const,stats*)

LOGEST accepts the same four arguments as the LINEST function and returns a result array in the same fashion. If you set the optional *stats* argument to TRUE, the function also returns validation statistics.

> **NOTE** The LINEST and LOGEST functions return only the y-axis coordinates used for calculating lines and curves. The difference between them is that LINEST projects a straight line and LOGEST projects an exponential curve. You must be careful to match the appropriate function to the analysis at hand. The LINEST function might be more appropriate for sales projections, and the LOGEST function might be more suited to applications such as statistical analyses or population trends.

For more information about the LOGEST function's underlying equations and its arguments, see "The LINEST Function," page 536.

The GROWTH Function

Whereas the LOGEST function returns a mathematical description of the exponential regression curve that best fits a set of known data, the GROWTH function lets you find points that lie along that curve. The GROWTH function works exactly like its linear counterpart, TREND, and takes the form

=GROWTH(*known_y's,known_x's,new_x's,const*)

For more information about the GROWTH function's arguments, see "The TREND Function," page 538.

Chapter 15

What-If Analysis

One of the most important benefits of spreadsheet software is that it lets you perform a what-if analysis quickly and easily. You can change key variables and instantly see the effect. For example, if you're using Microsoft Excel to decide whether to lease or purchase a car, you can test your financial model with different assumptions about interest rates and down payments, and you can see the effects of varying rates on "bottom-line" costs, such as the total interest you will pay.

Automatic recalculation provides you with instant feedback on your what-if experiments. When your model is set to recalculate automatically, you can change a value in a cell and watch as all cells whose values depend on the edited value are immediately recalculated.

Excel augments this basic capability with a number of advanced what-if features, which are also discussed in this chapter.

Data Tables

A data table, or *sensitivity table,* summarizes the impact of one or two variables on formulas that use those variables. You can use the Table command on the Data menu to create two kinds of data tables: a table based on a single input variable that tests the variable's impact on more than one formula, or a table based on two input variables that tests their impact on a single formula.

Data Tables Based on One Input Variable

Suppose you're considering buying a house that requires you to take on a 30-year, $200,000 mortgage, and you need to calculate monthly payments on the loan for several interest rates. A one-variable data table will give you the information you need.

To create this table, follow these steps:

1. Start by entering the inputs (that is, the interest rates) you want to test in a fresh worksheet. For this example, enter *6, 6.5, 7, 7.5, 8,* and *8.5* percent in cells B3:B8. (We'll call this range the *input range,* because it contains the input values we want to test.)

2. Next enter the formula that uses the input variable. In this case, enter the formula

   ```
   =PMT(A2/12,360,200000)
   ```

   in cell C2. In this formula, A2/12 is the monthly interest rate, 360 is the term of the loan in months, and 200000 is the loan principal. Notice that this formula refers to cell A2, which is currently blank. (Microsoft Excel assigns a value of 0 to a blank cell referenced in a numeric formula.) As you can see in Figure 15-1, because A2 is blank, the function returns a spurious result: the payment required to amortize the loan at an interest rate of 0 percent. Cell A2 is a placeholder through which Excel will feed the values in the input range. Excel never actually changes the underlying value of this cell, so this placeholder can be any cell in the worksheet outside the table range. You'll see in a moment why this formula refers to cell A2.

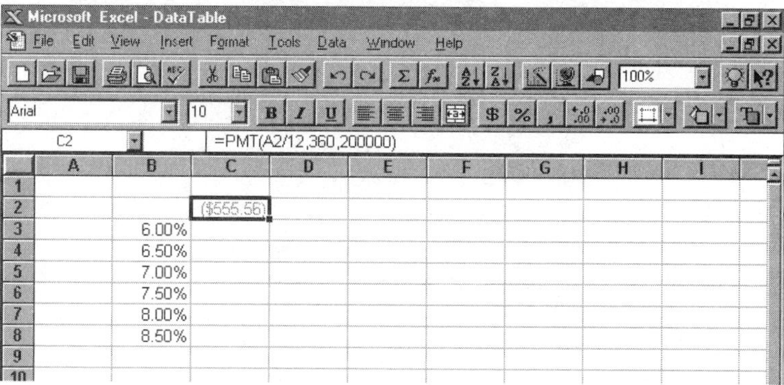

FIGURE 15-1
Begin building the data table by entering the interest rates and the PMT function in the worksheet.

3. Select the data table range — the smallest rectangular block that includes the formula and all the values in the input range. In this case, select the range B2:C8.

4. Choose Table from the Data menu. In the Table dialog box, shown in Figure 15-2, specify the location of the input cell in the Row Input Cell or Column Input Cell edit box. The input cell is the placeholder cell referred to by the table formula — in this example, A2. For a data table to work properly, you must enter the input cell reference in the correct edit box. If the input values are arranged in a row, enter the input cell reference in the Row Input Cell edit box. If the values in the input range are arranged in a column, use the Column Input Cell edit box. In this example, the input values are arranged in a column, so enter $A$2 in the Column Input Cell edit box.

Table
Row Input Cell:
Column Input Cell:
OK
Cancel

FIGURE 15-2
Use the Table dialog box to specify the input cell.

5. Click OK. Excel enters the results of the table formula (one result for each input value) in the available cells of the data table range. In this example, Excel enters six results in the range C3:C8, as shown in Figure 15-3.

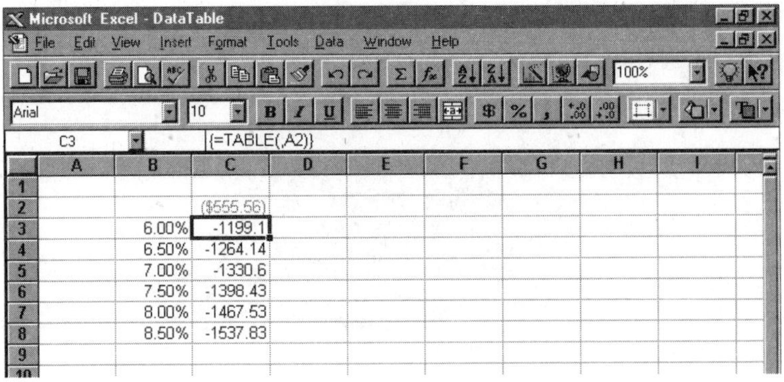

FIGURE 15-3
The monthly loan payments for each interest rate now appear in the data table.

	A	B	C
1			
2			($555.56)
3		6.00%	-1199.1
4		6.50%	-1264.14
5		7.00%	-1330.6
6		7.50%	-1398.43
7		8.00%	-1467.53
8		8.50%	-1537.83

When you create this data table, Excel enters the array formula

{=TABLE(,A2)}

in each cell in the range C3:C8 (the *results range*). In the sample table, the TABLE formula computes the results of the PMT function using each of the interest rates in column B. For example, the formula in cell C5 computes the payment at a rate of 7 percent.

The TABLE function used in the formula takes the form

=TABLE(*row input cell,column input cell*)

Because the one-input table in the example is arranged in a columnar format, Excel uses the column input reference, A2, as the function's second argument and leaves the first argument blank, using a comma to indicate that an argument has been omitted.

After you've built the table, you can change the table formula or any of the values in the input range to create a different set of results. For example, suppose you decide to borrow only $185,000 to buy your house. If you change the formula in cell C2 to

=PMT(A2/12,360,185000)

the values in the results range change as shown in Figure 15-4.

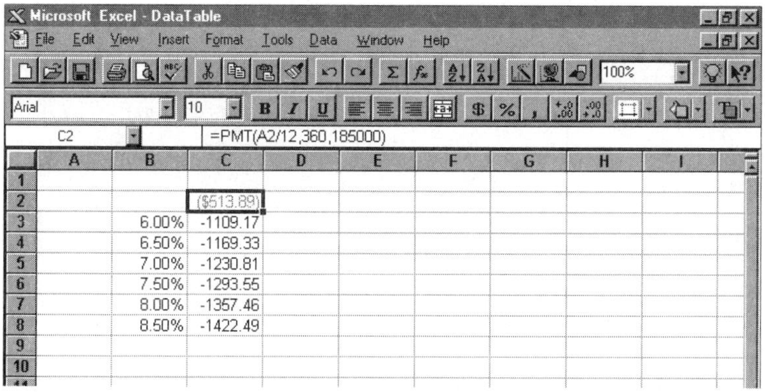

Microsoft Excel - DataTable

C2 =PMT(A2/12,360,185000)

	A	B	C
1			
2			($513.89)
3		6.00%	-1109.17
4		6.50%	-1169.33
5		7.00%	-1230.81
6		7.50%	-1293.55
7		8.00%	-1357.46
8		8.50%	-1422.49

FIGURE 15-4
When you change the loan amount, Excel recalculates the table.

Single-Variable Tables with More Than One Formula

You can include as many output formulas as you want when you create a single-variable data table. If your input range is in a column, enter the second output formula directly to the right of the first one, the third to the right of the second, and so on. You can use different formulas for different columns, but they must all use the same input cell.

Suppose you're also thinking about buying a house that would require you to take out a $180,000 mortgage. You want to know what your monthly payments would be on that mortgage at each of the interest rates in the input range, and you want to be able to compare these payments with those for the $200,000 mortgage calculated in Figure 15-3. You can expand the table in Figure 15-3 to include both formulas.

To add a new formula to the existing data table, follow these steps:

1. In the cell to the right of the existing formula — in this case, cell D2 — enter the new formula. For this example, enter

   =PMT(A2/12,360,180000)

   Notice that, like the first formula, this formula refers to cell A2, the same input cell as in the first formula. (Remember to restore the mortgage amount in the original formula to $200,000.)

2. Select the table range — in this case, B2:D8.
3. Choose the Table command, and enter the input cell reference $A$2 in the Column Input Cell edit box. Figure 15-5 on the next page shows the result.

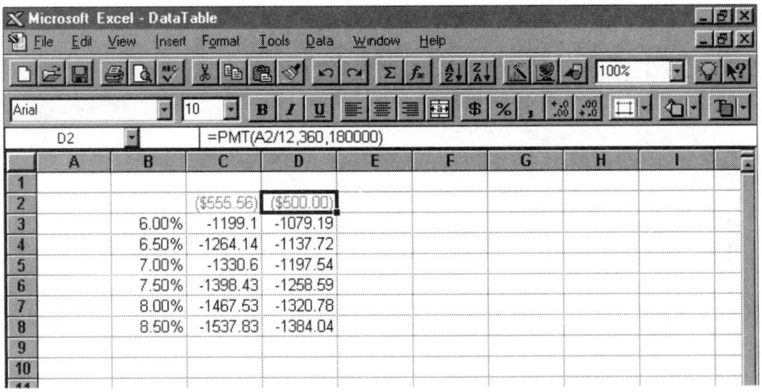

FIGURE 15-5
This data table computes the monthly payments on two different loan amounts at various interest rates.

	A	B	C	D	E	F	G	H	I
1									
2			($555.56)	($500.00)					
3		6.00%	-1199.1	-1079.19					
4		6.50%	-1264.14	-1137.72					
5		7.00%	-1330.6	-1197.54					
6		7.50%	-1398.43	-1258.59					
7		8.00%	-1467.53	-1320.78					
8		8.50%	-1537.83	-1384.04					
9									
10									

As before, each cell in the range C3:D8 contains the formula

{=TABLE(,A2)}

These formulas compute the results of the formulas in cells C2 and D2 at each interest rate in the input range. For example, the formula in cell D4 computes the result of the formula in cell D2 at the rate in cell B4, 6.5 percent.

Data Tables Based on Two Input Variables

The data tables considered so far compute the effect of a single variable on one or more formulas. You can also create tables that compute the effects of two variables on a single formula.

Suppose you want to build a data table that computes the monthly payment on a $200,000 mortgage, but this time you want to vary not only the interest rate but also the term of the loan. You want to know what effect changing the interest rate to 6, 6.5, 7, 7.5, 8, or 8.5 percent and changing the term to 15, 20, 25, or 30 years (180, 240, 300, or 360 months) will have on your monthly payment.

To create this table, follow these steps:

1. Enter the first set of input values you want to test in a column-oriented range. As before, enter the six interest rates in cells B3:B8.
2. Enter the second set of input values in a row-oriented range above and to the right of the first set. In this case, enter the different terms in cells C2:F2.
3. Now you can create the table formula. Because this is a two-variable table, the output formula must be entered in the cell at the intersection of the row and column that contain the two sets of input values — cell B2, in this example. Although you can include as many formulas as you want in a single-variable data table, you can include only one

output formula in a two-variable table. The formula for the table in this example is

=PMT(A2/12,B1,200000)

Figure 15-6 shows the result so far. The formula returns the #DIV/0! error value because the two blank cells, when used as arguments, produce a number either too large or too small for Excel to represent. As you'll see, this spurious result will not affect the performance of the table.

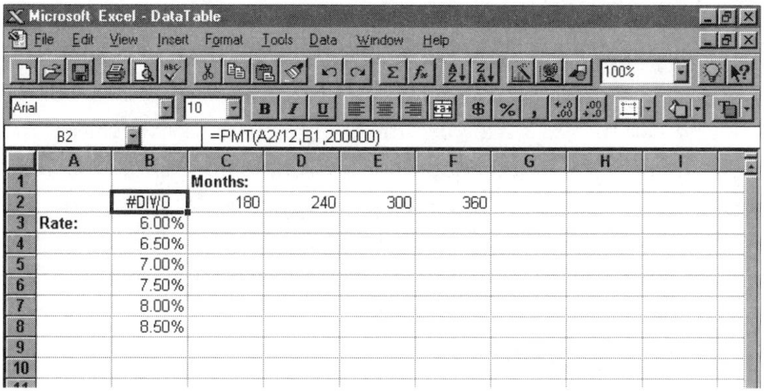

	A	B	C	D	E	F
1			**Months:**			
2		#DIV/0	180	240	300	360
3	**Rate:**	6.00%				
4		6.50%				
5		7.00%				
6		7.50%				
7		8.00%				
8		8.50%				

FIGURE 15-6
Cell B2 contains the formula for this two-variable table.

4. Select the data table range — the smallest rectangular block that includes all the input values and the table formula. In this example, the table range is B2:F8.
5. Choose the Table command from the Data menu and specify the input cells. Because this is a two-variable table, you must define two input cells: one for the first set of input values and one for the second set. For this example, enter the reference for the first input cell, $B$1, in the Row Input Cell edit box and then enter the reference for the second input cell, $A$2, in the Column Input Cell edit box.
6. Press Enter or click OK to compute the table. Figure 15-7 on the next page shows the result.

As in the previous examples, Excel enters TABLE array formulas in the results range C3:F8. Because this table has two sets of variables, the TABLE formula includes two references:

{=TABLE(B1,A2)}

The values in the results range are the monthly payments required to amortize the mortgage at each combination of interest rates and terms. For example, the value in cell D6, –1611.19, is the payment required to amortize a $200,000 mortgage over 240 months at an interest rate of 7.5 percent.

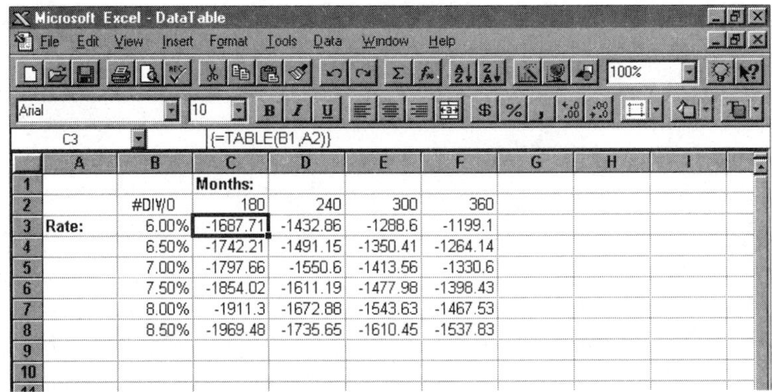

	A	B	C	D	E	F	G	H	I
1			Months:						
2		#DIV/0	180	240	300	360			
3	Rate:	6.00%	-1687.71	-1432.86	-1288.6	-1199.1			
4		6.50%	-1742.21	-1491.15	-1350.41	-1264.14			
5		7.00%	-1797.66	-1550.6	-1413.56	-1330.6			
6		7.50%	-1854.02	-1611.19	-1477.98	-1398.43			
7		8.00%	-1911.3	-1672.88	-1543.63	-1467.53			
8		8.50%	-1969.48	-1735.65	-1610.45	-1537.83			
9									
10									

FIGURE 15-7
This data table calculates the monthly payments using various interest rates and terms.

Be careful not to reverse the input cells in a two-variable table. If you do, Excel uses the input values in the wrong place in the table formula, which creates a set of meaningless results. For example, if you reverse the input cells in the previous example, Excel uses the values in the input range C2:F2 as interest rates and the values in the input range B3:B8 as terms.

Editing Tables

Although you can edit the input values or formulas in the left column or top row of a table, you can't edit the contents of any individual cell in the results range because the data table is an array. For example, if you try to clear cell D7 in Figure 15-7, Excel displays an alert box with the message *Cannot change part of a table.* If you make a mistake when you set up a data table, you must select all the results, use the Clear command on the Edit menu, and then recompute the table.

You can copy the table results to a different part of the worksheet. You might want to do this to save the table's current results before you change the table formula or variables. To copy the results of the sample table in Figure 15-7 from the range C3:F8 to the range C10:F15, select cells C3:F8, choose the Copy command from the Edit menu, select cell C10, and then choose the Paste command. (You can also copy the results using direct cell manipulation or the Copy and Paste buttons on the Standard toolbar.) As Figure 15-8 shows, the values in C10:F15 are constants, not array formulas. Excel changes the results of the table from a set of array formulas to their numeric values when you copy the results out of the table range.

For more information about direct cell manipulation, see "Moving and Copying with the Mouse," page 232.

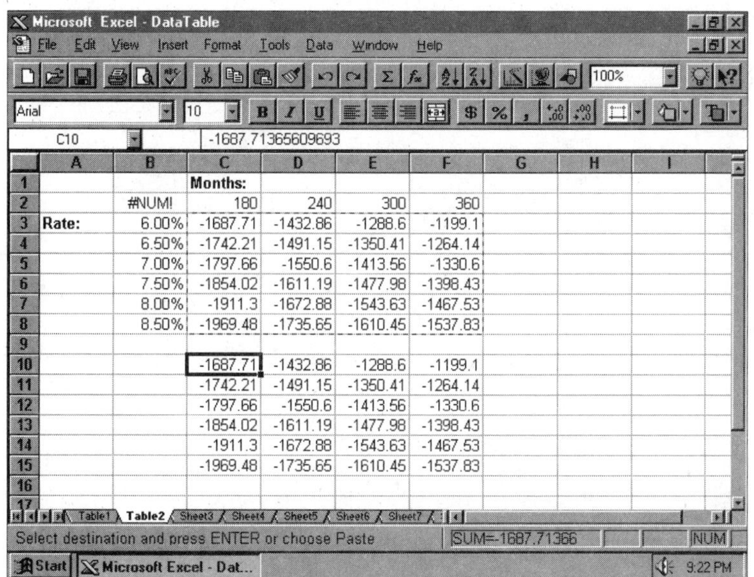

	A	B	C	D	E	F
1			Months:			
2		#NUM!	180	240	300	360
3	Rate:	6.00%	-1687.71	-1432.86	-1288.6	-1199.1
4		6.50%	-1742.21	-1491.15	-1350.41	-1264.14
5		7.00%	-1797.66	-1550.6	-1413.56	-1330.6
6		7.50%	-1854.02	-1611.19	-1477.98	-1398.43
7		8.00%	-1911.3	-1672.88	-1543.63	-1467.53
8		8.50%	-1969.48	-1735.65	-1610.45	-1537.83
9						
10			-1687.71	-1432.86	-1288.6	-1199.1
11			-1742.21	-1491.15	-1350.41	-1264.14
12			-1797.66	-1550.6	-1413.56	-1330.6
13			-1854.02	-1611.19	-1477.98	-1398.43
14			-1911.3	-1672.88	-1543.63	-1467.53
15			-1969.48	-1735.65	-1610.45	-1537.83

FIGURE 15-8
Copying the results range to another part of the worksheet transfers the numeric values, not the formulas used to compute them.

The Scenario Manager

Data tables are fine for relatively simple situations that involve only one or two variables, but real-world decisions usually involve many more unknowns. To model more complicated problems that involve as many as 32 variables, you can call on the services of the Scenario Manager by choosing the Scenarios command from the Tools menu.

Before we get started, we'll define some terms so we're all speaking the same language. A *scenario* is a named combination of values assigned to one or more variable cells in a what-if model. A *what-if model* is any worksheet, like the example in Figure 15-9 on the next page, in which you can substitute different values for *variables,* such as Average Customer Visits, in order to see the effect on other values, such as Operating Profit, that are computed by formulas dependent on the variables. The Scenario Manager identifies the cells that contain values you want to use as variables as *changing cells.*

You can use the Scenario Manager to create as many scenarios as your what-if model requires, and you can then print reports detailing all the changing cells and result cells. The Scenario Manager includes the following features:

- You can define a scenario by simply selecting cells and typing a name with the Scenarios box on the WorkGroup toolbar.
- You can create multiple scenarios for a single what-if model, each with its own sets of variables.

FIGURE 15-9
We'll use the Scenario Manager to model the effects of changing values in D2:D3, D5, and E8:E13 of this worksheet.

	A	B	C	D	E	F	G
1				**Total per week**	**Total per year**		
2		Revenues per Customer Visit		34.78			
3		Direct Costs per Customer Visit		30.12			
4		Gross Profit per Customer Visit		4.66			
5		Average Customer Visits		33,759			
6		**Gross Profit**		**157,317**	**8,180,481**		
7		Overhead Costs					
8			*Payroll*		3,494,046		
9			*Facilities*		1,635,511		
10			*Depreciation*		453,305		
11			*Advertising*		291,647		
12			*Supplies*		496,944		
13			*Other*		1,295,828		
14		**Subtotal**			**7,667,281**		
15		**Operating Profit**			**513,200**		

- You can distribute a what-if model to other members of your group so that they can add their own scenarios. Then you can collect the multiple versions and merge all the scenarios into a single worksheet.
- You can track changes made to scenarios easily with Scenario Manager's version control features by recording the date and the user name each time a scenario is added or modified.
- You can password-protect scenarios from modification, and even hide them from view.
- You can examine relationships between scenarios with different sets of variables created by multiple users by using the PivotTable report option. This adds another dimension to what-if analyses.

To understand how the Scenario Manager works, imagine that you manage a grocery store whose profit picture is modeled by the worksheet in Figure 15-9. The numbers in D2:D3, D5, and E8:E13 are recent historic averages. You're interested in testing the impact of changes in these cells on the bottom line, which is shown in cell E15. Nine variables are far too many for the Table command, but the Scenario Manager can help.

TIP Before you begin using the Scenario Manager, it's a good idea to name the cells you plan to use for your variables, as well as any cells containing formulas whose values depend on your variable cells. This step is not required, but it makes the scenario reports, as well as some of the dialog boxes, more intelligible.

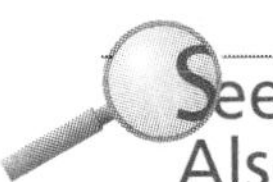

For more information about pivot tables, see Chapter 22, "Using the PivotTable Wizard," page 787.

Defining Scenarios

To define a scenario, follow these steps:

1. Choose Scenarios from the Tools menu.
2. In the Scenario Manager dialog box, shown in Figure 15-10, click the Add button.

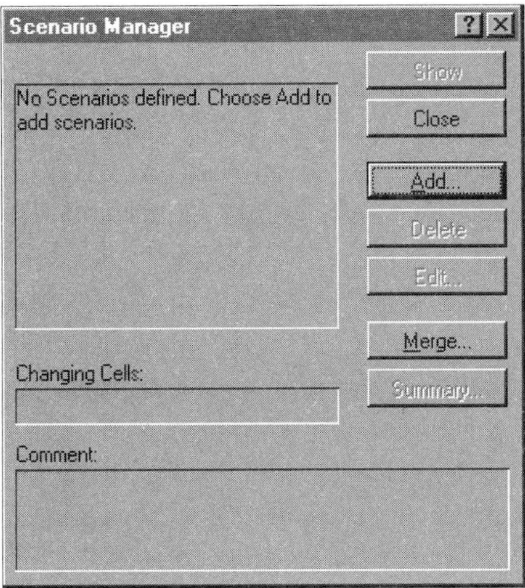

FIGURE 15-10
Choosing Scenarios from the Tools menu displays this Scenario Manager dialog box.

3. In the Add Scenario dialog box, shown in Figure 5-11 on the next page, type a name for your scenario.
4. In the Changing Cells edit box, indicate which cells you plan to vary. By default, this edit box displays the reference of the cell or range that was selected when you chose the Scenarios command, but you can change it by typing new references or names or by selecting cells with the mouse. (If the Add Scenario dialog box is in your way, drag it to one side.) You can indicate nonadjacent cells and ranges by separating their references or names with commas, as shown in Figure 15-11 on the next page.
5. Click OK to create the first scenario.

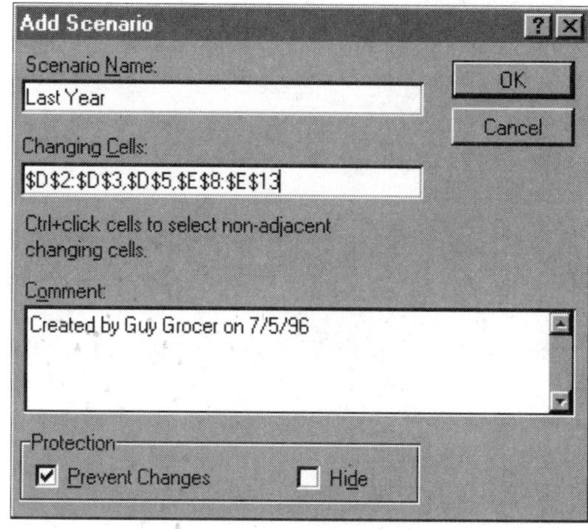

FIGURE 15-11

Here we entered the references of the changing cells individually by selecting each one with the mouse and separating one reference from the next with a comma.

6. The Scenario Values dialog box appears, displaying an edit box for each changing cell. If you have named the changing cells, the names are displayed adjacent to the edit boxes, as shown in Figure 15-12; otherwise, the references of the changing cells are displayed. The edit boxes contain the corresponding values currently entered in the worksheet. To complete a scenario, you simply edit these values, but for this example, we'll leave the starting values for the model as they are and just click OK.

   In each edit box, you can enter either a constant or a formula. For example, to increase the value of the first variable in Figure 15-12, click in front of the value in the first variable's edit box and type *=1.1** to create a formula that multiplies the current value by 1.1. (Note that although you can enter formulas in the Scenario Values dialog box, Excel alerts you that the formulas are converted to their resulting values when you click OK.) The Scenario Values dialog box displays only five variables at a time; use the scroll bar to the right of the edit boxes to display edit boxes for additional changing cells.

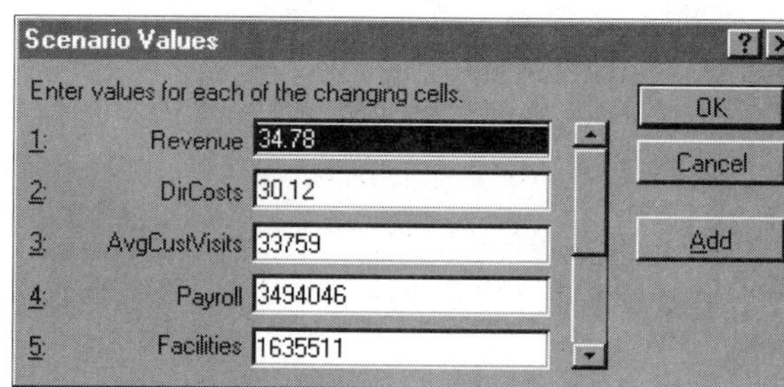

FIGURE 15-12

Enter a value for each changing cell. Because we previously named each changing cell, the names appear in the Scenario Values dialog box.

7. To create another scenario, click Add to return to the Add Scenario dialog box. (You can create as many scenarios as you want at this time.) When you have finished creating scenarios, click OK to return to the Scenario Manager dialog box. To return to the worksheet, click Close in the Scenario Manager dialog box. You can return to the Scenario Manager at a later time to create more scenarios or edit existing ones.

TIP It's a good idea to define the values you start with as a scenario before changing any of them. You can name this scenario something like *Starting Values* or *Last Year*, as we did in the example. If you don't name the starting scenario, you'll lose your original what-if assumptions when you display the new changing cell values in your worksheet.

Using the Show Button to View Scenarios

After you've created a few scenarios, you'll probably want to start testing their effects on your worksheet. To do so, choose the Scenarios command, select a scenario name in the Scenario Manager dialog box, and click Show. The Scenario Manager replaces the variable values currently in the worksheet with the values you specified when you created the selected scenario. Figure 15-13 on the next page shows how your worksheet might appear if you used the Show button with a scenario that increased average customer visits by 5 percent and decreased revenues per customer visit by the same percentage.

CAUTION Always save your worksheet before experimenting with the Scenario Manager's Show button. The Show button replaces your worksheet's current values with the values of the selected scenario. If you didn't save your original values or if you made changes to your worksheet after you saved it, the values or changes could be lost. You can use the Edit menu's Undo Show command to reverse this action when you return to the worksheet, but if you examined the impact of two or more scenarios, the Undo command reverses the effect of only the most recently shown scenario.

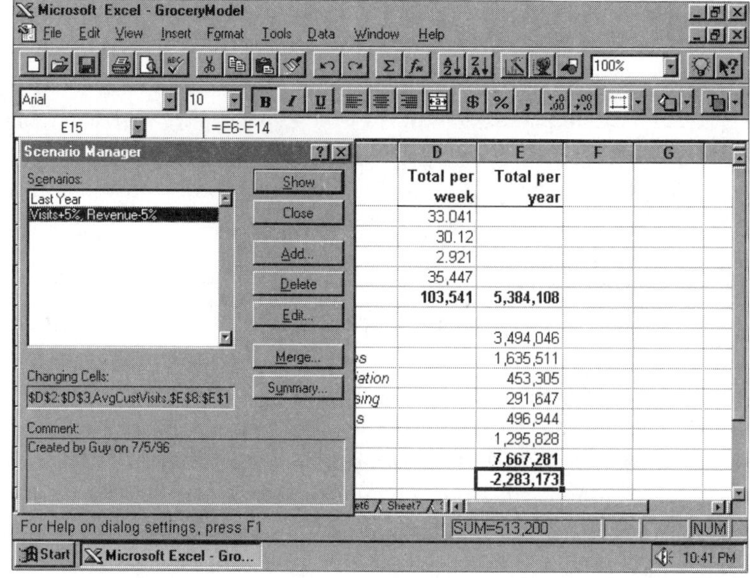

FIGURE 15-13 Clicking the Show button replaces your current worksheet values with the values of a specified scenario.

The Scenario Manager dialog box remains on screen when you use the Show button so that you can look at the results of other scenarios without returning to the worksheet. When you click Close or press Esc to close the Scenario Manager dialog box, the last scenario you looked at remains in the worksheet. As long as you have not made any other changes in the worksheet, you can reverse the effects of the last shown scenario by choosing the Edit menu's Undo Show command.

Adding, Editing, and Deleting Scenarios

Scenarios are saved with all other worksheet data when you use the File menu's Save command. Each worksheet in a workbook can contain its own set of scenarios, and each time you load a workbook, any scenarios associated with a particular worksheet are available. In the Scenario Manager dialog box, you add new scenarios by clicking Add, and you edit existing scenarios by clicking Edit.

Clicking the Edit button in the Scenario Manager dialog box displays the Edit Scenario dialog box, which is identical to the Add Scenario dialog box shown in Figure 15-11 on page 554. You can change the name of the selected scenario, add changing cells, remove existing changing cells, or specify a completely different set of changing cells. When you click OK, the Scenario Values dialog box appears so that you can edit the changing cell values.

As time goes by, you'll probably want to prune your scenario list. To erase a scenario, simply select the scenario's name in the Scenario Manager dialog box and click Delete.

How the Scenario Manager Tracks Changes

When someone edits an existing scenario, Excel adds a *Modified by* entry to the Comment box in the Scenario Manager dialog box, beneath the *Created by* entry that appears when a scenario is first added (see Figure 15-11 on page 554). Each time a scenario is modified, Excel adds another entry with the name of the user and the date of the modification. This information is particularly helpful if you route your what-if models to others and then merge their scenarios into a single what-if model, as discussed in the next section.

Merging Scenarios

If part of your job is to develop what-if models or projections for your company, you probably spend a lot of time gathering information from your coworkers about trends and market forces that might come to bear upon the company in the future. Often you need input from several people, each of whom knows the most about a particular aspect of the business, such as payroll costs or sales trends. In Excel, you can create scenarios with different sets of changing cells on the same worksheet. For example, you could create separate "best case" and "worst case" scenarios for payroll costs and sales trends. In addition, Excel includes two features that can make this sort of information-gathering task far more manageable: document routing and scenario merging.

If you are connected to a network that uses a compatible electronic mail system, you can use the Add Routing Slip command (or the Routing Slip button on the WorkGroup toolbar) to attach the current workbook to an electronic mail message to be sent to one or more of your coworkers. Compatible electronic mail systems include Microsoft Mail, Lotus cc:Mail, and any other electronic mail application that complies with the MAPI (Messaging Application Programming Interface) or VIM (Vendor Independent Messaging) standards.

If you are not connected to a network with a compatible electronic mail system, you can make copies of the worksheet containing your what-if model and distribute the copies to your coworkers the old-fashioned way — on floppy disks.

For example, suppose you want to distribute a what-if model to several of your coworkers: Vicki has expertise on customer trends, Max knows the payroll story, and Regina keeps track of advertising. You can consolidate their contributions in three ways: First, you can ask each person in turn to add his or her scenarios to the model in your original worksheet. Second, you can distribute a workbook with duplicates of the original model on four

The Scenario Express

The quickest and easiest way to define and display scenarios is to use the Scenarios box on the WorkGroup toolbar, shown here:

To display the WorkGroup toolbar, choose Toolbars from the View menu, select WorkGroup, and click OK.

To use the Scenarios box, first enter new values in the changing cells, select them, click the Scenarios box, type a name for the new scenario, and press Enter. Using this technique, you can define as many scenarios as you want, without ever using the Scenario Manager dialog box.

When you want to display a scenario, click the down arrow next to the Scenarios box and select the name of the scenario you want to show from the drop-down list.

You can also redefine scenarios using the Scenarios box. First select the name of the scenario you want to redefine from the Scenarios drop-down list to display its changing cell values. Next enter new values in the changing cells and again select the same scenario name from the Scenarios drop-down list. A dialog box appears, asking you to confirm that you want to redefine the scenario. (If you modify any of the current changing cell values, be careful not to inadvertently redefine the current scenario by selecting its name from the Scenarios drop-down list.)

separate worksheets — one for you and one for each of them. To create this workbook, you name each worksheet and select the worksheets as a group. Select the data to copy, and choose Fill and then Across Worksheets from the Edit menu to copy all the data, formulas, and formats from the original model to the other three worksheets, as shown in Figure 15-14. You can then pass the workbook to each person in turn, with a request that they create their scenarios on their respective worksheets.

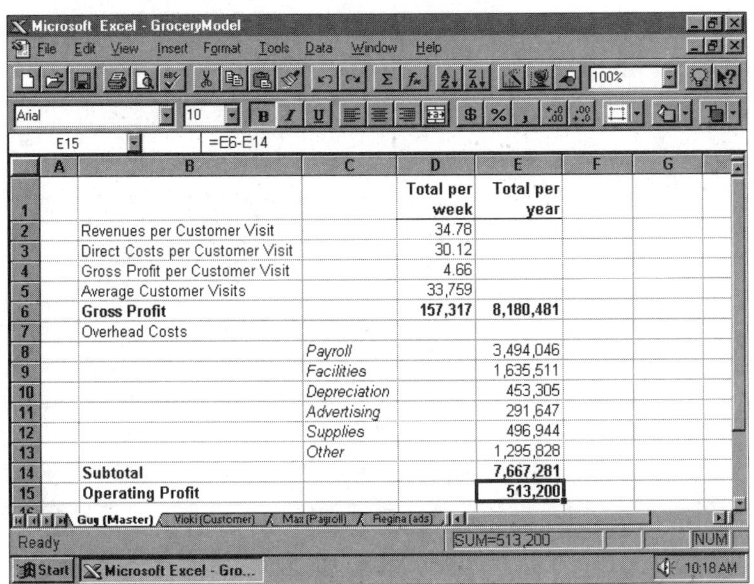

FIGURE 15-14
We set up this workbook for distribution to several coworkers, with a separate sheet for each person to use for his or her scenarios.

The third possibility is to make copies of the original workbook, each with a unique filename, so that each person can add his or her scenarios to a separate file.

With the second or third technique, after your coworkers add their what-if scenarios and return the workbook (or their copies of the workbook), you can merge the scenarios into a master worksheet. Simply open all of the workbooks containing the desired scenarios, activate the worksheet you wish to contain the merged scenarios, and use the Merge button in the Scenario Manager dialog box.

When you click the Merge button, a dialog box like the one in Figure 15-15 appears.

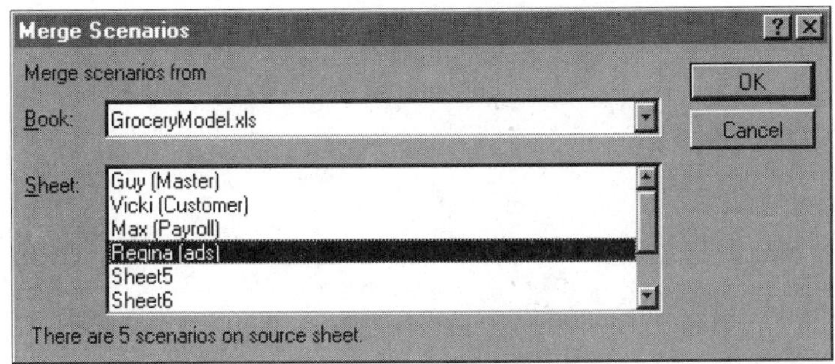

FIGURE 15-15
Clicking Merge in the Scenario Manager dialog box displays the Merge Scenarios dialog box, with which you can import scenarios from any sheet in any open workbook.

TIP Merging scenarios works best if the basic structure of all the worksheets is identical. Although this uniformity is not a strict requirement, merging scenarios from worksheets that are laid out differently can cause changing cell values to appear in unexpected locations. For this reason, and because it's generally difficult to ascertain the skill level of everyone contributing data, you might try a fourth approach. Distribute a "questionnaire" requesting only the data you need, use external cell references to link the requested data with the appropriate locations in your master worksheet, and create the scenarios yourself or with a macro. For more information on external cell references, see "Three Dimensional Names," page 134 and "Defining Sheet-Level Names," page 130.

In the Merge Scenarios dialog box, you select the workbook and worksheet from which you want to merge scenarios. As shown in Figure 15-15, when you select a worksheet from the Sheet list, a message at the bottom of the dialog box tells you how many scenarios exist on that worksheet. When you click OK, the scenarios on that worksheet are copied to the active worksheet. (The OK button is dimmed if you try to merge a scenario from the active worksheet or from a worksheet on which there are no scenarios.)

After merging all the scenarios from your coworkers, the Scenario Manager dialog box for this example looks like the one shown in Figure 15-16.

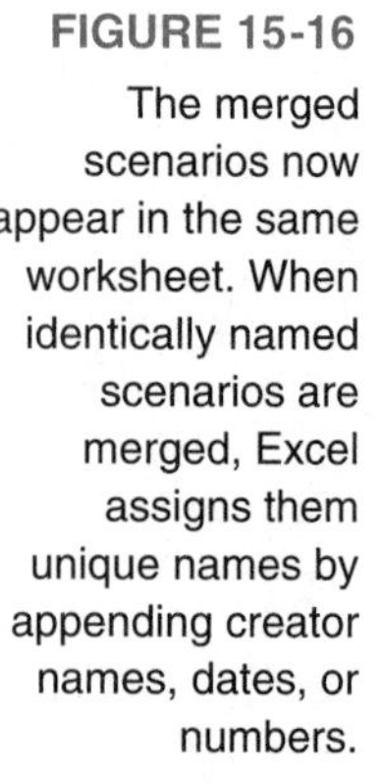

FIGURE 15-16
The merged scenarios now appear in the same worksheet. When identically named scenarios are merged, Excel assigns them unique names by appending creator names, dates, or numbers.

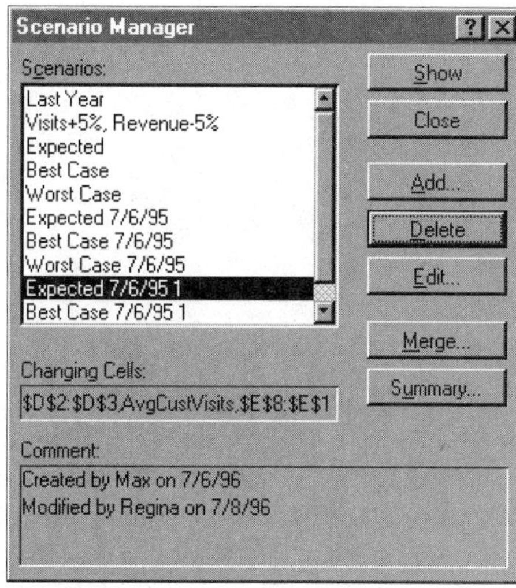

Notice in Figure 15-16 that the Comment box displays the name of the creator and modifier of the selected scenario. Notice also that the Scenarios list includes similarly named scenarios. In this example, all of the coworkers used the same three names — Expected, Best Case, and Worst Case — for their scenarios, and Excel avoided conflicts by appending the creator name and date when it encountered duplicate scenario names. (Excel might also use numbers to distinguish merged scenarios that were created on the same date.) You can use the Edit button to rename the scenarios if you want, but you might find it useful to retain the creator names and dates.

Each group of scenarios provided by the coworkers uses different changing cells. Vicki's scenarios change the values in cells D2, D3, and D5, while Max's scenarios change only the value in E8 and Regina's scenarios change only the value in E11. You can display these different scenarios together and watch how the combinations affect the bottom line. For example, some of the values in Guy's original scenarios have been changed in Vicki's, Max's, and Regina's scenarios. You could start out by displaying one of Guy's scenarios and then observe the effect of adding each of the other sets of changing cells to the model. The possibilities are virtually limitless.

For more information about Excel's file-sharing capabilities, see "Routing Workbooks to a Workgroup Using Electronic Mail," page 81.

For more information about the Fill and Across Sheets commands, see "The Across Worksheets Command," page 269.

For more information about group editing, see "Editing Groups of Sheets Simultaneously," page 326.

Creating Scenario Reports

The Grocery workbook with its merged scenarios has become quite a complex what-if model. However, you can create far more complex models that include as many scenarios as you want (or as many as your computer can handle) with up to 32 variables per scenario. The Scenario Manager's summary reports give you a way to keep track of all the possibilities, and the PivotTable report option gives you additional what-if functionality by allowing you to manipulate the elements of the report itself.

Clicking the Summary button in the Scenario Manager dialog box displays a dialog box with which you create a new worksheet containing a report that shows the values each scenario assigns to each changing cell. Optionally, this report can also show the impact of each scenario on one or more result cells.

Figure 15-17 shows the dialog box that appears when you click the Summary button while working in the Grocery workbook.

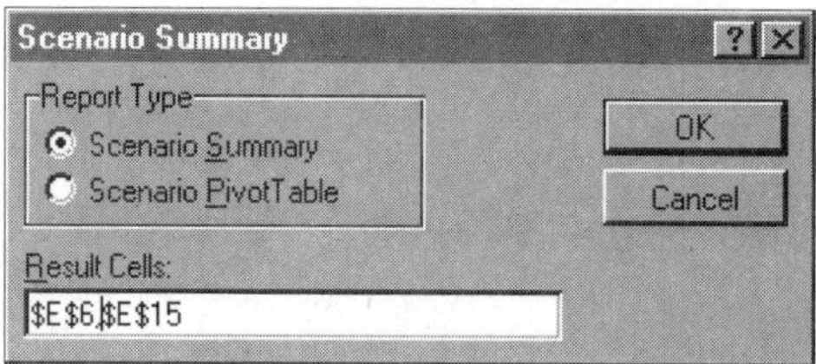

FIGURE 15-17
Use the Scenario Summary dialog box to specify the type of report and the result cells you want to see.

In the top section of this dialog box, you select the type of report you want. At the bottom of the dialog box, you can optionally identify any result cells that you want to appear in the report, separated by commas. For result cells, you want the cell that happens to be the final dependent of the changing cells — in this case, the Operating Profit value in cell E15 as well as cell E6 — the yearly Gross Profit value.

The Scenario Summary Report

After you specify the result cells and click OK, the Scenario Manager creates a report in a new worksheet. If you selected the Scenario Summary option in the Report Type section of the Scenario Summary dialog box, a worksheet named Scenario Summary is inserted next to the active worksheet in your workbook, as shown in Figure 15-18. You can then move the worksheet if you want. (We hid

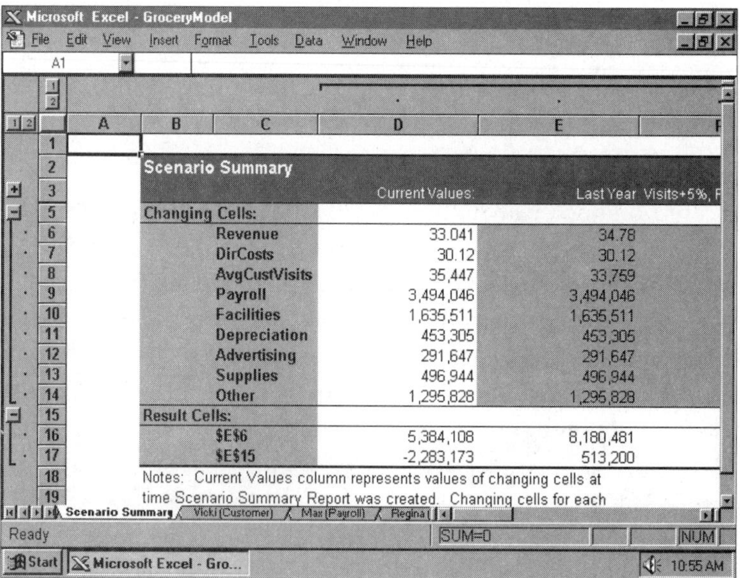

FIGURE 15-18
The Summary option creates a report in a new worksheet named Scenario Summary.

the toolbars and adjusted some of the column widths in the report in Figure 15-18 to display more of the report on the screen.)

Notice that the summary lists the changing cells and result cells by name if you have assigned names to them. The names of the scenarios appear as column headings, and the columns appear in the order in which the scenarios were defined. You might want to add a scenario description to each column by typing text in new rows inserted below the column headings, by creating text boxes, or by using the Note command on the Insert menu.

In Figure 15-18, notice that all the changing cell values in columns E and F are shaded in gray, but some of the values in column G are not. The shading indicates the cells that were designated as changing cells in the Add Scenario dialog box when the scenario whose name appears at the top of the column was created. This way, you can tell at a glance which scenarios control which cells in your what-if model.

Also notice that outlining symbols appear above and to the left of the summary report, allowing you to show and hide details. In Figure 15-18, the show detail symbol to the left of row 3 indicates that something is hidden here. Clicking this symbol displays the hidden data — the contents of the Comment box in the Scenario Manager dialog box, including the creation and modification date of each scenario. In Figure 15-19, we have hidden the changing cell details so that we can focus on the "bottom lines" of each scenario.

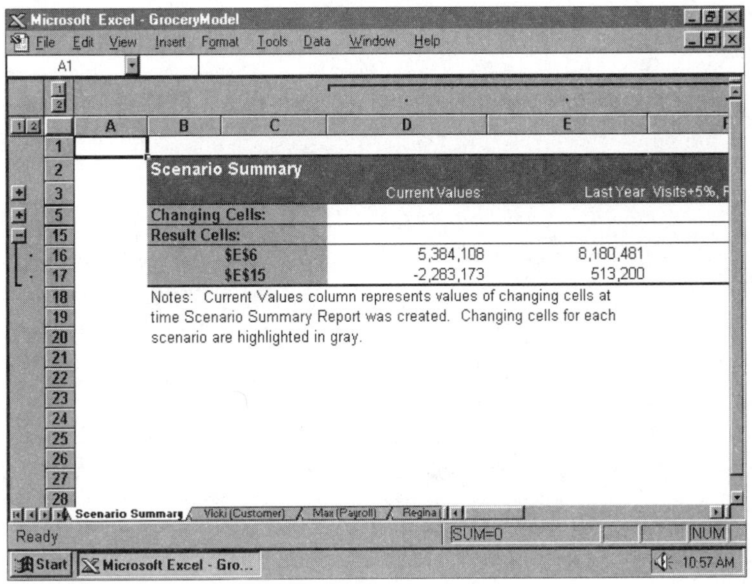

FIGURE 15-19
The outlining symbols in the Scenario Summary report let you manipulate your view of the data.

For information about working with worksheet outlines, see "Outlining Your Worksheets," page 217.

For information about adding notes to worksheets, see "Adding Notes to Cells," page 288.

For information about moving worksheets in workbooks, see "Working with Sheets," page 309.

For information about sorting data, see "Sorting Lists and Other Ranges," page 718.

The PivotTable Report

The other report option in the Scenario Summary dialog box is Scenario PivotTable. Like the Scenario Summary option, the Scenario PivotTable option inserts a new worksheet in your workbook. However, pivot tables are what-if tools in their own right, allowing you to use direct mouse manipulation techniques to mix and match different scenarios in the report and watch the effects on result cells.

Pivot tables are powerful analysis tools best suited to complex what-if models that include scenarios with different sets of changing cells created by different people. The more one-dimensional your what-if model, the less useful a PivotTable report becomes. Pivot tables take longer to create and consume more memory than Summary reports. If you create all the scenarios yourself and use the same set of changing cells in each, you might find it easier to use the Scenario Summary option because you won't be able to make use of the advantages offered by the PivotTable report.

Figure 15-20 shows a PivotTable report created from a version of the merged-scenario Grocery workbook. When you display a PivotTable report, the Query And Pivot toolbar appears.

The report cells containing numeric data represent the result cells as they would appear given the scenarios as they are currently displayed in the report. The row fields initially display the changing cells, whose names appear in shaded boxes above the names of each scenario in which the changing cells are included. The result cells initially appear across the top of the table. To try a different arrangement, you simply drag any of the shaded boxes from one area to another. The boxes in the upper left corner of the report are drop-down lists with the names of the scenario creators. By default, the All option is selected, but you can select any individual name.

For more information about pivot tables and the Query And Pivot toolbar, see Chapter 22, "Using the PivotTable Wizard," page 787.

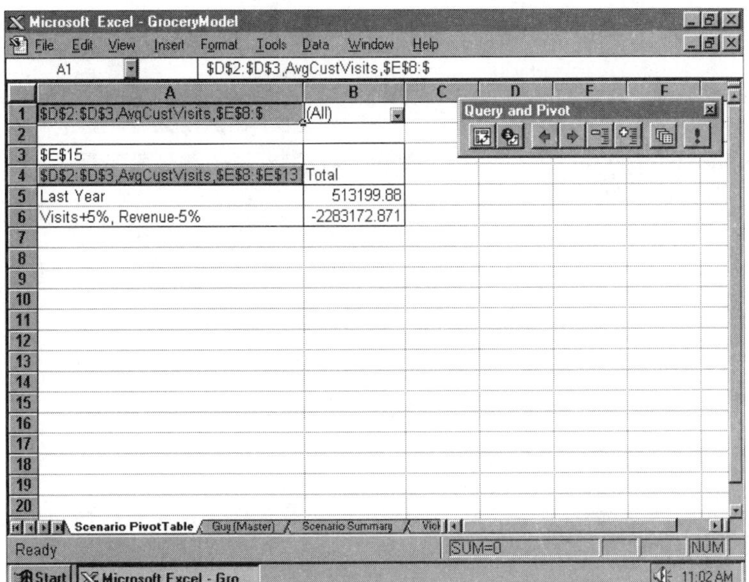

FIGURE 15-20

The Scenario PivotTable report lets you manipulate the actual data in the report.

The Goal Seek Command

With the Tools menu's Goal Seek command, you can compute an unknown value that will produce a desired result. For example, suppose you want to know the maximum 30-year mortgage you can afford if the interest rate is 6.5 percent and if you must limit your monthly payments to $2,000. To use the Goal Seek command to answer this question, follow these steps:

1. Set up the problem with trial values. For example, in the maximum-mortgage problem shown in Figure 15-21 at the top of the next page, a $500,000 mortgage would require monthly payments in excess of the $2,000 target. To define names for the cells B1:B4, select cells A1:B4 and choose Name from the Insert menu and then Create. Check the Left Column option and click OK.
2. Make the formula cell — in this case, B4 — the active cell. (This isn't absolutely necessary, but it simplifies the process.)
3. From the Tools menu, choose the Goal Seek command.
4. In the Goal Seek dialog box, shown in Figure 15-22 on the next page, accept the value in the Set Cell edit box (the absolute reference of the active cell).

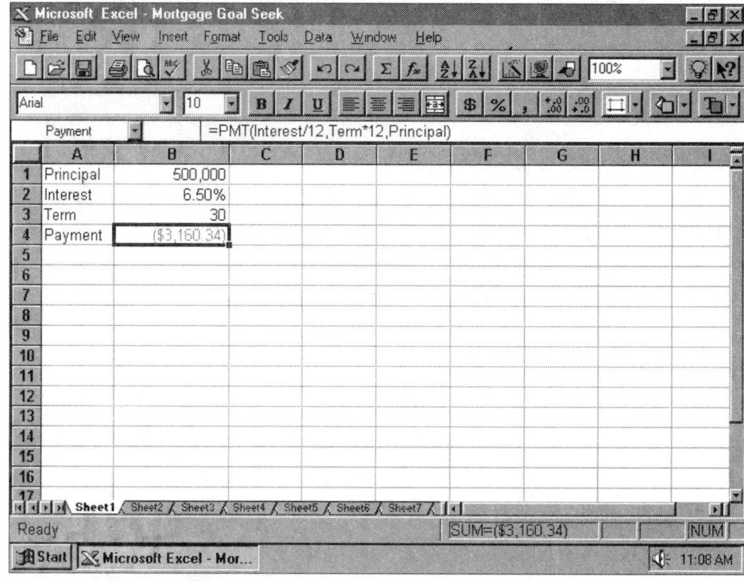

FIGURE 15-21

Use the Goal Seek command to find the maximum mortgage you can borrow if you want to keep your payments under a certain limit.

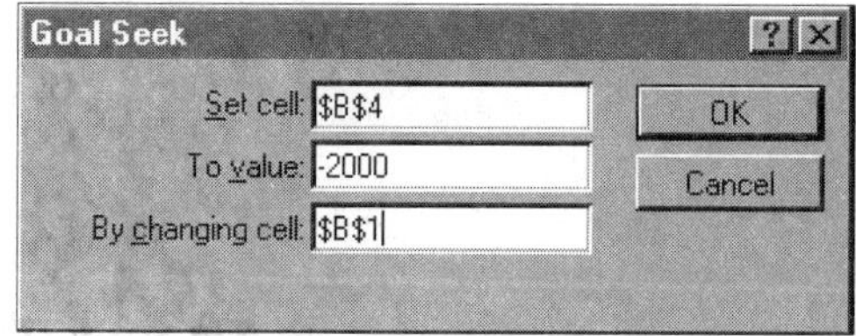

FIGURE 15-22

To use goal seeking, complete the Goal Seek dialog box.

5. In the To Value edit box, type the maximum value you want as the result of the formula — in this case, *–2000*. (You enter *–2000* because you are willing to pay $2000.)
6. In the By Changing Cell edit box, type the reference or click the cell in the worksheet whose value is unknown — in this case, cell B1 (the Principal value). (Alternatively, if you have assigned a name such as *Principal* to cell B1, you can type that name in the By Changing Cell edit box.)
7. Click OK or press Enter. Microsoft Excel displays the Goal Seek Status dialog box shown in Figure 15-23. The answer you are looking for appears in the cell specified in the By Changing Cell edit box. In this example, the result 316,422 appears in cell B1.

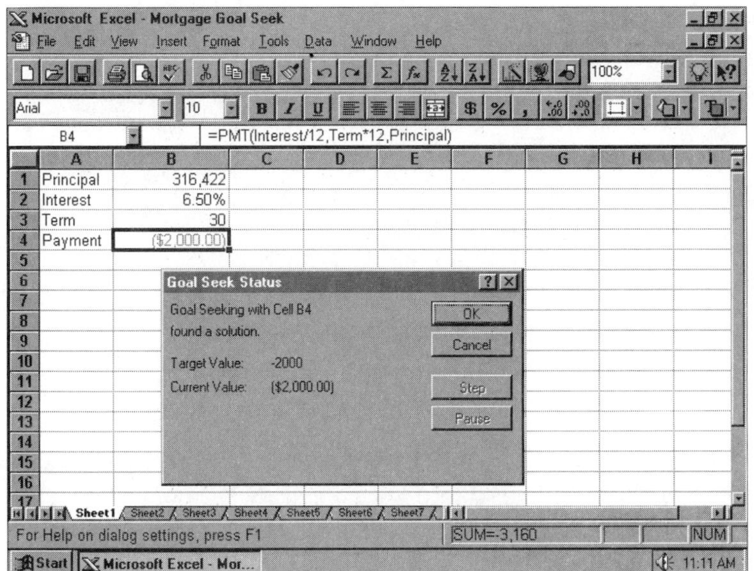

FIGURE 15-23

The Goal Seek Status dialog box informs you when a solution is found.

8. To retain this value, click OK in the Goal Seek Status dialog box. To restore the value that was in B1 before you used the Goal Seek command, click Cancel.

Excel uses an iterative technique to perform goal seeking. It tries one value after another for the variable cell specified in the By Changing Cell edit box until it arrives at the solution you requested. The mortgage problem we just looked at can be solved quickly. Other problems might take longer, and some might not be solvable at all.

While Excel is working on a complex goal-seeking problem, you can click Pause in the Goal Seek Status dialog box to interrupt the calculation and then click Step to display the results of each successive iteration. A Continue button appears in the dialog box when you are solving a problem in this stepwise fashion. To resume full-speed goal seeking, click Continue.

Precision and Multiple Solutions

Suppose you enter the formula =A2^2 in cell A1 of a blank worksheet and then use the Goal Seek command to find the value of A2 that will make A1 equal to 4. The result, shown in Figure 15-24 at the top of the next page, might be a little surprising. Excel seems to be telling you that the closest value it can find to the square root of 4 is 2.000023.

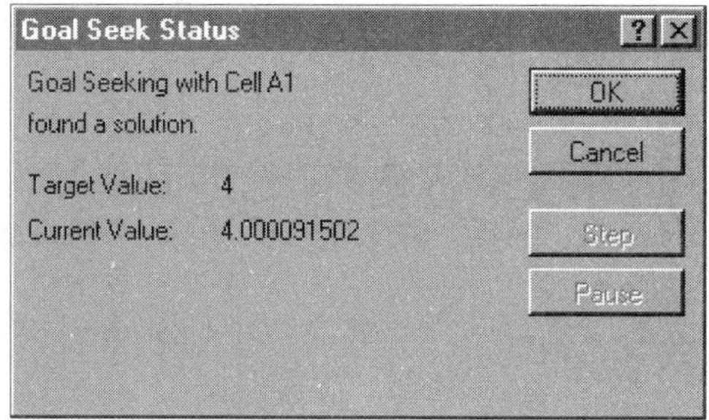

FIGURE 15-24
The Goal Seek command returns this result when asked to find the square root of 4.

By default, the Goal Seek command stops when it has either performed 100 iterations (trial solutions) or found an answer that comes to within 0.001 of your specified target value. If you need greater precision than this, you can change the default limits by choosing the Options command from the Tools menu, clicking the Calculation tab, and changing the Maximum Iterations value to a number higher than 100, the Maximum Change value to a number less than 0.001, or both.

This example illustrates another factor you should be aware of when you use the Goal Seek command. The Goal Seek command finds only one solution, even though your problem might have several. In this case, the value 4 has two square roots: +2 and –2. In situations like this, the Goal Seek command gives you the solution with the same sign as the starting value. For instance, if you start with a value of –1 in cell A2, the Goal Seek command reports the solution as –1.99992, instead of +2.000023.

For more information about worksheet calculation options, see "Calculating the Worksheet," page 146.

The Solver

The Goal Seek command is handy for problems that involve an exact target value that depends on a single unknown value. For more complex problems, you should use the Solver. The Solver can handle problems that involve many variable cells and can help you find combinations of variables that maximize or minimize a target cell. It also lets you specify one or more constraints — conditions that must be met for the solution to be valid.

The Solver is an add-in. If you performed a full installation of Excel, the Tools menu includes the Solver command. If you don't find that command on the Tools menu, choose the Add-Ins command instead and select Solver Add-In in the Add-Ins Available list box. If Solver isn't on the list, you'll need to install the Solver by running the Microsoft Excel Setup program and selecting the Complete/Custom installation.

This section provides only an introduction to the Solver. A complete treatment of this powerful tool is beyond the scope of this book. For more details, including an explanation of the Solver's error messages, see Excel's online Help system. For background material on optimization, we recommend two textbooks: *Management Science,* by Andrew W. Shogan (Englewood Cliffs, New Jersey: Prentice-Hall, 1988) and *Operations Research, Applications and Algorithms,* by Wayne L. Winston (Boston: PWS-Kent Publishing Co., 1991).

As an example of the kind of problem that the Solver can tackle, imagine you are planning an advertising campaign for a new product. Your total budget for print advertising is $12,000,000; you want to expose your ads at least 800 million times to potential readers; and you've decided to place ads in six publications — we'll call them Pub1 through Pub6. Each publication reaches a different number of readers and charges a different rate per page. (To keep this analysis simpler, we'll ignore the issue of quantity discounts.) Your job is to reach the readership target at the lowest possible cost with the following additional constraints:

- At least six advertisements should run in each publication.
- No more than a third of your advertising dollars should be spent on any one publication.
- Your total cost for placing advertisements in Pub3 and Pub4 must not exceed $7,500,000.

Figure 15-25 shows one way to lay out the problem.

Ad Campaign

	A	B	C	D	E	F	G
1	**Publication**	**Cost per Ad**	**Audience per ad (millions)**	**Number of ads placed**	**Total cost**	**Percent of total**	**Total audience (millions)**
2	*Pub1*	$147,420	9.9	6	$884,520	26.3%	59
3	*Pub2*	$124,410	8.4	6	$746,460	22.2%	50
4	*Pub3*	$113,100	8.2	6	$678,600	20.2%	49
5	*Pub4*	$70,070	5.1	6	$420,420	12.5%	31
6	*Pub5*	$53,000	3.7	6	$318,000	9.5%	22
7	*Pub6*	$52,440	3.6	6	$314,640	9.4%	22
8	**Total**				**$3,362,640**		**233**
9	**Total Pub3 + Pub4**				**$1,099,020**		
10							
11		**Constraints:**			Total advertising budget		$12,000,000
12					Total budget for Pub3 and Pub4		$7,500,000
13					Minimum total audience (millions)		800
14					Maximum % of budget spent on any publication		33.33%
15					Minimum number of ads per publication		6
16							

Sheet1 / Sheet2 / Sheet3 / Sheet4 / Sheet5 / Sheet6 / Sheet7

FIGURE 15-25
You can use the Solver to determine how many advertisements to place in each publication in order to meet your objectives at the lowest possible cost.

You might be able to work out this problem yourself by substituting many alternatives for the values currently in D2:D7, keeping your eye on the constraints, and noting the impact of your changes on the total expenditure figure in E8. In fact, that's what the Solver will do for you — but it will do it much more rapidly, and it will use some analytic techniques to home in on the optimal solution without having to try every conceivable alternative.

To use the Solver, choose the Solver command from the Tools menu. The dialog box shown in Figure 15-26 appears. To complete this dialog box, you must give the Solver three pieces of information: your objective, or *target* (to minimize total expenditure), your variables or *changing cells* (the number of advertisements you will place in each publication), and your *constraints* (the conditions summarized at the bottom of the worksheet in Figure 15-25).

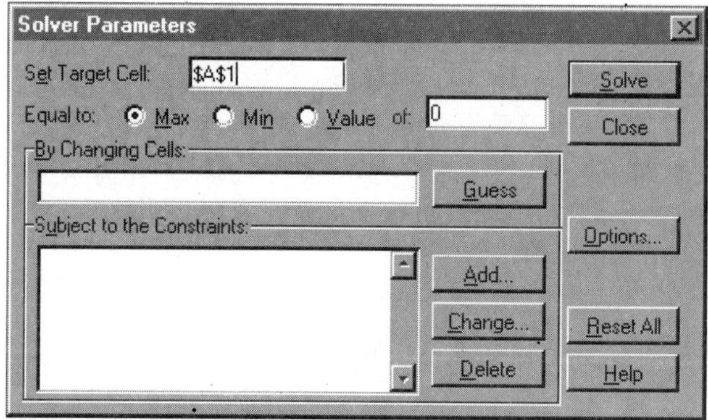

FIGURE 15-26 Use the Solver Parameters dialog box to set up your problem.

Stating the Objective

In the Set Target Cell edit box, you indicate the goal, or *target,* you want Solver to achieve. In this example, you want to minimize your total cost — the value in cell E8 — so you specify your objective by entering *E8* in the Set Target Cell edit box and selecting Min as the Equal To option.

You can enter your objective in the Set Target Cell edit box by typing a cell's coordinates, typing a name that has been assigned to a cell, or by clicking a cell in the worksheet. If you assign a name to the target cell, the Solver uses that name in its reports even if you specify the cell's coordinates instead of its name in the Set Target Cell edit box. If you don't name the cells, the Solver's reports construct names based on the nearest column-heading and row-heading text, but these constructed names don't appear in the Solver dialog boxes. For clarity, it's a good idea to name all the important cells of your model before you put the Solver to work.

In this example, you want the Solver to set your target cell to its lowest possible value, so you select Min. In other problems, you might want to raise a target cell to its highest possible value by selecting the Max option — for example, if your target cell expresses profits. Or you might want the Solver to find a solution that makes your target cell equal to some particular value, in which case you would select the Value Of option and enter an amount (or a cell reference) in the adjacent edit box. (Note that by selecting the Value Of option, specifying only one variable cell, and specifying no constraints, you can use the Solver as a glorified Goal Seek command.)

You don't have to specify an objective. If you leave the Set Target Cell edit box blank, click the Options button, and select the Show Iteration Results option, you can use the Solver to step through some or all of the combinations of variable cells that meet your constraints. You will then get an answer that solves the constraints but is not necessarily the optimal solution.

See Also For more information about the Show Iteration Results option, see "The Show Iteration Results Option," page 578.

Specifying Variable Cells

The next step is to tell the Solver which cells to change — that is, you need to specify your variable cells, or *changing cells*. In the advertisement campaign example, the cells whose values can be adjusted are those that specify the number of advertisements to be placed in each publication. These cells lie in the range D2:D7. As usual, you can provide this information by typing cell coordinates, typing cell names, or selecting cells in the worksheet. If the variables are not in adjacent cells, you can separate variable cells (or ranges) with commas. (If you click nonadjacent cells to enter their references, hold down Ctrl while you select each cell or range.) Alternatively, you can click Guess, and Solver will propose the appropriate changing cells based on the target cell you specified.

You must specify at least one variable cell; otherwise, the Solver will have nothing to do. If you specify a target cell (as you will in most cases), you must specify variable cells that are *precedents* of the target cell; that is, cells that the formula in the target cell depends on for its calculation. If the target cell's value does not depend on the variables, the Solver will not be able to solve anything.

Specifying Constraints

The last step, specifying constraints, is optional. To specify a constraint, click the Add button in the Solver Parameters dialog box and complete the Add Constraint dialog box. Figure 15-27 shows how you express the constraint that total advertising expenditures (the value in cell E8 in the model) must be less than or equal to the total budget (the value in cell G11).

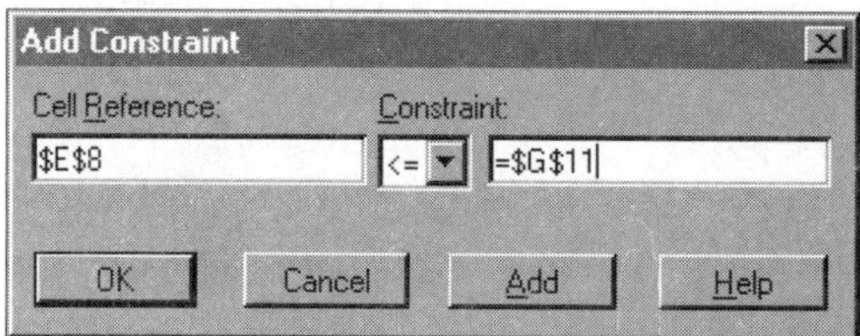

FIGURE 15-27 Click the Add button in the Solver Parameters dialog box to add constraints.

As you can see, a constraint consists of three components: a cell reference, a comparison operator, and a constraint value. You specify the cell reference in the Cell Reference edit box, select a comparison operator from the drop-down list in the middle of the dialog box, and specify the constraint value in the edit box on the right. After specifying a constraint in this manner, you can either click OK to return to the Solver Parameters dialog box or click Add to specify another constraint.

Figure 15-28 shows how the Solver Parameters dialog box looks after all your constraints have been specified. Notice that the constraints are listed in alphabetic order, not necessarily in the order in which you defined them.

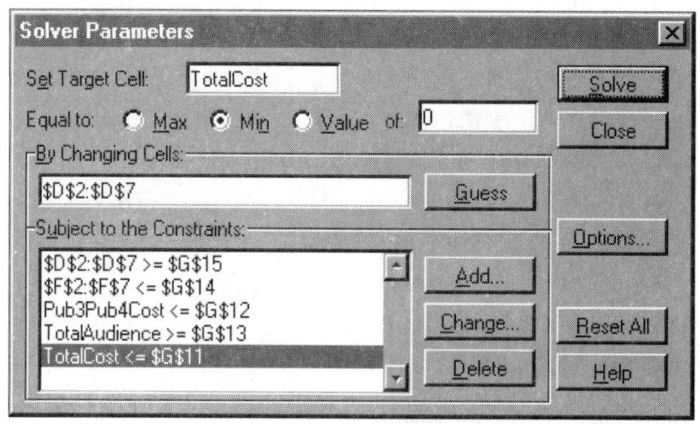

FIGURE 15-28 The Solver lists the constraints in alphabetic order and uses defined cell and range names whenever possible.

Also notice that two of the constraints have range references on the left side of the comparison operator. The expression $D$2:$D$7>=$G$15 stipulates that the value of each cell in D2:D7 must be 6 or greater, and the expression $F$2:$F$7<=$G$14 stipulates that the value of each cell in F2:F9 must be no greater than 33.30 percent. Each of these expressions is a shortcut way of stating six separate constraints. If you use this kind of shortcut, the constraint value on the right side of the comparison operator must be a range of the same dimensions as the range on the left side, a single cell reference, or a constant value.

After completing the Solver Parameters dialog box, click Solve. As the Solver works, messages appear in the status bar. The Solver plugs trial values into your variable cells, recalculates the worksheet, and then tests the results. By comparing the outcome of each iteration with that of preceding iterations, the Solver homes in on a set of values that meets your objective and satisfies your constraints.

In the advertisement campaign example, the Solver succeeds in finding an optimal value for the objective cell while meeting all the constraints and displays the dialog box shown in Figure 15-29. The values displayed in your worksheet at that time result in the optimal solution. You can leave these values in the worksheet by selecting the Keep Solver Solution option and clicking OK, or you can restore the values that your variables held before you activated the Solver by clicking Cancel or by selecting the Restore Original Values option and clicking OK. You also have the option of assigning the solution values to a named scenario.

The solution values shown in Figure 15-29 indicate that you can keep your advertisement campaign costs to a minimum by placing 6 ads in Pub1, 6 in Pub2, 33 in Pub3, 53.3 in Pub4, 34 in Pub5, and 6 in Pub6. This combination of placements will expose your target audience to your advertisements 800 million times (assuming the publications' readership

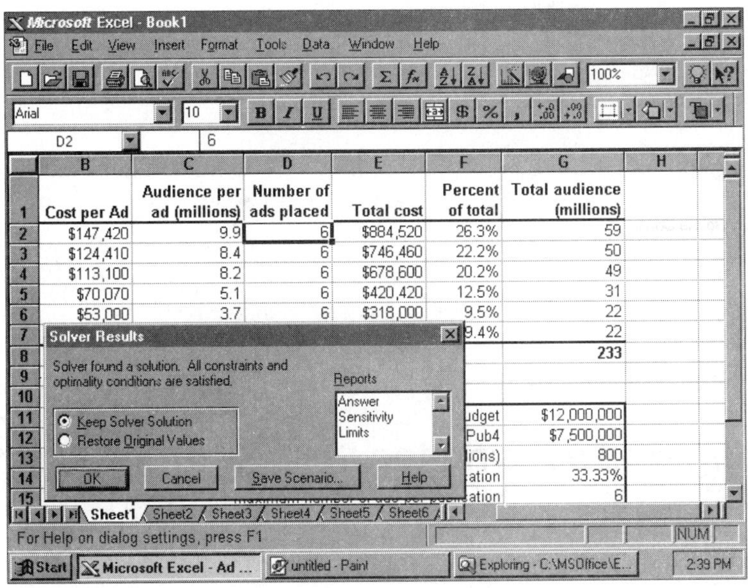

FIGURE 15-29

When the Solver succeeds, it presents the Solver Results dialog box.

numbers are correct). Unfortunately, because it's not possible to run three-tenths of an advertisement, the solution is not practical. In fact, Pub4 is not the only publication for which the Solver is recommending a noninteger number of advertisement placements. The solution value for Pub3 is slightly more than 33, and that for Pub5 is slightly below 34, but these values appear to be whole numbers when displayed to one decimal point of precision.

You can cope with the noninteger results in one of two ways: by rounding, or by adding new constraints that force the results to be whole numbers. Rounding Pub4 upward produces a readership number of 803 million at a cost of $11,267,347, which appears to be an acceptable accommodation in this case. The next section discusses what happens if you constrain the Solver to give an integer solution.

Specifying Integer Constraints

To stipulate that your advertisement placement variables be restricted to whole numbers, you invoke the Solver as usual and click the Add button in the Solver Parameters dialog box. In the Add Constraint dialog box, you select the range that holds your ad placement numbers — D2:D7. Next display the drop-down list in the middle of the dialog box and select the last item, *int*. The Solver inserts the word *integer* in the Constraint edit box, as shown in Figure 15-30. Click OK to return to the Solver Parameters dialog box.

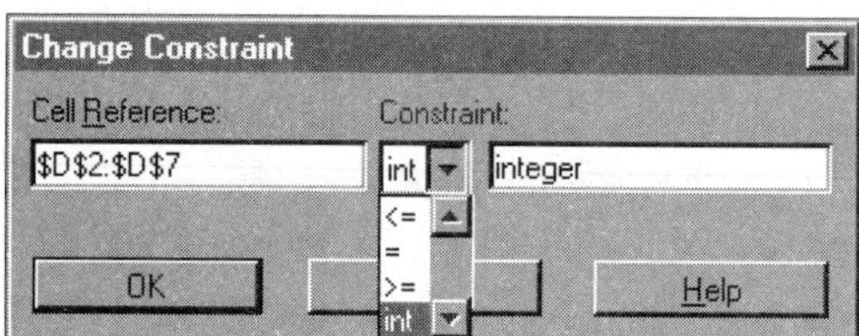

FIGURE 15-30 To specify an integer constraint, select the item labeled *int* in the drop-down list.

When you click the Solve button in the Solver Parameters dialog box to run the problem with the new integer constraint, the results indicate that rounding up the Pub4 ad placements does not produce the best solution. It turns out that you can achieve a better whole-number solution by decreasing the Pub4 placements from 53.3 to 53.0 and increasing the Pub5 placements from 34 to 35. These values generate a readership of 802 million at a cost of $11,246,630 — a savings of $20,717 over the simple integer rounding solution.

Saving and Reusing the Solver Parameters

When you save a workbook after using the Solver, all the values you entered in the Solver's dialog boxes are saved along with your worksheet data. You

Do You Need Integer Constraints?

Adding integer constraints to a Solver problem can geometrically increase the problem's complexity, resulting in possibly unacceptable delays. The example discussed in this chapter is relatively simple and does not take an inordinate amount of time to solve, but a more complex problem with integer constraints might pose more of a challenge for the Solver.

Certain problems can only be solved using integer constraints. In particular, integer solutions are essential for problems in which variables can assume only two values, such as 1 or 0 (yes or no).

do not need to respecify the problem if you want to continue working with it during a later Excel session.

Each worksheet in a workbook can store one set of Solver parameter values. To store more than one set of Solver parameters with a given worksheet, you must use the Solver's Save Model option. To use this option, follow these steps:

1. Choose Solver from the Tools menu.
2. Click the Options button and then in the Solver Options dialog box shown in Figure 15-31, click Save Model. Excel prompts you for a cell or range in which to store the Solver parameters on the worksheet.

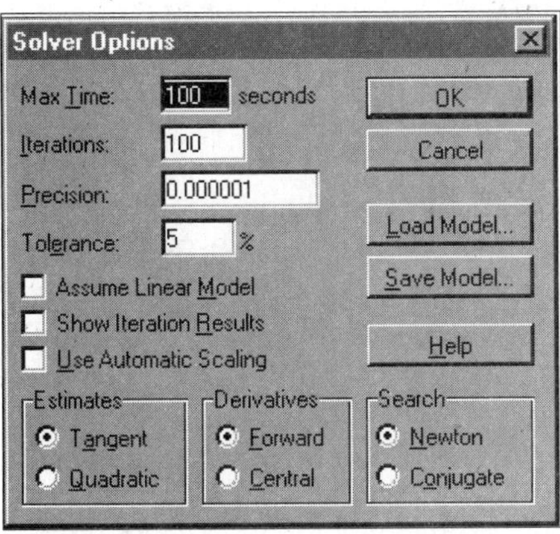

FIGURE 15-31
The Load Model and Save Model buttons in the Solver Options dialog box provide a way to store and retrieve your Solver parameters.

3. Specify a blank cell by clicking it or typing its reference and then click OK. If you specify a single cell, the Solver pastes in the save model range, starting at the indicated cell and inserting formulas in as many of the cells below it as necessary. (Be sure that the cells below the

indicated cell do not contain data.) If you specify a range, the Solver fills only the specified cells with the model parameters. If the range is too small, some of your parameters will not be saved.

4. To reuse the saved parameters, click Options in the Solver Parameters dialog box, click Load Model, and then specify the range in which you stored the Solver parameters.

You'll find it easiest to save and reuse Solver parameters if you assign a name to each save model range immediately after you use the Save Model option. You can then specify that name when you use the Load Model option.

Assigning the Solver Results to Named Scenarios

An even better way to save your Solver parameters is to save them as named scenarios using the Scenario Manager. As you might have noticed, the Solver Results dialog box shown earlier in Figure 15-29 includes a Save Scenario button. Clicking this button activates the Scenario Manager and lets you assign a scenario name to the current values of your variable cells. This option provides an excellent way to explore and perform further what-if analysis on a variety of possible outcomes.

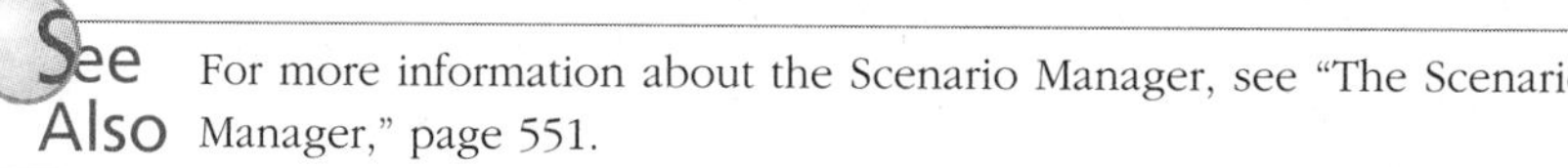
See Also For more information about the Scenario Manager, see "The Scenario Manager," page 551.

Other Solver Options

The Solver Options dialog box shown in Figure 15-31 contains several options that might need some explanation. With the Max Time and Iterations edit boxes, you tell the Solver, in effect, how hard to work on the solution. If the Solver reaches either the time limit or the number of iterations limit before finding a solution, calculation stops and Excel asks you whether you want to continue. The default settings are usually sufficient for solving most problems, but if you don't reach a solution with these settings, you can try adjusting them.

The Precision setting is used by the Solver to determine how close by you want values in the constraint cells to match your constraints. The closer this setting is to the value 1, the lower the precision. Specifying a setting that is less than the default 0.000001 results in a longer solution time.

The Tolerance setting applies only to problems that use integer constraints and represents a percentage of error allowed in the solution.

The Estimates, Derivatives, and Search options are best left at their default settings, unless you understand linear optimization techniques. If you want more information about these options, refer to Excel's online Help system.

The Assume Linear Model Option

A *linear* optimization problem is one in which the value of the target cell is a linear function of each variable cell; that is, if you plot XY charts of the target cell's value against all meaningful values of each variable cell, your charts are straight lines. If some of your plots produce curves instead of straight lines, the problem is nonlinear.

The Assume Linear Model option can be activated only for what-if models in which all the relationships are linear. Models that use simple addition and subtraction and worksheet functions such as SUM are linear in nature. However, most models are *nonlinear*. They are generated by multiplying changing cells by other changing cells, by using exponentiation or growth factors, or by using nonlinear worksheet functions such as PMT.

The Solver can handle both linear and nonlinear optimization problems. It can solve linear problems more quickly if you click the Options button in the Solver Parameters dialog box and then select the Assume Linear Model option. If you select this option for a nonlinear problem and then try to solve the problem, however, the Solver Results dialog box displays the message *The conditions for Assume Linear Model are not satisfied*. If you are not sure about the nature of your model, it's best not to use this option.

If you select the Assume Linear Model option and then select the Sensitivity report option, the Solver produces a Sensitivity report in a slightly different form than for nonlinear problems.

The Importance of Using Appropriate Starting Values

If your problem is nonlinear, you must be aware of one very important detail: Your choice of starting values can affect the solution generated by the Solver. With nonlinear problems you should always do the following:

- Set your variable cells to reasonable approximations of their optimal values before running the problem.
- Test alternative starting values to see what impact, if any, they have on the Solver's solution.

See Also For more information about Sensitivity reports, see "The Sensitivity Report," page 578.

The Show Iteration Results Option

If you're interested in exploring many combinations of your variable cells, rather than only the combination that produces the optimal result, you can take advantage of the Solver's Show Iteration Results option. Simply click the Options button in the Solver Parameters dialog box and select the Show Iteration Results option in the Solver Options dialog box. After each iteration, the Show Trial Solution dialog box appears, which allows you to save the scenario and then either stop or continue with the next iteration.

You should be aware that when you use the Show Iteration Results option, the Solver pauses for solutions that do not meet all your constraints as well as for suboptimal solutions that do.

Generating Reports

In addition to inserting optimal values in your problem's variable cells, the Solver can summarize its results in three reports: Answer, Sensitivity, and Limits. To generate one or more reports, select the names of the reports in the Solver Results dialog box shown earlier in Figure 15-29. Select the reports you want and then click OK. (Hold down Ctrl to select more than one.) Each report is saved on a separate worksheet in the current workbook, with the tab identified with the name of the report.

The Sensitivity Report

The Sensitivity report provides information about how sensitive your target cell is to changes in your constraints. This report has two sections: one for your variable cells and one for your constraints. The right column in each section provides the sensitivity information.

Each changing cell and constraint cell is listed in a separate row. The Changing Cell section includes a Reduced Gradient value that indicates how the target cell would be affected by a one-unit increase in the corresponding changing cell. Similarly, the Lagrange Multiplier column in the Constraints section indicates how the target cell would be affected by a one-unit increase in the corresponding constraint value.

The Linear Model Sensitivity Report If you select the Assume Linear Model option in the Solver Options dialog box, the Sensitivity report includes several additional columns of information.

For changing cells, the Reduced Cost column shows the increase in target cell value per unit of change in the changing cell value. The Objective Coefficient column shows the degree to which the changing cell and the target cell are related. The Allowable Increase and Allowable Decrease columns show the amount that the Objective Coefficient must change before the changing cells are affected.

For constraints, the Shadow Price column indicates the increase in the target value for each unit that the constraint increases. The Constraint RH Side column simply displays the constraint values used in the problem. And the Allowable Increase and Allowable Decrease columns show the amount that the constraint value (shown in the Constraint RH Side column) must change before the changing cells are affected.

The Answer Report

The Answer report lists the target cell, the variable cells, and the constraints. This report also includes information about the status of and slack value for each constraint. The status can be Binding, Not Binding, or Not Satisfied. The slack value is the difference between the solution value of the constraint cells and the number that appears on the right side of the constraint formula. A binding constraint is one for which the slack value is 0. A nonbinding constraint is a constraint that was satisfied with a nonzero slack value.

The Limits Report

The Limits report tells you how much the values of your variable cells can be increased or decreased without breaking the constraints of your problem. For each variable cell, this report lists the optimal value as well as the lowest and highest values that can be used without violating constraints.

When the Solver Is Unable to Solve

The Solver is powerful but not miraculous. It might not be able to solve every problem you give it. If the Solver can't find the optimal solution to your problem, it presents an unsuccessful completion message in the Solver Solution dialog box.

The most common unsuccessful completion messages are the following:

- *Solver could not find a feasible solution.* The Solver is unable to find a solution that satisfies all your constraints. This can happen if the constraints are logically conflicting (for example, if in separate constraints you ask that Pub1 be greater than 5 and less than 3) or if not all the constraints can be satisfied (for example, if you insist that your advertising campaign reach 800 million readers on a $1 million budget).

  In some cases, the Solver also returns this message if the starting values of your variable cells are too far from their optimal values. If you think your constraints are logically consistent and your problem is solvable, try changing your starting values and rerunning the Solver.

- *The maximum iteration limit was reached; continue anyway?* To avoid tying up your computer indefinitely with an unsolvable problem, the Solver is designed to pause and present this message when it has performed its default number of iterations without arriving at a solution. When you see this message, you can resume the search for a solution by clicking Continue, or you can quit by clicking Stop. (You can also assign the current values to a named scenario.)

If you click Continue, the Solver begins solving again and does not stop until it finds a solution, gives up, or reaches its maximum time limit. If your problems frequently exceed the Solver's iteration limit, you can increase the default setting by choosing the Solver command from the Tools menu, clicking the Options button, and entering a new value in the Iterations edit box.

- *The maximum time limit was reached; continue anyway?* This message is similar to the iteration-limit message. The Solver is designed to pause after a default time period has elapsed. You can increase this default by choosing the Solver command, clicking Options, and modifying the Max Time value.

See Also For information about assigning Solver values to scenarios, see "Assigning the Solver Results to Named Scenarios," page 576.

Part 4

Charts

Chapter 16

Basic Charting Techniques

With Microsoft Excel, you can create sophisticated charts from your worksheet data. You can choose from nine two-dimensional and six three-dimensional chart types, each of which is available in several variations. For example, if you're creating a column chart, you can choose overlapped, clustered, stacked, or 100 percent-stacked columns. You can also combine the basic chart types. For example, you can lay a line chart over a column chart to plot a stock's price together with its sales volume. You can even create "picture" charts that use graphic images instead of ordinary bars and lines to represent values. All of these chart types, combined with Excel's custom formatting options, provide you with a virtually endless variety of charting possibilities.

In Excel, a chart can reside either on the worksheet from which it is derived or on a separate chart sheet that is part of a workbook. A chart that appears directly on a worksheet is called an *embedded chart* and is a type of graphic object. Like arrows, geometric shapes, pictures, and other graphic objects, embedded charts can be placed anywhere on the worksheet, even on top of your worksheet data. You can also resize them and manipulate them in other ways.

In this chapter, we show you how to create, save, and print both embedded charts and charts that reside on separate chart sheets. We also discuss all the available chart types. Chapter 17 covers customizing charts. Chapter 18 provides more details about working with chart data, and Chapter 19 describes Excel 7's new mapping features.

See Also For more information about graphic objects, see Chapter 9, "Graphics," page 345.

Data Series and Categories

Before you begin working with charts, you should understand two terms: data series and categories. Let's start with data series.

A *data series* is simply a set of values you want to chart, or plot. If you want to plot a company's sales revenue for the past decade, your data series is the set of sales revenue values. If you want to plot profits for each of a company's regions, your data series is the set of profit values. And if you want to plot average daily temperatures for the month of July, your data series is the set of average daily temperature values. Each data series in a chart can have as many as 4000 values, or *data points*. You can plot as many as 255 data series, but a single chart is limited to 32,000 total data points.

You use *categories* to arrange, or organize, the values in a data series. In the case of the series of sales revenue values for the past decade, the categories are the years in the decade. For example, if the first year is 1987, the categories are 1988, 1989, 1990, and so on through 1996. In the case of the series of profit values for each of a company's regions, the categories are the regions. And in the case of the series of average daily temperature values for the month of July, the categories are the days of the month: July 1, July 2, July 3, and so forth.

TIP In a chart that plots the changes in a value over time — a time-series chart — the categories are always the time intervals: years, months, days, or some other appropriate time interval.

Sometimes the difference between a data series and a category can be confusing. The key distinction is this: The data series is the set of values you're plotting, and the categories are the "headings" under which the values are arranged. When you understand what data series and categories are, creating charts is easy.

TIP If you can't distinguish the data series from the categories, answer the question "What am I plotting?" with one word. Your answer will almost certainly identify the data series.

Creating Embedded Charts

The ChartWizard button on the Standard toolbar makes creating embedded charts a straightforward process. To create an embedded chart, you simply select the data you want to plot and click the ChartWizard button, which looks like a wand about to anoint a column chart. You then tell Microsoft Excel where you want to embed the chart and you fill out a series of dialog boxes.

NOTE The ChartWizard button is also available on the Chart toolbar — the toolbar that appears when an embedded chart is selected or when you're working in a chart sheet in a workbook. You can also start the ChartWizard by choosing the Chart command from the Insert menu. Then, to create an embedded chart, choose the On This Sheet command from the Chart submenu.

Suppose you're working with the sales-goals worksheet shown in Figure 16-1. In this case, two data series of sales-goals values are arranged in categories by region.

To embed a column chart from this data in columns D through I, follow these steps:

1. Select the range containing the data to be plotted — in this case A3:C8 — and click the ChartWizard button (or choose the Chart command from the Insert menu and then choose the On This Sheet command from the Chart submenu). As shown in Figure 16-2 on the next page, Excel draws a marquee around the selected data, changes the mouse pointer to a cross hair with a miniature chart, and displays the following message in the status bar: Drag in document to create a chart.
2. Position the mouse pointer in one corner (approximately D2) of the worksheet area where you want to embed the chart, hold down the mouse button, and drag to the opposite corner (approximately I13). As you drag, an outline shows where your chart will appear. (Don't worry about precision when staking out the chart area. You can always resize the chart or drag it to a new position after you've created it.)

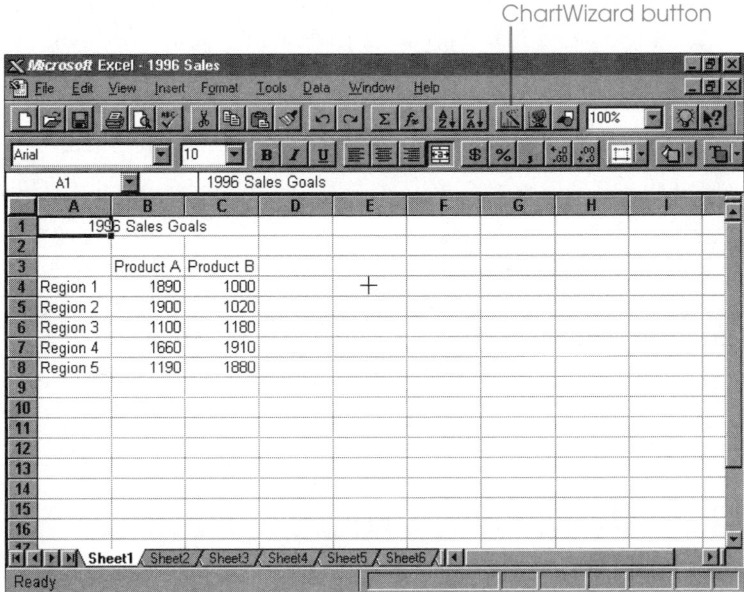

FIGURE 16-1

We'll use the ChartWizard to create an embedded chart of this data.

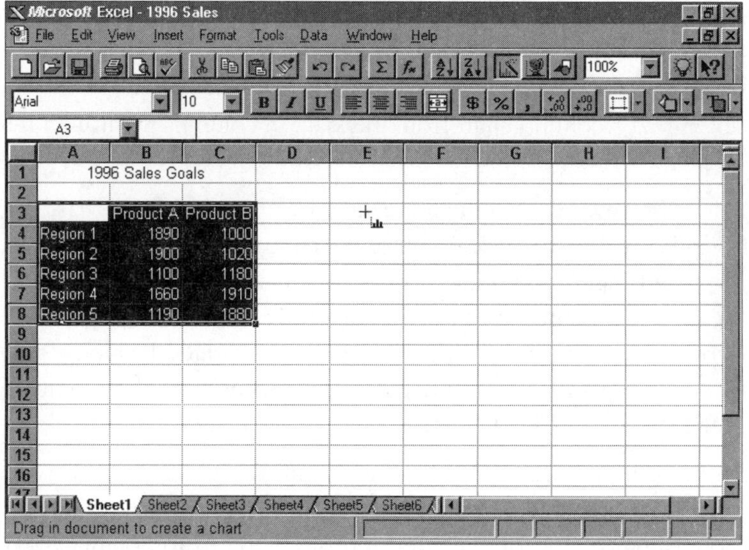

FIGURE 16-2
After you click the ChartWizard button, a message in the status bar prompts you to define the area where you want to embed your chart.

Manipulating Embedded Charts

If you hold down Shift while dragging the rectangle that tells the ChartWizard where you want to embed your chart, Excel constrains the rectangle to a square. If you hold down Alt while dragging the rectangle, Excel aligns the rectangle with the gridlines of your worksheet.

You can make an embedded chart as large as you want. To extend the rectangle that will contain the chart beyond the limits of your screen, drag the mouse pointer across the border of the worksheet window as you create the rectangle.

Usually you'll want to place an embedded chart in a blank worksheet area, but you can place it anywhere, including directly over other graphic objects or over worksheet data. To change the chart's position, click the chart to select it, position the mouse pointer anywhere within the chart, and drag it to its new location.

To change the chart's size, select the chart and then drag one of the handles around its border outward to increase the size of the chart or inward to reduce its size.

To remove an embedded chart, select it and then choose the All command on the Clear submenu of the Edit menu or simply press Del.

3. Release the mouse button. You then see a dialog box similar to the one in Figure 16-3.

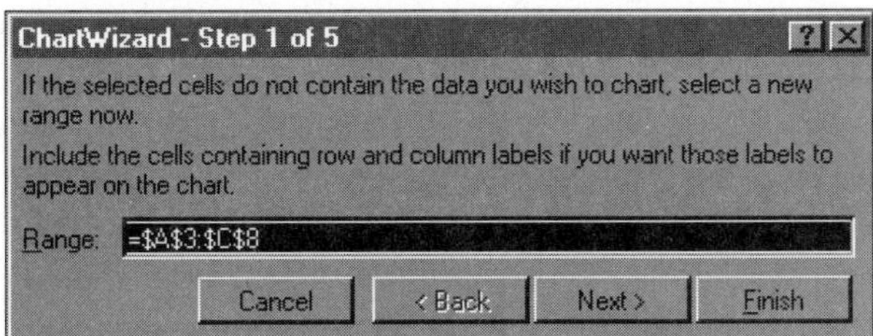

FIGURE 16-3
In the ChartWizard's first dialog box, you specify the data to be plotted.

4. Follow the steps in the dialog boxes. We will lead you through these steps over the next few pages.

Creating a chart with the ChartWizard tool is a five-step process. After completing each step, you move forward by clicking Next or you move backward by clicking Back. You can bail out at any time by clicking Cancel. You can also click Finish to skip the remaining steps and draw a chart based on the information you've given so far.

Specifying the Data to Plot

The ChartWizard's first dialog box asks you to confirm or specify the data you want to plot. In the example in Figure 16-2, you selected the data before clicking the ChartWizard button, so the Range edit box already contains the reference of the range where the data is stored. However, you don't have to preselect the plot range; if you prefer, you can click the ChartWizard button first and then either type a range reference, preceded by an equal sign, in the Range edit box or select the plot range with the mouse. (If the ChartWizard's dialog box is in your way, drag its title bar to move it.)

When you specify a plot range, it's a good idea to include any labels that identify the data series and categories to be plotted — such as the labels in column A (the names of the categories) and row 3 (the names of the data series) in Figure 16-2. As you'll see in a moment, the ChartWizard then incorporates this text into your chart. However, unless you're plotting a single column or row, don't include a chart title in the plot range because the ChartWizard cannot tell the difference between a title and a data point. Instead, add the title later in one of the ChartWizard's dialog boxes.

When the first ChartWizard dialog box displays the correct reference for the data, click the Next button to move on to the second dialog box.

TIP In this example, we plot a single range of worksheet cells. If you need to plot data from two or more separated ranges, you can outline your worksheet, hide the intervening columns or rows, plot a multiple selection, or add a new series to an existing chart.

For more information about selecting ranges, see "Moving Around the Worksheet," page 88.

For more information about hiding columns and rows, see "Controlling Column Width," page 192.

For more information about outlining, see "Outlining Your Worksheets," page 217.

For more information about adding series, see "Adding Data Series and Data Points to a Chart," page 672.

Choosing a Chart Type and Format

The ChartWizard's second dialog box presents the gallery of chart types shown in Figure 16-4. For this example, you want to create a column chart of your sales-target data, so select the third box in the top row, if it is not already selected. Then click the Next button.

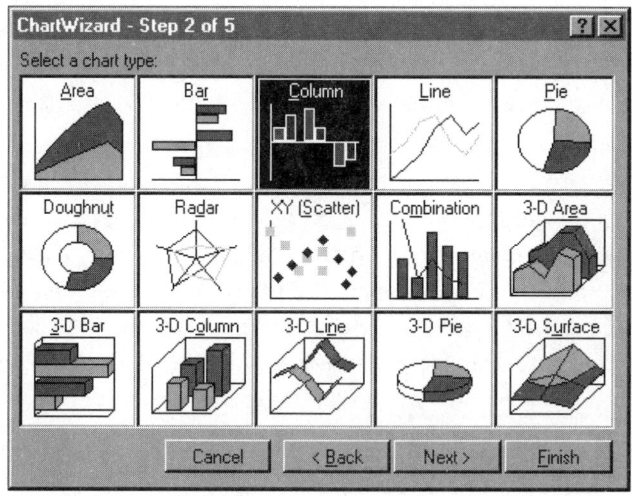

FIGURE 16-4
In the ChartWizard's second dialog box, you select a basic chart type from Excel's 15 options.

The ChartWizard presents another gallery, this time displaying the built-in formatting variants, called *autoformats,* available for the selected chart type. A chart autoformat is simply a set of chart formatting rules, such as "Use horizontal gridlines, don't use vertical gridlines, and add a legend to the right of the chart." Figure 16-5 shows the autoformat gallery for column charts.

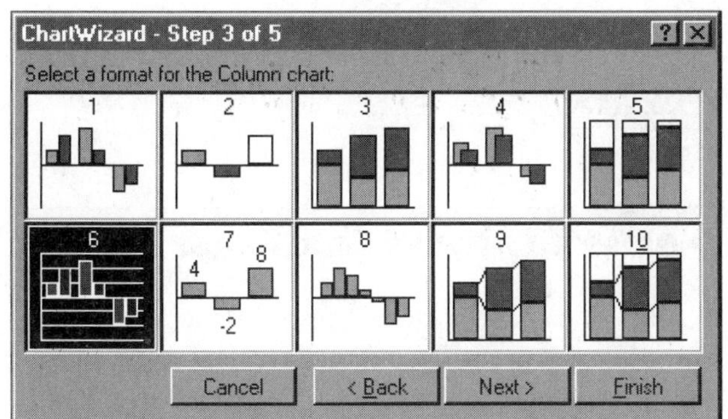

FIGURE 16-5
In the ChartWizard's third dialog box, you select one of the built-in autoformats available for the selected chart type.

The default autoformat for column charts, option 6, produces a nonoverlapping clustered chart with gridlines. Other options produce various kinds of stacked and overlapping charts. For this example, select option 6 and click Next.

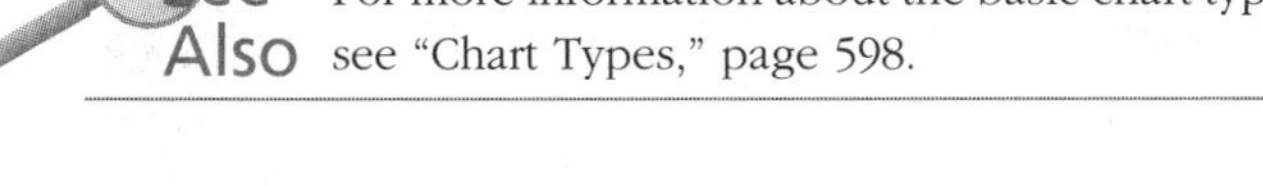

For more information about the basic chart types and their autoformats, see "Chart Types," page 598.

Telling the ChartWizard How to Interpret Your Data

The ChartWizard's fourth dialog box, shown in Figure 16-6 on the next page, displays a preview of your graph. Use this dialog box to be sure the ChartWizard interprets your data correctly. Use the Data Series In option to specify how the data series are organized — by row or by column. You use the Use First Column(s) For Category (X) Axis Labels option to specify which column (if any) contains the category names. And you use the Use First Row(s) For Legend Text option to specify which row (if any) contains the data series names.

NOTE If your data series are stored in rows and your categories are arranged in columns, Excel changes the edit box names to Use First Row(s) For Category (X) Axis Labels and Use First Column(s) For Legend Text.

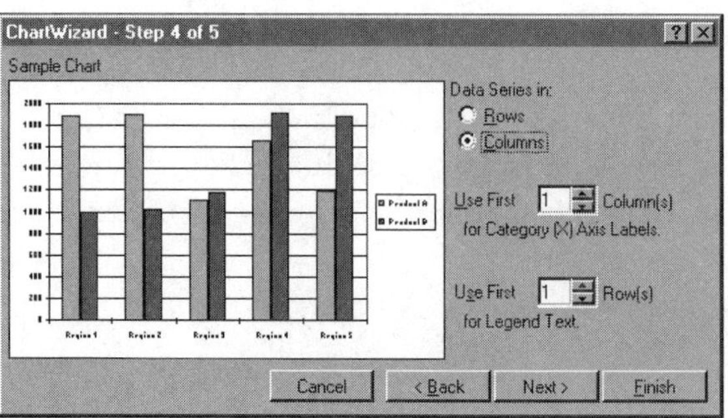

FIGURE 16-6
In the ChartWizard's fourth dialog box, you specify the orientation of your data series and identify any category and data series names.

How Excel Helps You Identify Data Series

Excel assumes that your data includes fewer data series than categories and takes a guess as to whether your data series are in rows or columns and whether you've provided data series and category names. If you plot a range that has more columns than rows, Excel makes each row a data series. If the range has more rows than columns, Excel makes each column a data series. If the range has the same number of columns as rows, Excel makes each row a data series.

When the range includes row and column labels, as the range A3:C8 shown earlier in Figure 16-2 does, Excel uses those labels in your chart. The labels associated with the data series become data series names and appear in the chart's legend. The labels associated with the categories become category names and appear along the chart's x-axis. For naming purposes, Excel treats any date entries in the top row or left column of the range as labels. You can also use a column of values as category names.

For example, in the range A3:C8 in Figure 16-2, the data series are arranged in columns and the categories are arranged in rows. The column labels — Product A and Product B — will be used as data series names and will appear in the chart's legend. The row labels — Region 1, Region 2, and so on — will be used as category names and will appear along the chart's x-axis.

If you plot a range without including labels for the data series, Excel assigns a dummy name to each series. The first series is called Series1, the second Series2, and so on. You can modify these names by editing the SERIES formulas used to create the chart. (For more information about SERIES formulas, see "Editing SERIES Formulas," page 676.)

You can enter any value in the edit boxes, so you aren't limited to using only the first column for category names or only the first row for data series names. For example, you can specify two columns or five rows. You don't have to spend a lot of time puzzling over these details, however; the Sample Chart at the left side of the dialog box immediately reflects your choices. In most cases, the ChartWizard anticipates your needs before you arrive at this step, and all you need to do is confirm its suggestions and click Next. For this example, the ChartWizard's suggestions are correct, so click Next to move to the next step.

Adding a Legend and Titles

In the ChartWizard's fifth dialog box, which is shown in Figure 16-7, you add a legend, a title for the chart itself, titles for each axis, and an overlay title (for combination chart types). Again, you can see the impact of your decisions before you leave the dialog box.

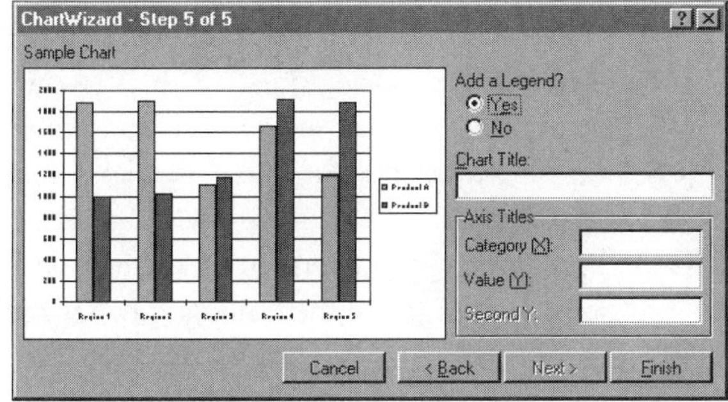

FIGURE 16-7
In the last ChartWizard dialog box, you can add a legend and titles.

If you include a legend, the ChartWizard positions it to the right of your chart, as shown in the Sample Chart section of the ChartWizard's fifth dialog box. You can change the legend's position later, but you can't change it within the ChartWizard.

To add a title, simply type it in the appropriate edit box. Any text you enter is inserted in your chart in the default font; if you want to change the content or appearance of the title, you can do so later with editing and formatting commands. If you want your titles to change to reflect changes in underlying worksheet cells, you can link the titles and the corresponding cells after you've created the chart, but you cannot use the ChartWizard to make the links.

To leave the ChartWizard and embed your chart, click the Finish button. Excel displays the chart in the range you selected. The chart is selected, so you can move it and make other changes if necessary. To return to the worksheet, click anywhere outside the chart.

See Also For more information about adding and linking chart titles, see Chapter 17, "Customizing Charts," page 619.

Modifying an Embedded Chart

When an embedded chart is selected, Excel displays the Chart toolbar. (If you don't see the Chart toolbar, use the Toolbars command on the View menu to make it visible.) You use the first button on the Chart toolbar to change the chart type. Simply select the chart if necessary and then click the Chart Type drop-down arrow. Excel displays a tear-off palette of chart types, as shown in Figure 16-8. (We discuss chart types later in this chapter.) If you change the chart type and then want to change it back to a column chart, click the Default Chart button on the Chart toolbar.

You can resize an embedded chart in the chart window by selecting the chart and dragging one of the eight handles in the direction you want to increase or decrease the chart size.

The other buttons on the toolbar allow you to manipulate the embedded chart in various ways. Clicking the ChartWizard button starts the ChartWizard; you can then use the ChartWizard to modify any of the chart settings you made when creating the chart. Clicking the Horizontal Gridlines button — the one that shows a chart with horizontal lines — adds and removes gridlines. And clicking the Legend button adds and removes the legend that identifies the chart's data series. When you have finished working with the embedded chart, simply click anywhere in the worksheet.

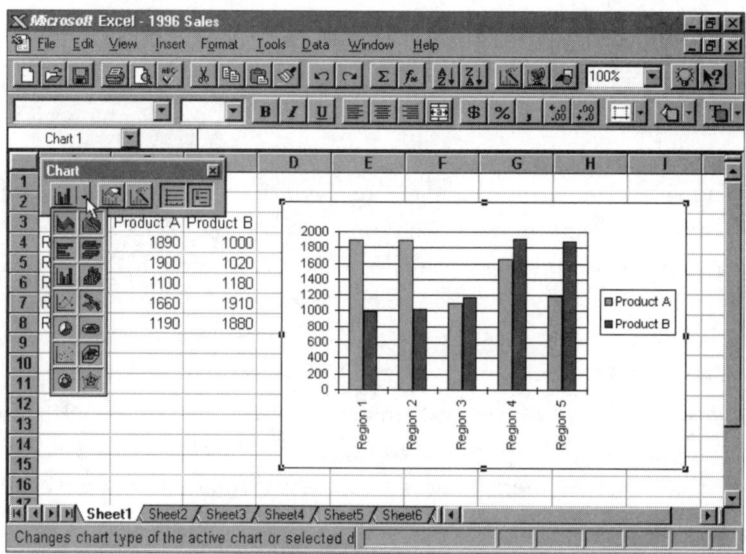

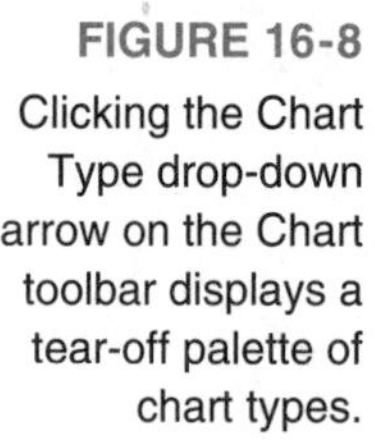

FIGURE 16-8
Clicking the Chart Type drop-down arrow on the Chart toolbar displays a tear-off palette of chart types.

To customize and make more extensive changes to an embedded chart, you need to activate it.

For more information about customizing charts, see Chapter 17, "Customizing Charts," page 619.

Creating Charts on Chart Sheets

To create a new chart on a separate sheet in a workbook, follow these steps:

1. Select the data you want to plot.
2. From the Insert menu, choose Chart and then As New Sheet. Microsoft Excel displays the first ChartWizard dialog box, shown in Figure 16-3 on page 589.
3. Complete the five ChartWizard dialog boxes as described in the preceding sections.

Excel inserts the chart sheet before the current worksheet, as shown in Figure 16-9.

When a chart sheet is active or an embedded chart is activated, Excel displays the Chart toolbar, as shown in Figure 16-9, and changes some of the commands on the Edit, View, Insert, and Format menus to the commands you are likely to use with charts.

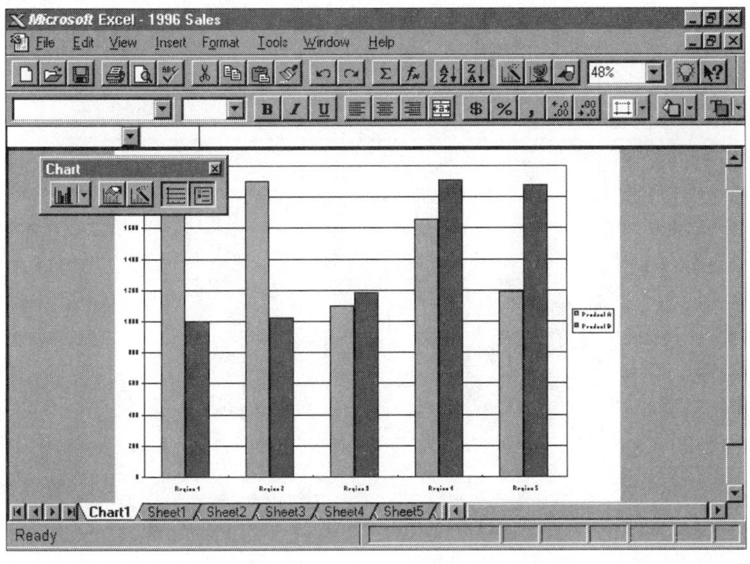

FIGURE 16-9
When you choose the As New Sheet command from the Chart submenu of the Insert menu, Excel plots the selected worksheet data on a separate chart sheet in the workbook.

TIP The quickest way to create a chart is to select your data and press the F11 key. The resulting chart uses the default chart type and autoformat. It appears on a separate chart sheet as shown in Figure 16-9.

You can size the chart in a chart sheet so that it fills the entire window, as shown in Figure 16-10. Simply choose the Sized With Window command from the View menu. Because the chart resides in its own window, you can print it independently of the source worksheet and the other workbook sheets.

Although you can print the chart sheet independently, it remains linked to the worksheet because Excel uses linking formulas based on the SERIES function to connect the chart to its source data. As a result, if you modify the underlying data, Excel updates the chart immediately to reflect the new source values.

Excel creates an appropriate SERIES formula for each data series when you select a range of data and insert a new chart sheet, so you seldom have to deal with these formulas yourself. On occasion, however, you might want to edit a SERIES formula.

See Also For more information about SERIES formulas, see "Editing SERIES Formulas," page 676.

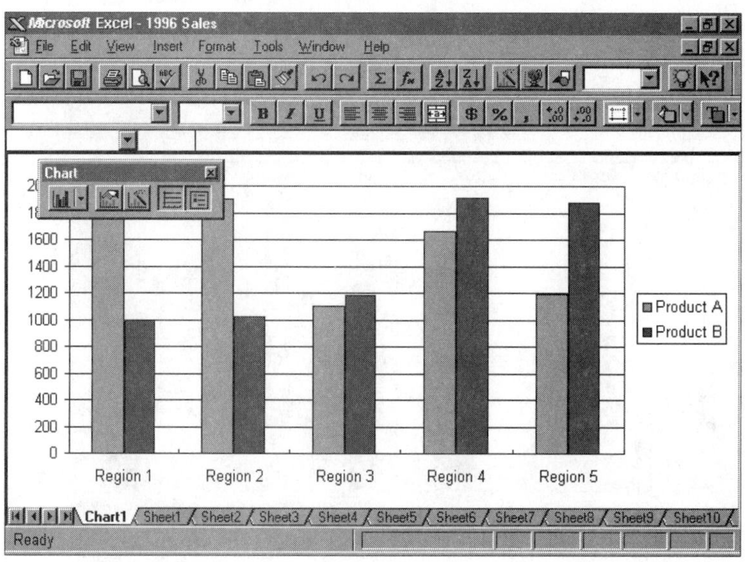

FIGURE 16-10 When you choose the Sized With Window command from the View menu, Excel expands the chart so that it fills the entire window.

Adding a Title Without the ChartWizard

Usually, you'll use the ChartWizard to build most parts of a chart. However, you can add a title to a selected embedded chart or to a chart shown in a chart sheet without using the ChartWizard. Follow these steps:

1. If you are adding a title to an embedded chart, double-click the chart to activate it.
2. From the Insert menu, choose the Titles command.
3. In the Titles dialog box, select the Chart Title option, as shown in Figure 16-11.

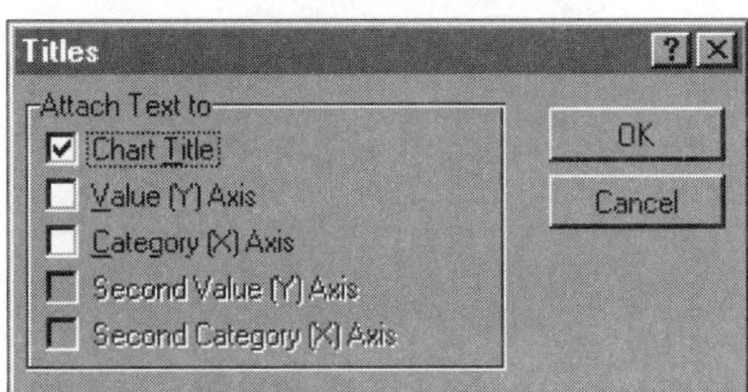

FIGURE 16-11
The Titles dialog box lets you assign titles to the chart itself, the x-axis, and the y-axis.

4. Click OK. The word *Title* appears with selection handles at the top of the chart, as shown in Figure 16-12. (Notice that Excel reduces the height of the chart slightly to make room for the title.)

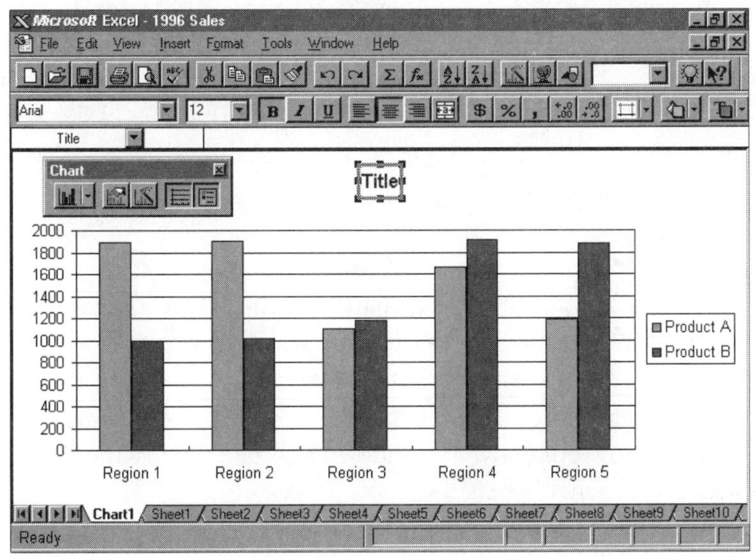

FIGURE 16-12
When you add a chart title, Excel initially displays the default text *Title.*

5. Replace the default title *Title* just as you would edit text in an edit box. Click outside the title to finish editing.

You can also create a formula to link the title to the text in a cell or in a range on your worksheet by typing an equal sign in the formula bar and then clicking on the cell. For example, Figure 16-13 shows a title that reflects the text in cell A1 of the worksheet shown earlier in Figure 16-1. If you change the text in that cell, the chart's title also changes.

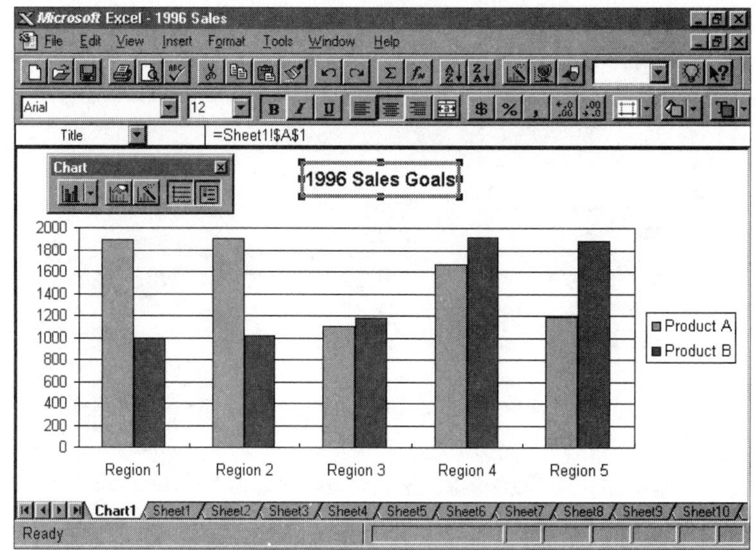

FIGURE 16-13
We used a formula to link the chart's title to cell A1 of the source worksheet.

See Also For more information about linking titles to cells, see "Linking a Chart Title to a Worksheet Cell," page 625.

Chart Types

So far, we've looked only at column charts, which is Microsoft Excel's default chart type. Excel provides 14 other chart types, and it even lets you combine chart types, creating hybrid, or combination, charts.

As you begin using charts as tools for analyzing and communicating, you'll want to know both how to decide which chart type is appropriate and how to change the chart type.

NOTE You can use the Options command on the Tools menu to specify a different default chart type. See "Changing the Default Chart Type and Autoformat," page 615.

Choosing and Changing Chart Types

The easiest way to change a chart's type is to click the Chart Type drop-down arrow on the Chart toolbar to display a tear-off palette with the different chart types. The tear-off palette includes a set of buttons, one for each of Excel's basic chart types: Area, Bar, Column, Line, Pie, XY (Scatter), Doughnut, 3-D Area, 3-D Bar, 3-D Column, 3-D Line, 3-D Pie, 3-D Surface, and Radar. When you click one of these chart type buttons, Excel reformats the selected chart according to your specification. You can use the Chart Type button to change the chart type of both embedded charts and chart sheet charts.

If you're working with a chart on a chart sheet or you've temporarily opened a window for an embedded chart by double-clicking the chart, you can use the Chart Type command on the Format menu to change the chart type. When you choose this command, a Chart Type dialog box appears from which you can select the basic chart type and, if you want, one of its formatting variants. Figure 16-14 shows the Chart Type dialog box with the 2-D option in the Chart Dimension section selected and examples of the available two-dimensional chart types displayed. You can display examples of the three-dimensional chart types by clicking the 3-D option in the Chart Dimension section. To specify a chart type, simply click it.

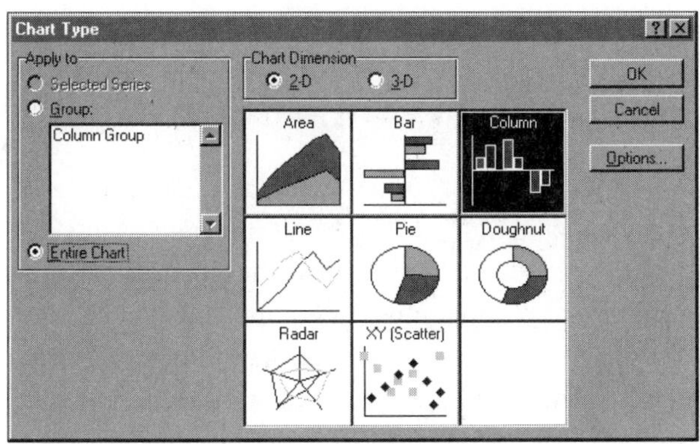

FIGURE 16-14
You can choose basic chart types using the Format menu's Chart Type command, which displays the Chart Type dialog box.

See Also For information about changing chart defaults, see "Changing the Default Chart Type and Autoformat," page 615.

Choosing and Changing Chart Autoformats

When you create a chart using the ChartWizard, you select an autoformat in the third ChartWizard dialog box. You can later change the autoformat without using the ChartWizard. Follow these steps:

1. Activate the chart sheet or the embedded chart with the autoformat you want to change. (If you're modifying an embedded chart, you activate the chart by double-clicking it to display the thick border and the chart commands.)
2. Choose the AutoFormat command from the Format menu. Excel displays the AutoFormat dialog box, like the one shown in Figure 16-15, with examples of the autoformats available for the selected chart's type. Figure 16-15 shows the 10 autoformats available for a column chart.

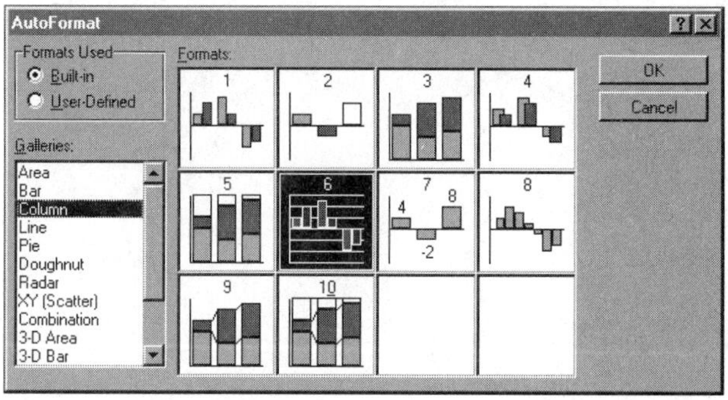

FIGURE 16-15
In the AutoFormat dialog box, you can select autoformats for each of the basic chart types.

Select a Chart Type and Autoformat Before You Customize

Autoformats let you make a set of formatting changes quickly and easily. However, if you make individual formatting changes to your chart and then change the chart's autoformat, the new autoformat might override your custom formatting. For example, if you change the colors and scaling of your axes and then use the AutoFormat command to switch from a column chart to a bar chart, Excel restores the default settings for color and axis scaling. It's always a good idea to select a chart type and autoformat before you apply any custom formatting.

TIP By default Excel displays only built-in autoformats — those that come with Excel. You can add your own custom formats. (See "Changing the Default Chart Type and Autoformat" on page 615.) You can then select the User-Defined option in the Formats Used section of the AutoFormat dialog box to see them. (When you select the User-Defined option, Excel adds a Customize button to the dialog box. You can use it to add and delete user-defined autoformats.)

3. Select the autoformat you want by clicking it, and then click OK.

TIP Using the Galleries list box in the AutoFormat dialog box, you can indicate the chart type for which you want to see autoformats. Selecting a different chart type in the Galleries list and then selecting an autoformat changes both the type and the autoformat.

See Also For information about changing chart defaults, see "Changing the Default Chart Type and Autoformat," page 615.

Column and Bar Charts

In Excel, vertically oriented bar charts are referred to as column charts, and horizontally oriented bar charts are referred to as bar charts. Figure 16-15 shows the autoformats available for column charts, including clustered, overlapping, and stacked options. Figure 16-16 shows the autoformats available for bar charts.

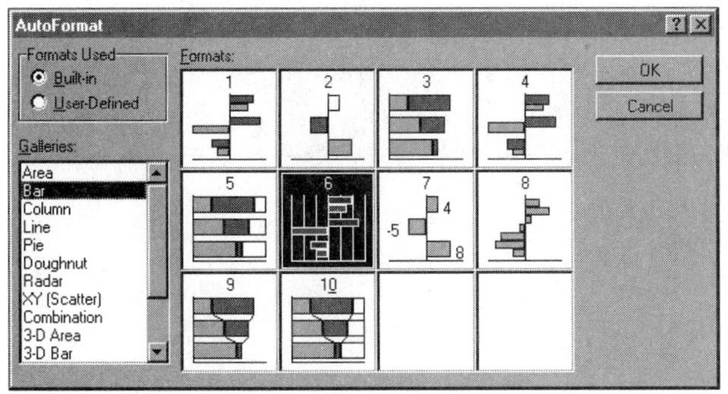

FIGURE 16-16

The Bar chart autoformats include clustered, overlapping, and stacked options.

Column and bar charts are useful for comparing discrete values from two or more data series. Because the individual points in a data series are not connected, these charts are less effective than line charts at showing trends.

Options 1 and 6 in the Column and Bar galleries display the points from each series in side-by-side clusters. Option 4 is similar, but the points in each cluster overlap, which means you can display more points in the same amount of space.

Options 3 and 9 stack the bars to picture each cluster's aggregate value. Options 5 and 10 produce *100-percent* charts, in which the values in each cluster are stacked and proportioned so that you can see the percentage each data point contributes to the cluster's total.

Option 2 is for single-series charts. If you select this option, Excel draws each point in a different color or shade. Option 7 is like option 2, except that Excel displays numerals to indicate the value of each point. Option 8, which produces a *step chart,* is like option 1, except that the space between the clusters is removed.

Line and High-Low Charts

Line charts are useful for showing the continuity between individual points in a series. You can use them to illustrate trends over time. High-low charts are variations of line charts that plot the value range over which events vary. For example, you might use a high-low chart to show average, high, and low rainfall values by month. Excel also offers high-low-close and open-high-low-close charts, which you can use to track the prices of securities. Figure 16-17 shows the Line autoformats.

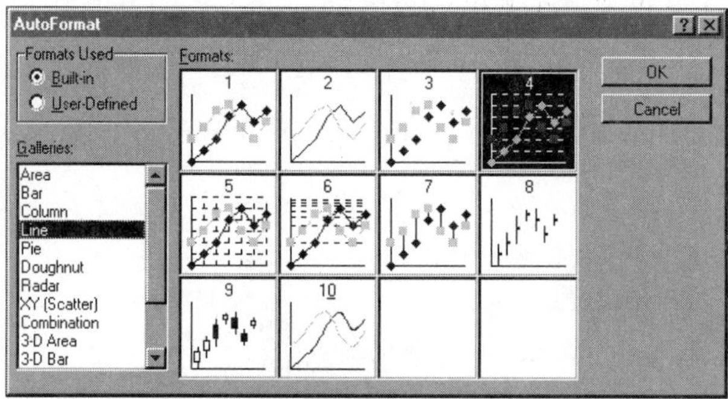

FIGURE 16-17
The Line autoformats include high-low options as well as connected and disconnected line charts.

Option 1 results in a connected line chart, and option 3 results in an unconnected line chart. In these charts, a square or diamond-shaped marker identifies each point. Option 2 generates a connected line chart with no markers. Options 4 and 5 are like option 1, except that gridlines are included: horizontal gridlines in option 4 and both horizontal and vertical gridlines in option 5. Option 6 applies logarithmic scaling to the y-axis.

Option 7 is a simple high-low chart in which a vertical line connects all points for each cluster. The picture in the dialog box shows only two points per cluster, but you can have as many as you need.

Option 8 is a high-low-close chart suitable for stock price tracking. To create this kind of chart, set up a data range in high-low-close order. In other words, if your prices are arranged in columns, put high prices in the first column, low prices in the second, and closing prices in the third. Follow the same order if your data is arranged by row. This chart can display only three data series. No additional series you specify will appear in the chart, but they will show up if you switch to a different kind of line chart or a different chart type.

Option 9 creates an open-high-low-close chart. To use this line chart option, arrange your data in four columns (or rows), in open-high-low-close order. Excel plots the high and low values for each point as a vertical line and the open and close values as a rectangle. One color (white by default) is used for periods when the close is higher than the open, and a contrasting color (black by default) is used for periods when the open is higher than the close.

Finally, option 10 resembles option 2, except Excel smooths the line it draws. Compare options 2 and 10, and you'll see the difference. In option 2,

TIP When you use logarithmic scaling in a chart, Excel plots the data points as powers of ten; that is, 10 shows as 1 because 10^1 equals 10, 100 shows as 2 because 10^2 equals 100, and so on. While the logarithms can seem confusing — at least initially — a logarithmically scaled chart provides a unique perspective, in that it shows the rate of change. For example, a plotted line showing revenues for a company that is growing 50 percent annually appears much steeper than a plotted line showing revenues for a company that is growing 5 percent annually. This is true even when the actual revenues of the two companies are markedly different in size.

Excel plots the data points and draws straight lines between the points, and in option 10, Excel draws a line through the same data points but curves the line to eliminate any zigzagging.

Area Charts

An area chart is a line chart in which the space between the line and the x-axis is filled. Figure 16-18 shows the gallery for this chart type.

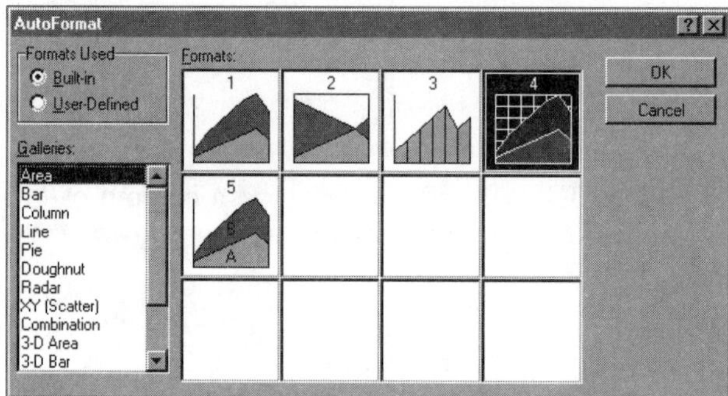

FIGURE 16-18
The Area gallery includes five autoformats.

With options 1, 3, 4, and 5, Excel stacks the values for each cluster. Like a stacked column chart, this kind of area chart can reveal the trends of aggregate values while giving you a rough idea of each series' contribution to the whole. The area chart, however, emphasizes the continuity between points much more than the stacked column chart.

The differences between options 1, 3, 4, and 5 in the area chart gallery are minimal. Option 3 adds vertical gridlines, option 4 adds both horizontal and vertical gridlines, and option 5 displays series names within the chart (obviating the need for a legend).

Option 2 is quite another story, however. Like the 100 percent options (options 5 and 10) in the Column and Bar galleries, option 2 shows the percentage that each data point contributes to each cluster's total.

Pie Charts

Unlike the other chart types discussed so far, a pie chart plots only one data series. Any additional series you specify are ignored, although they appear if you switch to a different chart type.

Pie charts are designed to show the relative contribution of each data point to the series total. Figure 16-19 shows the seven autoformats available for pie charts.

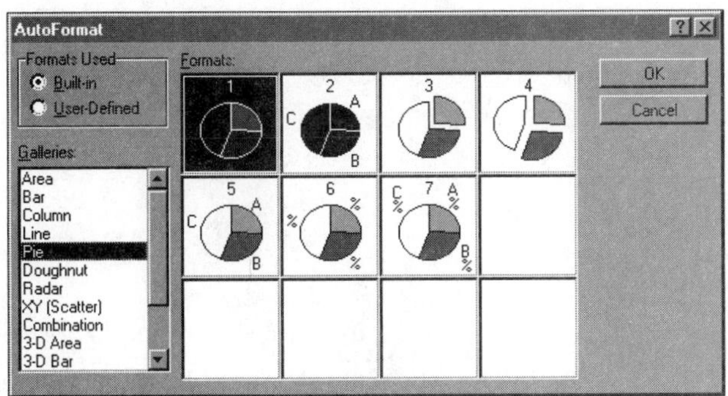

FIGURE 16-19
Pie charts show the relative contribution of each member of a series to the series total.

In option 1, the pie is fully assembled (all slices are in place), and no labels are assigned to the slices. In options 2 and 5, each slice is labeled. To create a labeled pie chart, select both a column of labels and a column of numbers (or a row of each). All the slices in option 2 are the same color or shade (black, by default); each slice in all other options is a different color. You can change the colors of slices individually. For example, you might select option 2 and add color to one or two slices while leaving the remaining slices black.

In option 6, Excel computes the percentage contributions of all slices and displays them around the perimeter of the pie. In option 7, both labels and percentages are displayed.

Options 3 and 4 are exploded pies, which means the slices are separated. In option 3, only one slice — the first point in the data series — is exploded; in option 4, the entire pie is exploded. If you want more than one but not all slices exploded, or if you want to explode any single slice other than the first point in the data series, you can drag slices with the mouse.

TIP When you plot data in a pie chart, keep two design issues in mind. First, note that the more data points you plot, the more difficult it becomes to distinguish slices. People use various rules of thumb for limiting the number of plotted data points, but we think plotting more than about half a dozen data points in a pie often risks illegibility.

Second, note that the first data point, which is plotted starting at the 12 o'clock position, is the dominant slice of the pie. If you want to emphasize a pie slice — particularly a small pie slice — be sure you make its data point the first in the series.

For information about changing the color or pattern of slices, see "Formatting Data Point Markers," page 639.

For information about exploding pies, see "Exploding Pie and Doughnut Slices," page 642.

Doughnut Charts

Doughnut charts resemble pie charts, with a major difference. A doughnut chart has a hole in the middle and its data markers appear as segments of a ring. Unlike the pie chart type, a doughnut chart allows you to plot more than one data series, with each series plotted in its own ring, or doughnut.

Like pie charts, doughnut charts are designed to show the relative contribution of each data point to the series total. Figure 16-20 shows the seven Doughnut autoformats, which mirror the pie chart autoformats.

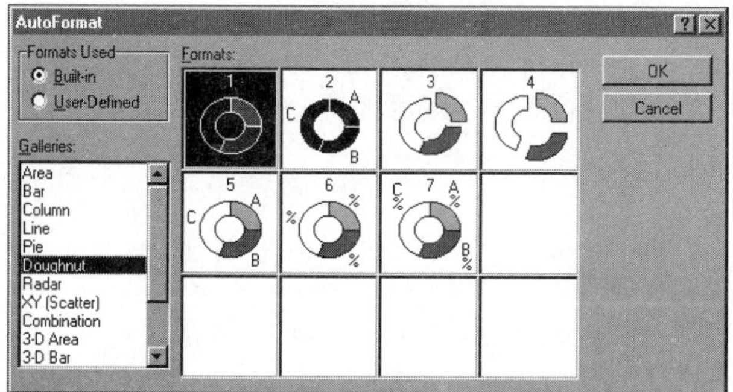

FIGURE 16-20
Like pie charts, doughnut charts show the relative contribution of each member of a series to the series total.

In option 1, the doughnut is fully assembled. Options 2 and 5 add category labels to identify the doughnut slices. To create a labeled doughnut chart, include the category labels in your selection. All the doughnut slices in option 2 are the same color or shade (black, by default); each slice in all other options is a different color. You can change the colors of slices individually. For example, you might select option 2 and add color to one or two slices while leaving the remaining slices black.

In option 6, Excel computes the percentage contributions of all doughnut slices and displays them around the doughnut's outer edge. In option 7, both labels and percentages are displayed.

Options 3 and 4 are exploded doughnuts, which means the slices are separated out. In option 3, only one slice — the first point in the data series — is exploded; in option 4, the entire doughnut is exploded. If you want more than one but not all doughnut slices exploded, or if you want to explode any single slice other than the first point in the data series, you can drag slices with the mouse.

For information about changing the color or pattern of slices, see "Formatting Data Point Markers," page 639.

For information about exploding doughnuts, see "Exploding Pie and Doughnut Slices," page 642.

Radar Charts

In a radar chart, the value of each point is indicated by its radial distance from a central origin. The angle of the radius is determined by the point's position within the data series.

For example, the radar chart in Figure 16-21 plots three series of 12 points. The chart's value (y) axis is a vertical line drawn through the chart's origin. Each point in the series has its own category (x) axis, but because these category axes are spaced at equal angles, the angular position of a data point is not particularly meaningful. The magnitude of each point is represented by its distance from the origin.

Radar charts are useful for showing or comparing the aggregate values of whole data series, rather than the values of individual points. Provided all the values in a series have the same sign (positive or negative), the absolute value of the aggregate is proportional to the area enclosed by the chart.

Seasonal fluctuations are also easily shown in radar charts. For example, Figure 16-21 shows that customer visits generally increase each year, but the sales staff can handle only about 800 customers each month.

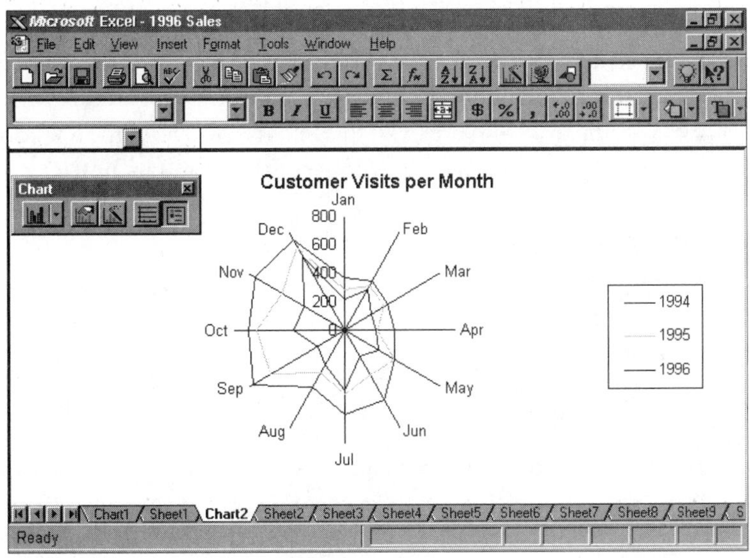

FIGURE 16-21
In a radar chart, the value of each point is represented by its distance from the origin.

Figure 16-22 shows the six autoformats in the Radar gallery. Option 1 produces a chart in which points along a series are marked and connected, and the category axes are displayed. Option 2, the autoformat used in the chart in Figure 16-21, is like option 1 but without the markers. Option 4 connects the category axes with gridlines. Option 5 is like option 4, except that the value axis is scaled logarithmically. Option 6 colors the interior areas created by the plot lines. Option 3 eliminates everything but the plot lines, so you can compare plot areas at a glance, but you're left guessing about absolute values.

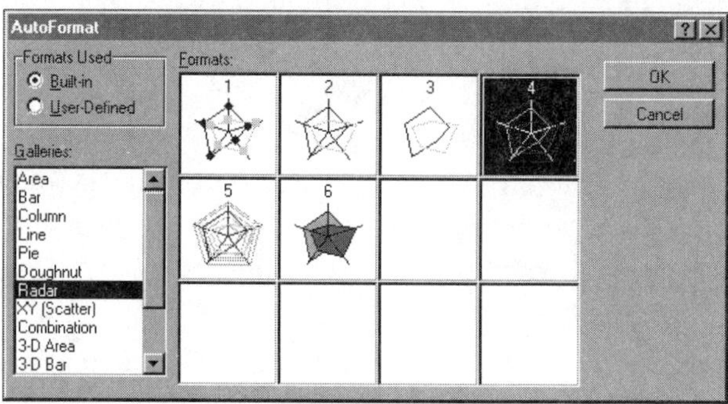

FIGURE 16-22
The Radar gallery includes six autoformats.

XY (Scatter) Charts

Most of the chart types we've seen so far display values along one axis and category names along another. Usually the vertical, or y, axis is the value axis, and the horizontal, or x, axis is the category axis. (The reverse is true for bar charts.) In an XY chart, both axes measure values.

Typically, XY charts are used to depict what kind of relationship — if any — exists between two data series. For example, Figure 16-23 shows a chart that plots the historical relationship between advertising expenditures and sales revenue for a company. A glance at this chart tells you that, historically, revenues rise with increasing advertising expenditures, but not in a strictly linear way.

An XY chart plots each point using a pair of coordinates, one from an x series and one from a y series. The top row (or left column) of your data selection represents the x series, and each succeeding row (or column) represents a y series.

Figure 16-24 displays the six XY (Scatter) autoformats. The chart in Figure 16-23 uses option 2, in which a straight line connects pairs of points. Option 6 resembles option 2 except that with option 6, Excel smooths the line connecting the data points. None of the remaining options connects the points.

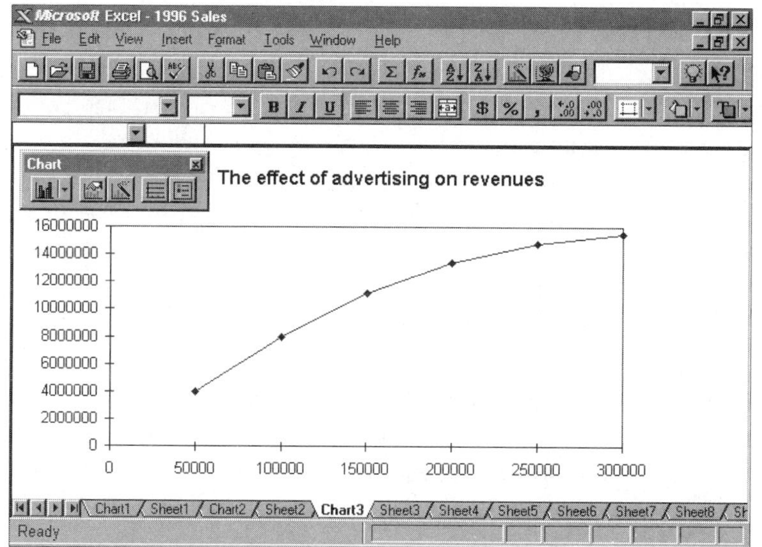

FIGURE 16-23

XY charts can help you determine if a predictable correlation exists between two or more data series.

Option 1 displays the data points without gridlines. Option 3 uses horizontal and vertical gridlines and linear scaling. Option 4 applies logarithmic scaling and gridlines to the y-axis. Option 5 uses logarithmic scaling and gridlines on both axes.

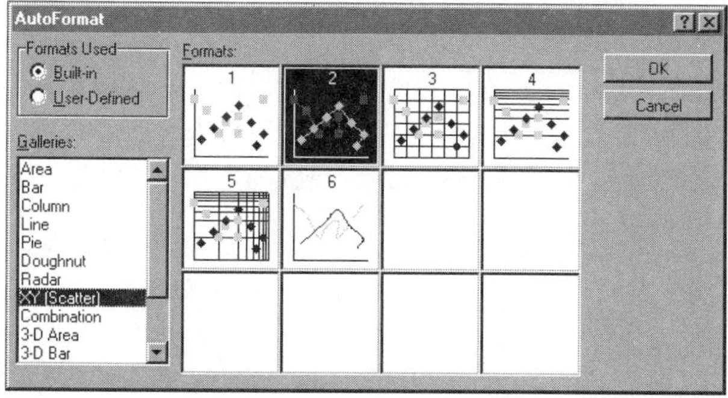

FIGURE 16-24

The XY autoformats include standard, semilogarithmic, and full logarithmic scaling.

TIP An XY chart depicts the correlation between two data series. To measure and empirically test any correlation, you should use regression analysis. For more information about regression analysis, see "Linear and Exponential Regression," page 534.

Combination Charts

A combination chart either uses two chart types or has a secondary x-axis or y-axis. Combination charts that use two chart types are useful for contrasting one or more series with the remaining series. For example, you might plot a salesperson's performance figures as a column chart together with quotas as a line chart. Combination charts that have a secondary x-axis or y-axis are valuable when some of your data series vary within one range of values and others vary within a markedly different range.

For some kinds of data, it is convenient to use two chart types *and* a secondary y-axis. For example, you might want to combine an open-high-low-close chart with a column chart to track stock prices and transaction volumes in a single chart. Because volumes can number in the millions and prices are likely to vary within a lower range, you need to plot the prices against one y-axis and the volumes against another. Figure 16-25 shows the Combination autoformats.

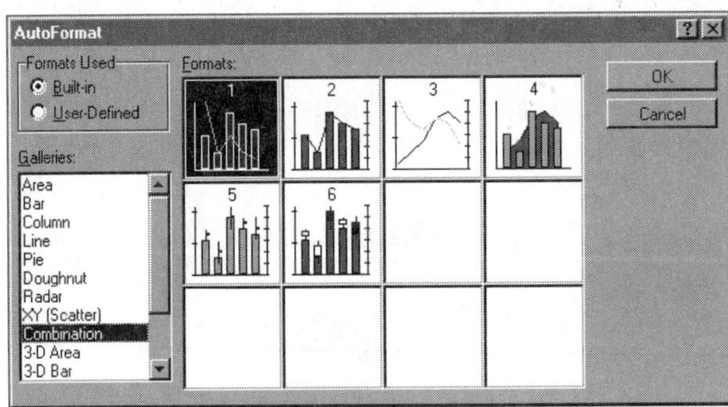

FIGURE 16-25
Six Combination autoformats are available.

The AutoFormat dialog box offers six Combination autoformats: a column/line chart with a single y-axis (option 1); a column/line chart with two y-axes (option 2); a line chart with two y-axes (option 3); a column/area chart with one y-axis (option 4); a high-low-close/volume chart (option 5); and an open-high-low-close/volume chart (option 6). With options 1, 2, 3, and 4, Excel divides the data series equally between the two chart types (or the two axes). For example, if you plot four data series using a column/line chart with two y-axes, the first and second series are plotted as columns against the primary (left) y-axis, and the third and fourth series are plotted as lines against the secondary (right) y-axis. With options 5 and 6, Excel assumes that the first series is the volumes and the remaining series are the prices. (You need to have five data series to use option 6.)

As you'll see in Chapter 18, you can build many kinds of combination charts in addition to the combination chart autoformats shown in Figure 16-25.

Three-Dimensional Column Charts

The eight autoformats in the 3-D Column gallery, shown in Figure 16-26, fall into two broad categories. Options 1 through 4 and option 8 are similar to options 1, 3, 5, and 6 in the 2-D Column gallery, except that the columns appear as solid shapes. These charts display columns from each data series in side-by-side clusters, just as the two-dimensional column charts do.

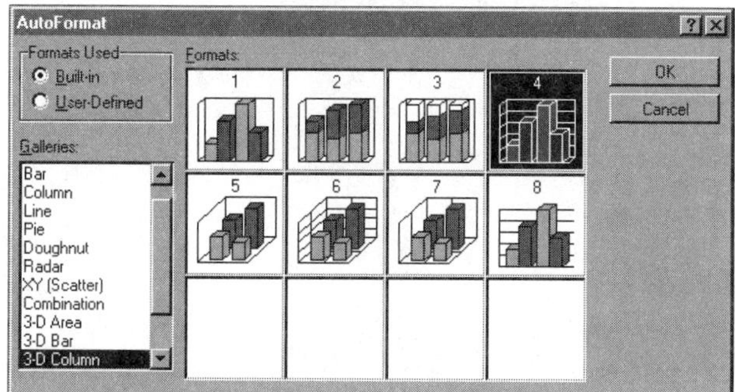

FIGURE 16-26
Five of the 3-D Column autoformats plot solid bars in side-by-side clusters. The remaining three autoformats plot each series on a separate plane.

Options 5 through 7, on the other hand, display each data series on a *separate plane* by adding a third axis — the *z-axis* — to the chart. Category names appear along the first axis, series names along the second, and values along the third. The additional axis eliminates the need for a legend, although you can add one if you want.

The only differences between options 5, 6, and 7 in the 3-D Column gallery have to do with gridlines. Option 5 has none; option 6 has x-, y-, and z-axis gridlines; and option 7 has x- and y-axis gridlines only.

Like a family portrait, a three-dimensional chart created with option 5, 6, or 7 in the 3-D Column gallery works best if the tall members stand behind the short ones. Otherwise, the short members become nearly invisible. However, as you'll see in Chapter 17, in most cases you can avoid having one series obscure another, because Excel makes it easy to modify the viewing angle of a three-dimensional chart.

For more information about viewing angles, see "Changing Three-Dimensional Viewing Angles," page 668.

Three-Dimensional Bar Charts

Although bar charts are horizontal counterparts of column charts, the 3-D Bar gallery, shown in Figure 16-27, has only five options. These options are similar to options 1, 3, 5, and 6 in the 2-D Bar gallery, except that the bars are solid shapes. Excel does not allow you to create three-dimensional bar charts with each series plotted on a separate plane.

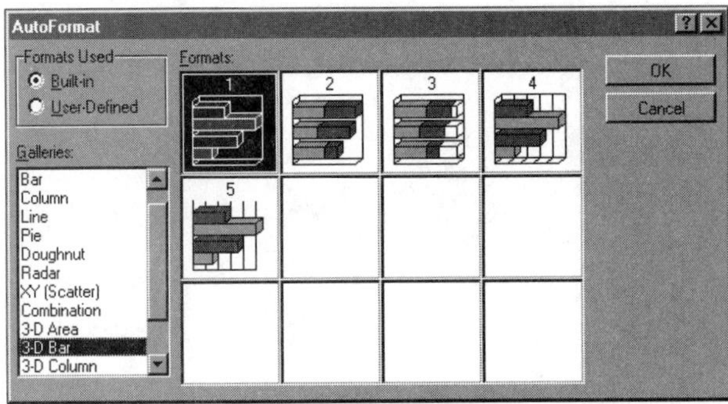

FIGURE 16-27
The 3-D Bar autoformats do not include options for plotting data series on separate planes.

Three-Dimensional Area Charts

The options for three-dimensional area charts are similar to those for three-dimensional column charts. The first four are solid-shape counterparts to four of the two-dimensional area chart options, and the remaining three plot each data series on a separate plane. Figure 16-28 shows the 3-D Area autoformats.

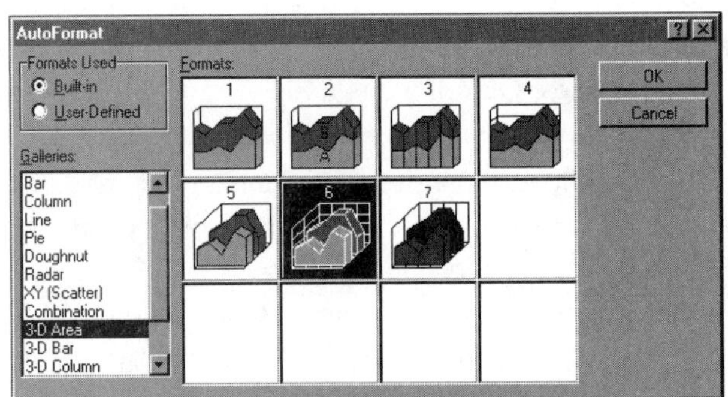

FIGURE 16-28
Four of the 3D Area autoformats plot data series as solid blocks. The remaining three autoformats plot each series on a separate plane.

Three-Dimensional Line Charts

In a three-dimensional line chart, each series is drawn as a solid line, or ribbon, which appears on its own plane. Figure 16-29 shows the four 3-D Line autoformats.

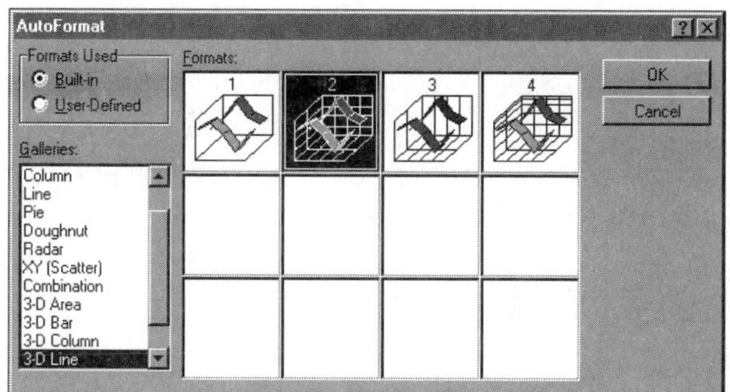

FIGURE 16-29

Each series in a three-dimensional line chart is drawn as a solid ribbon.

Your autoformat selection for a three-dimensional line chart depends on whether you want gridlines and logarithmic scaling. Option 2 includes x-, y-, and z-axis gridlines, and option 3 includes x- and y-axis gridlines. Option 4 is like option 2, except that the vertical z-axis is scaled logarithmically.

Three-Dimensional Pie Charts

In a three-dimensional pie chart, your pie is drawn as a solid disk. By default, you look down on this disk from a 15-degree angle above the horizon. Figure 16-30 shows the seven 3-D Pie autoformats. If you compare Figure 16-30 with Figure 16-19 (shown on page 605), you can see that these options correspond exactly to the options in the 2-D Pie gallery.

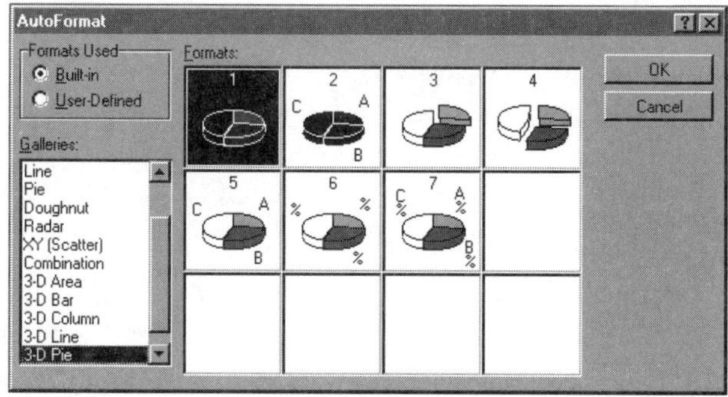

FIGURE 16-30

In a three-dimensional pie chart, the pie is drawn as a solid disk.

TIP Take care when using three-dimensional pie charts. To give the illusion of depth, Excel tilts the pie so that part of it appears in the foreground and part in the background. Because pie slices in the background seem smaller than they really are, you can't compare two pieces if one is in the foreground and one is in the background.

Three-Dimensional Surface Charts

In a three-dimensional surface chart, Excel plots two or more data series using a two-dimensional or three-dimensional surface. To do this, Excel draws lines for each data series and then visually connects the lines using either color or wire mesh. Figure 16-31 shows the 3-D Surface autoformats.

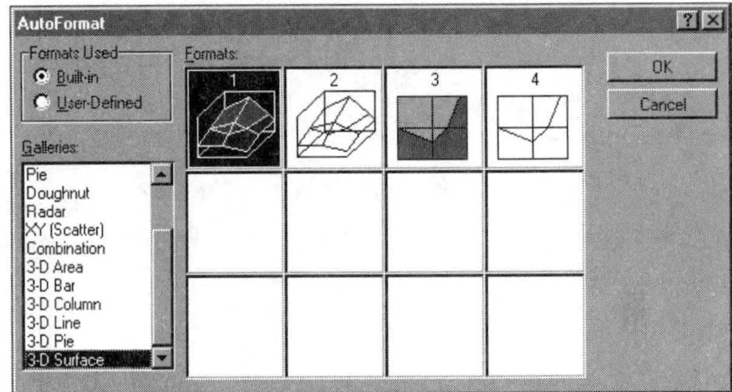

FIGURE 16-31
The 3-D Surface autoformats plot data series using a two-dimensional or three-dimensional surface.

In the first three-dimensional surface chart format, Excel connects the data series lines using a colored surface. In the second three-dimensional surface chart format, Excel connects the lines using a wire mesh. For both the first and second three-dimensional surface chart formats, the chart appears three dimensional.

The third and fourth three-dimensional surface chart formats are actually two dimensional. For both surface formats, the surface chart appears as if you were looking down at the chart from above. In the third three-dimensional surface chart format, Excel connects the data series lines using a colored surface. In the fourth three-dimensional surface chart format, Excel connects the data series lines using a wire mesh.

For both the first and third three-dimensional surface chart formats, Excel uses color not to identify data series — which is the way color is used for other charts — but to help calibrate the plotted values. In a colored three-dimensional surface chart, Excel uses color to show the tick-mark ranges on the major value axes.

For more information about previewing angles, see "Changing Three-Dimensional Viewing Angles," page 668.

Changing the Default Chart Type and Autoformat

Every chart you create initially appears in Microsoft Excel's default chart type and autoformat: a simple column chart. If you use another type of chart more often than the column type, you can change the default. To do this, follow these steps:

1. Use the AutoFormat command on the Format menu to select the chart type and autoformat you want and click OK.
2. Make any special formatting changes to your chart you want as part of your default chart type using the usual methods.
3. Choose the Options command from the Tools menu to display the Options dialog box.
4. Click the Chart tab to display the Chart options, as shown in Figure 16-32.

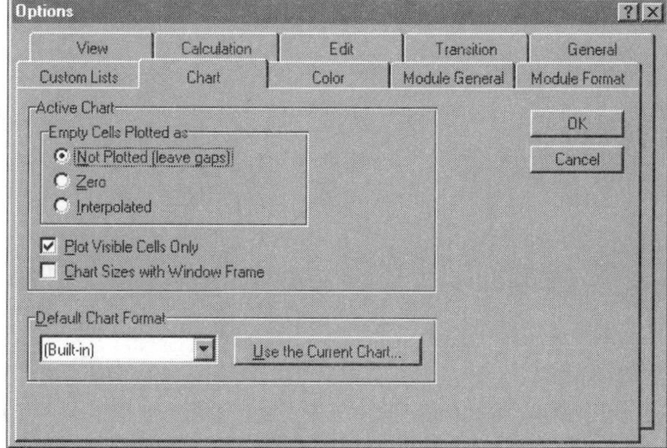

FIGURE 16-32
You use the Chart tab of the Options dialog box to specify the default chart type and autoformat.

5. Click the Use The Current Chart button.
6. When Excel prompts you for a name for the new chart type and autoformat, type a name in the Format Name edit box and click OK. Click OK to close the Options dialog box.

The new default format possesses every characteristic of the chart that was active when you selected the Use The Current Chart button.

TIP You can always return to the original default chart type and autoformat by resetting the Default Chart Format option to (Built-In).

Saving, Opening, and Protecting Charts

Charts are saved with the workbook in which they reside. To save a chart, simply save the workbook file by choosing either Save or Save As from the File menu. The chart is available whenever the workbook is open, so to open a chart, simply open its workbook.

After you create a chart, you can use the Protection command on the Tools menu to lock the worksheet or chart sheet containing the chart. Then other people can't change the sheet and, therefore, the chart. The Protection command works the same way for both worksheets and chart sheets.

For more information about file management, see Chapter 3, "Managing Files," page 51.

For more information about protecting charts, see "Protecting Your Data," page 106.

Printing Charts

Chapter 10 discusses the basic techniques for printing Microsoft Excel documents. To print an embedded chart, follow the procedures described in that chapter for printing worksheets.

You can print an embedded chart independently of its worksheet data. Double-click the embedded chart to activate it, and then choose Print from the File menu. The Selected Chart option in the Print What section is automatically selected. The embedded chart prints when you click OK.

Printing a chart on a chart sheet is the same as printing a chart embedded in a worksheet, with a few minor differences.

The Page Setup Command

To print a selected chart sheet, first choose the Page Setup command from the File menu and then click the Chart tab in the Page Setup dialog box. Excel displays options that let you define the layout of the page on which you will be printing and the printing quality.

Use the Printed Chart Size options — Use Full Page, Scale To Fit Page, and Custom — to tell Excel how large the printed chart should be. The Use Full Page option, the default setting, tells Excel to fill the entire page, regardless of the height-to-width ratio of the chart. Scale To Fit Page instructs Excel to print the chart as large as possible without losing the height-to-width ratio shown on the screen. If you want to control the dimensions of the printed chart manually, select the Custom option. This option tells Excel to print your chart exactly as it appears on the screen. To vary the size of the screen image, you can resize the window containing the chart just as you would resize a worksheet window.

The Print Preview Command

To see what your chart looks like before you print it, choose the Print Preview command (or click Print Preview in the Print dialog box). As in the worksheet environment, Excel displays the chart as it will appear on the printed page.

All the Print Preview features described in Chapter 10 work the same way in the chart environment as they do in the worksheet environment. You can zoom in for a close-up view, modify margin settings with the mouse, and directly access the Page Setup dialog box to change its settings. To print the chart, click Print.

The Print Command

When you choose the File menu's Print command, you see a dialog box like the one that appears when you choose the Print command in the worksheet environment. The Pages option in the Print dialog box does not apply when you are working with a chart sheet because all your charts fit on one page. However, you can use the Copies edit box to indicate the number of copies of the chart you want to print.

Chapter 17

Customizing Charts

In Chapter 16, we surveyed the steps involved in creating a chart and selecting a basic chart type and an autoformat. Now we'll look at the ways in which Microsoft Excel can help you tailor the appearance of your charts to suit your tastes and presentation needs.

Customizing Embedded Charts

When you select an embedded chart, Microsoft Excel displays the Chart toolbar (unless you have used the Toolbars command on the View menu to instruct Excel not to display it). This toolbar includes buttons for applying commonly used formatting. You can use the buttons on the Chart toolbar to change the chart type — from a column chart to a bar chart or pie chart, for example. However, even with this toolbar, the extent to which you can customize an embedded chart is limited. To apply more extensive formatting, the first step is to double-click the embedded chart to make it active. Excel displays a thick border around the chart and changes the menu bar to offer chart-related commands. You can then customize your chart with any of the procedures described in this chapter. When you've finished customizing, simply click anywhere outside the embedded chart.

TIP When you double-click an embedded chart that is too large to fit entirely within the current workbook window, Excel displays the chart temporarily in a new window. When you have finished editing the chart, click the Close button or press Ctrl-W to close this chart-editing window and return to your worksheet.

Selecting Chart Objects

A *chart object* is a component of a chart, such as an axis, a data point, a title, or a legend. Microsoft Excel divides a chart into the following classes of objects, each of which you can select and format:

- Chart area
- Plot area
- Floor (three-dimensional chart types only)
- Walls (three-dimensional chart types only)
- Legend

- Axes
- Text
- Arrows
- Gridlines
- First data series
- Second and subsequent data series
- Drop lines
- High-low lines
- Up bars
- Down bars
- Series lines

Some object classes consist of two or more separate objects. For example, most charts have at least two axes, and most data series consist of two or more data points. You can select and format the objects within a class separately.

With the mouse, you can usually select the object you want to format by clicking it. For example, to select a chart's y-axis so that you can change its scale, click that axis. If a selected object consists of still other objects, you can select a component object by clicking again. For example, you can select a data marker in a currently selected data series by clicking the marker.

In many cases, you can select an object and open a formatting dialog box at the same time by double-clicking the object. Double-clicking a legend, for example, selects the legend, opens the Format Legend dialog box, and displays the Patterns tab, where you can specify a background color and pattern for the box that contains the legend, add a drop shadow, and so on.

TIP Another way to format an object is to click it with the right mouse button and choose the Format command from the shortcut menu.

To select an object with the keyboard, use the direction keys. Pressing the Up and Down direction keys cycles you through the various objects, and pressing the Left and Right direction keys moves you from object to object within an object.

Whether you use the mouse or the keyboard, Excel provides two ways to distinguish the object you selected: The object's name appears in the Name box at the left end of the formula bar, and the object itself is surrounded by handles.

Excel abbreviates the names of some objects. For example, series are identified as S1, S2, and so on. The first data point in series 1 is called S1P1; the second data point in series 3 is called S3P2; and so on. If you find these abbreviations confusing, you can ignore them and use the handles to determine what's currently selected. For example, you might not remember which axis is axis 1, but when you see handles at the ends of your y-axis, you'll know which element of the chart you're about to format.

When you finish formatting an object, it remains selected so that you can continue working with it. To deselect the object, press Esc, select another object, or click anywhere near the four edges of the chart.

Using Graphic Objects on Your Charts

Any graphic object you can place on a worksheet can be placed on a chart. Lines, circles, polygons, rectangles, and buttons are all available, and any of them can be linked to Visual Basic macros. Each of these topics is covered in other chapters of this book.

See Also For more information about Excel's graphic objects, see Chapter 9, "Graphics," page 345.

For more information about Visual Basic, see Chapter 25 "An Overview of Visual Basic," page 861.

Adding Text to Charts

You can annotate your charts with text. For example, you can add a title to the entire chart, descriptions beside the y-axis and below the x-axis, and words or numbers next to individual data points. You can also add floating text annotations wherever you want.

Adding a Chart Title

To add a title to your chart, follow these steps:

1. Activate the chart. From the Insert menu, choose Titles. Excel displays the Titles dialog box shown in Figure 17-1 on the next page.

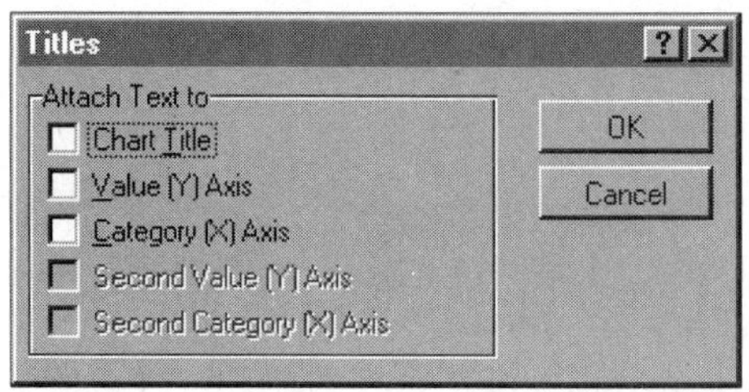

FIGURE 17-1 Use the Titles dialog box to add a title to a chart or chart axis.

2. Select the type of title you want to add — in this case, the Chart Title option — and click OK. Excel displays the dummy text Title, centered near the top of your chart or next to the axis. Handles appear around the dummy text.
3. Replace the dummy text by typing your own title. Your entry appears in the formula bar as you type.
4. Press Enter. Excel displays your title on the chart but leaves the handles in place in case you want to do anything further, such as select a different font.

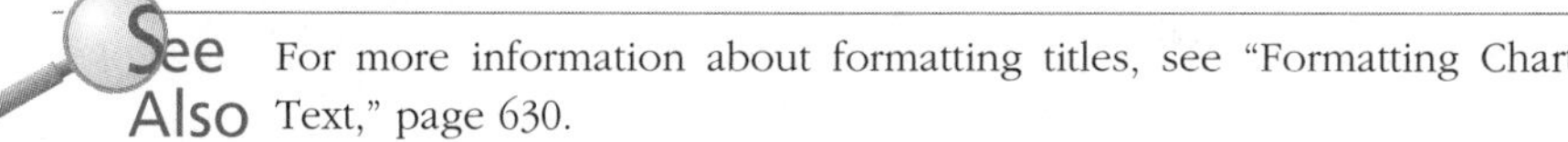

For more information about formatting titles, see "Formatting Chart Text," page 630.

Breaking a Chart Title into Two or More Lines

Excel normally displays the chart title on a single line. To break it into two or more lines, select the title, then place the insertion point in the text box where you want a line break, and press Enter. You can edit the title just as you would edit any text box.

Multiline titles are centered by default, but you can select left or right alignment by clicking the appropriate buttons on the Formatting toolbar. You can also change the alignment of titles with menu commands.

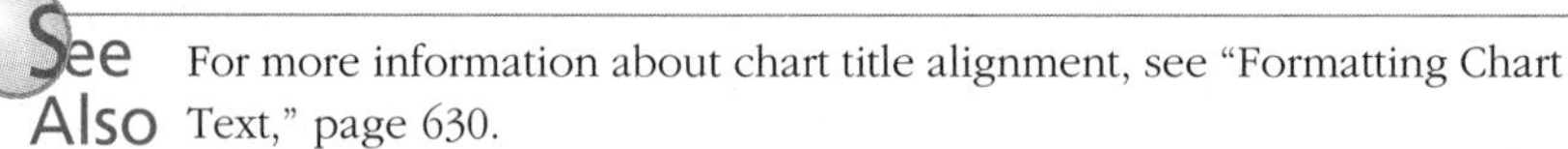

For more information about chart title alignment, see "Formatting Chart Text," page 630.

Adding Automatic Chart Titles

Under certain circumstances, Excel creates a title when you open a new chart window. Excel creates a title if the data to be plotted is in a single worksheet column and you include a column heading in the selected range, or if the data to be plotted is in a single row and you include a row heading.

For example, using the worksheet shown in Figure 17-2, select A3:B8 and create a column chart. Because the chart has only one series, the column heading, Product A, is treated as a chart title as well as a series name only. If the chart had more than one series, the heading Product A would be treated as a series name only. If you subsequently add another data series into this chart, Excel removes the title and uses the column heading as a series name instead.

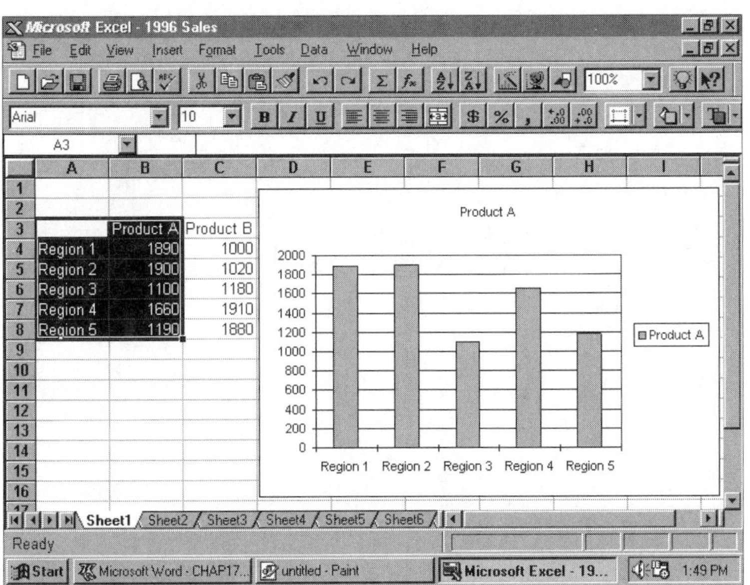

FIGURE 17-2
When a chart consists of a single series, Excel uses any column or row heading in the selected range as a default chart title.

Linking a Chart Title to a Worksheet Cell

You can link a chart title to the contents of a worksheet cell so that cell changes are automatically reflected in the title. To make this link, follow these steps:

1. Use the Titles dialog box to create a dummy title, as described on page 624.
2. Instead of replacing the dummy title with text, create a formula. For example, to link the title of a chart to cell A1 in Sheet1, select the dummy title and enter the formula

   =Sheet1!$A$1

   in the formula bar.

You can either type this formula directly in the formula bar or type the equal sign, click twice in the worksheet cell to which you want to link the title, and press Enter. If you subsequently move the worksheet cell somewhere else on the same worksheet, Excel updates the formula so that the title continues to reflect the entry in the cell.

You can link a title to a cell that contains numeric or text data. If you link it to a cell that contains numeric data, Excel uses the cell's current numeric format to display the title.

For more information about creating formulas, see Chapter 5, "Building Formulas," page 111.

Adding Labels to Chart Axes

Adding a label to a chart axis is similar to adding a title to the chart itself. Start by choosing Titles from the Insert menu. In the Titles dialog box, select the option for the axis you want to label and then click OK.

In most two-dimensional charts, the vertical axis is called the value or y-axis, and the horizontal axis is called the category or x-axis. The three exceptions are bar charts, in which the category axis is vertical and the value axis is horizontal, and pie and doughnut charts, which have no axes.

In three-dimensional charts (excluding three-dimensional pie charts, which have no axes), the vertical axis is still the value axis, but it's called the z-axis. The category axis remains the x-axis; the *series* axis (if your chart plots separate data series on separate planes) is the y-axis.

No question that this terminology is hard to remember. When you select an axis option in the Titles dialog box and click OK, Excel displays a dummy label surrounded with handles so you can see immediately which axis you're about to label. You can replace the dummy label with your own text or cell reference, and you can edit the label just as you would edit a chart title.

Excel centers axis labels between the end points of the axis. If you want the labels to appear somewhere else — above the y-axis, for example — use floating text instead of titles.

For more information about floating text, see "Adding Floating Text," page 629.

Adding Labels to Data Points

The easiest way to attach text to a data point is to select the data point and then choose the Data Labels command from the Insert menu. For example, suppose you want to add labels to the monthly earnings chart shown in Figure 17-3, and you want the labels to identify the high point for the year, which occurs in April, and the low point for the year, which occurs in August.

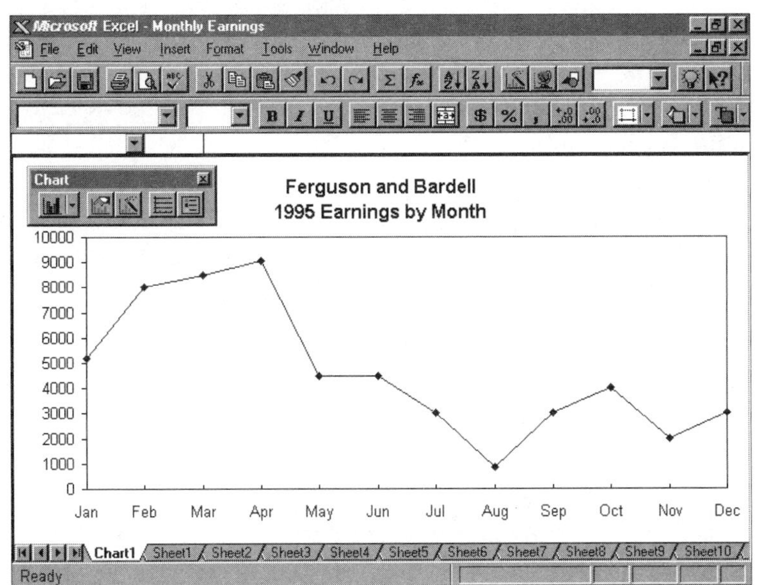

FIGURE 17-3
We want to label the high and low points in this line chart.

To add values as data-point labels, follow these steps:

1. Click the April data point one time to select the series, and then again to select the data point itself. Excel marks the point with a handle and displays S1P4 (an abbreviation for series 1 point 4) in the Name box at the left end of the formula bar.

   NOTE If you want to add labels to all the data points, simply click the data point once.

2. From the Insert menu, choose Data Labels. Excel displays the Data Labels dialog box, shown in Figure 17-4.
3. Click Show Value to tell Excel to label the data point with its plotted value.
4. Click OK. Excel displays the data label beside the data point.

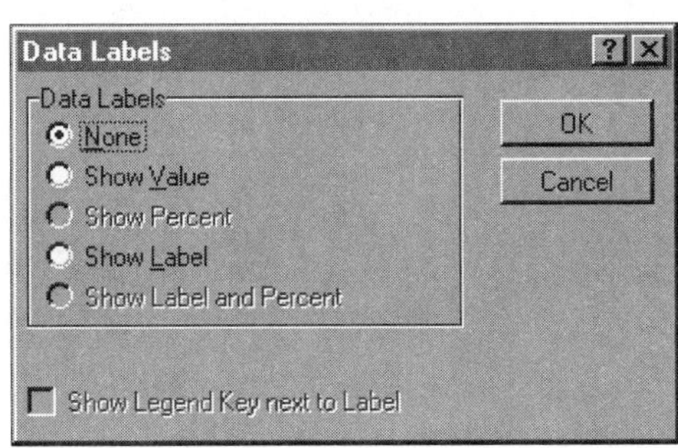

FIGURE 17-4
The Data Labels dialog box lets you label data points — for example, with their values.

5. Repeat these steps to annotate the August data point.

Figure 17-5 shows how the chart from Figure 17-3 looks with labels attached to both the April and August data points and formatted with a transparent background.

You aren't limited to using values as data-point labels. You can use the Show Label option to tell Excel to label the data point with the category name. If you want to change a value or category name label, simply select the label, click the formula bar, and make your changes.

> **TIP** If you edit a data-point label, the Data Labels dialog box changes to include the Automatic Text option. To return the label to its source-data value or category name, select the Automatic Text box.

If you're labeling the slices of a pie chart or doughnut chart, you can use the Show Percent and Show Label And Percent options in the Data Labels dialog box to use percentages as labels. (Excel calculates the percentage by dividing the data point's value by the data series total.)

FIGURE 17-5
We attached labels to show the values of the April and August data points. If the values of these points change, the labels also change.

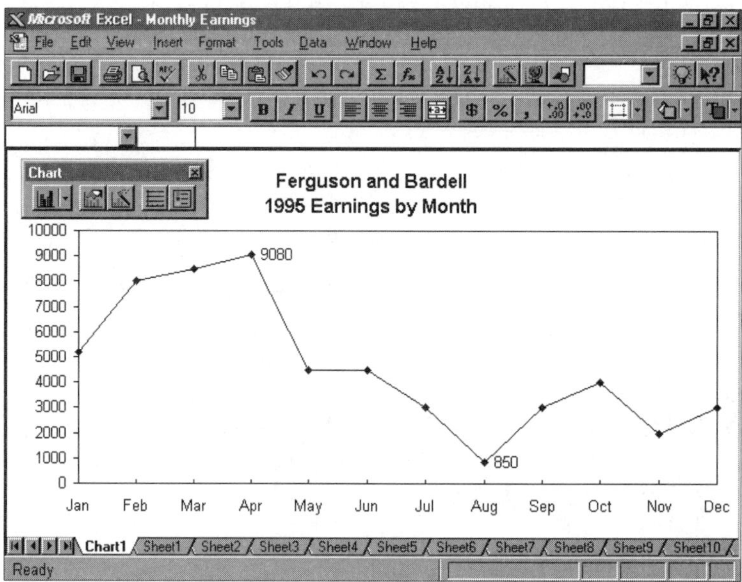

To display a legend next to labeled data points, select the Show Legend Key Next To Label option. Excel then displays next to the data point label a small square or line of the pattern or color you've applied to the corresponding data marker. This option can be a handy alternative to a chart legend when you're short of space.

Adding Floating Text

To add floating text to a chart, check that you haven't selected any chart objects (the Name box should be empty) and then type the text in the formula bar. Press Ctrl-Enter to begin a new line if you want your text to appear on more than one line. Press Enter to lock in your entry.

CAUTION If a chart object — particularly a data point or text — is selected when you add floating text, you can inadvertently destroy information in your chart.

When you lock in your entry, the text box initially appears in the middle of the plot area, which may make it difficult to read on the screen. You can drag the text to an empty area of the chart window so that it is more legible. Figure 17-6 shows the line chart from Figure 17-5 after we added some text.

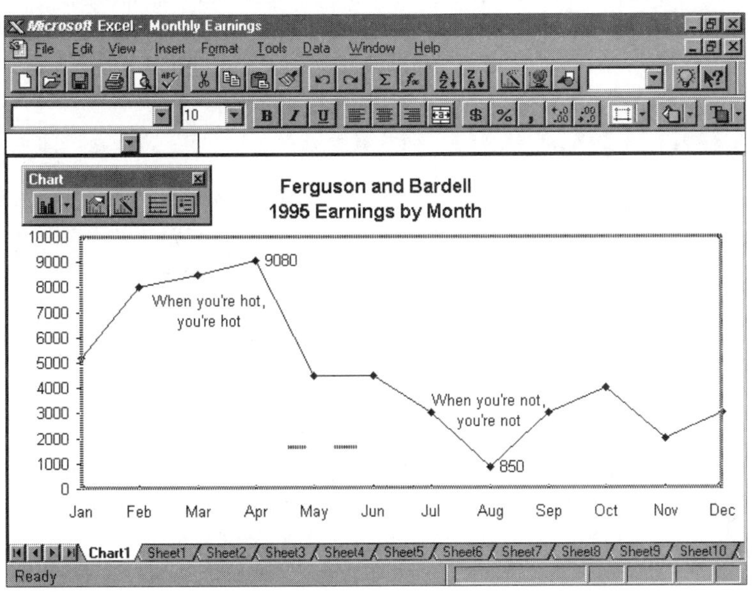

FIGURE 17-6
We annotated this line chart with floating text.

You can also change the proportions of the text box by dragging one of its handles. To change its height or width, drag one of the side handles; to change the height and width simultaneously, drag one of the corner handles.

When the positioning box is larger than the block of text, the text is centered within the box. When the positioning box is smaller than the block of text, Excel displays as much text as it has room for. The effects of resizing a text box are particularly important when you use the Patterns tab of the Format Object dialog box to place borders around the text.

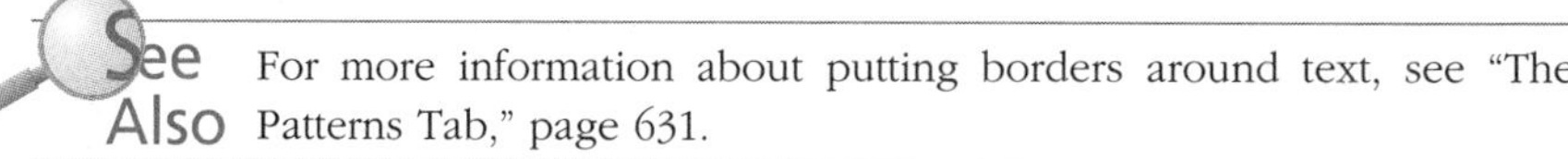

See Also For more information about putting borders around text, see "The Patterns Tab," page 631.

Editing and Removing Text

To change the contents of a text box, click the box to select it and then click it again to edit the contents directly. Follow the same procedures you use to directly edit a worksheet cell. When you finish, click anywhere outside the text box to lock in the edited text.

To remove any text box, select it and press Del or choose All from the Clear submenu of the Edit menu.

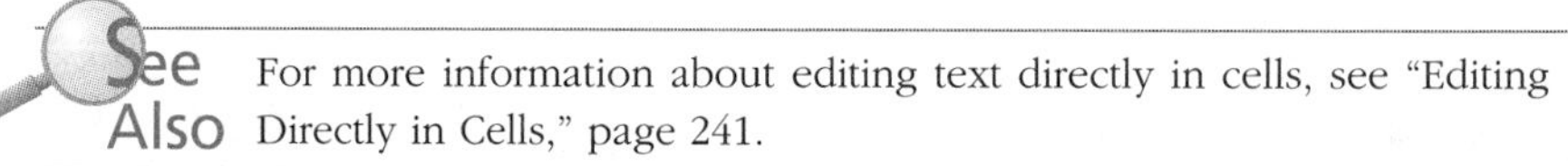

See Also For more information about editing text directly in cells, see "Editing Directly in Cells," page 241.

Formatting Chart Text

You can change the appearance of chart text by using the Selected command on the Format menu. The exact wording of the command that appears on the Format menu and the name of the dialog box it opens depend on the type of object you select. When you select title text and choose the Selected command, Microsoft Excel displays the corresponding Format dialog box with tabs for the object's properties.

TIP You can double-click a chart object to display the appropriate Format dialog box. You can also use the buttons on the Formatting toolbar to apply formatting to chart text.

The Patterns Tab

You use the options on the Patterns tab to customize the rectangle that contains a text box. Figure 17-7 shows the Patterns tab of the Format Title dialog box, which appears when you select the chart title and then choose the Selected command from the Format menu.

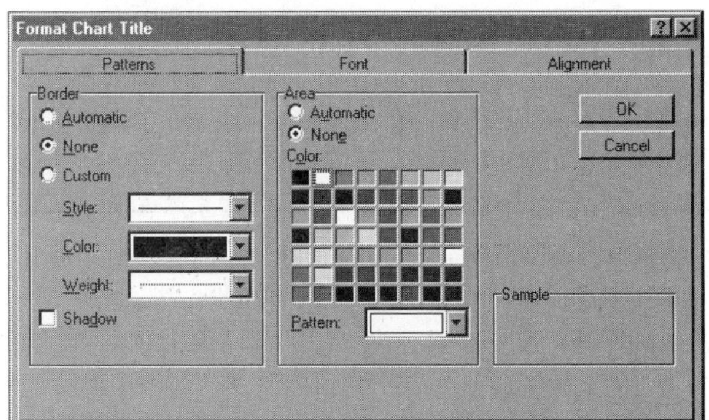

FIGURE 17-7
The Patterns tab options let you add a border and background pattern to a text box.

NOTE The options on the Patterns tab differ slightly for floating text boxes. Excel replaces the Area options with Fill options. These options work in the same basic way as the Area options. Excel also provides a Round Corners option. (As you'll see later in this chapter, the Patterns tab presents some different options when you select chart objects other than text.)

The Patterns tab shown in Figure 17-7 has two main sections: Border and Area. You use the options in the Border section to put a border around your text, with or without a shadow. You use the options in the Area section to add a pattern and color to the text block's background area.

In the lower right corner of the dialog box is a Sample box that shows what the selected text box will look like when Excel implements your selections.

The default setting for both Border and Area is None. To specify a border style, color, and weight, select from the three corresponding drop-down list boxes. Excel deselects None and selects Custom as soon as you open one of these lists. To remove a border, simply click the None option.

To include a shadow along the bottom and right edges of your border, select the Shadow option. Excel draws the shadow in black, regardless of the other colors you select on the Patterns tab.

To use rounded corners for the border of a floating text box, select the Round Corners option on the Patterns tab of the Format dialog box. (You can't round the corners of title text boxes, so this option does not appear in the Format Chart Title dialog box.)

If you want your text to appear against a colored or patterned background, select options from the Area section of the dialog box. Choose a color from the palette and a pattern from the drop-down list. To change the color of your text, select the Font tab and choose the color you want.

To change the color of only a portion of a title — a particular word, for example — first select the portion you want to change. Then choose the Format Selected command. The Font dialog box appears, in which you can specify the color you want.

TIP About one in ten men suffers from color blindness, meaning he can't differentiate, or can't *easily* differentiate, colors such as red and green or yellow, blue, and gray. One useful technique for ensuring that a viewer's color blindness doesn't destroy a chart's usefulness is to shy away from color sets that color-blind people commonly confuse, such as red and green.

The Font Tab

The default chart fonts are 12-point Arial bold for the chart title, 10-point Arial bold for axis labels, and regular 10-point Arial for all other text.

When you select a label or text box, choose the Selected command from the Format menu, and then select the Font tab, you see the options shown in Figure 17-8. (The fonts listed might be different on your system.) Many of the options in this dialog box will be familiar because you've used them to format worksheet text.

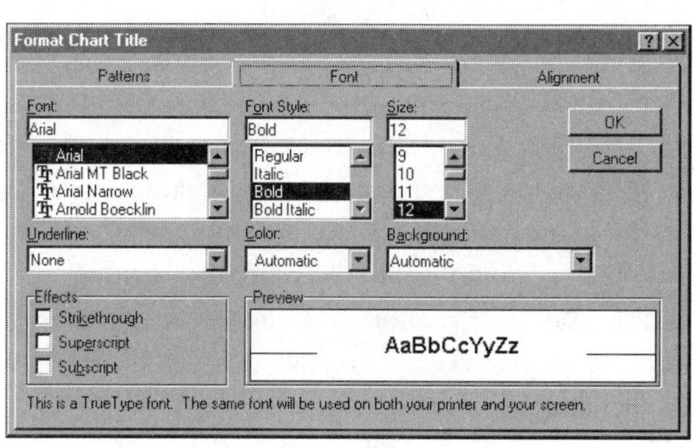

FIGURE 17-8
The Font tab options let you change the typeface, style, size, color, and background of chart text.

You use the Font, Font Style, and Size options to specify the typeface and format for the selected text. The Underline options let you underline text with one or two lines.

You use the Color options to change the color of the selected text for emphasis. (Be sure to select a color for your text that contrasts sufficiently with the Area or Fill color you selected on the Patterns tab.)

With the Background drop-down list box, you specify whether the text box's background pattern shows through the title text. This option has no effect unless you add a background pattern using the Patterns tab. If you do, however, you can tell Excel to show the background pattern beneath the chart title by selecting Transparent. With the Effects options, you can draw a line through the text (strikethrough). You can also use superscript and subscript characters.

See Also For more information about formatting in general, see Chapter 6, "Formatting a Worksheet," page 155.

For information about changing the default chart font, see "Formatting and Sizing Background Areas," page 665.

The Alignment Tab

The Alignment tab, shown in Figure 17-9, controls the alignment of chart text, its horizontal and vertical orientation, and the use of Excel's automatic labeling features.

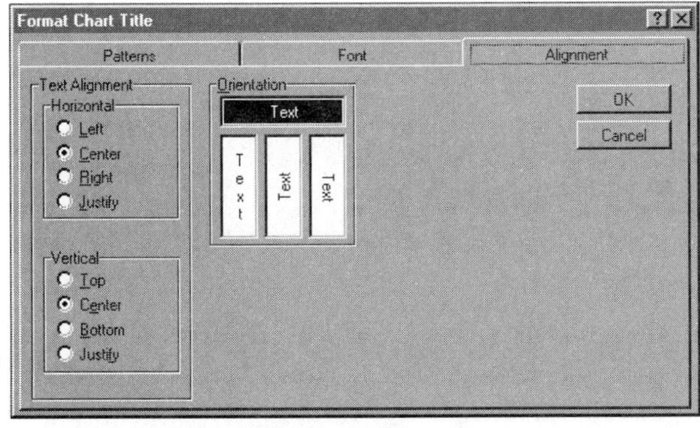

FIGURE 17-9
Use the Alignment tab options to change the alignment and orientation of chart text and to select automatic labeling.

Unless you specify otherwise, Excel prints all attached and unattached text horizontally, except for text attached to vertical axes. Text attached to a vertical axis on the left or right side of a chart is rotated 90 degrees counterclockwise.

If you have long category labels that won't fit horizontally on the chart, Excel might rotate them unless you tell it not to by selecting Justify.

To specify a different orientation for any block of attached or unattached text, select one of the options in the Alignment tab's Orientation section.

If you select a text box, an additional option appears on the Alignment tab of the Format dialog box: Automatic Size. When the Automatic Size option is in effect, the text box fits exactly around the text block. The advantage of this option is that Excel adjusts the size of the text box whenever you edit the text or use the options on the Font tab to change the display characteristics of the text.

Automatic Size is selected by default, but Excel deselects it if you manually resize a text box. After you manually resize the box, you can use this option to revert to automatic sizing.

See Also For information about formatting a chart's axes, see "Formatting and Scaling Axes," page 653.

The Protection Tab

Excel lets you lock floating text boxes so that when the sheet is protected, they can't be moved and their contents can't be changed. To lock a text box, select the Protection tab of the Format dialog box. Then select the Locked option to lock the text box's position, and select the Lock Text option to lock the text box's contents.

Adding, Positioning, and Formatting Legends

As discussed in Chapter 16, you can use the ChartWizard to add a legend to a chart. You can also use the Insert menu's Legend command. If the Chart toolbar is visible, you can add a legend simply by clicking the Legend button. The legend appears on the right side of your chart, framed by a set of handles. Microsoft Excel redraws the chart to make room for the legend.

See Also For more information about adding a legend to a chart, see "Adding a Legend and Titles," page 593.

Moving the Legend

The easiest way to move a legend is to drag it to a new location. Alternatively, you can select it, choose the Selected command from the Format menu, and then click the Placement tab, which is shown in Figure 17-10.

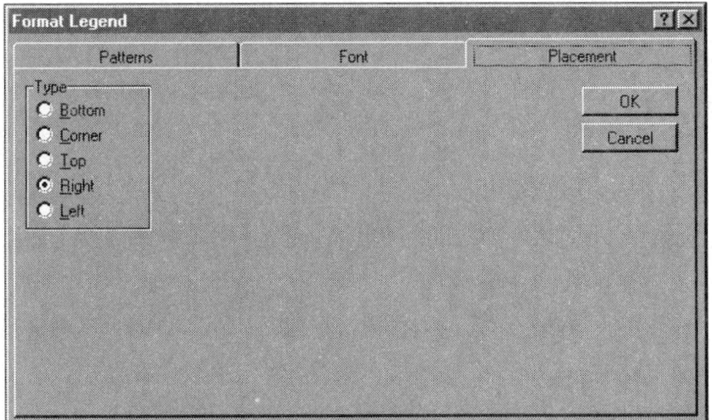

FIGURE 17-10
The Placement tab of the Format Legend dialog box lets you position a legend.

If you select Bottom, Excel positions the legend as one line at the bottom of the chart, where it is less conspicuous and takes up less room. If you select Corner, Excel moves the legend to the upper right corner of the chart. If you select Top, Excel uses a horizontal format for the legend and centers it above the chart. The Right and Left options center the legend along the right and left edges of the chart.

The advantage of dragging the legend with the mouse is that you're not limited to the five fixed-position options listed on the Placement tab. You can put the legend wherever you want it, even within the chart itself. Because displaying the legend alongside, above, or below the chart reduces the size of the chart's plot area, you might choose to place the legend within the chart. Figure 17-11 on the next page shows a legend positioned within a column chart.

TIP After you have moved the legend, you might want to resize the plot area to recover the blank space on the right of the chart.

When you first add a legend to a chart, Excel displays the series names one above another in a vertical format. To switch to a horizontal format so

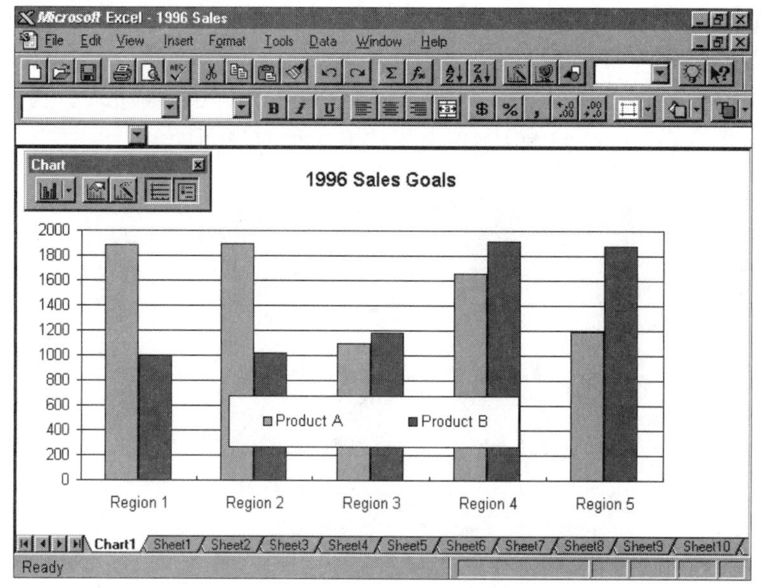

FIGURE 17-11

You can use the mouse to position a legend inside the plot area of your chart.

Excel displays the series names side by side, as in Figure 17-11, resize the legend so that its width is greater than its height.

For more information about sizing the plot area, see "Formatting and Sizing Background Areas," page 665.

Changing the Legend Text

You cannot edit the contents of the legend box. To change the text in the legend box, you must edit the cells of the worksheet that contain the series labels. You can also select the appropriate series and then use the Format menu's Selected Series command to change the legend text.

If your chart doesn't include series names (that is, if you didn't include cells that contain labels in the range you selected for your data series), Excel displays the legend labels Series1, Series2, and so on in the legend box. Again, you can replace these legend labels with more meaningful text by selecting the series and using the Format menu's Selected command.

For more information about changing legend text, see "Changing Series Descriptions," page 673.

Formatting the Legend or Legend Entries

You can change the appearance of the text of the entire legend or one of its entries. Click the legend once to select the legend as a whole; click a second time to select an individual entry. Then choose the Selected command from the Format menu. The Font tab of the Format Legend dialog box works the same way with legends and legend entries as it does with chart text. You can also apply the bold and italic styles by selecting the legend or legend entry and then clicking the appropriate buttons on the Formatting toolbar. You can use the Patterns tab to add a background color and a shadow to the legend, but not to a single entry.

See Also For more information about using the Patterns and Font tabs, see "Formatting Chart Text," page 630.

Removing a Legend

Removing a legend is easy. First, select the legend. Then, from the Edit menu, choose Clear and then All. Or, even easier, select the legend and press Del. If the Chart toolbar is visible, you can also delete a legend by clicking the Legend button.

Working with Arrows and Lines

Arrows are an effective way to draw attention to key information. To add an arrow to a chart, follow these steps:

1. Click the Drawing button on the Standard toolbar and then the Arrow button on the Drawing toolbar.
2. Move the cross-hair pointer to the place where you want the end of the arrow and click.
3. Drag the pointer to the place where you want the beginning, or head, of the arrow and release the mouse button.

   Microsoft Excel draws a black arrow, as shown in Figure 17-12.

The arrow's head is initially a solid equilateral triangle. You can change the length and position of the arrow, as well as the style and color of both the shaft and the head. You can even eliminate the arrowhead, turning the arrow into a simple straight line.

To adjust the length and angle of the arrow, select it and then drag the handle at either end with the mouse. When you drag the handle at one end,

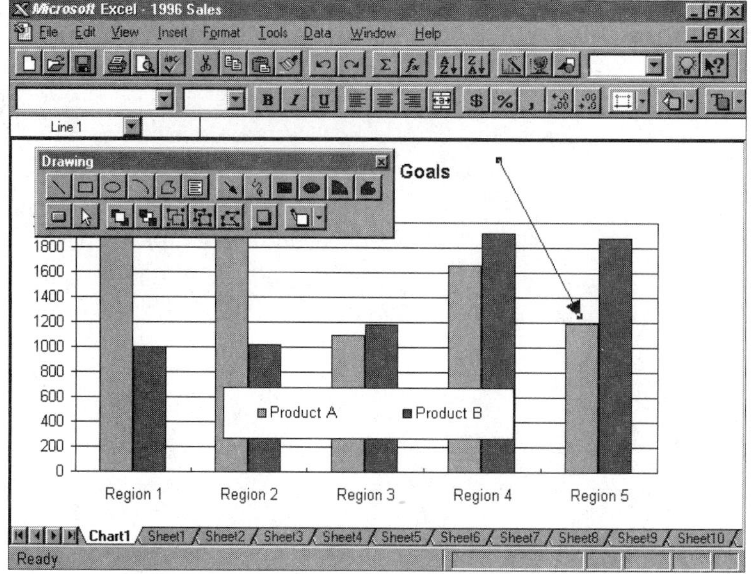

FIGURE 17-12

Add arrows to your charts using the Arrow button on the Drawing toolbar.

the handle at the other end remains anchored. You can move the entire arrow in any direction by dragging the shaft of the arrow.

Changing an Arrow's Style, Color, and Weight

To format an arrow, either select it and choose the Format menu's Selected command or double-click the arrow. Excel displays the Format Object dialog box with the Patterns tab showing, as shown in Figure 17-13.

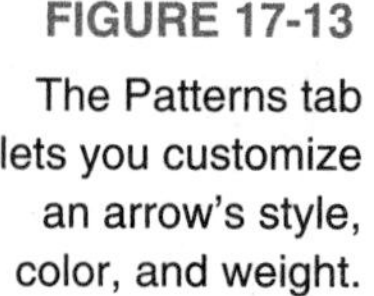

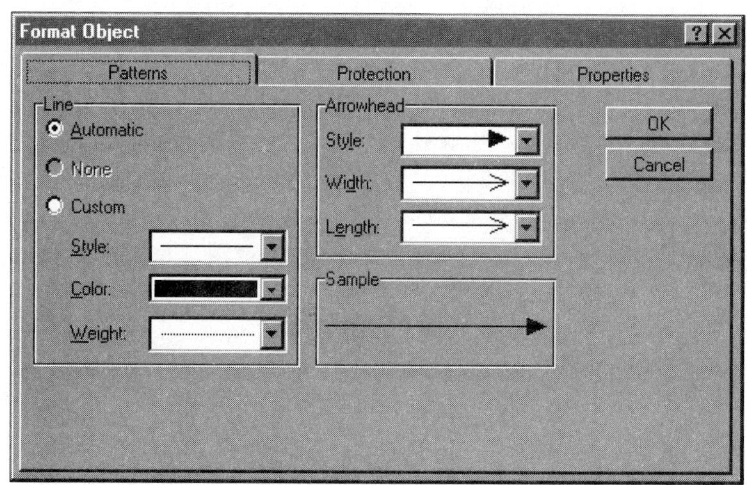

FIGURE 17-13

The Patterns tab lets you customize an arrow's style, color, and weight.

The Line section of this dialog box looks and works much like the Border section of the Patterns tab for formatting chart text. The only differences are that the None option is dimmed — you can't have an arrowhead without a line — and the Shadow option is not available.

You use the drop-down list boxes in the Arrowhead section of the Patterns tab to select a style, width, and length for the arrowhead. (The color of the arrowhead is the same as that of the shaft.) Five styles are available: no head, an open head, a filled head, open heads at both ends, and filled heads at both ends. You can combine the open or the filled head with any of the width and length options in the Arrowhead section; the results are displayed in the Sample box. If you select no head, you can add straight lines to your chart.

TIP To delete an arrow, select it and either choose the All command from the Clear submenu of the Edit menu or press the Del key.

See Also For more information about the Border area of the Patterns tab, see "The Patterns Tab," page 631.

Formatting Data Point Markers

In Microsoft Excel terminology, a *marker* is any symbol that represents a data point on a chart. In a column chart, for example, each column is a marker; in a line or radar chart, the little squares, triangles, and other symbols that appear along its lines are markers; in a pie chart, each slice is a marker; and so on.

To change the border, color, and pattern of any marker, either select a data point and choose the Selected command from the Format menu or double-click the data point. Excel then displays the Patterns tab of the Format Data Point dialog box, whose options are similar to those of the Patterns tab for text.

See Also For more information about the Pattern tab's options, see "The Patterns Tab," page 631.

Selecting Markers

In all chart types except area charts, three-dimensional area charts, and three-dimensional surface charts, you can select either an individual marker or all markers for a given series. When you click a marker once, Excel selects that marker and all others in the same series. If you click the same marker again, Excel selects the individual marker.

To select an entire series of markers with the keyboard, press the Up or Down direction key until you see the appropriate identifier in the Name box in the formula bar. The identifier for the first series is S1, for the second series S2, and so on. To select a single marker in a series, select the series and then press the Right direction key until the marker is selected.

Whether you use the mouse or the keyboard to make a selection, you can usually tell what has been selected by looking at the handles. When you select an entire series, for example, two or more of the series' markers have handles. When you select an individual marker, handles appear around only that marker. With line charts and XY charts, however, it's sometimes difficult to distinguish between the handles and the markers. In all cases, you can rely on the Name box in the formula bar to display your selection's reference. If you select an entire series, the Name box area displays the series identifier — S1, S2, S3, and so on. If you select an individual marker, the Name box displays the marker identifier. For example, if you select the second data point in the third series, the Name box area displays S3P2.

When you select an individual marker in certain kinds of charts, you can adjust the value of the data point with the mouse, and Excel will change the value in the source cell to match.

For more information about changing worksheet values, see "Changing Underlying Worksheet Values," page 681.

Formatting Individual Markers and Entire Series

When you select an individual marker and choose the Selected command from the Format menu, Excel displays the Format Data Point dialog box, as shown in Figure 17-14. The Patterns tab shown is for a marker in a two-dimensional or three-dimensional bar or column chart. For an area, doughnut, pie, three-dimensional line, and three-dimensional pie marker, the Patterns tab looks similar except that it lacks the Invert If Negative option. The Patterns tab for doughnut charts also does not have the Invert If Negative option, but it

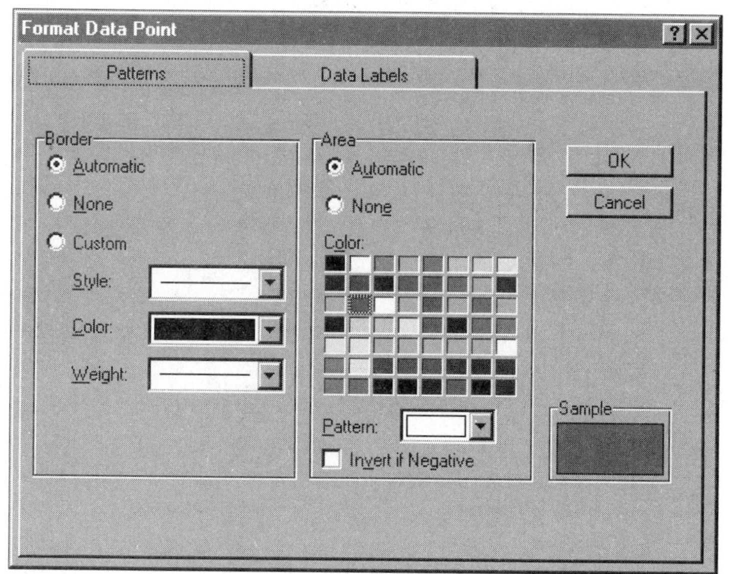

FIGURE 17-14
You can use the Patterns tab of the Format Data Point dialog box to format the data-point markers in your charts.

includes a Shadow option. For a line, XY, or radar marker, the Patterns tab offers several additional options.

Most of the options in the dialog box shown in Figure 17-14 are similar to those in the Patterns tab for text. You use the Border section of the tab to select a style, color, and weight for the line that surrounds your marker. In the Area section you specify a color and pattern for the body of the marker.

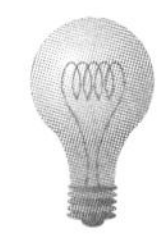

TIP You can double-click an individual data-point marker to display the Format Data Point dialog box.

For more information about the Patterns tab's options, see "The Patterns Tab," page 631.

The Invert If Negative Option

If you select the Invert If Negative option, Excel reverses the Color and Pattern selections for your marker when the corresponding value is less than zero. The background color becomes the pattern color and vice versa. This option is available only with two-dimensional and three-dimensional bar and column charts.

Options for Line, Radar, and XY Charts

If you select a marker in a line, radar, or XY chart and choose Selected Object from the Format menu, Excel replaces the Border and Area sections of the Patterns tab with the Line and Marker sections. The Line section controls the appearance of the line that connects the marker with the one before it; the Marker section controls the appearance of the markers themselves. You can select any of nine possible shapes and sizes from the Style drop-down list box. You can select the None option in the Line or Marker section to remove segments or markers in a series.

Adjusting Colors in Three-Dimensional Surface Charts

Excel doesn't assign colors to the data series in a three-dimensional surface chart because it doesn't use color to identify series; instead, Excel uses color to show major tick-mark ranges on the value axis. To change the color used for a value range, select a legend key (the colored square in the legend entry), choose the Selected command from the Format menu, and use the Patterns tab.

Exploding Pie and Doughnut Slices

An exploded pie or doughnut marker, or slice, is pulled away from the center of the chart, usually for emphasis. To explode a two-dimensional or three-dimensional pie slice or doughnut slice, select the slice and drag it with the mouse. You can explode as many slices as you want.

NOTE As you move pie and doughnut slices away from the center of the pie or doughnut, the overall chart becomes smaller in order to retain the proportions of the original chart.

Formatting All the Markers in a Group

The Group command on the Format menu also lets you control formatting of a chart's data markers. Because different formatting choices are appropriate for different data markers, Excel changes the Group command name to reflect the data marker type. Similarly, the name of the dialog box that appears when you choose the Group command depends on the type of chart displayed. If a column chart is displayed, for example, the last command on the Format menu is Column Group. If you choose this command, Excel displays the Format Column Group dialog box shown in Figure 17-15.

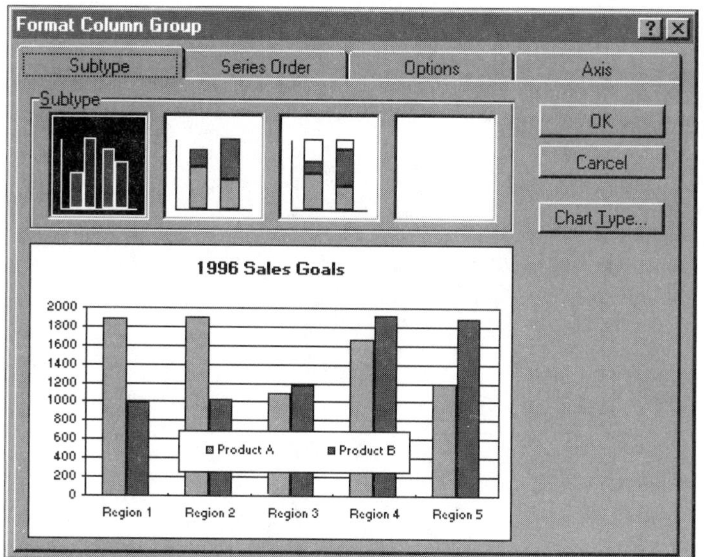

FIGURE 17-15
You use the Format Column Group dialog box to format data markers.

NOTE Some charts have more than one type of data marker. In this situation, Excel provides more than one Group command.

Stacking Data Markers

You can stack data markers in line charts as well as in two-dimensional and three-dimensional area, bar, and column charts so that the values plotted for the second and subsequent data series are cumulative. To stack the markers, you use the Subtype tab of the corresponding Format Group dialog box. Simply select a chart format that depicts the markers stacked on top of each other.

TIP You can draw lines to connect two-dimensional stacked bars or stacked columns. Choose the Group command from the Format menu, select the Options tab, and then select the Series Lines option.

Changing the Data Series Order

You can change the order in which Excel plots the data series in all charts. Normally, the first data series in the selected range is the first set of data markers, the second data series is the second set of data markers, and so on. To change this order, click the Series Order tab in the Format Group dialog box, as shown in Figure 17-16 on the next page. Then use the Series Order list box and the Move Up and Move Down buttons to reorder the data series' markers. Excel updates the dialog box's sample chart so you can preview your changes.

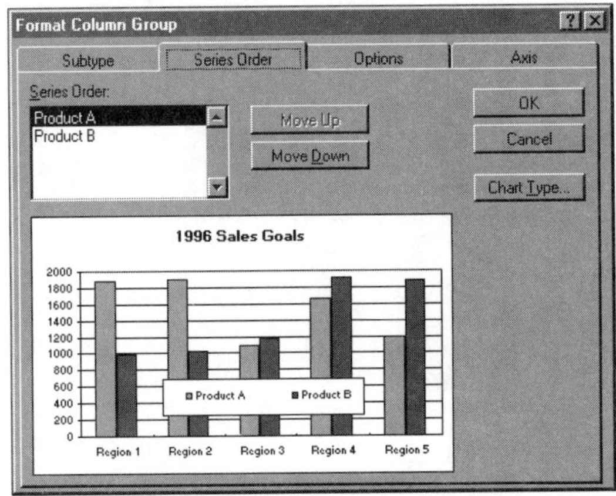

FIGURE 17-16
The Series Order tab lets you change the order in which your data is displayed.

Because two-dimensional and three-dimensional pie charts only chart the first series, changing the order of the series in these charts changes which series is charted. The Format Pie Group dialog box does not contain a Series Order tab, but you can easily change the order by editing the SERIES formula or by temporarily changing the chart type.

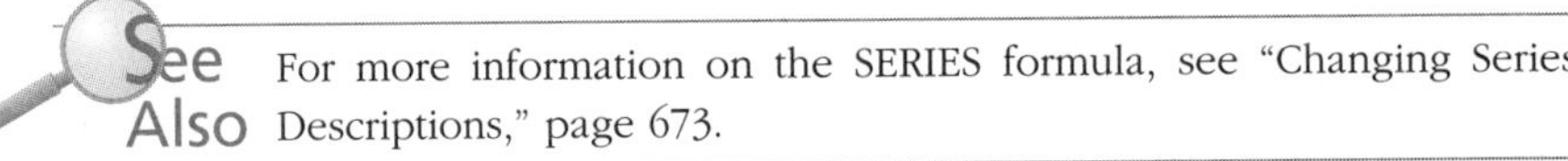

For more information on the SERIES formula, see "Changing Series Descriptions," page 673.

Positioning Bars and Columns

You use the Options tab of the Format Group dialog box to increase or decrease the space between markers in a bar or column chart. The Overlap option controls the distribution of markers within a cluster, and the Gap Width option determines the space between clusters.

The default settings for the column chart shown earlier in Figure 17-11 are 0 percent overlap and 150 percent gap width. As a result, Excel displays markers within a cluster side by side with no overlap and no space between them, and the space between clusters equals one-and-one-half the width of an individual marker.

To create a bar or column chart in which the markers overlap, either type or use the up and down arrows to enter a positive number (0 through 100) in the Overlap edit box. To separate markers within a cluster, enter a negative number (0 through –100) in the Overlap edit box.

Note that if you specify a 100 percent overlap, Excel displays all the markers in a given cluster on top of one another, but it doesn't stack them. When you select a stacked bar or column chart, however, the default Overlap value is 100 percent. By entering a number less than 100, you can create bar or column charts that are both stacked and staggered.

To change the amount of space between clusters, enter a value from 0 through 500 in the Gap Width edit box. The smaller the gap width, the wider your bars or columns. By specifying a 0 percent gap width, you can create a step chart — a bar or column chart in which all markers are lined up next to each other, with no intervening spaces.

You can adjust the gap width for three-dimensional bar and column charts as well. The default spacing between clusters is 150 percent in both cases.

Adjusting the Shape and Spacing of Three-Dimensional Markers

The shape and spacing of markers in three-dimensional bar and column charts are determined by three settings — Gap Depth, Gap Width, and Chart Depth — on the Options tab. Figure 17-17 illustrates these three settings.

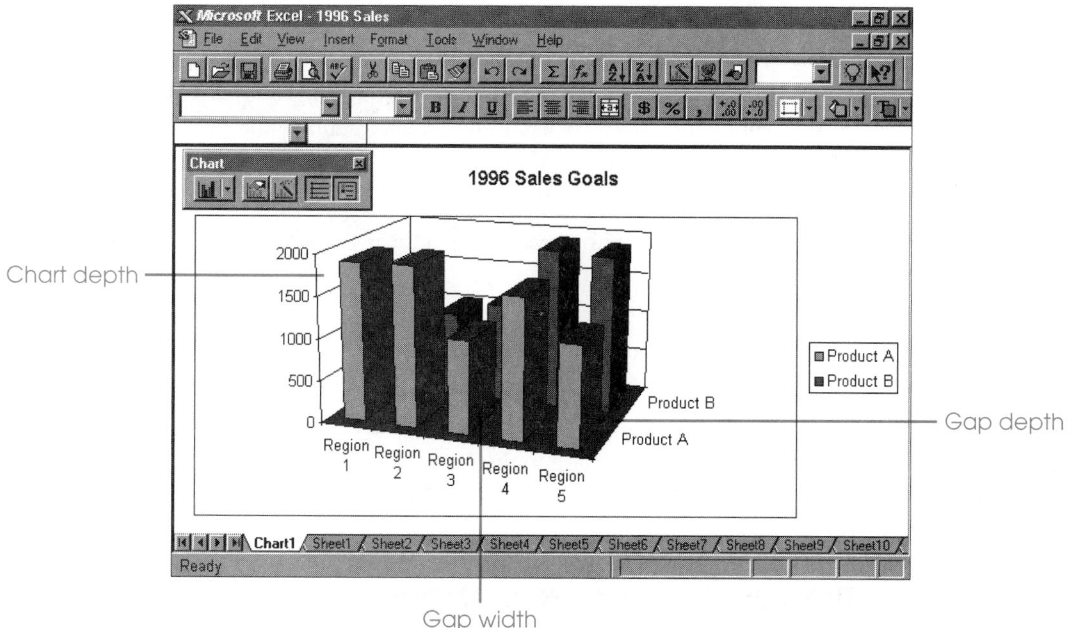

FIGURE 17-17

The Gap Depth and Gap Width settings determine the space between markers, the former along the category axis and the latter along the series axis. The Chart Depth setting determines the shape of each marker.

Excel normally leaves a 150 percent space — a space equal to one-and-one-half column widths — between bars or columns along both the category and series axes. To change the spacing along the category axis, change the Gap Width setting, and to change the spacing along the series axis, change the Gap Depth setting. You can select values from 0 through 500 in both cases.

If your three-dimensional chart does not plot separate data series on separate planes, the default value for Gap Depth is 0. Increasing the value increases the size of the floor on which the data markers rest.

As Figure 17-17 shows, Excel usually draws three-dimensional bar or column markers so that the top of each column is rectangular. To square the column tops so each column's depth is equal to its width, enter *100* in the Chart Depth edit box. To give the columns a flatter appearance, enter a value less than 100; the minimum value is 20. To make the columns even thicker, enter a number greater than the default of 200; the maximum value is 2000. (You can also use the Chart Depth setting to modify the appearance of three-dimensional area, line, and surface markers.)

Rotating a Pie or Doughnut Chart

Excel normally draws pie and doughnut charts so that the first data marker begins with a line that radiates straight up from the center of the chart. Excel then draws the chart in a clockwise fashion. For example, if the first data point amounts to 25 percent of the series total, its slice begins with a line that points straight up (due north) and ends with a line that points straight to the right (due east). The slice for the second data point begins where the slice for the first ends, and so on.

You can change this system using the Options tab in the Format Group dialog box. By entering a value greater than 0 and less than 360 in the Angle Of First Slice edit box, you can rotate the chart to a different starting point. For example, to tell Excel to begin the first slice with a horizontal radius that points to the right, enter 90 in the Angle Of First Slice edit box.

If you're working with a doughnut chart, you can also adjust the size of the hole by entering a value in the Doughnut Hole Size edit box on the Options tab. The hole size can be as small as 10 percent of the doughnut and as large as 90 percent.

The Vary Colors By Point Option

Select the Vary Colors By Point (or Vary Colors By Slice option for pie or doughnut charts) to display each marker of a series chart in a different color or pattern. The Vary Colors By Point option is available for many chart types. Typically, you'll want to use this option in a single-series chart.

Adding Drop Lines and High-Low Lines

Drop lines are straight lines that extend from a data point to the category (x) axis. You can add them to two-dimensional and three-dimensional area and line charts by selecting Drop Lines on the Options tab of the corresponding Format Group dialog box.

Drop lines are most useful in area charts. Because markers in these charts blend with the background, drop lines can help clarify where one marker ends and the next begins. Figure 17-18 shows an example of a three-dimensional area chart with drop lines.

High-low lines are straight lines that extend between the highest and lowest points in a cluster. You can use them to indicate the range over which a value varies. Figure 17-19 on the next page illustrates the use of high-low lines.

High-low lines are available only in two-dimensional line charts. To use them, select High-Low Lines on the Options tab of the Format Group dialog box.

TIP You can change the color and line style of drop lines and high-low lines in the same basic way you change color and line styles for arrows and lines. See "Changing an Arrow's Style, Color, and Weight," page 638.

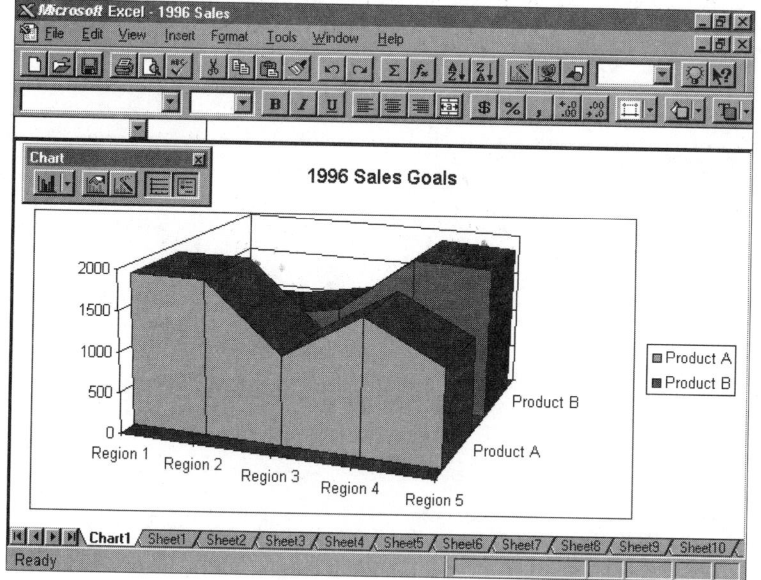

FIGURE 17-18
Drop lines can clarify area charts by showing where one marker ends and the next begins.

FIGURE 17-19
High-low lines show the range over which a value varies.

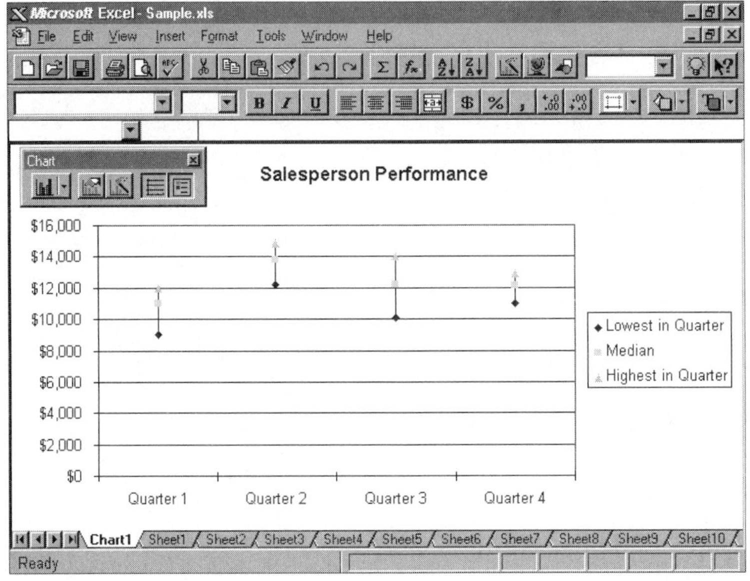

Adding Up and Down Bars

Up and down bars are useful primarily in charts that track price movements. You can add up and down bars to any line chart that includes at least two series of data by selecting Up-Down Bars on the Options tab of the Format Group dialog box. Figure 17-20 shows a standard open-high-low-close chart with up and down bars — the rectangles that bracket the opening (first) and closing (last) prices. By

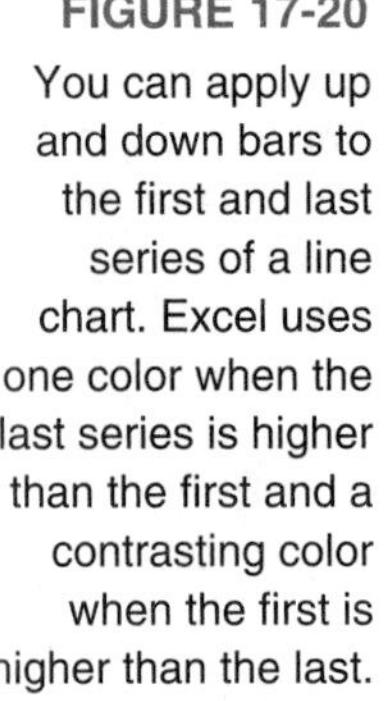

FIGURE 17-20
You can apply up and down bars to the first and last series of a line chart. Excel uses one color when the last series is higher than the first and a contrasting color when the first is higher than the last.

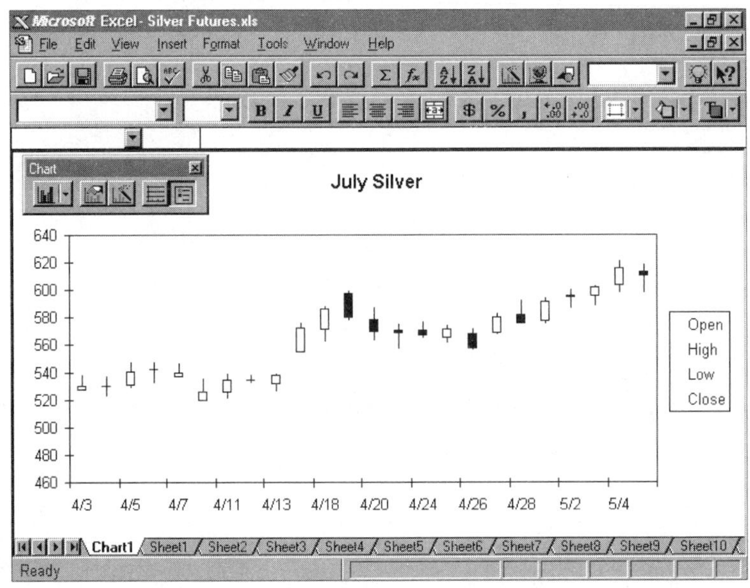

default, Excel draws up bars (when the last series is higher than the first) in white and down bars (when the first series is higher than the last) in black.

When you select the Up-Down Bars option, Excel also lets you modify the gap width. This option is normally available only with bar and column charts, but Excel treats a line chart with up and down bars as a column chart. Increasing the Gap Width number in the edit box makes the up and down bar rectangles narrower, and decreasing the number makes the bars wider.

Replacing Markers with Pictures

Another way to customize markers is to replace them with graphic images, thereby creating a picture chart. Figure 17-21 gives you a basic idea of what you can do with this feature.

Any graphic image that can be copied to the Clipboard can serve as the basis for a picture chart. You can create such images using Excel's drawing tools or with the help of other applications. Then, to create a picture chart, follow these steps:

1. Create a bar, column, line, radar, or XY chart.
2. Copy the graphic image you want to use to the Clipboard.
3. Return to your Excel chart, select the individual marker or the series you want to replace with the graphic image, and choose the Paste command from the Edit menu.

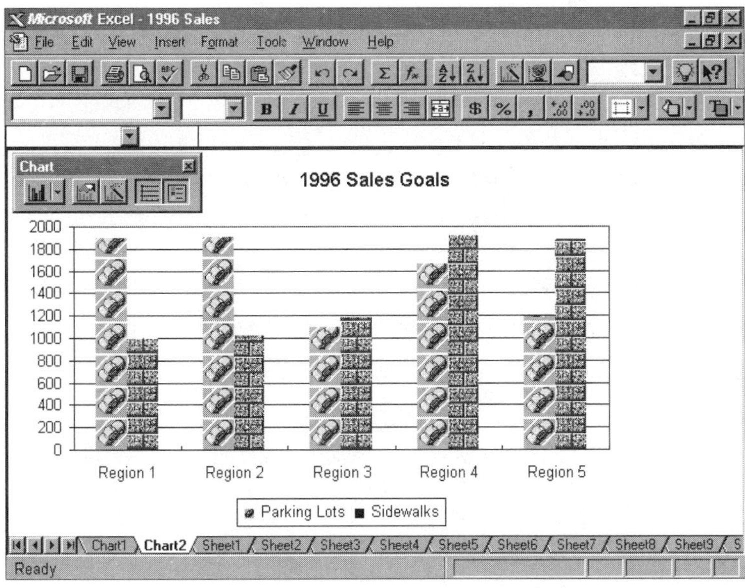

FIGURE 17-21

You can transform bar, column, line, radar, or XY charts into picture charts.

Excel replaces either the individual marker or every marker in the series with your image.

If you replace bar or column markers, the image initially stretches to fill the space formerly occupied by the marker. You can change the size of the graphic images in your chart by choosing the Selected command from the Format menu. Figure 17-22 shows the Patterns tab of the dialog box that appears.

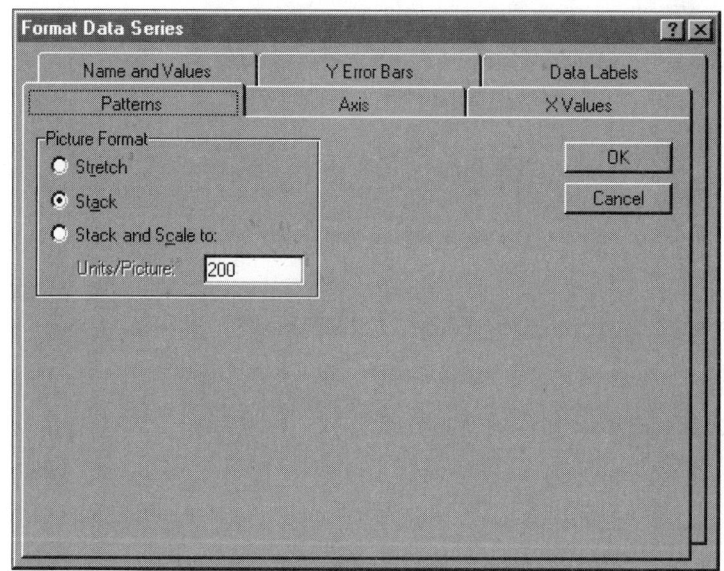

FIGURE 17-22
You can size graphic images in bar and column charts using the three Picture Format options on the Patterns tab.

The default option, Stretch, stretches the image to fit the chart data. If you select Stack, Excel displays the image in its original size and uses as many copies as necessary to fill the bar or column. The last copy in the marker is usually cropped. (The Stack option is used in Figure 17-21.) Excel also repeats and stacks the image if you select the Stack And Scale To Units/Picture option, but in this case, you can specify the magnitude of each unit in the stack.

If you replace markers in a line, radar, or XY chart, the image appears in its original size and shape and cannot be changed.

NOTE You can use the Insert menu's Picture command to insert a picture as a graphic object on a chart sheet, just as you can on a worksheet. (See "The Picture Command," page 368.)

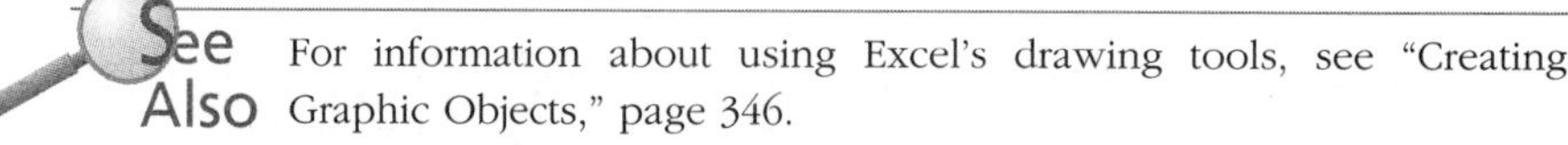

For information about using Excel's drawing tools, see "Creating Graphic Objects," page 346.

Working with Trendlines and Error Bars

You can further describe a plotted data series in an area, bar, column, line, or XY chart by adding trendlines and error bars. A trend line is either a regression line that best fits the plotted data or a moving averages line. An error bar is a high-low line that depicts possible errors in the data.

Adding Trendlines

To add a trendline to a data series in an area, bar, column, line, or XY chart, you select the data series and choose the Trendline command from the Insert menu. Excel displays the Trendline dialog box shown in Figure 17-23.

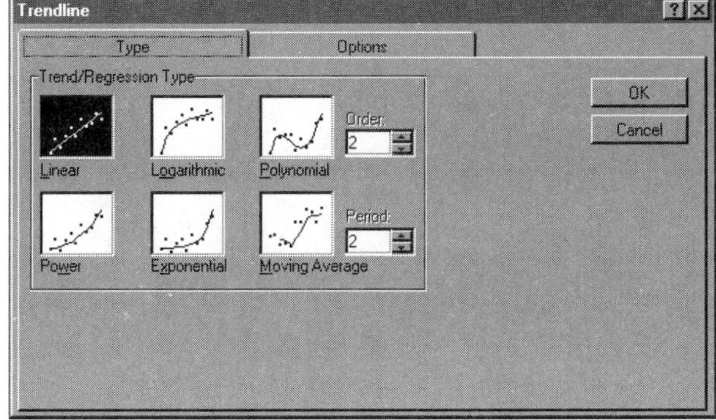

FIGURE 17-23
Use the Trendline dialog box to specify how Excel should create and format a data series trendline.

To specify how Excel should draw the trendline, select one of the Trend/Regression Type options. If you select Polynomial, indicate the highest power (from 2 through 6) for the independent variable in the adjacent Order edit box. If you select Moving Average, indicate how many periods Excel should use in its calculations in the adjacent Period edit box.

After you've indicated the type of trend/regression line Excel should draw, select the Options tab if you want to name this trendline specification. As long as you're not working with a moving averages trendline, you can also specify in the Forecast section whether the trendline should be calculated by looking backward and forecasting forward or by looking forward and forecasting backward. For linear, polynomial, and exponential trendlines, you can set the y-intercept in the Set Intercept edit box. If you want, you can also display the regression equation and the R-squared value on the trendline's chart for all but moving averages.

Adding Error Bars

When charting statistical data, it is often helpful to visually show the confidence level of your data. Excel's error bar makes this easy. To add error bars to a data series in an area, bar, column, line, or XY chart, you select the data series and choose the Error Bars command from the Insert menu. Excel then displays the Error Bars dialog box shown in Figure 17-24.

Error bars can be shown as the actual data point value plus some amount, minus some amount, or both plus and minus some amount. Use the options in the Display section to indicate which of these error bar styles you want.

You use the Error Amount options — Fixed Value, Percentage (of the data point value), Standard Deviation(s), Standard Error, and Custom (a manually specified amount) — to calculate the amount depicted by the error bar.

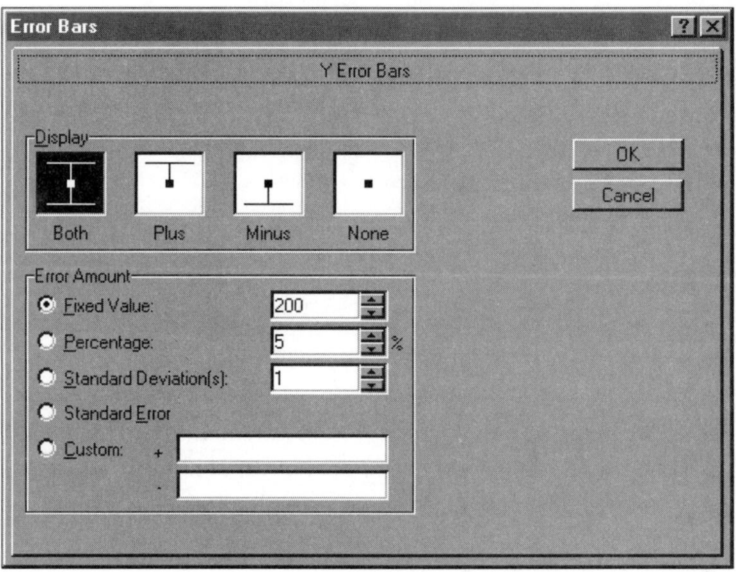

FIGURE 17-24
Use the Error Bars dialog box to specify how Excel should create error bars for a data series.

Suppose, for example, that you are tracking the President's approval rating over the past year. If the approval rating has a margin of error of 3 percent, you select the Percentage option and type *3* in the edit box.

TIP To make changes to a trendline or error bar, select it and choose either the Trendline or Error Bars command from the Insert menu. To remove a trendline or error bar, select it and either choose the All command from the Clear submenu of the Edit menu or press Del. To format a trendline or error bar, select it and choose the Selected command from the Format menu.

Formatting and Scaling Axes

Microsoft Excel gives you a great deal of control over the format, position, and scale of your chart's axes. After selecting the axis and choosing the Selected command from the Format menu to display the Format Axis dialog box, you can use the Patterns tab to specify the style, color, and weight of the axis, as well as the presence or absence of tick marks and tick labels. The Scale tab lets you switch between normal and logarithmic scaling (if appropriate) and lets you scale an axis manually. With the Font tab, you can select the font, style, and size used for tick labels. The Number tab lets you specify numeric formatting for the axis. The Alignment tab lets you override Excel's default orientation for tick-label text (changing vertical labels to horizontal, for example).

Suppressing the Display of an Axis

Before we launch into a detailed discussion of formatting and scaling axes, we should tell you how to suppress the display of axes in your charts. When you choose the Axes command from the Insert menu, Excel displays one of the dialog boxes shown in Figure 17-25. (The one on the right appears if the current chart is three-dimensional.) By deselecting the options in the Axes dialog box, you can suppress one or all of the axes in your chart.

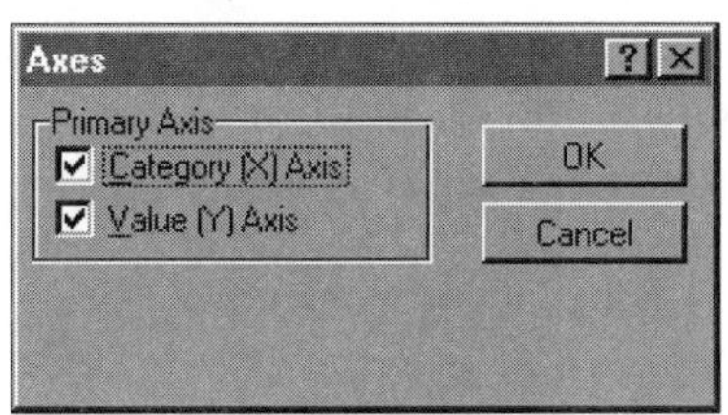

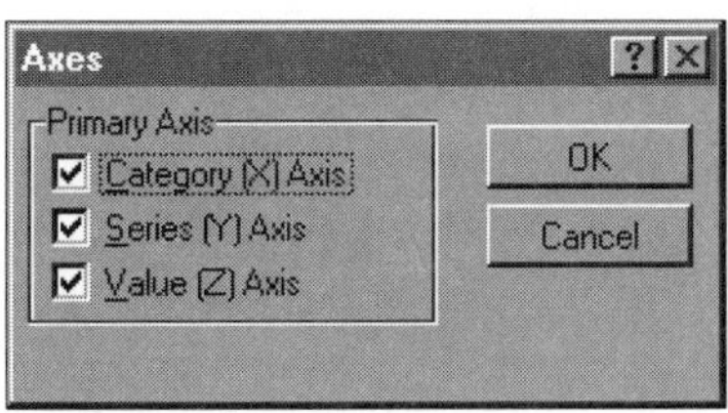

FIGURE 17-25
If you deselect options in the Axes dialog box, you suppress the display of axes in your charts.

When you suppress display of an axis, Excel removes not only the axis lines but also any associated labels. Removing axes often simplifies the display and gives Excel more space in which to draw the chart. When you want to call a viewer's attention to a single detail in a chart, you can suppress one or more of the axes and then use a text box, with or without an arrow, to make that detail stand out.

See Also For more information about adding text blocks, see "Adding Floating Text," page 629.

Selecting Line Style, Color, and Weight

To assign a style, color, or weight to any axis line, you can use the Patterns tab of the Format Axis dialog box, shown in Figure 17-26. The Axis section of this tab presents the same options used with text and legends.

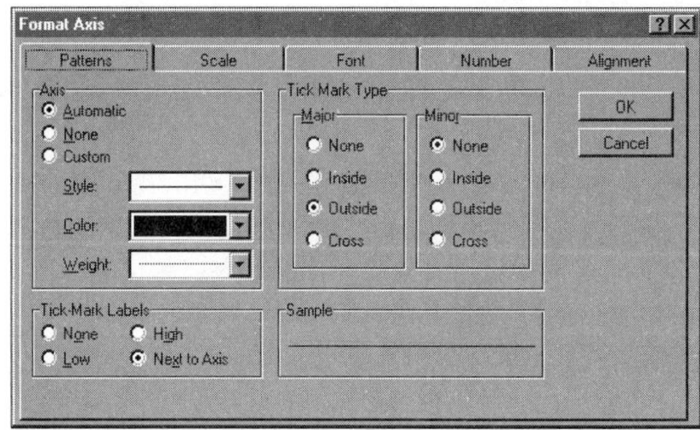

FIGURE 17-26 The Patterns tab of the Format Axis dialog box lets you customize an axis.

See Also For more information about the Axis section's options, see "The Patterns Tab," page 631.

Specifying the Position of Tick Marks

Tick marks are short lines that either cross or abut an axis line at regular intervals. Like the lines that mark inches and fractions of an inch along a ruler, tick marks help define the axis scale. For example, in Figure 17-19 (shown on page 648), major tick marks appear along the y-axis at $2,000, $4,000, $6,000, and so on. Major tick marks appear along the x-axis between the quarter names.

By default, Excel displays major tick marks on each axis but doesn't display minor tick marks. You can override this setting by selecting a Minor option in the Tick Mark Type section on the Patterns tab. You can position either major or minor tick marks inside, outside, or across the axis line. In Figure 17-19, the major tick marks cross the axes.

Using the Scale tab of the Format Axis dialog box, you can also control the interval at which both major and minor tick marks appear.

See Also For more information about scaling axes, see "Scaling the Value Axis Manually," page 658, and "Scaling the Category Axis Manually," page 660.

Formatting Tick Labels

Tick labels appear beside or below major tick marks. For example, in Figure 17-19 (shown earlier), the numbers $2,000, $4,000, and so on are tick labels; so are the chart's category names (Quarter 1, Quarter 2, and so on). You can format tick labels in a variety of ways by selecting options on the Patterns, Font, Number, and Alignment tabs in the Format Axis dialog box.

Specifying Position

You use the Tick-Mark Labels section of the Patterns tab in the Format Axis dialog box (shown earlier in Figure 17-26) to specify the position of tick labels relative to their axis lines. The default option for all axes is Next To Axis.

If you select None, Excel suppresses the display of tick labels. You might find this option useful if you plot a range of data that doesn't include column or row labels, in which case Excel displays the dummy category names 1, 2, 3, and so on below the x-axis. If those numbers are meaningless, you can eliminate them with the None option.

The Low option is handy in charts that plot both negative and positive numbers. As Figure 17-27 at the top of the next page illustrates, the default position of tick labels doesn't always produce the most satisfying results when the x-axis crosses the y-axis anywhere but at the end points of the y-axis. In a case like this, you can select Low on the Patterns tab in the Format Axis dialog box to make your chart look more like the one in Figure 17-28 at the bottom of the next page.

The Low option ensures that your x-axis labels appear at the bottom of the chart and your y-axis labels appear at the left edge, regardless of where the axes cross. The High option does the opposite; it displays x-axis labels at the top of the chart and y-axis labels at the right edge. When you use the Scale tab to reverse the direction in which axes are scaled, low labels appear above or to the right of the chart and high labels appear below or to the left of the chart.

FIGURE 17-27
By default, Excel draws tick labels next to axes, even when point markers obscure the labels.

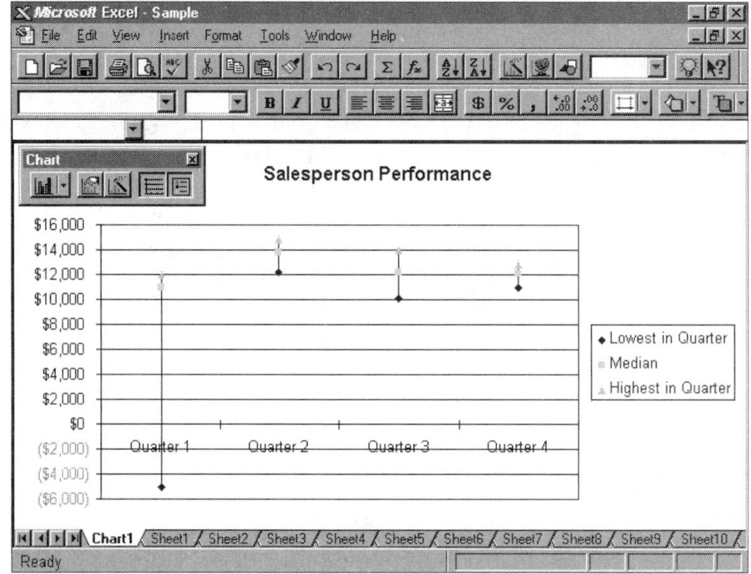

FIGURE 17-28
You can eliminate the conflict between labels and markers by selecting the Low option on the Patterns tab of the Format Axis dialog box.

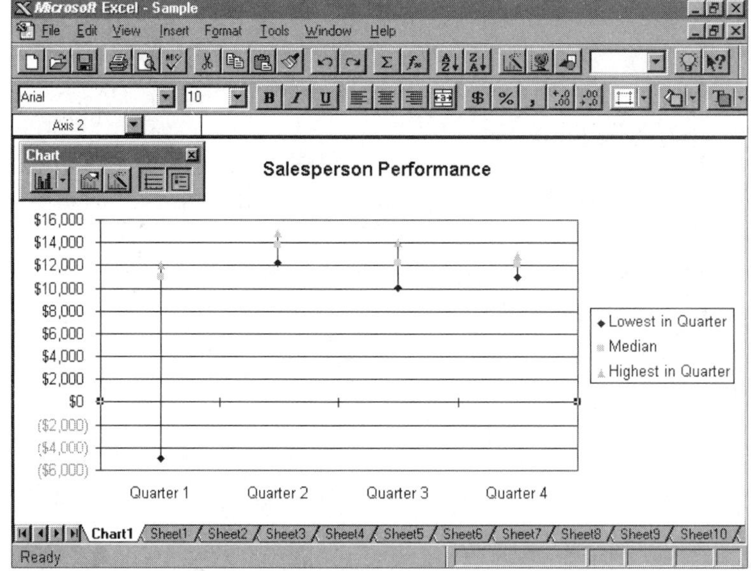

See Also For information about reversing the axis scaling direction, see "Reversing the Value-Axis Scale," page 660, and "Reversing the Category-Axis Scale," page 662.

Changing the Numeric Format of Tick Labels

You can use the Number tab of the Format Axis dialog box to control the formatting of the numbers shown on the value axis. The Number tab works the same way for formatting value axis tick labels as it does for formatting worksheet cells.

X-Axis Tick Labels

Sometimes Excel can't provide a satisfactory x-axis label display. The program doesn't know how to hyphenate, it won't stagger labels, and it won't switch to a smaller point size.

You can make these adjustments, however. For example, on the Scale tab of the Format Axis dialog box, you can tell Excel to display every other label, or every third, or every fourth, and so on — by changing the entry in the Number Of Categories Between Tick-Mark Labels edit box. On the Font tab, you can select a smaller point size or a more compact typeface. (See "Scaling the Category Axis Manually," page 660.)

If all else fails, you can modify the text of labels by changing the worksheet labels from which the x-axis labels were generated. Or you can specify new text altogether by editing the chart's SERIES formulas. (See "Editing SERIES Formulas," page 676.)

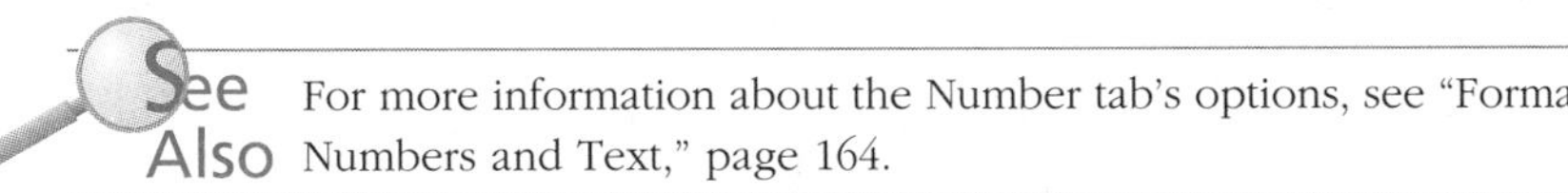
See Also For more information about the Number tab's options, see "Formatting Numbers and Text," page 164.

Choosing a Font and Color

To assign a new typeface, style, size, color, or effect to a set of tick labels, use the options on the Font tab of the Format Axis dialog box.

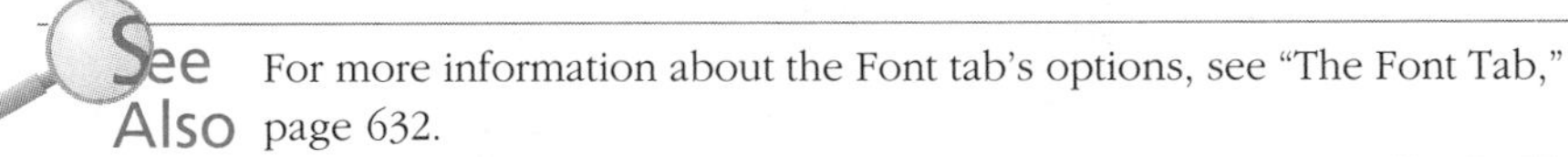
See Also For more information about the Font tab's options, see "The Font Tab," page 632.

Adjusting the Orientation

Excel displays tick labels horizontally whenever it can and rotates them 90 degrees counterclockwise when necessary to avoid overlapping. You can specify a nondefault orientation by selecting an option in the Orientation section on the Alignment tab of the Format Axis dialog box. (The four Orientation options are the same as those shown in Figure 17-9 on page 633.)

For example, you can edit the worksheet to display the full month names as the x-axis labels. If you then select the vertical option on the Alignment tab, you can make this chart look like the one in Figure 17-29.

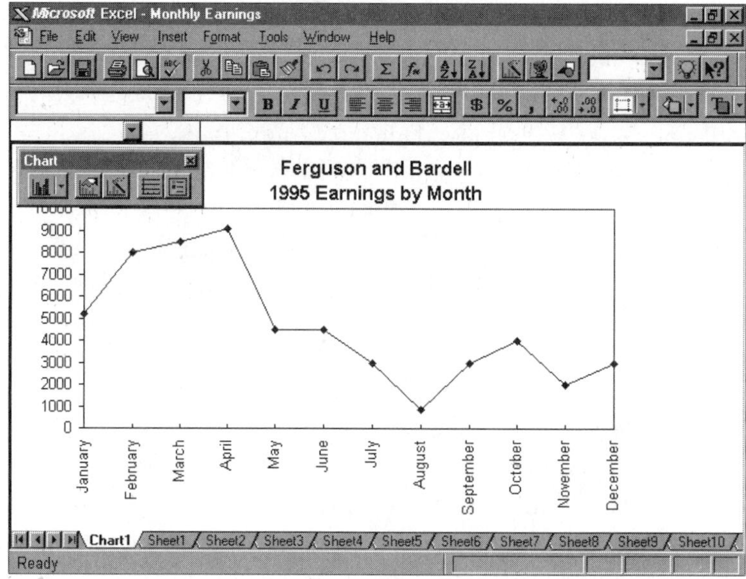

FIGURE 17-29 You can use the Alignment tab to apply vertical orientation to the month names.

Scaling the Value Axis Manually

Value axis is a generic term for any chart axis that is scaled by value instead of by category or by series. Examples include the vertical axes in column, line, and area charts, and both axes in XY charts. Excel usually creates a satisfactory scale for your value axes automatically, but you can easily alter the default scale by using the options on the Scale tab of the Format Axis dialog box for a value axis, which is shown in Figure 17-30.

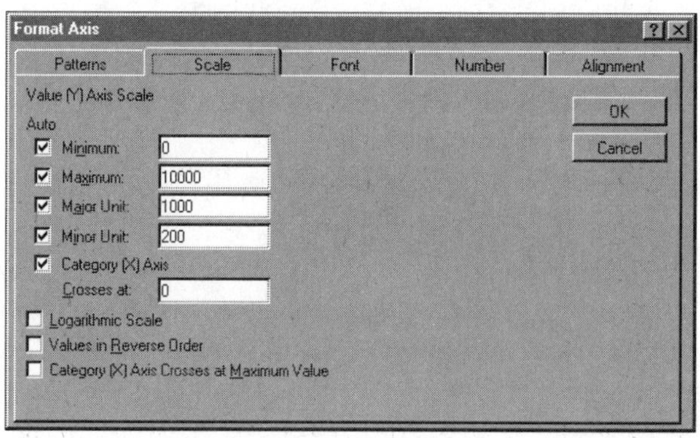

FIGURE 17-30 You can use the Scale tab options to alter the default scale for a value axis.

Setting Minimum and Maximum Values

When all the values in your chart data are positive, Excel's default value axis usually begins at 0 and ends at (or just above) the highest value in the chart. If all the chart values are negative, the scale normally begins at (or just below) the lowest value and ends at 0. If the chart includes both negative and positive values, the default scale starts at (or just below) the lowest value and ends at (or just above) the highest value.

In a chart with only positive values, you can zoom in on the plot area by changing the minimum scale value from 0 to a number that approximates the lowest value in the chart. In a chart with only negative values, you can zoom in on the plot area by making a similar change to the maximum value. To change either end point of the scale, simply enter the value of your choice in the Minimum or Maximum edit box on the Scale tab.

When you change the Minimum or Maximum value, Excel deselects the Auto check box to the left of the option. To restore the automatic Minimum or Maximum value, reselect the appropriate Auto check box.

Changing the Position of Tick Marks and Gridlines

The Major Unit and Minor Unit values on the Scale tab determine the position of major and minor tick marks. By default, Excel displays major tick marks but not minor ones. However, if you use options on the Patterns tab of the Format Axis dialog box to display minor tick marks, they appear at the interval specified in the Minor Unit edit box.

The Major Unit and Minor Unit values also determine the position of major and minor gridlines if you choose to display them. For example, to increase the space between gridlines, increase the Major Unit value, the Minor Unit value, or both by typing new values in the Major Unit and Minor Unit edit boxes.

When you change the Major Unit or Minor Unit value, Excel deselects the Auto check box to the left of the option. To restore automatic values, reselect the appropriate Auto check box.

See Also For more information about formatting gridlines, see "Displaying and Formatting Gridlines," page 664.

Changing the Intersection of the Category Axis

Normally, the category axis crosses the value axis at 0. To position it elsewhere, enter a value other than 0 in the Category (X) Axis Crosses At edit box on the Scale tab. Excel then deselects the associated Auto check box. To restore the normal position of the category axis, reselect the Auto check box.

You can also modify the position of the category axis by selecting the Category (X) Axis Crosses At Maximum Value option. Excel then displays the category axis at the high end of the value-axis scale (unless you also select the Values In Reverse Order option).

Using Logarithmic Scaling

In a logarithmic scale, each power of 10 is separated by the same distance. For example, in a logarithmic scale that runs from 1 to 10,000, the numbers 1, 10, 100, 1000, and 10,000 are equally spaced. Scientific and other types of technical charts often use logarithmic scaling.

To use logarithmic scaling, select the Logarithmic Scale option on the Scale tab of the Format Axis dialog box. To restore linear scaling, deselect this option.

In a logarithmic scale, the lowest value is typically 1. Negative and 0 values cannot be plotted. If you apply logarithmic scaling to a chart that contains negative or 0 values, Excel displays an error message and removes those values from the chart. To restore them, simply restore linear scaling.

Reversing the Value-Axis Scale

You can turn the value-axis scale upside down so that the highest values appear near the bottom of the chart and the lowest values appear near the top. This option is convenient if all your chart values are negative and you're interested primarily in the absolute values of each point. To reverse the scale, select the Values In Reverse Order option on the Scale tab.

Scaling the Category Axis Manually

Category axis is a generic term for any chart axis that is scaled by category instead of by value or by series. Examples include the horizontal axes in column, line, and area charts. Excel usually creates a satisfactory scale for your category axes automatically, but you can easily alter the default scale by using the options on the Scale tab of the Format Axis dialog box, shown in Figure 17-31.

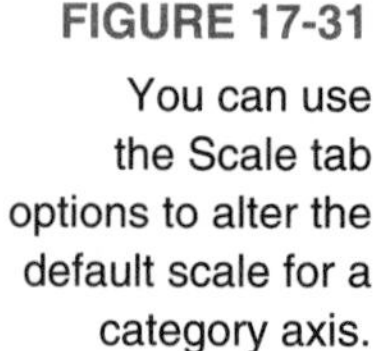

FIGURE 17-31

You can use the Scale tab options to alter the default scale for a category axis.

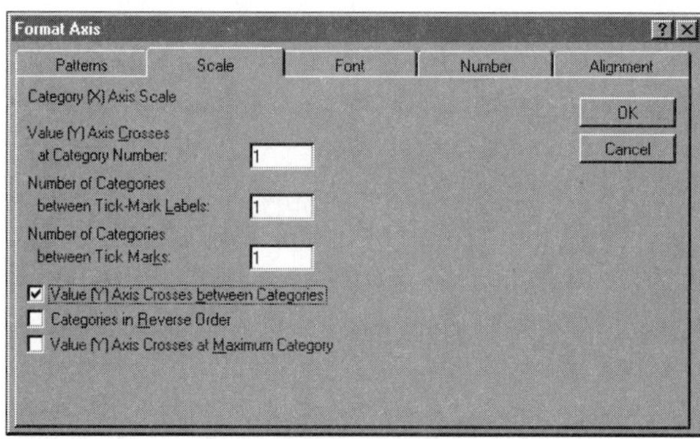

Changing the Intersection of the Value Axis

Normally, the value axis crosses the category axis to the left of the first category's data markers. You can position it elsewhere, however. Simply enter a value other than 1 in the Value (Y) Axis Crosses At Category Number edit box on the Scale tab of the Format Axis dialog box. To restore the normal position of the value axis, change the value back to 1.

You can also modify the position of the value axis by selecting the Value (Y) Axis Crosses At Maximum Category option. Excel then displays the value axis at the right side of the chart, unless you also select the Categories In Reverse Order option.

See Also For information about reversing the axis scaling directions, see "Reversing the Category-Axis Scale," page 662.

Changing the Intervals Between Category Labels

Category labels are displayed along the category axis to identify data clusters. For example, in Figure 17-18 (shown earlier), Region 1, Region 2, and so on are category labels.

Excel often displays a category label for each data cluster (or for each data point in a single-series chart). If you have many data points in each series, this default arrangement can make your labels difficult to read. You can alleviate congestion along the category axis by entering a value other than 1 in the Number Of Categories Between Tick-Mark Labels edit box on the Scale tab of the Format Axis dialog box. If you enter 2, for example, Excel displays a label for every other category. If you enter 3, Excel displays a label for every third category, and so on.

Changing the Intervals Between Tick Marks and Gridlines

The values in the Number Of Categories Between Tick Marks edit box determines the position of major tick marks along the category axis. By default, Excel creates a major tick mark for every category name. You can make them appear less frequently if you enter a value greater than 1 in this edit box.

The presence or absence of tick marks along the category axis doesn't have much of an impact on the appearance of your chart. But major gridlines emanate from major tick marks, so if you display major category-axis gridlines, you can control the frequency at which they appear by altering the interval between tick marks.

Excel draws minor category-axis gridlines halfway between each pair of major gridlines. You cannot customize this interval independently.

For more information about gridlines, see "Displaying and Formatting Gridlines," page 664.

Changing Where the First Point Appears

The Value (Y) Axis Crosses Between Categories option determines where the first point in each series appears, relative to the value axis. This option is selected by default for bar and column charts and deselected for area and line charts. As a result, Excel draws bar and column charts with a little space between the axis and the first marker, and area and line charts with their first markers flush against the value axis.

Reversing the Category-Axis Scale

You can invert the category-axis scale so that the first category appears on the right side of the chart and the last category appears on the left. This option is convenient if you want to emphasize the last category. To reverse the scale, select the Categories In Reverse Order option on the Scale tab.

In bar charts, reversing the category-axis scale places the first category at the top of the axis and the last category at the bottom. For example, if we display the chart shown earlier in Figure 17-2 as a bar chart, Region 1 appears at the bottom of the vertical axis, and Region 5 appears at the top. If you prefer reading the axis in a downward direction, you can select the Categories In Reverse Order option.

Scaling the Series Axis Manually

The series axis appears only in certain three-dimensional area, column, and line charts. When each series appears on a separate plane, Excel displays two axes along the floor of the chart and a third axis that rises straight up from the floor. One of the axes along the floor of the chart becomes the category (x) axis, and the other becomes the series (y) axis. The axis that rises up from the floor is the value (z) axis. Figure 17-32 shows all three axes in a three-dimensional area chart.

You can change the scale of a series axis by selecting it and using the options on the Scale tab of the Format Axis dialog box, as shown in Figure 17-33.

As you can see, the options for scaling the series axis are few and simple. To increase the space between series labels, enter a number greater than 1 in the Number Of Series Between Tick-Mark Labels edit box. To increase the space between tick marks (and gridlines, if you choose to display them), enter a value

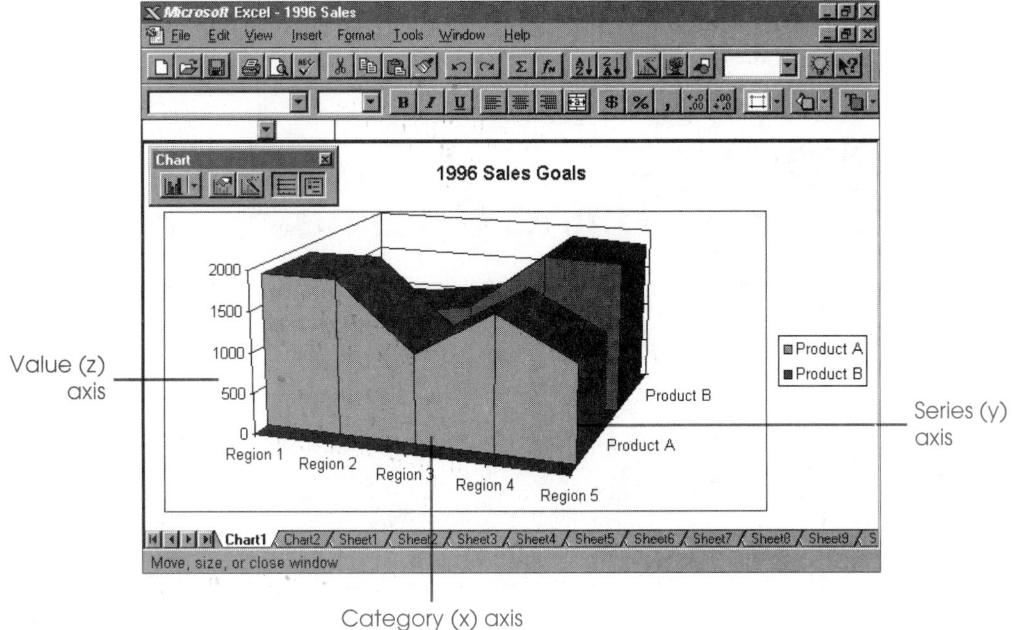

FIGURE 17-32
This three-dimensional area chart has a series axis as well as value and category axes.

greater than 1 in the Number Of Series Between Tick Marks edit box. To reverse the order in which Excel plots the series, select the Series In Reverse Order option.This last option might be useful if the points in your first series obscure those in subsequent series. (You can also deal with that problem by rotating the chart.)

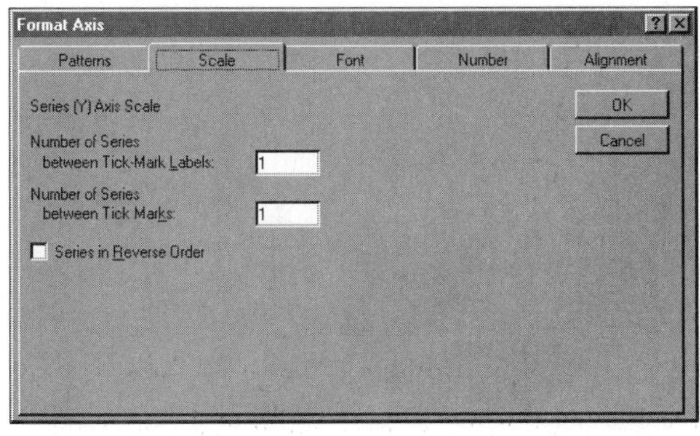

FIGURE 17-33
You can use the Scale tab options to alter the default scale for a series axis.

For information about rotating charts, see "Changing Three-Dimensional Viewing Angles," page 668.

Displaying and Formatting Gridlines

Gridlines are horizontal or vertical lines that help clarify the position of data markers relative to axis scales. Figure 17-34 shows a chart with both category-axis and value-axis gridlines.

FIGURE 17-34

Gridlines can clarify a chart.

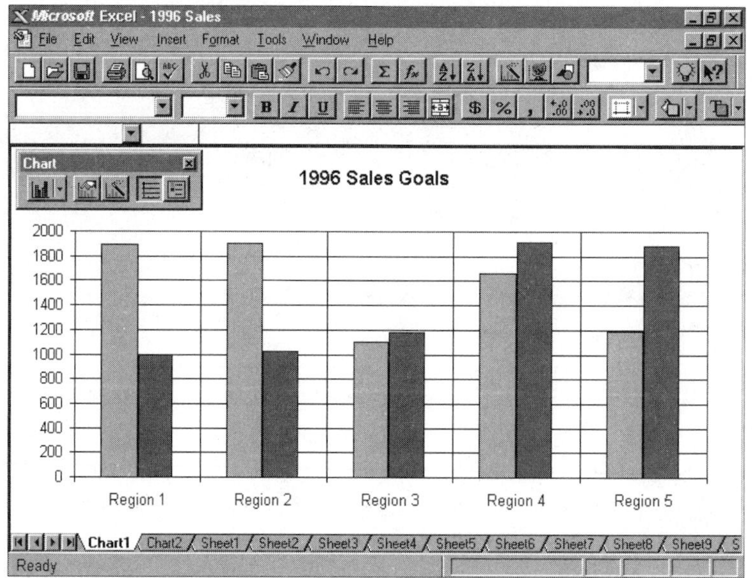

To add gridlines to your chart, choose the Gridlines command from the Insert menu. You'll see one of the dialog boxes shown in Figure 17-35. Select the type of gridlines you want to display and click OK.

Major gridlines emanate from major tick marks, and minor gridlines emanate from minor tick marks. You can change the position of both kinds of tick marks (and thus the number of gridlines that appear) on the Scale tab of the Format Axis dialog box.

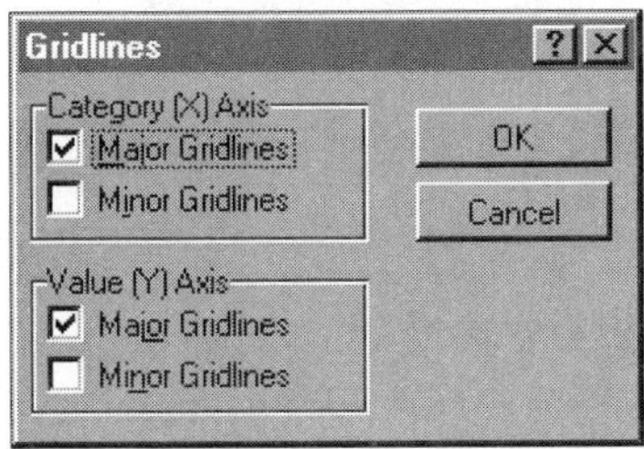

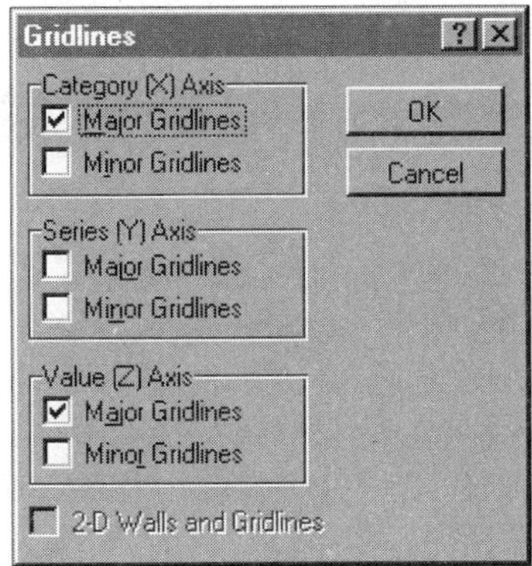

FIGURE 17-35

Excel can display major and minor gridlines from each chart axis.

Select the 2-D Walls And Gridlines option if you don't want walls and gridlines to be displayed in a three-dimensional bar chart. (They are displayed by default.) This option is available only if you're working with a three-dimensional chart that doesn't use a series axis.

To format a set of gridlines, select one of the gridlines, choose the Selected command from the Format menu, and then click the Patterns tab. (Alternatively, you can double-click one of the gridlines you want to format.) On the Patterns tab, specify a style, color, and weight for the selected gridlines.

For more information about changing the position of tick marks, see "Changing the Position of Tick Marks and Gridlines," page 659, and "Changing the Intervals Between Tick Marks and Gridlines," page 661.

Formatting and Sizing Background Areas

Every chart has two background areas that you can format independently: a larger one called the *chart area* and a smaller one called the *plot area*. Figure 17-36 on the next page shows the position of these two areas. Three-dimensional area, line, and column charts have two additional background areas called *walls* and *floors*, which can also be formatted.

Figure 17-37 on page 667 shows the walls and floor of a three-dimensional column chart.

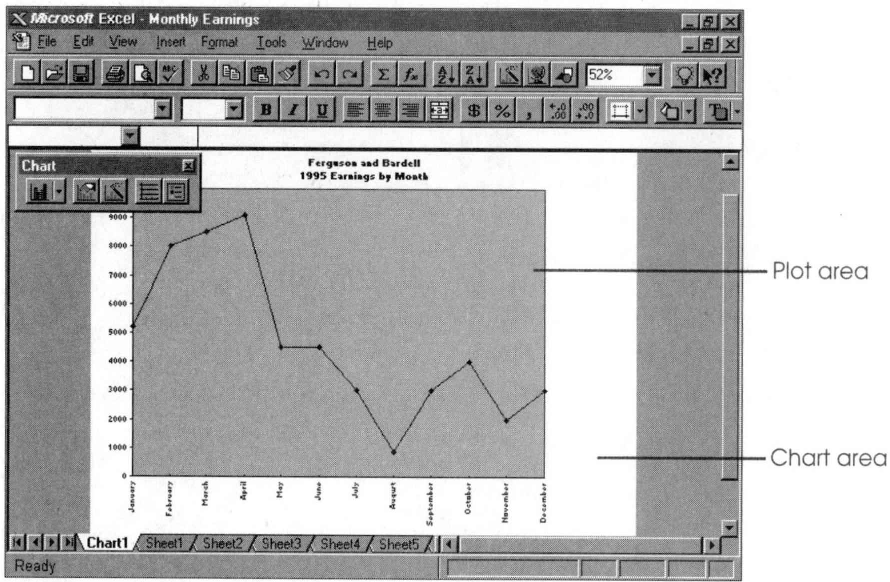

FIGURE 17-36

Every chart has two background areas: a larger one called the *chart area* and a smaller one called the *plot area.*

To format any of these areas, select the area, choose the Selected command from the Format menu, and then click the Patterns tab. Alternatively, you can double-click the area to go straight to the Patterns tab of the Format dialog box.

The Patterns tab for background areas presents many of the same options as the Patterns tabs for other objects. For example, you can add a border (in any style, color, and weight) to any of the background areas, and you can fill in any area with a color and pattern of your choice. And you can add a shadow to the right and lower edges of the border that surrounds the chart area.

You can also change the default font for all text in your chart. To do this, select the chart area, choose the Selected command from the Format menu, and then click the Font tab. Any font settings you make on the Font tab for individual chart objects take precedence over your default settings.

You can change the size of the chart area by choosing the Full Screen or the Sized With Window command. (Figure 17-37 is not sized with the window, but Figure 17-38 is.) When the chart area is sized with the window, you can alter the chart area size and shape by altering the window. To change the size and shape of the plot area, simply select it and use your mouse to drag one of its sizing handles.

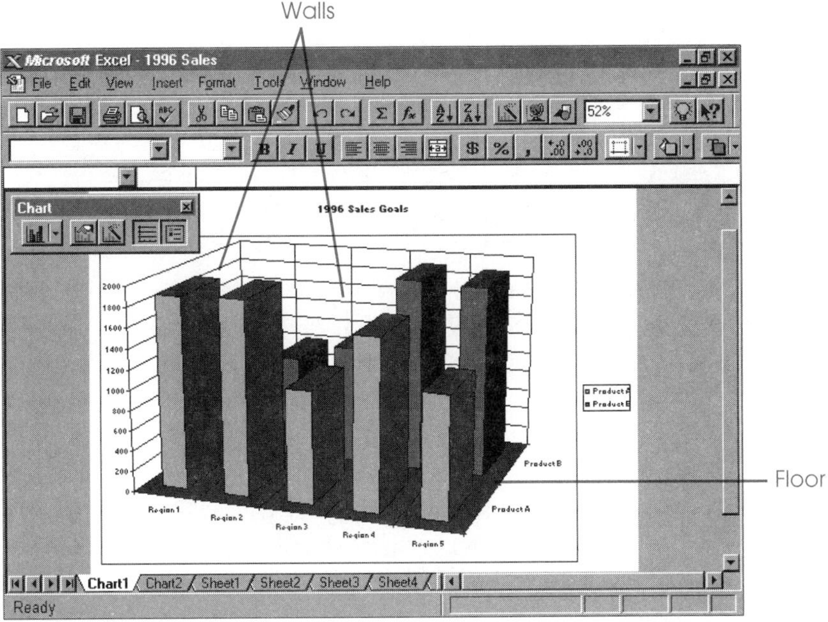

FIGURE 17-37
A three-dimensional column chart has walls and a floor as well as a plot area and a chart area.

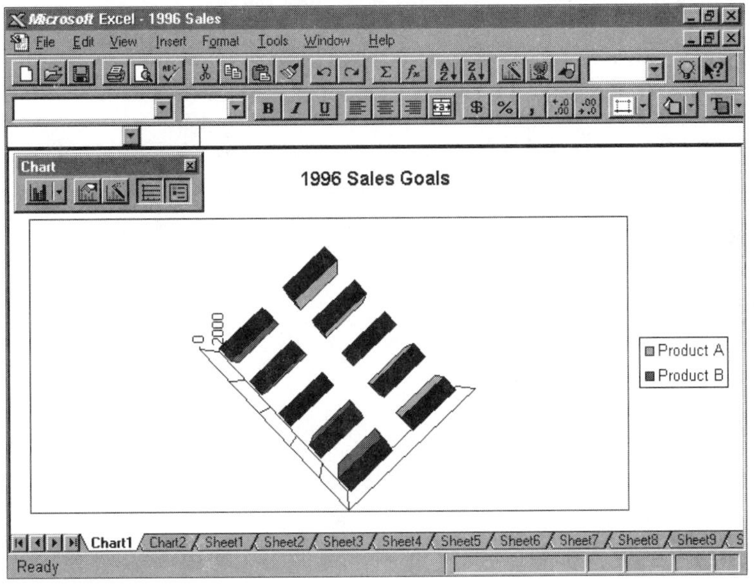

FIGURE 17-38
With direct manipulation, you can transform the appearance of three-dimensional charts in dramatic ways. If your efforts prove too dramatic, as shown here, you can click the Default button in the 3-D View dialog box to restore the original view.

Changing Three-Dimensional Viewing Angles

The simplest way to change the viewing angle of a three-dimensional chart is to select one of the chart's corner handles and drag it with the mouse. While you're dragging, Microsoft Excel displays an outline of the chart. (If you want to see the chart, hold down the Ctrl key.)

This direct-manipulation approach is simple, but it also lets you easily turn an intelligible chart into something quite the opposite. A mere flick of the wrist, for example, is all it takes to transform Figure 17-37 into Figure 17-38.

Fortunately, the dialog box that appears when you choose the 3-D View command from the Format menu includes a Default button, which you can click to return a chart to its original viewing angle. The 3-D View command also lets you fine-tune the appearance of your chart by modifying its elevation, rotation, perspective, and height. Figure 17-39 shows the Format 3-D View dialog box.

The Format 3-D View dialog box also includes a preview box and an Apply button that let you preview the effect of formatting changes.

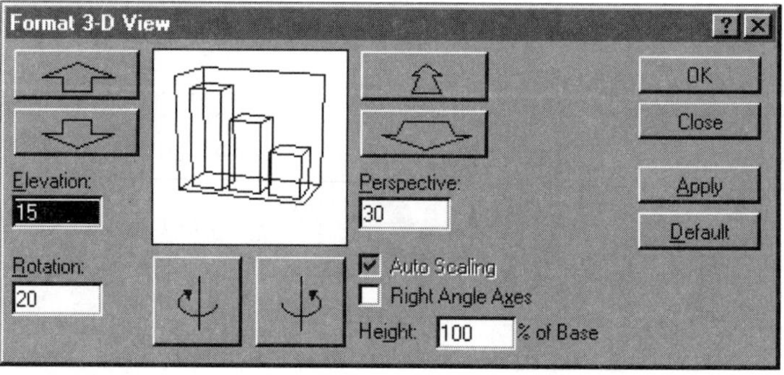

FIGURE 17-39 The Format 3-D View dialog box lets you rotate, tilt, and stretch your three-dimensional charts.

Adjusting the Elevation

The Elevation setting in the Format 3-D View dialog box changes your viewing angle relative to the floor of the chart. The default setting is 15, and you can specify any value from –90 through 90. (With three-dimensional pie charts, you're limited to a value from 10 through 80.) A setting of 90 places you directly above the chart, as if you were looking down on the tops of the markers. With a –90 setting, you look up through the chart's floor (which, incidentally, is always transparent regardless of how you format it). To change the elevation, type a number in the Elevation edit box or click the large up and down arrow in the upper left corner of the dialog box.

Increasing a chart's elevation can help make all data series visible when some series would otherwise be hidden. The three-dimensional column chart shown earlier in Figure 17-37 uses this technique. In that chart, we increased the elevation from the default setting of 15 to 20 and decreased the rotation from 20 to 10.

Changing the Rotation

Imagine that your chart is anchored to a turntable. The Rotation setting in the Format 3-D View dialog box allows you to spin the turntable. Technically, the rotation setting specifies the angle formed by the category axis and a line drawn horizontally across your screen. The default angle is 20 degrees (except for pie charts, where it's 0). You can specify any rotation value from 0 through 360 by entering it in the Rotation edit box or by clicking the clockwise and counter-clockwise buttons to the right of the edit box. The Rotation setting is especially useful if some markers are obscured by others at the default viewing angle.

Changing the Height

The Height setting in the Format 3-D View dialog box changes a chart's value-axis-to-category-axis ratio. The default is 100 percent; you can select any value from 5 through 500. The higher the value, the taller your chart. This option is unavailable for three-dimensional bar charts.

Changing the Perspective

The Perspective setting in the Format 3-D View dialog box determines the apparent depth of three-dimensional area, column, line, and surface charts (as long as the Right Angle Axes option is not selected). The default setting is 30, and you can specify any value from 0 through 100. Low values make the chart look flatter, as though you were looking at the chart through a telescope or a telephoto lens. High values have the opposite effect, as though you were looking through the wrong end of a pair of binoculars or a wide-angle lens.

The default setting, 30, specifies that the far side of the chart is 30 percent smaller than the near side. This means that with a rotation of 0, the back of the floor is 30 percent narrower than the front of the floor. Similarly, if the elevation is 90, the bottom of the tallest column in a three-dimensional column chart is about 30 percent smaller than the top of the column.

To change the Perspective setting, enter a new number in the Perspective edit box or click the up or down arrow above the Perspective option. You can also eliminate all perspective from a chart by selecting the Right Angle Axes option.

Changing the Axis Angle and Scale

The Right Angle Axes option sets the axes at right angles independent of chart rotation or elevation. To see axes in perspective, turn off this option. For three-dimensional bar charts, this option is always turned on.

Auto Scaling is available only if the Right Angle Axes option is selected. When you change a two-dimensional chart into a three-dimensional chart, it is sometimes drawn smaller. For charts with right-angle axes and a rotation of less than 45 degrees, the Auto Scaling option scales the three-dimensional chart so that it is closer in size to the two-dimensional version.

Chapter 18

Editing Chart Data

Charts have a way of changing over time. New data arrives, old data becomes irrelevant, new visual comparisons become meaningful. In this chapter, we'll take a look at Excel's procedures for working with the data that drives your charts. We'll see how to add new points and series to a chart, how to change the order in which series are plotted, and how to plot multilevel categories of information. We'll also take a look at the SERIES formulas that Excel uses to link charts with worksheet data.

Adding Data Series and Data Points to a Chart

Sometimes you won't have a complete data set when you first create a chart, and you'll want to add data as it becomes available. You can add data — albeit awkwardly — by copying the data from a worksheet and pasting it into a chart. But you have much simpler ways to add data series and data points to charts.

The easiest way to add a data series to an embedded chart is to select the data series range in the worksheet and then drag it to the chart. You can also use the Insert menu's New Data command to add a data series to either a chart that is embedded or to a chart sheet. To use this command, follow these steps:

1. Display and activate the chart to which you want to add a data series.
2. Choose the New Data command from the Insert menu. Excel displays the New Data dialog box shown in Figure 18-1.

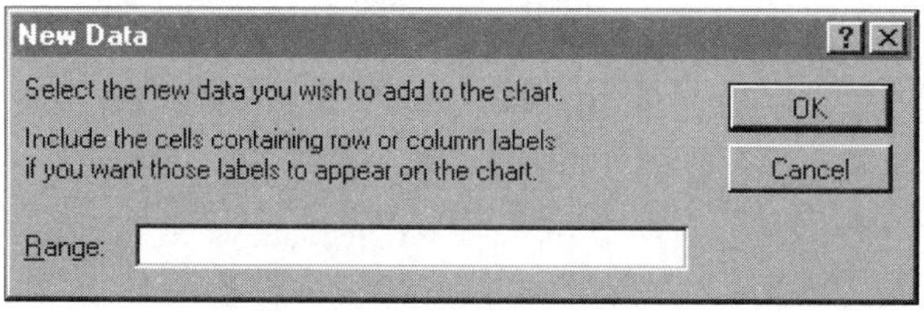

FIGURE 18-1
In the New Data dialog box, you can specify the range with the series you want to add.

3. Display the worksheet containing the data you want to add and then select the data range. (You might need to drag the dialog box out of the way.) Include the data series name if it appears in the worksheet. As you select the data range, Excel enters its reference in the Range edit box.
4. Click OK. Excel adds the data series to the chart.

NOTE If Excel cannot determine how to add the data series to the chart, the Paste Special dialog box appears. Complete steps 5–8 on the next page to add the data series to the chart.

Another way to add a data series to an existing chart is to use the Copy and Paste Special commands on the Edit menu. You can also use this method to add data points to a series by following these steps:

1. Select the worksheet range that holds the new data points.
2. Choose Copy from the Edit menu or click the Copy button on the Standard toolbar.
3. Display the chart sheet containing the chart you want to modify or select the embedded chart you want to modify.
4. Choose Paste Special. Excel displays the Paste Special dialog box shown in Figure 18-2.

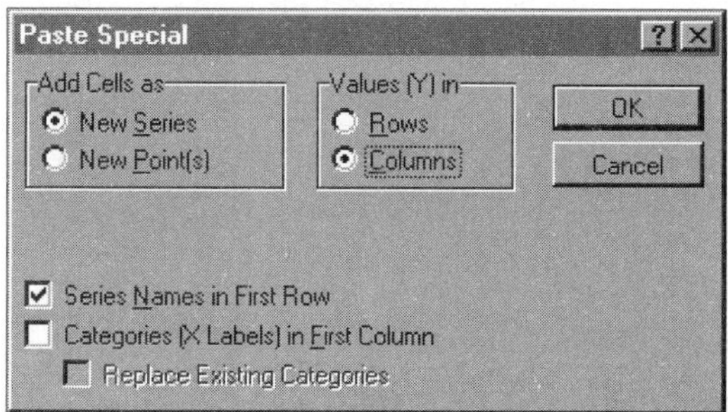

FIGURE 18-2
The Paste Special dialog box lets you add data series and data points to existing charts.

5. In the Add Cells As section, indicate that you want to add the values in the selected range as new data points by selecting New Point(s).
6. In the Values (Y) In section, indicate whether the data series are stored in rows or columns in the worksheet. (Excel uses this information to adjust the names of the options in the lower half of the dialog box.)
7. If the first row or column of the selected range holds category labels, select the Categories (X Labels) In First Column option.
8. Click OK to close the dialog box. Excel adds the selected data points to your existing chart.

Changing Series Descriptions

Microsoft Excel uses SERIES formulas (formulas built with the SERIES function) to link charts to underlying worksheet cells. By modifying these formulas with the Selected Series command on the Format menu, you can change the labels used in chart legends, change the labels assigned to the category axis, add or delete data points, change the order in which series are plotted, delete existing series, and add new series to a chart.

Before we explore using the Selected Series command to change series descriptions, we need to take a quick look at the SERIES function.

The SERIES Function

The SERIES function takes the form

=SERIES(*name_ref,categories,values,plot_order*)

The *name_ref* argument is the name of the data series being charted. The *categories* argument locates your category labels in the worksheet, and the *values* argument locates the data-point values in the worksheet. The *plot_order* argument determines the order in which your data series appear on the chart.

When you create a chart, Excel creates one SERIES formula for each of the chart's data series. For example, if you plot the data in cells A3:D7 of the worksheet in Figure 18-3, Excel creates the chart shown in Figure 18-4, which we can use to illustrate the mechanics of the SERIES function.

FIGURE 18-3
We used the data in this worksheet to plot the sample chart in Figure 18-4.

Microsoft Excel - Book1

	A	B	C	D
1				
2				
3		Product A	Product B	Product C
4	Quarter 1	100	123	110
5	Quarter 2	125	150	135
6	Quarter 3	140	105	130
7	Quarter 4	131	100	115

The formula bar in Figure 18-4 indicates that the SERIES formula for the first data series is

=SERIES(Sheet1!$B$3,Sheet1!$A$4:$A$7,Sheet1!$B$4:$B$7,1)

The *name_ref* argument in this formula is Sheet1!$B$3. The *categories* and *values* arguments are Sheet1!$A$4:$A$7 and Sheet1!$B$4:$B$7. As you can see, Excel uses the worksheet name followed by an exclamation point to indicate on which sheet the data series, category labels, and data-point values are located. Excel also uses absolute cell references in these arguments.

The *plot_order* argument, 1, in this SERIES formula tells Excel to plot this data series before any other series in this chart. As you'll see, you can change the order in which Excel plots data series simply by changing the *plot_order* argument at the end of the formula.

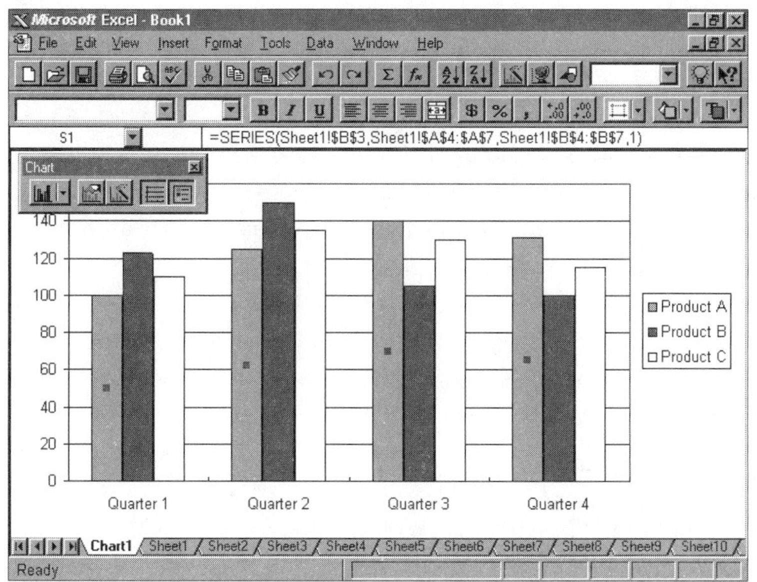

FIGURE 18-4

This sample chart shows the SERIES function in the formula bar.

The *name_ref* and *categories* arguments don't always appear in the SERIES formula. Excel uses these arguments only if you select cells that contain series and category labels. For example, if you select only cells B4:D7 in the worksheet in Figure 18-3, Excel creates a chart like the one shown in Figure 18-5.

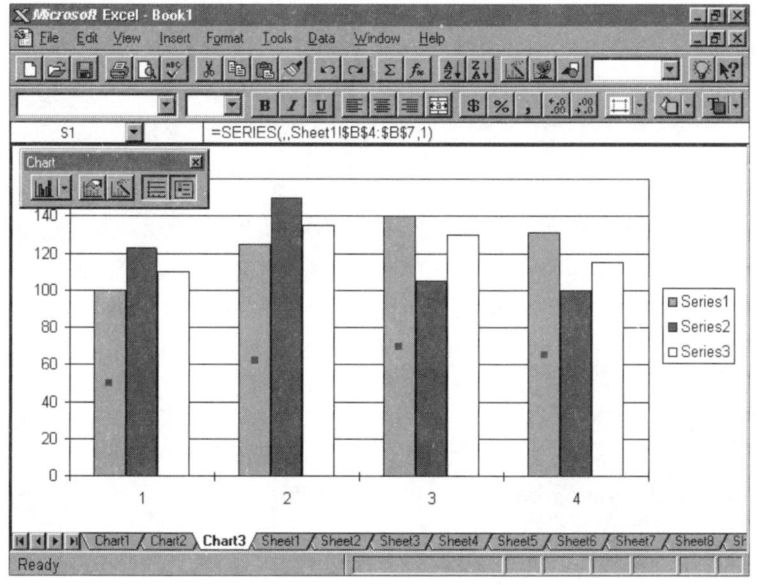

FIGURE 18-5

The SERIES formulas in this chart include neither series names nor category labels.

The SERIES formula for the first series in this chart is

=SERIES(,,Sheet1!$B$4:$B$7,1)

Notice that the first two arguments — *name_ref* and *categories* — are missing. Because the formula does not include a *name_ref* argument, Excel uses dummy names — Series 1, Series 2, and so on — in the legend, and because the formula does not include a *categories* argument, Excel uses dummy labels — 1, 2, 3, and 4 — for the category axis.

For more information about references to other worksheets, see "References to Other Worksheets in the Same Workbook," page 117.

Editing SERIES Formulas

You can edit SERIES formulas as you would edit other types of formulas. For example, to change the plot order of a data series, select the series and then modify the *plot_order* argument by editing the SERIES formula in the formula bar. You can add a new series to a chart by typing a new SERIES formula, and you can delete a series from a chart by deleting its SERIES formula.

Because the SERIES function takes four arguments (three of which are likely to be sheet references), building or modifying SERIES formulas manually is tedious and difficult to do accurately. Thanks to the Format menu's Selected Data Series command, this manual work is also unnecessary.

Replacing a Data Series or Changing Its Name

You can easily replace a data series or change its name using the Selected Series command. Follow these steps:

1. In the chart, select the data series you want to replace or rename.
2. Choose the Selected Data Series command from the Format menu. The Format Data Series dialog box appears as shown in Figure 18-6.
3. Select the Name And Values tab.
4. In the Name edit box, specify the cell reference of the data series name. First highlight any existing entry. Then either type a reference to the cell or click the edit box, display the worksheet containing the data series name, and click the cell containing the name. (You might need to drag the dialog box out of your way to select the data.)

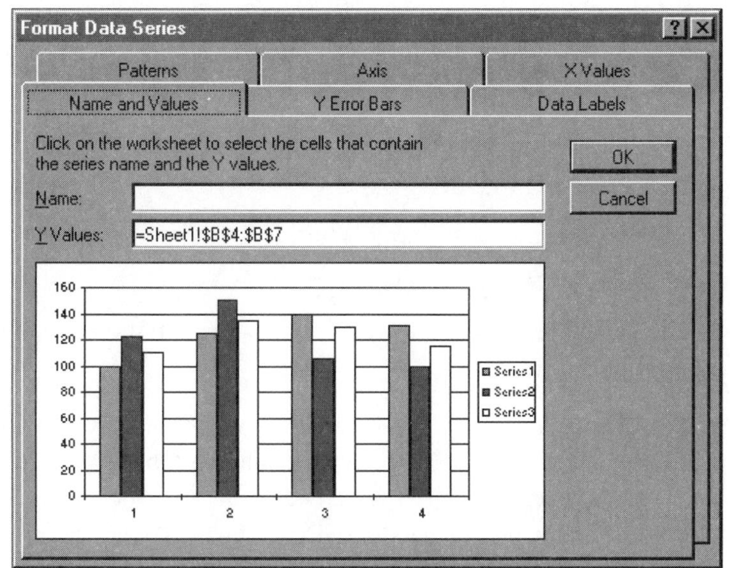

FIGURE 18-6
The options on the Name And Values tab of the Format Data Series dialog box let you replace or rename a data series.

5. In the Y Values edit box, specify the worksheet range containing the data series. Highlight the current entry and then type a reference to the range; or click the edit box, display the worksheet containing the data series, and then select the data range.
6. Click OK to rename or replace the data series.

TIP The data series name doesn't have to be stored in a worksheet cell. You can enter an independent data series name in the Name edit box. Don't enclose the name in quotation marks; Excel will add them for you.

Changing a Chart's Category Labels

The labels that appear along a chart's category axis are determined by the *categories* argument in the SERIES formula for the chart's first data series. If you omit this argument, Excel uses 1, 2, 3, and so on as dummy category names. Excel ignores the *categories* arguments for the second and subsequent data series; they have no effect on the chart's appearance.

Although only the first series' *categories* argument is significant, when you create a chart in the customary manner, Excel assigns the same *categories* argument to each series. (By "customary manner," we mean plotting a worksheet range that includes column and row headings as well as numbers.) Excel includes the argument in all series so that you can rearrange the series' plot order later.

To change a chart's category labels, follow these steps:

1. Select the first data series.
2. Choose the Selected Data Series command from the Format menu.
3. Select the X Values tab.
4. Click the X Values edit box and type the text of the new labels or enter a reference to the worksheet cells containing the new labels. If you enter the labels directly, type labels for each data point in the first series, separating the labels with commas. To enter a worksheet reference, the simplest method is to use the mouse to select the range containing the labels.

Adding Data Points to a Series

The most efficient way to add new data to your charts is to include one blank row or column at the end of each series. You can then add data by inserting new rows above the blank row or new columns to the left of the blank column. The range reference in the SERIES formula will automatically expand to include the inserted rows or columns.

TIP Although Excel uses range references as arguments in the SERIES function, you can also use range names. Using range names ensures that the SERIES function is automatically updated any time you redefine the range name, which you might do when you add data points.

An alternative (and slightly more difficult) way to add data to a series is to choose the Selected Series command from the Format menu and change the contents of the X Values and Y Values edit boxes.

Whichever method you use, you'll probably want to include the same number of data points in each of your chart's series.

TIP To remove any data series from a chart, select the series and press Del. Alternatively, you can select the series and delete the SERIES formula from the formula bar.

Controlling Plotted Worksheet Data

Microsoft Excel follows a set of rules when it uses worksheet data to draw a chart. If you include empty cells in the selected data range, for example, Excel ignores those cells. (You can tell Excel to treat empty cells as zero values or interpolate values for the cells, instead.) Excel also ignores any hidden cells included in the selected data range. If you want to change these charting rules, follow these steps:

1. Display the chart to which Excel should apply new charting rules.
2. Choose the Options command from the Tools menu.
3. Click the Chart tab.
4. Use the options in the Empty Cells Plotted As section to tell Excel how it should treat empty cells. The default treatment is to ignore them. You can also treat empty cells as if they contain zeros. You can have Excel interpolate values for the cells and then plot them, for example, by drawing a line segment between the previous and following values in a line chart.
5. Use the Plot Visible Cells Only option to indicate whether values in cells in hidden rows and columns should be included as part of a data series.
6. Use the Chart Sizes With Window Frame option to tell Excel whether it should adjust the chart's size when the document window's size changes.

Using Multilevel Categories

Microsoft Excel lets you categorize your categories. This sounds redundant, but a quick example will illustrate this technique. Suppose you want to plot the data shown in Figure 18-7 at the top of the next page. Here, the data series are months and the categories are the sales offices located in different cities. However, the categories — the city sales offices — are further classified, or categorized, by state.

FIGURE 18-7
This worksheet uses multilevel categories: City sales offices are grouped by the states in which the cities are located.

Microsoft Excel - Book1

A1 Salespeople by office

	A	B	C	D	E
1	Salespeople by office				
2					
3			January	February	March
4	Washington	Seattle	13	13	14
5	Washington	Spokane	6	8	10
6	Oregon	Portland	12	12	12
7	Oregon	Eugene	2	2	2
8	California	San Francisco	11	13	15
9	California	Los Angeles	14	18	2
10	California	San Diego	16	16	11

To plot the data in Figure 18-7 in a chart with multilevel categories, select the range A3:E10 and press F11 to plot the data in the simple column chart shown in Figure 18-8. Excel displays both the city names and the state names below the category axis.

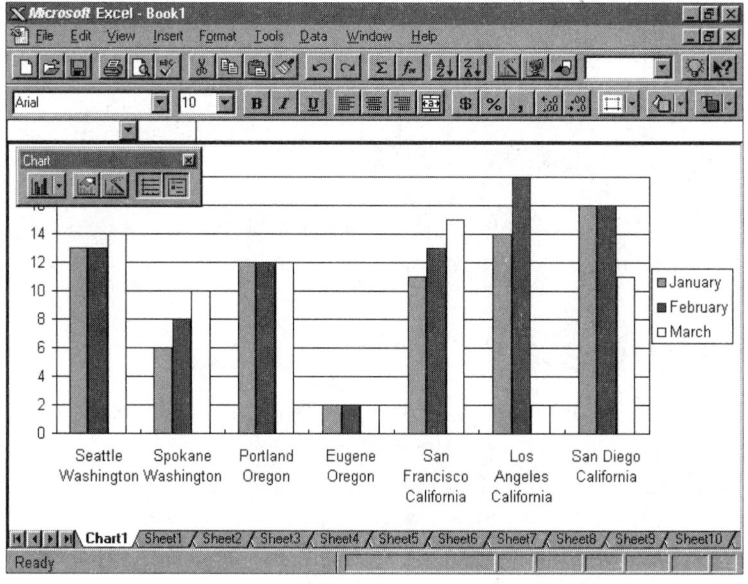

FIGURE 18-8
A multilevel category chart uses two or more sets of category names to label the category axis.

Changing Underlying Worksheet Values

Because charts are usually linked to worksheet cells, you can use charts to construct visual "what-if" scenarios with your data. For example, if you set up a break-even analysis in a worksheet and then plot fixed costs, variable costs, total costs, and gross margin in a chart, you can change fixed-cost assumptions in the worksheet and immediately see the effect on the gross-margin line in the chart.

You can also reverse this what-if process in two-dimensional bar, column, line, and XY charts. You can drag chart data markers — including picture markers — upward or downward and have Excel adjust the underlying worksheet. In the break-even analysis, for example, you can drag the chart's gross-margin line upward so that it crosses 0 at a different point and then find out on the worksheet exactly how much you would need to reduce your fixed costs to achieve the increase in profit.

Let's look at a simple example. Suppose that after examining the chart in Figure 18-9 you decide that the fourth-quarter data doesn't look quite right. Product B appears to lag behind Products A and C in that quarter, when in fact you expected B to do better than C — if not quite as well as A. Instead of going back to the worksheet and entering new values, you can change the chart directly.

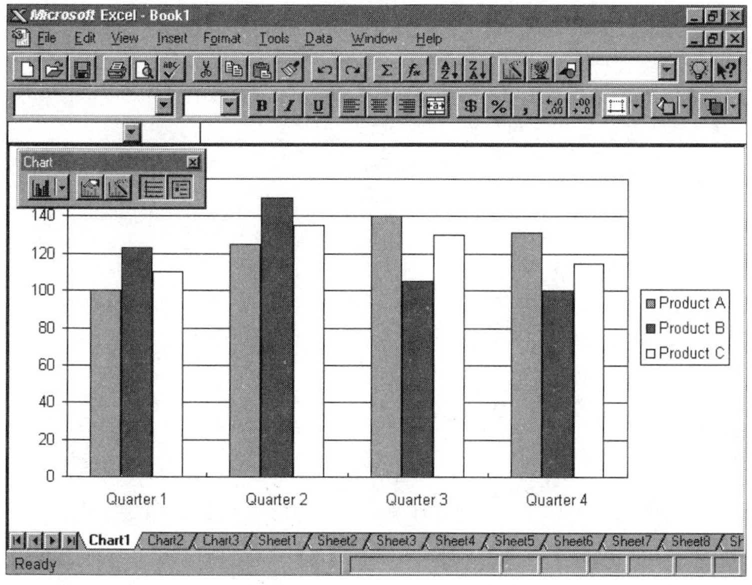

FIGURE 18-9
We'll use this simple chart to demonstrate Excel's reverse what-if capabilities.

To adjust the worksheet's values from the chart, follow these steps:

1. Select the data marker you want to adjust. Black handles appear on the marker. In our example, you would select the fourth-quarter marker for Product B.

2. Point to the top center black handle. The pointer becomes a double-headed arrow. Drag the marker upward until the marker's height is somewhere between that of Product A and Product C. As you drag Product B's marker, your screen looks similar to Figure 18-10.

   While you drag the marker, notice that both the Name box in the formula bar and an indicator on the value axis change to reflect what the marker's value will be if you release the mouse button at that point.

3. Release the mouse button when the data marker reflects the value you want. In Figure 18-10, the Name box displays 117.3. An indicator also appears on the value axis at 117.3. (It's difficult to see in Figure 18-10.) If you continue dragging until the data marker's value is 123.7 and then release the mouse button, the underlying value in the worksheet changes to 123.7, as shown in Figure 18-11.

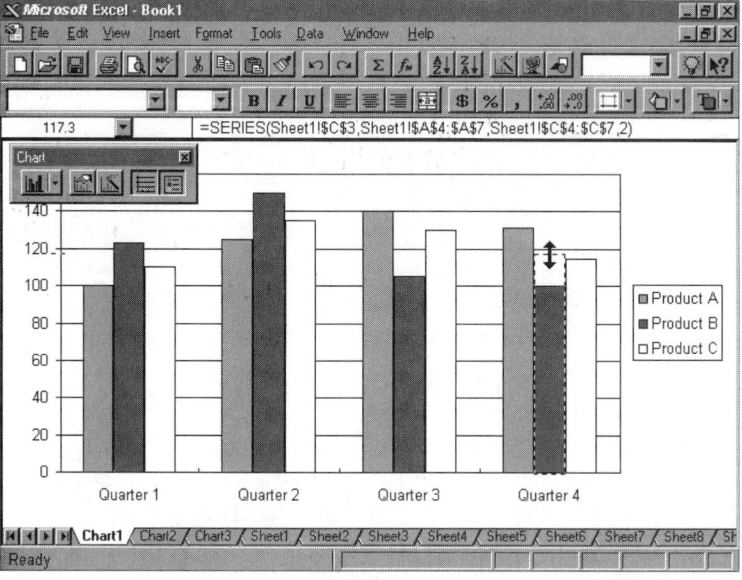

FIGURE 18-10
As you drag Product B's marker, the Name box in the formula bar displays the marker's new value.

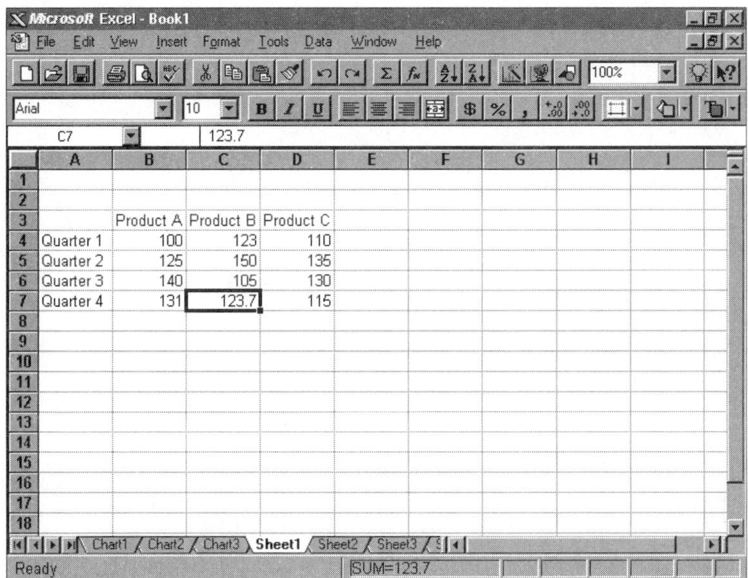

FIGURE 18-11

When you release the mouse button, Excel changes the fourth-quarter value for Product B to 123.7 in both the chart and the supporting worksheet.

In this example, all Excel has to do to make the chart display the new value we requested is modify cell C7 in the underlying worksheet. If cell C7 contains a formula instead of a constant, however, the situation is different. Excel understands that you want the result of the formula producing the data point value to change but don't want to replace the formula with a constant. To clarify your intentions, Excel presents the Goal Seek dialog box — the same dialog box you see when you use the Goal Seek command on the Formula menu. In the Goal Seek dialog box, you specify what value the formula should return and which formula input the Goal Seek command should adjust.

See Also For more information about the Goal Seek command, see "The Goal Seek Command," page 565.

Chapter 19

Mapping Geographical Data

In the past, applications that allowed you to display data in a geographical context were highly specialized, very expensive, and relatively complex to operate. Excel brings this capability down to earth with Microsoft Data Map — a robust add-in application that you can use to make geographical information highly presentable.

Like all Excel charts, data maps allow you to present rows and columns of information in a more immediately understandable format. You can use data maps in many ways. Perhaps the most obvious application is the display of inherently geographical statistics such as census or environmental data. You can display certain specific features, depending on the map, including highways, cities, airports, and rivers. And you can display data by country, state, province, or even by zip code.

NOTE Microsoft Data Map is an installation option. It is not installed if you performed a "typical" installation. You might have to rerun Setup to install it. For more information about installation, see Appendix B.

Split Personality

The term "add-in" refers to a separate module that performs specific tasks and is designed to run more or less seamlessly with Excel. One of the less "seamless" aspects of the Data Map add-in is that, when activated, it takes over most of the screen: the commands on the Edit, View, Insert, Tools, and Help menus are replaced by Data Map commands, a new Map menu appears, the regular Excel toolbars are hidden, and a special Data Map toolbar is displayed. When you edit a map, you activate this user interface, and Excel's interface is, in effect, pushed to the background. But it's easy to move back and forth between these "split personalities."

- Double-click the map object to activate the Data Map add-in's menus and commands.
- To return to the Excel menus and commands, click any part of the worksheet surrounding the map.

The Data Map add-in includes the following maps: World Countries, United States, Canadian Provinces, European Countries, United Kingdom, Australian States, and Mexican States. If you purchased Excel on compact disc, you may have additional maps available. You can order additional maps and "map enhancers" directly from MapInfo Corporation, the developer of the Data Map add-in. To get the scoop on additional map products, choose Data Map Help Topics from the Help menu in Data Map (while the add-in is active). Click the Contents tab, click Introduction, and then double-click "Where can I obtain more maps?"

Preparing Your Data

The first step in creating a data map is to make sure your worksheet data is organized in a way that makes sense for mapping. A geographical data table doesn't need to be very complex, but you do need to apply labels to your data that the Data Map add-in can understand. Therefore, your worksheet should include a column listing state names, country names, or postal codes. You can use the standard spellings of state or country names, or you can use standard abbreviations. Note that the Data Map add-in requires that these map "feature names" be in a column. You cannot use a transposed table layout in which the feature names appear across the top in a single row.

To begin constructing a data map, you first select the worksheet data you want to use. Figure 19-1 shows a sample worksheet that is organized for data mapping, with cells A3:F10 selected. Your selection should include the row and column headers and, of course, the data itself. The Data Map add-in scans the column containing the geographic locations and automatically determines the necessary map to use.

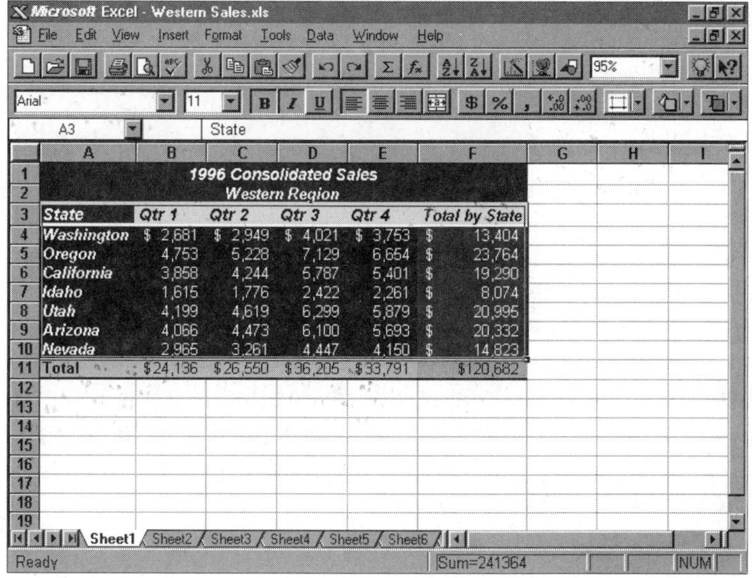

FIGURE 19-1

A geographic data table includes a column containing location names or postal codes.

TIP Excel normally doesn't display the leading zeros that many postal codes use. To create a data map using postal codes, therefore, enter the postal codes as text. One way to do this is by preceding the postal code number with an apostrophe, which tells Excel to treat the entire cell entry as text. Alternatively, you can select the entire column, press Ctrl-1, click the Number tab, click the Special category, and then select one of the Zip Code formats.

Creating a Data Map

After you select the worksheet data, click the Map button on the standard toolbar. The cursor changes to a small cross. As you do with the ChartWizard button, after you click the Map button, you use the cross to drag a box that describes the size of an embedded data map anywhere on the worksheet. When you release the mouse button, the Data Map add-in begins to build the map. Before it actually appears, you might have to answer a few questions. Figure 19-2 shows a dialog box that appears if more than one map exists that makes sense for your data.

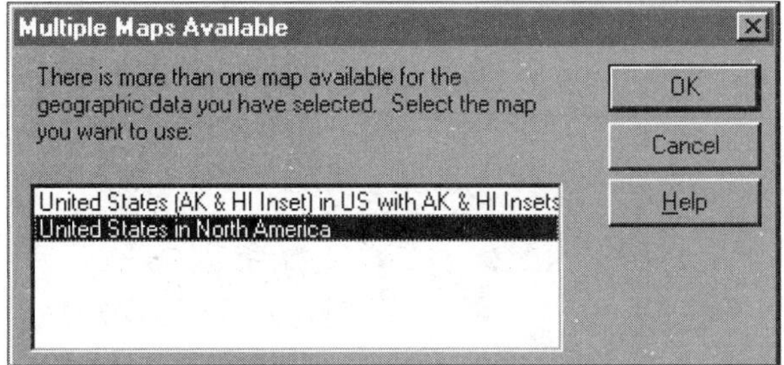

FIGURE 19-2
If more than one map is available for your data, choose the one you want.

Figure 19-3 shows a dialog box that appears if the Data Map add-in can't figure out the geographic locations listed in your table. This can happen because of misspelling, or if you simply forgot to select the column containing the locations before you clicked the Map button. In either case, it's easier at this point to cancel and correct the spelling error or select the necessary cell range. To create a blank data map, don't select a data table before clicking the map button, which is the same thing that happens if you click OK in the Unable To Create Data Map dialog box.

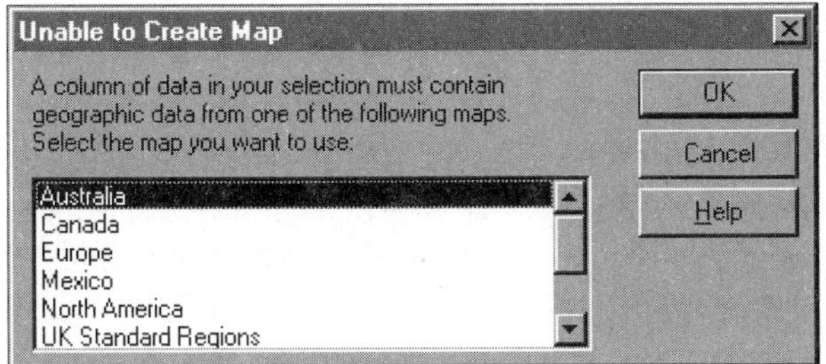

FIGURE 19-3

If Data Map has a problem interpreting the geographic locations in your data table, this dialog box appears.

You can adjust the amount of time allotted to the matching of your geographic data using the Options command on the Data Map add-in's Tools menu. As you can see in the dialog box shown in Figure 19-4, the Time Limit associated with the Thorough matching option is normally 5 seconds. You can increase this number to as much as 120 seconds if you are having trouble getting the results you need. If you have a large worksheet or database you are using to create a map, and if you are certain that your geographic location names are valid, increasing the time limit could solve the problem. Use the Quick matching option if you have a small amount of data or are using either postal codes or abbreviations as your geographic names.

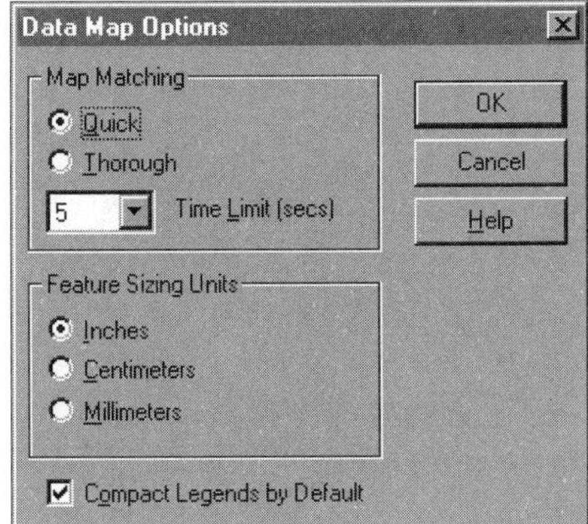

FIGURE 19-4

The Map Matching options control the amount of time spent matching maps to geographic names.

Once the Data Map add-in has the necessary information, the map appears on the worksheet and the Data Map Control dialog box appears, as shown in Figure 19-5 on the next page.

In Figure 19-5, you can see three distinct areas in the Data Map Control dialog box. At the top of the United States tab are *column buttons* — gray boxes with names like "Qtr 1" and "Total By State," which correspond to names of columns in the data table that you can display in the map. On the lower left of the dialog box are six *format buttons* you use to determine the way the data is to be displayed in the map. To see what the buttons mean, move the mouse cursor over a button. A ScreenTip appears showing you its name. (We'll discuss the various formats later.) The white area at the bottom of the dialog box is where you specify the format and column you want to use. The two dotted boxes, labeled "Format" and "Column," simply indicate what the icons above them signify. In Figure 19-5, the icon above the Format box is the Value Shading format button. The icon above the Column box indicates that Qtr 1 is the column of data currently displayed in the map. If you want to change the map to display Total By State rather than Qtr 1, simply click the Total By State box and drag it over the Qtr 1 box in the white area of the dialog box.

TIP If it's not clear exactly what a column button at the top of the Data Map Control dialog box refers to on the worksheet, double-click it to display the corresponding sheet and range reference. (Notice that when you double-click column buttons that appear in the white active area at the bottom of the dialog box, the add-in displays the Value Shading Options dialog box rather than the reference.)

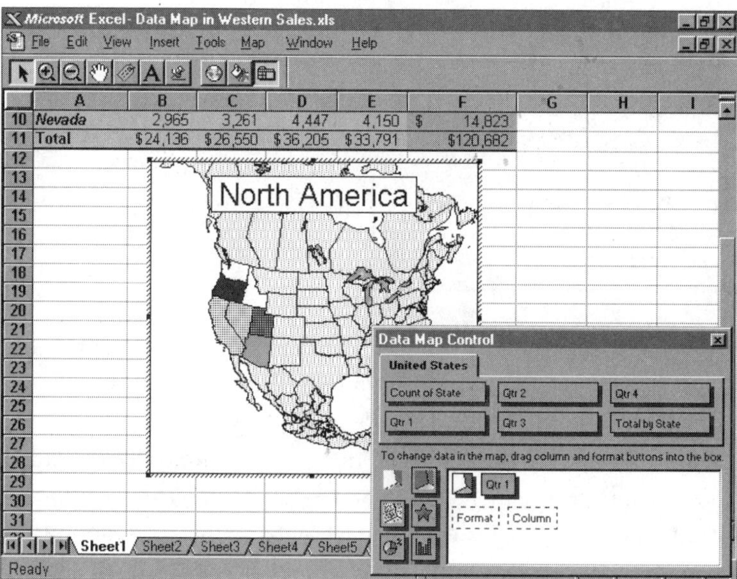

FIGURE 19-5
As soon as the map is drawn, you can modify it to suit your needs.

Single-Series Map Formats

The Value Shading, Category Shading, Dot Density, and Graduated Symbol formats can describe only one data series, while the Pie Chart and Column Chart formats can display multiple related data series. The default map format is Value Shading, which divides the values in the specified column into ranges and then color codes each map region according to where its corresponding value falls in the total range.

To illustrate this a little more clearly, click the right mouse button on the legend at the bottom of the map and choose the Compact command. The command normally appears with a check mark next to it, indicating that the legend is currently displayed in compact format. After choosing the command, the check mark disappears and the legend expands to its full size, showing the ranges used in the map and their corresponding colors, as shown in Figure 19-6. The expanded legend includes a number in parentheses following each value range. These handily indicate the number of states in the map that fall into each value range.

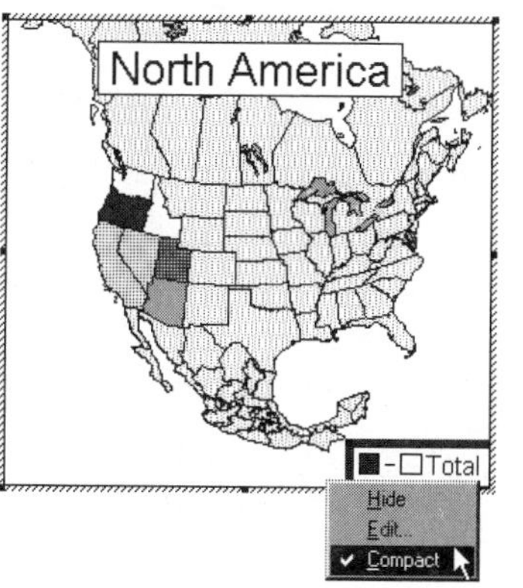

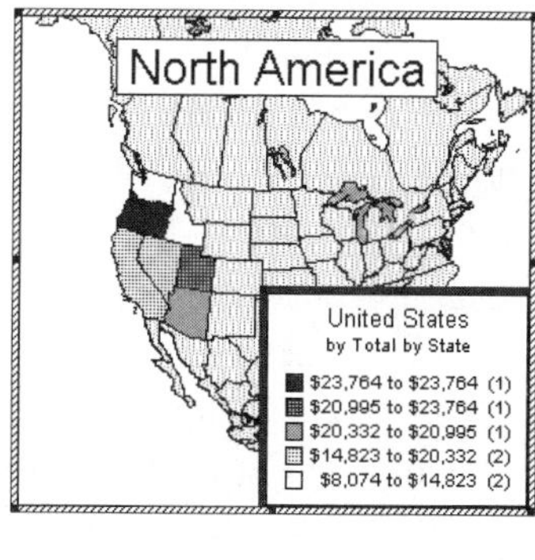

FIGURE 19-6
The expanded legend of a map in Value Shading format shows the color-coded value ranges.

TIP If you'd prefer your maps to be created with expanded legends rather than compact ones, choose the Options command from the Tools menu and deselect the Compact Legends By Default option. (See Figure 19-5.)

You can adjust the number of value ranges and how they are determined by double-clicking the Value Shading button while it is in the active white area of the Data Map Control dialog box. When you do so, the Value Shading Options dialog box appears, as shown in Figure 19-7 on the next page.

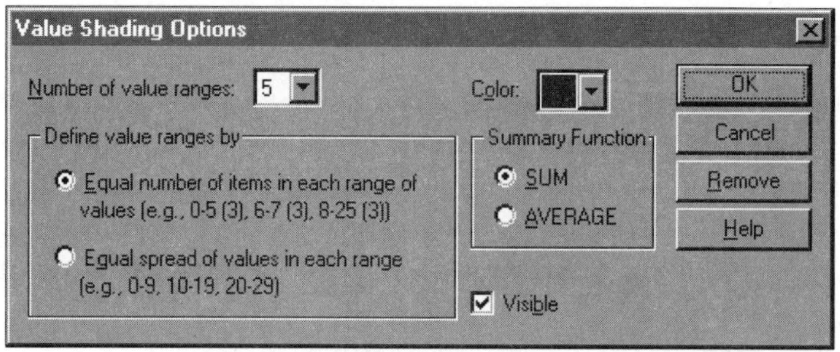

FIGURE 19-7 When a Value Shading map is active, choose the Value Shading Options command on the Map menu to display this dialog box.

The Number Of Value Ranges "spinner" control allows you to choose the number of ranges you want. Using the Color drop-down list, you select the base color to be used to indicate the different value ranges on the map. Only one color is used, and the different value ranges are achieved using variations on this base color. Use the Define Value Ranges By options to choose between two approaches: dividing the ranges into equal numbers of geographic locations or into equal ranges of values.

For example, in Figure 19-6, the expanded legend shows five ranges; three that include one state, and two that include two states. This is as close as Data Map could get to the "equal number of items in each range" option, since there are five ranges and seven states. If there were an even number of states displayed, you could adjust the number of value ranges until an even spread was possible.

You change the format of a map the same way you change a data series. Drag one of the format buttons on the lower left of the Data Map Control dialog box over an existing button in the white active area. For a single data series like the one in our example, you can use the Value Shading, Dot Density, and Graduated Symbols formats. The latter two formats are shown in Figure 19-8, using the same sample data.

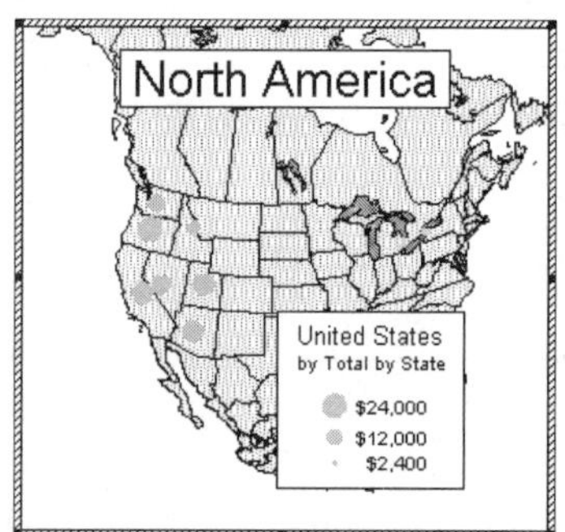

FIGURE 19-8 The Dot Density format on the left shows concentration. The Graduated Symbol format on the right shows relative size.

Both the Dot Density and the Graduated Symbol formats are useful when creating maps showing geographic concentrations. Each dot in a Dot Density map represents a fixed amount; more dots are added to represent a higher value in a geographic region. Each geographic region in a Graduated Symbol map is represented by a single symbol. Each symbol is sized proportionally according to the region's corresponding value.

NOTE If your source data includes a column of five-digit postal codes, the Data Map add-in automatically scans this column and positions the dots or symbols accordingly.

The Category Shading format is a bit different, in that it is designed to group geographic regions into subgroups that share a common characteristic. You could try using the Category Shading format button on our example map, but in this case it wouldn't make much sense. Because each state in our data table has a unique sales total associated with it, each state becomes a different category. But when our sample data includes a column listing the name of the sales representative for that state, we can create a map showing each representative's sales region, as shown in Figure 19-9.

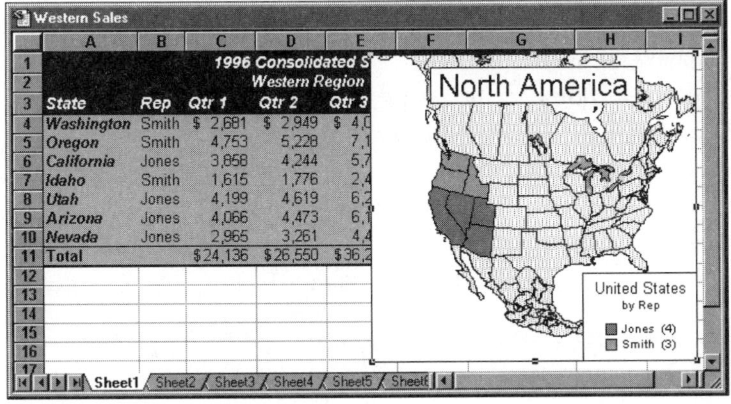

FIGURE 19-9
We added a Rep column and used the Category Shading format to show sales representatives' regions.

Changing the Look of a Map

So far, our sample map looks a little silly with only seven states active on a big North American map. But we can customize the map to feature the Western region a little more closely. The Data Map toolbar shown in Figure 19-10 on the next page includes several buttons we can use.

You use the Grabber button to drag the map around inside the object box, as if you were sliding a piece of paper around inside a frame to position it for cropping. The Select Objects button is active when you first start the Data Map add-in. You use it to reposition titles and legends by dragging, and to resize titles, legends, and the map object box itself using objects' selection handles.

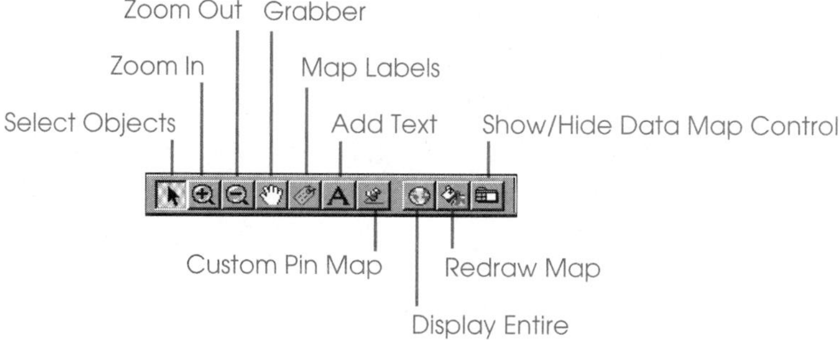

FIGURE 19-10

Control the display of the Data Map toolbar using the Toolbar command on the Data Map add-in's View menu.

The Zoom In button works in two ways. When you click the Zoom In button and then click somewhere on the map, the view enlarges 200%, centered on the point on the map where you click. (The Zoom Out button works in exactly the opposite fashion.) If you click the Zoom In button and then drag an outline around the area you want to enlarge, however, the area you outline fills the map object box as closely as it can, depending on the relative proportions of the map object box and the shape of outline box you drag. To create a better fit for the region you want to zoom in on, you can change the shape of the object box by dragging the handles that appear at the corners and at the middle of each side. You cannot drag an outline with the Zoom Out button.

Using the toolbar buttons, you can reorient the map to best display the area you want to focus on, as shown in Figure 19-11.

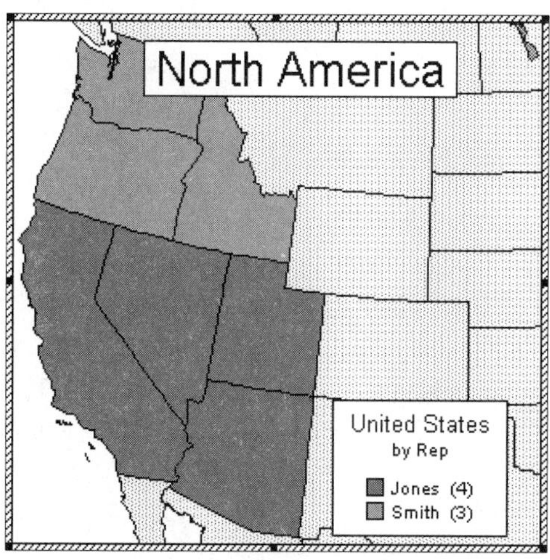

FIGURE 19-11

Change your map's point of view using the Zoom buttons and the Grabber button.

It's easy to edit the text in the title — just double-click the title object to activate it, and then edit it as you want. You can control the display of the title using the Title command on the View menu. This command is a toggle, so you can turn it on and off to try different effects. The View menu also includes the Subtitle command, which, as you might expect, adds a smaller title box beneath the title that you can also edit and display until you get the effect you want.

As shown in Figure 19-12, double-click the legend to display the Edit Legend dialog box, with which you control more than just the text content. You can change the fonts used for each element in the legend, specify whether currency format should be used for numeric values, and even specify a different title for the legend when it is displayed in "compact" format. Figure 19-12 shows the Edit Legend dialog box and the Edit Legend Entry subdialog box. Figure 19-13 shows our sample map with more meaningful titles and legend text.

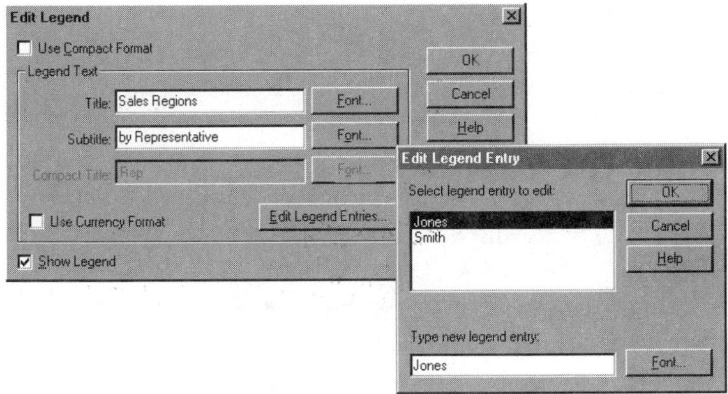

FIGURE 19-12
The Edit Legend dialog boxes offer total control over the way legends appear.

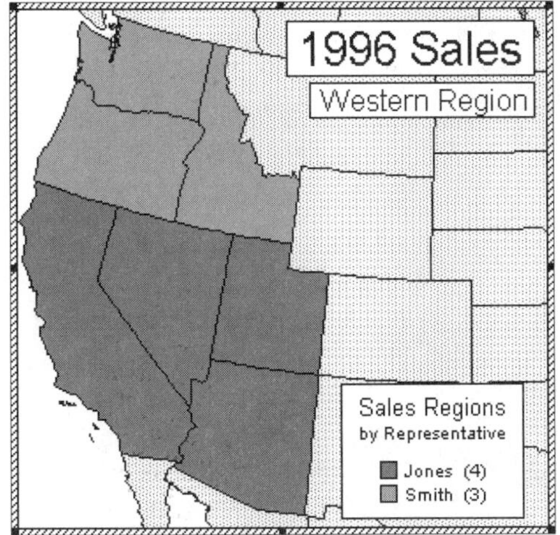

FIGURE 19-13
You can add a subtitle, edit the title, and position the titles and legend to help your map communicate more clearly.

Adding New Layers to a Map

Each row of icons in the active white area of the Data Map Control dialog box represents one map layer. You can usually add more than one layer to a data map by dragging format and column icons to a new row below the existing ones in the white area. Certain types of data can peacefully coexist in layers on a map, and others cannot. The Data Map Control dialog box is smart about this — most of the time it doesn't let you do things that don't make sense. Pairs of format symbols in the dialog box (ones adjacent to each other) cannot coexist in the same layer. Other behavior is not permitted, such as adding more than one column to the same layer in a Value Shading map. (You *can* do this, however, when you have a Pie or Column Chart format map displayed, which we'll discuss a bit later.)

TIP To remove a layer from the map, open the Data Map Control dialog box and drag the corresponding buttons in the white active area outside the dialog box.

We can get more information into our sample map in Figure 19-13 by adding an additional layer. Right now, this map uses the Category Shading format to show sales regions. We can add a separate layer using the Graduated Symbol format. To do this, click the Graduated Symbol button and drag it to the white area of the dialog box, below the existing row containing the Category Format and Rep column buttons. Next, drag the Total By State column button to the same row. After a little recalculating time, you'll see the symbols appear on the map. But they might not look like what you had in mind. So to edit the symbols, double-click the Graduated Symbols button to display the Graduated Symbols Options dialog box shown in Figure 19-14.

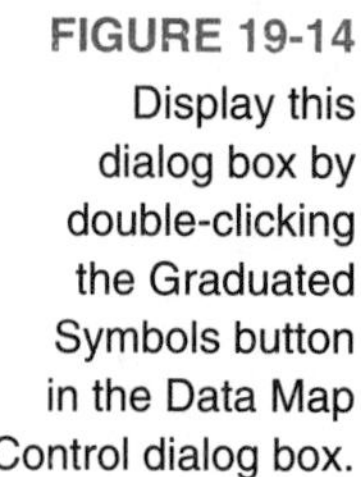

FIGURE 19-14 Display this dialog box by double-clicking the Graduated Symbols button in the Data Map Control dialog box.

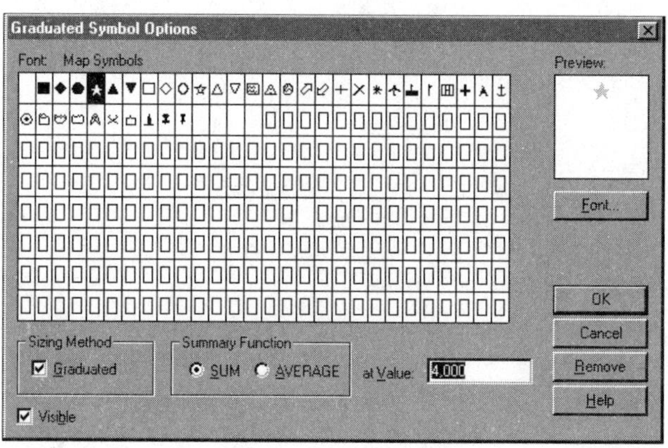

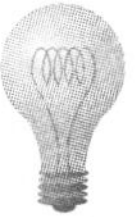

TIP Each format button in the Data Map Control dialog box has an associated options dialog box that you display by double-clicking the button. Note, however, that you can only display these dialog boxes when the format button, along with an associated column button, is in the active white area of the Data Map Control dialog box. Besides double-clicking the button, you can also display these dialog boxes by choosing commands. For each format currently active in the map, a corresponding command appears at the bottom of the Map menu.

With the Graduated Symbols Options dialog box, you can select a different symbol, change from summary calculation (the default) to averaging, switch from graduated symbols to fixed-size symbols, or remove the symbols altogether. The number in the At Value edit box is a rounded-up approximation of the highest value in the column used for the calculation. The size of symbols is determined by this number — symbols whose values match this number are the same size as the symbol you select in the dialog box. Symbols are scaled according to the relative value associated with a geographic location. If you want to make the symbols appear larger or smaller on the map, adjust the font size using the Font button. For the map shown in Figure 19-15, we selected a star symbol 36-point size from the Map Symbols font.

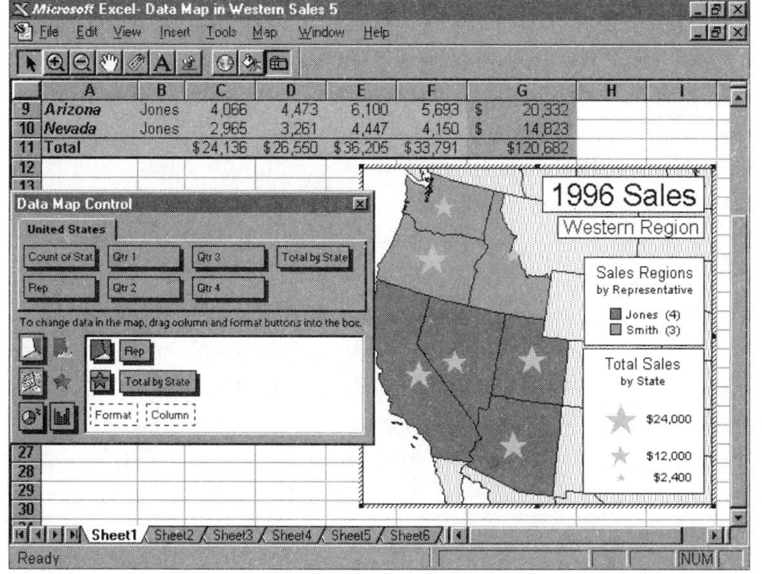

FIGURE 19-15

A Graduated Symbol format layer added to the map communicates more information in the same amount of space.

TIP Use the font size, not the At Value number, to determine symbol sizing. It's true that you can type a smaller number in the At Value box, which causes larger values to scale the associated symbol proportionately larger than the selected point size. However, each time the map is opened or recalculated, this number is reset to encompass the largest value.

You can see in Figure 19-15 that there are now two legends, one for each layer. We double-clicked the new legend to display the Edit Legend dialog box and used it to modify the text of the legend title and subtitle. We also repositioned the two legends within the map object box.

TIP To hide graduated symbols, deselect the Visible check box in the Graduated Symbols Options dialog box. When you do so, the symbols and the legend both disappear from the map, but they are easily restored by reselecting the option.

The Data Map Control Dialog Box

The Data Map Control dialog box doesn't really behave like a dialog box at all. It actually acts more like a toolbar. You can work on the map while the "dialog box" is displayed. When you switch to the worksheet by clicking a cell, the "dialog box" disappears, and then it reappears when you double-click the map to reactivate the Data Map add-in. Finally, you can resize the "dialog box" by dragging its borders.

If you drag several formats and columns into the active white area of the Data Map Control dialog box, scroll bars appear if there is not enough room to display everything. Similarly, scroll bars appear in the area at the top of the dialog box if there are too many column buttons to display at once.

Adding Map Features

If states, provinces, or countries aren't enough, you can add some additional map details, such as airports, highways, and cities. Click the Features command on the Map menu to display the Map Features dialog box, shown in Figure 19-16. This dialog box lists most of the features available for the current map. For each item, you can use a small check box to control its display. To see all the features available for all maps, click the Add button. When you choose to add a feature from the Add Map Feature dialog box, it becomes a resident of the Map Features dialog box, and its check box is automatically selected.

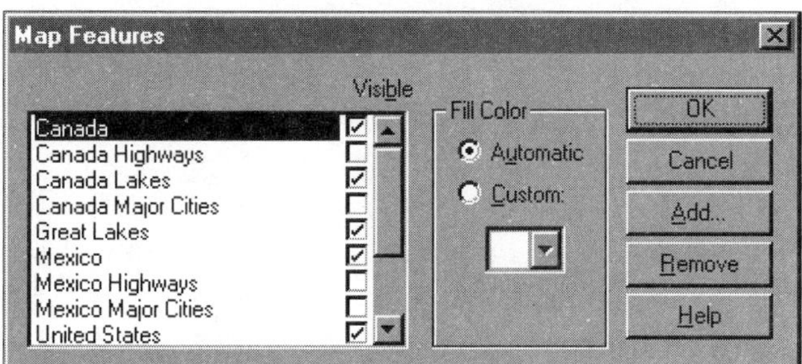

FIGURE 19-16
Use the Map Features dialog box to add more detail to a map.

For example, to add U.S. cities to a map, click the Add button and double-click the "US Cities (AK&HI Inset)" feature. The middle area of the dialog box shows the properties of the map feature. You can modify the feature's appearance by clicking the Custom option and then clicking the button below. For symbols, a dialog box appears similar to the Graduated Symbols Options dialog box shown in Figure 19-14. You can use also this dialog box to select a font for the city names.

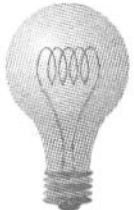

TIP Contrary to what you might expect, the various "Cities" features include many fine cities, but they do *not* include the major cities. To display symbols for all the cities available for a geographic region, select both the "Cities" and "Major Cities" features.

When you finish, symbols appear on your map, although no city names are displayed. Don't worry — this is for your own good, as you'll see. In a small map like our example, city names would be stacked up so thickly in places like Southern California that you wouldn't be able to read them at all. For this reason, the Labeler feature was created so you can choose exactly which feature names to show in your map. Click the Map Labels button on the toolbar to display the dialog box shown in Figure 19-17. (The Tools menu includes the Labeler command, which also displays this dialog box.)

FIGURE 19-17

Use the Map Labels dialog box to add selected labels to a map.

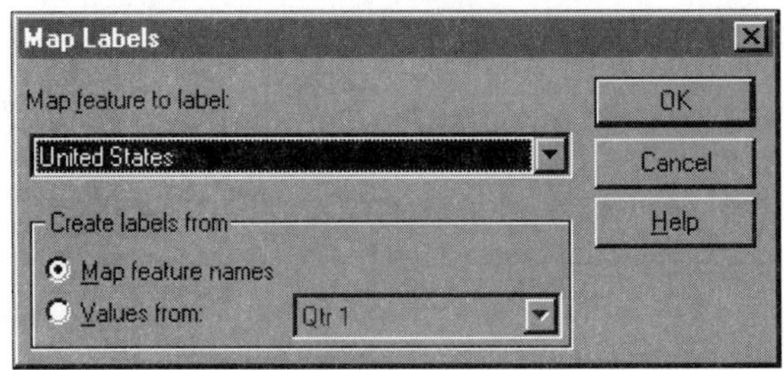

Features displayed on the current map are listed in the Map Feature To Label drop-down list. You can also add labels based on the entries in the worksheet columns, which are listed in the Values From drop-down list. Once you select a feature to label and click OK, it seems as if nothing happens to the map. But when you move the mouse pointer over a feature symbol on the map, the name of the feature — in this case, the name of the city — appears as long as the pointer stays over the symbol. If you want to affix a label to the map, click the mouse button when the label is visible. A small text object box appears containing the city name. This way, you can choose only the labels you want to add. When created, you can drag the text label to a better viewing position on the map, if necessary. Figure 19-18 shows what the map looks like with city symbols added, and then with selected labels added and symbols removed.

FIGURE 19-18

You can add or remove labels selectively, as shown on this map.

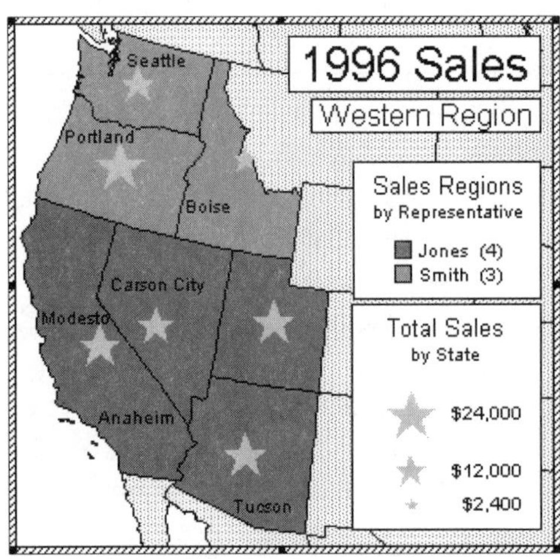

TIP If you want to add labels for more than one feature (for instance, "Cities" and "Major Cities"), you'll need to use the Labeler separately for each one.

You can copy, paste, edit, and delete labels. If labels are too long, break them into two labels. To change the font, click the right mouse button on a selected label and choose the Format Font command from the shortcut menu. If the Labeler doesn't provide exactly what you need, you can use the Add Text toolbar button to create your own labels.

TIP Be careful about adding too much to your maps. There is a fine line between good communication and "chart junk." It's better to create several separate maps that are clear and easy to understand than to cram everything into one.

Refreshing the Map

A map recalculates each time you open the worksheet, unless you turn off automatic calculation in Excel's Options dialog box (not Data Map's). Even though this recalculation occurs, the map drawing itself does not change. Instead, a small icon appears in the upper left corner of the map object, as shown in Figure 19-19, letting you know that you need to activate and refresh the map.

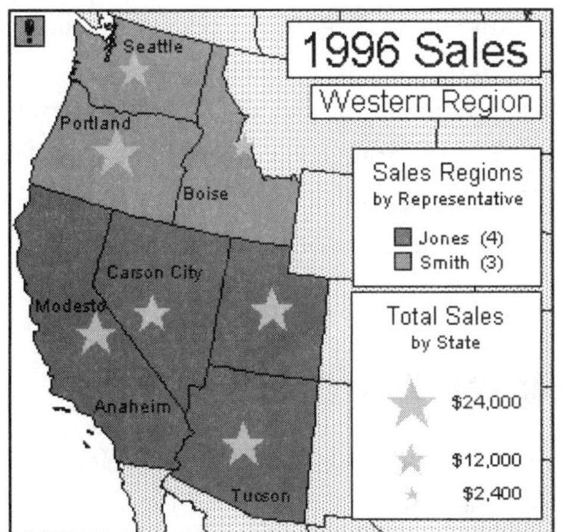

FIGURE 19-19
The exclamation-point icon in the upper left corner tells you that the map needs to be refreshed.

To refresh the map, double-click it to activate the Data Map add-in, then click the exclamation-point icon. Or you can refresh while you are editing a map by choosing the Refresh command on the Map menu. If the Refresh command is grayed, or if the exclamation-point icon is not visible, then Data Map has determined that the map is as current as it can be.

Saving the Map Template

When you've spent your hard-earned brain cells getting the map just the way you want it, you can save yourself the trouble of re-creating it next time by using the Save Map Template command on the Map menu. When you do, the dialog box in Figure 19-20 appears.

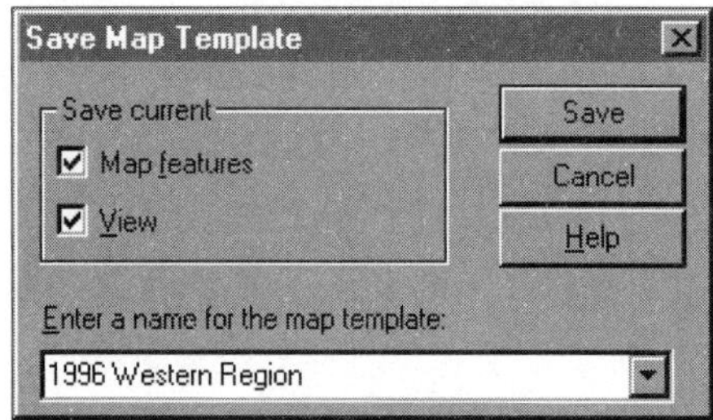

FIGURE 19-20
Save your map as a template so you can use it again as the basis for other maps.

When you save a map template, you can give it a new name that is then added to the list of available maps. For example, suppose you create and name a template similar to the United States map used in our examples. The new template name appears in the Multiple Maps Available dialog box (shown earlier in this chapter in Figure 19-2) the next time you create a map containing geographic location names that apply to this area.

Note that the overall format of the map is not saved since the type of data you select when creating the map determines the format. For example, if you save a template while a multiple-series map is displayed, the charts are not part of the template and will need to be reapplied. Only the map features you add and the current view are saved with the template.

Use the Delete Map Template command on the Map menu to remove unwanted templates.

Multiple-Series Map Formats

The Pie Chart and Column Chart formats can display multiple data series that are related in the sense of parts-to-the-whole. Using our sample data, we can add column charts that show the relative quarterly sales for each state in the map. To start with, we removed the graduated symbols from the map by dragging the Graduated Symbol button outside the white box in the Data Map Control dialog box. (When you do this, the associated column button is also removed.) Next, we dragged the Column Chart button and the four quarterly sales column buttons to the same row in the active white area of the Data Map Control dialog box. The result is shown in Figure 19-21, where we also displayed the full-sized legend and edited its title.

TIP If the Data Map Control dialog box is not currently visible, click the Show/Hide Data Map Control button on the toolbar. Click the toolbar button again to hide the dialog box.

As with all formats added to a map, a command appears at the bottom of the Map menu that allows you to choose options associated with the format. Choose the Column Chart Options command to display the dialog box shown in Figure 19-22 on the next page. (You can also double-click the Column Chart button in the active white area to display this dialog box.)

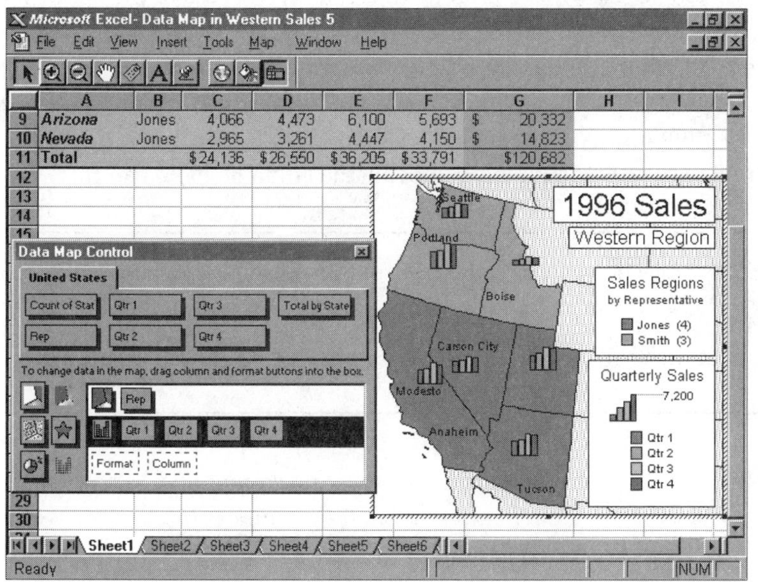

FIGURE 19-21

The Column Chart format illustrates the relative values of several columns of data in each geographic region.

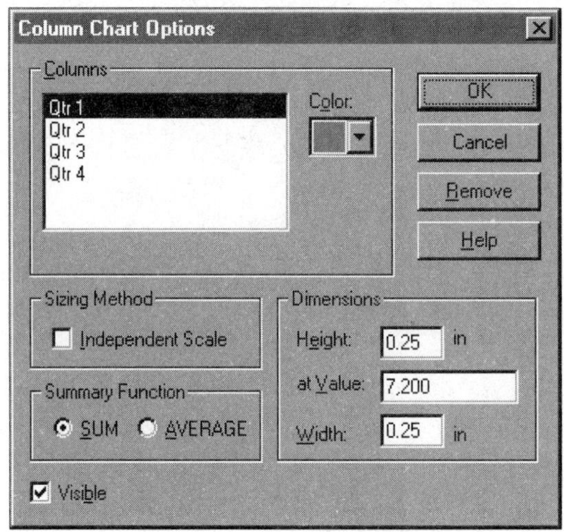

FIGURE 19-22 Double-click the Column Chart button to display the Column Chart Options dialog box.

The Independent Scale option is useful if each column button you drag into the active white area represents a different type of data. For example, you could show the number of customers per state, total sales per state, and average sale amount per customer in the same column chart. Because these are each very different units of measure, the Independent Scale option would be helpful. In our example, however, the column data are all related, so independent scaling is not recommended. The Summary Function options give you the choice of summing or averaging the data, and the Dimensions options allow you to control the size of the column charts on the map. Clicking the Remove button is the same as dragging the Column Chart button outside the Data Map Control dialog box, completely removing the column chart layer from the map.

TIP If you want to use units of measure other than inches for the dimensions options, choose the Options command from the Tools menu and select Centimeters or Millimeters. (See Figure 19-5 on page 690.)

Instead of using column charts, you can use the Pie Chart format button if your data might be better expressed in this manner. For example, you could show how each quarter contributed to the total "pie" for each state. The Pie Chart Options dialog box is identical to the Column Chart Options dialog box, except that the Height and Width edit boxes in the Dimensions group are replaced with a single Diameter edit box, and the Independent Scale check box is replaced by a Graduated check box. You use the Graduated check box to specify that the pie charts are scaled like graduated symbols — the larger the total for each geographic region, the larger the pie itself. If your data is based on percentages, such as demographic data showing the ethnic breakdown within a population, the Graduated option might not be desirable.

A Demographic Database

If you work with data that involves people, there are times you might like some perspective. For instance, if you want to gauge the potential market for a product, it might be helpful to know some details about the population in a particular area. While this sort of information is sliced and diced every way imaginable by the advertising industry, it isn't always readily available to most of us.

The Data Map add-in comes with a workbook entitled Mapstats, located in the Program Files\Common Files\Microsoft Shared\Datamap\Data folder, which contains a wealth of helpful demographic information. For example, Mapstats contains such detailed information as the total population of females between the ages of 15 and 64 in Angola, and the median household income in Wyoming. It also has worksheets containing data for the United States, Mexico, and Australia by state; Europe and the World by country; the United Kingdom by Standard Regions; and Canada by Province. One helpful aspect of the Mapstats workbook is that it is a spelling reference for all the state, province, region, and country names recognized by Data Map, along with their valid abbreviations.

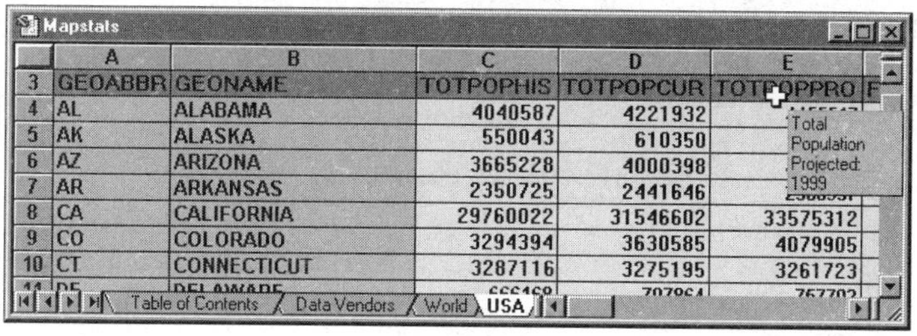
Mapstats
Total Population Projected 1999
Table of Contents
Data Vendors
World
USA

	A	B	C	D	E
3	GEOABBR	GEONAME	TOTPOPHIS	TOTPOPCUR	TOTPOPPRO
4	AL	ALABAMA	4040587	4221932	
5	AK	ALASKA	550043	610350	
6	AZ	ARIZONA	3665228	4000398	
7	AR	ARKANSAS	2350725	2441646	
8	CA	CALIFORNIA	29760022	31546602	33575312
9	CO	COLORADO	3294394	3630585	4079905
10	CT	CONNECTICUT	3287116	3275195	3261723

As you see in the illustration, you move the cursor over column titles in Mapstats to see screen tips describing the data.

Even if you can't apply this information to your work, it's fun and interesting to create data maps using the Mapstats data itself, plus it's a great tool for school projects.

Inserting Data into a Map

The Data Map add-in's Insert menu includes two commands, Data and External Data, that allow you to import data into your map that you didn't originally select when you first created the map.

TIP You can actually create a blank map by clicking the Map button without first selecting any data at all. You can then use the Insert menu commands to add data to the blank map.

When you choose the Data command from the Insert menu, the dialog box shown in Figure 19-23 appears. You can add data from any open workbook using this command. Simply type the worksheet name and cell reference into the edit box. A more foolproof method of entering the reference is to either click the sheet tab (if the data is in the active workbook) or use the Window menu to activate another open workbook, and then select the range you want to include. You can do all this while the Data Map dialog box is open. This way, the reference is automatically entered in the correct syntax. You can also use a named range instead of a cell reference. As shown in Figure 19-23, the name of the sheet is "USA," and the name of the range we want to use is also "USA."

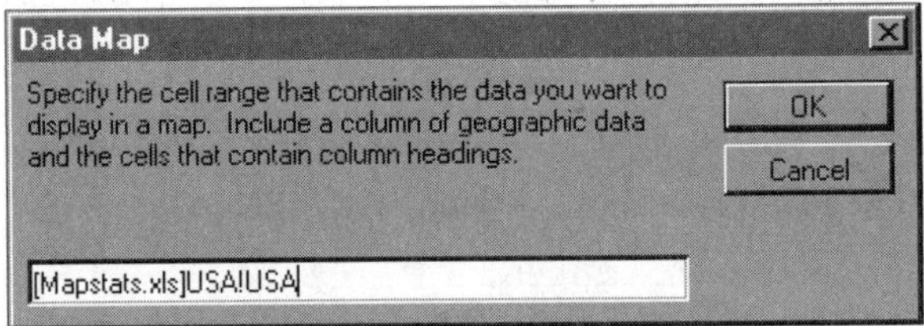

FIGURE 19-23
Use the Data command to display this dialog box, in which you enter a range or name from any open workbook.

TIP If you know the name of the range you want to add, click the sheet tab or choose the workbook from the Window menu, and then select any cell on the worksheet where the name is defined. Then simply delete the range reference and type the range name in its place.

After you indicate the new data range and click OK, a new column button is added to the Data Map Control dialog box for each column in the new range. As you can see in Figure 19-24, a scroll bar appears if there are too many column buttons to display. (In this case, we added a total of 34 new columns from the Mapstats workbook.) At the same time, the first column in the new data range is added to the map, using the format deemed most appropriate. In this case, Dot Density is the desired format, but a different column button was chosen. Also in Figure 19-24, the legend is shown expanded and edited to explain that the dots indicate total households with income over $50,000.

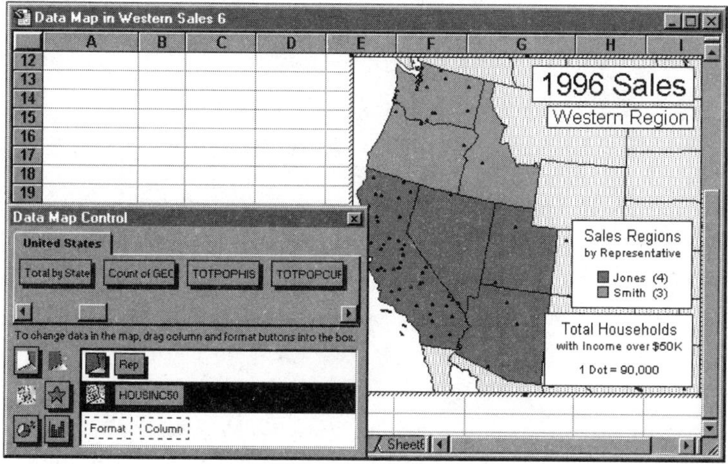

FIGURE 19-24
You can add different kinds of data from other worksheets and workbooks to a map.

The External Data command on the Insert menu performs similarly, except that instead of using open workbooks, it first presents you with the "file open" type of dialog box you use to open files created by database programs such as Microsoft Access. Note that you'll need to include a column of geographical information from your database so that the Data map add-in knows where to put the data.

Creating Custom Pin Maps

A custom pin map is like an overlay. You create a pin map using the Custom Pin Map button on the toolbar. The first time you click the button, the Custom Pin Map dialog box appears and asks you to provide a name for the pin map you are about to create, as shown in Figure 19-25 on the next page.

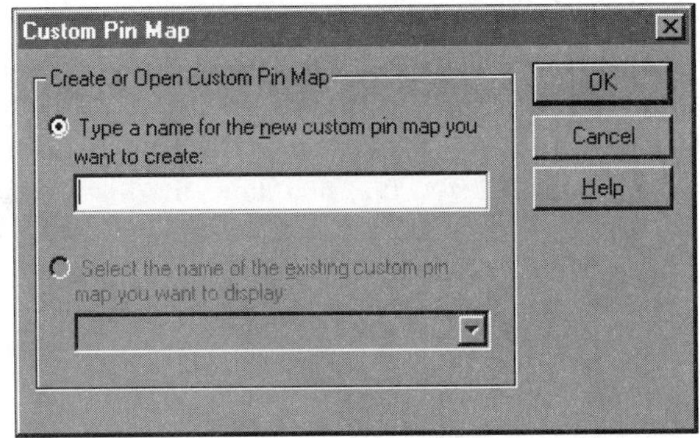

FIGURE 19-25 The Custom Pin Map dialog box is used for both creating and opening custom pin maps.

After you name the pin map and click OK, the mouse cursor changes to the "push-pin" cursor you use to add pins or other symbols to the map. Each time you click the mouse, another pin is added to the map at the place the cursor is when you click.

As soon as you add a pin to the map, type a label for it. You probably can't see it, but when you add a pin to the map, a text label box is added at the same time, to the right of the pin. If you simply begin typing while a pin is still selected, the label becomes apparent. Note that the pin symbol and label are linked so that when you drag the pin symbol, the label moves along with it. So if you want to reposition the label with respect to the pin symbol, you must drag the label's text box.

You format pins by clicking the right mouse button on the pin and choosing the Format command from the shortcut menu. In the custom pin map shown in Figure 19-26, pins and labels have been formatted so that they stand out on the map, and the titles have been edited to indicate the significance of the map.

FIGURE 19-26 Create a custom pin map to indicate special locations or points of interest.

TIP The pin images that appear when you first use the Custom Pin Map button might not look quite how you'd like them. To avoid unnecessary work, add one pin to your map, then format it immediately. Subsequent pins you add will be displayed in the same format, so you won't need to format each one individually.

The Map menu has three commands — Open Custom Pin Map, Close Custom Pin Map, and Delete Custom Pin Map — that you use to manage your pin map collection. You can create different pin maps for different purposes, and you can save them and apply them to any other maps you create.

TIP Note that you cannot open more than one pin map at a time. But if you want, you can include several different types of symbols in the same pin map. For example, you can use different symbols to indicate sales offices, distribution warehouses, and subsidiaries in the same pin map. You can format each with a different symbol, color, and label font.

Part 5

Database and List Management

Chapter 20

Managing Information in Lists

One of the tasks most commonly performed with spreadsheets is the management of lists — phone lists, client lists, task lists, lists of transactions, lists of assets and liabilities, you name it. Accordingly, Microsoft Excel, with a richer set of list-management features than any other spreadsheet on the market, makes it easy to organize and analyze this kind of information. We'll look at Excel's list-management features in this chapter and the two following chapters. In this chapter we'll also look at the Template Wizard, a new feature in Excel 7. The Template Wizard makes it easy to convert any workbook into a reusable template.

Building and Maintaining a List

To function effectively, a list should have the following characteristics:

- Each column should contain the same kind of information. In a personnel list, for example, you might devote one column to employees' ID numbers, another to their last names, a third to first names, a fourth to date of hire, and so on.
- The top one or two rows of the list should consist of labels, with each label describing the contents of the column beneath it.
- Blank rows and blank columns within the list should be avoided.
- Ideally, the list should occupy a worksheet by itself. If that's not possible, the list should be separated from any other information on the same worksheet by at least one blank row and one blank column.
- If you plan to filter your list, don't place any other information on the rows occupied by the list.

TIP Excel 7's new Shared Lists feature lets two or more users work with the same list at the same time. For details, see "Sharing Workbooks on a Network," page 77.

Figure 20-1 shows an example of a seven-column list. Notice that the column headings in the first row appear to be underscored. In actuality, we used Excel's Freeze Panes command to lock the top row so that it would remain visible as we scrolled through the list, and Excel marked the pane boundary with a rule.

If you want to underscore your headings, use the Font or Border tab of the Format Cells dialog box. (You can access this dialog box by choosing Cells

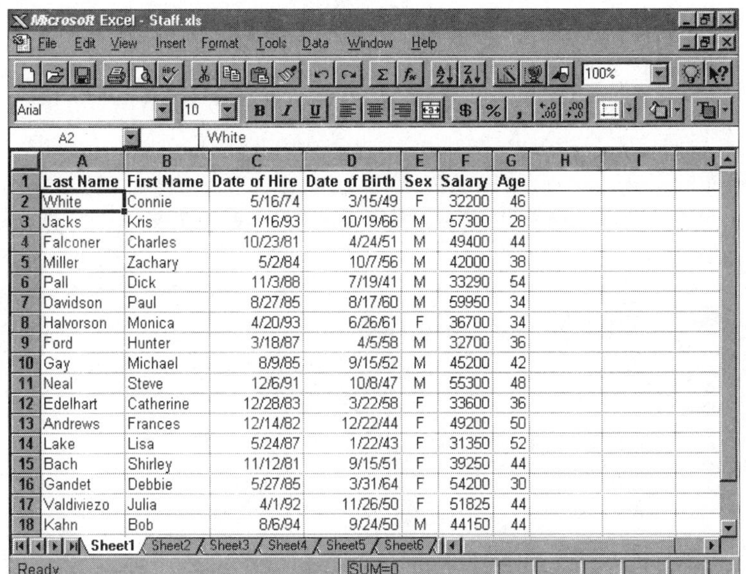

	A	B	C	D	E	F	G
1	Last Name	First Name	Date of Hire	Date of Birth	Sex	Salary	Age
2	White	Connie	5/16/74	3/15/49	F	32200	46
3	Jacks	Kris	1/16/93	10/19/66	M	57300	28
4	Falconer	Charles	10/23/81	4/24/51	M	49400	44
5	Miller	Zachary	5/2/84	10/7/56	M	42000	38
6	Pall	Dick	11/3/88	7/19/41	M	33290	54
7	Davidson	Paul	8/27/85	8/17/60	M	59950	34
8	Halvorson	Monica	4/20/93	6/26/61	F	36700	34
9	Ford	Hunter	3/18/87	4/5/58	M	32700	36
10	Gay	Michael	8/9/85	9/15/52	M	45200	42
11	Neal	Steve	12/6/91	10/8/47	M	55300	48
12	Edelhart	Catherine	12/28/83	3/22/58	F	33600	36
13	Andrews	Frances	12/14/82	12/22/44	F	49200	50
14	Lake	Lisa	5/24/87	1/22/43	F	31350	52
15	Bach	Shirley	11/12/81	9/15/51	F	39250	44
16	Gandet	Debbie	5/27/85	3/31/64	F	54200	30
17	Valdiviezo	Julia	4/1/92	11/26/50	F	51825	44
18	Kahn	Bob	8/6/94	9/24/50	M	44150	44

FIGURE 20-1

Each column in a list should contain a particular kind of information, and the first row should consist of labels describing the columns' contents.

from the Format menu.) Don't create a separate row and fill it with hyphens or equal signs because Excel might treat your "underscores" as data.

TIP Excel has a Text To Columns command that makes it easy to build lists from data stored in text files. This command is described in "Parsing Pasted Text with the Convert Text To Columns Wizard," page 894.

TIP You can use Excel's new AutoComplete and Pick From List features to simplify data entry in lists. For details, see "Let Excel Help with the Typing," page 279.

For more information about filtering, see "Using Filters to Analyze a List," page 726.

For more information about the Freeze Panes command, see "Freezing Panes," page 320.

For more information about the Format Cells dialog box, see Chapter 6, "Formatting a Worksheet," page 155.

Using a Form to Add, Change, or Delete Rows

You can always append new information to a list simply by moving to the first blank row below the list and typing. But you may find it easier to use Excel's Form command, which displays your list one row at a time. To use this command, select any single cell in your list and choose Form from the Data menu. Figure 20-2 shows the form display for the list illustrated in Figure 20-1.

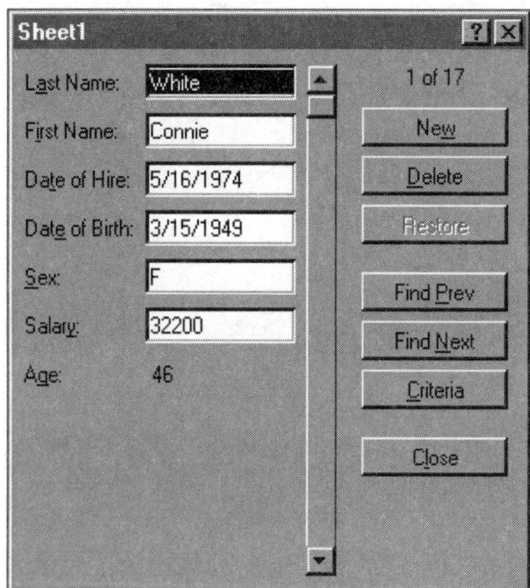

FIGURE 20-2
The Form command displays lists one row at a time.

CAUTION Be sure you have selected only one cell in the list when you choose the Form command from the Data menu. Otherwise, Excel might not present the correct column headings in the form.

TIP If you are also using Microsoft Access 7.0 (or later), you can create forms in Access to help you enter data in an Excel list. Access forms offer some advantages over the standard Excel forms. For example, you can add data-validation formulas to fields in an Access form. For more information, see the Access Links topic in the Excel Help file.

At the top of the form, Excel displays the name of the worksheet (not the workbook) that contains the list on which the form is based. Immediately below this title bar are all the list's column headings. If you've already entered some rows in your list, you'll see the entries for your first row of data alongside the column headings.

In the upper right corner of the form is a notation that tells you which row is currently displayed and how many rows the list contains. Notice that the headings row is excluded from this accounting. At the right side of the form are several command buttons that let you work with your list.

The form provides an edit box next to each column heading, unless the column contains values calculated by formulas. In our example, the values in the Age column are calculated by formulas, so the Age heading does not have an edit box.

To add a new row to your list, click the New button. Excel displays a blank form, in which you can enter the values for your new row. To add another new row, click New again; to return to the worksheet, click Close.

Naming a List

If you assign the name Database to your entire list (including the column headings) and use the Form command's New button to add rows to the list, Excel automatically adjusts the definition of the name Database to include the new rows. Excel does not automatically adjust the definitions of any names other than *Database,* however.

Assigning a name to a list and updating the definition of that name as the list grows can be very useful. Among other things, you can then use worksheet formulas based on the INDEX function to reference particular values in the list. For example, the formula

```
=INDEX(Database,ROWS(Database),2)
```

would give you the last value in column 2 of a list named Database. The formula

```
=MAX(INDEX(Database,2,3):INDEX(Database,
ROWS(Database),3))
```

would report the highest value in column 3, and so on.

For more information about the INDEX function, see Chapter 11, "Common Worksheet Functions," page 397.

When you add new rows to your list with the Form command, Excel expands the list downward without affecting any cells outside the list. If expanding the list will overwrite existing data, Excel alerts you that the list cannot be expanded.

To change a value in the list (other than a value that results from a formula), use the scroll bar in the Form dialog box to move to the row that contains the value you want to change and then make your changes in the appropriate edit box. To delete a row in the list, use the scroll bar to move to that row and then click Delete. You cannot undo deletions made in the Form dialog box, so Excel displays a confirmation prompt when you click the Delete button.

See Also For information about using the Form command as a tool for finding particular rows in your list, see the sidebar titled "Using a Form to Find List Information," page 744.

Sorting Lists and Other Ranges

Excel provides numerous ways to sort worksheet ranges regardless of whether Excel considers those ranges to be lists. You can sort by rows or columns, in ascending or descending order, and with capitalization considered or ignored. (When you sort by rows, the rows of your list are rearranged, while the columns remain in the same order. When you sort by columns, the opposite kind of rearrangment occurs.) You can even define custom sorting sequences so that, for example, your company's division names always appear in the order North, South, East, and West, rather than in alphabetic order. And issuing a sort command is easy in Excel.

A Simple Example

To sort a list, start by selecting one cell anywhere in the list. Then choose the Sort command from the Data menu. Excel examines your data to determine the extent of the list, makes a judgment about whether the list includes a heading row that should not be sorted, and then displays the Sort dialog box.

To demonstrate how the Sort command works, we'll use the unsorted list shown in Figure 20-3. To sort this list by recipient, select any single cell (not a range of cells) in the list, and then choose Sort from the Data menu. Excel responds with the dialog box shown in Figure 20-4.

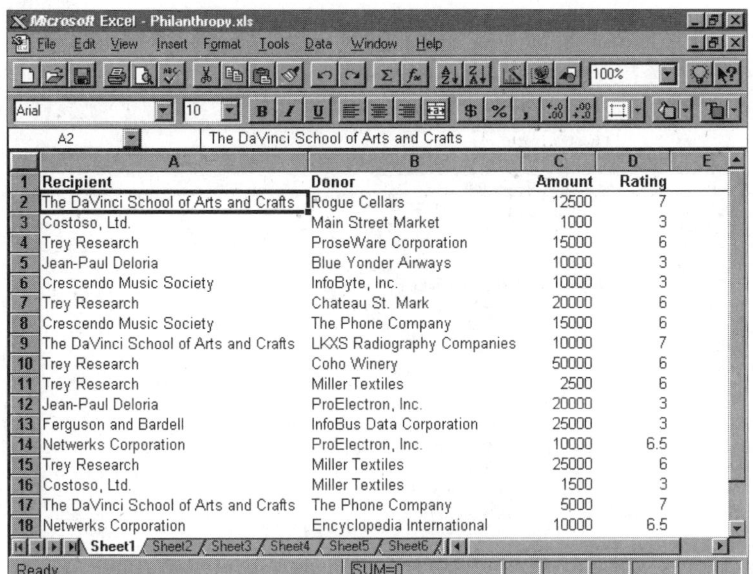

	A	B	C	D	E
1	Recipient	Donor	Amount	Rating	
2	The DaVinci School of Arts and Crafts	Rogue Cellars	12500	7	
3	Costoso, Ltd.	Main Street Market	1000	3	
4	Trey Research	ProseWare Corporation	15000	6	
5	Jean-Paul Deloria	Blue Yonder Airways	10000	3	
6	Crescendo Music Society	InfoByte, Inc.	10000	3	
7	Trey Research	Chateau St. Mark	20000	6	
8	Crescendo Music Society	The Phone Company	15000	6	
9	The DaVinci School of Arts and Crafts	LKXS Radiography Companies	10000	7	
10	Trey Research	Coho Winery	50000	6	
11	Trey Research	Miller Textiles	2500	6	
12	Jean-Paul Deloria	ProElectron, Inc.	20000	3	
13	Ferguson and Bardell	InfoBus Data Corporation	25000	3	
14	Netwerks Corporation	ProElectron, Inc.	10000	6.5	
15	Trey Research	Miller Textiles	25000	6	
16	Costoso, Ltd.	Miller Textiles	1500	3	
17	The DaVinci School of Arts and Crafts	The Phone Company	5000	7	
18	Netwerks Corporation	Encyclopedia International	10000	6.5	

FIGURE 20-3
This list is now unsorted. We'll use the Sort command to sort it by recipient.

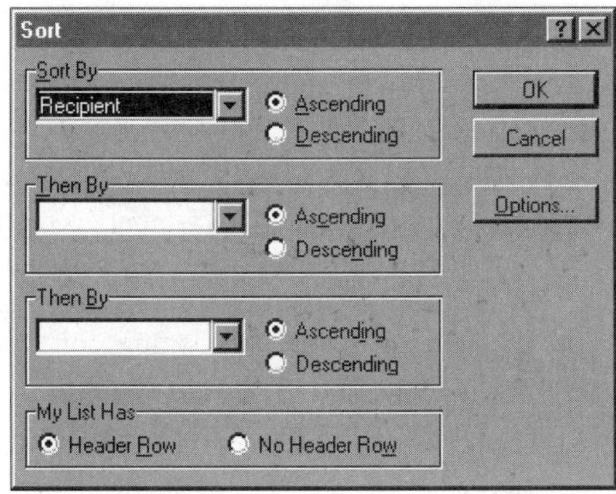

FIGURE 20-4
You can use the options in the Sort dialog box to tell Excel how you want your list sorted.

In the Sort By drop-down list box, make sure Recipient, the heading for the column on which you want to sort the list, is selected. To sort in ascending order (that is, A before Z and 1 before 2), leave the Ascending option selected. To sort in the opposite order, select the Descending option. Be sure the Header Row option at the bottom of the Sort dialog box is selected and then click OK. Excel reorders the list, as shown in Figure 20-5 on the next page. Notice that because the Header Row option was selected, the column headings were not included in the sort. Instead, the headings remain at the top of the list after the sort is performed.

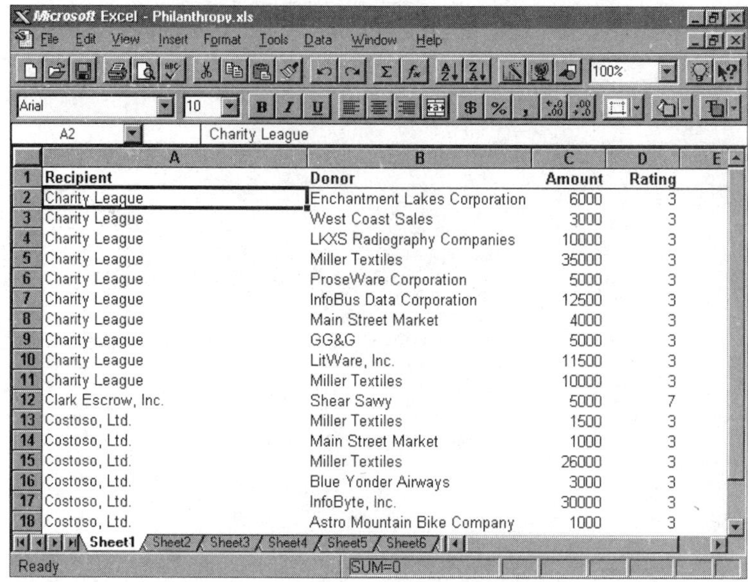

	A	B	C	D
1	Recipient	Donor	Amount	Rating
2	Charity League	Enchantment Lakes Corporation	6000	3
3	Charity League	West Coast Sales	3000	3
4	Charity League	LKXS Radiography Companies	10000	3
5	Charity League	Miller Textiles	35000	3
6	Charity League	ProseWare Corporation	5000	3
7	Charity League	InfoBus Data Corporation	12500	3
8	Charity League	Main Street Market	4000	3
9	Charity League	GG&G	5000	3
10	Charity League	LitWare, Inc.	11500	3
11	Charity League	Miller Textiles	10000	3
12	Clark Escrow, Inc.	Shear Sawy	5000	7
13	Costoso, Ltd.	Miller Textiles	1500	3
14	Costoso, Ltd.	Main Street Market	1000	3
15	Costoso, Ltd.	Miller Textiles	26000	3
16	Costoso, Ltd.	Blue Yonder Airways	3000	3
17	Costoso, Ltd.	InfoByte, Inc.	30000	3
18	Costoso, Ltd.	Astro Mountain Bike Company	1000	3

FIGURE 20-5

After an ascending sort on the Recipient column, the list shown in Figure 20-3 looks like this.

TIP Check the result of a sort immediately. If you don't like what you see, use the Undo command on the Edit menu to restore the previous order.

If you want to be able to restore the previous order of a list after several sort operations, create a row-number column before you perform the first sort. Simply add a new column to the list and fill that column with a numeric sequence. Then, to restore the previous order after sorting, sort again on the row-number column.

Sorting on More Than One Column

In our simple example, we sorted the list shown in Figure 20-3 on just one column, the Recipient column. We now have rows grouped by recipient, and the recipients are in alphabetical order. But within each group, the rows are in no meaningful sequence.

Suppose we had wanted the recipients in ascending alphabetical order, and within each recipient group, the amount values in descending order. To produce this arrangement, we would have to sort on two separate columns:

the Recipient and Amount columns. Figure 20-6 shows the resulting Sort dialog box, and Figure 20-7 shows the list after the two-column sort was performed.

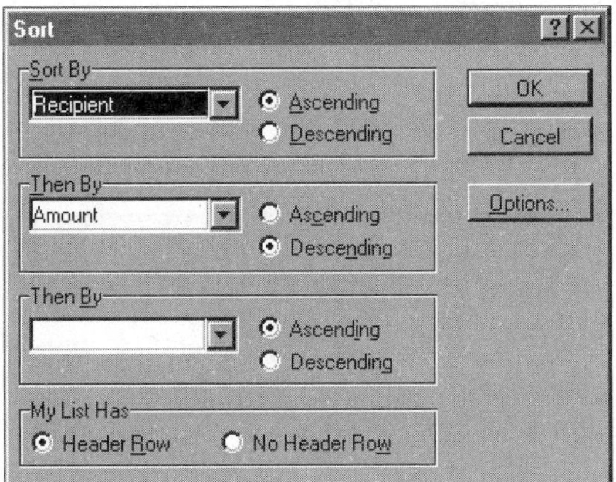

FIGURE 20-6

To sort on two columns, we supplied the names of the column headings in the Sort By and Then By drop-down list boxes.

We could even specify a third sort column in the Sort dialog box. For example, by entering the Donor heading in the second Then By drop-down list box, we could ensure that any rows with duplicate recipient and amount values will appear in ascending (or descending) alphabetic order.

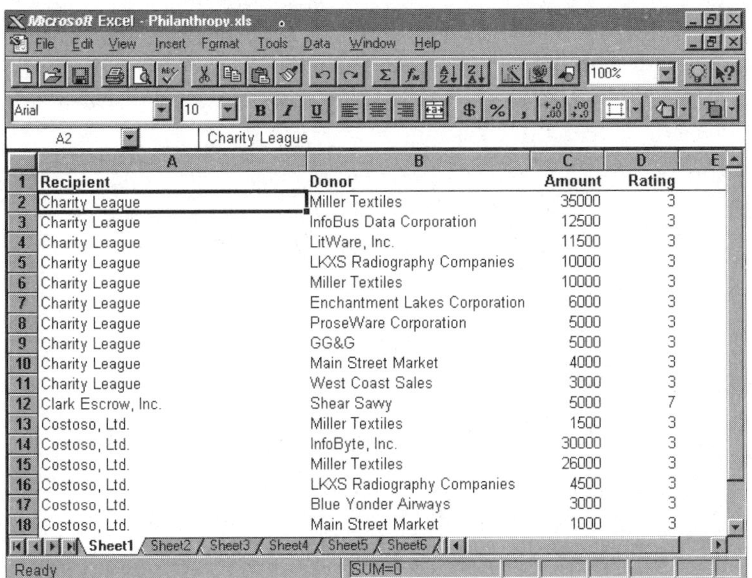

	Recipient	Donor	Amount	Rating
2	Charity League	Miller Textiles	35000	3
3	Charity League	InfoBus Data Corporation	12500	3
4	Charity League	LitWare, Inc.	11500	3
5	Charity League	LKXS Radiography Companies	10000	3
6	Charity League	Miller Textiles	10000	3
7	Charity League	Enchantment Lakes Corporation	6000	3
8	Charity League	ProseWare Corporation	5000	3
9	Charity League	GG&G	5000	3
10	Charity League	Main Street Market	4000	3
11	Charity League	West Coast Sales	3000	3
12	Clark Escrow, Inc.	Shear Sawy	5000	7
13	Costoso, Ltd.	Miller Textiles	1500	3
14	Costoso, Ltd.	InfoByte, Inc.	30000	3
15	Costoso, Ltd.	Miller Textiles	26000	3
16	Costoso, Ltd.	LKXS Radiography Companies	4500	3
17	Costoso, Ltd.	Blue Yonder Airways	3000	3
18	Costoso, Ltd.	Main Street Market	1000	3

FIGURE 20-7

A sort on two columns produced this list. The recipients are in ascending alphabetic order. Within each group of identical recipients, the rows are sorted by Amount in descending numeric order.

TIP To find out the sum, average, count, maximum, or minimum of any group of entries in a list, simply select those entries. Excel displays in the status bar the number you're interested in. For example, if you select cells C2:C11 in figure 20-5, the status bar reports "SUM=10200". To see the average or count instead, right-click the status bar and choose from the list that appears.

Sorting on More Than Three Columns

Excel allows you to sort a worksheet on up to three columns at once, and in most applications that's plenty. If you should ever need to sort on more than three columns, you can do so by performing successive single-column or multiple-column sorts. Simply sort the least important column first, repeat the sort on the next-least important column, and so on.

Sorting Only Part of a List

If you select a single cell before choosing the Sort command, Excel scans the area surrounding the selected cell, highlights the entire contiguous range of cells, and assumes you want to sort that entire range. If you want to sort only part of a list (a subset of a contiguous range), select only those rows and columns you want to sort. Then choose the Sort command from the Data menu. To sort rows 10 through 20 in Figure 20-3 (on page 719), for example, you would start by selecting A10 through D20.

Note that you can't specify a sort range in the Sort dialog box; you must select the range before you open the dialog box. Also note that the dialog box itself doesn't indicate what Excel is about to sort. Check your worksheet immediately after a sort and use the Undo command if you don't like what you get.

CAUTION Be sure to select all columns when you're sorting part of a list by rows. In Figure 20-3, if you selected A10 through B17 instead of A10 through D17, Excel would rearrange the rows in the first two columns and leave the rows in the third and fourth columns alone. The result would be a scrambled list.

The Header Row Option

Whether you ask Excel to sort a complete list or only part of a list, the program always looks for a row of column-heading labels at the top of the sort area. If Excel finds such a row, the Header Row option in the My List Has section of the Sort dialog box is selected by default. If you accept this default, Excel sorts the body of your list without moving the column headings.

To determine whether your list includes column headings, Excel examines the top two rows of the list. If the first row differs from the second in terms of data type, font, underscoring, alignment, or capitalization, Excel assumes the first row is a header. If the first and second rows are alike in these respects, Excel compares the second row with the third. If those rows differ, the first two rows are assumed to be headers and both are excluded from the sort.

The upshot of this is that in nearly all cases, Excel will correctly determine whether or not it should include the top one or two rows in the sort. Just to be sure the program doesn't let you down, though, it's a good idea to verify the options at the bottom of the Sort dialog box.

Sorting by Columns

All the examples presented so far have been sorted by row, or top to bottom. That is, we've rearranged the rows of a list, while leaving the order of the columns alone. Excel also allows you to sort by columns, while leaving the order of the

Watch Out for Formulas!

When you sort lists and ranges, watch out for cells that contain formulas.

If you sort by row (top to bottom), references to other cells in the same row will be correct after the sort. References to cells in *other* rows of the list will no longer be correct after the sort.

Similarly, if you sort by column (left to right), references to other cells in the same columns will be correct after the sort. References to cells in other columns will no longer be correct after the sort.

The following before-and-after illustrations demonstrate the shortcomings of sorting lists and ranges that contain formulas. Row 5 of the worksheet calculates the year-to-year change in profit, using relative-reference formulas. Cell C5, for example, uses the formula =C4–B4 to calculate the difference between 1990's profit and 1991's.

Watch Out for Formulas!

Microsoft Excel - Revenue and Expenses, 1990 - 1994.xls

C5 =C4-B4

	A	B	C	D	E	F
1		1990	1991	1992	1993	1994
2	Revenue	$97,000	$102,000	$107,000	$119,000	$128,000
3	Expenses	$42,000	$ 50,000	$ 52,000	$ 63,000	$ 67,000
4	Profit	$55,000	$ 52,000	$ 55,000	$ 56,000	$ 61,000
5	Y/Y Change		$ (3,000)	$ 3,000	$ 1,000	$ 5,000

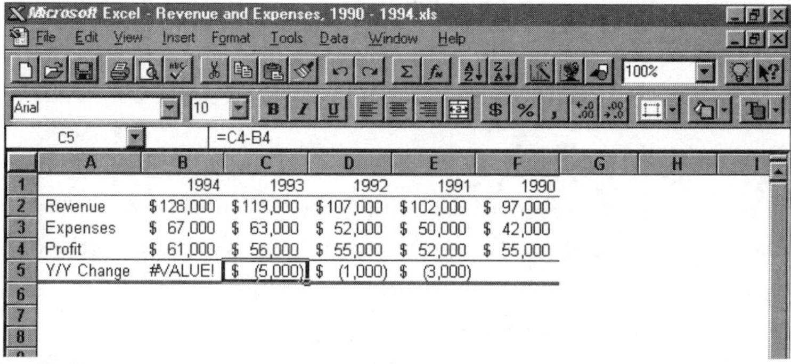

Microsoft Excel - Revenue and Expenses, 1990 - 1994.xls

C5 =C4-B4

	A	B	C	D	E	F
1		1994	1993	1992	1991	1990
2	Revenue	$128,000	$119,000	$107,000	$102,000	$ 97,000
3	Expenses	$ 67,000	$ 63,000	$ 52,000	$ 50,000	$ 42,000
4	Profit	$ 61,000	$ 56,000	$ 55,000	$ 52,000	$ 55,000
5	Y/Y Change	#VALUE!	$ (5,000)	$ (1,000)	$ (3,000)	

After sorting by column, the formula in C5 is still =C4–B4, but it's now incorrect! To continue reporting year-to-year changes, C5 would have to contain the formula =C4–D4. The other formulas in row 5 are also incorrect.

To avoid the problems associated with sorting lists and ranges that contain formulas, observe the following rules:

- In formulas that depend on cells outside the list, use only absolute references.
- When sorting by row, avoid formulas that reference cells in other rows.
- When sorting by column, avoid formulas that reference cells in other columns.

rows alone. To sort by columns, click the Options button in the Sort dialog box and select the Sort Left To Right option. Figure 20-8 and Figure 20-9 show a worksheet before and after a left-to-right sort.

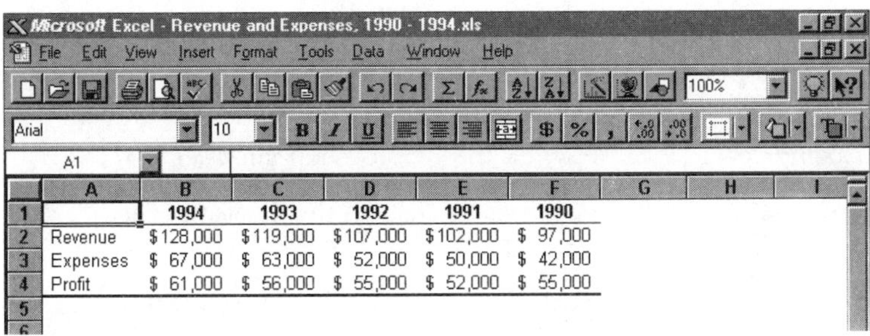

FIGURE 20-8
A simple financial worksheet.

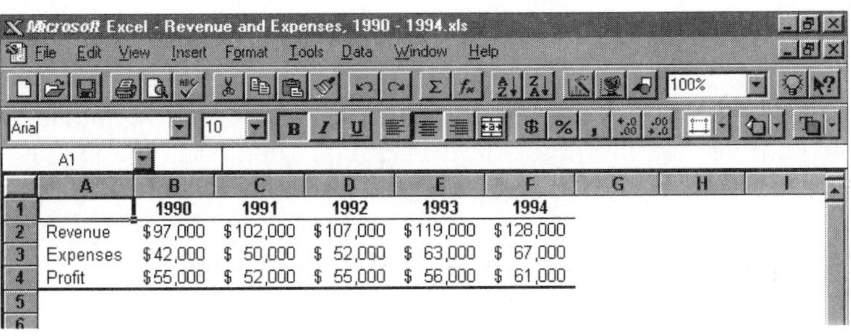

FIGURE 20-9
We used the Sort Left To Right option to reorder the years on the financial worksheet.

When performing a column, or left-to-right, sort, you should start by selecting all the data you want to sort. If you select a single cell in the worksheet shown in Figure 20-8, Excel will propose to sort everything in the worksheet, including the labels in column A. (In other words, Excel doesn't recognize row headings in column-oriented sorts.)

Creating and Using Custom Sort Orders

Excel doesn't limit you to the standard sorting sequence. If you want a set of labels to be sorted in a particular nonalphabetic order, you can define a custom sorting series. Excel has already defined the days of the week and the months of the year as custom sort orders, as you can see by choosing the Sort command, clicking the Options button, and opening the First Key Sort Order drop-down list box.

To create a new custom sort order, follow these steps:

1. Choose the Options command from the Tools menu and click the Custom Lists tab.
2. Select NEW LIST from the Custom Lists list.
3. In the List Entries section of the dialog box, type the items of your list in the order you want them sorted, placing each item on a new line or using commas to separate the items. Then click OK.

To delete a custom list, select the list on the Custom Lists tab and click the Delete button.

The items in your custom list can include spaces. For example, you could create the following list: Pitcher, Catcher, First Base, Second Base, Third Base, Shortstop, Left Field, Center Field, Right Field, Designated Hitter. Remember to separate the items with commas or place each item on a separate line.

To use a custom list, choose the Sort command from the Data menu and click the Options button in the Sort dialog box. Then open the First Key Sort Order drop-down list box and select the list.

Importing a Custom List from the Worksheet

If the items in your custom list already appear in the desired order as text in your worksheet, you don't have to type them on the Custom Lists tab of the Options dialog box. Simply select the list before choosing the Options command from the Tools menu. Your selection will appear in the edit box at the bottom of the dialog box, and you can simply click the Import button to add the new sequence to Excel's repertoire of custom lists.

Using Filters to Analyze a List

To *filter* a list means to hide all the rows except those that meet specified criteria. Excel provides two filtering commands — AutoFilter, for simple criteria, and Advanced Filter, for more complex criteria.

The AutoFilter Command

To use the AutoFilter command, start by selecting any single cell in your list. Then choose AutoFilter from the Filter submenu of the Data menu. Excel responds by displaying drop-down arrows next to each of the column headings in your list. Clicking the arrow next to any heading reveals a list of that heading's unique values, which you can use to specify filtering criteria.

TIP If you plan to use only one column for your filtering criteria, you can eliminate the drop-down arrows for the other columns. Select the heading cell for the column you want to use and hold down the Shift key while pressing Ctrl and the Down direction key. Then choose the AutoFilter command.

Let's look at an example. Suppose that from the list shown earlier in Figure 20-7, we'd like to see only those rows in which the donor is Miller Textiles. To generate this subset, we would choose the AutoFilter command and then select Miller Textiles from the drop-down list next to the Donor heading. The result would look like Figure 20-10.

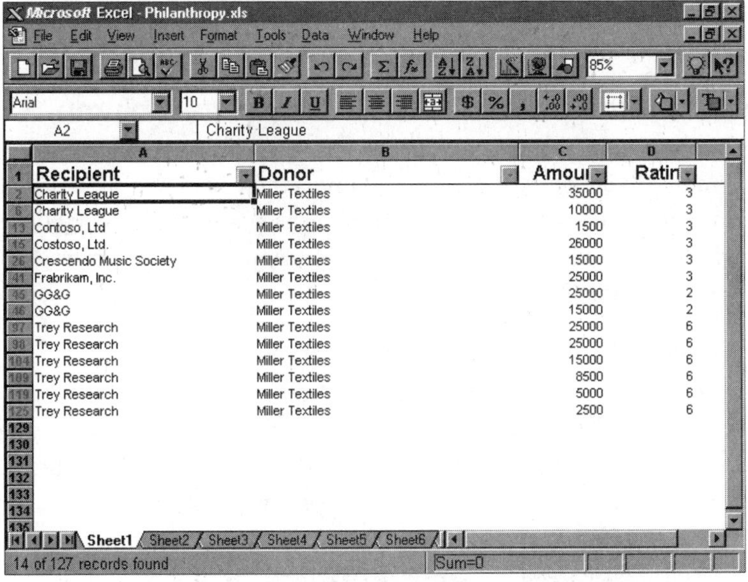

FIGURE 20-10
We used the AutoFilter command to display only those rows for which the donor is Miller Textiles.

CAUTION Because Excel creates filters by hiding rows, any data stored alongside a list might be hidden by the filtering process. Of course, you can restore this data to view by removing the filter, but it's simpler to avoid the problem altogether by placing your lists on worksheets by themselves. If you want to include other information in the same worksheet as the list, place the information above or below the list.

TIP You can use Excel's Subtotals command to analyze the rows that pass your filter. For more information, see "Using Subtotals to Analyze a List," page 743.

Notice the row-number gaps in Figure 20-10. When you use the AutoFilter command or the Advanced Filter command to display a subset of your list, Excel simply hides all the rows that don't meet your criteria. To remind you that you have filtered your list, Excel also displays the filtered row numbers in a contrasting color, and a reminder appears in the status bar.

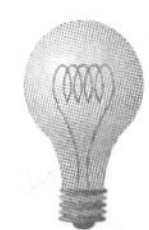

TIP When you first filter a list, Excel lets you see at a glance how many rows have met your filtering criteria. Excel displays the number of records found out of the total in the status bar.

Using AutoFilter Criteria in More Than One Column

You can specify AutoFilter criteria for your list in as many columns as you want. Simply filter your list on one column, then filter the resulting list on another column, and so on. For example, to show only the $25,000 donations made by Miller Textiles, we could open the Amount drop-down list in Figure 20-10 and select 25000.

Using AutoFilter to Find the Top Ten

You can use AutoFilter to find the top or bottom *n* items in a list, or those items that make up the top or bottom *n* percent of a column's total. Click the drop-down arrow for the column you're interested in, and then choose Top 10 from the list. Excel displays the dialog box shown in Figure 20-11.

FIGURE 20-11
Excel's Top 10 option lets you zero in on the top or bottom *n* list items.

The dialog box has three drop-down lists. In the first, you can choose either Top or Bottom. In the second, you can specify any number between 1 and 500. And in the third, you can choose either Items or Percent.

Using AutoFilter to Find Blank Cells

At the bottom of each AutoFilter drop-down list, you'll find the entries Blanks and NonBlanks. If you want to locate those rows in which a particular column has no entry, specify Blanks as your AutoFilter criterion. If you want to eliminate rows with blank entries from the filtrate, specify NonBlanks.

Using the Custom Option to Specify More Complex Criteria

The example shown in Figure 20-10 used a single equality comparison for its criterion. That is, we asked Excel to display only those rows in which the Donor column was equal to a particular value. With the help of the Custom option, you can filter on the basis of an inequality or find rows that fall within a range of values. To use the Custom option, open the drop-down list for the column you're interested in, scroll through the drop-down list, and select Custom. You'll see a dialog box similar to the one shown in Figure 20-12.

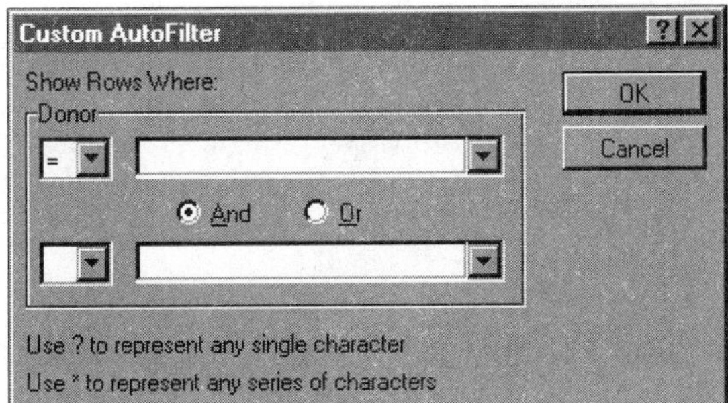

FIGURE 20-12
The Custom option lets you specify more complex AutoFilter criteria.

You can enter one or two criteria in the Custom AutoFilter dialog box, and you can select from a full range of Excel's relational operators. The small drop-down list boxes on the left side of the dialog box provide a selection of operators (=, >, <, and so on), and the large drop-down list boxes allow you to select the values that appear in your list.

Suppose, for example, that you want to see all the entries in Figure 20-7 in which the Amount value is greater than $100,000. First open the drop-down list box in the upper left corner of the Custom AutoFilter dialog box and select the > (greater-than) operator. Then open the large drop-down list box near the top of the dialog box and select 100000. (You could also type 100000 directly in the edit box.) You could also find all donations that fall within the range $50,000 to $100,000 by filling out the Custom AutoFilter dialog box, as shown in Figure 20-13 on the next page.

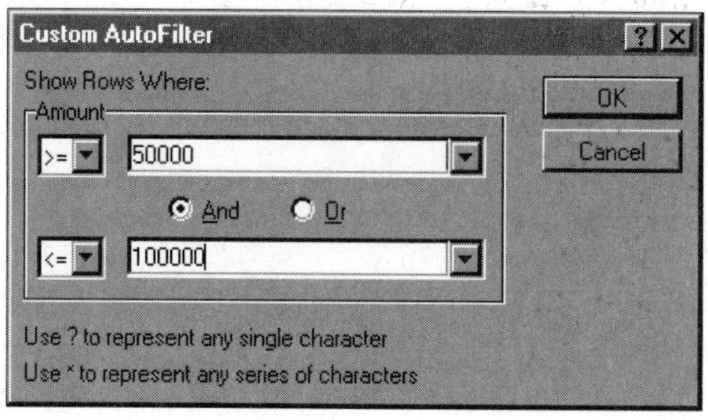

FIGURE 20-13 Filling out the Custom AutoFilter dialog box as shown here would produce a list of all donations between $50,000 and $100,000, inclusive.

Notice that we selected the And option in Figure 20-13, not the Or option. If we selected Or, our filtered list would no longer be a subset of the original list, because all donations in that list are either less than $100,000 or greater than $50,000.

Finding All Text Values Within a Particular Alphabetic Range

To find all the text values in a column that fall within a particular alphabetic range, use the AutoFilter command's Custom option and specify two criteria joined by And. For example, to find all the donors whose names begin with B, you would filter the Donor column and specify

>B

and

<C

in the Custom AutoFilter dialog box. In this case, the values B and C would probably not be found in the drop-down list boxes, so you would simply type them in the edit boxes.

Using Wildcards in Custom Criteria

As Figures 20-12 and 20-13 show, the Custom AutoFilter dialog box accepts two kinds of wildcard criteria:

- Use the asterisk character (*) as a proxy for any sequence of characters.
- Use the question-mark character (?) as a proxy for any single character.

The following table shows examples of wildcard specifications and the values that would pass through the resulting filters:

The Entry	Filters Out Everything Except
=Sm?th	Smith, Smyth
=H??t	Hart, Heit, Hurt
=S*n	Stevenson, Svenson, Smithson

Note that you can combine these wildcards in just about any imaginable way. You can even use multiple asterisks in the same criterion. For example, filtering the Recipient column of Figure 20-5, shown earlier, with the specification =*Music* would result in all rows whose recipient values include the word Music, such as Crescendo Music Society.

TIP If you want to include a literal question mark (?) or asterisk (*) in a filter, precede the ? or * with a tilde (~).

Removing AutoFilters

To remove an AutoFilter for a particular column, open the column's drop-down list and select (All). To remove all AutoFilters currently in effect from the Data menu, choose Filter and then Show All. To remove all AutoFilters and the drop-down arrows, choose the AutoFilter command again — thereby removing the check mark next to its name on the Filter submenu of the Data menu.

Copying AutoFiltered Data to Another Location

At times you might want to copy, or extract, the rows that meet AutoFilter criteria to some other part of your worksheet or to another worksheet altogether. You can copy autofiltered rows like any other type of worksheet data by using the Copy and Paste commands on the Edit menu.

If you want to extract selected rows in a single step, without having to use the Copy and Paste commands, you can use the Advanced Filter command, which is described in the next section. Note, however, that the Advanced Filter command will not automatically copy selected rows to a new file or to a new worksheet within the current workbook. To perform these tasks, you must still use the Copy and Paste commands.

The Advanced Filter Command

In contrast to the AutoFilter command, the Advanced Filter command allows you to do the following:

- Specify criteria involving two or more columns and the conjunction OR. For example, you could restrict your personnel list to all employees who are either older than 50 or earning more than $50,000. (You could also use Advanced Filter if you wanted to see rows that met both criteria, >50 and >$50,000, but it would be simpler to use the AutoFilter command twice in succession.)
- Specify three or more criteria for a particular column, where at least one OR conjunction is involved. For example, you could list the names of all employees in Division A, Division C, or Division D.
- Specify computed criteria. For example, you could list only those employees whose salaries are more than 25 percent greater than the median salary.

In addition, the Advanced Filter command can be used to extract rows from the list, placing copies of those rows in another part of the current worksheet. You can create extracts with the AutoFilter command as well, but you have to do the copying and pasting yourself. The Advanced Filter command will offer to do it for you.

Specifying a Criteria Range

The Advanced Filter command, unlike AutoFilter, requires that you specify filtering criteria in a worksheet range separate from your list. Because entire rows are hidden when the filter is executed, it's inadvisable to put the criteria range alongside the list. Instead, put it above or below the list. If you think your list may get longer over time, you'll probably find it more convenient to store the criteria above the list.

A criteria range must consist of at least two rows. You enter one or more column headings in the top row and your filtering criteria in the second and subsequent rows. With the exception of computed criteria, the headings in your criteria range must exactly match those in your list. To ensure accuracy, the best way to create these headings is by selecting the column headings in your list and then using the Copy and Paste commands on the Edit menu to paste copies of the headings into the top row of the criteria range.

Keep in mind that a criteria range does not have to include headings for every column in the list. Columns that are not involved in the selection process can be eliminated.

TIP If you use two or more sets of criteria regularly to filter the same list, it's a good idea to set them up in separate criteria ranges. Assigning names to these criteria ranges and then specifying the names, instead of the range addresses, in the Advanced Filter dialog box will make it easy to switch between filters.

See Also For more information about computed criteria, see "Using Computed Criteria," page 738.

An Example Using Two Columns Joined by OR Suppose that from the personnel list shown earlier in Figure 20-1 on page 715, you want to see the names of employees who are either earning salaries of more than $50,000 or over 50 years of age. To create this filter, follow these steps:

1. Insert some new rows at the top of the worksheet to make room for the criteria range.
2. Create the criteria range shown in Figure 20-14.
3. Choose the Advanced Filter command from the Filter submenu of the Data menu and enter the information in the Advanced Filter dialog box as shown in Figure 20-15 at the top of the next page.

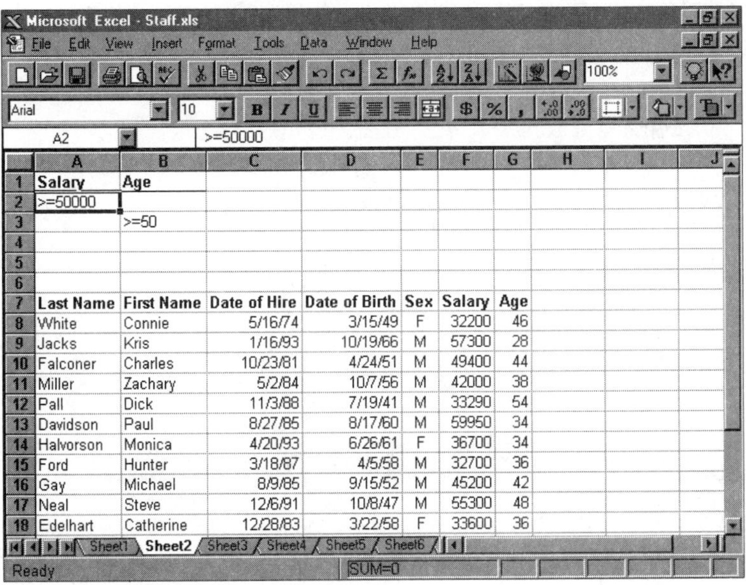

	A	B	C	D	E	F	G	H	I	J
1	Salary	Age								
2	>=50000									
3		>=50								
4										
5										
6										
7	Last Name	First Name	Date of Hire	Date of Birth	Sex	Salary	Age			
8	White	Connie	5/16/74	3/15/49	F	32200	46			
9	Jacks	Kris	1/16/93	10/19/66	M	57300	28			
10	Falconer	Charles	10/23/81	4/24/51	M	49400	44			
11	Miller	Zachary	5/2/84	10/7/56	M	42000	38			
12	Pall	Dick	11/3/88	7/19/41	M	33290	54			
13	Davidson	Paul	8/27/85	8/17/60	M	59950	34			
14	Halvorson	Monica	4/20/93	6/26/61	F	36700	34			
15	Ford	Hunter	3/18/87	4/5/58	M	32700	36			
16	Gay	Michael	8/9/85	9/15/52	M	45200	42			
17	Neal	Steve	12/6/91	10/8/47	M	55300	48			
18	Edelhart	Catherine	12/28/83	3/22/58	F	33600	36			

FIGURE 20-14
The criteria range in cells A1:B3 will filter the list to show only those employees who earn $50,000 or more or who are at least 50 years of age.

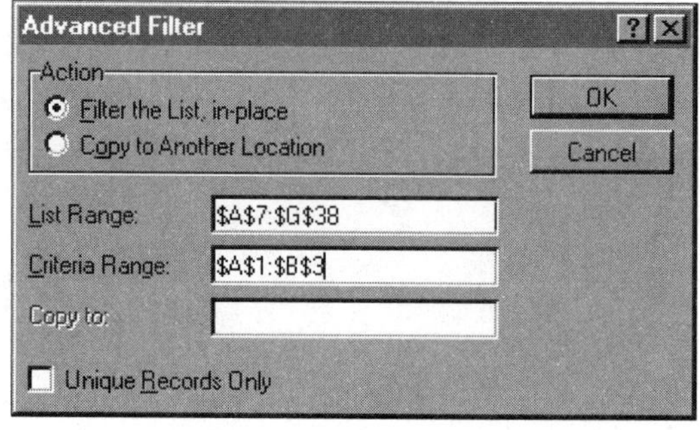

FIGURE 20-15 Enter the locations of your list and criteria range in the Advanced Filter dialog box.

4. Be sure the Filter The List In-Place option is selected and then click OK. Figure 20-16 shows the results.

Like AutoFilter, the Advanced Filter command will hide all rows that don't pass the filter. It also displays the qualifying row numbers in a contrasting color and the number of records found in the status bar.

TIP Immediately after you perform an advanced filter, the status bar reports the number of rows that have met the filtering criteria.

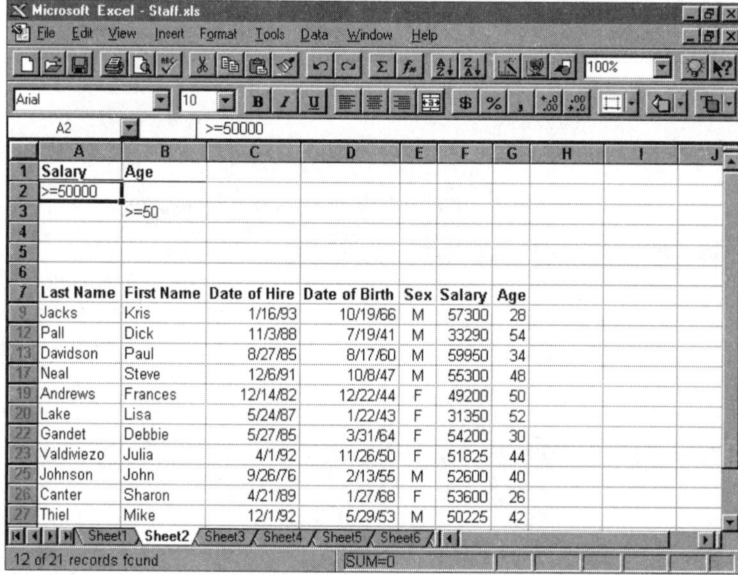

	A	B	C	D	E	F	G
1	Salary	Age					
2	>=50000						
3		>=50					
4							
5							
6							
7	Last Name	First Name	Date of Hire	Date of Birth	Sex	Salary	Age
9	Jacks	Kris	1/16/93	10/19/66	M	57300	28
12	Pall	Dick	11/3/88	7/19/41	M	33290	54
13	Davidson	Paul	8/27/85	8/17/60	M	59950	34
17	Neal	Steve	12/6/91	10/8/47	M	55300	48
19	Andrews	Frances	12/14/82	12/22/44	F	49200	50
20	Lake	Lisa	5/24/87	1/22/43	F	31350	52
22	Gandet	Debbie	5/27/85	3/31/64	F	54200	30
23	Valdiviezo	Julia	4/1/92	11/26/50	F	51825	44
25	Johnson	John	9/26/76	2/13/55	M	52600	40
26	Canter	Sharon	4/21/89	1/27/68	F	53600	26
27	Thiel	Mike	12/1/92	5/29/53	M	50225	42

FIGURE 20-16 After we created the criteria range as shown in Figure 20-14 and completed the Advanced Filter dialog box shown in Figure 20-15, Excel displayed this list.

In Figure 20-14, notice that the criteria in cells A1:B3 are entered as ordinary labels. You simply type

>=50000

under the Salary heading and

>=50

under the Age heading.

Notice also that the two criteria must be specified on separate lines. If you put both criteria on the same line, you'd be asking Excel to display only those rows where both criteria are met — that is, the rows for employees who earn more than $50,000 a year and are over 50 years of age.

You can enter as many criteria as you like in a criteria range. Excel interprets the range according to these rules:

- Criteria on the same line are considered to be joined by AND.
- Criteria on separate lines are considered to be joined by OR.

TIP When you specify a criteria range in the Advanced Filter dialog box, Excel assigns the name *Criteria* to that range. You can use this name as a navigation aid. For example, if you need to return to the range to change the criteria, press F5 and select Criteria from the Go To dialog box.

CAUTION A blank cell in a criteria range means "accept any value for this column." If you include a blank row in the criteria range, you will get an unfiltered list. To avoid this, be careful when removing criteria rows from a range. If you no longer need a row, it's not enough simply to delete the row's contents. You must also change the criteria range in the Advanced Filter dialog box to show the reduced range.

An Example Using Three ORs on a Column Now let's suppose that you want the list shown in Figure 20-1 (on page 715) to display only those employees whose names begin with A, F, or M. In this case, you would include the Last Name heading in your criteria range, and you would enter the letters A, F, and M in the three rows immediately below that heading. After you choose the

Advanced Filter command and enter the locations of the list and criteria range in the Advanced Filter dialog box, Excel displays the list shown in Figure 20-17.

An Example Using Both OR and AND What if we need the employees whose last names begin with A, F, or M and who are also at least 40 years of age? In this case, we would set up the criteria range as shown in Figure 20-18 on the next page. Notice that the criterion >=40 must be repeated in each row of the range because for each alphabetic category (A, F, and M) we want only those employees who meet two criteria — the alphabetic criterion *and* the age criterion.

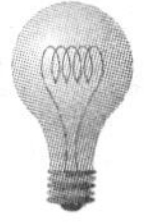

TIP Each time you use the Advanced Filter command, Excel reexamines the entire list rather than only the current filtrate. Therefore, you don't have to use the Show All command before changing the filter.

So far, our examples have involved only what are called *comparison* criteria. No computations were required. We'll give some examples of *computed* criteria in a moment. But first, we need to look more closely at the way Excel handles text criteria.

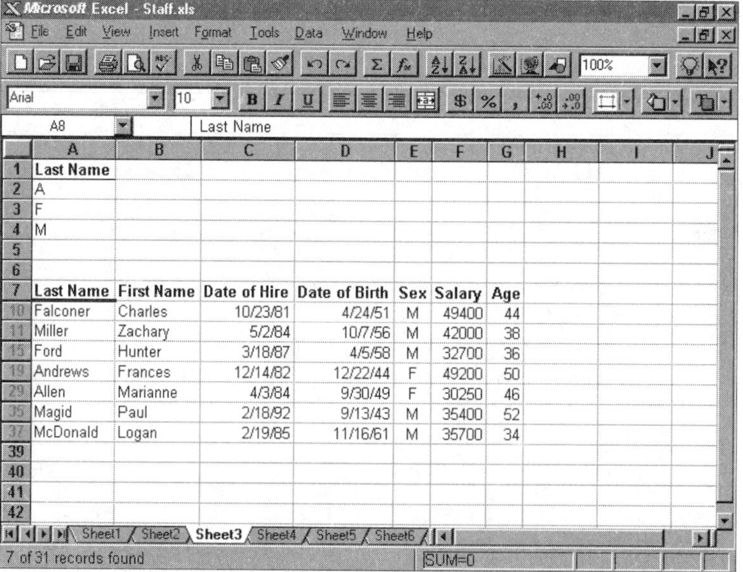

	A	B	C	D	E	F	G
1	Last Name						
2	A						
3	F						
4	M						
5							
6							
7	Last Name	First Name	Date of Hire	Date of Birth	Sex	Salary	Age
10	Falconer	Charles	10/23/81	4/24/51	M	49400	44
11	Miller	Zachary	5/2/84	10/7/56	M	42000	38
15	Ford	Hunter	3/18/87	4/5/58	M	32700	36
19	Andrews	Frances	12/14/82	12/22/44	F	49200	50
29	Allen	Marianne	4/3/84	9/30/49	F	30250	46
35	Magid	Paul	2/18/92	9/13/43	M	35400	52
37	McDonald	Logan	2/19/85	11/16/61	M	35700	34
39							
40							
41							
42							

FIGURE 20-17
Using the criteria range in cells A1:A4, we reduced the list to those employees whose last names start with A, F, or M.

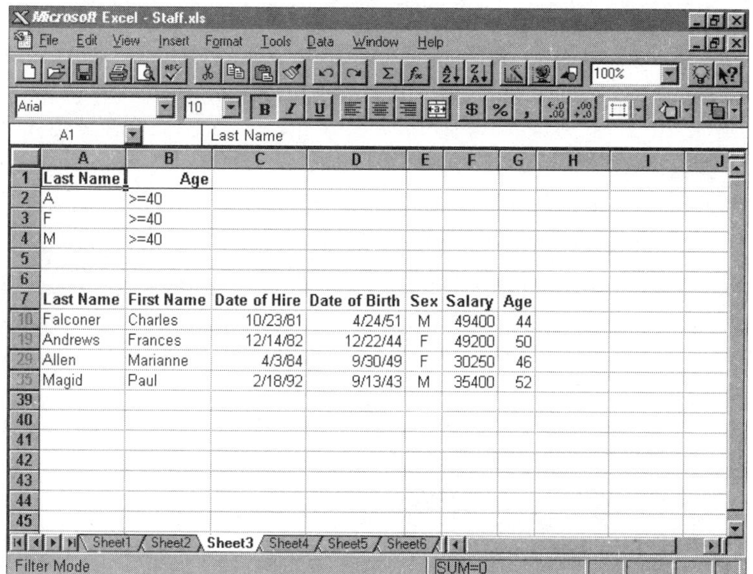

FIGURE 20-18

To display a list of employees whose names start with A, F, or M and who also belong to the over-forty set, we need to repeat the >=40 criterion in each line of the criteria range.

Specifying Text Criteria

The rules for specifying text criteria are not as obvious as you might like. The following paradigms should help you think the way Excel does:

- A single letter means "Accept any value that starts with this letter." Example: Entering M returns Mary, Martha, and Mr. Rogers.
- Greater-than and less-than symbols mean "Accept any value that falls after or before this point in the alphabet." Example: Entering >*M* under a Last Name heading returns all last names that begin with M through Z. Conversely, <M returns all last names that begin with A through L.
- The formula ="=text" means "Accept only those rows that contain the value *text*." Example: Specify *="=Smith"* to return the exact match Smith. If you specify Smith without the formula, Excel returns Smith, Smithsonian, Smithy, and so on.

Wildcards are permitted. Wildcards work the same way in an Advanced Filter as they do in an AutoFilter.

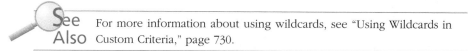

See Also For more information about using wildcards, see "Using Wildcards in Custom Criteria," page 730.

Using Computed Criteria

Computed criteria are criteria that involve any test other than a simple comparison of a column's value to a constant. Asking Excel to find employees with salaries above $50,000 does not require a computed criterion. Asking for employees with salaries greater than the median salary does.

Even experienced Excel users can get tripped up when using computed criteria. Here are three rules to help you stay on your feet:

- The column heading above a computed criterion must *not* be a copy of a column heading in the list. The criteria-range heading can be blank or it can contain anything else you like. (Note that this requirement is the exact opposite of what noncomputed criteria require.)
- References to cells outside the list should be absolute.
- References to cells within the list should be relative.

This last rule has one exception, as you'll see. Now for some examples.

Referencing a Cell Outside the List Figure 20-19 shows an advanced filter that finds all employees with salaries greater than the median salary. In setting up this filter, we first stored the formula

=MEDIAN(F8:F38)

outside the list, in cell H2. Then, in cell A2, we entered a computed criterion that references this "outside" cell. The criteria range is A1:A2, and the computed criterion formula in cell A2 reads =F8>$H$2.

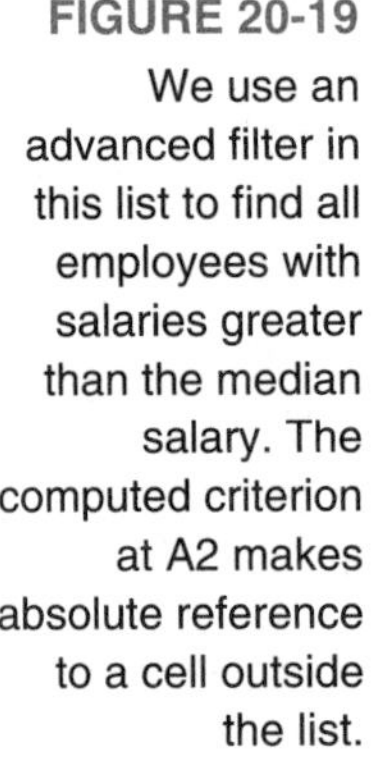

FIGURE 20-19
We use an advanced filter in this list to find all employees with salaries greater than the median salary. The computed criterion at A2 makes absolute reference to a cell outside the list.

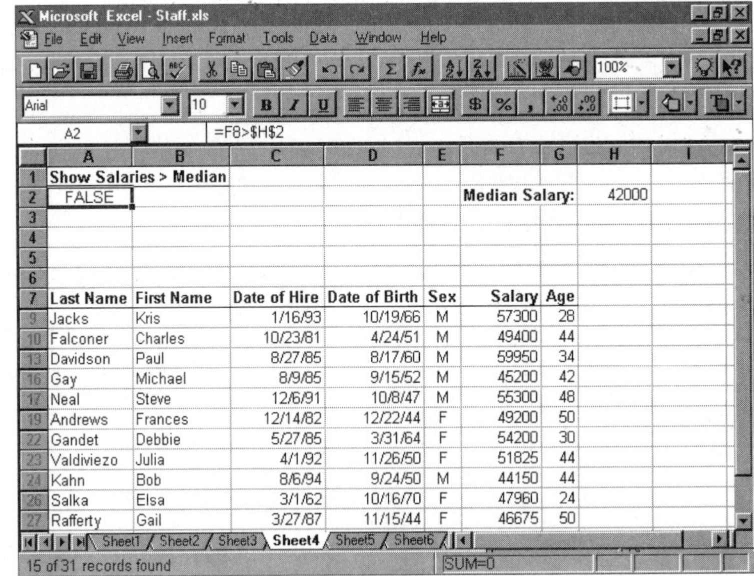

Microsoft Excel - Staff.xls
File Edit View Insert Format Tools Data Window Help
A2 =F8>$H$2
Show Salaries > Median
FALSE
Median Salary: 42000
Last Name First Name Date of Hire Date of Birth Sex Salary Age
Jacks Kris 1/16/93 10/19/66 M 57300 28
Falconer Charles 10/23/81 4/24/51 M 49400 44
Davidson Paul 8/27/85 8/17/60 M 59950 34
Gay Michael 8/9/85 9/15/52 M 45200 42
Neal Steve 12/6/91 10/8/47 M 55300 48
Andrews Frances 12/14/82 12/22/44 F 49200 50
Gandet Debbie 5/27/85 3/31/64 F 54200 30
Valdiviezo Julia 4/1/92 11/26/50 F 51825 44
Kahn Bob 8/6/94 9/24/50 M 44150 44
Salka Elsa 3/1/62 10/16/70 F 47960 24
Rafferty Gail 3/27/87 11/15/44 F 46675 50
Sheet1 Sheet2 Sheet3 Sheet4 Sheet5 Sheet6
15 of 31 records found
SUM=0

As the status bar in Figure 20-19 indicates, this filter admits 15 of the original 31 rows. In other words, just under half the employees have salaries above the median — which is exactly what you would expect.

In the previous example, note the following:

- The heading for the criteria range does not duplicate any of the headings in the list. (If it did, the filter would not work correctly.)

TIP As mentioned, the column heading in a computed criterion can be blank, or it can contain text, as long as the text is not a duplicate of any other heading in the list. If the column heading is blank, you must still include it in the criteria range when you specify the range in the Advanced Filter dialog box.

- The criterion formula compares cell F8 with cell H2. Cell F8 is the first cell in the Salary column of the unfiltered list, and the computed criterion formula instructs Excel to evaluate this first cell in the column. As Excel processes the filter, it substitutes each member of the list, in turn, for this first value; that is, Excel evaluates F8, followed by F9, followed by F10, and so on until it reaches the end of the list.
- The reference to cell H2 is absolute. In cell A2 of the criteria range, if we entered the formula =F8>H2 (that is, if we used a relative reference to H2), Excel would compare F8 with H2. Then it would compare F9 with H3, and so on. All tests except the first would be invalid.

TIP If you want to see the formula in the criteria range, open a new window and turn on the Formulas display option. (First choose New Window from the Window menu. Then, in the new window, choose Options from the Tools menu, click the View tab, and select the Formulas option.) You can size and position the two windows so that the formula remains visible while you work with the list.

- The value returned by the criterion formula itself is irrelevant. In our example, the formula returns FALSE — but only because the first employee in our unfiltered list happens to make less than the median salary.

Referencing Cells Within the List The advanced filter in Figure 20-20 subtracts the date of birth from the date of hire and compares the result against the product of 18 and 365 — to determine if any employee joined the firm before turning 18. The results returned by the filter reveal a flagrant violation of the child labor laws! (But at least she's well paid.)

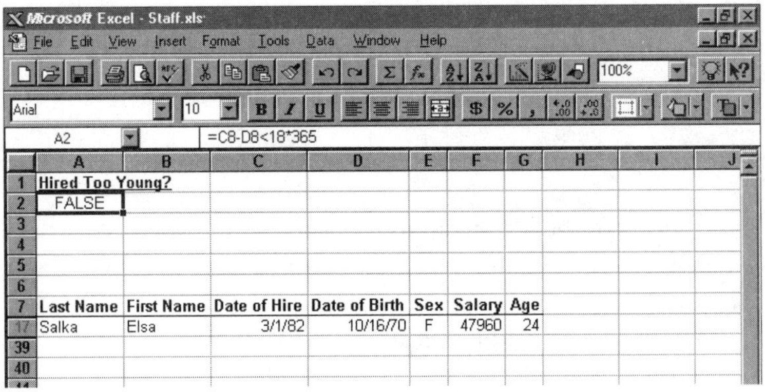

FIGURE 20-20
The computed criterion in this example uses only relative references.

The criterion formula

=C8–D8<18*365

uses only relative references because we want Excel to first subtract D8 from C8, then D9 from C9, and so on.

An Exception to the Rule Like the worksheet shown earlier in Figure 20-19, the worksheet in Figure 20-21 contains a filtered list displaying records of employees with salaries above the median. But the formula in this case,

=F8>MEDIAN($F$8:$F$38)

makes direct reference to the Salary column, rather than referencing an outside cell. According to the rules listed earlier on page 738, references to cells within the list should be relative; however, the references to cells F8 through F38 are absolute. We used absolute references because we want Excel to evaluate the same range of cells at each step of the filtering process. That is, we want Excel to compare F8 with the median of F8:F38, then F9 with the median of F8:F38, and so on. If we used a relative reference to F8:F38, only the first comparison would be valid.

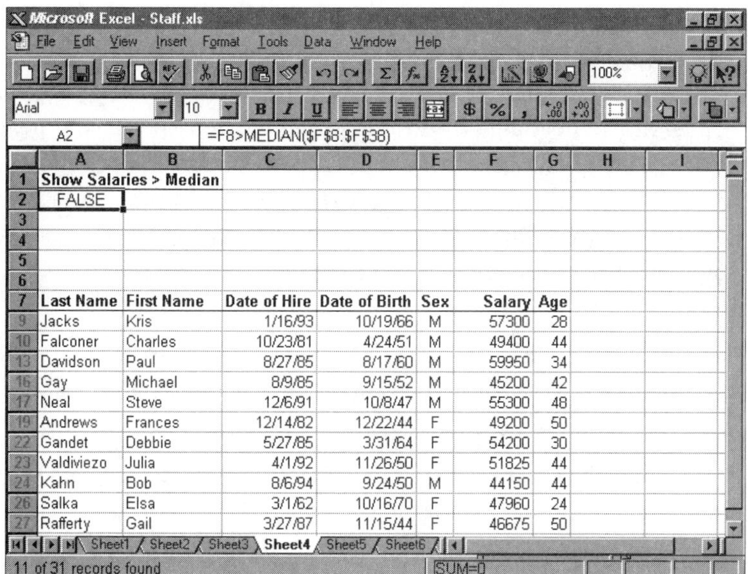

	A	B	C	D	E	F	G
1	Show Salaries > Median						
2	FALSE						
3							
4							
5							
6							
7	Last Name	First Name	Date of Hire	Date of Birth	Sex	Salary	Age
9	Jacks	Kris	1/16/93	10/19/66	M	57300	28
10	Falconer	Charles	10/23/81	4/24/51	M	49400	44
13	Davidson	Paul	8/27/85	8/17/60	M	59950	34
16	Gay	Michael	8/9/85	9/15/52	M	45200	42
17	Neal	Steve	12/6/91	10/8/47	M	55300	48
19	Andrews	Frances	12/14/82	12/22/44	F	49200	50
22	Gandet	Debbie	5/27/85	3/31/64	F	54200	30
23	Valdiviezo	Julia	4/1/92	11/26/50	F	51825	44
24	Kahn	Bob	8/6/94	9/24/50	M	44150	44
26	Salka	Elsa	3/1/62	10/16/70	F	47960	24
27	Rafferty	Gail	3/27/87	11/15/44	F	46675	50

FIGURE 20-21

References to cells within the list are usually relative. In this case, however, the reference to F8:F38 must be absolute.

Copying Filtered Rows to Another Worksheet Location

The Advanced Filter dialog box, shown earlier in Figure 20-15 (on page 734), includes an option for copying the selected rows to another worksheet location, instead of displaying a filtered list. To copy rows rather than display them, select the Copy To Another Location option in the Advanced Filter dialog box and supply the name or address of the range where you want the information to appear in the Copy To edit box.

The easiest way to specify the Copy To range is to click a blank cell in your worksheet where you want the range to start. Be sure that the cell has plenty of blank space below and to the right of it. Excel will then copy your list's column headings and all the rows that meet the advanced filter criteria to the range that begins with the cell you specified. Be careful, though: Any data already stored in the selected range will be overwritten.

TIP When you specify a Copy To range in the Advanced Filter dialog box, Excel assigns the name *Extract* to the range. You can use this name as a navigation aid. For example, when you need to return to the range to change column headings, press F5 and select Extract from the Go To dialog box.

Alternatively, if you specify a range of cells, Excel will copy the rows that pass the filter but stop when the range is full.

To copy only certain columns of your list to a new worksheet range, create copies of the headings for those columns. Then specify the headings (not only the first cell in the copied headings row, but the entire set of copied headings) as your Copy To range. For example, to filter the personnel list shown earlier in Figure 20-1 (on page 715) and copy only the Last Name, First Name, and Salary columns to the range beginning at cell A100, follow these steps:

1. Copy the Last Name, First Name, and Salary headings to A100:C100. (You can copy the headings in any order, depending on how you want your filtered data to appear.)
2. Choose the Advanced Filter command from the Filter submenu of the Data menu.
3. When the Advanced Filter dialog box appears, specify your list and criteria ranges and then type *A100:C100* in the Copy To edit box and click OK.

The Unique Records Only Option The Unique Records Only option in the Advanced Filter dialog box adds an additional filter to whatever you specify in your criteria range. It eliminates rows that are exact duplicates. (Keep in mind that the Unique Records Only option works only in conjunction with the Copy To Another Location option.)

For example, suppose that from the list shown earlier in Figure 20-7 (on page 721), you want to see the names of all recipients who have a rating of 3. You don't need to see every row in which the rating-3 recipients appear; you just want a simple list that shows each recipient once. To create this list, follow these steps:

1. Above or below the list, set up a criteria range consisting of the number 3 in the cell below the Rating heading.
2. In another, blank, region of the worksheet, enter the heading *Recipient.* The cell in which you do this is your Copy To range.
3. Choose the Advanced Filter command from the Filter submenu of the Data menu.
4. Enter the list and criteria ranges in the Advanced Filter dialog box. Select the Copy To Another Location option and the Unique Records Only option and then click OK. Figure 20-22 shows the results.

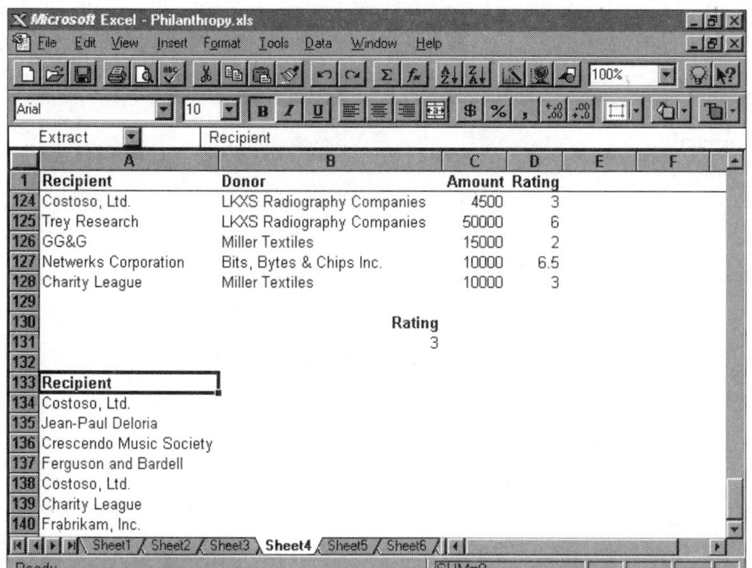

FIGURE 20-22

This list was filtered using the Unique Records Only option.

Using Subtotals to Analyze a List

After you've sorted your list properly and filtered out any information you don't (for the moment) need, you can use the Subtotals command on the Data menu to provide many kinds of summary details. The Subtotals command can do as its name suggests — add subtotal lines for each group of entries in your list. It can also supply other aggregate calculations at a group level. For example, you can use the Subtotals command to calculate the average of the values in a particular column for each group of rows, the number of rows in each group, the number of blank items in each group, the standard deviation for each group, and so on.

The Subtotals command also creates grand totals. That is, it applies the aggregation function you use, such as SUM or AVERAGE, to the entire body of your list, as well as to subgroups within the list. You can even choose whether you want the grand totals to appear above or below the list. (With long lists, you may find it more convenient to place this "bottom-line" calculation on top so you won't have to scroll to the end of the list.)

You shouldn't have to do much scrolling in any case, though, because Microsoft Excel builds an outline of your list when it creates subtotals. You can then click the outline symbols to see whatever level of detail you need.

Using a Form to Find List Information

Filters are an effective way to find list information, but they're not the only way. You can also use the Form command to locate rows that meet stated criteria. Here's how:

1. Select any cell in your list.
2. Choose the Form command from the Data menu, and when the dialog box appears, click the Criteria button.
3. Complete the edit boxes in the form as though you were creating a criteria range.

   The accompanying figure shows how you might complete the form if you wanted to see the names and other particulars for all male employees under the age of 40.

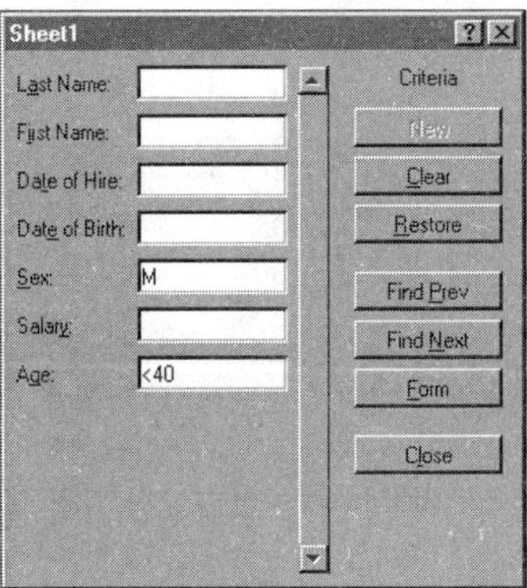

4. Click the Find Next button to display the first row in the list that meets your criteria.
5. Continue clicking Find Next to see subsequent rows or click Find Prev to return to previous rows.

To show you how the Subtotals command works, we'll use the list in Figure 20-23, which displays financial transactions imported from Microsoft Money. The list has columns for date, payee, budget category, and amount, and it is currently sorted by date.

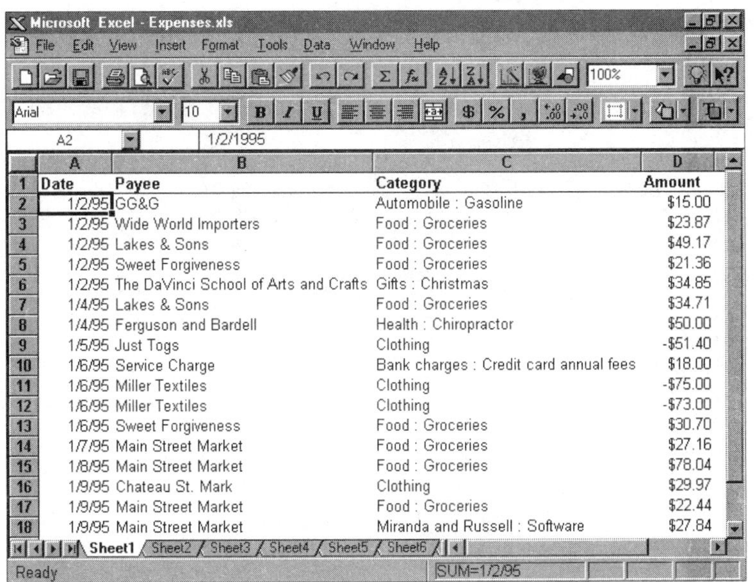

	A	B	C	D
1	Date	Payee	Category	Amount
2	1/2/95	GG&G	Automobile : Gasoline	$15.00
3	1/2/95	Wide World Importers	Food : Groceries	$23.87
4	1/2/95	Lakes & Sons	Food : Groceries	$49.17
5	1/2/95	Sweet Forgiveness	Food : Groceries	$21.36
6	1/2/95	The DaVinci School of Arts and Crafts	Gifts : Christmas	$34.85
7	1/4/95	Lakes & Sons	Food : Groceries	$34.71
8	1/4/95	Ferguson and Bardell	Health : Chiropractor	$50.00
9	1/5/95	Just Togs	Clothing	-$51.40
10	1/6/95	Service Charge	Bank charges : Credit card annual fees	$18.00
11	1/6/95	Miller Textiles	Clothing	-$75.00
12	1/6/95	Miller Textiles	Clothing	-$73.00
13	1/6/95	Sweet Forgiveness	Food : Groceries	$30.70
14	1/7/95	Main Street Market	Food : Groceries	$27.16
15	1/8/95	Main Street Market	Food : Groceries	$78.04
16	1/9/95	Chateau St. Mark	Clothing	$29.97
17	1/9/95	Main Street Market	Food : Groceries	$22.44
18	1/9/95	Main Street Market	Miranda and Russell : Software	$27.84

FIGURE 20-23
We'll use the Subtotals command to analyze this list of transactions.

Now suppose we want to know how much money we've spent in each budget category. The following steps will elicit this information:

1. Select a cell in the Category column and choose the Sort command from the Data menu to sort the list by category.
2. Choose the Subtotals command from the Data menu.
3. Complete the Subtotal dialog box as shown in Figure 20-24.

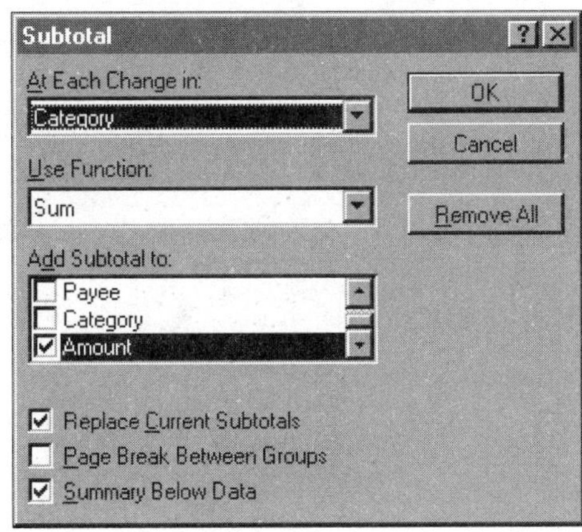

FIGURE 20-24
Filling out the Subtotal dialog box as shown here produces subtotals for each budget category.

4. Be sure the Replace Current Subtotals and Summary Below Data options are selected and then click OK. Figure 20-25 shows the results.

By completing the Subtotal dialog box as shown in Figure 20-24, we asked Excel to do the following:

- Create a new aggregation formula for each change in the Category column.
- Build the formula with the SUM function and apply it to the Amount column (that is, add up the amounts in each group).
- Place the subtotals below each group and the grand total at the bottom of the list.

In Figure 20-25, notice that Excel has also outlined the list. We can use this outline as follows:

- To see only the grand total, click the row 1 level symbol.
- To see only the subtotals and grand total, click the row 2 level symbol.
- To see the list in full detail, click the row 3 level symbol.

We can also use the outline to sort the list by the values of the subtotals. For example, if we wanted to rearrange the list so that the budget categories that put the biggest dent in our wallets appeared at the top, we could do the following:

1. Click the row 2 level symbol to make the outline display the subtotals and grand total only.

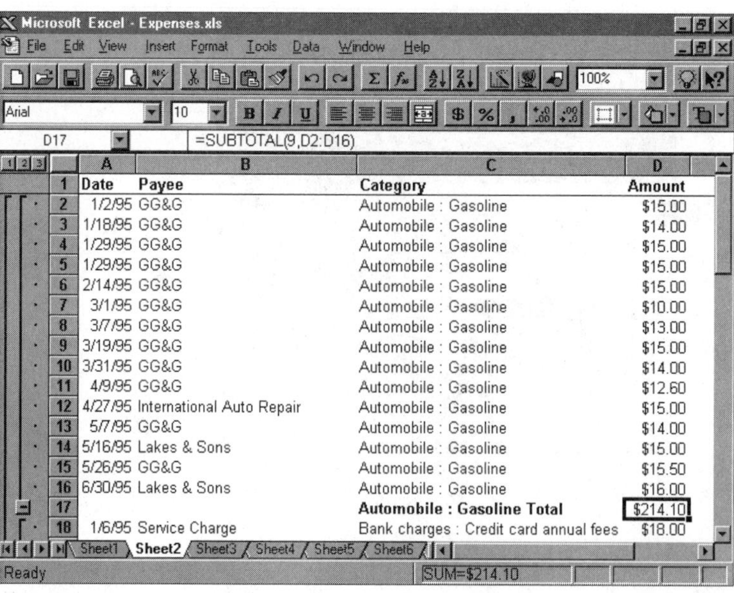

	A	B	C	D
1	Date	Payee	Category	Amount
2	1/2/95	GG&G	Automobile : Gasoline	$15.00
3	1/18/95	GG&G	Automobile : Gasoline	$14.00
4	1/29/95	GG&G	Automobile : Gasoline	$15.00
5	1/29/95	GG&G	Automobile : Gasoline	$15.00
6	2/14/95	GG&G	Automobile : Gasoline	$15.00
7	3/1/95	GG&G	Automobile : Gasoline	$10.00
8	3/7/95	GG&G	Automobile : Gasoline	$13.00
9	3/19/95	GG&G	Automobile : Gasoline	$15.00
10	3/31/95	GG&G	Automobile : Gasoline	$14.00
11	4/9/95	GG&G	Automobile : Gasoline	$12.60
12	4/27/95	International Auto Repair	Automobile : Gasoline	$15.00
13	5/7/95	GG&G	Automobile : Gasoline	$14.00
14	5/16/95	Lakes & Sons	Automobile : Gasoline	$15.00
15	5/26/95	GG&G	Automobile : Gasoline	$15.50
16	6/30/95	Lakes & Sons	Automobile : Gasoline	$16.00
17			**Automobile : Gasoline Total**	$214.10
18	1/6/95	Service Charge	Bank charges : Credit card annual fees	$18.00

FIGURE 20-25
The transactions list now contains subtotals for each budget category. Notice the row level symbols on the left.

2. Sort the "collapsed" list in descending order on the Amount column.

All the detail rows would still be associated with the appropriate summary rows after the sort.

TIP Outline level symbols eat valuable screen real estate, pushing columns out of view. You can restore the columns to view by using the Zoom command on the View menu. Alternatively, you can hide the outline symbols. From the Tools menu, choose Options. Then click the View tab and deselect Outline Symbols.

See Also For more information about importing files from other programs, see Chapter 27, "Importing and Exporting," page 909.

For more information about using outlines, see "Outlining Your Worksheets," page 217.

How Subtotal Formulas Are Built

The formula in cell D17 in Figure 20-25 provides an example of how Excel calculates subtotals. It uses the SUBTOTAL function, rather than the SUM function, and its first argument, 9, indicates the kind of calculation that is being performed. The important things to know about the SUBTOTAL function are:

- You don't have to worry about how it works because the Subtotals command automatically creates it for you.
- You do have to be careful not to apply your own aggregation formulas "by hand" to a range that includes SUBTOTAL formulas. For example, if you moved to a cell below the subtotaled list and created your own SUM formula to calculate a grand total, the SUM formula would add up everything in the range — details, subtotals, and the existing grand total. It would not "skip over" the SUBTOTAL formulas.

Using Automatic Page Breaks

The Page Break Between Groups option in the Subtotal dialog box is handy if you plan to print your subtotaled list. When you select this option, Excel prints each group on a separate page.

TIP If you apply the AutoFormat command to a subtotaled list, Excel will give each subtotal formula a contrasting format, making it easy for you to see both details and summary data at a glance.

Applying More Than One Aggregation Formula to a Column

After looking at the list shown earlier in Figure 20-25, we might be curious to know what the average expenditure in each category was. We can do that by simply repeating the Subtotal command, selecting Average as our aggregation function, and deselecting the Replace Current Subtotals option. Figure 20-26 shows the results.

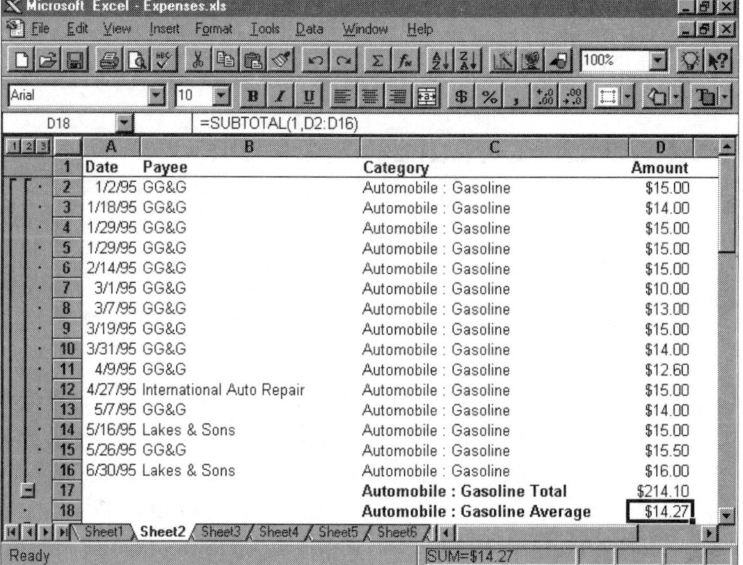

FIGURE 20-26
In addition to the SUM function, we applied the AVERAGE function to the Category column in this list.

Removing or Replacing Subtotals

To remove the subtotals as well as the outline, open the Subtotal dialog box and choose Remove All. To replace the current subtotals with different subtotal calculations, open the Subtotal dialog box and be sure that the Replace Current Subtotals option is selected.

Subtotals Within Subtotals

Subtotals can be *nested*. That is, you can create subtotals within subtotals. Suppose, for example, that after seeing the totals by category shown in Figure 20-25, we want to know how much of each category's outlay went to each payee. Here's how we can find out:

1. Choose the Subtotals command from the Data menu. When the Subtotal dialog box appears, click the Remove All button to remove the current subtotals.
2. Choose the Sort command and sort the list in ascending order first by Payee and then by Category.
3. Choose the Subtotals command again. Select Payee from the At Each Change In drop-down list box, select Sum from the Use Function drop-down list box, and select Amount from the Add Subtotal To list box. Click OK.
4. Repeat step 3, but this time select Category from the At Each Change In drop-down list box. Be sure the Replace Current Subtotals option is deselected and then click OK.

The resulting list, shown in Figure 20-27, has a new outline level and a new set of subtotals.

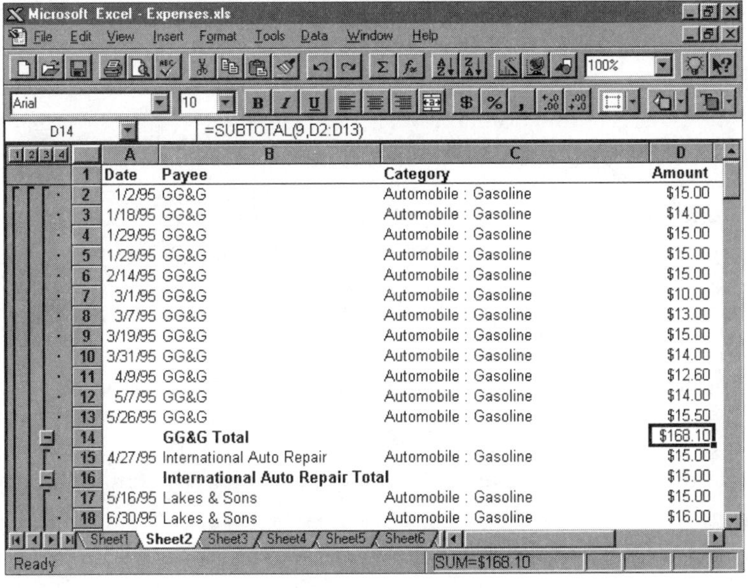

	A	B	C	D
1	Date	Payee	Category	Amount
2	1/2/95	GG&G	Automobile : Gasoline	$15.00
3	1/18/95	GG&G	Automobile : Gasoline	$14.00
4	1/29/95	GG&G	Automobile : Gasoline	$15.00
5	1/29/95	GG&G	Automobile : Gasoline	$15.00
6	2/14/95	GG&G	Automobile : Gasoline	$15.00
7	3/1/95	GG&G	Automobile : Gasoline	$10.00
8	3/7/95	GG&G	Automobile : Gasoline	$13.00
9	3/19/95	GG&G	Automobile : Gasoline	$15.00
10	3/31/95	GG&G	Automobile : Gasoline	$14.00
11	4/9/95	GG&G	Automobile : Gasoline	$12.60
12	5/7/95	GG&G	Automobile : Gasoline	$14.00
13	5/26/95	GG&G	Automobile : Gasoline	$15.50
14		**GG&G Total**		$168.10
15	4/27/95	International Auto Repair	Automobile : Gasoline	$15.00
16		**International Auto Repair Total**		$15.00
17	5/16/95	Lakes & Sons	Automobile : Gasoline	$15.00
18	6/30/95	Lakes & Sons	Automobile : Gasoline	$16.00

FIGURE 20-27
By deselecting the Replace Current Subtotals option, you can create new subtotals within groups that have already been subtotaled.

Using Functions to Analyze a List

Microsoft Excel offers 14 functions — COUNTIF, SUMIF, DAVERAGE, DCOUNT, DCOUNTA, DGET, DMAX, DMIN, DPRODUCT, DSTDEV, DSTDEVP, DSUM, DVAR, and DVARP — that are tailored for working with lists. Each of these functions returns information about the elements in a range that meet some criterion or criteria.

TIP COUNTBLANK is another important function to know about. The formula =COUNTBLANK(*range*) returns the number of cells in *range* that are either empty or contain formulas that return null strings. If your application would be invalidated by the presence of blank elements in particular columns of a list, you might want to create some COUNTBLANK formulas as "flags." Format the COUNTBLANK cells to display a contrasting color if the formulas return any value other than 0.

Using the COUNTIF and SUMIF Functions

The COUNTIF and SUMIF functions are easier to use than the other list-oriented functions because they let you specify your criteria directly within the formula. With both functions, however, you're limited to simple comparison criteria.

The COUNTIF function takes the form

=COUNTIF(*range,criteria*)

where *range* is the range whose values you want to count and *criteria* is a text value expressing the required criterion. To count the number of women employees in the list shown earlier in Figure 20-1, for example, you could use the formula

=COUNTIF(E2:E38,"F")

To count the number of employees who are 45 or older, you could use

=COUNTIF(G2:G38,">=45")

Note that the criteria argument can be applied only to the range that you are counting.

The SUMIF function takes the form

=SUMIF(*range, criteria, sum_range*)

Here the *criteria* argument is applied to *range,* while *sum_range* is the range whose values you want to add. For example, in Figure 20-1, to calculate the total spent on salaries for workers below the age of 30, you could use the formula

=SUMIF(G2:G38,"<30",F2:F38)

Because an average is a sum divided by a count, you can use the SUMIF and COUNTIF functions together to calculate averages. For example, the formula

=SUMIF(G2:G38,"<30",F2:F38)/COUNTIF(G2:G38,"<30")

returns the average salary paid to employees under 30 years of age.

Using the D Functions

The remaining list-oriented functions belong to a group known as the D functions. The D Functions are DAVERAGE, DCOUNT, DCOUNTA, DGET, DMAX, DMIN, DPRODUCT, DSTDEV, DSTDEVP, DSUM, DVAR, and DVARP.

Each of these functions, with the exception of DGET, is the counterpart of a "normal" statistical function. The DSUM function, for example, is the counterpart of the SUM function; the DSTDEV function is the counterpart of the STDEV function; and so on.

The difference between the D functions and their counterparts is that the D functions operate only on those members of a range that meet stated criteria. In Figure 20-28, for example, we used the formula

=DAVERAGE(A7:G38,"Salary",A1:A2)

Microsoft Excel - Staff.xls

F4 =DAVERAGE(A7:G38,"Salary",A1:A2)

	A	B	C	D	E	F	G
1	Age						
2	>=40						
3							
4		Average salary for Employees over 40:				$41,401	
5							
6							
7	Last Name	First Name	Date of Hire	Date of Birth	Sex	Salary	Age
8	White	Connie	5/16/74	3/15/49	F	32200	46
9	Jacks	Kris	1/16/93	10/19/66	M	57300	28
10	Falconer	Charles	10/23/81	4/24/51	M	49400	44
11	Miller	Zachary	5/2/84	10/7/56	M	42000	38
12	Pall	Dick	11/3/88	7/19/41	M	33290	54
13	Davidson	Paul	8/27/85	8/17/60	M	59950	34
14	Halvorson	Monica	4/20/93	6/26/61	F	36700	34
15	Ford	Hunter	3/18/87	4/5/58	M	32700	36
16	Gay	Michael	8/9/85	9/15/52	M	45200	42
17	Neal	Steve	12/6/91	10/8/47	M	55300	48
18	Edelhart	Catherine	12/28/83	3/22/58	F	33600	36

Sheet1 / Sheet2 / Sheet3 / Sheet4 / Sheet5 / Sheet6

Ready SUM=$41,401

FIGURE 20-28

The database statistical functions are useful for analyzing list information that meets particular criteria. Here we used DAVERAGE to find the average salary of workers 40 and over.

to calculate the average salary of employees 40 and over.

Note the following points about the form of the D functions:

- The first argument specifies the entire list, not just a particular column.
- The second argument identifies the column you want to sum, average, count, or otherwise calculate.
- For the second argument, you can use the column heading, expressed as a text value. Or you can use a number representing the column's position in the list. For example, in the formula in Figure 20-28, the second argument could have been 6 (the quotation marks aren't necessary when a number is used rather than text) because Salary is the sixth column in the list.
- The third argument specifies a criteria range.

Because the D functions require a criteria range, they're a bit more difficult to use than the SUMIF and COUNTIF functions. However, they allow you to perform more complex calculations. While SUMIF and COUNTIF are limited to simple comparison criteria, the D functions can use any criteria that can be expressed in a criteria range.

For more information about statistical functions, see Chapter 14, "Statistical Analysis," page 503.

For more information about criteria ranges, see "The Advanced Filter Command," page 732.

The DGET Function

The DGET function returns the value of any cell in a column that meets the criteria expressed in a criteria range. If no cell meets the criteria, the function returns the #VALUE! error value. If more than one cell meets the criteria, the function returns the #NUM! error value.

Using the Template Wizard to Create Templates and Databases

Excel 7 includes a Template Wizard that can turn any worksheet into a reusable template and create a database to track the entries in particular fields of the template. The wizard's data-tracking feature allows you to designate particular cells of interest in your template and have whatever values you enter in those cells automatically posted to a database file. The database can be a list in an Excel worksheet or it can be another ODBC-supported data format, such as an Access file, a dBase file, or a FoxPro file.

If you've installed this add-in, you'll find a Template Wizard command on your Data menu. If you haven't, you can install it by choosing Add-Ins from the Tools menu, and then selecting the item labeled Template Wizard With Data Tracking.

NOTE If you want to turn a worksheet into a template without also creating a tracking database, simply save the worksheet as an .XLT file. (See "Using Template Files," page 206).

For example, suppose you want to build a template that others can use for creating expense reports. Suppose also that you want certain entries on expense reports — such as the reporting period, the employee name, the employee department number, and the various line-item totals — to be posted automatically to an expense database. That way you can analyze expenses by period, by employee, and so on, with the help of Excel's (or another program's) list-management features.

To create this application, start by setting up a worksheet to act as your template. Figure 20-29 shows how you might do this.

TIP When setting up the worksheet that will act as your template, assign names to the cells whose values you want to track. This will simplify the creation of your tracking database.

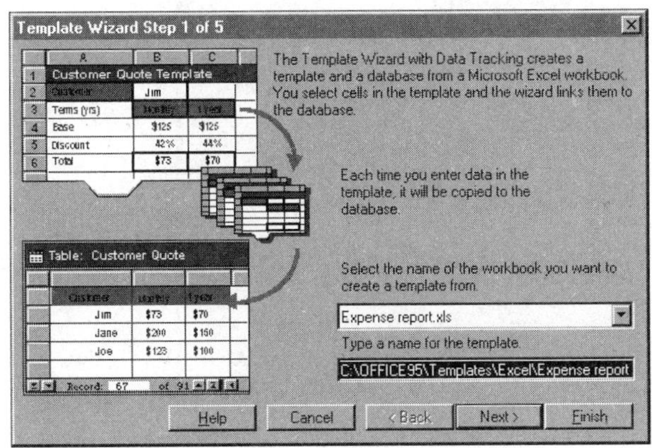

FIGURE 20-29
We'll use the Template Wizard to turn this worksheet into a reusable template. The wizard will also create a separate database file to record entries made in particular template cells.

When you have the worksheet set up to your satisfaction, follow these steps to create the template:

1. Choose Template Wizard from the Data menu.
2. In the wizard's first dialog box, enter the name of the worksheet from which you're creating your template, as well as the name you want Excel to use for the template that it will create. Then click Next.

   Excel supplies useful defaults for these names, so you may only have to confirm the values that already appear in the dialog box.
3. In the wizard's second dialog box, choose the type of database you want to create. Also specify the filename under which you want your database created.

   The wizard's default database type is "Microsoft Excel Workbook." But you can choose a different type by opening the drop-down list in the wizard's second dialog box.
4. In the wizard's third dialog box, specify each cell of your worksheet that you want to track. Also specify the field name under which you want each cell to be tracked in the completed database.

   Figure 20-30 shows how you might begin filling out the wizard's third dialog box for the expense-report application. In the figure, you see that cell B2 will be tracked under the field name Employee_Name. Cell B3 will be tracked under the field name Department_Name, and so on. Note that if you have assigned names to the worksheet cells that you want to track, the wizard automatically proposes those names as field names. All you need to do to fill out the third dialog box, then, is to point to the various cells you want to track.

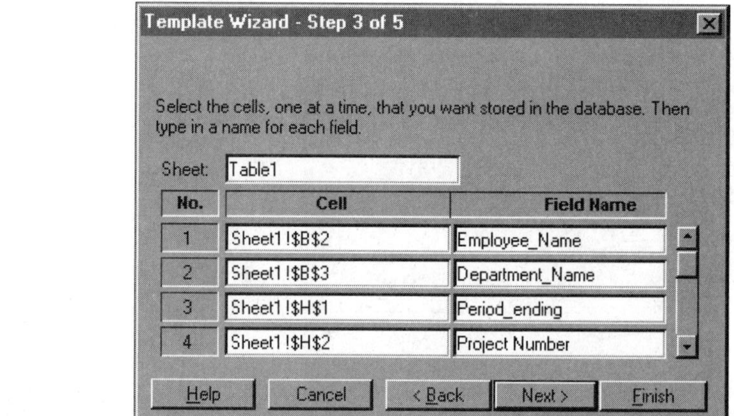

FIGURE 20-30
In the Template Wizard's third dialog box, you specify which cells you want to track and the field names you want your database to use.

5. In the wizard's fourth dialog box, specify any existing worksheets that you want tracked in the database you're about to create. If you've already got a stock of expense reports, and you want to add values from these reports to your database, this is your opportunity to do so. The existing reports must be structured identically with the template you're creating, however.
6. In the wizard's fifth and final database, you can opt to attach a routing slip to your new template. If you create a routing slip, the template will be circulated to the names on the slip each time anyone creates and saves a new worksheet based on the template.

Chapter 21

An Introduction to Microsoft Query

Microsoft Query, a program shipped with Microsoft Excel, lets you tap into external data sources. You can use it as a stand-alone tool, or you can call it from an Excel worksheet. Either way, you can connect to a data file stored on disk, query that file to get just the information you need, and then sort, format, and analyze the information. If you launch Query from within Excel, a simple command appears in Query's menu bar that lets you transfer the data from Query back to your Excel worksheet. There you can continue working with the data, using any of the list-management features described in Chapter 20. You can also have Query refresh the imported data periodically, keeping your worksheet current as the external data source changes.

Data Sources Supported by Microsoft Query

With Microsoft Query, you can connect to any data source for which you have installed a *full-conformance ODBC (Open Database Connectivity)* driver. The ODBC driver is a software layer that provides applications such as Query with a common standard for communicating with diverse databases. The ODBC driver, typically supplied by the database vendor, translates generic instructions from the application to SQL (Structured Query Language) code appropriate for the database, much the way your printer driver converts generic printing instructions to printer-specific code. Excel 7 includes drivers for Microsoft FoxPro, Microsoft Access, Paradox, dBASE, and SQL server.

Using Microsoft Query with Excel Tables

You can also use Microsoft Query to read data stored in Excel worksheet tables. You might want to do this (in preference to simply opening an Excel table with the File Open command) under the following circumstances:

- When the data file is particularly large. Query brings into memory only those portions of the file that meet stated criteria.
- When the data file is shared or likely to be updated by others. Tapping into a data file via Query helps your Excel worksheet stay in step as others use and update the database.
- When you need to join two or more data tables. Unlike Excel's own Data-menu commands, Query can join tables that share common fields.

Installing the Microsoft Query Add-In

You can access Microsoft Query from within Microsoft Excel in two ways: by choosing the Get External Data command from Excel's Data menu or by choosing the PivotTable command from the Data menu and specifying an external data source.

We discuss the PivotTable command, which can use either internal or external data sources, in Chapter 22. For now, we'll focus our attention on the Get External Data command.

If your Data menu does not include the Get External Data command, you need to install the add-in file XLquery.xla by following these steps:

1. Choose the Add-Ins command from the Tools menu. When the Add-Ins dialog box appears, select the MSQuery Add-In option and click OK.
2. If the Add-Ins dialog box does not include the MSQuery Add-In option, click Browse, move to the Library subfolder of your Excel program folder, and then move to the MSQuery folder and select XLQuery.xla.
3. Click OK to return to the Add-Ins dialog box, select the MSQuery Add-In option and then click OK to return to the worksheet.

Microsoft Query Terminology

Term	Definition
Data source	A collection of one or more tables. Depending on which ODBC driver you're using, a data source can be either a disk directory containing table files or a collection of tables stored in a single file.
Field	Equivalent to a column in an Excel list. (Microsoft Query uses the terms *field* and *column* interchangeably.)
Field name	Equivalent to a column heading in an Excel list.
Record	Equivalent to a row in an Excel list.
Result set	The set of records that meet your current criteria. Query displays the result set in the data pane.
SQL	Structured Query Language. The language used by Query to get information from your data source.
Table	A collection of information on a single topic, organized into fields and records. Equivalent to a list in Excel.

If you don't find XLQuery.xla in your MSQuery folder, you'll have to install this file from the Microsoft Office 95 CD-ROM. You can install the XLQuery.xla file by double-clicking the Office setup icon, choosing the Add/Remove installation tab, and selecting the Data Access option from Converters, Filters, and Data Access.

TIP You can run Microsoft Query as a standard application. Double-click the Microsoft Query program icon to start Query. When you start Query in this way, however, the Return Data To Excel button doesn't appear on the toolbar, and the Return Data To Microsoft Excel command doesn't appear on the File menu.

See Also For information about the PivotTable command, see Chapter 22, "Using the PivotTable Wizard," page 787.

Connecting to a Data Source

To begin working with external data, choose the Get External Data command from the Data menu. After Microsoft Query is activated, it presents the Select Data Source dialog box. Here you'll find a list of the data sources that you've been using. To reuse a data source, simply double-click its name, or select it and click the Use button. Query then displays the Add Tables dialog box, where you can tell Query which table you want to work with.

MS Query Cue Cards

Microsoft Query includes a separate MS Query Cue Cards window. These cue cards provide easy access to online Help for Query. Click the Menu button to view a list of topics related to designing a query. If you click the Search button, the Search dialog box appears, from which you can navigate to all Query-related topics. You might need to move or close the MS Query Cue Cards window to see the entire results of your query.

Defining a New Data Source

To use a data source that's not listed in the Select Data Source dialog box, click the Other button. Query then displays the ODBC Data Sources dialog box, which, like the Select Data Source dialog box, is simply a list of named data sources. If the data source you need isn't listed here, click the New button to display the Add Data Source dialog box, shown in Figure 21-1.

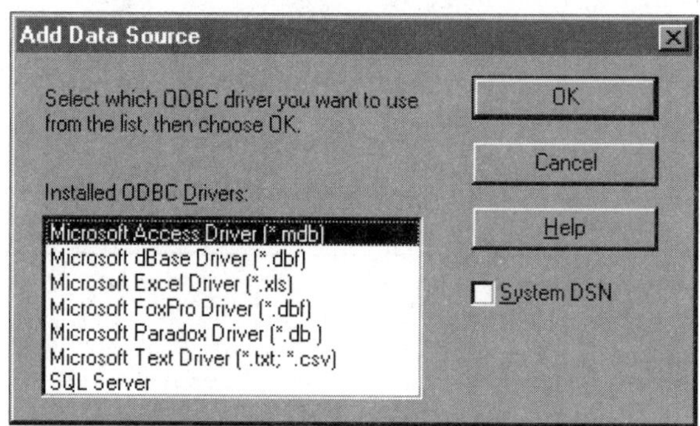

FIGURE 21-1
The first step in making a new data source available to Query is to identify which ODBC driver you'll be using.

In the Add Data Source dialog box, select the ODBC driver that your data source will need. For example, if your data source is a directory of dBASE files, select dBase Files and then click OK.

Notice that some of the entries in the Installed ODBC Drivers list box include the word *Files*. These entries represent programs that store tables in separate files. The remaining entries in the Installed ODBC Drivers list box store related tables in a single file.

After you select a driver from the Add Data Source dialog box, Query takes you to the corresponding ODBC Setup dialog box, where you can enter a name and a description for your data source. The name you supply is the one that will appear in the ODBC Data Sources dialog box. The description is optional and for your own edification only. Other options in this dialog box vary with ODBC drivers. In some cases, for example, you are prompted to supply a path to your database server as well as the sign-on information required by that server.

After you've filled out the Setup dialog box and clicked Select Directory, a standard file selection dialog box appears. Specify either the folder that contains your table files or the name of a database file. When you complete this task, your new data source is added to the list in the ODBC Data Sources dialog box. You can then double-click the name of your data source to return to the Select Data Source dialog box and double-click again in the Select Data Source dialog box to open the Add Tables dialog box.

Adding Tables

After you connect to your data source, Microsoft Query opens a new query window and displays the Add Tables dialog box. Here you can specify the table or tables you want to work with. In the examples that follow, we'll focus on single-table operations, but you can also use Query to join multiple tables.

To work with a single table, double-click its name in the Add Tables dialog box and click the Close button. (To work with multiple tables, double-click the name of each table you want before you click the Close button.) You can now work with your query window, which looks like the one shown in Figure 21-2.

The query window is divided into two sections: A table pane occupies the top section, and a data pane occupies the bottom section. As you'll soon see, your query window can include a criteria pane as well. Notice that you can have more than one query window open at a time.

TIP While you are working with your data source, you can click the Add Table(s) button on the toolbar to display the Add Tables dialog box.

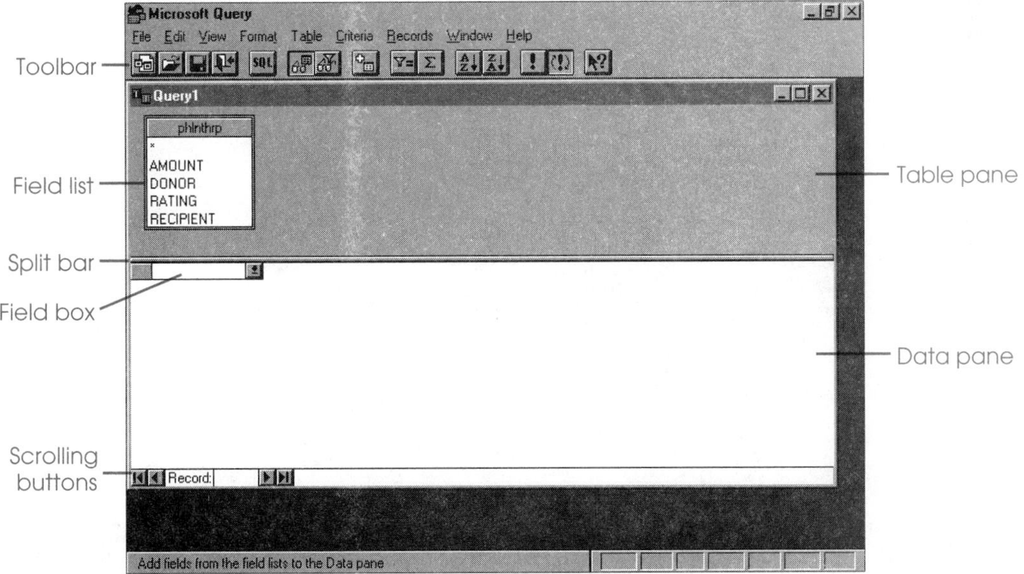

FIGURE 21-2

A new query window includes a table pane and a data pane. (When you specify filtering criteria, the query window includes a criteria pane as well.)

In the *table pane,* you'll see one or more field lists labeled with the name of the table you're working with and the fields each table contains. In our example, we have just one table: a dBASE file called Phlnthrp.dbf. As Figure 21-2 shows, the Phlnthrp.dbf table contains four fields: AMOUNT, DONOR, RATING, and RECIPIENT.

The *data pane* is where Query displays the records that meet the specified criteria. These records are known as the *result set.* Initially, the data pane displays one empty field box with a drop-down arrow beside it. As you add fields to your data pane, Query continues to display an empty field box so that you can add more fields to the query window.

TIP You can change the size of the panes in a query window by dragging the split bar that divides the table pane from the data pane. If your table has relatively few fields, for example, you can probably increase the default size of the data pane without covering up the information in the table pane. You can then see more records in the data pane.

As shown in Figure 21-3, Microsoft Query has its own toolbar, which you can use to perform queries and return data to your Excel worksheet.

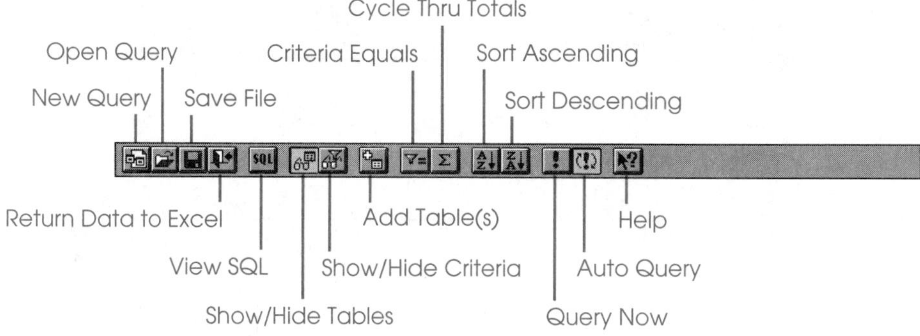

FIGURE 21-3

Microsoft Query has its own toolbar.

Choosing and Arranging Fields

You can ask Microsoft Query to display records from your table using some or all of the fields in the table, and you can arrange the fields in any order you want. You bring a field into view in one of four ways:

Automatic Query Versus Manual Query

By default, Microsoft Query updates the result set every time you add a new field to the data pane, rearrange the order of the existing fields in the data pane, change a sort specification, or change a filter criterion. In response to these actions, Query creates a new SQL statement and executes that statement against your data source. (You can see the SQL code by clicking the View SQL button on the toolbar.) If your data source is particularly large or network traffic is high, Automatic Query can cause annoying delays. You can turn off Automatic Query so that Query executes the current SQL statement only when you ask it to.

You can determine whether Automatic Query is on by looking at the Auto Query button on the toolbar. (See Figure 20-3.) If the button looks as if it has been pushed in, Automatic Query is on. You can turn off Automatic Query by clicking the Auto Query button or by choosing the Automatic Query command from the Records menu.

To execute the current query while you're in manual query mode, click the Query Now button or choose the Query Now command from the Records menu.

- In the table pane, double-click the name of the field you want.
- Drag the name of the field you want from the table pane to the empty field box at the top of the data pane.
- Click the drop-down arrow beside the data pane's empty field box and select the field you want.
- Choose the Add Column command from the Records menu and select the name of the field you want.

Adding All Fields to the Data Pane

To add all of your table's fields to the data pane, drag the asterisk in the table pane's field list box to the data pane's empty field box. (You can also double-click the asterisk, or choose the Add Column command and select the asterisk.) Query displays the fields in the order they appear in your database file, which might or might not reflect their alphabetic order in the field list. You can rearrange the fields after they appear in the data pane.

TIP After you have finished adding fields to the data pane, you might not need to see the table pane anymore. You can hide the table pane by clicking the Show/Hide Tables button on the toolbar. (See Figure 21-3.) When you want to redisplay the table pane, simply click the Show/Hide Tables button again.

Rearranging Fields

You can move fields in the data pane by dragging them with the mouse. Click a field heading to select the field, and then drag the field to its new position.

Removing Fields

If you decide that you no longer need a particular field, you can remove it from the data pane. Simply select the field heading and press the Del key.

Resizing and Hiding Columns

You can change the width of the column in which a field is displayed by employing the same techniques you use to resize a column in an Excel worksheet. Simply drag the column border to the right of the field heading. For more precise positioning, you can choose the Column Width command on the Format menu.

To make a column just wide enough to accommodate its longest entry, double-click the border to the right of the column heading. Alternatively, you select the column, choose the Column Width command from the Format menu, and click the Best Fit button. Note that in adjusting column widths, the Best Fit command takes into account only those records currently displayed in the result set, not all the records in your database. When the result set changes, you might need to reuse Best Fit.

To hide a column, drag it to zero width, or select the column and choose the Hide Columns command from the Format menu. To restore a hidden column to view, choose the Show Columns command from the Format menu.

See Also For more information about resizing columns, see "Controlling Column Width," page 192.

Renaming Columns

By default, Microsoft Query uses the names of your fields as field headings. If these field names are short and cryptic, you might want to supply different headings. First select the column you want to change and choose the Edit Column command from the Records menu (or simply double-click the field heading). Then type a new name in the Column Heading edit box and click OK. (Note that this action has no effect on the underlying database; it simply supplies a different heading for display purposes.)

Navigating the Data Pane

Figure 21-4 shows all four fields of the first 13 records in the Phlnthrp table. At the bottom of the data pane, Microsoft Query displays a record number bordered by scrolling buttons. You can use these buttons to move through the records of your database. Alternatively, you can use the scroll bar to the right of the data pane. Note, however, that scrolling with the scroll bar does not change the selection; it only moves different records into view.

Some of Excel's navigation keystrokes also work in Query. For example, you can move directly to the last record in your database by pressing Ctrl-End, or to the first record by pressing Ctrl-Home. The End key maneuvers (the End key used in combination with the Up or Down direction key) do not work in Query, however.

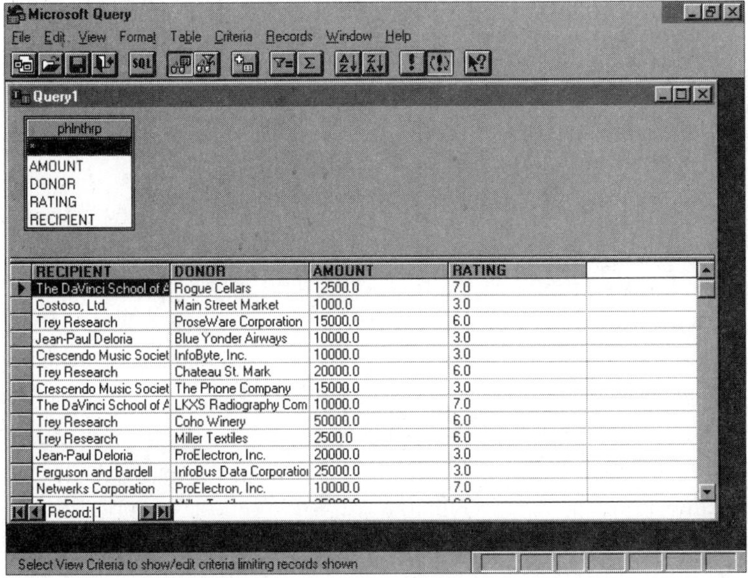

FIGURE 21-4

You can use the scrolling buttons at the bottom of the data pane to move between records.

Sorting the Result Set

Microsoft Query initially displays records in the order in which they're stored in the underlying database. You can use sorting commands to change their order in the result set without affecting the order of the underlying database. You can sort by using the Sort command or by clicking buttons on the toolbar.

Using the Sort Command

Suppose we want to see the result set shown in Figure 21-4 in ascending order by donor. We start by choosing the Sort command from the Records menu to display the Sort dialog box shown in Figure 21-5.

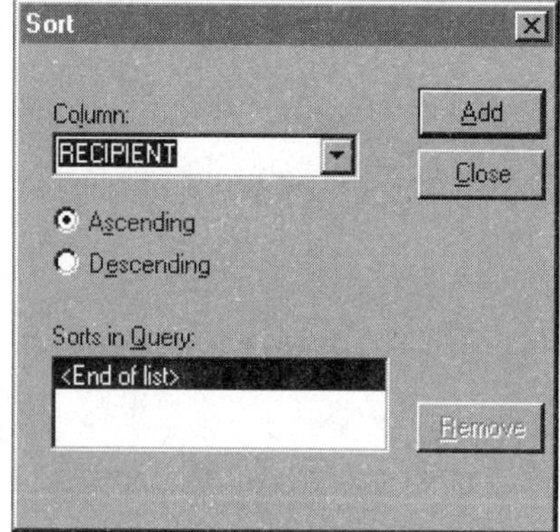

FIGURE 21-5
The Sort dialog box displays the current sort order and lets you add fields from a drop-down list.

The Sorts In Query list box in the Sort dialog box indicates what sort specification, if any, is currently in effect. In Figure 21-5, the Sorts In Query list box is empty except for the <End Of List> entry, indicating that the result set is currently unsorted. The Column drop-down list box at the top of the Sort dialog box lists all the table fields available for sorting.

To sort the result set by donor, we simply select DONOR from the Column drop-down list box and then click the Add button. Query adds the DONOR heading to the Sorts In Query list box, preceding it with (Asc) to indicate that we've sorted on the DONOR column in ascending order. If Automatic Query is in effect, Query sorts the result set by donor but leaves the Sort dialog box open in case we want to specify another sort field. Figure 21-6 shows how the dialog box and result set look after this initial sort.

Now suppose we want to sort the records with identical DONOR fields by the values in their AMOUNT fields, with the highest amounts at the top of each group. To sort the records in this order, we need to specify two sort fields:

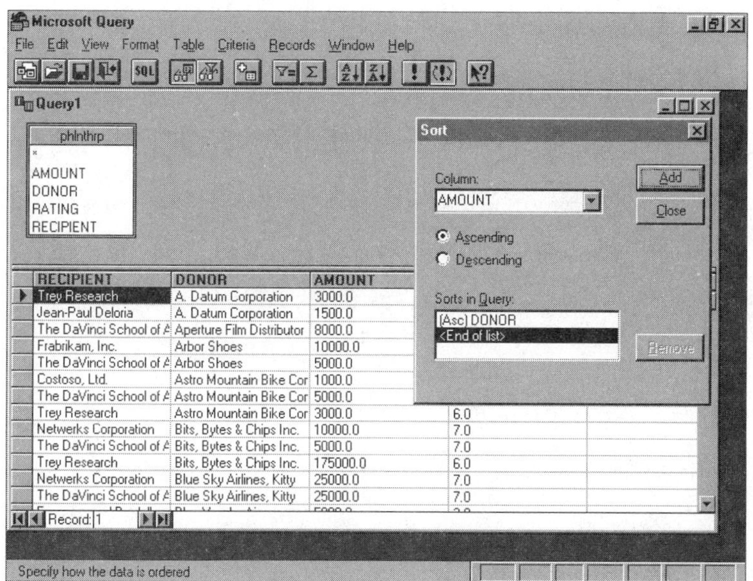

FIGURE 21-6
After you add a field to the sort specification, Query re-sorts the result set and updates the Sort dialog box, leaving the dialog box open in case you want to do additional sorting.

DONOR and AMOUNT. DONOR will be our primary sort field because we want Query to sort the entire table by the DONOR field. AMOUNT will be our secondary field because we want Query to sort AMOUNT values only within groups of matching DONOR fields. If we wanted to sort matching AMOUNT values by another field — RATING or RECIPIENT — that additional field would be a tertiary sort field.

You can sort on as many fields as you like in Query. Simply add fields to the Sorts In Query list box in descending order of precedence. That is, add your primary sort field first, then your secondary sort field, and so on.

In our example, we have already sorted on the DONOR field. To sort on the AMOUNT field, we need to add this field to the Sorts In Query list box after the DONOR field. To add the AMOUNT field after the DONOR field, we can do the following:

1. With the Sort dialog box shown in Figure 21-6 still open, select <End Of List> in the Sorts In Query list box.
2. Select AMOUNT from the Column drop-down list box and then select the Descending option.
3. Click the Add button.

Query adds (Desc) AMOUNT to the Sorts In Query list box and re-sorts the result set. Figure 21-7 on the next page shows how the Sort dialog box and result set look after this secondary sort.

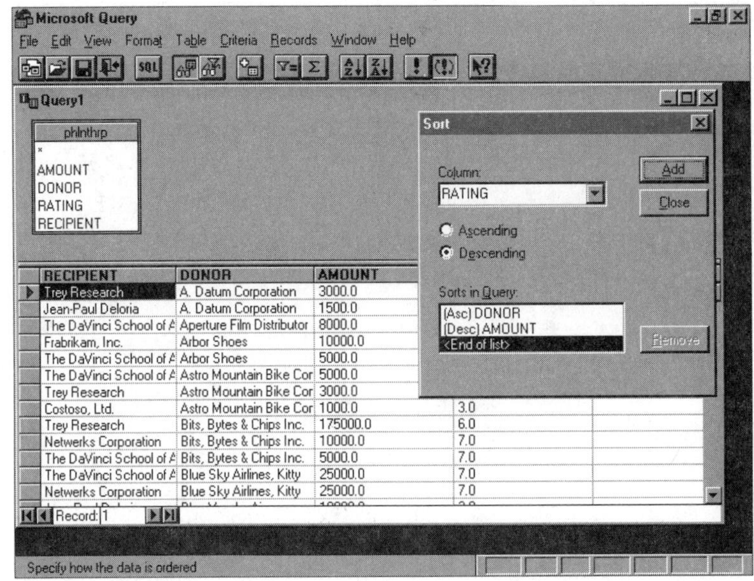

FIGURE 21-7 This list was first sorted by DONOR and then by AMOUNT. Notice that the primary sort field appears first in the Sorts In Query list box, followed by the secondary field, and so on.

Rearranging Sort Fields

When you click the Add button in the Sort dialog box, Query adds your new sort field above the currently selected field in the Sorts In Query list box. If you accidentally add a sort field in the wrong order, select the field and click the Remove button. Then add the field in the correct position.

Sorting with the Toolbar

Sorting with the buttons on the toolbar is a little simpler than sorting with the Sort command, although you don't get the benefit of seeing the names of any fields on which the result set is already sorted. To sort our example table first on DONOR (in ascending order), and then on AMOUNT (in descending order), we would do the following:

1. Select any cell in the DONOR field.
2. Click the Sort Ascending button. (See Figure 21-3 on page 764.)
3. Select any cell in the AMOUNT field.
4. Hold down Ctrl and click the Sort Descending button.

When you click a sort button without holding down Ctrl, Query replaces any current sort specification with your new sort. In other words, it applies your new sort to the records as they are ordered in the underlying database.

When you hold down Ctrl and click a sort button, Query sorts the records on the new sort field after it sorts them on the previous sort fields.

Filtering the Result Set

Microsoft Query provides a variety of methods by which you can filter the result set so that it lists only the records you're actually interested in. As with Microsoft Excel's own list-filtering features, you create a filter by specifying one or more criteria — conditions that particular fields must meet.

See Also For more information about Excel's list-filtering features, see Chapter 20, "Managing Information in Lists," page 713.

Exact-Match Criteria

The simplest kind of criterion is one in which you stipulate that a field exactly equal some value. Query makes it extremely easy to create such criteria:

1. Select a field value that already meets your exact-match criterion.
2. Click the Criteria Equals button on the toolbar. (See Figure 21-3.)

For example, suppose we want to filter the result set shown earlier in Figure 21-4 so that it displays only those records in which the RATING field equals 7.0. To do this, we simply select any record in the RATING field that already equals 7.0 (such as the eighth record in Figure 21-4) and click the Criteria Equals button. Query responds by displaying the criteria pane (if it's not already displayed) and applying the new filter to the table, as shown in Figure 21-8 on the next page.

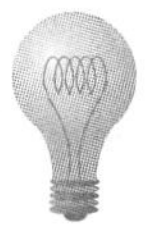

TIP After you use the Criteria Equals button to specify an exact-match criterion, Query leaves your match value selected in the criteria pane. You can quickly switch to a different match by typing a new value to replace the current one. For example, to change the result set shown in Figure 21-8 to show records with RATING values of 6.0, simply type *6* and press Enter.

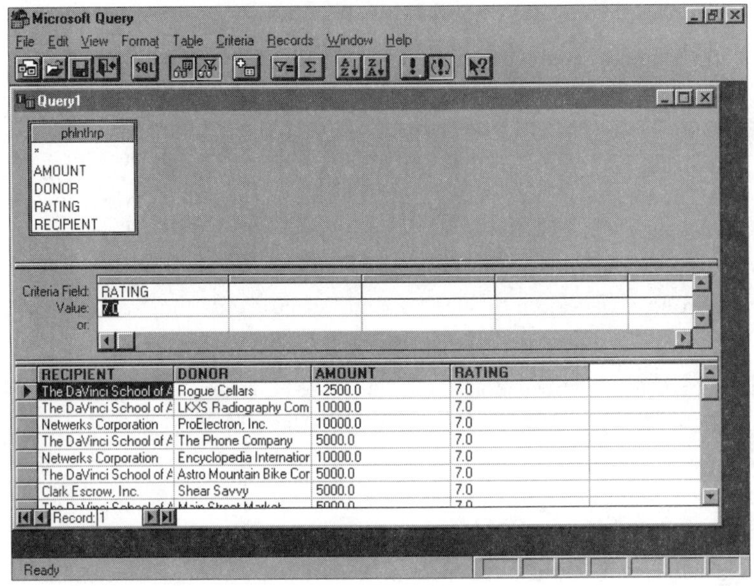

FIGURE 21-8
When we clicked the Criteria Equals button, Query displayed the criteria pane and applied the filter to the result set.

If you've used Excel's Advanced Filter command, you'll notice that the *criteria pane* in the query window looks a lot like a criteria range in an Excel worksheet. Field headings appear in the top row, and criteria are stated in subsequent rows. Although you can enter new criteria or edit existing criteria directly in the criteria pane, it's not necessary because Query's menu commands take care of filling out the criteria pane for you. In fact, you don't need to have the criteria pane on your screen at all.

TIP To make more room for the result set, you can remove the criteria pane by clicking the Show/Hide Criteria button on the toolbar or by choosing the Criteria command from the View menu.

For more information about the Advanced Filter command, see "The Advanced Filter Command," page 732.

Using Multiple Exact-Match Criteria

Suppose we want to see records in which the DONOR field is Shear Savvy and the RATING field is 7.0. We can do this by simply adding another exact-match criterion, as follows:

1. Select a cell in which the DONOR field is Shear Savvy. (The seventh record in Figure 21-8 will do.)
2. Click the Criteria Equals button on the toolbar.

As Figure 21-9 shows, Query adds the new criterion to the criteria pane, placing it in the same row as the first criterion. As in an advanced filter criteria range in Excel, criteria that appear in the same row of the criteria pane are said to be joined by AND; the filter admits only those records that meet both criteria.

To see records in which the RATING field equals *either* 7.0 *or* 6.0, we can do the following, starting with the result set shown in Figure 21-4:

1. Turn off Automatic Query by clicking the Auto Query button or by choosing the Automatic Query command from the Records menu.
2. In the RATING field, select a cell that equals 7.0 and click the Criteria Equals button.
3. In the RATING field, select a record that equals 6.0 and click the Criteria Equals button.
4. Turn on Automatic Query by clicking the Auto Query button or by choosing Automatic Query from the Records menu.

When you use the Criteria Equals button to add two or more values from the same field to the criteria pane, Query creates a filter in which the criteria are said to be joined by OR; the filter admits records that meet either criteria.

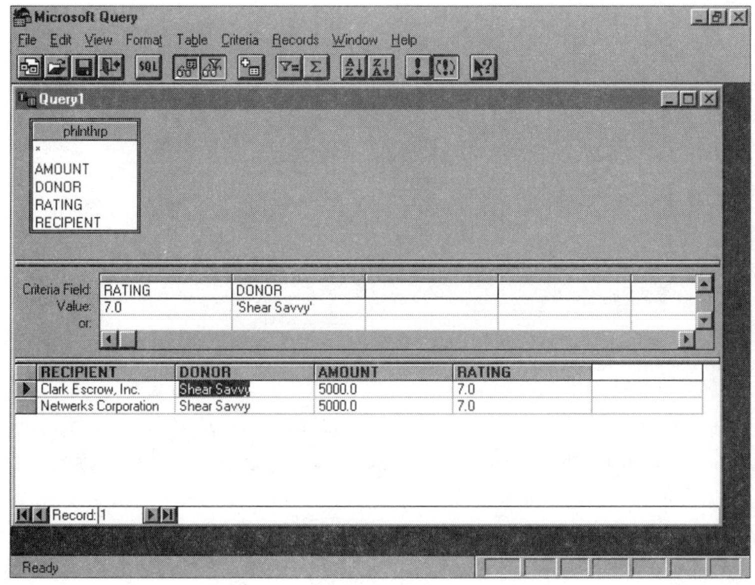

FIGURE 21-9
When you use the Criteria Equals button in two separate fields, Query's filter admits only those records that meet both criteria.

Specifying Exact-Match Criteria Without a Mouse

If you don't have a mouse or if you prefer to use menu commands rather than toolbar buttons, you can specify an exact-match criterion as follows:

1. Select a field value that meets your specification. (You can use the keyboard to navigate to that value.)
2. Choose the Add Criteria command from the Criteria menu and when the Add Criteria dialog box appears, press Enter. (The Add Criteria dialog box should already contain the correct settings when you choose the Add Criteria command.)

Removing Criteria

The simplest way to remove a filter criterion is to select the criterion's heading in the criteria pane and press the Del key. Then select something else — another cell in the criteria pane or a cell in the result set, for example. As soon as you move the selection away from the deleted criterion's location, Query updates the result set (assuming Automatic Query is turned on).

To remove all criteria and restore the unfiltered result set, choose the Remove All Criteria command from the Criteria menu.

Comparison Criteria

To specify a comparison criterion, start by choosing the Add Criteria command from the Criteria menu. You'll see a dialog box similar to the one shown in Figure 21-10.

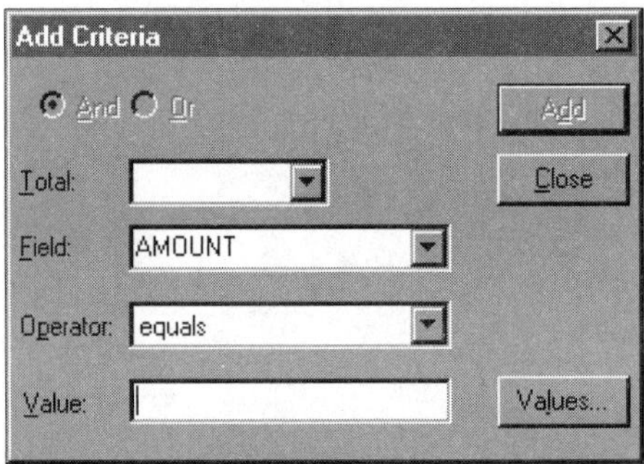

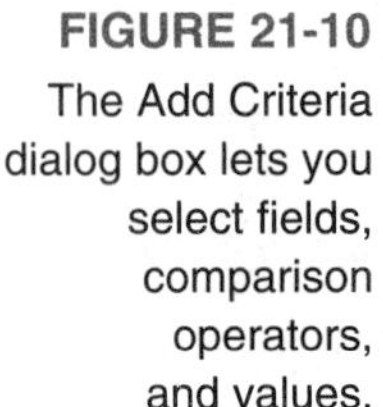

FIGURE 21-10 The Add Criteria dialog box lets you select fields, comparison operators, and values.

In the Add Criteria dialog box, you can construct your criteria by selecting options from various drop-down list boxes. For example, you can select a field from the Field drop-down list box and then select an operator, such as *Is Greater Than,* from the Operator drop-down list box. You can also enter a value in the Value edit box by typing it or by clicking the Values button and selecting the value you want. When you click the Values button, a list containing all the entries for the selected field is displayed. In many cases, however, it's easier to type the value rather than select it. For example, to filter out amounts greater than 100,000, simply select *Is Greater Than* from the Operator drop-down list box and then type *100000* in the Value edit box.

> **NOTE** For comparison criteria that don't involve computed fields, be sure the Total drop-down list box in the Add Criteria dialog box is blank, as it is in Figure 21-10. (We'll discuss the Total drop-down list box later in this chapter in the section titled "Filtering on Calculated Fields," page 782.)

After you complete the Add Criteria dialog box, click the Add button. Query responds by creating the appropriate entry in the criteria pane and (if Automatic Query is on) executing the new query. The Add Criteria dialog box remains open so that you can specify more criteria. To add another criterion, select the And option or the Or option at the top of the dialog box and then enter the remaining information as before. When you've finished entering criteria, click the Close button.

The And and Or Options

A criterion added with the And option selected appears in the criteria pane on the same row as the previously added criterion. A criterion added with the Or option selected appears on a new row.

As mentioned earlier, when Query evaluates the criteria pane, it treats all entries sharing a common row as a single criterion. As a result, the filter admits only those records that satisfy every entry on the row. When criteria appear on separate rows, the filter admits all records that satisfy the entries on any row. Note that Query interprets the information in a criteria pane in exactly the same way that Excel's Advanced Filter command interprets the information in a criteria range.

If an entry in the criteria pane is not arranged the way you want it, you can delete the entry and use the Add Criteria dialog box to reenter it. Or you can use the Cut and Paste commands on the Edit menu to position the entry on the row where it belongs.

See Also For more information about the Advanced Filter command, see "The Advanced Filter Command," page 732.

For more information about cutting and pasting, see "Cutting and Pasting," page 251.

Comparison Operators

To use an operator, simply select it from the Operator drop-down list box in the Add Criteria dialog box. As you can see in the following list, Query offers a rich set of comparison operators:

- Equals
- Does Not Equal
- Is Greater Than
- Is Greater Than Or Equal To
- Is Less Than
- Is Less Than Or Equal To
- Is One Of
- Is Not One Of
- Is Between
- Is Not Between
- Begins With
- Does Not Begin With
- Ends With
- Does Not End With
- Contains
- Does Not Contain
- Like
- Not Like
- Is Null
- Is Not Null

Although most of these comparison operators are self-explanatory, you might want to keep the following points in mind.

Begins With, Ends With, Contains, Does Not Contain When you select the comparison operator Begins With, Ends With, Contains, or Does Not Contain from the Add Criteria dialog box, Query automatically creates entries using the % wildcard character. For example, if you want to find all RECIPIENT values from the PHLNTHRP table that contain the word *America,* you can select Contains as your operator and type *America* in the Value edit box. In the criteria pane, Query expresses this entry as

```
Like '%America%'
```

where Like is equivalent to Contains.

TIP If you want to use the _ wildcard character, you can select an operator such as Like or Not Like and then type an entry in the Value edit box. For example, to find all RECIPIENT values in the Phlnthrp table that contain either *America* or *Amerika,* you can select the Like operator and type *Ameri_a* in the Value edit box.

Is One Of, Is Not One Of When you use Is One Of or Is Not One Of, you can select as many values in the Values list as you want. Simply click the Values button, select each value, and then click the OK button. (To deselect a value you've already selected, click it again.) If you're typing values directly in the Value edit box or criteria pane, separate your values with commas.

Is Between, Is Not Between The Is Between and Is Not Between operators require exactly two values. Click the two values you want in the Values list. If you're typing them directly into the Value edit box, you can separate the two values by a comma or by the word *and.*

Is Null, Is Not Null To find blank or nonblank entries, select the Is Null or Is Not Null operator. Query dims the Value edit box when you select either of these operators.

Filtering on Fields That Are Not in the Result Set

Your filter criteria can be based on fields that are not currently displayed in the result set. For example, if you want a list of all the recipients from the Phlnthrp table who were given donations greater than $50,000, you can do the following, assuming the query window is already open:

1. Show only the RECIPIENT field in the data pane.
2. Choose the Add Criteria command from the Criteria menu.
3. When the Add Criteria dialog box appears, select AMOUNT from the Field drop-down list box, select Is Greater Than from the Operator drop-down list box, and type *50000* in the Value edit box.

When you click the Add button, Query lists the recipient of each donation greater than $50,000, displaying one record for each donation.

Limiting the Result Set to Unique Entries

In a case like the preceding example, you would probably rather see each recipient's name listed only once, no matter how many donations greater than $50,000 that recipient received. To limit the result set, choose Query Properties from the View menu. In the dialog box shown in Figure 21-11, select Unique Values Only. You can make this selection before or after you create your filter.

FIGURE 21-11
The Unique Values Only option eliminates duplicate entries.

Performing Aggregate Calculations

You can analyze your result set thoroughly after you get into your Excel worksheet. If you prefer, however, you can have Microsoft Query do some of the calculating for you. With Query, you can make *aggregate calculations* the basis of filtering criteria — as you'll see in a moment. First we'll consider some details about how to perform the calculations.

Query refers to all calculations as *totals,* although summing values is only one of the functions Query has to offer. The other aggregate functions that are common to all ODBC drivers are AVG (Average), COUNT, MIN (Minimum), and MAX (Maximum). Your driver might support additional functions as well.

Using the Totals Button

One way to perform aggregate calculations is by clicking the Cycle Thru Totals button on the toolbar. (See Figure 21-3 on page 764.) For example, to find the total amount of all donations recorded in the Phlnthrp table, you can do this:

1. With the query window open, display only the AMOUNT field in the data pane and remove all filtering criteria from the criteria pane.
2. Select the AMOUNT column and click the Cycle Thru Totals button.

As shown in Figure 21-12, Query then displays the donation total in the data pane.

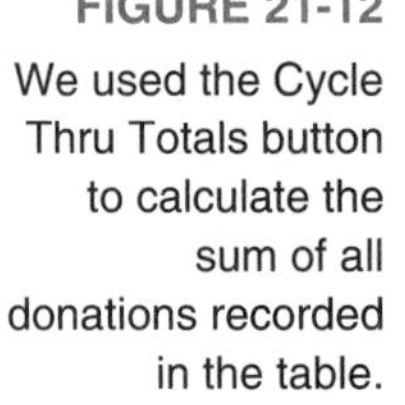

FIGURE 21-12
We used the Cycle Thru Totals button to calculate the sum of all donations recorded in the table.

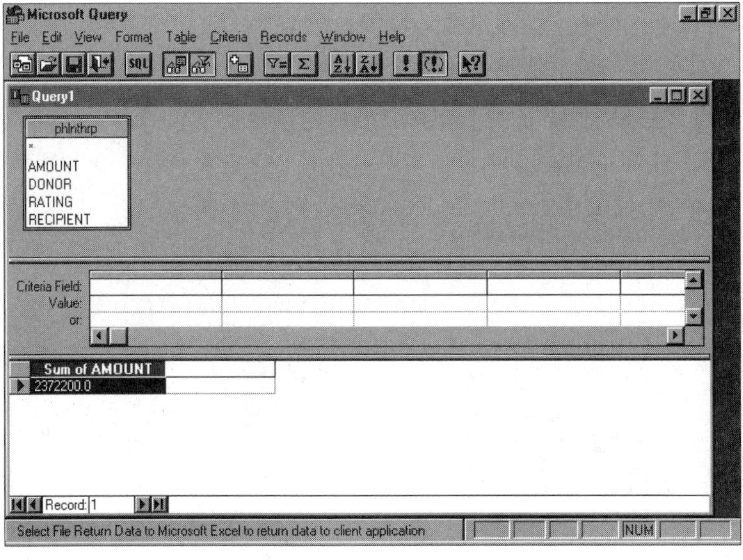

Cycling Through the Functions

In the previous example, clicking the Cycle Thru Totals button a second time changes the aggregation function from SUM to AVG, and the amount shown in the data pane then changes to reflect the average of all the donations recorded in the PHLNTHRP table rather than the sum. Successive clicks on the Cycle Thru Totals button result in the count of all donations, the minimum donation, and the maximum donation, as the button cycles through the other aggregate functions. One more click returns the result set to its original, unaggregated state.

> **NOTE** Not all of the aggregate functions are available for every field type.

Using Menu Commands

If you prefer to use menu commands rather than toolbar buttons, you can use the Edit Column command. First choose Edit Column from the Records menu. Then, when the Edit Column dialog box appears, select the function you want from the Total drop-down list box, as shown in Figure 21-13.

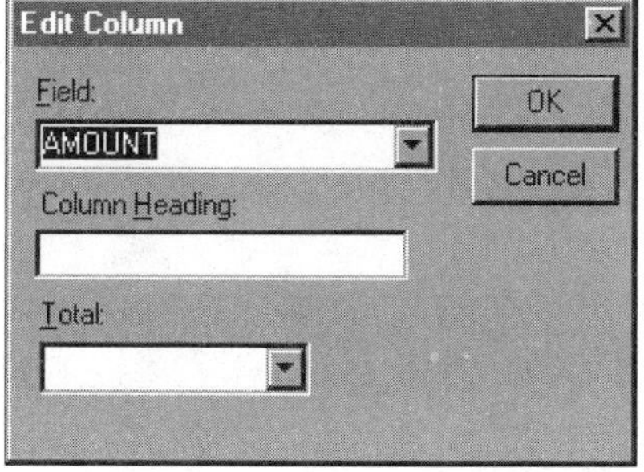

FIGURE 21-13
Instead of clicking the Cycle Thru Totals button, you can use the Edit Column command to perform calculations on your result set.

TIP To quickly access the Edit Column dialog box, double-click the field heading in the data pane.

Changing the Displayed Field Heading

As mentioned earlier, you can also use the Edit Column dialog box to change field headings. For example, if you want to use Grand Total rather than Sum of AMOUNT for your field heading, simply type *Grand Total* in the Column

Heading edit box. (Remember, this action has no effect on the underlying database; it simply changes the heading for display purposes in the query window.)

Aggregating Groups of Records

In addition to grand totals, you can also calculate totals for groups of records. For example, suppose you want to calculate the total amount of donations made for each value of the RATING field in the PHLNTHRP table. (The RATING field in this table categorizes recipient organizations by their political philosophies, using values ranging from 2 to 8.) Follow these steps:

1. In the data pane, display the RATING column first, followed by the AMOUNT column.
2. Select the AMOUNT column and click the Cycle Thru Totals button on the toolbar.

As Figure 21-14 shows, Query displays one record for each rating value and shows the sum of all donations made to organizations in each rating category.

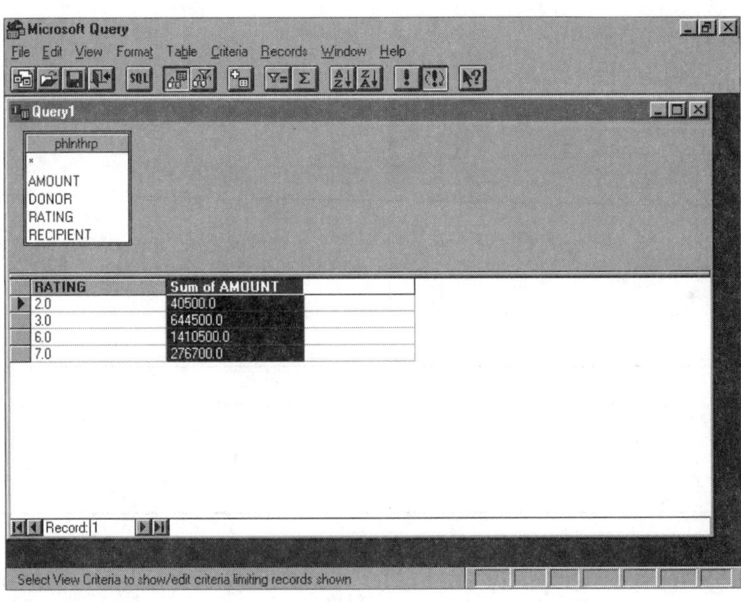

FIGURE 21-14 You can apply aggregate calculations to groups of records. Here we calculated the total amount of donations made to recipients in each rating category.

Aggregating Subgroups

By adding the RECIPIENT field to the data pane, between the RATING field and the Sum of AMOUNT field, we can make Query tally the total amount donated to each recipient within each rating category. The result of that calculation is shown in Figure 21-15.

For more information about adding and moving fields, see "Choosing and Arranging Fields," page 764.

Using More Than One Aggregate Field

You can add as many aggregate fields to your result set as you need. For example, to display average donations as well as total donations in Figure 20-15, you can drag the AMOUNT heading from the field list box in the table pane to the empty field box in the data pane. Then simply click the Cycle Thru Totals button until you display the Avg Of Amount heading.

Sorting on an Aggregate Field

Notice that the records in Figure 21-14 and Figure 21-15 are sorted in ascending order, first on the leftmost column and then on the next column. Query performs these sorts automatically. Depending on the capabilities of your ODBC driver, you might also be able to sort the records yourself, using the aggregate field. For example, you might want to sort the result set in Figure 21-15 on the Sum of AMOUNT column rather than the RATING field.

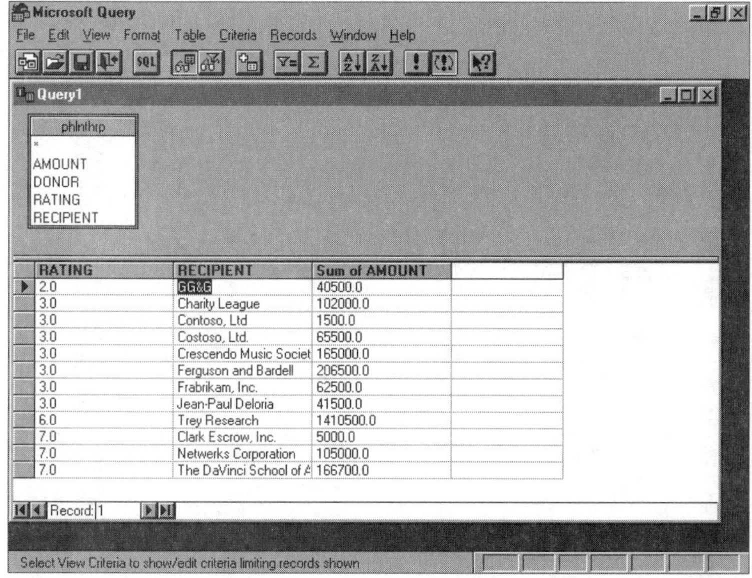

FIGURE 21-15

When an aggregate field appears to the right of two other fields, Query aggregates groups within groups. This result set shows the total donated to each recipient in each rating group.

If your ODBC driver does not allow this kind of sort, you can always sort the data after you return it to your worksheet.

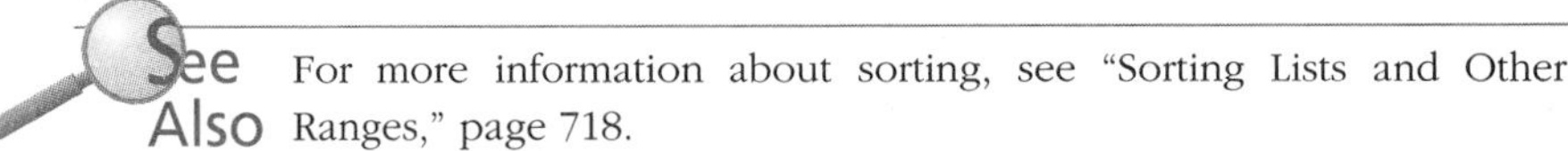

See Also For more information about sorting, see "Sorting Lists and Other Ranges," page 718.

Filtering on Calculated Fields

A field that performs an aggregate calculation is also known as a *calculated field*. You can use calculated fields as the basis for filtering criteria. For example, in Figure 21-16, the result set shows the names of all recipients in the Phlnthrp table who have received at least 10 donations totaling at least $50,000.

To create the filter shown in Figure 21-16, follow these steps:

1. In the data pane, add the RECIPIENT field to the empty field box. Then add the AMOUNT field twice.
2. Select the first AMOUNT field and click the Cycle Thru Totals button to display the SUM function.
3. Select the second AMOUNT field and click the Cycle Thru Totals button until you arrive at the COUNT function.

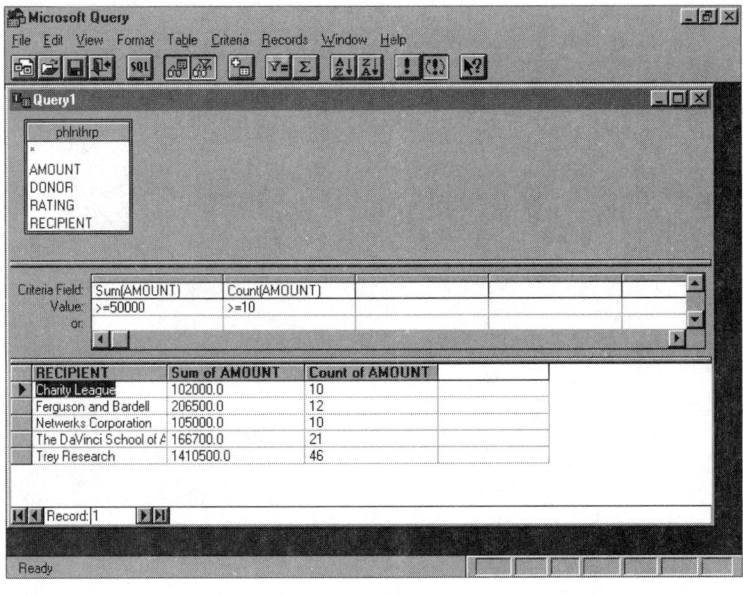

FIGURE 21-16
We used calculated fields as the basis for filters, restricting the result set to recipients who have received 10 or more donations totaling at least $50,000.

4. Complete the Add Criteria dialog box as shown in Figure 21-17. Be sure to select the SUM function in the Total drop-down list box and then click the Add button.

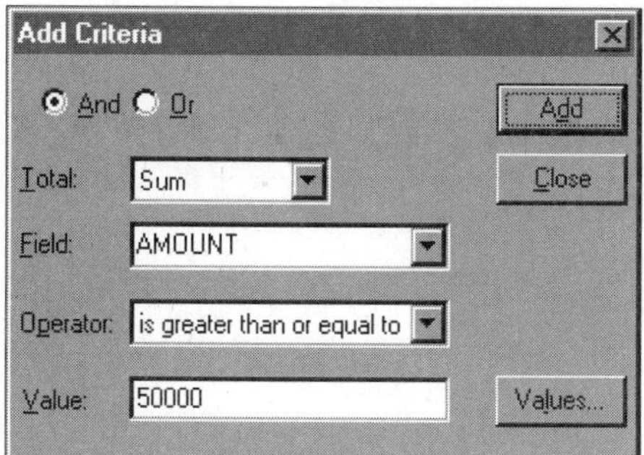

FIGURE 21-17
To filter on a calculated field, select the calculation function in the Total drop-down list box and the name of the uncalculated field in the Field drop-down list box.

5. With the Add Criteria dialog box still open, select COUNT in the Total drop-down list box, type *10* in the Value edit box, and click Add again.
6. Click Close to return to the query window.

Joining Tables

You can use Microsoft Query to extract data from multiple tables that share common fields. In database terminology, this kind of operation is called a *join*. Figure 21-18 shows a simple join example.

In this example, the CLIENTS and INVOICES tables have a common field named CLIENT_NUM. In the result set, the NAME field is derived from the CLIENTS table, and the DATE and AMOUNT fields come from the INVOICES table. Because we asked Query to join the tables on the common field, each record in the result set has the same CLIENT_NUM value in both tables.

To join tables in this manner, start by adding both tables to the query window, following the procedure described earlier in this chapter. If both tables share a primary key common field, those fields are automatically joined. As shown in Figure 21-18, Query indicates common fields by connecting them with a line in the table pane. If the two tables are not automatically joined, you can do the joining yourself. Using the example in Figure 21-18 at the top of the next page, follow these steps to manually join the CLIENTS and INVOICES tables:

1. Select CLIENT_NUM in the CLIENTS field list.
2. Hold down the mouse button and drag to the CLIENT_NUM field in the INVOICES field list.
3. Release the mouse button.

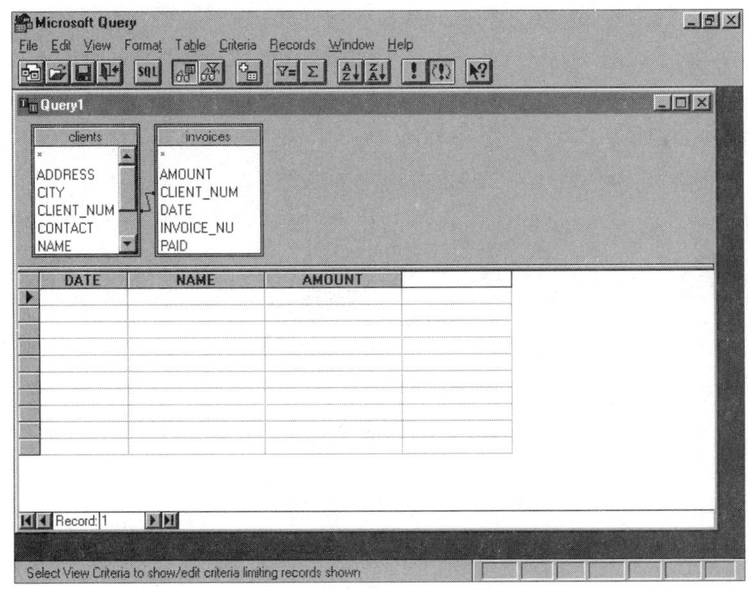

FIGURE 21-18 We joined two tables that share a common CLIENT_NUM field. In the result set, the NAME field is from the CLIENTS table, while the DATE and AMOUNT fields are from the INVOICES table.

Query draws a line connecting the two tables to confirm the join.

After you join the tables, you can add fields to the data pane, sort the result set, filter the result set, and perform calculations on the result set, following the same procedures you would use for a single table. To help avoid confusion when more than one table is involved, Query's sorting and filtering dialog boxes list the table names as prefixes to the field names, as shown in the Add Criteria dialog box in Figure 21-19.

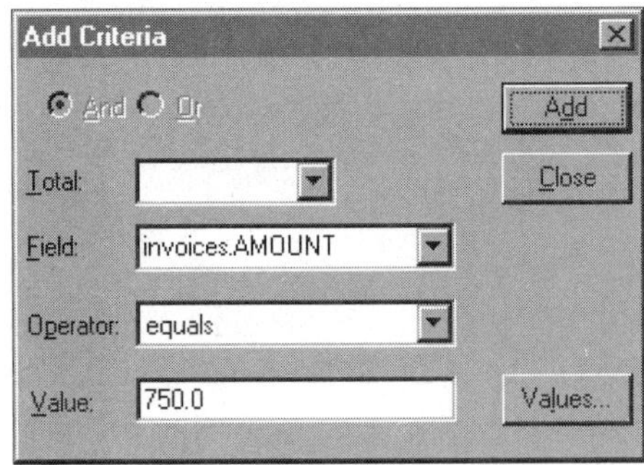

FIGURE 21-19 When you work with more than one table, Query's dialog boxes use table names as prefixes for field names.

See Also For more information about adding tables to the query window, see "Adding Tables," page 763.

Returning the Result Set to Microsoft Excel

When Query has been invoked from within Excel (as opposed to being run as a stand-alone program), its File menu includes the Return Data To Microsoft Excel command and the Return Data To Excel button appears on the toolbar. To transport your result set back to the Excel worksheet, simply choose this command or click the toolbar button. The Get External Data dialog box, shown in Figure 21-20, appears.

In the Destination edit box of the Get External Data dialog box, Excel proposes to store your data at the current worksheet location. You can accept that place or specify a different one.

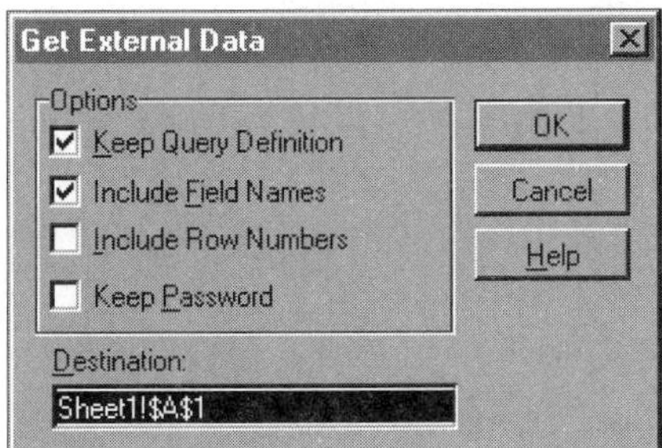

FIGURE 21-20
Excel presents this dialog box when you use Query's Return Data To Microsoft Excel command.

Select the Keep Query Definition option if you want to be able to refresh your result set from within Excel. Deselect this option if you're sure you'll never need to refresh the result set.

Select the Include Field Names option if you want Query to write the field names on your worksheet. If you already have field names on your worksheet, you might want to deselect this option.

Select the Include Row Numbers option if you want Query to number the records it writes to your Excel worksheet. If you select this option and also select the Include Field Names option, your field name row will be numbered 0. The remaining rows in the imported result set will be numbered consecutively, beginning at 1.

Select Keep Password to save the password for the external data source. Clear this option if you want to re-enter the password each time you connect to the external data source and update the result set.

TIP You can save your query by choosing either Save or Save As from the File menu or by clicking the Save File button on the toolbar. Enter a name in the File Name edit box and click OK. You can retrieve your query by starting Microsoft Query and clicking the Open Query button on the toolbar. Alternatively, you can choose the Open Query command on the File menu.

Refreshing the Result Set from Within Microsoft Excel

To update your query from within Excel, choose the Refresh Data command from Excel's Data menu. Excel will reactivate Microsoft Query, if Query is not already running, and Query will reexecute your query. Query will then send the updated records back to your worksheet, replacing the records currently stored on your worksheet.

Closing Microsoft Query

When you choose the Return Data To Microsoft Excel command from Query's File menu or click the Return Data button, Query itself remains open on your desktop, making it easy for you to refresh your data or create a new query. When you no longer need to work with an external database, close Query by choosing the Exit command on Query's File menu.

Chapter 22

Using the PivotTable Wizard

A pivot table is a special kind of table that summarizes information from particular fields of a list or database. When you create a pivot table using the PivotTable Wizard, you specify which fields you're interested in, how you want the table organized, and what kinds of calculations you want the table to perform. After you have built the table, you can rearrange it to view your data from alternative perspectives. This ability to "pivot" the dimensions of your table — for example, to transpose column headings to row positions and vice versa — gives the pivot table its name and makes the PivotTable Wizard a powerful analytic tool.

Pivot tables are "warm linked" to the data from which they're derived. As the source data changes, the table is not automatically recalculated. But you can "refresh" the table at any time by clicking a button on the Query And Pivot toolbar, which appears by default when you create a pivot table.

A Simple Example

Figure 22-1 shows a list of sales figures for a small publishing firm. (We have hidden the Formatting toolbar in this chapter to display more data.) The list is organized by year, quarter, catalog number, distribution channel, units sold, and sales receipts. The data spans a period of eight quarters (1994 and 1995), and the firm uses three distribution channels — domestic, international, and mail order. With the PivotTable Wizard, we can quickly turn this "flat" list into a table that's easy to read and understand. One possible arrangement for the table is shown in Figure 22-2 on the next page.

Microsoft Excel - Books.xls

File Edit View Insert Format Tools Data Window Help

A1 Year

	A	B	C	D	E	F	G	H
1	Year	Quarter	CatalogNo	Channel	Units	Sales		
2	1994	1	23524	International	149	349.11		
3	1994	1	23524	Mail Order	72	1,436.40		
4	1994	1	23524	Domestic	-468	(4,554.87)		
5	1994	1	26059	International	851	12,050.00		
6	1994	1	26059	Mail Order	55	1,361.25		
7	1994	1	26059	Domestic	10995	140,909.23		
8	1994	1	30782	International	896	12,678.40		
9	1994	1	30782	Mail Order	93	2,301.75		
10	1994	1	30782	Mail Order	29	703.25		
11	1994	1	30782	Domestic	5872	80,188.00		
12	1994	1	41210	Domestic	6208	77,600.00		
13	1994	1	41210	International	741	10,485.15		
14	1994	1	41210	Mail Order	100	2,475.00		
15	1994	1	50724	Domestic	6453	80,662.50		
16	1994	1	50724	International	620	15,345.00		
17	1994	1	50724	Mail Order	15	212.25		
18	1994	1	50751	Domestic	1078	13,475.00		
19	1994	1	50751	International	968	13,697.20		
20	1994	1	50751	Mail Order	5	123.75		

List

Ready SUM=0

FIGURE 22-1

It's difficult to see the bottom line in a flat list like this. The PivotTable Wizard can help.

In Figure 22-2, the Year and Quarter fields have been positioned along the table's *column axis,* and the CatalogNo and Channel fields have taken up positions along the *row axis.* The body of the table displays the total sales numbers for each column-and-row intersection. Cell H4, for example, shows that the total domestic sales in the first quarter of 1995 for the book whose catalog number is 23524 were a negative $488 — meaning that returns outnumbered sales for that title in that time period.

Rows 7, 11, and 15 in Figure 22-2 display subtotals for the various items in the catalog number field. Column G displays subtotals for the four quarters of 1994. Beyond the boundaries of the figure lie additional subtotals, and at the outer edges the PivotTable Wizard has created a grand total column and a grand total row. If you scrolled the table in Figure 22-2 to the bottom cell in column C, for example, you would find the total Q194 sales for all titles across all distribution channels. The PivotTable Wizard creates these subtotals and grand totals automatically, unless you tell it not to.

The pivot table shown in Figure 22-2 makes it easy to find almost all the information recorded in Figure 22-1's list. The only details that do not appear are the unit sales. Had we wanted to make the table a bit more complex, we could have shown those also. We have displayed the Query And Pivot toolbar and named the worksheet to make it easier to modify the table.

Suppose, however, that instead of more detail, we want less. The PivotTable Wizard can easily accommodate that need as well. Figure 22-3 shows one of the many ways in which the table in Figure 22-2 can be

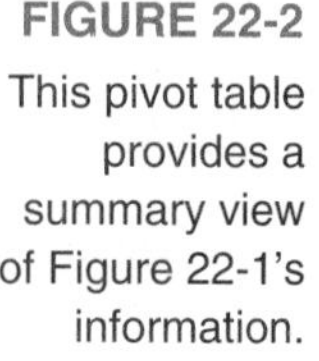

FIGURE 22-2
This pivot table provides a summary view of Figure 22-1's information.

Microsoft Excel - Books.xls

	A	B	C	D	E	F	G	H
1	Sum of Sales		Year	Quarter				
2			1994				1994 Total	1995
3	CatalogNo	Channel	1	2	3	4		1
4	23524	Domestic	-4555	-3796	-1331	115245	105564	-488
5		International	349	678	134	3113	4274	-34770
6		Mail order	1436	20	319	50	1825	1257
7	23524 Total		-2769	-3098	-877	118408	111663	-34001
8	26059	Domestic	140909	109931	93317	97381	441538	-48616
9		International	12050	10217	1073	472	23812	3206
10		Mail order	1361	1312	910	758	4342	117
11	26059 Total		154320	121461	95300	98612	469692	-45293
12	30782	Domestic	80188	371831	159791	167544	779354	3040
13		International	12678	11000	7040	651	31369	6976
14		Mail order	3005	1188	1955	1850	7999	293
15	30782 Total		95871	384019	168786	170045	818721	10310
16	41210	Domestic	77600	40750	23950	1925	144225	310755
17		International	10485	9636	7202	10414	37738	5802

Pivot Table / List

Ready SUM=0

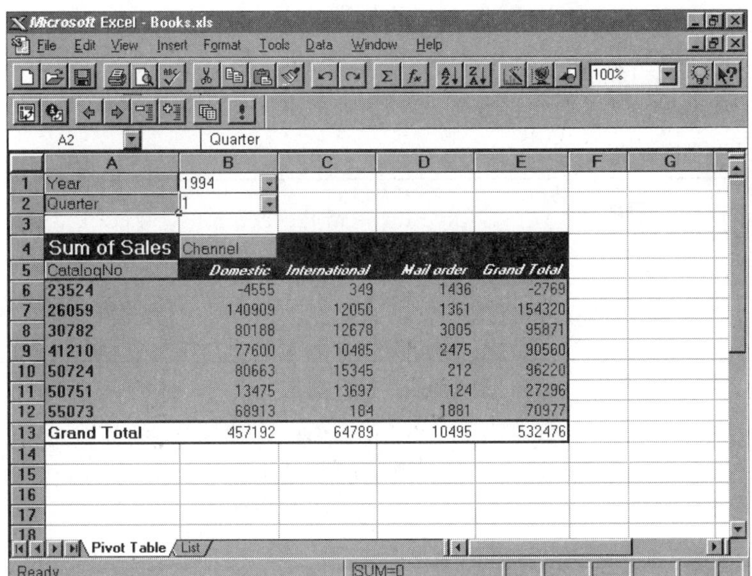

	A	B	C	D	E
1	Year	1994			
2	Quarter	1			
3					
4	Sum of Sales	Channel			
5	CatalogNo	*Domestic*	*International*	*Mail order*	*Grand Total*
6	23524	-4555	349	1436	-2769
7	26059	140909	12050	1361	154320
8	30782	80188	12678	3005	95871
9	41210	77600	10485	2475	90560
10	50724	80663	15345	212	96220
11	50751	13475	13697	124	27296
12	55073	68913	184	1881	70977
13	Grand Total	457192	64789	10495	532476

FIGURE 22-3

Using the PivotTable Wizard, you can also focus on a particular section of data in a table.

modified to let us focus on a particular section of the data. Here we have transposed the Channel field from the row axis to the column axis and moved both the Year and Quarter fields to the *page axis*. Moving these fields to the page axis lets us "zoom in" on the numbers for a particular year and quarter. When we want to see a different time period, we can simply select a different year or quarter from the drop-down lists next to the Year and Quarter field headings.

Pivot Table Basics

In the following section, we introduce you to the basics of pivot tables. We start by showing you how to create a pivot table, and then we move on to some of the finer points, such as assigning numeric formats to the data in pivot tables; refreshing, or recalculating, pivot tables; and sorting. Along the way, we show you how to rearrange, add, delete, and rename fields and items in pivot tables.

Creating a Pivot Table

Let's look at the steps involved in creating the pivot table in Figure 22-2 from the list shown in Figure 22-1. Then we'll format the pivot table so that it looks like Figure 22-2 .

1. Choose the PivotTable command from the Data menu.

   The PivotTable Wizard displays the first of its four dialog boxes. Here you specify the kind of data you want to use to build your table.

Your choices are an Excel list or database in the current workbook or elsewhere; an external data source, such as a dBASE table; two or more consolidation ranges; and another pivot table. In this example, we'll use an Excel list. Later in the chapter, we'll look at the other three options.

TIP If your source list is in the current workbook, select a single cell in the list before choosing the PivotTable command. Excel will then correctly fill out the PivotTable Wizard's second dialog box for you.

2. Leave the Microsoft Excel List Or Database option selected and click the Next button. The second PivotTable Wizard dialog box appears, asking you to specify the range occupied by your source data.

Pivot Table Terminology

Term	Definition
Axis	A dimension in a pivot table, such as a column, row, or page.
Data source	The list or table from which the pivot table is derived.
Field	A category of information. Equivalent to a column in a list.
Field heading	A label describing the contents of a field. You can pivot a pivot table by dragging its field headings.
Item	A member of a field. In Figure 22-2, 1994 and 1995 are items in the Year field.
Pivot	To rearrange a pivot table by repositioning one or more fields.
Summary function	The worksheet function used by the PivotTable Wizard to calculate values in the body of the table. The default summary function is SUM for numeric values and COUNT for text. You can select from a list of alternative functions.
Refresh	To recalculate the pivot table so that its values reflect the current state of the data source. You can refresh a pivot table by clicking the Refresh Data button on the Query And Pivot toolbar.

3. If the Step 2 dialog box already specifies your source data, click the Next button. If not, indicate the source by typing a range name or range reference, or by pointing to the data.

   If your source is in another Excel file that's not open in memory, you can use the Browse button in the Step 2 dialog box to find the file. You will still need to type a range name or reference after specifying the file, however.

TIP If you're likely to insert new rows in your data source, you should assign a range name to the source and then specify the name (rather than a range reference) in the Step 2 dialog box. If you don't identify the source by name, the PivotTable Wizard might not evaluate all of your source data when you refresh the table. For more information about refreshing pivot tables, see "Refreshing a Pivot Table," page 796.

The Pivot Table Wizard displays a third dialog box, shown in Figure 22-4. Here you specify the layout of your new table.

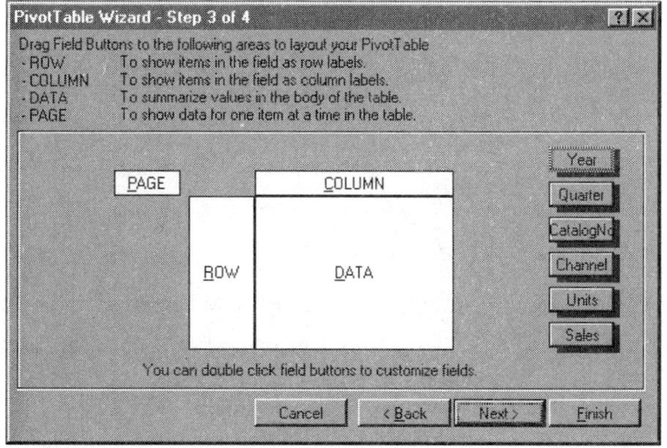

FIGURE 22-4
In the Step 3 dialog box, you specify the layout of your table by dragging field headings to the Row, Column, Data, and Page areas.

4. Drag the Year and Quarter field headings to the Column area of the Step 3 dialog box.
5. Drag the CatalogNo and Channel field headings to the Row area.
6. Drag the Sales field heading to the Data area.

   At this point, the Step 3 dialog box looks like Figure 22-5. When you click Next, the PivotTable Wizard displays the Step 4 dialog box.

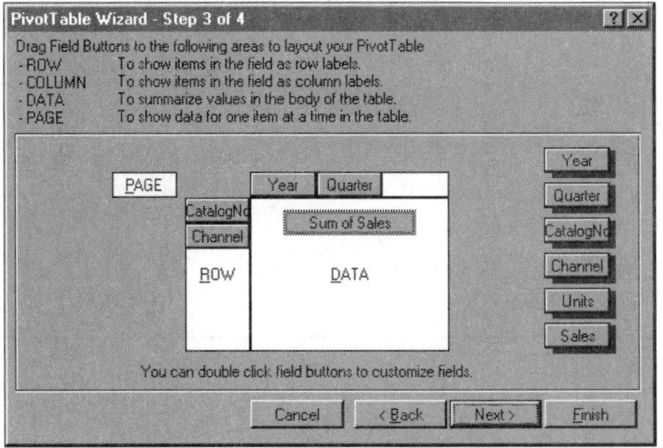

FIGURE 22-5 This dialog box will produce a pivot table with two fields on the column axis and two fields on the row axis. Sales figures will be summed.

TIP By default, the PivotTable Wizard applies the SUM function to numeric values in the Data area and applies the COUNT function to nonnumeric values. To use a different summary function, double-click the field heading after you drag it to the Data area and then select a function from the list of available functions in the PivotTable Field dialog box. For more information about using other functions, see "Using Other Summary Functions," page 811.

7. In the Step 4 dialog box, point to the cell where you want the upper left corner of the pivot table to appear (or type a cell name or reference). Then type a descriptive name for the table (if you don't like the default name) and click Finish.

When you click Finish, the PivotTable Wizard creates your table. If your source data is of modest dimensions and your computer is quick, the table might appear almost instantly. If not, you might need to wait a moment or two.

TIP If you leave the PivotTable Starting Cell edit box blank and the current worksheet is blank, Excel enters the current cell's reference by default in the PivotTable Starting Cell edit box in the Step 4 dialog box. If the current worksheet is not blank, Excel inserts a new worksheet in front of the current worksheet and places the pivot table on the new worksheet. You might also want to give the sheet tab a descriptive name, such as Pivot Table.

Saving Data with the Pivot Table Layout

By default, Excel stores a hidden copy of your pivot table's source data with the pivot table. This hidden data allows Excel to recalculate the table quickly whenever you modify the table's layout, add totals or subtotals, or add new fields to the table. The hidden data also uses memory, however. If your table's data source is large or if your memory resources are small, you might want to create the table without storing the hidden source data. You can do that by deselecting the Save Data With Table Layout option in the PivotTable Wizard's Step 4 dialog box.

If you do not save the data with the table layout, you can modify and refresh your pivot table, but Excel will need to reevaluate the data source when you do so. If your data source is an external database or an Excel worksheet not currently in memory, Excel might take a little longer to update your table.

Assigning Numeric Formats to Pivot Table Data

You can assign any of Excel's AutoFormats to your pivot table. Excel maintains this formatting even if you rearrange the table.

It's possible, however, that your favorite autoformat will not give you the numeric format you prefer. For example, the Classic 3 AutoFormat option we used to format the table shown in Figure 22-2 (on page 790) does not round numeric entries. To make the table more compact we decided to use an integer format instead.

You can change the numeric format of the data in your pivot table by following these steps:

1. Select any cell with a sales figure — for example, cell C4 in Figure 22-2.
2. Display the Query And Pivot toolbar and click the PivotTable Field button or choose the PivotTable Field command from the Data menu.
3. In the dialog box that appears, click the Number button, select the format you want, and then click OK twice.

If you assign a numeric format to the data in your pivot table using the PivotTable Field button or command, the format remains in place no matter how you manipulate the table. In contrast, if you assign a numeric format by first selecting the cells that contain the data and then choosing the Cells command from the Format menu, Excel reformats the cells every time it recalculates the table.

TIP Certain kinds of source data produce pivot tables with lots of zero values. If you have "sparse" data of this sort, you might want to assign a custom numeric format that suppresses the display of zeros. For example, you can enter the format *0;-0;;* to hide zeros and display everything else as integers. For more information about custom numeric formats, see "Creating Custom Numeric Formats," page 170.

See Also For more information about the AutoFormat command, see "Using AutoFormat," page 162.

Refreshing a Pivot Table

To refresh, or recalculate, a pivot table, simply click the Refresh Data button on the Query And Pivot toolbar or choose the Refresh Data command from the Data menu.

Rearranging Fields

At the top of your pivot table's column and row areas, Excel displays buttons for your field headings. You can pivot, or rearrange, your table by simply dragging these heading buttons. To move a field heading from the column axis to the row axis, for example, simply drag the heading from the column area to the row area.

In addition to transposing columns and rows, you can also change the order in which fields are displayed on either the column or row axis of the pivot table. Using Figure 22-2 (on page 790) as our starting point, for example, we dragged the Channel heading to the left of the CatalogNo heading and widened Column A. As shown in Figure 22-6, the catalog number items now appear within channel groups, and subtotals summarize the receipts in each channel.

Positioning Fields on the Page Axis

You can move fields in your pivot table to the page axis in order to get a closer look at the information in those fields. To move fields to the page axis, simply drag the field headings above the upper left corner of the table. As you drag the headings, your mouse pointer changes to three cascading pages. When you see this distinctive pointer shape, you can release the mouse button and drop the field

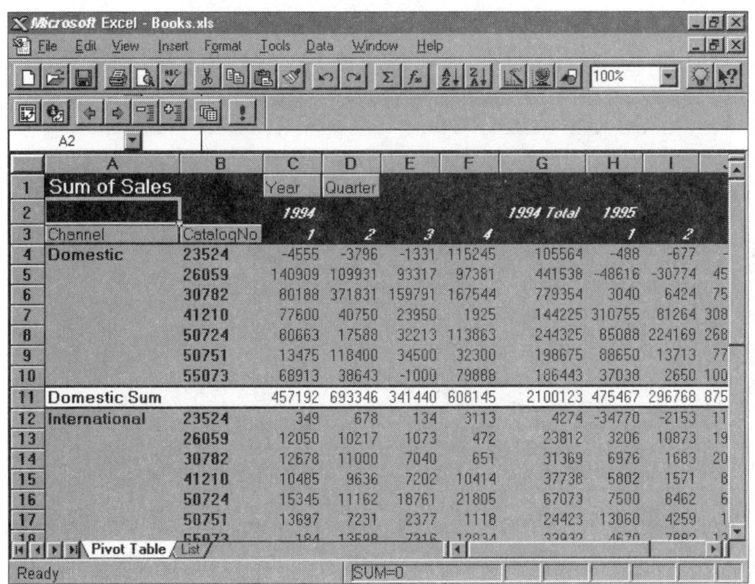

FIGURE 22-6 By dragging the Channel heading to the left of the CatalogNo heading, we changed the organization of information on the table's row axis.

headings into place on the Page area. (If you drop a heading on the wrong area by mistake, simply click the heading and drag it to the correct area.)

In Figure 22-3 (on page 791), for example, we moved the Year and Quarter fields from the Column area in Figure 22-2 (on page 790) to the Page area so that we could focus on the information for a particular year and quarter.

Cycling Through Items on the Page Axis When you display a field on either the row axis or column axis, you can see all of that field's items just by scrolling through the table. On the page axis, however, each field can show only one item at a time. In Figure 22-3, we see only the 1994 item for the Year field and the 1 item for the Quarter field. To see other items in a field, we need to select from that field's drop-down list. By clicking each entry in the list in turn, you can see a two-dimensional (column and row) "slice" corresponding to each value in the field in the Page area.

Displaying Totals for a Field in the Page Area At the bottom of each field's drop-down list box, you'll find the (All) option. You can select this option to display total values for each field on the page axis. Figure 22-7 shows the result of selecting the (All) option for the Year and Quarter fields in Figure 22-3.

Moving Page Fields to Separate Workbook Pages Even though a pivot table might include a page axis, the table is stored only on one workbook page. By clicking the Show Pages button on the Query And Pivot toolbar, however, you can create a series of linked pivot tables, each of which can show one item in a page field. (If the Query And Pivot toolbar is not displayed on your screen, press the

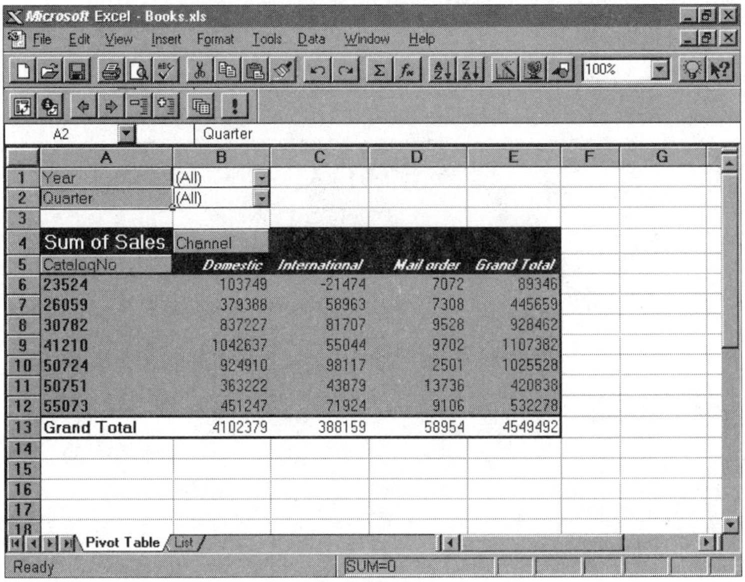

FIGURE 22-7

Select (All) in a field's drop-down list box to insert total values for that field. Here we see the sales figures for all quarters of all years, broken out by distribution channel and catalog number.

Year	(All)			
Quarter	(All)			
Sum of Sales	Channel			
CatalogNo	Domestic	International	Mail order	Grand Total
23524	103749	-21474	7072	89346
26059	379388	58963	7308	445659
30782	837227	81707	9528	928462
41210	1042637	55044	9702	1107382
50724	924910	98117	2501	1025528
50751	363222	43879	13736	420838
55073	451247	71924	9106	532278
Grand Total	4102379	388159	58954	4549492

right mouse button while the mouse cursor is over your pivot table. Then choose Show Pages from the shortcut menu.) For example, in Figure 22-8, we used the Show Pages button to create a separate copy of our pivot table for each item in the Year field. Notice that Excel creates a new worksheet for each item in the Year field, positions the new worksheets in front of the original pivot table worksheet, and assigns names to the sheets based on the items in the Year field.

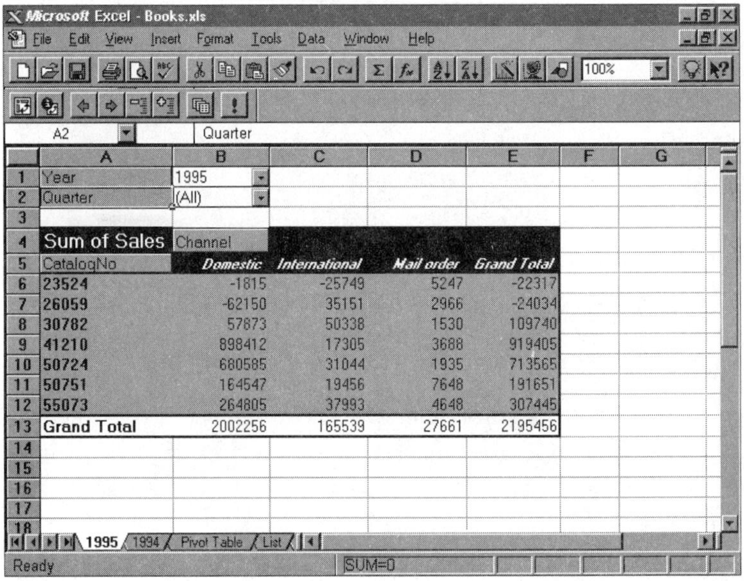

FIGURE 22-8

We used the Show Pages button to create separate copies of the pivot table for each item in the Year field.

Year	1995			
Quarter	(All)			
Sum of Sales	Channel			
CatalogNo	Domestic	International	Mail order	Grand Total
23524	-1815	-25749	5247	-22317
26059	-62150	35151	2966	-24034
30782	57873	50338	1530	109740
41210	898412	17305	3688	919405
50724	680585	31044	1935	713565
50751	164547	19456	7648	191651
55073	264805	37993	4648	307445
Grand Total	2002256	165539	27661	2195456

For information about how to hide the items on the page axis, see "Hiding and Showing Details," page 803.

Adding and Deleting Fields

To add new fields to a pivot table or delete existing ones, start by selecting any cell in the table. Then choose the PivotTable command from the Data menu or click the PivotTable Wizard button on the Query And Pivot toolbar. Excel displays the PivotTable Wizard's Step 3 dialog box in which you originally specified the field layout for your table.

To add a new field, simply drag its heading to the appropriate table area. To remove a field, drag it out of the table.

Note that the areas of your pivot table, including the Data area, can contain as many fields as you want. In Figure 22-9, we added the Units field to the Data area of the pivot table shown earlier in Figure 22-2 (on page 790).

Notice that with two fields in the Data area, Excel displays subtotals for each field. Also notice that the table now includes a new field heading called Data. As with other field headings, you can further rearrange the table layout by dragging the new field heading, as Figure 22-10 on the next page shows.

			Year	Quarter			
			1994				1994 Total
CatalogNo	Channel	Data	1	2	3	4	
23524	Domestic	Sum of Sales	-4555	-3796	-1331	115245	105564
		Sum of Units	-468	-390	-67	7683	6758
	International	Sum of Sales	349	678	134	3113	4274
		Sum of Units	149	1	51	220	421
	Mail order	Sum of Sales	1436	20	319	50	1825
		Sum of Units	72	1	16	2	91
23524 Sum of Sales			-2769	-3098	-877	118408	111663
23524 Sum of Units			-247	-388	0	7905	7270
26059	Domestic	Sum of Sales	140909	109931	93317	97381	441538
		Sum of Units	10995	8883	1476	7857	29211
	International	Sum of Sales	12050	10217	1073	472	23812
		Sum of Units	851	717	3008	169	4745
	Mail order	Sum of Sales	1361	1312	910	758	4342
		Sum of Units	55	53	36	39	183

FIGURE 22-9
We added a second field, Units, to the Data area.

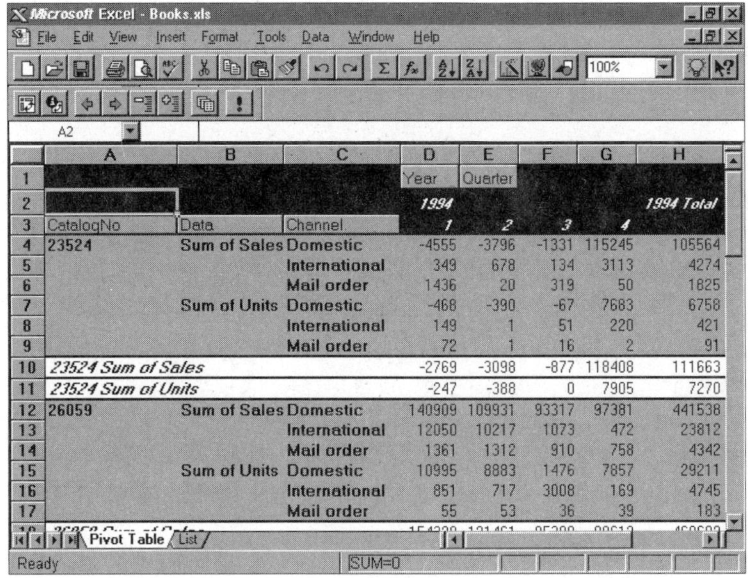

FIGURE 22-10 The Data field heading, which appears whenever the Data area has two or more fields, can be repositioned just as any other field heading can. Here we've moved it to the left of the Channel heading.

Renaming Fields and Items

You don't have to use the field and item names supplied by the PivotTable Wizard. You can change these names by simply editing the field heading or any occurrence of the item in the pivot table. When you change the name of an item in this manner, all other occurrences of the item are changed as well. For example, you can change the CatalogNo heading to Title by selecting the heading in cell A3, typing *Title,* and pressing Enter.

CAUTION Don't change a field heading in your pivot table to the name of another field in your data source. If you do, Excel will insert that field in the pivot table, if it's not already there. If the field is already there, Excel will think that you want to rearrange the existing fields. In either case, using a duplicate field name will almost certainly have unintended consequences.

Sorting Items

The PivotTable Wizard sorts items in ascending order. For example, the Channel items in Figure 22-10 appear in ascending alphabetic order—Domestic followed by International followed by Mail Order. The PivotTable Wizard also recognizes any custom sort orders you have defined. So, for example, the months of the year will automatically be arranged in their chronological, not alphabetic, sequence.

If you want to sort field items in descending order or if you want to sort the items based on values in the data field, you can use the Sort command on the Data menu. You can also rearrange items simply by moving them with the mouse.

See Also For more information about custom sort orders, see "Creating and Using Custom Sort Orders," page 725.

Sorting on the Basis of Item Labels

To perform a descending sort on the items in a pivot table field, follow these steps:

1. Select any item in the field you want to sort. For example, to sort the items in the Year field (1994 and 1995) shown in Figure 22-2 (on page 790), we could select cell C2 or H2.
2. Choose the Sort command from the Data menu.
3. When the Sort dialog box appears, select the Descending option and click OK.

Sorting on the Basis of Data Field Values

You can also use the Sort command to perform a sort based on particular values in the data field. For example, in Figure 22-3 shown on page 791, we could sort the sales figures by grand total rather than by catalog number. To perform a sort based on data field values, follow these steps:

1. Select any cell in the column that contains the values you want to sort by, excluding the cell that contains the column heading. In Figure 22-3 (on page 791), we could select any cell in the Grand Total column, with the exception of cell E5.
2. Choose the Sort command from the Data menu.
3. When the Sort dialog box appears, select Ascending or Descending, as desired, and click OK.

NOTE When the page axis in a pivot table contains fields, as the page axis in Figure 22-3 does, the Sort command affects the items on the current page only. In Figure 22-3, if you want the sales figures for other years and quarters to be sorted by their grand totals, you would have to perform a sort on each page.

TIP You can use the Sort Ascending and Sort Descending buttons on the Standard toolbar to sort items in a pivot table field. Simply select any item in the field you want to sort and click the appropriate button.

Rearranging Items with the Mouse

When neither an ascending nor a descending sort is exactly what you want, you can use the Options command on the Tools menu to create a custom sort order and then refresh your pivot table, or more simply, you can use the mouse to drag items in your pivot table to the desired positions.

For example, suppose that you want the Channel items shown in Figure 22-2 (on page 790) arranged in this order: Domestic, Mail Order, International. You could define Domestic, Mail Order, International as a custom sort order, but the following is a much simpler method:

1. Select any Mail Order heading in the pivot table. (For example, select cell B6.)
2. Position the mouse pointer on the edge of the cell border and, when the pointer changes to an arrow, drag the Mail Order heading to the cell containing the International heading (in this example, cell B5). Release the mouse button.

TIP If you have turned off Excel's drag-and-drop feature, you can reorder items in your pivot table by typing over existing labels. For example, to place Mail Order items ahead of International items, you can select any International label in the table and type *Mail Order*. When you overtype an existing item label with the name of another item label, Excel interprets your action as a command to swap the two labels. You can also use this technique to rearrange entire fields.

Excel responds by reordering all the Mail Order and International items in the pivot table.

See Also For more information about using custom sort orders, see "Creating and Using Custom Sort Orders," page 725.

Hiding and Showing Details

Moving fields to the page axis is one way to modify a pivot table so that you can focus on particular details. In this section, we discuss the other options Microsoft Excel offers for both hiding and showing details in your pivot table.

See Also For more information about moving fields to the page area, see "Positioning Fields on the Page Axis," page 796.

Hiding and Showing Field Items

You can hide particular field items in your pivot table by double-clicking a field heading and, in the resulting dialog box, selecting the names of the items you want to hide. For example, to eliminate the international sales figures from the pivot table shown in Figure 22-2 (on page 790), follow these steps:

1. Double-click the Channel field heading to display the dialog box shown in Figure 22-11.

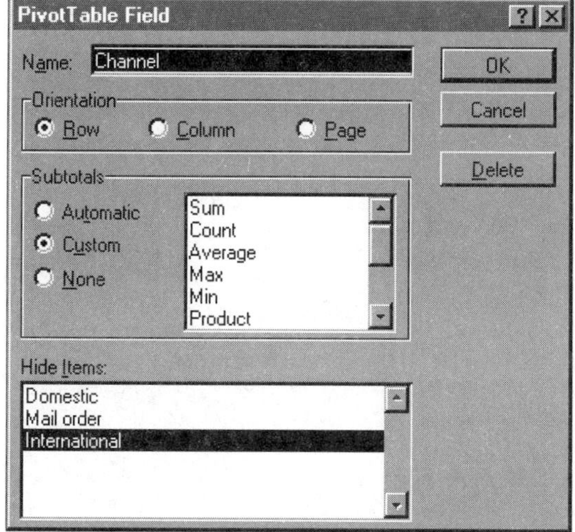

FIGURE 22-11 The PivotTable Field dialog box lets you hide particular field items in the pivot table.

   Alternatively, you can select the Channel field heading and click the PivotTable Field button on the Query And Pivot toolbar, or select the Channel field heading and choose the PivotTable Field command from the Data menu.

2. In the Hide Items list box, select the name of the item you want to hide — in this case, International — and then click OK.

You can select as many items as you want. To deselect an item that's already selected, simply select it a second time.

NOTE Subtotals and grand totals in your pivot table are based only on the currently displayed items. As a result, hidden items are excluded from these totals.

To redisplay items that have been hidden, return to the PivotTable Field dialog box and deselect those items in the Hide Items list box.

Hiding and Showing Inner Field Items

In the pivot table shown earlier in Figure 22-2 (on page 790), CatalogNo and Year are *outer* fields, while Channel and Quarter are *inner* fields. The pivot table repeats the items of the inner field for each item in the outer field. You can suppress a set of inner field items by double-clicking the associated outer field item.

For example, to hide the quarterly detail for 1994 in Figure 22-2, you can simply double-click the 1994 heading. Figure 22-12 shows the result. To redisplay the inner field detail, double-click the outer field heading a second time.

Displaying the Details Behind a Data Value

By double-clicking a data value, you "drill down" to the details behind that value. Excel copies the detail figures to a new workbook page.

Figure 22-13 sshows an example of this process. We've double-clicked the 1994 Total cell for catalog number 23524 (cell G7) shown in Figure 22-2 (on page 790). Excel then responded by listing all the entries from the data source that contributed to that pivot table value.

Grouping Items

The PivotTable Wizard automatically groups inner field items under each outer field heading and, if requested, creates subtotals for each group of inner field items. You might find it convenient to group items in additional ways — for example, to collect monthly items into quarterly groups, or sets of numbers into larger numeric categories. The PivotTable Wizard provides several options for grouping items.

Creating Groupings

Suppose that after looking at Figure 22-2 (on page 790), you decide you'd like to see the Domestic and International sales figures grouped into a category called Retail. To create this group, follow these steps:

1. Select the Domestic and International headings anywhere in the table (for example, cells B4 and B5 in Figure 22-2 on page 790).
2. Click the Group button on the Query And Pivot toolbar, or choose the Group command from the Group And Outline submenu of the Data menu.

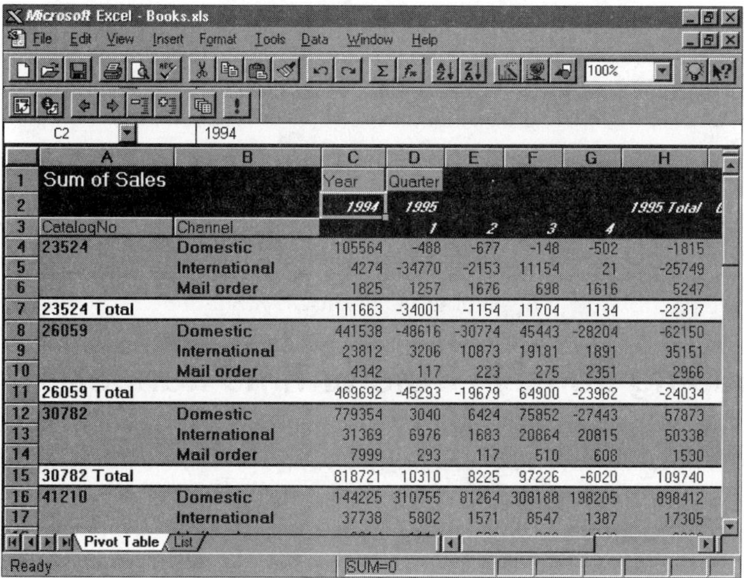

Sum of Sales		Year	Quarter				
		1994	1995				1995 Total
CatalogNo	Channel		1	2	3	4	
23524	Domestic	105564	-488	-677	-148	-502	-1815
	International	4274	-34770	-2153	11154	21	-25749
	Mail order	1825	1257	1676	698	1616	5247
23524 Total		111663	-34001	-1154	11704	1134	-22317
26059	Domestic	441538	-48616	-30774	45443	-28204	-62150
	International	23812	3206	10873	19181	1891	35151
	Mail order	4342	117	223	275	2351	2966
26059 Total		469692	-45293	-19679	64900	-23962	-24034
30782	Domestic	779354	3040	6424	75852	-27443	57873
	International	31369	6976	1683	20864	20815	50338
	Mail order	7999	293	117	510	608	1530
30782 Total		818721	10310	8225	97226	-6020	109740
41210	Domestic	144225	310755	81264	308188	198205	898412
	International	37738	5802	1571	8547	1387	17305

FIGURE 22-12

You can hide the 1994 quarterly detail by double-clicking the 1994 heading.

Year	Quarter	CatalogNo	Channel	Units	Sales
1994	1	23524	Domestic	-468	-4554.87
1994	2	23524	Domestic	-390	-3795.92
1994	3	23524	Domestic	-67	-1330.68
1994	4	23524	Domestic	7683	115245
1994	1	23524	International	149	349.11
1994	2	23524	International	1	678.23
1994	3	23524	International	51	134.08
1994	4	23524	International	220	3113
1994	1	23524	Mail order	72	1436.4
1994	2	23524	Mail order	1	19.95
1994	3	23524	Mail order	16	319.2
1994	4	23524	Mail order	2	49.5

FIGURE 22-13

When we double-clicked the 1994 total for catalog number 23524 (cell G7) in Figure 22-2, Excel created this new workbook page, containing all the rows in the data source that contributed to the selected cell.

Excel responds by creating a new field heading called Channel2 and grouping the selected items into a new item called Group1. Figure 22-14 illustrates these developments.

3. Select any cell that says Group1 and type the new name for Group1: *Retail.*

At this point, the group is named appropriately, but the pivot table still shows both the group and the items that comprise the group. You can suppress the detail behind the group by double-clicking the new group heading anywhere it appears in the table. To see the group's component values again, simply double-click the group heading a second time.

If you want to eliminate the group's component values — in this case, Channel — from the table entirely, click the PivotTable Wizard button or choose the Data menu PivotTable command. Then, in the Step 3 dialog box, drag the innermost field heading off the diagram. When you click the Finish button, Excel rebuilds the pivot table as shown in Figure 22-15.

Grouping Items in Date or Time Ranges

The table we used as a source for our examples in the first part of this chapter was already summarized by quarter. However, when the source table is raw data, the default options in the PivotTable Wizard often produce a pivot table that is unmanageable.

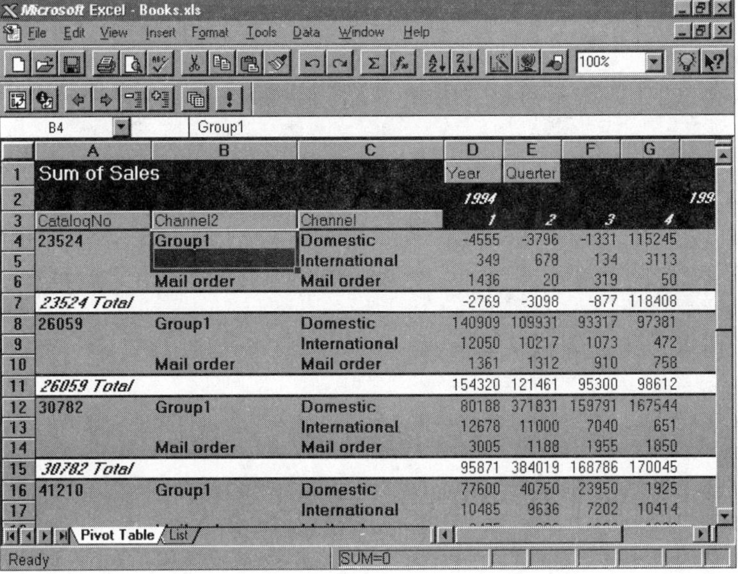

Microsoft Excel - Books.xls
File Edit View Insert Format Tools Data Window Help
100%
B4 Group1
Sum of Sales Year Quarter
1994
CatalogNo Channel2 Channel 1 2 3 4
23524 Group1 Domestic -4555 -3796 -1331 115245
International 349 678 134 3113
Mail order Mail order 1436 20 319 50
23524 Total -2769 -3098 -877 118408
26059 Group1 Domestic 140909 109931 93317 97381
International 12050 10217 1073 472
Mail order Mail order 1361 1312 910 758
26059 Total 154320 121461 95300 98612
30782 Group1 Domestic 80188 371831 159791 167544
International 12678 11000 7040 651
Mail order Mail order 3005 1188 1955 1850
30782 Total 95871 384019 168786 170045
41210 Group1 Domestic 77600 40750 23950 1925
International 10485 9636 7202 10414
Pivot Table List
Ready SUM=0

FIGURE 22-14 We created a group comprising the Domestic and International items in the Channel field.

Figure 22-16 shows a pivot table derived from the expense list depicted in Chapter 20's Figure 20-22 (on page 743). As you can see, the PivotTable Wizard has created a separate item in the Date field for each date on which a transaction occurred. This results in an extremely sparse table, populated almost entirely by zeros. The table would be considerably more useful if we grouped the date items into monthly or quarterly blocks.

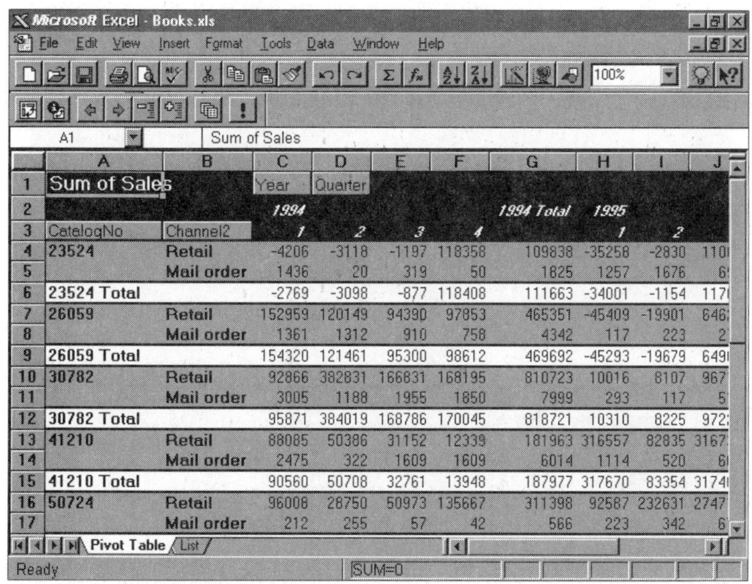

	A	B	C	D	E	F	G	H	I	J
1	Sum of Sales		Year	Quarter						
2			1994				1994 Total	1995		
3	CatalogNo	Channel2	1	2	3	4		1	2	
4	23524	Retail	-4206	-3118	-1197	118358	109838	-35258	-2830	110
5		Mail order	1436	20	319	50	1825	1257	1676	6
6	23524 Total		-2769	-3098	-877	118408	111663	-34001	-1154	117
7	26059	Retail	152959	120149	94390	97853	465351	-45409	-19901	646
8		Mail order	1361	1312	910	758	4342	117	223	2
9	26059 Total		154320	121461	95300	98612	469692	-45293	-19679	649
10	30782	Retail	92866	382831	166831	168195	810723	10016	8107	967
11		Mail order	3005	1188	1955	1850	7999	293	117	5
12	30782 Total		95871	384019	168786	170045	818721	10310	8225	972
13	41210	Retail	88085	50386	31152	12339	181963	316557	82835	3167
14		Mail order	2475	322	1609	1609	6014	1114	520	6
15	41210 Total		90560	50708	32761	13948	187977	317670	83354	3174
16	50724	Retail	96008	28750	50973	135667	311398	92587	232631	2747
17		Mail order	212	255	57	42	566	223	342	6

FIGURE 22-15
We removed the original Channel grouping from the pivot table shown in Figure 22-14.

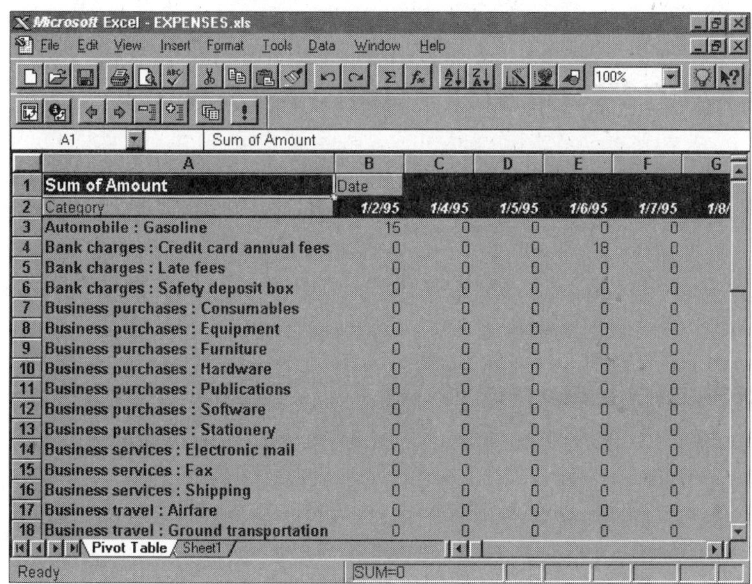

	A	B	C	D	E	F	G
1	Sum of Amount	Date					
2	Category	1/2/95	1/4/95	1/5/95	1/6/95	1/7/95	1/8/
3	Automobile : Gasoline	15	0	0	0	0	
4	Bank charges : Credit card annual fees	0	0	0	18	0	
5	Bank charges : Late fees	0	0	0	0	0	
6	Bank charges : Safety deposit box	0	0	0	0	0	
7	Business purchases : Consumables	0	0	0	0	0	
8	Business purchases : Equipment	0	0	0	0	0	
9	Business purchases : Furniture	0	0	0	0	0	
10	Business purchases : Hardware	0	0	0	0	0	
11	Business purchases : Publications	0	0	0	0	0	
12	Business purchases : Software	0	0	0	0	0	
13	Business purchases : Stationery	0	0	0	0	0	
14	Business services : Electronic mail	0	0	0	0	0	
15	Business services : Fax	0	0	0	0	0	
16	Business services : Shipping	0	0	0	0	0	
17	Business travel : Airfare	0	0	0	0	0	
18	Business travel : Ground transportation	0	0	0	0	0	

FIGURE 22-16
Grouping the items in the Date field into monthly or quarterly blocks would make this pivot table more useful.

To group date items, follow these steps:

1. Select any item in the field you want to group (for example, cell B2 in Figure 22-16).
2. Click the Group button on the Query And Pivot toolbar, or choose the Group command from the Group And Outline submenu of the Data menu.
3. When the Grouping dialog box appears, select a date or time interval from the By list box and then click OK. For example, in the Grouping dialog box shown in Figure 22-17, we selected Months.

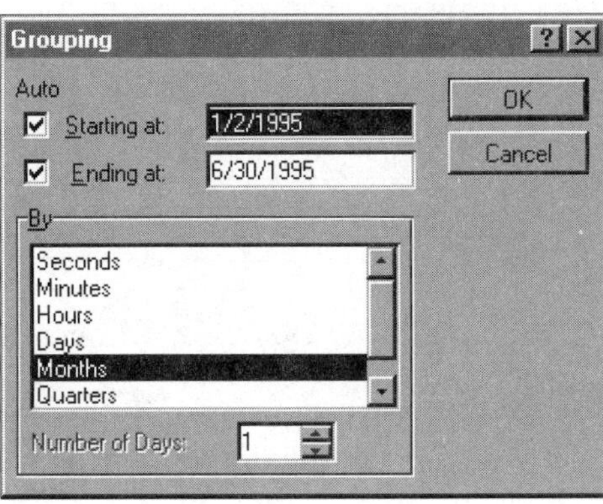

FIGURE 22-17
You can use the Grouping dialog box to gather date or time items into meaningful groups.

You can select more than one interval in the Grouping dialog box. Figure 22-18 on the next page shows the pivot table that would result if we selected both Months and Quarters.

Grouping Items in Numeric Ranges

If your pivot table includes numeric items, such as part numbers, you might want to gather those items into groups. You can group numeric items in the same way that you would group date items: Select an item in the field you want to group, and then click the Group button on the Query And Pivot toolbar. When the Grouping dialog box appears, specify the interval you want to use, as well as the lowest (Starting At) and highest (Ending At) values you want to include in the group.

Removing Groups

To remove any group and restore a field to its ungrouped state, simply select a grouped item and click the Ungroup button on the Query And Pivot toolbar. You can also select a grouped item and choose the Ungroup command from the Group And Outline submenu of the Data menu.

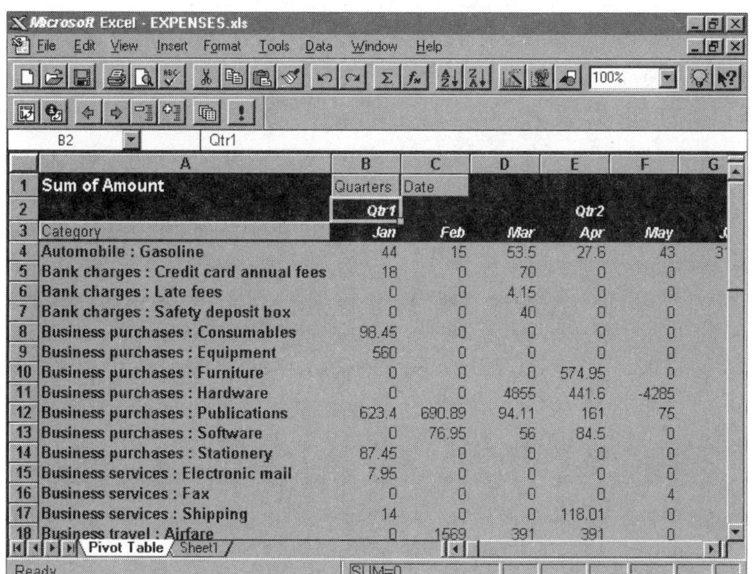

FIGURE 22-18

We grouped daily transactions into monthly totals and monthly totals into quarterly totals.

Other Pivot Table Functions

In each of the previous examples, we used the SUM function to calculate values in the pivot table's Data area. Microsoft Excel provides a number of functions that allow you to count text entries, summarize numeric data, show data relationships, and provide grand totals, subtotals, and block totals.

Counting Text Values in the Data Area

SUM is the default summary function for numeric values in the Data area, while COUNT is the default summary function for nonnumeric, or text, values. Figures 22-19 and 22-20 on the next page provide an example of how you might use the COUNT function. Figure 22-19 is a slightly expanded version of the personnel list shown in Chapter 20's Figure 20-1 (shown on page 715). The pivot table in Figure 22-20 performs a head count of this personnel list, broken out by division and department. To create this pivot table, we followed the steps described earlier, and when the Step 3 dialog box appeared, we placed the Dept. field on the column axis, the Division field on the row axis, and the Last Name field in the Data area. Because Last Name is a text field, the PivotTable Wizard gave us a count by default.

Note that when you use the COUNT function in a pivot table, the field in your Data area does not have to contain unique values. For example, we could have used Sex instead of Last Name in the Data area of Figure 22-20, and the results would have been the same. The pivot table simply reports the number of instances in which each Division item intersects with each Dept. item.

FIGURE 22-19
We used this list to generate a pivot table showing the number of employees in each department and division.

Last Name	First Name	Date of Hire	Date of Birth	Sex	Division	Dept.	Salary	Age
White	Connie	5/16/73	3/15/48	F	East	3	32200	47
Jacks	Kris	1/17/92	10/19/65	M	South	1	57300	30
Falconer	Charles	10/23/80	4/24/50	M	South	1	49400	45
Miller	Zachary	5/3/83	10/8/55	M	North	1	42000	40
Pall	Dick	11/4/87	7/19/40	M	North	2	33290	55
Davidson	Paul	8/27/84	8/18/59	M	East	4	59950	36
Halvorson	Monica	4/20/92	6/26/60	F	North	1	36700	35
Ford	Hunter	3/18/86	4/5/57	M	North	4	32700	38
Gay	Michael	8/9/84	9/16/51	M	West	2	45200	44
Neal	Steve	12/6/90	10/8/46	M	North	1	55300	49
Edelhart	Catherine	12/28/82	3/22/57	F	East	1	33600	38
Andrews	Frances	12/14/81	12/23/43	F	East	3	49200	52
Lake	Lisa	5/24/86	1/22/42	F	North	3	31350	53
Bach	Shirley	11/12/80	9/15/50	F	East	1	39250	45
Gandet	Debbie	5/27/84	4/1/63	F	South	1	54200	32
Valdiviezo	Julia	4/2/91	11/26/49	F	West	4	51825	46
Kahn	Bob	8/7/83	9/24/49	M	South	1	44150	46
Walkenbach	Janice	2/18/90	12/23/68	F	East	3	39725	27
Salka	Elsa	3/1/81	10/16/69	F	South	2	47950	26

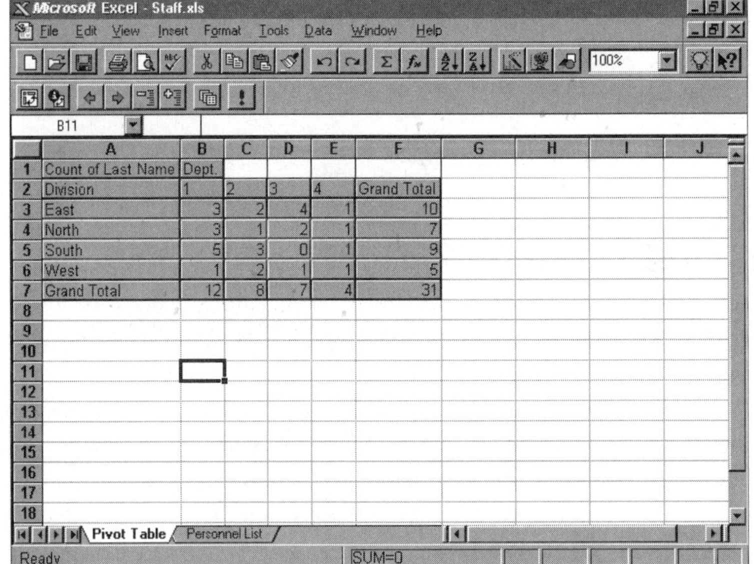

Count of Last Name	Dept.				
Division	1	2	3	4	Grand Total
East	3	2	4	1	10
North	3	1	2	1	7
South	5	3	0	1	9
West	1	2	1	1	5
Grand Total	12	8	7	4	31

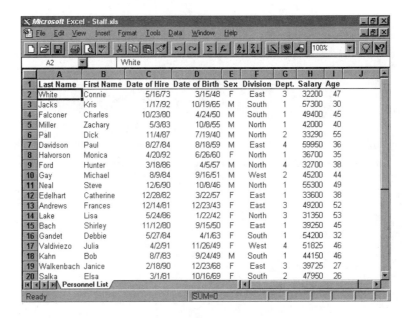

FIGURE 22-20
Because we placed a text field in the Data area of the table, the PivotTable Wizard used COUNT as its summary function.

See Also For more information about creating a pivot table, see "Creating a Pivot Table," page 791.

Using Other Summary Functions

To change the summary function that Excel uses to calculate a data field, select an item in the data field and click the PivotTable Field button on the Query And Pivot toolbar or choose the PivotTable Field command from the Data menu. Excel then displays the available functions in the PivotTable Field dialog box, shown in Figure 22-21.

You can use any of the following functions to calculate your data field: SUM, COUNT, AVERAGE, MAX, MIN, PRODUCT, STDEV, STDEVP, VAR, and VARP. The Summarize By list box also includes a Count Nums item, which returns a COUNT of the numeric values only.

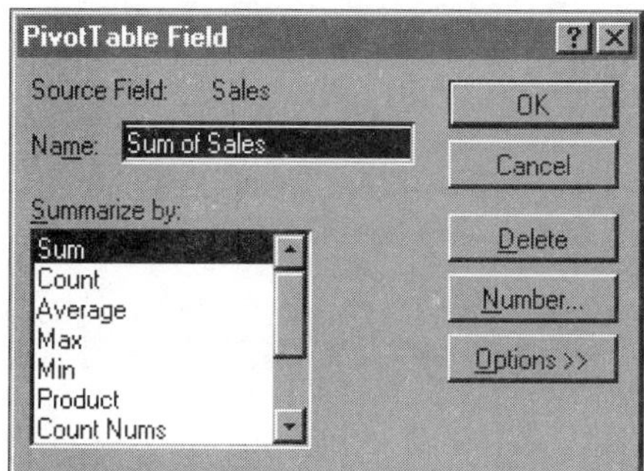

FIGURE 22-21
By selecting a Data area's item and clicking the PivotTable Field button or choosing the PivotTable Field command, you can change the data field's summary function.

For more information about functions, see Chapter 11, "Common Worksheet Functions," page 397.

Calculating Relationships Between Items

In addition to summarizing items in a field — for example, calculating sums, averages, or standard deviations — the PivotTable Wizard can calculate relationships between different items. For example, you can use the PivotTable Wizard to report the cumulative (running) total of an item, the period-to-period differences in an item, or the percentage that each item contributes to the total of all items in a field.

In Figure 22-2 (on page 790), for instance, we could find the quarter-to-quarter differences in book sales along with the sales figures themselves by doing the following:

1. Click the PivotTable Wizard button or choose the PivotTable command from the Data menu to display the wizard's Step 3 dialog box.

2. Drag the Sales field heading to the Data area of the table diagram. The diagram displays a second data field heading, labeled Sum Of Sales2.
3. Double-click the Sum Of Sales2 field heading.

   When you double-click a data field heading in the Step 3 dialog box, the PivotTable Field dialog box opens so that you can select a summary function or another calculation option.
4. In the PivotTable Field dialog box, click the Options button. The dialog box expands as shown in Figure 22-22.

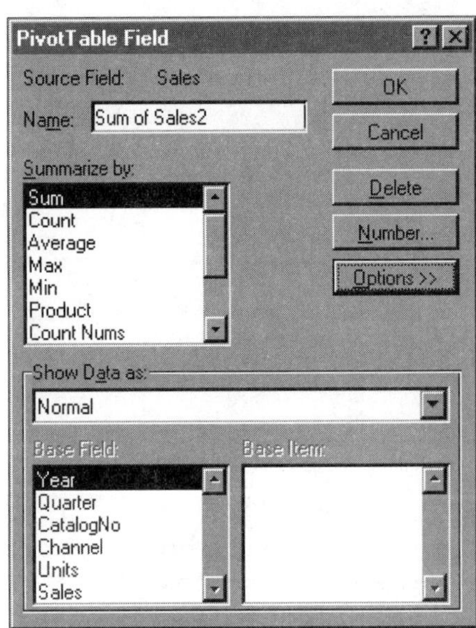

FIGURE 22-22
You can use the PivotTable Field dialog box to calculate relationships between items.

5. In the Show Data As drop-down list box, select Difference From and in the Base Field list box, select Quarter.
6. In the Base Item list box, select (Previous). To format this field similarly to the other data in the table, click Number, select the appropriate Format Code, and click OK.
7. Click OK in the PivotTable Field dialog box and then click the Finish button at the bottom of the Step 3 dialog box. Figure 22-23 shows the results.

Note that this procedure produces a data field that calculates dollar differences from quarter to quarter. By choosing % Difference From instead of Difference From in the Show Data As drop-down list box, we could calculate the differences as percentages instead of dollars.

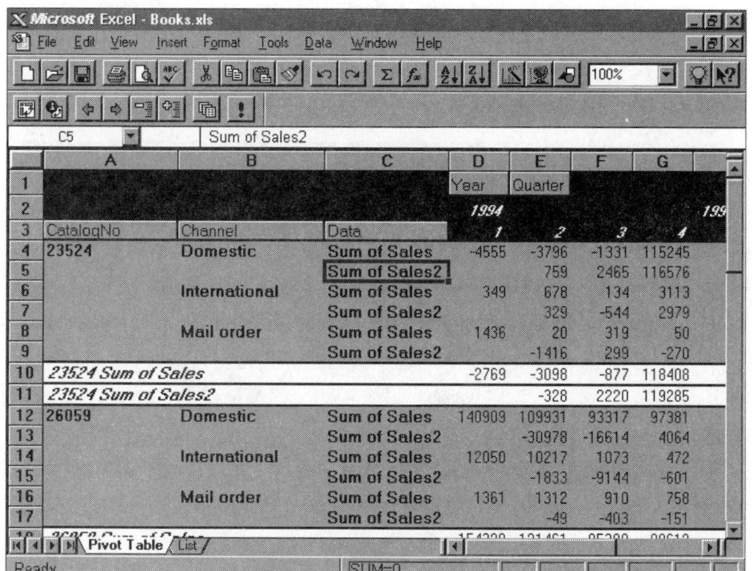

FIGURE 22-23
This pivot table shows the quarter-to-quarter differences in book sales.

Using Grand Totals, Subtotals, and Block Totals

By default, the PivotTable Wizard generates grand totals for all outer fields in your table and subtotals for all inner fields except the innermost field. You can suppress the default totals, and you can also generate subtotals (called *block totals*) for the innermost fields.

Grand Totals

If you use more than one data field, the PivotTable Wizard generates separate grand totals for each data field. A grand total always uses the same summary function as the data field that it totals.

For example, in Figure 22-24 on the next page, the numbers in column M and row 32 are grand totals for the Sales field. Because the Sales field values have been calculated with the SUM function, the SUM function is also used for these grand totals. If we had used the AVERAGE function to calculate the Sales field values instead of the SUM function, the Grand Total column and row would report "grand averages" instead of "grand sums."

To create a pivot table without grand totals, deselect the Grand Totals For Columns and Grand Totals For Rows options in the Step 4 dialog box. To remove grand totals from an existing pivot table, follow these steps:

1. Select any cell in the pivot table.

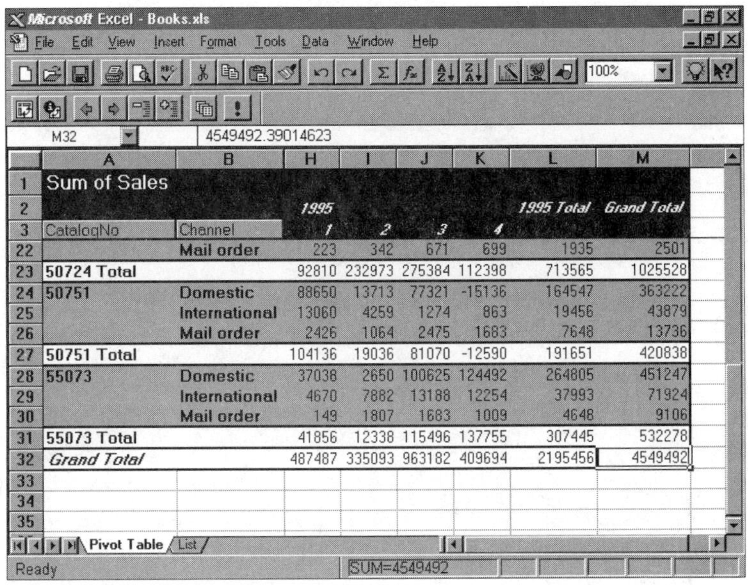

FIGURE 22-24 Grand totals appear in the rightmost column and bottom row of your pivot table by default.

2. Click the PivotTable Wizard button on the Query And Pivot toolbar or choose the PivotTable command from the Data menu.
3. Click the Next button to get to the Step 4 dialog box and then deselect one or both of the Grand Totals options.
4. Click the Finish button to re-create your table.

Subtotals

By default, the PivotTable Wizard creates subtotals for each field on the column and row axes of the pivot table, with the exception of the innermost fields. For example, in Figure 22-2 (on page 790), column G displays subtotals for the items in the Year field, and rows 7, 11, and 15, display subtotals for the items in the CatalogNo field. The PivotTable Wizard does not create subtotals for the items in the Channel and Quarter fields because these are the innermost fields on their respective axes.

As with grand totals, the PivotTable Wizard generates one subtotal line for each data field in the table, and the subtotals, by default, use the same summary function as the associated data field. The subtotals in Figure 22-2 were calculated using the SUM function because the SUM function was used to calculate the numbers in the Data area of the table.

In the case of subtotals, however, you can override the default summary function, and you can use more than one summary function. You can also suppress the generation of subtotals for particular fields. The steps for each of these actions follow.

To override the default summary function or use multiple functions, follow these steps:

1. Double-click the field heading (not an item in the field).

   Alternatively, you can select the field heading and click the PivotTable Field button or choose the PivotTable Field command from the Data menu.

2. In the PivotTable Field dialog box, select one or more functions and then click OK.

You can also suppress subtotals for a field altogether. To remove subtotals for a field, follow these steps:

1. Double-click the field heading (not an item in the field).

   Alternatively, you can select the field heading and click the PivotTable Field button or choose the PivotTable Field command from the Data menu.

2. In the PivotTable Field dialog box, select the None option and then click OK.

If you decide later that you want the subtotals to appear after all, you can redisplay them. Follow these steps:

1. Double-click the field heading (not an item in the field).

   Alternatively, you can select the field heading and click the PivotTable Field button or choose the PivotTable Field command from the Data menu.

2. In the PivotTable Field dialog box, select the Automatic option and click OK.

Block Totals

Block totals are subtotals for the innermost field on the pivot table's column or row axis. Although the PivotTable Wizard does not generate block totals by default, you can specify as many as you like, and you can use multiple summary

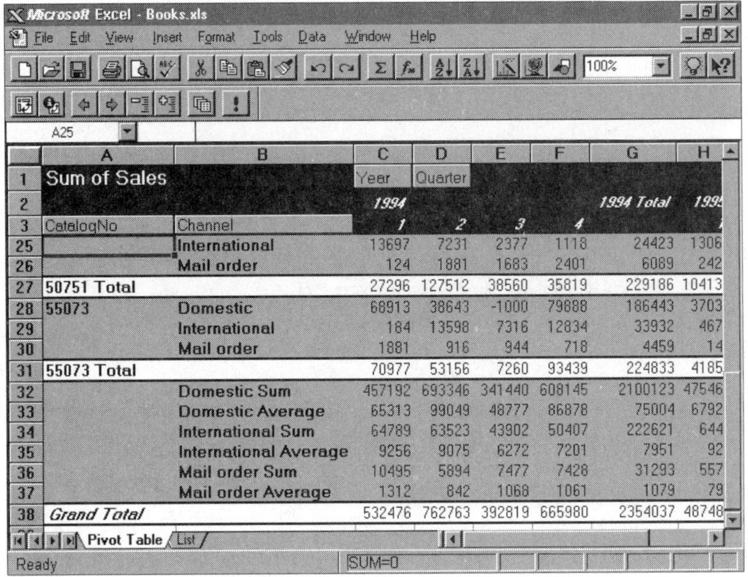

	A	B	C	D	E	F	G	H
1	Sum of Sales		Year	Quarter				
2			*1994*				*1994 Total*	*199*
3	CatalogNo	Channel	*1*	*2*	*3*	*4*		
25		International	13697	7231	2377	1118	24423	1306
26		Mail order	124	1881	1683	2401	6089	242
27	50751 Total		27296	127512	38560	35819	229186	10413
28	55073	Domestic	68913	38643	-1000	79888	186443	3703
29		International	184	13598	7316	12834	33932	467
30		Mail order	1881	916	944	718	4459	14
31	55073 Total		70977	53156	7260	93439	224833	4185
32		Domestic Sum	457192	693346	341440	608145	2100123	47546
33		Domestic Average	65313	99049	48777	86878	75004	6792
34		International Sum	64789	63523	43902	50407	222621	644
35		International Average	9256	9075	6272	7201	7951	92
36		Mail order Sum	10495	5894	7477	7428	31293	557
37		Mail order Average	1312	842	1068	1061	1079	79
38	*Grand Total*		532476	762763	392819	665980	2354037	48748

FIGURE 22-25

Block totals are subtotals applied to an inner field. Here we generated block totals for the Channel field, using the SUM and AVERAGE functions.

functions. Block totals, if present, appear at the bottom or right edge of the pivot table, just above or to the left of the grand totals. Figure 22-25 shows examples of block totals.

TIP If you copy a pivot table and paste it somewhere else using the Copy and Paste commands on the Edit menu (or the Copy and Paste buttons on the Standard toolbar), Excel creates a second pivot table. If you want to "freeze" the table rather than copy it, first copy the table as usual and then use the Paste Special command and select the Values option.

To generate block totals, follow these steps:

1. Double-click an inner field heading (not an item in the field).

   Alternatively, select the field heading and click the PivotTable Field button or choose the PivotTable Field command from the Data menu.

2. In the PivotTable Field dialog box, select one or more functions and then click OK.

Creating a Chart from a Pivot Table

You can create a chart from a pivot table just as you would from any other type of worksheet data by using the ChartWizard button on the Standard toolbar or by choosing the Chart command from the Insert menu. In addition, if you create a chart from a pivot table and subsequently pivot the table, Microsoft Excel reorganizes the chart so that it reflects the "pivoted" table.

For best results when charting pivot table data, observe the following guidelines:

- Remove subtotals, block totals, and grand totals from the table.
- Be sure the table has no more than two fields on the column and row axes.
- Hide all items except the ones you're interested in.

Figures 22-26 through 22-29 on this and the following pages illustrate the process of creating and updating a chart from a pivot table.

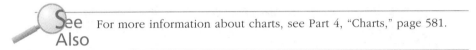

See Also For more information about charts, see Part 4, "Charts," page 581.

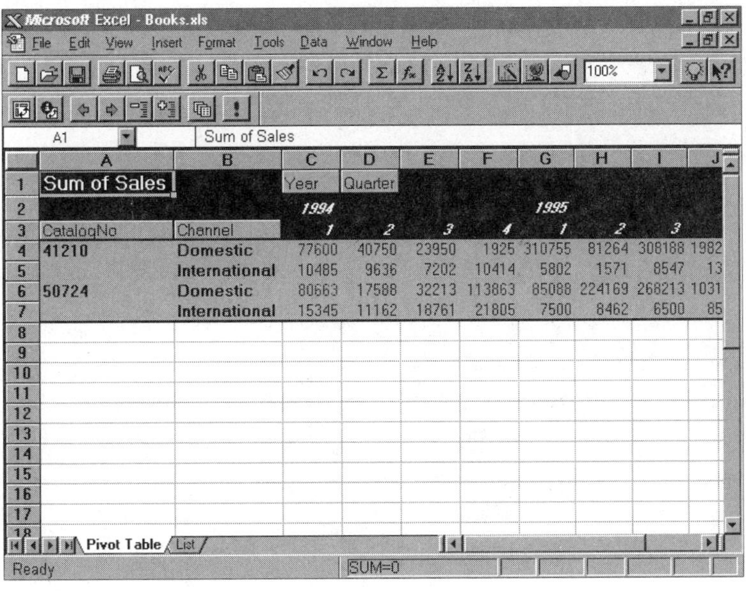

FIGURE 22-26
We'll use this pivot table to create a simple column chart. Notice that we have removed subtotals and grand totals from the pivot table and that the table has just two fields on the column and row axes.

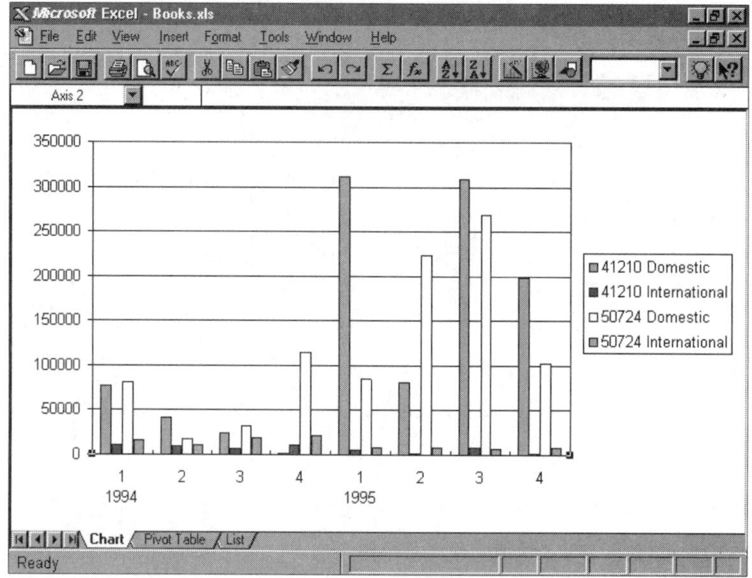

FIGURE 22-27 This chart was created from the pivot table data shown in Figure 22-26.

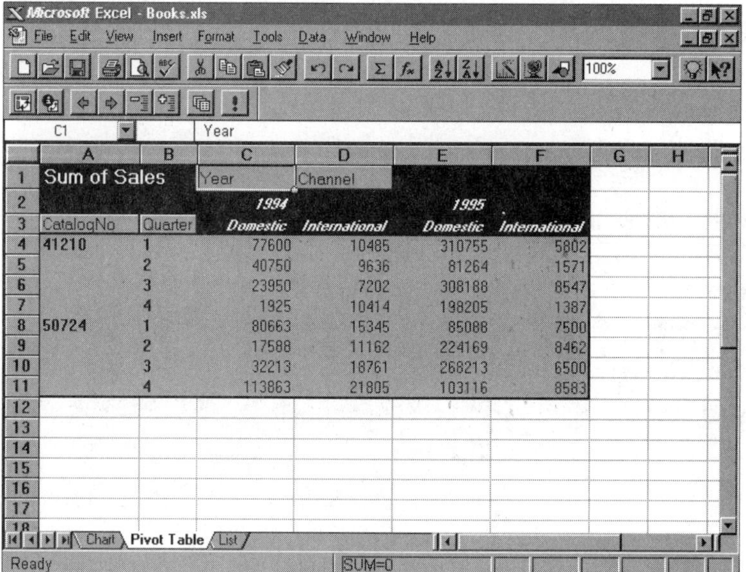

Sum of Sales		Year	Channel		
		1994		1995	
CatalogNo	Quarter	Domestic	International	Domestic	International
41210	1	77600	10485	310755	5802
	2	40750	9636	81264	1571
	3	23950	7202	308188	8547
	4	1925	10414	198205	1387
50724	1	80663	15345	85088	7500
	2	17588	11162	224169	8462
	3	32213	18761	268213	6500
	4	113863	21805	103116	8583

FIGURE 22-28 We transposed the Channel and Quarter fields.

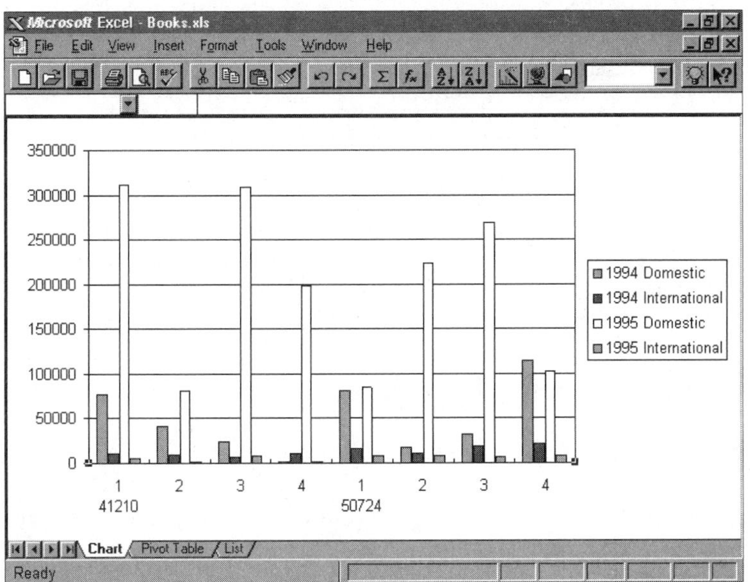

FIGURE 22-29
Excel automatically updates the chart to reflect the reorganized pivot table shown in Figure 22-28.

Creating a Pivot Table from External Data

To use an external table or database as the source for your pivot table, select the External Data Source option in the PivotTable Wizard Step 1 dialog box and then click the Next button. In the Step 2 dialog box, click the Get Data button to activate Microsoft Query, which you can use to select one or more tables, apply filtering criteria, and so on.

When Microsoft Query's result set contains the data you want to use, choose the Return Data To Microsoft Excel command from Query's File menu or click the Return Data button on the toolbar. At this point, Excel returns you to the PivotTable Wizard's Step 2 dialog box. Click Next and then follow the steps described in "Creating a Pivot Table," page 791, to complete the creation of your pivot table.

To modify the layout of your table, simply follow the steps outlined throughout this chapter. To change the query used to retrieve your external data — for example, to apply a different filtering criterion or to add another field to the table — follow these steps:

1. Click the PivotTable Wizard button on the Query And Pivot toolbar or choose the PivotTable Wizard command from the Data menu.
2. Click the Back button to return to the Step 2 dialog box and then click the Get Data button to return to Microsoft Query.

3. Modify the result set as desired and choose the Return Data To Microsoft Excel command from Microsoft Query's File menu or click the Return Data toolbar button.
4. Complete the PivotTable Wizard's remaining dialog boxes and click the Finish button.

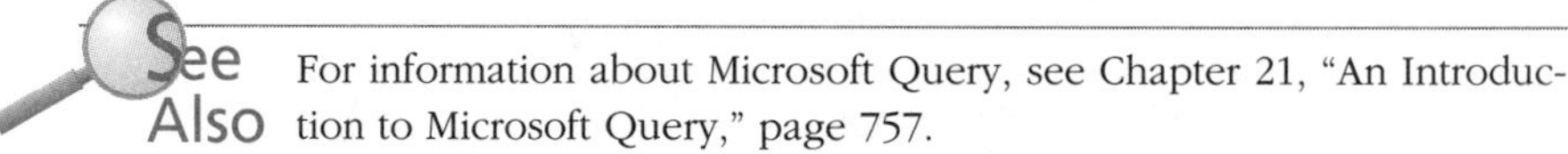

For information about Microsoft Query, see Chapter 21, "An Introduction to Microsoft Query," page 757.

Building a Pivot Table from Another Pivot Table

To use one pivot table as the data source for a second pivot table, select the Another PivotTable option in the PivotTable Wizard Step 1 dialog box and then click Next. In the Step 2 dialog box, select from the list of available pivot tables.

The pivot table that you use as your data source must be located in the same workbook in which you are creating the second pivot table. To use a pivot table stored in another workbook, first copy that table to the current workbook.

Using a Pivot Table to Consolidate Ranges

You can use the PivotTable Wizard to consolidate data in separate Excel ranges. In the resulting pivot table, each source range can be displayed as an item on the page axis. By using the drop-down list on the page axis, you can see each source range at a glance, as well as the table that consolidates the ranges.

For example, Figure 22-30 shows quarterly examination scores. The data is stored in four separate worksheets, named Exams 1, Exams 2, Exams 3, and Exams 4.

To generate a consolidation pivot table from these worksheets, use the following steps:

1. Choose the PivotTable command from the Data menu. When the Step 1 dialog box appears, select the Multiple Consolidation Ranges option and click Next.

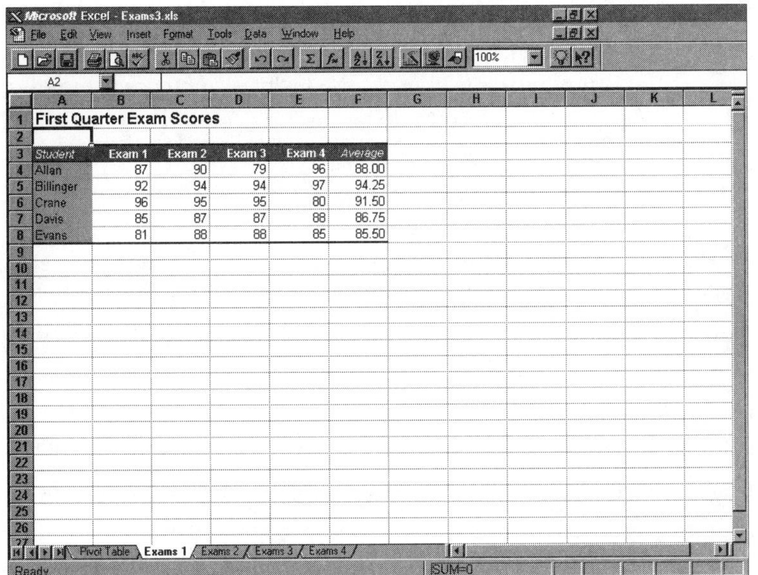

Figure 22-30
We'll use the PivotTable Wizard to consolidate the four worksheets in this workbook.

2. When the Step 2a dialog box appears, accept the Create A Single Page Field For Me option (the default option in the Step 2a dialog box). Excel displays the Step 2b dialog box, shown in Figure 22-31.

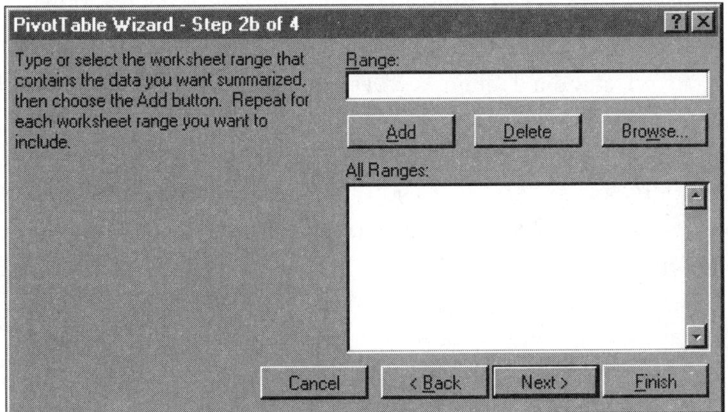

FIGURE 22-31
In the Step 2b dialog box, specify each data range that you want your pivot table to consolidate.

3. Select the first data range that you want the pivot table to consolidate, and then click the Add button. In this example, the first range we want to consolidate is 'Exams 1'!A3:E8, and we also want to consolidate 'EXAMS 2'!A3:E8, 'EXAMS 3'!A3:E9, and 'EXAMS 4'!A3:E7.

TIP When specifying ranges to consolidate, include column and row headings, but do not include summary columns and rows. In other words, do not include columns and rows in the source range that calculate totals or averages.

4. Repeat step 3 for each additional source range. When you have specified all your source ranges, click Next to move to the Step 3 dialog box.

   The Step 3 dialog box for a consolidation pivot table looks similar to the Step 3 dialog box shown earlier in Figure 22-4 (on page 793), except that Excel does not identify fields by name. You can easily provide descriptive field names after Excel has created the pivot table.

5. If you want your consolidation pivot table to total the values in your source ranges, click the Next button. If you want to use a different summary function, double-click the Sum of Value heading, select the function you want, and then click Next.

6. When the Step 4 dialog box appears, select a destination for your pivot table and click Finish. (If the PivotTable Start Cell edit box is empty and there is data on the current worksheet, the PivotTable Wizard adds a new sheet for the pivot table.)

Figure 22-32 shows the finished and formatted pivot table. Notice that the current page-axis item is (All). This page shows the consolidated exam scores. Every other item on the page axis displays an unconsolidated source range, in effect duplicating the four source ranges within the pivot table. If your source ranges are in separate workbook files, you can see these ranges much more easily by stepping through the page axis of the pivot table than by opening each source file.

In this example, we selected the Create A Single Page Field For Me option in the PivotTable Wizard Step 2a dialog box. Let's look now at an example in which you might want to select the I Will Create The Page Fields option.

Figure 22-33 shows a workbook in which each of seven worksheets displays unit and sales figures for a particular year and quarter, broken out by catalog number. In consolidating these eight worksheets we would like to have two page-axis fields, Year and Quarter.

To create this pivot table, follow these steps:

1. Choose the PivotTable command from the Data menu, and when the Step 1 dialog box appears, select the Multiple Consolidation Ranges option and click Next.

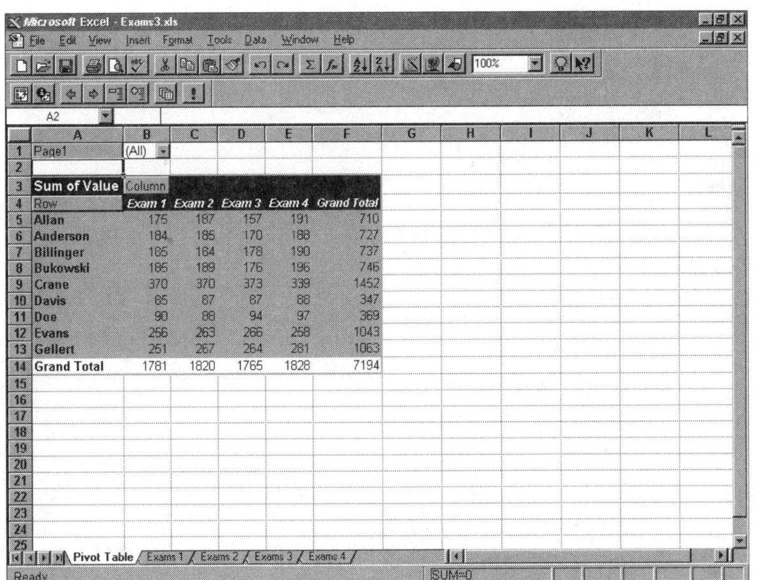

Page1	(All)				
Sum of Value	Column				
Row	Exam 1	Exam 2	Exam 3	Exam 4	Grand Total
Allan	175	187	157	191	710
Anderson	184	185	170	188	727
Billinger	185	184	178	190	737
Bukowski	185	189	176	196	746
Crane	370	370	373	339	1452
Davis	85	87	87	88	347
Doe	90	88	94	97	369
Evans	256	263	266	258	1043
Gellert	251	267	264	281	1063
Grand Total	1781	1820	1765	1828	7194

FIGURE 22-32
The (All) item on the page axis displays the consolidated exam scores.

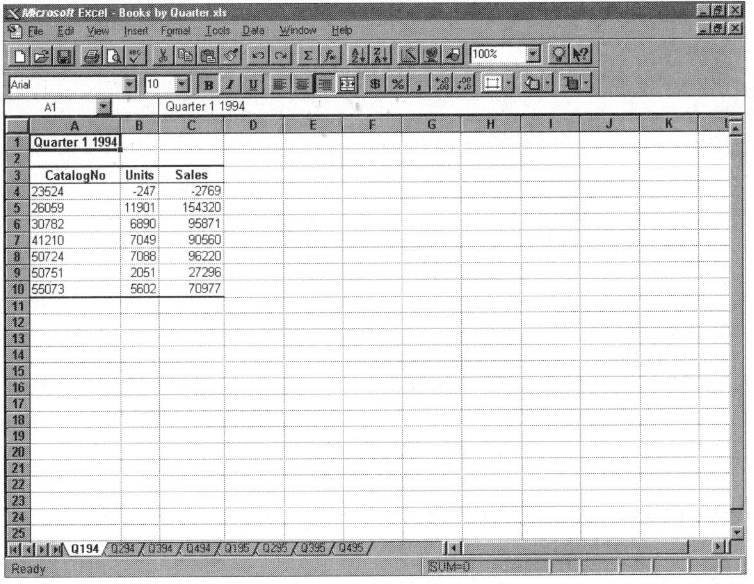

Quarter 1 1994

CatalogNo	Units	Sales
23524	-247	-2769
26059	11901	154320
30782	6890	95871
41210	7049	90560
50724	7088	96220
50751	2051	27296
55073	5602	70977

FIGURE 22-33
Each of the worksheets in this workbook displays quarterly unit and sales figures for each book in the catalog.

2. When the Step 2a dialog box appears, select the I Will Create The Page Fields option, and click Next.

   Excel displays the Step 2b dialog box, shown in Figure 22-34 on the next page. Because you selected the I Will Create Page Fields option, this version of the Step 2b dialog box is slightly more complex than the one shown earlier in Figure 22-31.

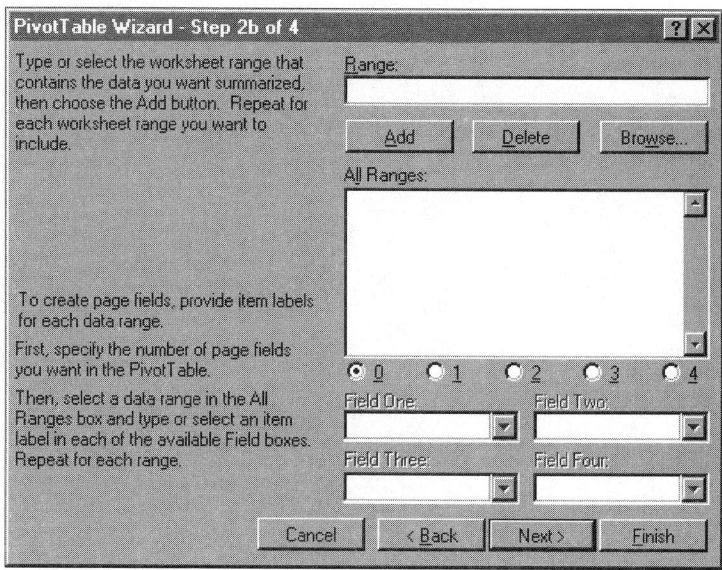

FIGURE 22-34 When you create your own page fields, the Step 2b dialog box requires some additional information from you.

3. In the Step 2b dialog box, select the first data range that you want the pivot table to consolidate, and then click the Add button.
4. Repeat step 3 for each additional source range.
5. When you have identified all your source ranges, select the 2 option button.

   You select 2 in this case because you want to create two page-axis fields. You are allowed to create as many as four page-axis fields. Figure 22-35 shows the Step 2b dialog box after we have identified our data sources and selected the 2 option button.
6. Select the first range in the All Ranges list. Then enter *1994* in the Field One box. Next enter *Q1* in the Field Two box.
7. Select the second range in the All Ranges list. Enter *1995* and *Q1* in the Field One and Field Two boxes. Continue in this manner until you have identified each range specified in the All Ranges list box. Then click Next.

TIP You will find it much easier to identify your source ranges if they are stored on separate named worksheets. In Figure 22-35, for example, the worksheet names Q194, Q294, and so on, make it easy to tell which worksheets store which source ranges.

8. If you want your consolidation pivot table to total the values in your source ranges, click the Next button. If you want to use a different

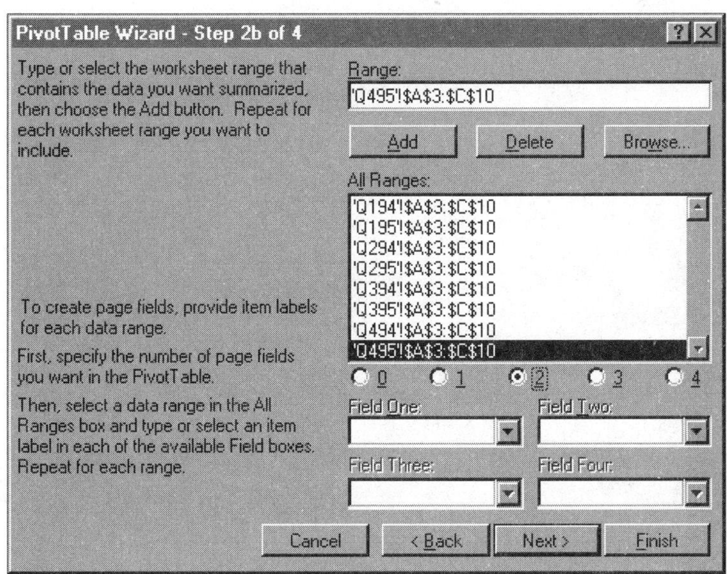

FIGURE 22-35
After you identify your data sources and specify how many page-axis fields you want, you complete the Step 2b dialog box by telling Excel which source ranges should be associated with which page-axis fields.

summary function, double-click the Sum Of Value heading, select the function you want, and then click Next.

9. When the Step 4 dialog box appears, select a destination for your pivot table and click Finish.

Figure 22-36 shows the pivot table you would see after completing step 9 and formatting the table. The table now shows a complete consolidation of

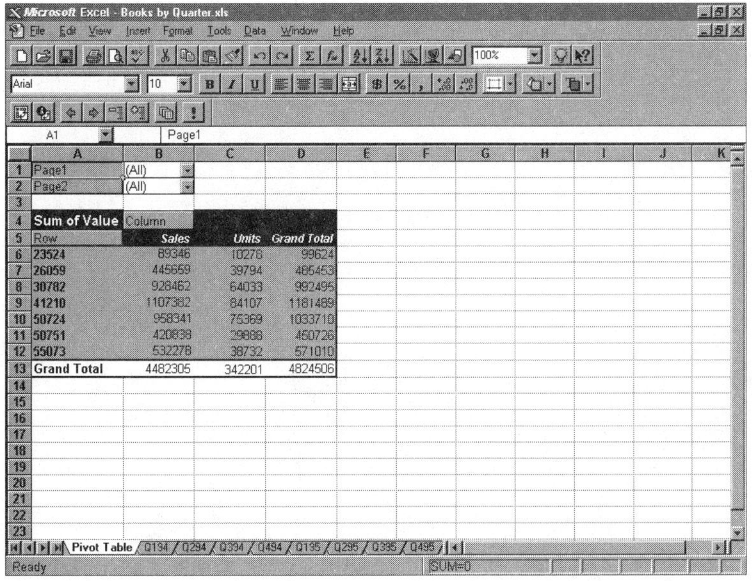

FIGURE 22-36
This consolidation pivot table has two page-axis fields.

the source ranges. By working with the drop-down list boxes beside the two page-axis field headings, you can make the table show various perspectives on your data. For example, in Figure 22-37, we changed the Quarter field on the page axis to display Q4, while keeping the Year field at (All). In this view, we see a consolidation of the fourth-quarter sales across all years. (In Figure 22-37, we also renamed the field headings and deleted the grand totals for rows.)

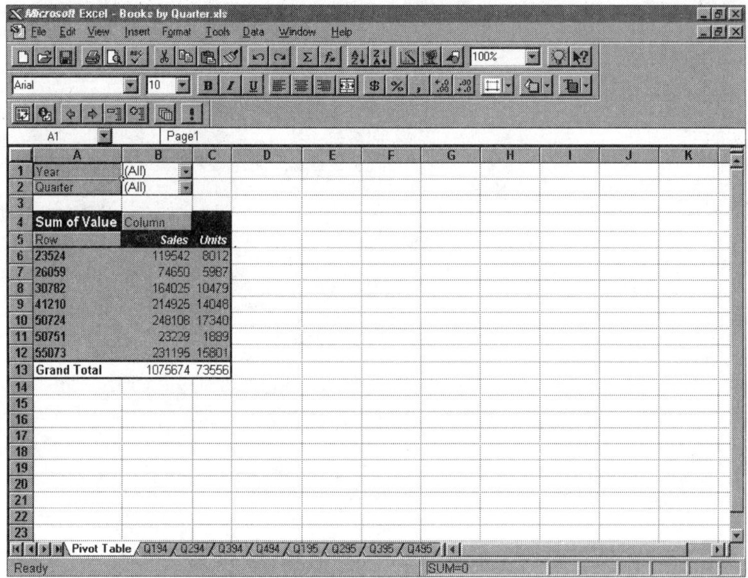

FIGURE 22-37

In this view we see fourth-quarter sales consolidated across all years.

Part 6

Macros and Visual Basic

Chapter 23

Creating Macros

A macro is a set of instructions that tell Microsoft Excel to perform an action for you. Macros are like computer programs, but they run completely within Excel. You can use them to automate tedious or frequently repeated tasks.

Macros can carry out sequences of actions much more quickly than you could do yourself. For example, you can create a macro that enters a series of dates across one row of a worksheet, centers the date in each cell, and then applies a border format to the row. Or you can create a macro that defines special print settings in the Page Setup dialog box and then prints the document. Macros can be very simple or extremely complex. They can even be interactive; that is, you can write macros that request information from the user and then act upon that information.

There are two ways to create a macro: You can record it, *or you can build it by entering instructions in an Excel sheet called a* module. To enter instructions in a module, you use a special programming language called *Visual Basic*. Visual Basic is a powerful language that has become increasingly common in Windows and Macintosh applications, and it offers some definite advantages over other macro programming languages. For example, with Visual Basic, you have to learn only one language to control many different applications, and you can develop macros that work with more than one application. Using Visual Basic, you can write a series of macros that extracts stock price data from an information service, import the data into an Excel worksheet, apply a series of special calculations to the data, prepare a stock price chart, and then move the chart to a report in Microsoft Word.

In this chapter, we'll show you how to record a simple macro, and we'll introduce you to Visual Basic along the way. (However, we save a detailed discussion of Visual Basic until Chapter 25.) Next we'll show you how to view the recorded macro and make it more useful by doing some simple editing. Finally we'll discuss using absolute and relative references and subroutines in your macros as well as various ways to activate macros.

Recording Macros

Rather than type macros character by character, you can have Microsoft Excel create a macro by recording the menu commands, keystrokes, and other actions needed to accomplish a task.

After you've recorded a series of actions, you can run the macro to perform the task again. As you might expect, this playback capability is most useful with macros that automate long or repetitive processes, such as entering and formatting tables or printing a certain section of a worksheet.

The overall process for recording a macro consists of three steps. First you start the macro recorder and supply a name for the macro. Next you perform the actions you want to record, such as choosing menu commands, selecting cells, and entering data. Finally you stop the macro recorder.

Let's investigate this process by creating a simple macro that inserts a company name and address in a worksheet. Begin by saving and closing all open workbooks, and then open a new workbook. Also, choose Options from the Tools menu, click the Edit tab, and make sure the Move Selection After Enter option is not set. Next, follow these steps:

1. Choose Record Macro and then Record New Macro from the Tools menu. Excel displays a dialog box; if you click the Options button, the dialog box expands to reveal more options, as shown in Figure 23-1.

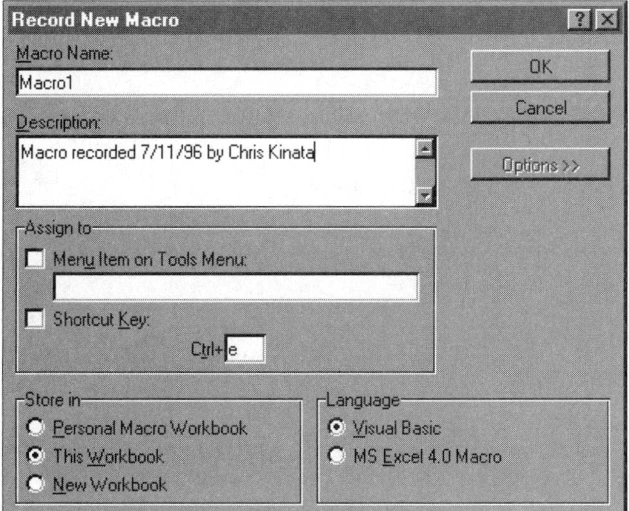

FIGURE 23-1
The Record New Macro dialog box.

2. Assign a name to the macro. You can accept Excel's suggestion (Macro1) or enter your own name — let's use CompanyAddress.
3. Enter a description for the macro in the Description box; in this case, type *Enter company address.*
4. If you want, you can assign the macro to an item on the Tools menu by selecting the Menu Item On Tools Menu check box. Then enter the item name in the Menu Item On Tools Menu edit box. (If you want, you can precede a character in the item name with an ampersand to create an accelerator key for the resulting menu command.) Then choosing that item from the Tools menu will run the macro. In this case, select the check box and type Company Address in the edit box.

5. Assign a key combination to the macro by selecting the Shortcut Key check box and entering a letter — in this case uppercase *A* — in the edit box.
6. Store the macro in the currently active workbook by selecting the This Workbook option.

   A macro stored in the Personal Macro Workbook is available every time you start Excel, but one stored in any other workbook requires that that workbook be opened before the macro can be used. There are advantages to each method, as discussed later in this chapter.
7. To begin recording, click OK. Excel displays the message *Recording* in the status bar, and the Stop Recording Macro button appears on the Stop Recording toolbar, shown in Figure 23-2.

FIGURE 23-2
The Stop Recording toolbar.

8. Select cell A6 and type

   Consolidated Confetti Company

   Press the Down direction key to select cell A7 and type

   3012 West Beaujolais Street

   Press the Down direction key to select cell A8 and type

   Walla Walla, WA 98107

   Then press Enter.
9. Click the Stop Recording Macro button on the Stop Recording toolbar, or choose Record Macro and then Stop Recording from the Tools menu. This step is important; if you don't stop the macro recorder, Excel continues to record your actions indefinitely.

To test the new macro, clear the worksheet and then choose the Company Address menu item from the Tools menu or press Ctrl-Shift-A. Excel runs the macro and performs the sequence of actions in the same way you recorded them.

Viewing a Macro Behind the Scenes

Now that you've recorded your macro, let's find out what Excel actually did. When you clicked OK in the Record Macro dialog box, Excel inserted a type of sheet called a *module* at the end of the active workbook. As you entered the company name and address in the active worksheet, Excel recorded your actions and inserted the corresponding Visual Basic code in the module.

The new module appears to the right of the last sheet in the workbook so that it doesn't interfere with the actions you record. If you switch to the module now, you'll see the macro shown in Figure 23-3. At this point, it might be a good idea to drag the tab for the module to the left and place it between Sheet1 and Sheet2 in the workbook. Doing this will let you switch more easily between the module and the worksheet in which you've entered the address.

The first and last lines of code act as the beginning and end points for the macro you've recorded; a Sub statement starts the macro and names it, and an End Sub statement ends the macro. If you have a color monitor, you'll notice that special Visual Basic terms, called *keywords,* are displayed in blue. (You can view the colors assigned to various elements of a Visual Basic macro by choosing Options from the Tools menu and selecting the Module Format tab.) You can get detailed information about a keyword by clicking the word and pressing F1. In Figure 23-3, if you place the insertion point in the keyword Sub and press F1, Excel presents a Help screen containing an entry for the Sub statement, as shown in Figure 23-4 on the next page.

The next statement,

```
Range("A6").Select
```

illustrates an important characteristic of Visual Basic code: The syntax of many statements first specifies an *object,* and then an action upon that object. An object can be a range, a worksheet, a graphic object, a workbook — any of the more than 100 types of objects in Excel. Here, we specify a *Range* object — cell A6 — and an action to perform — select the range.

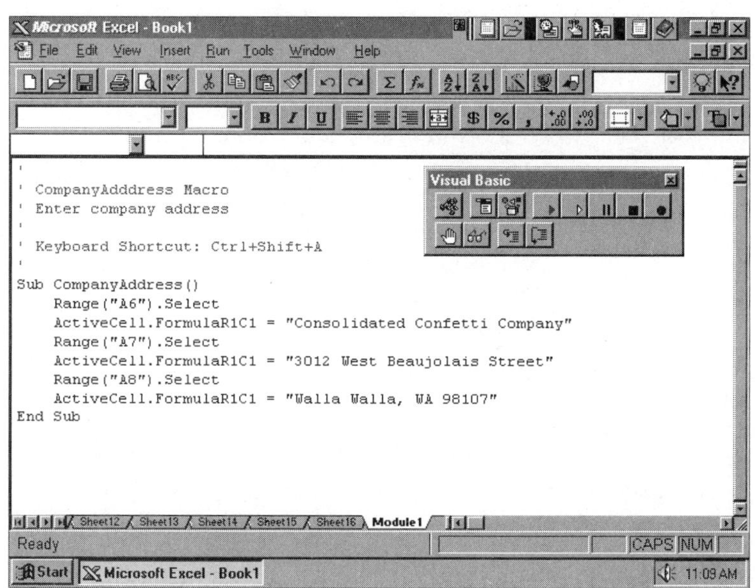

FIGURE 23-3

Excel translated each action you performed into Visual Basic code and inserted it in the module.

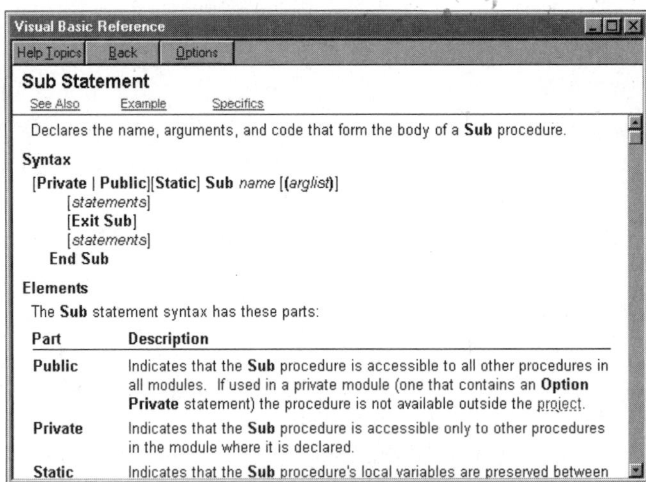

FIGURE 23-4 The Help reference for the Sub statement.

In Visual Basic, any action that a given object is capable of performing is referred to as a *method*. To understand this concept, let's say we are programming a robotic dog through Visual Basic: To cause the dog to bark, we might use the "statement"

```
Dog.Bark
```

Robotic dogs, however, are (or ought to be) capable of more than just barking. For example, you might want the dog to understand

```
Dog.Sit
Dog.RollOver
Dog.Fetch
```

The list of methods an object can perform depends on the object. A Range object, for example, supports almost 80 different methods that you can use to copy and paste cells, sort, add formatting, and so on.

Looking back at Figure 23-3, you'll see that Excel has recorded references as absolute references in the A1-text format. In Visual Basic, cell selections are recorded as absolute references unless you choose the Use Relative References command from the Record Macro submenu of the Tools menu.

The third statement in our CompanyAddress macro,

```
ActiveCell.FormulaR1C1 = "Consolidated Confetti Company"
```

takes the active cell and changes one of its properties. A *property* is a characteristic or attribute that belongs to an object, and you set it by following the property with an equal sign and a variable. Continuing our robotic dog example, we could set the length of the dog's tail with

```
Dog.TailLength = 10
```

where TailLength is a property of the Dog object.

In the case of our macro, the FormulaR1C1 property consists of the contents of the active cell, which we set to the name of the company, Consolidated Confetti Company.

TIP You can watch the macro recording process by opening another window for the workbook, choosing Arrange from the Window menu, and then selecting the Tiled option in the Arrange dialog box so that both the worksheet and the module are visible. As you record your actions, you'll see the corresponding Visual Basic statements appear in the module window.

Quality Control

In some spreadsheet programs, if you type a word incorrectly or choose the wrong command, both the mistake and your efforts to correct it are recorded. Excel's macro recorder does not record an action until you complete it. For example, the macro recorder does not record a cell as being selected until you perform some action in the cell, such as choosing a formatting or editing command. Similarly, the macro recorder does not record a menu command that calls up a dialog box until you click OK in the dialog box. If you click Cancel instead, the macro recorder does not include the command in the macro.

Inserting Code in an Existing Macro

Suppose you've recorded a macro that enters a series of labels, sets their font, and draws a border around them. Then you discover that you forgot a step or that you recorded a step incorrectly — the wrong border format, for example. What do you do?

Excel provides a way to edit an existing macro by recording your subsequent actions at a location you specify in the macro. To add instructions to a macro, you use the Mark Position For Recording and the Record At Mark commands on the Record Macro submenu.

For example, to add to the CompanyAddress macro a step that sets font options for the company's name, follow these steps:

1. Click at the beginning of the line containing the statement

   ```
   Range("A7").Select
   ```

   to create an insertion point.

2. Choose Record Macro and then Mark Position For Recording from the Tools menu.

3. Switch to the worksheet containing the address you entered earlier and select cell A6, which contains the name of the company.

4. Start recording by choosing Record At Mark from the Record Macro submenu. Excel displays the Stop Recording toolbar.

5. Choose the Cells command from the Format menu and click the Font tab. On the Font tab, select Arial (or any other installed font), 14 point font size, and the Bold Italic style. Then click OK to apply the formats.

6. Click the Stop Recording button on the Stop Recording toolbar.

You can test the edited macro by choosing Company Address from the Tools menu or by pressing Ctrl-Shift-A. When you run the macro this time, Excel not only enters the address but also applies the font formats you specified. When you switch to the module containing your macro, you'll see that the new Visual Basic code has been inserted, as shown in the following listing:

```
Sub CompanyAddress()
  Range("A6").Select
  ActiveCell.FormulaR1C1 = "Consolidated Confetti Company"
  With Selection.Font
    .Name = "Arial"
    .FontStyle = "Bold Italic"
    .Size = 14
    .Strikethrough = False
    .Superscript = False
    .Subscript = False
    .OutlineFont = False
    .Shadow = False
    .Underline = xlNone
    .ColorIndex = xlAutomatic
  End With
  Range("A7").Select
  ActiveCell.FormulaR1C1 = "3012 West Beaujolais Street"
  Range("A8").Select
  ActiveCell.FormulaR1C1 = "Walla Walla, WA 98107"
End Sub
```

The With and End With statements specify a series of properties belonging to an object — in this case, the font of the current selection. (In the CompanyAddress macro, the active cell and the selection are the same — cell A6. Because you can apply a series of font formatting options to an entire range, Excel records the action with Selection rather than ActiveCell.)

Using Absolute and Relative References

When you pulled down the Record Macro submenu earlier, you may have noticed the Use Relative References command. After you choose this command, a check appears before the command name to show that the command is active. This command lets you specify whether you want to record cell references as relative references or absolute references. (You can toggle back and forth between relative and absolute references at any time — even while recording a macro.) Regardless of which command you choose, references are recorded in the A1 format.

Suppose that instead of inserting the company's name and address in cells A6:A8 of the active worksheet, you'd like to insert the address in whichever cell happens to be active when you run the macro. In order to do this, we need to create a new CompanyAddress macro that uses relative references instead of absolute references:

1. Switch to the module containing the CompanyAddress macro, select the Visual Basic statements between (not including) the Sub and End Sub statements, and choose Cut from the Edit menu.
2. Add a line after the End Sub statement and type

   ```
   Sub CompanyAddressOriginal
   ```

3. Press Enter, choose Paste from the Edit menu, and type *End Sub*. This preserves a copy of the original macro so that we can compare the two versions.

   This second copy of the macro now has the name Company-AddressOriginal. To assign a new menu item and key combination to this macro, you can choose Macro from the Tools menu, select the name of the macro in the Macro Name/Reference list box, click the Options button, and then set the options you want.

4. Click an insertion point at the beginning of the End Sub statement in the first copy of the macro.
5. Choose Record Macro and then Mark Position For Recording from the Tools menu.

6. Switch back to the worksheet, clear the worksheet, and select cell A6.
7. Choose Record Macro and then Use Relative References from the Tools menu. Then choose Record Macro and then Record At Mark from the Tools menu.
8. Choose Cells from the Format menu and select 14-point Arial bold italic. Enter the text

   Consolidated Confetti Company

   Then press the Down direction key once and type

   3012 West Beaujolais Street

   Press the Down direction key again and type

   Walla Walla, WA 98107

   Then press Enter.
9. Click the Stop Recording button.

If you switch back to the module, you'll see the new macro, which is shown in the following listing:

```
Sub CompanyAddress()
  ActiveCell.FormulaR1C1 = "Consolidated Confetti Company"
  With Selection.Font
    .Name = "Arial"
    .FontStyle = "Bold Italic"
    .Size = 14
    .Strikethrough = False
    .Superscript = False
    .Subscript = False
    .OutlineFont = False
    .Shadow = False
    .Underline = xlNone
    .ColorIndex = xlAutomatic
  End With
  ActiveCell.Offset(1, 0).Range("A1").Select
  ActiveCell.FormulaR1C1 = "3012 West Beaujolais Street"
  ActiveCell.Offset(1, 0).Range("A1").Select
  ActiveCell.FormulaR1C1 = "Walla Walla, WA 98107"
End Sub
```

The original macro enters the address in the range A6:A8, regardless of which cell is active when you start the macro. The new macro, on the other hand, enters the address in the active cell, no matter where that cell is located.

If you compare the two versions of the macro, you'll see that the only difference between them lies in the statements used to select cells. For example, the new version of the macro does not include a statement for selecting the first cell because it uses relative references and the first cell is already selected.

In addition, to select the second cell, the original macro uses the statement

```
Range("A7").Select
```

whereas the new version uses

```
ActiveCell.Offset(1, 0).Range("A1").Select
```

To move from the active cell to the cell below it in the new macro, Visual Basic starts with the Selection object to which it applies the Offset method. The Range keyword then returns a range having the same dimensions as its argument. In this case, the argument "A1" specifies that we want a range consisting of a single cell. Finally, the Select method selects the range, as in the original macro.

Obviously, the position of the active cell makes a great deal of difference when you use a macro that was recorded with relative references. Before you run the macro, be sure to select the cell in which you want to enter the address. Otherwise, the address is entered wherever the active cell happens to be.

The major difference between using cell references in a worksheet and in a module is this: In a worksheet, you use the $ symbol to indicate that a column or row reference is absolute, but in a module, all references are absolute. As a result, relative references in modules can be constructed only by using the Offset method on an absolute Range object.

Which form is better — absolute or relative? It depends. Absolute references are useful when you want to perform the same action in exactly the same spot in several worksheets, or when you want to perform the same action repeatedly in the same part of one worksheet. Relative references are useful when you want to perform an action anywhere in a worksheet.

Macro Subroutines

Suppose you're creating a complex macro and you discover that, among other things, you want the macro to perform a task that you've already recorded under a different name. Or suppose you discover that a task you've recorded as part of a macro is actually something you'd like to use by itself. In our CompanyAddress macro, for example, it might be nice if we could quickly and easily apply the font formats of the company name to other items in a worksheet.

With Visual Basic, you can conveniently divide large macros into a series of smaller macros, and you can easily string together a series of small macros to create one large macro. A macro that is used by another macro is called a *subroutine*. Macro subroutines can simplify your macros because you have to write only one set of instructions rather than repeat the instructions over and over again. To use a macro subroutine in another macro, you *call* the subroutine by using its name in the other macro.

To demonstrate, let's split the CompanyAddress macro into two parts:

1. Switch to the CompanyAddress macro and select the statements that format the font of the company's name:

```
With Selection.Font
   .Name = "Arial"
   .FontStyle = "Bold Italic"
   .Size = 14
   .Strikethrough = False
   .Superscript = False
   .Subscript = False
   .OutlineFont = False
   .Shadow = False
   .Underline = xlNone
   .ColorIndex = xlAutomatic
End With
```

2. Choose Cut from the Edit menu.
3. Click an insertion point below the End Sub statement at the end of the CompanyAddress macro, type

    Sub CompanyFont( )

   and press Enter to start a new line.
4. Choose Paste from the Edit menu to reinsert the font formatting codes, type

    End Sub

   and then press Enter.

You've created a new CompanyFont macro by removing the font formatting codes from the CompanyAddress macro. As mentioned, to run one macro from within another, you must use the name of the second macro in the first. Update the CompanyAddress macro so that it uses the CompanyFont macro by following these steps:

1. Click an insertion point at the end of the statement

```
ActiveCell.FormulaR1C1 = "Consolidated Confetti Company"
```

   and press Enter to insert a new line.

2. Type *CompanyFont*.

When you've finished, the two macros should look like the ones in the following listing:

```
Sub CompanyAddress()
  ActiveCell.FormulaR1C1 = "Consolidated Confetti Company"
  CompanyFont
  ActiveCell.Offset(1, 0).Range("A1").Select
  ActiveCell.FormulaR1C1 = "3012 West Beaujolais Street"
  ActiveCell.Offset(1, 0).Range("A1").Select
  ActiveCell.FormulaR1C1 = "Walla Walla, WA 98107"
End Sub

Sub CompanyFont()
  With Selection.Font
    .Name = "Arial"
    .FontStyle = "Bold Italic"
    .Size = 14
    .Strikethrough = False
    .Superscript = False
    .Subscript = False
    .OutlineFont = False
    .Shadow = False
    .Underline = xlNone
    .ColorIndex = xlAutomatic
  End With
End Sub
```

When you activate the CompanyAddress macro by choosing Company Address from the Tools menu or by pressing Ctrl-Shift-A, Excel runs the first statement in the macro. When Excel reaches the statement that calls the CompanyFont macro, it switches to the first line of CompanyFont. When Excel reaches the End Sub statement at the end of CompanyFont, it returns to the statement in CompanyAddress below the one that called Company-Font and continues until it reaches the End Sub statement at the end of CompanyAddress.

Other Ways to Run Macros

Earlier in this chapter we assigned the CompanyAddress macro to the Company Address menu item at the bottom of the Tools menu and to the Ctrl-Shift-A key combination. Excel offers many other ways to run macros.

Using the Macro Dialog Box

You don't have to know a macro's menu assignment or key combination in order to run the macro. Instead, you can use the Macro dialog box, like this:

1. Choose Macro from the Tools menu to display the Macro dialog box, as shown in Figure 23-5.
2. Select the name of the macro and click the Run button.

FIGURE 23-5
You can run macros from the Macro dialog box.

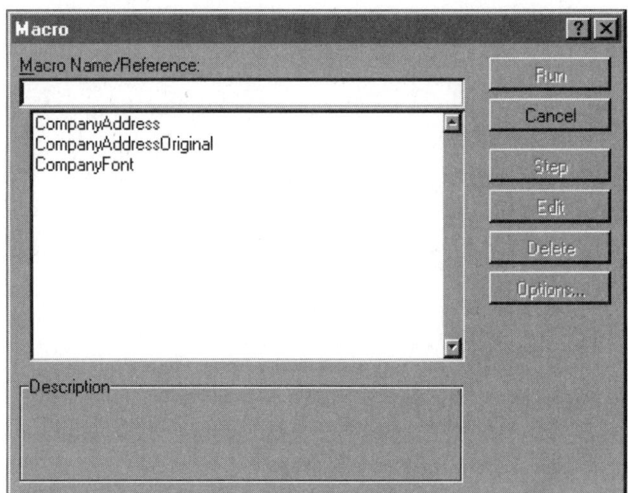

TIP You can also use the Macro dialog box to edit macros, or you can click the Options button to assign the macro to a Tools menu item or key combination. See "Recording Macros," page 830.

Using a Toolbar Button

You can also assign a macro to a button on a toolbar, making it available for use on any sheet in the workbook. Suppose you want to add a SmileyFace button to the Standard toolbar and then assign the CompanyAddress macro to it. You can do so by following these steps:

1. Position the mouse pointer over any displayed toolbar and click the right mouse button. When the shortcut menu appears, choose Customize.
2. In the Customize dialog box, select the Custom category to display a collection of toolbar buttons.

3. Drag the SmileyFace button to the Standard toolbar and position it between the last two buttons. When you release the mouse button, Excel inserts the SmileyFace button in the Standard toolbar and displays the Assign Macro dialog box.
4. Select the name of the macro you want to assign to the button and click OK.

You can also use the Assign Macro dialog box to simultaneously record a new macro and assign it to a button, or to jump to a macro already assigned to a button so that you can then edit the macro.

Using a Button on a Worksheet or Chart

Occasionally, you might want to associate a macro with a particular worksheet or chart in a workbook by assigning the macro to a "floating" button. For example, you might want to click a button on a chart to switch between two views of the data. To place a button on a worksheet or chart, perform the following steps:

1. Position the mouse pointer over any displayed toolbar, click the right mouse button, and choose Forms from the shortcut menu. Excel then displays the Forms toolbar, as shown in Figure 23-6.

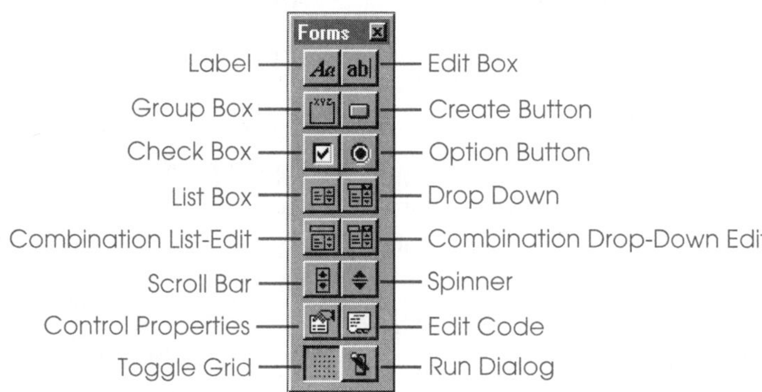

FIGURE 23-6
The Forms toolbar.

2. Click and release the Create Button button and then move the pointer to the location in the worksheet or chart where you want the new button to appear. Click and drag to draw the button.
3. When Excel displays the Assign Macro dialog box, select the name of the macro you want to assign to the button and click OK.

After you've assigned a macro to a button, you can edit the label on the button and format it with a different font and style.

Using a Drawing Object

You can also assign a macro to any drawing object. The process of assigning a macro to an object is almost identical to the process of assigning a macro to a button, as the steps below demonstrate:

1. Position the mouse pointer over any displayed toolbar, press the right mouse button, and then choose Drawing to display the Drawing toolbar.
2. Click any button on the Drawing toolbar (an oval, for example) and drag to the location in the worksheet or chart where you want the object to appear.
3. Position the mouse pointer on the object, click the right mouse button, and choose Assign Macro.
4. When Excel displays the Assign Macro dialog box, select the name of the macro you want to assign to the object and click OK.

Using the Personal Macro Workbook

When you recorded the CompanyAddress macro earlier in this chapter, we instructed you to place the macro in a module that belongs to the active workbook. A macro that has been placed in a module becomes available only when the workbook containing the macro is open.

If you'd like to make a macro available at all times, you can store it in the Personal Macro Workbook. Although the Personal Macro Workbook is normally hidden, you can unhide it by choosing the Unhide command from the Window menu and double-clicking Personal in the Unhide dialog box. If you have not yet recorded a macro in the Personal Macro Workbook, however, the Unhide command is dimmed, and the Personal file is not listed in the Unhide dialog box. The easiest way to get around this problem is to record a simple macro as described earlier and then select the Personal Macro Workbook option in the Record New Macro dialog box. Excel then creates the Personal Macro Workbook and places its file (Personal) in the main Excel directory.

The Personal Macro Workbook initially contains only one module, but you can add other modules — or even worksheets — to it. For example, you can use the Personal Macro Workbook to store modules that contain general purpose macros, such as macros that enter company and client addresses.

To transfer an existing macro to an unhidden Personal Macro Workbook, follow these steps:

1. Switch to the module containing the macro.
2. Select the macro (be sure to include the final End Sub statement and any statements that appear before the initial Sub statement) and then choose Cut from the Edit menu.
3. Switch to the Personal Macro Workbook, click an insertion point where you want the macro to appear in the workbook, and choose Paste from the Edit menu.
4. Finally, choose the Hide command from the Window menu to hide the Personal Macro Workbook. When you quit the current work session, Excel asks if you want to save changes to the Personal Macro Workbook. Click Yes to save the hidden workbook. (Be sure to choose the Hide command before you save the Personal Macro Workbook; otherwise, the workbook will appear each time you start Excel.)

Chapter 24

Custom Functions

Although Microsoft Excel includes a multitude of built-in worksheet functions, you probably perform calculations for which no function is available. Suppose your company uses a special mathematical formula for computing discounts for buyers of your product. Wouldn't it be convenient if you had a function named Discount that could compute the discount for you on any order? In this chapter, we'll show you how to create such custom functions.

Custom functions, also known as *user-defined functions,* are one of the most innovative and exciting features of Microsoft Excel. To create a custom function, you must write a special Visual Basic procedure, called a *function procedure,* that accepts information from the worksheet, performs calculations, and then returns a result to the worksheet. The types of information-handling and calculation tasks that you can simplify, generalize, or streamline with custom functions are virtually unlimited.

Like built-in functions, custom functions are initiated when Excel calculates the formulas in a worksheet or macro sheet. Custom functions make calculations and return values without performing actions in the workspace; because they don't perform actions, you cannot record a custom function as you can a macro. The value returned to the worksheet is typically numeric, but could also be a text value, a logical value, an error value, or an array of values.

After you create a custom function, you can use it the way you use any built-in function (except for the minor differences discussed in the section entitled "Custom Function Rules," page 854). For example, you can create a custom function that computes the interest paid to date on a loan or one that computes a weighted average for a range of numbers. Often, custom functions let you condense into one cell calculations that would otherwise occupy a large amount of space in a worksheet.

You can also add custom functions to Excel and use them in exactly the same way you would any of the built-in functions, by saving the workbook containing the custom function in the special Add-In format.

See Also For more information about add-ins, see "Converting to an Add-In Application," page 885.

For more information about Visual Basic keywords and syntax, see Excel's online Help.

Creating a Custom Function

Creating a custom function is a two-step process. First you create a new module or open an existing module to hold the Visual Basic code that defines the custom function. Second you type a series of Visual Basic statements that calculate the result you want to return to the worksheet.

In many spreadsheet programs, macros are stored in the cells of the related worksheet, but in Microsoft Excel, you create and store macros and custom functions in modules. Because the macros and custom functions are independent of a specific worksheet, you can use them with many worksheets. In fact, you can collect several macros and custom functions in one module and use it as a library.

To illustrate, let's build a simple custom function. Suppose your company offers a discount of 10 percent on the sale of a product, but only if the order is for more than 100 units. The worksheet in Figure 24-1 shows an order form that lists each item, the quantity, the price, the discount (if any), and the resulting charge.

To create a custom function — in this case, one that computes each discount — perform the following steps:

1. Insert a new module in the active workbook by choosing Macro and then Module from the Insert menu. Excel inserts a blank module and displays the Visual Basic toolbar, as shown in Figure 24-2 on the next page.

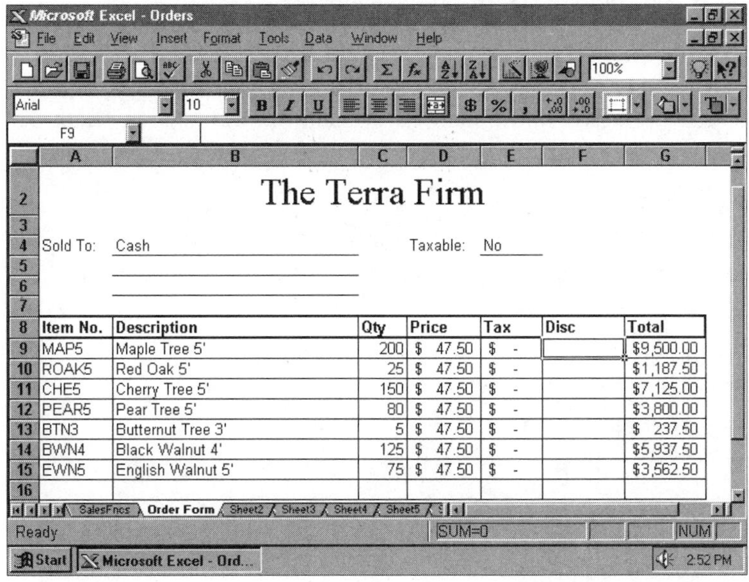

FIGURE 24-1
We want to calculate the discount for each item ordered.

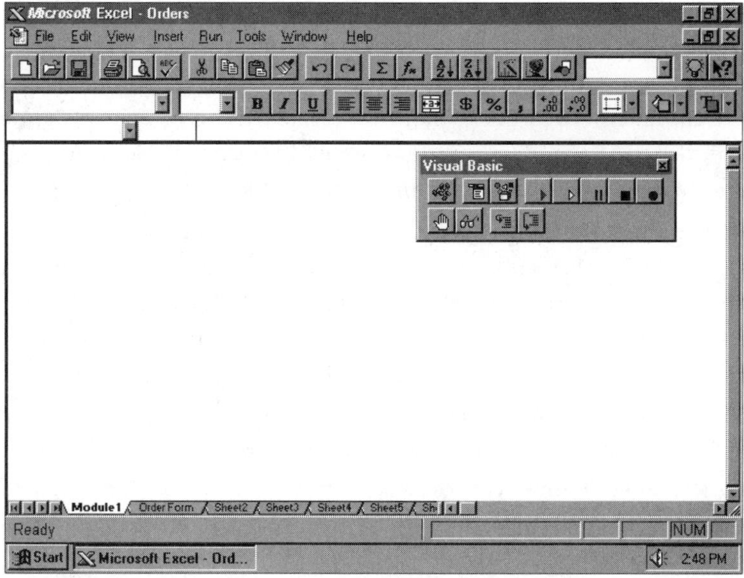

FIGURE 24-2 Choosing Macro and then Module from the Insert menu adds a module to the workbook. As you can see, modules are different from worksheets.

As you can see, a module doesn't look like a worksheet. Instead of a grid of columns and rows, you see a blank window much like the one you might see in a word processing program. The menu bar above the module includes a new Run menu, and Excel also displays the Visual Basic toolbar. In the new module you can enter, copy, move, insert, and delete Visual Basic statements and comments using techniques that are similar to those you use in a word processing program.

2. Give the module a name by choosing Rename from the Sheet submenu of the Edit menu and entering the name in the Rename Sheet dialog box — in this case, enter *SalesFncs*. (You can also double-click the tab for the module and enter a new name.)

3. In the module, enter the Visual Basic statements for the custom function. For this example, enter the following code, using the Tab key to indent lines:

```
Function Discount(quantity, price)
  If quantity >= 100 Then
    Discount = quantity * price * 0.1
  Else
    Discount = 0
  End If
  Discount = Application.Round(Discount,2)
End Function
```

The act of entering the function in a module defines the function's name (in this case, Discount) and makes it available to any open worksheet. If you have a color monitor, you'll notice as you enter the Visual Basic code that Excel displays certain terms in different colors so that the purposes of the various parts of the code or function are easier to understand.

When you press Enter at the end of a line of code, Excel checks the new code for simple errors in syntax. If you make a typing error or misuse a Visual Basic keyword, Excel might display a message box telling you the nature of the error. At this point, you might not understand many of these messages; instead of trying to figure out the problem, compare what you typed with the example code and enter the text exactly.

Figure 24-3 shows the module at this point.

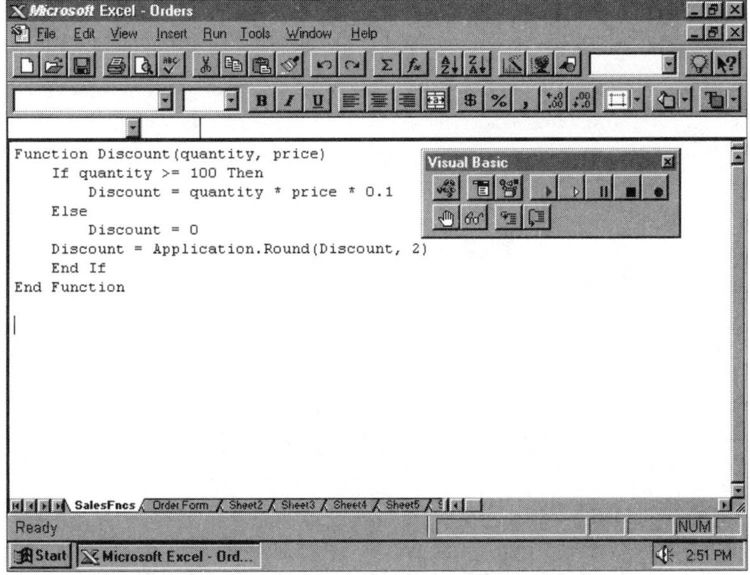

FIGURE 24-3
This custom function calculates the discount on a sales order.

Using Custom Functions

Now you're ready to use the new Discount function. Switch to the worksheet shown earlier in Figure 24-1, select cell F9, and enter

```
=Discount (C9,D9)
```

Notice that you don't have to identify the module containing the function procedure. The function's first argument, C9, identifies the cell that contains the quantity that corresponds to the function's *quantity* argument. The second argument, D9, identifies the cell that contains the price that corresponds to the function's *price* argument. When you press Enter, Microsoft Excel calculates and returns the correct discount for the arguments supplied: $950.00.

You can now assign a dollar format to cell F9 and copy the formula from cell F9 to cells F9:F15, as shown in Figure 24-4. To copy the formula, drag the AutoFill handle down six more cells. Because the references to cells C9 and D9 in the original formula are relative references, they change as the formula is copied to the new cells. For example, the formula in cell F14 is

```
=Discount(C14,D14)
```

If you change the values in cells C9:D15, the custom function immediately updates the discount calculations in cells F9:F5.

What's Happening

Let's consider how Excel interprets this function procedure. When you press Enter to lock in the formula in the worksheet, Excel looks for the name Discount in the current workbook and finds that it is a procedure in the SalesFncs module. The argument names enclosed in parentheses — *quantity* and *price* — are placeholders for the values upon which the calculation of the discount is based.

The If statement in the block of code

```
If quantity >= 100 then
  Discount = quantity * price * 0.1
Else
  Discount = 0
End If
```

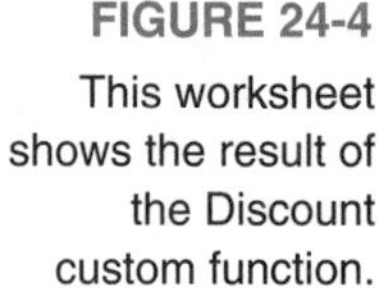

FIGURE 24-4

This worksheet shows the result of the Discount custom function.

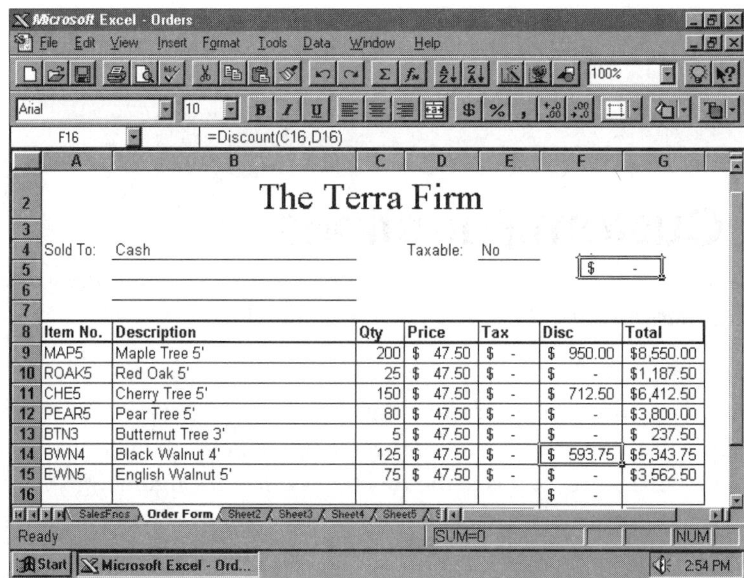

examines the *quantity* argument and determines whether the number of items sold is greater than or equal to 100. If it is, Excel executes the statement

```
Discount = quantity * price * 0.1
```

which multiplies the *quantity* value by the *price* value and then multiplies the result by 0.1 (the numerical equivalent of a 10 percent discount). The final result is stored as the variable *Discount.* A Visual Basic statement that stores a value in a variable is often called an *assignment statement,* because it evaluates the expression on the right of the equal sign and assigns the result to the variable name on the left. Because the variable *Discount* has the same name as the function procedure itself, the value stored in the variable is returned to the formula in cell F9 of the worksheet.

Notice that formulas entered in a worksheet and Visual Basic statements entered in a module are different in several ways. In a worksheet, a formula always begins with an equal sign, and the result of the formula is stored in the cell containing the formula. You can use the Define Name dialog box to assign a name to a cell containing a formula, thereby creating a *named reference.* You can also enter a formula in the Define Name dialog box to assign a name to the formula without storing the formula in a cell, thereby creating a *named formula.* (The simplest case of a named formula is when the formula is a constant; for example, you might assign the name *Pi* to the formula =3.14159.) Depending on how you have set up your worksheet, you can use a value elsewhere in the worksheet by entering the reference of the cell containing the formula that produces the value, the named reference of that cell, or the named formula (or constant). When Excel encounters a named formula, it evaluates the associated formula and uses the result.

In a Visual Basic module, values are stored in variables, which are never coupled with locations on a worksheet. In this sense, a variable in a module is similar to a named constant in a worksheet; when Excel encounters an assignment statement such as *Discount* = *quantity* * *price* * 0.1, it doesn't store the expression *quantity* * *price* * 0.1 in the variable, as you would expect if this were a worksheet. Instead, Excel evaluates the expression and stores only the result in the variable. If you use the variable name elsewhere in the function procedure, Excel uses the last value stored in the variable.

If quantity is less than 100, no discount is offered, and Excel executes the statement

```
Discount = 0
```

which simply sets *Discount* to 0.

The If...Else...End If sequence is called a *control structure;* If is a Visual Basic keyword that is analogous to the IF worksheet function. Control structures such as If...Else...End If let your macros and custom functions test for specific conditions on a worksheet or in the Excel environment and change the behavior of the procedure accordingly.

NOTE Control structures cannot be recorded. Being able to use them in macros and custom functions is one of the primary reasons to learn to write and edit Visual Basic procedures.

Finally, the statement

```
Discount = Application.Round(Discount,2)
```

rounds the value that represents the amount of the discount to two decimal places. Notice that Visual Basic has no Round function, but Excel does. Therefore, to use Round in this statement you tell Visual Basic to "look for the Round method (function) in the Application object (Excel)" by adding *Application.* before the word *Round.* Use this syntax whenever you need to access an Excel function from a Visual Basic module.

Custom Function Rules

Our example illustrates many of the characteristics of custom functions. First, a custom function must start with a Function statement and end with an End Function statement. You need not explicitly specify that a macro is a custom function and define its name. With Visual Basic, the act of typing the name of the custom function in a Function statement in a module defines it. In addition to the function name, the initial Function statement almost always specifies at least one argument, enclosed in parentheses. You can specify up to 13 arguments, using commas to separate them. (Technically, you can create a custom function that uses no data from a worksheet but returns a value; for example, you could create a function that takes no argument but returns the current time and date as a specially formatted text string.)

Second, custom functions include one or more statements in Visual Basic that make decisions and perform calculations using the arguments passed to the function. To return the result of a calculation to a worksheet formula that uses the custom function, you assign the result to a variable that has the same name as the custom function itself.

Third, you can use only the custom functions that are located in the modules of open workbooks. If you close a workbook that contains a custom function used in a formula in an open worksheet, the value returned by the function changes to the #REF! error value. To regenerate the correct value, reopen the workbook containing the module in which the custom function is defined.

Visual Basic Keywords Available to Custom Functions

The number of Visual Basic keywords you can use in custom functions is smaller than the number you can use in macros, because custom functions are not allowed to do anything other than return a value to a formula in a worksheet. For example, custom functions cannot resize windows, edit a formula in a cell, or change the font, color, or pattern options for the text in a cell or the cell itself. As a result, the Visual Basic keywords that change these options cannot be used in a custom function.

Documenting Macros and Custom Functions

Even simple macros and custom functions can be difficult to read. You can make them easier to understand by entering explanatory text in the form of comments. You add comments by preceding the explanatory text with a single quotation mark. For example, Figure 24-5 shows the Discount function with comments. Adding comments like these will enhance your understanding should you have to change the *Discount* procedure in the future.

A single quotation mark tells Excel to ignore everything to the right on the same line, so you can place a comment to the right of a Visual Basic statement. You can also insert comments between the statements in a macro or custom function. For example, you might begin a relatively lengthy block of code with a comment that identifies its overall purpose, and then use in-line comments to document individual statements.

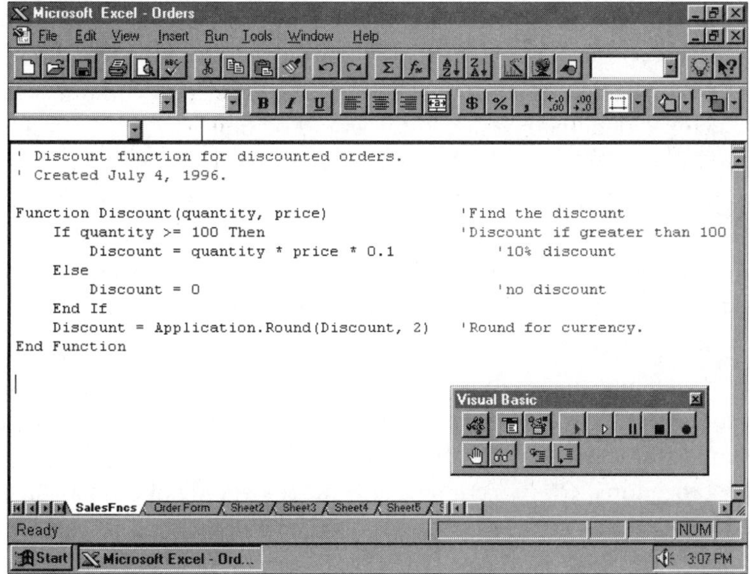

FIGURE 24-5
The Discount custom function now includes comments.

Another way to document your macros and custom functions is to give them descriptive names. For example, rather than name a macro Labels, you could name it RelMonthLabels, where Rel indicates that the macro uses relative references and MonthLabels describes the type of label the macro creates. Using descriptive names for macros and custom functions is essential when you've created many procedures, particularly if you create procedures that have similar, but not identical, purposes.

Deactivating Statements in Macros or Custom Functions

The essential difference between a statement in the Visual Basic programming language (which is executed) and a comment (which isn't) is that a comment is always preceded by a single quotation mark. Therefore, if you're building a macro or custom function and enter a statement that you don't want to be executed when you run the procedure, simply insert a single quotation mark before the statement to convert the statement into a comment. When you run the macro, Excel skips past the deactivated, or *commented out,* statement as if it weren't there. So, for example, if you are developing a macro that formats your worksheet and then prints it, you can comment out the print statement during development to save a few trees.

As a rule, you should give a custom function the shortest name that describes its purpose and yet sets it apart from other functions and Visual Basic keywords. For example, you might name a function that computes federal income taxes FederalIncomeTax, but it would be better to shorten that name to FedIncTax or FedTax. On the other hand, don't make the names of your custom functions so short that they aren't descriptive. For example, you probably wouldn't want to call your federal income tax function Tax because this name doesn't tell you what kind of tax the function computes. In addition, don't give your functions names that conflict with Visual Basic keywords such as End and Function.

How you document your macros and custom functions is a matter of personal preference. It doesn't matter which method you select, as long as you document them somehow. Documentation is most important for long and complex procedures, for procedures that you look at only once in a while, and for procedures that will be maintained by other people.

Editing Custom Functions

Let's create another custom function to gain some experience with editing procedures in a Visual Basic module.

Some of Excel's built-in worksheet functions let you omit certain arguments. For example, if you omit the *type* and *future value* arguments from the PV function, Excel still computes the result. However, if you omit an argu- ment from a custom function, Excel displays an error message unless you've specified that the argument is optional by using the Optional keyword and told your function procedure to test whether the argument has been supplied.

For example, suppose you want to create a simple custom function, called Triangle, that uses the Pythagorean theorem to compute the length of any side of a right triangle, given the lengths of the other two sides, as illustrated here:

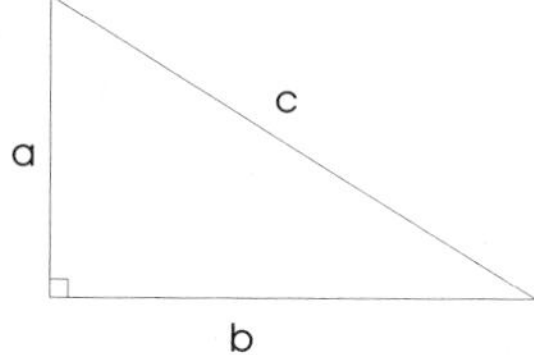

The equation that expresses the Pythagorean theorem is

$$a^2 + b^2 = c^2$$

where a and b are the short sides, and c is the hypotenuse.

Given any two sides, you can rewrite the equation in these three ways so that the unknown variable is always on the left of the equal sign:

$$a = \sqrt{c^2 - b^2}$$

$$b = \sqrt{c^2 - a^2}$$

$$c = \sqrt{a^2 + b^2}$$

The following custom function uses these three versions of the equation to return the length of the missing side:

```
Function Triangle(Optional short1, Optional short2, _
Optional longside)
  If Not (IsMissing(short1)) _
  And Not (IsMissing(short2)) Then
    Triangle = Sqr(short1 ^ 2 + short2 ^ 2)
  Else
    If Not (IsMissing(short1)) _
```

```
    And Not (IsMissing(longside)) Then
      Triangle = Sqr(longside ^ 2 - short1 ^ 2)
    Else
      If Not (IsMissing(short2)) _
      And Not (IsMissing(longside)) Then
        Triangle = Sqr(longside ^ 2 - short2 ^ 2)
      Else
        Triangle = Null
      End If
    End If
  End If
End Function
```

Note that in this function we cannot use the word *long* as an argument name because *long* is a reserved word in Visual Basic.

The first statement names the custom function and the optional arguments *short1, short2,* and *longside.* The following block of code contains a series of If statements that use the Visual Basic IsMissing function to test whether each possible pair of arguments has been supplied and to calculate and return the length of the third side.

For example, the statement

```
If Not (IsMissing(short1)) _
And Not (IsMissing(short2)) Then
  Triangle = Sqr(short1 ^ 2 + short2 ^ 2)
```

tests for the presence of *short1* and *short2;* the IsMissing function returns True if the argument has not been supplied. If *short1* is not missing and *short2* is not missing, then Excel computes the square root of the sum of the squares of the lengths of the two short sides and returns the length of the hypotenuse to the worksheet.

If fewer than two arguments are supplied, none of the If statements evaluates to True, and the statement

```
Triangle = Null
```

is executed. This statement returns the Visual Basic value Null, which becomes the #N/A error value in the worksheet.

Now let's see what happens when we use this custom function in a worksheet. The formula

=Triangle(,4,5)

returns the value 3, the length of the missing short side. Similarly, the formula

=Triangle(3,,5)

returns 4, the length of the other missing short side. And finally, the formula

```
=Triangle(3,4,)
```

returns 5, the length of the hypotenuse. If the lengths of the two short sides, 3 and 4, are stored in cells A4 and B4 and you enter the formula

```
=Triangle(A4,B4,)
```

in cell C4, Excel displays the result 5 in that cell.

If values for all three arguments are supplied, then the first of the If statements evaluates to True, and the custom function acts as if the value for the hypotenuse were not supplied. But what if you enter cell references for all three arguments? For example, suppose you enter the following function in cell D4 of a worksheet:

```
=Triangle(A4,B4,C4)
```

intending that the lengths of two of the triangle's sides will be entered in the referenced cells instead of in the function directly. If cells A4 and C4 contain the lengths of one short side and the hypotenuse but cell B4 is empty, you might expect Triangle to return the length of the other short side. However, the reference to the empty B4 evaluates to 0, not #N/A. Because the first two arguments have numeric values, the function attempts to calculate the hypotenuse of a right triangle in which one of the short sides has zero length and returns the square root of the sums of the squares of the short sides as usual. The result is the length of the short side you supplied in the worksheet, not the length of the missing side.

One way to deal with this potential problem is to change the If statements so that they test for zero values as well as #N/A error values. A right triangle cannot have a side of zero length, so if an argument evaluates to zero, that argument wasn't supplied.

This problem highlights one of the major issues that faces the designer of custom functions: You should design custom functions so that they work even when used in unexpected ways.

Chapter 25

An Overview of Visual Basic

Perhaps the best way to learn a computer language, or any language, is to simply jump in and start reading it. Visual Basic is no exception. By analyzing Visual Basic code that has already been written or recorded, in the context of a well-defined task, you can more easily understand the correspondence between the code and the task.

In this chapter, we'll take a high-speed reconnaissance flight over this terrain. As examples, we'll use a few macros and custom functions that together attempt to solve a common problem — transferring a series of stock market price quotations to Microsoft Excel, formatting the resulting data, and finally printing it as a chart. Along the way, the examples will illustrate the range and power of the Visual Basic language for formatting worksheets and charts, working with files, and modifying the user interface in various ways.

When we've finished assembling a collection of procedures that work together to solve a problem, we'll save the workbook containing the procedures in the special Add-in format. You can then make the fruit of your efforts available to others, without fear that prying eyes will discover your trade secrets.

Objects, Properties, and Methods

As mentioned in Chapter 23, Visual Basic is an object-oriented language, which means that every item in the Excel environment is considered an object rather than an abstract set of data structures or an arrangement of pixels on the screen. As shown in Figure 25-1, each object is a container for the objects within it (if any). The largest object is the Excel application itself; it contains all other objects.

Like objects in the "real" world, objects in Visual Basic have *properties*. If you think of objects as the nouns of Visual Basic, properties are its adjectives. A property is a quality or characteristic of the object, such as its color or pattern. In Chapter 23, we used the analogy of creating a robotic dog; characteristics such as its color, number of spots, the length of its tinny tail, and the loudness of its bark are this object's properties.

Visual Basic objects also have behaviors, or sets of actions, that they "know" how to perform. These behaviors are called the *methods* of the object. Methods are like verbs. The tricks our robodog can perform, such as barking, rolling over, fetching, and so on, are its methods.

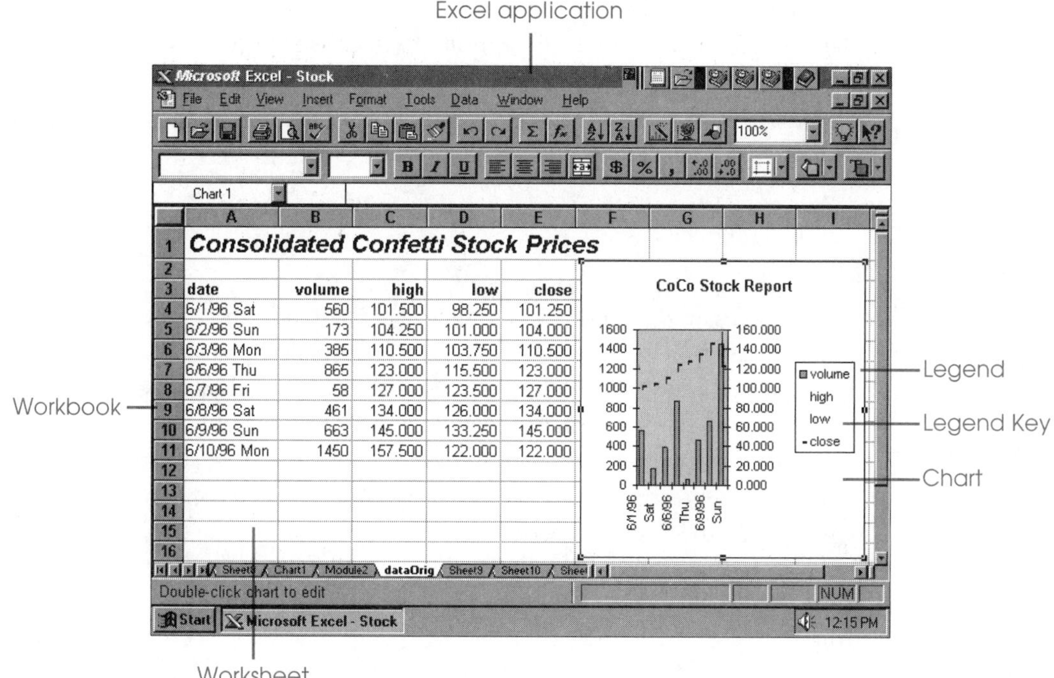

FIGURE 25-1

Each labeled object is a container for any object within it.

Naming Objects

You can have more than one instance of the same Visual Basic object; together, these instances comprise a collection. Each instance in a collection of objects is identified by its index or its name. For example, the collection of all robodogs might be

```
Robodogs()
```

and a specific instance of a robodog might be either

```
Robodogs(3)          'The third robodog in the collection.
```

or

```
Robodogs("Fido")     'A named instance of a robodog.
```

In Visual Basic, each item in a collection has its own index, but the range of index numbers might have gaps because if you delete one instance of an object, the indexes of the other instances might not be renumbered. For example, if you delete Robodogs(3) from a collection of 12 robodogs, there's no guarantee that Excel will renumber Robodogs(4) through Robodogs(12) to fill the gap.

In other programming languages, you might use a For...Next construction such as

```
For n = 1 to 12            'Make them all bark.
  Robodogs(n).Bark
Next n
```

to repeat an operation many times. If you run this code after deleting Robodogs(3), Visual Basic displays an error dialog box and stops the macro because Robodogs(3) no longer exists. To allow for nonconsecutive indexes, Visual Basic offers the For Each...Next statement, a control structure that applies a series of statements to each item in a collection, regardless of their index numbers. For example, to get all the robodogs to bark consecutively, you might use the following code:

```
For Each Robodog In Robodogs()
  Robodog.Bark
Next
```

You can send a message to or set a property of an object contained in another object by specifying the "subobject" as a series of nested objects. For example, if each instance of a robodog contains several objects, one of which is a tail, you might get the tail of a particular robodog to wag by using the statement

```
Robodogs("Fido").Tail.Wag
```

Naming Arguments to Methods

Many methods in Visual Basic have arguments that let you specify options for the action to be performed. If the Wag method of the Tail object has arguments (for example, *wagRate,* the number of wags per second; *wagTime,* the duration of wagging in seconds; and *wagArc,* the number of degrees of arc in each wag), you can specify them using one of two syntaxes.

In the first syntax, which is often called the *by-name syntax,* you name each argument you use, in any order; for example, the statement

```
Robodogs("Fido").Tail.Wag
  wagRate:= 3, _
  wagTime:= 3600, _
  wagArc:= 180
```

wags the tail three times per second for an hour, over an arc of 180 degrees. You assign a value to an argument by using a colon and an equal sign, and you separate arguments by using commas.

NOTE The underscore at the end of the first and second lines of code tells Visual Basic that the following line is part of the same statement. Using this symbol makes the list of supplied arguments easier to read and allows you to document individual arguments, if needed.

In the second syntax, which is often called the *by-position syntax,* you enter arguments in a prescribed order. (The order of arguments for each method is listed in the Excel online Help.) For example, the preceding statement expressed in the by-position syntax looks like this:

```
Robodogs("Fido").Tail.Wag(3,3600,180)
```

Notice that the list of arguments is surrounded by parentheses. The by-position syntax isn't as useful as the by-name syntax because you have to remember the order of arguments, and when you review the code at a later date, you won't have the argument names to refresh your memory about their settings.

NOTE Excel's macro recorder records arguments by position rather than by name, which can make it more difficult to understand recorded macros than manually created macros in which you've named the arguments.

TIP To get quick information about Visual Basic keywords, select the keyword and press the F1 key. Excel then displays a Help topic describing the by-position syntax for the keyword. Many Help topics for Visual Basic keywords include a button that, when clicked, displays another Help screen containing one or more examples of the keyword as it might be used in working Visual Basic code. If you want, you can copy this code, paste it into a module, and edit the resulting text to meet your own needs.

A Visual Basic Application

This section presents a series of sample macros and custom functions used to provide a Microsoft Excel solution to a typical spreadsheet problem: capturing as a text file stock prices from an information service such as CompuServe, transforming the data into a hi-lo chart, and printing the chart before the user gets up for breakfast in the morning. We'll call this solution the Stock Report system.

The following steps make up the Stock Report system, in order of execution:

1. Start the Windows HyperTerminal program and capture as a text file a series of stock quotes from an information service.
2. Open the text file from a macro, read its contents, and insert them into a new worksheet or database.
3. Copy the data to the permanent database.
4. Format the table containing the data. (For this task, we'll record Excel's AutoFormat feature.)
5. Chart the resulting data. (Again, this task is best recorded.)
6. Print the chart.

NOTE You can use any of the sample procedures independently of the others. For example, if you create another Excel application that needs to print a chart, you can simply call the chart printing procedure.

Of the six tasks, the first three cannot be recorded; instead, we must enter the code for the necessary Sub and Function procedures by hand.

To allow the user to run these procedures by choosing a command from a menu, we'll add a menu item backed up by a master-control procedure that manages the Stock Report system. When we're done, we'll package the group of routines as an add-in application that could be distributed to others.

You could adapt this system to track more than one stock. You could give commands within the HyperTerminal application to report on a series of stocks, capturing the resulting text into a series of files. You would then convert the information and insert each stock's data either in a separate worksheet in a single workbook or in a separate column in a single common worksheet.

Automatically Loading a Workbook

You can specify that a certain workbook, such as one containing a library of macros, be opened automatically each time Excel starts. This is accomplished by putting the document in Excel's XLStart folder, located in the folder that contains the Excel application.

To ensure that a workbook, such as the Stock Report system, is loaded automatically when you start Excel, do the following:

1. Choose New from the File menu, select Workbook, and click OK.
2. With the workbook active, choose Save from the File menu.

3. Locate and open Excel's XLStart folder.
4. Type the name of the workbook file — in this case, Stock.XLS — in the File Name edit box.
5. Click Save.

Opening the workbook ensures that the menu command for starting the Stock Report system (which we have not yet created) appears automatically when the user starts Excel.

For information about creating menu commands, see "Creating a Custom Menu Item," page 870.

Automatically Running a Macro

To run a macro automatically whenever the workbook containing the macro is opened, all you need do is name the macro Auto_Open. If you want to open the workbook and bypass the auto-open macro, you can choose Open from the File menu, select the filename from the list box, and hold down Shift while you click OK.

Similarly, to run a macro whenever a workbook is closed, all you need do is name the macro Auto_Close. Auto-close macros are useful for cleaning up after a system of macros has run its course, returning menu bars and toolbars to their original state, ensuring that the relevant files are closed, and so on. If you want to close the workbook without executing an auto-close macro, you can press Shift as you choose the Close command.

As an example of an auto-open macro, let's create a procedure that sets the path for the files generated by the Stock Report system. To begin, insert a new module — from the Insert menu choose Macro and then Module. Next enter the following auto-open procedure:

```
Public stockPath
Sub Auto_Open()
  stockPath = "C:\Stockreport"      'Path for temp files, etc.
End Sub
```

This procedure establishes *stockPath* as a *public variable* (often called a *global variable* in other programming languages) that is available to all procedures in all modules in the workbook. Unless you declare a variable as public, the variable "belongs" to the macro or custom function in which you use it, and no other procedure can use the value stored in that variable. In this example, the text value "C:\Stockreport" can be accessed by other procedures that need to know the location of Stock Report files.

Finally we need to ensure that the Stockreport folder will be there when we need it. Switch to the Windows Explorer, select the icon for the C: drive, choose New and then Folder from the File menu, and change the folder name to Stockreport.

Waiting for an Event

Sometimes you'd like a macro to run not at the moment the user initiates the macro (for example, by choosing a menu command, clicking on a toolbar button, or pressing a key combination associated with the macro), but when a specific event occurs in the Excel environment. Examples of these events are

- When the user presses a particular key combination
- When a worksheet is recalculated
- When a particular sheet or window is activated or deactivated
- When the user chooses the Undo or Repeat command from the Edit menu.
- At a particular time or on a particular date.

In the case of the Stock Report system, suppose you want Excel to wait until 2:00 A.M. before downloading the stock price information from the information service. The following procedures accomplish this task. Enter them in the Stock Report module after the auto-open macro.

```
'Wait for 2:00 AM before downloading.
Sub WaitForTime()
  'Make sure we want the report.
  answer = Notify("Download stock data tonight?")

  'If user clicks OK, run StockReport at 2:00am.
  If answer = vbOK Then
    Application.OnTime _
      EarliestTime:=TimeValue("2:00:00"), _
      Procedure:="StockReport"
  End If
End Sub

'Standard message box.
Function Notify(msg)
  'Title.
  msgboxTitle = "Stock Report System"
  'Buttons & icon.
  btns = vbOKCancel + vbQuestion + vbDefaultButton1
  Notify = MsgBox(CStr(msg), btns, msgboxTitle)
```

```
End Function

Sub StockReport()
   'Capture the stock prices.
   UseTerminalApp
   'Import and convert data.
   ImportStockFile
   'Format the resulting table.
   FormatStockData
   'Chart the data.
   FormatChart
   'Print the chart.
   PrintChart
End Sub
```

Of course, none of the procedures in the StockReport macro exists yet—we'll create them a little later.

The WaitForTime procedure calls the Notify procedure, which in turn uses the MsgBox function to ask the user whether to go ahead with the request. You use the MsgBox function to create simple dialog boxes. The first argument used in the MsgBox function specifies the message to display. The *btns* variable stores a series of Excel constants beginning with the text *vb* that specify the type of buttons to display, an icon, and which of the buttons to choose if the user presses Enter. The last argument specifies the title to use on the title bar of the dialog box.

For example, the MsgBox statement in the Notify procedure displays the dialog box shown in Figure 25-2. Clicking OK causes the MsgBox function to return TRUE. Clicking Cancel causes the function to return FALSE. These logical results are then used to branch to different parts of the macro, either ending or continuing the task. If the user clicks OK or presses Enter, the OnTime method posts a request to wait until 2:00 A.M., when Excel is to execute the StockReport macro, which calls the various procedures in the system, one by one.

FIGURE 25-2
The Notify procedure displays this alert box.

The OnTime method runs a macro at a specified date and time. You supply as the earliestTime argument a serial date value that represents the date and time at which you want the macro to run. (The TimeValue function converts a date as text to a serial date value.) If the value is less than 1, the specified macro runs every day.

Under some circumstances, Excel does not respond to the OnTime method as expected. If the module that contains the macro isn't open when the correct time arrives, Excel ignores the request. Similarly, if Excel isn't in Ready mode at the specified time or during the tolerance period, it waits until the tolerance period elapses and then cancels the macro's execution. And (of course), Excel must be running at the specified time in order for the event to be trapped.

TIP If you want to download the stock price file every evening, you can add the WaitForTime routine to the auto-open procedure described earlier in this chapter. As long as the workbook containing this auto-open procedure is in Excel's XLStart folder, all you will have to do is start Excel. The workbook will then open, and Excel will automatically run the procedure.

See Also For more information about calling one procedure from another, see "Macro Subroutines," page 839.

Creating a Custom Menu Item

You can add an item to a menu to allow the user to run a macro by choosing the item. To illustrate, let's create a new menu item called Get Stock Report on the Tools menu of the standard menu bar and tell Excel to run the WaitForTime macro when the user chooses the command.

To assign the WaitForTime macro to a menu command, do the following:

1. With the module active, choose Menu Editor from the Tools menu or Visual Basic toolbar.
2. Select the menu bar, the menu, and the menu item below which you want the new item to appear. In this case, select the Worksheet menu bar, the Tools menu, and then the End of Menu item in the Menu Items list, as shown in Figure 25-3.
3. Click Insert to create a space for the new menu item.
4. In the Caption edit box, type the name of the item — in this case, *&Download Stock Report.*

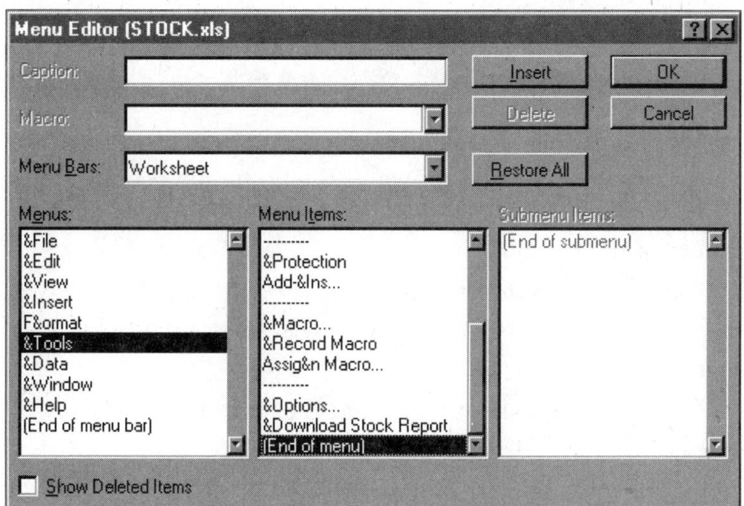

FIGURE 25-3

This Menu Editor dialog box specifies that a new item should be added to the bottom of the Tools menu on the Worksheet menu bar.

Customizing Menus from Visual Basic

In addition to using the Menu Editor to create custom menu bars, menus, commands, and submenu commands, you can use Visual Basic. You can also add a command to one of the shortcut menus that appear when the user clicks an active area of the screen with the right mouse button.

You can assign macros only to commands, submenu commands, and shortcut menu commands. You can add new commands to Excel's built-in menus, rename existing commands, dim them, put check marks next to them, and remove them. You can also create your own menus and add them to a built-in menu bar (such as the Chart menu bar) or to a new menu bar of your own design.

Many of the methods that belong to menu objects require that you identify the menu with which you want to work, either by its index or by its name, as text. For example, in the worksheet environment, you can use an index of 3 or the text "VIEW" to refer to the View menu — the third menu from the left — when a worksheet is open.

You use the Add method to add a new command to a menu. After Excel adds the command to the appropriate menu, it returns the new command's position number. As an argument to the Add

(continued)

(continued)

Customizing Menus from Visual Basic

method, you can supply the position number or name of the command above which you want to add the new command. If you omit this argument, Excel adds the new command to the bottom of the menu.

To dim a custom menu command, set the Enabled property to false. For example, to dim a custom Totals command on the Format menu, use the statement

```
Menubars("xlWorksheet").Menus("Format").MenuItems _
("Totals")Enabled = False
```

You cannot dim the built-in commands.

You set the Checked property to add or remove a check mark before a command. Check marks are useful for showing that a particular condition is in effect. For example, if you create a command and an accompanying command macro to display formulas in a worksheet, you can use a check mark to indicate when formula viewing is in effect.

You use the Delete method to remove a command from a specified menu. You can delete both built-in and custom commands. Suppose you want to prevent the user from choosing the Sort command on the Data menu. Because Sort is a built-in command, you cannot dim it. Instead you can use the statement

```
Menubars("xlWorksheet").Menus("Data").MenuItems _
("Sort...").Delete
```

to remove the command altogether.

If you want to develop an entire application within Excel, you can add new menus to built-in menu bars, and you can also create up to 15 completely new menu bars for custom menus and commands. You use the Add method to create new menu bars, menus, commands, and submenu commands. To make a menu bar appear, you use the Activate method; if the specified menu bar is not appropriate for the active document, an error occurs, and the macro stops. To eliminate a menu bar, you use the Delete method.

Typing an ampersand (&) in front of the D specifies that D is the accelerator key for the new menu command. To initiate the command, the user can either choose it from the Tools menu or press Alt-T-D.

5. In the Macro drop-down list box, select the WaitForTime procedure and then click OK.

Now that the basic structure of the Stock Report system is in place, in the following sections we'll create the various procedures used by the Stock-Report macro.

> **NOTE** The new menu command is stored with the workbook containing its macro. When the workbook is opened, the Download Stock Report command appears on the Tools menu automatically.

Controlling Another Application

Suppose you use the Windows HyperTerminal application every Friday night to connect to an information service such as CompuServe from which you capture stock prices as a text file. You need an Excel macro that can control the HyperTerminal application, send it logon commands, find the correct database, request the desired stock prices, and capture the data as a text file. This macro cannot be recorded because it doesn't involve Excel's internal features.

Excel offers four ways to control other Windows applications from a Visual Basic procedure: creating compound documents by linking and embedding objects, OLE Automation, Dynamic Data Exchange (DDE), and the Visual Basic SendKeys method.

When linking and embedding objects, you copy material in a source application — an Excel chart, for example — and paste the material into another application, such as Microsoft Word. A linked object exists as a separate file and is maintained by the application that created it. An embedded object exists only in the document created by the destination application. Visual Basic supports several keywords for inserting, updating, and deleting linked and embedded objects.

You can use Visual Basic's support of OLE Automation to directly access an object in another application without having to use the external OLE features of Excel. With OLE Automation, you can act upon any object that is listed in the application's object library, such as windows, toolbars, documents, or data. For example, you could transfer text from an Excel worksheet to Word, make use of Word's search and replace features, and transfer the text back to an Excel worksheet without the user knowing that Word was used. OLE Automation is not yet supported by every Windows application.

Dynamic Data Exchange lets you open a communications channel between two applications that support DDE, so that you can send data between two documents. DDE operates at a lower level than OLE Automation and is somewhat arcane. As OLE Automation becomes more common, a knowledge of DDE will be unnecessary.

Using any of these three techniques requires that the method be supported by both applications, and currently none of them is supported by every Windows application. The one technique that works with every Windows application is the SendKeys method. With it, you can simulate the action of a user typing at the keyboard.

The following procedure uses the SendKeys method to send a series of keystrokes that operate the HyperTerminal application as if a user were typing them at the keyboard. We'll use this procedure to perform the first step of the StockReport macro of our Stock Report system.

```
Sub UseTerminalApp()
    'Uses public var stockPath.
    'Path to HyperTerminal application.
    termPath = "C:\Program Files\Accessories\HyperTerminal\"
    returnVal = Shell(termPath + "Hypertrm", 1)
    'Activate HyperTerminal.
    AppActivate Title:="Hyperterminal"

    'Cancel New Connection dialog box.
    Application.SendKeys "{Esc}", True
    Application.Wait Now() + TimeValue("00:00:10")
    DoEvents

    'Alt-File-Open
    Application.SendKeys "%FO", True
    Application.SendKeys "infoserv", True

    'Send commands to download data to file
    'Alt Call/Connect.
    Application.SendKeys "%CC", True
    'Press Enter to initiate the connection.
```

```
    Application.SendKeys "{Enter}", True
    'STOCKDAT.TXT in path stockPath.

    'Let HyperTerminal process keystrokes.
    DoEvents

    'Wait 15 seconds.
    Application.Wait Now() + TimeValue("00:00:15")
    'Type my password.
    Application.SendKeys "GO MYSTOCK{ENTER}", True
    'Wait 15 seconds.
    Application.Wait Now() + TimeValue("00:00:15")
    'Alt-transfer-Receive Text File.
    Application.SendKeys "%TR", True
    'Text file in stockPath
    Application.SendKeys stockPath + "\stockdat.txt", _
        True
    'Choose OK
    Application.SendKeys "{ENTER}", True

    'Get to the stock information.
    Application.SendKeys "GET COCO{ENTER}", True
    'Wait 15 seconds
    Application.Wait Now() + TimeValue("00:00:15")
    'Alt-Transfer-Stop.
    Application.SendKeys "%TO", True
    'log off
    Application.SendKeys "bye", True
    'Alt-Phone-Hangup
    Application.SendKeys "%PH", True
    'Quit HyperTerminal.
    Application.SendKeys "%FX{esc}", True

    'Switch back to Excel.
    AppActivate Title:="Microsoft Excel"

End Sub
```

The SendKeys method takes two arguments. The first argument specifies the text to send to the destination application, and the second argument, if TRUE, causes Excel to wait for the designated action to be performed. You can use special codes to send certain key combinations, such as % for the Alt key and {ESC} for the Escape key.

NOTE For a complete list of the special codes used in the SendKeys method, read the topic for the SendKeys method in Excel's online Help system.

The DoEvents method lets the HyperTerminal application process the keystrokes that have been sent.

At certain points in the procedure, the macro must wait for a few seconds for HyperTerminal and the remote information service to catch up with the series of keystrokes the UseTerminalApp procedure is sending. The Wait method of the Application object pauses execution of the procedure for 15 seconds in each instance.

Working with Text Files

Excel's Text Import Wizard does an admirable job of importing files with formats other than those native to the Excel environment. For example, the text file of stock prices downloaded from the information service might look like this:

```
6/10/96    865     123       115 1/2    123
6/11/96    58      127       123 1/2    127
6/12/96    461     134       126        134
6/13/96    663     145       133 1/4    145
6/14/96    1450    157 1/2   122        122
```

Each line of text consists of the date and the volume, high, low, and closing prices for the stock. Each item is separated from the next by a tab character. Fractional numbers are represented by a numerator, a slash character, and a denominator.

For the Stock Report system, we need a procedure that can open and read the text for each day of data and can transfer each item of data to the correct location at the end of the database that contains previously captured stock prices. Figure 25-4 shows the database as it looks when we start recording the macro. Notice that we've been entering data manually for a few days. To create the ImportStockFile procedure, begin by recording the following actions:

1. In the module, enter the following programming stub:

```
Sub ImportStockFile()
  'Text Import Wizard actions.
End Sub
```

2. Click an insertion point at the beginning of the End Sub statement, and choose Record Macro and then Mark Position For Recording from the Tools menu.

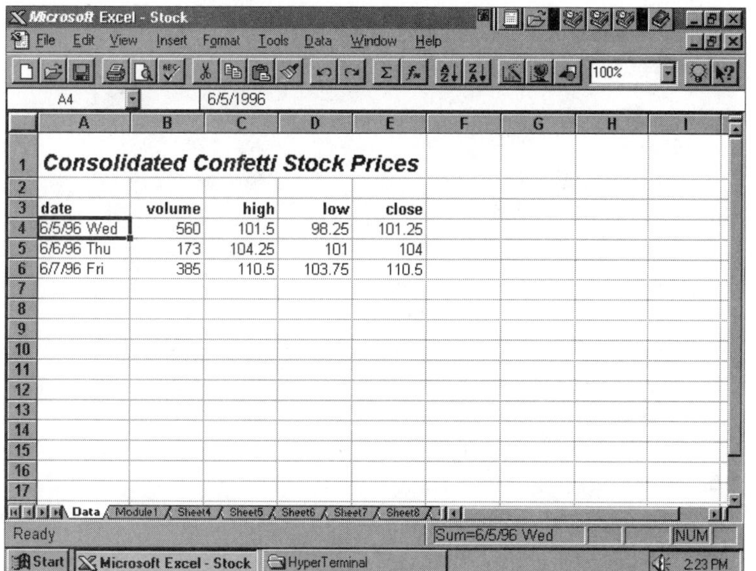

FIGURE 25-4

The database before we start recording the macro.

3. Switch to an empty sheet in the Stock workbook, and choose Record Macro and then Record At Mark from the Tools menu.
4. Choose Open from the File menu, find the Stockreport directory, and double-click the Stockdat file. (You may have to choose All Files from the Files Of Type drop-down list to see the file name.) Excel pauses for a moment and then presents the dialog box shown in Figure 25-5.
5. Click the Next button. Excel presents the dialog box shown in Figure 25-6 at the top of the next page.

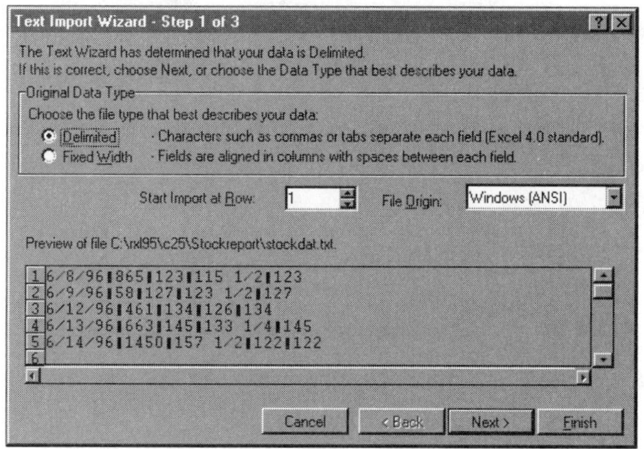

FIGURE 25-5

The first of three Text Import Wizard dialog boxes.

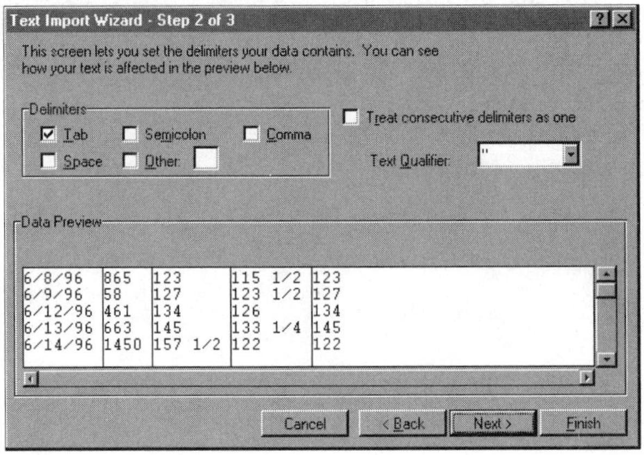

FIGURE 25-6

The second Text Import Wizard dialog box.

6. When you click the Next button again, Excel displays the third Text Import Wizard dialog box, shown in Figure 25-7.

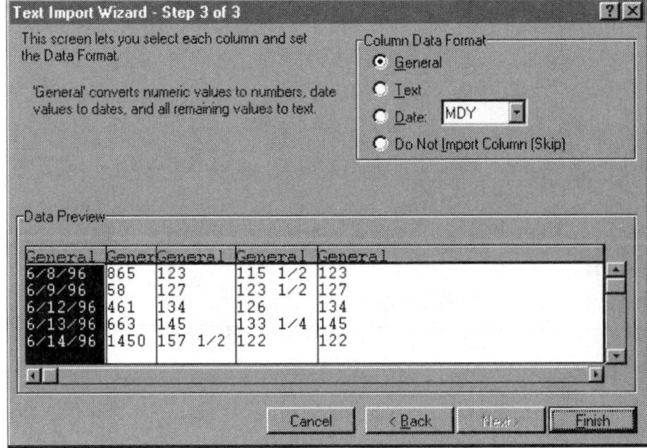

FIGURE 25-7

The third Text Import Wizard dialog box.

7. Click the Finish button. Excel opens a new workbook and inserts into the worksheet the text captured by the Text Import Wizard, as shown in Figure 25-8.

   Column A contains the dates for each day, and columns B through E contain the prices, formatted using one of the Fraction number formats.

8. Select the Go To command from the Edit menu, click the Special button, select the Current Region option, and click OK.

9. Choose Copy from the Edit menu.

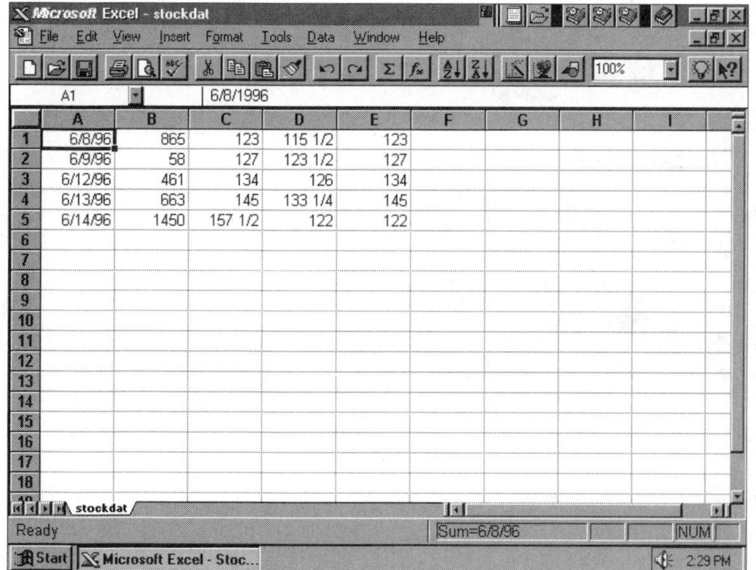

FIGURE 25-8
This is the Stockdat worksheet after the text file was converted using the Text Import Wizard.

10. Switch to the first worksheet of the Stock workbook, select the Date heading in column A (cell A3), and press Ctrl-Down Arrow to select the last non-empty cell in column A.
11. From the Tools menu, choose Record Macro and then Use Relative References.
12. Press the Down Arrow key once more to select the next empty cell in column A.
13. Choose Paste from the Edit menu. The worksheet then looks like Figure 25-9 as shown on the next page.
14. Switch back to the Stockdat worksheet and choose Close from the File menu. If Excel presents a dialog box asking whether you want to save the sheet, click No.
15. Choose Record Macro and then Stop Recording from the Tools menu.

When you switch back to the module containing the ImportStockFile macro, you'll see the following code (without the comments we've added as documentation):

```
Sub ImportStockFile()
    'Text Import Wizard actions.
    ChDir "C:\Stockreport"
```

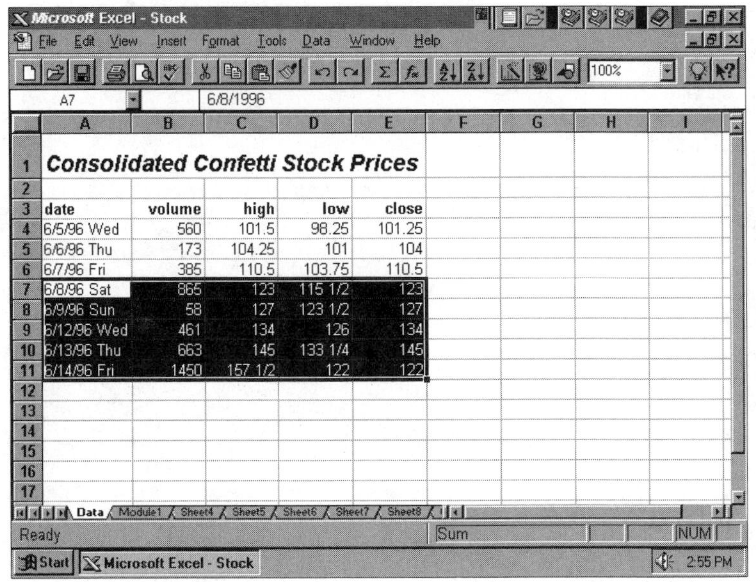

FIGURE 25-9 The stock price data after pasting into the Stock worksheet.

```
Workbooks.OpenText _
  Filename:="C:\Stockreport\stockdat.txt", _
  Origin:=xlWindows, StartRow:=1, DataType:=xlDelimited, _
  Text Qualifier:=xlDoubleQuote, _
  ConsecutiveDelimeter: =False, _
  Tab:=True, Semicolon:=False, _
  Comma:=False, Space:= False, Other:=False, _
  FieldInfo:=Array(Array(1, 1), Array(2, 1), _
  Array(3, 1), Array(4, 1), Array(5, 1))

'Select the current region and copy it.
Selection.CurrentRegion.Select
Selection.Copy

'Activate Stock.XLS workbook.
Windows("Stock.XLS").Activate
Sheets("Data").Select

'Select Date heading and find the end of the column.
 Range("A3").Select
Selection.End(xlDown).Select
```

```
    'Relative move one cell below and paşte new data.
    Active Cell.Offset(1, 0).Range("A1") Select
    ActiveSheet.Paste

    'Activate and close source workbook.
    Windows("Stockdat.txt").Activate
    ActiveWorkbook.Close
End Sub
```

You need to make only one significant change to this macro to make it more general-purpose. You must change the *Filename* argument of the OpenText method so that it looks for the file in the folder specified by the *stockPath* public variable. Change the line

```
Filename:="C:\Stockreport\stockdat.txt", _
```

to

```
Filename:=stockPath + "\Stockdat.txt", _
```

This edit isn't strictly necessary if the path to the Stockdat.txt file never changes. However, if the path might change, setting the path in the Public statement at the beginning of the module establishes the path for every procedure that needs to find the file.

Formatting a Worksheet

The simplest way to format a worksheet table from within a procedure is to turn on the macro recorder and use the Cells command on the Format menu, like this:

1. In the module, enter the following stub:

   ```
   Sub FormatStockData()

   End Sub
   ```

2. Choose Record Macro and then Use Relative References from the Tools menu to remove the check from the menu item and return to absolute references.

3. Click an insertion point in the empty line, before the End Sub statement. From the Tools menu, choose Record Macro and then Mark Position For Recording. Then switch to the Data worksheet and choose Record Macro and then Record At Mark from the Tools menu.

4. Select column A and choose Cells from the Format menu.
5. Select the Number tab. From the Category list, select Date, and then select the *m-d-yy* format.
6. Select the Alignment tab. In the Horizontal group, select the Left alignment option and click OK.
7. Select columns C through E and again choose Cells from the Format menu.
8. Select the Number tab. From the Category list, select Number and then specify 3 decimal places.
9. Click OK to close the Format Cells dialog box.
10. From the Tools menu, choose Record Macro and then Stop Recording.

Here is the resulting code, with comments added to indicate the various formats selected:

```
'Format the table.
Sub FormatStockData()
  'Select Column A and apply format.
  Columns("A:A").Select
  Selection.NumberFormat = "m/d/yy[space]ddd"
  With Selection
    .HorizontalAlignment = xlLeft
    .VerticalAlignment = xlBottom
    .WrapText = False
    .Orientation = xlHorizontal
    .AddIndent = False
  End With

  'Select column C through E and apply number format.
  Columns("C:E").Select
  Selection.NumberFormat = "0.000"
End Sub
```

Notice that Excel recorded every option set on the dialog box's Alignment tab. If you want, you can delete the uncommented lines in the With block, leaving only the specific option you want the procedure to set.

Creating a Chart

You can record the ChartWizard steps necessary to create and format a chart. For example, the following code is an unedited series of statements recorded through the ChartWizard that chart the daily stock prices generated by the Stock Report system.

1. Start by entering a stub for the new procedure:

```
Sub FormatChart()

End Sub
```

2. Click an insertion point before the End Sub statement and choose Record Macro and then Mark Position For Recording from the Tools menu. Switch to the Data worksheet, and then choose Record Macro and Record At Mark from the Tools menu.
3. Select cell A3, choose Record Macro then Use Relative References from the Tools menu, choose Go To from the Edit menu, click the Special button, select Current Region, and click OK.
4. From the Insert menu, choose Chart and then As New Sheet. The first ChartWizard dialog box appears.
5. Click the Next button.
6. In the second ChartWizard dialog box, select the Combination option, and click the Next button.
7. In the third dialog box, select charting option 5, and click the Next button.
8. In the fourth dialog box, click the Next button.
9. In the fifth dialog box, select No in the Add A Legend area. In the Chart Title edit box, enter *CoCo Stock Report*. Click the Finish button. The ChartWizard inserts a new chart in the workbook.
10. Choose Record Macro and then Stop Recording from the Tools menu.

The resulting chart looks like the one shown in Figure 25-10. (We chose Sized With Window from the View menu to make it easier to see.) Here's the resulting macro, with comments added:

```
Sub FormatChart()
  'Select current region.
  Range("A3").Select
  Selection.CurrentRegion.Select
  'Create a hi-lo chart from the data.
  Charts.Add
  ActiveChart.ChartWizardSource:=Sheets("Data").Range("A3:E11"), _
    Gallery:=xlCombination, Format:=5, PlotBy:=xlColumns, _
    CategoryLabels:=1, SeriesLabels:=1, HasLegend:=2, Title:= _
    "CoCo Stock Report", CategoryTitle:="", ValueTitle:="", _
    ExtraTitle:=""
End Sub
```

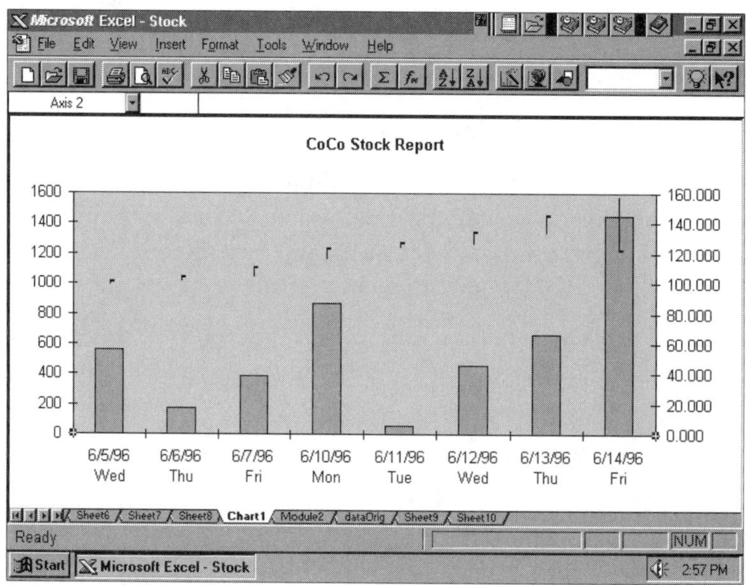

FIGURE 25-10
The resulting chart of daily stock prices.

Printing a Chart

Printing a chart involves the Visual Basic equivalent of choosing Page Setup from the File menu, setting a series of printing options, clicking the Print button, and clicking OK to print the document. Here is the PrintChart procedure for the Stock Report system:

```
Sub PrintChart()
  With ActiveSheet.PageSetup
    .LeftHeader = ""
    .CenterHeader = "&A"
    .RightHeader = ""
    .LeftFooter = ""
    .CenterFooter = "Page# &P"
    .RightFooter = ""
    .LeftMargin = Application.InchesToPoints(0.75)
    .RightMargin = _
      Application.InchesToPoints(0.75)
    .TopMargin = Application.InchesToPoints(1)
    .BottomMargin = Application.InchesToPoints(1)
    .HeaderMargin = _
      Application.InchesToPoints(0.5)
    .FooterMargin = _
      Application.InchesToPoints(0.5)
    .ChartSize = xlFullPage
    .CenterHorizontally = False
    .CenterVertically = False
```

```
        .Orientation = xlLandscape
        .Draft = False
        .PaperSize = xlPaperLetter
        .FirstPageNumber = xlAutomatic
        .BlackAndWhite = False
        .Zoom = 100
    End With
    ActiveWindow.SelectedSheets.PrintOut Copies:=1
End Sub
```

Converting to an Add-In Application

After you create and thoroughly debug a series of command and function macros that work well as a system, you can convert them to a format that makes them appear as if they are part of Microsoft Excel itself. Simply use the Make Add-In command on the Tools menu to save the active workbook in the Add-in format. When you open the resulting add-in, it is hidden and cannot be displayed with the Unhide command.

To protect the intellectual property of a developer of Excel macro applications, a workbook saved as an add-in is unreadable by anyone — even the developer. There are no passwords, and the data in the resulting file is stored in an unreadable format. It's a good idea to save a backup copy of the workbook containing your modules before you convert it to an add-in, just in case you need to make modifications in the future.

You can put an auto-open procedure in a workbook destined to become an add-in, and you can put the add-in itself in the XLStart folder so that Excel opens the add-in automatically. By careful use of an auto-open procedure in an add-in, you can even create an application that completely changes the standard appearance of Excel, replacing all the built-in menus and toolbars with those of your own design.

To save a workbook — in this case, the one containing the Stock Report system — as an add-in, perform the following steps:

1. With a module in the workbook active, choose Make Add-In from the Tools menu.
2. In the Make Add-In dialog box, enter the name you want to give the add-in file. Be careful to give the file a different name than that of the workbook itself; if you use the same name, Excel will overwrite the readable workbook with the unreadable add-in, and you'll have to reconstruct the workbook from scratch if you ever need to change it. For this example, enter Stock Addin.XLA.
3. Click Save.

Finally, because you now have both the original workbook and the add-in in the XLStart folder, you should move the Stock.XLS file to another folder to avoid automatically loading the same set of procedures twice.

TIP Some sets of procedures work in a Workbook but do not work when saved as an add-in. For example, Stock.xls does not work as an add-in. You cannot add data to an add-in file as you do in the Import Stock File procedure in Stock.xls because add-ins are hidden and don't have windows. Instead, you can store the data in a regular workbook and then create the chart in that workbook.

Part 7

Microsoft Excel and Other Applications

Chapter 26

Integrating Applications with the Clipboard and OLE

As you work with Microsoft Excel, you might need to transfer information from Excel to another application or from another application to Excel. For example, you might want to transfer a chart from Excel to a report you're writing in Microsoft Word for Windows.

Excel has several methods of exchanging data with other applications. You can use the Save As command to save a file in a format other applications can read. Or you can share data via the Clipboard with other applications that run under Microsoft Windows. You can also use OLE (formerly Object Linking and Embedding) to create links between documents created in different applications.

In this chapter, we'll show you some techniques for transferring information between Excel and other applications. We begin with a discussion of the Windows Clipboard and OLE. In Chapter 27, we'll discuss methods of converting Excel's files to other formats and for importing documents that were created in other spreadsheet and database applications into Excel.

Data Formats and the Clipboard

Using the Microsoft Windows Clipboard to copy or move information between Microsoft Excel and another Windows-based application is much the same as using it to copy or move data within Excel. In the same way that you use the Edit menu's Copy and Paste commands (or toolbar buttons) to reproduce a cell or range elsewhere in an Excel worksheet, you can use Excel's Copy command and another application's Paste command to reproduce a section of the worksheet in a document created with the other application — a report written with a word processor, for example. Or you can use another application's Copy command and Excel's Paste command to import data — a block of text, a table, a graphic image, or even a sound annotation — from another Windows-based application into Excel.

In all these cases, the Windows Clipboard acts as a way station for information in transit. The Copy command stores information on the Clipboard. (The Cut command does the same thing, but also removes the information from the source document.) And the Paste command fetches whatever the Clipboard is currently storing.

The only complexity arises because the Clipboard typically stores data in several formats at the same time. When you move information within or between Excel documents, you usually don't need to concern yourself with the format of the data you're moving. But when you use the Clipboard as a transfer medium between applications, it can be useful to know what formats are available.

When you copy a worksheet range from Excel to the Clipboard, Excel normally stores your data in 27 different formats, ready for you to paste. If you have installed the Windows 95 Clipboard Viewer application, you can see the names of these formats by opening the Clipboard and pulling down the viewer's Display menu. Figure 26-1 shows the names of Excel's Clipboard formats. (The dimmed items are formats that the Clipbook Viewer cannot display.)

When you use the Paste command, the application whose Paste command you use selects what it considers the most appropriate available format. (If none is appropriate, the application dims its Paste command.)

In some cases, the receiving application can receive data in only one format, so the issue of which format to paste does not arise. For example, if you copy data from Excel and paste it into Notepad (an application that handles only the simplest form of text), Notepad requests the Text format; you have no choice in the matter. Similarly, if you paste Excel data into a non–Windows-based program running under Windows, the non–Windows-based program pastes in the OEM Text format, which is similar to the Text format except that it uses the IBM PC extended-ASCII character set instead of the ANSI character set.

Many Windows-based applications can handle data in more than one format, however. For example, WordPad, the word processor shipped with Windows 95, can accept information in both text and graphic formats. When you choose the Paste command of such an application, often the format chosen by the receiving application is the one you want, but it might not always be.

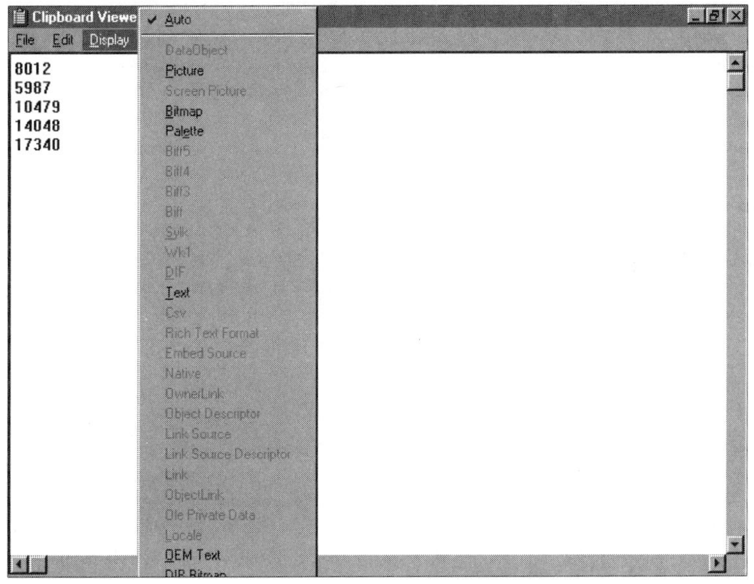

FIGURE 26-1
The Display menu of the Windows 95 Clipboard Viewer shows the formats available for data copied to the Clipboard using Excel's Copy command.

Choosing Formats with the Paste Special Command

Most Windows-based applications that can paste data in more than one format have a Paste Special command on the Edit menu. (In some applications, the command might have a slightly different name, such as Paste Format.) Whenever the Clipboard holds information in more than one usable format, these applications make their Paste Special commands available. If you choose the Paste command, the application pastes the data in its default format. If you choose the Paste Special command, a dialog box appears that lists all the available formats (including the default) so that you can take your pick.

You're probably accustomed to using Paste Special in Excel for pasting the formats assigned to a worksheet range without pasting the range's values, or for pasting the values without the formats. When the Clipboard holds data that originated outside Excel, however, Excel's Paste Special command changes. Like the Paste Special command of other applications, it lets you select an available Clipboard format. Figure 26-2 shows how Excel's Paste Special dialog box looks if the Clipboard holds text copied from Microsoft Word for Windows.

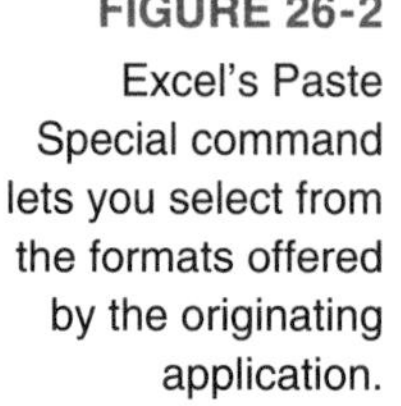

FIGURE 26-2
Excel's Paste Special command lets you select from the formats offered by the originating application.

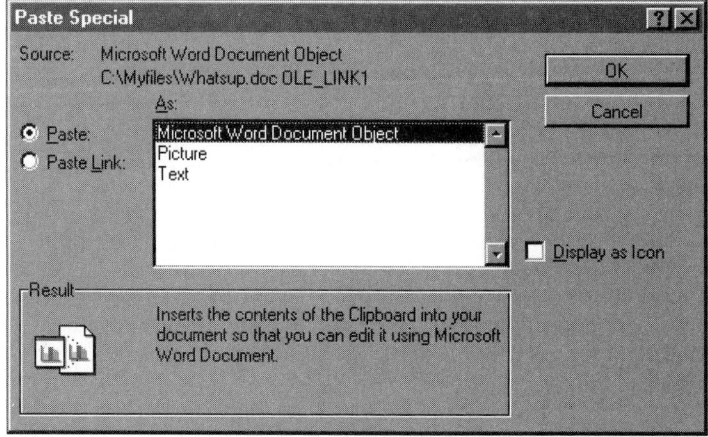

The following sections offer some basic guidelines to help you choose among the options you're most likely to encounter.

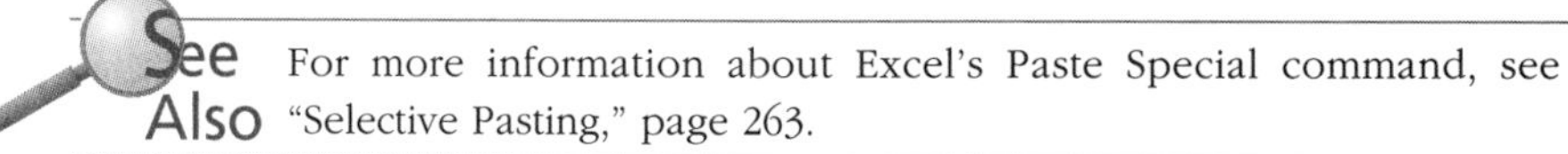

For more information about Excel's Paste Special command, see "Selective Pasting," page 263.

Exchanging Pasted Data with Text-Oriented Applications

Microsoft Windows-based applications that handle text, such as word processors and text editors, can usually paste Microsoft Excel worksheet data in either Text or Rich Text Format. In either case, any formulas in your worksheet are converted to their results.

When you paste in unformatted Text format, formatting characters such as dollar signs or percent signs are included, but font, size, alignment characteristics, column widths, shading, borders, and color are omitted. Tab characters separate the original columns of your Excel data, but unless all entries in each column happen to be the same width, you will probably need to adjust the tab settings in the receiving application to line up the columns.

When you paste in Rich Text Format (sometimes identified as RTF or Formatted Text), virtually all formatting characteristics are preserved. Typically, the receiving application responds to Excel data in Rich Text Format by setting up a table. If you paste Rich Text Format data into Microsoft Word for Windows, for example, Word creates a table that you can manipulate with commands on Word's Table menu.

Many Windows-based word processors can paste graphic information as well as text. For example, you can paste an Excel chart (a graphic) or a graphic object into a Word document as easily as you can paste a table of numbers from an Excel worksheet. In this context, the word processor behaves like a graphics-oriented application.

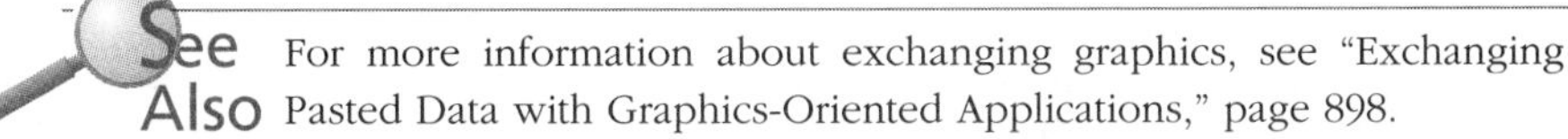
See Also For more information about exchanging graphics, see "Exchanging Pasted Data with Graphics-Oriented Applications," page 898.

Pasting from Text-Oriented Applications into Microsoft Excel

Microsoft Excel pastes text from the Windows Clipboard in various ways, depending on the context.

Pasting Text into Worksheet Cells

If the current selection is a worksheet cell or range, the Paste command imports words and numbers as unformatted text. In other words, it handles characters received from the Clipboard much as it would if you typed them at the keyboard. Each line of text copied to the Clipboard is pasted into Excel on a separate worksheet row, beginning at the current cell selection. (Excel might treat an entire paragraph as a single row depending on the application from which it was copied.) If the current selection encompasses a single column and multiple rows, Excel pastes only as many lines as the selection includes rows. If the selection encompasses multiple columns, in most cases you will be warned that the paste area is not the same shape as the data on the Clipboard and asked to confirm your intention. If the result is not what you want, you can use the Undo command.

Although Excel can copy text to the Clipboard in Rich Text Format, it cannot paste text in Rich Text Format. Text formatted with a word processor must be reformatted after you import it into Excel.

Excel normally treats tab characters in Clipboard text as a signal — called a *column delimiter* — to move to the next column. For example, if you paste a tabbed table from a word processor, Excel typically parses the text correctly into columns. (*Parsing* is the process of breaking data into smaller chunks.)

NOTE Excel can also interpret different column delimiter characters if you import files by choosing the Open command from the File menu. When you open text files in Excel, the Import Text Wizard appears automatically, giving you total control over parsing.

When you paste text into a worksheet cell or range, Excel does not, by default, treat the text as an embeddable object, even if its source is an OLE server application such as Word for Windows. If you want the text to be embedded, use the Paste Special command.

For more information about embedding and OLE, see "Linking and Embedding Objects," page 899.

Parsing Pasted Text with the Convert Text To Columns Wizard

If you don't want to open an entire text file in Excel, or if the data you want is not in a file that is saved in text format, you can cut and paste the data into a workbook and then parse it using the Text To Columns command on the Data menu. The Text To Columns command displays the Convert Text To Columns Wizard, a series of three dialog boxes that walk you through the process of converting your text strings into the proper columnar format.

For example, if you have comma-separated data in a word processor file, you can copy and paste it into Excel and then, while the pasted data is still selected, choose the Text To Columns command from the Data menu. The first dialog box displayed by the Convert Text To Columns Wizard is shown in Figure 26-3.

The wizard's first dialog box shows what the selected data looks like and allows you to choose between fixed-width and delimited data. In Figure 26-3, Excel correctly guesses that the data is separated by commas, so the Delimited option is selected. Select the Fixed Width option only when the fields (columns) of data are the same width in each record (row). Click the Next button to display the wizard's second dialog box, as shown in Figure 26-4.

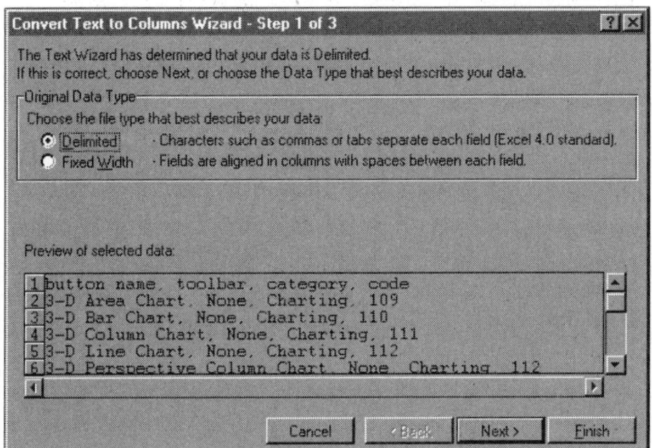

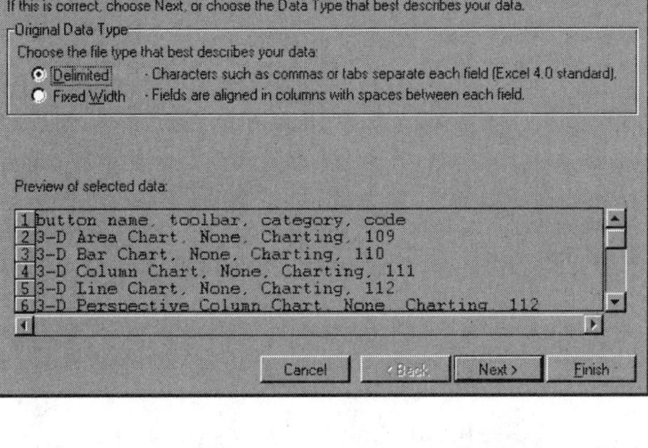

FIGURE 26-3

Choosing the Text To Columns command activates a wizard that helps you parse pasted data.

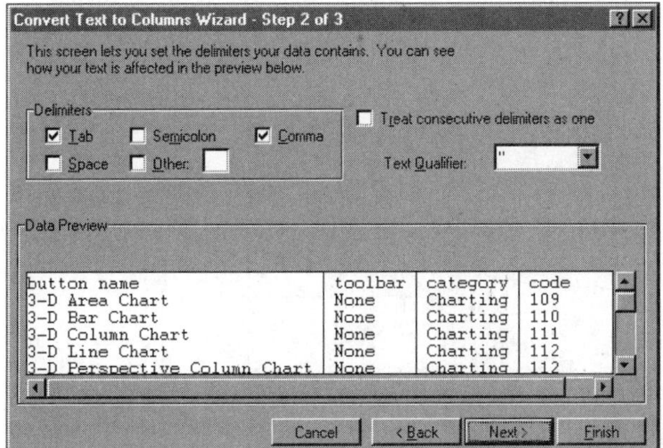

FIGURE 26-4

You can use the Convert Text To Columns Wizard to parse data separated with virtually any delimiter.

In the second dialog box, you select the delimiter used in the text file. In our example, commas are used, and selecting the Comma option causes the Data Preview section to display what appears to be the correct distribution of columns. To be sure, you can view all of the selected data by using the scroll bars below and to the right of the preview area.

In a data file, some fields might be empty, in which case two delimiters appear right next to each other, as in the following:

1234 Maypole Street,#11,Redmond,WA,91234

2345 Seeda Lane,,Seattle,WA,91234

The double comma in the second address indicates that the apartment number field is not used. When you parse these addresses normally, a separate column is created for apartment numbers, some cells of which will be empty. If you don't want empty cells, select the Treat Consecutive Delimiters As One option in the Convert Text To Columns Wizard's second dialog box, bearing in mind that columns of data might not align perfectly. In the example, selecting this option would cause the apartment number in the first address, #11, and the city in the second address, Seattle, to end up in the same column.

You can also specify one of three Text Qualifier options: double quotation marks, single quotation marks, or none. Text files are often created with these qualifiers surrounding any text or with them surrounding text strings that contain delimiter characters as part of the data itself. For example, in the name and address

"Bits, Bytes, & Chips, Inc." 1234 Maypole Street,#11,Redmond,WA,91234

the double quotation marks indicate that the entire text string they enclose is a single field. The comma contained within the quotes is to be considered not a delimiter but part of the text itself.

When you are satisfied that the delimiter options parse the text correctly into columns, click the Next button to display the Convert Text To Columns Wizard's final dialog box, shown in Figure 26-5.

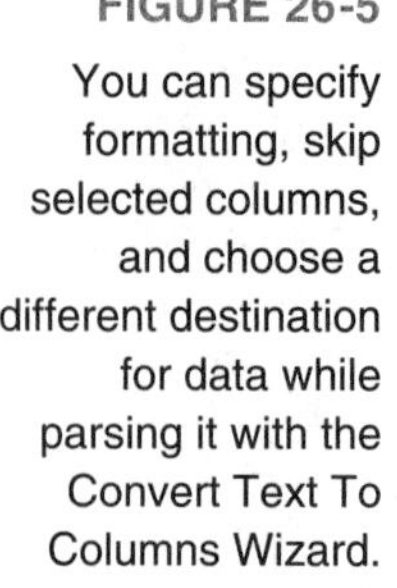

FIGURE 26-5

You can specify formatting, skip selected columns, and choose a different destination for data while parsing it with the Convert Text To Columns Wizard.

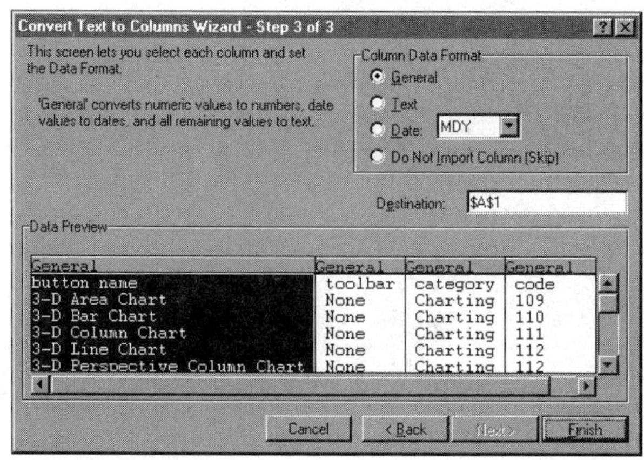

The third dialog box appears with the first column of data selected in the Data Preview section. With this dialog box, you can specify simple formatting for each column. The format name appears at the top of the column in the Data Preview section. The General format displays text or numeric values just as it would if you typed them in Excel. You can format a column as Text or select a Date format from the drop-down list box to ensure that dates are interpreted correctly. If you highlight a column in the Data Preview section and select the Do Not Import Column (Skip) option, that's exactly what happens: The column is skipped — a very handy feature for eliminating unnecessary data. The Destination edit box allows you to specify the first cell of the range that you want to contain the parsed data. When you specify a cell, the original unparsed data remains in the location where you first pasted it and a parsed copy is pasted beginning at the indicated cell.

CAUTION Any data in the cells within the destination range are overwritten when Excel pastes the data and parses it into separate columns, so be careful. If you inadvertently lose data, you can always recover it by using the Undo command or button immediately after the data is pasted.

Figure 26-6 shows a worksheet where the first eight rows contain pasted, comma-delimited data, and the second eight rows contain the same data after

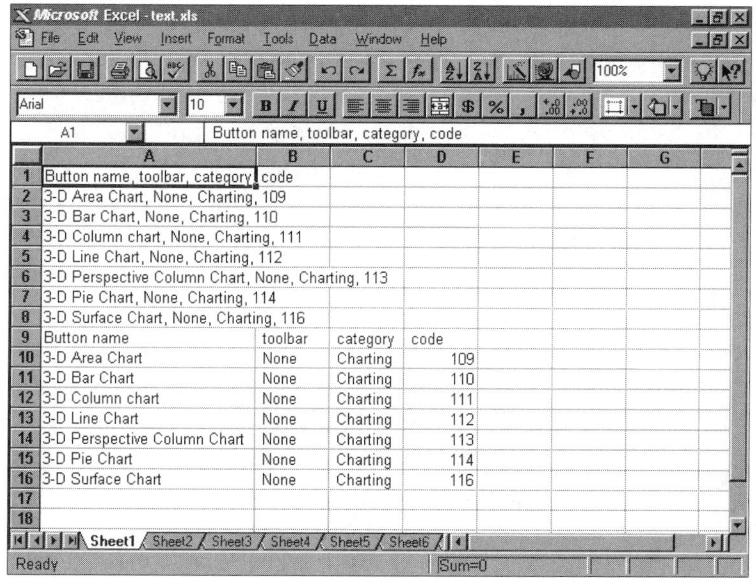

FIGURE 26-6
Rows 1 through 8 contain unparsed data; rows 9 through 16 contain the same data, parsed using the Convert Text To Columns Wizard.

parsing with the Convert Text To Columns Wizard and specifying cell A9 in the Destination edit box.

Pasting Text into Worksheet Objects

If you paste text that originated in an OLE application and if the current selection is a graphic object, Excel's Paste command embeds the text as an object that looks like an icon. If the current selection lies within a text box or a button object, and a flashing text insertion point is visible, Excel pastes the text into the box or button, even if it came from an OLE application.

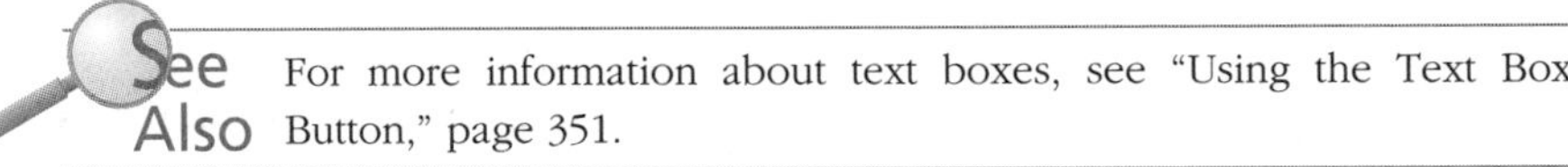

For more information about text boxes, see "Using the Text Box Button," page 351.

Pasting Text into Charts

If you paste text when a chart sheet is active or when an embedded chart is selected, the text is pasted as a graphic object. You can also paste text into a chart sheet's formula bar. For example, to use a heading from a word processor document as text for a chart, copy the heading to the Clipboard, click the chart sheet's formula bar, and choose the Paste command.

Exchanging Pasted Data with Graphics-Oriented Applications

Microsoft Excel's Copy command puts three graphic formats on the Clipboard: Picture, Bitmap, and Device-Independent Bitmap. Most applications that handle graphics information accept any of these formats from the Clipboard but use the Picture format by default. In most cases, you must use the Paste Special (or equivalent) command to paste bit-mapped data.

The essential difference between the Picture and the two bitmap formats is that the bitmap formats provide an exact reproduction, bit for bit, of the pixels that make up the visual presentation of your data in Excel, whereas the Picture format is a translation of the image into commands. For example, a straight line in Bitmap format includes a specification of each individual point along the line. In Picture format, the same image includes only the end-point specifications and other characteristics of the line.

The principal advantage of the Picture format is that it is designed to be scalable. You can also scale images in Bitmap format, but they usually suffer serious distortion in the process. In particular, you are much more likely to get a satisfactory printout from an image in Picture format than from one in Bitmap format. You will probably find little reason to use the Bitmap format to paste an image into an application that can accept the Picture format.

The Copy Picture Command

You can use Excel's Copy Picture command to put your selection on the Clipboard as a picture or a bitmap. The Copy Picture command replaces the normal Copy command when you hold down Shift before you pull down the Edit menu. When you choose the Copy Picture command, a dialog box appears allowing you to specify whether to copy selected cells as they appear on the screen or as they appear when printed, based on the settings in the Page Setup dialog box.

You might find the Copy Picture command useful for pasting a "snapshot" of a worksheet range in another (or the same) Excel workbook. You can also use the Camera button to copy a linked picture of worksheet cells to another workbook location.

See Also For more information about the Page Setup command, see "Controlling the Appearance of Your Pages," page 377.

For more information about the Camera button, see "Taking Pictures of Your Worksheets," page 364.

Pasting from Graphics-Oriented Applications into Microsoft Excel

Excel can paste two kinds of graphic formats: Picture and Bitmap. If the source application supports OLE, the Object format might also be available. As with copying from Excel, you'll generally get the best results with the Picture format. If you use the Paste Special command on the Edit menu, you can select one of the available formats to paste; otherwise, the Paste command selects one for you.

Linking and Embedding Objects

All the Clipboard transfers described so far produce what might be called *static results*. A block of text copied into a Microsoft Excel worksheet from Notepad, for example, simply becomes a range of words or numbers on the receiving worksheet, just as if you had entered the data directly from the keyboard. In particular, the pasted data has no link to its source application. If the document in which those words and numbers were first generated happens to change, you have to repeat the Copy and Paste procedure to keep the Excel worksheet in step.

The Microsoft Toolbar

Using the Microsoft toolbar, you can easily activate other Microsoft applications while you're working in Excel. To display the Microsoft toolbar, choose Toolbar from the View menu, and choose Microsoft from the list. You'll see the toolbar shown here:

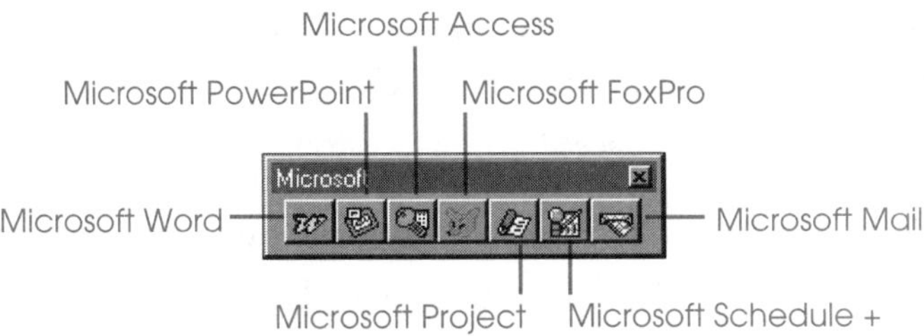

The operation of the buttons on this toolbar is pretty simple: When you click a button, you switch to the associated application. If the application is not already running, clicking the button loads the application and then activates it. To return to Excel, you can press Alt-Tab until Excel reappears, or if the other application also has a toolbar or button similar to Excel's Microsoft toolbar, you can use it to reactivate Excel.

For those times when static results don't meet your needs, Excel supports the Windows OLE protocol, which lets you copy and paste data in such a way that the data remains associated with its source. OLE is a superset of the earlier Dynamic Data Exchange (DDE) transfer protocol. Excel still supports DDE, and Copy and Paste Link procedures between Excel and other DDE-supporting applications still work well. But OLE gives you some valuable new ways to integrate data across applications.

Clients, Servers, and Objects

OLE involves an exchange of information between two parties, called a *server* and a *client*. The server is the application in which the data originates. The client is the one that receives the data. If you embed an Excel chart in a Microsoft Word for Windows document, for example, the server is Excel and the client is Word.

Excel and a growing number of other Windows-based applications support OLE as both server and client. Some applications support OLE in only one mode or the other, however, and some applications do not support OLE at all. Some older programs that don't support OLE do support DDE; when using such programs with Excel, you can link but not embed.

In an OLE transaction, any data item managed by an OLE server application is called the *object*. For example, a block of text from Microsoft Word for Windows, a sound annotation recorded in Sound Recorder, or an image created in Microsoft Paint can each be an object. One way in which OLE represents an advance over earlier methods of data exchange is that the client application doesn't have to know how to render the embedded or linked data object. For example, if you embed a sound annotation in an Excel worksheet, Excel displays an icon to represent the embedded object. When you want to "play" the annotation, the OLE mechanism invokes the server application, and the server renders the object — in this case, Sound Recorder plays the annotation.

Linking Versus Embedding

OLE has two components: *linking* and *embedding*. The difference between them is crucial. When you create a link to Excel data from another application, that application stores a set of pointers to the data's source in Excel; it does not store the data itself. If the source data changes, the document containing the link is updated, either automatically or on demand. In contrast, when you embed Excel data in another application, a copy of the embedded data is incorporated into the receiving document, and this embedded information is not updated if the source data changes. Typically, embedded data requires more disk space; linked data requires less disk space but also requires that the source document remain available.

Why and How to Embed

You should embed, rather than link, when you want the server data in its current form to become a permanent part of the client document or when the server document will no longer be available to the client document. For example, suppose you plan to create a report in Microsoft Word for Windows that incorporates several Excel pivot tables and charts, and you need to take this report on the road. On your portable computer's hard disk, you have Excel and Word, but you keep your Excel data files on a file server at the office. In this case, it is appropriate to embed the Excel material in your Word document. While on the road, if you want to reformat or edit the Excel data, you can simply double-click it in your Word document to invoke Excel and then edit your Excel data.

You might also want to use embedding when you want to be able to call on an OLE server for some simple ad hoc procedure. For example, MS Office comes with an equation editor that can act as an OLE server application. While you work in Excel, you might want to use this equation editor to create a text box that shows some Excel formula in traditional (nonspreadsheet) mathematic notation. With embedding, you don't need to start the equation editor, create the equation, copy it to the Clipboard, and paste or link it into Excel. Instead, you can invoke the equation editor with Excel's Object command (which we discuss in a moment), create your equation, and then use the editor's Update command to embed your work in the Excel document. You need not save the equation itself in its own file.

You can embed an object in two ways: by using the Copy and Paste (or Paste Special) commands and buttons, or by using the Insert Object (or equivalent) command. To embed a data object with the Copy and Paste commands, follow these steps:

1. Copy the data from the server application to the Clipboard as usual.
2. Use the client application's Paste or Paste Special command. In many situations, if the data on the Clipboard originated in an OLE server, the client application's Paste command automatically embeds the object. But this is not always the case. To be sure that you're actually embedding the data, you might want to use Paste Special, instead of Paste. In the list of formats that appears, choose the one that includes the word *object*.

Most OLE client applications offer an Insert Object command, typically on their Edit menus. In Excel's case, the Object command appears on the Insert menu. When you choose this command, a dialog box lists all the types of embeddable data objects known to your system. For example, if you use Excel's Object command, you might see a listing similar to the one shown in Figure 26-7.

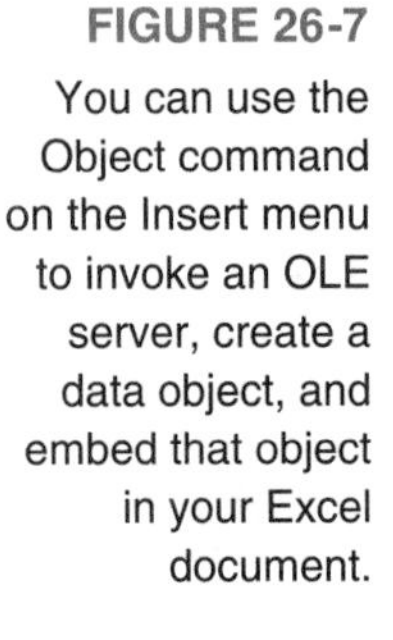

FIGURE 26-7
You can use the Object command on the Insert menu to invoke an OLE server, create a data object, and embed that object in your Excel document.

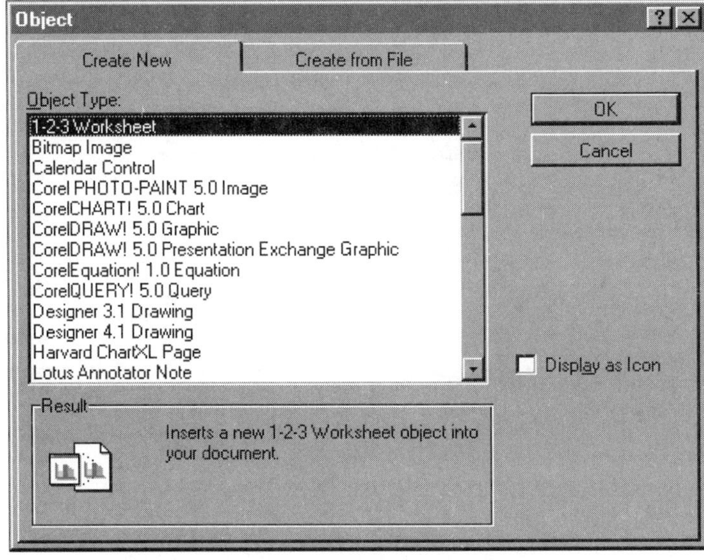

By selecting the type of object you want to embed and clicking OK, you start the server application associated with that kind of object. After you create the object in the server application, you can use the server's Update command (typically on the File menu) to embed the data in your client document. (You can also embed the data by quitting the server application and answering Yes to an update prompt.)

For example, to use Microsoft Paint to create a visual adornment for an Excel worksheet, follow these steps:

1. From the Insert menu, choose the Object command.
2. In the Object dialog box, select Paintbrush Picture and then click OK.

   The menus and toolbars change and Paint provides a drawing area in the Excel window.
3. Create the graphic, and when you are finished, click outside the drawing area to return to Excel. The Excel menus and toolbars reappear.

The Paint image is embedded as a picture at the current cell location in the Excel worksheet.

When you embed any form of data into Excel, Excel renders it as a graphic object and identifies it with a formula based on the EMBED function. For example, Figure 26-8 shows an Excel worksheet with two embedded objects: a graphic created with Microsoft Paint and a block of text from Microsoft Word for Windows. The Word object is selected. As you can see,

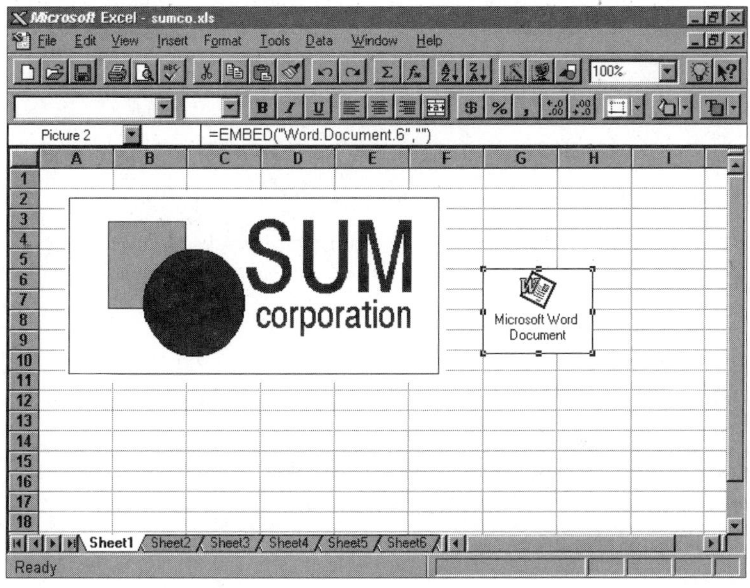

FIGURE 26-8
This Excel worksheet has two embedded objects: a graphic from Paintbrush and a block of text from Word for Windows, displayed as an icon.

the Name box at the left end of the formula bar identifies this object as Picture 2, and the formula bar displays the object's EMBED formula.

> **NOTE** The designation Picture 2 does not imply that the embedded data is in any way graphic. Rather it means that the data is represented in the Excel worksheet by a graphic object (an icon). This object is in every way a normal Excel worksheet object. You can size it, move it, and manipulate it just as you would other worksheet objects.

If you're embedding information from Excel into a document created in a different OLE application, whether or not that data is represented as an icon depends entirely on the abilities and predilections of the client application.

To hear an embedded sound object or play an embedded video, double-click the icon representing that object. To edit an embedded sound or video object, right-click it, choose the Object command from the shortcut menu that appears, and then choose Edit from the next menu. To see or edit text embedded as an icon, double-click the icon.

See Also For more information about embedding objects in Excel, see "Using Graphics from Other Programs," page 367.

Why and How to Link

You should link rather than embed data in the following situations:

- When you want to use a data object in several client documents and you need to ensure that the data will be identical in each.
- When the data object is likely to change over time and you want to maintain it in its source application.
- When you simply want to avoid enlarging the client document.

For example, suppose you want an Excel worksheet to use sales information recorded in an OLE server document that's stored on a network file server. This data is frequently updated in the source document, and you want your Excel worksheet always to have access to the current values. In this case, you should create a link. As we'll see, you can designate the link as either *automatic,* in which case the changes to the data source are always reflected in the Excel worksheet, or *manual,* in which case the changes are read into the Excel document only when you ask for them.

You can create links either with server applications that support OLE or with older Windows-based programs that support DDE but not OLE. The procedures for creating and maintaining the links are the same in both cases, and whether the application supports OLE or only DDE, the document that supplies the data is called a *server,* and the document into which the data is linked is called the *client*.

To create a link in Excel, follow these steps:

1. Save the document in the server application. Most server programs cannot copy a linkable format to the Clipboard from a document that has never been saved because such a document does not have a filename.
2. Copy the data to the Clipboard, just as you would if you were performing a static transfer.
3. Switch to your workbook and choose the Paste Special command from the Edit menu to display the dialog box shown earlier in Figure 26-2 on page 892. Excel creates automatic links by default. Depending on the server application, you might be able to select from several data formats as well as specify the automatic/manual status of the link. When you select a format that can be linked, the Paste Link option becomes available. Choose this option and click OK. When you click OK, the data is added in the selected cell. In the formula bar, the application name, file name, and the word OLE help you identify that the object is a link.

If you link data from Excel to another application, we recommend that you name the Excel range that contains your linked data before you create the link. If you do not name the range and you subsequently rearrange your worksheet, the odds are good that your client document will no longer be linked to the correct data. When a worksheet rearrangement causes the client document to be linked to an entirely new set of numbers, it's easy to overlook the fact that the link has, in effect, become corrupted.

When you name the Excel range before you create the link, the client application might not identify the server range by its name. Some applications insist on using the column and row coordinates even when the range has a name. Fortunately, you can use the client application's link-editing procedure to see how the link is identified and to change it if necessary.

For more information about link editing, see "Editing Links," page 908.

Automatic Versus Manual Links

As mentioned earlier, links are either automatic (updated whenever data changes) or manual (updated on demand). Some applications use other terms — such as *hot* and *cold, hot* and *warm,* or *active* and *inactive* — but the concepts are the same. No other forms of linkage exist.

To update a manual link, you typically choose a command with a name similar to Links from the File or Edit menu. (In Excel, the Links command is on the Edit menu.) As shown in Figure 26-9, the Links dialog box lists all links to the current document and provides a set of command buttons. Clicking the button labeled Update, Activate, or something similar, produces the latest values for the link. (In Excel, the button is labeled Update Now.)

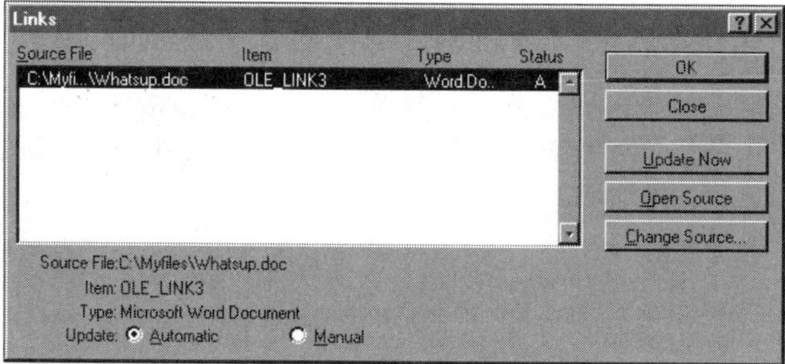

FIGURE 26-9
This dialog box lets you update, edit, or cancel a link, switch between automatic and manual linking, and open the server for the linked data.

In most applications, the same dialog box that lets you update a manual link also lets you change a link's status from manual to automatic or vice versa. In Excel, you change a link's status by choosing Links from the Edit menu, selecting the link to be changed, and clicking either the Automatic or Manual option.

Opening a File That Contains Links

When you open a workbook that contains a remote reference to a document in another application, Excel asks whether you want to reestablish the link and update references to the server document. If you click Yes, Excel attempts to reestablish the link; if you click No, Excel freezes the linked references and displays the values shown when you last saved the workbook.

Suspending Links

To suspend a link temporarily, choose Options from the Tools menu, click the Calculation tab, and deselect the Update Remote References option. Excel then displays in the linked cells the last set of values received from the supporting document.

In addition to initiating remote requests to other applications, Excel can also receive DDE requests. Excel automatically responds to any DDE request it receives. If you want to close Excel to DDE requests, choose the Options command from the Tools menu, click the General tab, and select the Ignore Other Applications option.

For information about procedures for creating external references to Excel from within another application, see the documentation for that application.

How Links Are Identified in Microsoft Excel

Linked data is identified by three elements: the server application, the server document's filename, and the location of the data within the server document. In formal OLE parlance, these elements are referred to as the *application,* the *topic,* and the *item.*

When you link data to an Excel worksheet, Excel identifies the link with a *remote reference* by creating a formula that looks like this:

=*Application* | *Topic*'!'*Item*

For example, the link shown in Figure 26-19 would look like this:

=Word.Document.6|'C:\MYFILES\WHATSUP.DOC'!'OLE_LINK3'

You can create links manually by entering a remote reference formula in any worksheet cell. However, the only practical reason for creating a link manually is if you want to set up a link at a time when the server application or document isn't available. Otherwise, you'll probably find it simpler to use the Copy and Paste technique.

Linking Text Versus Linking Objects or Pictures

If the server application is a sophisticated word processor that handles both text and graphics, its Copy command probably supplies the Clipboard with data in both text and graphic formats. If you use Excel's Paste Special command with the Paste Link option selected, Excel links the default format, which is probably either an OLE object format or a picture (if the server does not support OLE).

If you don't need to see the linked text in your worksheet, the icon representation provided by the Display As Icon option in the Paste Special dialog box is a more compact way to annotate your worksheets. Users who want to read the annotation can simply double-click the icon; those who don't are not distracted by the entire text.

To see the text, choose Paste Special from the Edit menu, select the Text format, select the Paste Link option, and click OK. Each line of text in the server document appears on a separate row in Excel, and Excel turns the link formula into an array that spans the entire range occupied by the text. (Depending on the server, Excel might treat an entire paragraph as a single line of text and display it in one row.) If you select a single cell before creating the link, Excel uses as many rows as it needs to paste the server data.

Activating a Link

If the server application supports OLE, you can "activate" the link by double-clicking it. Windows then launches the server application (if it isn't already running). The server in turn loads the linked document and presents the linked item.

CAUTION If the client application is Excel, double-clicking a cell containing a link formula might produce unexpected results. If the Edit Directly In Cell option is turned on, double-clicking activates the cell for editing. If the cell contains a note and the Edit Directly In Cell option is turned off, the Cell Note dialog box appears. Consequently, the most predictable way to display the Links dialog box is to choose the Links command from the Edit menu. (For more information, see "Editing Directly in Cells," page 241, and "Adding Notes to Cells," page 288.)

As an alternative to double-clicking — one that works with applications that don't support OLE as well as with OLE servers — you can choose Links (or its equivalent) from the File or Edit menu. (In some applications, this command is called Edit Links or something similar.) A dialog box lists all linked items and provides some command buttons. Select the item and then look for a command button called Open, Activate, or something similar. (In Excel, the button is called Open Source.)

Editing Links

The principal hazard with linking (as opposed to embedding) is that the server data might get moved or renamed. When that happens, the client document either reports an error (if you're lucky) or becomes linked to the wrong information. Most client applications, Excel included, provide commands to help you repair such damaged links. Typically you choose the Links command from the File or Edit menu (again, this command might be called Edit Links or something similar), select the damaged link in the list box, and then click a Change or Edit command button. (In Excel, the button is called Change Source.) Typically, the application then provides a dialog box in which you can edit the link.

Chapter 27

Importing and Exporting

In this chapter, we discuss the sharing of information between Microsoft Excel 7 and specific programs, including Lotus 1-2-3, Quattro Pro, dBase, Microsoft Multiplan, and other versions of Microsoft Excel. Although Microsoft Excel 7 is a versatile file exchanger, foreign relations are never entirely uncomplicated. If you're moving to Excel from another spreadsheet application, such as Lotus 1-2-3, you'll be pleased to know that most of your worksheets and macros will work immediately in Excel. But Lotus 1-2-3 and Excel are different applications in many respects. This chapter explains some of the differences and how they affect the process of importing and exporting worksheets and charts.

General Procedures

In this section, we discuss briefly the two File menu commands used for all your importing and exporting operations. You should already be familiar with both of these commands, so you can consider the following a refresher course.

Using the Open Command to Import Files

To import a file from another application or from an earlier version of Excel, choose the Open command from the File menu (or click the Open button on the Standard toolbar) and select the file you want to import from the list of files in the Open dialog box. You can use the Files Of Type drop-down list box in the lower left corner of the Open dialog box to display files with a particular extension, such as .WK* files. Keep in mind that it is not necessary to include a default filename extension when you import a file because Excel determines the format of the file by examining the file's contents, not its name.

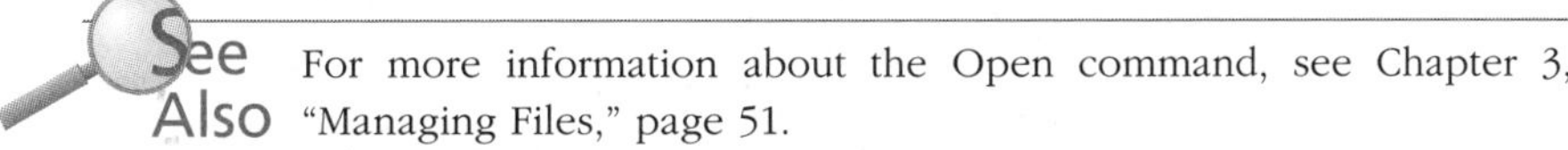

See Also For more information about the Open command, see Chapter 3, "Managing Files," page 51.

Using the Save As Command to Export Files

To export a Microsoft Excel file to another application or to an earlier version of Excel, choose the Save As command from the File menu (or, if you're saving the file for the first time, click the Save button on the Standard toolbar). Then select the format of the application you're exporting to from the Save As Type drop-down list box. Note that when you select a format from the Save As Type drop-down list box, Excel automatically changes the .XLS extension of the file you're exporting to the default filename extension of the application.

See Also For more information about the Save As command, see Chapter 3, "Managing Files," page 51.

Importing .WKS, .WK1, and .WR1 Files

Microsoft Excel can import two-dimensional (single-sheet) Lotus 1-2-3 spreadsheets in the following formats:

- .WKS (Lotus 1-2-3 Release 1A)
- .WK1 (Lotus 1-2-3 Release 2.0, 2.01, 2.2, 2.3, and 2.4)
- .WR1 (Symphony)

If you have used the Lotus 1-2-3 Impress, WYSIWYG, or Allways add-ins to format your Lotus 1-2-3 worksheets, the formatting information is stored in separate files with the same base names as your worksheets. For example, Impress or WYSIWYG formatting information for a worksheet named NUMBERS.WK1 is stored in a file named NUMBERS.FMT. Allways formatting information is stored in a file named NUMBERS.ALL.

Excel's import routine looks for associated .FMT and .ALL files and automatically translates those files into Excel formatting attributes. All you have to do to import the formatting is ensure that the .FMT or .ALL file associated with your worksheet is stored in the same directory as the worksheet.

If the imported Lotus 1-2-3 worksheet includes graphs that are not embedded on the worksheet, Excel converts the graphs and stores each one on a separate sheet. The current graph (the one that Lotus 1-2-3 displays when you press F10 or use the /Graph View command) appears on a page named Current.

If the imported Lotus 1-2-3 worksheet includes graphs that are embedded on the worksheet, Excel embeds the graphs on the converted worksheet, in the same sizes and positions as the originals. In this case, the graphs are not stored on separate Excel sheets.

A few Impress and WYSIWYG formatting commands cannot be translated correctly by Excel. Format codes within cell entries (such as codes to change the font or color for particular words in a label) appear as unreadable characters in Excel. As a result, you have to edit these codes out of the imported file and substitute the appropriate Excel commands manually. Drop shadows and objects drawn on top of charts are not translated. Double underlines and wide underlines are converted to single underlines.

Excel translates most Lotus 1-2-3 numeric formats into standard or custom Excel formats. The only Lotus 1-2-3 formats Excel can't translate are +/– and Text, which it converts to the General format.

Formula Conversion

The precedence of arithmetic operators in Excel is different from that in Lotus 1-2-3. In Excel, the negation operator takes precedence over the exponentiation operator. In Lotus 1-2-3, the exponentiation operator takes precedence over the negation operator. Thus, the formula –2^2 returns 4 in Excel but –4 in Lotus 1-2-3. You can overcome this difference by careful use of parentheses.

Excel supports only natural-order calculation; that is, it recalculates any precedents for a formula before it recalculates the formula itself. In addition to natural-order calculation, Lotus 1-2-3 supports by-column and by-row calculation. When you import a Lotus 1-2-3 worksheet into Excel, recalculation is set to natural, regardless of the original Lotus 1-2-3 setting.

All Lotus 1-2-3 Release 2.x functions have counterparts in Excel. Some functions have slightly different names, but they are otherwise identical. For example, the function that computes the average of a set of values is AVERAGE in Excel and @AVG in Lotus 1-2-3. When you import a Lotus 1-2-3 worksheet, Excel automatically changes the names of the functions.

In a few cases, an Excel function and its Lotus 1-2-3 counterpart don't work in exactly the same way. Excel usually overcomes these differences during translation. For example, both Excel and Lotus 1-2-3 have CHOOSE functions. In Excel, the CHOOSE function takes the form

=CHOOSE(*index_num,value1,value2,...*)

In Lotus 1-2-3, the CHOOSE function takes the form

@CHOOSE(*offset,value0,value1,...*)

The difference between these functions is that the first value in the Excel function has an index value of 1, whereas the first value in the Lotus 1-2-3 function has an offset (index) value of 0. In other words, the formula

=CHOOSE(1,100,200,300)

returns 100 in Excel, but the formula

@CHOOSE(1,100,200,300)

returns 200 in Lotus 1-2-3.

Excel overcomes this difference by adding 1 to the offset value when it loads a Lotus 1-2-3 worksheet into Excel or by subtracting 1 from the index value when it converts an Excel CHOOSE function to Lotus 1-2-3. Excel uses the same technique with the VLOOKUP and HLOOKUP functions and with all database statistical functions (DSUM, DAVERAGE, and so on).

In Excel, the *payment* and *principal* arguments of the PV, FV, and PMT functions are negative. In Lotus 1-2-3, the same arguments are positive. For this reason, when Excel translates one of these functions from Excel to Lotus 1-2-3 or from Lotus 1-2-3 to Excel, it changes the sign of the *payment* and *principal* arguments.

Finally, whereas the Excel IRR function takes the form

=IRR(*values,guess*)

the Lotus 1-2-3 @IRR function takes the form

@IRR(*guess,values*)

To account for this difference, Excel always transposes the *values* and *guess* arguments when it translates an IRR function.

For more information about creating formulas in Excel, see Chapter 5, "Building Formulas," page 111.

For more information about functions, see Chapter 11, "Common Worksheet Functions," page 397.

Linked Files

Lotus 1-2-3 formulas that reference external worksheets are translated into external-reference formulas in Excel. After Excel translates a file that contains such formulas, it displays a dialog box asking whether you want to update your automatic links, or external references. If you select No, Excel uses the formulas' most recent values. If you select Yes, Excel reads the supporting documents on disk and updates the external-reference formulas.

Dates

Excel and Lotus 1-2-3 use the same serial date system for calculating date and time values. However, the Excel DATE function accepts *year* arguments from 0 through 178, whereas the Lotus 1-2-3 @DATE function accepts *year* arguments from 0 through 199. As long as the *year* argument of an imported Lotus 1-2-3 @DATE function is less than 179, Excel converts the function correctly. If the *year* argument of an @DATE function is outside this range, Excel does not recognize it as a date value.

Tables

If your Lotus 1-2-3 worksheet contains a data table, Excel imports the input values, table formulas, and results of the table. However, the definition of the table is lost. You must use the Table command on the Data menu to redefine the table in Excel.

Excel data tables are slightly different from those in Lotus 1-2-3. First, the results of an Excel data table are defined by an array formula; arrays are not supported in Lotus 1-2-3. In addition, Excel data tables are calculated automatically whenever you calculate the worksheet, just like other formulas. In Lotus 1-2-3, you must choose a command or press a function key to calculate your data tables. Finally, Excel allows more flexibility with the input values in a one-input table: They can be in either the first column or the first row of the table. In Lotus 1-2-3, input values must be in the first column.

Transition Formula Evaluation and Entry Options

Certain other differences between Excel and Lotus 1-2-3 present more difficult translation issues. For example, in some contexts, Lotus 1-2-3 (Release 2.01 and later) treats both blank cells and cells containing text as equivalent to 0. Excel treats blank cells as equivalent to 0, but it regards text as a separate data type that cannot be referenced with a numeric value. These differences can cause the same worksheet to produce divergent results in the two applications.

Suppose cell A1 contains text and cell A2 contains the value 100. The following formulas produce one set of results in Excel and something quite different in Lotus 1-2-3:

Excel Formula	Returns	Equivalent Lotus 1-2-3 Formula	Returns
=2*A1	#VALUE!	+2*A1	0
=MIN(A1:A2)	100	@MIN(A1..A2)	0
=AVERAGE(A1:A2)	100	@AVG(A1..A2)	50
=COUNT(A1:A2)	1	@COUNT(A1..A2)	2

Excel and Lotus 1-2-3 also differ in the way they handle text as the first argument of a VLOOKUP or HLOOKUP function. If you use text values in the first column of a vertical lookup table or the first row of a horizontal lookup table, Excel requires that you order the text values alphabetically. Excel then searches through the first column or first row until it finds a value "greater than" the text supplied as the first argument of the function. When it finds such a value, it returns to the previous item in that column or row and uses that item as an index to the lookup table. Lotus 1-2-3, in contrast, does not insist on an alphabetically ordered index column or row, but if the first argument of the lookup function doesn't match an index value exactly, the function returns the ERR error value.

For example, suppose your lookup table (named TABLE) contains the following information:

Johannesburg	10
New Delhi	90
Beijing	45

The formula =VLOOKUP("Madras",TABLE,2) would return 10, the value opposite Johannesburg. If you had the same table in Lotus 1-2-3, the formula @VLOOKUP("Madras",TABLE,2) would return ERR because the argument "Madras" does not exactly match an entry in the index column of the table.

Other small differences between the two spreadsheet applications affect the outcome of INT and MOD functions, the behavior of computed criteria in database criteria ranges, and the values returned by logical formulas.

The Transition tab of the Options dialog box in Excel includes a Transition Formula Evaluation option. When selected, this option causes Excel to interpret worksheet formulas in exactly the same way the comparable formulas would be interpreted in a Lotus 1-2-3 worksheet. If you regularly work with both native Excel files and imported files from any version of Lotus 1-2-3, it is vitally important that you be aware of the state of this option. As you can imagine from the previous examples, turning this option on or off will change the values returned in your worksheet.

Excel's import routine automatically turns on the Transition Formula Evaluation option for any imported Lotus 1-2-3 file. To change the setting of this option for the current worksheet, choose the Options command from the Tools menu, click the Transition tab, and select or deselect the Transition Formula Evaluation option. Your setting affects the current worksheet only and is saved as an attribute of that worksheet.

Another option provided for compatibility with Lotus 1-2-3 is called Transition Formula Entry. This option primarily affects the way range names are handled. With Transition Formula Entry turned on, range names are automatically applied to formulas. If you subsequently delete a range name, any formula references to that name revert to the underlying cell coordinates, as they do by default in Lotus 1-2-3 Release 2.x. In contrast, Excel formulas that reference deleted range names normally return #NAME?.

By default, Excel's import routine turns on the Transition Formula Entry option for imported worksheets that include one or more backslash-named ranges (ranges with names such as \a) because these ranges are customarily assigned to macro code, and your macros might depend on Lotus 1-2-3's default behavior. The Transition Formula Entry option is normally turned off for imported worksheets that do not include a range name that begins with a backslash. To change the setting of this option for the current worksheet, choose the Options command from the Tools menu, click the Transition tab, and select or deselect the Transition Formula Entry option. Your setting affects the current worksheet only and is saved as an attribute of that worksheet.

For more information about the Lotus 1-2-3 transition options, see "Lotus 1-2-3 Transition Options," page 152.

Using the Lotus 1-2-3 Macro Interpreter

Excel's Lotus 1-2-3 macro interpreter lets you run most macros written for Lotus 1-2-3 Release 2.01 without change and without a separate translation step. Simply import your .WK1 file into Excel. If Excel's import routine finds a Lotus 1-2-3 range name that consists of a backslash (\) followed by a single letter, it creates a similar name in the translated Excel worksheet, turns on the Transition Formula Evaluation and Transition Formula Entry options, and makes the macro interpreter available. To run your Lotus 1-2-3 macro, press Ctrl plus the letter associated with the macro's range name. For example, if your Lotus 1-2-3 macro is stored in a range named \A, you would run this macro by pressing Ctrl-A. Note that you press only the Ctrl key and the letter — do not press the Shift key, even if you assigned an uppercase letter as the name in Lotus 1-2-3.

While your Lotus 1-2-3 macro is running, you will see the designation MI (for *macro interpreter*) in the status bar of your Excel application window. In response to interactive macro commands, such as {GETLABEL}, the interpreter will display an edit box. Custom Lotus 1-2-3 menus appear in dialog boxes.

In response to the {?} command, the interpreter simply pauses and displays *MI Pause* in the status bar. Macro execution resumes when you press Enter. While the macro is paused, all Excel menus are dimmed except for the application and document control menus. Thus, you can move and size an imported Lotus 1-2-3 document while its macro awaits input from you. (You can even close the document or quit Excel.) But you can't use any Excel-specific features that require access to the menu bar.

You can interrupt a Lotus 1-2-3 macro by pressing Ctrl-Break, even if that macro includes a {BREAKOFF} command. Single-step execution of Lotus 1-2-3 macros is not available.

Excel's Transition Formula Evaluation option is automatically turned on whenever you import a Lotus 1-2-3 worksheet that contains a backslash-named macro range. Even if you turn off this option after importing, Excel turns it back on for you while the macro is running. As a result, Lotus 1-2-3 macro expressions such as

```
{WAIT @NOW+@TIME(0,0,5)}
```

work correctly, regardless of how you set the Transition Formula Evaluation option. For sanity's sake, however, it's best to leave the option in one mode or the other.

Limitations and Caveats

Be sure to test all your imported macros carefully before you commit your data to them. Here are some issues to be aware of as you work with imported Lotus 1-2-3 macros:

- The macro interpreter lets you activate only those macros in ranges named with a backslash and a single letter. You cannot use Alt-F3 to activate other macro ranges. Backslash-named macros can, however, call subroutines and other macros that do not have backslash names.
- The macro interpreter cannot import macros from Lotus .MLB macro-library files.
- Navigation commands in imported macros work as they do in Lotus 1-2-3. However, the effects of commands such as {BIGRIGHT} and {BIGLEFT} are measured relative to the current window dimensions. Before you run an imported macro, you might want to be sure that the window displays 20 rows by 8 columns, the size of the normal Lotus 1-2-3 display.
- Macros that depend on Lotus 1-2-3 add-ins, including Allways and WYSIWYG, do not work.
- An imported macro must not end in a menu.
- The macro interpreter supports the menu system of Lotus 1-2-3 Release 2.01. Thus, for example, a macro can use /FR (File Retrieve) but not /FO (File Open) because /FR is included in the Release 2.01 command set, whereas /FO was not introduced until Release 3.
- Some Lotus 1-2-3 commands, such as /File Admin, do not work in Excel because Excel cannot duplicate them.

- If your macro turns off the worksheet frame with {BORDERSOFF} or {FRAMEOFF}, you must deliberately turn the frame back on again with {BORDERSON} or {FRAMEON}. Unlike Lotus 1-2-3, Excel's macro interpreter does not automatically redisplay the frame at the end of a macro run.
- The following Lotus 1-2-3 macro commands are not supported and may generate a syntax error: {APPENDBELOW}, {APPENDRIGHT}, {FORM}, {FORMBREAK}, and {MENU}.

Exporting .WKS and .WK1 Files

To export a Microsoft Excel file to Lotus 1-2-3 Release 1A, choose the Save As command from the File menu and select the WKS (1-2-3) (*.wks) option in the Save As Type drop-down list box. To export an Excel file to Lotus 1-2-3 Release 2.x, choose the Save As command and select WK1,FMT (1-2-3) (*.wk1), WK1,ALL (1-2-3) (*.wk1), or WK1 (1-2-3) (*.wk1) in the Save As Type drop-down list box. All of these options save only the current sheet.

The WK1,FMT (1-2-3) option stores formatting information (fonts, underscores, and shading, among other things) in a .FMT file, for use with the Impress or WYSIWYG add-ins. WK1,ALL (1-2-3) stores formatting information in an .ALL file that can be read by the Allways add-in. WK1 (1-2-3) creates a Lotus 1-2-3 document without an associated formatting file. In this case, numeric formats, column widths, and alignment attributes are saved (because these details are controlled by Lotus 1-2-3, not by Impress, WYSIWYG, or Allways), but other formatting characteristics are lost.

When you export Excel charts in any of the .WK1 formats, the charts are saved as named graphs in Lotus 1-2-3. Even if you don't have the Impress, WYSIWYG, or Allways add-ins, you can display your Excel charts by using the /Graph Name Use command. If an Excel chart type is not available in Lotus 1-2-3, it is converted to an alternative type. For example, Excel doughnut charts become Lotus 1-2-3 pie graphs.

Numeric Format Conversion

Most built-in Excel numeric formats have Lotus 1-2-3 counterparts and convert properly. Those Excel formats that do not have Lotus 1-2-3 equivalents (the fractional formats, for example) are assigned the General format in the .WK1 file. Note that these untranslatable formats do *not* acquire the Lotus 1-2-3 global default format. If you use the /Worksheet Global Format command to change the global default format — from General to one of Lotus 1-2-3's Currency formats, for example — your untranslatable Excel formats remain in the General format.

If you defined custom numeric formats in your Excel worksheet, Excel attempts to convert those formats to Lotus 1-2-3 formats. For example, Excel converts the custom format $#,##0.000_);($#,##0.000) to Currency with three decimal places. However, if Excel can't convert the format for a particular cell, that cell is assigned the General format in the Lotus 1-2-3 worksheet. For example, the custom format dddd, mmmm d, yyyy displays Excel dates in the following form: Saturday, January 1, 1996. This format has no counterpart in Lotus 1-2-3, so the resulting cell in a Lotus 1-2-3 2.3 worksheet is formatted as General.

External-Reference Formulas

Lotus 1-2-3 Release 2.2, Release 2.3, and Release 2.4 support only the most rudimentary form of external-reference formulas. In these applications, you can reference a single external cell, but you cannot perform calculations within the external-reference formula. If you restrict your external-reference formulas similarly in Excel, you can translate them to the .WK1 format. (Note, however, that Lotus 1-2-3 Release 2.01 does not support any form of external referencing, so even correctly translated external-reference formulas return *ERR* in Release 2.01.) Before you export an Excel worksheet that contains external-reference formulas, be sure to save all the supporting worksheets in .WK1 format.

Differences and Incompatibilities

When you export any Excel formula that involves arrays or uses a discontiguous selection as an argument, the formula is converted to its current value. In addition, some Excel functions and their Lotus 1-2-3 equivalents don't work in exactly the same way. In most of these cases, Excel overcomes the differences during translation. In a few cases, however, the conversion might not work. For example, the Excel PV and PMT functions can take as many as five arguments, but Lotus 1-2-3 doesn't support the fourth *(future value)* and fifth *(type)* arguments. When you export an Excel worksheet that contains a PV or PMT function with no more than three arguments, Excel converts the formula properly. When you export a worksheet that contains a PV or PMT function with more than three arguments, Excel replaces the formula with a constant.

The Excel NPV function is similar to the Lotus 1-2-3 @NPV function, except that the Excel function accepts many *cash flow* arguments, whereas the Lotus 1-2-3 function accepts only one. Excel converts the formula to a constant. Formulas that involve functions without a Lotus 1-2-3 counterpart are also converted to constants.

When you export an Excel worksheet to Lotus 1-2-3, all AND, OR, and NOT functions change to #AND#, #OR#, and #NOT# operators. For example, the AND function in this Excel formula

```
=AND(A1>100,A1<200)
```

converts to the #AND# operator in this Lotus 1-2-3 formula

```
(A1>100#AND#A1<200)
```

The conversion from the Excel function to the Lotus 1-2-3 operator does not affect the formula's result, however.

Excel supports seven error values: #DIV/0!, #N/A, #NAME?, #NULL!, #NUM!, #REF!, and #VALUE! These values can appear as constants in cells and formulas and also as the results of formulas. Lotus 1-2-3 supports only two error values — ERR and NA — both of which appear only as the results of formulas. When you export an Excel worksheet to Lotus 1-2-3, any error value translates to ERR. When you import a Lotus 1-2-3 worksheet into Excel, any NA value translates to the #N/A error value, and any ERR value translates to the #VALUE! value.

Lotus 1-2-3 does not support Excel's intersection *(space)* operator. Excel translates any formula that contains an intersection operator to a constant.

An Excel worksheet includes 16,384 rows. Lotus 1-2-3 Release 2.0 and later worksheets include only 8,192 rows. If your Excel worksheet includes data beyond row 8192, break it up before you export it. Excel's export routine does not generate warning messages when it translates references outside Lotus 1-2-3's 8,192-row limit.

Pivot tables in Excel are translated as static worksheet data. That is, they become a set of labels and numeric constants in the exported worksheet.

In Excel, you can assign names to cells or ranges in the worksheet or to constant values and formulas that aren't entered in cells. In Lotus 1-2-3, on the other hand, you can assign names only to cells or ranges and not to multiple areas, constant values, or formulas. Any formula that contains a reference to a named cell or range converts properly from Excel to Lotus 1-2-3. If you convert a worksheet that contains formulas that use named constants or formulas, however, Excel converts those named constants and formulas to constant values. For example, suppose you assigned the name Test to the constant 100 in an Excel worksheet and then used that name in the formula

```
=Test*A1
```

When Excel converts this formula, the name Test changes to the value 100. If you convert a worksheet to a 1-2-3 format using formulas that refer to named multiple areas, Excel displays an alert box warning you that it cannot translate the name.

Excel and Lotus 1-2-3 both support manual and automatic calculation. However, Lotus 1-2-3's Automatic calculation option is equivalent to Excel's Automatic Except Tables calculation option. When you export worksheets from Excel to Lotus 1-2-3, Automatic remains Automatic, Manual remains Manual, and Automatic Except Tables becomes Automatic. Although Lotus 1-2-3 accepts Excel's Maximum Iterations setting, it ignores the Maximum Change setting when an Excel file is converted.

When your Excel worksheet contains a data table, the table formula and the input values (variables) are usually converted properly for Lotus 1-2-3. Keep in mind that Lotus 1-2-3 requires your input values to appear in the first column of the table range, however. The results in an Excel data table are array formulas; these formulas are changed to constant values during the conversion. In addition, you must redefine the table range and the input cell or cells before you use the table in Lotus 1-2-3.

Excel and Lotus 1-2-3 both support cell protection. In Excel, however, a cell can be both locked (protected from accidental change) and hidden. In Lotus 1-2-3, cells can only be locked. Thus, when you export an Excel worksheet to Lotus 1-2-3, all locked cells are locked in the Lotus 1-2-3 worksheet, but all hidden cells are unhidden unless you used Excel's Hidden number format.

.WK1 files can use only eight fonts. Therefore, only the first eight fonts in your Excel worksheets are translated to equivalent WYSIWYG formatting.

Finally, outlines, graphic objects (other than embedded charts), and macros are not translated when you export an Excel file to Lotus 1-2-3.

Importing .WK3 and .WK4 Files

Microsoft Excel can import the .WK3 files created by Lotus 1-2-3 Release 3.x, as well as the .WK4 files created by Lotus 1-2-3 for Windows Release 4 and Release 5. Each sheet in your .WK3 or .WK4 file is imported as a separate worksheet in Excel. WYSIWYG formatting in .WK3 files is converted to Excel formatting, provided Excel can find a like-named file with an .FM3 extension in the same directory as the .WK3 file. A few formatting commands assigned with WYSIWYG might not be translated. Graphs that are not embedded on Lotus 1-2-3 worksheets are stored on separate chart sheets in Excel. Embedded 1-2-3 graphs appear as embedded charts in Excel.

Limitations

Excel's Lotus 1-2-3 macro interpreter handles the macro language of 1-2-3 Release 2.01. Any macros that depend on later macro commands (such as the user-interface commands introduced with 1-2-3 for Windows Release 4) cannot be translated.

Excel does not preserve alternative range information recorded with Lotus 1-2-3's Version Manager. The range values displayed when your .WK4 was last saved are the ones that will appear in your converted Excel file.

Maps and other OLE objects embedded in .WK4 files are not imported. Most drawing objects are imported, but rotated text and drawing objects appear without rotation in Excel. Lotus 1-2-3 "design frames" are not imported. Gradient fills are imported as solid fills.

Exporting .WK3 and .WK4 Files

To export a Microsoft Excel file to Lotus 1-2-3 Release 3.x or Lotus 1-2-3 for Windows, choose the Save As command from the File menu and select the appropriate file type from the Save As Type drop-down list. Choose WK3,FM3 (1-2-3) to save a file for use in 1-2-3 Release 3.x and preserve the file's formatting. Choose WK3 (1-2-3) if you want to use an Excel file in 1-2-3 Release 3.x but don't want to preserve all formatting details. Choose WK4 (1-2-3) to save a file for use in 1-2-3 for Windows Release 4 or Release 5.

Importing and Exporting .WQ1 and .WB1 Files

Microsoft Excel can import and export two Quattro Pro file formats: .WQ1, the format used by Quattro Pro for DOS versions 4 and earlier, and .WB1, the format used by Quattro Pro for Windows versions 1 and 5. Excel does not support the .WQ2 format used by Quattro Pro for DOS version 5 or the .WB2 format used by Quattro Pro for Windows version 6.

Importing and Exporting .DBF Files

Microsoft Excel can import .DBF files from three versions of dBASE: dBASE II, dBASE III, and dBASE IV. Excel creates a list from the imported file, placing the dBASE field names in the first row as column headings. The dBASE records appear in rows immediately below the field names. Excel sets the worksheet column width to match the width of the corresponding dBASE fields.

Note that you can also use Microsoft Query to import information stored in .DBF files. When you use the Open command on the File menu to import a dBASE file, Excel imports the entire file. In contrast, when you use Query to import a dBASE file, you can import only specific records or fields, or you can import the entire file.

To export an Excel file to dBASE, choose Save As from the File menu and select one of the following formats: DBF 4 (dBASE IV) (*.dbf), DBF 3 (dBASE III) (*.dbf), or DBF 2 (dBASE II) (*.dbf). In each case, you must first create a list and name it Database. Excel exports only the information in this list.

For more information about Microsoft Query, see Chapter 21, "An Introduction to Microsoft Query," page 757.

For more information about creating lists, see Chapter 20, "Managing Information in Lists," page 713.

Importing and Exporting Text Files

To export an Excel file as a text file, choose Save As from the File menu and select one of the following seven text formats:

- Formatted Text (Space delimited) (*.prn)
- Text (Tab delimited) (*.txt)
- CSV (Comma delimited) (*.csv)
- Text (Macintosh) (*.txt)
- Text (OS/2 or MS-DOS) (*.txt)
- CSV (Macintosh) (*.csv)
- CSV (OS/2 or MS-DOS) (*.csv)

With all of these formats, Excel saves only the current sheet. Formatting assigned with the Number tab of the Format Cells dialog box is preserved, but all other formatting is removed.

Formatted Text (Space delimited) creates a file in which column alignment is preserved by means of space characters. You might want to use this kind of file when communicating via modem with a recipient who does not have Excel.

Text (Tab delimited) separates the cells of each row with tab characters. Any cell in which a comma appears is surrounded by quotation marks.

With CSV (Comma delimited), Excel separates the cells of each row with commas. Comma-delimited files are preferable to tab-delimited files for importing into database management programs. (Many database management programs can accept either form of text file, but some accept only .CSV files.) Also, many word processing applications can use .CSV files to store the information for form letters.

The differences between the normal, Macintosh, and OS/2 or MS-DOS variants of each file type have to do only with characters that lie outside the normal 7-bit ASCII range. The normal Text and CSV options use the ANSI character set. You should select one of these options if you intend to import your text file into a Windows-based application, such as Microsoft Word for Windows. The Macintosh options use the Macintosh character set; select one of these options if you intend to transfer your file to a Macintosh application. The MS-DOS and OS/2 options use the IBM PC extended character set — the same character set your computer uses when it's not running Windows. (The documentation for some Windows-based programs or for Windows itself might refer to this character set as OEM text.) Select one of these options if you intend to import your text file into a non-Windows–based application, such as XyWrite, or into an OS/2 application.

Importing and Exporting Multiplan Files

To import a file from Multiplan version 3.04 or earlier, first save the file in the SYLK format. Then load Excel, choose Open from the File menu, select SYLK Files (*.slk) in the List Files Of Type drop-down list box, and select the desired file.

To import a file from Multiplan version 4.0 or later, first save the file in Multiplan as an Excel 2.1 file. You can then open the file in Excel like any other .XLS file.

Excel does a good job of importing Multiplan worksheets. Most of the basic data in the worksheets, including all numeric and text entries, names, formats, and protection status, are converted correctly. Multiplan formulas are converted to Excel formulas.

To export an Excel file to Multiplan 3.04 or earlier, choose Save As from the File menu and select SYLK (Symbolic Link) (*.slk) in the Save As Type drop-down list box. To export an Excel file to Multiplan 4.0 or later, choose Save As from the File menu and select Microsoft Excel 2.1 Worksheet (*.xls) in the Save As Type drop-down list box.

Exporting Files to Earlier Versions of Microsoft Excel

Microsoft Excel versions 5 and 7 use the same file format. Therefore, the files you save in Excel 7 can be used without a translation step in Excel 5, and vice versa.

Microsoft Excel's Save As command provides four options for exporting files to earlier versions of Excel. Select Microsoft Excel 4.0 Workbook to save all worksheets in the current .XLS file to an .XLW file suitable for use in Excel 4. Select Microsoft Excel 4.0 Worksheet, Microsoft Excel 3.0 Worksheet, or Microsoft Excel 2.1 Worksheet to save the current sheet as an .XLS file suitable for use in an earlier version.

Charts in Excel 7 documents can be saved in the Excel 4.0 formats only. Pivot tables can be exported only as static data. (Note that an Excel 7 pivot table cannot be exported as an Excel 4 crosstab.)

Exporting Files to VisiCalc

To export a Microsoft Excel file to VisiCalc, choose Save As from the File menu and select DIF (Data Interchange Format) (*.dif) from the Save As Type drop-down list box. This option saves values only, not the formulas that produce them. When you use this option to save a worksheet, Excel saves the file with the .DIF extension.

Sharing Data with Microsoft Excel for the Macintosh

The Windows and Macintosh versions of Microsoft Excel share data easily. All numbers and text — and most formulas and cell formats — are converted without problems. A document's protection status, calculation, iteration, and display settings are also converted.

To exchange data between a PC and a Macintosh, simply transfer files from one computer to the other. (You can accomplish this with a special cable or with a modem.) If your computer uses a disk drive that accepts 3½-inch disks, you can also use a utility program to transfer data between Windows and the Macintosh. If you're connected to a network that supports both Windows and the Macintosh, you'll probably be able to transfer files from one computer to another without any extra equipment or software.

Importing Macintosh Files

To import Macintosh files to your PC, follow these steps:

1. Transfer the file to your PC (via a cable, modem, disk, or network).
2. Start the Windows version of Excel, choose Open from the File menu, and type the name of the document you want to open. Because the Macintosh does not add filename extensions when you save a file, you can zero in on the Macintosh files by typing a wildcard and the null filename extension, such as *. in the File Name edit box and then pressing Enter. Excel lists all the available files without extensions.
3. Select the file you want to import and click OK. Excel loads the selected file.

Exporting Microsoft Excel for Windows Files

Exporting files from a Windows version of Excel to the Macintosh version is just as easy as importing Macintosh files. First transfer the file from the PC to the Macintosh (via a cable, modem, disk, or network). Next start Excel on the Macintosh and then use the Open command to load the file just as you would to load a file in Excel for Windows.

Adjusting Date Values

Although the Windows and Macintosh versions of Excel share many characteristics and capabilities, they do not use the same date system. In the Windows version of Excel, the base date is January 1, 1900. In the Macintosh version of Excel, the base date is January 2, 1904. When you transfer files either to or from the Macintosh, Excel maintains the date type by selecting or deselecting the 1904 Date System option on the Calculation tab of the Options dialog box. Although this technique is usually acceptable, it can cause problems when a date from a Macintosh file is compared with a date from a PC file. For this reason, we suggest that you use the same date setting on all your machines.

Part 8

Appendixes

Appendix A

Toolbar Buttons and Boxes

Microsoft Excel includes an incredible number of toolbar buttons you can use to help lighten the daily workload. And, as if that weren't enough, Excel also provides features and techniques you can employ to create even more buttons. In this appendix, we'll acquaint you with the plethora of prefab buttons Excel provides for you.

See Also For more information about customizing toolbars and creating your own buttons, see Chapter 2, "Toolbars and Buttons," page 33.

Reference to Toolbar Buttons and Boxes

The following table is an alphabetic list of each toolbar button and box included with Microsoft Excel, along with its name; the name of the toolbar on which the button or box resides (or *None,* if it appears only in the Customize dialog box); the category or categories to which the button or box belongs; the code number, which is the number used to refer to the button or box in macro formulas; a brief description of the button or box's operation; and, if applicable, how the button's operation changes when you press Shift while clicking the button.

Button/ Box	Name	Toolbar	Category	Code	Description
	3-D Area Chart AutoFormat	None	Charting	109	Creates a default 3-D area chart.
	3-D Bar Chart AutoFormat	None	Charting	110	Creates a default 3-D bar chart.
	3-D Column Chart AutoFormat	None	Charting	111	Creates a default 3-D column chart.
	3-D Line Chart AutoFormat	None	Charting	113	Creates a default 3-D line chart.
	3-D Perspective Column Chart AutoFormat	None	Charting	112	Creates a default 3-D column chart with a 3-D plot area.
	3-D Pie Chart AutoFormat	None	Charting	114	Creates a 3-D pie chart with percentage labels.
	3-D Surface Chart AutoFormat	None	Charting	116	Creates a default 3-D surface chart.
	Align Left	Formatting	Text Formatting	63	Aligns the text in the selection flush left.
	Align Right	Formatting	Text Formatting	65	Aligns the text in the selection flush right.
	Arc	Drawing	Drawing	85	Draws an arc. Shift-click draws a filled arc. Press Shift after click to create a quarter circle.
	Area Chart AutoFormat	None	Charting	103	Creates a default area chart.
	Arrow	Drawing	Drawing	77	Draws a line with an arrow at the point you release the mouse button. Press Shift to constrain along horizontal, vertical, and diagonal lines.
	Attach Note	Auditing	Auditing	154	Displays the Cell Note dialog box.
	AutoFilter	None	Data	168	Performs an AutoFilter analysis from the active cell.

(continued)

continued

Button/ Box	Name	Toolbar	Category	Code	Description
	AutoFormat	None	Formatting	52	Applies last-used table format from the AutoFormat dialog box. Shift-click cycles through formats.
	AutoSum	Standard	Formula/ Utility	39	Inserts the SUM function and automatically selects a range.
	Bar Chart AutoFormat	None	Charting	104	Creates a default bar chart.
	Bold	Formatting	Text Formatting	58	Applies bold formatting to the selection.
	Borders	Formatting	Formatting	198	Displays a tear-off palette of available borders.
	Bottom Border	None	Formatting	47	Adds or removes a border at the bottom edge of the selection.
	Bottom Double Border	None	Formatting	48	Adds or removes a double border at the bottom edge of the selection.
	Bring To Front	Drawing	Drawing	95	Moves selected objects to the foreground. Shift-click sends objects to the background.
	Calculate Now	None	Utility	126	Recalculates all open workbooks or the formula bar.
	Camera	None	Utility	125	Makes a linked copy of the selection.
	Center Across Columns	Formatting	Text Formatting	67	Centers text across selected columns.
	Center	Formatting	Text Formatting	64	Center-aligns the text in the selection.
	Chart Type	Chart	Charting	234	Displays a tear-off palette of available chart types.
	ChartWizard	Standard/ Chart	Charting	121	Starts the ChartWizard, which lets you create or edit a chart.
	Check Box	Forms	Forms	140	Lets you create a check box control.

(continued)

continued

Button/ Box	Name	Toolbar	Category	Code	Description
	Clear Contents	None	Edit	15	Deletes only formulas and values from the selection, or deletes selected objects.
	Clear Formats	None	Edit	16	Deletes only formats from the selection.
	Colon	None	Formula	35	Inserts a colon (:) at the insertion point in the formula bar.
	Color	Formatting	Drawing	233	Displays a tear-off palette of colors you can apply to cells, charts, and objects.
	Column Chart AutoFormat	None	Charting	105	Creates a default column chart.
	Combination Drop-Down Edit	Forms	Forms	197	Lets you create a drop-down control linked to an edit control.
	Combination List-Edit	Forms	Forms	188	Lets you create a list box control linked to an edit control.
	Comma	None	Formula	36	Inserts a comma at the insertion point in the formula bar.
	Comma Style	Formatting	Formatting	55	Applies a Comma format with two decimal places to the selection.
	Constrain Numeric	None	Formula	42	Restricts the handwriting recognition for Pen Windows to digits and punctuation.
	Control Properties	Forms	Forms	238	Lets you change control properties.
	Copy	Standard	Edit	13	Copies the selection to the Clipboard.
	Create Button	Drawing/ Forms	Drawing/ Utility	80	Creates a button to which you can assign a macro.
	Currency Style	Formatting	Formatting	53	Applies a Currency format with two decimal places to the selection.

(continued)

continued

Button/ Box	Name	Toolbar	Category	Code	Description
	Cut	Standard	Edit	12	Cuts the selection and places it on the Clipboard.
	Cycle Font Color	None	Text Formatting	62	Cycles the selected text through each color in the color palette.
	Dark Shading	None	Formatting/ Drawing	49	Adds a dark shading pattern to the selection.
	Decrease Decimal	Formatting	Formatting	57	Removes a decimal place from the format of the selection. Shift-click to add a decimal place.
	Decrease Font Size	None	Text Formatting	72	Changes the text in the selection to the next smallest built-in font size. Shift-click changes to the next largest font size.
	Default Chart	Chart	Charting	120	Creates an embedded chart in the default format.
	Delete	None	Edit	19	Removes the selected cells and shifts the adjacent cells to fill in the space. Shift-click inserts cells.
	Delete Column	None	Edit	21	Removes the selected columns. Shift-click inserts columns.
	Delete Row	None	Edit	20	Removes the selected rows. Shift-click inserts rows.
	Division Sign	None	Formula	31	Inserts a forward slash (/) at the insertion point in the formula bar.
	Dollar Sign	None	Formula	38	Inserts a dollar sign at the insertion point in the formula bar.
	Double Underline	None	Text Formatting	176	Applies a double-underline to the selected text.
	Doughnut Chart Autoformat	None	Charting	145	Creates a doughnut chart with percentage labels.
	Drawing	Standard	Drawing	240	Displays the Drawing toolbar.

(continued)

continued

Button/ Box	Name	Toolbar	Category	Code	Description
	Drawing Selection	Drawing	Drawing	184	Selects an object or group of objects.
	Drop-Down	Forms	Forms	182	Lets you create a drop-down control.
	Drop Shadow	Drawing	Drawing	51	Adds a drop-shadow effect to the selected cells or objects.
	Edit Box	Forms	Forms	142	Lets you create an edit control.
	Edit Code	Forms	Forms	244	Lets you edit an object macro or create a new one.
	Ellipse	Drawing	Drawing	84	Draws an oval. Shift-click to draw a filled circle. Press Shift after click to create a circle.
	Equal Sign	None	Formula	27	Inserts an equal sign at the insertion point in the formula bar.
	Exponentiation Sign	None	Formula	32	Inserts a caret (^) at the insertion point in the formula bar.
	Fill Down	None	Edit	26	Copies values, formulas, and formats in the top row of the selection down, to fill the selection. Shift-click copies from the bottom up.
	Fill Right	None	Edit	25	Copies values, formats, and formulas in the leftmost column of the selection to the right, to fill the selection. Shift-click copies from right to left.
	Filled Arc	Drawing	Drawing	90	Draws a filled arc. Shift-click draws an unfilled quarter circle. Press Shift after click to create a filled quarter circle.
	Filled Ellipse	Drawing	Drawing	89	Draws a filled oval. Shift-click draws an unfilled circle. Press Shift after click to create a filled circle.

(continued)

continued

Button/ Box	Name	Toolbar	Category	Code	Description
	Filled Freeform	Drawing	Drawing	92	Draws a filled polygon that is a combination of freehand and straight lines. Click the beginning point to complete the drawing. Shift-click draws an unfilled polygon.
	Filled Polygon	None	Drawing	91	Draws a filled polygon using straight lines. Click the beginning point to complete the drawing. Shift-click draws an unfilled polygon.
	Filled Rectangle	Drawing	Drawing	88	Draws a filled rectangle. Shift-click draws an unfilled square. Press Shift after click to create a filled square.
	Find File	WorkGroup	File	177	Displays the Find File or Search dialog box, depending on whether you previously defined a search.
	Font box	Formatting	Text Formatting	68	Lists the available fonts.
	Font Color	Formatting	Text Formatting	236	Displays a tear-off palette of colors you can apply to the selected text.
	Font Size box	Formatting	Text Formatting	69	Lets you enter or select a font size.
	Format Painter	Standard	Edit	185	Copies and pastes the formats of the selected cells or objects.
	Freeform	Drawing	Drawing	87	Draws a polygon that is a combination of freehand and straight lines. Click the beginning point to complete the drawing. Shift-click to draw a filled freehand polygon.
	Freehand	Drawing	Drawing	78	Draws a freehand line. Shift-click draws a filled freehand line.

(continued)

continued

Button/ Box	Name	Toolbar	Category	Code	Description
	Freeze Panes	None	Utility	137	Freezes windows that are already split into panes, or splits and freezes panes above and to the left of the active cell. Click again to unfreeze or remove the panes.
	Full Screen	Full Screen	Utility	241	Toggles between full screen and default display.
	Function Wizard	Standard	Formula/ Macro/ Utility	40	Displays the Function Wizard dialog box.
	Group	Query And Pivot	Data	130	Groups the selected rows or columns. Also used for outlining.
	Group Box	Forms	Forms	181	Lets you create a group box control.
	Group Objects	Drawing	Drawing	93	Joins selected objects together as a single object. Shift-click separates grouped objects.
	Help	Standard	Utility	128	Displays an online Help topic. Double-click to display Help's Search dialog box.
	Help Topics	Utility	Utility	248	Invokes the Answer Wizard.
	Hide Detail	Query And Pivot	Data	175	Summarizes the data underlying the current selection.
	Horizontal Gridlines	Chart	Charting	122	Adds or removes the major gridlines on the value axis.
	Increase Decimal	Formatting	Formatting	56	Adds a decimal place to the format of the selection. Shift-click removes a decimal place.
	Increase Font Size	None	Text Formatting	71	Changes the text in the selection to the next largest built-in font size. Shift-click changes to the next smallest font size.

(continued)

continued

Button/ Box	Name	Toolbar	Category	Code	Description
	Insert	None	Edit	22	Inserts cells at the selected location and shifts the adjacent cells to accommodate the insertion. Shift-click deletes cells.
	Insert Chart Sheet	None	File	8	Inserts a new chart sheet.
	Insert Column	None	Edit	24	Inserts columns at the selected location and shifts the adjacent columns to accommodate the insertion. Shift-click deletes columns.
	Insert Dialog	None	File	245	Inserts a new dialog sheet to the left of the selected sheet.
	Insert Module	Visual Basic	File/Macro	190	Inserts a new Visual Basic module.
	Insert MS Excel Macro	None	File	6	Inserts a new Microsoft Excel (.XLM) macro sheet.
	Insert Row	None	Edit	23	Inserts rows at the selected location and shifts the adjacent rows to accommodate the insertion. Shift-click deletes rows.
	Insert Worksheet	None	File	7	Inserts a new worksheet.
	Instant Watch	Visual Basic	Macro	194	Displays the value of the selected expression.
	Italic	Formatting	Text Formatting	59	Applies italic formatting to the selection.
	Justify Align	None	Text Formatting	66	Aligns text in the selection flush right and flush left, adding space between words where necessary.
	Label	Forms	Forms	199	Lets you create a dialog label.
	Left Border	None	Formatting	44	Adds or removes a border at the left edge of the selection.

(continued)

continued

Button/ Box	Name	Toolbar	Category	Code	Description
	Left Parenthesis	None	Formula	33	Inserts an open parenthesis at the insertion point in the formula bar.
	Legend	Chart	Charting	124	Adds or removes a chart legend.
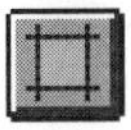	Light Shading	None	Formatting/ Drawing	50	Adds a light shading pattern to the selection.
	Line	Drawing	Drawing	76	Draws a straight line. Press Shift to constrain along horizontal, vertical, and diagonal lines.
	Line Chart AutoFormat	None	Charting	107	Creates a default line chart.
	Line/Column Chart AutoFormat	None	Charting	118	Creates a default line/column chart.
	List Box	Forms	Forms	144	Lets you create a list box control.
	Lock Cell	None	Utility	136	Locks and unlocks selected cells and objects.
	Map	Standard	Drawing	246	Creates a map of your data.
	Menu Editor	Visual Basic	Macro	192	Displays the Menu Editor dialog box.
	Microsoft Access	Microsoft	Utility	216	Switches to Microsoft Access.
	Microsoft FoxPro	Microsoft	Utility	160	Switches to Microsoft FoxPro.
	Microsoft Mail	Microsoft	Utility	203	Switches to Microsoft Mail.
	Microsoft PowerPoint	Microsoft	Utility	204	Switches to Microsoft PowerPoint.
	Microsoft Project	Microsoft	Utility	205	Switches to Microsoft Project.
	Microsoft Schedule+	Microsoft	Utility	227	Switches to Microsoft Schedule+.

(continued)

continued

Button/ Box	Name	Toolbar	Category	Code	Description
	Microsoft Word	Microsoft	Utility	202	Switches to Microsoft Word.
	Minus Sign	None	Formula	29	Inserts a minus sign at the insertion point in the formula bar.
	Multiplication Sign	None	Formula	30	Inserts an asterisk (*) at the insertion point in the formula bar.
	New Workbook	Standard	File	9	Creates a new workbook.
	Object Browser	Visual Basic	Macro	191	Displays procedures, objects, methods, and properties.
	Open	Standard	File	1	Displays the File Open dialog box.
	Option Button	Forms	Forms	141	Lets you create an option button control.
	Outline Border	None	Formatting	43	Adds or removes border at the outside edges of the selection.
	Paste	Standard	Edit	14	Pastes the contents of the Clipboard.
	Paste Formats	None	Edit	17	Pastes only the formats of the copied cells. Shift-click pastes only the values and formulas.
	Paste Names	None	Formula/ Macro/Utility	41	Displays the Paste Name dialog box.
	Paste Values	None	Edit	18	Pastes only the values and formulas of the copied cells. Shift-click pastes only the formats.
	Pattern	Drawing	Drawing	232	Displays a tear-off palette of available patterns.
	Percent Sign	None	Formula	37	Inserts a percent sign at the insertion point in the formula bar.
	Percent Style	Formatting	Formatting	54	Applies a percent format with no decimal places to the selection.

(continued)

continued

Button/ Box	Name	Toolbar	Category	Code	Description
	Pie Chart AutoFormat	None	Charting	108	Creates a pie chart with percentage labels.
	PivotTable Field	Query And Pivot	Data	171	Allows changes to the current pivot table field's properties.
	PivotTable Wizard	Query And Pivot	Data	167	Creates or modifies a pivot table.
	Plus Sign	None	Formula	28	Inserts a plus sign at the insertion point in the formula bar.
	Polygon	None	Drawing	86	Draws a polygon using straight lines. Click the beginning point to complete the drawing. Shift-click draws a filled polygon.
	Print	Standard	File	3	Prints the active workbook. Shift-click displays a preview of the workbook.
	Print Preview	Standard	File	4	Displays a preview of the current workbook. Shift-click prints the active workbook.
	Radar Chart AutoFormat	None	Charting	117	Creates a default radar chart.
	Record Macro	Visual Basic	Macro	98	Records your actions as a new macro.
	Rectangle	Drawing	Drawing	83	Draws a rectangle. Shift-click draws a filled square. Press Shift after click to create an unfilled square.
	Refresh Data	Query And Pivot	Data	170	Updates the pivot table with the most current data.
	Remove All Arrows	Auditing	Auditing	153	Removes all tracer arrows.
	Remove Dependent Arrows	Auditing	Auditing	147	Removes one level of dependent tracer arrows.
	Remove Precedent Arrows	Auditing	Auditing	149	Removes one level of precedent tracer arrows.

(continued)

continued

Button/ Box	Name	Toolbar	Category	Code	Description
	Repeat	Standard	Edit	11	Repeats the last command or action.
	Reshape	Drawing	Drawing	82	Lets you adjust the shape of polygons and freehand lines.
	Resume Macro	Visual Basic	Macro	102	Resumes running a paused macro.
	Right Border	None	Formatting	45	Adds or removes a border at the right edge of the selection.
	Right Parenthesis	None	Formula	34	Inserts a close parenthesis at the insertion point in the formula bar.
	Rotate Text Down	None	Text Formatting	75	Rotates text vertically, reading from top to bottom.
	Rotate Text Up	None	Text Formatting	74	Rotates text vertically, reading from bottom to top.
	Routing Slip	WorkGroup	File	162	Displays the Add Routing Slip dialog box.
	Run Dialog	Forms	Forms	187	Runs the current dialog box.
	Run Macro	Visual Basic	Macro	100	Runs the selected macro starting at the insertion point.
	Save	Standard	File	2	Saves the active document.
	Scenarios	WorkGroup	Utility	166	Lets you define and select named scenarios.
	Scroll Bar	Forms	Forms	143	Lets you create a scroll bar control.
	Select Current Region	None	Utility	133	Selects all the adjacent cells in a rectangular area, bounded by blank rows, columns, and worksheet borders.
	Select Visible Cells	None	Utility	132	Selects the visible cells in the selection, ignoring any hidden cells.

(continued)

continued

Button/ Box	Name	Toolbar	Category	Code	Description
	Selection	None	Drawing	81	Selects groups of objects.
	Send Mail	WorkGroup	File	163	Displays the dialog box for your mail program.
	Send To Back	Drawing	Drawing	96	Moves selected objects to the background. Shift-click brings objects to the foreground.
	Set Print Area	None	File	5	Defines the print area based on the current selection.
	Shape	None	Drawing	235	Displays a tear-off palette of available drawing tools.
	Show Detail	Query And Pivot	Data	173	Displays the data underlying the current selection.
	Show Info Window	Auditing	Auditing	243	Displays the Info Window.
	Show Outline Symbols	None	Utility	131	Displays or hides outline symbols. If no outline exists, asks if you want to create one.
	Show Pages	Query And Pivot	Data	172	Creates one pivot table for each item in a Page field.
	Sort Ascending	Standard	Utility/Data	134	Sorts the selected cells in alphabetic order, using the active cell as the sort key. Shift-click sorts in descending order.
	Sort Descending	Standard	Utility/Data	135	Sorts the selected cells in reverse alphabetic order, using the active cell as the sort key. Shift-click sorts in ascending order.
	Spelling	Standard	Utility	127	Checks the spelling of the text in the worksheet or the formula bar.

(continued)

continued

Button/ Box	Name	Toolbar	Category	Code	Description
	Spinner	Forms	Forms	183	Lets you create a spinner control.
	Stacked Column Chart AutoFormat	None	Charting	106	Creates a default stacked column chart.
	Step Into	Visual Basic	Macro	195	Executes the next macro statement, stepping into procedure.
	Step Macro	Visual Basic	Macro	101	Steps through the selected macro starting at the insertion point or lets you pick a macro to run.
	Step Over	Visual Basic	Macro	196	Executes the next macro statement, stepping over procedure.
	Stop Recording Macro	Visual Basic/Stop Recording	Macro	99	Stops the execution or recording of a macro.
	Strikethrough	None	Text Formatting	61	Applies strikeout formatting to the text in the selection.
	Style box	None	Formatting/ Text Formatting	70	Lets you select or define a style.
	Tab Order	None	Forms	186	Lets you change the order of controls.
	Text box	Standard/ Drawing	Drawing/ Utility	79	Draws a box in which text can be typed or adds an unattached text box to a chart.
	TipWizard	Standard	TipWizard	179	Shows or hides the TipWizard toolbar.
	TipWizard box	TipWizard	TipWizard	178	Suggests shortcuts or features related to what you are doing.
	Toggle Breakpoint	Visual Basic	Macro	193	Sets or clears a breakpoint at the insertion point.

(continued)

continued

Button/ Box	Name	Toolbar	Category	Code	Description
	Toggle Grid	Forms	Forms	239	Switches between displaying and hiding gridlines.
	Toggle Read Only	WorkGroup	File	165	Switches file status between read-only and read-write.
	Top Border	None	Formatting	46	Adds or removes a border at the top edge of the selection.
	Trace Dependents	Auditing	Auditing	148	Shows the formulas that refer to the selected cell.
	Trace Error	Auditing	Auditing	174	Shows the cells causing an error in the selected cell.
	Trace Precedents	Auditing	Auditing	242	Shows the cells referred to by the selected formula.
	Underline	Formatting	Text Formatting	60	Applies a single underline to the text in the selection.
	Undo	Standard	Edit	10	Undoes the last command or action.
	Ungroup	Query And Pivot	Data	129	Ungroups the selected rows or columns. Also used in outlining.
	Ungroup Objects	Drawing	Drawing	94	Separates previously grouped objects. Shift-click groups objects.
	Update File	WorkGroup	File	164	Updates a read-only file to the last-saved value.
	Vertical Gridlines	None	Charting	123	Adds or removes the major gridlines on the category axis.
	Vertical Text	None	Text Formatting	73	Stacks text vertically in cells.
	Volume/High-Low-Close Chart AutoFormat	None	Charting	119	Creates a default combination chart for stock prices.
	XY (Scatter) Chart AutoFormat	None	Charting	115	Creates a default XY (scatter) chart.

(continued)

continued

Button/ Box	Name	Toolbar	Category	Code	Description
	Zoom Control box	Standard	Utility	189	Lets you select or specify a zoom percentage for the current worksheet.
	Zoom In	None	Utility	138	Displays the document at the next highest magnification. Shift-click zooms out.
	Zoom Out	None	Utility	139	Displays the document at the next lowest magnification. Shift-click zooms in.
	Custom	None	Custom	237	Blank button for assigning a macro.
	Custom	None	Custom	201	Blank button for assigning a macro.
	Custom	None	Custom	214	Blank button for assigning a macro.
	Custom	None	Custom	206	Blank button for assigning a macro.
	Custom	None	Custom	207	Blank button for assigning a macro.
	Custom	None	Custom	208	Blank button for assigning a macro.
	Custom	None	Custom	228	Blank button for assigning a macro.
	Custom	None	Custom	209	Blank button for assigning a macro.
	Custom	None	Custom	210	Blank button for assigning a macro.
	Custom	None	Custom	200	Blank button for assigning a macro.
	Custom	None	Custom	215	Blank button for assigning a macro.
	Custom	None	Custom	213	Blank button for assigning a macro.

(continued)

continued

Button/ Box	Name	Toolbar	Category	Code	Description
	Custom	None	Custom	217	Blank button for assigning a macro.
	Custom	None	Custom	97	Blank button for assigning a macro.
	Custom	None	Custom	218	Blank button for assigning a macro.
	Custom	None	Custom	219	Blank button for assigning a macro.
	Custom	None	Custom	220	Blank button for assigning a macro.
	Custom	None	Custom	225	Blank button for assigning a macro.
	Custom	None	Custom	226	Blank button for assigning a macro.
	Custom	None	Custom	229	Blank button for assigning a macro.
	Custom	None	Custom	230	Blank button for assigning a macro.
	Custom	None	Custom	231	Blank button for assigning a macro.
	Custom	None	Custom	211	Blank button for assigning a macro.
	Custom	None	Custom	212	Blank button for assigning a macro.
	Custom	None	Custom	221	Blank button for assigning a macro.
	Custom	None	Custom	222	Blank button for assigning a macro.
	Custom	None	Custom	223	Blank button for assigning a macro.
	Custom	None	Custom	224	Blank button for assigning a macro.

Appendix B

Installing Microsoft Excel

Whether you install Excel from diskettes or from CD-ROM, as a stand-alone application or as part of the Microsoft Office suite, the Excel setup program is extraordinarily easy to use.

Hardware Requirements and Memory Considerations

To run Microsoft Excel for Windows 95, version 7, you need a system that runs Windows 95. You need an IBM-compatible computer with an Intel 80386 or higher microprocessor and at least 6 megabytes (MB) of memory. We recommend a minimum of 8 megabytes. In addition, your system must include Microsoft Windows 95, one 3½-inch floppy-disk drive, and a hard disk.

Optional Components

The following components can increase your speed and efficiency as you work in Excel. These components are optional, based on your personal requirements.

Printers and Plotters

Excel supports a number of printers, including Hewlett-Packard LaserJet and DeskJet series printers, the Apple LaserWriter series (or any PostScript-compatible printer), and many other printers compatible with Microsoft Windows 95. You might also want to use a plotter to print high-quality color charts and graphs. Excel supports the Hewlett-Packard 7470A plotter and all other plotters compatible with Windows 95.

For more information about printer support, see the Microsoft Windows 95 documentation.

A Mouse or Other Pointing Device

Excel uses a graphical interface, taking advantage of drop-down menus and icons to let you make selections quickly and easily. Although a mouse is still technically considered an optional accessory, many of the features available in Excel 7 require one. For example, most of the toolbar buttons can be accessed only with a mouse.

You can use a track ball or other pointing device as a substitute for a mouse if you prefer.

Networks

You can install Excel on a computer attached to a network so that two or more users can share data stored on a common network drive. Networking also allows two or more users to share printing resources.

Excel supports any network compatible with Microsoft Windows 95, but your network might need a version of MS-DOS later than 3.1. Check with your dealer for details about your network system.

Additional Memory

Although you can operate Excel with 6 MB of memory, the more memory you have, the more efficiently Excel runs. With additional memory, you can build larger worksheets and carry out commands and calculations more quickly.

Math Coprocessor

If you're using a computer with an 80386 microprocessor, a math coprocessor can increase the speed at which Excel performs certain calculations—particularly those involving financial and trigonometric functions.

Installing Microsoft Excel

To install Microsoft Excel, choose Settings from the Windows 95 Start menu. Then choose Control Panel. Double-click the Control Panel item labeled Add/Remove Programs. Insert your first diskette in your floppy disk drive or the Microsoft Office CD-ROM in your CD-ROM drive. Then click the Install button and follow the instructions that appear.

TIP If you're installing Excel from diskettes, it's a good idea to make backup copies of your diskettes before you begin the installation. Save your backup copies in case your original disks are misplaced or damaged.

Removing Components

The Excel 7 setup program allows you to remove installed components when you choose the Complete/Custom installation option. Leave selected the components you want to keep and deselect the components you want to remove. Be sure that the already-installed items (such as Microsoft Excel!) are still checked, or they'll be removed.

Add-Ins

The Excel setup program can install several auxiliary programs called *add-ins*. In essence, add-ins are macro sheets that make additional commands and functions available to Excel. (You can also create add-ins, allowing you to customize Excel for your own needs.) If you select the Complete/Custom option, Setup installs the following add-ins on your hard disk:

Add-In Name	Filename	Commands or Features Added	See
AccessLinks	Acclink.xla	Access Form, Access Report, and Convert to Access (Data Menu)	Chapter 20
Analysis ToolPak	Analysis.xll Atpvbaen.xla	Data Analysis command (Tools menu), plus a number of financial and engineering functions	Chapters 13 and 14
AutoSave	Autosave.xla	AutoSave command (Tools menu)	Chapter 3
Report Manager	Reports.xla	Report Manager command (View menu)	Chapter 10
Solver	Solver.xla	Solver command (Tools menu)	Chapter 15
Template Wizard with Data Tracking	Wztemplt.xla	Template Wizard (Data Menu)	Chapter 20
View Manager	Views.xla	View Manager command (View menu)	Chapter 8

If you select the Typical or Laptop (Minimum) installation setup options, the .XLA files listed in the table above might not be available on your hard disk. You can install them later by rerunning the setup program.

If, after installation, any of the add-in commands do not appear on your menus, choose the Add-Ins command from the Tools menu and click the Browse button to find the missing .XLA files in your Library folder.

NOTE In a typical Office installation, programs such as Microsoft Query and Data Map are installed in the Programs folder, in a subfolder named Common Files.

See Also For information about Microsoft Query, see Chapter 21, "An Introduction to Microsoft Query," page 757.

PSS Q&A

Troubleshooting Tips from Microsoft Product Support Services

Formatting Worksheets

Why does the formula bar show the percent sign when I enter a value with a percent sign in a cell? It used to display the number as a decimal.

This behavior is new to Microsoft Excel 7 and is by design. Excel 7 makes it convenient to enter another value in the cell that contains the Percentage number formatting. For example, in versions of Excel earlier than version 7, when you entered the value 0.41 on your worksheet and formatted the cell as a percentage, the value was displayed as 41%. If you then entered the value 56 in that same cell, the value was displayed as 5600%, instead of 56%, as you may have intended.

Why aren't the gridlines printing on my worksheet?

This behavior is different from the default behavior in earlier versions of Excel. In Excel 7, when you create a new worksheet, the worksheet is displayed in print preview and is printed without gridlines. However, when you open a worksheet or workbook that was created in a previous version of Excel, the file behaves as it did in the previous version; in other words, the file is printed and displayed in print preview with gridlines if it was printed with gridlines in the earlier version of Microsoft Excel.

To print your worksheet with gridlines in Microsoft Excel 7, follow these steps:

1. On the File menu, click Page Setup, and then click the Sheet tab.
2. Under Print, click the Gridlines check box.
3. Click OK.

To print all worksheets in new workbooks with gridlines by default, create a workbook autotemplate, BOOK.XLT. Follow these steps:

1. In a new workbook, select all of the worksheets.
2. On the File menu, click Page Setup, and then click the Sheet tab.
3. Under Print, click the Gridlines check box, and then click OK.
4. On the File menu, click Save As. In the File Name box, enter *Book*. In the Save As Type list, click Template.
5. In the Save In list, click the MSOffice folder. In the list of folders, double-click the Excel folder, and then double-click the XLStart folder. Click Save.
6. Close and then restart Excel.

I've been trying to print multiple worksheets to a PostScript printer and have experienced trouble with settings I pick in the Layout option. I've tried printing both by selecting individual sheets and by printing the entire workbook, and the Layout option for individual sheets seems to be ignored. I formatted one of my worksheets to print in the "1 up" Layout option, and it printed with the "4 up" Layout option instead. How can I fix this?

The Layout option, available when you print to a PostScript printer, applies to the entire print job. When you print multiple worksheets at one time, or when you print one print job, each of the sheets is printed with the Layout option that is applied to the first selected sheet. For example, if you click the Sheet1 sheet tab, press the Ctrl key, and select the Sheet2 sheet tab, when you print using the Selected Worksheet(s) print option, the worksheets are printed using the Layout option applied to Sheet1.

To print multiple worksheets that have different Layout options, print each sheet individually by selecting one worksheet at a time and then choosing Print on the File menu or the Print button on the Standard toolbar.

Other printing options, such as orientation, scaling, and paper size, are applied individually to each worksheet, even when you print selected worksheets or the entire workbook. If you print a workbook that contains a worksheet in portrait orientation and a worksheet in landscape orientation, for example, the worksheets are printed the way you expect.

When I open the Format Cells dialog box and click the Number tab, I can't use the scrollbar in the Category list. When I click an item in the Category list, different lists appear in the Format Cells dialog box, and most lists contain a scrollbar. The only scrollbar that I can use, however, is the scrollbar that appears in the Type list when I click the Custom category. What's up?

This behavior occurs because only one of the lists on the Number tab in the Format Cells dialog box contains enough items to make the scrollbar in the list active. The other lists are too short, yet the scrollbar is still visible. Note that lists in foreign-language versions of Excel, when you select Date, Time, Fraction, or Special in the Category list, may contain additional items. The scrollbar is necessary for these lists, even if it you cannot use it for some lists in the U.S. version.

Can you tell me more about how I can create a data map object using zip codes as the geographical data? Is there a special format I need to use?

Numeric postal codes or zip codes must be formatted with the special Zip Code number format. If a column of nonformatted zip codes is selected and you insert a data map object, you see the error message "A column of data in your selection must contain geographical data." This happens to prevent the possible misinterpretation of numeric data as zip codes.

Use the following steps to properly format a range of zip codes:

1. Click Cells on the Format menu.
2. Select the Number Tab.
3. From the catagory list box, select Special.
4. From the Type list box, select either the Zip Code or Zip Code + 4 format.

Managing Files and Worksheets

When I open a template file, Excel opens the actual template instead of a copy of the template — what's wrong?

In previous versions of Excel, when you open a template file (such as SHEET.XLT), a copy of the file, SHEET1, is opened. However, in Excel 7, when you open a template file, the file is opened for editing (as if you opened a regular workbook file). Now you can edit any template file by using the Open command or the Open button on the Standard toolbar. You don't have to hold down the Shift key to open the file for editing as you do in previous versions of Excel.

To create a new worksheet, chart, macro, or workbook file based on a template file in Excel 7, follow these steps:

1. On the File menu, click the New command.
2. Click one of the tabs.
3. Click the template file you want, and then click OK.

When I display the Pick From list, it doesn't show all of the entries in the column I'm editing. When I enter data in a cell on my worksheet with the AutoComplete feature enabled, if the first few letters I type match an existing entry in the column, the existing entry may not be automatically entered in the cell as I expected.

This happens if the values in the column in which you are entering data are not within the "current region." The AutoComplete feature and the Pick From list use only the entries in the active column in the current region. The "current region" is bounded by any combination of blank rows and blank columns. For example, when you select cell A6 below, the current region is A4:A6, and the Pick List only includes the values east and west, as here:

A1: north

A2: south

A3:

A4: east

A5: west

A6:

The Pick From list may not contain all of the values in the column if the column contains blank cells. To include more values from the column in the Pick From list and the AutoComplete list, avoid having blank cells in the column in which you are entering data.

To locate the current region on your worksheet, follow these steps:

1. On the Edit menu, click Go To.
2. In the Go To dialog box, click Special.
3. In the Go To Special dialog box, click the Current Region option, and then click OK. The current region on the worksheet is selected.

When I insert or delete a row or column on my worksheet, the row or column may be added or removed without animation, even if the Animate Insertion And Deletion check box is selected on the Edit tab of the Options dialog box.
Usually, when you select the Animate Insertion And Deletion check box on the Edit tab of the Options dialog box, you can see how the worksheet changes when you insert or delete rows or columns. However, when you have multiple windows open for the same workbook, you do not see this animated effect. This occurs whether you view the windows at the same time (tile or cascade), or you view one window of the workbook at a time. Animation still occurs, however, when you change the width of a column or the height of a row, even if multiple windows are open for the same workbook.

To work around this behavior, close all but one of the windows for the workbook before you insert or delete the row or column on your worksheet. The effect of this behavior is only visual; that is, the row or column is inserted or deleted as expected.

When I enter a text value that contains an extended character in a cell and a value that I previously entered in the same column begins with the same character, the AutoComplete feature doesn't complete the entry in the cell.
This occurs when you enter a value such as the character é ("e" with the acute accent, Alt+130), and an entry in the column containing the corresponding ASCII character in the same position is sorted *after* the value you enter.

For example, when you enter é in cell A3 like this:

```
A1: egg
A2: ebc (where the "e" is the character e with the acute accent)
A3:
```

the AutoComplete feature does not fill in the rest of the value "ebc" as expected. AutoComplete behaves as if the first characters in cell A1 and A2 were equal.

However, when you enter the character "e" with the acute accent in cell A3 as follows

```
A1: egg
A2: egh (where the "e" is the character e with the acute accent)
A3:
```

the AutoComplete feature completes the value "egh" as expected.

When I edit a map on my worksheet using the buttons on the Data Map toolbar, the button doesn't release when I complete the edit. When I click the button, it remains depressed until I click another button on the Data Map toolbar.

The Select Object, Zoom In, Zoom Out, Grabber, Label, Text, and Custom Pin Map buttons are "sticky," which means they remain selected until you click another button on the Data Map toolbar. This might cause unexpected results when you click your map. The button stays selected even if you deactivate the map, select another object on your worksheet, and then reactivate the map. The button that was selected when you deactivated the map is selected when you activate the map again.

To turn off a map feature, such as the labeler, click another button on the Data Map toolbar. Note that pressing the Esc key does not turn off the selected map editing button.

I've noticed that data map objects, unlike objects such as charts, do not update automatically when associated data is changed. How come?

Data map objects don't update automatically because of the potentially prohibitive time required to update the objects associated with large amounts of data.

A data map object can be updated either manually by activating the object and clicking the Update button or through a Visual Basic for Applications procedure. Here's a macro you might use. Type the following in a module sheet; we've added some comments to let you know what the program is doing:

```
Sub Update_DataMap_Object()

 'Assign DataMap Object Name to a Variable
 MapName = "Picture 1"

 'Update DataMap Object
 ActiveSheet.OLEObjects(MapName).Object.Refreshmap

End Sub
```

I seem to get math errors when I'm working with floating-point numbers. Am I doing something wrong?

Many combinations of arithmetic operations on floating-point numbers may produce results that appear to be incorrect by very small amounts. For example, the expression (.5-.4-.1) evaluates to the quantity (2.8E-17) or .000000000000000028. This behavior is not a bug or limitation of Excel; it results because the IEEE 754 floating-point standard requires that numbers be stored in binary format.

The IEEE 754 standard is a method of storing floating-point numbers in a compact way that is easy to manipulate. This standard is used by Intel coprocessors and most PC-based programs that implement floating-point math. IEEE standard 754 specifies that numbers be stored in binary format to reduce storage requirements and allow the built-in binary arithmetic instructions available on all microprocessors to process the data relatively rapidly. However, some simple, nonrepeating decimal numbers convert into repeating binary numbers and cannot be stored with perfect accuracy. For example, the number 1/10 can be represented in a decimal number system with a simple decimal

```
.1
```

However, the same number in binary format becomes the repeating binary decimal

```
.0001100011000111000111 (and so on)
```

and can be repeated as far as you want. This binary number cannot be represented in a finite amount of space. Therefore, it will be rounded down by approximately -2.8E-17 when it is stored. If several arithmetic operations are performed to obtain a given result, these rounding errors may build up until the effect is noticeable.

I have WinFax by Delrina installed on my computer and am experiencing some strange behavior. Excel 7 keeps opening new workbooks. What can I do to fix this?

Delrina's WinFax Pro version 4.0 software installs two Microsoft Excel type macros that allow faxing directly from Excel. These macros were designed for Excel 4 and Excel 5. Opening the MSEXCEL4.XLM file will cause Excel version 7 to repeatedly open new workbooks. The macro will continue to open books until it is halted or the computer runs low of memory. The MSEXCEL5.XLM file does not affect Excel 7 in this matter, but also will not work in Excel 7 because it is designed for a 16-bit application.

To prevent the macros from continuously opening the workbooks when launching Excel, remove both the MSEXCEL4.XLM and MSEXCEL5.XLM from the XLStart directory. This problem has been documented in the XLREADME.TXT file that ships with Excel 7.

When I remove a floppy disk or disconnect from a network drive that contains a workbook file that I'm editing, an error message appears when I continue editing the workbook. Can you provide some more information about this?

The error message that you receive depends on the data contained in the workbook you are editing and the types of changes you make to the workbook. Here's summary of these error messages and when you receive them.

- If the workbook contains a linked or embedded object, when you edit the object or create another object, you receive the following error messages:

  "Editing or inserting an embedded or linked object"
  "Cannot start source application"
  "Pasting a new linked or embedded object"
  "Cannot paste data"

- If the workbook contains a Visual Basic module and you try to run a procedure contained in the module or to insert a new module in the workbook, you receive the following error message:

  "Unable to read from the disk"

- If the workbook contains a pivot table and you attempt to edit the pivot table, the following error message appears:

  "Unable to obtain PivotTable data from disk"

  NOTE You can create a new pivot table in the workbook under the above conditions without receiving an error message, even if the workbook already contains a pivot table.

- When you save a workbook file to another location, such as your hard disk drive, the following error message appears if the workbook file contains a pivot table, a linked or embedded object, or a Visual Basic module and you do not have access to the disk that contains the workbook file:

  "Document not saved"

  When you save a workbook that contains a Visual Basic module, you may also receive the following error message:

  "Unable to write to the disk"

  In Excel 7, workbook files are not stored entirely in memory. Some elements of the workbook are stored on the disk your file is stored on. This is a change from the way earlier versions of Excel stored files. Now, when you create a pivot table, an OLE object, or a Visual Basic module in a workbook, you must have continuous access to the drive that contains the workbook because these items are stored on the drive.

  To avoid running into problems when you are working on files from a floppy or a network drive, do not remove the floppy or disconnect from the network drive until you have closed the file you are working on.

  To avoid receiving an error message in any of the above situations, you must insert the floppy disk or connect to the network drive that contains the workbook file. You can then edit and create OLE objects, pivot tables, and Visual Basic modules, and you can also save the workbook file.

Using Shared Worksheets

When I try to save or close a shared file, I receive the error message "File is locked. Please try again." Why?

This happens when the file you are saving or closing is open in Microsoft Quick View. Quick View, which ships with Microsoft Windows 95, is an application that you can use to view a document without opening it in the application used to create the document. When a nonshared file is open in Excel, you cannot open the same file in Quick View because the file is locked by Excel. However, when a shared file is open in Excel, the file is not locked (to allow for sharing). It can thus be viewed in Quick View. When you save or close a shared file, Excel locks the file for saving. If you save or close a shared file in Excel while the file is open in Quick View, you receive the error message you're asking about because in this case the file is locked by Quick View.

To avoid receiving the "File is locked" error message when you save or close a shared file in Excel, you must first close the file in Quick View.

Why can't I show the Conflict History on a shared file?

When a file is open read-only, you cannot change the status of the Multi-User Editing feature. When you change the status of the Multi-User Editing feature in a file, Excel requires that you then save the file. When a file is open read-only, you cannot display the Shared Lists dialog box.

Although you cannot display the Shared Lists dialog box in a read-only file, you can display the Conflict History by running the following procedure in a Visual Basic module

```
Sub Conflict_History()
' In the following commands, replace BOOK1.XLS
' with the name of the file that is open read-only
Workbooks("BOOK1.XLS").Activate
Workbooks("BOOK1.XLS").ShowConflictHistory = True
End Sub
```

When I save changes to a shared file and click the Use These Changes button in the Conflict Resolution dialog box, the value that's entered in the conflicting cell is not always the value that was displayed in the Conflicting Changes By box. Why not?

The Conflicting Changes By box shows the value contained in the conflicting cell when the conflict first occurs. If the other user continues to make changes, you are not prompted multiple times for changes in the same conflicting cell. Although the Conflicting Changes By box shows only the first conflicting change, when you click the Use These Changes button, the value entered in the conflicting cell is the current value contained in that cell — the value entered most recently by the other user.

For example, suppose User1 and User2 are both editing Sheet1 in the shared file BOOK1. User1 enters the value "1/2/1995" in cell A1, saves the file, and then changes the value in cell A1 to "January" and saves the file. When User2 enters a value in cell A1 and saves the file, the Conflict Resolution dialog box appears as expected. However, the Conflicting Changes By User1 box contains the original value "1/2/1995" instead of the current value "January." If User1 clicks the Use These Changes button, the current value "January" is entered in cell A1 as expected.

When I click the Allow Multi-User Editing check box on the Editing tab of the Shared Lists dialog box, the Save As dialog box displays "Microsoft Excel Workbook" as the only option listed in the Save As Type box. Why?

This occurs when you click the Allow Multi-User Editing check box in a workbook that hasn't been saved or that is saved in a file format other than Microsoft Excel workbook. This is by design because you cannot share a file in Microsoft Excel unless it is saved in the Excel workbook format. Also, you cannot save a file in Excel to a file format other than Excel workbook and still maintain the multiuser editing feature.

When I click the Allow Multi-User Editing check box in a Microsoft Excel workbook file, it displays the message "This operation will result in a save. Continue?" What should I do?

You should continue. When you choose OK, the file is saved again as a Microsoft Excel workbook, and the Multi-User Editing feature is enabled. However, when you click the Allow Multi-User Editing check box in a file that has not been saved or in a file that has been saved in a file format other than Microsoft Excel workbook, the Save As dialog box appears as you describe. If you do not save the file as a Microsoft Excel workbook, the Multi-User Editing feature is not enabled for the file.

When I save a file that has the Multi-User Editing feature turned on, this feature may not be turned on in the saved file. Why?

This occurs when you use the Save As command to save the file and you change either the file format or the filename. If you change the file format, the Multi-User Editing feature is not turned on in the new file because you can only share a Microsoft Excel workbook file.

If you change only the filename, the Multi-User Editing feature is not turned on because typically when you save a shared file you do so to make your own local copy. Therefore, the Multi-User Editing feature is not "saved" to the new copy of the file.

To work around this behavior, you can turn on the Multi-User Editing feature in the new file. Follow these steps:

1. On the File menu, click Shared Lists, and then click the Editing tab.
2. Click the Allow Multi-User Editing check box.

If the format of this file is not Microsoft Excel workbook, the Save As dialog box appears. You must save the file in the Microsoft Excel workbook format in order to save the file with the Multi-User Editing feature turned on.

When I display the Shared Lists dialog box in a shared workbook to view the list of users who currently have the workbook open, the list contains an incorrect user name — one that doesn't match the current user name in any of the copies of Microsoft Excel in which the file is open. How can this happen?

The Status tab of the Shared Lists dialog box contains a list of users that currently have the shared workbook open, along with the date and time that the file was opened. The user name is taken from the User Name box on the General tab of the Options dialog box in the copies of Excel in which the file is open. However, if you change the user name in the Options dialog box while you have a shared workbook file open, the new name is not immediately reflected on the Status tab.

When you open a shared file, the user name is attached to the file itself. That is, as long as you have the file open, the user name that appeared on the General tab of the Options dialog box when you opened the file is the name that appears on the Status tab in the Shared Lists dialog box for your open copy of the file.

To display the correct name for any shared files that you have open after you change the user name in the Options dialog box, you must close the files and then open them again.

The Conflict Resolution dialog box appeared when I saved a shared workbook. When I click the Use All Remaining Changes From My Session button or the Use All Remaining Changes From The Other Session button, the mouse pointer changes to the hourglass and Excel appears to hang. Help!

This might occur when the changes you made to the shared file conflict with the changes saved in the same file by another user. The Conflict Resolution dialog box appears in this case, prompting you to resolve the conflicts. If you click the Use All Remaining Changes From My Session button or the Use All Remaining Changes From The Other Session button, the conflicts are resolved without prompting you for each conflicting cell. If there are many changes to resolve, this process can take a long time, a matter of minutes, and there is no indication that Excel is processing any changes. No dialog box or status bar indicator shows the percentage of the process that is complete, and the Excel window is not updated (no screen updates) as the conflicts are being resolved. Additionally, if you press Ctrl+Alt+Delete to display the Close Program dialog box, the text "Not Responding" appears following the Excel item in the list of programs.

If the Conflict Resolution dialog box appears when I save a shared workbook, the change information in the Your Changes On Sheet '<sheetname>' box is exactly the same as the information in the Conflicting Changes By <Username> box. Is this okay?

Typically, when you receive the Conflict Resolution dialog box, the change information in the Your Changes On Sheet '<sheetname>' box is different from the information in the Conflicting Changes By <username> box because your changes conflict with the changes another user made to the same workbook. However, if you have edited information on the worksheet by dragging cells, the Conflict Resolution dialog box appears when you save the file even if the other user editing the file made the exact same changes by dragging the same cells. In this case, the information in the Conflict Resolution dialog box confirms that the changes you made are the same as the changes the other user made.

When two actions performed in a shared workbook by two different users are exact, one of the actions loses "silently," or without displaying the Conflict Resolution dialog box. However, if a change made by moving cells is followed by exactly the same change, the Conflict Resolution dialog box appears when the file is saved to avoid checking to see whether a long list of actions are the same. When this occurs, you can choose to accept either your changes to the file or the other user's changes because they are the same.

When I add a value to the end of a list in a shared workbook file that conflicts with a value added in the same cell by another user, the Conflict Resolution dialog box appears instead of the value being added to the list as expected. Why? And what should I do?

This behavior occurs if the worksheet in the shared workbook contains data in a row below the last row of data in the list. For example, when you enter a value in a cell, for example, cell A4, at the end of a list in column A in a shared workbook, and another user has entered a different value in cell A4 on the same worksheet and saved the file, the Conflict Resolution dialog box appears if there is a value on the worksheet in cell E25.

Normally, when you enter a value in a cell at the end of a list in a workbook shared with another user, an additional row is inserted in the list for the value that you entered, and the value that the other user entered is added to the end of the list. For example, if one user enters the value "d" in cell A4, at the end of this list

```
A1: a
A2: b
A3: c
```

and then saves the file, when you enter the value e in cell A4 on the same worksheet, the list appears as follows when you save the file:

```
A1: a
A2: b
A3: c
A4: e
A5: d
```

The Conflict Resolution dialog box does not appear in this case. However, if data appears on the worksheet below the last row of data in the list, a new row is not inserted in the list because of the possibility of pushing the data that appears below the list off the last row on the worksheet.

To avoid receiving the Conflict Resolution dialog box in a shared file when you add data to the end of a list, make sure that the worksheet that contains the list does not contain any data below the last row of data in the list.

When I use the shared lists feature by clicking the Allow Multi-User Editing check box on the Editing tab of the Shared Lists dialog box, some of the commands and features that I normally use in my workbook are not available.

This behavior occurs because when you share a workbook file you cannot use some of the Excel features that you normally use. This is by design because of the way a shared file is saved. For example, you cannot change cell formatting in a shared workbook.

Programming Excel

I've created some custom dialog boxes in Excel 7 and noticed that they don't look the same when I use them in Excel 5. The fonts used in the dialog boxes have a bolder appearance in Excel 5 and the font spacing in text labels is misaligned from their original design. What's up?

Excel 7 uses a thinner font than the system font in order to comply with Microsoft Windows 95 standards for dialog boxes. Previous versions of Excel use a system font that is bolder in its appearance. Because spacing for the text labels is based on the thinner font, the labels may look misaligned or cut off behind other objects in the dialog box when the dialog box is opened in Excel 5. Dialog boxes created in Excel 5 appear correctly in Excel 7.

If you need to run dialog boxes created with Excel 7 in both Excel 5 and 7, you should design the dialogs with enough spacing between the labels and objects to compensate for the change in font type.

I know that in earlier versions of Excel, you couldn't control the appearance of the mouse pointer while running a macro. Can you do this in Excel 7?
Yes. In Excel 5, the mouse pointer is normally displayed as an hourglass when you run a macro. The exception is when you run a macro from a control in a custom dialog box, in which case the mouse pointer continues to be displayed as an arrow and does not give you an indication that the macro is running.

In Excel 7, however, you can use the Visual Basic for Applications Cursor property to display the mouse pointer as an arrow, an hourglass, an I-beam (displayed when editing text), or the default pointer. The following built-in constants correspond to each of the available cursor shapes:

xlNorthwestArrow	The northwest-arrow pointer
xlWait	The hourglass pointer
xlIBeam	The I-beam pointer
xlNormal	The default pointer

(When you type in the constant for the I-beam pointer, the letter that follows the "xl" prefix is an "I"—for I-beam.)

Index

Special Characters

A

B

C

E

F

G

H

I

J

K

L

M

N

O

P

Q

S

T

U

V

W

X

Y

Z

The manuscript for this book was prepared and submitted to Microsoft Press in electronic form. Text files were prepared using Microsoft Word 6.0 for Windows. Pages were composed by Editorial Services of New England using Ventura Publisher for Windows 4.2 with text in ITC Garamond and display type in Avant Garde Demi. Composed pages were delivered to the printer as color-separated electronic prepress files.

Cover Designer
Rebecca Geisler

Cover Color Separator
Color Service Inc.

Interior Graphic Designers
Kim Eggleston, Amy Peppler Adams — designlab

Principal Typographers
Peter Whitmer, Mark Heffernan

Principal Word Processor
Sean Donahue

Principal Proofreader
Bettina Burch

Indexer
Matthew Spence

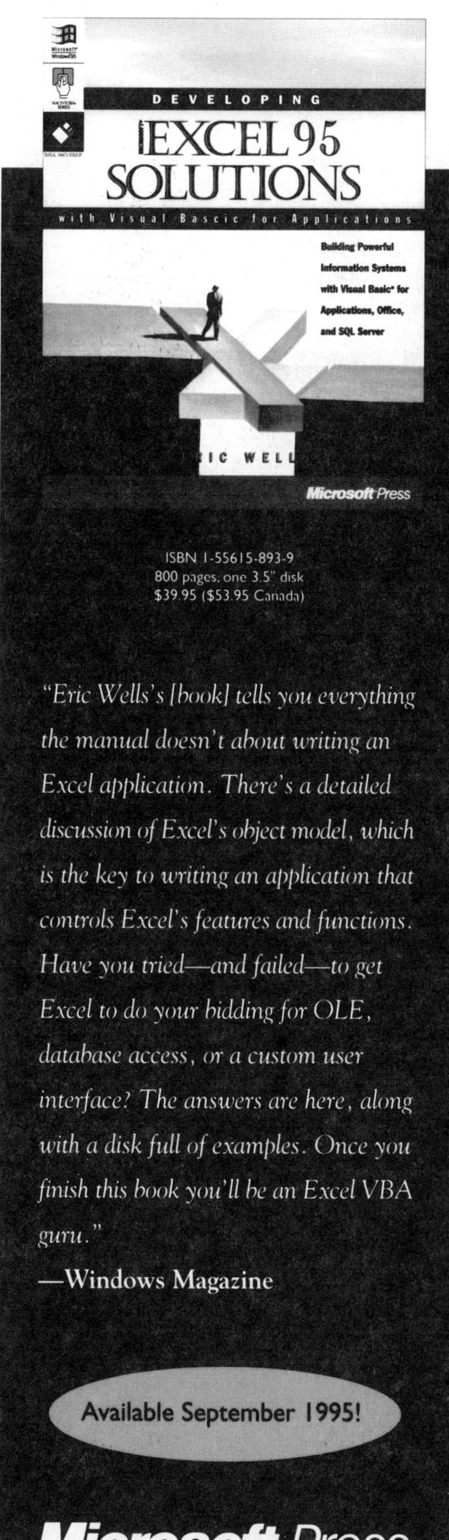

Create industrial-strength business applications for Windows® and the Macintosh® in the Microsoft® Excel object model and in Visual Basic® for Applications.

This book will teach you how to use the powerful tools in Microsoft Excel to create business applications that turn raw data into meaningful, useful information—in a way that could previously be done only by using a high-end development tool such as C or COBOL. You'll save time and money by being able to quickly and efficiently build, maintain, and update these applications within Microsoft Excel, using easy-to-write Visual Basic for Applications macros.

You Have a Powerful Development Tool at Your Fingertips—Microsoft Excel

Microsoft Excel contains more than 125 advanced data analysis objects that you can piece together to create business applications. Not only can you rely on these objects, but because Microsoft Excel supports OLE, you can also integrate a variety of objects from other applications (such as Microsoft Word and Microsoft Access) into your applications.

Learn to Use the Power

After an overview of the Excel object model and Visual Basic for Applications features, you'll learn how to:

- Develop information systems and design custom interfaces
- Take advantage of the powerful Jet database engine to develop database solutions in Excel that can be used with Microsoft Access and Visual Basic
- Develop custom applications with Microsoft Office and other products that support OLE
- Distribute your applications
- Enhance the performance of your applications

Benefit from Expert Advice and Insight

Written by a member of the Microsoft Excel technical team, DEVELOPING MICROSOFT EXCEL 95 SOLUTIONS WITH VISUAL BASIC® FOR APPLICATIONS, delivers inside strategies, tips, and tricks you won't find anywhere else. The companion disk includes sample Visual Basic for Applications macros and applications covered in the book. This is the only reference you'll need to start creating your own professional-quality data-access and decision-making tools in Microsoft Excel right away.

The Map feature allows you to display geographically oriented data in a graphic format.

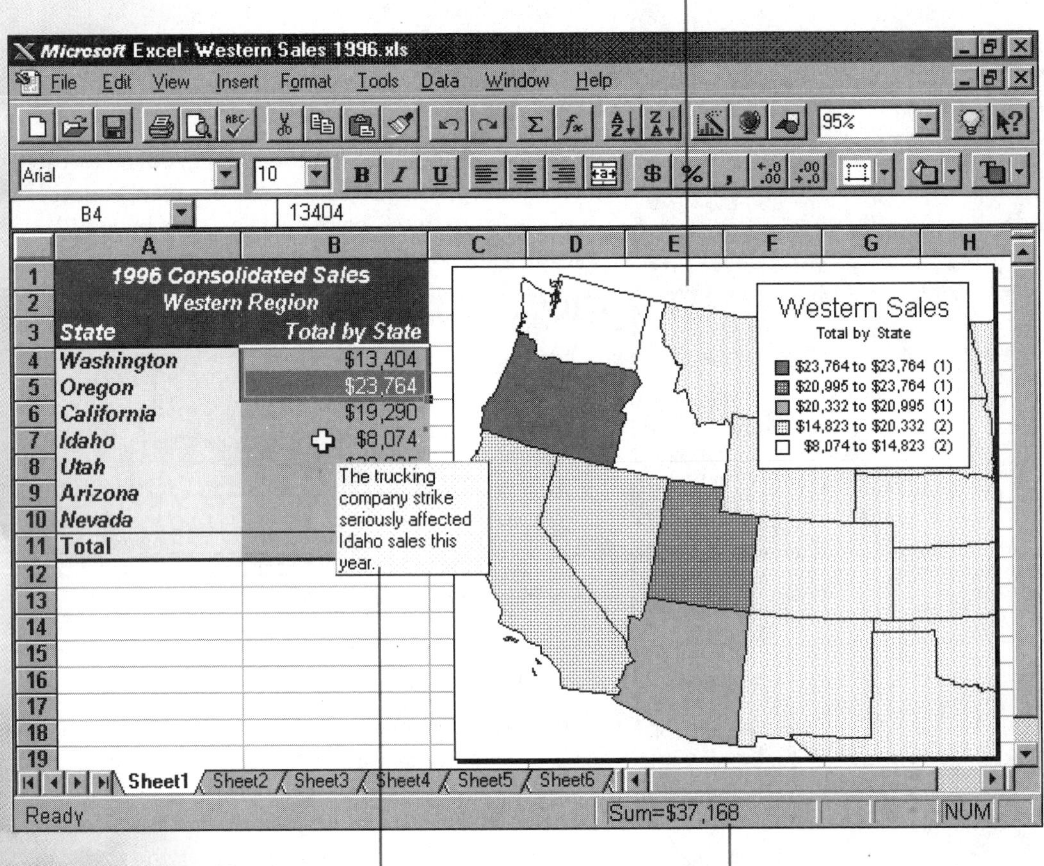

Cell notes now appear as Cell Tips, which are displayed when you move the cursor over a cell with a note attached.

AutoCalculate instantly displays the sum, average, count, maximum, or minimum value of the selected cells.